Explorations: An Open Invitation to Biological Anthropology, 2nd Edition

D1611280

EXPLORATIONS: AN OPEN INVITATION TO BIOLOGICAL ANTHROPOLOGY, 2ND EDITION

BETH SHOOK, PH.D.; KATIE NELSON, PH.D.; KELSIE AGUILERA, M.A.; AND LARA BRAFF, PH.D.

American Anthropological Association
Arlington

CONTENTS

PREFACE

We (the editors) are delighted to release the second edition of our Open Educational Resources (OER) textbook, *Explorations: An Open Invitation to Biological Anthropology*. Since the publication of the first edition of *Explorations* in 2019, there have been a number of discoveries, scientific advancements, and, of course, a global pandemic that resulted in significant shifts within our discipline and societies. These influences have led to changes to the norms and pedagogical/andragogical standards within Anthropology, including increased emphasis on diversity, equity, inclusion, anti-racism, accessibility, as well as primate conservation and welfare. To this end, our work on the second edition was guided by the following commitments:

1. **Diversity, equity, and inclusion.** We recognize that higher education has, and continues to be, an inequitable space of learning, particularly for historically underrepresented groups. We are committed to creating inclusive learning materials that better reflect our diverse student readers. We are motivated to redress the historic exclusion from science of several groups of people, including women, marginalized racial and ethnic groups, Indigenous communities, queer communities, early career researchers, among others. Following the guidance set forth by Academic Senate for California Community Colleges Open Educational Resources Initiative (ASCCC OERI)'s Inclusion, Diversity, Equity, and Anti-Racism (IDEA) Framework, this edition integrates constructivist theories of learning, culturally responsive, and anti-racist pedagogical approaches, as well as more inclusive content.

2. **Primate welfare.** Following the guidelines of the International Union for Conservation of Nature (IUCN) Species Survival Commission (SSC), Primate Specialist Group Section on Human Primate Interaction, we are committed to promoting appropriate primate treatment, conservation, and welfare. We recognize that two-thirds of all primate species throughout the world are in decline or threatened; that primates are frequently killed or captured by humans for use in research or the pet trade; and that primate-human interactions run the risk of zoonotic disease transmission (see Appendix B) . We are dedicated to raising awareness of the threats to primates and promoting appropriate primate-human interaction through education. For example, in the second edition, we eliminated images of people in close proximity to primates, opting instead for images that portray researchers viewing primates from afar or with protective equipment.

3. **Human remains.** We recognize the rights of descendant and related living communities to determine the disposition and portrayal of affiliated human remains. Some of these rights are protected under U.S. law and others are supported by ethical standards established by professional anthropological associations.

4. **Informed consent.** We respect the rights of all people to participate (or not participate) in research and publications. We have therefore eliminated images or blurred the faces of individuals in photographs throughout the second edition when documented informed consent could not be acquired.

5. **Decolonizing anthropology.** We acknowledge that biological anthropology was originally built on colonialism, scientific racism, and elitism. The terminology and language of our scholarship has the potential to either reinforce or combat racism, ethnocentrism, and structural inequalities. We have therefore been intentional about removing potentially harmful words and concepts in favor of more equity-minded terminology.

6. **Student perspectives.** Our textbook is written, first and foremost, for our students, who come to us to learn about human origins and evolution, bringing with them their unique backgrounds and perspectives . Over the years, students have written to us, expressing their reactions to, and suggestions for, chapters of this book. Their invaluable feedback was supplemented by that of formally recruited and paid student reviewers in order to produce a more student-centered book.

7. **Accessibility.** In order to make this OER fully accessible to diverse learners, it has undergone multiple comprehensive accessibility reviews . The eBook was created using Pressbooks' accessibility resources, including their Voluntary Product Accessibility Template [VPAT®] and their Accessibility Standards and Commitments. Ancillary materials underwent Microsoft build-in accessibility checks. The entire project was submitted to the OERI for a professional accessibility review. We have corrected all known accessibility issues.

Summary of Second Edition Updates

Like the first edition, this peer-reviewed OER is available free-of-charge online for students, instructors, and the public. The second edition was funded by the ASCCC OERI and the California State University, Chico – University Foundation. It was also supported by the American Anthropological Association (AAA) and California State University Affordable Learning Solutions (AL$) program.

The first edition was made possible by grants from Minnesota State Educational Innovations Grant, the ASCCC OERI, and the Society for Anthropology in Community Colleges (SACC).

In response to instructor and student feedback, in addition to formal peer reviews, we have made substantive changes to the second edition, including

1. More concise chapters (8000-10000 words, not including call out boxes);
2. Up-to-date chapters that include current discoveries and events;
3. Diversity, equity, inclusion, and anti-racism principles applied to the text and images;
4. The implementation of updated accessibility standards;
5. An instructor guide detailing how to adapt the book to fit your course;
6. A new chapter two on the history of evolutionary thought;
7. The first edition's chapter two is now chapter 17, which focuses on biopolitics;
8. Chapter 15 now focuses on forensic anthropology and points readers to other OER for more on archaeology and bioarchaeology;
9. The ancient DNA special topic that was featured in chapter 11 is now Appendix D;
10. Updated ancillary materials.

An OER for YOU

This book is grounded in the OER movement that emerged in response to the skyrocketing costs of traditional textbooks. These costs, along with increased tuition, create serious barriers to student learning and success, especially for students with financial constraints. As anthropologists concerned with social equity, we find that OER can begin to level the playing field within academia by enabling all students, regardless of socioeconomic status, to access materials they need to succeed in their courses.

Students: This textbook has been created for you with your success in mind. The editors and authors are experienced instructors who hope to engage your curiosity and answer your questions about humankind. Our textbook is available to you for FREE! We hope that it sparks your interest in scientific inquiry and anthropological discoveries.

Instructors: We commend you for making the inspired choice to adopt this textbook, which is written, reviewed, and edited by anthropology instructors just like you. Explorations offers you the academic freedom to align it with your own pedagogy, course content, and areas of expertise. Rather than conform your course to the chapters of a conventional textbook, you are free to modify, supplement, or add to this textbook. This is why we chose to publish Explorations with a Creative Commons Attribution-NonCommercial 4.0 International License (CC BY-NC 4.0), which allows anyone to remix, adapt, transform, and build upon the contents. You can use this book as it is, or alter it by reorganizing, omitting chapters or sections of chapters, assigning only some chapters, or curating chapter selections. The only requirement is that you credit the authors and source, specify the license, and indicate any changes made. In the spirit of open education, this textbook and the content within cannot be used for commercial purposes. To learn more about OER and Creative Commons licensing, as well as specific guidance on how to adapt this book, please see the Instructor's Guide, located at the end of our book.

This textbook started as a grassroots endeavor by four full-time college instructors, brought together by their shared goals of saving students money and piquing student interest in biological anthropology. We were inspired by previous OER creators including the editors of *Perspectives: An Open Invitation to Cultural Anthropology*. With support from our professional communities, colleagues, students, and especially the wonderful authors that wrote the chapters, we published *Explorations* in 2019 and released the second edition in 2023.

This project of love is dedicated to our students, but we are happy that others have benefited as well. This is also an ongoing project. If you see errors or have suggestions please let us know by using the corresponding form on our website (https://explorations.americananthro.org/) or by sending an email to explorationstextbook@gmail.com.

Explorations: Mission and Organization

Mission Statement: To provide a high-quality introductory biological anthropology textbook that is readable, engaging, and accessible to all students. With chapters written by experienced instructors and subject area specialists, this textbook addresses the question of what it means to be human by exploring the origins, evolution, and diversification of primates, especially that of our species, *Homo sapiens*.

Anthropology is the study of humanity, in all its biological and cultural aspects, past and present. It is a four-field discipline comprising biological anthropology, cultural anthropology, archaeology, and linguistic anthropology. The focus of this book is biological anthropology, which explores who we are from biological, evolutionary, and adaptive perspectives.

We lay the foundation for this inquiry in the first four chapters by introducing the discipline of anthropology, evolutionary theory, molecular biology and genetics, and the forces of evolution. Chapters 5–8 consider the evolutionary, biological, and social aspects of our closest living relatives, nonhuman primates, with whom we share millions of years of evolution. We also learn about how fossils provide material insight into our past. Chapters 9–12 describe prior hominin species and the emergence of Homo sapiens, us! Finally, the last five chapters (Chapters 13–17) explore human biological variation and the concept of race, bioarchaeology and forensic anthropology, human biology and health, and biopolitics of heredity. We include further readings on osteology (Appendix A), primate conservation (Appendix B), human behavioral ecology (Appendix C), and ancient DNA (Appendix D). To guide your reading, each chapter begins with learning objectives and ends with review questions, along with a list of key terms.

We are honored that you have chosen to use *Explorations: An Open Invitation to Biological Anthropology* in your course(s) and hope that you will enjoy the second edition. If you have any questions, please do not hesitate to reach out.

Sincerely,

Beth Shook, Lara Braff, Katie Nelson, and Kelsie Aguilera

Acknowledgements

We (the editors) are enormously grateful for the community of people who contributed to the development of the second edition of this textbook. In particular, we wish to thank all the authors who were willing to update content or produce new content. We also thank the peer and student reviewers for the time and thought they put into chapter reviews. We thank the International Union for Conservation of Nature (IUCN) SSC Primate Specialist Group for their guidance on the use of images of primates to promote appropriate primate treatment, conservation and welfare.

This edition would not have been possible without the financial support of The Academic Senate for California Community College Open Educational Resources Initiative (ASCCC OERI), and the California State University Chico – University Foundation's Governor's Award.

Copyeditor

Mayumi Shimose Poe

Peer Reviewers:

Belkis Abufau

Bridget Alex

Francisca Alves Cardoso

Amanda Barnes-Kenned

Victoria Berezowski

Samantha Blatt

Jennifer Byrnes

Amy Carattini

Keith Chan

Caroline Clark Rivera

Megan Cleary

Shannon Clinkinbeard

Karen Daar

Elizabeth Doyle

Alejandra Estrin Dashe

Heather Gill-Frerking

Janeal Godfrey

Alexis Gray

Laura Greathouse

Corinna Guenther

Lindsay Hunter

Kelsie Johnson

Suzanne Kempke

Katie King

Sarah Lacy

David S. Leitner

Lydia Light

Vasiliki Louka

Christopher Loy

Ashley Magana

Giovanni Magginetti

Ashley Maxwell

Roxanne Mayoral

Jayashree Mazumder

Thomas McIlwraith

Carolyn Orbann

Andrew Petto

Jessica Proctor

Alexandra Rocca

Daniela Rodrigues

Ben Schaefer

Yasmine Shereen

Victoria Swenson

Lauren Taylor-Hill

Amy Todd

Lori Tremblay

Alberto Vigil

Erin Waxenbaum

Amanda Williams

Kristin Wilson

Heather Worne

Jessica Yann

Bonnie Yoshida-Levine

Aaron Young

Samantha Young

Jennifer Zovar

California Community College Regional Liaisons

David Leitner

Ashley Magana

Kristin Wilson

Samantha Young

Student Reviewers

Abdikhaliq Ali

Rebecca Buckler

Joseph DiGerlando

Jessalyn Fowler

Brooke Gorman

Emily Lindsay

Kuba Maldonado

Ramon Martinez

Alisandria Ramirez

Dufault, Randy

Savannah Suarez

Hannah Swartzel-Rausch

Naomi Tracy-Hegg

Billy Utecht

Cover art

Adapted from Stewart William's first edition cover design by Katie Nelson

Illustrator

Mary Nelson

Cartography

Students and Faculty of Geo Place, California State University, Chico

DEDICATION

This text is dedicated to our students.

INSTRUCTORS' GUIDE FOR EXPLORATIONS

Explorations: An Adaptable Open Educational Resource

Open Educational Resources (OER)

Unlike a traditional textbook, *Explorations* is an Open Educational Resources (OER). OER are teaching, learning, and research materials that have been openly licensed and that come in many forms: books, case studies, software, reference materials, assessments, assignments, tutorials, slides, videos, and more.

OER emerged in response to rising textbook costs in higher education. According to the Bureau of Labor Statistics, there has been a 1,041% percent increase in textbook prices from January 1977 to June 2015. Students often feel compelled to buy these expensive textbooks to succeed in their courses. Recognizing that textbook costs exacerbate existing socioeconomic and racial disparities in education, some instructors and institutions have sought to provide *free,* high-quality teaching and learning resources. As more instructors adopt OER, students are saving hundreds of dollars every semester, and large systems, like the University System of Georgia, calculate cumulative savings to be in the millions of dollars.

In addition to cost savings, OER have the added benefits of coming in a variety of accessible formats, being available on the first day of class, and having an open license that permits reuse and adaptation without a need to obtain permission from the copyright holder. For more information on OER and its benefits, we suggest The OER Starter Kit and Affordable Learning Georgia.

Creative Commons Licenses

Copyright law automatically protects all creative works, but a copyright holder may waive some or all rights by placing them under an open license or in the public domain. The most commonly used license types are Creative Commons(CC) licenses. The Creative Commons was established in 2001 to allow copyright holders a standardized, flexible, and legally sound way to express the conditions under which others can use the work.

Creative Commons offers six copyright licenses. Each license requires users to provide attribution (BY) to the creator when the material is used and shared. The most permissive CC license requires only this attribution (CC BY). Beyond that, creators may select additional limitations including Share Alike (SA), Non Commercial (NC), and No Derivatives (ND). The six licenses, and descriptions of the limiting terms are provided in the image below (Figure 1), and more information can be found on Creative Commons website.

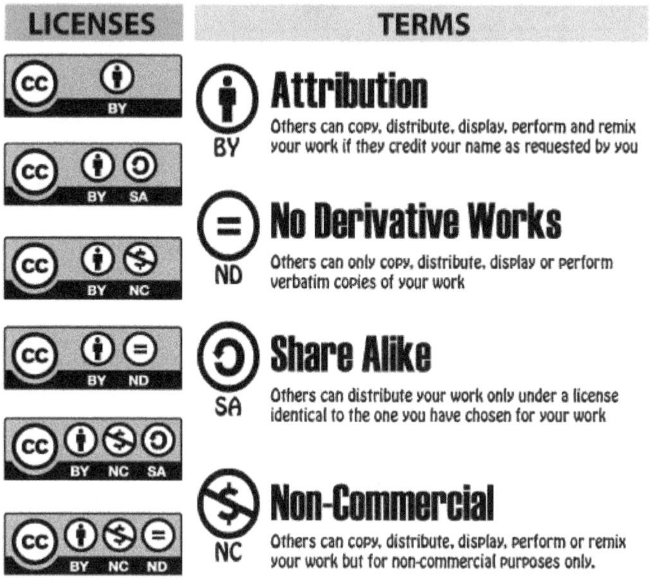

Figure 1: Creative Commons licenses and their terms. Credit: Understanding Creative Commons Licenses (Figure 3.1) by Das and Kinjilal 2015 is under a CC BY-SA 3.0 License.

**Figure 2: Creative Commons licenses from least restrictive (top) to most restrictive (bottom).
Credit: Adapted from Icons by The Noun Project.by Creative Commons and is under a CC BY
4.0 License**

License	Terms
CC 0	**All Rights Granted/Public Domain:** Licensors waive all rights and place a work in the public domain.
CC BY	**Attribution:** Others can copy, distribute, display, perform and remix your work if they credit your name as requested by you. This is the most accommodating of licenses offered. Recommended for maximum dissemination and use of licensed materials.
CC BY-SA	**Attribution-ShareAlike:** This license lets others remix, adapt, and build upon your work even for commercial purposes, as long as they credit you and license their new creations under the identical terms. This license is often compared to "copyleft" free and open source software licenses. All new works based on yours will carry the same license, so any derivatives will also allow commercial use. This is the license used by Wikipedia, and is recommended for materials that would benefit from incorporating content from Wikipedia and similarly licensed projects.
CC BY-ND	**Attribution-NoDerivs** This license lets others reuse the work for any purpose, including commercially; however, it cannot be shared with others in adapted form, and credit must be provided to you.
CC BY-NC	**Attribution-NonComercial:** This license lets others remix, adapt, and build upon your work non-commercially, and although their new works must also acknowledge you and be non-commercial, they don't have to license their derivative works on the same terms.
CC BY-NC-SA	**Attribution-NonComercial-ShareAlike:** This license lets others remix, adapt, and build upon your work non-commercially, as long as they credit you and license their new creations under the identical terms.
CC BY-NC-ND	**Attribution-NonComercial-NoDerivs:** This license is the most restrictive of our six main licenses, only allowing others to download your works and share them with others as long as they credit you, but they can't change them in any way or use them commercially.

The Creative Commons also has a Public Domain dedication (CC0 or CC Zero), which allows creators to give up their copyright and place works in the worldwide public domain to be used without any restrictions (Figure 2).

Figure 3: Creative Commons Public Domain
license (CC0 or CC Zero). Credit: CC0 "No Rights
Reserved" Marker by Creative Commons is
under a CC BY 4.0 License.

CC licenses come at no cost, and works do not need to be registered. CC licensing an original work only requires selecting the license that suits the creator's needs, communicating them clearly to the reader, and including a link to that Creative Commons license. It can be as simple as adding the following statement to the title page: "© 2022. This work is licensed under a CC BY-NC 4.0 license."

CC Licenses and OER

According to <u>David Wiley's definition of "openness,"</u> true OER grant legal permission to engage in the "five R activities": reuse, retain, revise, remix, and redistribute.

- Retain: make, own, and control a copy of the resource.
- Revise: edit, adapt, and modify your copy of the resource.
- Remix: combine your original or revised copy of the resource with other existing material to create something new.
- Reuse: use your original, revised, or remixed copy of the resource publicly.
- Redistribute: share copies of your original, revised, or remixed copy of the resource with others.

The following image (Figure 3) characterizes the six CC licenses on a scale of most to least freedom.

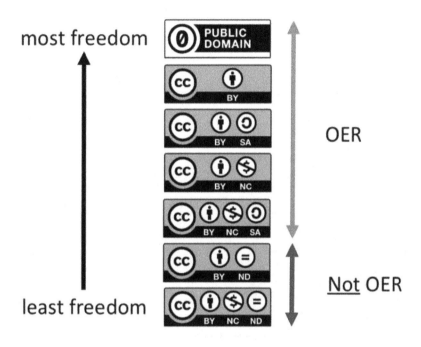

Figure 4: A graphic rendering how much liberty different Creative Commons licenses grant. Credit: Spectrum of open licenses by Cable Green is used under a CC BY 4.0 License.

Note that CC licensed materials that include "No Derivatives (ND)" are not considered OER because they do not allow the public to revise or remix the material and share them publicly. Therefore, such materials do not meet the 5R criteria (or any of the major OER definitions).

For more information, see the <u>Open Access and OER Handout</u> by Anita Walz.

Adapting OER

OER support academic freedom because they promote adapting content by revising and remixing material. When you adapt content, you are able to customize the resource(s) to the topics you teach, the order in which you teach them, your teaching style, and the preparation of your students.

Adaptation refers to modifying, revising, expanding, contracting, or otherwise altering the text. Perhaps you disagree with how a theory is presented, or you wish to replace one example with another one you know better, or you want to shorten a chapter. The changes you make may be small or large scale. For example, you could:

- make word-level edits to make the writing more accessible to your readers;

- remove some sections or highlight boxes;
- use only a portion of the text;
- update with current information;
- add media or links to other resources;
- add your own (or other openly licensed) case studies;
- translate the entire manuscript into another language; or
- use open pedagogy, a method that engages students as creators of information.

Unlike copyrighted materials that forbid the manipulation of the work, OER encourage it. *Explorations* has a CC BY-NC 4.0 License that permits users to *distribute, remix, adapt, and build upon the material in any medium or format for noncommercial purposes* (as long as attribution is given to the creator). We encourage you to customize this resource for your classroom needs.

To learn more about OER Adaptation, we recommend the BC Campus Open Education Adaptation Guide. Here, we discuss how to adapt *Explorations* using two different platforms: Pressbooks and LibreTexts.

Pressbooks: Cloning a Book or Importing Content

Explorations is published using the Pressbooks platform. To access Pressbooks to publish your own version, you either need to have an account through your academic institution or you can become a Self-Publisher for a reasonable monthly cost. You then have two options: You can clone and adapt Explorations, or you can create your own book and import chapters from Explorations (and other sources) and then remix and/or revise them. Pressbooks is easy to use and creates EPUB and PDF exports that are simple for students to access and read.

Cloning

Cloning a book involves making a new copy of it. During the cloning process, the book that you copy is called the source book. The new copy, called the target book, is added to your Pressbooks network (account). Only a public, openly licensed book that is published in a Pressbooks network—such as Explorations—can be cloned.

Once the book has been cloned, you are free to delete sections or chapters, edit content, or add new material. For more information on cloning, including step-by-step instructions on how to clone a book, see the chapter "Clone a Book" in the Pressbooks User Guide.

Importing

The import tool enables you to add content from one or more sources into a book that you have created. You might add a chapter or two (or more!) from Explorations, or you might have material of your own that you have created in a different file format that you now want to add to your book. This is a good option if, for example, you wanted to create a four-fields anthropology book (perhaps including content from our sister OER Perspectives and Traces), or perhaps an upper-division biological anthropology book, with some Explorations content for background.

The import tool in Pressbooks can work with the following file formats:

- EPUB (.epub)
- Word document (.docx)
- OpenOffice documents (.odt)

- Pressbooks/WordPress XML (.xml or .wxr)
- Web page (.html or URL).

You may need to clean up the formatting of material that you use before adding it to your book. Also, be aware that you need to create at least the shell of a book before you start importing content. You cannot import content (including an entire book) directly into the network; you can import it only into an existing book.

For more information on importing, including step-by-step instructions on how to use the import tool, see Bring Your Content into Pressbooks in the Pressbooks User Guide.

This Pressbooks section is adapted from CUNY Pressbooks Guide by Andrew McKinney, Rachael Nevins, and Elizabeth Arestyl. It is licensed under a CC BY-NC 4.0 License.

LibreTexts Remixer

LibreTexts houses a large free repository of OER organized by discipline. You can find *Explorations* by going to LibreTexts, then click: Explore the Libraries > Social Sciences > Bookshelves > Anthropology > Biological Anthropology > Explorations.

To adapt *Explorations* for your course, you must:

1. Establish a free account for LibreTexts
2. Fork the page(s) you wish to edit
3. Make changes and save

We will now explore each of these steps.

1. Establish your account.

After you open *Explorations*, you will notice a gray bar across the top of the page. Click "Sign in," on the right hand side, to request a free account using your .edu email address. Once LibreTexts receives your request and creates your account, you will receive an email with a prompt to change your password and finish setting up your account (be sure to check your spam folder if you don't receive this email within 24–48 hours after submitting your request). If you need help, please contact info@libretexts.org.

You can access your account from the Tools link, in the blue toolbar, on the left-hand side of the screen. When you are in your account, the menu bar turns black, displaying options to edit content:

- Edit: Allows you to edit the page you are on.
- New: Allows you to create a new book, chapter, unit, or page.
- Remixer: Redirects you to the LibreTexts Remixer where you can mix content from across LibreTexts libraries to create new OER.
- Downloads: Redirects you to the Download Center for the library you are in. The Download Center contains pre-formatted copies of every text in the LibreTexts libraries for easy printing at sites such as lulu.com or Amazon.

Note: Accounts are library specific. You can only save text to a library in which you have an account and you can only edit a text housed within that library. However, content from another library can be accessed and integrated into whichever library you are working in. For example, if you are working within the Social Sciences library and want to add content from the Humanities library, you may do so. But, with a Social Sciences account, you would not be able to edit a book housed within the Humanities library.

2.   Fork the section you wish to edit.

After you select the Remixer tool, you will notice the Forker icon. Once a page, chapter, or book in LibreTexts has been added to your sandbox, it remains connected to its original source. If you want to edit the content, you must break that connection through a process referred to as "forking." Forking makes a copy of a page that is no longer connected to the original source so your edits will not alter the original source material and changes to the original source material will not alter your work. Note that forking happens at the page level, so it is limited to the sections you wish to modify. If a page has not yet been "forked," you will see the fork icon next to the title. The advantage of forking is that you maintain complete control over the content you are editing.

3.   Editing pages in LibreTexts.

After forking the page, you will be able to edit, add, delete, and/or import content. When you have finished your edits, you can save and share the page(s) you've modified.

For more information about the Remixer Tool, see the LibreTexts Construction Guide.

A Word of Caution

When adapting OER, please be aware that some CC licenses cannot be mixed. It is important to identify the license you plan to apply to your material and the licenses of the materials (both text and images) you intend to use. The license you apply to your final product needs to maintain the limitations of the licenses of the content you use. For example, if you use content from *Explorations*, your product must be similarly licensed as CC BY-NC or by a license that maintains those limitations (like CC BY-NC-SA). While the overall text in *Explorations* is CC BY-NC, some images are individually licensed with a stricter license (oftentimes, CC BY-NC-SA); in such cases, the image license is included in its attribution.

For more information, see: Creating OER and Combining Licenses by TheOGRepository.

Explorations: More Than a Textbook

Because *Explorations* is written for students, we have developed resources with them—and their instructors—in mind.

Accessibility

OER creators and OER publishing platforms (like Pressbooks and LibreText) typically prioritize accessibility. Both the eBook and PDF versions of *Explorations* were created using Pressbooks, and the Pressbooks Accessibility page provides resources about this product including their Voluntary Product Accessibility Template [VPAT®] and their Accessibility Standards and Commitments. *Explorations* editors have made their best efforts to meet the requirements of the Americans with Disabilities Act (42 U.S.C. § 12100 et seq.) and section 508 of the Rehabilitation Act of 1973, as amended (29 U.S.C. § 794d).

Explorations adheres to the following accessibility recommendations put forth by the Academic Senate for California Community Colleges *Open Educational Resources Initiative*:

• Pages use structured headings [Heading 1, Heading 2, etc.] and styles accessible to a screen reader.

- Text is easily readable in terms of font, color contrast, and spacing.
- Lists are created using the bullet or numbered list tool and not formatted manually.
- Videos are accurately captioned.
- Audio files have a complete and accurate transcript.
- All images have appropriate alternative texts that connect the image to the context and content on the page.
- Alternative text does not contain "image of," "picture of," or file extensions.
- Objects (including tables and charts) have alternative text that connects the resource to the learning in a meaningful manner.
- Tables have correct column and row header designation so that screen readers can read table cells in correct order.
- Color is not used as the only method to convey meaning.
- Hyperlink text is unique and meaningful.
- Interactive content [H5P, Slides, etc.] is created in an accessible format.

In addition, *Explorations* is available in the following accessible formats:

- eBook
- PDF
- Print (for a cost on Amazon or other publishing platforms).

Ancillary Materials

As with the first edition, we are pleased to offer the following materials to help instructors teach *Explorations, 2nd edition* and help students master the content:

- Slides: Presentation slides for each chapter and appendix can be downloaded from our website.
- Test bank: Using this form, faculty may request a copy of the test bank for *Explorations*. To protect the integrity of this test bank, we request verification information before we release it to faculty (the testbank is never distributed to students). A file is not currently available for adding the test bank to learning management systems (LMS).
- Matrix Notes: These notes are based on a guided reading system that is backed by research and developed by Inver Hills Community College Reading Instructor Kathryn Klopfleish. Available for download as chapter-specific Google Docs, the note-taking form is tailored to help college students develop strong reading and comprehension skills.
- Lab and activities manual: Our manual includes labs or activities for each chapter and appendix. Each lab or activity is under a CC BY-NC 4.0 License and includes: learning objectives, a list of required supplies, instructions for faculty, estimated duration, and student worksheets. The labs and activities can be individually printed by faculty for in-class use or packaged into course lab books for the term. Many labs are designed to be easily adapted for online learning courses.

How you decide to use *Explorations* and its ancillary materials is completely up to you! We intentionally gave our book a Creative Commons license in order to provide students with a free, high learning resource, while giving instructors the flexibility to adapt the textbook. Feel free to assign the entire textbook or just the chapters (or parts of chapters) that support your course learning objectives and your approach to teaching biological anthropology. We would love to hear from you: reach out to us (using the Feedback form on our *Explorations* website) with suggestions and updates to help us improve the next edition!

References

Das, Anup Kumar and Uma Kinjilal. 2015. *"Open Access for Library Schools, Module 1: Introduction to Open Access."* In Introduction to Open Access. Edited by Sanjaya Mishra and M.P. Satija. *Paris: UNESCO.*

1.

INTRODUCTION TO BIOLOGICAL ANTHROPOLOGY

Katie Nelson, Ph.D., Inver Hills Community College

Lara Braff, Ph.D., Grossmont College

Beth Shook, Ph.D., California State University, Chico

Kelsie Aguilera, M.A., University of Hawai'i: Leeward Community College

This chapter is a revision from "Chapter 1: Introduction to Biological Anthropology" by Katie Nelson, Lara Braff, Beth Shook, and Kelsie Aguilera. In Explorations: An Open Invitation to Biological Anthropology, first edition, edited by Beth Shook, Katie Nelson, Kelsie Aguilera, and Lara Braff, which is licensed under CC BY-NC 4.0.

Learning Objectives

- Describe anthropology and the four subdisciplines.
- Explain the main anthropological approaches.
- Define biological anthropology, describe its key questions, and identify major subfields.
- Explain key components of the scientific method.
- Differentiate between hypotheses, theories, and laws.
- Differentiate science from other ways of knowing.

Diving in caves along the Caribbean coast of Mexico, archaeologist Octavio del Rio and his team spotted something unusual in the sand 26 feet below the ocean surface. As they swam closer, they suspected it could be a bone—and likely a very ancient one, as this cave system is inaccessible today without modern diving equipment. However, in the distant past, these caves were dry land formations high above the ocean. The divers ended up recovering not just one but many bones from the site. Eventually they were able to reconstruct an 80% complete human skeleton that they named "Eve of Naharon." Dated to 13,600 years ago, she is (as of today) the oldest known North American skeleton (TANN 2018).

Who was Eve? What was her life like? How did she end up in the cave? What can we learn about her from the bones she left behind? Anthropologists have determined that Eve was 4.6 feet tall, had a broken back, and died in her early 20s. Although it is rare to find an ancient, nearly complete skeleton in the ocean depths, Eve is not the only such find. In underwater caves along Mexico's Yucatan Peninsula, archaeologists have found eight well-preserved skeletons dated between 9,000 to 13,000 years old. With each new discovery—whether it is a skeleton in North America, fossil footprints in Tanzania, or a mandible with teeth in China—we come another step closer to understanding the evolution of our species.

Biological anthropologists study when and how human beings evolved; their intriguing findings are the focus of this book. Biological anthropology is one of four **subdisciplines** within anthropology; the others are cultural anthropology, archaeology, and linguistic anthropology. All anthropological subdisciplines seek to better understand what it means to be human.

What is Anthropology?

Why are people so diverse (Figure 1.1)? Some people live in the frigid Arctic tundra, others in the arid deserts of sub-Saharan Africa, and still others in the dense forests of Papua New Guinea. Human beings speak more than 6,000 distinct languages. Some people are barely five feet tall while others stoop to fit through a standard door frame. What makes people, around the world, look, speak, and behave differently from one another? And what do all humans share in common?

Figure 1.1: Despite superficial differences among individuals, humans are 99.9% genetically similar to one another. Credit: Humans (Figure 1.1) original to Explorations: An Open Invitation to Biological Anthropology is a collective work under a CC BY-NC-SA 4.0 License. [Includes Untitled by Mission de l'ONU au Mali – UN Mission in Mali/Gema Cortes, CC BY-NC-SA 2.0; Untitled in Middle East by Mark Fischer, CC-BY-SA 2.0; Smiling Blonde Girl by Egor Gribanov, CC BY 2.0; UNDP Supports Mongolian Herders by United Nations Photo, CC BY-NC-ND].

Anthropology is a discipline that explores human differences and similarities by investigating our biological and cultural complexity, past and present. Derived from Greek, the word –*anthropos* means "human" and –*logy* refers to the "study of." Therefore, anthropology is, by definition, the study of humans. Anthropologists are not the only scholars to focus on the human condition; biologists, sociologists, psychologists, and others also examine human nature and societies. However, anthropology is a uniquely dynamic, multifaceted discipline that emerged from a deep-seated curiosity about who we are as a species.

The Subdisciplines

In the United States, the discipline of anthropology includes four subdisciplines: cultural anthropology, biological anthropology, archaeology, and linguistic anthropology. In addition, applied anthropology is sometimes called the fifth subdiscipline (Figure 1.2). Each of the subdisciplines provides a distinct perspective on the human experience. Some (like biological anthropology) use the scientific method to develop theories about human origins, evolution, material remains, or behaviors. Others (like cultural anthropology) use humanistic and interpretive approaches to understand human beliefs, languages, behaviors, cultures, and societies. Findings from all subdisciplines, together, contribute to a multifaceted appreciation of human biocultural experiences, past and present.

Cultural Anthropology

Cultural anthropologists focus on similarities and differences among living persons and societies. They suspend their sense of what is expected in their own culture in order to understand other perspectives without judging them (**cultural relativism**). They learn these perspectives through **participant-observation** fieldwork. Beyond describing another way of life, cultural anthropologists ask broader questions about humankind: Are human emotions universal or culturally distinct? Is maternal behavior learned or innate? How and why do groups migrate to new places? For cultural anthropologists, no aspect of human life is outside their purview: They study art, religion, medicine, migration, natural disasters, even video gaming. While many cultural anthropologists are intrigued by human diversity, they recognize that people around the world share much in common.

One famous U.S. cultural anthropologist, Margaret Mead (1901–1978, Figure 1.3), conducted cross-cultural studies of gender

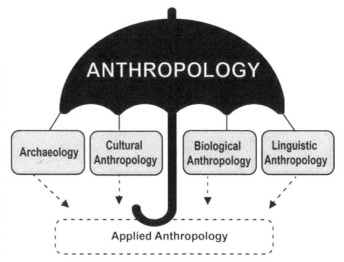

Figure 1.2: The discipline of anthropology has four subdisciplines: archaeology, cultural anthropology, biological anthropology, and linguistic anthropology, as well as an applied dimension. Credit: Subdisciplines of anthropology (Figure 1.8) original to Explorations: An Open Invitation to Biological Anthropology by Mary Nelson is under a CC BY-NC 4.0 License.

and socialization. In the early twentieth century, people in the U.S. wondered if the emotional turbulence exhibited by American adolescents was caused by the biology of puberty, and thus natural and universal. To find out, Mead went to the Samoan Islands, where she lived for several months getting to know Samoan teenagers. She learned that Samoan adolescence was relatively tranquil and happy. Based on her fieldwork, Mead wrote *Coming of Age in Samoa*, a best-selling book that was both sensational and scandalous (Mead 1928). In it, she critiqued U.S. parenting as restrictive in contrast to Samoan parenting, which allowed teenagers to freely explore their community and even their sexuality. Ultimately, she argued that nurture (i.e., socialization) more than nature (i.e., biology) shaped adolescent development. Despite her expressed relativism, she has been critiqued recently for exploiting the people she studied.

Figure 1.3: Margaret Mead, circa 1948. Credit: Margaret Mead by Internet Archive Book Images has been designated to the public domain (CC0). [Image from page 47 of "A brief expedition into science at the American Museum of Natural History" (1969).]

Cultural anthropologists do not always travel far to learn about human experiences. In the 1980s, American anthropologist Philippe Bourgois (1956–) asked how pockets of extreme poverty persist in the United States, a country widely perceived as wealthy with an overall high quality of life compared to other countries. To answer this question, he lived with Puerto Rican drug dealers in East Harlem, contextualizing their experiences both historically and presently, in terms of ongoing social marginalization and institutional racism. Rather than blame drug dealers for their choices, Bourgois argued that both individual choices and social inequality can trap people in the overlapping worlds of drugs and poverty (Bourgois 2003).

Linguistic Anthropology

The study of people is incomplete without attending to language, a defining trait of human beings. While other animals have communication systems, only humans have complex symbolic languages—and more than 6,000 of them! Human language makes it possible to teach and learn, plan and think abstractly, coordinate our efforts, and contemplate our own demise. Linguistic anthropologists ask questions like: How did language first emerge? How has it evolved and diversified over time? How has language helped our species? How can linguistic style convey social identity? How does language influence our worldview? Some linguistic anthropologists track the emergence and diversification of languages, while others focus on language use in social context. Still others explore how language is crucial to socialization: children learn their culture and identities through language and nonverbal forms of communication (Ochs and Schieffelin 2017; Figure 1.4).

One line of linguistic anthropological research focuses on the relationships among language, thought, and culture. For example, Benjamin Whorf (1897–1941) observed that whereas the English language has grammatical tenses to indicate past, present, and future, the Hopi language does not; instead, it indicates whether or not something has "manifested." Whorf argued that this grammatical difference causes English and Hopi speakers to think about time in distinct ways: English speakers think about time in a linear way, while Hopi think about time in terms of a cycle of things or events that have manifested or are manifesting (Whorf 1956). Based on his research, Whorf developed a strong version of the **Sapir-Whorf hypothesis** (also known as linguistic relativity), which states that language shapes thought. Some critics, like German American linguist Ekkehart Malotki (1938–), recognized that English and Hopi tenses differ but argued against Whorf by claiming that the Hopi language does, in fact, have linguistic terms for time and that a linear sense of time may be universal (Malotki 1983). Nevertheless, anthropological linguists tend to see human languages as a unique form of communication, linked to our ability to think and process our world.

Figure 1.4: From the moment they are born, children learn through language and nonverbal forms of communication. Credit: Babytalk by Torbein Rønning is under a CC BY-NC-ND 2.0 License.

Archaeology

Archaeologists focus on material remains—tools, pottery, rock art, shelters, seeds, bones, and other objects—to better understand people and societies. Archaeologists ask specific questions like: How did people in a particular area live? How did they utilize their environment? What happened to their society? They also ask general questions about humankind: When did our ancestors begin to walk on two legs? How and why did they leave Africa? Why did humans first develop agriculture? How did the first cities develop?

One critical method that archaeologists use to answer these questions is excavation, which involves carefully digging and removing sediment to uncover material remains while recording their context. Take the example of Kathleen Kenyon (1906–1978), a British archaeologist and one of few female archaeologists in the 1940s. While excavating at Jericho, which dates back to 10,000 BCE (Figure 1.5), she discovered city structures and cemeteries built during the Early Bronze Age (3,200 YBP in Europe). Based on her findings, she argued that Jericho is the oldest city continuously occupied by different groups of people for thousands of years (Kenyon 1979).

Figure 1.5: Archaeologists, including Kathleen Kenyon, have helped unearth the foundations of ancient dwellings at Jericho. Credit: Jerycho8 by Abraham Sobkowski has been designated to the public domain (CC0).

While most archaeologists study the past, some excavate at contemporary sites to gain new perspectives on present-day societies. For example, participants in the Garbage Project, which began in the 1970s in Tucson, Arizona, excavate modern landfills as if they were a conventional dig site. They have found that what people say they throw out differs from what is actually in the trash. The landfill holds large amounts of paper products (that people claim to recycle) as well as construction debris (Rathje and Murphy 1992). This finding indicates the need to create more environmentally conscious waste-disposal practices.

Biological Anthropology

Biological anthropology—the focus of this book—is the study of human evolution and biological variation. Some biological anthropologists study our closest living relatives—monkeys and apes—to learn how nonhuman and human primates are alike and how they differ both biologically and behaviorally (Figure 1.6). Other biological anthropologists focus on extinct human species and subspecies, asking questions like: What did they look like? What did they eat? When did they start to speak? How did they adapt to new environments? Still other biological anthropologists focus on modern human diversity, asking questions about the evolution of traits, like lactose tolerance or skin color, that differ between populations. Throughout this book, we will learn about biological anthropological research that explores our nonhuman primate cousins, the origins of **hominins** (i.e. humans and fossil human relatives), how they adapted over time, and how we – modern humans – continue to change.

Figure 1.6: Chimpanzees are the nonhuman primate that is most closely related to humans. Credit: Chimpanzees by Klaus Post is under a CC BY 2.0 License.

Applied Anthropology

Sometimes considered the fifth subdiscipline, applied anthropology involves the practical application of anthropological theories, methods, and findings to solve real-world problems. Applied anthropologists span the subdisciplines. An applied archaeologist might work in cultural resource management to assess a potentially significant archaeological site unearthed during a construction project. An applied cultural anthropologist could work for a technology company that seeks to understand how people interact with their products in order to design them better. Applied anthropologists are employed outside of academic settings, in public and private sectors, including business firms, advertising companies, city government, law enforcement, hospitals, nongovernmental organizations, and even the military.

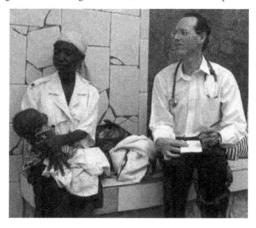

Figure 1.7: Paul Farmer in Haiti. Credit: PEF-with-mom-and-baby—Quy-Ton-12-2003 1-1-310 by Cjmadson is under a CC BY 3.0 License.

Trained as both a physician and anthropologist, Paul Farmer (1959–2022, Figure 1.7) demonstrated the potential of applied anthropology to improve lives. As a college student in North Carolina, Farmer became interested in the Haitian migrants working on nearby farms. This led him to visit Haiti, the most resource-poor country in the Western Hemisphere, where he was struck by the deprived state of its health care facilities. Years later, he would return to Haiti, as a physician, to treat diseases that had been largely eradicated in the United States, such as tuberculosis and cholera. Drawing on his anthropological training, he also did fieldwork and wrote books that contextualize the suffering of Haitians in relation to historical, social, and political conditions (Farmer 2006). Finally, as an applied anthropologist, he took action by co-founding Partners in Health, a nonprofit organization that establishes health clinics in resource-poor countries and trains local staff to administer care.

Anthropological Approaches

Each of the four main anthropological subdisciplines contributes to our understanding of humankind by exploring cultures, languages, material remains, and biological adaptations. To study these phenomena, anthropologists draw upon distinct research approaches, including **holism**, comparison, dynamism, and fieldwork.

Holism

Anthropologists are interested in the *whole* of humanity. We look at the interactions among several aspects of our complex bodies or societies, rather than focusing on a singular aspect (Figure 1.8). For example, a biological anthropologist studying the social behaviors of a monkey species in South America may not only observe how they interact with one another, but also how physical adaptations, foraging patterns, ecological conditions, and habitat changes also affect their behaviors. By focusing on only one factor, the anthropologist would attain an incomplete understanding of the species' social life. A cultural anthropologist studying marriage in a small village in India would not only consider local gender norms but also family networks, laws regarding marriage, religious rules, and economic factors. All of these aspects can influence marital practices in a given context. In both examples, the anthropologist is using a holistic approach by considering the multiple interrelated and intersecting factors that comprise a given phenomena.

Figure 1.8: By using a holistic approach, anthropologists learn how different aspects of humanity interact with and influence one another. Credit: Holism (Figure 1.2) original to *Explorations: An Open Invitation to Biological Anthropology* by Mary Nelson is under a CC BY-NC 4.0 License.

Comparison

Anthropologists use comparative approaches to compare and contrast data from different populations, from groups within a population, or from the same group over time. For example: How do humans today differ from prior *Homo sapiens* populations? How does Egyptian society today compare to ancient Egyptian society? How do male and female behaviors differ within a given human society or a particular primate group? Comparative analyses help us understand commonalities and differences within or across species, groups, or time.

Dynamism

Comparative analysis is facilitated by the fact that humans are extremely dynamic. Our ability to change, both biologically and culturally, has enabled us to persist over millions of years and to thrive in different environments. Anthropologists ask about all kinds of changes: short-term and long-term, temporary and permanent, cultural and biological. For example, a cultural anthropologist might look at how people in a relatively isolated society are affected by globalization. A linguistic anthropologist might explore how a hybrid form of language, like Spanglish, emerged. An archaeologist might study how climate change influenced the emergence of agriculture. A biological anthropologist might consider how diseases affecting our ancestors led to physical changes that persist today. All of these examples highlight the dynamic nature of human bodies and societies.

Fieldwork

Figure 1.9: Anthropologist Katie Nelson conducting fieldwork with undocumented Mexican immigrant college students. Credit: Ethnographic interview by Luke Berhow is under a CC BY-NC 4.0 License.

Throughout this book, you will read examples of anthropological research from around the world. Anthropologists do not only work in laboratories, libraries, or offices. To collect data, they travel to where their data lives, whether it is a city, village, cave, tropical forest, or desert. At their field sites, anthropologists collect data that, depending on subdiscipline, may include interviews with local peoples (Figure 1.9), examples of language in use, skeletal features, or cultural remains like stone tools. While anthropologists ask an array of questions and use diverse methods to answer their research questions, they share this commitment to conducting research in the field.

What is Biological Anthropology?

Biological anthropology uses a scientific and evolutionary approach to answer many of the same questions that all anthropologists are concerned with: What does it mean to be human? Where do we come from? Who are we today? Biological anthropologists are concerned with exploring how humans vary biologically, how humans adapt to their changing environments, and how humans have evolved over time and continue to evolve today. Some biological anthropologists also study what humans and nonhuman primates have in common and how we differ.

You may have heard biological anthropology referred to by another name—physical anthropology. Physical anthropology is a discipline that dates to as far back as the eighteenth century, when it focused mostly on physical variation among humans. Some early physical anthropologists were also physicians or anatomists interested in comparing and contrasting the human form. These researchers dedicated themselves to measuring bodies and skulls (anthropometry and craniometry) in great detail (Figure 1.10). Many also acted under the misguided racist belief that human biological races existed and that it was possible to differentiate between, or even rank, such races by measuring differences in human anatomy. Anthropologists today agree that there are no biological human races and that all humans alive today are members of the same species, *Homo sapiens*, and subspecies, *Homo sapiens sapiens*. We recognize that the differences we can see between peoples' bodies are due to a wide variety of factors, including environment, diet, activities, and genetic makeup.

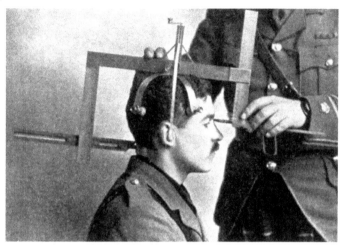

Figure 1.10: An anthropometric device used to measure a subject's head, circa 1913. Credit: Head-Measurer of Tremearne (side view) by A.J.N. Tremearne, Man 15 (1914): 87–88 is in the public domain.

The subdiscipline has changed a great deal since these early years. Biological anthropologists no longer identify human differences in order to assign people to groups, like races. The focus is instead on understanding how and why human and primate variation developed through evolutionary processes. The name for the subdiscipline has transitioned in recent years (from *physical anthropology* to *biological anthropology*) to reflect these changes. Many believe the term *biological anthropology* better reflects the subdiscipline's focus today, which includes genetic and molecular research.

The Scope of Biological Anthropology

Just as anthropology as a discipline is wide ranging and holistic, so too is the subdiscipline of biological anthropology. There are at least six **subfields** within biological anthropology (Figure 1.11): primatology, paleoanthropology, molecular anthropology, bioarchaeology, forensic anthropology, and human biology. Each subfield focuses on a different dimension of what it means to be human from a biological perspective. Through their varied research in these subfields, biological anthropologists try to answer the following key questions:

- What is our place in nature? How are we related to other organisms? What makes us unique?
- What are our origins? What influenced our evolution?
- How and when did we move/migrate across the globe?
- How are humans around the world today different from and similar to each other? What influences these patterns of variation? What are the patterns of our recent evolution and how do we continue to evolve?

The terms *subfield* and *subdiscipline* are very similar and are often used interchangeably. In this book we use *subdiscipline* to refer to the four major areas of focus that make up the discipline of anthropology: biological anthropology, cultural anthropology, archaeological anthropology, and linguistic anthropology. When we use the term *subfield* we are referring to the different specializations within biological anthropology.

Primatology

Primatologists study the anatomy, behavior, ecology, and genetics of living and extinct nonhuman primates, including apes, monkeys, tarsiers, lemurs, and lorises. Primatology research gives us insights into how evolution has shaped our species, since nonhuman primates are our closest living biological relatives. Through such studies, we have learned that all primates share a suite of traits. Primates, for instance, have nails instead of claws, possess hands that can grasp and manipulate objects (Figure 1.12), invest great amounts of time and energy in raising a small number of offspring, and employ complex social behaviors. Behavioral studies, such as those by Jane Goodall of wild chimpanzees and others, reveal that great apes are like humans in that they have families and form strong maternal-infant relationships. Gorillas mourn the deaths of their group members, and they exhibit behaviors similar to humans such as playing and tickling. Importantly, the work of Goodall, Karen B. Strier (see Appendix B), and others focus on primate conservation: They have brought attention to the fact that 60% of primates are currently threatened with extinction (Estrada et al. 2017).

Figure 1.11: Biological anthropology has at least six subfields. Credit: Subfields of biological anthropology (Figure 1.16) original to *Explorations: An Open Invitation to Biological Anthropology* by Mary Nelson is under a CC BY-NC 4.0 License.

Paleoanthropology

Paleoanthropologists study human ancestors from the distant past to learn how, why, and where they evolved. Because these ancestors lived before there were written records, paleoanthropologists have to rely on various types of physical evidence to come to their conclusions. This evidence includes fossilized remains (particularly fossilized bones; Figure 1.13), DNA, artifacts such as stone tools, and the contexts in which these items are found. In recent years, paleoanthropologists have made some monumental discoveries about hominin evolution.

Figure 1.12: A mountain gorillas feeds on insects. Their fingers and fingernails are very similar to that of humans. Credit: **Mountain gorilla finger detail.KMRA** by Kurt Ackermann (username KMRA) is under a CC BY 2.5 License.

Figure 1.13: Donald Johanson and an Australopithecus fossil skull. Credit: **Donald Johanson 2009** by Julesasu has been designated to the public domain (CC0).

These findings helped us learn that human evolution did not occur in a simple, straight line but, rather, branched out in many directions. Most branches were evolutionary "dead ends." Humans are now the only living hominins left on planet Earth. Paleoanthropologists frequently work together with other scientists such as archaeologists, geologists, and paleontologists to interpret and understand the evidence they find. Paleoanthropology is a dynamic subfield of biological anthropology that contributes to our understanding of human origins and evolution.

Molecular Anthropology

Molecular anthropologists use molecular techniques (primarily genetics) to compare ancient and modern populations as well as to study living populations of humans or nonhuman primates. By examining DNA sequences, molecular anthropologists can estimate how closely related two populations are, as well as identify population events, like a population decline, that explain the observed genetic patterns. This information helps scientists trace patterns of migration and identify how people have adapted to different environments over time.

Several molecular anthropologists have recently attracted international recognition for their groundbreaking work. For instance, in 2022, Svante Pääbo won the Nobel Prize in physiology (medicine) for his work extracting the DNA from 40,000-year-old Neanderthal bones and producing the first complete genome of *Homo neanderthalensis*. This was a challenging task because ancient DNA does not preserve well and older extraction techniques tended to become contaminated by the researcher's and other environmental DNA. Pääbo and his team designed specialized clean rooms for handling ancient DNA and made advances in DNA sequencing. Their research helped scientists identify genetic differences between modern humans and Neanderthals and analyze how those differences influence how diseases, such as COVID-19, affect our bodies. Molecular anthropology is a quickly changing field as new techniques and discoveries shape our understanding of ourselves, our ancestors, and our nonhuman primate relatives.

Bioarchaeology

Bioarchaeologists study human skeletal remains along with the surrounding soils and other materials. They use the research methods of skeletal biology, mortuary studies, osteology, and archaeology to answer questions about the lifeways of past populations. Through studying the bones and burials of past peoples, bioarchaeologists search for answers to how people lived and died, including their health, nutrition, diseases, and/or injuries. Most bioarchaeologists study not just individuals but entire populations to reveal biological and cultural patterns.

People have always been intrigued by the remains of the dead, however historically, human bodies were often studied isolated from the ground and location where they were found. Bioarchaeologists emphasize the context in and around where the remains are found, using a biocultural approach that studies humans through an understanding of the interconnectedness of biology, culture, and environment.

Forensic Anthropology

Forensic anthropologists use many of the same techniques as bioarchaeologists to develop a biological profile for unidentified individuals, including estimating sex, age at death, height, ancestry, or other unique identifying features such as skeletal trauma or diseases. They may also go to a crime or accident scene to assist in the search and recovery of human remains, aiding law enforcement teams (Figure 1.14). The popular television show *Bones* told the fictional story of a forensic anthropologist, Dr. Temperance Brennan, who brilliantly interpreted clues from victims' bones to help solve crimes. While the show includes forensic anthropology techniques and responsibilities, it also includes many inaccuracies. For example, forensic anthropologists do not collect trace evidence like hair or fibers, run DNA tests, carry weapons, or solve criminal cases.

Figure 1.14: A remembrance of the victims of El Mozote Massacre in El Salvador. Forensic anthropologists played an important role in identifying the victims of this massacre during the Salvadoran Civil War. Credit: Untitled by Presidencia El Salvador has been designated to the public domain (CC0).

Forensic anthropology is considered an applied area of biological anthropology, because it involves a practical application of anthropological theories, methods, and findings to solve real-world problems. While some forensic anthropologists are academics that work for colleges and universities, others are employed by public safety and law agencies.

Human Biology

Many biological anthropologists do work that falls under the label of "human biology." This type of research explores how the human body is affected by different physical environments, cultural influences, and nutrition. These include studies of **human variation** or the physiological differences among humans around the world. Some of these anthropologists study **human adaptations** to extreme environments, which includes physiological responses and genetic advantages to help them survive. Others are interested in how nutrition and disease affect human growth and development. Biological anthropologists engage in a wide range of research that spans the breadth of human biological diversity.

The six subfields of biological anthropology—primatology, paleoanthropology, molecular anthropology, bioarchaeology, forensic anthropology, and human biology—all help us to understand what it means to be biologically human. From molecular analyses of our cells to studies of our changing skeleton, to research on our nonhuman primate cousins, biological anthropology assists in answering the central question of anthropology: What does it mean to be human? Despite their different foci, all biological anthropologists share a commitment to using a scientific approach to study how we became the complex, adaptable species we are today.

Anthropologists as Scientists

Biological anthropologists use the scientific method as a way of learning about the world around them. Many people think of science as taking place in a sterile laboratory, but in biological anthropology it is just as likely to occur somewhere else, such as at a research station in Ethiopia, a field site in Tanzania, or a town in El Salvador. To understand how information in this field is established, it is important to recognize what science is and is not, as well as to understand how the scientific method actually works.

Recognizing Science

Science combines our natural curiosity with our ability to experiment so we can understand the world around us and address needs in our communities. Thanks to science, meteorologists can predict the weather, it takes a relatively small number of farmers to grow enough food to feed our large population, our medicine continues to improve, and over half of the world's population owns a cell phone.

Anyone can participate in science—not just academics. In fact, children are often some of the best scientists (Figure 1.15). An early, well-known psychologist, Jean Piaget (1896–1980), argued that a child is a "little scientist," internally motivated to experiment and explore their world. This can be seen when an infant repeatedly drops a toy to see if the parent will pick it up, or when a four-year-old sincerely asks "why" again and again. Maria Montessori (1870–1952), an Italian doctor and educator, was interested in how children learn. Through her research, she also recognized that children have natural scientific tendencies. Children have a desire to explore their environment, ask questions, use their imaginations, and learn by doing. In 1907, Montessori opened a school to foster children's natural desire to learn this way. This developed a child-centered teaching method that has spread around the world and is being used in over 22,000 schools today. In anthropology and other scientific fields, the process of learning is more formalized, but scientists still benefit from the curiosity that motivates children and still experience the thrill of discovery.

Science represents both a body of knowledge and the process for learning that knowledge (the scientific method). Scientific claims can, at times, be difficult to distinguish from other information. Science also incorporates a broad range of methods to collect data, adding to the difficulty of knowing what science really is. This section will address four key characteristics that help us define and recognize science: (1) science studies the physical and natural world and how it works, (2) scientific explanations must be testable and refutable, (3) science relies on **empirical** (observable) evidence, and (4) science involves the scientific community.

Figure 1.15: Children are true scientists as they explore and test the world around them through sight and touch. Credit: Child Scientist at Window original to Explorations: An Open Invitation to Biological Anthropology (2nd ed.) by Beth Shook is under a CC BY-NC 4.0 License.

Science Studies the Physical and Natural World and How It Works

Our physical and natural universe ranges from very small (e.g., electrons) to very large (e.g., Earth itself and the galaxies beyond it). Scientists often design their research to address how and why natural forces influence our physical and natural world. In biological anthropology, we focus our questions on humans as well as other primate species, both living and extinct. We ask questions like: What influences a primate's diet? Why do humans walk on two legs? And did Neanderthals and modern humans interbreed?

There are very few questions that are considered off-limits in science. That being said, the scope of scientific investigation is generally focused on *natural* phenomena and *natural* processes and excludes the supernatural. People often regard the supernatural, whether it be a ghost, luck, or god, as working outside the laws of the universe, which makes it difficult to study with a scientific approach. Science neither supports nor contradicts the existence of supernatural powers—it simply does not include the supernatural in its explanations.

Scientific Explanations Must Be Testable and Refutable

The goal of scientists is to identify a research question and then identify the best answer(s) to that question. For example, an excavation of a cemetery may reveal that many people buried there had unhealed fractures when they died, leading the anthropologist to ask: "Why did this population experience more broken bones than their neighbors?" There might be multiple explanations to address this question, such as a lack of calcium in their diets, participation in dangerous work, or violent conflict with neighbors; these explanations are considered hypotheses. In the past, you might have learned that a **hypothesis** is an "educated guess," but in science, hypotheses are much more than that. A scientific hypothesis reflects a scientist's knowledge-based experiences and background research. A hypothesis is better defined as an explanation of observed facts; hypotheses explain how and why observed phenomena are the way they are.

Scientific hypotheses should generate expectations that are *testable*. For example, if the best explanation regarding our cemetery population was that they were experiencing violent conflict with their neighbors, we should expect to find clues, like weapons or protective walls around their homes, in the anthropological record to support this. Alternatively, if this population did not experience violent conflict with their neighbors, we may eventually be able to gather enough evidence to rule out (refute) this explanation. An important part of science is rigorous testing. Science *does not prove* any hypothesis. However, a strong hypothesis is one that has strong supporting evidence and has not yet been disproven.

Science Relies on Empirical Evidence

The word *empirical* refers to experience that is verified by observation (rather than evidence that derives primarily from logic or theory). In anthropology, much evidence about our world is collected by observation through fieldwork or in a laboratory. The most reliable studies are based on accurately and precisely recorded observations. Scientists value studies that explain exactly what methods were used so that their data collection and analysis processes are reproducible. This allows for other scientists to expand the study or provide new insights into the observations.

Science Involves the Scientific Community

Contrary to many Hollywood science fiction films, good science is not carried out in isolation in a secret basement laboratory; rather, it is done as part of a community. Scientists pay attention to what others have done before them, present new ideas to each other, and publish in scientific journals. Most scientific research is collaborative, bringing together researchers with different types of specialized knowledge to work on a shared project. Today, thanks to technology, scientific projects can bring together researchers from different backgrounds, experiences, locations, and perspectives. Most big anthropological questions such as "Where did modern humans develop?," "What genetic changes make us uniquely human?," and "How did cooperative behavior evolve?" cannot be addressed with one simple study but are tested with different lines of evidence and by different scientists over time.

Working within a scientific community supports one of the most valuable aspects of science: that *science is self-correcting*. Science that is openly communicated with others allows for a system with checks and balances: competing explanations can be proposed and questionable studies can be reevaluated. Ultimately, the goal is that through science the best explanations will stand the test of time.

How Science Works: The Scientific Method

Most students have learned the scientific method as a simple linear, or perhaps circular, process (see, e.g., Figure 1.16). Typically, the process is said to begin with making observations about the natural world. This leads to the development of a scientific hypothesis. From the hypothesis a set of predictions can be made, which are then tested by experimentation or by making additional observations. Scientific predictions are often phrased as "if... then..." statements, such as "If hypothesis A is true, then this experiment will show outcome B." The results of a scientific study should then either support or reject the hypothesis.

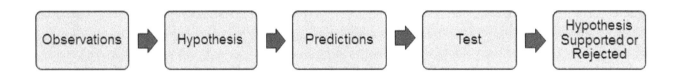

Figure 1.16: Simple depiction of the scientific method. Credit: Simple depiction of the scientific method (Figure 1.23) original to Explorations: An Open Invitation to Biological Anthropology is under a CC BY-NC 4.0 License.

This simple version of the scientific method is valuable because it highlights the key aspects that should be present in any scientific research experiment or scientific paper. However, this simplistic view does not accurately represent the dynamic and creative side of science, nor does it identify the complex steps that are incorporated into a scientist's routine.

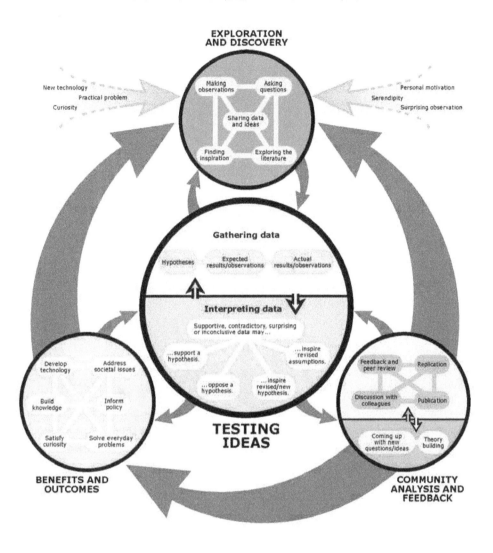

Figure 1.17: Complex flow of the scientific method. A full text description is available from Understanding Science.
Credit: **Complex Science Flowchart (2022)** by Understanding Science, University of California Museum of Paleontology is used by permission and available here under a CC BY-NC 4.0 License.

Figure 1.17 provides an alternative representation of the scientific method that emphasizes the many paths to scientific discovery. While still incorporating the key components of making observations, testing ideas, and interpreting results, this chart shows that scientific ideas have many possible starting points and influences, and scientists often repeat steps and circle back around. Gathering evidence does not always rest on experiments in the laboratory. Evaluating data is not always clear-cut, and results are sometimes surprising or inconclusive. Many important discoveries were in fact made by mistake. For example, engineer Percy Spencer accidentally melted a chocolate bar in his pocket with a magnetron, which became the first microwave, and Spencer Silver invented the adhesive for 3M Post-it ® notes while trying to develop a strong glue. The real scientific process is more similar to the philosophy of the animated television character Ms. Frizzle from *The Magic School Bus*, "Take chances, make mistakes, get messy."

Two key components lacking in the simple version of the scientific method are exploration and discovery. There are many reasons that a scientist might choose a particular research question: they may be motivated by personal experience, struck by something they read, or inspired by a student's question in class. Often scientific research reveals more questions than answers, so experienced researchers rarely lack problems to solve. But identifying a research question is just part of the process; most scientists spend more time exploring the literature, sharing ideas, asking questions, and planning their research project than conducting the test itself.

Science itself is a social enterprise that is influenced by cultural issues and values, as well as funding priorities. For example, corporations are the biggest funders of scientific research, followed by government agencies such as the National Science Foundation (which also fund many research projects done at colleges and universities). Those organizations have great influence on what is considered valuable research at any given time. For example, the World Health Organization (WHO) has classified many diseases as "neglected tropical diseases," including dengue, leprosy, rabies, and hookworm. Together these diseases affect an estimated one billion people, mostly in impoverished areas. While these debilitating tropical diseases can be as deadly as diseases that receive more attention, like AIDS and tuberculosis, they receive comparatively little funding due to political priorities (Farmer et al. 2013).

Also important to the scientific process are interactions within the scientific community. Scientific collaboration can take place through informal discussion over a cup of coffee as well as more formal interactions, such as presenting at conferences and engaging in **scholarly peer review**. Scholarly peer review describes the process whereby an author's work must pass the scrutiny of other experts in the field before being accepted for publication in a journal or book. This helps keep scientists accountable for ethically responsible research projects and papers. Additionally, presenting data at conferences and in articles and books allows researchers to receive critical feedback from academic peers and others to test these ideas and further the field of science toward identifying the best explanations. It is important that the scientific field include researchers with diverse identities, backgrounds, and experiences so that researchers ask new questions, innovate, and problem solve more effectively.

Hypotheses, Theories, and Laws

Scientific investigation occurs at many levels, from investigating individual cases (e.g., "What is causing this child's mysterious illness?") to understanding processes that affect most of us ("What is the ideal amount of sleep for an adult?"). All of these questions are important and will generate different types of testable scientific explanations. So far, we have used the term *hypothesis* to describe these scientific ideas about why observed phenomena are the way they are. Hypotheses are typically explanations that address a narrow set of phenomena, such as (in anthropology) a particular human population or primate species.

In science, a **theory** is an explanation of observations that addresses a wide range of phenomena. Like hypotheses, theories also explain how or why something occurs, rely on empirical evidence, and are testable and able to be refuted. Because the term *theory* is often used casually outside of science, you may hear people try to dismiss a scientific claim as "just a theory." In science there are often multiple competing theories, but over time some are eliminated, leaving standing the theory or theories that best explain the most evidence. Scientific theories that have stood the test of time are thus supported by many lines of evidence and are usually reliable. Some well-tested theories accepted by most scientists include the theory of general relativity, which explains the law of gravitation and its relation to other forces, and evolutionary theory, which describes how heritable traits can change in a population over time.

While scientific hypotheses and theories share many characteristics, laws are quite different. A **law** is a *prediction* about what will happen given certain conditions, *not* an explanation for how or why it happens. A law is not a "mature" version of a theory. For example, Newton's universal law of gravity allows us to predict the gravitational force (F) between any two objects using the equation $F=G(m_1m_2)/r^2$, but it does not explain *why* gravity works. Laws are often mathematical, and some well-known laws include Newton's three laws of motion and Mendel's laws of genetic inheritance. Laws are important, and their discovery often promotes the development of theories.

To demonstrate how important laws can be—and to show how unusual things can inspire scientific discoveries—we can use the story of the ancient Greek mathematician and inventor Archimedes (Figure 1.18). Archimedes's buoyancy principle is a law that is useful for many things, including density calculations and designing ships. Purportedly, he made this discovery when he noticed the water level rise in the bathtub when he climbed in it. Realizing its importance, he is said to have shouted "Eureka" and proceeded to run naked through the city of Syracuse. While this fun story may or may not be true, it does remain that scientific laws, alongside scientific hypotheses and theories, have a very important role in the scientific process and in generating scientific explanations about our natural world.

Figure 1.18: Archimedes is portrayed here having just discovered his Principle of Buoyancy. The vignette is by Count Giammaria Mazzuchelli (1707–1765). Credit: Eureka! Archimede by Science and Society Piture Library Prints is in the public domain. [This image is a faithful photographic reproduction of "Archimedes' Principle" vignette from "Historical and Critical Information about the Life, Inventions and Writings of Archimedes of Syracuse" by Count Giammaria Mazzuchelli (1707–1765), published in Brescia, Italy in 1737.]

Ways of Knowing: Science, Faith, and Anthropology

In anthropology, we recognize that there are many ways of knowing things. For instance, you might know that fingernails are softer than metal because as a child you accidentally stapled through your fingernail while doing an art project (a coauthor of this textbook once experienced this). This would be an example of knowledge you gained through experience. You might also know that inserting a knife into an electrical outlet is dangerous and could greatly harm you. Hopefully you learned this not from personal experience but through instruction from parents, teachers, and others in your social group. The degree to which humans rely on and benefit from the experiential knowledge of others is an important characteristic of what makes us human.

A unified way of knowing that is shared by a group of people and used to explain and predict phenomena is called a **knowledge system**. Human knowledge systems are diverse and reflect the wide range of cultures and societies throughout the world and through time.

Science and religion are both knowledge systems. Yet they differ in important ways. The type of knowledge gained from science is often called **scientific understanding**. As we have explored in the previous section, scientific understanding can change and relies on evidence and rigorous, repeated testing. Religious or spiritual ways of knowing are called **belief**, which is different from scientific understanding because they do not require repeated testing or validation (although they can rely on observations and experiences). Instead, belief relies on trust and **faith**.

Different individuals, cultures, and societies may place more value on one type of knowing than another, although most use a combination that includes science, empiricism, and religion. In fact, Bronisław Malinowski (1884–1942), an important anthropologist of the early twentieth century, concluded that all societies use both religion *and* science in some way or another, because they are both common ways that humans experience the world.

In contemporary societies such as the United States, science and (some) religions conflict on the topic of human origins. Nearly every culture and society has a unique origin story that explains where they came from and how they came to be who they are today. These stories are often integrated into the culture's religious belief system. Many anthropologists are interested in faith-based origin stories and other beliefs because they show us how a particular group of people explain the world and their place in it. Anthropologists also value scientific understanding as the basis for how humans vary biologically and change over time. In other words, anthropologists value the multiple knowledge systems of different groups and use them to understand the human condition in a broad and inclusive way.

It is also important to note that scientists often depend on the local knowledge of the people with whom they work to understand elements of the natural or physical world that science has not yet investigated. Many groups, including **Indigenous** peoples, know about the world through prolonged relationships with the environment. Indigenous knowledge systems—specific to an Indigenous community or group—are informed by their own empirical observation of a specific environment and passed down over generations.

While religion and Indigenous knowledge systems may play a complementary role in helping anthropologists understand the human condition, they are distinct from science. The anthropological subdiscipline of biological anthropology is based on scientific ways of knowing about humans and human origins. In this volume, we will exclusively explore what science tells us about how humans came to be and why we are the way we are today. Therefore, you do not need to *believe* in evolution to master this material, because belief is not a scientific way of knowing. For this textbook, you only need to *understand* the scientific perspectives of evolution.

Throughout our lives, each of us work to reconcile our worldview with the different ways we have of knowing things. This is part of our lifelong intellectual journey. It is also, in our opinion, one of the most exciting parts of learning. We are pleased you have joined us on this journey of knowledge about humanity and yourself!

Review Questions

- What are some key approaches to anthropological research?
- What are some similarities and differences between the subdisciplines? How does the "fifth subdiscipline" of applied anthropology fit within the larger discipline of anthropology?
- What are the subfields of biological anthropology and their unique contributions?
- What is science? What is the scientific method? How does science compare to other ways of knowing?

Key Terms

Belief: A firmly held opinion or conviction typically based on spiritual apprehension rather than empirical proof.

Cultural relativism: The anthropological practice of suspending judgment and seeking to understand another culture on its own terms sympathetically enough so that the culture appears to be a coherent and meaningful design for living.

Empirical: Evidence that is verifiable by observation or experience instead of relying primarily on logic or theory.

Faith: Complete trust or confidence in the doctrines of a religion, typically based on spiritual apprehension rather than empirical proof.

Holism: The idea that the parts of a system interconnect and interact to make up the whole.

Hominins: Species that are regarded as human, directly ancestral to humans, or very closely related to humans.

Human adaptation: The ways in which human bodies, people, or cultures change, often in ways better suited to the environment or social context.

Human variation: The range of forms of any human characteristic, such as body shape or skin color.

Hypothesis: Explanation of observed facts; details how and why observed phenomena are the way they are. Scientific hypotheses rely on empirical evidence, are testable, and are able to be refuted.

Indigenous: Refers to people who are the original settlers of a given region and have deep ties to that place. Also known as First Peoples, Aboriginal Peoples, or Native Peoples, these populations are in contrast to other groups who have settled, occupied, or colonized the area more recently.

Knowledge system: A unified way of knowing that is shared by a group of people and used to explain and predict phenomena.

Law: A prediction about what will happen given certain conditions; typically mathematical.

Participant observation: A research method common in cultural anthropology that involves living with, observing, and participating in the same activities as the people one studies.

Sapir-Whorf hypothesis: The principle that the language you speak allows you to think about some things and not other things. This is also known as the linguistic relativity hypothesis.

Scholarly peer review: The process whereby an author's work must pass the scrutiny of other experts in the field before being published in a journal or book.

Scientific understanding: Knowledge accumulated by systematic scientific study, supported by rigorous testing and organized by general principles.

Subdisciplines: The four major areas that make up the discipline of anthropology: biological anthropology, cultural anthropology, archaeology, and linguistic anthropology. Applied anthropology is sometimes considered to be a fifth subdiscipline.

Subfield: In this textbook, *subfield* refers to the different specializations within biological anthropology, including primatology, paleoanthropology, molecular anthropology, bioarchaeology, forensic anthropology, and human biology.

Theory: An explanation of observations that typically addresses a wide range of phenomena.

About the Authors

Katie Nelson, Ph.D.

Inver Hills Community College, kanelson@inverhills.edu

Katie Nelson is an instructor of anthropology and sociology at Inver Hills Community College. She is the recipient of the 2022 Minnesota State Board of Trustees Educator of the Year award. Her research focuses on migration, identity, belonging, and citizenship(s) in human history and in the contemporary United States, Mexico, and Morocco.

She received her B.A. in anthropology and Latin American studies from Macalester College, her M.A. in anthropology from the University of California, Santa Barbara, an M.A. in education and instructional technology from the University of Saint Thomas, and her Ph.D. from CIESAS Occidente (Centro de Investigaciones y Estudios Superiores en Antropología Social –Center for Research and Higher Education in Social Anthropology), based in Guadalajara, Mexico.

Katie views teaching and learning as central to her practice as an anthropologist and is co-founder and Associate Editor of *Teaching and Learning Anthropology Journal*. She has contributed to several open access textbook projects, both as an author and an editor, and views the affordability of quality learning materials as an important piece of the equity and inclusion puzzle in higher education.

Lara Braff, Ph.D.

Grossmont College, Lara.Braff@gcccd.edu

Lara Braff is a professor of anthropology at Grossmont College, where she teaches courses in cultural and biological anthropology. She received her B.A. in anthropology and Spanish from the University of California at Berkeley, and her M.A. and Ph.D. in comparative human development from the University of Chicago, where she specialized in medical anthropology.

Lara's research, teaching, and involvement in open access projects (like this textbook) are rooted in concerns about social equity. In an effort to make college more accessible to all students, she serves as an Open Educational Resources (OER) coordinator at Grossmont College and Liaison for the Academic Senate for California Community Colleges—Open Educational Resources Initiative.

Beth Shook, Ph.D.

California State University, Chico, bashook@csuchico.edu

Beth Shook is a lecturer in the anthropology department at California State University, Chico. She received her B.A. in anthropology and in molecular biology from Cornell College (in Mount Vernon, Iowa) and her M.A. and Ph.D. in anthropology from the University of California, Davis. While she is broadly trained in anthropology, her research has focused on utilizing DNA in forensic and anthropological contexts.

Beth enjoys teaching a variety of anthropology courses and mentoring graduate students in teaching. Additionally, she leads Chico State's Affordable Learning Solutions (CAL$) program, is committed to programs that prioritize diversity, and serves on the Society for Anthropology in Community Colleges (SACC) Executive Board.

Kelsie Aguilera, M.A.

Leeward Community College, kelsieag@hawaii.edu

Kelsie Aguilera is an associate professor of anthropology at Leeward Community College. Located on the island of O'ahu, Leeward Community College is part of the University of Hawai'i System and holds a special commitment to Native Hawaiian education. At Leeward, Kelsie teaches anthropology courses in all of the subdisciplines.

Kelsie received her B.A. in anthropology from the University of Miami and her M.A. in anthropology from Binghamton University. She is active within the American Anthropological Association and the Society for Anthropology in Community Colleges. She continues to work hard toward making anthropology accessible and relevant for her students.

For Further Exploration

American Anthropological Association website.

American Association of Biological Anthropologists website.

Partners in Health.

Understanding Science website (a project of the University of California Museum of Paleontology.

Anticole, Matt. n.d. "What's the Difference between a Scientific Law and Theory?" TedEd Lesson. Accessed January 28, 2023.

Chan, Keith. 2021. "Icebreaker Science." In *Explorations: Lab and Activities Manual*, edited by Beth Shook, Katie Nelson, Kelsie Aguilera, and Lara Braff. Arlington, VA: American Anthropological Association.

Chizmeshya, Sydney Quinn, and Katherine E. Brent. 2021. "Knowing and Believing." In *Explorations: Lab and Activities Manual*, edited by Beth Shook, Katie Nelson, Kelsie Aguilera, and Lara Braff. Arlington, VA: American Anthropological Association.

Pfister, Anne E. 2021. "Science and Belief: Just Because We Can, Doesn't Always Mean We Should." In *Explorations: Lab and Activities Manual* edited by Beth Shook, Katie Nelson, Kelsie Aguilera, and Lara Braff. Arlington, VA: American Anthropological Association.

References

Binford, Leigh. 2016. *The El Mozote Massacre: Human Rights and Global Implications.* Revised and expanded edition. Tucson: University of Arizona Press.

Estrada, Alejandro, Paul A. Garber, Anthony B. Rylands, Christian Roos, Eduardo Fernandez-Duque, Anthony Di Fiore, K. Anne-Isola Nekaris, et al. 2017. "Impending Extinction Crisis of the World's Primates: Why Primates Matter." *Science Advances* 3(229): 1–16.

Farmer, Paul. 2006. *AIDS and Accusation: Haiti and the Geography of Blame.* Berkeley: University of California Press.

Farmer, Paul, Matthew Basilico, Vanessa Kerry, Madeleine Ballard, Anne Becker, Gene Bukhman, Ophelia Dahl, et al. 2013. "Global Health Priorities for the Early Twenty-first Century." In *Reimagining Global Health: An Introduction,* edited by Paul Farmer, Jim Yong Kim, Arthur Kleinman, and Matthew Basilico, 302–339. Berkeley: University of California Press.

Kenyon, Kathleen. 1979. *Archaeology in the Holy Land.* New York: W.W. Norton.

Malotki, Ekkehart. 1983. *Hopi Time: A Linguistic Analysis of the Temporal Concepts in the Hopi Language.* Berlin: De Gruyter.

Mead, Margaret. 1928. *Coming of Age in Samoa.* Oxford: Morrow.

Ochs, Elinor and Bambi Schieffelin. 2017. "Language Socialization: An Historical Overview." In *Encyclopedia of Language and Education, Volume 8,* edited by Patricia Duff, 3-16. New York: Springer.

Rathje, William and Cullen Murphy. 1992. "Five Major Myths about Garbage, and Why They're Wrong." *Smithsonian* 23, no. 4: 113-122.

TANN. 2018. "Mexican Anthropologists Put Face on Nearly 14,000-Year-Old Woman." *Archaeology News Network,* August 19, 2018. Accessed on November 16, 2022.

Whorf, Benjamin. 1956. *Language, Thought, and Reality.* Cambridge: MIT Press.

Acknowledgment

We are grateful to the anonymous reviewers for their many insightful comments and suggestions.

2.

A HISTORY OF EVOLUTIONARY THOUGHT

Joylin Namie, Ph.D., Truckee Meadows Community College

Learning Objectives

- Identify and describe the major developments in scientific thought that led to the discovery of evolutionary processes.
- Explain how natural selection works and results in evolutionary change over time.
- Explain what is meant by the "Modern Synthesis" and its impacts on evolutionary thought.
- Discuss the teaching of human evolution in the U.S. and abroad.

The Beginnings of Evolutionary Thinking

Throughout our evolutionary history, humans have developed an understanding of the natural world as they interacted with and extracted resources from it. To survive, our earliest ancestors possessed an understanding of the physical environment, including weather patterns, animal behavior, edible and medicinal plants, locations of water, and seasonal cycles. Many ancient cultures, including those of the Americas (Dunbar-Ortiz 2014), Mesopotamia, and Egypt, left writings, hieroglyphics, and stories passed down through oral tradition detailing their understanding of the natural environment, human and zoological anatomy, botany, and medical practices (Moore 1993).

Figure 2.1a-b: Aristotle was the first to publish that a. octopuses can change their colors when disturbed and b. elephants use their trunks as a snorkel when crossing deep water. Credit: a. Octopus macropus by SUBnormali Team (originally from Yoruno) is under a CC-BY-SA 3.0 License. b. Elephant swimming, Botswana (cropped) by Jorge Láscar from Australia (uploaded by Peter D. Tillman) is under a CC BY 2.0 License.

There are also over 2,000 years of organized thought and writing regarding **evolution**, including contributions from Greek, Roman, and Islamic scholars. Three examples of note are included here. The Greek philosopher Aristotle (384–322 BCE) studied the natural world, publishing several volumes on animals based on systematic observations, rather than attributing what he observed to divine intervention, as his contemporaries were doing (Figure 2.1). Aristotle's system for the biological classification of nearly 500 species of animals was based on his own observations and dissections, interviews with specialists such as beekeepers and fishermen, and accounts of travelers. His nine book *History of Animals*, published in the 4th century BC (n.d.), was one of the first zoological taxonomies ever created. Aristotle's primary contribution to the classification of biological species was to recognize that natural groups are based on structure, physiology, mode of reproduction, and behavior (Moore 1993, 39).

Aristotle's *History of Animals* also placed animals in a hierarchy, ranking animals above plants due to what he claimed were their abilities to sense the world around them and to move. He also graded animals according to their modes of reproduction. Those giving birth to live young were placed above those who laid eggs. Warm-blooded animals ranked above invertebrates. This concept of "higher" and "lower" organisms was expanded upon by scholars in the Medieval period to form the *Scala Naturae* (Latin for "ladder of being"). This "Great Chain of Being," depicting a hierarchy of beings with God at the top and minerals at the bottom (Figure 2.2), was thought by medieval Christians to have been decreed by God; in this Great Chain, humans were placed closer to God than other species. Aristotle's works were rediscovered by Islamic scholars in the ninth century and translated into Arabic, Syriac, Persian, and later into Latin, becoming part of university curriculum in 13th-century Europe (Lindberg 1992), allowing Aristotle's works and ideas to influence other thinkers for 2,000 years.

Figure 2.2: The Great Chain of Being by Didacus Valades. Credit: Great Chain of Being by Didacus Valades (Diego Valades 1579), print from Rhetorica Christiana (via Getty Research), is in the public domain.

Figure 2.3: An image from Kitāb
al-ḥayawān (Book of the Animals) by
Al-Jahiz. Credit: Al-Jahiz by Al-Jahiz [in
Kitāb al-ḥayawān (Book of the Animals),
15th century] is in the public domain.

Science also owes a debt to many Arabic scholars. One such Islamic scholar and writer, who built upon the ideas of Aristotle, was Abū ʿUthman ʿAmr ibn Baḥr al-Kinānī al-Baṣrī / al-Jāḥiẓ, known as Al-Jahiz (776–868 CE), who authored over 200 books (El-Zaher 2018; Figure 2.3). His most well-known work was the seven-volume *Kitab al-Hayawan* or *Book of Animals*, in which he described over 350 species in zoological detail. Importantly, Al-Jahiz introduced the idea and mechanisms of biological evolution 1,000 years before Darwin proposed the concept of **natural selection** in 1859 (Love 2020). For instance, Al-Jahiz wrote about the struggle for existence, the transformation of species over time, and environmental factors that influence the process, all ideas that were later espoused by western European scientists in the 19th century. Al-Jahiz wrote:

> Animals engage in a struggle for existing, and for resources, to avoid being eaten, and to breed. Environmental factors influence organisms to develop new characteristics to ensure survival, thus transforming them into new species. Animals that survive to breed can pass on their successful characteristics to their offspring. [Masood 2009]

Figure 2.4: Drawing of Ibn al-Haytham.
Credit: Ibn al-Haytham by Sopianwar is
under a CC BY-SA 4.0 License.

Another important early Islamic scientist is Ibn al-Haytham (965–1040), a 10th-century Islamic scholar who contributed a great deal to our understanding of optics and how human vision works (Figure 2.4; Lindberg 1992, 177–180). Born in what is now Iraq, al-Haytham was a scholar of many disciplines, including mathematics, physics, mechanics, astronomy, philosophy, and medicine. He authored some 200 books in his lifetime and was an expert on Aristotle's natural philosophy, logic, and metaphysics. In relation to evolution, al-Haytham's methodology of investigation—specifically, using experiments to verify theory—is similar to what later became known as the modern scientific method. He is most famous for discovering the laws of reflection and refraction over 1,000 years ago and inventing the camera obscura, which was incredibly important for the eventual development of photography. His work is credited for its influence on astronomy, mathematics, and optics, inspiring Galileo, Johannes Kepler, and Sir Isaac Newton (Tasci 2020). As an inspirational scientific figure, al-Haytham was celebrated in 2016 by UNESCO as a trailblazer and the founder of modern optics (Figure 2.5). An International Year of Light was named in his honor and a scholarly conference on his contributions was held to coincide with the 1,000th anniversary of the publication of his *Kitāb al-Manāẓir* (Book of Optics; UNESCO.org 2015).

The writings of these Islamic scholars as well as similar scientific texts from other cultures were unknown to or unacknowledged by Western scientists until recently. Fortunately, many science teachers are now incorporating this content into their classes (Love 2020).

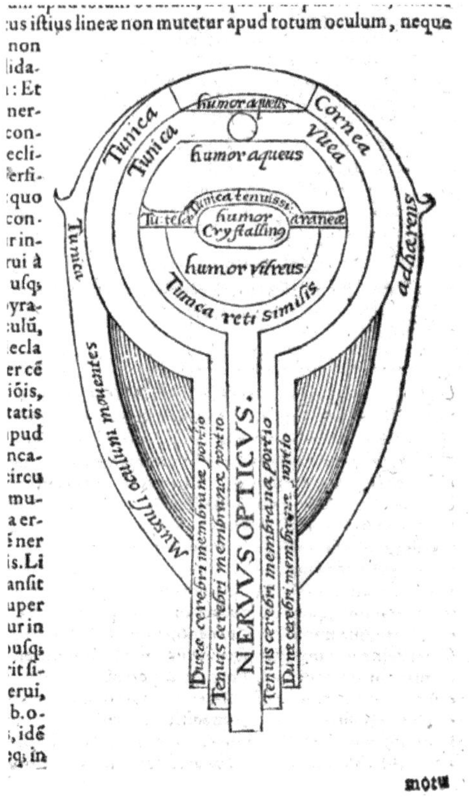

Western European Evolutionary Thought

Although there have been many different scientific traditions throughout world history, a new global discourse around science emerged in Western Europe in the 19th century. Europeans pointed to the continuing expansion of their colonial power, as well as their military and technological success, as evidence of the efficacy of Western science, which came to dominate on a global scale (Elshakry 2010). The movement toward a global science centered in Western Europe began with formulation of the **Scientific Method**.

The Scientific Method was first codified by Francis Bacon (1561–1626), an English politician who was likely influenced by the methods of inquiry established by Ibn al-Haytham centuries prior (Tbakhi and Amr 2007). Bacon has been called the founder of **empiricism** for proposing a system for weighing the truthfulness of knowledge based solely on inductive reasoning and careful observations of natural phenomena. Ironically, he died as a result of trying to scientifically observe the effects of cold on the putrefaction of meat. On a journey out of London, he purchased a chicken and stuffed it with snow for observation, catching a chill in the process. One week later, he died of bronchitis (Urbach, Quinton, and Lea 2023).

Figure 2.5: Diagram of the Human Eye by Ibn al-Haytham. Credit: Diagram of the eye by Ibn Al [Alhazen] Haitham (16th Century) has been modified (cropped) and is under a CC BY 4.0 License. This image is available from Wellcome Images 3044 (under the photo number L0011969).

The second important development with regard to evolution was the concept of a **species**. John Ray (1627–1705), an English parson and naturalist, was the first person to publish a biological definition of species in his *Historia Plantarum* (*History of Plants),* a three volume work published in 1686, 1688, and 1704. Ray defined a *species* as a group of morphologically similar organisms arising from a common ancestor. However, we now define a species as a group of similar organisms capable of producing fertile offspring. In keeping with the scientific method, Ray classified plants according to similarities and differences that emerged from observation. He claimed that any seed from the same plant was the same species, even if it had slightly different traits.

The modern period of biological classification began with the work of Carl von Linne ("Carolus Linnaeus") (1707–1778), a Swedish scientist who laid the foundations for the modern scheme of taxonomy used today. He established the system of **binomial nomenclature**, in which a species of animal or plant receives a name consisting of two terms: the first term identifies the genus to which it belongs and the second term identifies the species. His original *Systema Naturae*, published in 1736, went through several editions. By the tenth edition in 1758, mammals incorporated primates, including apes and humans, and the term *Homo sapiens* was introduced to signify the latter (Paterlini 2007).

Georges-Louis Leclerc, Comte de Buffon (1707–1788), was a prominent French naturalist whose work influenced prominent scientists in the second half of the 18th century. Buffon's idea that species change over time became a cornerstone of modern evolutionary theory. His technique of comparing similar structures across different species, called **comparative anatomy**, is still in use today in the study of evolution. He published 36 volumes of *Histoire Naturelle* during his lifetime and heavily influenced two prominent French thinkers who were to have significant impacts on our understanding of evolution, Georges Cuvier and Jean-Baptiste Lamarck.

Figure 2.6: Cuvier with one of his drawings of a fossil quadruped. Credit: Cuvier and a fossil quadruped original to Explorations: An Open Invitation to Biological Anthropology (2nd ed.) is a collective work under a CC BY-NC-SA 4.0 License. [Includes Georges Cuvier 3 by François-André Vincent (artist), public domain; Mammoth skeleton in OpenClipart, public domain (CC0).]

Georges Cuvier (1769–1832) was a paleontologist and comparative anatomist (Figure 2.6). One of his first major contributions to the field of evolution was proof that some species had become **extinct** through detailed and comprehensive analyses of large fossil quadrupeds (Moore 1993, 111). The idea of extinction was not new, but it was challenging to demonstrate if a fossil species was truly extinct or still had living relatives elsewhere. It was also challenging in that it ran counter to religious beliefs of the time. The Bible's Book of Genesis was interpreted as saying that all species had been created by God in the seven days it took to create the world and that all created species have survived to this day. Extinction was interpreted as implying imperfection, suggesting God's work was flawed. Also, given that the Earth was calculated to have been created in 4004 B.C.E., based on biblical genealogies, there would not have been enough time for species to disappear (Moore 1993, 112).

Cuvier was so knowledgeable in this field that he became famous for his ability to reconstruct what an extinct animal looked like from fragmentary remains. He demonstrated that fossil mammoths differed from similar living creatures, such as elephants. His many examples of fossils telling the stories of animals that lived and then disappeared were taken as incontrovertible proof of extinctions (PBS 2001). Where Cuvier went awry was his hypothesis of how extinction worked and its causes. As part of his study of comparative anatomy, Cuvier made observations of stratified layers of rock, or sediment, each containing different species. From this, he drew conclusions that species were "fixed" and did not evolve, but then went extinct, and that different assemblages of fossils occurred at different times in the past, as evidenced by the sedimentary layers (Moore 1993, 118). Cuvier explained this through a theory of **catastrophism**, which stated that successive catastrophic deluges (akin to Biblical floods) swept over parts of the Earth periodically, exterminating all life. When the waters receded from a particular region, lifeforms from unaffected regions would repopulate the areas that were destroyed, giving rise to a new layer of species that looked different from the layer below it. This theory implied that species were fixed in place and did not evolve and that the Earth was young. In fact, Cuvier postulated that the last catastrophe was a deluge he believed occurred five to six thousand years ago, paving the way for the advent of humans (Moore 1993, 118). Cuvier's catastrophism became part of an ongoing and vociferous debate between two schools of geology. The catastrophists believed the present state of the earth was the consequence of a series of violent catastrophes of short duration, while the uniformitarians thought it was the result of slow acting geological forces that continue to shape the earth.

James Hutton (1726–1797) was one prominent proponent of **uniformitarianism**. Based on evidence he found at sites in his native Scotland, Hutton argued that the Earth was much older than previously thought. Examining the geology of Siccar Point, a cliff site on the eastern coast of Scotland (Figure 2.7), Hutton concluded that the intersection of the vertical and horizontal rocks represented a gap in time of many millions of years, during which the lower rocks had been deformed and eroded before the upper layers were deposited on top. From this, Hutton argued sediments are deposited primarily in the oceans, where they become strata, or layers of sedimentary rock. Volcanic action uplifts these strata to form mountains, which are then subject to erosion from rain, rivers, and wind, returning sediment to the oceans (Moore 1993, 121). Hutton's *Theory of the Earth* (1788) demanded vast periods of time (known as "deep time") for such slow-working forces to shape the earth. At the time, he was heavily criticized for this view, as it contradicted the biblical version of the history of creation.

Figure 2.7: Siccar Point, Aberdeen, UK. Credit: Siccar Point by Anne Burgess is under a CC BY-SA 2.0 License.

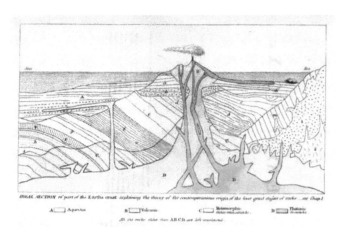

Figure 2.8: The frontispiece from Charles Lyell's Principles of Geology (2nd American edition, 1857), showing the origins of different rock types. Credit: Lyell Principles frontispiece by Charles Lyell (Principles of Geology, 2nd American edition, 1857) is in the public domain.

Another Scotsman, who was to become a highly influential geologist and a close friend of Darwin, was Charles Lyell (1797–1875). Lyell was originally a lawyer who began his studies of Geology at Oxford under the tutelage of catastrophist William Buckland, from whom he diverged when Buckland tried to find physical evidence of Noah's flood from the Christian Bible. Lyell was instead intent on establishing geology as a science based on observation. Building upon Hutton's ideas (published 50 years earlier), Lyell traveled throughout Europe, documenting evidence of uniformitarianism. During his travels, he cataloged evidence of sea level rise and fall and of volcanoes positioned atop much older rocks. He also found evidence of valleys formed through erosion, mountains resulting from earthquakes, and volcanic eruptions that had been witnessed or documented in the past (University of California Berkeley Museum of Paleontology n.d.). Lyell also espoused the principle that "rocks and strata (layers of rock) increase in age the further down they are in a geological sequence.

Barring obvious upheavals or other evidence of disturbance, the same principle must apply to any fossils contained within the rock. The lower down in a sequence of rocks a fossil is, the older it is likely to be (Wood 2005, 12)."

Lyell published the first edition of his three-volume *Principles of Geology* in 1830–1833 (Figure 2.8). It established geology as a science, underwent constant revisions as new scientific evidence was discovered, and was published in 12 editions during Lyell's lifetime. In it, he espoused the key concept of uniformitarianism—that "the present is the key to the past." What this meant was that geological remains from the distant past can be explained by reference to geological processes now in operation and directly observable.

Jean-Baptiste Lamarck (1744–1829) was the first Western scientist to propose a mechanism explaining why and how traits changed in species over time, as well as to recognize the importance of the physical environment in acting on and shaping physical characteristics. Lamarck's view of how and why species changed through time, known as the "Theory of Inheritance of Acquired Characteristics," was first presented in the introductory lecture to students in his invertebrate zoology class at the Museum of Natural History in Paris in 1802 (Burkhardt 2013). It was based on the idea that as animals adapted to their environments through the use and disuse of characteristics, their adaptations were passed on to their offspring through reproduction (Figure 2.9). Lamarck was right about the environment having an influence on characteristics of species, as well as about variations being passed on through reproduction. He simply had the mechanism wrong.

Figure 2.9a-b: Inheritance of Acquired Characteristics and Natural Selection. Credit: Lamarckian Evolution (Figure 4.2A and 4.2B) original to Explorations: An Open Invitation to Biological Anthropology by Mary Nelson is under a CC BY-NC 4.0 License.

Lamarck's theory involved a three-step process. Step one involves an animal experiencing a radical change in its environment. Step two is the animal (either individual or species) responding with a new kind of behavior. Step three is how the behavioral change results in morphological (meaning physical) changes to the animal that are successfully passed on to subsequent generations (Ward 2018, 8). Lamarck's most famous example was the proposition that giraffes actively stretched their necks to reach leaves on tall trees to eat. Over their lifetimes, the continuation of this habit resulted in gradual lengthening of the neck. These longer necks were then passed on to their offspring. Lamarck's theory was disproved when evolutionary biologist August Weismann published the results of an experiment involving mice (Figure 2.10). Weismann amputated the tails of 68 mice and then successively bred five generations of them, removing the tails of all offspring in each generation, eventually producing 901 mice, all of whom had perfectly healthy long tails in spite of having parents whose tails were missing (Weismann 1889).

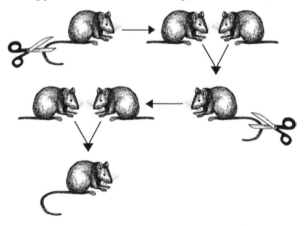

Figure 2.10: Weismann's mouse-tail experiment showing that offspring do not inherit traits that the parents acquired during their lifetimes. Credit: Weismann's mouse-tail experiment (Figure 4.3) original to Explorations: An Open Invitation to Biological Anthropology by Mary Nelson is under a CC BY-NC 4.0 License.

How giraffes actually ended up with long necks is a different story. In an environment where the food supply is higher off the ground, and perhaps less available to competing species, giraffes who happened to have slightly longer necks (due to random individual variation and genetic mutation) would be more likely to survive. These giraffes would then be able to reproduce, passing along the slight variation in neck length that would allow their offspring to do the same. Over time, individuals with longer necks would be overrepresented in the population, and neck lengths overall would increase among giraffes. Unfortunately, Lamarck's ideas challenged the scientific establishment of the time and were rejected. He was discredited and harassed "to the point of loss of money, reputation, and then health" (Ward 2018, 9).

The final piece in the evolutionary puzzle leading up to the theory of natural selection was put forth by Thomas Malthus (1766–1834), who published *An Essay on Population* in 1798. Malthus lived in England during the time of the Industrial Revolution. It was a time of great poverty and misery when many people migrated from the countryside to squalid, disease-ridden cities to work extremely long hours in dangerous conditions in factories, coal mines, and other industrial workplaces. Birth rates were high and starvation and disease were rampant. Malthus struggled to explain why. His answer was basically the idea of **carrying capacity**, an ecological concept still in use today. Malthus suggested the rate of population growth exceeded the rate of increase of the human food supply. In other words, people were outgrowing the available food crops. He also suggested that populations of animals and plants were naturally constrained by the food supply, resulting in reductions in population in times of scarcity, "restraining them within the prescribed bounds" (Moore 1993, 147). But, despite significant challenges, some individuals always survived. This was the key to later understandings of evolutionary change in species over time.

The Journey to Natural Selection

In Western European thought, the individual most closely associated with evolution is Charles Darwin (1809–1882). However, as one can see from the individuals and ideas presented in the prior section, he was not the first person to explore evolution and how it might work. In fact, Darwin built upon and synthesized many of the ideas—from geology to biology, ecology, and economy—discussed above. He was simply in the right place at the right time. If he had not worked out his ideas when he did, someone else would have. As a matter of fact, as noted below, someone else did, forcing Darwin to publicly reveal his theory.

Darwin's journey to the discovery of natural selection began during a childhood spent being curious, experimenting, and collecting natural specimens. When Darwin was 12 years old, his nickname was "Gas" because of the foul-smelling chemistry experiments he and his older brother, Erasmus, performed late into the evenings in their makeshift laboratory in the garden of their parent's home (Costa 2017). Darwin was also a lifelong collector of biological and geological specimens, most famously beetles, at times going to great lengths in pursuit of a new specimen, as one of his personal letters relates,

> I will give a proof of my zeal: one day, on tearing off some old bark, I saw two rare beetles, and seized one in each hand; then I saw a third and new kind, which I could not bear to lose, so that I popped the one which I held in my right hand into my mouth. Alas! it ejected some intensely acrid fluid, which burnt my tongue so that I was forced to spit the beetle out, which was lost, as was the third one. [Darwin 2001 (1897), 50].

Darwin continued his observations and experiments during his formal education, culminating in his graduation from Cambridge in 1831, at which point he was invited to become a gentleman naturalist for a British Royal Navy surveying mission of the globe aboard the H.M.S. *Beagle*. It is worth noting that Darwin was only 22 years old and the captain's third choice for the position (Costa 2017), but he proved extremely curious and methodical. The mission departed in December of 1831 and returned five years later (Figure 2.11). During this time, Darwin produced copious notebooks, observations, drawings, and reflections on the natural phenomena he encountered and the experiments he performed.

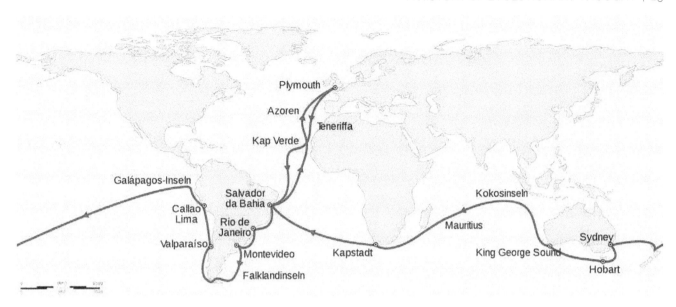

Figure 2.11: Map of the voyage of the H.M.S. Beagle. Credit: Voyage of the Beagle-de by Succu is under a CC BY-SA 3.0 License. [Image Description].

Discussing all of Darwin's work aboard the *Beagle* is beyond the scope of this chapter, but his primary interests were in cataloging new varieties of plant and animal life and examining the geology of the places the ship made landfall. Part of Darwin's success with regard to both ventures was due to his extreme seasickness, which began before the ship even left Plymouth Harbor. It never let up, encouraging Darwin to go ashore at every available opportunity. "In fact, of the nearly five years of the voyage, Darwin was actually on board the ship for just a year and a half altogether" (Costa 2017, 18).

During the voyage, the young Darwin tried to make sense of what he saw through the lens of the scientific paradigms he held when he left England, but he continually made observations that challenged these paradigms. For example, while the *Beagle* crewmen were charting the coast of Argentina, Darwin conducted fieldwork on land. There he observed species that were new to him, like armadillos. He also collected fossils, including those of extinct armadillos. Meaning, he had found both **extant** and extinct members of the same species in the same geographic location, which challenged the theory of catastrophism put forth by Cuvier, who argued that each variant of an animal, living or extinct, was its own distinct species (Moore 1993, 144). Darwin also observed geographic variation in the same species all along the east coast of South America, from Brazil to the southern tip of Argentina. He noted that some species were found in multiple localities and differed from place to place. Those living closer to each other exhibited only slight variations, while those living further apart might be cataloged as entirely different species if one did not know better.

He made similar observations in the Galapagos Islands located off the northwest coast of Ecuador, with regard to giant tortoises and finches (Figure 2.12). A local resident of the islands explained to Darwin that each island had its own variety of tortoise and that locals could discern which island a tortoise came from simply by looking at it. Darwin noted other such examples in both plants and animals, meaning geographic variation was occurring on separate, neighboring islands.

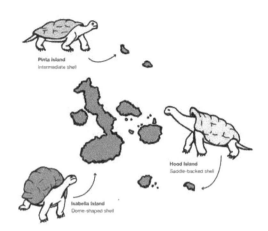

Figure 2.12: Variation in giant tortoises in the Galapagos Islands. Credit: Giant Tortoises of the Galapagos Islands original to Explorations: An Open Invitation to Biological Anthropology (2nd ed.) by Mary Nelson and Katie Nelson is under a CC BY-NC 4.0 License.

Prevailing views of time argued that variations in living species, and even the fossil armadillos and the living armadillos, were the result of separate creation events. According to this view, each variation, no matter how slight, was a different species. Challenging these ideas would mean challenging not only catastrophism, but the **Fixity of Species** and other well-accepted ideas of the time. Darwin was aware that he was a young, unestablished naturalist. He was also aware of the ruin that befell Lamarck when his theories were rejected. Lastly, Lyell, who was a good friend of Darwin's, rejected evolution altogether. It is no wonder that Darwin published a great deal about the geological and fossil data he collected when he returned from the voyage, but not his early hypotheses about evolution.

Upon Darwin's return to England, it took another twenty years of data collection and experimentation before he was ready to share his conclusions about evolution. Much of this work was conducted at Down House, his home of forty years, where he performed all sorts of experiments that laid the groundwork for his ideas about evolution. Darwin's home was his laboratory, and he engaged the help of his children, neighbors, friends, and servants in collecting, dissecting, and experimenting. At one point in the 1850s, sheets of moistened paper covered with frogs eggs lined the hallways of the house, while flocks of sixteen different pigeon breeds cooed outside, glass jars filled with salt water and floating seeds filled the cellar, and the smell of dissected pigeon skeletons pervaded the air inside the house. There were also ongoing experiments in the yard, including piles of dissected flowers, beekeeping, and fenced-off plots of land where seedlings were under study. Darwin was a keen experimental scientist, observer, and a prolific writer and presenter of scientific papers. He regarded his work as "one long argument" that never really ended. In fact, Darwin published ten books after *On the Origin of Species*, addressing such far-ranging topics as animal behavior, orchids, and domestication, among others (Costa 2017).

Darwin may not have published *Origins* in 1859 had it not been for receiving a paper in June of 1858 from Alfred Russel Wallace, an English naturalist working in Malaysia, espousing the same ideas. Wallace had sent the paper to Darwin asking if it was worthy of publication and requesting he forward it to Lyell and the English botanist, Joseph Hooker. Darwin wrote to Lyell and Hooker about Wallace's paper, entitled *On the Tendency of Varieties to Depart Indefinitely from the Original Type*. In recognition that both Wallace and Darwin had arrived at the same discovery, a "joint" paper composed of four parts (none of them actually coauthored) was read to the Linnaean Society by Lyell, then secretary of the Society, on July 1, 1858, and published on August 20. Darwin published *On the Origin of Species* 15 months later. (The original composite paper read before the Linnaean society is available to read for free from the Alfred Russell Wallace Website, on the 1858 Darwin-Wallace paper page.)

The Mechanism of Natural Selection

On the subject of natural selection and how it works, let's hear from Darwin himself from the original publication of *On the Origin of Species* (1859):

> A struggle for existence inevitably follows from the high rate at which all organic beings tend to increase. Every being, which during its natural lifetime produces several eggs or seeds, must suffer destruction during some period of its life, and during some season or occasional year, otherwise, on the principle of geometric increase, its numbers would quickly become so inordinately great that no country could support the product. Hence, as more individuals are produced than can possibly survive, there must in every case be a struggle for existence...It is the doctrine of Malthus applied with manifold force to the whole animal and vegetable kingdoms...There is no exception to the rule that every organic being naturally increases at so high a rate, that if not destroyed, the earth would soon be covered by the progeny of a single pair. ...Owing to this struggle for life, any variation, however slight and from whatever cause proceeding, if it be in any degree profitable to an individual of any species...will tend to the preservation of that individual, and will be inherited by its offspring. The offspring, also, will thus have a better chance of surviving, for, of the many individuals of any species which

are periodically born, but a small number can survive. I have called this principle, by which slight variation, if useful, is preserved, by the term Natural Selection. [Darwin 1859, 61–62]

Let us take a moment here to explore the mechanism of natural selection in more detail. Before we begin, it is important to recognize that Darwin defined evolution as descent with modification, by which he meant that species share a common ancestor yet change over time, giving rise to new species. Descent with modification refers to the fact that offspring from two parents look different from each of their parents, and from each other, meaning they descend with slight differences ("modifications"). If you have ever observed a litter of puppies or a field of flowers and stopped to examine each individual closely, you have seen that each differs from the next, and none look exactly like their parents. These variations are random, not specific, and may or may not be present in the following generations.

Darwin struggled to explain why some slight differences were preserved over time, while others were not. He turned to what he knew of animal breeding (**artificial selection**) for an explanation (Richards 1998). Darwin bred different breeds of pigeons at Down House, carefully documenting phenotypic differences across generations, including slight anatomical variations he observed through dissection. He also grew and crossbred species of flowers and dissected those too. Darwin was also very fond of hunting and of hunting dogs. In an early draft of his theory on speciation, he used greyhounds as an example of adaptation and selection, "noting how its every bone and muscle, instinct and habit, were fitted to run down hare (rabbits) (University of Cambridge n.d.)." In each case of plant and animal breeding Darwin observed, he noted that humans were selecting variants in each generation that had characteristics humans desired (i.e., sweetness of fruits, colors of flowers, fur type and color of animals). Breeders then continually bred plants and animals with the desired variants, over and over again. These small changes added up over time to create new species of plants and breeds of animals. Darwin also noted that artificial selection does not necessarily render plants or animals better adapted to their original environments. The characteristics humans desire often result in plants less likely to survive in the wild and animals more likely to suffer from certain behavioral or health problems. One has only to examine high rates of hip dysplasia in several modern breeds of dogs to observe what Darwin was referring to.

From his studies of artificial selection, Darwin drew the conclusion that nature also acts upon variations among members of the same species. Instead of human intervention, the forces of nature, such as heat, cold, predation, disease, and now climate change, determine which offspring, with which variants, survive and reproduce. These individuals then pass down these favorable variants to their own offspring. In this way, nature selects for traits that are beneficial within a particular environment and selects against traits that are disadvantageous within a particular environment. Over many generations, populations of a species become more and more adapted (or, in evolutionary terms, "fit") for their specific environments. Darwin named this process natural selection.

This theory explained the variations in tortoises Darwin had observed years earlier in the Galapagos Islands (see Figure 2.12). Tortoises who lived on larger islands with lush vegetation to feed on were larger than those on smaller islands. They also had shorter necks and dome-shaped shells as their food was close to the ground. Tortoises on smaller, drier islands fed on cacti, which grew much taller. These tortoises had longer necks, longer front legs, and saddle-shaped shells, which allowed them to successfully stretch to reach the edible cactus pads that grew on the tops of the plants. How did these observable differences in the two tortoise populations emerge? Darwin would argue that, over time, small, random variations in the tortoises were differentially selected for by the distinct natural environments on different islands.

In addition to the biogeographical evidence Darwin offered from his research aboard the *Beagle*, as well as the evidence he documented from the artificial selection of plants and animals, he also relied, where possible, on fossil evidence. One example, mentioned above, were the fossil findings of extinct armadillos in Argentina in the same locations as living armadillos. Unfortunately, as Darwin himself noted, the geological record was incomplete, most often missing the transitional fossil forms that bridge extinct and living species. That issue has since been resolved with scientific research in geochronology and paleontology, among other fields. It is now well-established that life is far more ancient than was believed in Darwin's time and that these ancient forms of life were the ancestors to all life on this planet (Kutschera and Niklas 2004).

What Darwin was Missing

Although the theory of evolution by natural selection gained traction in scientific circles in the decades after Darwin's publication of *Origins*, he was never able to discover the mechanisms that caused variation within members of the same species or the means by which traits were inherited. This began later in 1892 with the publication of *The Germ-Plasm: A Theory of Heredity* by August Weismann, the same Weismann of the mouse tail experiment presented earlier in this chapter. In his book, Weissman proposed a theory of germ-plasm, which was a precursor to the later discovery and understanding of DNA. Weismann specialized in cytology, a branch of biology devoted to understanding the function of plant and animal cells. Germ-plasm, he proposed, was a substance in the germ cells (what we would call gametes, or sex cells, today) that carried hereditary information. He predicted that an offspring inherits half of its germ-plasm from each of its parents, and claimed that other cells (e.g. somatic, or body, cells) could not transmit genetic information from parents to offspring. This thereby erased the possibility that acquired traits (which he argued resided in somatic cells) could be inherited (Zou 2015). This contribution to evolutionary theory was an important step toward understanding genetic inheritance, but a connection between genetics and evolution was still lacking.

A series of lectures by a deceased Augustinian monk named Gregor Mendel (1822–1884), originally published in 1865, changed that perspective (Moore 1993, 285). Although Darwin was unknown to Mendel, he began a series of experiments with pea plants shortly after the publication of Darwin's *Origins*, aiming to add to evolutionary understandings of heredity. As Mendel bred different generations of pea plants that had differences in seed shape and color, pod shape and color, flower position, and stem length, he documented consistent expression of some variations over others in subsequent generations. He meticulously documented the statistics of each crossing of plants and the percentages of **phenotypes** that resulted, eventually discovering the concept of dominance and recessiveness of characteristics. He also documented that there is no blending of inherited characteristics. For example, pea pod colors in the offspring of two parent plants, one with yellow pods and one with green, were *either* yellow or green, not yellowish green. Mendel also discovered that characteristics are inherited and expressed independently of each other, meaning the color of the pea pod was not necessarily expressed in conjunction with the pod being wrinkled or smooth. The recognition of the importance of Mendel's work began with its rediscovery by Hugo de Vries and Carl Correns, both of whom were working on hypotheses regarding heredity in plants and had arrived at conclusions similar to Mendel's. Both published papers supporting Mendel's conclusions in 1900 (Moore 1993). Research into the inheritance of characteristics continued through the next three decades, and by the close of the 1930s, no major scientific questions remained regarding the transmission of heredity through **genes**, although what genes did and what chemicals they were made of were still under investigation.

The **Modern Synthesis** refers to the merging of Mendelian genetics with Darwinian evolution that took place between 1930 and 1950. The basic principles of the synthetic theory were influenced by scientists working in many different fields, including genetics, zoology, biology, paleontology, botany, and statistics. Although there were differences of opinion among them, evolution came to be defined as changes in allele frequencies within populations. Genetic mutations, changes in the genetic code that are the original source of variation in every living thing, were believed to be random, the sources of phenotypic variation, and transmitted through sexual reproduction. These assertions were supported by a growing body of field and laboratory research, as well as new work in mathematics in the field of population genetics that defined evolution as numerical changes in gene frequencies within an interbreeding population from one generation to the next (Corning 2020). These changes in gene frequencies were argued to be the result of natural selection, mutation, migration (**gene flow**), and **genetic drift**, or random chance. Empirical research and mathematics demonstrated that very small selective forces acting over a relatively long time were able to generate substantial evolutionary change, including speciation (Plutynski 2009). Thus, the Modern Synthesis encompassed both **microevolution**, which refers to changes in gene frequencies between generations within a population, and **macroevolution**, longer-term changes in a population that can eventually result in speciation, wherein individuals from different populations are no longer able to successfully interbreed and produce viable offspring.

Figure 2.13: Theodosius Dobzhansky (1943). Credit: Dobzhansky no Brasil em 1943 by unknown creator via Cely Carmo at Flickr is in the public domain.

Genetics and the Origin of Species, published in 1937 by Theodosius Dobzhansky (Figure 2.13), was a cornerstone of the modern synthesis, applying genetics to the study of natural selection in wild populations, appealing to both geneticists and field biologists. Dobzhansky was interested in **speciation**, particularly in finding out what kept one species distinct from another and how speciation occurred. His research involved fruit flies, the species *Drosophila pseudoobscura*. At the time he began in the 1920s, biologists assumed all members of the same species had nearly identical genes. Dobzhansky traveled from Canada to Mexico capturing wild members of *D.pseudoobscura*, discovering that different populations had different combinations of **alleles** (forms of a **gene**) that distinguished them from other populations, even though they were all members of the same species. What, then, led to the creation of new species? Dobzhansky realized it was sexual selection. Members of the same species are more likely to live among their own kind and to recognize, and prefer, them as mates. Over time, as a result of random mutations, natural selection in a given environment, and **genetic drift**, meaning random changes in allele frequencies, members of the same population accumulate mutations distinct to their own **gene pool**, eventually becoming genetically distinct from other populations. What this means is that they have become a new **species.**

From these studies, Dobzhansky and others developed the Bateson-Dobzhansky-Muller model, also known as Dobzhansky-Muller model (Figure 2.14). It is a model of the evolution of genetic incompatibility. Combining genetics with natural selection, the model is important in understanding the role of reproductive isolation during speciation and the role of natural selection in bringing it about. Due to sexual selection (mate preference), populations can become reproductively isolated from one another. Eventually, novel mutations may arise and be selected for in one or both populations, rendering members of each genetically incompatible with the other, resulting in two distinct species.

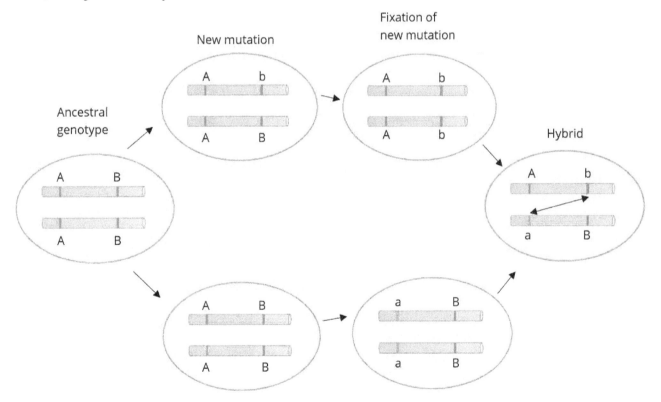

Figure 2.14: The Dobzhansky-Muller Model: In the ancestral population the genotype is AABB. When two populations become isolated from each other, new mutations can arise. In one population uppercase A evolves into lowercase a, and in the other uppercase B evolves into lowercase b. When the two populations hybridize, it is the first time a and b interact with each other. When these alleles are incompatible, they represent Dobzhansky-Muller incompatibilities. Credit: **Bateson-Dobzhansky-Muller model** by OrientationEB is under a **CC BY-SA 4.0 License.**

Evolution and Natural Selection Observable Today

Figure 2.15: Puerto Rican Crested Anole photographed in Picard, Dominica. Credit: Anolis cristatellus in Picard, Dominica-2012 02 15 0339 by Postdif is under a CC BY-SA 3.0 Unported License.

Although this chapter primarily focuses on the past, it is important to remember that natural selection and evolution are still ongoing processes. Climate change, deforestation, urbanization, and other human impacts on the planet are influencing evolution among many contemporary species of plants and animals. One such example occurs among crested anoles (*Anolis cristatellus*), small lizards of the Caribbean jungle that are increasingly making their home in cities (Figure 2.15).

As urban sprawl continues across the planet, shrinking the availability of wilderness habitat, many wild species have come to make their homes in cities. "Urbanization has dramatically transformed landscapes around the world—changing how animals interact with nature, creating "heat islands" with higher temperatures, and hurting local biodiversity. Yet many organisms survive and even thrive in these urban environments, taking advantage of new habitats created by humans (National Science Foundation 2023). A recent example of lizards in Puerto Rico demonstrates evolution happening quickly in both behavior and genes that has come about as a result of the pressures of urban life (Winchell et al. 2023). Crested anoles, who once lived only in forests, now scurry around towns and cities throughout the Caribbean. As a result of having to sprint across large open spaces, like hot streets and parking lots, they have developed longer limbs. City-living lizards also now sport longer toe pads with special scales that allow them to cling to smooth surfaces, like windows and walls (as well as the plastic patio furniture pictured in Figure 2.15), rather than to the rough surfaces of bark and rock that their forest-living relatives climb. These adaptations enhance their ability to escape predators and survive in cities.

Researchers were curious to see if these changes were the result of genetic changes in urban populations, so they captured 96 male lizards in three Puerto Rican regions and compared their genomes to each other and to forest specimens in each location. They found that members of the three city-living populations were genetically distinct from each other, as well as from forest populations in their respective regions. In total, 33 genes in the urban lizards' genomes were different from their forest-living counterparts and were linked to urbanization. These changes are estimated to have occurred just within the last 30 to 80 generations, suggesting that selective pressures related to survival in urban environments is strong. As study coauthor Kristen Winchell put it, "We are watching evolution as it is unfolding" (National Public Radio 2023). (If you are interested in hearing more about the study, see "How Lizards Adapt to Urban Living," an episode of Science Sessions, a free podcast from the Proceedings of the National Academy of Sciences (PNAS 2023) featuring Dr. Winchell and her work.)

Misconceptions About Evolution Through Natural Selection

After many years of teaching about evolution and natural selection, it continues to surprise me how many misconceptions exist about how the process works. If you do a web image search for "human evolution," the following image is likely to appear (Figure 2.16).

Figure 2.16: An artist's visual representation of the process of human evolution. Credit: Human evolution scheme by M. Garde is under a CC BY-SA 3.0 License.

What is wrong with this picture? First, it implies that humans evolved from chimpanzees, which is incorrect. Although, as primates, we share a common ancestor very far back in time, we split from other primates, including our closest relatives, the nonhuman apes, several million years ago. This image also suggests that evolution is gradual and progressive; that it is intentional and directional; and that there is an end to it—a stopping point. As you will be learning, evolution takes place in fits and starts, depending on the physical environment, changes in climate, food supply, predation, reproductive success, and other factors. It is also not intentional, in the sense that there is no predetermined end; in fact, if environmental conditions change, species can evolve in different directions or even go extinct. Evolution also does not necessarily progress in the same direction over time. One example is the eel-like creature *Qikiqtania wakei* that lived 375 million years ago. It was originally a fish that evolved to walk on land, then evolved to live back in the water. Early tetrapods like *Qikiqtania* were likely spending more and more time out of the water during this period. The arrangement of bones and joints in their fins was starting to resemble arms and legs, which would have allowed them to prop themselves up in shallow water and survive on mudflats. *Qikiqtania's* skeletal morphology, however, suggests that it then evolved from having rudimentary fingers and toes back to fins that allowed them to again swim in open water (Stewart et al. 2022).

There is also the misperception that natural selection can create entirely new anatomical structures out of thin air in response to changes in environmental pressures. For example, when asked if they can think of ways in which modern humans are continuing to evolve biologically, students often postulate that, as a result of climate change, humans might rapidly develop gills, webbed hands and feet, and learn to breathe underwater in response to rising sea levels. Unfortunately, natural selection can only act on slight variations in anatomy that are already present, and we have no rudimentary physiological system for breathing underwater. Given that natural selection can only act upon existing variation, humans have evolved in such a way that many parts of our bodies are prone to injury. Our knees are one example. The anterior cruciate ligament (ACL) in our knees is "vulnerable to tearing in humans because our upright bipedal posture forces it to endure much more strain than it is designed to" (Lents 2018, 23). When our ancestors made the transition from quadrupedalism to upright walking, we shifted from four bent legs to two straight legs, relying more on our bones than our muscles to support our weight. This is functional for normal walking and running in a straight line, but sudden shifts in direction and momentum, combined with the sizes and weights of modern humans, result in tears in an ACL that is simply not strong enough to bear the stress. If evolution had the capability to engineer a knee from scratch, it would look quite different, and any ligaments involved would likely be larger, stronger, and more flexible. For an interesting look at what anatomically modern humans might look like if we had evolved to withstand the stresses our bodies undergo in our present environment, see "This is what the perfect body looks like – according to science," which was proposed by biological anthropologist Alice Roberts (Harrison 2018).

Another misperception about evolution is that some species are "more evolved" than others. Every species currently alive on the planet today is the result of millennia of natural selection that has rendered current members of that species well-adapted to their respective environments. Humans are no more "evolved" than fruit flies or yeast. What sets us apart are our cultural and technological abilities, which have allowed us to successfully survive in a wide variety of physical environments, many of which are now becoming too hot, too wet, or too dry to sustain human life without a great deal of technological intervention (IPCC 2022).

There is also some confusion about what "fitness" actually means and a failure to grasp that it changes as environmental conditions change. Evolutionary "fitness" is different from physical fitness. "Fitness" in evolutionary terms refers to an individual's ability to survive and reproduce viable offspring who also survive and reproduce. Evolutionary fitness and reproductive success are highly dependent on specific environmental conditions, which can shift over time, greatly affecting the relative fitness of individuals in a population. Recent research on the impacts of climate change on dragonflies will serve to illustrate the point (Figure 2.17).

Pictured here is a male dragonfly, who, you will notice, has distinctive black markings on its wings. This is due to melanization. Males control breeding, and those with more ornamentation tend to attract more mates and to successfully ward off male competitors. Higher levels of melanization, however, have negative consequences for males in warming climates. The black markings absorb heat, elevating body temperatures, which can cause overheating, reduce

Figure 2.17: Adult male Common Whitetail Dragonfly, *Libellula lydia*. Credit: **Common Whitetail Dragonfly – Plathemis lydia** by Bruce Marlin is under a CC BY-SA 2.5 License.

male fighting ability, and even lead to death (Moore et al. 2021). Females are not as adversely affected because they spend more time in shaded areas, while males are more often flying in sunlit areas, fending off rivals. However, as highly melanized males become less viable, wing coloration is undergoing selection in males. In other words, what constitutes being "fit" for males has changed, favoring those who have fewer of the black markings and, therefore, are less negatively impacted by warming temperatures. Note that natural selection acts on individuals, "selecting" those who happen to be fit for particular environmental conditions at a particular point in time. Evolution, though, happens at the level of the population. If the climate continues to warm, populations of dragonflies who inhabit warming areas will increasingly exhibit less ornamentation in males.

Lastly, natural selection can only act on characteristics that influence reproductive success. Deleterious traits that have nothing to do with one's ability to reproduce and successfully rear offspring to reproductive age will continue to be passed on. For example, the author of this chapter is a natural redhead, and redheads are predisposed genetically to a number of conditions that can negatively affect health (Colliss Harvey 2015), but some of these conditions are not diagnosed until later in life. One example is Parkinson's disease (Chen et al. 2017), which is a degenerative neurological disorder. The average age of diagnosis of Parkinson's is 60 years of age, meaning redheads may encounter such a diagnosis well past childbearing age, having already passed on the genetic predisposition. Thus, Parkinson's disease cannot be selected out from the redhead family tree.

Dig Deeper: Teaching Evolution Around the World

Evolution is recognized as a central organizing principle for all scientific disciplines and accepted without controversy among scientists and educated people around the world. The United States has historically been the exception (Lerner 2000). In some parts of the U.S. the teaching of evolution to K-12 students continues to evoke controversy, related to politics and religion. The problem is compounded by the degree of control individual states and local school boards exercise over curriculum in the nation's public schools (Lerner 2000).

Figure 2.18: Crowds attend the Scopes trial, Dayton, Tennessee, July 20, 1925. Credit: Clarence S. Darrow interrogating William Jennings Bryan, Scopes trial (1925) by William Silverman via Smithsonian Institution has no known copyright restrictions. [Smithsonian Institution archives, Acc. 10-042, William Silverman Photographs, 1925, Image ID: 2009-21077.]

The debate over teaching evolution in schools in the United States first came to a head in 1925 after several states attempted to legislate a ban against its teaching. The state of Tennessee eventually did pass such a ban, and the American Civil Liberties Union (ACLU) offered to defend any science teacher who agreed to break the law. John Scopes, who taught in a small, rural Tennessee school, continued to teach evolution, resulting in the "Scopes Monkey Trial," one of the most famous media trials in American history (Figure 2.18). The entire nation listened to its broadcast live on the radio and read about it daily in hundreds of newspapers. Scopes was defended by Clarence Darrow, the most famous lawyer in the country at the time; Scopes was eventually convicted, though the conviction was later overturned. The pro-Evolution movement benefited greatly from Darrow's questioning of those on the anti-Evolution side, whose responses were perceived negatively by well-educated listeners in northern cities. The teaching of evolution was also bolstered by a Supreme Court decision in 1947 overriding states' rights to make decisions on church-state issues and by the launching of Sputnik, the first Soviet (Russian) satellite, in 1957, making science education a national priority. During the 1960s to 1970s, **creationism** and **intelligent design** began to take hold as courts ruled in favor of "academic freedom" (Pew Research Center 2019). Since that time, states, and even local school boards, have pushed for the removal of evolution from science curriculum and textbooks or for teaching evolution on equal footing with concepts such as creationism and intelligent design (Masci 2019).

Partly in response to chronically low scores by students in the United States on international measures of ability in science, math, and reading (Desilver 2017), development of the Next Generation Science Standards (NGSS) for K-12 education began in 2011 and were implemented in 2013 in public schools across the nation (nextgenscience.org). The standards were developed collaboratively by The National Research Council (NRC; a branch of the National Academy of Sciences), the National Science Teachers Association, the American Association for the Advancement of Science, and Achieve, an independent, nonpartisan, nonprofit education-reform organization dedicated to working with states to raise academic standards and graduation rates. Twenty-six states also partnered together in the development of the standards. However, due to a number of issues, including funding and support for teachers, adoption of the standards has varied by state. States were also allowed to alter the curriculum. One of the main issues in several states with the original curriculum was the teaching of evolution (Pew Research Center 2014). One prominent aspect to note is that the NGSS do not specify that human evolution be taught, and high school standards do not require teaching about all of the forces of evolution, only mutation and natural selection.

The situation regarding teaching evolution has changed greatly in recent years. A 2007 survey found that only one in three public high school biology teachers in the United States presented evolution consistently with the recommendations of the nation's leading scientific authorities, and 13% of these teachers emphasized creationism as a valid scientific alternative to modern evolutionary biology (Plutzer, Branch, and Reid 2020). A repeat of the survey in 2019 demonstrated marked improvement in the amount of time teachers devoted to teaching evolution, as well as more teacher training and preparedness to teach evolution. Such improvements were attributed to the need to meet the Next Generation Science Standards, as well as continuing outreach by the National Science Teaching Association, the National Association of Biology Teachers, and the National Academy of Sciences in producing classroom resources and providing professional development opportunities to advance the inclusion of evolution in the nation's classrooms.

Public acceptance of evolution has also substantially improved in recent years (Miller et al. 2022). National samples of American adults have been asked at regular intervals since 1985 to agree or disagree with the following statement: "Human beings, as we know them today, developed from earlier species of animals (Miller et al. 2022)" During the last decade, the percentage of U.S. adults agreeing with this statement increased from 40% to 54%—a majority for the first time. This level of acceptance of evolution in the United States is atypically low for a developed nation. In a study of the acceptance of evolution in 34 developed nations in 2005, only Turkey—at 27%—scored lower than the United States (Miller, Scott and Okamoto 2006). There are also distinct differences among members of the U.S. population in terms of acceptance of evolution, with 68% of those ages 18–24, 58% of those with college degrees, and 65% of those who have taken four or more college-level science courses the most accepting of evolution. An increasing number of parents also report changing their unfavorable views of evolution due to helping their children with science homework and science fair projects.

Approaches to teaching evolution vary across the globe, with considerable differences within and between nations. One example is the United Kingdom, home of Darwin and Wallace. There, evolution is not introduced until ages 14–16, which is considered quite late by some educators. And, although evolution is taught in biology classes, it is addressed as a separate topic, rather than integrated into the curriculum as a foundational concept. As in the United States, there is also considerable variation between public and private schools, and between religious and secular institutions, in their treatment of the topic and the inclusion of alternative viewpoints, such as creationism (Harmon 2011). There are similar differences across the European Union, including within different populations in member countries.

There are also differences in the teaching of evolution across many predominantly Muslim nations. Salman Hameed, Professor of Integrated Science and Humanities at Hampshire College and Director of the Center for the Study of Science in Muslim Societies (SSiMS), whose research focuses on the acceptance of evolution among Muslims, has uncovered a great deal of variation among Muslims regarding beliefs about evolution. He points out that there is no central position within Islam regarding evolution, leaving it up to governments, textbook authors, and other entities to decide whether, and how, to address evolution in education. Saudi Arabia, Oman, Algeria, Morocco, and Lebanon all ban the teaching of evolution on religious grounds. Other Islamic nations, including Egypt, Malaysia, Syria, and Turkey, include evolutionary concepts like natural selection in their science curriculum but refrain from discussing human evolution (Asghar, Hameed, and Farahani 2014).

Impeding acceptance of evolution in science classes around the world is the adoption of textbooks from the E.U., the U.K., and the U.S. that include examples that are not culturally relevant to local populations (Harmon 2011). One classic example Hameed cites is that of the peppered moths in England whose predominant color pattern evolved from mostly white to mostly black due to pollutants darkening the tree bark of their habitat during the Industrial Revolution. Historical examples like this have little relevance for 21st-century students who grew up in non-Western countries and know little of England's history or of the species that live there. It also privileges Western science over local science, to which many individuals in former European colonies and territories object (Jones 2017). Hameed suggests customizing textbooks to include local fossils and species whenever possible (Harmon 2011).

Are We Still Evolving?

After reading this chapter, many students are curious to know if humans are still evolving. The answer is yes. As a species, we continue to respond to selective pressures biologically and culturally. This final section will focus on three contemporary examples of human evolution. Before beginning, let's review the conditions necessary for natural selection to operate on a trait. First, the trait must be heritable, meaning it is transmitted genetically from generation to generation. There must also be variation of the trait within the population and the trait must influence reproductive success. Three examples of traits that meet these criteria are immunity to the Human Immunodeficiency Virus (HIV), height, and wisdom teeth (Andrews, Kalinowski, and Leonard 2011).

AIDS is a potentially fatal infectious disease caused by HIV, a zoonosis believed to be derived from Simian Immunodeficiency Viruses (SIVs) found in chimpanzees and monkeys and most likely transmitted to humans through the butchering of infected animals (Sharp and Hahn 2011). In total, 40 million people have died from AIDS-related illnesses since the start of the global epidemic in the 1980s. There were 38.4 million people around the world living with AIDS as of 2021, including 1.5 million new cases and 650,000 deaths in that year alone (UNAIDS 2021). A disease causing this level of morbidity and mortality represents a major selective pressure, especially given that infection can occur before birth (Goulder et al. 2016), thereby affecting future reproductive success.

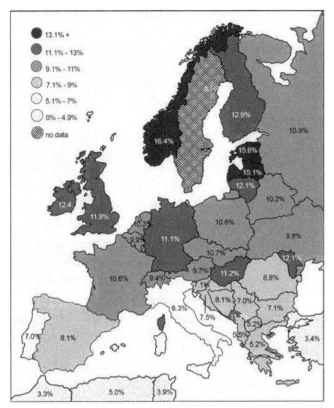

The majority of people in the world are highly susceptible to HIV infection, but some are not. These latter individuals are homozygous for a rare, recessive allele at the CCR5 locus that makes them immune to HIV. Heterozygotes who inherit a single copy of this allele are more resistant to infection and, when infected, the disease takes longer to progress in the event that they are infected. The mechanism by which the allele prevents infection involves a 32-base pair deletion in the DNA sequence of the CCR5 gene, creating a nonfunctioning receptor on the surface of the cell that prevents HIV from infecting the cell. The allele is inherited as a simple Mendelian trait, and there is variation in its prevalence, ranging as high as 14% of the population in northern Europe and Russia (Novembre, Galvani, and Slatkin 2005; see Figure 2.19). What is interesting about the allele's geographic distribution is that it does not map onto parts of the world with the highest rates of HIV infection (Figure 2.20), suggesting that AIDS was not the original selective pressure favoring this allele (see Figures 2.19 and 2.20).

Figure 2.19: Map of CCR5-delta32 allele distribution. Credit: **Map of CCR5-delta32 allele distribution (Figure 16.10)** original to **Explorations: An Open Invitation to Biological Anthropology** by Katie Nelson is a collective work under a **CC BY-NC 4.0 License**. [Includes **Europe Map Western Political 32847** by Clker-Free-Vector-Images, Pixabay License; data from Solloch et al. 2017.] [Image Description].

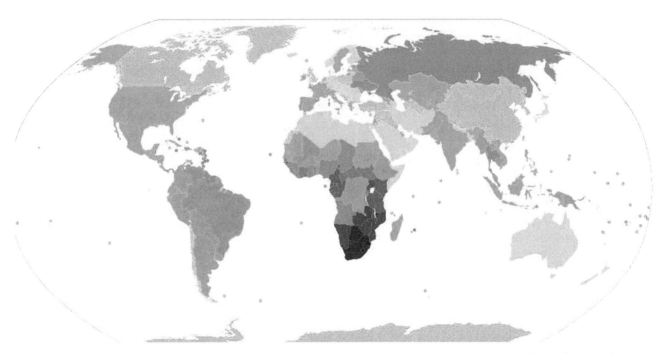

Figure 2.20: World map of countries shaded according to their HIV/AIDS adult prevalence rate in 2020. Credit: **World map of countries by HIV-AIDS adult prevalence rate (2020)** by LuccaSSC has been designated to the **public domain (CC0 1.0)**. [Image Description].

Given its current geographic distribution, the bubonic plague, which ravaged Europe repeatedly from the 14th to the 19th centuries (Pamuk 2007), was initially proposed as the selective agent. Subsequent research suggests smallpox, which killed up to 400,000 people annually in 18th-century Europe (Hays 2005), was more likely the selective pressure (Novembre, Galvani, and Slatkin 2005). Given the mortality rates for smallpox (Crosby 2003), an allele that conferred immunity was highly advantageous, as it is for those faced with the threat of HIV infection today.

Height is another example of a trait experiencing selective pressure. If you have ever toured a historical site, you have likely hit your head on a doorframe or become claustrophobic trying to squeeze down a narrow hallway under a lower-than-average ceiling. It is not your imagination. Humans have gotten taller in recent centuries. In fact, the average height of people in industrialized nations has increased approximately 10 centimeters (about four inches) in the past 150 years. This increase has been attributed to improvements in nutrition, sanitation, and access to medical care (Hatton 2014). But this is only part of the story.

Height is highly heritable. Studies indicate 80% of variation in height within populations is due to genetics, with 697 different genetic variances identified as having an effect on adult stature (Devuyst 2014). Multiple studies also demonstrate a positive relationship between height and reproductive success for men (Andrews, Kalinowsky, and Leonard 2011). This is primarily due to sexual selection and nonrandom mating, namely women's preferences for taller men, which may explain why height is one characteristic men often lie about on dating websites (Guadagno, Okdie, and Kruse 2012). Sexual selection also plays out with regard to economic success in Western cultures, with taller men more likely to be in higher-level positions that pay well. Research demonstrates an inch of height is worth an additional $789 per year in salary, meaning a man who is six feet tall will earn on average $5,525 more per year than an identical man who is five foot five purely due to heightism bias (Gladwell 2007). Over the course of a career, this can add up to hundreds of thousands of dollars, likely allowing taller men to attract more potential mates, increasing their reproductive success.

Wisdom teeth are also undergoing evolutionary pressure. Have you or anyone in your family had their wisdom teeth removed? While it can be a painful and expensive process, it is a common experience in Western nations. It begs the question as to why there is no longer room in our mouths for all of our teeth? Biological anthropologist Daniel Lieberman offers several reasons, including that modern humans are growing faster and maturing earlier, which could be leading to impaction if skeletal growth takes place faster than dental growth. He also argues that the soft diets many modern humans consume generate insufficient strain to stimulate enough growth in our jaws to accommodate all of our teeth. Lastly, as the human brain has expanded over the past hundreds of thousands of years, it is taking up more space in the skull, causing the jaw to shrink, leaving no room for third molars (Lieberman 2011).

Conversely, do you know anyone whose wisdom teeth never came in? That is fairly common in some populations, suggesting evolutionary pressure favoring the absence of wisdom teeth has been culturally influenced. The oldest fossil evidence of skulls missing third molars was found in China and is 300,000 to 400,000 years old, suggesting the earliest mutation selecting against the eruption of wisdom teeth arose in Asia (Main 2013). Since that time, jaws have continued to decrease in size to the point they often cannot accommodate third molars, which can become impacted, painful, and even infected, a condition physical anthropologist Alan Main argues might have interfered with the ability to survive and reproduce in ancestral populations (Main 2013). As we have learned, a mutation that positively influences reproductive success—such as being born without the trait to develop wisdom teeth—would likely be selected for over time. Evidence in modern humans suggests that this is the case, with 40% of modern Asians and 45% of Native Alaskans and Greenlanders (populations descended from Asian populations) lacking wisdom teeth. The percentage among those of European descent ranges from 10 to 25% and for African Americans is 11% (Main 2013). Later chapters of this textbook emphasize that directional selection progresses along a particular path until the environment changes and a trait is no longer advantageous. In the case of wisdom teeth, the ability of modern dentistry to preempt impaction through surgery may, in fact, be what is preventing natural selection from doing away with wisdom teeth altogether.

Key Developments in Evolutionary Thought

- Aristotle (384–322 BCE): "Founder of Biology." Publishes *History of Animals*, a biological classification system of over 500 animals based on structure, physiology, reproduction, and behavior. Also creates the "Great Chain of Being," ranking species and placing humans closest to God.

- Al-Jahiz (776–868 CE): Writes seven-volume *Book of Animals*, which includes animal classifications and food chains. Introduces concept of biological evolution and its mechanisms.

- Ibn al-Haythem (965–1040 CE): "Father of Modern Optics." Uses experimental science to catalog how vision works and discovers laws of reflection and refraction. Publishes *Book of Optics* and invents *camera obscura*, the foundation for modern photography.

- Francis Bacon (1561–1626): "Father of Empiricism." Publishes *The Novum Annum*, formulating the scientific method based on observation and inductive reasoning.

- John Ray (1627–1705): First to publish a biological definition of *species* in *History of Plants*.

- Comte de Buffon (1707–1788): Publishes *Histoire Naturelle*, comparing anatomical structures across species using methods still in use today. Inspires Lamarck and Cuvier.

- Carl von Linne (Carolus Linnaeus) (1707–1778): Introduces system of binomial nomenclature. Publishes *Systema Naturae*, the tenth edition of which introduces the designation *Homo sapiens* for humans.

- James Hutton (1726–1797): "Father of Geology." Publishes *Theory of the Earth*; introduces idea of Deep Time; explains how features of the earth were formed through the actions of rain, wind, rivers, and volcanic eruptions.

- Thomas Malthus (1766–1834): Economist and "Father of Statistics." Publishes *An Essay on Population*; introduces concept of carrying capacity; explains how populations outstrip the food supply, leaving some individuals to die off; inspires Darwin's idea of "natural selection."

- Jean-Baptiste Lamarck (1744–1829): Publishes theory of the Inheritance of acquired characteristics; is the first Western scientist to propose a mechanism explaining how traits change in species over time and to recognize the importance of the physical environment in acting on species and their survival.

- Georges Cuvier (1769–1832): Paleontologist/comparative anatomist; proved species went extinct; proposed the Theory of Catastrophism.

- Charles Lyell (1797–1875): Establishes geology as a science. Publishes first edition of *The Principles of Geology* (1830–33); issuing 12 total editions in his lifetime, each updated according to new scientific data.

- Alfred Russel Wallace (1823–1913): Sends scientific paper to Darwin titled "On the Tendency of Varieties to Depart Indefinitely from the Original Type," essentially espousing the concept of natural selection; a reading of the papers by both Wallace and Darwin to the Linnaean Society is conducted by Lyell.

- Charles Darwin (1809–1882): Publishes *On the Origin of Species by Means of Natural Selection* (1859).

- Gregor Mendel (1822–1884): Publishes *Experiments in Plant Hybridization* (1865), outlining the fundamentals of genetic inheritance.

- August Weismann (1834–1914): Publishes *Essays Upon Heredity* (1889), disproving the inheritance of acquired characteristics. Publishes *The Germ Plasm* (1892), postulating an early idea of inheritance through sexual reproduction.

- Theodosius Dobzhansky (1900–1975): One of the founders of the Modern Synthesis of biology and genetics. Publishes *Genetics and the Origin of Species* (1937). Documents a genetic model of speciation through reproductive isolation.

Review Questions

- Summarize the major scientific developments that led to the formulation of the theory of natural selection.

- Explain how natural selection operates and how it leads to evolution in populations.
- Explain the importance of genetics to an understanding of human evolution.
- Have you observed current examples of evolution taking place where you live? In which species? Which forces of evolution are involved?

Key Terms

Allele: A nonidentical DNA sequence found in the same gene location on a homologous chromosome, or gene copy, that codes for the same trait but produces a different phenotype.

Artificial selection: The identification by humans of desirable traits in plants and animals, and the subsequent steps taken to enhance and perpetuate those traits in future generations.

Binomial nomenclature: A system of classification in which a species of animal or plant receives a name consisting of two terms: the first identifies the genus to which it belongs, and the second identifies the species.

Carrying capacity: The number of living organisms, including animals, crops, and humans, that a geographic area can support without environmental degradation.

Catastrophism: The theory that the Earth's geology has largely been shaped by sudden, short-lived, violent events, possibly worldwide in scope. Compare to uniformitarianism.

Comparative anatomy: Georges-Louis Leclerc's technique of comparing similar anatomical structures across different species.

Creationism: The belief that the universe and all living organisms originate from specific acts of divine creation, as in the Biblical account, rather than by natural processes such as evolution.

Empiricism: The idea that all learning and knowledge derives from experience and observation. It became prominent in the 17th and 18th centuries in western Europe due to the rise of experimental science.

Evolution: In a biological sense, this term refers to cumulative inherited change in a population of organisms through time. More specifically, *evolution* is defined as a change in allele (gene) frequencies from one generation to the next among members of an interbreeding population.

Extant: Still in existence; surviving.

Extinct: Said of a species, family, or other group of animals or plants that has no living members; no longer in existence.

Fixity of Species: The idea that a species, once created, remains unchanged over time.

Gene: A sequence of DNA that provides coding information for the construction of proteins.

Genetic drift: Random changes in allele frequencies within a population from one generation to the next.

Gene flow: The introduction of new genetic material into a population through interbreeding between two distinct populations.

Gene pool: The entire collection of genetic material in a breeding community that can be passed from one generation to the next.

Genotype: The genotype of an organism is its complete set of genetic material—its unique sequence of DNA. Genotype also refers to the alleles or variants an individual carries in a particular gene or genetic location.

Hybrid: Offspring of parents that differ in genetically determined traits.

Intelligent design: A pseudoscientific set of beliefs based on the notion that life on earth is so complex that it cannot be explained by the scientific theory of evolution and therefore must have been designed by a supernatural entity.

Macroevolution: Large and often-complex changes in biological populations, such as species formation.

Microevolution: Changes in the frequency of a gene or allele in an interbreeding population.

Modern synthesis: The mid–20th century merging of Mendelian genetics with Darwinian evolution that resulted in a unified theory of evolution.

Natural selection: The natural process by which the survival and reproductive success of individuals or groups within an interbreeding population that are best adjusted to their environment leads to the perpetuation of genetic qualities best suited to that particular environment at that point in time.

Phenotype: The detectable or visible expression of an organism's *genotype*.

Scientific method: A method of procedure that has characterized natural science since the 17th century, consisting of systematic observation, measurement, experimentation, and the formulation, testing, and modification of hypotheses.

Speciation: The process by which new genetically distinct species evolve from the main population, usually through geographic isolation or other barriers to gene flow.

Species: A group of living organisms consisting of similar individuals capable of exchanging genes or interbreeding. The species is the principal natural taxonomic unit, ranking below a genus and denoted by a Latin binomial (e.g., *Homo sapiens*).

Uniformitarianism: The theory that changes in the earth's crust during geologic history have resulted from the action of continuous and uniform processes—such as wind, precipitation, evaporation, condensation, erosion, and volcanic action—that continue to act in the present. Compare to *catastrophism*.

About the Author

Joylin Namie, Ph.D.

Truckee Meadows Community College, jnamie@tmcc.edu

Joylin Namie is Professor of Anthropology at Truckee Meadows Community College, where she teaches courses in biological and cultural anthropology. Her current research interest is in (un)sustainable tourism in desert environments, particularly in the country of Jordan and the U.S. state of Nevada. She was awarded a fellowship to Jordan from the Council of American Overseas Research Centers (CAORC) in 2020 to explore this topic, including visiting Petra and other important tourism destinations in Jordan. Dr. Namie's favorite things in life are teaching, traveling, and spending time with her dog, Charley.

For Further Exploration

Costa, James T. 2017. *Darwin's Backyard: How Small Experiments Led to a Big Theory*. New York: W.W. Norton.

Darwin, Charles. 1905. *The Voyage of the Beagle*. (Originally published in 1839 as *Journal and Remarks*). [Author's note: Several editions exist with different publishers, including illustrated editions, paperback editions, and e-books.]

Moore, John A. 1993. *Science as a Way of Knowing: The Foundations of Modern Biology*. Cambridge, MA: Harvard University Press.

References

Al-Haytham, Ibn. 1011-1021. *Kitāb al-Manāẓir* (Book of Optics). Cairo, Egypt.

Al-Jahiz. 776–868 CE. *Kitab al-Hayawan* (*Book of Animals*).

Andrews, Tessa M., Steven T. Kalinowski, and Mary J. Leonard. 2011. "Are Humans Evolving? A Classroom Discussion to Change Students' Misconceptions Regarding Natural Selection." *Evolution: Education and Outreach* 4 (3): 456–466.

Aristotle. 384-322 BCE. *History of Animals*.

Asghar, Anila, Salman Hameed, and Najme Kashani Farahani. 2014. "Evolution in Biology Textbooks: A Comparative Analysis of Five Muslim Countries." *Religion & Education* 41 (1). Accessed February 12, 2023. https://www.tandfonline.com/doi/abs/10.1080/15507394.2014.855081.

Associated Press. January 10, 2023. "Forest Lizards Have Genetically Morphed To Survive Life In The City, Researchers Say." *National Public Radio (NPR)*. Retrieved February 19, 2023 from https://www.npr.org/2023/01/10/1148150056/forest-lizards-genetically-morphed-cities.

Burkhardt, Richard W. 2013. "Lamarck, Evolution, and the Inheritance of Acquired Characters." *Genetics* 194 (4): 793–805.

Chen, Xiqun, Danielle Feng, Michael A. Schwartzchild, and Xiang Gao. 2017. "Red Hair, MC1R Variants, and Risk for Parkinson's Disease—A Meta-Analysis." *Annals of Clinical and Translational Neurology* 4 (3): 212–216.https://doi.org/10.1002/acn3.381.

Colliss Harvey, Jacky. 2015. *Red: A History of the Redhead*. New York: Black Dog & Levanthal.

Corning, Peter A. 2020. "Beyond the Modern Synthesis: A Framework for a More Inclusive Biological Synthesis." *Progress in Biophysics and Molecular Biology* 153: 5–12.

Costa, James T. 2017. *Darwin's Backyard: How Small Experiments Led to a Big Theory*. New York: W. W. Norton.

Crosby, Alfred W., Jr. 2003. *The Columbian Exchange: Biological and Cultural Consequences of 1492*. 30th Anniversary Edition. Westport, CT: Praeger.

Darwin, Charles. 1859. *On the Origin of Species by Means of Natural Selection, or the Preservation of Favoured Races in the Struggle for Life*. First Edition. London: John Murray.

Darwin, Francis, ed. 2001[1897]. *The Life & Letters of Charles Darwin*, vol. 2. Honolulu: University Press of the Pacific.

Desilver, Drew. 2017. "U.S. Students' Academic Achievement Still Lags That of Their Peers in Many Other Countries." Pew Research Center, February 15. Accessed May 25, 2022. https://www.pewresearch.org/fact-tank/2017/02/15/u-s-students-internationally-math-science/.

Devuyst, Olivier. 2014. "High Time for Human Height." *Peritoneal Dialysis International* 34 (7):685–686.

Dobzhansky, Theodosius. 1937. *Genetics and the Origin of Species*. Columbia University Biological Series (Volume 11). New York: Columbia University Press.

Dunbar-Ortiz, Roxanne. 2014. *An Indigenous Peoples' History of the United States*. Boston: Beacon.

El-Zaher, Sumaya. 2018. "The Father of the Theory of Evolution: Al-Jahiz and His Book of Animals." MVSLIM.com, October 9. Accessed August 27, 2022. https://mvslim.com/the-father-of-the-theory-of-evolution-al-jahiz-and-his-book-of-animals/.

Elshakry, Marwa. 2010. "When Science Became Western: Historiographical Reflections." *ISIS* 101 (1). Accessed November 20, 2022. https://www.journals.uchicago.edu/doi/10.1086/652691.

Gladwell, Malcolm. 2007. *Blink: The Power of Thinking without Thinking*. New York: Back Bay

Guadagno, Rosanna E., Bradley M. Okdie, and Sara A. Kruse. 2012. "Dating Deception: Gender, Online Dating, and Exaggerated Self-Presentation." *Computers in Human Behavior* 28 (2): 642–647.

Harmon, Katherine. 2011. "Evolution Abroad: Creationism Evolves in Science Classrooms around the Globe." *Scientific American,* March 3. Accessed May 25, 2022. https://www.scientificamerican.com/article/evolution-education-abroad/.

Harrison, Ellie. 2018. "This is What the Perfect Body Looks Like – According to Science." *Radiotimes.com*. Accessed June 14, 2023. https://www.radiotimes.com/tv/documentaries/this-is-what-the-perfect-body-looks-like-according-to-science/.

Hatton, Tim. 2014. "Why Did Humans Grow Four Inches in 100 Years? It Wasn't Just Diet." *The Conversation*, May 1. https://theconversation.com/why-did-humans-grow-four-inches-In-100-years-it-wasnt-just-diet-25919.

Hays, J. N. 2005. *Epidemics and Pandemics: Their Impacts on Human History*. Santa Barbara, CA: ABC-CLIO.

Hutton, James. 1788. *Theory of the Earth*. Transactions of the Royal Society of Edinburgh, Volume 1. Scotland: Royal Society of Edinburgh.

IPCC. 2022. *Climate Change 2022: Impacts, Adaptation, and Vulnerability*. Contribution of Working Group II to the Sixth Assessment Report of the Intergovernmental Panel on Climate Change, edited by H.-O. Pörtner, D.C. Roberts, M. Tignor, E.S. Poloczanska, K. Mintenbeck, A. Alegría, M. Craig, S. Langsdorf, S. Löschke, V. Möller, A. Okem, and B. Rama. Cambridge: Cambridge University Press. https://www.ipcc.ch/report/ar6/wg2/.

Jones, Stephen. 2017. "Religion, Science, and Evolutionary Theory"[an interview with Salman Hameed]. Podcast, *The Religious Studies Project*, January 30. Accessed May 29, 2023. https://www.religiousstudiesproject.com/podcast/religion-science-and-evolutionary-theory/.

Kutschera, Ulrich, and Karl J. Niklas. 2004. "The Modern Theory of Biological Evolution: An Expanded Synthesis." *Naturwissenschaften* 91: 255–276.

Leclerc, Georges-Louis, Comte de Buffon. 1749-1804. *Histoire Naturelle*. Volumes 1-36. Paris: *Imprimerie Royale* (Royal Printing House).

Lents, Nathan H. 2018. *Human Errors: A Panorama of Our Glitches, from Pointless Bones to Broken Genes*. Boston: Houghton Mifflin Harcourt.

Lerner, Lawrence S. 2000. *Good Science, Bad Science: Teaching Evolution in the States*. Washington, DC: Thomas B. Fordham Foundation.

Lieberman, Daniel E. 2011. *The Evolution of the Human Head*. Cambridge, MA: Harvard University Press.

Lindberg, David C. 1992. *The Beginnings of Western Science: The European Scientific Tradition in Philosophical, Religious, and Institutional Context, 600 B.C. to A.D. 1450*. Chicago: The University of Chicago Press.

Linnaeus, Carl. 1736. *Systema Naturae*. First Edition. Stockholm: Laurentius Salvius.

Love, Shayla. 2020. "A Thousand Years before Darwin, Islamic Scholars Were Writing about Evolution." VICE World News, October 5. Accessed August 27, 2022. https://www.vice.com/en/article/ep4ykn/a-thousand-years-before-darwin-islamic-scholars-were-writing-about-natural-selection.

Main, Douglas. 2013. "Ancient Mutation Explains Missing Wisdom Teeth." *Live Science*, March 13. https://www.livescience.com/27529-missing-wisdom-teeth.html.

Malthus, Thomas Robert. 1798. *An Essay on the Principle of Population*. London: J. Johnson.

Masci, David. 2019. "For Darwin Day, 6 Facts About the Evolution Debate." Pew Research Center. Accessed June 14, 2023. https://www.pewresearch.org/short-reads/2019/02/11/darwin-day/.

Masood, Ehsan. 2009. "Islam's Evolutionary Legacy." *The Guardian*, March 1. Accessed February 13, 2023. https://www.theguardian.com/commentisfree/belief/2009/feb/27/islam-religion-evolution-science.

Miller, Jon D., Eugenie C. Scott, Mark S. Ackerman, Belen Laspra, Glenn Branch, Carmelo Polino, and Jordan S. Huffaker. 2022. "Public Acceptance of Evolution in the United States, 1985–2020." *Public Understanding of Science* 31 (2): 223–238.

Miller, Jon D., Eugenie C. Scott, and Shinji Okamoto. 2006, August 11. "Public Acceptance of Evolution." *Science* 313 (5788): 765-766. DOI: 10.1126/science.1126746.

Moore, John A. 1993. *Science as a Way of Knowing: The Foundations of Modern Biology.* Cambridge, MA: Harvard University Press.

Moore, Michael P., Kaitlyn Hersch, Chanont Sricharoen, Sarah Lee, Caitlin Reice, Paul Rice, Sophie Kronick, Kim A. Medley, and Kasey D. Fowler-Finn. 2021. "Sex-Specific Ornament Evolution Is a Consistent Feature of Climatic Adaptation across Space and Time in Dragonflies." *PNAS* 118 (28): e2101458118. https://doi.org/10.1073/pnas.210145818.

National Public Radio. 2023. "Forest Lizards Have Genetically Morphed to Survive Life in the City, Researchers Say." *National Public Radio (NPR),* January 10. Accessed February 19, 2023. https://www.npr.org/2023/01/10/1148150056/forest-lizards-genetically-morphed-cities.

National Science Foundation. 2023. "Urban Lizards Share Genomic Markers Not Found in Forest-Dwellers." National Science Foundation, February 7. Accessed May 25, 2023. https://beta.nsf.gov/news/urban-lizards-share-genomic-markers-not-found.

Novembre, John, Alison P. Galvani, and Montgomery Slatkin. 2005. "The Geographic Spread of the CCR5 Δ32 HIV-Resistance Allele." *PLoS Biology* 3 (11): e339.

Pamuk, Şevket. 2007. "The Black Death and the Origins of the 'Great Divergence' across Europe, 1300–1600." *European Review of Economic History* 11 (3): 289–317.

Paterlini, Marta. 2007. "There Shall Be Order: The Legacy of Linnaeus in the Age of Molecular Biology." *EMBO Reports* 8 (9): 814–816. https://doi.org/10.1038/sj.embor.7401061.

Pew Research Center. 2019. "Darwin in America: The Evolution Debate in the United States." Pew Research Center, February 6, 2019. Accessed June 13, 2023. https://www.pewresearch.org/religion/2019/02/06/darwin-in-america-2/.

Pew Research Center. 2014. "Fighting Over Darwin, State by State." Pew Research Center, February 4, 2009; updated February 3, 2014. Accessed May 25, 2022. https://www.pewresearch.org/religion/2009/02/04/fighting-over-darwin-state-by-state/.

Plutynski, Anya. 2009. "The Modern Synthesis." *Routledge Encyclopedia of Philosophy*, November 15 (updated December 14, 2009). Accessed November 27, 2022. http://philsci-archive.pitt.edu/15335/.

Plutzer, Eric, Glenn Branch, and Ann Reid. 2020. "Teaching Evolution in the U.S. Public Schools: A Continuing Challenge." *Evolution: Education and Outreach* 13: Article 14. https://evolution-outreach.biomedcentral.com/articles/10.1186/s12052-020-00126-8.

Proceedings of the National Academy of Sciences (PNAS). 2023. "How Lizards Adapt to Urban Living." *Science Sessions Podcast,* February 13, . Accessed February 19, 2023. https://www.pnas.org/post/podcast/lizards-adapt-urban-living.

Public Broadcasting System. 2001. "Georges Cuvier." *WGBH Evolution Library.* Accessed May 26, 2022. https://www.pbs.org/wgbh/evolution/library/02/1/l_021_01.html#   :~:text=With%20elegant%20studies%20of%20the,as%20incontrovertible%20proof%20of%20extinctions.

Ray, John. 1686-1704. *Historia plantarum.* London: Clark. Volume 1 (1686), Volume II (1688), Volume III (1704).

Richards, Richard A. 1998. "Darwin, Domestic Breeding, and Artificial Selection." *Endeavour* 22 (3): 106–109.

Solloch, Ute V., Kathrin Lang, Vinzenz Lange, and Irena Böhme. 2017. "Frequencies of Gene Variant CCR5-Δ32 in 87 Countries Based on Next-Generation Sequencing of 1.3 Million Individuals Sampled from 3 National DKMS Donor Centers." *Human Immunology* 78 (11–12): 701-717.

Stewart, Thomas A., Justin B. Lemberg, Ailis Daly, Edward B. Daeschler, and Neil H. Shubin. 2022. "A New Epistostegalian from the Late Devonian of the Canadian Arctic." *Nature* 608 (7923): 563–568.

Tasci, Ufuk Necat. 2020. "How a 10-Century Muslim Physicist Discovered How Humans See." *TRT World*, May 25. Accessed May 18, 2022. https://www.trtworld.com/magazine/how-a-10th-century-muslim-physicist-discovered-how-humans-see-36620.

Tbakhi, Abdelghani, and Samir S. Amr. 2007. "Ibn Al-Haytham: Father of Modern Optics." *Annals of Saudi Medicine* 27 (6): 464–467. UNAIDS. 2021. "Global HIV & AIDS Statistics—Fact Sheet." https://www.unaids.org/en/resources/fact-sheet.

UNESCO.org. 2015. "International Year of Light: Ibn al Haytham, Pioneer of Modern Optics celebrated at UNESCO." UNESCO, September 8. Accessed May 18, 2022. https://www.unesco.org/en/articles/international-year-light-ibn-al-haytham-pioneer-modern-optics-celebrated-unesco.

University of California Berkeley Museum of Paleontology. N.d. "The History of Evolutionary Thought—Uniformitarianism: Charles Lyell." *Understanding Evolution* website. Accessed February 13, 2023. https://evolution.berkeley.edu/the-history-of-evolutionary-thought/1800s/uniformitarianism-charles-lyell/.

University of Cambridge. N.d. "Darwin and Dogs." *The Darwin Correspondence Project* website. Accessed February 17, 2023. https://www.darwinproject.ac.uk/commentary/curious/darwin-and-dogs.

Urbach, Peter Michael, Anthony M. Quinton, and Kathleen Marguerite Lea. "Francis Bacon: British Author, Philosopher, and Statesman." *Encyclopaedia Britannica*. Last updated May 12, 2023. https://www.britannica.com/biography/Francis-Bacon-Viscount-Saint-Alban.

Ward, Peter. 2018. *Lamarck's Revenge: How Epigenetics Is Revolutionizing Our Understanding of Evolution's Past and Present.* New York: Bloomsbury.

Weismann, August. 1892. *Das Keimplasma: Eine Theorie der Vererbung* (*The Germ Plasm: a Theory of Inheritance*). Jena (Germany): Fischer.

Weismann, August. 1889. Translations. *Essays upon Heredity.* Oxford: Clarendon. Accessed November 27, 2022. E-copy available at http://www.esp.org/books/weismann/essays/facsimile/.

Winchell, Kristen M., Shane C. Campbell-Staton, Jonathan B. Losos, and Anthony Geneva. 2023. "Genome-Wide Parallelism Underlies Contemporary Adaptation In Urban Lizards." *PNAS* 120 (3): e2216789120. https://doi.org/10.1073/pnas.2216789120.

Wood, Bernard. 2005. *Human Evolution: A Very Short Introduction.* Oxford: Oxford University Press.

Zou, Yawen. 2015. "The Germ-Plasm: a Theory of Heredity (1893), by August Weismann." *Embryo Project Encyclopedia*, January 26. Accessed February 18, 2023. http://embryo.asu.edu/handle/10776/8284.

Image Descriptions

Figure 2.11: A simple world map with a line depicting the ocean route that the H.M.S. Beagle took, and the ports visited. Leaving Plymouth (Europe), the ship traveled south past Africa, around most of the coastline of South America, then around the southern sides of Australia and Africa, before returning briefly to South America and then Europe. Ports noted on the map include Plymouth (Europe); Teneriffa (Africa), Kap Verde, Salvador da Bahia, Rio de Janeiro, Montevideo, Falklandinseln, Valparaiso, Callao Lima, Galápagos-Inseln Kap Verde (South America); Sydney, Hobart, King George Sound (Australia), Kokosinseln, Mauritius (Southeast Asian Islands); Kapstadt (Africa); Salvador da Bahia (South America); Azoren (Atlantic Island); Plymouth (Europe).

Figure 2.19: Grayscale political map of Europe on a blue background. The percentage of individuals with the CCR5-delta 32 allele is printed on each nation. Albania: 5.5%; Algeria: 5.0%; Armenia: 3.3%; Austria: 9.7%; Azerbaijan: 4.0%; Belarus: 10.2%; Belgium: 9.9%; Bosnia-Herzegovina: 8.1%; Bulgaria: 7.1%; Chile:12.0%; Croatia : 7.5%; Czech Republic: 10.7%; Denmark: 12.3%; Eritrea: 0.3%; Estonia: 15.6%; Faroe Islands: 9.9%;

Finland: 12.9%; France: 10.6%; Georgia: 4.2%; Germany: 11.1%; Greece: 5.2%; Hungary: 11.2%; Ireland: 12.4%; Italy: 6.3%; Kazakhstan: 10.3%; Latvia: 15.1%; Lithuania: 12.1%; Luxembourg: 9.2%; Macedonia: 5.2%; Morocco: 3.3%; Moldova: 12.1%; Montenegro: 11.1%; Netherlands: 10.3%; Norway: 16.4%; Poland: 10.6%; Romania: 8.8%; Russia: 10.9%; Serbia: 7.0%; Slovakia: 9.4%; Slovenia: 7.1%; Spain: 8.1%; Switzerland: 9.4%; Tunisia: 3.9%; Turkey: 3.4%; Ukraine: 9.8%; United Kingdom: 11.8%.

Figure 2.20: Political map of the world on a white oval background. Unlabeled nations are color coded by the percentage of individuals with HIV/AIDS. Colors range from no-data (gray), and shades of pink and red. Categories are from lightest pink: x < 0.2%, 0.2% ≤ x < 0.5%, 0.5% ≤ x < 1%, 1% ≤ x < 2%, 2% ≤ x < 3%, 3% ≤ x < 5%, 5% ≤ x < 10%, 10% ≤ x < 15%, 15% ≤ x < 20%, 20% ≤ x. The lightest shades of pink are in North Africa, the Middle east, Australia, and parts of Europe. The darkest shades are found in sub saharan Africa, particularly in the most southern and eastern regions.

3.

MOLECULAR BIOLOGY AND GENETICS

Hayley Mann, M.A., Binghamton University

This chapter is a revision from "Chapter 3: Molecular Biology and Genetics" by Hayley Mann, Xazmin Lowman, and Malaina Gaddis. In Explorations: An Open Invitation to Biological Anthropology, first edition, edited by Beth Shook, Katie Nelson, Kelsie Aguilera, and Lara Braff, which is licensed under CC BY-NC 4.0.

Learning Objectives

- Explain and identify the purpose of both DNA replication and the cell cycle.
- Identify key differences between mitosis and meiosis.
- Outline the process of protein synthesis, including transcription and translation.
- Use principles of Mendelian inheritance to predict genotypes and phenotypes of future generations.
- Explain complexities surrounding patterns of genetic inheritance and polygenic traits.
- Discuss challenges to and bioethical concerns of genetic testing.

I [Hayley Mann] started my Bachelor's degree in 2003, which was the same year the Human Genome Project released its first draft sequence. I initially declared a genetics major because I thought it sounded cool. However, upon taking an actual class, I discovered that genetics was *challenging*. In addition to my genetics major, I signed up for biological anthropology classes and soon learned that anthropology could bring all those molecular lessons to life. For instance, we are composed of cells, proteins, nucleic acids, carbohydrates, and lipids. Anthropologists often include these molecules in their studies to identify how humans vary; if there are meaningful differences, they propose theories to explain them. Anthropologists study biomolecules in both living and ancient individuals. Ancient biomolecules can also be found on artifacts such as stone tools and cooking vessels. Over the years, scientific techniques for studying organic molecules have improved, which has unlocked new insights into the deep human past.

This chapter provides the basics for understanding human variation and how the evolutionary process works. A few advanced genetics topics are also presented because biotechnology is now commonplace in health and society. Understanding the science behind this remarkable field means you will be able to participate in bioethical and anthropological discussions as well as make more informed decisions regarding genetic testing.

Cells and Molecules

Molecules of Life

All organisms are composed of four basic types of molecules that are essential for cell structure and function: proteins, lipids, carbohydrates, and nucleic acids (Figure 3.1). **Proteins** are crucial for cell shape and nearly all cellular tasks, including receiving signals from outside the cell and mobilizing intra-cellular responses. **Lipids** are a class of organic compounds that include fats, oils, and hormones. As discussed later in the chapter, lipids are also responsible for the characteristic phospholipid bilayer structure of the cell membrane. **Carbohydrates** are sugar molecules and serve as energy to cells in the form of glucose. Lastly, **nucleic acids**, including **deoxyribonucleic acid (DNA)**, carry genetic information about a living organism.

Figure 3.1: Information about the four biomolecules. Credit: Biomolecules Table original to Explorations: An Open Invitation to Biological Anthropology (2nd ed.) by Hayley Mann is under a CC BY-NC 4.0 License.

Molecule	Definition	Example
Proteins	Composed of one or more long chains of amino acids (i.e., basic units of protein) Often folded into complex 3D shapes that relate to function Proteins interact with other types of proteins and molecules	Proteins come in different categories including structural (e.g., collagen, keratin, lactase, hemoglobin, cell membrane proteins), defense proteins (e.g, antibodies), enzymes (e.g., lactase), hormones (e.g., insulin), and motor proteins (e.g., actin)
Lipids	Insoluble in water due to hydrophilic (water-loving) head and a hydrophobic (water-repelling) tail	Fats, such as triglycerides, store energy for your body Steroid hormones (e.g., estrogen and testosterone) act as chemical messengers to communicate between cells and tissues, as well as biochemical pathways inside of the cell
Carbohydrates	Large group of organic molecules that are composed of carbon and hydrogen atoms	Starches and sugars, including blood glucose, provide cells with energy
Nucleic Acids	Carries the genetic information of an organism	DNA RNA

Cells

In 1665, Robert Hooke observed slices of plant cork using a microscope. Hooke noted that the microscopic plant structures he saw resembled *cella,* meaning "a small room" in Latin. Approximately two centuries later, biologists recognized the cell as being the most fundamental unit of life and that all life is composed of cells. Cellular organisms can be characterized as two main cell types: **prokaryotes** and **eukaryotes** (Figure 3.2).

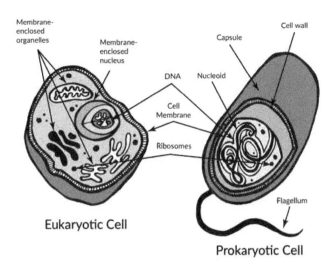

Prokaryotes include bacteria and archaea, and they are composed of a single cell. Additionally, their DNA and **organelles** are not surrounded by individual membranes. Thus, no compartments separate their DNA from the rest of the cell (see Figure 3.2). It is well known that some bacteria can cause illness in humans. For instance, *Escherichia coli* (*E. coli*) and *Salmonella* contamination can result in food poisoning symptoms. Pneumonia and strep throat are caused by *Streptococcal* bacteria. *Neisseria gonorrhoeae* is a sexually transmitted bacterial disease. Although bacteria are commonly associated with illness, not all bacteria are harmful. For example, researchers are studying the relationship between the **microbiome** and human health. The bacteria that are part of the healthy human microbiome perform beneficial roles, such as digesting food, boosting the immune system, and even making vitamins (e.g., B12 and K).

Eukaryotes can be single-celled or multi-celled in their body composition. In contrast to prokaryotes, eukaryotes possess membranes that surround their DNA and organelles. An example of a single-celled eukaryote is the microscopic algae found in ponds (phytoplankton), which can produce oxygen from the sun. Yeasts are also single-celled, and fungi can be single- or multicellular. Plants and animals are all multicellular.

Although plant and animal cells have a surprising number of similarities, there are some key differences (Figure 3.3). For example, plant cells possess a thick outer cell membrane made of a fibrous carbohydrate called cellulose. Animal and plant cells also have different **tissues**. A tissue is an aggregation of cells that are morphologically similar and perform the same task. For most plants, the outermost layer of cells forms a waxy cuticle that helps to protect the cells and to prevent water loss. Humans have skin, which is the outermost cell layer that is predominantly composed of a tough protein called keratin. Overall, humans have a diversity of tissue types (e.g., cartilage, brain, and heart).

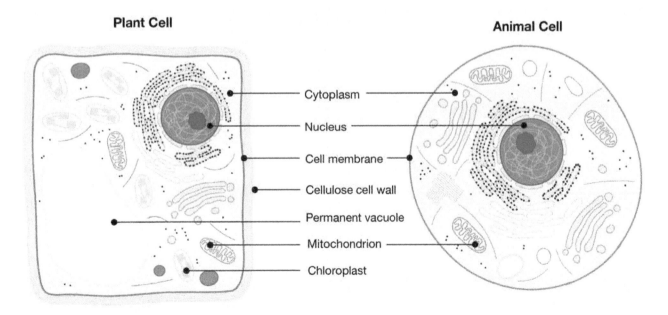

Animal Cell Organelles

An animal cell is surrounded by a double membrane called the **phospholipid bilayer** (Figure 3.4). A closer look reveals that this protective barrier is made of lipids and proteins that provide structure and function for cellular activities, such as regulating the passage of molecules and ions (e.g., H_2O and sodium) into and out of the cell. **Cytoplasm** is the jelly-like matrix inside of the cell membrane. Part of the cytoplasm comprises organelles, which perform different specialized tasks for the cell (Figure 3.5). An example of an organelle is the **nucleus**, where the cell's DNA is located.

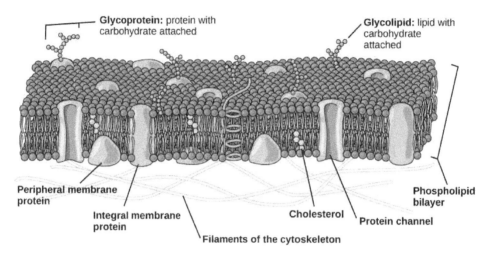

Figure 3.4: A phospholipid bilayer with membrane-bound carbohydrates and proteins. Credit: Cell Membrane (Anatomy & Physiology, Figure 3.4) by OpenStax is under a CC BY 4.0 License. [Image Description].

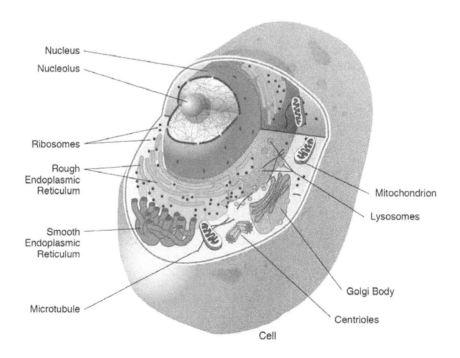

Figure 3.5: An animal cell with membrane-enclosed organelles. Credit: Organelle by NIH National Human Genome Research Institute is in the public domain. [Image Description].

Another organelle is the **mitochondrion**. Mitochondria are often referred to as "powerhouse centers" because they produce energy for the cell in the form of **adenosine triphosphate (ATP)**. Depending on the species and tissue type, multicellular eukaryotes can have hundreds to thousands of mitochondria in each of their cells. Scientists have determined that mitochondria were once *symbiotic* prokaryotic organisms (i.e., helpful bacteria) that transformed into cellular organelles over time. This evolutionary explanation helps explain why mitochondria also have their own DNA, called **mitochondrial DNA (mtDNA)**. All organelles have important physiological functions and disease can occur when organelles do not perform their role optimally. Figure 3.6 lists other organelles found in the cell and their specialized cellular roles.

Figure 3.6: This table depicts the names of organelles and their cellular functions. Credit: Cell Structure table (Figure 3.11) original to Explorations: An Open Invitation to Biological Anthropology by Hayley Mann, Xazmin Lowman, and Malaina Gaddis is under a CC BY-NC 4.0 License.

Cell structure	Description
Centrioles	Assist with the organization of mitotic spindles, which extend and contract for the purpose of cellular movement during mitosis and meiosis.
Cytoplasm	Gelatinous fluid located inside of cell membrane that contains organelles.
Endoplasmic reticulum (ER)	Continuous membrane with the nucleus that helps transport, synthesize, modify, and fold proteins. Rough ER has embedded ribosomes, whereas smooth ER lacks ribosomes.
Golgi body	Layers of flattened sacs that receive and transmit messages from the ER to secrete and transport proteins within the cell.
Lysosome	Located in the cytoplasm; contains enzymes to degrade cellular components.
Microtubule	Involved with cellular movement including intracellular transport and cell division.
Mitochondrion	Responsible for cellular respiration, where energy is produced by converting nutrients into ATP.
Nucleolus	Resides inside of the nucleus and is the site of **ribosomal RNA (rRNA)** transcription, processing, and assembly.
Nucleopore	Pores in the **nuclear envelope** that are selectively permeable.
Nucleus	Contains the cell's DNA and is surrounded by the nuclear envelope.
Ribosome	Located in the cytoplasm and also the membrane of the rough endoplasmic reticulum. Messenger RNA (mRNA) binds to ribosomes and proteins are synthesized.

Introduction to Genetics

Genetics is the study of heredity. Biological parents pass down their genetic traits to their offspring. Although children resemble their parents, genetic traits often vary in appearance or molecular function. For example, two parents with normal color vision can sometimes produce a son with red-green colorblindness. Patterns of genetic inheritance will be discussed in a later section. **Molecular geneticists** study the biological mechanisms responsible for creating variation between individuals, such as DNA **mutations** (see Chapter 4), cell division, and genetic regulation.

Molecular anthropologists use genetic data to test anthropological questions. Some of these anthropologists utilize **ancient DNA (aDNA)**, which is DNA that is extracted from anything once living, including human, animal, and plant remains. Over time, DNA becomes degraded (i.e., less intact), but specialized laboratory techniques can make copies of short degraded aDNA segments, which can then be reassembled to provide more complete DNA information. A recent example of an aDNA study is provided in Special Topic: Native American Immunity and European Diseases, and aDNA is also explored in Appendix D.

DNA Structure

The discovery, in 1953, of the molecular structure of deoxyribonucleic acid (DNA) was one of the greatest scientific achievements of all time. Using X-ray crystallography, Rosalind Franklin (Figure 3.7) provided the image that clearly showed the double helix shape of DNA. However, due to a great deal of controversy, Franklin's colleague and outside associates received greater publicity for the discovery. In 1962, James Watson, Francis Crick, and Maurice Wilkins received a Nobel Prize for developing a biochemical model of DNA. Unfortunately, Rosalind Franklin had passed away in 1958 from ovarian cancer. In current times, Franklin's important contribution and her reputation as a skilled scientist are widely acknowledged.

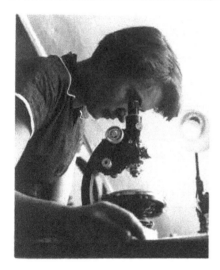

Figure 3.7: Chemist and X-ray crystallographer Rosalind Franklin. Credit: **Rosalind Franklin** from the personal collection of Jenifer Glynn by MRC Laboratory of Molecular Biology is under a CC BY-SA 4.0 License.

The double helix shape of DNA can be described as a twisted ladder (Figure 3.8). More specifically, DNA is a double-stranded molecule with its two strands oriented in opposite directions (i.e., antiparallel). Each strand is composed of **nucleotides** with a **sugar phosphate backbone**. There are four different types of DNA nucleotides: adenine (A), thymine (T), cytosine (C), and guanine (G). The two DNA strands are held together by nucleotide **base pairs**, which have chemical bonding rules. The complementary base-pairing rules are as follows: A and T bond with each other, while C and G form a bond. The chemical bonds between A-T and C-G are formed by "weak" hydrogen atom interactions, which means the two strands can be easily separated. A DNA sequence is the order of nucleotide bases (A, T, G, C) along only one DNA strand. If one DNA strand has the sequence CATGCT, then the other strand will have a complementary sequence GTACGA. This is an example of a short DNA sequence. In reality, there are approximately three billion DNA base pairs in human cells.

DNA Is Highly Organized within the Nucleus

If you removed the DNA from a single human cell and stretched it out completely, it would measure approximately two meters (about 6.5 feet). Therefore, DNA molecules must be compactly organized in the nucleus. To achieve this, the double helix configuration of DNA undergoes coiling. An analogy would be twisting a string until coils are formed and then continuing to twist so that secondary coils are formed, and so on. To assist with coiling, DNA is first wrapped around proteins called **histones**. This creates a complex called **chromatin,** which resembles "beads on a string" (Figure 3.9). Next, chromatin is further coiled into a **chromosome**. Another important feature of DNA is that chromosomes can be altered from tightly coiled (chromatin) to loosely coiled (**euchromatin**). Most of the time, chromosomes in the nucleus remain in a euchromatin state so that DNA sequences are accessible for regulatory processes to occur.

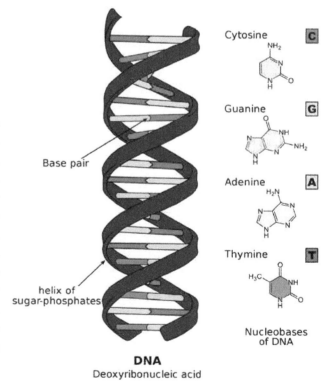

Figure 3.8: Structural components that form double-stranded nucleic acid (DNA). Credit: **Difference DNA RNA-EN** by **Sponk** (translation by **Sponk**, cropped by Katie Nelson) is under a CC BY-NC-SA 4.0 License.

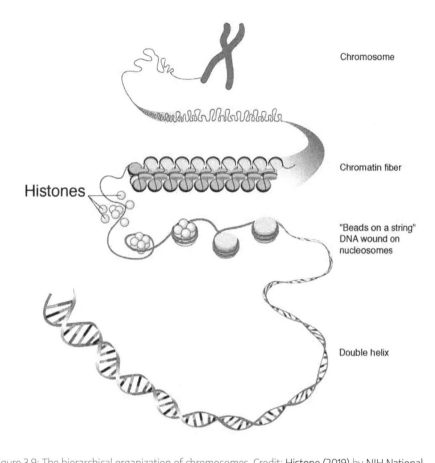

Figure 3.9: The hierarchical organization of chromosomes. Credit: Histone (2019) by NIH National Human Genome Research Institute is in the public domain. [Image Description].

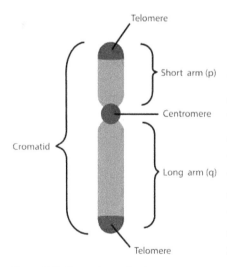

Figure 3.10: The regions of a chromosome. Credit: Chromosome (Figure 3.16) original to Explorations: An Open Invitation to Biological Anthropology by Katie Nelson is under a CC BY-NC 4.0 License.

Human body cells typically have 23 pairs of chromosomes, for a total of 46 chromosomes in each cell's nucleus. An interesting fact is that the number of chromosomes an organism possesses varies by species, and this figure is not dependent upon the size or complexity of the organism. For instance, chimpanzees have a total of 48 chromosomes, while hermit crabs have 254. Chromosomes also have a distinct physical structure, including **centromeres** (the "center") and **telomeres** (the ends) (Figure 3.10). Because of the centromeric region, chromosomes are described as having two different "arms," where one arm is long and the other is shorter. Centromeres play an important role during cell division, which will be discussed in the next section. Telomeres are located at the ends of chromosomes; they help protect the chromosomes from degradation after every round of cell division.

Special Topic: Native American Immunity and European Diseases—A Study of Ancient DNA

Figure 3.11a: Tsimshian Native Americans of the Pacific Northwest Coast. Credit: A group of Tsimshian people having a tea party in a tent, Lax Kw'alaams (formerly Port Simpson), B.C., c. 1890 by unknown photographer is in the Public Domain. This image is available from the Library and Archives Canada, item number 3368729.

Beginning in the early fifteenth century, Native Americans progressively suffered from high mortality rates as the result of colonization from foreign powers. European-borne diseases such as measles, tuberculosis, influenza, and smallpox are largely responsible for the population collapse of indigenous peoples in the Americas. Many Europeans who immigrated to the Americas had lived in large sedentary populations, which also included coexisting with domestic animals and pests. Although a few prehistoric Native American populations can be characterized as large agricultural societies (especially in Mesoamerica), their overall culture, community lifestyle, and subsistence practices were markedly different from that of Europeans. Therefore, because they did not share the same urban living environments as Europeans, it is believed that Native Americans were susceptible to many European diseases.

In 2016, a *Nature* article published by John Lindo and colleagues was the first to investigate whether pre-contact Native Americans possessed a genetic susceptibility to European diseases. Their study included Tsimshians, a First Nation community from British Columbia (Figure 3.11a-b). DNA from both present-day and ancient individuals (who lived between 500 and 6,000 years ago) was analyzed. The research team discovered that a change occurred in the *HLA-DQA1* gene, which is a member of the major histocompatibility complex (MHC) immune system molecules. MHC molecules are responsible for detecting and triggering an immune response against pathogens. Lindo and colleagues (2016) concluded that *HLA-DQA1* gene helped Native Americans adapt to their local environmental ecology. However, when European-borne epidemics occurred in the Northwest during the 1800s, a certain *HLA-DQA1* **DNA sequence** variant (allele) associated with ancient Tsimshian immunity was no longer adaptive. As the result of past selective pressures from European diseases, present-day Tsimshians have different *HLA-DQA1* allele frequencies. The precise role that *HLA-DQA1* plays in immune adaptation requires further investigation. But overall, this study serves as an example of how studying ancient DNA from the remains of deceased individuals can help provide insight into living human populations and historical events.

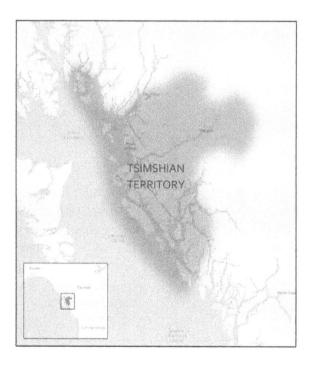

Figure 3.11b: Tsimshian territory in present-day British Columbia. Credit: Tsimshian Territory map (Figure 3.12b) original to Explorations: An Open Invitation to Biological Anthropology by Elyssa Ebding at GeoPlace, California State University, Chico is under a CC BY-NC 4.0 License.

DNA Replication and Cell Division

For life to continue and flourish, cells must be able to divide. Tissue growth and cellular damage repair are also necessary to maintain an organism throughout its life. All these rely on the dynamic processes of **DNA replication** and the **cell cycle**. The mechanisms highlighted in this section are tightly regulated and represent only part of the life cycle of a cell.

DNA Replication

DNA replication is the process by which new DNA is copied from an original DNA template. It is one phase of the highly coordinated cell cycle, and it requires a variety of enzymes with special functions. The creation of a complementary DNA strand from a template strand is described as **semi-conservative replication**. The result of semi-conservative replication is two separate double-stranded DNA molecules, each of which is composed of an original "parent" template strand and a newly synthesized "daughter" DNA strand.

DNA replication progresses in three steps referred to as **initiation**, **elongation,** and **termination**. During initiation, enzymes are recruited to specific sites along the DNA sequence (Figure 3.12). For example, an initiator enzyme, called **helicase**, "unwinds" DNA by breaking the hydrogen bonds between the two parent strands. The unraveling of the helix into two separated strands exposes the strands and creates a fork, which is the active site of DNA replication.

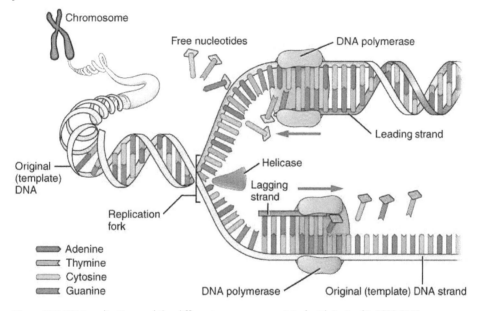

Figure 3.12: DNA replication and the different enzymes associated with it. Credit: 0323 DNA Replication by OpenStax is under a CC BY 4.0 License. [Image Description].

Elongation is the assembly of new DNA daughter strands from the exposed original parent strands. The two parent strands can further be classified as **leading strand** or **lagging strand** and are distinguished by the direction of replication. Enzymes called **DNA polymerases** read parent template strands in a specific direction. Complementary nucleotides are added, and the newly formed daughter strands will grow. On the leading parent strand, a DNA polymerase will create one continuous strand. The lagging parent strand is created in several disconnected sections and other enzymes fill in the missing nucleotide gaps between these sections.

Finally, termination refers to the end of DNA replication activity. It is signaled by a stop sequence in the DNA that is recognized by machinery at the replication fork. The end result of DNA replication is that the number of chromosomes are doubled so that the cell can divide into two.

DNA Mutations

DNA replication should result in the creation of two identical DNA nucleotide sequences. However, although DNA polymerases are quite precise during DNA replication, copying mistakes are estimated to occur every 10^7 DNA nucleotides. Variation from the original DNA sequence is known as a mutation. The different types of mutations will be discussed in greater detail in Chapter 4. Briefly, mutations can result in single nucleotide changes, as well as the insertion or deletion of nucleotides and repeated sequences. Depending on where they occur in the genome, mutations can be **deleterious** (harmful). For example, mutations may occur in regions that control cell cycle regulation, which can result in cancer (see Special Topic: The Cell Cycle and Immortality of Cancer Cells). Many other types of mutations, however, are not harmful to an organism.

Regardless of their effect, the cell attempts to reduce the frequency of mutations that occur during DNA replication. To accomplish this, there are polymerases with proofreading capacities that can identify and correct mismatched nucleotides. These safeguards reduce the frequency of DNA mutations so that they only occur every 10^9 nucleotides.

Mitotic Cell Division

There are two types of cells in the body: **germ cells** (sperm and egg) and **somatic cells**. The body and its various tissues comprises somatic cells. Organisms that contain two sets of chromosomes in their somatic cells are called **diploid** organisms. Humans have 46 chromosomes and they are diploid because they inherit one set of chromosomes (n = 23) from each parent. As a result, they have 23 matching pairs of chromosomes, which are known as **homologous chromosomes**. As seen in Figure 3.13, homologous chromosome pairs vary in size and are generally numbered from largest (chromosome 1) to smallest (chromosome 22) with the exception of the 23rd pair, which is made up of the sex chromosomes (X and Y). Typically, the female sex is XX and the male sex is XY. Individuals inherit an X chromosome from their chromosomal mother and an X or Y from their chromosomal father.

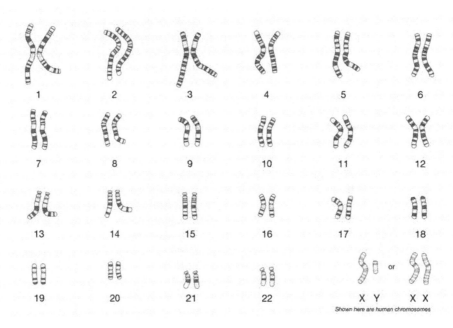

Figure 3.13: The 23 human chromosome pairs. Credit: Genome (2019) by NIH National Human Genome Research Institute is in the public domain.

To grow and repair tissues, somatic cells must divide. As discussed previously, for cell division to occur, a cell must first replicate its genetic material. During DNA replication, each chromosome produces double the amount of genetic information. The duplicated arms of chromosomes are known as **sister chromatids,** and they are attached at the centromeric region. To elaborate, the number of chromosomes stays the same (n = 46); however, the amount of genetic material is doubled in the cell as the result of replication.

Mitosis is the process of somatic cell division that gives rise to two diploid daughter cells. Figure 3.14 includes a brief overview of mitosis. Once DNA and other organelles in the cell have finished replication, mitotic spindle fibers physically align each chromosome at the center of the cell. Next, the spindle fibers divide the sister chromatids and move each one to opposite sides of the cell. At this phase, there are 46 chromosomes on each side of a human cell. The cell can now divide into two fully separated daughter cells.

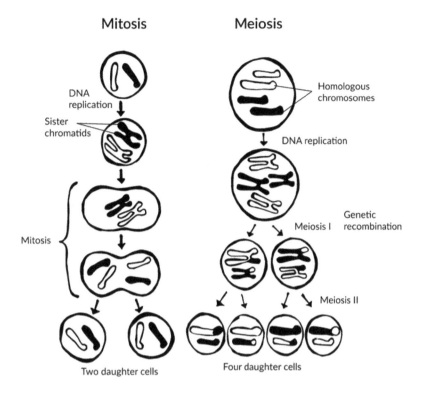

Figure 3.14: The steps of mitotic cell division and meiotic cell division. Credit: Mitosis and meiosis original to Explorations: An Open Invitation to Biological Anthropology (2nd ed.) by Katie Nelson is a collective work under a CC BY-NC 4.0 License. [Includes Mitosis (Figure 3.20) and Meiosis (Figure 3.21) by Mary Nelson; CC BY-NC 4.0 License.]

Meiotic Cell Division

Gametogenesis is the production of **gametes** (sperm and egg cells); it involves two rounds of cell division called **meiosis**. Similar to mitosis, the parent cell in meiosis is diploid. However, meiosis has a few key differences, including the number of daughter cells produced (four cells, which require two rounds of cell division to produce) and the number of chromosomes each daughter cell has (see Figure 3.14).

During the first round of division (known as meiosis I), each chromosome (n = 46) replicates its DNA so that sister chromatids are formed. Next, with the help of spindle fibers, homologous chromosomes align near the center of the cell and sister chromatids physically swap genetic material. In other words, the sister chromatids of matching chromosomes cross over with each other at matching DNA nucleotide positions. The occurrence of homologous chromosomes crossing over, swapping DNA, and then rejoining segments is called **genetic recombination**. The "genetic shuffling" that occurs in gametes increases organismal genetic diversity by creating new combinations of genes on chromosomes that are different from the parent cell. Genetic mutations can also arise during recombination. For example, there may be an unequal swapping of genetic material that occurs between the two sister chromatids, which can result in deletions or duplications of DNA nucleotides. Once genetic recombination is complete, homologous chromosomes are separated and two daughter cells are formed.

The daughter cells after the first round of meiosis are **haploid**, meaning they only have one set of chromosomes (n = 23). During the second round of cell division (known as meiosis II), sister chromatids are separated and two additional haploid daughter cells are formed. Therefore, the four resulting daughter cells have one set of chromosomes (n = 23), and they also have a genetic composition that is not identical to the parent cells nor to each other.

Although both sperm and egg gamete production undergo meiosis, they differ in the final number of viable daughter cells. In the case of spermatogenesis, four mature sperm cells are produced. Although four egg cells are also produced in oogenesis, only one of these egg cells will result in an ovum (mature egg). During fertilization, an egg cell and sperm cell fuse, which creates a diploid cell that develops into an embryo. The ovum also provides the cellular organelles necessary for embryonic cell division. This includes mitochondria, which is why humans, and most other multicellular eukaryotes, have the same mtDNA sequence as their mothers.

Chromosomal Disorders: Aneuploidies

During mitosis or meiosis, entire deletions or duplications of chromosomes can occur due to error. For example, homologous chromosomes may fail to separate properly, so one daughter cell may end up with an extra chromosome while the other daughter cell has one less. Cells with an unexpected (or abnormal) number of chromosomes are known as **aneuploid**. Adult or embryonic cells can be tested for chromosome number (**karyotyping**). Aneuploid cells are typically detrimental to a dividing cell or developing embryo, which can lead to a loss of pregnancy. However, the occurrence of individuals being born with three copies of the 21st chromosome is relatively common; this genetic condition is known as Down Syndrome. Moreover, individuals can also be born with aneuploid sex chromosome conditions such as XXY, XXX, and XO (referring to only one X chromosome).

Special Topic: The Cell Cycle and Immortality of Cancer Cells

DNA replication is part of a series of preparatory phases that a cell undergoes prior to cell division, collectively known as **interphase** (Figure 3.15). During interphase, the cell not only doubles its chromosomes through DNA replication, but it also increases its metabolic capacity to provide energy for growth and division. Transition into each phase of the cell cycle is tightly controlled by proteins that serve as checkpoints. If a cell fails to pass a checkpoint, then DNA replication and/or cell division will not continue. Some of the reasons why a cell may fail at a checkpoint is DNA damage, lack of nutrients to continue the process, or insufficient size. In turn, a cell may undergo **apoptosis**, which is a mechanism for cell death.

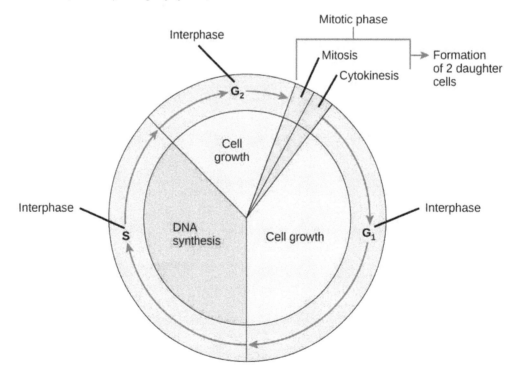

Figure 3.15: The phases and checkpoints of the cell cycle. Credit: Cell cycle (Biology 2e, Figure 10.5) by OpenStax is under a CC BY 4.0 License. [Image Description].

Unchecked cellular growth is a distinguishing hallmark of cancer. In other words, as cancer cells grow and proliferate, they acquire the capacity to avoid death and replicate indefinitely. This uncontrolled and continuous cell division is also known as "immortality." As previously mentioned, most cells lose the ability to divide due to shortening of telomeres on the ends of chromosomes over time. One way in which cancer cells retain replicative immortality is that the length of their telomeres is continuously protected. Chemotherapy, often used to treat cancer, targets the cell cycle (especially cell division) to halt the propagation of genetically abnormal cells. Another therapeutic approach that continues to be investigated is targeting telomere activity to stop the division of cancer cells.

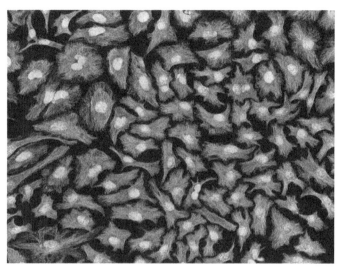

Figure 3.16: A microscopic slide of HeLa cancer cells. Credit: HeLa-III by National Institutes of Health (NIH) is in the public domain.

Researchers have exploited the immortality of cancer cells for molecular research. The oldest immortal cell line is HeLa cells (Figure 3.16), which were harvested from Henrietta Lacks, an African American woman diagnosed with cervical cancer in 1955. At that time, extracted cells frequently died during experiments, but surprisingly HeLa cells continued to replicate. Propagation of Lacks's cell line has significantly contributed to medical research, including contributing to ongoing cancer research and helping to test the polio vaccine in the 1950s. However, Lacks had not given her consent for her tumor biopsy to be used in cell culture research. Moreover, her family was unaware of the extraction and remarkable application of her cells for two decades. The history of HeLa cell origin was first revealed in 1976. The controversy voiced by the Lacks family was included in an extensive account of HeLa cells published in Rebecca Skloot's 2010 book, *The Immortal Life of Henrietta Lacks*. A film based on the book was also released in 2017 (Wolfe 2017).

Protein Synthesis

At the beginning of the chapter, we defined *proteins* as strings of **amino acids** that fold into complex 3-D shapes. There are 20 standard amino acids that can be strung together in different combinations in humans, and the result is that proteins can perform an impressive amount of different functions. For instance, muscle fibers are proteins that help facilitate movement. A special class of proteins (immunoglobulins) help protect the organism by detecting disease-causing pathogens in the body. Protein hormones, such as insulin, help regulate physiological activity. Blood hemoglobin is a protein that transports oxygen throughout the body. **Enzymes** are also proteins, and they are catalysts for biochemical reactions that occur in the cell (e.g., metabolism). Larger-scale protein structures can be visibly seen as physical features of an organism (e.g., hair and nails).

Transcription and Translation

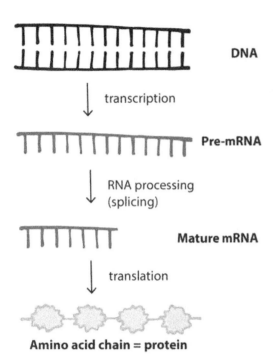

Figure 3.17: The major steps of protein synthesis. Credit: Protein synthesis original to Explorations: An Open Invitation to Biological Anthropology (2nd ed.) by Mary Nelson is under a CC BY-NC 4.0 License. [Image Description].

Nucleotides in our DNA provide the coding instructions on how to make proteins. Making proteins, also known as **protein synthesis**, can be broken down into two main steps referred to as **transcription** and **translation**. The purpose of transcription, the first step, is to make an **ribonucleic acid (RNA)** copy of our genetic code. Although there are many different types of RNA molecules that have a variety of functions within the cell, we will mainly focus on **messenger RNA (mRNA)**. Transcription concludes with the processing (**splicing**) of the mRNA. The second step, translation, uses mRNA as the instructions for chaining together amino acids into a new protein molecule (Figure 3.17).

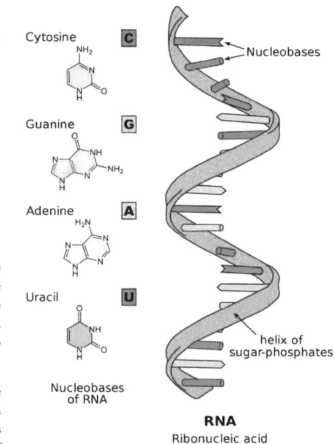

Figure 3.18: Structural components that form ribonucleic acid (RNA). Credit: Difference DNA RNA-EN by Sponk (translation by Sponk, cropped by Katie Nelson) is under a CC BY-NC-SA 4.0 License. [Image Description].

Unlike double-stranded DNA, RNA molecules are single-stranded nucleotide sequences (Figure 3.18). Additionally, while DNA contains the nucleotide thymine (T), RNA does not—instead its fourth nucleotide is uracil (U). Uracil is complementary to (or can pair with) adenine (A), while cytosine (C) and guanine (G) continue to be complementary to each other.

For transcription to proceed, a **gene** must first be turned "on" by the cell. A gene is a segment of DNA that codes for RNA, and genes can vary in length from a few hundred to as many as two million base pairs in length. The double-stranded DNA is then separated, and one side of the DNA is used as a coding template that is read by **RNA polymerase.** Next, complementary free-floating RNA nucleotides are linked together (Figure 3.19) to form a single-stranded mRNA. For example, if a DNA template is TACGGATGC, then the newly constructed mRNA sequence will be AUGCCUACG.

Genes contain segments called **introns** and **exons**. Exons are considered "coding" while introns are considered "noncoding"—meaning the information they contain will not be needed to construct proteins. When a gene is first transcribed into pre-mRNA, introns and exons are both included (Figure 3.20). However, once transcription is finished, introns are removed in a process called splicing. During splicing, a protein/RNA complex attaches itself to the pre-mRNA. Next, introns are removed and the remaining exons are connected, thus creating a shorter mature mRNA that serves as a template for building proteins.

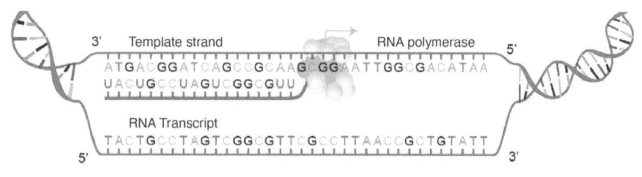

Figure 3.19: RNA polymerase catalyzing DNA transcription. Credit: Transcription (2019) by NIH National Human Genome Research Institute has been modified (cropped and labels changed by Katie Nelson) and is under a CC BY-NC 4.0 License. [Image Description].

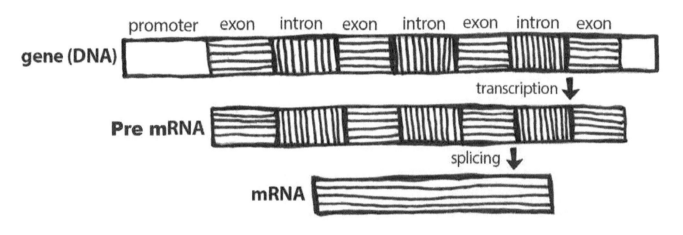

Figure 3.20: RNA processing is the modification of RNA, including the removal of introns, called splicing, between transcription and translation. Credit: Protein synthesis (Figure 3.23) original to Explorations: An Open Invitation to Biological Anthropology by Mary Nelson is under a CC BY-NC 4.0 License. [Image Description].

As described above, the result of transcription is a single-stranded mRNA copy of a gene. Translation is the process by which amino acids are chained together to form a new protein. During translation, the mature mRNA is transported outside of the nucleus, where it is bound to a **ribosome** (Figure 3.21). The nucleotides in the mRNA are read in triplets, which are called **codons**. Each mRNA codon corresponds to an amino acid, which is carried to the ribosome by a **transfer RNA** (tRNA). Thus, tRNAs is the link between the mRNA molecule and the growing amino acid chain.

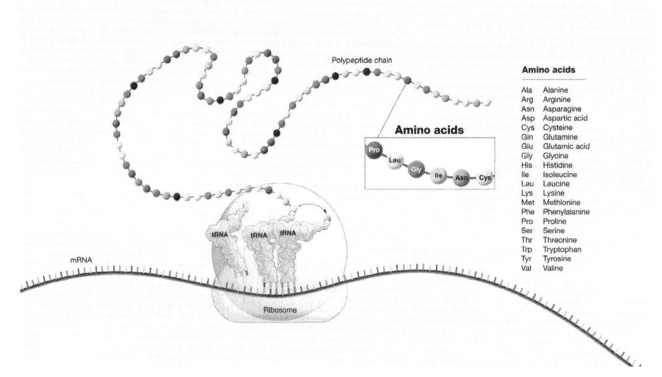

Figure 3.21: Translation of mRNA into a polypeptide chain composed of the twenty different types of amino acids. Credit: **Amino Acids** by NIH National Human Genome Research Institute is in the **public domain**. [Image Description].

Continuing with our mRNA sequence example from above, the mRNA sequence AUG-CCU-ACG codes for three amino acids. Using a codon table (Figure 3.22), AUG is a codon for methionine (Met), CCU is proline (Pro), and ACG is threonine (Thr). Therefore, the protein sequence is Met-Pro-Thr. Methionine is the most common "start codon" (AUG) for the initiation of protein translation in eukaryotes. As the ribosome moves along the mRNA, the growing amino acid chain exits the ribosome and folds into a protein. When the ribosome reaches a "stop" codon (UAA, UAG, or UGA), the ribosome stops adding any new amino acids, detaches from the mRNA, and the protein is released. Depending upon the amino acid sequence, a linear protein may undergo additional "folding." The final three-dimensional protein shape is integral to completing a specific structural or functional task.

Dig Deeper: Protein Synthesis

To see protein synthesis in animation, please check out the From DNA to Protein video on YourGenome.org.

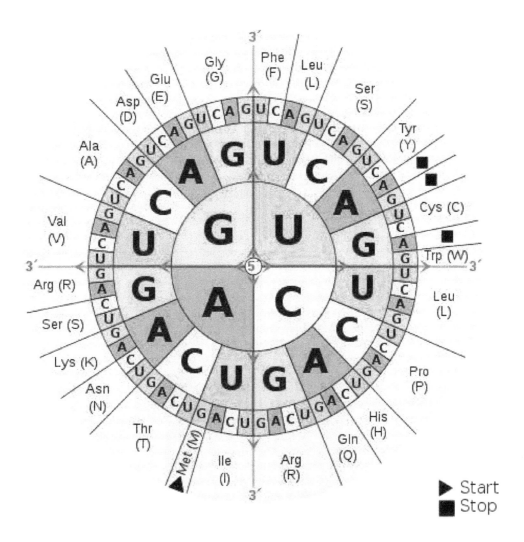

Figure 3.22: This table can be used to identify which mRNA codons (sequence of three nucleotides) correspond with each of the 20 different amino acids. For each mRNA codon, you work in the 5' to 3' direction (inside the circle to outside). For example, if the mRNA codon is CAU, you look at the inner circle for the "C," the middle circle for "A," and outside circle for "U," indicating that the CAU codon corresponds with the amino acid "histidine" (abbreviated "His" or "H"). The table also indicates that the "start codon" (AUG) correlates with Methionine, and the three "stop" codons are UAA, UAG, and UGA. Credit: **Aminoacids table** by **Mouagip** has been designated to the **public domain (CC0)**. [Image Description].

Special Topic: Genetic Regulation of the Lactase (LCT) Gene

The *LCT* gene codes for a protein called lactase, an enzyme produced in the small intestine. It is responsible for breaking down the sugar "lactose," which is found in milk. Lactose intolerance occurs when not enough lactase enzyme is produced and, in turn, digestive symptoms occur. To avoid this discomfort, individuals may take lactase supplements, drink lactose-free milk, or avoid milk products altogether.

The *LCT* gene is a good example of how cells regulate protein synthesis. The **promoter** region of the *LCT* gene helps regulate whether it is transcribed or not transcribed (i.e., turned "on" or "off," respectively). Lactase production is initiated when a regulatory protein known as a **transcription factor** binds to a site on the *LCT* promoter. RNA polymerases are then recruited; they read DNA and string together nucleotides to make RNA molecules. An *LCT* pre-mRNA is synthesized (made) in the nucleus, and further chemical modifications flank the ends of the mRNA to ensure the molecule will not be degraded in the cell. Next, a spliceosome complex removes the introns from the *LCT* pre-mRNA and connects the exons to form a mature mRNA. Translation of the *LCT* mRNA occurs and the growing protein then folds into the lactase enzyme, which can break down lactose.

Most animals lose their ability to digest milk as they mature due to the decreasing transcriptional "silence" of the *LCT* gene over time. However, some humans have the ability to digest lactose into adulthood (also known as "lactase persistence"). This means they have a genetic mutation that leads to continuous transcriptional activity of *LCT*. Lactase persistence mutations are common in populations with a long history of pastoral farming, such as northern European and North African populations. It is believed that lactase persistence evolved because the ability to digest milk was nutritionally beneficial. More information about lactase persistence will be covered in Chapter 14.

Mendelian Genetics

Figure 3.23: Statue of Mendel located at the Mendel Museum, located at Masaryk University in Brno, Czech Republic. Credit: Mendel´s statue by Coeli has been designated to the public domain (CC0).

Gregor Johann Mendel (1822–1884) is often described as the "Father of Genetics." Mendel was a monk who conducted pea plant breeding experiments in a monastery located in the present-day Czech Republic (Figure 3.23). After several years of experiments, Mendel presented his work to a local scientific community in 1865 and published his findings the following year. Although his meticulous effort was notable, the importance of his work was not recognized for another 35 years. One reason for this delay in recognition is that his findings did not agree with the predominant scientific viewpoints on inheritance at the time. For example, it was believed that parental physical traits "blended" together and offspring inherited an intermediate form of that trait. In contrast, Mendel showed that certain pea plant physical traits (e.g., flower color) were passed down separately to the next generation in a statistically predictable manner. Mendel also observed that some parental traits disappeared in offspring but then reappeared in later generations. He explained this occurrence by introducing the concept of "dominant" and "recessive" traits. Mendel established a few fundamental laws of inheritance, and this section reviews some of these concepts. Moreover, the study of traits and diseases that are controlled by a single gene is commonly referred to as **Mendelian genetics**.

Seed		Flower	Pod		Stem	
Form	Cotyledons	Color	Form	Color	Place	Size
ROUND	YELLOW	WHITE	FULL	YELLOW	AXIAL FLOWERS	TALL
WRINKLED	GREEN	PURPLE	CONSTRICTED	GREEN	TERMINAL FLOWERS	SHORT

Figure 3.24: Various phenotypic characteristics of pea plants resulting from different genotypes. Credit: Mendels peas by Mariana Ruiz LadyofHats has been designated to the public domain (CC0 1.0).

The physical appearance of a trait is called an organism's **phenotype**. Figure 3.24 shows pea plant (*Pisum sativum*) phenotypes that were studied by Mendel, and in each of these cases the physical traits are controlled by a single gene. In the case of Mendelian genetics, a phenotype is determined by an organism's **genotype**. A genotype consists of two gene copies, wherein one copy was inherited from each parent. Gene copies are also known as **alleles** (Figure 3.25), which means they are found in the same gene location on homologous chromosomes. Alleles have a nonidentical DNA sequence, which means their phenotypic effect can be different. In other words, although alleles code for the same trait, different phenotypes can be produced depending on which two alleles (i.e., genotypes) an organism possesses. For example, Mendel's pea plants all have flowers, but their flower color can be purple or white. Flower color is therefore dependent upon which two color alleles are present in a genotype.

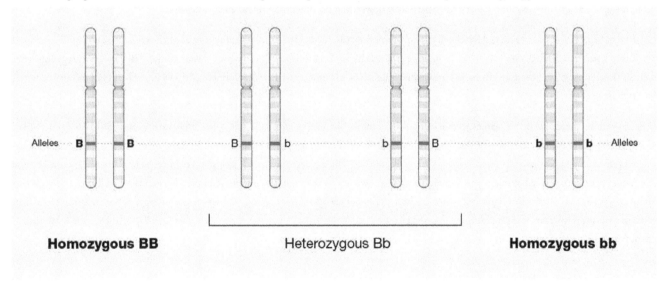

Figure 3.25: Homozygous refers to having the same alleles (e.g. two capital Bs or two lowercase bs). Heterozygous refers to having two different alleles (e.g. one capital B and one lowercase b). Credit: Homozygous by NIH National Human Genome Research Institute is in the public domain.

A Punnett square is a diagram that can help visualize Mendelian inheritance patterns. For instance, when parents of known genotypes mate, a Punnett square can help predict the ratio of Mendelian genotypes and phenotypes that their offspring would possess. When discussing genotype, biologists use upper and lower case letters to denote the different allele copies. Figure 3.26 is a Punnett square that includes two **heterozygous** parents for flower color (Bb). A heterozygous genotype means there are two different alleles for the same gene. Therefore, a pea plant that is heterozygous for flower color has one purple allele and one white allele. When an organism is **homozygous** for a specific trait, it means their genotype consists of two copies of the same allele. Using the Punnett square example, the two heterozygous pea plant parents can produce offspring with two different homozygous genotypes (BB or bb) or offspring that are heterozygous (Bb).

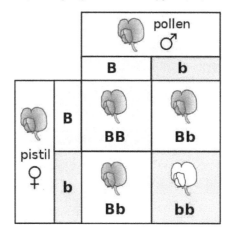

Figure 3.26: Punnett square depicting the possible genetic combinations of offspring from two heterozygous parents. Credit: **Punnett square mendel flowers** by Madeleine Price Ball (**Madprime**) is under a CC BY-SA 3.0 License. [Image Description].

A pea plant with purple flowers could be heterozygous (Bb) or homozygous (BB). This is because the purple color allele (B) is **dominant** to the white color allele (b), and therefore it only needs one copy of that allele to phenotypically express purple flowers. Because the white flower allele is **recessive**, a pea plant must be homozygous for the recessive allele in order to have a white color phenotype (bb). As seen by the Punnett square example (Figure 3.26), three of four offspring will have purple flowers and the other one will have white flowers.

The Law of Segregation was introduced by Mendel to explain why we can predict the ratio of genotypes and phenotypes in offspring. As discussed previously, a parent will have two alleles for a certain gene (with each copy on a different homologous chromosome). The Law of Segregation states that the two copies will be segregated from each other and will each be distributed to their own gamete. We now know that the process where that occurs is meiosis.

Offspring are the products of two gametes combining, which means the offspring inherits one allele from each gamete for most genes. When multiple offspring are produced (like with pea plant breeding), the predicted phenotype ratios are more clearly observed. The pea plants Mendel studied provide a simplistic model to understand single-gene genetics. While many traits anthropologists are interested in have a more complicated inheritance (e.g., are informed by many genes), there are a few known Mendelian traits in humans. Additionally, some human diseases also follow a Mendelian pattern of inheritance (Figure 3.27). Because humans do not have as many offspring as other organisms, we may not recognize Mendelian patterns as easily. However, understanding these principles and being able to calculate the probability that an offspring will have a Mendelian phenotype is still important.

Figure 3.27: Examples of human diseases with their gene names that follow a Mendelian pattern of inheritance.

Mendelian disorder	Gene
Alpha Thalassemia	HBA1
Cystic Fibrosis	CFTR
Fragile X Syndrome	FMR1
Glucose-6-Phosphate Dehydrogenase Deficiency	G6PD
Hemophilia A	F8
Huntington disease	HTT
Mitochondrial DNA Depletion Syndrome	TYMP
Oculocutaneous Albinism: Type 1	TYR
Polycystic Kidney Disease	PKHD1
Sickle-cell anemia	HBB
Spinal Muscular Atrophy: SMN1 Linked	SMN1
Tay-Sachs Disease	HEXA
Wilson Disease	ATP7B

Example of Mendelian Inheritance: The ABO Blood Group System

In 1901, Karl Landsteiner at the University of Vienna published his discovery of ABO blood groups. While conducting blood immunology experiments in which he combined the blood of individuals who possess different blood cell types, he observed an agglutination (clotting) reaction. The presence of agglutination implies there is an incompatible immunological reaction; no agglutination will occur in individuals with the same blood type. This work was clearly important because it resulted in a higher survival rate of patients who received blood transfusions. Blood transfusions from someone with a different type of blood causes agglutinations, and the resulting coagulated blood can not easily pass through blood vessels, resulting in death. Landsteiner received the Nobel Prize (1930) for his discovery and explaination of the ABO blood group system.

Blood **cell surface antigens** are proteins that coat the surface of red blood cells, and **antibodies** are specifically "against" or "anti" to the antigens from other blood types. Thus, antibodies are responsible for causing agglutination between incompatible blood types. Understanding the interaction of antigens and antibodies helps to determine ABO compatibility amongst blood donors and recipients. To better comprehend blood phenotypes and ABO compatibility, blood cell antigens and plasma antibodies are presented in Figure 3.28. Individuals that are blood type A have A antigens on the red blood cell surface, and anti-B antibodies, which will bind to B antigens should they come in contact. Alternatively, individuals with blood type B have B antigens and anti-A antibodies. Individuals with blood type AB have both A and B antigens but do not produce antibodies for the ABO system. This does not mean type AB does not have any antibodies present, just that specifically anti-A and anti-B antibodies are not produced. Individuals who are blood type O have nonspecific antigens and produce both anti-A and anti-B antibodies.

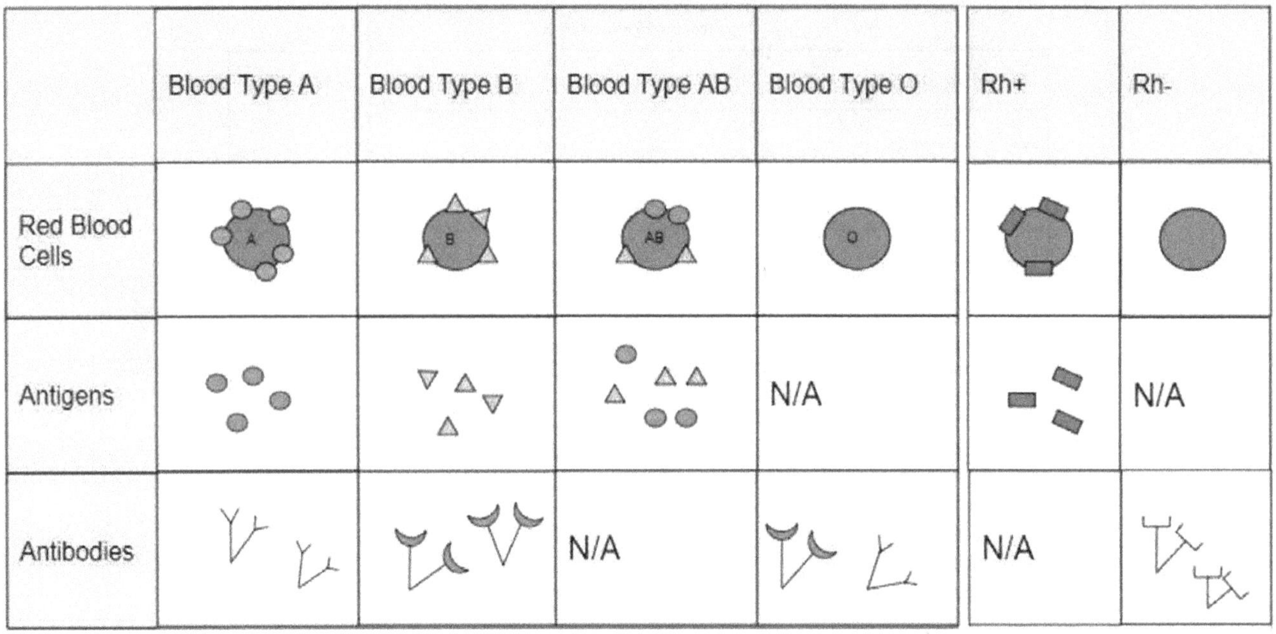

Figure 3.28: The different ABO and Rhesus blood types with their associated antibodies and antigens. Credit: Different Blood Types by Michael540170 has been modified (antibodies images swapped) and is under a CC BY-NC-SA 4.0 License. [Image Description].

Figure 3.29 shows a table of the ABO allele system, which has a Mendelian pattern of inheritance. Both the A and B alleles function as dominant alleles, so the A allele always codes for the A antigen, and the B allele codes for the B antigen. The O allele differs from A and B, because it codes for a nonfunctional antigen protein, which means there is no antigen present on the cell surface of O blood cells. To have blood type O, two copies of the O allele must be inherited, one from each parent, thus the O allele is considered recessive. Therefore, someone who is a heterozygous AO genotype is phenotypically blood type A, and a genotype of BO is blood type B. The ABO blood system also provides an example of **codominance**, which is when both alleles are observed in the phenotype. This is true for blood type AB: when an individual inherits both the A and B alleles, then both A and B antigens will be present on the cell surface.

	A	B	O
A	AA	AB	AO
B	AB	BB	BO
O	AO	BO	OO

Figure 3.29: The different combinations of ABO blood alleles (A, B, and O) to form ABO blood genotypes. Credit: ABO Blood Genotypes (Figure 3.33) original to Explorations: An Open Invitation to Biological Anthropology by Katie Nelson is under a CC BY-NC 4.0 License. [Image Description].

Also found on the surface of red blood cells is the rhesus group antigen, known as "Rh factor." In reality, there are several antigens on red blood cells independent from the ABO blood system, however, the Rh factor is the second most important antigen to consider when determining blood donor and recipient compatibility. Rh antigens must also be considered when a pregnant mother and her baby have incompatible Rh factors. In such cases, a doctor can administer necessary treatment steps to prevent pregnancy complications and hemolytic disease, which is when the mother's antibodies break down the newborn's red blood cells.

An individual can possess the Rh antigen (be Rh positive) or lack the Rh antigen (be Rh negative). The Rh factor is controlled by a single gene and is inherited independently of the ABO alleles. Therefore, all blood types can either be positive (O+, A+, B+, AB+) or negative (O-, A-, B-, AB-).

Individuals with O+ red blood cells can donate blood to A+, B+, AB+, and O+ blood type recipients. Because O- individuals do not have AB or Rh antigens, they are compatible with all blood cell types and are referred to as "universal donors." Individuals that are AB+ are considered to be "universal recipients" because they do not possess antibodies against other blood types.

Mendelian Patterns of Inheritance and Pedigrees

A **pedigree** can be used to investigate a family's medical history by determining if a health issue is inheritable and will possibly require medical intervention. A pedigree can also help determine if it is a Mendelian recessive or dominant genetic condition. Figure 3.30 is a pedigree example of a family with Huntington's disease, which has a Mendelian dominant pattern of inheritance. In a standard pedigree, males are represented by a square and females are represented by a circle. Biological family members are connected to a horizontal line, with biological parents above and offspring below. When an individual is affected with a certain condition, the square or circle is filled in as a solid color. With a dominant condition, at least one of the parents will have the disease and an offspring will have a 50% chance of inheriting the affected chromosome. Therefore, dominant genetic conditions tend to be present in every generation. In the case of Huntington's, some individuals may not be diagnosed until later in adulthood, so parents may unknowingly pass this dominantly inherited disease to their children.

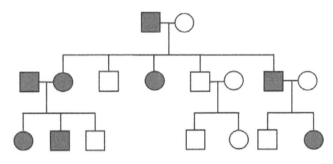

Figure 3.30: A pedigree depicting an example of dominant Mendelian inheritance like Huntington's. Offspring with the trait will have at least one parent with the same trait. Credit: Mendelian dominant pattern of inheritance (Figure 3.34) original to Explorations: An Open Invitation to Biological Anthropology by Beth Shook is under a CC BY-NC 4.0 License.

Because the probability of inheriting a disease-causing recessive allele is more rare, recessive medical conditions can skip generations. Figure 3.31 is an example of a family that carries a recessive cystic fibrosis mutation. A parent that is heterozygous for the cystic fibrosis allele has a 50% chance of passing down their affected chromosome to the next generation. If a child has a recessive disease, then it means both of their parents are **carriers** (heterozygous) for that condition. In most cases, carriers for recessive conditions show no serious medical symptoms. Individuals whose family have a known medical history for certain conditions sometimes seek family planning services (see the Genetic Testing section).

Pedigrees can also help distinguish if a health issue has either an **autosomal** or **X-linked** pattern of inheritance. As previously discussed, there are 23 pairs of chromosomes and 22 of these pairs are known as autosomes. The provided pedigree examples (Figure 3.30–31) are autosomally linked genetic diseases. This means the genes that cause the disease are on one of the chromosomes numbered 1 to 22. The conditions caused by genes located on the X chromosome are referred to as X-linked diseases.

Figure 3.32 depicts a family in which the mother is a carrier for the X-linked recessive disease Duchenne Muscular Dystrophy (DMD). The mother is a carrier for DMD, so daughters and sons will have a 50% chance of inheriting the **pathogenic** *DMD* allele. Because females have two X chromosomes, females who inherit only one copy will not have the disease (although in rare cases, female carriers may show some symptoms of the disease). On the other hand, males who inherit a copy

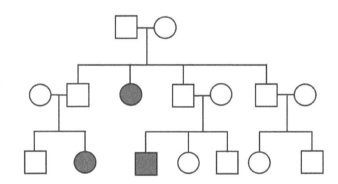

Figure 3.31: A pedigree depicting an example of recessive Mendelian inheritance like cystic fibrosis. Individuals may have a trait not observed in the previous generation. Credit: Mendelian recessive pattern of inheritance (Figure 3.35) original to Explorations: An Open Invitation to Biological Anthropology by Beth Shook is under a CC BY-NC 4.0 License.

of an X-linked pathogenic *DMD* allele will typically be affected with the condition. Thus, males are more susceptible to X-linked conditions because they only have one X chromosome. Therefore, when evaluating a pedigree, if a higher proportion of males are affected with the disease, this could suggest the disease is X-linked recessive.

Compared to the X chromosome, the Y chromosome is smaller with only a few genes. Y-linked traits are therefore rare and can only be passed from a chromosomal father to a biological XY child.

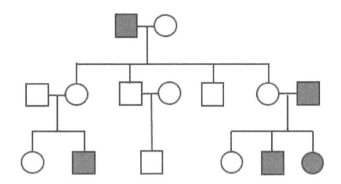

Figure 3.32: A pedigree depicting an example of X-linked Mendelian inheritance like Duchenne Muscular Dystrophy (DMD). Credit: X-linked recessive pattern of inheritance (Figure 3.36) original to Explorations: An Open Invitation to Biological Anthropology by Beth Shook is under a CC BY-NC 4.0 License.

Other Patterns of Inheritance

Complexity Surrounding Mendelian Inheritance

Pea plant trait genetics are relatively simple compared to what we know about genetic inheritance today. The vast majority of genetically controlled traits are not strictly dominant or recessive, so the relationship among alleles and predicting phenotype is often more complicated. For example, traits that exhibit **incomplete dominance** occur when a heterozygote exhibits a phenotype that is an intermediate phenotype of both alleles. In snapdragon flowers, the red flower color (R) is dominant and white is recessive (r). Therefore, the homozygous dominant RR is red and homozygous recessive rr is white. However, because the R allele is not completely dominant, the heterozygote Rr is a blend of red and white, which results in a pink flower (Figure 3.33).

An example of incomplete dominance in humans is the enzyme β-hexosaminidase A (Hex A), which is encoded by the gene *HEXA*. Patients with two dysfunctional *HEXA* alleles are unable to metabolize a specific lipid-sugar molecule (GM2 ganglioside); because of this, the molecule builds up and causes damage to nerve cells in the brain and spinal cord. This condition is known as Tay-Sachs disease, and it usually appears in infants who are three to six months old. Most children with Tay-Sachs do not live past early childhood. Individuals who are heterozygous for the functional type *HEXA* allele and one dysfunctional allele have reduced Hex A activity. However, the amount of enzyme activity is still sufficient, so carriers do not exhibit any neurological phenotypes and appear healthy.

Some genes and alleles can also have higher **penetrance** than others. Penetrance can be defined as the proportion of individuals who have a certain allele and also express an expected phenotype. If a genotype always produces

Figure 3.33: Snap dragons with different genotypes resulting in different flower color phenotypes. Credit: Antirrhinum a.k.a. Snap dragon at lalbagh 7112 by Rameshng is under a CC BY-SA 3.0 License.

an expected phenotype, then those alleles are said to be fully penetrant. However, in the case of incomplete (or reduced) penetrance, an expected phenotype may not occur even if an individual possesses the alleles that are known to control a trait or cause a disease.

A well-studied example of genetic penetrance is the cancer-related genes *BRCA1* and *BRCA2*. Mutations in these genes can affect crucial processes such as DNA repair, which can lead to breast and ovarian cancers. Although *BRCA1* and *BRCA2* mutations have an autosomal dominant pattern of inheritance, it does not mean an individual will develop cancer if they inherit a pathogenic allele. Several lifestyle and environmental factors can also influence the risk for developing cancer. Regardless, if a family has a history of certain types of cancers, then it is often recommended that genetic testing be performed for individuals who are at risk. Moreover, publically available genetic testing companies are now offering health reports that include *BRCA1* and *BRCA2* allele testing (see the Genetic Testing section).

Polygenic Traits

While Mendelian traits tend to be influenced by a single gene, the vast majority of human phenotypes are **polygenic traits**. The term *polygenic* means "many genes." Therefore, a polygenic trait is influenced by many genes that work together to produce the phenotype. Human phenotypes such as hair color, eye color, height, and weight are examples of polygenic traits. Hair color, for example, is largely determined by the type and quantity of a pigment called melanin, which is produced by a specialized cell type within the skin called melanocytes. The quantity and ratio of melanin pigments determine black, brown, blond, and red hair colors. *MC1R* is a well-studied gene that encodes a protein expressed on the surface of melanocytes that is involved in the production of eumelanin pigment. Typically, people with two functional copies of *MC1R* have brown hair. People with reduced functioning *MC1R* allele copies tend to produce pheomelanin, which results in blond or red hair. However, *MC1R* alleles have variable penetrance, and studies are continually identifying new genes (e.g., *TYR*, *TYRP1*, *SLC24A5*, and *KITLG*) that also influence hair color. Individuals with two nonfunctioning copies of the gene *TYR* have a condition called oculocutaneous albinism—their melanocytes are unable to produce melanin so these individuals have white hair, light eyes, and pale skin.

In comparison to Mendelian diseases, **complex diseases** (e.g., Type II diabetes, coronary heart disease, Alzheimer's, and schizophrenia) are more prevalent in humans. Complex diseases are polygenic, but their development is also influenced by physical, environmental, sociocultural, and individual lifestyle factors. Families can be more predisposed to certain diseases; however, complex diseases often do not have a clear pattern of inheritance.

Although research of complex traits and diseases continue, geneticists may not know all of the genes involved with a given complex disease. Additionally, how much genetic versus nongenetic determinants contribute to a disease phenotype can be difficult to decipher. Therefore, predicting individual medical risk and risk across different human populations is often a significant challenge. For instance, cardiovascular diseases (CVDs) continue to be one of the leading causes of death around the world. Development of CVDs has been linked to nutrient exposure during fetal development, high fat and sedentary lifestyles, drug usage, adverse socioeconomic conditions, and various genes. Human environments are diverse, and public health research including the field of Human Biology can help identify risk factors and behaviors associated with chronic diseases. Large-scale clinical genetic studies with powerful bioinformatic approaches can also help elucidate some of these complex relationships.

Genomics and Epigenetics

A **genome** is all of the genetic material of an organism. In the case of humans, this includes 46 chromosomes and mtDNA. The human genome contains approximately three billion base pairs of DNA and has regions that are both noncoding and coding. Scientists now estimate that the human genome contains 20,000–25,000 protein-coding genes, with each chromosome containing a few hundred to a few thousand genes. As our knowledge of heredity increases, researchers have begun to realize the importance of **epigenetics**, or changes in gene expression that do not result in a change of the underlying DNA sequence. Epigenetics research is also crucial for unraveling gene regulation, which involves complex interactions between DNA, RNA, proteins, and the environment.

Genomics

The vast majority of the human genome is noncoding, meaning there are no instructions to make a protein or RNA product in these regions. Historically, noncoding DNA was referred to as "junk DNA" because these vast segments of the genome were thought to be irrelevant and nonfunctional. However, continual improvement of DNA **sequencing** technology along with worldwide scientific collaborations and consortia have contributed to our increased understanding of how the genome functions. Through these technological advances and collaborations, we have since discovered that many of these noncoding DNA regions are involved in dynamic genetic regulatory processes.

Genomics is a diverse field of molecular biology that focuses on genomic evolution, structure, and function; gene mapping; and **genotyping** (determining the alleles present). Evolutionary genomics determined that humans share about 98.8% percent of their DNA with chimpanzees. Given the phenotypic differences between humans and chimpanzees, having a DNA sequence difference of 1.2% seems surprising. However, a lot of genomics research is also focused on understanding how noncoding genomic regions influence how individual genes are turned "on" and "off" (i.e., regulated). Therefore, although DNA sequences are identical, regulatory differences in noncoding genetic regions (e.g., promoters) are believed to be largely responsible for the physical differences between humans and chimpanzees.

Further understanding of genomic regulatory elements can lead to new therapies and personalized treatments for a broad range of diseases. For example, targeting the regulatory region of a pathogenic gene to "turn off" its expression can prevent its otherwise harmful effects. Such molecular targeting approaches can be personalized based on an individual's genetic makeup. Genome-wide association studies (GWAS), which seek to determine genes that are linked to complex traits and diseases, typically require significant computational efforts. This is because millions of DNA sequences must be analyzed and GWAS sometimes include thousands of participants. During the beginning of the genomics field, most of the large-scale genomics studies only included North American, European, and East Asian participants and patients. Researchers are now focusing on increasing ethnic diversity in genomic studies and databases. In turn, accuracy of individual disease risk across all human populations will be improved and more rare disease–causing alleles will be identified.

Epigenetics

All cells within your body have the same copy of DNA. For example, a brain neuron has the same DNA blueprint as does a skin cell on your arm. Although these cells have the same genetic information, they are considered specialized. The reason all cells within the body have the same DNA but different morphologies and functions is that different subsets of genes are turned "on" and "off" within the different cell types. A more precise explanation is that there is differential expression of genes among different cell types. In the case of neuronal cells, a unique subset of genes are active that allow them to grow axons to send and receive messages. This subset of genes will be inactive in non-neuronal cell types such as skin cells. Epigenetics is a branch of genetics that studies how these genes are regulated through mechanisms that do not change the underlying DNA sequence. "Special Topics: Epigenetics and X Chromosome Inactivation" details a well-known example of epigenetics regulation.

The prefix *epi-* means "on, above, or near," and epigenetic mechanisms such as **DNA methylation** and histone modifications occur on, above, or near DNA. The addition of a methyl group (— CH_3) to DNA is known as DNA methylation (Figure 3.34). DNA methylation and other modifications made to the histones around which DNA are wrapped are thought to make chromatin more compact. This DNA is inaccessible to transcription factors and RNA polymerases, thus preventing genes from being turned on (i.e., transcribed). Other histone modifications have the opposite effect by loosening chromatin, which makes genes accessible to transcription factors.

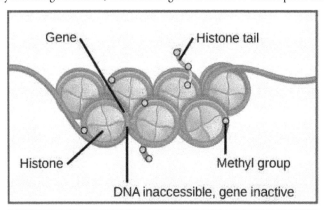

Methylation of DNA and histones causes nucleosomes to pack tightly together. Transcription factors cannot bind the DNA, and genes are not expressed.

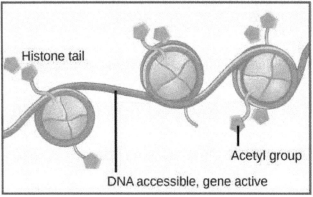

Histone acetylation results in loose packing of nucleosomes. Transcription factors can bind the DNA and genes are expressed.

Figure 3.34: Different types of epigenetic histone tail modifications that can tighten (top) and loosen (bottom) the chromatin of DNA. Credit: Epigenetic Control (Biology 2e, Figure 16.7) by OpenStax is under a CC BY 4.0 License. [Image Description].

It is important to note that environmental factors can alter DNA methylation and histone modifications and also that these changes can be passed from generation to generation. For example, someone's **epigenetic profile** can be altered during a stressful time (e.g., natural disasters, famine, etc.), and those regulatory changes can be inherited by the next generation. Moreover, our epigenetic expression profile changes as we age. For example, certain places in our genome become "hyper" or "hypo" methylated over time. Identical twins also have epigenetic profiles that become more different as they age. Researchers are only beginning to understand what all of these genome-wide epigenetic changes mean. Scientists have also discovered that changes in epigenetic modifications can alter gene expression in ways that contribute to diseases. It is also important to note that, unlike DNA mutations (which permanently change the nucleotide sequence), epigenetic changes can be easily reversed. A lot of research now focuses on how drugs can alter or modulate changes in DNA methylation and histone modifications to treat diseases such as cancer.

Special Topic: Epigenetics and X Chromosome Inactivation

Mary Lyon was a British geneticist who presented a hypothesis for X chromosome inactivation (called the *Lyon hypothesis*) based on her work and other studies of the day. Females inherit two X chromosomes, one from each parent. Males have one functional X chromosome; however, this does not mean females have more active genes than males. During the genetic embryonic development of many female mammals, one of the X chromosomes is inactivated at random, so females have one functional X chromosome. The process of X chromosome inactivation in females occurs through epigenetic mechanisms, such as DNA methylation and histone modifications. Recent studies have analyzed the role of a long noncoding RNA called X-inactive specific transcript (XIST), which is largely responsible for the random silencing of one of the X chromosomes. The presence of two X chromosomes is the signal for XIST RNA to be expressed so that one X chromosome can be inactivated. However, some cells may have an active paternal X chromosome while other cells may have an active maternal X chromosome. This phenomenon is easily seen in calico and tortoiseshell cats (Figure 3.35). In cats, the gene that controls coat color is found on the X chromosome. During early embryo development, random inactivation of X chromosomes gives rise to populations of cells that express black or orange, which results in the unique coat patterning. Therefore, calico cats are typically always female.

Figure 3.35: A multicolored coat pattern as the result of X chromosome inactivation during development. Credit: "Rue" the calico cat by Hayley Mann is under a CC BY-NC 4.0 License.

Genetic Testing

To assist with public health efforts, newborn screening for genetic diseases has been available in the United States for over 50 years. One of the first available genetic tests was to confirm a phenylketonuria (PKU) diagnosis in infants, which is easily treatable with a dietary change. Currently, each state decides what genes are included on newborn screening panels and some states even have programs to help with infant medical follow-ups.

There are now hundreds of laboratories that provide testing for a few thousand different genes that can inform medical decisions for infants and adults. What has made this industry possible are the advancements in technology and decreased cost to patients. Moreover, genetic testing has been made available publicly to anyone without the assistance of medical professionals.

Clinical Testing

Clinical genetics tests assist patients with making medically informed decisions about family planning and health. Applications of this technology include assistance with *in vitro* fertilization (IVF) procedures, embryo genetic screening, and personalized medicine such as matching patients to cancer therapies. To ensure accuracy of patient genetic screening, it is important that all clinical laboratories are regulated. The Clinical Laboratory Improvement Amendments (CLIA) are United States federal standards that all human laboratory testing clinics must follow. A major benefit provided by some clinical genetic testing companies is access to genetic counselors, who have specialized education and training in medical genetics and counseling. For individuals with a family history of genetic disease, a physician may recommend genetic carrier screening to see if there is a risk for passing on a disease to a child. Genetic counselors provide expertise with interpretation of genetic testing results, as well as help guide and support patients when making impactful medical decisions.

Direct-to-Consumer (DTC) Genetic Testing

Genetic testing that is performed without the guidance of medical professionals is called direct-to-consumer (DTC) genetic testing. Companies that sell affordable genome sequencing products to the public continue to increase in popularity. These companies have marketing campaigns typically based on the notion of personal empowerment, which can be achieved by knowing more about your DNA. For example, if you are identified as having a slightly increased risk for developing celiac disease (Figure 3.36), then you may be motivated to modify your dietary consumption by removing gluten from your diet. Another scenario is that you could test positive for a known pathogenic *BRCA1* or *BRCA2* cancer-predisposing allele. In this case, you may want to follow up with a physician and obtain additional clinical testing, which could lead to life-altering decisions. DNA sequencing products for entertainment and lifestyle purposes are also available. For example, some DTC companies offer customized genetic reports for health and fitness, wherein recommendations for optimal exercise workout and meal plans are provided.

People with this result have a slightly increased risk of developing celiac disease. Lifestyle and other factors can also affect your risk.

1 variant detected

in the HLA-DQB1 gene

Figure 3.36: A positive result for a genetic allele associated with an increased risk for celiac disease. Credit: Positive carrier result for celiac disease allele by Hayley Mann is under a CC BY-NC 4.0 License.

European	91.6%
● British & Irish	32.9%
United Kingdom	
● Scandinavian	5.9%
● Iberian	4.3%
● French & German	1.6%
Netherlands	
● Ashkenazi Jewish	0.5%
● Broadly Northwestern European	34.6%
● Broadly Southern European	6.0%
● Broadly European	5.8%
East Asian & Native American	**7.8%**
● Native American	6.4%
Mexico	
We predict you had ancestors that lived in Mexico within the last 200 years.	
● Broadly East Asian	0.1%
● Broadly East Asian & Native American	1.4%
South Asian	**0.2%**
● Broadly South Asian	0.2%
Sub-Saharan African	**0.1%**
● West African	0.1%
Unassigned	**0.4%**

Figure 3.37: An example of ancestry percentage results provided to customers. Credit: DNA ancestry percentage test results by Hayley Mann is under a CC BY-NC 4.0 License.

DTC testing typically lacks genetic counselor services to consumers, and regulations for nonclinical laboratories are not as strict. This has led to some controversies regarding company genetic products that provide health information. The company 23andMe was the first on the market to offer DTC health testing, and in 2013, the U.S. Food and Drug Administration (FDA) intervened. 23andMe worked toward complying with FDA regulations and then gained approval to offer testing on a few medically related genes. In 2017, 23andMe offered a "Late-Onset Alzheimer's Disease" genetic risk report. Such offerings have been criticized because customers could receive results they may not fully be able to interpret without professional assistance and advice. In turn, this could increase the stress of participants (sometimes called the "burden of knowing") and could lead to unnecessary medical intervention.To address this issue, 23andMe now provides disclaimers and also interactive learning modules that customers must complete if they wish to view certain genotyping results. However, individuals who tested positive for a disease-causing allele have also been able to successfully seek medical help. The potential for harm and the proposed benefits of DTC testing continue to be a topic of debate and investigation.

Ancestry percentage tests are also widely popular (Figure 3.37). Customers are genotyped and their alleles are assigned to different groups from around the world (Chapter 4 will discuss human biological variation in further detail). However, the scientific significance and potential harm of ancestry percentage tests have been called into question. For example, most alleles tested are not exclusive to one population, and populations may be defined differently depending on the testing companies. If an allele is assigned to the "Irish" population, there is a good chance that the allele may have evolved in a different cultural group or region that pre-dates the formation of the country Ireland. In other words, genetic variation often pre-dates the origins of the population and geographical names of the region used by genetic testing companies. Another critique is that someone's identity need not include biological relationships. In using the tests, customers have the option to find and connect online with other individuals with whom they share portions of their genome, which has resulted in both positive and negative personal experiences. Another interesting development in this field is that law enforcement is currently developing forensic techniques that involve mining DTC genomic databases for the purpose of identifying suspects linked to crimes. Regardless of these various considerations, there are now millions of individuals worldwide who have "unlocked the secrets" of their DNA, and the multibillion-dollar genomics market only continues to grow.

As you have seen in this chapter, DNA provides instructions to our cells, which results in the creation and regulation of proteins. Understanding these fundamental mechanisms is important to being able to understand how the evolutionary process works (see Chapter 4) and how humans vary from one another (see Chapters 13 and 14). In addition, advancement in genetic technologies—including ancient DNA studies, genomics, and epigenetics—has led to new anthropological understandings about our biological relationships to other living (extant) and extinct primates. Many of these genetic discoveries will be covered in the chapters to come.

Special Topic: Genetic Biotechnology

Polymerase Chain Reaction (PCR) and Sanger Sequencing

One of the most important inventions in the genetics field was **polymerase chain reaction (PCR)**. In order for researchers to visualize and therefore analyze DNA, the concentration must meet certain thresholds. In 1985, Kary Mullis developed PCR, which can amplify millions of copies of DNA from a very small amount of template DNA (Figure 3.38). For example, a trace amount of DNA at a crime scene can be amplified and tested for a DNA match. Also, aDNA is typically degraded, so a few remaining molecules of DNA can be amplified to reconstruct ancient genomes. The PCR assay uses similar biochemical reactions to our own cells during DNA replication.

In **Sanger sequencing**, PCR sequences can be analyzed at the nucleotide level with the help of fluorescent labeling. Several different types of alleles and genetic changes can be detected in DNA by using this analysis. Figure 3.39 shows someone who is heterozygous for a single nucleotide allele. These methods continue to be used extensively alongside larger-scale genome technologies.

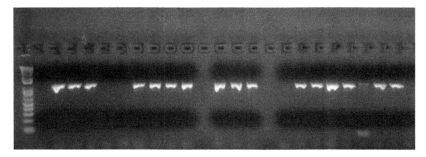

Figure 3.38: Gel electrophoresis is used to analyze DNA after PCR amplification. DNA is loaded into wells at the top, and an electric current applied to pull negatively charged DNA through the gel. Small DNA fragments move more quickly, separating DNA by size. Credit: PCR electrophoresis gel by Hayley Mann is under a CC BY-NC 4.0 License.

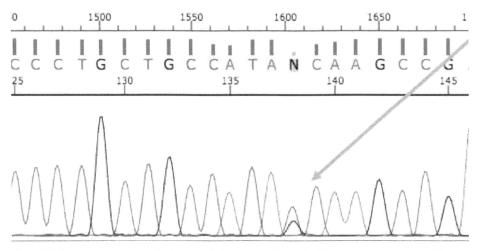

Figure 3.39: Sanger sequencing results showing a heterozygous DNA nucleotide. The sequencer detected the presence of both G (black) and C (blue) bases, as seen in the peaks at the bottom. The software records the base as N (undetermined) since both C and G bases are present. Credit: Sanger sequencing with heterozygous result by Hayley Mann is under a CC BY-NC 4.0 License.

Genetic innovations are transforming the healthcare industry. However, the different types of technology and the results of these tests often include a learning curve for patients, the public, and medical practitioners. **Microarray technology**, by which DNA samples are genotyped (or "screened") for specific alleles, has been available for quite some time (Figure 3.40). Presently, microarray chips can include hundreds of alleles that are known to be associated with various diseases. The microarray chip only binds with a DNA sample if it is "positive" for that particular allele and a fluorescent signal is emitted, which can be further analyzed.

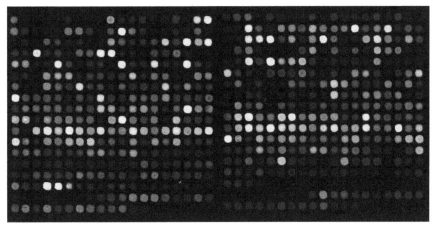

Figure 3.40: Microarray chip with fluorescent labeled probes that hybridize with DNA to detect homozygous and heterozygous nucleotides throughout the genome. Credit: **Cdnaarray** by Mangapoco (cropped from www.sgn.cornell.edu) is under a CC BY-SA 3.0 License.

Next-generation sequencing (NGS) is a newer technology that can screen the entire genome by analyzing millions of sequences within a single machine run. If a patient is suspected of having a rare genetic condition that cannot be easily diagnosed or the diagnosis is entirely unknown, whole genome sequencing may be recommended by a doctor. However, sequencing the entire genome is still not a cost-effective healthcare approach. Therefore, clinical NGS genetic testing typically only includes a smaller subset of the genome known to have pathogenic disease-causing mutations (i.e., the gene-coding, or "exonic," regions of the genome). Sequencing cancer tumor genomes is another significant application of this technology. To better understand how genetic mutations affect gene expression patterns, tumor genomic analysis also often involves RNA sequencing (known as the "transcriptome"). The primary goal of this complex "multi-omics" analysis is to provide personalized medicine, where patient outcome can be improved by administering tailored targeted therapies.

Review Questions

- What is the purpose of DNA replication? Explain in a few sentences what happens during DNA replication. When do DNA mutations happen? And how does this create phenotypic variation (i.e., different phenotypes of the same physical trait)?
- Using your own words, what are homologous chromosomes and sister chromatids? What are the key differences between mitosis and meiosis?
- Determine if the pedigree diagram below (Figure 3.41) represents an autosomal dominant, autosomal recessive, or X-linked recessive pattern of inheritance. You should write the genotype (i.e., AA, Aa, or aa) above each square to help you (note: there may sometimes be two possible answers for a square's genotype). Please also explain why you concluded a particular pattern of inheritance.

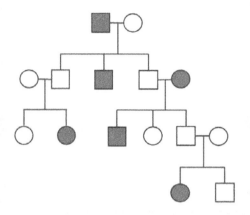

Figure 3.41: A four generation pedigree depicting a trait with an undetermined inheritance pattern. Credit: X-linked recessive pattern of inheritance (Figure 3.46) original to Explorations: An Open Invitation to Biological Anthropology by Beth Shook is under a CC BY-NC 4.0 License.

- Use base pairing rules to transcribe the following DNA template sequence into mRNA: GTAAAGGTGCTGGCCATC. Next, use the protein codon table (see Figure 3.21) to translate the sequence. In regard to transcription, explain what the significance is of the first and last codon/protein in the sequence.
- In your opinion, what do you think the benefits are of direct-to-consumer (DTC) genetic testing? What are the drawbacks and/or greater ethical concerns? Do you think benefits outweigh concerns?
- Imagine that you submit your DNA sample to a genetic testing company and among the various diseases for which they test, there is an allele that is associated with late-onset Alzheimer's disease. You have the option to view your Alzheimer's result or to not view your result. What do you do and why?

Key Terms

Adenosine triphosphate (ATP): A high-energy compound produced by mitochondria that powers cellular processes.

Allele: A nonidentical DNA sequence found in the same gene location on a homologous chromosome, or gene copy, that codes for the same trait but produces a different phenotype.

Amino acids: Organic molecules that are the building blocks of protein. Each of the 20 different amino acids have their own unique chemical property. Amino acids are chained together to form proteins.

Ancient DNA (aDNA): DNA that is extracted from organic remains and that often dates from hundreds to thousands of years ago. Also, aDNA is typically degraded (i.e., damaged) due to exposure to the elements such as heat, acidity, and humidity.

Aneuploid: A cell with an unexpected amount of chromosomes. The loss or gain of chromosomes can occur during mitotic or meiotic division.

Antibodies: Immune-related proteins that can detect and bind to foreign substances in the blood such as pathogens.

Apoptosis: A series of molecular steps that is activated leading to cell death. Apoptosis can be activated when a cell fails checkpoints during the cell cycle; however, cancer cells have the ability to avoid apoptosis.

Autosomal: Refers to a pattern of inheritance in which an allele is located on an autosome (non sex chromosome).

Base pairs: Chemical bonding between nucleotides. In DNA, adenine (A) pairs with thymine (T) and cytosine (C) pairs with guanine (G); in RNA, adenine (A) always pairs with uracil (U).

Carbohydrate: Molecules composed of carbon and hydrogen atoms that can be broken down to supply energy.

Carrier: An individual who has a heterozygous genotype that is typically associated with a disease.

Cell cycle: A cycle the cell undergoes with checkpoints between phases to ensure that DNA replication and cell division occur properly.

Cell surface antigen: A protein that is found on a red blood cell's surface.

Centromere: A structural feature that is defined as the "center" of a chromosome and that creates two different arm lengths. This term also refers to the region of attachment for microtubules during mitosis and meiosis.

Chromatin: DNA wrapped around histone complexes. During cell division, chromatin becomes a condensed chromosome.

Chromosome: DNA molecule that is wrapped around protein complexes, including histones.

Codominance: The effects of both alleles in a genotype can be seen in the phenotype.

Codons: A sequence that comprises three DNA nucleotides that together code for a protein.

Complex diseases: A category of diseases that are polygenic and are also influenced by environment and lifestyle factors.

Cytoplasm: The "jelly-like" matrix inside of the cell that contains many organelles and other cellular molecules.

Deleterious: A mutation that increases an organism's susceptibility to disease.

Deoxyribonucleic acid (DNA): A molecule that carries the hereditary information passed down from parents to offspring. DNA can be described as a "double helix'" shape. It includes two chains of nucleotides held together by hydrogen bonds with a sugar phosphate backbone.

Diploid: Refers to an organism or cell with two sets of chromosomes.

DNA methylation: Methyl groups bind DNA, which modifies the transcriptional activity of a gene by turning it "on" or "off."

DNA polymerase: Enzyme that adds nucleotides to existing nucleic acid strands during DNA replication. These enzymes can be distinguished by their processivity (e.g., DNA replication).

DNA replication: Cellular process in which DNA is copied and doubled.

DNA sequence: The order of nucleotide bases. A DNA sequence can be short, long, or representative of entire chromosomes or organismal genomes.

Dominant: Refers to an allele for which one copy is sufficient to be visible in the phenotype.

Elongation: The assembly of new DNA from template strands with the help of DNA polymerases.

Enzymes: Proteins responsible for catalyzing (accelerating) various biochemical reactions in cells.

Epigenetic profile: The methylation pattern throughout a genome—that is, which genes (and other genomic sites) are methylated and unmethylated.

Epigenetics: Changes in gene expression that do not result in a change of the underlying DNA sequence. These changes typically involve DNA methylation and histone modifications. These changes are reversible and can also be inherited by the next generation.

Euchromatin: Loosely coiled chromosomes found within the nucleus that are accessible for regulatory processing of DNA.

Eukaryote: Single-celled or multicelled organism characterized by a distinct nucleus, with each organelle surrounded by its own membrane.

Exon: Protein-coding segment of a gene.

Gametes: Haploid cells referred to as an egg and sperm that will fuse together during sexual reproduction to form a diploid organism.

Gene: Segment of DNA that contains protein-coding information and various regulatory (e.g., promoter) and noncoding (e.g., introns) regions.

Genetic recombination: A cellular process that occurs during meiosis I in which homologous chromosomes pair up and sister chromatids on different chromosomes physically swap genetic information.

Genome: All the genetic information of an organism.

Genotype: The combination of two alleles that code for or are associated with the same gene.

Genotyping: A molecular procedure that is performed to test for the presence of certain alleles or to discover new ones.

Germ cells: Specialized cells that form gametes (egg and sperm cells).

Haploid: Cell or organism with one set of chromosomes ($n = 23$).

Helicase: A protein that breaks the hydrogen bonds that hold double-stranded DNA together.

Heterozygous: Genotype that consists of two different alleles.

Histones: Proteins that DNA wraps around to assist with DNA organization within the nucleus.

Homologous chromosomes: A matching pair of chromosomes wherein one chromosome is maternally inherited and the other is paternally inherited.

Homozygous: Genotype that consists of two identical alleles.

Incomplete dominance: Heterozygous genotype that produces a phenotype that is a blend of both alleles.

Initiation: The recruitment of proteins to separate DNA strands and begin DNA replication.

Interphase: Preparatory period of the cell cycle when increased metabolic demand allows for DNA replication and doubling of the cell prior to cell division.

Introns: Segment of DNA that does not code for proteins.

Karyotyping: The microscopic procedure wherein the number of chromosomes in a cell is determined.

Lagging strand: DNA template strand that is opposite to the leading strand during DNA replication. This strand is created in several disconnected sections and other enzymes fill in the missing nucleotide gaps between these sections.

Leading strand: DNA template strand in which replication proceeds continuously.

Lipids: Fatty acid molecules that serve various purposes in the cell, including energy storage, cell signaling, and structure.

Meiosis: The process that gametes undergo to divide. The end of meiosis results in four haploid daughter cells.

Mendelian genetics: A classification given to phenotypic traits that are controlled by a single gene.

Messenger RNA (mRNA): RNA molecule that is transcribed from DNA. Its tri-nucleotide codons are "read" by a ribosome to build a protein.

Microarray technology: A genotyping procedure that utilizes a microarray chip, which is a collection of thousands of short nucleotide sequences attached to a solid surface that can probe genomic DNA.

Microbiome: The collective genomes of the community of microorganisms that humans have living inside of their bodies.

Mitochondrial DNA (mtDNA): Circular DNA segment found in mitochondria that is inherited maternally.

Mitochondrion: Specialized cellular organelle that is the site for energy production. It also has its own genome (mtDNA).

Mitosis: The process that somatic cells undergo to divide. The end of mitosis results in two diploid daughter cells.

Molecular anthropologists: Individuals who use molecular techniques (primarily genetics) to compare ancient and modern populations and to study living populations of humans and nonhuman primates.

Molecular geneticists: Biologists that study the structure and function of genes.

Mutation: A nucleotide sequence variation from the template DNA strand that can occur during replication. Mutations can also happen during recombination.

Next-generation sequencing: A genotyping technology that involves producing millions of nucleotide sequences (from a single DNA sample) that are then read with a sequencing machine. It can be used for analyzing entire genomes or specific regions and requires extensive program-based applications.

Nuclear envelope: A double-layered membrane that encircles the nucleus.

Nucleic acid: A complex structure (like DNA or RNA) that carries genetic information about a living organism.

Nucleotide: The basic structural component of nucleic acids, which includes DNA (A, T, C, and G) and RNA (A, U, C, and G).

Nucleus: Double-membrane cellular organelle that helps protect DNA and also regulates nuclear activities.

Organelle: A structure within a cell that performs specialized tasks that are essential for the cell. There are different types of organelles, each with its own function.

Pathogenic: A genetic mutation (i.e., allele) that has a harmful phenotypic disease-causing effect.

Pedigree: A diagram of family relationships that indicates which members may have or carry certain genetic and/or phenotypic traits.

Penetrance: The proportion of how often the possession of an allele results in an expected phenotype. Some alleles are more penetrant than others.

Phenotype: The physical appearance of a given trait.

Phospholipid bilayer: Two layers of lipids that form a barrier due to the properties of a hydrophilic (water-loving) head and a hydrophobic (water-repelling) tail.

Polygenic trait: A phenotype that is controlled by two or more genes.

Polymerase chain reaction (PCR): A molecular biology procedure that can make copies of genomic DNA segments. A small amount of DNA is used as a starting template and is then used to make millions of copies.

Prokaryote: A single-celled organism characterized by the lack of a nucleus and membrane-enclosed organelles.

Promoter: The region of a gene that initiates transcription. Transcription factors can bind and DNA methylation may occur at a promoter site, which can modify the transcriptional activities of a gene.

Protein: Chain of amino acids that folds into a three-dimensional structure that allows a cell to function in a variety of ways.

Protein synthesis: A multi-step process by which amino acids are strung together by RNA machinery read from a DNA template.

Recessive: Refers to an allele whose effect is not normally seen unless two copies are present in an individual's genotype.

Ribonucleic acid (RNA): Single-stranded nucleic acid molecule. There are different RNAs found within cells and they perform a variety of functions, such as cell signaling and involvement in protein synthesis.

Ribosomal RNA (rRNA): A ribosome-bound molecule that is used to correctly assemble amino acids into proteins.

Ribosome: An organelle in the cell found in the cytoplasm or endoplasmic reticulum. It is responsible for reading mRNA and protein assemblage.

RNA polymerase: An enzyme that catalyzes the process of making RNA from a DNA template.

Sanger-sequencing: A process that involves the usage of fluorescently labeled nucleotides to visualize DNA (PCR fragments) at the nucleotide level.

Semi-conservative replication: DNA replication in which new DNA is replicated from an existing DNA template strand.

Sequencing: A molecular laboratory procedure that produces the order of nucleotide bases (i.e., sequences).

Sister chromatids: During DNA replication, sister chromatids are produced on the chromosome. In cell division, sister chromatids are pulled apart so that two cells can be formed. In meiosis, sister chromatids are also the sites of genetic recombination.

Somatic cells: Diploid cells that comprise body tissues and undergo mitosis for maintenance and repair of tissues.

Splicing: The process by which mature mRNAs are produced. Introns are removed (spliced) and exons are joined together.

Sugar phosphate backbone: A biochemical structural component of DNA. The "backbone" consists of deoxyribose sugars and phosphate molecules.

Telomere: A compound structure located at the ends of chromosomes to help protect the chromosomes from degradation after every round of cell division.

Termination: The halt of DNA replication activity that occurs when a DNA sequence "stop" codon is encountered.

Tissue: A cluster of cells that are morphologically similar and perform the same task.

Transcription: The process by which DNA nucleotides (within a gene) are copied, which results in a messenger RNA molecule.

Transcription factors: Proteins that bind to regulatory regions of genes (e.g., promoter) and increase or decrease the amount of transcriptional activity of a gene, including turning them "on" or "off."

Transfer RNA (tRNA): RNA molecule involved in translation. Transfer RNA transports amino acids from the cell's cytoplasm to a ribosome.

Translation: The process by which messenger RNA codons are read and amino acids are "chained together" to form proteins.

X-linked: Refers to a pattern of inheritance where the allele is located on the X or Y chromosome.

About the Author

Hayley Mann, M.A.

Binghamton University, hmann3@binghamton.edu

Hayley Mann received her bachelor's degree in Genetics from the University of California, Davis, and continued her graduate studies in Biological and Molecular Anthropology at the California State University, Sacramento. She is currently a Ph.D. candidate at Binghamton University, where her dissertation focus is on studying genetic variation of Pacific Islanders (Republic of Vanuatu) and also changes in health as the result of colonization. Hayley also works in clinical molecular carrier screening and specializes in DNA-sequencing procedures.

For Further Exploration

National Human Genome Research Institute

Genetics Home Reference

Genetics Generation

yourgenome

NOVA. 2018. Gene Sequencing Speeds Diagnosis of Deadly Newborn Diseases. NOVA, March 7, 2018. Accessed January 31, 2023. http://www.pbs.org/wgbh/nova/next/body/newborn-gene-sequencing/.

Zimmer, Carl. N.d. "Carl Zimmer's Game of Genomes." STATnews. Accessed January 31, 2023. https://www.statnews.com/feature/game-of-genomes/season-one/.

Illumina. 2016. "Illumina Sequencing by Synthesis." YouTube.com, October 5, 2016. Accessed January 31, 2023. https://www.youtube.com/watch?v=fCd6B5HRaZ8.

References

Aartsma-Rus, Annemieke, Ieke B. Ginjaar, and Kate Bushby. 2016. "The Importance of Genetic Diagnosis for Duchenne Muscular Dystrophy." Journal of Medical Genetics 53 (3): 145–151.

Acuna-Hidalgo, Rocio, Joris A. Veltman, and Alexander Hoischen. 2016. "New Insights into the Generation and Role of De Novo Mutations in Health and Disease." Genome Biology 17 (241): 1–19.

Albert, Benjamin, Susanna Tomassetti, Yvonne Gloor, Daniel Dilg, Stefano Mattarocci, Slawomir Kubik, Lukas Hafner, and David Shore. 2019. "Sfp1 Regulates Transcriptional Networks Driving Cell Growth and Division through Multiple Promoter-Binding Modes." Genes & Development 33 (5–6): 288–293.

Almathen, Faisal, Haitham Elbir, Hussain Bahbahani, Joram Mwacharo, and Olivier Hanotte. 2018. "Polymorphisms in Mc1r and Asip Genes Are Associated with Coat Color Variation in the Arabian Camel." Journal of Heredity 109 (6): 700–706.

Ballester, Leomar Y., Rajyalakshmi Luthra, Rashmi Kanagal-Shamanna, and Rajesh R. Singh. 2016. "Advances in Clinical Next-Generation Sequencing: Target Enrichment and Sequencing Technologies." Expert Review of Molecular Diagnostics 16 (3): 357–372.

Baranovskiy, Andrey G., Vincent N. Duong, Nigar D. Babayeva, Yinbo Zhang, Youri I. Pavlov, Karen S. Anderson, and Tahir H. Tahirov. 2018. "Activity and Fidelity of Human DNA Polymerase Alpha Depend on Primer Structure." Journal of Biological Chemistry 293 (18): 6824–6843.

Brezina, Paulina R., Raymond Anchan, and William G. Kearns. 2016. "Preimplantation Genetic Testing for Aneuploidy: What Technology Should You Use and What Are the Differences?" Journal of Assisted Reproduction and Genetics 33 (7): 823–832.

Bultman, Scott J. 2017. "Interplay Between Diet, Gut Microbiota, Epigenetic Events, and Colorectal Cancer." Molecular Nutrition & Food Research 61 (1):1–12.

Cutting, Garry R. 2015. "Cystic Fibrosis Genetics: From Molecular Understanding to Clinical Application." Nature Reviews Genetics 16 (1): 45–56.

D'Alessandro, Giuseppina., and Fabrizio d'Adda di Fagagna. 2017. "Transcription and DNA Damage: Holding Hands or Crossing Swords?" Journal of Molecular Biology 429 (21): 3215–3229.

De Craene, Johan-Owen, Dimitri L. Bertazzi, Séverine Bar, and Sylvie Friant. 2017. "Phosphoinositides, Major Actors in Membrane Trafficking and Lipid Signaling Pathways." International Journal of Molecular Sciences 18 (3): 1–20.

Deng, Lian, and Shuhua Xu. 2018. "Adaptation of Human Skin Color in Various Populations." Hereditas 155 (1): 1–12.

Dever, Thomas E., Terri G. Kinzy, and Graham D. Pavitt. 2016. "Mechanism and Regulation of Protein Synthesis in Saccharomyces Cerevisiae." Genetics 203 (1): 65–107.

Eme, Laura, Anja Spang, Jonathan Lombard, Courtney W. Stairs, and Thijs J. G. Ettema. 2017. "Archaea and the Origin of Eukaryotes." Nature Reviews Microbiology 15 (12): 711–723.

Gomez-Carballa, Alberto, Jacobo Pardo-Seco, Stefania Brandini, Alessandro Achilli, Ugo A. Perego, Michael D. Coble, Toni M. Diegoli, et al. 2018. "The Peopling of South America and the Trans-Andean Gene Flow of the First Settlers." Genome Research 28 (6): 767–779.

Gvozdenov, Zlata, Janhavi Kolhe, and Brian C. Freeman. 2019. "The Nuclear and DNA-Associated Molecular Chaperone Network." Cold Spring Harbor Perspectives in Biology 11 (10): a034009.

Harkins, Kelly M., and Anne C. Stone. 2015. "Ancient Pathogen Genomics: Insights into Timing and Adaptation." Journal of Human Evolution 79: 137–149.

Jackson, Maria, Leah Marks, Gerhard H. W. May, and Joanna B. Wilson. 2018. "The Genetic Basis of Disease." Essays in Biochemistry 62 (5): 643–723.

Lenormand, Thomas, Jan Engelstadter, Susan E. Johnston, Erik Wijnker, and Christopher R. Haag. 2016. "Evolutionary Mysteries in Meiosis." Philosophical Transactions of the Royal Society B 371: 1–14.

Levy, Shawn E., and Richard M. Myers. 2016. "Advancements in Next-Generation Sequencing." Annual Review of Genomics and Human Genetics 17: 95–115.

Lindo, John, Emilia Huerta-Sánchez, Shigeki Nakagome, Morten Rasmussen, Barbara Petzelt, Joycelynn Mitchell, Jerome S. Cybulski, et al. 2016. "A Time Transect of Exomes from a Native American Population Before and After European Contact." Nature Communications 7: 1–11. https://doi.org/10.1038/ncomms13175.

Lu, Mengfei, Cathryn M. Lewis, and Matthew Traylor. 2017. "Pharmacogenetic Testing through the Direct-to-Consumer Genetic Testing Company 23andme." BMC Medical Genomics 10 (47): 1–8.

Ly, Lundi, Donovan Chan, Mahmoud Aarabi, Mylene Landry, Nathalie A. Behan, Amanda J. MacFarlane, and Jacquetta Trasler. 2017. "Intergenerational Impact of Paternal Lifetime Exposures to Both Folic Acid Deficiency and Supplementation on Reproductive Outcomes and Imprinted Gene Methylation." Molecular Human Reproduction 23 (7): 461–477.

Ma, Wenxiu, Giancarlo Bonora, Joel B. Berletch, Xinxian Deng, William S. Noble, and Christine M. Disteche. 2018. "X-Chromosome Inactivation and Escape from X Inactivation in Mouse." Methods in Molecular Biology 1861: 205–219.

Machiela, Mitchell J., Weiyin Zhou, Eric Karlins, Joshua N. Sampson, Neal D. Freedman, Qi Yang, Belynda Hicks, et al. 2016. "Female Chromosome X Mosaicism Is Age-Related and Preferentially Affects the Inactivated X Chromosome." Nature Communications 7: 1–9. https://doi.org/10.1038/ncomms11843.

Mahdavi, Morteza, Mohammadreza Nassiri, Mohammad M. Kooshyar, Masoume Vakili-Azghandi, Amir Avan, Ryan Sandry, Suja Pillai, Alfred K. Lam, and Vinod Gopalan. 2019. "Hereditary Breast Cancer; Genetic Penetrance and Current Status with BRCA." Journal of Cellular Physiology 234 (5): 5741–5750.

McDade, Thomas W., Calen P. Ryan, Meaghan J. Jones, Morgan K. Hoke, Judith Borja, Gregory E. Miller, Christopher W. Kuzawa, and Michael S. Kobor. 2019. "Genome-Wide Analysis of DNA Methylation in Relation to Socioeconomic Status During Development and Early Adulthood." American Journal of Physical Anthropology 169 (1): 3–11.

Migeon, Barbara R. 2017. "Choosing the Active X: The Human Version of X Inactivation." Trends in Genetics 33 (12): 899–909.

Myerowitz, Rachel. 1997. "Tay-Sachs Disease-Causing Mutations and Neutral Polymorphisms in the Hex A Gene." Human Mutation 9 (3): 195–208.

Onufriev, Alexey V., and Helmut Schiessel. 2019. "The Nucleosome: From Structure to Function through Physics." Current Opinion in Structural Biology 56: 119–130.

Quillen, Ellen E., Heather L. Norton, Esteban J. Parra, Frida Lona-Durazo, Khai C. Ang, Florin M. Illiescu, Laurel N. Pearson, et al. 2019. "Shades of Complexity: New Perspectives on the Evolution and Genetic Architecture of Human Skin." American Journal of Physical Anthropology 168 (67): 4–26.

Raspelli, Erica, and Roberta Fraschini. 2019. "Spindle Pole Power in Health and Disease." Current Genetics 65 (4): 851–855.

Ravinet, M., R. Faria, R. K. Butlin, J. Galindo, N. Bierne, M. Rafajlovic, M. A. F. Noor, B. Mehlig, and A. M. Westram. 2017. "Interpreting the Genomic Landscape of Speciation: A Road Map for Finding Barriers to Gene Flow." Journal of Evolutionary Biology 30 (8): 1450–1477.

Regev, Aviv, Sarah A. Teichmann, Eric S. Lander, Ido Amit, Christophe Benoist, Ewan Birney, Bernd Bodenmiller, et al. 2017. "The Human Cell Atlas." Elife 6e27041: 1–30. https://doi.org/10.7554.eLife.27041.

Roberts, Andrea L., Nicole Gladish, Evan Gatev, Meaghan J. Jones, Ying Chen, Julia L. MacIsaac, Shelley S. Tworoger, et al. 2018. "Exposure to Childhood Abuse Is Associated with Human Sperm DNA Methylation." Translational Psychiatry 8 (194): 1–11.

Roger, Andrew J., Sergio A. Muñoz-Gómez, and Ryoma Kamikawa. 2017. "The Origin and Diversification of Mitochondria." Current Biology 27 (21): R1177–R1192. https://www.sciencedirect.com/science/article/pii/S096098221731179X?via%3Dihub#!

Ségurel, Laure, and Céline Bon. 2017. "On the Evolution of Lactase Persistence in Humans." Annual Review of Genomics and Human Genetics 18: 297–319.

Sheth, Bhavisha P., and Vrinda S. Thaker. 2017. "DNA Barcoding and Traditional Taxonomy: An Integrated Approach for Biodiversity Conservation." Genome 60 (7): 618–628.

Skloot, Rebecca. 2010. The Immortal Life of Henrietta Lacks. New York: Crown Publishing Group.

Snedeker, Jonathan, Matthew Wooten, and Xin Chen. 2017. "The Inherent Asymmetry of DNA Replication." Annual Review of Cell and Developmental Biology 33: 291–318.

Sullivan-Pyke, Chantae, and Anuja Dokras. 2018. "Preimplantation Genetic Screening and Preimplantation Genetic Diagnosis." Obstetrics and Gynecology Clinics of North America 45 (1): 113–125.

Szostak, Jack W. 2017. "The Narrow Road to the Deep Past: In Search of the Chemistry of the Origin of Life." Angewandte Chemie International Edition 56 (37): 11037–11043.

Tessema, Mathewos, Ulrich Lehmann, and Hans Kreipe. 2004. "Cell Cycle and No End." Virchows Archiv European Journal of Pathology 444 (4): 313–323.

Tishkoff, Sarah A., Floyd A. Reed, Alessia Ranciaro, Benjamin F. Voight, Courtney C. Babbitt, Jesse S. Silverman, Kweli Powell, et al. 2007. "Convergent Adaptation of Human Lactase Persistence in Africa and Europe." Nature Genetics 39 (1): 31–40.

Visootsak, Jeannie, and John M. Graham, Jr. 2006. "Klinefelter Syndrome and Other Sex Chromosomal Aneuploidies." Orphanet Journal of Rare Diseases 1:42. https://doi.org/10.1186/1750-1172-1-42.

Wolfe, George C., dir. 2017. The Immortal Life of Henrietta Lacks. HBO Films, April 22, 2017. TV Movie.

Yamamoto, Fumi-ichiro, Henrik Clausen, Thayer White, John Marken, and Sen-itiroh Hakomori. 1990. "Molecular Genetic Basis of the Histo-Blood Group ABO System." Nature 345 (6272): 229–233.

Zlotogora, Joël. 2003. "Penetrance and Expressivity in the Molecular Age." Genetics in Medicine 5 (5): 347–352.

Zorina-Lichtenwalter, Katerina, Ryan N. Lichtenwalter, Dima V. Zaykin, Marc Parisien, Simon Gravel, Andrey Bortsov, and Luda Diatchenko. 2019. "A Study in Scarlet: MC1R as the Main Predictor of Red Hair and Exemplar of the Flip-Flop Effect." Human Molecular Genetics 28 (12): 2093-2106.

Zwart, Haeh. 2018. "In the Beginning Was the Genome: Genomics and the Bi-Textuality of Human Existence." New Bioethics 24 (1): 26–43.

Image Descriptions

Figure 3.2: Two cells drawn with openings so the inside organelles can be viewed and labeled. The eukaryotic cell is square shaped with a thick cell membrane around the outside. DNA is inside a circular membrane-enclosed nucleus. Labeled arrows point to different shaped membrane-enclosed organelles and ribosomes (represented by small dots). The prokaryotic cell has a capsule shape and a flagellum (tail). The thick cell wall is labeled, as is the cell membrane underneath it. DNA is loosely coiled in the nucleoid, ribosomes are represented by small dots.

Figure 3.3: Two cells are depicted with different shaped organelles inside them. The plant cell is square with a thick cellulose cell wall outside the cell membrane. The cytoplasm inside holds many chloroplasts (green ovals), two mitochondrion (brown ovals with wavy lines inside), and a circular nucleus containing loose DNA strands. A large permanent vacuole (empty space) is shown. The animal cell is round, with a thin cell wall. The cytoplasm holds different shaped organelles including a few mitochondria and a circular nucleus containing loose DNA strands.

Figure 3.4: The phospholipid bilayer is constructed of two sheet-like layers of lipid molecules. The individual lipid molecules have hydrophobic tails and hydrophilic heads. The tail-side of the two sheets form the middle of the bilayer, with the heads forming the outsides of the bilayer. Under the bilayer are filaments of the cytoskeleton (drawn as thick wavy lines). Imbedded in the phospholipid bilayer are:

- Glycoproteins: proteins with carbohydrate attached,
- Glycolipid: lipid with carbohydrate attached,
- Peripheral membrane proteins (fit in only one layer),
- Integral membrane proteins (that extend all the way through the bilayer),
- Cholesterol (small molecules in only one layer), and
- Protein channels (hat extend all the way through the bilayer)

Figure 3.5: A three-dimensional cell is partly opened to expose various labeled organelles. These include:

- A sphere shaped nucleus containing a smaller sphere shaped nucleolus,
- Ribosomes depicted as small dots,
- Rough endoplasmic reticulum shown as long thin membranes outside of the nucleus,
- Smooth endoplasmic reticulum near the rough ER,

- Mitochondria shown as small oval organelles with a wavy membrane inside. Some have microtubules (lines) extending from them.
- Tube like centrioles,
- Golgi body appearing as a stacked membrane, and
- Lysosomes appear as small dots outside the nucleus.

Figure 3.9: The DNA double helix is shown wound around nucleosomes. Each nucleosome is made of clustered spherical histones and the DNA wraps around it twice. The DNA wound around nucleosomes resembles "beads on a string." Many wrapped and condensed nucleosomes form chromatin fiber, which are further wound into an X-shaped chromosome.

Figure 3.12: Original (template) DNA extends from an X shaped chromosome, and its two strands are separated at the replication fork by helicase (an enzyme depicted as a triangle). The bottom original template strand has DNA polymerase moving away from the replication fork to create a new lagging strand DNA by adding free nucleotides. On the upper strand of original DNA, DNA polymerase works toward the replication fork, adding free nucleotides to build the leading strand.

Figure 3.15: This pie chart shows the proportion of time spent in each cell phase. The shortest phases are the mitotic phases (mitosis followed by cytokinesis) which lead to the formation of two daughter cells. This is followed by a long cell growth (G1, interphase), DNA synthesis (S, interphase), and cell growth (G2, interphase), before returning to the mitotic phase.

Figure 3.17: Image depicts protein synthesis as divided into three phases, and shows the molecules involved at each phase, and that are used to help create the following document. First, in transcription, DNA (double stranded) is used as a template to create pre-mRNA (single stranded). Second, in RNA processing (also called splicing), pre-mRNA is modified to form a shorter mature mRNA. Lastly, in translation, mature mRNA is used as instructions to link together spherical amino acids in a chain, or protein.

Figure 3.18: The single-stranded structure of RNA is shown with a backbone of sugar-phosphates in a helical shape and nucleobases are shown as rungs on a ladder. On the left side of the figure, the chemical structure of each nucleobase is depicted: cytosine (C), guanine (G), adenine (A), and uracil (U).

Figure 3.19: A stretch of double stranded DNA is depicted in the process of transcription. The two strands are pulled apart in the middle, the top strand forms the template strand. RNA polymerase (a bubble shaped enzyme) sits on the template strand and adds free nucleotides to a growing RNA transcript. The DNA template strand reads ATGACGGATCAG... and the RNA strand is complementary and contains uracil (U; UACUGCCUAGUC...).

Figure 3.20: At the top of the diagram, sections of a gene (DNA) are labeled: a promoter region followed by alternating sections of exons (filled in with horizontal lines) and introns (vertical lines). In the middle of the diagram, the pre mRNA transcription contains copies of the alternating exon and intron portions with lines drawn in. The bottom strand (mature mRNA) shows the introns removed and the exons (all horizontal lines) connected.

Figure 3.21: A roughly circular ribosome sits on a mRNA strand and facilitates the transfer of amino acids (dots) carried by tRNA to a growing amino acid (peptide) chain. Amino acids appear as different colored dots on a string. Their abbreviations and full names are listed.

alanine – ala

arginine – arg

asparagine – asn

aspartic acid – asp

cysteine – cys

glutamine – gln

glutamic acid – glu

glycine – gly

histidine – his

isoleucine – ile

leucine – leu

lysine – lys

methionine – met

phenylalanine – phe

proline – pro

serine – ser

threonine – thr

tryptophan – trp

tyrosine – tyr

valine – val

Figure 3.22

Accessible full text RNA codon to amino acid table

Figure 3.26: Grid illustration of the pollen of a purple-flowered pea plant (heterozygous genotype of capital B and lowercase b) mixing with the pistol (also a heterozygous genotype of capital B and lowercase b) could create combinations of genotypes: two capital B alleles (purple flower), capital B and lowercase B alleles (purple flower), or two lower case b alleles (white flower).

Figure 3.28: A grid format uses images of circles for the red blood cells, covered with smaller shapes, to depict antigens on blood types. Shapes that fit against the antigen shapes like puzzle pieces depict antibodies that can bind antigens.

For ABO blood types:

- A has circular (A) antigens on the cell, and V-shaped antibodies capable of binding B antigens.
- B has triangular (B) antigens on the cell, and moon-shaped antibodies capable of binding A antigens.
- AB has circular (A) and triangle (B) antigens. No corresponding antibodies.
- O has no antigens, and both V-shaped and moon-shaped antibodies capable of binding A and B antigens.

For Rh Blood types:

- Rh+ has rectangular (Rh) antigens on the cell. No corresponding antibodies.
- Rh- has no specific antigens, and box-shaped antibodies capable of binding Rh antigens.

Figure 3.29: A 3×3 Punnett-square grid showing the genotypes that result when the different ABO blood type alleles come together. A, B, and O constitute both the row and column headers. The cells are the resulting genotype (two combined alleles).

Top row: AA, AB, AO

Middle row: AB, BB, BO

Bottom row: AO, BO, OO

Figure 3.34: Two images each show DNA wrapped around a series of histones.

The top image shows DNA wrapped around seven tightly clustered histones. Many methyl groups (small dots) are on the DNA and on histone tails. A portion of the DNA tucked between two histones is highlighted as a gene and labeled "DNA inaccessible, gene inactive". Text reads: Methylation of DNA and histones causes nucleosomes to pack tightly together. Transcription factors cannot bind the DNA, and genes are not expressed.

The bottom image shows DNA wrapping around three widely spaced histones, with a highlighted active gene (where the DNA is accessible between two histones). Acetyl groups are attached to histone tails. Text reads: Histone acetylation results in loose packing of nucleosomes. Transcription factors can bind the DNA and genes are expressed.

4.

FORCES OF EVOLUTION

Andrea J. Alveshere, Ph.D., Western Illinois University

This chapter is a revision from "Chapter 4: Forces of Evolution" by Andrea J. Alveshere. In Explorations: An Open Invitation to Biological Anthropology, first edition, edited by Beth Shook, Katie Nelson, Kelsie Aguilera, and Lara Braff, which is licensed under CC BY-NC 4.0.

Learning Objectives

- Outline a 21st-century perspective of the Modern Synthesis.
- Define populations and population genetics as well as the methods used to study them.
- Identify the forces of evolution and become familiar with examples of each.
- Discuss the evolutionary significance of mutation, genetic drift, gene flow, and natural selection.
- Explain how allele frequencies can be used to study evolution as it happens.
- Contrast micro- and macroevolution.

It's hard for us, with our typical human life spans of less than 100 years, to imagine all the way back, 3.8 billion years ago, to the **origins of life**. Scientists still study and debate how life came into being and whether it originated on Earth or in some other region of the universe (including some scientists who believe that studying evolution can reveal the complex processes that were set in motion by God or a higher power). What we do know is that a living single-celled organism was present on Earth during the early stages of our planet's existence. This organism had the potential to reproduce by making copies of itself, just like bacteria, many amoebae, and our own living cells today. In fact, with modern technologies, we can now trace genetic lineages, or **phylogenies**, and determine the relationships between all of today's living organisms—eukaryotes (animals, plants, fungi, etc.), archaea, and bacteria—on the branches of the **phylogenetic tree of life** (Figure 4.1).

Looking at the common sequences in modern genomes, we can even make educated guesses about the likely genetic sequence of the **Last Universal Common Ancestor (LUCA)** of all living things. Through a wondrous series of mechanisms and events over nearly four billion years, that ancient single-celled organism gave rise to the rich diversity of species that fill the lands, seas, and skies of our planet. This chapter explores the mechanisms by which that amazing transformation occurred and considers some of the crucial scientific experiments that shaped our current understanding of the evolutionary process.

Updating the Modern Synthesis: Tying it All Together

Chapter 2 examined the roles played by many different scientists, and their many careful scientific experiments, in providing the full picture of evolution. The term **Modern Synthesis** describes the integration of these various lines of evidence into a unified theory of evolution.

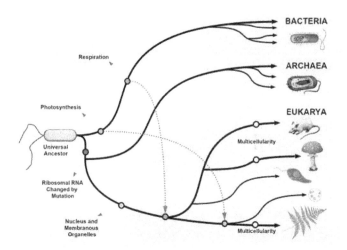

Figure 4.1: Phylogenetic tree of life illustrating probable relationships between the single-celled Last Universal Common Ancestor (LUCA) and select examples of bacteria, archaea, and eukaryotes. Major evolutionary developments, including independent evolution of multicellularity, photosynthesis, and respiration, are indicated along the branches. Credit: Cladograma dos Dominios e Reinos by MarceloTeles has been modified (English labels replace Portuguese) and is under a CC BY-SA 4.0 License. [Image Description].

Looking at the common sequences in modern genomes, we can even make educated guesses about the likely genetic sequence of the **Last Universal Common Ancestor (LUCA)** of all living things. Through a wondrous series of mechanisms and events over nearly four billion years, that ancient single-celled organism gave rise to the rich diversity of species that fill the lands, seas, and skies of our planet. This chapter explores the mechanisms by which that amazing transformation occurred and considers some of the crucial scientific experiments that shaped our current understanding of the evolutionary process.

Updating the Modern Synthesis: Tying it All Together

Chapter 2 examined the roles played by many different scientists, and their many careful scientific experiments, in providing the full picture of evolution. The term **Modern Synthesis** describes the integration of these various lines of evidence into a unified theory of evolution.

While the biggest leap forward in understanding how evolution works came with the joining (synthesis) of Darwin's concept of natural selection with Mendel's insights about particulate inheritance (described in detail in Chapter 3), there were some other big contributions that were crucial to making sense of the variation that was being observed. Mathematical models for evolutionary change provided the tools to study variation and became the basis for the study of population genetics (Fisher 1919; Haldane 1924). Other experiments revealed the existence of **chromosomes** as carriers of collections of genes (Dobzhansky 1937; Wright 1932).

Studies on wild butterflies confirmed the mathematical predictions and also led to the definition of the concept of **polymorphisms** to describe multiple forms of a trait (Ford 1949). These studies led to many useful advances such as the discovery that human blood type polymorphisms are maintained in the human population because they are involved in disease resistance (Ford 1942; see also the Special Topic box on Sickle Cell Anemia below).

Population Genetics

Defining Populations and the Variations within Them

One of the major breakthroughs in understanding the mechanisms of evolutionary change came with the realization that evolution takes place at the level of populations, not within individuals. In the biological sciences, a **population** is defined as a group of individuals of the same **species** who are geographically near enough to one another that they can breed and produce new generations of individuals.

For the purpose of studying evolution, we recognize populations by their even smaller units: genes. Remember, a **gene** is the basic unit of information that encodes the proteins needed to grow and function as a living organism. Each gene can have multiple **alleles**, or variants—each of which may produce a slightly different protein. Each individual, for genetic inheritance purposes, carries a collection of genes that can be passed down to future generations. For this reason, in population genetics, we think of populations as **gene pools**, which refers to the entire collection of genetic material in a breeding community that can be passed on from one generation to the next.

For genes carried on our human chromosomes (our nuclear DNA), we inherit two copies of each, one from each parent. This means we may carry two of the same alleles (a **homozygous genotype**) or two different alleles (a **heterozygous genotype**) for each nuclear gene.

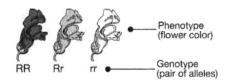

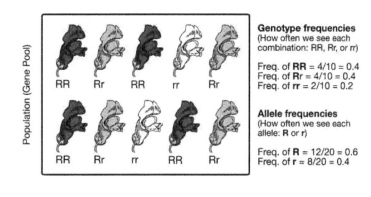

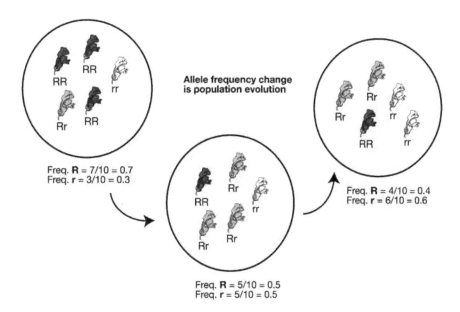

Figure 4.2: Population evolution can be measured by allele frequency changes. This diagram illustrates the differences between genotype frequencies and allele frequencies, as well as how they can be measured in a population of snapdragon flowers. The lower portion of the diagram also depicts how evolution is recognized as allele frequencies change in a population over time. Credit: Population evolution original to Explorations: An Open Invitation to Biological Anthropology (2nd ed.) by Katie Nelson and Beth Shook is a collective work under a CC BY-NC 4.0 License. [Includes Snapdragon-flower-pink-lilac by OpenClipart-Vectors, public domain (CC0) under a Pixabay License.] [Image Description].

Defining Evolution

In order to understand evolution, it's crucial to remember that evolution is always studied at the population level. Also, if a population were to stay exactly the same from one generation to the next, it would not be evolving. So evolution requires both a population of breeding individuals and some kind of a genetic change occurring within it. Thus, the simple definition of **evolution** is a change in the allele frequencies in a population over time. What do we mean by allele frequencies? **Allele frequencies** refer to the ratio, or percentage, of one allele (one variant of a gene) compared to the other alleles for that gene within the study population (Figure 4.2). By contrast, **genotype frequencies** are the ratios or percentages of the different homozygous and heterozygous genotypes in the population. Because we carry two alleles per **genotype**, the total count of alleles in a population will usually be exactly double the total count of genotypes in the same population (with the exception being rare cases in which an individual carries a different number of chromosomes than the typical two; e.g., Down syndrome results when a child carries three copies of Chromosome 21).

The Forces of Evolution

Today, we recognize that evolution takes place through a combination of mechanisms: mutation, genetic drift, gene flow, and natural selection. These mechanisms are called the "forces of evolution"; together they account for all the genotypic variation observed in the world today. Keep in mind that each of these forces was first defined and then tested—and retested—through the experimental work of the many scientists who contributed to the Modern Synthesis.

Mutation

The first force of evolution we will discuss is mutation, and for good reason: mutation is the original source of all the genetic variation found in every living thing. Imagine all the way back in time to the very first single-celled organism, floating in Earth's primordial sea. Based on what we observe in simple, single-celled organisms today, that organism probably spent its lifetime absorbing nutrients and dividing to produce cloned copies of itself. While the numbers of individuals in that population would have grown (as long as the environment was favorable), nothing would have changed in that perfectly cloned population. There would not have been variety among the individuals. It was only through a copying error—the introduction of a **mutation**, or change, into the genetic code—that new alleles were introduced into the population.

After many generations have passed in our primordial population, mutations have created distinct chromosomes. The cells are now amoeba-like, larger than many of their tiny bacterial neighbors, who have long since become their favorite source of nutrients. Without mutation to create this diversity, all living things would still be identical to LUCA, our universal ancestor (Figure 4.3).

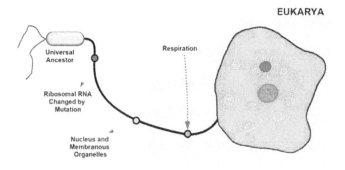

Figure 4.3: Key mutational differences between Last Universal Common Ancestor and an amoeba-like primordial cell. Credit: Key differences between LUCA and a primordial cell original to Explorations: An Open Invitation to Biological Anthropology (2nd ed.) by Andrea J. Alveshere is a collective work under a CC BY-NC-SA 4.0 License. [Includes Cladograma dos Dominios e Reinos by MarceloTeles (cropped, labels and color changed), CC BY-SA 4.0; Amoeba Proteus TK-UT by Tomáš Kebert and umimeto.org (cropped and color changed), CC BY-SA 4.0.] [Image Description].

When we think of genetic mutation, we often first think of **deleterious mutations**—the ones associated with negative effects such as the beginnings of cancers or heritable disorders. The fact is, though, that every genetic adaptation that has helped our ancestors survive since the dawn of life is directly due to **beneficial mutations**—changes in the DNA that provided some sort of advantage to a given population at a particular moment in time. For example, a beneficial mutation allowed chihuahuas and other tropical-adapted dog breeds to have much thinner fur coats than their cold-adapted cousins the northern wolves, malamutes, and huskies.

Every one of us has genetic mutations. Yes, even you. The DNA in some of your cells today differs from the original DNA that you inherited when you were a tiny, fertilized egg. Mutations occur all the time in the cells of our skin and other organs, due to chemical changes in the nucleotides. Exposure to the UV radiation in sunlight is one common cause of skin mutations. Interaction with UV light causes **UV crosslinking**, in which adjacent thymine bases bind with one another (Figure 4.4). Many of these mutations are detected and corrected by **DNA repair mechanisms**, enzymes that patrol and repair DNA in living cells, while other mutations may cause a new freckle or mole or, perhaps, an unusual hair to grow. For people with the **autosomal recessive** disease **xeroderma pigmentosum**, these repair mechanisms do not function correctly, resulting in a host of problems especially related to sun exposure, including severe sunburns, dry skin, heavy freckling, and other pigment changes.

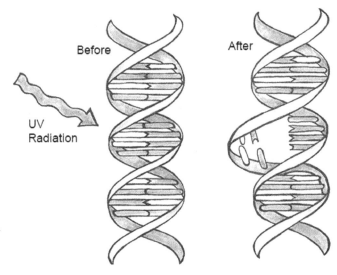

Figure 4.4: A crosslinking mutation in which a UV photon induces a bond between two thymine bases. Credit: UV-induced Thymine dimer mutation (Figure 4.6) original to Explorations: An Open Invitation to Biological Anthropology by Mary Nelson is under a CC BY-NC 4.0 License. [Image Description].

Most of our mutations exist in **somatic cells**, which are the cells of our organs and other body tissues. Those will not be passed onto future generations and so will not affect the population over time. Only mutations that occur in the **gametes**, the reproductive cells (i.e., the sperm or egg cells), will be passed onto future generations. When a new mutation pops up at random in a family lineage, it is known as a **spontaneous mutation**. If the individual born with this spontaneous mutation passes it on to his offspring, those offspring receive an **inherited mutation**. Geneticists have identified many classes of mutations and the causes and effects of many of these.

Point Mutations

A **point mutation** is a single-letter (single-nucleotide) change in the genetic code resulting in the substitution of one nucleic acid base for a different one. As you learned in Chapter 3, the DNA code in each gene is translated through three-letter "words" known as **codons**. So depending on how the point mutation changes the "word," the effect it will have on the protein may be major or minor or may make no difference at all.

If a mutation does not change the resulting protein, then it is called a **synonymous mutation**. Synonymous mutations do involve a letter (nucleic acid) change, but that change results in a codon that codes for the same "instruction" (the same amino acid or stop code) as the original codon. Mutations that do cause a change in the protein are known as **nonsynonymous mutations.** Nonsynonymous mutations may change the resulting protein's amino acid sequence by altering the DNA sequence that encodes the mRNA or by changing how the mRNA is spliced prior to translation (refer to Chapter 3 for more details).

Insertions and Deletions

In addition to point mutations, another class of mutations are **insertions** and **deletions**, or **indels**, for short. As the name suggests, these involve the addition (insertion) or removal (deletion) of one or more coding sequence letters (nucleic acids). These typically first occur as an error in DNA replication, wherein one or more nucleotides are either duplicated or skipped in error. Entire codons or sets of codons may also be removed or added if the indel is a multiple of three nucleotides.

Frameshift mutations are types of indels that involve the insertion or deletion of any number of nucleotides that is not a multiple of three (e.g., adding one or two extra letters to the code). Because these indels are not consistent with the codon numbering, they "shift the reading frame," causing all the codons beyond the mutation to be misread. Like point mutations, small indels can also disrupt splice sites.

Transposable elements, or **transposons**, are fragments of DNA that can "jump" around in the genome. There are two types of transposons: **retrotransposons** are transcribed from DNA into RNA and then "reverse transcribed," to insert the copied sequence into a new location in the DNA, and **DNA transposons**, which do not involve RNA. DNA transposons are clipped out of the DNA sequence itself and inserted elsewhere in the genome. Because transposable elements insert themselves into existing DNA sequences, they are frequent gene disruptors. At certain times, and in certain species, it appears that transposons became very active, likely accelerating the mutation rate (and thus, the genetic variation) in those populations during the active periods.

Chromosomal Alterations

The final major category of genetic mutations are changes at the chromosome level: crossover events, nondisjunction events, and translocations. **Crossover events** occur when DNA is swapped between homologous chromosomes while they are paired up during meiosis I. Crossovers are thought to be so common that some DNA swapping may happen every time chromosomes go through meiosis I. Crossovers don't necessarily introduce new alleles into a population, but they do make it possible for new combinations of alleles to exist on a single chromosome that can be passed to future generations. This also enables new combinations of alleles to be found within siblings who share the same parents. Also, if the fragments that cross over don't break at exactly the same point, they can cause genes to be deleted from one of the homologous chromosomes and duplicated on the other.

Nondisjunction events occur when the homologous chromosomes (in meiosis I) or sister chromatids (in meiosis II and mitosis) fail to separate after pairing. The result is that both chromosomes or chromatids end up in the same daughter cell, leaving the other daughter cell without any copy of that chromosome (Figure 4.5). Most nondisjunctions at the gamete level are fatal to the embryo. The most widely known exception is Trisomy 21, or Down syndrome, which results when an embryo inherits three copies of Chromosome 21: two from one parent (due to a nondisjunction event) and one from the other (Figure 4.6). **Trisomies** (triple chromosome conditions) of Chromosomes 18 (Edwards syndrome) and 13 (Patau syndrome) are also known to result in live births, but the children usually have severe complications and rarely survive beyond the first year of life.

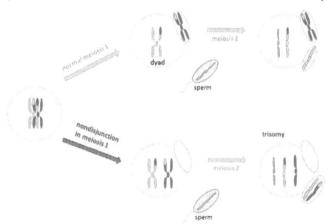

Sex chromosome trisomies (XXX, XXY, XYY) and X chromosome **monosomies** (inheritance of an X chromosome from one parent and no sex chromosome from the other) are also survivable and fairly common. The symptoms vary but often include atypical sexual characteristics, either at birth or at puberty, and often result in sterility. The X chromosome carries unique genes that are required for survival; therefore, Y chromosome monosomies are incompatible with life.

Chromosomal translocations involve transfers of DNA between nonhomologous chromosomes. This may involve swapping large portions of two or more chromosomes.

Figure 4.5: Illustration of an egg cell (oocyte) undergoing normal meiosis 1, resulting in a diploid daughter cell, compared to an egg cell undergoing nondisjunction during meiosis 1, resulting in a trisomy in the daughter cell. Credit: Trisomy due to nondisjunction in maternal meiosis 1 by Wpeissner has been modified (labels deleted by Katie Nelson) and is under a CC BY-NC-SA 4.0 License.

Figure 4.6: Amy Bockerstette, a competitive golfer and disabilities advocate, also has Down Syndrome. Credit: Amy Bockerstette Headshot by Bucksgrandson is under a CC BY-SA 4.0 License.

The exchanges of DNA may be balanced or unbalanced. In **balanced translocations**, the genes are swapped, but no genetic information is lost. In **unbalanced translocations**, there is an unequal exchange of genetic material, resulting in duplication or loss of genes. Translocations result in new chromosomal structures called **derivative chromosomes**, because they are derived or created from two different chromosomes. Translocations are often found to be linked to cancers and can also cause infertility. Even if the translocations are balanced in the parent, the embryo often won't survive unless the baby inherits both of that parent's derivative chromosomes (to maintain the balance).

Genetic Drift

The second force of evolution is commonly known as genetic drift. This is an unfortunate misnomer, as this force actually involves the drifting of alleles, not genes. **Genetic drift** refers to *random* changes ("drift") in allele frequencies from one generation to the next. The genes are remaining constant within the population; it is only the alleles of the genes that are changing in frequency. The random nature of genetic drift is a crucial point to understand: it specifically occurs when none of the variant alleles confer an advantage.

Let's imagine far back in time, again, to that ancient population of amoeba-like cells, subsisting and occasionally dividing, in the primordial sea. A mutation occurs in one of the cells that changes the texture of the cell membrane from a relatively smooth surface to a highly ruffled one (Figure 4.7). This has absolutely no effect on the cell's quality of life or ability to reproduce. In fact, eyes haven't evolved yet, so no one in the world at the time would even notice the difference. The cells in the population continue to divide, and the offspring of the ruffled cell inherit the ruffled membrane. The frequency (percentage) of the ruffled allele in the population, from one generation to the next, will depend entirely on how many offspring that first ruffled cell ends up having, and the random events that might make the ruffled alleles more common or more rare (such as population bottlenecks and founder effects, which are discussed below).

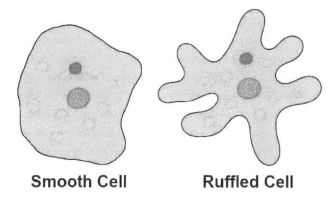

Smooth Cell   **Ruffled Cell**

Figure 4.7: Smooth and ruffled amoeba-like cells. Credit: Smooth and ruffled amoeba-like cells original to Explorations: An Open Invitation to Biological Anthropology (2nd ed.) by Andrea J. Alveshere is a collective work under a CC BY-NC-SA 4.0 License. [Includes Amoeba Proteus TK-UT by Tomáš Kebert and umimeto.org (modified), CC BY-SA 4.0.]

Sexual Reproduction and Random Inheritance

Tracking alleles gets a bit more complicated in our primordial cells when, after a number of generations, a series of mutations have created populations that reproduce sexually. These cells now must go through an extra round of cell division (meiosis) to create haploid gametes. The combination of two gametes is now required to produce each new diploid offspring.

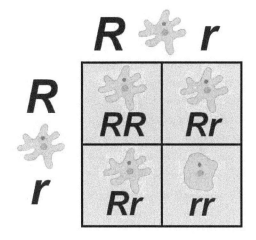

Figure 4.8: A Punnett square demonstrating the sexual inheritance pattern of ruffled (dominant) and smooth amoeba-like primordial cells. Credit: Punnett square of primordial cells original to Explorations: An Open Invitation to Biological Anthropology (2nd ed.) by Andrea J. Alveshere is a collective work under a CC BY-NC-SA 4.0 License. [Includes Amoeba Proteus TK-UT by Tomáš Kebert and umimeto.org (modified), CC BY-SA 4.0; Punnett Hetero x Hetero by Purpy Pupple (modified), CC BY-SA 3.0].

In the earlier population, which reproduced via **asexual reproduction**, a cell either carried the smooth allele or the ruffled allele. With **sexual reproduction**, a cell inherits one allele from each parent, so there are homozygous cells that contain two smooth alleles, homozygous cells that contain two ruffled alleles, and heterozygous cells that contain one of each allele (Figure 4.8). If the new, ruffled allele happens to be dominant (and we'll imagine that it is), the heterozygotes will have ruffled cell **phenotypes** but also will have a 50/50 chance of passing on a smooth allele to each offspring. As long as neither phenotype (ruffled nor smooth) provides any advantage over the other, the variation in the population from one generation to the next will remain completely random.

In sexually reproducing populations (including humans and many other animals and plants in the world today), that 50/50 chance of inheriting one or the other allele from each parent plays a major role in the random nature of genetic drift.

Population Bottlenecks

A **population bottleneck** occurs when the number of individuals in a population drops dramatically due to some random event. The most obvious, familiar examples are natural disasters. Tsunamis and hurricanes devastating island and coastal populations and forest fires and river floods wiping out populations in other areas are all too familiar. When a large portion of a population is randomly wiped out, the allele frequencies (i.e., the percentages of each allele) in the small population of survivors are often much different from the frequencies in the predisaster, or "parent," population.

If such an event happened to our primordial ocean cell population—perhaps a volcanic fissure erupted in the ocean floor and only the cells that happened to be farthest from the spewing lava and boiling water survived—we might end up, by random chance, with a surviving population that had mostly ruffled alleles, in contrast to the parent population, which had only a small percentage of ruffles (Figure 4.9).

One of the most famous examples of a population bottleneck is the prehistoric disaster that led to the extinction of dinosaurs, the **Cretaceous–Paleogene extinction** event (often abbreviated K–Pg; previously K-T). This occurred approximately 66 million years ago. Dinosaurs and all their neighbors were going about their ordinary routines when a massive asteroid zoomed in from space and crashed into what is now the Gulf of Mexico, creating an impact so enormous that populations within hundreds of miles of the crash site were likely immediately wiped out. The skies filled with dust and debris, causing temperatures to plummet worldwide. It's estimated that 75% of the world's species went extinct as a result of the impact and the deep freeze that followed (Jablonski and Chaloner 1994).

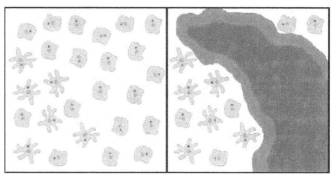

Figure 4.9: Illustration of a population of amoeba-like cells shifting from primarily smooth phenotypes (at left) to mostly ruffled phenotypes due to eruption of a volcanic fissure (at right) that exterminated the nearest cells. Credit: Population of amoeba-like cells and volcanic fissure original to Explorations: An Open Invitation to Biological Anthropology (2nd ed.) by Andrea J. Alveshere is a collective work under a CC BY-NC-SA 4.0 License. [Includes Amoeba Proteus TK-UT by Tomáš Kebert and umimeto.org (modified), CC BY-SA 4.0.]

The populations that emerged from the K-Pg extinction were markedly different from their predisaster communities. Surviving mammal populations expanded and diversified, and other new creatures appeared. The ecosystems of Earth were filled with new organisms and have never been the same (Figure 4.10).

Much more recently in geological time, during the colonial period, many human populations experienced bottlenecks as a result of the fact that imperial powers were inclined to slaughter communities who were reluctant to give up their lands and resources. This effect was especially profound in the Americas, where Indigenous populations faced the compounded effects of brutal warfare, exposure to new bacteria and viruses (against which they had no immunity), and ultimately segregation on resource-starved reservations. The populations in Europe, Asia, and Africa had experienced regular gene flow during the 10,000-year period in which most kinds of livestock were being domesticated, giving them many generations of experience building up immunity against zoonotic diseases (those that can pass from animals to humans). In contrast, the residents of the Americas had been almost completely isolated during those millennia, so all these diseases swept through the Americas in rapid succession,

Figure 4.10: The Cretaceous–Paleogene extinction event, which led to the fall of the dinosaurs and rise of the mammals. Credit: The Cretaceous–Paleogene extinction event (Figure 4.12) original to Explorations: An Open Invitation to Biological Anthropology by Mary Nelson is under a CC BY-NC 4.0 License.

creating a major loss of genetic diversity in the Indigenous American population. It is estimated that between 50% and 95% of the Indigenous American populations died during the first decades after European contact, around 500 years ago (Livi-Bacci 2006).

An urgent health challenge facing humans today involves human-induced population bottlenecks that produce antibiotic-resistant bacteria. **Antibiotics** are medicines prescribed to treat bacterial infections. The typical prescription includes enough medicine for ten days. People often feel better much sooner than ten days and sometimes decide to quit taking the medicine ahead of schedule. This is often a big mistake. The antibiotics have quickly killed off a large percentage of the bacteria—enough to reduce the symptoms and make you feel much better. However, this has created a bacterial population bottleneck. There are usually a small number of bacteria that survive those early days. If you take the medicine as prescribed for the full ten days, it's quite likely that there will be no bacterial survivors. If you quit early, though, the survivors—who were the members of the original population who were most resistant to the antibiotic—will begin to reproduce again. Soon the infection will be back, possibly worse than before, and now all of the bacteria are resistant to the antibiotic that you had been prescribed.

Other activities that have contributed to the rise of antibiotic-resistant bacteria include the use of antibacterial cleaning products and the inappropriate use of antibiotics as a preventative measure in livestock or to treat infections that are viral instead of bacterial (viruses do not respond to antibiotics). In 2017, the World Health Organization published a list of twelve antibiotic-resistant pathogens that are considered top priority targets for the development of new antibiotics (World Health Organization 2017).

Founder Effects

Founder effects occur when members of a population leave the main or "parent" group and form a new population that no longer interbreeds with the other members of the original group. Similar to survivors of a population bottleneck, the newly founded population often has allele frequencies that are different from the original group. Alleles that may have been relatively rare in the parent population can end up being very common due to the founder effect. Likewise, recessive traits that were seldom seen in the parent population may be seen frequently in the descendants of the offshoot population.

One striking example of the founder effect was first noted in the Dominican Republic in the 1970s. During a several-year period, eighteen children who had been born with female genitalia and raised as girls suddenly grew penises at puberty. This culture tended to value sons over daughters, so these transitions were generally celebrated. They labeled the condition *guevedoces*, which translates to "penis at twelve," due to the average age at which this occurred. Scientists were fascinated by the phenomenon.

Genetic and hormonal studies revealed that the condition, scientifically termed **5-alpha reductase deficiency,** is an autosomal recessive syndrome that manifests when a child having both X and Y sex chromosomes inherits two nonfunctional (mutated) copies of the *SRD5A2* gene (Imperato-McGinley and Zhu 2002). These children develop testes internally, but the 5-alpha reductase 2 steroid, which is necessary for development of male genitals in babies, is not produced. In absence of this male hormone, the baby develops female-looking genitalia (in humans, "female" is the default infant body form, if the full set of the necessary male hormones are not produced). At puberty, however, a different set of male hormones are produced by other fully functional genes. These hormones complete the male genital development that did not happen in infancy. This condition became quite common in the Dominican Republic during the 1970s due to founder effect—that is, the mutated *SRD5A2* gene happened to be much more common among the Dominican Republic's founding population than in the parent populations. (The Dominican population derives from a mixture of Indigenous Americans [Taino] peoples, West Africans, and Western Europeans.) Five-alpha reductase syndrome has since been observed in other small, isolated populations around the world.

Founder effect is closely linked to the concept of inbreeding, which in population genetics does not necessarily mean breeding with immediate family relatives. Instead, **inbreeding** refers to the selection of mates exclusively from within a small, closed population—that is, from a group with limited allelic variability. This can be observed in small, physically isolated populations but also can happen when cultural practices limit mates to a small group. As with the founder effect, inbreeding increases the risk of inheriting two copies of any nonfunctional (mutant) alleles.

The Amish in the United States are a population that, due to their unique history and cultural practices, emerged from a small founding population and have tended to select mates from within their groups. The **Old Order Amish** population of Lancaster County, Pennsylvania, has approximately 50,000 current members, all of whom can trace their ancestry back to a group of approximately 80 individuals. This small founding population immigrated to the United States from Switzerland in the mid-1700s to escape religious persecution. Since the Amish keep to themselves and almost exclusively select mates from within their own communities, they have more recessive traits compared to their parent population.

One of the genetic conditions that has been observed much more frequently in the Lancaster County Amish population is **Ellis-van Creveld syndrome**, which is an autosomal recessive disorder characterized by short stature (dwarfism), polydactyly (the development of more than five digits [fingers or toes] on the hands or feet], abnormal tooth development, and heart defects (Figure 4.11). Among the general world population, Ellis-van Creveld syndrome is estimated to affect approximately 1 in 60,000 individuals; among the Old Order Amish of Lancaster County, the rate is estimated to be as high as 1 in every 200 births (D'Asdia et al. 2013).

One important insight that has come from the study of founder effects is that a limited gene pool carries a much higher risk for genetic diseases. Genetic diversity in a population greatly reduces these risks.

Figure 4.11: A person displaying polydactyly. Credit: 6 Finger by Wilhelmy is under a CC BY-SA 4.0 License.

Gene Flow

The third force of evolution is traditionally called gene flow. As with genetic drift, this is a misnomer, because it refers to flowing alleles, not genes. (All members of the same species share the same genes; it is the alleles of those genes that may vary.) **Gene flow** refers to the movement of alleles from one population to another. In most cases, gene flow can be considered synonymous with migration.

Returning again to the example of our primordial cell population, let's imagine that, after the volcanic fissure opened up in the ocean floor, wiping out the majority of the parent population, two surviving populations developed in the waters on opposite sides of the fissure. Ultimately, the lava from the fissure cooled into a large island that continued to provide a physical barrier between the populations (Figure 4.12).

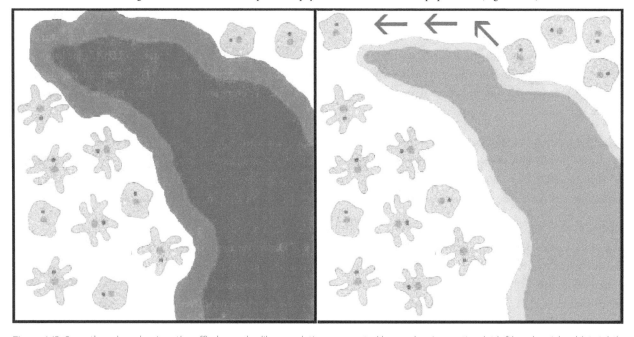

Figure 4.12: Smooth and predominantly ruffled amoeba-like populations separated by a volcanic eruption (at left) and an island (at right) with unidirectional gene flow moving from east to west with ocean currents. Credit: Population of amoeba-like cells separated by volcanic eruption original to Explorations: An Open Invitation to Biological Anthropology (2nd ed.) by Andrea J. Alveshere is a collective work under a CC BY-NC-SA 4.0 License. [Includes Amoeba Proteus TK-UT by Tomáš Kebert and umimeto.org (modified), CC BY-SA 4.0.]

In the initial generations after the eruption, due to founder effect, isolation, and random inheritance (genetic drift), the population to the west of the islands contained a vast majority of the ruffled membrane alleles while the eastern population carried only the smooth alleles. Ocean currents in the area typically flowed from east to west, sometimes carrying cells (facilitating gene flow) from the eastern (smooth) population to the western (ruffled) population. Due to the ocean currents, it was almost impossible for any cells from the western population to be carried eastward. Thus, for inheritance purposes, the eastern (smooth) population remained isolated. In this case, the gene flow is unidirectional (going only in one direction) and unbalanced (only one population is receiving the new alleles).

Among humans, gene flow is often described as **admixture.** In forensic cases, anthropologists and geneticists are often asked to estimate the ancestry of unidentified human remains to help determine whether they match any missing persons' reports. This is one of the most complicated tasks in these professions because, while "race" or "ancestry" involves simple checkboxes on a missing person's form, among humans today there are no truly distinct genetic populations. All modern humans are members of the same fully breeding compatible species, and all human communities have experienced multiple episodes of gene flow (admixture), leading all humans today to be so genetically similar that we are all members of the same (and only surviving) human subspecies: *Homo sapiens sapiens.*

Gene flow between otherwise isolated nonhuman populations is often termed **hybridization..** One example of this involves the hybridization and spread of **Scutellata honey bees** (a.k.a. "killer bees") in the Americas. All honey bees worldwide are classified as *Apis mellifera.* Due to distinct adaptations to various environments around the world, there are 28 different subspecies of *Apis mellifera.*

During the 1950s, a Brazilian biologist named Warwick E. Kerr experimented with hybridizing African and European subspecies of honey bees to try to develop a strain that was better suited to tropical environments than the European honey bees that had long been kept by North American beekeepers. Dr. Kerr was careful to contain the reproductive queens and drones from the African subspecies, but in 1957, a visiting beekeeper accidentally released 26 queen bees of the Scutellata subspecies (*Apis mellifera scutellata*) from southern Africa into the Brazilian countryside. The Scutellata bees quickly interbred with local European honey bee populations. The hybridized bees exhibited a much more aggressively defensive behavior, fatally or near-fatally attacking many humans and livestock that ventured too close to their hives. The hybridized bees spread throughout South America and reached Mexico and California by 1985. By 1990, permanent colonies had been established in Texas, and by 1997, 90% of trapped bee swarms around Tucson, Arizona, were found to be Scutellata hybrids (Sanford 2006).

Another example involves the introduction of the **Harlequin ladybeetle**, *Harmonia axyridis*, native to East Asia, to other parts of the world as a "natural" form of pest control. Harlequin ladybeetles are natural predators of some of the aphids and other crop-pest insects. First introduced to North America in 1916, the "biocontrol" strains of Harlequin ladybeetles were considered to be quite successful in reducing crop pests and saving farmers substantial amounts of money. After many decades of successful use in North America, biocontrol strains of Harlequin ladybeetles were also developed in Europe and South America in the 1980s.

Over the seven decades of biocontrol use, the Harlequin ladybeetle had never shown any potential for development of wild colonies outside of its native habitat in China and Japan. New generations of beetles always had to be reared in the lab. That all changed in 1988, when a wild colony took root near New Orleans, Louisiana. Either through admixture with a native ladybeetle strain, or due to a spontaneous mutation, a new allele was clearly introduced into this population that suddenly enabled them to survive and reproduce in a wide range of environments. This population spread rapidly across the Americas and had reached Africa by 2004.

In Europe, the invasive, North American strain of Harlequin ladybeetle admixed with the European strain (Figure 4.13), causing a population explosion (Lombaert et al. 2010). Even strains specifically developed to be flightless (to curtail the spreading) produced flighted offspring after admixture with members of the North American population (Facon et al. 2011). The fast-spreading, invasive strain has quickly become a disaster, out-competing native ladybeetle populations (some to the point of extinction), causing home infestations, decimating fruit crops, and contaminating many batches of wine with their bitter flavor after being inadvertently harvested with the grapes (Pickering et al. 2004).

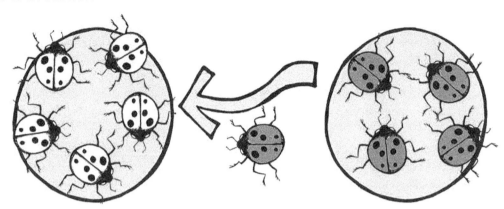

Figure 4.13: Gene flow between two populations of ladybeetles (ladybugs). Credit: Ladybug Gene Flow (Figure 4.14) original to *Explorations: An Open Invitation to Biological Anthropology* by Mary Nelson is under a CC BY-NC 4.0 License.

Natural Selection

The final force of evolution is natural selection. This is the evolutionary process that Charles Darwin first brought to light, and it is what the general public typically evokes when considering the process of evolution. **Natural selection** occurs when certain phenotypes confer an advantage or disadvantage in survival and/or reproductive success. The alleles associated with those phenotypes will change in frequency over time due to this selective pressure. It's also important to note that the advantageous allele may change over time (with environmental changes) and that an allele that had previously been benign may become advantageous or detrimental. Of course, dominant, recessive, and codominant traits will be selected upon a bit differently from one another. Because natural selection acts on phenotypes rather than the alleles themselves, deleterious (disadvantageous) alleles can be retained by heterozygotes without any negative effects.

In the case of our primordial ocean cells, up until now, the texture of their cell membranes has been benign. The frequencies of smooth to ruffled alleles, and smooth to ruffled phenotypes, has changed over time, due to genetic drift and gene flow. Let's now imagine that the Earth's climate has cooled to a point that the waters frequently become too cold for survival of the tiny bacteria that are the dietary staples of our smooth and ruffled cell populations. The way amoeba-like cells "eat" is to stretch out the cell membrane, almost like an arm, to encapsulate, then ingest, the tiny bacteria. When the temperatures plummet, the tiny bacteria populations plummet with them. Larger bacteria, however, are better able to withstand the temperature change.

The smooth cells were well-adapted to ingesting tiny bacteria but poorly suited to encapsulating the larger bacteria. The cells with the ruffled membranes, however, are easily able to extend their ruffles to encapsulate the larger bacteria. They also find themselves able to stretch their entire membrane to a much larger size than their smooth-surfaced neighbors, allowing them to ingest more bacteria at a given time and to go for longer periods between feedings (Figure 4.14).

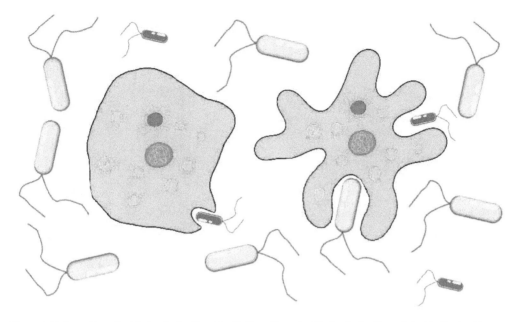

Figure 4.14: Smooth and ruffled cells feeding. Credit: Smooth and ruffled cells feeding original to Explorations: An Open Invitation to Biological Anthropology (2nd ed.) by Andrea J. Alveshere is a collective work under a CC BY-NC-SA 4.0 License. [Includes Cladograma dos Dominios e Reinos by MarceloTeles (modified), CC BY-SA 4.0; Amoeba Proteus TK-UT by Tomáš Kebert and umimeto.org (modified), CC BY-SA 4.0.]

The smooth and ruffled traits, which had previously offered no advantage or disadvantage while food was plentiful, now are subject to natural selection. During the cold snaps, at least, the ruffled cells have a definite advantage. We can imagine that the western population that has mostly ruffled alleles will continue to do well, while the eastern population is at risk of dying out if the smaller bacteria remain scarce and no ruffled alleles are introduced.

A classic example of natural selection involves the study of an insect called the **peppered moth** (*Biston betularia*) in England during the Industrial Revolution in the 1800s. Prior to the Industrial Revolution, the peppered moth population was predominantly light in color, with dark (pepper-like) speckles on the wings. The "peppered" coloration was very similar to the appearance of the bark and lichens that grew on the local trees (Figure 4.15). This helped to camouflage the moths as they rested on a tree, making it harder for moth-eating birds to find and snack on them. There was another phenotype that popped up occasionally in the population. These individuals were heterozygotes that carried an overactive, dominant pigment allele, producing a solid black coloration. As you can imagine, the black moths were much easier for birds to spot, making this phenotype a real disadvantage.

The situation changed, however, as the Industrial Revolution took off. Large factories began spewing vast amounts of coal smoke into the air, blanketing the countryside, including the lichens and trees, in black soot. Suddenly, it was the light-colored moths that were easy for birds to spot and the black moths that held the advantage. The frequency of the dark pigment allele rose dramatically. By 1895, the black moth phenotype accounted for 98% of observed moths (Grant 1999).

Figure 4.15: Dark and light peppered moth variants and their relative camouflage abilities on clean (top) and sooty (bottom) trees. Credit: Peppered moths c2 by Khaydock is under a CC BY-SA 3.0 License.

Thanks to new environmental regulations in the 1960s, the air pollution in England began to taper off. As the soot levels decreased, returning the trees to their former, lighter color, this provided the perfect opportunity to study how the peppered moth population would respond. Repeated follow-up studies documented the gradual rise in the frequency of the lighter-colored phenotype. By 2003, the maximum frequency of the dark phenotype was 50% and in most parts of England had decreased to less than 10% (Cook 2003).

Directional, Balancing/Stabilizing, and Disruptive/Diversifying Selection

Natural selection can be classified as directional, balancing/stabilizing, or disruptive/diversifying, depending on how the pressure is applied to the population (Figure 4.16).

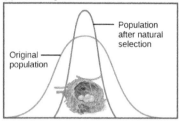

(a) Stabilizing selection

Robins typically lay four eggs, an example of stabilizing selection. Larger clutches may result in malnourished chicks, while smaller clutches may result in no viable offspring.

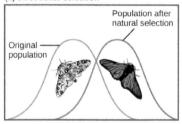

(b) Directional selection

Light-colored peppered moths are better camouflaged against a pristine environment; likewise, dark-colored peppered moths are better camouflaged against a sooty environment. Thus, as the Industrial Revolution progressed in nineteenth-century England, the color of the moth population shifted from light to dark, an example of directional selection.

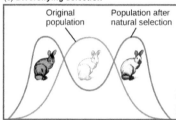

(c) Diversifying selection

In a hyphothetical population, gray and Himalayan (gray and white) rabbits are better able to blend with a rocky environment than white rabbits, resulting in diversifying selection.

Figure 4.16: Lines depict the affects of (a) Balancing/Stabilizing, (b) Directional, and (c) Disruptive/Diversifying selection on populations. Credit: Biology (ID: 185cbf87-c72e-48f5-b51e-f14f21b5eabd@9.17) by CNX OpenStax is used under a CC BY 4.0 License. [Image Description].

Both of the above examples of natural selection involve **directional selection**: the environmental pressures favor one phenotype over the other and cause the frequencies of the associated advantageous alleles (ruffled membranes, dark pigment) to gradually increase. In the case of the peppered moths, the direction shifted three times: first, it was selecting for lighter pigment; then, with the increase in pollution, the pressure switched to selection for darker pigment; finally, with reduction of the pollution, the selection pressure shifted back again to favoring light-colored moths.

Balancing selection (a.k.a. stabilizing selection) occurs when selection works against the extremes of a trait and favors the intermediate phenotype. For example, humans maintain an average birth weight that balances the need for babies to be small enough not to cause complications during pregnancy and childbirth but big enough to maintain a safe body temperature after they are born. Another example of balancing selection is found in the genetic disorder called sickle cell anemia (see "Special Topic: Sickle Cell Anemia").

Disruptive selection (a.k.a. diversifying selection), the opposite of balancing selection, occurs when both extremes of a trait are advantageous. Since individuals with traits in the mid-range are selected against, disruptive selection can eventually lead to the population evolving into two separate species. Darwin believed that the many species of finches (small birds) found in the remote Galapagos Islands provided a clear example of disruptive selection leading to speciation. He observed that seed-eating finches either had large beaks, capable of eating very large seeds, or small beaks, capable of retrieving tiny seeds. The islands did not have many plants that produced medium-size seeds. Thus, birds with medium-size beaks would have trouble eating the very large seeds and would also have been inefficient at picking up the tiny seeds. Over time, Darwin surmised, this pressure against mid-size beaks may have led the population to divide into two separate species.

Sexual Selection

Sexual selection is an aspect of natural selection in which the selective pressure specifically affects reproductive success (the ability to successfully breed and raise offspring) rather than survival. Sexual selection favors traits that will attract a mate. Sometimes these sexually appealing traits even carry greater risks in terms of survival.

A classic example of sexual selection involves the brightly colored feathers of the peacock. The **peacock** is the male sex of the peafowl genera *Pavo* and *Afropavo*. During mating season, peacocks will fan their colorful tails wide and strut in front of the peahens in a grand display. The peahens will carefully observe these displays and will elect to mate with the male that they find the most appealing. Many studies have found that peahens prefer the males with the fullest, most colorful tails. While these large, showy tails provide a reproductive advantage, they can be a real burden in terms of escaping predators. The bright colors and patterns as well as the large size of the peacock tail make it difficult to hide. Once predators spot them, peacocks also struggle to fly away, with the heavy tail trailing behind and weighing them down (Figure 4.17). Some researchers have argued that the increased risk is part of the appeal for the peahens: only an especially strong, alert, and healthy peacock would be able to avoid predators while sporting such a spectacular tail.

Figure 4.17: Showy peacock tail disadvantages (becoming easier prey) and advantages (impressing peahens). Credit: Peacock tail advantage and disadvantages (Figure 4.18) original to Explorations: An Open Invitation to Biological Anthropology by Mary Nelson is under a CC BY-NC 4.0 License.License.

It's important to keep in mind that sexual selection relies on the trait being present throughout mating years. Reflecting on the NF1 genetic disorder (see "Special Topic: Neurofibromatosis Type 1 [NF1]"), given how disfiguring the symptoms can become, some might find it surprising that half of the babies born with NF1 inherited it from a parent. Given that the disorder is autosomal dominant and fully penetrant (meaning it has no unaffected carriers), it may seem surprising that sexual selection doesn't exert more pressure against the mutated alleles. One important factor is that, while the neurofibromas typically begin to appear during puberty, they usually emerge only a few at a time and may grow very slowly. Many NF1 patients don't experience the more severe or disfiguring symptoms until later in life, long after they have started families of their own.

Some researchers prefer to classify sexual selection separately, as a fifth force of evolution. The traits that underpin mate selection are entirely natural, of course. Research has shown that subtle traits, such as the type of pheromones (hormonal odors related to immune system alleles) someone emits and how those are perceived by the immune system genotype of the "sniffer," may play crucial and subconscious roles in whether we find someone attractive or not (Chaix, Cao, and Donnelly 2008).

Special Topic: Neurofibromatosis Type 1 (NF1)

Neurofibromatosis Type 1, also known as **NF1**, is a genetic disorder that illustrates how a mutation in a single gene can affect multiple systems in the body. Surprisingly common, more people have NF1 than cystic fibrosis and muscular dystrophy combined. Even more surprising, given how common it is, is how few people have heard of it. One in every 3,000 babies is born with NF1, and this holds true for all populations worldwide (Riccardi 1992). This means that, for every 3,000 people in your community, there is likely at least one person living with this disorder. NF1 is an **autosomal dominant** condition, which means that everyone born with a mutation in the gene, whether inherited or spontaneous, has a 50/50 chance of passing it on to each of their own children.

The NF1 disorder results from mutation of the *NF1* gene on Chromosome 17. Almost any mutation that affects the sequence of the gene's protein product, neurofibromin, will cause the disorder. Studies of individuals with NF1 have identified over 3,000 different mutations of all kinds (including point mutations, small and large indels, and translocations). The *NF1* gene is one of the largest known genes, containing at least 60 **exons** (protein-encoding sequences) in a span of about 300,000 nucleotides.

We know that neurofibromin plays an important role in preventing tumor growth because one of the most common symptoms of the NF1 disorder is the growth of **benign** (noncancerous) tumors, called **neurofibromas**. Neurofibromas sprout from nerve sheaths—the tissues that encase our nerves—throughout the body, usually beginning around puberty. There is no way to predict where the tumors will occur, or when or how quickly they will grow, although only about 15% turn **malignant** (cancerous). The two types of neurofibromas that are typically most visible are **cutaneous neurofibromas**, which are spherical bumps on, or just under, the surface of the skin (Figure 4.18), and **plexiform neurofibromas**, growths involving whole branches of nerves, often giving the appearance that the surface of the skin is "melting" (Figure 4.19).

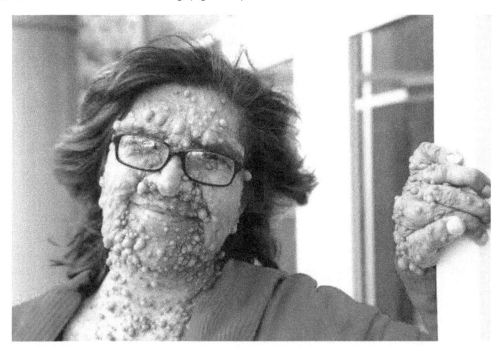

Figure 4.18: A woman with many cutaneous neurofibromas, a common symptom of Neurofibromatosis Type 1. Credit: Woman with cutaneous neurofibromas (symptom of NF1) by Rick Guidotti of Positive Exposure is used with permission and is available here under a CC BY-NC 4.0 License.

Figure 4.19: Photo on the left is of a man with large plexiform neurofibroma, another symptom of Neurofibromatosis Type 1. Photo on the right is a childhood photo of the same man, illustrating the progressive nature of the NF1 disorder. Credit: Man with plexiform neurofibroma (symptom of NF1) from Ashok Shrestha is used by permission and available here under a CC BY-NC 4.0 License. Childhood photo of the same man with NF1 disorder from Ashok Shrestha is used by permission and available here under a CC BY-NC 4.0 License.

Unfortunately, there is currently no cure for NF1. Surgical removal of neurofibromas risks paralysis, due to the high potential for nerve damage, and often results in the tumors growing back even more vigorously. This means that patients are often forced to live with disfiguring and often painful neurofibromas. People who are not familiar with NF1 often mistake neurofibromas for something contagious. This makes it especially hard for people living with NF1 to get jobs working with the public or even to enjoy spending time away from home. Raising public awareness about NF1 and its symptoms can be a great help in improving the quality of life for people living with this condition.

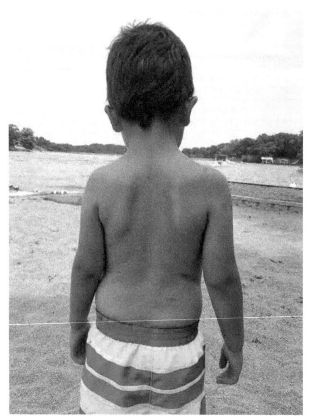

Figure 4.20: Image of a child with café-au-lait macules (birthmarks) typical of the earliest symptoms of NF1. Credit: Child with café-au-lait macules (birthmarks) typical of the earliest symptoms of NF1 by Andrea J. Alveshere is under a CC BY-NC 4.0 License.

One of the first symptoms of NF1 in a small child is usually the appearance of **café-au-lait spots**, or **CALS**, which are flat, brown birthmark-like spots on the skin (Figure 4.20). CALS are often light brown, similar to the color of coffee with cream, which is the reason for the name, although the shade of the pigment depends on a person's overall complexion. Some babies are born with CALS, but for others the spots appear within the first few years of life. Having six or more CALS larger than five millimeters (mm) across is a strong indicator that a child may have NF1.

Other common symptoms include the following: gliomas (tumors) of the optic nerve, which can cause vision loss; thinning of bones and failure to heal if they break (often requiring amputation); low muscle tone (poor muscle development, often delaying milestones such as sitting up, crawling, and walking); hearing loss, due to neurofibromas on auditory nerves; and learning disabilities, especially those involving spatial reasoning. Approximately 50% of people with NF1 have some type of speech and/or learning disability and often benefit greatly from early intervention services. Generalized developmental disability, however, is not common with NF1, so most people with NF1 live independently as adults. Many people with NF1 live full and successful lives, as long as their symptoms can be managed.

Based on the wide variety of symptoms, it's clear that the neurofibromin protein plays important roles in many biochemical pathways. While everyone who has NF1 will exhibit some symptoms during their lifetime, there is a great deal of variation in the types and severity of symptoms, even between individuals from the same family who share the exact same NF1 mutation. It seems crazy that a gene with so many important functions would be so susceptible to mutation. Part of this undoubtedly has to do with its massive size—a gene with 300,000 nucleotides has ten times more nucleotides available for mutation than does a gene of 30,000 bases. This also suggests that the mutability of this gene might provide some benefits, which is a possibility that we will revisit later in this chapter.

Special Topic: Sickle Cell Anemia

Sickle cell anemia is an autosomal recessive genetic disorder that affects millions of people worldwide. It is most common in Africa, countries around the Mediterranean Sea, and eastward as far as India. Populations in the Americas that have high percentages of ancestors from these regions also have high rates of sickle cell anemia. In the United States, it's estimated that 72,000 people live with the disease, with one in approximately 1,200 Hispanic-American babies and one in every 500 African-American babies inheriting the condition (World Health Organization 1996).

Sickle cell anemia affects the hemoglobin protein in red blood cells. Normal red blood cells are somewhat doughnut-shaped—round with a depression on both sides of the middle. They carry oxygen around the bloodstream to cells throughout the body. Red blood cells produced by the mutated form of the gene take on a stiff, sickle-like crescent shape when stressed by low oxygen or dehydration (Figure 4.21). Because of their elongated shape and the fact that they are stiff rather than flexible, they tend to form clumps in the blood vessels, inhibiting blood flow to adjacent areas of the body. This causes episodes of extreme pain and can cause serious problems in the oxygen-deprived tissues. The sickle cells also break down much more quickly than normal cells, often lasting only 20 days rather than the 120 days of normal cells. This causes an overall shortage of blood cells in the sickle cell patient, resulting in low iron (anemia) and problems associated with it such as extreme fatigue, shortness of breath, and hindrances to children's growth and development.

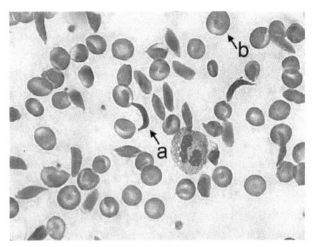

Figure 4.21: Sickle cell anemia. Arrows indicate (a) sickled and (b) normal red blood cells. Credit: Sickle-cell smear 2015-09-10 by Paulo Henrique Orlandi Mourao has been modified (contrast modified and labels added) and is under a CC BY-NC-SA 4.0 License.

The devastating effects of sickle cell anemia made its high frequency a pressing mystery. Why would an allele that is so deleterious in its homozygous form be maintained in a population at levels as high as the one in twelve African Americans estimated to carry at least one copy of the allele? The answer turned out to be one of the most interesting cases of balancing selection in the history of genetic study.

While looking for an explanation, scientists noticed that the countries with high rates of sickle cell disease also shared a high risk for another disease called **malaria**, which is caused by infection of the blood by a ***Plasmodium*** parasite. These parasites are carried by mosquitoes and enter the human bloodstream via a mosquito bite. Once infected, the person will experience flu-like symptoms that, if untreated, can often lead to death. Researchers discovered that many people living in these regions seemed to have a natural resistance to malaria. Further study revealed that people who carry the sickle cell allele are far less likely to experience a severe case of malaria. This would not be enough of a benefit to make the allele advantageous for the sickle cell homozygotes, who face shortened life spans due to sickle cell anemia. The real benefit of the sickle cell allele goes to the heterozygotes.

People who are heterozygous for sickle cell carry one normal allele, which produces the normal, round, red blood cells, and one sickle cell allele, which produces the sickle-shaped red blood cells. Thus, they have both the sickle and round blood cell types in their bloodstream. They produce enough of the round red blood cells to avoid the symptoms of sickle cell anemia, but they have enough sickle cells to provide protection from malaria.

When the *Plasmodium* parasites infect an individual, they begin to multiply in the liver, but then must infect the red blood cells to complete their reproductive cycle. When the parasites enter sickle-type cells, the cells respond by taking on the sickle shape. This prevents the parasite from circulating through the bloodstream and completing its life cycle, greatly inhibiting the severity of the infection in the sickle cell heterozygotes compared to non–-sickle cell homozygotes. See Chapter 14 for more discussion of sickle cell anemia.

Special Topic: The Real Primordial Cells—*Dictyostelium Discoideum*

The amoeba-like primordial cells that were used as recurring examples throughout this chapter are inspired by actual research that is truly fascinating. In 2015, Gareth Bloomfield and colleagues reported on their genomic study of the social amoeba **Dictyostelium discoideum** (a.k.a. "slime molds," although technically they are amoebae, not molds). Strains of these amoebae have been grown in research laboratories for many decades and are useful in studying the mechanisms that amoeboid single-celled organisms use to ingest food and liquid. For simplification of our examples in this chapter, our amoeba-like cells remained ocean dwellers. Wild *Dictyostelium discoideum*, however, live in soil and feed on soil bacteria by growing ruffles in their membranes that reach out to encapsulate the bacterial cell. Laboratory strains, however, are typically raised on liquid media (agar) in Petri dishes, which is not suitable for the wild-type amoebae. It was widely known that the laboratory strains must have developed mutations in one or more genes to allow them to ingest the larger nutrient particles in the agar and larger volumes of liquid, but the genes involved were not known.

Bloomfield and colleagues performed genomic testing on both the wild and the laboratory strains of *Dictyostelium discoideum*. Their discovery was astounding: every one of the laboratory strains carried a mutation in the *NF1* gene, the very same gene associated with Neurofibromatosis Type 1 (NF1) in humans. The antiquity of this massive, easily mutated gene is incredible. It originated in an ancestor common to both humans and these amoebae, and it has been retained in both lineages ever since. As seen in *Dictyostelium discoideum*, breaking the gene can be advantageous. Without a functioning copy of the neurofibromin protein, the cell membrane is able to form much-larger feeding structures, allowing the *NF1* mutants to ingest larger particles and larger volumes of liquid. For these amoebae, this may provide dietary flexibility that functions somewhat like an insurance policy for times when the food supply is limited.

Dictyostelium discoideum are also interesting in that they typically reproduce asexually, but under certain conditions, one cell will convert into a "giant" cell, which encapsulates surrounding cells, transforming into one of three sexes. This cell will undergo meiosis, producing gametes that must combine with one of the other two sexes to produce viable offspring. This ability for sexual reproduction may be what allows *Dictyostelium discoideum* to benefit from the advantages of *NF1* mutation, while also being able to restore the wild type *NF1* gene in future generations.

What does this mean for humans living with NF1? Well, understanding the role of the neurofibromin protein in the membranes of simple organisms like *Dictyostelium discoideum* may help us to better understand how it functions and malfunctions in the sheaths of human neurons. It's also possible that the mutability of the NF1 gene confers certain advantages to humans as well. Alleles of the NF1 gene have been found to reduce one's risk for alcoholism (Repunte-Canonigo Vez et al. 2015), opiate addiction (Sanna et al. 2002), Type 2 diabetes (Martins et al. 2016), and hypomusicality (a lower-than-average musical aptitude; Cota et al. 2018). This research is ongoing and will be exciting to follow in the coming years.

Studying Evolution in Action

The Hardy-Weinberg Equilibrium

This chapter has introduced you to the forces of evolution, the mechanisms by which evolution occurs. How do we detect and study evolution, though, in real time, as it happens? One tool we use is the **Hardy-Weinberg Equilibrium**: a mathematical formula that allows estimation of the number and distribution of dominant and recessive alleles in a population. This aids in determining whether allele frequencies are changing and, if so, how quickly over time, and in favor of which allele? It's important to note that the Hardy-Weinberg formula only gives us an estimate based on the data for a snapshot in time. We will have to calculate it again later, after various intervals, to determine if our population is evolving and in what way the allele frequencies are changing. To learn how to calculate the Hardy-Weinberg formula, see "Special Topic: Calculating the Hardy-Weinberg Equilibrium" at the end of the chapter.

Interpreting Evolutionary Change: Nonrandom Mating

Once we have detected change occurring in a population, we need to consider which evolutionary processes might be the cause of the change. It is important to watch for nonrandom mating patterns, to see if they can be included or excluded as possible sources of variation in allele frequencies.

Nonrandom mating (also known as assortative mating) occurs when mate choice within a population follows a nonrandom pattern.

Positive assortative mating patterns result from a tendency for individuals to mate with others who share similar phenotypes. This often happens based on body size. Taking as an example dog breeds, it is easier for two Chihuahuas to mate and have healthy offspring than it is for a Chihuahua and a St. Bernard to do so. This is especially true if the Chihuahua is the female and would have to give birth to giant St. Bernard pups.

Negative assortative mating patterns occur when individuals tend to select mates with qualities different from their own. This is what is at work when humans choose partners whose pheromones indicate that they have different and complementary immune alleles, providing potential offspring with a better chance at a stronger immune system.

Among domestic animals, such as pets and livestock, assortative mating is often directed by humans who decide which pairs will mate to increase the chances of offspring having certain desirable traits. This is known as **artificial selection.**

Among humans, in addition to phenotypic traits, cultural traits such as religion and ethnicity may also influence assortative mating patterns.

Defining a Species

Species are organisms whose individuals are capable of breeding because they are biologically and behaviorally compatible to produce viable, fertile offspring. **Viable offspring** are those offspring that are healthy enough to survive to adulthood. **Fertile offspring** are able to reproduce successfully, resulting in offspring of their own. Both conditions must be met for individuals to be considered part of the same species. As you can imagine, these criteria complicate the identification of distinct species in fossilized remains of extinct populations. In those cases, we must examine how much phenotypic variation is typically found within a comparable modern-day species; we can then determine whether the fossilized remains fall within the expected range of variation for a single species.

Some species have subpopulations that are regionally distinct. These are classified as separate **subspecies** because they have their own unique phenotypes and are geographically isolated from one another. However, if they do happen to encounter one another, they are still capable of successful interbreeding.

There are many examples of sterile hybrids that are offspring of parents from two different species. For example, horses and donkeys can breed and have offspring together. Depending on which species is the mother and which is the father, the offspring are either called mules, or hennies. Mules and hennies can live full life spans but are not able to have offspring of their own. Likewise, tigers and lions have been known to mate and have viable offspring. Again, depending on which species is the mother and which is the father, these offspring are called either ligers or tigons. Like mules and hennies, ligers and tigons are unable to reproduce. In each of these cases, the mismatched set of chromosomes that the offspring inherit produce an adequate set of functioning genes for the hybrid offspring; however, once mixed and divided in meiosis, the gametes don't contain the full complement of genes needed for survival in the third generation.

Micro- to Macroevolution

Microevolution refers to changes in allele frequencies within breeding populations—that is, within single species. **Macroevolution** describes how the similarities and differences between species, as well as the phylogenetic relationships with other taxa, lead to changes that result in the emergence of new species.. Consider our example of the peppered moth that illustrated microevolution over time, via directional selection favoring the peppered allele when the trees were clean and the dark pigment allele when the trees were sooty. Imagine that environmental regulations had cleaned up the air pollution in one part of the nation, while the coal-fired factories continued to spew soot in another area. If this went on long enough, it's possible that two distinct moth populations would eventually emerge—one containing only the peppered allele and the other only harboring the dark pigment allele.

When a single population divides into two or more separate species, it is called **speciation**. The changes that prevent successful breeding between individuals who descended from the same ancestral population may involve chromosomal rearrangements, changes in the ability of the sperm from one species to permeate the egg membrane of the other species, or dramatic changes in hormonal schedules or mating behaviors that prevent members from the new species from being able to effectively pair up.

There are two types of speciation: allopatric and sympatric. **Allopatric speciation** is caused by long-term **isolation** (physical separation) of subgroups of the population (Figure 4.22). Something occurs in the environment—perhaps a river changes its course and splits the group, preventing them from breeding with members on the opposite riverbank. Over many generations, new mutations and adaptations to the different environments on each side of the river may drive the two subpopulations to change so much that they can no longer produce fertile, viable offspring, even if the barrier is someday removed.

Figure 4.22: Isolation leading to speciation: a. original population before isolation; b. a barrier divides the population and prevents interbreeding between the two groups; c. time passes, and the populations become genetically distinct; d. after many generations, the two populations are no longer biologically or behaviorally compatible, thus can no longer interbreed, even if the barrier is removed. Credit: Isolation Leading to Speciation (Figure 4.19) original to Explorations: An Open Invitation to Biological Anthropology by Mary Nelson is under a CC BY-NC 4.0 License.

Sympatric speciation occurs when the population splits into two or more separate species while remaining located together *without* a physical barrier. This typically results from a new mutation that pops up among some members of the population that prevents them from successfully reproducing with anyone who does not carry the same mutation. This is seen particularly often in plants, as they have a higher frequency of chromosomal duplications.

One of the quickest rates of speciation is observed in the case of adaptive radiation. **Adaptive radiation** refers to the situation in which subgroups of a single species rapidly diversify and adapt to fill a variety of ecological niches. An **ecological niche** is a set of constraints and resources that is available in an environmental setting. Evidence for adaptive radiations is often seen after population bottlenecks. A mass disaster kills off many species, and the survivors have access to a new set of territories and resources that were either unavailable or much coveted and fought over before the disaster. The offspring of the surviving population will often split into multiple species, each of which stems from members in that first group of survivors who happened to carry alleles that were advantageous for a particular niche.

The classic example of adaptive radiation brings us back to Charles Darwin and his observations of the many species of finches on the Galapagos Islands. We are still not sure how the ancestral population of finches first arrived on that remote Pacific Island chain, but they found themselves in an environment filled with various insects, large and tiny seeds, fruit, and delicious varieties of cactus. Some members of that initial population carried alleles that gave them advantages for each of these dietary niches. In subsequent generations, others developed new mutations, some of which were beneficial. These traits were selected for, making the advantageous alleles more common among their offspring. As the finches spread from one island to the next, they would be far more likely to find mates among the birds on their new island. Birds feeding in the same area were then more likely to mate together than birds who have different diets, contributing to additional assortative mating. Together, these evolutionary mechanisms caused rapid speciation that allowed the new species to make the most of the various dietary niches (Figure 4.23).

Figure 4.23: Darwin's finches demonstrating Adaptive Radiation. Credit: **Darwin's finches (Figure 4.20)** original to *Explorations: An Open Invitation to Biological Anthropology* by Mary Nelson is under a CC BY-NC 4.0 License.

In today's modern world, understanding these evolutionary processes is crucial for developing immunizations and antibiotics that can keep up with the rapid mutation rate of viruses and bacteria. This is also relevant to our food supply, which relies, in large part, on the development of herbicides and pesticides that keep up with the mutation rates of pests and weeds. Viruses, bacteria, agricultural pests, and weeds have all shown great flexibility in developing alleles that make them resistant to the latest medical treatment, pesticide, or herbicide. Billion-dollar industries have specialized in trying to keep our species one step ahead of the next mutation in the pests and infectious diseases that put our survival at risk.

Special Topic: Calculating the Hardy-Weinberg Equilibrium

In the Hardy-Weinberg formula, p represents the frequency of the dominant allele, and q represents the frequency of the recessive allele. Remember, an allele's frequency is the proportion, or percentage, of that allele in the population. For the purposes of Hardy-Weinberg, we give the allele percentages as decimal numbers (e.g., 42% = 0.42), with the entire population (100% of alleles) equaling 1. If we can figure out the frequency of one of the alleles in the population, then it is simple to calculate the other. Simply subtract the known frequency from 1 (the entire population): $1 - p = q$ and $1 - q = p$.

The Hardy-Weinberg formula is $p^2 + 2pq + q^2$, where:

p^2 represents the frequency of the homozygous dominant genotype;

$2pq$ represents the frequency of the heterozygous genotype; and

q^2 represents the frequency of the homozygous recessive genotype.

It is often easiest to determine q^2 first, simply by counting the number of individuals with the unique, homozygous recessive phenotype (then dividing by the total individuals in the population to arrive at the "frequency"). Once we have this number, we simply need to calculate the square root of the homozygous recessive phenotype frequency. That gives us q. Remember, $1 - q$ equals p, so now we have the frequencies for both alleles in the population. If we needed to figure out the frequencies of heterozygotes and homozygous dominant genotypes, we'd just need to plug the p and q frequencies back into the p^2 and $2pq$ formulas.

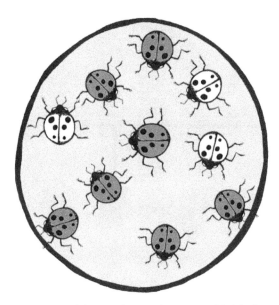

Figure 4.24: Ladybug population with a mixture of dark (red) and light (orange) individuals. Credit: Ladybug mix (Figure 4.21) original to Explorations: An Open Invitation to Biological Anthropology by Mary Nelson is under a CC BY-NC 4.0 License.

Let's imagine we have a population of ladybeetles that carries two alleles: a dominant allele that produces red ladybeetles and a recessive allele that produces orange ladybeetles. Since red is dominant, we'll use *R* to represent the red allele, and *r* to represent the orange allele. Our population has ten beetles, and seven are red and three are orange (Figure 4.24). Let's calculate the number of genotypes and alleles in this population.

Of ten total beetles, we have three orange beetles3/10 = .30 (30%) frequency—and we know they are homozygous recessive (*rr*). So:

> *rr* = *.3*; therefore, *r* = √.3 = .5477
>
> *R* = 1 – .5477 – .4523
>
> Using the Hardy-Weinberg formula:
>
> $1 = .4523^2 + 2 \times .4523 \times .5477 + .5477^2 = .20 + .50 + .30 = 1$
>
> Thus, the genotype breakdown is 20% *RR*, 50% *Rr*, and 30% *rr*
>
> (2 red homozygotes, 5 red heterozygotes, and 3 orange homozygotes).

Since we have 10 individuals, we know we have 20 total alleles: 4 red from the *RR* group, 5 red and 5 orange from the *Rr* group, and 6 orange from the *rr* group, for a grand total of 9 red and 11 orange (45% red and 55% orange, just like we estimated in the 1 – *q* step).

Reminder: The Hardy-Weinberg formula only gives us an estimate for a snapshot in time. We will have to calculate it again later, after various intervals, to determine if our population is evolving and in what way the allele frequencies are changing.

Review Questions

- Summarize the Modern Synthesis and provide several examples of how it is relevant to questions and problems in our world today.

- You inherit a house from a long-lost relative that contains a fancy aquarium, filled with a variety of snails. The phenotypes include large snails and small snails; red, black, and yellow snails; and solid, striped, and spotted snails. Devise a series of experiments that would help you determine how many snail species are present in your aquarium.

- Match the correct force of evolution with the correct real-world example:
  a. Mutation i. 5-alpha reductase deficiency
  b. Genetic Drift ii. Peppered Moths
  c. Gene Flow iii. Neurofibromatosis Type 1
  d. Natural Selection iv. Scutellata Honey Bees

- Imagine a population of common house mice (*Mus musculus*). Draw a comic strip illustrating how mutation, genetic drift, gene flow, and natural selection might transform this population over several (or more) generations.

- The many breeds of the single species of domestic dog (*Canis familiaris*) provide an extreme example of microevolution. Discuss why this is the case. What future scenarios can you imagine that could potentially transform the domestic dog into an example of macroevolution?

- The ability to roll one's tongue (lift the outer edges of the tongue to touch each other, forming a tube) is a dominant trait. In a small town of 1,500 people, 500 can roll their tongues. Use the Hardy-Weinberg formula to determine how many individuals in the town are homozygous dominant, heterozygous, and homozygous recessive.

Key Terms

5-alpha reductase deficiency: An autosomal recessive syndrome that manifests when a child having both X and Y sex chromosomes inherits two nonfunctional (mutated) copies of the SRD5A2 gene, producing a deficiency in a hormone necessary for development in infancy of typical male genitalia. These children often appear at birth to have female genitalia, but they develop a penis and other sexual characteristics when other hormones kick in during puberty.

Adaptive radiation: The situation in which subgroups of a single species rapidly diversify and adapt to fill a variety of ecological niches.

Admixture: A term often used to describe gene flow between human populations. Sometimes also used to describe gene flow between nonhuman populations.

Allele frequency: The ratio, or percentage, of one allele compared to the other alleles for that gene within the study population.

Alleles: Variant forms of genes.

Allopatric speciation: Speciation caused by long-term isolation (physical separation) of subgroups of the population.

Antibiotics: Medicines prescribed to treat bacterial infections.

Artificial selection: Human-directed assortative mating among domestic animals, such as pets and livestock, designed to increase the chances of offspring having certain desirable traits.

Asexual reproduction: Reproduction via mitosis, whereby offspring are clones of the parents.

Autosomal dominant: A phenotype produced by a gene on an autosomal chromosome that is expressed, to the exclusion of the recessive phenotype, in heterozygotes.

Autosomal recessive: A phenotype produced by a gene on an autosomal chromosome that is expressed only in individuals homozygous for the recessive allele.

Balanced translocations: Chromosomal translocations in which the genes are swapped but no genetic information is lost.

Balancing selection: A pattern of natural selection that occurs when the extremes of a trait are selected against, favoring the intermediate phenotype (a.k.a. stabilizing selection).

Beneficial mutations: Mutations that produce some sort of an advantage to the individual.

Benign: Noncancerous. Benign tumors may cause problems due to the area in which they are located (e.g., they might put pressure on a nerve or brain area), but they will not release cells that aggressively spread to other areas of the body.

Café-au-lait spots (CALS): Flat, brown birthmark-like spots on the skin, commonly associated with Neurofibromatosis Type 1.

Chromosomal translocations: The transfer of DNA between nonhomologous chromosomes.

Chromosomes: Molecules that carry collections of genes.

Codons: Three-nucleotide units of DNA that function as three-letter "words," encoding instructions for the addition of one amino acid to a protein or indicating that the protein is complete.

Cretaceous–Paleogene extinction: A mass disaster caused by an asteroid that struck the earth approximately 66 million years ago and killed 75% of life on Earth, including all terrestrial dinosaurs. (a.k.a. K-Pg Extinction, Cretatious-Tertiary Extinction, and K-T Extinction).

Crossover events: Chromosomal alterations that occur when DNA is swapped between homologous chromosomes while they are paired up during meiosis I.

Cutaneous neurofibromas: Neurofibromas that manifest as spherical bumps on or just under the surface of the skin.

Deleterious mutation: A mutation producing negative effects to the individual such as the beginnings of cancers or heritable disorders.

Deletions: Mutations that involve the removal of one or more nucleotides from a DNA sequence.

Derivative chromosomes: New chromosomal structures resulting from translocations.

Dictyostelium discoideum: A species of social amoebae that has been widely used for laboratory research. Laboratory strains of *Dictyostelium discoideum* all carry mutations in the *NF1* gene, which is what allows them to survive on liquid media (agar) in Petri dishes.

Directional selection: A pattern of natural selection in which one phenotype is favored over the other, causing the frequencies of the associated advantageous alleles to gradually increase.

Disruptive selection: A pattern of natural selection that occurs when both extremes of a trait are advantageous and intermediate phenotypes are selected against (a.k.a. diversifying selection).

DNA repair mechanisms: Enzymes that patrol and repair DNA in living cells.

DNA transposons: Transposons that are clipped out of the DNA sequence itself and inserted elsewhere in the genome.

Ecological niche: A set of constraints and resources that are available in an environmental setting.

Ellis-van Creveld syndrome: An autosomal recessive disorder characterized by short stature (dwarfism), polydactyly (the development of more than five digits [fingers or toes] on the hands or feet), abnormal tooth development, and heart defects. Estimated to affect approximately one in 60,000 individuals worldwide, among the Old Order Amish of Lancaster County, the rate is estimated to be as high as one in every 200 births.

Evolution: A change in the allele frequencies in a population over time.

Exons: The DNA sequences within a gene that directly encode protein sequences. After being transcribed into messenger RNA, the introns (DNA sequences within a gene that do not directly encode protein sequences) are clipped out, and the exons are pasted together prior to translation.

Fertile offspring: Offspring that can successfully reproduce, resulting in offspring of their own.

Founder effect: A type of genetic drift that occurs when members of a population leave the main or "parent" group and form a new population that no longer interbreeds with the other members of the original group.

Frameshift mutations: Types of indels that involve the insertion or deletion of any number of nucleotides that is not a multiple of three. These "shift the reading frame" and cause all codons beyond the mutation to be misread.

Gametes: The reproductive cells, produced through meiosis (a.k.a. germ cells or sperm or egg cells).

Gene: A sequence of DNA that provides coding information for the construction of proteins.

Gene flow: The movement of alleles from one population to another. This is one of the forces of evolution.

Gene pool: The entire collection of genetic material in a breeding community that can be passed on from one generation to the next.

Genetic drift: Random changes in allele frequencies within a population from one generation to the next. This is one of the forces of evolution.

Genotype: The set of alleles that an individual has for a given gene.

Genotype frequencies: The ratios or percentages of the different homozygous and heterozygous genotypes in the population.

Guevedoces: The term coined locally in the Dominican Republic for the condition scientifically known as 5-alpha reductase deficiency. The literal translation is "penis at twelve."

Hardy-Weinberg Equilibrium: A mathematical formula ($1=p^2 + 2pq + q^2$) that allows estimation of the number and distribution of dominant and recessive alleles in a population.

Harlequin ladybeetle: A species of ladybeetle, native to East Asia, that was introduced to Europe and the Americas as a form of pest control. After many decades of use, one of the North American strains developed the ability to reproduce in diverse environments, causing it to spread rapidly throughout the Americas, Europe, and Africa. It has hybridized with European strains and is now a major pest in its own right.

Heterozygous genotype: A genotype comprising two different alleles.

Homozygous genotype: A genotype comprising an identical set of alleles.

Hybridization: A term often used to describe gene flow between nonhuman populations.

Inbreeding: The selection of mates exclusively from within a small, closed population.

Indels: A class of mutations that includes both insertions and deletions.

Inherited mutation: A mutation that has been passed from parent to offspring.

Insertions: Mutations that involve the addition of one or more nucleotides into a DNA sequence.

Isolation: Prevention of a population subgroup from breeding with other members of the same species due to a physical barrier or, in humans, a cultural rule.

Last Universal Common Ancestor (LUCA): The ancient organism from which all living things on Earth are descended.

Macroevolution: Changes that result in the emergence of new species, how the similarities and differences between species, as well as the phylogenetic relationships with other taxa, lead to changes that result in the emergence of new species.

Malaria: A frequently deadly mosquito-borne disease caused by infection of the blood by a *Plasmodium* parasite.

Malignant: Cancerous. Malignant tumors grow aggressively and their cells may metastasize (travel through the blood or lymph systems) to form new, aggressive tumors in other areas of the body.

Microevolution: Changes in allele frequencies within breeding populations—that is, within a single species.

Modern Synthesis: The integration of Darwin's, Mendel's, and subsequent research into a unified theory of evolution.

Monosomies: Conditions resulting from a nondisjunction event, in which a cell ends up with only one copy of a chromosome. In humans, a single X chromosome is the only survivable monosomy.

Mutation: A change in the nucleotide sequence of the genetic code. This is one of the forces of evolution.

Natural selection: An evolutionary process that occurs when certain phenotypes confer an advantage or disadvantage in survival and/or reproductive success. This is one of the forces of evolution, and it was first identified by Charles Darwin.

Negative assortative mating: A pattern that occurs when individuals tend to select mates with qualities different from their own.

Neurofibromas: Nerve sheath tumors that are common symptoms of Neurofibromatosis Type 1.

Neurofibromatosis Type 1: An autosomal dominant genetic disorder affecting one in every 3,000 people. It is caused by mutation of the *NF1* gene on Chromosome 17, resulting in a defective neurofibromin protein. The disorder is characterized by neurofibromas, café-au-lait spots, and a host of other potential symptoms.

NF1: An abbreviation for Neurofibromatosis Type 1. When italicized, *NF1* refers to the gene on Chromosome 17 that encodes the neurofibromin protein.

Nondisjunction events: Chromosomal abnormalities that occur when the homologous chromosomes (in meiosis I) or sister chromatids (in meiosis II and mitosis) fail to separate after pairing. The result is that both chromosomes or chromatids end up in the same daughter cell, leaving the other daughter cell without any copy of that chromosome.

Nonrandom mating: A scenario in which mate choice within a population follows a nonrandom pattern (a.k.a. assortative mating).

Nonsynonymous mutation: A point mutation that causes a change in the resulting protein.

Old Order Amish: A culturally isolated population in Lancaster County, Pennsylvania, that has approximately 50,000 current members, all of whom can trace their ancestry back to a group of approximately eighty individuals. This group has high rates of certain genetics disorders, including Ellis-van Creveld syndrome.

Origins of life: How the first living organism came into being.

Peacock: The male sex of the peafowl, famous for its large, colorful tail, which it dramatically displays to attract mates. (The female of the species is known as a peahen.)

Peppered moth: A species of moth (*Biston betularia*) found in England that has light and dark phenotypes. During the Industrial Revolution, when soot blackened the trees, the frequency of the previously rare dark phenotype dramatically increased, as lighter-colored moths were easier for birds to spot against the sooty trees. After environmental regulations eliminated the soot, the lighter-colored phenotype gradually became most common again.

Phenotype: The observable traits that are produced by a genotype.

Phylogenetic tree of life: A family tree of all living organisms, based on genetic relationships.

Phylogenies: Genetically determined family lineages.

Plasmodium: A genus of mosquito-borne parasite. Several *Plasmodium* species cause malaria when introduced to the human bloodstream via a mosquito bite.

Plexiform neurofibromas: Neurofibromas that involve whole branches of nerves, often giving the appearance that the surface of the skin is "melting."

Point mutation: A single-letter (single-nucleotide) change in the genetic code, resulting in the substitution of one nucleic acid base for a different one.

Polymorphisms: Multiple forms of a trait; alternative phenotypes within a given species.

Population: A group of individuals who are genetically similar enough and geographically near enough to one another that they can breed and produce new generations of individuals.

Population bottleneck: A type of genetic drift that occurs when the number of individuals in a population drops dramatically due to some random event.

Positive assortative mating: A pattern that results from a tendency for individuals to mate with others who share similar phenotypes.

Retrotransposons: Transposons that are transcribed from DNA into RNA, and then are "reverse transcribed," to insert the copied sequence into a new location in the DNA.

Scutellata honey bees: A strain of honey bees that resulted from the hybridization of African and European honey bee subspecies. These bees were accidentally released into the wild in 1957 in Brazil and have since spread throughout South and Central America and into the United States. Also known as "killer bees," they tend to be very aggressive in defense of their hives and have caused many fatal injuries to humans and livestock.

Sexual reproduction: Reproduction via meiosis and combination of gametes. Offspring inherit genetic material from both parents.

Sexual selection: An aspect of natural selection in which the selective pressure specifically affects reproductive success (the ability to successfully breed and raise offspring).

Sickle cell anemia: An autosomal recessive genetic disorder that affects millions of people worldwide. It is most common in Africa, countries around the Mediterranean Sea, and eastward as far as India. Homozygotes for the recessive allele develop the disorder, which produce misshapen red blood cells that cause iron deficiency, painful episodes of oxygen-deprivation in localized tissues, and a host of other symptoms. In heterozygotes, though, the sickle cell allele confers a greater resistance to malaria.

Somatic cells: The cells of our organs and other body tissues (all cells except gametes) that replicate by mitosis.

Speciation: The process by which a single population divides into two or more separate species.

Species: Organisms whose individuals are capable of breeding because they are biologically and behaviorally compatible to produce viable, fertile offspring.

Spontaneous mutation: A mutation that occurs due to random chance or unintentional exposure to mutagens. In families, a spontaneous mutation is the first case, as opposed to mutations that are inherited from parents.

Subspecies: A distinct subtype of a species. Most often, this is a geographically isolated population with unique phenotypes; however, it remains biologically and behaviorally capable of interbreeding with other populations of the same species.

Sympatric speciation: When a population splits into two or more separate species while remaining located together without a physical (or cultural) barrier.

Synonymous mutation: A point mutation that does not change the resulting protein.

Transposable elements: Fragments of DNA that can "jump" around in the genome.

Transposon: Another term for "transposable element."

Trisomies: Conditions in which three copies of the same chromosome end up in a cell, resulting from a nondisjunction event. Down syndrome, Edwards syndrome, and Patau syndrome are trisomies.

Unbalanced translocations: Chromosomal translocations in which there is an unequal exchange of genetic material, resulting in duplication or loss of genes.

UV crosslinking: A type of mutation in which adjacent thymine bases bind to one another in the presence of UV light.

Viable offspring: Offspring that are healthy enough to survive to adulthood.

Xeroderma pigmentosum: An autosomal recessive disease in which DNA repair mechanisms do not function correctly, resulting in a host of problems especially related to sun exposure, including severe sunburns, dry skin, heavy freckling, and other pigment changes.

About the Author

Andrea J. Alveshere, Ph.D.

Western Illinois University, a-alveshere@wiu.edu, Andrea Alveshere: Archaeologist & Biological Anthropologist

Dr. Andrea Alveshere is an associate professor of anthropology and chemistry at Western Illinois University. Her research focuses on relationships between humans and their environments, including cultural and biological adaptations surrounding ancient diet, health, and knowledge systems; genetic disorders such as Neurofibromatosis Type 1 (NF1); effects of environmental factors on the preservation of bones, plant remains, and the molecules within them; and the comparative utility of field and laboratory techniques to produce informative archaeological, nutritional, and forensic data.

Dr. Alveshere earned her B.A. in anthropology at the University of Washington with an emphasis in archaeology and an undergraduate research focus on the analysis of skeletal remains and geoarchaeological deposits. At the University of Minnesota, she completed her Ph.D. in anthropology, with a minor in human genetics. Her graduate thesis investigated factors that influence the preservation and detection of DNA in ancient and forensic specimens.

Dr. Alveshere also worked for several years as a forensic scientist in the DNA/Biology section of the Minnesota Bureau of Criminal Apprehension Forensic Science Laboratory. She led the WIU Archaeological Field School, on alternate summers since 2017, and conducted archaeological excavations in Israel, South Africa, and throughout the midwestern United States.

For Further Exploration

Explore Evolution on HHMI's Biointeractive website.

Teaching Evolution through Human Examples, Smithsonian Museum of Natural History websites.

References

Bloomfield, Gareth, David Traynor, Sophia P. Sander, Douwe M. Veltman, Justin A. Pachebat, and Robert R. Kay. 2015. "Neurofibromin Controls Macropinocytosis and Phagocytosis in *Dictyostelium*." *eLife* 4:e04940.

Chaix, Raphaëlle, Chen Cao, and Peter Donnelly. 2008. "Is Mate Choice in Humans MHC-Dependent?" *PLoS Genetics* 4 (9): e1000184.

Cook, Laurence M. 2003. "The Rise and Fall of the *Carbonaria* Form of the Peppered Moth." *The Quarterly Review of Biology* 78 (4): 399–417.

Cota, Bruno Cézar Lage, João Gabriel Marques Fonseca, Luiz Oswaldo Carneiro Rodrigues, Nilton Alves de Rezende, Pollyanna Barros Batista, Vincent Michael Riccardi, and Luciana Macedo de Resende. 2018. "Amusia and Its Electrophysiological Correlates in Neurofibromatosis Type 1." *Arquivos de Neuro-Psiquiatria* 76 (5): 287–295.

D'Asdia, Maria Cecilia, Isabella Torrente, Federica Consoli, Rosangela Ferese, Monia Magliozzi, Laura Bernardini, Valentina Guida, et al. 2013. "Novel and Recurrent EVC and EVC2 Mutations in Ellis-van Creveld Syndrome and Weyers Acrofacial Dyostosis." *European Journal of Medical Genetics* 56 (2): 80–87.

Dobzhansky, Theodosius. 1937. *Genetics and the Origin of Species.* Columbia University Biological Series. New York: Columbia University Press.

Facon, Benoît, Laurent Crespin, Anne Loiseau, Eric Lombaert, Alexandra Magro, and Arnaud Estoup. 2011. "Can Things Get Worse When an Invasive Species Hybridizes? The Harlequin Ladybird *Harmonia axyridis* in France as a Case Study." *Evolutionary Applications* 4 (1): 71–88.

Fisher, Ronald A. 1919. "The Correlation between Relatives on the Supposition of Mendelian Inheritance." *Transactions of the Royal Society of Edinburgh* 52 (2): 399–433.

Ford, E. B. 1942. *Genetics for Medical Students.* London: Methuen.

Ford, E. B. 1949. *Mendelism and Evolution.* London: Methuen.

Grant, Bruce S. 1999. "Fine-tuning the Peppered Moth Paradigm." *Evolution* 53 (3): 980–984.

Haldane, J. B. S. 1924. "A Mathematical Theory of Natural and Artificial Selection (Part 1)." *Transactions of the Cambridge Philosophical Society* 23 (2):19–41.

Imperato-McGinley, J., and Y.-S. Zhu. 2002. "Androgens and Male Physiology: The Syndrome of 5 Alpha-Reductase-2 Deficiency." *Molecular and Cellular Endocrinology* 198 (1-2): 51–59.

Jablonski, David, and W. G. Chaloner. 1994. "Extinctions in the Fossil Record." *Philosophical Transactions of the Royal Society of London B: Biological Sciences* 344 (1307): 11–17.

Livi-Bacci, Massimo. 2006. "The Depopulation of Hispanic America after the Conquest." *Population Development and Review* 32 (2): 199–232.

Lombaert, Eric, Thomas Guillemaud, Jean-Marie Cornuet, Thibaut Malausa, Benoît Facon, and Arnaud Estoup. 2010. "Bridgehead Effect in the Worldwide Invasion of the Biocontrol Harlequin Ladybird." *PLoS ONE* 5 (3): e9743.

Martins, Aline Stangherlin, Ann Kristine Jansen, Luiz Oswaldo Carneiro Rodrigues, Camila Maria Matos, Marcio Leandro Ribeiro Souza, Juliana Ferreira de Souza, Maria de Fátima Haueisen Sander Diniz, et al. 2016. "Lower Fasting Blood Glucose in Neurofibromatosis Type 1." *Endocrine Connections* 5 (1): 28–33.

Pickering, Gary, James Lin, Roland Riesen, Andrew Reynolds, Ian Brindle, and George Soleas. 2004. "Influence of *Harmonia axyridis* on the Sensory Properties of White and Red Wine." *American Journal of Enology and Viticulture* 55 (2): 153–159.

Repunte-Canonigo Vez, Melissa A. Herman, Tomoya Kawamura, Henry R. Kranzler, Richard Sherva, Joel Gelernter, Lindsay A. Farrer, Marisa

Roberto, and Pietro Paolo Sanna. 2015. "NF1 Regulates Alcohol Dependence-Associated Excessive Drinking and Gamma-Aminobutyric Acid Release in the Central Amygdala in Mice and Is Associated with Alcohol Dependence in Humans." *Biological Psychiatry* 77 (10): 870–879.

Riccardi, Vincent M. 1992. *Neurofibromatosis: Phenotype, Natural History, and Pathogenesis.* Baltimore: Johns Hopkins University Press.

Sanford, Malcolm T. 2006. "The Africanized Honey Bee in the Americas: A Biological Revolution with Human Cultural Implications, Part V—Conclusion." *American Bee Journal* 146 (7): 597–599.

Sanna, Pietro Paolo, Cindy Simpson, Robert Lutjens, and George Koob. 2002. "ERK Regulation in Chronic Ethanol Exposure and Withdrawal." *Brain Research* 948 (1–2): 186–191.

World Health Organization. 1996. "Control of Hereditary Disorders: Report of WHO Scientific meeting (1996)." WHO Technical Reports 865. Geneva: World Health Organization.

World Health Organization. 2017. "Global Priority List of Antibiotic-Resistant Bacteria to Guide Research, Discovery, and Development of New Antibiotics." Global Priority Pathogens List, February 27. Geneva: World Health Organization. https://www.who.int/medicines/publications/WHO-PPL-Short_Summary_25Feb-ET_NM_WHO.pdf.

Wright, Sewall. 1932. "The Roles of Mutation, Inbreeding, Crossbreeding, and Selection in Evolution." *Proceedings of the Sixth International Congress on Genetics* 1 (6): 356–366.

Acknowledgment

Many thanks to Dr. Vincent M. Riccardi for sharing his vast knowledge of neurofibromatosis and for encouraging me to explore it from an anthropological perspective.

Image Descriptions

Figure 4.1: The universal ancestor (left) is depicted as a blue capsule with two tails. From it, lines branch right indicating the evolution of bacteria (top), archaea (middle), and eukarya (bottom). The bacteria branch notes "photosynthesis" and "respiration." Archaea and Eukarya share "ribosomal RNA changed by mutation" before splitting into their two branches. The Eukarya branch also notes "nucleus and membranous organelles" and "respiration" before diverging into five separate branches with respective images of a mouse, mushroom, parasite, green algae, and a fern frond. Multicellularity is noted as independently evolving on the mouse, mushroom, and fern branches.

Figure 4.2: Snapdragons are used to illustrate phenotypes, genotypes, and alleles in a three part diagram.

Top diagram: At the top, three snapdragons are each labeled with a pair of letters:

- Red snapdragon – Two uppercase Rs
- Pink snapdragon – One upper case R and one lower case r
- White snapdragon – Two lower case rs

The set of three has two labels:

- phenotype (flower color)
- genotype (pair of alleles)

Middle diagram: A rectangle labeled "population (gene pool)" contains ten different snapdragons with corresponding genotypes: four red snapdragons (two uppercase Rs), four pink (one upper case R, one lower case r), and two white (two lower case rs).

Text on the side reads:

- Genotype frequencies (How often we note each combination: RR, Rr, or rr).
  - Freq. of RR = 4/10 = 0.4
  - Freq. of Rr = 4/10 = 0.4
  - Freq. of rr = 2/10 = 0.2
- Allele frequencies (How often we see each allele: R or r
  - Freq. of R = 12/20 = 0.6
  - Freq. of r = 8/20 = 0.4

Bottom diagram: Three circles, connected by arrows, each surround a population of five snapdragons with their genotype labels (two letters for each snapdragon). A label reads: Allele frequency change is population evolution. Underneath each population is the corresponding allele frequencies.

- First population contains three red (RR), one pink (Rr), and one white (rr) snapdragons.
  - Freq. R = 7/10 = 0.7
  - Freq. r = 3/10 = 0.3
- Second population contains one red (RR), three pink (Rr), and one white (rr) snapdragons.
  - Freq. R = 5/10 = 0.5
  - Freq. r = 5/10 = 0.5
- Third population contains one red (RR), two pink (Rr), and two white (rr) snapdragons.
  - Freq. R = 4/10 = 0.4
  - Freq. r = 6/10 = 0.6

Figure 4.3: A capsule shaped universal ancestor is linked to a cell with smoothly rounded edges and different colored organelles by a thin black line. The line is labeled Eukarya branch (reminding the reader of Figure 4.1). Along the branch dots represent evolutionary events: ribosomal RNA changed by mutation, nucleus and membranous organelles, and respiration.

Figure 4.4: Two DNA double helix shapes are drawn. The left one, labeled "Before" shows an arrow labeled "UV radiation" pointing towards its middle. The right one, labeled "After" bulges in the middle showing that the nucleotides on the same strand have bonded together, instead of to their complements on the other strand as they should.

Figure 4.16: Three line graphs illustrate population change as a result of different types of selection. A blue line represents the original population, the red line represents the population after natural selection. While unlabeled, the X axis represents different phenotypes in the population, and the Y axis represents the frequency of each of those phenotypes. An image placed in the box of the line graph visualizes the trait being represented.

Stabilizing selection:

Text reads: Robins typically lay four eggs, an example of stabilizing selection. Larger clutches may result in malnourished chicks, while smaller clutches may result in no viable offspring.

Line graph indicates a narrower range of phenotypes – or many middle sized clutches – after selection on a population with more diverse clutch sizes. Image of eggs in a nest.

Directional selection:

Text reads: Light-colored peppered moths are better camouflaged against a pristine environment; likewise dark-colored peppered moths are better camouflaged against sooty environments. Thus, as the Industrial Revolution progressed in nineteenth century England, the color of the moth population shifted from light to dark, an example of directional selection.

Both the before and after population are bell-shaped curves, but the after population has shifted to the right indicating more dark-colored moths and few light-colored moths.

Diversifying selection:

Text reads: In a hypothetical population, gray and Himalayan (gray and white) rabbits are better able to blend with a rocky environment than white rabbits, resulting in diversifying selection.

Image shows the before population as a bell-shaped curve with white rabbits (in the middle) as the most common. The after population shows more gray and Himalayan rabbits (the extremes on each side) as more populous than the white rabbit in the middle.

5.

MEET THE LIVING PRIMATES

Stephanie Etting, Ph.D., Sacramento City College

This chapter is a revision from "Chapter 5: Meet the Living Primates" by Stephanie Etting. In Explorations: An Open Invitation to Biological Anthropology, first edition, edited by Beth Shook, Katie Nelson, Kelsie Aguilera, and Lara Braff, which is licensed under CC BY-NC 4.0.

Learning Objectives

- Describe how studying nonhuman primates is important in anthropology.
- Compare two ways of categorizing taxa: grades and clades.
- Define different types of traits used to evaluate primate taxa.
- Identify key ways that primates differ from other mammals.
- Distinguish between the major primate taxa using their key characteristics.
- Describe your place in nature by learning your taxonomic classification.

You may be wondering why a field dedicated to the study of humans includes discussions of nonhuman animals. Our primary goal in biological anthropology is to understand how humans are similar to and different from the rest of the natural world, why we have the traits we have, and how we got to be the way we are. But to fully grasp our place in nature, we must look to our closest living relatives, the nonhuman primates. In this chapter, we focus on the organization and diversity within the Order Primates.

Studying Primates in Biological Anthropology

Primates are one of at least twenty Orders belonging to the Class Mammalia, and probably one of the oldest. One genetic estimate puts the origin of primates at approximately 91 million years ago (mya), predating the extinction of the dinosaurs (Bininda-Emonds et al. 2007). Today, the Order Primates is a diverse group of animals that includes lemurs and lorises, tarsiers, monkeys, apes, and humans, all of which are united in sharing a suite of anatomical, behavioral, and life history characteristics. While nonhuman primates are fascinating animals in their own right, their close relationship to humans makes them ideal for studying humans via **homology,** looking at traits that are shared between taxa because they inherited the trait from a common ancestor. For example, humans (genus *Homo*) and chimpanzees (genus *Pan*) both share the trait of male cooperation in hunting. This trait—along with many others that chimpanzees and humans share—is likely homologous, meaning it was probably passed down from the last common ancestor of *Homo* and *Pan,* which lived about 6–8 million years ago.

Nonhuman primates also make excellent comparators for learning about humans via **analogy**. Many nonhuman primates live in environments similar to those in which our ancestors lived and therefore exhibit traits similar to what we see in humans. For example, baboons and humans both have long legs. In humans, this is because about 1.7 million years ago, our ancestors moved into savanna habitats where longer legs helped them move more efficiently over long distances. Baboons, who also live in savanna habitats, independently evolved longer arms and legs for the same reason—to be able to cover more ground, more efficiently. This means that having long legs is an analogous trait in baboons and humans: —that is, this adaptation evolved independently in the two species but for the same purpose. Using homology and analogy, our closest living relatives provide the critical context in which to understand human biology, morphology, and behavior. It is only by studying how humans compare with our primate relatives that we can fully comprehend our place in nature.

Ways of Organizing Taxa

You learned in Chapter 2 about Linnaeus and the hierarchical nature of taxonomic classification. Our goal in classifying taxa is to create categories that reflect clade relationships. A **clade** is a grouping of organisms based on relatedness that reflects a branch of the evolutionary tree. Clade relationships are determined using traits shared by groups of taxa as well as genetic similarities. An example of a clade would be a grouping that includes humans, chimpanzees, bonobos, and gorillas (Figure 5.1). These taxa are in what is referred to as the **African clade** of hominoids (a taxonomic group you will learn about later in this chapter). The African clade grouping reflects how humans, chimpanzees, bonobos, and gorillas all share a more recent ancestor with each other than any of them do with other species—that is, we are on the same branch of the evolutionary tree. We know members of the African clade are most closely related based on shared morphological traits as well as genetic similarities. Excluded from this grouping is the orangutan, which is considered a member of the **Asian clade** of hominoids.

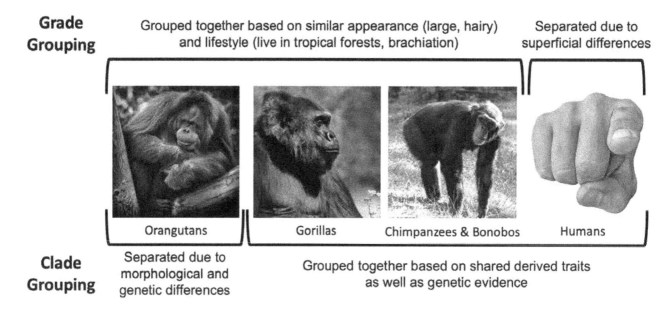

Figure 5.1: Grades vs. Clades. A grade grouping of apes places orangutans, gorillas, chimpanzees, and bonobos together based on their similar appearance and lifestyle, but excludes humans. Clade classification is based on shared derived traits and genetic evidence (both reflecting close evolutionary relationships). A clade grouping of apes places humans with gorillas, chimpanzees, and bonobos., whereas orangutans are separated. Credit: Grades vs. clades comparison (Figure 5.12) original to Explorations: An Open Invitation to Biological Anthropology by Stephanie Etting is a collective work under a CC BY-NC-SA 4.0 License. [Includes Orangutan on a tree (Unsplash) by Dawn Armfield, public domain (CC0 1.0); Gorilla Profile (17997840570) by Charlie Marshall from Bristol UK, modified (cropped), CC BY 2.0 License; Chimpanzee (14679767561) by Magnus Johansson, modified (cropped), CC BY-SA 2.0; Pointing finger (1922074) by truthseeker08, Pixabay License.]

In contrast, **grades** are groupings that reflect levels of adaptation or overall similarity and not necessarily evolutionary relationships. An example of a grade would be placing orangutans, gorillas, bonobos, and chimpanzees into a group, and excluding humans. Grouping in this way is based on the superficial similarities of the apes in being large-bodied, having lots of body hair, living in tropical forests, climbing and sleeping in trees, and so on. According to these criteria, humans seem to be unusual in that we differ in our morphology, behavior, and ecology. Separating humans from the large-bodied apes is the system that was used historically. We now know that grouping orangutans, gorillas, bonobos, and chimpanzees and excluding humans does not accurately reflect our true evolutionary relationships. Since our goal in taxonomic classification is to organize animals to reflect their evolutionary relationships, we prefer to use clade classifications.

Types of Traits

When evaluating relationships between taxa, we use key traits that allow us to determine which species are most closely related to one another. Traits can be either ancestral or derived. **Ancestral traits** are those that a taxon has because it has inherited the trait from a distant ancestor. For example, all primates have body hair because we are mammals and all mammals share an ancestor hundreds of millions of years ago that had body hair. This trait has been passed down to all mammals from a shared ancestor, so all mammals alive today have body hair. **Derived traits** are those that have been more recently altered. This type of trait is most useful when we are trying to distinguish one group from another because derived traits tell us which taxa are more closely related to each other. For example, humans walk on two legs. The many adaptations that humans possess that allow us to move in this way evolved after humans split from the Genus *Pan*. This means that when we find fossil taxa that share derived traits for walking on two legs, we can conclude that they are likely more closely related to humans than to chimpanzees and bonobos.

There are a couple of other important points about ancestral and derived traits that will become apparent as we discuss primate diversity. First, the terms *ancestral* and *derived* are relative terms, meaning that a trait can be either one depending on the taxa being compared. For example, in the previous paragraph, body hair was used as an example for an ancestral trait among primates. All mammals have body hair because we share a distant ancestor who had this trait. The presence of body hair therefore doesn't allow you to distinguish whether monkeys are more closely related to apes or lemurs because they all share this trait. However, if we are comparing mammals to birds and fish, then body hair becomes a derived trait of mammals. It evolved after mammals diverged from birds and fish, and it tells us that all mammals are more closely related to each other than they are to birds or fish. The second important point is that very often when one lineage splits into two, one taxon will stay more similar to the last common ancestor in retaining more ancestral traits, whereas the other lineage will usually become more different from the last common ancestor by developing more derived traits. This will become very apparent when we discuss the two suborders of primates, Strepsirrhini and Haplorrhini. When these two lineages diverged, strepsirrhines retained more ancestral traits (those present in the earliest primates) and haplorrhines developed more derived traits (became more different from ancestral primates).

There are two other types of traits that will be relevant to our discussions here: generalized and specialized traits. **Generalized traits** are those characteristics that are useful for a wide range of things. Having **opposable thumbs** that go in a different direction than the rest of your fingers is a very useful, generalized trait. You can hold a pen, grab a branch, peel a banana, or text your friends all thanks to your opposable thumbs! **Specialized traits** are those that have been modified for a specific purpose. These traits may not have a wide range of uses, but they will be very efficient at their job. Hooves in horses are a good example of a specialized trait: they allow horses to run quickly on the ground on all fours. You can think of generalized traits as a Swiss Army knife, useful for a wide range of tasks but not particularly good at any one of them. That is, if you're in a bind, then a Swiss Army knife can be very useful to cut a rope or fix a loose screw, but if you were going to build furniture or fix a kitchen sink, then you'd want specialized tools for the job. As we will see, most primate traits tend to be generalized.

What Makes Something a Primate?

The Order Primates is distinguished from other groups of mammals in having a *suite of characteristics*. This means that there is no individual trait that you can use to instantly identify an animal as a primate; instead, you have to look for animals that possess a collection of traits. What this also means is that each individual trait we discuss may be found in nonprimates, but if you see an animal that has most or all of these traits, there is a good chance it is a primate.

Primates are most distinguishable from other organisms in traits related to our vision. Our Order relies on vision as a primary sense, which is reflected in many areas of our anatomy and behavior. All primates have eyes that face forward with convergent (overlapping) visual fields. So if you cover one eye with your hand, you can still see most of the room with your other one. This also means that we cannot see on the sides or behind us as well as some other animals can. In order to protect the sides of the eyes from the muscles we use for chewing, all primates have at least a **postorbital bar,** a bony ring around the outside of the eye (Figure 5.2). Primate taxa with more convergent eyes need extra protection, so animals with greater orbital convergence will have a **postorbital plate** or **postorbital closure** in addition to the bar (Figure 5.2). The postorbital bar is a derived trait of primates, appearing in our earliest ancestors.

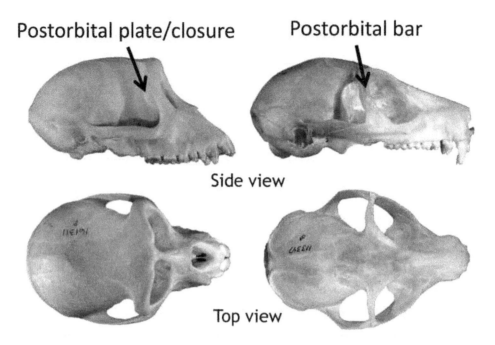

Figure 5.2: All primates have bony protection around their eyes. Some have a postorbital bar only (right), but many have full postorbital closure, also called a postorbital plate, that completely protects the back of the eye socket (left). Credit: Postorbital bar/Postorbital closure (Figure 5.1) a derivative work original to Explorations: An Open Invitation to Biological Anthropology by Stephanie Etting is under a CC BY-NC-SA 4.0 License. [Includes Otolemur crassicaudatus (greater galago) by Animal Diversity Web, CC BY-NC-SA 3.0; Macaca fascicularis (long-tailed macaque) by Animal Diversity Web, CC BY-NC-SA 3.0.]

Another distinctive trait of our Order is that many primates have **trichromatic color vision**, the ability to distinguish reds and yellows in addition to blues and greens. Birds, fish, and reptiles are **tetrachromatic** (they can see reds, yellows, blues, greens, and even ultraviolet), but most mammals, including some primates, are only **dichromatic** (they see only in blues and greens). It is thought that the nocturnal ancestors of mammals benefited from seeing better at night rather than in color, and so dichromacy is the ancestral condition for mammals. Trichromatic primates are known to use their color vision for all sorts of purposes: finding young leaves and ripe fruits, identifying other species, and evaluating signals of health and fertility.

The primate visual system uses a lot of energy, so primates have compensated by cutting back on other sensory systems, particularly our sense of smell. Compared to other mammals, primates have reduced snouts, another derived trait that appears even in the earliest primate ancestors. There is variation across primate taxa in how much snouts are reduced. Those with a better sense of smell usually have poorer vision than those with a relatively dull sense of smell. The reason for this is that all organisms have a limited amount of energy to spend on running our bodies, so we make **evolutionary trade-offs**, as energy spent on one trait cuts back on energy spent on another. So primates with better vision are spending more energy on vision and thus have a poorer smell (and shorter snout), and those who spend less energy on vision will have a better sense of smell (and a longer snout).

Primates also differ from other mammals in the size and complexity of our brains. On average, primates have brains that are twice as big for their body size when compared to other mammals. Not unexpectedly, the visual centers of the brain are larger in primates and the wiring is different from that in other animals, reflecting our reliance on this sense. The neocortex, which is used for higher functions like consciousness and language in humans, as well as sensory perception and spatial awareness, is also larger in primates relative to other animals. In nonprimates this part of the brain is often smooth, but in primates it is made up of many folds, which increase the surface area. It has been proposed that the more complex neocortex of primates is related to diet, with fruit-eating primates having larger relative brain sizes than leaf-eating primates, due to the more challenging cognitive demands required to find and process fruits (Clutton-Brock and Harvey 1980). An alternative hypothesis argues that larger brain size is necessary for navigating the complexities of primate social life, with larger brains occurring in species who live in bigger, more complex groups relative to those living in pairs or solitarily (Dunbar 1998). There seems to be support for both hypotheses, as large brains are a benefit under both sets of selective pressures.

Animals with large brains usually have extended life history patterns, and primates are no exception. **Life history** refers to the pace at which an organism grows, reproduces, and ages. Some animals grow very quickly and reproduce many offspring in a short time frame but do not live very long. Other animals grow slowly, reproduce few offspring, reproduce infrequently, and live a long time. Primates are all in the "slow lane" of life history patterns. Compared to animals of similar body size, primates grow and develop more slowly, have fewer offspring per pregnancy, reproduce less often, and live longer. Primates also invest heavily in each offspring. With a few exceptions, most primates only have one offspring at a time. A group of small-bodied monkeys in South America regularly give birth to twins, and some lemurs can give birth to multiple offspring at a time, but these primates are the exception rather than the rule. Primates also reproduce relatively infrequently. The fastest-reproducing primates will produce offspring about every six months, while the slowest, the orangutan, reproduces only once every seven to nine years. This very slow reproductive rate makes the orangutan the slowest-reproducing animal on the planet! Primates are also characterized by having long lifespans. The group that includes humans and large-bodied apes has the most extended life history patterns among all primates, with some large-bodied apes estimated to live up to 58 years in the wild (Robson et al. 2006).

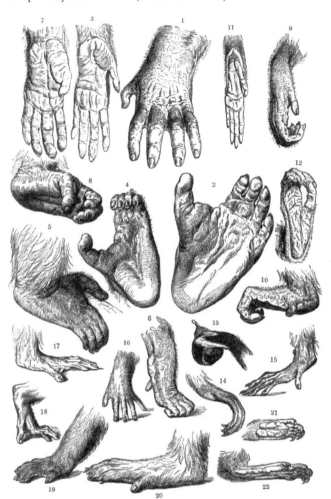

HANDS AND FEET OF APES AND MONKEYS.

1, 2, Gorilla ; 3–8, Chimpanzee ; 9, 10, Orang ; 11, 13, Gibbon ; 14, 15, Guereza ; 16–18, Macaque ; 19, 20, Baboon ; 21, 22, Marmoset.

Figure 5.3: These drawings of the hands and feet of different primates show the opposable thumbs and big toes, pentadactyly, flattened nails, and tactile pads characteristic of our Order. Credit: PrimateFeet by Richard Lydekker, original from The Royal Natural History 1:15 (1893), is in the public domain.

Primates also differ from other animals in our hands and feet. The Order Primates is a largely **arboreal** taxonomic group, meaning that most primates spend a significant amount of their time in trees. As a result, the hands and feet of primates have evolved to move in a three-dimensional environment. Primates have the generalized trait of **pentadactyly**— possessing five digits (fingers and toes) on each limb. Many nonprimates, like dogs and horses, have fewer digits because they are specialized for high-speed, **terrestrial** (on the ground) running. Pentadactyly is also an ancestral trait, one that dates back to the earliest four-footed animals. Primates today have opposable thumbs and, with the exception of humans, opposable big toes (Figure 5.3). Opposable thumbs and toes are a derived trait that appeared in the earliest primate fossils about 55 million years ago. Having thumbs and big toes that go in a different direction from the rest of the fingers and toes allow primates to be excellent climbers in trees as well as to manipulate objects. Our ability to manipulate objects is further enhanced by the flattened nails on the backs of our fingers and toes that we possess in the place of the claws and hooves that many other mammals have. On the other side of our digits, we have sensitive **tactile pads** that allow us to have a fine sense of touch. Primates use this fine sense of touch for handling food and, in many species, grooming themselves and others. In primates, grooming is an important social currency, through which individuals forge and maintain social bonds.

Lastly, primates are very social animals. All primates, even those that search for food alone, establish strong social networks within species. Unlike many animals, primates do not migrate: they stay in a relatively stable area for their whole life, often interacting with the same individuals for their long lives. The long-term relationships that primates form with others of their species lead to complex and fascinating social behaviors (see Chapter 6). Finally, nonhuman primates show a clear preference for tropical regions of the world. Most primates are found between the Tropic of Cancer and the Tropic of Capricorn, with only a few taxa living outside these regions. Figure 5.4 shows a summary of primate traits.

Key Traits Used to Distinguish Between Primate Taxa

When placing primate species into specific taxonomic groups, we focus on dental characteristics, behavioral adaptations, and locomotor adaptations. Differences in these characteristics across groups reflect constraints of evolutionary history as well as variation in adaptations.

Dental Characteristics

Teeth may not seem like the most exciting topic with which to start, but we can learn a tremendous amount about an organism from its teeth. First, teeth are vital to survival. Wild animals do not have the benefit of knives and forks; they rely on their teeth to process their food. Because of this, teeth of any species have evolved to reflect what that organism eats and therefore have a lot to tell us about their diet. Second, variation in tooth size, shape, and number reveals an organism's evolutionary history. Some taxa have more teeth than others or

Figure 5.4: Primate Traits at a Glance: This table summarizes the suite of traits that differentiate primates from other mammals. Credit: Primate at a glance table (Figure 5.3) by Stephanie Etting original to Explorations: An Open Invitation to Biological Anthropology is under a CC BY-NC 4.0 License.

Primate suite of traits
Convergent eyes
Postorbital bar
Many have trichromatic color vision
Short snouts
Opposable thumbs and big toes
Pentadactyly
Flattened nails
Tactile pads
Highly arboreal
Large brains
Extended life histories
Live in the tropics

different forms of teeth. Furthermore, differences in teeth between males and females can tell us about competition over mates (see Chapter 6). Lastly, teeth are overly represented in the fossil record. Enamel is hard, and there is little meat on jaws so carnivores and scavengers often leave them behind. Sometimes, the only remains we have from an extinct taxon is its teeth!

Figure 5.5: This picture of an open-mouthed Hamadryas baboon demonstrates the diastema between his upper canine and front teeth. This space is taken up by his lower canine when he closes his mouth. Credit: Ha,ha,ha .... (14986571843) by Rolf Dietrich Brecher from Germany is under a CC BY-SA 2.0 License.

Like other mammals, primates are **heterodont**: they have multiple types of teeth that are used for different purposes. We have **incisors** for slicing; **premolars** and **molars** for grinding up our food; and **canines**, which most primates (not humans) use as weapons against predators and each other. The sizes of canines vary across species and can often be **sexually dimorphic**, with males tending to have larger canines than females. Some nonhuman primates **hone**, or sharpen, their canines by gnashing the teeth together to sharpen the sides. The upper canine sharpens on the first lower premolar and the lower canine sharpens on the front of the upper canine. As canines get larger, they require a space to fit in order for the jaws to close. This space between the teeth is called a **diastema** (Figure 5.5).

We use a **dental formula** to specify how many incisors, canines, premolars, and molars are in each quadrant of the mouth (half of the top or bottom). For example, Figure 5.6 shows half of the lower teeth of a human. You can see that in half of the mandible, there are two incisors, one canine, two premolars, and three molars. This dental formula is written as 2:1:2:3. (The first number represents the number of incisors, followed by the number of canines, premolars, and molars).

To determine the dental formula, you need to be able to identify the different types of teeth. You can recognize incisors because they often look like spatulas with a flat, blade-like surface. Premolars and molars can be differentiated by the number of **cusps** that they have. Cusps are the bumps that you can feel with your tongue on the surface of your back teeth. Premolars are smaller than molars and, in primates, often have one or two cusps on them. Molars are bigger, providing a larger chewing surface, and have more cusps. Depending on the species and whether you're looking at upper or lower teeth, primate molars can have between three and five cusps. Molar cusps can also vary between taxa in how they are arranged; you will learn more about this later in this chapter. Canines are often easy to distinguish because, in most taxa, they are much longer and more conical than the other teeth.

Teeth also directly reflect an organism's diet. Primates are known to eat a wide range of plant parts, insects, gums, and, rarely, meat. While all primates eat a variety of foods, what differs among primates are the proportions of each of these food items in the diet. That is, two primates living in the same forest may be eating the same foods but in vastly different proportions, and so we would categorize them as different dietary types. The most common dietary types among primates are those whose diets consist primarily of fruit (**frugivores**), those who eat mostly insects (**insectivores**), and those who eat primarily leaves (**folivores**). A few primate taxa are **gummivores**, specializing in eating gums and saps, but we will only focus on the adaptations found in the three primary dietary groups.

Frugivores

Plants want animals to eat their fruits because, in doing so, animals eat the seeds of the fruit and then disperse them far away from the parent plant. Therefore, plants often "advertise" fruits by making them colorful and easy to spot, full of easy-to-digest sugars that make them taste good and, often, easy to chew and digest (not being too fibrous or tough). For these reasons, frugivores often do not need a lot of specialized traits to consume a diet rich in fruits

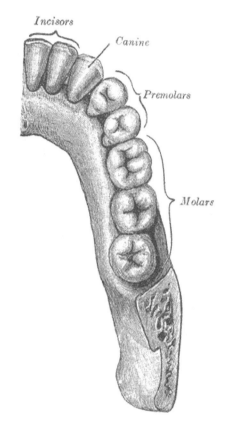

Figure 5.6: This drawing shows half of the human mandible. With the four types of teeth labeled, you can determine that the dental formula is 2:1:2:3. Credit: Gray997 by Henry Vandyke Carter, original in Henry Gray (1918) Anatomy of the Human Body, Plate 997, is in the public domain.

(Figure 5.7). Their molars usually have a broad chewing surface with low, rounded cusps (referred to as **bunodont** molars). Frugivores have large incisors for slicing through the outer coatings on fruit, and they tend to have stomachs, colons, and small intestines that are intermediate in terms of size and complexity between insectivores and folivores (Chivers and Hladik 1980). They are also usually of intermediate body size between the other two dietary types. Because fruit does not contain protein, frugivores must supplement their diet with protein from insects, leaves, and/or seeds. Frugivores who get protein by eating seeds evolved to have thicker enamel on their teeth to protect them from excessive wear.

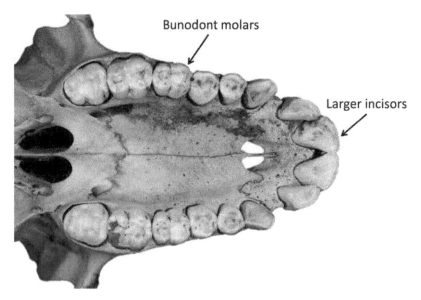

Figure 5.7: Frugivores are characterized by large incisors, bunodont molars, and digestive tracts that are intermediate in complexity between the other two dietary types. Credit: Papio papio (Guinea baboon).jpg by Phil Myers on Animal Diversity Web is under a CC BY-NC-SA 3.0 License.

Insectivores

While insects can be difficult to find and catch, they are easy to chew and digest. As a result, insectivorous primates usually have small molars with pointed cusps to puncture the exoskeleton of the insects (Figure 5.8), and they have simple stomachs and colons with a long small intestine to process the insects. Nutritionally, insects provide a lot of protein and fat but are not plentiful enough in the environment to support large-bodied animals, so insectivores are usually the smallest of the primates.

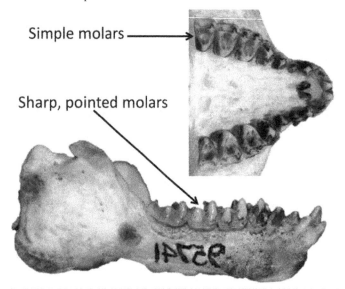

Figure 5.8: Insectivores need sharp, pointed molar cusps to break through the exoskeletons of insects. Insects are easy to digest, so these primates have simple digestive tracts. Credit: Tarsier (an insectivor)'s teeth original to Explorations: An Open Invitation to Biological Anthropology (2nd ed.) by Stephanie Etting is a collective work under a CC BY-NC-SA 3.0 License. [Includes Lower_lateral1942 by Phil Myers on Animal Diversity Web, CC BY-NC-SA 3.0; Ventral by Phil Myers on Animal Diversity Web, CC BY-NC-SA 3.0.]

Folivores

Plants rely on leaves to get energy from the sun, so plants do not want animals to eat their leaves (unlike their fruit). As a result, plants evolved to try to discourage animals from eating their leaves. Leaves often carry toxins, taste bitter, are very fibrous and difficult to chew, and are made of large cellulose molecules that are difficult to break down into usable sugars. Thus, animals who eat leaves need a lot of specialized traits (Figure 5.9). Folivorous primates have broad molars with high, sharp cusps connected by **shearing crests**. These molar traits allow folivores to physically break down fibrous leaves when chewing. Folivores then chemically break down cellulose molecules into usable energy. To do this, some folivores have complex stomachs with multiple compartments, while others have large, long intestines and special gut bacteria that can break up cellulose. Folivores are usually the largest bodied of all primates, and they tend to spend a large portion of their day digesting their food, so they are less active than frugivores or insectivores.

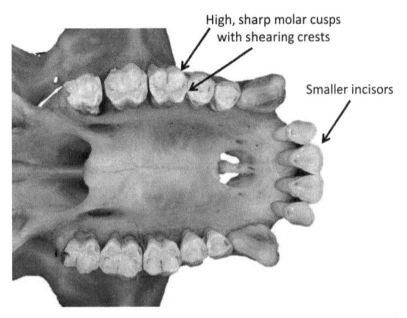

Figure 5.9: To derive energy from leaves, folivores, like this Trachypithecus (dusky leaf monkey), have smaller incisors and high sharp molar cusps connected by shearing crests. Credit: Trachypithecus obscurus (dusky leaf monkey) upper teeth by Phil Myers on Animal Diversity Web has been modified (background removed, labels added by Stephanie Etting) is under a CC BY-NC-SA 3.0 License.

Behavioral Adaptations

Since Chapter 6 is dedicated to primate behavior, we will only briefly discuss variations in activity patterns, social grouping, and habitat use. Primate groups differ in **activity patterns**: whether they are active during the day (**diurnal**), at night (**nocturnal**), or through the 24-hour period (**cathemeral**). Primate taxa vary in social groupings: some are primarily solitary, others live in pairs, and still others live in groups of varying sizes and compositions. Lastly, some taxa are primarily arboreal while others are more terrestrial.

Locomotor Adaptations

Finally, primate groups vary in their adaptations for different forms of **locomotion**, or how they move around. Living primates are known to move by vertical clinging and leaping, quadrupedalism, brachiation, and bipedalism.

Vertical clinging and leaping is when an animal grasps a vertical branch with its body upright, pushes off with long hind legs, and then lands on another vertical support branch (Figure 5.10a). Animals who move in this way usually have longer legs than arms, long fingers and toes, and smaller bodies. Vertical clinger leapers also tend to have elongated ankle bones, which serve as a lever to help them push off with their legs and leap to another branch (Figure 5.10b).

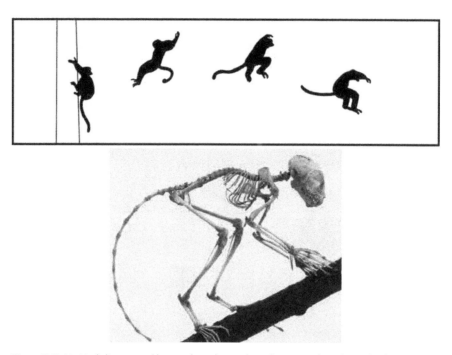

Figure 5.10: Vertical clingers and leapers have longer legs than arms, long lower backs, and long fingers and toes. They also have elongated ankle bones to help them push off when leaping. Credit: a. **Propithecus vertical clinging and leaping** by Terpsichores is under a **CC BY-SA 3.0 License**. b. **Tarsier skeleton** by Emőke Dénes has been modified (background removed) by Stephanie Etting and is under a **CC BY-SA 4.0 License**. Original Spectral tarsier (Tarsius tarsier) skeleton at the Cambridge University Museum of Zoology, England.)

Quadrupedalism, walking on all fours, is the most common form of locomotion among primates. Quadrupedal animals usually have legs and arms that are about the same length and a tail for balance. Arboreal quadrupeds (Figure 5.11a) usually have shorter arms and legs and longer tails, while terrestrial quadrupeds (Figure 5.11b) have longer arms and legs and, often, shorter tails. These differences relate to the lower center of gravity needed by arboreal quadrupeds for balance in trees and the longer tail required for better balance when moving along the tops of branches. Terrestrial quadrupeds have longer limbs to help them cover more distance more efficiently.

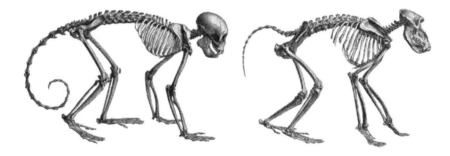

Figure 5.11: Two examples of quadrupedal primates. The capuchin monkey skeleton on the left (a) is a typical arboreal quadruped with shorter arms and legs, longer fingers and toes, and a long tail. The baboon skeleton on the right (b) is a terrestrial quadruped with relatively long arms and legs, shorter fingers and toes, and a short tail. Credit: a. **Capuchin monkey skeleton** by Henri-Marie Ducrotay de Blainville is in the **public domain**. b. **Baboon** by Henri-Marie Ducrotay de Blainville is in the **public domain**.

The third form of locomotion seen in primates is **brachiation**, the way of moving you used if you played on "monkey bars" as a child. Brachiation involves swinging below branches by the hands (Figure 5.12a). To be an efficient brachiator, a primate needs to have longer arms than legs, flexible shoulders and wrists, a short lower back, and no tail (Figure 5.12b). Some primates move via **semi-brachiation**, in which they swing below branches but do not have all of the same specializations as brachiators. Semi-brachiators have flexible shoulders, but their arms and legs are about the same length, which is useful because they are quadrupedal when on the ground. They also use long **prehensile tails** as a third limb when swinging (Figure 5.13). The underside of the tail has a tactile pad, resembling your fingerprints, for better grip.

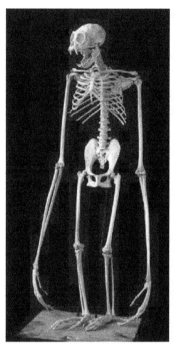

Figure 5.12: a. Example of brachiation. b. Skeleton of a typical brachiator, showing longer arms than legs, short back, and lack of a tail. Credit: a. Brachiator (Figure 5.9b) original to Explorations: An Open Invitation to Biological Anthropology by Mary Nelson is under a CC BY-NC 4.0 License. b. Skeleton of Gibbon (Giboia) by Joxerra Aihartza is under a Free Art License.

Figure 5.13. Spider monkeys are considered semi-brachiators, as they can swing below branches but use their tails as a third limb. On the ground they move via quadrupedal locomotion. Credit: Ateles-fusciceps 54724770b by LeaMaimone is under a CC BY 2.5 License.

Lastly, humans move around on two feet, called **bipedalism**. Some nonhuman primates will occasionally travel on two feet but do so awkwardly and never for long distances. Among mammals, only humans have evolved to walk with a striding gait on two legs as a primary form of locomotion.

Primate Diversity

As we begin exploring the different taxa of primates, it is important to keep in mind the hierarchical nature of taxonomic classification and how this relates to the key characteristics that will be covered. Figure 5.14 summarizes the major taxonomic groups of primates that you will learn about here. If you locate humans on the chart, you can trace our classification and see all of the categories getting more inclusive as you work your way up to the Order Primates. This means that humans will have the key traits of each of those groups. It is a good idea to refer to the figure to orient yourself as we discuss each taxon.

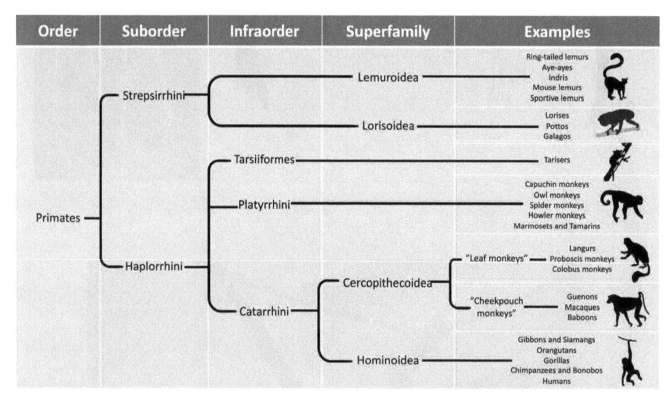

Figure 5.14: This taxonomy chart shows the major groups of primate taxa, starting with the largest category (Order) and moving to more specific categories and examples. Credit: Primate taxonomy char (Figure 5.11) original to Explorations: An Open Invitation to Biological Anthropology by Stephanie Etting is a collective work under a CC BY-NC 4.0 License. [Includes Lemur catta Linnaeus, 1759 by Roberto Díaz Sibaja, CC BY 3.0; Lorisoidea original to Explorations: An Open Invitation to Biological Anthropology by Katie Nelson, CC BY-NC 4.0; Tarsiiformes original to Explorations: An Open Invitation to Biological Anthropology by Mary Nelson, CC BY-NC 4.0; Cebinae Bonaparte, 1831 by Sarah Werning, CC BY 3.0; Colobus guereza Ruppell, 1835 by Yan Wong, designated to the public domain (CC0); Papio cynocephalus by Owen Jones, designated to the public domain (CC0); animals silhouette wolf elephant (2755766) by mohamed_hassan, Pixabay License.] [Image Description].

Suborder Strepsirrhini

Figure 5.15: (Clockwise from top right) sifaka, black-and-white ruffed lemur, loris, galago, slender loris, mouse lemur, aye-aye, and ring-tailed lemur. Credit: Extant Strepsirrhini a collective work by **Mark Dumont** is under a CC BY-SA 3.0 License. [Includes **Katta család** by Veszprémi Állatkert, CC BY-SA 3.0; Aye-aye at night in the wild in Madagascar by Frank Vassen, CC BY 2.0; Diademed ready to push off by Michael Hogan, designated to the **public domain (CC0)**; Juvenile Black-and-White Ruffed Lemur, Mantadia, Madagascar by Frank Vassen, CC BY 2.0; Microcebus murinus -Artis Zoo, Amsterdam, Netherlands-8a by Arjan Haverkamp, CC BY 2.0; Slow Loris by Jmiksanek, CC BY-SA 3.0; Slender Loris by Kalyan Varma (Kalyanvarma), CC BY-SA 4.0; Garnett's Galago (Greater Bushbaby) by Mark Dumont, CC BY 2.0.]

The Order Primates is subdivided into Suborder Strepsirrhini and Suborder Haplorrhini, which, according to molecular estimates, split about 70–80 million years ago (Pozzi et al. 2014). The strepsirrhines include the groups commonly called lemurs, lorises, and galagos (Figure 5.15). Strepsirrhines differ from haplorrhines in many ways, most of which involve retaining ancestral traits from the earliest primates. Strepsirrhines do have two key derived traits that evolved after they diverged from the haplorrhines: the **grooming claw** (Figure 5.16) on the second digit of each foot, and the **tooth comb** (or **dental comb**) located on the lower, front teeth (Figure 5.17). In most strepsirrhines, there are six teeth in the toothcomb—four incisors and two canines. Other than the tooth comb, the teeth of strepsirrhines are fairly simple and are neither large or distinctive relative to haplorrhines.

Figure 5.16: The foot of a ring-tailed lemur showing its grooming claw on the second digit. Credit: Lemur catta toilet claw by Alex Dunkel (Maky) is under a CC BY 3.0 License.

Compared to haplorrhines, strepsirrhines rely more on nonvisual senses. Strepsirrhines get their name because they have wet noses (**rhinariums**) like cats and dogs, a trait that, along with a longer snout, reflect strepsirrhines' greater reliance on olfaction relative to haplorrhines. Many strepsirrhines use **scent marking**, including rubbing scent glands or urine on objects in the environment to communicate with others. Additionally, many strepsirrhines have mobile ears that they use to locate insect prey and predators. While strepsirrhines have a better sense of smell than haplorrhines, their visual adaptations are more ancestral. Strepsirrhines have less convergent eyes than haplorrhines and therefore all have postorbital bars, whereas haplorrhines have full postorbital closure (see Figure 5.2). All strepsirrhines have a **tapetum lucidum**, a reflective layer at the back of the eye that reflects light and thereby enhances the ability to see in low-light conditions. It is the same layer that causes your dog or cat to have "yellow eye" when you take photos of them with the flash on. This is a trait thought to be ancestral among mammals as a whole.

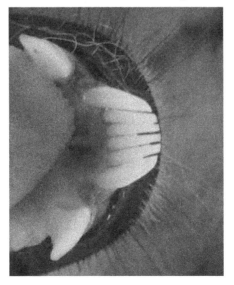

Figure 5.17: The lower front teeth of a ring-tailed lemur showing the six teeth of the tooth comb: four incisors and two canines. The teeth that superficially look like canines are premolars. Credit: Lemur catta toothcomb by Alex Dunkel (Maky) is under a CC BY 3.0 license.

Strepsirrhines also differ from haplorrhines in some aspects of their ecology and behavior. The majority of strepsirrhines are solitary, traveling alone to search for food; a few taxa are more social. Most strepsirrhines are also nocturnal and arboreal. Strepsirrhines are, on average, smaller than haplorrhines, and so many of them have a diet consisting of insects and fruit, with few taxa eating primarily leaves. Lastly, most strepsirrhines are good at leaping, with several taxa specialized for vertical clinging and leaping. In fact, among primates, all but one of the vertical clinger leapers belong to the Suborder Strepsirrhini.

Strepsirrhines can be found all across Asia, Africa, and on the island of Madagascar (Figure 5.18). The Suborder Strepsirrhini is divided into two groups: (1) the lemurs of Madagascar and (2) the lorises, pottos, and galagos of Africa and Asia. By molecular estimates, these two groups split about 65 million years ago (Pozzi et al. 2014).

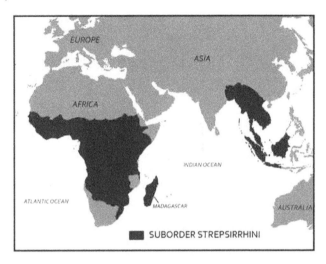

Figure 5.18: Geographic distribution of living strepsirrhines. Lemurs live only on Madagascar, while lorises and galagos live across Central Africa and South and Southeast Asia. Credit: **Geographic distribution of living strepsirrhines (Figure 5.16)** original to **Explorations: An Open Invitation to Biological Anthropology** by Elyssa Ebding at GeoPlace, California State University, Chico is under a CC BY-NC 4.0 License.

Lemurs of Madagascar

Madagascar is an island off the east coast of Africa, and it is roughly the size of California, Oregon, and Washington combined. It has been separated from Africa for about 130 million years and from India for about 85 million years, which means it was already an island when strepsirrhines got there approximately 60–70 million years ago. Only a few mammal species ever reached Madagascar, and so when lemurs arrived they were able to flourish into a variety of forms.

The lemurs of Madagascar are much more diverse compared to their mainland counterparts, the lorises and galagos. While many Malagasy strepsirrhines are nocturnal, plenty of others are diurnal or cathemeral. They range in body size from the smallest of all primates, the mouse lemur, some species of which weigh a little over an ounce (see Figure 5.15), up to the largest of all strepsirrhines, the indri, which weighs up to about 20 pounds (Figure 5.19). Lemurs include species that are insectivorous, frugivorous, and folivorous. A couple of members of this group have unusual diets for primates, including the gummivorous fork-marked and bamboo lemurs, who are able to metabolize the cyanide in bamboo. The most unique lemur is the aye-aye (depicted in Figure 5.15). This nocturnal lemur has rodent-like front teeth that grow continuously and a long-bony middle finger that it uses to fish grubs out of wood. It has a very large brain compared to other strepsirrhines, which it fuels with a diet that includes bird's eggs and other animal matter. Based on genetic estimates and morphological studies, it is believed that aye-ayes were the first lemurs to separate from all other strepsirrhines and to evolve on their own since strepsirrhines arrived in Madagascar (Matsui et al. 2009).

Figure 5.19: Indris, the largest of the lemurs. These folivorous lemurs are vertical clingers and leapers and live in pairs. Credit: Indri indri 0003 by Christophe Germain is under a CC BY-SA 4.0 License.

Lemurs are also diverse in terms of social behavior: Many lemurs are solitary foragers, some live in pairs, others in small groups, still others in larger groups, and some, like the red-ruffed lemur, live in unique and complex social groups (Vasey 2006). Lemurs include some of the best vertical clingers and leapers, and while many lemurs are quadrupedal, even the quadrupedal lemurs are quite adept at leaping. Malagasy strepsirrhines also exhibit a few unusual traits. They are highly seasonal breeders, often mating only during a short window once a year (Wright 1999). Female ring-tailed lemurs, for example, come into estrus one day a year for a mere six hours. Unlike most primates, where males are typically large and dominant, Malagasy strepsirrhines feature socially dominant females that are similar in size to males and have priority access to resources.

Lorises, Pottos, and Galagos of Asia and Africa

Figure 5.20: This slow loris, like all others in this taxonomic group, is solitary and nocturnal, with a diet heavy in insects and fruit. Credit: Nycticebus coucang 002 by David Haring / Duke Lemur Center is under a CC BY-SA 3.0 License.

Unlike the lemurs of Madagascar, lorises, pottos, and galagos live in areas where they share their environments with monkeys and apes, who often eat similar foods. Lorises live across South and Southeast Asia, while pottos and galagos live across Central Africa. Because of competition with larger-bodied monkeys and apes, mainland strepsirrhines are more restricted in the niches they can fill in their environments and so are less diverse than the lemurs.

The strepsirrhines of Africa and Asia are all nocturnal and solitary, with little variation in body size and diet. For the most part, the diet of lorises, pottos, and galagos consists of fruits and insects. A couple of species eat more gum, but overall the diet of this group is narrow when compared to the Malagasy lemurs. Lorises (Figure 5.20) and pottos are known for being slow, quadrupedal climbers, moving quietly through the forests to avoid being detected by predators. These strepsirrhines have developed additional defenses against predators. Lorises, for example, eat a lot of caterpillars, which makes their saliva slightly toxic. Loris mothers bathe their young in this toxic saliva, making the babies unappealing to predators. In comparison to the slow-moving lorises and pottos, galagos are active quadrupedal runners and leapers that scurry about the forests at night. Galagos make distinctive calls that sound like a baby crying, which has led to their nickname "bushbabies." Figure 5.21 summarizes the key differences between these two groups of strepsirrhines.

Figure 5.21: Strepsirrhini at a glance: This table summarizes the key differences between the two groups of strepsirrhines. Credit: Strepsirrhines at a glance table (Figure 5.19) original to Explorations: An Open Invitation to Biological Anthropology by Stephanie Etting is a collective work under a CC BY-NC-SA 4.0 License. [Includes Ringtailed Lemurs in Berenty by David Dennis, CC BY-SA 2.0; Komba ušatá by Petr Hamerník, CC BY-SA 4.0.]

	 Lemurs	 Lorises, Pottos, and Galagos
Geographic range	Madagascar	South and Southeast Asia Central Africa
Activity patterns	Diurnal, nocturnal, or cathemeral	Nocturnal
Dietary types	Insectivore, frugivore, or folivore	Insectivore, frugivore
Social groupings	Solitary, pairs, or small to large groups	Solitary
Forms of locomotion	Vertical clinger leapers, quadrupedal	Slow quadrupedal climbers and active quadrupedal runners

Suborder Haplorrhini

When the two primate suborders split from one another, strepsirrhines retained more ancestral traits while haplorrhines developed more derived traits, which are discussed below.

As mentioned earlier, haplorrhines have better vision than strepsirrhines. This is demonstrated by the full postorbital closure protecting the more convergent eyes that haplorrhines possess (with one exception seen in Figure 5.2). Most haplorrhines are trichromatic, and all have a **fovea**, a depression in the retina at the back of the eye containing concentrations of cells that allows them to see things very close up in great detail. The heavier reliance on vision over olfaction is also reflected in the shorter snouts ending with the **dry nose** (no rhinarium) of haplorrhines. All but two genera of living haplorrhines are active during the day, so this group lacks the tapetum lucidum that is so useful to nocturnal species. On average, haplorrhines also have larger brains relative to their body size when compared with strepsirrhines.

The Haplorrhini differ from the Strepsirrhini in their ecology and behavior as well. Haplorrhines are generally larger than strepsirrhines, and they tend to be folivorous and frugivorous. This dietary difference is reflected in the teeth of haplorrhines, which are broader with more surface area for chewing. The larger body size of this taxon also influences locomotion. Only one haplorrhine is a vertical clinger and leaper. Most members of this suborder are quadrupedal, with one subgroup specialized for brachiation. A few haplorrhine taxa are **monomorphic**, meaning males and females are the same size, but many members of this group show moderate to high sexual dimorphism in body size and canine size. Haplorrhines also differ in social behavior. All but two haplorrhines live in groups, which is very different from the primarily solitary strepsirrhines. Differences between the two suborders are summarized in Figure 5.22.

Figure 5.22: Suborders at a glance: This table summarizes the key differences between the two primate suborders. Credit: Suborders at a glance table (Figure 5.20) original to Explorations: An Open Invitation to Biological Anthropology by Stephanie Etting is a collective work under a CC BY-NC-SA 4.0 License. [Includes Black-and-White Ruffed Lemur, Mantadia, Madagascar by Frank Vassen, CC BY 2.0; Crab eating macaque face by Bruce89, CC BY-SA 4.0.]

	 Suborder Strepsirrhini	 Suborder Haplorrhini
Sensory adaptations	Rhinarium Longer snout Eyes less convergent Postorbital bar Tapetum lucidum Mobile ears	No rhinarium Short snout Eyes more convergent Postorbital plate No tapetum lucidum Many are trichromatic Fovea
Dietary differences	Mostly insectivores and frugivores, few folivores	Few insectivores, mostly frugivores and folivores
Activity patterns and Ecology	Mostly nocturnal, few diurnal or cathemeral Almost entirely arboreal	Only two are nocturnal, rest are diurnal Many arboreal taxa, also many terrestrial taxa
Social groupings	Mostly solitary, some pairs, small to large groups	Only two are solitary, all others live in pairs, small to very large groups
Sexual dimorphism	Minimal to none	Few taxa have little/none, many taxa show moderate to high dimorphism

Suborder Haplorrhini is divided into three infraorders: Tarsiiformes, which includes the tarsiers of Asia; Platyrrhini, which includes the monkeys of Central and South America; and Catarrhini, a group that includes the monkeys of Asia and Africa, apes, and humans. According to molecular estimates, tarsiers split from the other haplorrhines close to 70 million years ago, and platyrrhines split from catarrhines close to 46 million years ago (Pozzi et al. 2014).

Infraorder Tarsiiformes of Asia

Figure 5.23: Tarsiers are the only living representatives of this Infraorder. Credit: Tarsier Sanctuary, Corella, Bohol (2052878890) by yeowatzup is under a CC BY 2.0 License.

Today, the Infraorder Tarsiiformes includes only one genus, *Tarsius* (Figure 5.23). Tarsiers are small-bodied primates that live in Southeast Asian forests (Figure 5.24) and possess an unusual collection of traits that have led to some debate about their position in the primate taxonomy. They are widely considered members of the haplorrhine group because they share several derived traits with monkeys, apes, and humans, including dry noses, a fovea, not having a tapetum lucidum, and eyes that are more convergent. Tarsiers also have some traits that are more like strepsirrhines and some that are unique. Tarsiers are the only haplorrhine that are specialized vertical clinger leapers, a form of locomotion only otherwise seen in some strepsirrhines. Tarsiers actually get their name because their ankle (tarsal) bones are elongated to provide a lever for vertical clinging and leaping. Tarsiiformes are also small, with most species weighing between 100 and 150 grams. Like strepsirrhines, tarsiers are nocturnal, but because they lack a tapetum lucidum, tarsiers compensate by having enormous eyes. In fact, each eye of a tarsier is larger than its brain. These large eyes allow enough light in for tarsiers to still be able to see well at night without the reflecting layer in their eyes. To protect their large eyes, tarsiers have a partially closed postorbital plate that appears somewhat intermediate

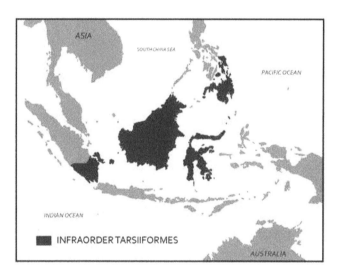

Figure 5.24: Tarsiiformes are found in the tropical forests of multiple islands in Southeast Asia including Sumatra, Borneo, Celebes, and the Philippines. Credit: Infraorder Tarsiiformes of Asia map (Figure 5.22) original to Explorations: An Open Invitation to Biological Anthropology by Elyssa Ebding at GeoPlace, California State University, Chico is under a CC BY-NC 4.0 License.

between the postorbital bar of strepsirrhines and the full postorbital closure of other haplorrhines (Figure 5.25). Tarsiers have different dental formulas on their upper and lower teeth. On the top, the dental formula is 2:1:3:3, but on the bottom it is 1:1:3:3. Other unusual traits of tarsiers include having two grooming claws on each foot and the ability to rotate their heads around 180 degrees, a trait useful in locating insect prey. The tarsier diet is considered **faunivorous** because it consists entirely of animal matter, making them the only primate not to eat any vegetation. They are only one of two living haplorrhines to be solitary, the other being the orangutan. Most tarsiers are not sexually dimorphic, like strepsirrhines, although males of a few species are slightly larger than females.

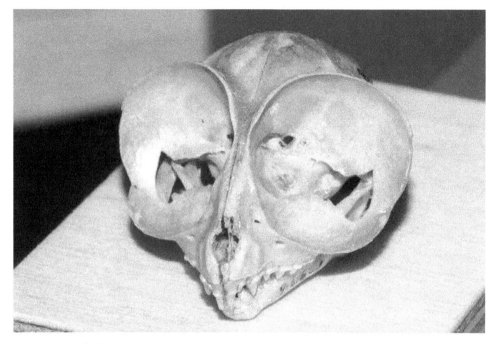

Figure 5.25: Skull of a tarsier showing very large eye sockets and partially closed postorbital plates. Credit: Tarsier skull by Andrew Bardwell is under a CC BY-SA 2.0 License.

Two alternative classifications have emerged due to the unusual mix of traits that tarsiers have. Historically, tarsiers were grouped with lemurs, lorises, and galagos into a suborder called Prosimii. This classification was based on tarsiers, lemurs, lorises, and galagos all having grooming claws and similar lifestyles. Monkeys, apes, and humans were then separated into a suborder called the Anthropoidea. These suborder groupings were based on *grade* rather than *clade*. Today, most people use Suborders Strepsirrhini and Haplorrhini, which are clade groupings based on the derived traits that tarsiers share with monkeys, apes, and humans. The Strepsirrhini/Haplorrhini dichotomy is also supported by the genetic evidence that indicates tarsiers are more closely related to monkeys, apes, and humans (Jameson et al. 2011). Figure 5.26 summarizes the unusual mix of traits seen in tarsiers.

Figure 5.26: Tarsiers at a glance: Tarsiers have a mix of traits that lead to debate about their classification. While they have some unique characteristics, they also have traits that superficially resemble strepsirrhines, and many derived traits shared with haplorrhines. Credit: Tarsiers at a glance table (Figure 5.24) original to Explorations: An Open Invitation to Biological Anthropology by Stephanie Etting is under a CC BY-NC 4.0 License.

Like Strepsirrhini	Unique	Like Haplorrhini
Very small		Almost full PO closure
Nocturnal	Two grooming claws	More convergent eyes
Highly insectivorous	2:1:3:3/1:1:3:3 dental formula	No tapetum lucidum
Solitary	Do not eat vegetation	No rhinarium
Vertical clinger-leapers	Can rotate their heads nearly 180 degrees	Genetic evidence
Little/no sexual dimorphism		Fovea

Infraorder Platyrrhini of Central and South America

Figure 5.27: Geographic distribution of the platyrrhines across the southern part of Central America and the tropical and termporate regions of South America. Credit: Infraorder Platyrrhini map original to Explorations: An Open Invitation to Biological Anthropology by Elyssa Ebding at GeoPlace, California State University, Chico is under a CC BY-NC 4.0 License.

The platyrrhines are the only nonhuman primates in Central and South America (Figure 5.27) and so, like the lemurs of Madagascar, have diversified into a variety of forms in the absence of competition. Infraorder Platyrrhini get their name from their distinctive nose shape. "Platy" means flat and "rhini" refers to noses, and, indeed, platyrrhines have noses that are flat and wide, with nostrils that are far apart, facing outward, and usually round in shape (Figure 5.28). This nose shape is very different from what we see in catarrhines.

On average, platyrrhines are smaller and less sexually dimorphic than catarrhines, and they have retained the more ancestral primate dental formula of 2:1:3:3. Platyrrhines are all highly arboreal, whereas many catarrhines spend significant time on the ground. The monkeys in Central and South America also differ in having less well-developed vision. This is reflected in the wiring in the visual system of the brain as well as in their **polymorphic color vision**. The genes that enable individuals to distinguish reds and yellows from blues and greens are on the X chromosome. Different genes code for being able to see different wavelengths of light so to distinguish between them you need to be heterozygous for seeing color. The X chromosomes of platyrrhines each carry the genes for seeing one wavelength, so male platyrrhines (with only one X chromosome) are always dichromatic. Female platyrrhines can be dichromatic (if they are homozygous for one version of the color vision gene) or trichromatic (if they are heterozygous) (Kawamura et al.

2012). We currently know of two exceptions to this pattern among platyrrhines. Nocturnal owl monkeys are **monochromatic**, meaning that they cannot distinguish any colors. The other exception are howler monkeys, which have evolved to have two color vision genes on each X chromosome. This means that both male and female howler monkeys are able to see reds and yellows. By contrast, catarrhine males and females are all trichromatic.

Platyrrhines include the smallest of the monkeys, the marmosets and tamarins (Figure 5.29), all of which weigh less than one kilogram and live in cooperative family groups, wherein usually only one female reproduces and everyone else helps carry and raise the offspring. They are unusual primates in that they regularly produce twins. Marmosets and tamarins largely eat gums and saps, so these monkeys have evolved claw-like nails that enable them to cling to the sides of tree trunks like squirrels as well as special teeth that allow them to gnaw through bark. Except for the Goeldi's monkey, these small monkeys have one fewer molar than other platyrrhines, giving them a dental formula of 2:1:3:2.

Figure 5.28: A capuchin monkey demonstrating a typical platyrrhine nose shape with round nostrils pointing outward on a flat nose. Credit: CARABLANCA – panoramio by Manuel Velazquez is under a CC BY 3.0 License.

Figure 5.29: Clockwise from top right: golden-headed lion tamarin, pygmy marmoset, Goeldi's monkey, bare-eared marmoset, emperor tamarin, and common marmoset. Credit: Callitrichinae genus by Miguelrangeljr is a collective work under a CC BY-SA 3.0 License. [Includes Weißbüschelaffe_(Callithrix_jacchus) by Raymond, CC BY-SA 4.0; Leontopithecus chrysomelas (portrait) by Hans Hillewaert, CC BY-SA 4.0; Emperor_Tamarin_portrait_2_edit1 by Brocken Inaglory, CC BY-SA 4.0; Dværgsilkeabe_Callithrix_pygmaea by Malene Thyssen (User Malene), GNU Free Documentation License; Mico_argentatus_(portrait) by Hans Hillewaert, CC BY-SA 4.0; Titi Monkey by Jeff Kubina, CC BY-SA 2.0].]

The largest platyrrhines are a family that include spider monkeys, woolly spider monkeys, woolly monkeys, and howler monkeys (Figure 5.30). These monkeys can weigh up to 9–15 kg and have evolved prehensile tails that can hold their entire body weight. It is among this group that we see semi-brachiators, like the spider monkey (see Figure 5.13). To make them more efficient in this form of locomotion, spider monkeys evolved to not have thumbs so that their hands work more like hooks that can easily let go of branches while swinging. Howler monkeys are another well-known member of this group, earning their name due to their loud calls, which can be heard miles away. To make these loud vocalizations, howler monkeys have a specialized vocal system that includes a large larynx and hyoid bone. Howler monkeys are the most folivorous of the platyrrhines and are known for spending a large portion of their day digesting their food.

Figure 5.30: Clockwise from top right: howler monkey, woolly monkey, woolly spider monkey, and spider monkey. Credit: Atelidae Family by Miguelrangeljr is a collective work under a CC BY-SA 3.0 License. [Includes Ateles marginatus (Sao Paulo zoo) by Miguelrangeljr, CC BY-SA 3.0; Alouatta caraya male by Miguelrangeljr, CC BY-SA 3.0; Lagothrix lagotricha (walking) by Hans Hillewaert, CC BY-SA 3.0; Brachyteles hypoxanthus2 by Paulo B. Chaves, CC BY 2.0.]

There are many other monkeys in Central and South America, including the gregarious capuchins (see Figure 5.28) and squirrel monkeys, the pair-living titi monkeys, and the nocturnal owl monkeys. There are also the seed-eating saki monkeys and uakaris. In many areas across Central and South America, multiple species of platyrrhines share the forests, with some even traveling together in association. According to molecular evidence, the diversity of platyrrhines that we see today seems to have originated about 25 million years ago (Schneider and Sampaio 2015). Figure 5.31 summarizes the key traits of platyrrhines relative to the other infraorders of Haplorrhini.

Figure 5.31: Platyrrhini at a glance: Summary of the key traits we use to distinguish platyrrhines. Traits indicated with an * are those with exceptions detailed in the text. Credit: Platyrrhini at a glance table (Figure 5.29) original to Explorations: An Open Invitation to Biological Anthropology by Stephanie Etting is under a CC BY-NC 4.0 License.

Platyrrhini traits
Flat nose with rounded nostrils pointing to the side
Highly arboreal
Less sexually dimorphic on average
2:1:3:3 dental formula*
Polymorphic color vision*

Infraorder Catarrhini of Asia and Africa

Infraorder Catarrhini includes Superfamily Cercopithecoidea (the monkeys of Africa and Asia) and Superfamily Hominoidea (apes and humans). Nonhuman catarrhines are found all over Africa and South and Southeast Asia, with some being found as far north as Japan. The most northerly and southerly catarrhines are cercopithecoid monkeys. In contrast, apes are less tolerant of drier, more seasonal environments and so have a relatively restricted geographic range.

Relative to other haplorrhine infraorders, catarrhines are distinguished by several characteristics. Catarrhines have a distinctive nose shape, with teardrop-shaped nostrils that are close together and point downward (Figure 5.32) and one fewer premolar than most other primates, giving us a dental formula of 2:1:2:3 (Figure 5.33). On average, catarrhines are the largest and most sexually dimorphic of all primates. Gorillas are the largest living primates, with males weighing up to 220 kg. The most sexually dimorphic of all primates are mandrills. Mandrill males not only have much more vibrant coloration than mandrill females but also have larger canines and can weigh up to three times more (Setchell et al. 2001). The larger body size of catarrhines is related to the more terrestrial lifestyle of many members of this infraorder. In fact, the most terrestrial of living primates can be found in this group. Among all primates, vision is the most developed in catarrhines. Catarrhines independently evolved the same adaptation as howler monkeys in having each X chromosome with genes to distinguish both reds and yellows, so all male and female catarrhines are trichromatic, which is useful for these diurnal primates.

Figure 5.32: A Wolf's guenon demonstrating a typical catarrhine nose with teardrop-shaped nostrils close together and pointed downward. Credit: Wolf's Guenon Picking Up Food (19095137693) by Eric Kilby is under a CC BY-SA 2.0 License.

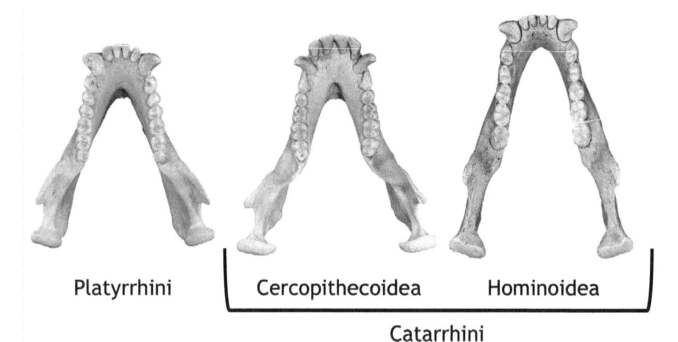

Platyrrhini   Cercopithecoidea   Hominoidea

Catarrhini

Figure 5.33: Catarrhines have two premolars whereas most other primate taxa (including platyrrhini) have three premolars. This image also shows one of the derived traits of cercopithecoids, their bilophodont molars, which differ from the more ancestral Y-5 molars of apes and humans. Credit: Platyrrhini vs. Catarrhini dentition original to Explorations: An Open Invitation to Biological Anthropology by Stephanie Etting is a collective work under a CC BY-NC-SA 4.0 License. [Includes Cebus apella (brown capuchin) at Animal Diversity Web by Phil Myers, CC BY-NC-SA 3.0; Lophocebus albigena (gray-cheeked mangaby) at Animal Diversity Web by Phil Myers, CC BY-NC-SA 3.0; Symphalangus syndactylus (siamang) at Animal Diversity Web by Phil Myers, CC BY-NC-SA 3.0.]

The two superfamilies of catarrhines—Superfamily Cercopithecoidea, the monkeys of Africa and Asia, and Superfamily Hominoidea, which includes apes and humans—are believed to have split about 32 million years ago based on molecular evidence (Pozzi et al. 2014). This fits with the fossil record, which shows evidence of these lineages by about 25 million years ago (see Chapter 8).

Superfamily Cercopithecoidea of Africa and Asia

Figure 5.34: The second derived trait of cercopithecoids are their ischial callosities, shown here on a crested black macaque. Credit: Sulawesi trsr DSCN0572 v1 by T. R. Shankar Ramanis is under a CC BY-SA 3.0 License.

Compared to hominoids, cercopithecoids have an ancestral quadrupedal body plan with two key derived traits. The first derived trait of cercopithecoids is their **bilophodont** molars ("bi" meaning two, "loph" referring to ridge, and "dont" meaning tooth). If you refer back to Figure 5.33, you will see how the molars of cercopithecoids have four cusps arranged in a square pattern and have two ridges connecting them. It is thought that this molar enabled these monkeys to eat a wide range of foods, thus allowing them to live in habitats that apes cannot. The other key derived trait that all cercopithecoids share is having **ischial callosities** (Figure 5.34). The ischium is the part of your pelvis that you are sitting on right now (see Appendix A: Osteology). In cercopithecoids, this part of the pelvis has a flattened surface that, in living animals, has callused skin over it. These function as seat pads for cercopithecoids, who often sit above branches when feeding and resting.

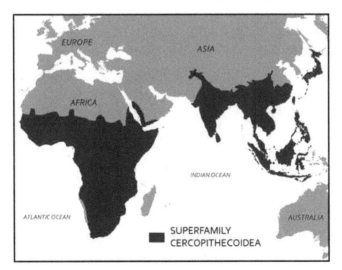

Figure 5.35: Geographic distribution of the cercopithecoid monkeys. Catarrhines have the widest geographic distribution due to the success of cercopithecoids who are found all across subsaharan Africa and southern Asia. Credit: Superfamily Cercopithecoidea map (Figure 5.33) original to Explorations: An Open Invitation to Biological Anthropology by Elyssa Ebding at GeoPlace, California State University, Chico is under a CC BY-NC 4.0 License.

Cercopithecoid monkeys are the most geographically widespread group of nonhuman primates (Figure 5.35). Since their divergence from hominoids, this monkey group has increased in numbers and diversity due, in part, to their fast reproductive rates. On average, cercopithecoids will reproduce every one to two years, whereas hominoids will reproduce once every four to nine years, depending on the taxon.

Cercopithecoidea is split into two groups, the leaf monkeys and the cheek-pouch monkeys. Both groups coexist in Asia and Africa; however, the majority of leaf monkey species live in Asia with only a few taxa in Africa. In contrast, only one genus of cheek-pouch monkey lives in Asia, and all the rest of them in Africa. As you can probably guess based on their names, the two groups differ in terms of diet. Leaf monkeys are primarily folivores, with some species eating a significant amount of seeds. Cheek-pouch monkeys tend to be more frugivorous or omnivorous, with one taxon, geladas, eating primarily grasses. The two groups also differ in some other interesting ways. Leaf monkeys tend to produce infants with **natal coats**—infants whose fur is a completely different color from their parents (Figure 5.36). Leaf monkeys are also known for having odd noses (Figure 5.37), and so they are sometimes called "odd-nosed monkeys." Cheek-pouch monkeys are able to pack food into their cheek pouches (Figure 5.38), thus allowing them to move to a location safe from predators or aggressive individuals of their own species where they can eat in peace.

Figure 5.36: Silver leaf monkey infants are born with orange fur, dramatically contrasting the adult coat color of their mothers. After a few months, the infants gradually change color to that of their parents. Credit: Silverleaf Monkey (Kuala Lumpur) by Andrea Lai from Auckland, New Zealand, is under a CC BY 2.0 License.

Figure 5.37: Proboscis monkeys are one of several "odd-nosed" leaf monkeys. Male proboscis monkeys, like this one, have large, pendulous noses, while females have much smaller noses. Credit: Proboscis monkey (Nasalis larvatus) male head by Charles J Sharp creator QS:P170,Q54800218 is under a CC BY-SA 4.0 License.

Figure 5.38: This bonnet macaque has filled its cheek pouches with food, an adaptation that is useful in transporting food to a safer location to eat. Credit: Bonnet macaque DSC 0893 by T. R. Shankar Raman is under a CC BY-SA 4.0 License.

Superfamily Hominoidea of Africa and Asia

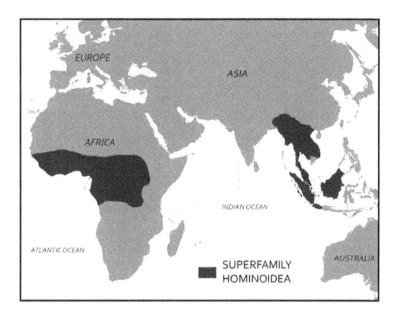

Figure 5.39: Geographic distribution of apes across Central and West Africa and Southeast Asia. Hominoids overlap geographically with cercopithecoid monkeys but have a lower tolerance for seasonal environments and so are found only in tropical forests across these regions. Credit: Superfamily Hominoidea map (Figure 5.38) original to Explorations: An Open Invitation to Biological Anthropology by Elyssa Ebding at GeoPlace, California State University, Chico is under a CC BY-NC 4.0 License.

Superfamily Hominoidea of Africa and Asia (Figure 5.39) includes the largest of the living primates: apes and humans. Whereas cercopithecoid monkeys have bilophodont molars, hominoids have the more ancestral **Y-5 molars**, which feature five cusps separated by a "Y"-shaped groove pattern (see Figure 5.33). The Y-5 molar was present in the common ancestors of hominoids and cercopithecoids, thus it is the more ancestral molar pattern of the two. Hominoids differ the most from other primates in our body plans, due to the unique form of locomotion that hominoids are adapted for: brachiation (Figure 5.40).

To successfully swing below branches, many changes to the body needed to occur. Hominoid arms are much longer than the legs to increase reach, and the lower back is shorter and less flexible to increase control when swinging. The torso, shoulders, and arms of hominoids have evolved to increase range of motion and flexibility (see again Figure 5.12). The clavicle, or collar bone, is longer to stabilize the shoulder joint out to the side, thus enabling us to rotate our arms 360 degrees. Hominoid rib cages are wider side to side and shallower front to back than those of cercopithecoids and we do not have tails, as tails are useful for balance when running on all fours but generally not useful while swinging. Hominoids also have modified ulnae, one of the two bones in the forearm (see Appendix A: Osteology). At the elbow end of the ulna, hominoids have a short **olecranon process**, which allows for improved extension in our arms. At the wrist end of the ulna, hominoids have a short **styloid process**, which enables us to have very flexible wrists, a trait critical for swinging. Both the olecranon process and styloid process are long in quadrupedal animals who carry much of their weight on their forelimbs when traveling and who therefore need greater stability rather than flexibility in those joints.

Figure 5.40: Quadrupedalism vs. brachiation: Summary of the key anatomical differences between a quadrupedal primate and one adapted for brachiation. To view these traits using photos of bones, check out the interactive skeletal websites in "Further Explorations" below. Credit: Quadrupedalism vs. Brachiation table (Figure 5.39) original to Explorations: An Open Invitation to Biological Anthropology by Stephanie Etting is under a CC BY-NC 4.0 License.

	Quadrupedalism	Brachiation
Arm length vs. leg length	About equal	Arms are longer
Shoulder position	More on the front	Out to the side
Ribcage shape	Deep front-to-back Narrow side-to-side	Shallow front-to-back Wide side-to-side
Length of lower back	Long	Short
Collar bone length	Short	Long
Ulnar olecranon process	Long	Short
Ulnar styloid process	Long	Short
Tail	Short to long	None

Apes and humans also differ from other primates in behavior and life history characteristics. Hominoids all seem to show some degree of female dispersal at sexual maturity but, as you will learn in Chapter 6, it is more common that males leave. Some apes show males dispersing in addition to females, but the hominoid tendency for female dispersal is a bit unusual among primates. Our superfamily is also characterized by the most extended life histories of all primates. All members of this group take a long time to grow and reproduce much less frequently compared to cercopithecoids. The slow pace of this life history is likely related to why hominoids have decreased in diversity since they first evolved. Figure 5.41 summarizes the key traits of Infraorder Catarrhini and its two superfamilies. Today, there are only five types of hominoids left: gibbons and siamangs, orangutans, gorillas, chimpanzees and bonobos, and humans.

Figure 5.41a: Catarrhini at a glance: Summary of key traits of the Infraorder Catarrhini. Credit: Catarrhini at a glance (Figure 5.40) original to Explorations: An Open Invitation to Biological Anthropology by Stephanie Etting is a collective work under a CC BY-NC 4.0 License. [Includes Duskyleafmonkey1 by Robertpollai, CC BY 3.0 AT; Male Bornean Orangutan – Big Cheeks by Eric Kilby, CC BY-SA 2.0.]

Infraorder Catarrhini
Downward facing, tear-drop shaped nostrils, close together
Arboreal and more terrestrial taxa
On average, largest primates
On average, most sexually dimorphic taxonomic group
2:1:2:3 dental formula
All trichromatic

Figure 5.41b: Characteristics used to distinguish between the two Catarrhini superfamilies. Credit: Catarrhini at a glance (Figure 5.40) original to *Explorations: An Open Invitation to Biological Anthropology* by Stephanie Etting is a collective work under a CC BY-NC 4.0 License. [Includes Duskyleafmonkey1 by Robertpollai, CC BY 3.0 AT; Male Bornean Orangutan – Big Cheeks by Eric Kilby, CC BY-SA 2.0.]

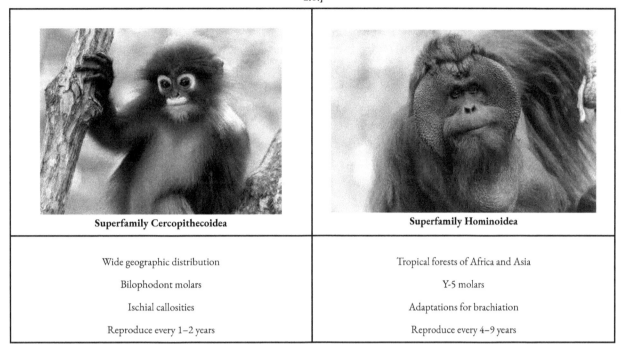

Superfamily Cercopithecoidea	Superfamily Hominoidea
Wide geographic distribution	Tropical forests of Africa and Asia
Bilophodont molars	Y-5 molars
Ischial callosities	Adaptations for brachiation
Reproduce every 1–2 years	Reproduce every 4–9 years

Family Hylobatidae *of Southeast Asia*

The number of genera in this group has been changing in recent years, but the taxa broadly encompasses gibbons and siamangs. Both are found across Southeast Asian tropical forests. Gibbons weigh, on average, about 13 pounds and tend to be more frugivorous, whereas siamangs are larger than gibbons and also more folivorous. Unlike the larger-bodied apes (orangutans, chimps, bonobos, and gorillas) who make nests to sleep in every night, gibbons and siamangs will develop callused patches on their ischium resembling ischial callosities. Gibbon species are quite variable in their coloration and markings, while siamangs are all black with big throat sacs that are used in their exuberant vocalizations (Figure 5.42). Both gibbons and siamangs live in pairs with very little sexual dimorphism, although males and females do differ in coloration in some gibbon species.

Figure 5.42: Siamangs are the largest of the Hylobatidae family. They are all black with a throat sac that can become inflated to give out loud calls. Credit: Shout (373310729) by su neko is under a CC BY-SA 2.0 License.

Pongo *of Southeast Asia*

The Genus *Pongo* refers to orangutans. These large red apes are found in Southeast Asia, with the two well-known species each living on the islands of Borneo and Sumatra. A third, very rare species, was recently discovered in Southern Sumatra (Nater et al. 2017). Orangutans are highly frugivorous but will supplement their diet with leaves and bark when fruit is less available. As mentioned earlier, orangutans are the only diurnal, solitary taxon among primates and are extremely slow to reproduce, producing only one offspring about every seven to nine years. They are highly sexually dimorphic (Figure 5.43 a and b), with fully developed, "flanged" males being approximately twice the size of females. These males have large throat sacs; long, shaggy coats; and cheek flanges. The skulls of male orangutans often feature a **sagittal crest**, which is believed to function as additional attachment area for chewing muscles as well as a trait used in sexual competition (Balolia, Soligo, and Wood 2017). An unusual feature of orangutan biology is **male bimaturism**. Male orangutans are known to delay maturation until one of the more dominant, flanged males disappears. The males that delay maturation are called "unflanged" males, and they can remain in this state for their entire life. Unflanged males resemble females in their size and appearance and will sneak copulations with females while avoiding the bigger, flanged males. Flanged and unflanged male orangutans represent alternative reproductive strategies, both of which successfully produce offspring (Utami et al. 2002).

Figure 5.43: (a) A female orangutan eating fruit with her infant nearby and (b) a flanged adult male eating leaves. Male orangutans are about twice the size of females and have a longer coat length, cheek flanges, and throat sac. Credit: a. Orang Utan (Pongo pygmaeus) female with baby (8066259067) by Bernard DUPONT is under a CC BY-SA 2.0 Licence. b. Orangutan -Zoologischer Garten Berlin-8a by David Forsman is under a CC BY 2.0 License.

Gorilla *of Africa*

There are several species of gorillas that can be found across Central Africa. Gorilla males, like orangutan males, are about twice the size of female gorillas (Figure 5.44a and b). When on the ground, gorillas use a form of quadrupedalism called **knuckle-walking**, wherein the fingers are curled under and the weight is carried on the knuckles. Male gorillas have a large sagittal crest and large canines compared with females. Adult male gorillas are often called "silverbacks" because when they reach about twelve to thirteen years old, the hair on their backs turns silvery gray. Gorillas typically live in groups of one male and several females. Gorillas are considered folivorous, although some species can be more frugivorous depending on fruit seasonality (Remis 1997).

Figure 5.44: (a) A female gorilla with her two offspring and (b) a silverback adult male. Male gorillas are about twice the size of females. They also differ from females in having a large sagittal crest and a silver back, which appears as they mature. Credit: a. **Enzo naomi echo** by Zoostar is under a **CC BY 3.0 License**. b. **Male gorilla in SF zoo** by Brocken Inaglory is under a **CC BY-SA 3.0 License**.

Pan *of Africa*

Figure 5.45: Bonobo (Pan paniscus). You can see the distinctive hair-part on this bonobo. Credit: **Bonobo male Jasongo 15yo Twycross 582a (2014 11 14 01 04 18 UTC)** by William H. Calvin is under a **CC BY-SA 4.0 License**.

The Genus *Pan* includes two species: *Pan troglodytes* (the common chimpanzee) and *Pan paniscus* (the bonobo). These species are separated by the Congo River, with chimpanzees ranging across West and Central Africa and bonobos located in a restricted area south of the Congo River. Chimpanzees and bonobos both have broad, largely frugivorous diets. The two species differ morphologically in that bonobos are slightly smaller, have their hair parted down the middle of their foreheads, and are born with dark faces (Figure 5.45). In contrast, chimpanzees do not have the distinctive parted hair and are born with light faces that darken as they mature (Figure 5.46). Chimpanzees and bonobos live in a grouping called a fission-fusion community, which you will learn more about in Chapter 6. Both species are moderately sexually dimorphic, with males about 20% larger than females. When on the ground, chimpanzees and bonobos knuckle-walk like gorillas do.

Figure 5.46: A common chimpanzee (Pan troglodytes) female (center) and her offspring. Note the pink face of the youngest individual. Bonobos are born with dark-skinned faces, but chimpanzees are born with pink faces that darken with age. Credit: Chimpanzees in Uganda (5984913059) by USAID Africa Bureau uploaded by Elitre is in the public domain.

Homo

The last member of the Hominoidea to discuss is our own taxon, Genus *Homo*. Later chapters will discuss the many extinct species of *Homo*, but today there is only one living species of *Homo*, our own species, *sapiens*. While it is interesting to focus on how humans differ from apes in many aspects of our morphology, behavior, and life history, one objective of this chapter, and of biological anthropology in general, is to understand our place in nature. This means looking for aspects of human biology that link us to the taxonomic diversity we have discussed. To that end, here we will focus on similarities humans share with other hominoids.

Like other hominoids, humans lack a tail and possess upper-body adaptations for brachiation. While our lower body has been modified for a bipedal gait, we are still able to swing from branches and throw a baseball, all thanks to our mobile shoulder joint. Humans, like other hominoids, also have a Y-5 cusp pattern on our molars. All hominoids, including humans, have an extended life history, taking time to grow and develop, and reproducing slowly over a long life span. Lastly, while humans show a great deal of variation across cultures, many human societies show tendencies for female dispersal (Burton et al. 1996).

Among the hominoids, humans show particular affinities with other members of the African Clade, *Pan* and *Gorilla*. Humans share over 96% of our DNA with gorillas (Scally et al. 2012), and over 98% with *Pan* (Ebersberger et al. 2002). Even without this strong genetic evidence, the African Clade of hominoids share many morphological similarities, including having wide-set eye sockets and backward-sweeping cheekbones. Today, *Pan* and *Gorilla* knuckle-walk when on the ground, and it has been suggested the last common ancestor of chimpanzees, bonobos, gorillas, and humans did as well (Richmond, Begun, and Strait 2001). Further, humans, chimpanzees, and bonobos all live in fission-fusion social groups characterized by shared behaviors, like male cooperation in hunting and territoriality, as well as tool use.

Special Topic: Primates in Culture and Religion

One of the best parts of teaching anthropology for me is getting to spend time watching primates at zoos. What I also find interesting is watching people watch primates. I have very often heard a parent and child walk up to a chimpanzee enclosure and exclaim "Look at the monkeys!" The parent and child often don't know that a chimpanzee is not a monkey, nor are they likely to know that chimpanzees share more than 98% of their DNA with us. What strikes me as significant is that, although most people do not know the difference between a monkey, an ape, and a lemur, they nonetheless recognize something in the animals as being similar to themselves. In fact, recognition of similarities between humans and other primates is very ancient, dating back far earlier than Linnaeus. For many of us, we only ever get to see primates in zoos and animal parks, but in many areas of the world, humans have coexisted with these animals for thousands of years. In areas where humans and primates have a long, shared history, nonhuman primates often play key roles in creation myths and cultural symbolism.

Hamadryas baboons feature significantly in Ancient Egyptian iconography. Ancient Egyptian deities and beliefs transformed over time, as did the role of hamadryas baboons. Early on, baboons were thought to represent dead ancestors, and one monkey deity, called Babi or Baba, was thought to feed off of dead souls. Later, baboons became the totem animal for Thoth, the deity of science, writing, wisdom, and measurement, who also wrote the Book of the Dead. Sunbathing hamadryas baboons led ancient Egyptians to associate them with Ra, the sun god, who was the son of Thoth. During mummification, human organs were removed and put into canopic jars, one of which was topped with the head of the baboon-headed god, Hapi. Hamadryas baboons were also often kept as pets, as depicted in hieroglyphics, and occasionally mummified as well.

On Madagascar, indris and aye-ayes play roles in the creation myths and omens of local people.There are many myths regarding the origins of indris and their relationship to humans, including one where two brothers living in the forest separated, with one brother leaving the forest and becoming a human while the other stayed in the forest to become the indri. Like humans, indris have long legs, no tail, and upright posture. They are considered sacred and are therefore protected. Unfortunately, the aye-aye is not treated with the same reverence. Because of their unusual appearance (see Figure 5.15), aye-ayes are seen as omens of death.They are usually killed when encountered because it is believed that someone will die if an aye-aye points at them.

In India, monkeys play a key role in the Hindu religion. Hanuman, who resembles a monkey, is a key figure in the Ramayana. Hanuman is thought to be a guardian deity, and so local monkeys like Hanuman langurs and macaques are protected in India (Figure 5.47). In Thailand, where Hinduism is also practiced, the Hindu reverence for monkeys extends to "monkey feasts," where large quantities of food are spread out in gratitude to the monkeys for bringing good fortune.

Figure 5.47: Because of important monkey-like figures in the Hindu religion, macaques are protected in India and often live near temples where they are fed by local peoples. Credit: Macaque India 4 by Thomas Schoch (Mosmas) is under a CC BY-SA 3.0 License.

The people of Japan have coexisted with Japanese macaques for thousands of years, and so monkeys play key roles in both of the major Japanese religions. In the Shinto religion, macaques are thought of as messengers between the spirit world and humans, and monkey symbols are thought to be good luck. The other major religion in Japan is Buddhism, and monkeys play a role in symbolism of this religion as well. The "Three Wise Monkeys" who see no evil, speak no evil, and hear no evil derive from Buddhist iconography of monkeys.

In Central and South America, monkeys feature often in Mayan and Aztec stories. In the Mayan creation story, the Popol Vuh, the "hero brothers," are actually a howler monkey and a spider monkey, who represent ancestors of humans in the story. In the Aztec religion, spider monkeys are associated with the god of arts, pleasure, and playfulness. A spider monkey is also represented in a Peruvian Nazca geoglyph, a large design made on the ground by moving rocks.

In many of these regions today, the relationships between humans and nonhuman primates are complicated. The bushmeat and pet trades make these animals valuable at the expense of many animals' lives, and in some areas, nonhuman primates have become pests who raid crop fields and consume valuable foods. All of this has led to the development of a new subarea of anthropology called **Ethnoprimatology**, which involves studying the political, economic, symbolic, and practical relationships between humans and nonhuman primates.This field highlights the particular challenges for humans of having to coexist with animals with whom we share so much in common. It also provides insight into some of the challenges facing primate conservation efforts (see Appendix B: Primate Conservation).

Conclusion

The Order Primates is a diverse and fascinating group of animals united in sharing a suite of characteristics—visual specialization, grasping hands and feet, large brains, and extended life histories—that differentiates us from other groups of mammals. In this chapter, we surveyed the major taxonomic groups of primates, discussing where humans fit among our close relatives as well as discovering that primates are interesting animals in their own right. We discussed a range of key traits used to distinguish between the many taxa of living primates, including dietary, locomotor, and behavioral characteristics. Because of our long, shared evolutionary history with these animals, nonhuman primates provide a crucial resource for understanding our current biology. In Chapter 6, you will discover the fascinating and complex social behaviors of nonhuman primates, which provide further insight into our evolutionary biology.

Review Questions

- Why does the field of anthropology, a field dedicated to the study of humans, include the study of nonhuman animals? What can we learn from nonhuman primates?
- Why is it important to try to place taxa into a clade classification rather than groupings based on grade? Can you think of an example?
- One of the important goals of an introductory biological anthropology course is to teach you about your place in nature. What is the full taxonomic classification of humans, and what are some of the traits we have of each of these categories?
- When you have seen primates in person, did you observe any facial expressions, behaviors, or physical traits that seemed familiar to you? If so, which ones and why?
- Draw out a tree showing the major taxonomic group of primates described here, making sure to leave room in between each level. Underneath each taxon, list some of the key features of this group so that you can compare traits between groups.

Key Terms

Activity pattern: Refers to the time of day an animal is typically active.

African clade: A grouping that includes gorillas, chimpanzees, bonobos, humans, and their extinct relatives.

Analogy: When two or more taxa exhibit similar traits that have evolved independently, the similar traits evolve due to similar selective pressures. (Also sometimes called convergent evolution, parallel evolution, or homoplasy.)

Ancestral trait: A trait that has been inherited from a distant ancestor.

Arboreal: A descriptor for an organism that spends most of its time in trees.

Asian clade: A grouping that includes orangutans and their extinct relatives.

Bilophodont: Molar pattern of cercopithecoid monkeys in which there are usually four cusps that are arranged in a square pattern and connected by two ridges.

Bipedalism: Walking on two legs.

Brachiation: A form of locomotion in which the organism swings below branches using the forelimbs.

Bunodont: Low, rounded cusps on the cheek teeth.

Canines: In most primates, these are the longest of the teeth, often conical in shape and used as a weapon against predators or others of their species.

Cathemeral: Active throughout the 24-hour period.

Clade: A grouping based on ancestral relationships; a branch of the evolutionary tree.

Cusps: The bumps on the chewing surface of the premolars and molars, which can be quite sharp in some species.

Dental formula: The number of each type of tooth in one quadrant of the mouth, written as number of incisors: canines: premolars: molars.

Derived trait: A trait that has been recently modified, most helpful when assigning taxonomic classification.

Diastema: A space between the teeth, usually for large canines to fit when the mouth is closed.

Dichromatic: Being able to see only blues and greens.

Diurnal: Active during the day.

Dry nose: The nose and upper lip are separated and the upper lip can move independently; sometimes referred to as a "hairy" or "mobile" upper lip.

Ethnoprimatology: A subarea of anthropology that studies the complexities of human-primate relationships in the modern environment.

Evolutionary trade-off: When an organism, which is limited in the time and energy it can put into aspects of its biology and behavior, is shaped by natural selection to invest in one adaptation at the expense of another.

Faunivorous: Having a diet consisting entirely of animal matter: insects, eggs, lizards, etc.

Folivore: Having a diet consisting primarily of leaves.

Fovea: A depressed area in the retina at the back of the eye containing a concentration of cells that allow one to focus on objects very close to one's face.

Frugivore: Having a diet consisting primarily of fruit.

Generalized trait: A trait that is useful for a wide range of tasks.

Grade: A grouping based on overall similarity in lifestyle, appearance, and behavior.

Grooming claw: A claw present on the second pedal digit in strepsirrhines.

Gummivore: Having a diet consisting primarily of gums and saps.

Heterodont: Having different types of teeth.

Homology: When two or more taxa share characteristics because they inherited them from a common ancestor.

Hone: When primates sharpen their canines by wearing them on adjacent teeth.

Incisors: The spatula-shaped teeth at the front of the mouth.

Insectivore: Having a diet consisting primarily of insects.

Ischial callosities: Modified seat bones of the pelvis that are flattened and over which calluses form; function as seat pads for sitting and resting atop branches.

Knuckle-walking: A form of quadrupedal movement used by *Gorilla* and *Pan* when on the ground, wherein the front limbs are supported on the knuckles of the hands.

Life history: Refers to an organism's pace of growth, reproduction, lifespan, etc.

Locomotion: How an organism moves around.

Male bimaturism: Refers to the alternative reproductive strategies in orangutans in which males can delay maturation, sometimes indefinitely, until a fully mature, "flanged" male disappears.

Molars: The largest teeth at the back of the mouth; used for chewing. In primates, these teeth usually have between three and five cusps.

Monochromatic: Being able to see only in shades of light to dark, no color.

Monomorphic: When males and females of a species do not exhibit significant sexual dimorphism.

Natal coat: Refers to the contrasting fur color of baby leaf monkeys compared to adults.

Nocturnal: Active at night.

Olecranon process: Bony projection at the elbow end of the ulna.

Opposable thumb or **opposable big toe**: Having thumbs and toes that go in a different direction from the rest of the fingers, allows for grasping with hands and feet.

Pentadactyly: Having five digits or fingers and toes.

Polymorphic color vision: A system in which individuals of a species vary in their abilities to see color. In primates, it refers to males being dichromatic and females being either trichromatic or dichromatic.

Postorbital bar: A bony ring that surrounds the eye socket, open at the back.

Postorbital closure/plate: A bony plate that provides protection to the side and back of the eye.

Prehensile tail: A tail that is able to hold the full body weight of an organism, which often has a tactile pad on the underside of the tip for improved grip.

Premolars: Smaller than the molars, used for chewing. In primates, these teeth usually have one or two cusps.

Quadrupedalism: Moving around on all fours.

Rhinariums: Wet noses; resulting from naked skin of the nose which connects to the upper lip and smell-sensitive structures along the roof of the mouth.

Sagittal crest: A bony ridge along the top/middle of the skull, used for attachment of chewing muscles.

Scent marking: The behavior of rubbing scent glands or urine onto objects as a way of communicating with others.

Semi-brachiation: A form of locomotion in which an organism swings below branches using a combination of forelimbs and prehensile tail.

Sexually dimorphic: When a species exhibits sex differences in morphology, behavior, hormones, and/or coloration.

Shearing crests: Sharpened ridges that connect cusps on a bilophodont molar.

Specialized trait: A trait that has been modified for a specific purpose.

Styloid process of ulna: A bony projection of the ulna at the end near the wrist.

Tactile pads: Sensitive skin at the fingertips for sense of touch. Animals with a prehensile tail have a tactile pad on the underside of the tail as well.

Tapetum lucidum: Reflecting layer at the back of the eye that magnifies light.

Terrestrial: A descriptor for an organism that spends most of its time on the ground.

Tetrachromatic: Having the ability to see reds, yellows, blues, greens, and ultraviolet.

Tooth comb or **dental comb**: A trait of the front, lower teeth of strepsirrhines in which, typically, the four incisors and canines are long and thin and protrude outward.

Trichromatic color vision: Being able to distinguish yellows and reds in addition to blues and greens.

Vertical clinging and leaping: A locomotor pattern in which animals are oriented upright while clinging to vertical branches, push off with hind legs, and land oriented upright on another vertical branch.

Y-5 molar: Molar cusp pattern in which five molar cusps are separated by a "Y"-shaped groove pattern.

About the Author

Stephanie Etting, Ph.D.

Sacramento City College and Sonoma State University, ettings@scc.losrios.edu

Dr. Etting became hooked on biological anthropology as a freshman at UC Davis when she took the "Introduction to Biological Anthropology" course. She obtained her Ph.D. in anthropology in 2011 from UC Davis, where she studied anti-predator behavior toward snakes in rhesus macaques, squirrel monkeys, and black-and-white ruffed lemurs. While in graduate school, Dr. Etting discovered her love of teaching and, since finishing her dissertation, has taught at UC Berkeley; Sonoma State University; UC Davis; California State University, Sacramento; and Sacramento City College.In addition to her interests in primate behavior, Dr. Etting is also very interested in primate evolution and functional anatomy.

For Further Exploration

Animal Diversity Web. This website is hosted by the Zoology Department at the University of Michigan. It has photographs of skulls, teeth, hands, arms, and feet of many primate species.

eSkeletons. This website is hosted by the Department of Anthropology at University of Texas, Austin. It is an interactive website where you can compare specific bones from different species of primates.

Fleagle, John G. 2013. *Primate Adaptation and Evolution*. Third edition. San Diego: Academic Press.

Fuentes, Agustín, and Kimberley J. Hockings. 2010. "The Ethnoprimatological Approach in Primatology." *American Journal of Primatology* 72 (10): 841–847.

Rowe, Noel. 1996. *Pictorial Guide to the Living Primates*. Charlestown, RI: Pogonias Press.

Whitehead, Paul F., William K. Sacco, and Susan B. Hochgraf. 2005. *A Photographic Atlas for Physical Anthropology*. Englewood, CO: Morton Publishing.

References

Balolia, Katharine L., Christophe Soligo, and Bernard Wood. 2017. "Sagittal Crest Formation in Great Apes and Gibbons." *Journal of Anatomy* 230 (6): 820–832.

Bininda-Emonds, Olaf R., Marcel Cardillo, Kate E. Jones, Ross D. E. MacPhee, Robin M. D. Beck, Richard Grenyer, Samantha A. Price, Rutger A. Vos, John L. Gittleman, and Andy Purvis. 2007. "The Delayed Rise of Present-Day Mammals." *Nature* 446 (7135): 507–512.

Burton, Michael L., Carmella C. Moore, John W. M. Whiting, A. Kimball Romney, David F. Aberle, Juan A. Barcelo, Malcolm M. Dow, et al. 1996. "Regions Based on Social Structure." *Current Anthropology* 37 (1): 87–123.

Chivers, David J., and C. M. Hladik. 1980. "Morphology of the Gastrointestinal Tract in Primates: Comparisons with Other Mammals in Relation to Diet." *Journal of Morphology* 166 (3): 337–386.

Clutton-Brock, T. H., and Paul H. Harvey. 1980. "Primates, Brains, and Ecology." *Journal of Zoology* 190 (3): 309–323.

Dunbar, Robin I. M. 1998. "The Social Brain Hypothesis." *Evolutionary Anthropology* 6 (5): 178–190.

Ebersberger, Ingo, Dirk Metzler, Carsten Schwarz, and Svante Pääbo. 2002. "Genomewide Comparison of DNA Sequences Between Humans and Chimpanzees." *American Journal of Human Genetics* 70 (6): 1490–1497.

Jameson, Natalie M., Zhuo-Cheng Hou, Kirstin N. Sterner, Amy Weckle, Morris Goodman, Michael E. Steiper, and Derek E. Wildman. 2011. "Genomic Data Reject the Hypothesis of a Prosimian Primate Clade." *Journal of Human Evolution* 61 (3): 295–305.

Kawamura, Shoji, Chihiro Hiramatsu, Amanda D. Melin, Colleen M. Schaffner, Filippo Aureli, and Linda M. Fedigan. 2012. "Polymorphic Color Vision in Primates: Evolutionary Considerations." In *Post-Genome Biology of Primates*, edited by H. Irai, H. Imai, and Y. Go, 93–120. Tokyo: Springer.

Matsui, Atsushi, Felix Rakotondraparany, Isao Munechika, Masami Hasegawa, and Satoshi Horai. 2009. "Molecular Phylogeny and Evolution of Prosimians Based on Complete Sequences of Mitochondrial DNAs." *Gene* 441 (1–2): 53–66.

Nater, Alexander, Maja P. Mattle-Greminger, Anton Nurcahyo, Matthew G. Nowak, Marc de Manuel, Tariq Desai, Colin Groves, et al. 2017. "Morphometric, Behavioral, and Genomic Evidence for a New Orangutan Species." *Current Biology* 27 (22): 3487–3498.

Pozzi, Luca, Jason A. Hodgson, Andrew S. Burrell, Kirstin N. Sterner, Ryan L. Raaum, and Todd R. Disotell. 2014. "Primate Phylogenetic Relationships and Divergence Dates Inferred from Complete Mitochondrial Genomes." *Molecular Phylogenetics and Evolution* 75: 165–183.

Remis, Melissa J. 1997. "Western Lowland Gorillas (*Gorilla gorilla gorilla*) as Seasonal Frugivores: Use of Variable Resources." *American Journal of Primatology* 43 (2): 87–109.

Richmond, Brian G., David R. Begun, and David S. Strait. 2001. "Origin of Human Bipedalism: The Knuckle-Walking Hypothesis Revisited." *American Journal of Physical Anthropology* 116 (S33): 70–105.

Robson, Shannen L., Carel P. van Schaik, and Kristen Hawkes. 2006. "The Derived Features of Human Life History." In *The Evolution of Human Life History, edited by Kristen Hawkes and Richard R. Paine,* 17–44. Santa Fe: SAR Press.

Scally, Aylwyn, Julien Y. Dutheil, LaDeana W. Hillier, Gregory E. Jordan, Ian Goodhead, Javier Herrero, Asger Hobolth, et al. 2012. "Insights into Hominid Evolution from the Gorilla Genome Sequence." *Nature* 483 (7388): 169–175.

Schneider, Horacio, and Iracilda Sampaio. 2015. "The Systematics and Evolution of New World Primates: A Review." *Molecular Phylogenetics and Evolution* 82 (B): 348–357.

Setchell, Joanna M., Phyllis C. Lee, E. Jean Wickings, and Alan F. Dixson. 2001. "Growth and Ontogeny of Sexual Size Dimorphism in the Mandrill (*Mandrillus sphinx*)." *American Journal of Physical Anthropology* 115 (4): 349–360.

Utami, Sri Suci, Benoît Goossens, Michael W. Bruford, Jan R. de Ruiter, and Jan A. R. A. M. van Hooff. 2002. "Male Bimaturism and Reproductive Success in Sumatran Orang-utans." *Behavioral Ecology* 13 (5): 643–652.

Vasey, Natalie. 2006. "Impact of Seasonality and Reproduction on Social Structure, Ranging Patterns, and Fission–Fusion Social Organization in Red Ruffed Lemurs." In *Lemurs: Ecology and Adaptation*, edited by Lisa Gould and Michelle L. Sauther, 275–304. New York: Springer.

Wright, Patricia C. 1999. "Lemur Traits and Madagascar Ecology: Coping with an Island Environment." *American Journal of Physical Anthropology* 110 (S29): 31–72.

Acknowledgments

The author would very much like to thank the editors for the opportunity to contribute to this textbook, along with anonymous reviewers who provided useful feedback on earlier drafts of this chapter. She would particularly like to thank Karin Enstam Jaffe for her support and encouragement during the writing of this chapter and its revision. Most of all, the author would like to thank all of the Introduction to Biological Anthropology students that she has had over the years who have listened to her lecture endlessly on these animals that she finds so fascinating and who have helped her to hone her pedagogy in a field that she loves.

Image Description

Figure 5.14: A branching diagram illustrates the classification level (order, suborder, infraorder and/or superfamily) and relationships of different types of primates. Primates (order) divide into Strepsirrhini and Haplorrhini (suborder). Strepsirrhini include Lemuroidea and Lorisoidea (superfamily). Haplorrhini include Tarsiiformes, Platyrrhini, and Catarrhini (Infraorder). Catarrhini include Cercopithecoidea (both leaf monkeys and cheek pouch monkeys) and Hominoidea (superfamily). Example primates include:

- Lemuroidea (Strepsirrhini): ring-tailed lemurs, aye-ayes, indris, mouse lemurs, sportive lemurs.
- Lorisoidea (Strepsirrhini): lorises, pottos, galagos.
- Tarsiiformes (Haplorrhini): tarsiers.
- Platyrrhini (Haplorrhini): capuchin monkeys, owl monkeys, spider monkeys, howler monkeys, marmosets, and tamarins.
- "Leaf monkeys" (Haplorrhini, Catarrhini, Cercopithecoidea): langurs, proboscis monkey, colobus monkey.
- "Cheek Pouch monkeys" (Haplorrhini, Catarrhini, Cercopithecoidea): guenons, macaques, baboons.
- Hominoidea (Haplorrhini, Hominoidea): gibbons and siamangs, orangutans, gorillas, chimpanzees and bonobos, humans.

6.

PRIMATE ECOLOGY AND BEHAVIOR

Karin Enstam Jaffe, Ph.D., Sonoma State University

This chapter is a revision from "Chapter 6: Primate Ecology and Behavior" by Karin Enstam Jaffe. In Explorations: An Open Invitation to Biological Anthropology, first edition, edited by Beth Shook, Katie Nelson, Kelsie Aguilera, and Lara Braff, which is licensed under CC BY-NC 4.0.

Learning Objectives

- Describe the variables that affect primate diets.
- Explain how primates interact with other organisms in their environment.
- Discuss why primates live in groups, types of primate groups, and components of their social systems.
- Describe the reproductive strategies of males and females.
- Explain the ways in which primates communicate.
- Discuss the evidence for primate cultural traditions.

I remember the summer after my first year of graduate school vividly. There I was, in Kenya, following wild monkeys through the bush. Finally! It was a dream come true for me. I have loved monkeys for as long as I can remember. As a child, I played with monkey stuffed animals instead of dolls. In high school, my AP history teacher gave me an introductory textbook about anthropology and I was overjoyed to learn that I could study my favorite animals in college and beyond. Now, roughly five years later, I was intently observing a group of about 50 patas monkeys (*Eyrthrocebus patas*) as they searched for food, played, and groomed one another. Suddenly, one of the monkeys gave a loud, staccato vocalization that sounded like "Nyow!" Soon, other individuals joined in. There I was, in the middle of the group, taking it all in and loving every second of it. That is until my advisor slowly approached me and pointed to the grass on the edge of the group. "Look," she said, "we need to go back to the car." I looked closely in the direction she was pointing and saw, crouching in the grass, a large lion. We slowly backed away and walked to our car. Looking back, I should have been scared, but I wasn't, I was thrilled. I would return a year later to study the same group's response to predators for two years.

Nonhuman primates (hereafter, "primates") are a fascinating group of animals, whose similarity to humans can be striking. Because of this similarity, studying primates helps anthropologists to gain insight into how our human ancestors may have behaved. It also allows us to better understand our own behavior through **comparison** (examining similarities and differences) with other primates as well as by comparing different species of primates to one another. In this way, studying primates helps anthropologists comprehend humanity from a biological perspective, which contributes to anthropology's commitment to **holism**, the idea that the parts of a system interconnect and interact to make up the whole.

Ethology is the study of animal behavior, while **primatology** is the study of primate behavior. People who study primates are called **primatologists**. Research on primates can be conducted in the field (i.e., on wild primates) or in captivity (i.e., zoos) and may or may not involve experiments, such as playing recorded alarm calls to see how individuals react. Unlike some other Science, Technology, Engineering, and Math (STEM) fields, primatology has a long history of research conducted by women (see "Special Topic: Women in Primatology"). Primatologists come from many different disciplines, have diverse backgrounds, and study primates for different reasons. Biologists study primates as examples of evolutionary theories like natural selection, and to understand behaviors as **adaptations**, or traits with a function that increases **fitness**, i.e. an individual's survival and/or reproduction. Primate intelligence is of interest to psychologists who want to learn more about deception or cooperation and to linguists interested in the principles of communication and language. Ecologists consider how primates interact with the habitats they occupy, and conservationists examine how primates are affected by deforestation, poaching, or illegal animal trade (see Appendix B: Primate Conservation for more information on these topics). Biological anthropologists, like myself (Figure 6.1), who study primates are interested in learning about their social complexity, and ecological and behavioral variation, to better understand the biological basis of human behavior. And, similar to biologists, we also explore how primate behavior is adaptive and contributes to individual fitness. Like other sciences, primatology is only as strong as its researchers, methods, and theories, and the field has benefitted recently from efforts to increase diversity and reckon with its colonialist past, as discussed below in "Special Topic: Women in Primatology."

Figure 6.1: The author observing patas monkeys from a distance in Laikipia, Kenya. Credit: Karin Enstam Jaffe observing patas monkeys in Laikipia, Kenya (Figure 6.5) by Rebecca Chancellor is under a CC BY-NC 4.0 License.

Humans share many traits in common with primates. As you learned in Chapter 5, some of these traits are similar due to **homology**, traits both species inherited from a common primate ancestor. For example, like most other primates, humans are social animals who live in groups. Group living did not evolve independently in humans and other primates. Rather, group living is a trait that evolved in a primate ancestor, and because it benefited survival, it was retained in the species' **descendants** (or the species that come after the ancestor species). In contrast, humans and other primates can have similar traits that evolved independently, which is called **analogy**. For example, both humans and Japanese macaques (*Macaca fuscata*) use natural hot springs (Figures 6.2a-b). Research on these monkeys indicates that sitting in hot springs reduces stress and helps keep them warm, much as it does for humans (Takeshita et al. 2018). But this behavior is not the result of humans and Japanese macaques having a shared ancestor who used hot springs. Rather, the behavior arose independently in two species that both occupy northerly environments and adapted to cold climates using a similar behavior. Studying the homologous traits we share with other primates, like living in groups, helps us develop hypotheses about human behaviors as adaptations, which in turn helps us develop models for the behavior of our human ancestors. Studying analogous traits, like hot springs use, allows us to better understand the effects of ecological variables on morphology and behavior of both primates and humans, living and extinct.

Figure 6.2a-b: Both humans (left) and Japanese macaques (right) use natural hot springs to reduce stress and relax. This similar trait arose independently in the two species, making it a good example of analogy. Credit: a. Hot Spring Landscape by Pexels has been modified (cropped) and has been designated to the **public domain (CC0)** under a Pixabay License. b. Jigokudani hotspring in Nagano Japan 001 by Yosemite is under a CC BY-SA 3.0 License.

Special Topic: Women in Primatology

While many STEM fields have traditionally been, and continue to be, dominated by men, primatology has a long history of significant research conducted by women. This is due, in part, to the fact that three of the most well-known primatologists are women. In the early 1960s, British paleoanthropologist Louis Leakey (discussed in Chapters 9 and 10) was looking for students to study the great apes in hopes of shedding light on the behaviors of our early ancestors. He chose Jane Goodall (Figure 6.3a) to study chimpanzees (*Pan troglodytes*), Birute Galdikas (Figure 6.3b) to study Bornean orangutans (*Pongo pygmaeus*), and Dian Fossey (Figure 6.3c) to study mountain gorillas (*Gorilla beringei beringei*). The work of these three women, sometimes referred to as Leakey's "Trimates," has transformed our understanding of ape (and primate) behavior.

Figure 6.3a-c: Louis Leakey's "Trimates" (left to right): a. Jane Goodall's research on the Gombe chimpanzees spans over half a century; b. Birute Galdikas's research and rescue work on behalf of orangutans spans 40 years; c. Dian Fossey studied mountain gorillas in Rwanda for almost 20 years, until her murder in 1985. Credit: a. **Jane Goodall HK** by Jeekc has been modified (cropped) and is under a **CC BY-SA 3.0 License**. b. **Dr Birute Galdikas** by **Simon Fraser University – University Communications** has been modified (cropped) and is under a **CC BY 2.0 License**. c. **US-223658 Dian Fossey** by **Mary-Lynn** has been modified (cropped) and is under a **CC BY 2.0 License**.

Arriving at the Gombe Stream Reserve in Tanzania in 1960, Jane Goodall was one of the first scientists to conduct a long-term study of wild nonhuman primates. Before then, most studies lasted less than a year and were often zoo-based. By 1961, she had made two astounding observations that forced us to reconsider what differentiates humans from the rest of the primate order. She observed chimpanzees eating a colobus monkey, the first reported evidence of meat eating in our closest relatives (she later observed them hunting and sharing meat). And she discovered that chimpanzees make and use tools by stripping leaves off twigs to "fish" for termites. Her work, spanning several decades, has produced long-term data on chimpanzee mating strategies, mother-infant bonds, and aggression. In the mid-1980s, Goodall transitioned from field researcher to conservationist and activist, advocating for the humane use of nonhuman animals (Stanford 2017).

Birute Galdikas began her study of orangutans in Kalimantan, Borneo, in 1971. Hers was the first long-term study conducted on the Bornean orangutan. Galdikas and her colleagues have collected over 150,000 hours of observational data, focusing on the life histories of individual orangutans. While conducting behavioral research, Galdikas discovered that the pet trade and habitat loss were adversely affecting the orangutan population. Eventually, Galdikas's conservation efforts began to extend beyond advocacy and into rehabilitation and forest preservation (Bell 2017). If you would like to learn more about primate conservation efforts, please see Appendix B: Primate Conservation.

In 1967, Dian Fossey began her long-term study of mountain gorillas and founded the Karisoke Research Center in Rwanda. Her and her colleagues' research, over several decades, revealed much about gorilla social behavior, ecology, and life history. Her efforts also led to the development of mountain gorilla conservation programs. However, she was a controversial figure, as discussed below. Fossey was murdered in December 1985; the case remains unsolved (Stewart 2017).

Decolonizing Primatology

Recently, the movement to **decolonize** primatology, by understanding and highlighting the theories and research of non-Western individuals and perspectives, has gathered steam. This movement draws attention to the maltreatment of local people by Western primatologists. For example, Michelle Rodrigues (2019) argues that it's time we stop focusing on the scientific and conservation contributions of Dian Fossey and acknowledge that her "active conservation" techniques included kidnapping and torturing local Rwandans who were known as, or suspected to be, gorilla poachers. Rodrigues (2019) argues:

> The image of Fossey, a white American woman, whipping and torturing black African poachers is evocative of the behavior of white slaveholders in the American South. It is appalling enough to think of that behavior occurring in the 1850s; there is no way we can explain Fossey's behavior in the 1970s as the product of "a different time." Yet, almost three decades later, the romantic notion of a noble martyr who died for her devotion to gorillas prevails, and these terrifying actions are often described as simply unorthodox methods. Perhaps these truths are softened due to fears that the reality of this legacy would harm gorilla conservation efforts. But memorializing her as a martyr and patron saint of gorilla conservation demands that we forget the cruel acts she advocated for and performed.

Further, Louis Leakey's installment of Goodall, Galdikas, and Fossey to study chimpanzees, orangutans, and mountain gorillas, respectively, is itself viewed as recapitulating the colonial legacy in Africa and Asia. Given that Leakey was the offspring of British missionaries, Rodrigues (2019) argues, it is no accident that he was willing to mentor British and American women, while overlooking women from Africa and Asia as potential researchers. This leads us to another level of the decolonizing movement, which aims to highlight the research of non-Western primatologists, particularly those living in what primatologists refer to as "habitat countries" that are home to living primates. As you will see in this chapter, scientists from diverse backgrounds are active contributors to exciting research on primates around the world.

Ecology

The more than 600 species and subspecies of living primates are highly diverse in their dietary preferences and the habitats they occupy. In this section we'll briefly discuss aspects of **ecology**, or the relationship between organisms and their physical surroundings, that impact a primate's life, the foods they eat, and the other species with whom they interact.

Primate Diets

Diet may be the most important variable influencing variation in primate morphology, behavior, and ecology. Most primates are **omnivores** who ingest a variety of foods in order to obtain appropriate levels of protein, carbohydrates, fats, and fluids, but one type of food often makes up the majority of each species' diet. You learned about the dental and digestive adaptations of **frugivores** (who feed primarily on fruit), **folivores** (whose diet consists mostly of leaves), and **insectivores** (who eat mainly insects) in Chapter 5, so we will not discuss them again here.

Body Size and Diet

Figure 6.4a-b: Primates eat different types of food. Small primates, like the spectral tarsier (left), eat mostly insects while large primates, like the mountain gorilla (right), eat mostly leaves. Credit: a. Spectral Tarsier Tarsius tarsier (7911549768) by Bernard DUPONT has been modified (cropped) and is under a CC BY-SA 2.0 License. b. Mountain gorilla (Gorilla beringei beringei) eating by Charles J Sharp (creator QS:P170,Q54800218) has been modified (cropped) and is under a CC BY-SA 4.0 License.

Insects are a high-quality food, full of easily digestible protein and high in calories that meet most of a primate's dietary needs. Although all primates will eat insects if they come upon them, those species that rely most heavily on insects tend to be the smallest. Why? Because larger primates simply cannot capture and consume enough insects every day to survive. Because of their small size (less than 150 g), spectral tarsiers (*Tarsius spectrum*) have a fast **metabolism**, which means they turn food to energy quickly, but they do not need to consume large amounts of food each day. It does not matter to a spectral tarsier that a grasshopper only weighs 300 mg, because the tarsier (*Tarsius*) itself is so small that one grasshopper is a good-size meal (Figure 6.4a). That same grasshopper is not even a snack for an adult male mountain gorilla (*Gorilla beringei beringei*), who may weigh up to 200 kg. Fortunately for gorillas (*Gorilla)*, their large body size means they have a slow metabolism, converting food into energy much more slowly, so they can eat lower quality food that takes longer to digest, provided there is a lot of it. For gorillas, leaves, which are hard to digest but plentiful, fit the bill (Figure 6.4b). Most medium-sized primates are highly frugivorous, and supplement their fruit based diet in ways that correspond with their size: Smaller frugivores tend to supplement with insects, while larger frugivores tend to supplement with leaves.

Food Abundance and Distribution

Nutrients are not the only dietary considerations primates must make. They must also ensure that they consume more calories than they use. The abundance and distribution of food affect energy expenditure and calorie intake because they determine how far animals must travel in search of food and how much they must compete to obtain it. **Abundance** refers to how much food is available in a given area while **distribution** refers to how food is spread out. In terms of abundance, food is either plentiful or scarce (Figure 6.5a–b). Food is distributed in one of three ways: uniformly (Figure 6.6a), in clumps (Figure 6.6b), or randomly (Figure 6.6c). In general, higher-quality foods, like fruit and insects, are less abundant and have patchier distributions than lower-quality foods, like leaves. Primates who eat fruit or insects usually have to travel farther to find food and burn more calories in the process. Abundance and distribution of food is another reason why larger primates tend to rely more heavily on leaves than either fruit or insects.

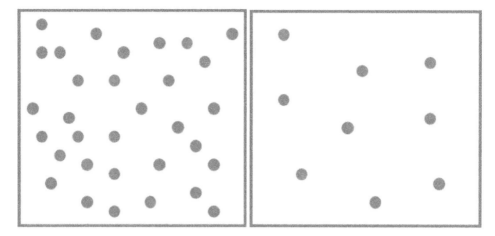

Figure 6.5a-b: Two types of food abundance. Food is plentiful when there is a lot of it in a given area (left). Food is scarce when there is not very much of it in a given area (right). Credit: **Food abundance and food scarcity (Figure 6.7)** by Karin Enstam Jaffe original to Explorations: An Open Invitation to Biological Anthropology is under a CC BY-NC 4.0 License.

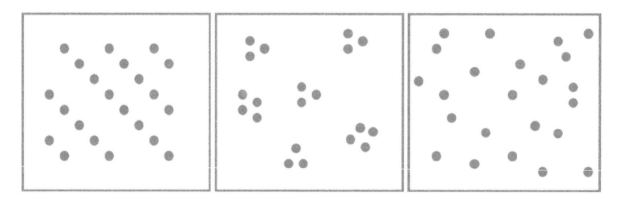

Figure 6.6a-c: Three types of food distribution. a. Food has a uniform distribution when it is spread out evenly in the environment. b. Food has a clumped distribution when it is found in patches. c. Food is randomly distributed when it has neither uniform nor clumped distribution. Credit: **Food distribution patterns (Figure 6.8)** by Karin Enstam Jaffe original to Explorations: An Open Invitation to Biological Anthropology is under a CC BY-NC 4.0 License.

Community Ecology

Primates are members of broader ecological communities composed of other species, including other primates, predators, parasites, and even humans. **Community ecology** deals with the relationships and interactions between different organisms that occupy the same habitat. Interactions with **conspecifics** (members of the same species) and **heterospecifics** (members of different species) are critical aspects of ecological communities. Some habitats support highly diverse **primate communities** consisting of 10 or more primate species. How can so many primate species occupy the same area and avoid competition? In most cases, the primate species that live together occupy different **niches**, which means they do not meet their needs for food and shelter in the exact same way. Two species can avoid competition by eating different kinds of food, living at different levels of a forest, or even searching for food at different times of day. Because tropical rainforests, like Manu National Park in Peru, are highly variable, with many habitats and many sources of food and shelter, there are many different niches for multiple species to exploit, and large primate communities can result (Figure 6.7).

Figure 6.7: Eight of the 14 primate species in Manu National Park, Peru. Top row, left to right: Goeldi's marmoset (Callimico goeldi), Rio Tapajós saki (Pithecia irrorata), tufted capuchin (Sapajus apella); middle row, left to right: emperor tamarin (Saguinus imperator), black-headed night monkey (Aotus nigriceps), Bolivian red howler (Alouatta sara); bottom row, left to right: black-capped squirrel monkey (Saimiri boliviensis), Peruvian spider monkey (Ateles chamek). Credit: Primate species in Manu National Park original to Explorations: An Open Invitation to Biological Anthropology (2nd ed.) by Karin Jaffe is a collective work under a CC BY-NC-SA 4.0 License. [Includes: Tamarin Baby/Goeldi's Monkey by stefan_fotos, CC BY 2.0 License; Pithecia irrorata -Brazil-8b by Ana_Cotta, modified (cropped), CC BY 2.0 License; Tufted Capuchin on a Branch in Singapor by Basile_Morin, modified (cropped), CC BY-SA 4.0 License; Tamarin Portrait by Brocken Inaglory, modified (cropped), CC BY-SA 3.0 License; Aotus nigriceps 1 by DuSantos, modified (cropped), CC BY 2.0 License; Aloutta sara (Bolivian Red Howler) by Raul Ignacio, modified (cropped), CC BY-SA 2.0 License; Black-Capped Squirrel Monkey (Chalalan) by Rodrigo Mariaca, modified (cropped), CC BY-SA 4.0 License; Maquisapa (Spider Monkey) by Ivan Mlinaric, modified (cropped), CC BY 2.0 License].

Competitive Interactions

Although species living in the same location often occupy different niches to avoid competition, when a resource that is important for survival or reproduction is scarce, individuals will compete to obtain that resource. This is a central tenet of Charles Darwin's theory of evolution by natural selection (see Chapter 2). Competition between primates takes two forms: Individuals engage in **direct competition**, which involves physical interaction between individuals (such as fighting), over resources that are large and worth defending (fruit is a good example of a food resource over which primates will fight). Individuals engage in **indirect competition**, in which there is no physical interaction between individuals, when a resource is small. Primates often engage in indirect competition for insects, like grasshoppers, that are eaten quickly, often before another individual arrives on the scene. Primates may engage in direct and/or indirect competition with members of their own group, with members of other groups of conspecifics, or with heterospecifics.

Predator-Prey Interactions

The plants and animals that primates eat are an important part of their ecological community. In addition to insects, many primates incorporate some **vertebrate** (animals with an internal spinal column or backbone) prey into their diet. Often, predation by primates is opportunistic, occurring because the prey happens to be in the right place at the right time. I've observed vervets (*Chlorocebus pygerythrus*) opportunistically killing lizards by smashing them against a rock or tree trunk and eating them. More rarely, hunting is deliberate and cooperative. In some chimpanzee (*Pan troglodytes*) populations, hunts involve multiple individuals, each of whom plays a specific role and is rewarded afterward with a share of the prey that has been captured (Samuni et al. 2018).

All primates are susceptible to predation by mammalian **carnivores** (animals whose diet consists primarily of animal tissue (e.g., Figure 6.8a), reptiles (e.g., Figure 6.8b), or birds of prey (e.g., Figure 6.8c). Although the specific predators found in an ecological community differ based on geography, smaller primates always fall prey to a wider range of predators. Because predators are diverse in their hunting tactics, primates have evolved a wide range of tactics to avoid or escape them. We will discuss some of these behavioral adaptations later in this chapter in the section titled "Why Do Primates Live in Groups?."

Figure 6.8a-c: Examples of primate predators: the Indian leopard (Panthera fusca) is an example of a mammalian carnivore (top left), the South African python (Python natalensis) is an example of a reptilian predator (bottom left), and the harpy eagle (Harpia harpyja) of Central and South America is an example of a bird of prey (right). Credit: a. **Leopard** by **Srikaanth Sekar** has been modified (cropped) and is under a CC BY-SA 2.0 License. b. **Python natalensis G. J. Alexander** by Graham J. Alexander, University of the Witwatersrand, USGS, is in the **public domain**. c. Harpy Eagle clutching captured bird – Itirapina Reserve by Jonathan Wilkins has been modified (cropped) and is under a CC BY-SA 3.0 License.

Mutualistic Interactions

So far, we've discussed competitive and predator-prey interactions in primate communities. But there are some interactions (between different primate species and between primates and other species) that are **mutualistic**, which is when organisms of different species work together, each benefiting from the interaction or relationship. One example is **seed dispersal**, which is the process by which seeds move away from the plant that produced them in preparation for germination and becoming a new plant. When seeds are dispersed by animals, like primates, it is an example of mutualism. The primate eats the fruit of a plant, which provides nutrients for its body, and in the process ingests the plant's seeds. Later, it deposits the seeds at another location as a pile of fertilizer.

Another example of mutualism is **polyspecific associations**, which are associations between two or more different species that are maintained by behavioral changes by at least one of the species. While some associations are short in duration, others are semi-permanent. The mutualistic benefits of polyspecific associations include one species gaining access to food that would otherwise have been inaccessible or being alerted to the presence of predators that they would not have not have known were present otherwise. In some cases, individuals seem to recognize and seek out specific members of another species. Twenty years of observations on chimpanzees and Western lowland gorillas (*Gorilla gorilla gorilla*) in the Republic of Congo has revealed social ties (some might call them friendships) between individual chimpanzees and gorillas that last for years and occur in a variety of social contexts, including play (Sanz et al. 2022).

Parasite-Host Interactions

Primates are hosts for a variety of **parasites**, which are organisms that live in or on another organism (the host). Parasites come in many forms and pose varying levels of danger to the host. Blood parasites cause diseases like yellow fever and malaria. Skin parasites include fleas and ticks, which feed on the host's blood, and botflies, which lay eggs in the host's flesh. Bot fly larvae feed on the host's flesh as they develop and eventually (if not removed) break through the skin at maturity. Gut parasites, like tapeworms, get into the intestines and feed off of the food that is being digested by the host. Because most primates live in groups (see the "Primate Societies" section of this chapter), the tendency for **social transmission** of parasites, or the transfer of parasites from one individual to another, is high. Primates have evolved mechanisms to avoid parasite infection, including switching sleeping and feeding sites so as to avoid parasites. Mandrills (*Mandrillus sphinx*) have been shown to avoid grooming infected conspecifics as well as to avoid their feces, which smell different than the feces of individuals who are not infected with parasites (Poirotte et al. 2017). Other primates, including chimpanzees, appear to self-medicate when infected with parasites by ingesting plants that have antiparasitic properties (Krief et al. 2005).

Human-Primate Interactions

Humans are part of many primate communities and our relationship with our closest relatives is often complicated. In some areas, humans hunt primates for their meat or as trophies, or so they can sell the infants as pets. As the human population increases in size, our demand for natural resources, like wood to build houses or land on which to grow food, also increases, often at the expense of pristine primate (and other animal) habitat. As their natural habitat shrinks, primates search for food in areas occupied by humans and may be shot as crop-raiding pests. While deforestation, hunting, and the pet trade are examples of ways in which humans negatively affect the lives of primates, some human-primate interactions are beneficial. In some parts of the world primates are central to **ecotourism**, which focuses on nature-based attractions to educate tourists and uses economically and ecologically sustainable practices. Perhaps one of the greatest success stories of ecotourism involves the mountain gorillas of Rwanda (see Figure 6.4b). After internal conflict plagued Rwanda during the 1990s, the Virunga Mountains area developed gorilla-based tourism to aid in socioeconomic development and to bring stability to the region. This process not only helped to increase mountain gorilla populations but was also able to generate enough income to cover the operation costs of three national parks and provide income and other benefits to people living in the area (Maekawa et al. 2013). You can learn more about human-primate interactions in Appendix B: Primate Conservation.

Primate Societies

Unlike many other animals, primates are highly social and many live in stable groups consisting of adult males and females, even outside the **breeding season**, when females are **receptive** and available for mating because they are not pregnant or nursing. Indeed, **sociality**, or the tendency to form social groups, is a key behavioral adaptation of the order primates (see Chapter 5). This has led primatologists to ask two questions: "Why do primates live in groups?" and "What types of groups do primates live in?"

Why Do Primates Live in Groups?

Primates live in groups when the benefits of doing so exceed the costs. Although there are many potential benefits to group living, enhanced feeding competition and predator avoidance are important benefits for many group living primates. When primates feed on high-quality, scarce food (like fruit), larger groups are more successful in competition with other groups. For example, in a long-term study of vervets in Kenya's Amboseli National Park, larger vervet groups had larger and better **home ranges**, which is the area in which a group regularly moves around as it performs its daily activities, including searching for food and water. Females in larger groups had higher average infant and female survival rates than the smallest group. Because pregnancy and nursing are energetically expensive for females, female **reproductive success**, or genetic contribution to future generations (measured by the number of offspring produced), is limited by access to food. Although living in a group means females compete with members of their own group for food, the benefits of being a member of a larger vervet group outweigh the costs (Cheney and Seyfarth 1987).

However, because they contain more individuals, larger groups are more likely to attract the attention of predators compared to smaller groups. This is one of the reasons that primates who rely on **crypsis**, or the ability to avoid detection by others, including predators, are often **solitary** (the term used to describe individuals who do not live together with other members of their species) and **nocturnal**, or active at night. If an animal is already hard to see because it is active at night, then moving quietly in small groups is a good strategy to avoid detection by predators.

The slow loris (*Nycticebus coucang*) of Southeast Asia is a good example of this strategy (Figure 6.9a). Nocturnal and solitary, the slow loris moves slowly and quietly as its primary strategy to avoid detection (Wiens and Zitzmann 2003). In contrast, primates who live in large groups and are **diurnal**, or active during the day (like gelada baboons [*Theropithecus gelada*]; Figure 6.9b) cannot avoid detection by predators. Instead, group-living primates rely on behaviors that alert others to the presence of danger and/or deter predators, including shared **vigilance** (watchful behavior to detect potential danger), **mobbing** (the act of cooperatively attacking or harassing a predator), and **alarm calling** (vocalizations emitted by social animals in response to danger). We will discuss alarm calls in the Communication section.

Figure 6.9a-b: Some primates, like the slow loris (left), are solitary and spend most of their time alone. However, most primates, like the gelada baboon (right), live in groups of varying sizes. Credit: a. Slow Loris by Jmiksanek is under a CC BY-SA 3.0 License. b. Field of baboons by mariusz kluzniak is under a CC BY-NC-ND 2.0 License.

What Types of Groups Do Primates Live In?

Primates vary with regard to the types of groups in which they live. A **social system** describes a set of social interactions and behaviors that is typical for a species. The components that make up a species' social system include:

- Group size, which refers to the number of individuals that typically live together. Primate group size can be highly variable, ranging from one or a few individuals, to a few dozen, upward to several hundred individuals.
- Group composition describes group membership in terms of age class (e.g., adult, juvenile, infant) and sex. In some primates, groups consist of a mother and her dependent offspring while in others, one adult male lives long-term with one adult female and their dependent offspring. In other species, one or more adult males live with multiple females and their offspring.
- A species' **mating system** refers to which male(s) and female(s) mate. The terms that describe a mating system (e.g., **polygyny**, in which one male mates with multiple females) are sometimes used to describe a primate species' social system, but a mating system is one component of the species' social system. For example, two species might both have polygynous mating systems, but in one species, the group is composed of one male and multiple females, while members of the other species live as solitary individuals.
- **Ranging behavior** refers to the way in which animals move about their environment. Most primate species have a home range, where they perform their daily activities. Some primates defend a **territory** which is the part of the home range that the group actively guards in an attempt to keep out conspecifics.
- **Dispersal** patterns describe which sex moves to a new group to reproduce. In most primate species, males disperse because the benefits of dispersal, including increased access to mates and reduced competition from other males, outweigh the costs of migrating into a new group, which often comes with aggression from current group members. For many female primates, the opposite is true: females usually benefit from remaining **philopatric**, or in the group of their birth. This allows them to maintain strong alliances with female relatives, which helps them compete successfully against other groups for food. In solitary species, offspring of both sexes leave their mother's home range and become solitary. If this did not happen, the species would not be solitary. Even though both sexes disperse in solitary species, males usually disperse farther than females.
- Social interactions describe the ways in which individuals interact with members of their own and other groups of conspecifics. **Affiliative** (i.e., friendly or nonaggressive) behaviors include **grooming** (picking through the fur of another individual), playing, or **coalitions**

(temporary alliances between individuals). **Agonistic** (i.e., aggressive) behaviors include fighting over food or fighting over access to mates. In groups that contain multiple adult individuals of the same sex, it is common to have a **dominance hierarchy**, or a group of individuals that can be ranked according to their relative amount of power over others in the hierarchy. Initially, dominance hierarchies are established through the outcome of conflicts. Individuals who lose conflicts with others are **subordinate** (or low rank) to those who win them. Those who win conflicts are **dominant** (or high rank). Dominant individuals gain access to resources, like food or mates, before subordinates. Once a hierarchy is established, agonism decreases because everyone "knows their place."

The main types of primate social systems are as follows: solitary; single-male, single-female; single-male, multi-female; multi-male, multi-female; fission-fusion; and multi-male, single-female. These types are discussed below.

Solitary

Recall that the term *solitary* is used to describe species in which individuals do not live or travel together with other members of the same species, except for mothers and unweaned offspring. Males typically occupy a large home range or territory that overlaps the home ranges of multiple females, with whom they mate (Figure 6.10a). Because one male mates with multiple females, the mating system of solitary primates is polygyny. Social interactions between adults are limited but because some males do not get to mate, competition between males is intense. When males compete physically, they benefit from large body size and weaponry. The result is **sexual dimorphism**, when males and females look different from one another. Both males and females disperse, although males move farther from their mother than females. The nocturnal West African potto (*Perodicticus potto*; Figure 6.10b) is solitary. Bornean orangutans, which are diurnal, are also solitary.

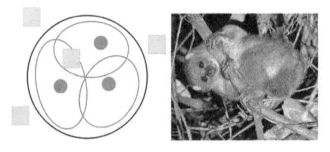

Figure 6.10a-b: Illustration of a solitary species' grouping pattern is shown on the left. Key: square = adult male; dot = adult female; open circle represents the outline of the male's home range; open oval represents individual female home ranges. The West African potto is a solitary primate (right). Credit: a. Polygyny in a Solitary Social System original to Explorations: An Open Invitation to Biological Anthropology (2nd ed.) by Karin Enstam Jaffe is under a CC BY-NC 4.0 License. b. West African Potto Perodicticus potto Kakum National Park, Ghana by Nik Barrow has been modified (cropped) and is under a CC BY-NC 2.0 License. [Image Description].

Single-Male, Single-Female

Primate species in which an adult male and adult female live together with their dependent offspring have a **single-male, single-female** social system, sometimes referred to as a "family," with group sizes between two and five individuals. The adult male and adult female engage in behaviors that strengthen their social relationship, or **pair bond**, including mutual grooming and resting together. The pair defend a territory (Figure 6.11a) and keep same-sex individuals away from their mate. The adult male and adult female mate with each other, so the mating system is **monogamy**, although mating outside the pair bond may occur. Species with monogamous mating systems are usually **sexually monomorphic** (males and females look similar) because competition for mates is relaxed since most males are able to obtain a mate. Males are usually confident that they are the father of their mate's infant, so they help with offspring care by carrying the infant when it is not nursing. Once offspring are sexually mature, both males and females disperse. As with solitary species, males disperse farther from their parents than females. Bolivian Gray titi monkeys (*Plecturocebus donacophilus*) are an example of a species that has a single-male, single-female social system. One of their signature behaviors is tail twining, when two individuals sit with their tails wrapped around each other (Figure 6.11b). This behavior reinforces the social bond among family members and is especially common between the adult male and female. Gibbons (*Hylobates*) and owl monkeys (*Aotus*) also live in single-male, single-female groups.

Single-Male, Multi-Female

Single-male, multi-female groups consist of one adult male living with multiple adult females and their dependent offspring (Figure 6.12a) . These groups can range from as few as five or ten individuals to as many as 50. Female social relationships are governed by the female dominance hierarchy. Females are usually philopatric and males disperse. Males who are unable to join a group of females may join a bachelor group with other males. Because a single male mates with multiple females, the mating system is polygyny. Species that form single-male, multi-female groups may or may not defend a territory, but the **resident male**, who lives with a group of females, is aggressive toward other males, who may try to take over the group and become the new resident male. Competition between males to be the resident male of a group is intense, and these species usually display sexual dimorphism, with males being larger than females and possessing large canines. Hanuman langurs (*Semnopithecus entellus*) of India form single-male, multi-female groups (Figure 6.12b). When a new male takes over a group of females and ousts the former resident male, he may commit **infanticide,** or kill the unweaned infants. This is especially likely if the new resident male has not yet mated with any of the females and thus cannot be the infants' father. This causes the females, who were nursing, to become sexually receptive sooner, increasing the new resident male's chances of producing offspring (Sharma, Ram, and Raipurohit 2010). Gorillas, patas monkeys, and golden snub-nosed monkeys (*Rhinopithecus roxellana*) also live in single-male, multi-female groups.

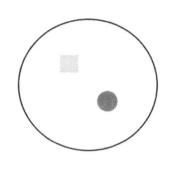

Figure 6.11a-b: Illustration of a single-male, single-female grouping pattern is shown on the left. Key: square = adult male; dot = adult female; open circle represents the outline of the group's territory, which the bonded pair defend against conspecifics. The titi monkey (right) is an example of a primate species with a single-male, single-female social system. Credit: a. Single-Male, Single-Female Social System original to Explorations: An Open Invitation to Biological Anthropology (2nd ed.) by Karin Enstam Jaffe is under a CC BY-NC 4.0 License. b. Two Red Titi Monkeys (Callicebus cupreus) sitting together with their tails intertwined at the London Zoo by Steven G. Johnson has been modified (cropped) and is under a CC BY-SA 3.0 License.

Multi-Male, Multi-Female

Multi-male, multi-female groups consist of multiple adult males living with multiple adult females and their dependent offspring. Although there is more than one adult male, there are more adult females than adult males in the group (Figure 6.13a). Multi-male, multi-female groups can range in size from about ten to as many as 500 individuals. They occupy a home range but may or may not defend a territory. In groups that contain multiple males and multiple females, it is not possible for one male to monopolize all the matings, so the mating system is **polygamy**, in which multiple males mate with multiple females. However, this does not mean that all males have an equal opportunity to mate with all females. In multi-male, multi-female groups, both males and females form a dominance hierarchy. The male dominance hierarchy determines their access to females for mating in much the same way that a female dominance hierarchy

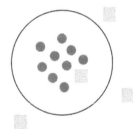

Figure 6.12a-b: An illustration of the one-male, multi-female grouping pattern is shown on the left. Key: square = adult male; dot = adult female; open circle represents the outline of the group's home range (or territory). The Hanuman langur (right) is an example of a species with a one-male, multi-female social system. Credit: a. Single-Male, Multi-Female Social System original to Explorations: An Open Invitation to Biological Anthropology (2nd ed.) by Karin Enstam Jaffe is under a CC BY-NC 4.0 License. b. Close-up of Two Grey Langurs by Amit Rai has been modified (cropped) and is free to use via Pexels.

determines a female's access to food. Because their place in the hierarchy can affect their reproductive success, males compete with each other, but because it is rare for males to be excluded from mating altogether, the level of competition and degree of sexual dimorphism are less extreme than what we see in polygynous species. Usually, females are philopatric and males disperse. Vervet monkeys (Figure 6.13b), ring-tailed lemurs (*Lemur catta*), white-faced capuchins (*Cebus capucinus*), and black-capped squirrel monkeys (*Saimiri boliviensis*) live in multi-male, multi-female groups.

Fission-Fusion

Fission-fusion is a fluid social system in which the size and composition of the social group changes, with groups splitting (fission) or merging (fusion) depending on food availability (Pinacho-Guendulain and Ramos-Fernández 2017). When key resources are scarce, individuals spread out (fission) and move and feed individually or in small subgroups (Figure 6.14a). When key food resources are plentiful, individuals come together (fusion) and individuals travel and feed as a more cohesive group (Figure 6.14a). Fission-fusion social structure is believed to reduce feeding competition when resources are scarce. Because group composition changes over time, species with fission-fusion social systems are referred to as a community. Communities consist of multiple adult males, multiple adult females, and offspring, and group size varies but typically ranges from ten to a few dozen individuals. Females typically disperse and males are philopatric. Thus, community males are related and display unusual

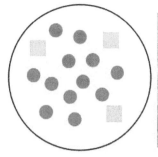

Figure 6.13a-b: An illustration of the multi-male, multi-female grouping pattern is shown on the left. Key: square = adult male; dot = adult female; open circle represents the outline of the group's home range (or territory). Vervet monkeys (right) are an example of a species that lives in multi-male, multi-female groups. Credit: a. Multi-Male, Multi-Female Social System original to Explorations: An Open Invitation to Biological Anthropology (2nd ed.) by Karin Enstam Jaffe is under a CC BY-NC 4.0 License. b. Vervet Monkeys (Chlorocebus pygerythrus) by Bernard DUPONT has been modified (cropped) and is under a CC BY-SA 2.0 License.

forms of cooperation. The mating system associated with fission-fusion is polygamy. Because males are not excluded from mating, competition for mates is relaxed and sexual dimorphism is moderate (males are slightly larger than females). Geoffroy's spider monkeys (*Ateles geoffroyi*) (Figure 6.14b) and chimpanzees both have fission-fusion social system.

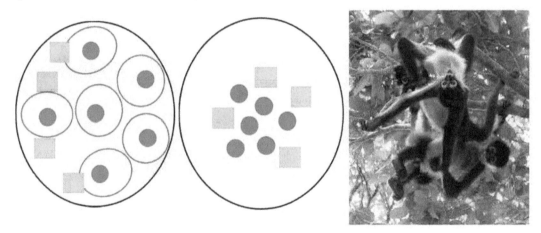

Figure 6.14a-b: An illustration of the fission-fusion grouping pattern appears on the left. The left illustration represents fission, when females travel and feed independently in individual home ranges within the community boundary. The right illustration represents fusion, when community members form a cohesive group. Key: square = adult male; dot = adult female; open circle represents the outline of the community boundary. Open ovals represent individual female home ranges when the group fissions. Credits: a. Fission-Fusion Social System original to Explorations: An Open Invitation to Biological Anthropology (2nd ed.) by Karin Enstam Jaffe is under a CC BY-NC 4.0 License. b. Geoffry's Spider Monkeys (Ateles geoffroyi) by Bernard DUPONT has been modified (cropped) and is under a CC BY-SA 2.0 License. [Image Description].

Multi-Male, Single-Female

In **multi-male, single-female** groups, two or more males live with one breeding female, her dependent offspring, and non-breeding females (Figure 6.15a). This type of social system is found in the **callitrichids**, the primate family that includes marmosets (*Callithrix*; Figure 6.15b) and tamarins (*Saguinus*) of Central and South America. Their groups rarely exceed 15 individuals, and each group actively defends their territory from conspecifics. Although more than one adult female may live in the group, the mating system is **polyandry** because there is only one breeding female who mates with all of the adult males. This is achieved through **reproductive suppression**, which involves the breeding female preventing other females from reproducing through physiological and/or behavioral means (Digby, Ferrari, and Salzman 2011). This limits the opportunities for other females in the group to become pregnant. Instead, these females, and the males in the group, help raise the breeding female's offspring. This is referred to as **cooperative breeding** and usually takes the form of carrying infants, grooming them, and protecting them from danger (de Oliveira Terceiro and Burkart 2019). Because reproductive opportunities for female tamarins and marmosets are limited, they are very competitive, and females are slightly larger than males, which helps them compete for the breeding spot in a group.

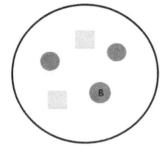

Figure 6.15a-b: An illustration of multi-male, single-female grouping pattern appears on the left. Key: square = adult male; B dot = breeding female; unmarked dot = non-breeding female; open circle represents the outline of the group's territory, which is defended against conspecifics. The common marmoset (Callithrix jacchus) is an example of a primate species that has this type of social system (right). Credit: a. Multi-Male, Single-Female Social System original to Explorations: An Open Invitation to Biological Anthropology (2nd ed.) by Karin Enstam Jaffe is under a CC BY-NC 4.0 License. b. Family of Common Marmoset – REGUA – Brazil MG 9480 (12930855765) by Francesco Veronesi has been modified (cropped) and is under a CC BY-SA 2.0 License.

Reproductive Strategies

Reproductive strategies have evolved to maximize individual reproductive success. These strategies can be divided into those that deal with offspring production and care (parental investment) and those that maximize mating success (sexual selection). Because the reproductive physiology of male and female primates differs, males and females differ with regard to parental investment and sexual selection strategies. Female strategies focus on obtaining the food necessary to sustain a pregnancy and choosing the best male(s) to father offspring. Male strategies focus on gaining access to receptive females.

Parental Investment

Figure 6.16: A female Japanese macaque nursing her infant. Credit: Snow monkey baby milk time by Daisuke Tashiro is under a CC BY-SA 2.0 License.

Biologically speaking, **parental investment** is any time or energy a parent devotes to the current offspring that enhances its survival (and eventual reproductive success) at the expense of the parent's ability to invest in the next offspring (Trivers 1972). Female primates invest more heavily in offspring than males. Even before conception, females produce energy-containing eggs, and they will be responsible for sustaining a fertilized egg until it implants in the uterus. After that, they invest in pregnancy and lactation (Figure 6.16). Because all of this investment requires a lot of energy, female primates can only produce one offspring (or litter) at a time. A species' **interbirth interval**, or the typical length of time between one birth and the next, is determined by the length of time necessary to maximize each offspring's survival without jeopardizing the female's ability to produce the greatest number of offspring possible. If a female invests too little (i.e., weans an offspring too early), she may give birth to many offspring, but very few (if any) of them will survive. If she invests too much (i.e., nurses an offspring even after it could be weaned), she ensures the survival of that individual offspring but will not be able to produce very many during her lifetime. To maximize her reproductive success, a female must invest *just* long enough to ensure the greatest number of offspring survive to reproduce. We often think of maternal care as an **innate** (or natural), instinctive behavior. Yet this is not the case. The "Special Topic: Is Maternal Behavior Innate?" dispels the myth that maternal behavior is solely instinctual and explains how female primates learn to be good mothers.

Sexual Selection

Sexual selection, or selection for traits that maximize mating success, comes in two forms. **Intrasexual selection** is selection for traits that enhance the ability of members of one sex to compete amongst themselves ("*intra*sexual" = within one sex). **Intersexual selection** is selection for traits that enhance the ability of one sex to attract the other ("*inter*sexual" = between the sexes).

Intrasexual selection most often operates on males. In the wild, adult females are either pregnant or lactating for most of their adult lives. So, in a given population, there are usually more males available and willing to mate than there are females. The result? Females are a scarce resource over which males compete. Intrasexual selection favors traits that help a male win fights with other males. In primates, these traits include large body size

(Figure 6.17a) and large canines (Figure 6.17b). Because females don't possess these same traits, males and females of some species look different; that is, they are sexually dimorphic (Figure 6.17a).

Figure 6.17a-b: a. Hamadryas baboons (Papio hamadryas) are sexually dimorphic. The male (left) is much bigger than the female (center) and also has different colored fur. b. Adult males, like this gelada baboon, also have larger canines than females. Credit: a. Dierenpark Emmen baboon (2679944324) by robin bos has been modified (cropped) and is under a CC BY 2.0 License. b. Olive Baboon Papio anubis, Picture Taken in Tanzania by Nevit Dilmen has been modified (cropped) and is under a CC BY-SA 3.0 License.

Intersexual selection also tends to operate on males, selecting traits that make a male more attractive to females. Females, in turn, choose among potential fathers. Because female primates invest more in offspring production and care than males (see the "Parental Investment" section, above), it is more costly for them if the offspring dies before maturity or reaches maturity but does not reproduce. Thus, it benefits a female primate to be choosy and try to pick the healthiest male as a mate. Males must display traits that tell a female why she should choose *him*, and not another male, as her mate.

What traits are female primates looking for? In humans, women may look for a mate who can provide important resources, such as food, paternal care, or protection. This is rare in other primates, though, since most females do not need males to provide resources. More commonly, female primates obtain genetic benefits for their offspring from choosing one male over another. Often the specific criteria by which females select mates is unknown. However, if a female chooses a healthy (as indicated by traits like a plush coat, bright coloration, or large body size) or older male, she may obtain genes for her offspring that code for health or long life. If a male's rank is determined by competitive ability that has a genetic component, females who choose males who win fights may acquire these genes (and qualities) for their offspring. Females in some species appear to prefer new immigrants, sometimes even "sneaking" copulations with males who are not established members of their groups. Such a preference may provide their offspring with novel genes and increase genetic variation (for more about the importance of genetic variation, see Chapter 4). Female choice is often more subtle than male-male competition, so it can be more difficult to study. However, as more research is conducted, we continue to improve our understanding of the ways that female primates exert their choice.

Special Topic: Is Maternal Behavior Innate?

Zoos almost always have nurseries where infants are cared for by zookeepers if their mothers will not care for them (Figure 6.18). These exhibits are among the most popular because the babies are so cute and so much fun to watch. And the caretaking positions in zoo nurseries are often among the most coveted by zoo personnel for the same reasons. But if maternal behavior is instinctive, why do zoo nurseries even exist? The answer is that in many species, including primates, maternal behavior is not purely instinctual; it is dependent on **social learning** (behavior learned by observing and imitating others), as well.

Figure 6.18: Newborn orangutan at Audubon Zoo being bottle-fed. Credit: Newborn orangutan born at Audubon Zoo being bottle fed (2022) by Audubon Nature Institute is used by permission.

Captive female primates, including gorillas and chimpanzees, who have not had the opportunity to observe their mother or other females care for infants do not know how to care for their own offspring. Although it is preferred that the primate mother care for her own infant, there are cases when she will not and humans must step in to ensure the offspring survives. When hand-rearing by humans is necessary, the infant is returned to the group as soon as possible in the hopes that it will learn species-typical behavior from its mother and other conspecifics. Observations such as these indicate that maternal behavior is learned, not innate, and that maternal care is critically important to the social and psychological development of young primates.

Communication

In its most basic form, communication occurs when one individual (the sender) emits a signal that conveys information, which is detected by another individual (the receiver). We have discussed several aspects of primate sociality in this chapter, all of which require the communication of information between individuals. But exactly *how* does a female chimpanzee communicate her sexual availability? *How* does a vervet monkey communicate the approach of a leopard or that a python is nearby? *How* do solitary, nocturnal primates, like the slow loris, communicate information about themselves to conspecifics? Primate communication comes in four forms: vocal, visual, olfactory, and tactile. Species vary in their reliance on each.

Vocal Communication

Primates use sound to communicate danger or threats, to claim and maintain a territory, or make contact with other group members. Alarm calls are given in response to predators. In some cases, alarm calls are used to alert members of the group to the presence of a predator so they can take evasive action. In other cases, they are directed at the predator itself, signaling that it has been detected. You can learn more about alarm calls as forms of vocal communication in the highlight box in this chapter entitled "Dig Deeper: Alarm Calls: Signals to Friends or Foes?."

Loud calls are designed to travel great distances and are used in territorial defense by many primate species including indris (*Indri indri*), orangutans, gibbons, and howler monkeys (*Alouatta*). In dense forest, where visual communication can be difficult, loud calls can be useful in signaling to conspecifics that a group or individual occupies a specific area. Howler monkeys are named for their loud calls, or "roars," which can be heard one kilometer or more away (Schön Ybarra 1986). Howler monkey roars may act to maintain distance between neighboring groups or keep extragroup males from entering the home range (Schön Ybarra 1986).

Other vocalizations are intended to communicate with individuals in one's own group. These include vocalizations given as part of threat displays or dominance interactions, as well as contact calls that provide information about one's location to other group members. Chacma baboons (*Papio ursinus*) have a rich repertoire of vocalizations for communicating with other group members (Fischer et al. 2008). Adult males give specific vocalizations during threat displays and physical confrontations. Subordinates "screech" when retreating from a dominant individual, signaling submission. Since baboons rely on membership in their group for finding food and detecting predators, a baboon separated from his group will vocalize in an attempt to regain contact. Young baboons emit their own contact calls when separated from their mothers.

Visual Communication

Figure 6.19a-b: Two female hamadryas baboons. The female on the left has a sexual swelling while the female on the right (in foreground, with infant clinging to her belly) does not. An adult male is behind her. Credit: a. Sexual swelling in female Hamadryas baboon by Mamoritai has been modified (cropped) and is under a CC BY-SA 2.0 License. b. Hamadryas baboon at Giza Zoo by Hatem Moushir 36 by Hatem Moushir has been modified (cropped) and is under a CC BY-SA 3.0 License.

Visual communication, which involves signals that can be seen, is an important component of nonhuman primate behavior, alone or in combination with other forms of communication. **Piloerection**, or raising one's hair or fur, is used in aggressive interactions to make an individual appear larger than it actually is. Female macaques (*Macaca*), baboons (*Papio*), and chimpanzees, signal sexual receptivity through changes in the size, shape, and, often, color of their hindquarters, called a **sexual swelling** (Figure 6.19a). The sexual swelling reaches its maximum size at ovulation. When females are not receptive, either because they are pregnant or are nursing, they do not display a sexual swelling (Figure 6.19b). Thus, the presence or absence of a sexual swelling signals a female's reproductive state.

Monkeys and apes use diverse facial expressions in visual communication. Showing your teeth in a "smile" sends a signal of friendship in humans. Displaying teeth in this way is a sign of anxiety or fear in primates. That male mandrill you see "yawning" at your local zoo is actually displaying his teeth to signal tension or to threaten a rival (Figure 6.20a). In addition to showing their canines, male gelada baboons use "lip flips," in which the gums and teeth are exposed by flipping the upper lip up over the nostrils (Figure 6.20b), and "raised eyelids," in which the pale eyelids are exposed by pulling the scalp back as threatening gestures (Aich, Moos-Heilen, and Zimmerman 1990). Submissive males respond by fleeing or presenting their hindquarters.

Figure 6.20a-b: Males use visual displays to communicate with other males. The male mandrill (left) is yawning to display his canines, and the male gelada baboon (right) enhances the yawn by flipping his upper lip back and raising his eyelids. Credit: a. **Mandrill** by **Mathias Appel** has been modified (cropped) and designated to the **public domain (CC0)**. b. BabouinGeladaAuReveil by **BluesyPete** has been modified (cropped) and is under a **CC BY-SA 3.0 License**.

Figure 6.22a-b: Many monkey species have colorful faces, including the bald uakari (Cacajao calvus; left) and the white-bellied spider monkey (Ateles belzebuth) (right). Credit: a. **Uakari** by Coada dragos has been modified (cropped) and is under a **CC BY-SA 4.0 License**. 6.22b **Ateles belzebuth (White-bellied spider monkey) 2** by **Ewa** (username: Ewcek65) has been modified (cropped) and is under a **CC BY 2.0 License**.

Primates also communicate through color. In female and male mandrills, facial coloration provides information about an individual's health, competitive ability, and reproductive state to conspecifics (Figure 6.21; Setchell et al. 2008; Setchell, Wickings, and Knapp 2006). Variation in facial coloration among monkeys of Central and South America ranges from very simple (Figure 6.22a) to complex (Figure 6.22b). Species living with larger numbers of other primate species have evolved more complex facial coloration patterns, suggesting that this trait evolved as a form of **species recognition**, or the ability to differentiate conspecifics from members of other species (Santana, Lynch Alfaro, and Alfaro 2012).

Olfactory Communication

All primates use scent to communicate. Females secrete chemicals from their **anogenital** region (the area of the anus and genitals) that provide males with information about their reproductive state. In some species, like macaques and chimpanzees, this olfactory signal is enhanced by a sexual swelling, as discussed above. **Olfactory communication**, or communicating through scent, is particularly important for monkeys of Central and South America, lemurs, and lorises. Male and female common squirrel monkeys (*Saimiri sciureus*) (Figure 6.23a) engage in "urine washing," in which an individual urinates on its hands and feet and then uses them to spread urine all over its body. Urine washing may be used to mark trails for others to follow, to control body temperature, as part of dominance displays, or to communicate reproductive state (Boinski 1992). During aggressive interactions with other males, male ring-tailed lemurs rub their tails with scent from glands on their wrists and chests. They use their "perfumed" tails in aggressive interactions with other males,

Figure 6.21: The colorful face of the male mandrill provides information about health and fitness to other mandrills.Credit: Mandrill by Mathias Appel has been modified (cropped) and designated to the public domain (CC0).

who may respond by waiving their own scented tail, with physical aggression, or by fleeing (Jolly 1966). Males also waive their tails, saturated in scent, to attract females (Shirasu et al. 2020). Males use scent glands in their wrists to mark territorial boundaries (Figure 6.23b; Mertl-Millhollen 1988).

Figure 6.23a-b: Some primates, like the common squirrel monkey (left) and the ring-tailed lemur (right), communicate using scent. Credit: a. Saimiri sciureus by Ruben Undheim is under a CC BY-SA 2.0 License. b. Lemur catta 004 by Maky has been modified (cropped) and is under a CC BY-SA 3.0 License.

Tactile Communication

Tactile communication, or communicating through touch, is very important in all primate species. Physical contact is used to comfort and reassure, is part of courtship and mating, and is used to establish dominance and alliances. Grooming is an important and clearly enjoyable form of tactile communication for all primates (Figure 6.24). Not only does grooming serve to clean the skin and fur, removing parasites and debris, but it is an important affiliative behavior that helps reinforce social bonds, repair relationships, and cement alliances.

Figure 6.24: Examples of grooming in Japanese macaques (upper left), tufted capuchins (Sapajus apella) (upper right), gelada baboons (lower left), and black-and-white ruffed lemurs (Varecia variegata; lower right). Credit: Examples of grooming original to Explorations: An Open Invitation to Biological Anthropology (2nd ed.) by Karin Jaffe is a collective work under a CC BY-NC-SA 4.0 License. [Includes Yakushima macaques grooming each other by Grendelkhan, CC BY-SA 4.0 License; Tufted capuchin monkeys grooming session III by Adrian Soldati, CC BY-SA 4.0 License; Baboons Wunania 012018 by Kim Toogood, CC BY-SA 4.0 License; Black-and-white ruffed lemur 03 by Mattis2412, public domain (CC0 1.0)].

Dig Deeper: Alarm Calls: Signals to Friends or Foes?

Alarm calls are common among group-living primates. They often serve to notify conspecifics of potential danger, as is the case with vervet monkeys. Research has shown that: (1) vervets classify predators based on hunting style; (2) alarm calls convey information to other vervets about that hunting style; and (3) other vervets respond in ways appropriate for evading that type of predator (Seyfarth, Cheney, and Marler 1980a). When a vervet gives a "leopard" alarm call (directed at mammalian carnivores like leopards, Figure 6.25a), monkeys on the ground climb the nearest tree, while monkeys already in trees stay there or climb higher. Since most mammalian carnivores hunt on the ground, getting into, and staying in, a tree is the best option for escape. When the "snake" alarm call is given, vervets stand on their hind legs and look down at the ground (Figure 6.25b). Since snakes are not pursuit predators, locating them quickly so as to avoid them is the best strategy. Lastly, when an "eagle" alarm call is given, vervets look up or run into bushes, both of which are useful responses for avoiding hawks and eagles, which attack from above (Figure 6.25c).

Vervets clearly understand the meaning of each type of alarm call, as they respond appropriately even when they do not see the actual predator (Seyfarth, Cheney, and Marler 1980b). Such **semantic communication**, which involves the systematic use of signals to refer to objects in the environment, was once believed to be unique to humans. It may be a precursor to the symbolic capacities of human language.

Figure 6.25a

Figure 6.25b

Figure 6.25a-c: Vervet monkeys respond in different ways to alarm calls for each of their three main predators (leopards, snakes, and eagles) which are appropriate to predator hunting strategies. Credit: Vervet Monkey Alarm Calls by Mary Nelson, original to Explorations: An Open Invitation to Biological Anthropology, 2nd edition, is under a CC BY-NC 4.0 License.

Research on other African monkeys indicates that some species use alarm calls to signal to the predator that it has been detected. Diana monkeys (*Cercopithecus diana*) give alarm calls to leopards (*Panthera pardus*) but not chimpanzees (Zuberbühler, Noë, and Seyfarth 1997). Because leopards are stealth predators, they rely on the element of surprise to sneak up on their prey (Figure 6.26a). Alarm calling at leopards appears to tell the leopard that it has been seen and therefore its chance of success will be low. Research shows leopards are more likely to stop hunting after an alarm call has been emitted. Unlike leopards, chimpanzees are pursuit predators and may even use alarm calls to locate potential prey (Figure 6.26b). With such a predator, prey are better off remaining as silent as possible so as not to alert the predator to their location (Zuberbühler et al. 1999).

Figure 6.26a-b: Because leopards (left) and chimpanzees (right) hunt differently, Diana monkeys react differently to them. Credit: a. **Crouching Leopard** by Thimindu Goonatillake is under a **CC BY-SA 2.0 License**. b. **Chimpanzee in the wild** by D.G. Kulakov is under a **CC BY-SA 4.0 License**.

The Question of Culture

It may be surprising in a chapter on nonhuman primates to see a discussion of culture. After all, culture is considered by many, including cultural anthropologists, to be a distinguishing characteristic of humans. Indeed, some anthropologists question claims of culture in primates and other animals. Definitions of animal culture focus on specific behaviors that are unique to one population. Anthropological definitions of human culture emphasize shared ideology (e.g., values, morals, beliefs) and symbols, not just behavior. Using this definition, some cultural anthropologists view primates as lacking culture because of the absence of symbolic life (e.g., religion). However, the longer we study primate groups and populations, the more insight we gain into primate behavioral variation. If we define **culture** as the transmission of behavior from one generation to the next through social learning, then we must view at least some of the behavioral variation we see in primates as forms of **cultural tradition**, or a distinctive pattern of behavior shared by multiple individuals in a social group that persists over time (Whiten 2001).

Chimpanzee Culture

Due to both their high level of intelligence and the large number of long-term studies on several different populations, chimpanzees provide the best example of cultural tradition in primates. Chimpanzees express cultural variation in multiple behavioral patterns, ranging from population-specific prey preferences and hunting strategies to tool-use techniques and social behaviors. For example, in Tanzania, chimpanzees fish for termites by stripping twigs and then poking the twigs into termite mounds. The termites react to the "invasion" by attacking the twig. The chimpanzee pulls the twig out, termites attached, and eats them. In Gambia, they use modified twigs to extract honey from holes in trees. In Fongoli, Sénégal, chimpanzees use sticks as "spears" that they stab into tree cavities to hunt for galagos (Figure 6.27). Multiple chimpanzee populations use a "hammer and anvil" to crack open nuts, but the specific techniques differ. Because the cultural traditions are so diverse and unique, if a researcher can observe enough of a chimpanzee's behavior, it is possible to assign that individual to a specific community, much in the same way a human being can be associated with a specific culture based on his or her behavior (Whiten 2011).

Figure 6.27a-d: Tool-assisted hunting by a chimpanzee at Fongoli, Sénégal. An adult male chimpanzee uses a tree branch with a modified end to (a–c) stab into a cavity within a hollow tree branch that houses a galago. He ultimately captures the galago as (d) his adolescent brother looks on. Credit: Pan troglodytes, tool use in Senegal by J. D. Pruetz, P. Bertolani, K. Boyer Ontl, S. Lindshield, M. Shelley, and E. G. Wessling is under a CC BY 4.0 License.

How do chimpanzee cultures develop, and how does cultural transmission occur? Although we do not know for sure how chimpanzee cultural traditions develop initially, it is possible that different groups invent, either accidentally or deliberately, certain behaviors that other individuals copy. **Immigration**, or movement of an individual into a new group or community, is an important avenue of cultural transmission in chimpanzees, much as it is between human cultures. Immigrants (typically females) may bring cultural traditions to their new community, which residents observe and learn. Conversely, immigrants may observe and learn a cultural tradition practiced in their new community (Whiten 2011).

Cultural Transmission in Macaques

Two monkey species are well-known for behavioral variation that has been called "pre-cultural" by some primatologists: Japanese macaques and tufted capuchins (*Sapajus apella*). The transmission of unique **foraging** (the act of searching for food) behaviors through the members of a provisioned group of Japanese macaques on Koshima Island is well known (Matsuzawa 2015). In an effort to keep the monkeys nearby, researchers provided them with piles of sweet potatoes. A juvenile female named Imo spontaneously washed a muddy sweet potato in a stream. This new food-processing technique first spread among other juveniles and then gradually to older individuals. Within 30 years, it had spread across generations, and 46 of 57 monkeys in the group engaged in the behavior. Another example comes from a group living far to the north, in Shiga-Heights, Nagano Prefecture. Researchers used apples to entice Japanese macaques to the area. Within a few years, monkeys visited the area regularly and were observed playing with the water in the hot springs. Soon, they climbed into the hot springs and learned to immerse themselves to keep warm and reduce stress when not foraging (Figure 6.28; Matsuzawa 2018; Takeshita et al. 2018; recall also our discussion of hot spring use as an example of analogous traits at the beginning of this chapter). These examples share several characteristics with human culture, including invention or modification of behavior, transmission of behavior between individuals, and the persistence of the behavior across generations (McGrew 1998).

Figure 6.28: Hot spring use by Japanese macaques is a culturally transmitted behavior. Credit: Oooh, This Feels Sooo Good! by Peter Theony – Quality HD Photography is under a CC BY-NC-SA 2.0 License.

Conclusion

Primates are socially complex, extremely intelligent, and highly adaptable. In this chapter we discussed aspects of primate ecology, including how body size and characteristics of food affect what primates eat and how primates interact with other species in their environment. We examined why primates live in groups, the types of groups in which they are found, and the reproductive strategies used by males and females to maximize reproductive success. Like other aspects of their behavior, primate communication is varied and complex, and we discussed how primates communicate using vocal, visual, olfactory, and tactile signals. Finally, we explored the question of culture among nonhuman primates and learned that some species have cultural traditions, distinctive patterns of behavior shared by multiple individuals in a social group that persist over time. Humans and other primates are similar in many ways. Learning about principles of primate ecology and behavior can help us better understand our own behavior and the behaviors of our extinct relatives.

Review Questions

- If anthropology is the study of humans, why do some anthropologists study primates?
- How does a primate's ecology affect their diet and interactions with other organisms?
- Why do primates live in groups and in what types of groups do they live?
- What is parental investment and sexual selection?
- What are some examples of primate communication?
- What is the evidence for cultural traditions in primates and how do primatologists think cultural transmission occurs in primates?

Key Terms

Abundance: How much food is available in a given area.

Adaptation: A trait with a function.

Affiliative: Nonaggressive social interactions and associations between individuals.

Agonistic: Conflict; aggressive interactions between individuals.

Alarm calling: Vocalizations emitted by social animals in response to danger.

Analogy: A similar trait found in different species that arose independently.

Anogenital: Relating to the anus and genitals.

Breeding season: The time of year when females are receptive to mating.

Callitrichids: The primate family that includes marmosets and tamarins.

Carnivores: Organisms whose diet consists primarily of animal tissue.

Coalition: A temporary alliance between individuals.

Community ecology: The branch of ecology that deals with the relationships and interactions between different organisms that occupy the same habitat.

Comparison: An examination of the similarities and differences between two things, such as two primate species.

Conspecifics: Members of the same species.

Cooperative breeding: When individuals other than the mother and father help raise the offspring.

Crypsis: The ability to avoid detection by other organisms, such as predators.

Cultural tradition: A distinctive pattern of behavior shared by multiple individuals in a social group, which persists over time and is acquired through social learning.

Culture: The transmission of behavior from one generation to the next through observation and imitation.

Decolonize: Understanding and highlighting the theory and research of non-Western individuals and perspectives.

Descendant: A species that comes after the ancestor species.

Direct competition: Competition that involves physical interaction between individuals, such as fighting.

Dispersal: To leave one's group or area. This may or may not involve joining another group.

Distribution: How food is spread out.

Diurnal: Active during the day.

Dominance hierarchy: The ranked organization of individuals established by the outcome of aggressive-submissive interactions.

Dominant: Being of high rank.

Ecology: The relationship between organisms and their physical surroundings.

Ecotourism: A form of tourism that focuses on nature-based attractions to provide learning opportunities and that uses economically and ecologically sustainable practices.

Ethology: The study of animal behavior.

Fission-fusion: Societies in which group composition is flexible, such as chimpanzee and spider monkey societies. Individuals may break up into smaller feeding groups (fission) and combine into larger groups (fusion).

Fitness: An individual's ability to survive and reproduce relative to other members of the same species.

Folivores: Organisms whose diet consists primarily of leaves.

Foraging: The act of searching for food.

Frugivores: Organisms whose diet consists primarily of fruit.

Grooming: Picking through the fur of another individual for cleaning or bonding purposes.

Heterospecifics: Members of different species.

Holism: The idea that the parts of a system interconnect and interact to make up the whole.

Home range: The area that a group or individual uses over a given period of time (often over a year).

Homology: A similar trait found in different species because it was inherited from a common ancestor.

Immigration: Movement of an individual into a new group or community.

Indirect competition: Competition that does not involve physical interaction between individuals, such as eating food before another individual arrives at the food site.

Infanticide: The killing of infants of one's own species.

Innate: Natural; as in behavior that comes naturally.

Insectivores: Organisms whose diets consist primarily of insects.

Interbirth interval: The typical length of time between one birth and the next for a species.

Intersexual selection: The selection for traits that enhance the ability of the members of one sex to attract the attention of the other.

Intrasexual selection: Selection for traits that enhance the ability of members of one sex to compete amongst themselves.

Mating system: A way of describing which male(s) and female(s) mate.

Metabolism: The chemical changes that take place in an organism that turn nutrients into energy.

Mobbing: Cooperatively attacking or harassing a predator.

Monogamy: A mating system in which one male mates with one female.

Multi-male, multi-female: A group that consists of multiple adult males, multiple adult females, and their dependent offspring.

Multi-male, single-female: A group that consists of two or more adult males, one breeding female, their dependent offspring, and non-breeding females.

Mutualistic/mutualism: When different species work together, with each benefiting from the interaction.

Niche: The role of a species in its environment; how it meets its needs for food, shelter, etc.

Nocturnal: Active at night.

Olfactory communication: Conveying information through scent.

Omnivores: Organisms whose diet consists of plant and animal matter.

Pair bond: A strong, long-term relationship between two individuals.

Parasite: An organism that lives in or on another organism.

Parental investment: Any time or energy a parent devotes to the current offspring that enhances its survival (and eventual reproductive success) at the expense of the parent's ability to invest in the next offspring.

Philopatric: Remaining in the group of one's birth.

Piloerection: Raising one's hair or fur in an effort to look bigger.

Polyandry: A mating system in which multiple males mate with a single breeding female.

Polygamy: A mating system in which multiple males mate with multiple females.

Polygyny: A mating system in which one male mates with multiple females.

Polyspecific association: An association between two or more different species that involves behavioral changes in at least one of them to maintain the association.

Primate community: All primate species that occur in an area.

Primatologist: A scientist who studies primate behavior and/or ecology.

Primatology: The scientific field that studies primate behavior and/or ecology.

Ranging behavior: Refers to the way in which animals move about their environment.

Receptive: A term used to describe females who are ready for sexual reproduction (i.e., not pregnant or nursing).

Reproductive success: An individual's genetic contribution to future generations, often measured through the number of offspring produced.

Reproductive suppression: The prevention or inhibition of reproduction of healthy adults.

Resident male: Term that describes the male who lives with a group of females.

Seed dispersal: The process by which seeds move away from the plant that produced them in preparation for germination and becoming a new plant.

Semantic communication: The systematic use of signals to refer to objects in the environment.

Sexual dimorphism: When males and females of a species have different morphological traits.

Sexual selection: The selection for traits that increase mating success. This occurs via intersexual selection and intrasexual selection.

Sexual swelling: Area of the hindquarters that change in size, shape, and often color over the course of a female's reproductive cycle, reaching maximum size at ovulation. Occurs in many primate species that live in Africa and Asia.

Sexually monomorphic: When males and females of a species have similar morphological traits.

Single-male, multi-female: A group that consists of one adult male, multiple adult female, and their dependent offspring.

Single-male, single-female: A group that consists of one adult male, one adult female, and their dependent offspring.

Social learning: The idea that new behaviors can be acquired by observing and imitating others.

Social system: A way of describing the typical number of males and females of all age classes that live together.

Social transmission: Transfer of something from one individual to another; this can include parasites, information, or cultural traditions.

Sociality: The tendency to form social groups.

Solitary: Living alone.

Species recognition: The ability to differentiate conspecifics from members of other species.

Subordinate: Being of low rank.

Tactile communication: Conveying information through touch.

Territory: A home range whose boundary is defended from intrusion by conspecifics.

Vertebrates: The group of animals characterized by an internal spinal column or backbone. This includes fish, amphibians, reptiles, birds, and mammals.

Vigilance: Watchful behavior used to detect potential danger, usually in the form of predators or potential competitors.

Visual communication: Conveying information through signals that can be seen.

Vocal communication: Conveying information through signals that can be heard.

About the Author

Karin Enstam Jaffe, Ph.D.

Sonoma State University, karin.jaffe@sonoma.edu

Dr. Karin Enstam Jaffe has loved primates since she was five years old. As an undergraduate at U.C. San Diego, she participated in projects studying orangutans, langurs, and Mona monkeys. She earned her Ph.D. in Anthropology from U.C. Davis studying vervet and patas monkey antipredator behavior in Kenya. She has been a faculty member in the Anthropology Department at Sonoma State University since August 2002. A dedicated teacher-scholar, Dr. Jaffe has won several teaching, scholarship, and mentoring awards, including SSU's Excellence in Teaching Award, Educational Experience Enhancement Award, and the President's Excellence in Scholarship Award. In addition to teaching, she has led student research projects on behavioral enrichment involving ring-tailed lemurs, chimpanzees, and sun bears, as well as a study of the social network of hamadryas baboons at Oakland Zoo.

For Further Exploration

Goodall, Jane. 1971. *In the Shadow of Man*. Boston: Houghton Mifflin.

Rowe, Noel, and Marc Myers, eds. 2016. *All the World's Primates*. Charleston, RI: Pogonias Press.

Strier, Karen B. 2017. *Primate Behavioral Ecology*. 5th ed. New York: Routledge.

Primate Info Net is an information service of the National Primate Research Center at the University of Wisconsin, Madison. It includes Primate Factsheets, primate news and publications, a list of primate-related jobs, and an international directory of primatology, among other information.

Primate Specialist Group is a collection of scientists and conservationists who work in dozens of African, Asian, and Latin American nations to promote research on primate conservation.

Short videos of some primate behaviors discussed in this chapter:

- Watch vervet monkeys respond to different types of predators: BBC One. n.d. "Vervet Monkey's Escape Plans – Talk to the Animals: Episode 2 Preview." Accessed December 16, 2022. https://www.youtube.com/watch?v=q8ZG8Dpc8mM.
- Watch male gelada baboons use the lip flip in competition with other males: Smithsonian Channel, June 9, 2017. "Why These Vegetarian Monkeys Have Sharp Predator Teeth." Accessed July 25, 2019. https://www.youtube.com/watch?time_continue=145&v=aC6iYj_EBjY.
- Watch (and listen to!) howler monkeys "roar": Science News. N.d. "Hear a Male Howler Monkey Roar." Accessed November 21, 2022. https://www.youtube.com/watch?v=PYar0dkZ6v8.
- Watch Japanese macaques using natural hot springs: National Geographic. N.d. "Meditative Snow Monkeys Hang Out in Hot Springs." Accessed July 25, 2019. https://www.youtube.com/watch?v=Aat9O85ynsI.
- Watch chimpanzees make and use tools: National Geographic. n.d. "Chimps and Tools." Accessed July 25, 2019. https://www.youtube.com/watch?v=o2TBicMRLtA.

References

Aich, H., R. Moos-Heilen, and E. Zimmermann. 1990. "Vocalizations of Adult Gelada Baboons (*Theropithecus gelada*): Acoustic Structure and Behavioural Context." *Folia Primatologica* 55 (3–4): 109–132.

Bell, Sarah A. 2017. "Galdikas, Birute." In *The International Encyclopedia of Primatology, Volume A–G*, edited by Agustín Fuentes, 445–446. Malden, MA: John Wiley & Sons.

Boinski, S. 1992. "Olfactory Communication among Costa Rican Squirrel Monkeys: A Field Study." *Folia Primatologica* 59 (3): 127–136.

Cheney, D. L., and R. M. Seyfarth. 1987. "The Influence of Intergroup Competition on the Survival and Reproduction of Female Vervet Monkeys." *Behavioral Ecology and Sociobiology* 21 (6): 375–386.

de Oliveira Terceiro, Francisco Edvaldo, and Judith M. Burkart. 2019. "Cooperative Breeding." In *Encyclopedia of Animal Cognition and Behavior*, edited by Jennifer Vonk and Todd Shackelford, 1–6. Edinburg, Scotland: Springer Cham.

Digby, Leslie J., Stephen F. Ferrari, and Wendy Saltzman. 2011. "Callitrichines: The Role of Competition in Cooperatively Breeding Species." In *Primates in Perspective*, edited by Christina J. Campbell, Austín Fuentes, Katherine C. MacKinnon, Simon K. Bearder, and Rebecca M. Stumpf, 91–10. 2nd edition. New York: Oxford University Press.

Fischer, Julia, Kurt Hammerschmidt, Dorothy L. Cheney, and Robert M. Seyfarth. 2008. "Acoustic Features of Female Chacma Baboon Barks." *Ethology* 107 (1): 33–54.

Jolly, Alison. 1966. *Lemur Behavior: A Madagascar Field Study*. Chicago: University of Chicago Press.

Krief, Sabrina, Claude Marcel Hladik, and Claudie Haxaire. 2005. "Ethnomedicinal and Bioactive Properties of Plants Ingested by Wild Chimpanzees in Uganda." *Journal of Ethnopharmacology* 110 (1–3): 1–15.

Maekawa, Mkio, Annette Lanjouw, Eugène Rutagarama, and Doublas Sharp. 2013. "Mountain Gorilla Tourism Generating Wealth and Peace in Post-Conflict Rwanda." *Natural Resources Forum* 37 (2): 127–137.

Matsuzawa, Tetsuro. 2015. "Sweet-Potato Washing Revisited: 50th Anniversary of the *Primates* Article." *Primates* 56: 285–287.

Matsuzawa, Tetsuro. 2018. "Hot-Spring Bathing of Wild Monkeys in Shiga-Heights: Origin and Propagation of a Cultural Behavior." *Primates* 59: 209–213.

McGrew, W. C. 1998. "Culture in Nonhuman Primates?" *Annual Review of Anthropology* 27: 301–328.

Mertl-Millhollen, Anne S. 1988. "Olfactory Demarcation of Territorial but Not Home Range Boundaries by *Lemur catta*." *Folia Primatologica* 50 (3–4): 175–187.

Pinacho-Guendulain, B., and G. Ramos-Fernández. 2017. "Influence of Fruit Availability on the Fission-Fusion Dynamics of Spider Monkeys (*Ateles geoffroyi*)." *International Journal of Primatology* 38: 466–484.

Poirotte, Clémence, François Massol, Anaïs Herbert, Eric Willaume, Pacelle M. Bomo, Peter M. Kappeler, and Marie J. E. Charpentier. 2017. "Mandrills Use Olfaction to Socially Avoid Parasitized Conspecifics." *Science Advances* 3 (4): e160172.

Rodrigues, Michelle. 2019. "It's Time to Stop Lionizing Dian Fossey as a Conservation Hero." *Lady Science* website, September 20. Accessed December 14, 2022. https://www.ladyscience.com/ideas/time-to-stop-lionizing-dian-fossey-conservation.

Samuni, Liran, Anna Preis, Tobias Deschner, Catherine Crockford, and Roman M. Wittig. 2018. "Reward of Labor Coordination and Hunting Success in Wild Chimpanzees." *Communications Biology* 1: 138.

Santana, Sharlene E., Jessica Lynch Alfaro, and Michael E. Alfaro. 2012. "Adaptive Evolution of Facial Colour Patterns in Neotropical Primates." *Proceedings of the Royal Society B: Biological Sciences* 279 (1736): 2204–2211.

Sanz, Crickette M., David Strait, Crepin Eyana Ayina, Jean Marie Massamba, Thierry Fabrice Ebombi, Severin Ndassoba Kialiema, Delon Ngoteni, et al. 2022. "Interspecific Interactions Between Sympatric Apes." i*Science* 25 (10): 105059.

Schön Ybarra, M. A. 1986. "Loud Calls of Adult Male Red Howling Monkeys (*Alouatta seniculus*)." *Folia Primatologica* 47 (4): 204–216.

Setchell, Joanna M., Tessa Smith, E. Jean Wickings, and Leslie A. Knapp. 2008. "Social Correlates of Testosterone and Ornamentation in Male Mandrills." *Hormones and Behavior* 54 (3): 365–372.

Setchell, Joanna M., E. Jean Wickings, and Leslie A. Knapp. 2006. "Signal Content of Red Facial Coloration in Female Mandrills (*Mandrillus sphinx*)." *Proceedings of the Royal Society B: Biological Sciences* 273 (1599): 2395–2400.

Seyfarth, R. M., D. L. Cheney, and P. Marler. 1980a. "Monkey Responses to Three Different Alarm Calls: Evidence of Predator Classification and Semantic Communication." *Science* 210 (4471): 801–803.

Seyfarth, Robert M., Dorothy L. Cheney, and Peter Marler. 1980b. "Vervet Monkey Alarm Calls: Semantic Communication in a Free-Ranging Primate." *Animal Behaviour* 28 (4): 1070–1094.

Sharma, Goutam, Chan Ram, and Lal Singh Rajpurohit. 2010. "A Case Study of Infantcide After Resident Male Replacement in *Semnopithecus entellus* around Jodhpur (India)." *Proceeding of the Zoological Society* 63 (2): 93–98.

Shirasu, Mika, Satomi Ito, Akihiro Itoigawa, Takashi Hayakawa, Kodzue Kinoshita, Isao Munechika, Hiroo Imai, and Kazushige Touhara. 2020. "Key Male Glandular Odorants Attracting Female Ring-Tailed Lemurs." *Current Biology* 30 (11): 2131–2138.

Stanford, Craig B. 2017. "Goodall, Jane." In *The International Encyclopedia of Primatology, Volume A–G*, edited by Agustín Fuentes, 471–472. Malden, MA: John Wiley & Sons.

Stewart, Kelly. 2017. "Fossey, Dian." In *The International Encyclopedia of Primatology, Volume A–G*, edited by Agustín Fuentes, 432–433. Malden, MA: John Wiley & Sons.

Takeshita, Rafaela S.C., Fred B. Bercovitch, Kodzue Kinoshita, and Michael A. Huffman. 2018. "Beneficial Effect of Hot Spring Bathing on Stress Levels in Japanese Macaques." *Primates* 59 (3): 215–225.

Trivers, Robert L. 1972. "Parental Investment and Sexual Selection." In *Sexual Selection and the Descent of Man, 1871–1971*, edited by Bernard Campbell, 136–179. Chicago: Aldine.

Whiten, Andrew. 2011. "The Scope of Culture in Chimpanzees, Humans and Ancestral Apes." *Philosophical Transactions of the Royal Society of London B: Biological Sciences* 366 (1567): 997–1007.

Wiens, Frank, and Annette Zitzmann. 2003. "Social Structure of the Solitary Slow Loris *Nycticebus coucang* (Lorisidae)." *Journal of Zoology* 261 (1): 35–46.

Zuberbühler, Klaus, David Jenny, and Redouan Bshary. 1999. "The Predator Deterrence Function of Primate Alarm Calls." *Ethology* 105 (6): 477–490.

Zuberbühler, Klaus, Ronald Noë, and Robert M. Seyfarth. 1997. "Diana Monkey Long-Distance Calls: Messages for Conspecifics and Predators." *Animal Behaviour* 53 (3): 589–604.

Acknowledgments

The author is grateful to the editors for the opportunity to contribute to this open-source textbook. She thanks Dr. Stephanie Etting for her encouragement and support during the revision of this chapter. Her suggestions, along with comments made by two anonymous reviewers on an earlier draft of this chapter, improved the final version considerably. Finally, she thanks all the primatologists who came before her, especially her advisor, Lynne A. Isbell, for their tireless efforts to understand the behavior and ecology of the living primates. Without their work, this chapter would not have been possible.

Image Descriptions

Figure 6.10a: Open circle contains three regions (open ovals), each of which have one dot (adult female). There is one square (adult male) that overlaps these three regions. Outside the circle are three squares (adult males).

Figure 6.14a: Top circle contains four squares (adult males) and six open ovals (female home range) each with a dot (adult female). Bottom circle contains six dots (adult females) and four squares (adult males).

7.

STONES AND BONES: STUDYING THE FOSSIL RECORD

Sarah S. King, Ph.D., Cerro Coso Community College

Kara Jones, M.A., Ph.D. student, University of Nevada Las Vegas

This chapter is a revision from "Chapter 7: Understanding the Fossil Context" by Sarah King and Lee Anne Zajicek. In Explorations: An Open Invitation to Biological Anthropology, first edition, edited by Beth Shook, Katie Nelson, Kelsie Aguilera, and Lara Braff, which is licensed under CC BY-NC 4.0.

Learning Objectives

- Identify the different types of fossils and describe how they are formed.
- Discuss relative and chronometric dating methods, the type of material they analyze, and their applications.
- Describe the methods used to reconstruct past environments.
- Interpret a site using the methods described in this chapter.

Fossil Study: An Evolving Process

Mary Anning and the Age of Wonder

Figure 7.1: An oil painting of Mary Anning and her dog, Tray, prior to 1845. The "Jurassic Coast" of Lyme Regis is in the background. Notice that Anning is pointing at a fossil. Credit: Mary Anning by B. J. Donne from the Geological Society/NHMPL is in the public domain.

Mary Anning (1799–1847) is likely the most famous fossil hunter you've never heard of (Figure 7.1). Anning lived her entire life in Lyme Regis on the Dorset coast in England. As a woman, born to a poor family, with minimal education (even by 19th-century standards), the odds were against Anning becoming a scientist (Emling 2009, xii). It was remarkable that Anning was eventually able to influence the great scientists of the day with her fossil discoveries and her subsequent hypotheses regarding evolution.

The time when Anning lived was a remarkable period in human history because of the Industrial Revolution in Britain. Moreover, the scientific discoveries of the 18th and 19th centuries set the stage for great leaps of knowledge and understanding about humans and the natural world. Barely a century earlier, Sir Isaac Newton had developed his theories on physics and become the president of the Royal Society of London (Dolnick 2011, 5). In this framework, the pursuit of intellectual and scientific discovery became a popular avocation for many individuals, the vast majority of whom were wealthy men (Figure 7.2).

Figure 7.2: A Walk at Dusk, 1830–1835, by Caspar David Friedrich, is a painting likely of a dolmen, a megalithic (large rock) tomb. Dolmens were built throughout Europe, five to six thousand years ago. Scholars were fascinated by the ancient world, which was an accepted part of Earth's history, even if explanation defied nonsecular thought. Credit: A Walk at Dusk object 93.PA.14 by Casper David Friedrich German, 1774–1840, Paul Getty Museum, is in the public domain and part of the Getty Open Content Program.

In spite of the expectations of Georgian English society to the contrary, Anning became a highly successful fossil hunter as well as a self-educated geologist and anatomist. The geology of Lyme Regis, with its limestone cliffs, provided a fortuitous backdrop for Anning's lifework. Now called the "Jurassic Coast," Lyme Regis has always been a rich source for fossilized remains (Figure 7.3). Continuing her father's passion for fossil hunting, Anning scoured the crumbling cliffs after storms for fossilized remains and shells. The work was physically demanding and downright dangerous. In 1833, while searching for fossils, Anning lost her beloved dog in a landslide and nearly lost her own life in the process (Emling 2009).

Figure 7.3: The "Jurassic Coast" of Lyme Regis: the home of fossil hunter Mary Anning. Credit: Lyme-regis-coast-sea-cliffs-924431 by jstarj has been designated to the public domain (CC0) under a Pixabay License.

Around the age of ten, Anning located and excavated a complete fossilized skeleton of an ichthyosaurus ("fish lizard"). She eventually found *Pterodactylus macronyx* and a 2.7-meter *Plesiosaurus*, considered by many to be her greatest discovery (Figure 7.4). These discoveries proved that there had been significant changes in the way living things appeared throughout the history of the world. Like many of her peers, including Darwin, Anning had strong religious convictions. However, the evidence that was being found in the fossil record was contradictory to the Genesis story in the Bible. In *The Fossil Hunter: Dinosaurs, Evolution, and the Woman Whose Discoveries Changed the World*, Anning's biographer Shelley Emling (2009, 38) notes, "the puzzling attributes of Mary's fossil [ichthyosaurus] struck a blow at this belief and eventually helped pave the way for a real understanding of life before the age of humans."

Intellectual and scientific debate now had physical evidence to support the theory of evolution, which would eventually result in Darwin's seminal work, *On the Origin of Species* (1859). Anning's discoveries and theories were appreciated and advocated by her friends, intellectual men who were associated with the Geological Society of London. Regrettably, this organization was closed to women, and Anning received little official recognition for her contributions to the fields of natural history and paleontology. It is clear that Anning's knowledge, diligence, and uncanny luck in finding magnificent specimens of fossils earned her unshakeable credibility and made her a peer to many antiquarians (Emling 2009).

Fossil hunting is still providing evidence and a narrative of the story of Earth. Mary Anning recognized the value of fossils in understanding natural history and relentlessly championed her theories to the brightest minds of her day. Anning's ability to creatively think "outside the box"—skillfully assimilating knowledge from multiple academic fields—was her gift to our present understanding of the fossil record. Given how profoundly Anning has shaped how we, in the modern day, think about the origins of life, it is surprising that her contributions have been so marginalized. Anning's name should be on the tip of everyone's tongue. Fortunately, at least in one sense of the word, it is. The well-known tongue twister, below, may have been written about Mary Anning:

> She sells sea-shells on the sea-shore.
>
> The shells she sells are sea-shells, I'm sure.
>
> For if she sells sea-shells on the sea-shore
>
> Then I'm sure she sells sea-shore shells.

—T. Sullivan (1908)

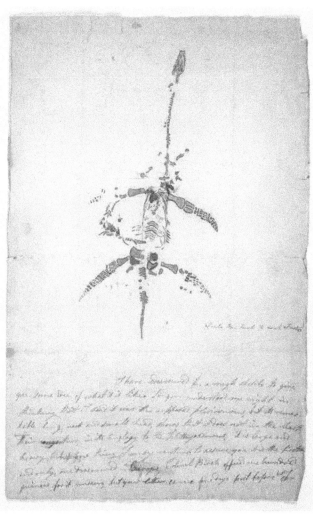

Figure 7.4: Plesiosaurus, illustrated and described by Mary Anning in an undated handwritten letter. Credit: **Autograph letter concerning the discovery of plesiosaurus** by Mary Anning (1799–1847) from the Wellcome Collection is under a CC BY 4.0 License.

Developing Modern Methods

As Mary Anning's story suggests, scientists in Europe were working at a time dominated by western Christian tradition. Literal interpretations of the bible did not allow for the long, slow processes of geological or evolutionary change to operate. However, many scientists were making observations that did not fit the biblical narrative. During the 18th century, Scotsman James Hutton's work on the formation of Earth provided a much longer timeline of events than previous biblical interpretations would allow. Hutton's theory of **Deep Time** was crucial to the understanding of fossils. Deep Time gave the history of Earth enough time—4.543 billion years—to encompass **continental drift**, the evolution of species, and the fossilization process. A second Scotsman, Charles Lyell, propelled Hutton's work into his own theory of **uniformitarianism**, the doctrine that

Earth's geologic formations are the work of slow geologic forces. Lyell's three-volume work, *Principles of Geology* (1830–1833), was influential to naturalist Charles Darwin (see Chapter 2 for more information on Darwin's work). In fact, Lyell's first volume accompanied Darwin on his five-year voyage around the world on the *HMS Beagle* (1831–1836). The concepts proposed by Lyell gave Darwin an opportunity to apply his working theories of evolution by natural selection and a greater length of time with which to work. These resulting theories were important scientific discoveries and paved the way for the "Age of Wonder" (Holmes 2010, xvi).

Figure 7.5: Murexsul (Miocene): This fossil was found at the Naval Weapons Center, China Lake, California, in 1945. The fossil was buried deep in the strata and was pulled out of the ground along with a crashed "Fat Boy" missile after atomic missile testing (S. Brubaker, personal communication, March 9, 2018). Credit: Murexsul (Figure 7.6) from the Maturango Museum, Ridgecrest, California, by Sarah S. King and Lee Anne Zajicek is under a CC BY-NC 4.0 License.

The work of Anning, Darwin, Lyell, and many others laid the foundation for the modern methods we use today. Though anthropology is focused on humans and our primate relatives (and not on dinosaurs, as many people wrongly assume), you will see that methods developed in paleontology, geology, chemistry, biology, and physics are often applied in anthropological research. In this chapter, you will learn about the primary methods and techniques employed by biological anthropologists to answer questions about **fossils**, the mineralized copies of once-living organisms (Figure 7.5). Ultimately, these answers provide insights into human evolution. Pay close attention to ways in which modern biological anthropologists use other disciplines to analyze evidence and reconstruct past activities and environments.

Earth: It's Older than Dirt

Scientists have developed precise and accurate dating methods based on work in the fields of physics and chemistry. Using these methods, scientists are able to establish the age of Earth as well as approximate ages of the organisms that have lived here. Earth is roughly 4.6 billion years old, give or take a few hundred million years. The first evidence for a living organism appeared around 3.5 billion years ago (**bya**). The scale of geologic time can seem downright overwhelming. In order to organize and make sense of Earth's past, geologists break up that time into subunits, which are human-made divisions along Earth's timeline. The largest subunit is the **eon.** An eon is further divided into **eras,** and eras are divided into **periods**. Finally, periods are divided into **epochs** (see Figure 7.6; Williams 2004, 37). Currently, we are living in the Phanerozoic eon, Cenozoic era, Quaternary period, and probably the Holocene epoch—though there is academic debate about the current epoch (see below).

Eon	Era	Period	Epoch	MYA	Life Forms	North American Events
Phanerozoic	Cenozoic (CZ) / Tertiary (T)	Quaternary (Q)	Holocene (H)	0.01	Extinction of large mammals and birds; Modern humans	Ice age glaciations; glacial outburst floods
			Pleistocene (PE)	2.6	Spread of grassy ecosystems (Age of Mammals)	Cascade volcanoes (W); Linking of North and South America (Isthmus of Panama); Columbia River Basalt eruptions (NW); Basin and Range extension (W)
		Neogene (N)	Pliocene (PL)	5.3		
			Miocene (MI)	23.0		
		Paleogene (PG)	Oligocene (OL)	33.9		Laramide Orogeny ends (W)
			Eocene (E)	56.0		
			Paleocene (EP)	66.0	Early primates — Mass extinction	
	Mesozoic (MZ) (Age of Reptiles)	Cretaceous (K)		145.0	Placental mammals; Early flowering plants	Laramide Orogeny (W); Western Interior Seaway (W); Sevier Orogeny (W)
		Jurassic (J)		201.3	Dinosaurs diverse and abundant	Nevadan Orogeny (W); Elko Orogeny (W)
		Triassic (TR)		251.9	Mass extinction; First dinosaurs; first mammals; Flying reptiles — Mass extinction	Breakup of Pangaea begins; Sonoma Orogeny (W)
	Paleozoic (PZ)	Permian (P)		298.9	(Age of Amphibians) Coal-forming swamps; Sharks abundant; First reptiles	Supercontinent Pangaea intact; Ouachita Orogeny (S); Alleghany (Appalachian) Orogeny (E); Ancestral Rocky Mountains (W)
		Pennsylvanian (PN)		323.2		
		Mississippian (M)		358.9	Mass extinction; First amphibians; First forests (evergreens)	Antler Orogeny (W); Acadian Orogeny (E-NE)
		Devonian (D)		419.2	(Fishes)	
		Silurian (S)		443.8	First land plants; Mass extinction; Primitive fish	Taconic Orogeny (E-NE)
		Ordovician (O)		485.4	(Marine Invertebrates) Trilobite maximum; Rise of corals	Extensive oceans cover most of proto-North America (Laurentia)
		Cambrian (C)		541.0	Early shelled organisms	
Proterozoic		Precambrian (PC, W, X, Y, Z)			Complex multicelled organisms	Supercontinent rifted apart; Formation of early supercontinent; Grenville Orogeny (E)
				2500	Simple multicelled organisms	First iron deposits; Abundant carbonate rocks
Archean				4000	Early bacteria and algae (stromatolites)	Oldest known Earth rocks
Hadean				4600	Origin of life; Formation of the Earth	Formation of Earth's crust

Figure 7.6: The Geologic time scale is shown here, with periods broken into eons, eras, periods, and in some cases epochs. Some life forms and geological events are noted for each period. Credit: **Geologic Time Scale**, by **National Park Service**, designed by Trista Thornberry-Ehrlich and Rebecca Port, adapted from ones from **USGS** and the International Commission on Stratigraphy, is in the **public domain**. [Image Description].

These divisions are based on major changes and events recorded in the geologic record. Events like significant shifts in climate or mass extinctions can be used to mark the end of one geologic time unit and the beginning of another. However, it is important to remember that these borders are not real in a physical sense; they are helpful organizational guidelines for scientific research. There can be debate regarding how the boundaries are defined. Additionally, the methods we use to establish these dates are refined over time, occasionally leading to shifts in established chronology (see the discussion on calibration in the radiocarbon dating section below). For instance, the current epoch has been traditionally known as the **Holocene**. It began almost twelve thousand years ago (**kya**) during the warming period after that last major ice age. Today, there is evidence to indicate human-driven climate change is warming the world and changing the environmental patterns faster than the natural cyclical processes. This has led some scientists within the stratigraphic community to argue for a new epoch beginning around 1950 with the Nuclear Age called the **Anthropocene** (Monastersky 2015; Waters et al. 2016). Nobel Laureate Paul Crutzen places the beginning of the Anthropocene much earlier—at the dawn of the Industrial Revolution, with its polluting effects of burning coal (Crutzen and Stoermer 2000, 17–18). Geologist William Ruddiman argues that the epoch began 5,000–8,000 years ago with the advent of agriculture and the buildup of early methane gasses (Ruddiman et al. 2008). Regardless of when the Anthropocene started, the major event that marks the boundary is the warming temperatures and mass extinction of nonhuman species caused by human activity (Figure 7.7). Researchers now declare that "human activity now rivals geologic forces in influencing the trajectory of the Earth System" (Steffen et al. 2018, 1).

Figure 7.7: The Chooz Nuclear Power, in a valley in Ardennes, France, is a reminder that human activity affects the planet greatly. Credit: Chooz Nuclear Power Plant-9361 by Raimond Spekking is under a CC BY-SA 4.0 License.

Fossils: The Taphonomic Process

Most of the evidence of human evolution comes from the study of the dead. To obtain as much information as possible from the remains of once-living creatures, one must understand the processes that occur after death. This is where **taphonomy** comes in (Figure 7.8). Taphonomy is the study of what happens to an organism after death (Komar and Buikstra 2008, 189; Stodder 2008). It includes the study of how an organism becomes a fossil. However, as you'll see throughout this book, the majority of organisms never make it through the full fossilization process.

Taphonomy is important in biological anthropology, especially in subdisciplines like bioarchaeology (the study of human remains in the archaeological record) and zooarchaeology (the study of faunal remains from archaeological sites). It is so important that many scientists have recreated a variety of burial and decay experiments to track taphonomic change in modern contexts. These contexts can then be used to understand the taphonomic patterns seen in the fossil record (see Reitz and Wing 1999, 122–141).

Taphonomic analysis can also give us important insights into the development of complex thought and ritual in human evolution. In Chapter 11, you will see the first evidence of recognized burial practices in hominins. Taphonomy helped to establish whether these burials were simply the result of natural processes or intentionally constructed by humans (Klein 1999, 395; Straus 1989). Deliberate burials often include the body placed in a specific position, such as supine (on the back) with arms crossed over the chest or in a flexed position (think fetal position) facing a particular direction. If bones have evidence of a carnivore or rodent gnawing on them, it can be inferred that the remains were exposed to scavengers after death.

Figure 7.8: Taphonomy focuses on what happens to the remains of an organism, like this coyote, after death. Credit: Coyote remains (Figure 7.14) by Sarah S. King is under a CC BY-NC 4.0 License.

Going back further in time, taphonomic evidence may tell us how our ancestors died. For instance, several australopithecine fossils show evidence of carnivore tooth marks and even punctures from saber-toothed cats, indicating that we weren't always the top of the food chain. The Bodo Cranium, a *Homo erectus* cranium from Middle Awash Valley, Ethiopia, shows cut marks made by stone tools, indicating an early example of possible defleshing activity in our human ancestors (White 1986). At the archaeological site of Zhoukoudian, researchers used taphonomy to show that the highly fragmented remains of at least 51 *Homo erectus* individuals were scavenged by Pleistocene cave hyenas (Boaz et al. 2004). The damage on Skull VI was described as "elongated, raking bite marks, isolated puncture bite marks, and perimortem breakage consistent with patterns of modern hyaenid bone modification" (Boaz et al. 2004). Additionally, a fresh burnt equid cranium was discovered which supports the theory of mobile hominid scavenging and fire use at the site (Boaz et al. 2004).

Special Topic: Bog Bodies and Mummies

Preservation is a key topic in anthropological research, since we can only study the evidence that gets left behind in the fossil and archaeological record. This chapter is concerned with the fossil record; however, there are other forms of preserved remains that provide anthropologists with information about the past. You've undoubtedly heard of mummification, likely in the context of Egyptian or South American mummies. However, bog bodies and ice mummies are further examples of how remains can be preserved in special circumstances. It is important to note that fossilization is a process that takes much longer than the preservation of bog bodies or mummies.

Bog bodies are good examples of wetland preservation. Peat bogs are formed by the slow accumulation of vegetation and silts in ponds and lakes. Individuals were buried in bogs throughout Europe as far back as 10 kya, with a proliferation of activity from 1,600 to 3,200 years ago (Giles 2020; Ravn 2010). When they were found thousands of years later, they resembled recent burials. Their hair, skin, clothing, and organs were exceptionally well preserved, in addition to their bones and teeth (Eisenbeiss 2016; Ravn 2010). Preservation was so good in fact that archaeologists could identify the individuals' last meals and re-create tattoos found on their skin.

Extreme cold can also halt the natural decay process. A well-known ice mummy is Ötzi, a Copper Age man dating to around 5,200 years ago found in the Alps (Vanzetti et al. 2012; Vidale et al. 2016). As with the bog bodies, his hair, skin, clothing, and organs were all well preserved. Recently, archaeologists were able to identify his last meal (Maixner et al. 2018). It was high in fat, which makes sense considering the extremely cold environment in which he lived, as meals high in fat assist in cold tolerance (Fumagalli et al. 2015).

In the Andes, ancient peoples would bury human sacrifices throughout the high peaks in a sacred ritual called Capacocha (Wilson et al. 2007). The best-preserved mummy to date is called the "Maiden" or "Sarita" because she was found at the summit of Sara Sara Volcano. Her remains are over 500 years old, but she still looks like the 15-year-old girl she was at the time of her death, as if she had just been sleeping for 500 years (Reinhard 2006).

Finally, arid environments can also contribute to the preservation of organic remains. As discussed with waterlogged sites, much of the bacteria that is active in breaking down bodies is already present in our gut and begins the putrefaction process shortly after death. Arid environments deplete organic material of the moisture that putrefactive bacteria need to function (Booth et al. 2015). When that occurs, the soft tissue like skin, hair, and organs can be preserved. It is similar to the way a food dehydrator works to preserve meat, fruit, and vegetables for long-term storage. There are several examples of arid environments spontaneously preserving human remains, including catacomb burials in Austria and Italy (Aufderheide 2003, 170, 192–205).

Fossilization

Fossils only represent a tiny fraction of creatures that existed in the past. It is extremely difficult for an organism to become a fossil. After all, organisms are designed to deteriorate after they die. Bacteria, insects, scavengers, weather, and environment all aid in the process that breaks down organisms so their elements can be returned to Earth to maintain ecosystems (Stodder 2008). **Fossilization**, therefore, is the preservation of an organism against these natural decay processes (Figure 7.9).

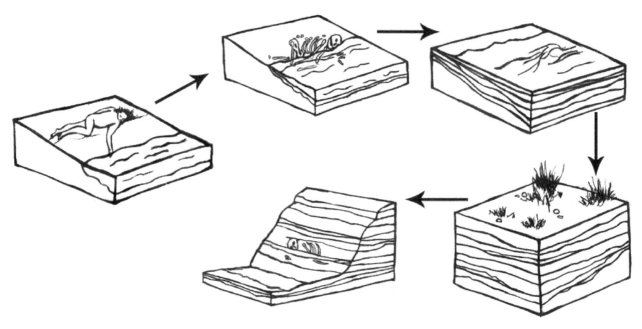

Figure 7.9: A simplified illustration of the fossilization process beginning at an organism's death. In this example, the individual begins to decompose and then is covered by water and sediments, both protecting it and creating an environment for permineralization. Sediments accumulate over time. Erosion eventually exposes the fossil, leading to its eventual discovery by paleoanthropologists. Credit: Fossilization process (Figure 7.15) original to Explorations: An Open Invitation to Biological Anthropology by Mary Nelson is under a CC BY-NC 4.0 License.

For fossilization to occur, several important things must happen. First, the organism must be protected from things like bacterial activity, scavengers, and temperature and moisture fluctuations. A stable environment is important. This means that the organism should not be exposed to significant fluctuations in temperature, humidity, and weather patterns. Changes to moisture and temperature cause the organic tissues to expand and contract repeatedly, which will eventually cause microfractures and break down (Stodder 2008). Soft tissue like organs, muscle, and skin are more easily broken down in the decay process; therefore, they are less likely to be preserved. Bones and teeth, however, last much longer and are more common in the fossil record (Williams 2004, 207).

Wetlands are a particularly good area for preservation because they allow for rapid permanent burial and a stable moisture environment. That is why many fossils are found in and around ancient lakes and river systems. Waterlogged sites can also be naturally **anaerobic** (without oxygen). Much of the bacteria that causes decay is already present in our gut and can begin the decomposition process shortly after death during putrefaction (Booth et al. 2015). Since oxygen is necessary for the body's bacteria to break down organic material, the decay process is significantly slowed or halted in anaerobic conditions.

The next step in the fossilization process is sediment accumulation. The sediments cover and protect the organism from the environment. They, along with water, provide the minerals that will eventually become the fossil (Williams 2004, 31). Sediment accumulation also provides the pressure needed for mineralization to take place. **Lithification** is when the weight and pressure of the sediments squeeze out extra fluids and replace the voids that appear with minerals from the surrounding sediments. Finally, we have **permineralization**. This is when the organism is fully replaced by minerals from the sediments. A fossil is really a mineral copy of the original organism (Williams 2004, 31).

Types of Fossils

Plants

Figure 7.10: An exquisite piece of petrified wood. Credit: PetrifiedWood at the Petrified Forest National Park by Jon Sullivan has been designated to the public domain (CC0).

Plants make up the majority of fossilized materials. One of the most common plants existing today, the fern, has been found in fossilized form many times. Other plants that no longer exist or the early ancestors of modern plants come in fossilized forms as well. It is through these fossils that we can discover how plants evolved and learn about the climate of Earth over different periods of time.

Another type of fossilized plant is **petrified wood**. This fossil is created when actual pieces of wood—such as the trunk of a tree—mineralize and turn into rock. Petrified wood is a combination of silica, calcite, and quartz, and it is both heavy and brittle. Petrified wood can be colorful and is generally aesthetically pleasing because all the features of the original tree's composition are illuminated through mineralization (Figure 7.10). There are a number of places all over the world where petrified wood "forests" can be found, but there is an excellent assemblage in Arizona, at the Petrified Forest National Park. At this site, evidence relating to the environment of the area some 225 **mya** is on display.

Human/Animal Remains

We are more familiar with the fossils of early animals because natural history museums have exhibits of dinosaurs and extinct mammals. However, there are a number of fossilized hominin remains that provide a picture of the fossil record over the course of our evolution from primates. The term **hominins** includes all human ancestors who existed after the evolutionary split from chimpanzees and bonobos, some six to seven mya. Modern humans are *Homo sapiens*, but hominins can include much earlier versions of humans. One such hominin is "Lucy" (AL 288-1), the 3.2 million-year-old fossil of *Australopithecus afarensis* that was discovered in Ethiopia in 1974 (Figure 7.11). Until recently, Lucy was the most complete and oldest hominin fossil, with 40% of her skeleton preserved (see Chapter 9 for more information about Lucy). In 1994, an *Australopithecus* fossil nicknamed "Little Foot" (Stw 573) was located in the World Heritage Site at Sterkfontein Caves ("the Cradle of Humankind") in South Africa. Little Foot is more complete than Lucy and possibly the oldest fossil that has so far been found, dating to at least 3.6 million years (Granger et al. 2015). The ankle bones of the fossil were extricated from the matrix of concrete-like rock, revealing that the bones of the ankles and feet indicate bipedalism (University of Witwatersrand 2017).

Both the Lucy and Little Foot fossils date back to the Pliocene (5.8 to 2.3 mya). Older hominin fossils from the late Miocene (7.25 to 5.5 mya) have been located, although they are much less complete. The oldest hominin fossil is a fragmentary skull named *Sahelanthropus tchadensis*, found in Northern Chad and dating to circa seven mya (Lebatard et al. 2008). It is through the discovery, dating, and study of primate and early hominin fossils that we find physical evidence of the evolutionary timeline of humans.

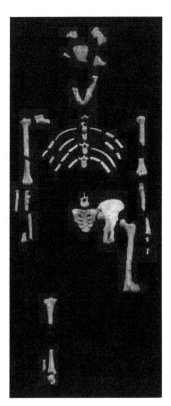

Figure 7.11: "Lucy" (AL 288-1), Australopithecus afarensis. Credit: Lucy blackbg by 120 is under a CC BY 2.5 License.

Asphalt

Figure 7.12: This is a recreation of how animals tragically came to be trapped in the asphalt lake at the La Brea Tar Pits. Credit: **Mammoth Tragedy at La Brea Tar Pits (5463657162)** by KimonBerlin is under a CC BY-SA 2.0 License.

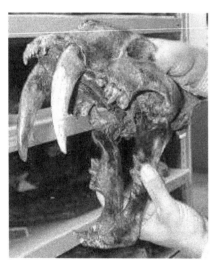

Figure 7.13: The fearsome jaws of the saber-toothed cat (Smilodon fatalis) found at the La Brea Tar Pits. Credit: **Smilodon saber-toothed tiger skull (La Brea Asphalt, Upper Pleistocene; Rancho La Brea tar pits, southern California, USA) 1** by James St. John is under a CC BY 2.0 License.

Asphalt, a form of crude oil, can also yield fossilized remains. Asphalt is commonly referred to in error as tar because of its viscous nature and dark color. A famous fossil site from California is La Brea Tar Pits in downtown Los Angeles (Figure 7.12). In the middle of the busy city on Wilshire Boulevard, asphalt (not tar) bubbles up through seeps (cracks) in the sidewalk. The La Brea Tar Pits Museum provides an incredible look at the both extinct and extant animals that lived in the Los Angeles Basin 40,000–11,000 years ago. These animals became entrapped in the asphalt during the Pleistocene and perished in place. Ongoing excavations have yielded millions of fossils, including **megafauna** such as American mastodons and incomplete skeletons of extinct species of dire wolves, *Canis dirus*, and the saber-toothed cat, *Smilodon fatalis* (Figure 7.13). Fossilized remains of plants have also been found in the asphalt. The remains of one person have also been found at the tar pits. Referred to as La Brea Woman, the remains were found in 1914 and were subsequently dated to around 10,250 years ago. The La Brea Woman was a likely female individual who was 17–28 years old at the time of her death, with a height of under five feet (Spray 2022). She is thought to have died from blunt force trauma to her head, famously making her Los Angeles's first documented homicide victim (Spray 2022). (Learn more about her in the Special Topic box, "Necropolitics," below.) Between the fossils of animals and those of plants, paleontologists have a good idea of the way the Los Angeles Basin looked and what the climate in the area was like many thousands of years ago.

Igneous Rock

Most fossils are found in sedimentary rock. This type of rock has been formed from deposits of minerals over millions of years in bodies of water on Earth's surface. Some examples include shale, limestone, and siltstone. Sedimentary rock typically has a layered appearance. However, fossils have been found in igneous rock as well. Igneous rock is volcanic rock that is created from cooled molten lava. It is rare for fossils to survive molten lava, and it is estimated that only 2% of all fossils have been found in igneous rock (Ingber 2012). Part of a giant rhinocerotid skull dating back 9.2 mya to the Miocene was discovered in Cappadocia, Turkey, in 2010. The fossil was a remarkable find because the eruption of the Çardak caldera was so sudden that it simply dehydrated and "baked" the animal (Antoine et al. 2012).

Trace Fossils

Depending on the specific circumstances of weather and time, even footprints can become fossilized. Footprints fall into the category of **trace fossils**, which includes other evidence of biological activity such as nests, burrows, tooth marks, and shells. A well-known example of trace fossils are the Laetoli footprints in Tanzania (Figure 7.14). More recently, archaeological investigations in North America have revealed fossil footprints which rewrite the history of people in the Americas at White Sands, New Mexico. You can read more about the Laetoli and White Sands footprints in the Dig Deeper box below.

Figure 7.14: A few early hominin footprints fossilized at Laetoli. Credit: NHM – Laetoli Fußspuren by Wolfgang Sauber is under a CC BY-SA 4.0 License.

Other fossilized footprints have been discovered around the world. At Pech Merle cave in the Dordogne region of France, archaeologists discovered two fossilized footprints. They then brought in indigenous trackers from Namibia to look for other footprints. The approach worked, as many other footprints belonging to as many as five individuals were discovered with the expert eyes of the trackers (Pastoors et al. 2017). These footprints date back 12,000 years (Granger Historical Picture Archive 2018).

Some of the more unappealing but still-fascinating trace fossils are bezoars and coprolite. **Bezoars** are hard, concrete-like substances found in the intestines of fossilized creatures. Bezoars start off like the hair balls that cats and rabbits accumulate from grooming, but they become hard, concrete-like substances in the intestines. If an animal with a hairball dies before expelling the hair ball mass *and* the organism becomes fossilized, that mass becomes a bezoar.

Coprolite is fossilized dung. One of the best collections of coprolites is affectionately known as the "Poozeum." The collection includes a huge coprolite named "Precious" (Figure 7.15). Coprolite, like all fossilized materials, can be **in matrix**—meaning that the fossil is embedded in secondary rock. As unpleasant as it may seem to work with coprolites, remember that the organic material in dung has mineralized or has started to mineralize; therefore, it is no longer soft and is generally not smelly. Also, just as a doctor can tell a lot about health and diet from a stool sample, anthropologists can glean a great deal of information from coprolite about the diets of ancient animals and the environment in which the food sources existed. For instance, 65 million-year-old grass *phytoliths* (microscopic silica in plants) found in dinosaur coprolite in India revealed that grasses had been in existence much earlier than scientists initially believed (Taylor and O'Dea 2014, 133).

Figure 7.15: An extremely large coprolite named "Precious." Credit: Precious the Coprolite Courtesy of the Poozeum by Poozeum is under a CC BY-SA 4.0 License.

Pseudofossils

Pseudofossils are not to be mistaken for fake fossils, which have vexed scientists from time to time. A fake fossil is an item that is deliberately manipulated or manufactured to mislead scientists and the general public. In contrast, pseudofossils are not misrepresentations but rather misinterpretations of rocks that look like true fossilized remains (S. Brubaker, personal communication, March 9, 2018). Pseudofossils are the result of impressions or markings on rock, or even the way other inorganic materials react with the rock. A common example is dendrites, the crystallized deposits of black minerals that resemble plant growth (Figure 7.16). Other examples of pseudofossils are unusual or odd-shaped rocks that include various concretions and nodules. An expert can examine a potential fossil to see if there is the requisite internal structure of organic material such as bone or wood that would qualify the item as a fossil.

Figure 7.16: A beautiful example of dendrites, a type of pseudofossil. It's easy to see how the black crystals look like plant growth. Credit: Dendrites (Figure 7.25) from the Maturango Museum, Ridgecrest, California, by Sarah S. King and Lee Anne Zajicek is under a CC BY-NC 4.0 License.

Dig Deeper: Trace Fossils

The Power of Poop

Coprolites found in Paisley Caves, Oregon, in the United States are shedding new light on some of the earliest occupants in North America. Human coprolites are distinguished from animal coprolites through the identification of fecal biomarkers using lipids, or fats, and bile acids (Shillito et al. 2020a). Paisley Caves have 16,000 years of anthropogenic, or human-caused, deposition, with some coprolites having been dated as old as 12.8kya (Blong et al. 2020). Over 285 radiocarbon dates have been recorded from the site (Shillito et al. 2020a), making Paisley Caves one of the most well-dated archaeological sites in the United States. Coprolite analysis can be summarized in three levels, macroscopic, microscopic, and molecular. This can also be understood as analyzing the morphology (macroscopic), contents (microscopic), and residues (molecular) (Shillito et al. 2020b). Each of these levels adds a different layer of information. Coprolite shape is informative through what can be seen macroscopically, such as ingestions of basketry or cordage, small gravels and grains, and general shape. The contents of coprolites may be of the most interest to scientists because certain plants and animals can signal past environments as well as food procurement methods. Coprolites from Paisley Caves have included small pebbles and obsidian chips from butchering game, grinding plants, and general food preparation as well as small bits of fire cracked rock likely from cooking in hearths (Blong 2020). Additionally, rodent bones in coprolites included crania and vertebrae, which suggests whole consumption (Taylor et al. 2020). Insect remains are present in the coprolites as well, such as ants, Jerusalem crickets, June beetles, and darkling beetles (Blong 2020). In all, the coprolites of Paisley Caves have provided an invaluable resource to anthropologists to study the past climate and lifeways of early humans in the Americas.

Coprolites can also signal past health, which is a study known as paleopathology. A study by Katelyn McDonough and colleagues (2022) focused on the identification of parasites in coprolites at Bonneville Estates Rockshelter in eastern Nevada and their link to the greater Great Basin during the Archaic, a period of time spanning 8,000–5,000 years ago. According to the study, parasites such as Acanthocephalans (thorny-headed worms) have been affecting the Great Basin for at least the last 10,000 years. Acanthocephalans are endoparasites, meaning parasites that live inside of their hosts. They are found worldwide and seem to have been concentrated in the Great Basin in the past. Bonneville Estates Rockshelter has been visited by humans for over 13,000 years, with parasite identification going back to nearly 7,000 years. The species identified at Bonneville Estates is *Moniliformis clarki*. This species parasitizes crickets and insects, a popular food source during the Archaic in the Great Basin. The parasite uses intermediate hosts to get to mammals and birds as definitive hosts. Crickets and beetles have been recorded as food materials in Paisley Caves as well. Insects have remained an important dietary staple for people of the Great Basin and are consumed raw, dried, brined, or ground into flour. Insects that remain uncooked or undercooked have a higher risk for transmission of parasites. Symptoms associated with Acanthocephalans infection are intense intestinal discomfort, anemia, and anorexia, leading to death. It is hypothesized that the consumption of basketry, cordage, and charcoal (which was also identified at Paisley Caves), sometimes associated with parasite-infected coprolites, may have been a method of treatment for the infection. Interestingly, present day infections from this parasite are rising after remaining quite rare, as detection of the parasite is occurring in insect farms.

Walking to the Past

In 1974, British anthropologist Mary Leakey discovered fossilized animal tracks at Laetoli (Figure 7.17), not far from the important paleoanthropological site at Olduvai Gorge in Tanzania. A few years later, a 27-meter trail of hominin footprints were discovered at the same site. These 70 footprints, now referred to as the Laetoli Footprints, were created when early humans walked in wet volcanic ash. Before the impressions were obscured, more volcanic ash and rain fell, sealing the footprints. These series of environmental events were truly extraordinary, but they fortunately resulted in some of the most famous and revealing trace fossils ever found. Dating of the footprints indicate that they were made 3.6 mya (Smithsonian National Museum of Natural History 2018).

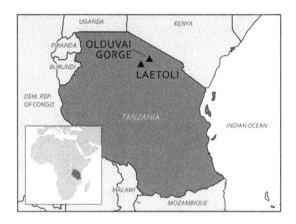

Figure 7.17: Location of Laetoli site in Tanzania, Africa, with Olduvai Gorge nearby. Credit: Laetoli and Olduvai Gorge sites (Figure 7.26) original to Explorations: An Open Invitation to Biological Anthropology by Elyssa Ebding at GeoPlace, California State University, Chico is under a CC BY-NC 4.0 License.

Just as forensic scientists can use footprints to identify the approximate build of a potential suspect in a crime, archaeologists have read the Laetoli Footprints for clues to these early humans. The footprints clearly indicate bipedal hominins who had similar feet to those of modern humans. Analysis of the gait through computer simulation revealed that the hominins at Laetoli walked similarly to the way we walk today (Crompton 2012). More recent analyses confirm the similarity to modern humans but also indicate a gait that involved more of a flexed limb than that of modern humans (Hatala et al. 2016; Raichlen and Gordon 2017). The relatively short stride implies that these hominins had short legs—unlike the longer legs of later early humans who migrated out of Africa (Smithsonian National Museum of Natural History 2018). In the context of Olduvai Gorge, where fossils of *Australopithecus afarensis* have been located and dated to the same timeframe as the footprints, it is likely that these newly discovered impressions were left by these same hominins.

The footprints at Laetoli were made by a small group of as many as three *Australopithecus afarensis*, walking in close proximity, not unlike what we would see on a modern street or sidewalk. Two trails of footprints have been positively identified with the third set of prints appearing smaller and set in the tracks left by one of the larger individuals. While scientific methods have given us the ability to date the footprints and understand the body mechanics of the hominin, additional consideration of the footprints can lead to other implications. For instance, the close proximity of the individuals implies a close relationship existed between them, not unlike that of a family. Due to the size variation and the depth of impression, the footprints seem to have been made by two larger adults and possibly one child. Scientists theorize that the weight being carried by one of the larger individuals is a young child or a baby (Masao et al. 2016). Excavation continues at Laetoli today, resulting in the discovery of two more footprints in 2015, also believed to have been made by *Au. afarensis* (Masao et al. 2016).

But it is not just human evolution studies that can benefit from the analysis of fossil footprints. A recent discovery of fossilized footprints has rewritten what we know about the peopling of the Americas. It was originally thought that humans had been in the Americas for at least the last 15,000 years by crossing through the ice-free corridor (IFC) between the Cordilleran and Laurentide ice sheets in present-day Alaska and Canada. However, fossil footprints from the Tularosa Basin of New Mexico (see Figure 7.18) discovered in 2021 have challenged this theory. The footprints, dated between 22,860 (∓320) and 21,130 (∓250) years ago (nps.gov) based on *Ruppia cirrhosa* grass seeds located above and below the footprints, have shown humans have been in the Americas for much longer than previously thought. These footprints represent an adolescent individual and toddler walking through the lakebed at White Sands (see Figure 7.19), New Mexico, alongside both giant ground sloths and mammoths (Barras 2022; Wade 2021). Also present in the lakebed are footprints of camels and dire wolves (nps.gov 2022; Wade 2021).

Figure 7.18: Tularosa Basin, New Mexico. Credit: Map of Tularosa Basin by the United States Geological Survey is in the public domain.

Figure 7.19: Excavation of fossil footprints from New Mexico. Credit: Images of White Sands National Park Study Site Footprints by the USGS Climate Research and Development Program is in the public domain.

The IFC model was upheld by a group of theorists known as "Clovis First," who believed the migration of people into the Americas was recent and was represented archaeologically through the Clovis projectile point toolkit. Subsequent discoveries at sites such as Cactus Hill on the east coast of the United States and Monte Verde, Chile, have demonstrated that this model wouldn't have worked. Because these sites are as old as 20,000 years and 18,500 years respectively, the IFC would have been frozen over and impassable (Gruhn 2020). Other models have been adopted to account for this, such as the coastal migration model down the west coast of North America. The more-likely migration scenario seems to be neither of these as more discoveries or antiquity continue to emerge. People may instead have migrated into the Americas before the last glacial maximum began, around 25,500–19,000 years ago. According to Indigenous knowledge, they have always been here. With the discovery of the White Sands footprints, it is known that humans have been in the Americas for at least 20,000 years.

This discovery also reveals the importance of recognizing knowledge beyond that which is produced by the European scientific tradition. Rather than framing science in a way that runs counter to Indigenous knowledge, it can be thought that science is catching up with it. For instance, the Acoma Pueblo people have the word for *camel* in their vocabulary. This was dismissed by scientists who assumed the word was for describing camels that were introduced to the United States in the past 100 years. However, the discovery of the White Sands footprints also included the footprints of Pleistocene camels in the same strata. Therefore, the fact that the Acoma Pueblo people have had a word for *camel* likely refers the Pleistocene-age megafauna camel, *Camelops hesternus,* rather than *Camelus dromedarius* or *Camelus bactrianus*, two present-day camel species (which are actually descendants of *Camelops hesternus*). Therefore, the existence of the Acoma Pueblo word for *camel* is not like an anomaly but rather a testament to the fact that Acoma Pueblo ancestors walked beside *C. hesternus* on this continent 20,000 years ago. These footprints challenge the "ice-free corridor" expansion model, as the bridge connecting present-day Alaska and Russia into Canada would have been covered in an impenetrable ice sheet at this time. The discovery of these footprints urges scientists to reconsider further investigations at well-known Terminal Pleistocene/Early Holocene dry lake beds in the Southwestern and Mojave deserts—and to include Indigenous knowledge in their work rather than ignore it.

Special Topic: Necropolitics

What are necropolitics? Necropolitics is an application of critical theory that describes how "governments assign differential value to human life" and similarly how someone is treated after they die (Verghese 2021). How is someone's death political?

Consider the La Brea Woman example from the section on asphalt above. The La Brea Woman's discovery was controversial, not because she is the only person to be found in the tar pits or because of her age but also because of necropolitics. The La Brea Woman was collected in 1914 and her body was housed on display at the George C. Page Museum in Los Angeles against the wishes of the Chumash and the Tongva, two tribes whose ancestral lands include Los Angeles. The museum decided to display a skull cast instead to meet the request of the tribes which included a separate postcranial skeleton from a different individual. The updated display itself was wrought with other ethical issues, as a cast of her skull was "attached to the ancient remains of a Pakistani female that was dyed dark bronze, the femurs shortened to approximate the stature of native people" (Cooper 2010). In both cases, neither the individuals or their descendent communities consented to the display or grotesque modification of human remains. According to an interview conducted by LA Weekly (Cooper 2010) with Cindi Alvitre, former chair of the Gabrielino-Tongva Tribal Council, the display of Indigenous human remains is akin to voyeurism. She states "It's disheartening to me because it's very inappropriate to display any human remains. The things we do to fill the imagination of visitors. It violates human rights." It is important to listen to the wishes of Indigenous people and center their values when conducting work with their ancestors. A good source for considering places to look for archaeological research ethics before conducting fieldwork (and ideally during your research design) is the Society for American Archaeology's ethics principle list, as well as following the Indigenous Archaeology Collective.

Indigenous remains are now protected in the United States due to legislation such as Native American Graves Protection and Repatriation Act (NAGPRA). You can read more about this in Chapter 15: Bioarchaeology and Forensic Anthropology. Before the passing of NAGPRA, tribes had little agency over how the bodies of their ancestors were treated by anthropologists and museums, including decisions about sampling and destructive tests. Now when archaeological field work is conducted on federal land, tribes must be consulted before work begins. This consultation process often includes what to do if human remains are encountered. Indigenous tribes are multifaceted and multivocal; each has its own rules about how to handle the remains of their ancestors. In some cases, all work on the project must be halted after the discovery of human remains. Other tribes allow for work to continue if the remains are moved and reburied. Some tribes are open to radiometric dating if it aligns with their beliefs in the afterlife. Each tribe is different, and each tribe deserves to have its wishes respected.

Voices From the Past: What Fossils Can Tell Us

Given that so few organisms ever become fossilized, any anthropologist or fossil hunter will tell you that finding a fossil is extremely exciting. But this is just the beginning of a fantastic mystery. With the creative application of scientific methods and deductive reasoning, a great deal can be learned about the fossilized organism and the environment in which it lived, leading to enhanced understanding of the world around us.

Dating Methods

Context is a crucial concept in paleoanthropology and archaeology. Objects and fossils are interesting in and of themselves, but without context there is only so much we can learn from them. One of the most important contextual pieces is the dating of an object or fossil. By being able to place it in time, we can compare it more accurately with other contemporary fossils and artifacts or we can better analyze the evolution of a fossil species or artifacts. To answer the question "How do we know what we know?," you have to know how archaeologists and paleoanthropologists establish dates for artifacts, fossils, and sites.

Though accurate dating is important for context and analysis, we must consider the impact. Many of the chronometric dating methods used by anthropologists require the removal of small samples from artifacts, bones, soils, and rock. Thus these techniques are considered destructive. How much of an artifact are you willing to destroy to get your date? Sharon Clough, a Senior Environmental Officer at Cotswold Archaeology, addressed this issue in a case study from her research. She stated that "the benefit of a date did not outweigh the destruction of a valuable and finite resource" (Clough 2020). The resource in question was human remains. When considering our dating options, we want to be sure that we do as little harm as possible, especially in the case of human remains (read more about this issue in the Special Topic box, "Necropolitics").

Dating techniques are divided into two broad categories: relative dating methods and chronometric (sometimes called absolute) dating methods.

Relative Dating

Relative dating methods are used first because they rely on simple observational skills. In the 1820s, Christian Jürgensen Thomsen at the National Museum of Denmark in Copenhagen developed the "three-age" system still used in European archaeology today (Feder 2017, 17). He categorized the artifacts at the museum based on the idea that simpler tools and materials were most likely older than more complex tools and materials. Stone tools must predate metal tools because they do not require special technology to develop. Copper and bronze tools must predate iron because they can be smelted or worked at lower temperatures, etc. Based on these observations, he categorized the artifacts into Stone Age, Bronze Age, and Iron Age.

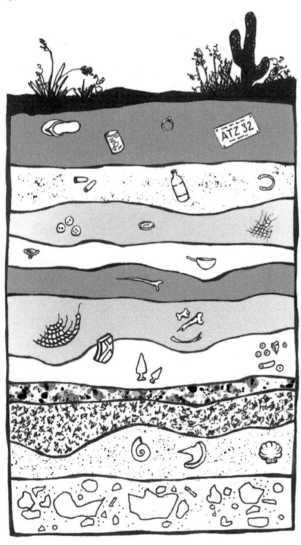

Figure 7.20: An illustration of a stratigraphic cross-section. The objects at a lower strata are older than the one above. Credit: Stratigraphic cross-section (Figure 7.28) original to Explorations: An Open Invitation to Biological Anthropology by Mary Nelson is under a CC BY-NC 4.0 License.

The restriction of relative dating is that you don't know specific dates or how much time passed between different sites or artifacts. You simply know that one artifact or fossil is older than another. Thomsen knew that Stone Age artifacts were older than Bronze Age artifacts, but he couldn't tell if they were hundreds of years older or thousands of years older. The same is true with fossils that have differences of ages into the hundreds of millions of years.

The first relative dating technique is **stratigraphy** (Figure 7.20). You might have already heard this term if you have watched documentaries on archaeological excavations. That's because this method is still being used today. It provides a solid foundation for other dating techniques and gives important context to artifacts and fossils found at a site.

Stratigraphy is based on the **Law of Superposition** first proposed by Nicholas Steno in 1669 and further explored by James Hutton (the previously mentioned "Father" of Deep Time). Essentially, superposition tells us that things on the bottom are older than things on the top (Williams 2004, 28). Notice on Figure 7.20 that there are distinctive layers piled on top of each other. It stands to reason that each layer is older than the one immediately on top of it (Hester et al. 1997, 338). Think of a pile of laundry on the floor. Over the course of a week, as dirty clothes get tossed on that pile, the shirt tossed down on Monday will be at the bottom of the pile while the shirt tossed down on Friday will be at the top. Assuming that the laundry pile was undisturbed throughout the week, if the clothes were picked up layer by layer, the clothing choices that week could be reconstructed in the order that they were worn.

Another relative dating technique is **biostratigraphy**. This form of dating looks at the context of a fossil or artifact and compares it to the other fossils and biological remains (plant and animal) found in the same stratigraphic layers. For instance, if an artifact is found in the same layer as wooly mammoth remains, you know that it must date to around the last ice age, when wooly mammoths were still abundant on Earth. In the absence of more specific dating techniques, early archaeologists could prove the great antiquity of stone tools because of their association with extinct animals. The application of this relative dating technique in archaeology was used at the Folsom site in New Mexico. In 1927, a stone spear point was discovered embedded in the rib of an extinct species of bison. Because of the undeniable association between the artifact and the ancient animal, there was scientific evidence that people had occupied the North American continent since antiquity (Cook 1928).

Similar to biostratigraphic dating is **cultural dating** (Figure 7.21). This relative dating technique is used to identify the chronological relationships between human-made artifacts. Cultural dating is based on artifact types and styles (Hester et al. 1997, 338). For instance, a pocket knife by itself is difficult to date. However, if the same pocket knife is discovered surrounded by cassette tapes and VHS tapes, it is logical to assume that the artifact came from the late 20th century like the cassette and VHS tapes. The pocket knife could not be dated earlier than the late 20th century because the tapes were made no earlier than 1977. In the Thomsen example above, he was able to identify a relative chronology of ancient European tools based on the artifact styles, manufacturing techniques, and raw materials. Cultural dating can be used with any human-made artifacts. Both cultural dating and biostratigraphy are most effective when researchers are already familiar with the time periods for the artifacts and animals. They are still used today to identify general time periods for sites.

Chemical dating was developed in the 19th century and represents one of the early attempts to use soil composition and chemistry to date artifacts. A specific type of chemical dating is **fluorine dating**, and it is commonly used to compare the age of the soil around bone, antler, and teeth located in close proximity (Cook and Ezra-Cohn 1959; Goodrum and Olson 2009). While this technique is based on chemical dating, it only provides the relative dates of items rather than their absolute ages. For this reason, fluorine dating is considered a hybrid form of relative and chronometric dating methods (which will be discussed next).

Soils contain different amounts of chemicals, and those chemicals, such as fluorine, can be absorbed by human and animal bones buried in the soil. The longer the remains are in the soil, the more fluorine they will absorb (Cook and Ezra-Cohn 1959; Goodrum and Olson 2009). A sample of the bone or antler can be processed and measured for its

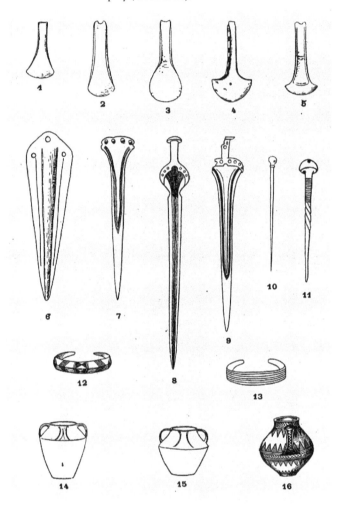

Figure 7.21: Charts of typology, like these representing items from the Bronze Age, are used to classify artifacts and illustrate cultural material assemblages. Credit: **Bronze Age implements, ornaments and pottery (Period II)** by Wellcome Collection is under a CC BY 4.0 License.

fluorine content. Unfortunately, this absorption rate is highly sensitive to temperature, soil pH, and varying fluorine levels in local soil and groundwater (Goodrum and Olson 2009; Haddy and Hanson 1982). This makes it difficult to get an accurate date for the remains or to compare remains between two sites. However, this technique is particularly useful for determining whether different artifacts come from the same burial context. If they were buried in the same soil for the same length of time, their fluorine signatures would match.

Chronometric Dating

Unlike relative dating methods, **chronometric dating** methods provide specific dates and time ranges. Many of the chronometric techniques we will discuss are based on work in other disciplines such as chemistry and physics. The modern developments in studying radioactive materials are accurate and precise in establishing dates for ancient sites and remains.

Many of the chronometric dating methods are based on the measurement of radioactive decay of particular elements. **Elements** are materials that cannot be broken down into more simple materials without losing their chemical identity (Brown et al. 2018, 48). Each element consists of an

atom that has a specific number of protons (positively charged particles) and electrons (negatively charged particles) as well as varying numbers of neutrons (particles with no charge). The protons and neutrons are located in the densely compacted nucleus of the atom, but the majority of the volume of an atom is space outside the nucleus around which the electrons orbit (see Figure 7.22).

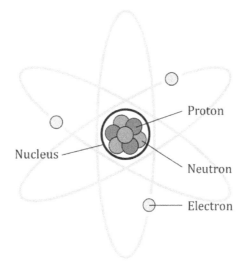

Figure 7.22: Simplified illustration of an atom. Credit: Atom Diagram by AG Caesar is under a CC BY-SA 4.0 License.

Elements are classified based on the number of protons in the nucleus. For example, carbon has six protons, giving it an atomic number 6. Uranium has 92 protons, which means that it has an atomic number 92. While the number of protons in the atom of an element do not vary, the number of neutrons may. Atoms of a given element that have different numbers of neutrons are known as **isotopes**.

The majority of an atom's mass is determined by the protons and neutrons, which have more than a thousand times the mass of an electron. Due to the different numbers of neutrons in the nucleus, isotopes vary by nuclear/atomic weight (Brown et al. 2018, 94). For instance, isotopes of carbon include carbon 12 (^{12}C), carbon 13 (^{13}C), and carbon 14 (^{14}C). Carbon always has six protons, but ^{12}C has six neutrons whereas ^{14}C has eight neutrons. Because ^{14}C has more neutrons, it has a greater mass than ^{12}C (Brown et al. 2018, 95).

Most isotopes in nature are considered **stable isotopes** and will remain in their normal structure indefinitely. However, some isotopes are considered **unstable isotopes** (sometimes called radioisotopes) because they spontaneously release energy and particles, transforming into stable isotopes (Brown et al. 2018, 946; Flowers et al. 2018, section 21.1). The process of transforming the atom by spontaneously releasing energy is called **radioactive decay**. This change occurs at a predictable rate for nearly all radioisotopes of elements, allowing scientists to use unstable isotopes to measure time passage from a few hundred to a few billion years with a large degree of accuracy and precision.

The leading chronometric method for archaeology is **radiocarbon dating** (Figure 7.23). This method is based on the decay of ^{14}C, which is an unstable isotope of carbon. It is created when nitrogen 14 (^{14}N) interacts with cosmic rays, which causes it to capture a neutron and convert to ^{14}C. Carbon 14 in our atmosphere is absorbed by plants during photosynthesis, a process by which light energy is turned into chemical energy to sustain life in plants, algae, and some bacteria. Plants absorb carbon dioxide from the atmosphere and use the energy from light to convert it into sugar that fuels the plant (Campbell and Reece 2005, 181–200). Though ^{14}C is an unstable isotope, plants can use it in the same way that they use the stable isotopes of carbon.

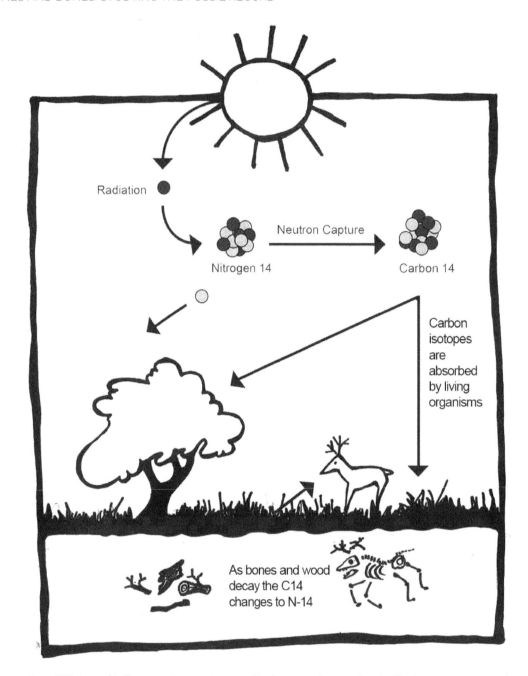

Figure 7.23: A graphic illustrating how 14C is created in the atmosphere, is absorbed by living organisms, and ends up in the archaeological record. Credit: Radiocarbon dating (Figure 7.32) original to Explorations: An Open Invitation to Biological Anthropology by Mary Nelson is under a CC BY-NC 4.0 License.

Animals get ^{14}C by eating the plants. Humans take it in by eating plants and animals. After death, organisms stop taking in new carbon, and the unstable ^{14}C will begin to decay. Carbon 14 has a half-life of 5,730 years (Hester et al. 1997, 324). That means that in 5,730 years, half the amount of ^{14}C will convert back into ^{14}N. Because the pattern of radioactive decay is so reliable, we can use ^{14}C to accurately date sites up to 55,000 years old (Hajdas et al. 2021). However, ^{14}C can only be used on the remains of biological organisms. This includes charcoal, shell, wood, plant material, and bone. This method involves destroying a small sample of the material. Earlier methods of radiocarbon dating required at least 1 gram of material, but with the introduction of accelerator mass spectrometry (AMS), sample sizes as small as 1 milligram can now be used (Hajdas et al. 2021). This significantly reduces the destructive nature of this method.

The use of radiocarbon dating at Denisova Cave in modern-day Russia revealed an astounding find, the first dated first-generation individual with a

Neanderthal mother and Denisovan father. Vivian Slon and colleagues (2018) sequenced the genome, which revealed the individual's hybrid genetic background, and radiocarbon dated the remains, revealing the sub-adult was over 50,000 years old (Slon et al. 2018).

As mentioned before, ^{14}C is unstable and ultimately decays back into [14]N. This decay is happening at a constant rate (even now, inside your own body!). However, as long as an organism is alive and taking in food, ^{14}C is being replenished in the body. As soon as an organism dies, it no longer takes in new [14]C. We can then use the rate of decay to measure how long it has been since the organism died (Hester et al. 1997, 324). However, the amount of ^{14}C in the atmosphere is not stable over time. It fluctuates based on changes to the earth's magnetic field and solar activity. In order to turn ^{14}C results into accurate calendar years, they must be calibrated using data from other sources. Annual tree rings (see discussion of **dendrochronology** below), **foraminifera** from stratified marine sediments, and microfossils from lake sediments can be used to chart the changes in ^{14}C as "calibration curves." The radiocarbon date obtained from the sample is compared to the established curve and then adjusted to reflect a more accurate calendar date (see Figure 7.24). The curves are updated over time with more data so that we can continue to refine radiocarbon dates (Törnqvist et al. 2016). The most recent calibration curves were released in 2020 and may change the dates for some existing sites by hundreds of years (Jones 2020).

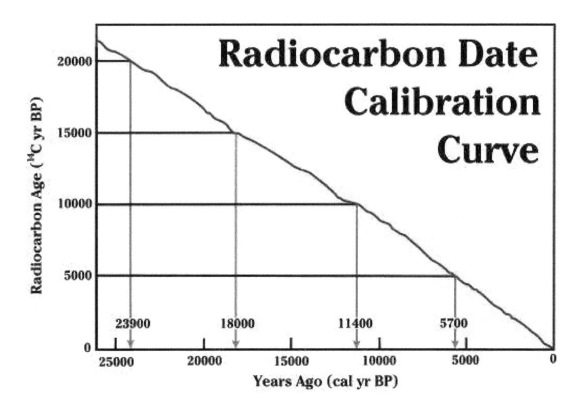

Figure 7.24: This is a simplified example of a calibration curve, showing how the radiocarbon age (y axis) is compared with the calibration curve to produce calibrated dates (x axis). Credit: Radiocarbon Date Calibration Curve by HowardMorland is under a CC BY-SA 3.0 License. [Based on information from Reimer et al. 2004. Radiocarbon 46: 1029-58.] [Image Description].

As you will see in the hominin chapters (Chapters 9–12), 55,000 years is only a tiny fragment of human evolutionary history. It is insignificant in the context of the age of our planet. In order to date even older fossils, other methods are necessary.

Potassium-argon (K-Ar) dating and **argon-argon (Ar-Ar) dating** can reach further back into the past than radiocarbon dating. Used to date volcanic rock, these techniques are based on the decay of unstable potassium 40 ([40]K) into argon 40 ([40]Ar) gas, which gets trapped in the crystalline structures of volcanic material. It is a method of indirect dating. Instead of dating the fossil itself, K-Ar and Ar-Ar dates volcanic layers around the fossil. It will tell you when the volcanic eruption that deposited the layers occurred. This is where stratigraphy becomes important. The date of the surrounding layers can give you a minimum and maximum age of the fossil based on where it is in relation to those layers. This technique was used at Gesher Benot Ya'aqo in the Jordan Valley, dating early stratigraphic deposits of basalt flows to 100,000 years old (Bar-Yosef and Belmaker 2011).

The site is unique because early layers of occupation with an Acheulean handaxe industry were made primarily of basalt, which is an uncommon material for this tool technology (see Chapter 10 for a full discussion of this tool technology). The benefit of this dating technique is that ^{40}K has a half-life of circa 1.3 billion years, so it can be used on sites as young as 100 kya and as old as the age of Earth. As you will see in later chapters, it is particularly useful in dating early hominin sites in Africa (Michels 1972, 120; Renfrew and Bahn 2016, 155). Another benefit to this technique is that it does not damage precious fossils because the samples are taken from the surrounding rock instead. However, this method is not without its flaws. A study by J. G. Funkhouser and colleagues (1966) and Raymond Bradley (2015) demonstrated that igneous rocks with fluid inclusions, such as those found in Hawai'i, can release gasses including radiogenic argon when crushed, leading to incorrectly older dates. This is an example of why it is important to use multiple dating methods in research to detect anomalies.

Uranium series dating is based on the decay chain of unstable isotopes of uranium. It uses mass spectrometry to detect the ratios of uranium 238 (^{238}U), uranium 234(^{234}U), and thorium 230 (^{230}Th) in carbonates (Wendt et al. 2021). Thorium accumulates in the carbonate sample through radiometric decay. Thus, the age of the sample is calculated from the difference between a known initial ratio and the ratio present in the sample to be dated. This makes uranium series ideal for dating carbonate rich deposits such as carbonate cements from glacial moraine deposits, speleothems (deposits of secondary minerals that form on the walls, floors, and ceilings of caves, like stalactites and stalagmites), marine and lacustrine carbonates from corals, caliche, and tufa, as well as bones and teeth (University of Arizona, n.d.; van Calsteren and Thomas 2006). Due to the timing of the decay process, this dating technique can be used from a few years up to 650k (Wendt et al. 2021). Since many early hominin sites occur in cave environments, this dating technique can be very powerful. This method has also been used to develop more accurate calibration curves for radiocarbon dating. However, the accuracy of this method depends on knowing the initial ratios of the elements and ruling out possible contamination (Wendt et al. 2021). It also involves the destruction of a small sample of material.

Fission track dating is another useful dating technique for sites that are millions of years old. This is based on the decay of radioactive uranium 238 (^{238}U). The unstable atom of ^{238}U fissions at a predictable rate. The fission takes a lot of energy and causes damage to the surrounding rock. For instance, in volcanic glasses we can see this damage as trails in the glass. Researchers in the lab take a sample of the glass and count the number of fission trails using an optical microscope. As ^{238}U has a half-life of 4,500 million years, it can be used to date rock and mineral material starting at just a few decades and extending back to the age of Earth. As with K-Ar, archaeologists are not dating artifacts directly. They are dating the layers around the artifacts in which they are interested (Laurenzi et al. 2007).

Luminescence dating, which includes thermoluminescence and a related technique called optically stimulated luminescence, is based on the naturally occurring background radiation in soils. Pottery, baked clay, and sediments that include quartz and feldspar are bombarded by radiation from the soils surrounding it. Electrons in the material get displaced from their orbit and trapped in the crystalline structure of the pottery, rock, or sediment. When a sample of the material is heated to 500°C (thermoluminescence) or exposed to particular light wavelengths (optically stimulated luminescence) in the laboratory, this energy gets released in the form of light and heat and can be measured (Cochrane et al. 2013; Renfrew and Bahn 2016, 160). You can use this method to date artifacts like pottery and burnt flint directly. When attempting to date fossils, you may use this method on the crystalline grains of quartz and feldspar in the surrounding soils (Cochrane et al. 2013). The important thing to remember with this form of dating is that heating the artifact or soils will reset the clock. The method is not necessarily dating when the object was last made or used but when it was last heated to 500°C or more (pottery) or exposed to sunlight (sediments). Luminescence dating can be used on sites from less than 100 years to over 100,000 years (Duller 2008, 4). As with all archaeological data, context is crucial to understanding the information.

Like thermoluminescence dating, **electron spin resonance dating** is based on the measurement of accumulated background radiation from the burial environment. It is used on artifacts and rocks with crystalline structures, including tooth enamel, shell, and rock—those for which thermoluminescence would not work. The radiation causes electrons to become dislodged from their normal orbit. They become trapped in the crystalline matrix and affect the electromagnetic energy of the object. This energy can be measured and used to estimate the length of time in the burial environment. This technique works well for remains as old as two million years (Carvajal et al. 2011, 115–116). It has the added benefit of being nondestructive, which is an important consideration when dealing with irreplaceable material.

Not all chronometric dating methods are based on unstable isotopes and their rates of decay. There are several other methods that make use of other natural biological and geologic processes. One such method is known as dendrochronology (Figure 7.25), which is based on the natural growth patterns of trees. Trees create concentric rings as they grow; the width of those rings depends on environmental conditions and season. The age of a tree can be determined by counting its rings, which also show records of rainfall, droughts, and forest fires.

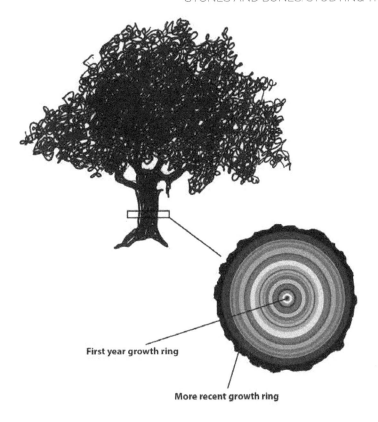

First year growth ring

More recent growth ring

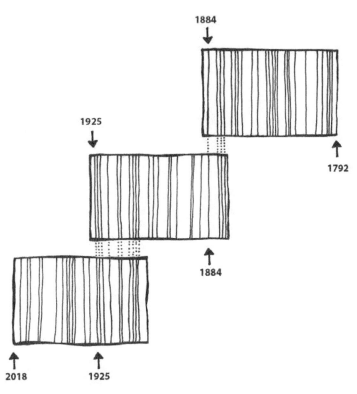

Figure 7.25: Dendrochronology uses the variations in tree rings to create timelines. Credit: **Dendrochronology (Figure 7.34)** original to **Explorations: An Open Invitation to Biological Anthropology** by Mary Nelson is under a **CC BY-NC 4.0 License**.

Tree rings can be used to date wood artifacts and ecofacts from archaeological sites. This first requires the creation of a profile of trees in a particular area. The Laboratory of Tree-Ring Research at the University of Arizona has a comprehensive and ongoing catalog of tree profiles (see University of Arizona n.d.). Archaeologists can then compare wood artifacts and ecofacts with existing timelines, provided the tree rings are visible, and find where their artifacts fit in the pattern. Dendrochronology has been in use since the early 20th century (Dean 2009, 25). The Northern Hemisphere chronology stretches back nearly 14,000 years (Reimer et al. 2013, 1870) and has been used successfully to date southwestern U.S. sites such as Pueblo Bonito and Aztec Ruin (Dean 2009, 26). Dendrochronological evidence has helped calibrate radiocarbon dates and even provided direct evidence of global warming (Dean 2009, 26–27).

In Australia, dendrochronology, along with other environmental reconstruction methods, has been used to show that the Indigenous people had sophisticated land management systems before the arrival of British invaders. According to the work of Michael-Shawn Fletcher and colleagues (2021), there was a significant encroachment of the rainforests and tree species into grasslands after the British invasion. Prior to this time, Indigenous people managed the landscape through controlled burns at regular intervals. This practice created climate-resistant grasslands that were biodiverse and provided predictable food supplies for humans and other animals. Under European land management, there have been negative impacts on biodiversity and climate resilience and an increase in catastrophic wildfires (Fletcher et al. 2021).

This dating method does have its difficulties. Some issues are interrupted ring growth, microclimates, and species growth variations. This is addressed through using multiple samples, statistical analysis, and calibration with other dating methods. Despite these limitations, dendrochronology can be a powerful tool in dating archaeological sites (Hillam et al. 1990; Kuniholm and Striker 1987).

Environmental Reconstruction

As you read in Chapter 2, Charles Darwin, Jean-Baptiste Lamarck, Alfred Russel Wallace, and others recognized the importance of the environment in shaping the evolutionary course of animal species. To understand what selective processes might be shaping evolutionary change, we must be able to reconstruct the environment in which the organism was living.

One of the ways to do that is to look at the plant species that lived in the same time range as the species in which you are interested. One way to identify ancient flora is to analyze **sediment cores** from water and other protected sources. Pollen gets released into the air and some of that pollen will fall on wetlands, lakes, caves, and so forth. Eventually it sinks to the bottom of the lake and forms part of the sediment. This happens year after year, so subsequent layers of pollen build up in an area, creating strata. By taking a core sample and analyzing the pollen and other organic material, an archaeologist can build a timeline of plant types and see changes in the vegetation of the area (Hester et al. 1997, 284). This can even be done over large areas by studying ocean bed cores, which accumulate pollen and dust from large swaths of neighboring continents.

While sediment coring is one of the more common ways to reconstruct past environments, there are a few other methods. These have been recently employed at Holocene Lake Ivanpah, a paleolake that straddles the California and Nevada border in the United States. This lake was originally thought to have been completely dry around 9,300–7,800 kya (Sims and Spaulding 2017). However, analyzing core samples using soil identification, sediment chemistry, subsurface stratigraphy, and **geomorphology** (the study of the physical characteristics of the Earth's surface) revealed deposition of three recent lake fillings during this period in the forms of additional hardpan, or lake bottom, playas, bedded or layered fine-grained (wetland) sediments, and buried beaches below the surface (Sims and Spaulding 2017; Spaulding and Sims 2018). These discoveries are important because they have not been integrated into interpretation of the local archaeological record, as it was assumed that the lake had been dry for thousands of years. Sedimentological analyses such as coring and those listed above can provide great insight into past climates and are accomplished in a minimally destructive way.

Another way of reconstructing past environments is by using stable isotopes. Unlike unstable isotopes, stable isotopes remain constant in the environment throughout time. Plants take in the isotopes through photosynthesis and ground water absorption. Animals take in isotopes by drinking local water and eating plants. Stable isotopes can be powerful tools for identifying where an organism grew up and what kind of food the organism ate throughout its life. They can even be used to identify global temperature fluctuations.

Global Temperature Reconstruction

Oxygen isotopes are a powerful tool in tracking global temperature fluctuations throughout time. The isotopes of Oxygen 18 (^{18}O) and Oxygen 16

(^{16}O) occur naturally in Earth's water. Both are stable isotopes, but ^{18}O has a heavier atomic weight. In the normal water cycle, evaporation takes water molecules from the surface to the atmosphere. Because ^{16}O is lighter, it is more likely to be part of this evaporation process. The moisture gathers in the atmosphere as clouds that eventually may produce rain or snow and release the water back to the surface of the planet. During cool periods like **glacial periods** (ice ages), the evaporated water often comes down to Earth's surface as snow. The snow piles up in the winter but, because of the cooler summers, does not melt off. Instead, it gets compacted and layered year after year, eventually resulting in large glaciers or ice sheets covering parts of Earth. Since ^{16}O, with the lighter atomic weight, is more likely to be absorbed in the evaporation process, it gets locked up in glacier formation. The waters left in oceans would have a higher ratio of ^{18}O during these periods of cooler global temperatures (Potts 2012, 154–156; see Figure 7.26).

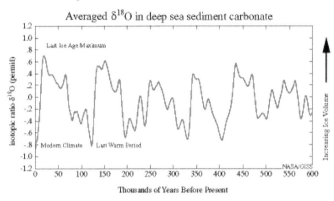

Figure 7.26: This graph depicts how temperatures of the sea have fluctuated greatly over the course of the history of the planet. Credit: Oxygen in deep sea sediment carbonate (Figure 2) by NASA Goddard Institute for Space Studies originally from "Science Briefs: Cold Climates, Warm Climates: How Can We Tell Past Temperatures?" by Gavin Schmidt, is in the public domain. [Image Description].

The microorganisms that live in the oceans, foraminifera, absorb the water from their environment and use the oxygen isotopes in their body structures. When these organisms die, they sink to the ocean floor, contributing to the layers of sediment. Scientists can extract these ocean cores and sample the remains of foraminifera for their ^{18}O and ^{16}O ratios. These ratios give us a good approximation of global temperatures deep into the past. Cooler temperatures indicate higher ratios of ^{18}O (Potts 2012, 154–156).

Diet Reconstruction

You may be familiar with the saying "you are what you eat." When it comes to your teeth and bones, this adage is literal. Stable isotopes can also be used to reconstruct animal diet and migration patterns. Living organisms absorb elements from ingested plants and water. These elements are used in tissues like bones, teeth, skin, hair, and so on. By analyzing the stable isotopes in the bones and teeth of humans and other animals, we can identify the types of food they ate at different stages of their lives.

Plants take in carbon dioxide from the atmosphere during photosynthesis. We've already discussed this using the example of the unstable isotope ^{14}C; however, this absorption also takes place with the stable isotopes of ^{12}C and ^{13}C. During photosynthesis, some plants incorporate carbon dioxide as a three-carbon molecule (C3 plants) and some as a four-carbon molecule (C4 plants). On the one hand, C3 plants include certain types of trees and shrubs that are found in relatively wet environments and have lower ratios of ^{13}C compared to ^{12}C. C4 plants, on the other hand, include plants from drier environments like savannahs and grasslands. C4 plants have higher ratios of ^{13}C to ^{12}C than C3 plants (Renfrew and Bahn 2016, 312). These ratios remain stable as you go up the food chain. Therefore, you can analyze the bones and teeth of an animal to identify the ^{13}C/^{12}C ratios and identify the types of plants that animal was eating.

The ratios of stable nitrogen isotopes ^{15}N and ^{14}N can also give information about the diet of fossilized or deceased organisms. Though initially absorbed from water and soils by plants, the nitrogen ratios change depending on the primary diet of the organism. An animal who has a mostly vegetarian diet will have lower ratios of ^{15}N to ^{14}N, while those further up the food chain, like carnivores, will have higher ratios of ^{15}N. Interestingly, breastfeeding infants have a higher nitrogen ratio than their mothers, because they are getting all of their nutrients through their mother's milk. So nitrogen can be used to track life events like weaning (Jay et al. 2008, 2). A marine versus terrestrial diet will also affect the nitrogen signatures. Terrestrial diets have lower ratios of ^{15}N than marine diets. In the course of human evolution, this type of analysis can help us identify important changes in human nutrition. It can help anthropologists figure out when meat became a primary part of the ancient human diet or when marine resources began to be used. The ratios of stable nitrogen isotopes can also be used to determine a change in status, as in the case of the Llullaillaco children (the "ice mummies") found in the Andes Mountains. For instance, the nitrogen values in hair from the Llullaillaco Maiden showed a significant positive shift that is associated with increased meat consumption in the last 12 months of her life (Wilson et al. 2007). Although the two younger children had little changes in their diets in the last year of their short lives, the changes in their nitrogen values were significant enough to suggest that the improvement in their diets may have been attributed to the Incas' desire to sacrifice healthy, high-status children" (Faux 2012, 6).

Migration

Stable isotopes can also tell us a great deal about where an individual lived and whether they migrated during their lifetime. The geology of Earth varies because rocks and soils have different amounts or ratios of certain elements in them. These variations in the ratios of isotopes of certain elements are called isotopic signatures. They are like a chemical fingerprint for a geographical region. These isotopes get into the groundwater and are absorbed by plants and animals living in that area. Elements like strontium, oxygen, and nitrogen, among others, are then used by the body to build bones and teeth. If you ate and drank local water all of your life, your bones and teeth would have the same isotopic signature as the geographical region in which you lived.

However, many people (and animals) move around during their lifetimes. Isotopic signatures can be used to identify migration patterns in organisms (Montgomery et al. 2005). Teeth develop in early childhood. If the isotopes of teeth are analyzed, these isotopes would resemble those found in the geographic area where an individual lived as a child. Bones, however, are a different story. Bones are constantly changing throughout life. Old cells are removed and new cells are deposited to respond to growth, healing, activity change, and general deterioration. Therefore, the isotopic signature of bones will reflect the geographical area in which an individual spent the last seven to ten years of life. If an individual has different isotopic signatures for their bones and teeth, it could indicate a migration some time during their life after childhood.

Figure 7.27: Stonehenge continues to provide clues to its mysterious existence with recent research using isotope ratios. Credit: Stonehenge (Figure 7.37) by Sarah S. King is under a CC BY-NC 4.0 License.

Recent work involving stable isotope analysis has been done on the cremation burials from Stonehenge, in Wessex, England (Figure 7.27). Much of the archaeological work at Stonehenge in the past focused on the building and development of the monument itself. That is partly because most of the burials at the monument were cremated remains, which are difficult to study because of their fragmentary nature and the chemical alterations that bone and teeth undergo when heated. The cremation process complicates the oxygen and carbon isotopes. However, the researchers determined that strontium would not be affected by heating and could still be analyzed in cranial fragments. Using the remains of 25 individuals, they compared their strontium signatures to the geology of Wessex and other regions of the UK. Fifteen of those individuals had strontium signatures that matched the local geology. This means that in the last ten or so years of their lives, they lived and ate food from around Stonehenge. However, ten of the individuals did not match the local geologic signature. These individuals had strontium ratios more closely aligned with the geology of west Wales. Archaeologists find this particularly interesting because in the early phases of Stonehenge's construction, the smaller "blue stones" were brought 200 km from Wales in a feat of early engineering. These larger regional connections show that Stonehenge was not just a site of local importance. It dominated a much larger region of influence and drew people from all over ancient Britain (Snoeck et al. 2018).

Special Topic: Cold Case Naia

Figure 7.28: Map of Mexico showing the Yucatan Peninsula and the locations of Hoyo Negro and Sistema Sac Actun. Credit: Hoyo Negro and Sistema Sac Actun, Mexic0 (Figure 7.38) original to Explorations: An Open Invitation to Biological Anthropology by Elyssa Ebding at GeoPlace, California State University, Chico is under a CC BY-NC 4.0 License.

In 2007, cave divers exploring the Sistema Sac Actun in the Yucatán Peninsula in Mexico (see Figure 7.28 and 7.29) discovered the bones of a 15- to 16-year-old female human along with the bones of various extinct animals from the Pleistocene (Collins et al. 2015). The site was named Hoyo Negro ("Black Hole"). The human bones belonged to a Paleo-American, later named "Naia" after a Greek water nymph. Examination of the partially fossilized remains revealed a great deal about Naia's life, and the radiocarbon dating of her tooth enamel indicated that she lived some 13,000 years ago (Chatters et al. 2014). Naia's arms were not overly developed, so her daily activities did not involve heavy carrying or grinding of grain or seeds. Her legs, however, were quite muscular, implying that Naia was used to walking long distances. Naia's teeth and bones indicate habitually poor nutrition. There is evidence of violent injury during the course of Naia's life from a healed spiral fracture of her left forearm. Naia also suffered from tooth decay and osteoporosis even though she appeared young and undersized. Dr. Jim Chatters hypothesizes that Naia entered the cave at a time when it was not flooded, probably looking for water. She may have become disoriented and fell off a high ledge to her death. The trauma to her pelvis is consistent with such an injury (Watson 2017).

Naia's skeleton is remarkably complete given its age. As divers were able to locate her skull, Naia's physical appearance in life could be interpreted. Surprisingly, in examining the skull, it was determined that Naia did not resemble modern Indigenous peoples in the region. However, the **mitochondrial DNA** (mtDNA) recovered from a tooth indicates that Naia shares her DNA with modern Indigenous peoples (Chatters et al. 2014). Though Naia's burial environment made chemical analysis difficult, researchers were able to recover carbon isotopes from her remains. The isotopes from Naia's tooth enamel suggest a diet of "cool-season grasses and/or broad-leaf vegetation" (Chatters et al. 2022, 68). Naia's teeth also displayed numerous dental caries and only light dental wear. Coupled with the isotopic data, she likely had a "softer, more sugar-rich diet" (Chatters et al. 2022, 68).

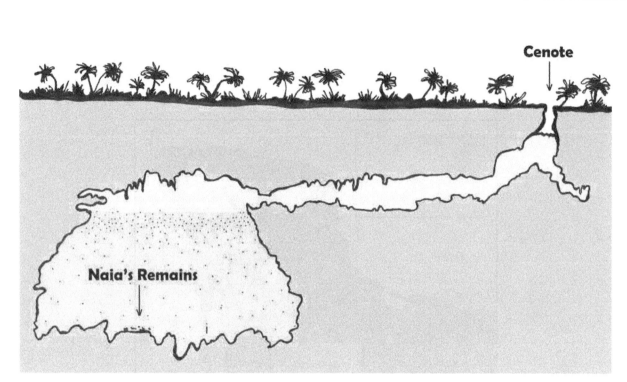

Figure 7.29: A diagram of the Sistema Sac Actun and the Hoyo Negro cenote where Naia rested underwater for roughly 13,000 years. The illustration depicts a cenote or hole in the ground leading to a long, narrow tunnel, ending in a large cavern. The cavern and tunnel are both filled with water. Credit: Hoyo Negro cenote (Figure 7.39) original to Explorations: An Open Invitation to Biological Anthropology by Mary Nelson is under a CC BY-NC 4.0 License.

Summary

With a timeline that extends back some 4.6 billion years, Earth has witnessed continental drift, environmental changes, and a growing complexity of life. Fossils, the mineralized remains of living organisms, provide physical evidence of life and the environment on the planet over the course of billions of years. In order to better understand the fossil record, anthropologists rely on the collaboration of numerous academic fields and disciplines. Anthropologists use a variety of scientific methods, both relative and chronometric, to analyze fossils to determine age, origins, and migration patterns as well as to provide insight into the health and diet of the fossilized organism. While each method has its advantages, disadvantages, and limited applications, these tools enable anthropologists to theorize how all living organisms evolved, including the evolution of early humans into modern humans, *H. sapiens*. The fossil record is far from complete, but our expanding understanding of the fossil context, with exciting new discoveries and improved scientific methods, enables us to document the history of our planet and the evolution of life on Earth.

Dating Methods Quick Guide

Method	Material	Effective date range
Stratigraphy	Soil layers	Relative
Biostratigraphy	Plant and animal remains	Relative
Cultural dating	Human-made objects	Relative
Fluorine	Bone, antler, teeth	Relative
Radiocarbon	Organic carbon bearing material (bones, teeth, antler, plant material, shell, charcoal)	Younger than 55,000 years
Potassium-argon and argon-argon	Volcanic rock	Older than 100,000 years
Uranium series	Carbonates such as stalactites, stalagmites, corals, caliche, and tufa	Younger than 650,000 years
Fission track	Volcanic glasses and crystalline minerals	Spans age of Earth
Luminescence	Pottery, baked clay, sediments	100 to older than 100,000 years
Electron spin resonance dating	Tooth enamel, shell, rock with crystalline structures	Younger than 2 million years
Dendrochronology	Wood (where tree rings are identifiable)	Dependent on location and available chronologies

Review Questions

- How do remains become fossils? What conditions are necessary for the fossilization process?
- What kind of information could you acquire from a single fossil? What could it tell you about the broader environment?
- What factors would you take into consideration when deciding which dating method to use for a particular artifact?
- What methods do anthropologists use to reconstruct past environments and lifestyles?

Key Terms

Anaerobic: An oxygen-free environment.

Anthropocene: The proposed name for our current geologic epoch based on human-driven climate change.

Argon-argon (Ar-Ar) dating: A chronometric dating method that measures the ratio of argon gas in volcanic rock to estimate time elapsed since the volcanic rock cooled and solidified. See also *potassium-argon dating*.

Atom: A small building block of matter.

Bezoars: Hard, concrete-like substances found in the intestines of fossil creatures.

Biostratigraphy: A relative dating method that uses other plant and animal remains occurring in the stratigraphic context to establish time depth.

Bya: Billion years ago.

Chronometric dating: Dating methods that give estimated numbers of years for artifacts and sites.

Continental drift: The slow movement of continents over time.

Coprolite: Fossilized poop.

Cultural dating: The relative dating method that arranges human-made artifacts in a time frame from oldest to youngest based on material, production technique, style, and other features.

Deep Time: James Hutton's theory that the world was much older than biblical explanations allowed. This age could be determined by gradual natural processes like soil erosion.

Dendrochronology: A chronometric dating method that uses the annual growth of trees to build a timeline into the past.

Electron spin resonance dating: A chronometric dating method that measures the background radiation accumulated in material over time.

Element: Matter that cannot be broken down into smaller matter.

Eon: The largest unit of geologic time, spanning billions of years and divided into subunits called *eras*, *periods*, and *epochs*.

Epochs: The smallest units of geologic time, spanning thousands to millions of years.

Eras: Units of geologic time that span millions to billions of years and that are subdivided into *periods* and *epochs*.

Fission track dating: A chronometric dating method that is based on the fission of ^{283}U.

Fluorine dating: A relative dating method that analyzes the absorption of fluorine in bones from the surrounding soils.

Foraminifera: Single-celled marine organisms with shells.

Fossilization: The process by which an organism becomes a fossil.

Fossils: Mineralized copies of organisms or activity imprints.

Geomorphology: The study of the physical characteristics of the Earth's surface.

Glacial periods: Periods characterized by low global temperatures and the expansion of ice sheets on Earth's surface.

Holocene: The geologic epoch from 10 kya to present. (See the discussion on "the Anthropocene" for the debate regarding the current epoch name.)

Hominin: The term used for humans and their ancestors after the split with chimpanzees and bonobos.

In matrix: When a fossil is embedded in a substance, such as igneous rock.

Isotopes: Variants of elements.

Kya: Thousand years ago.

Law of Superposition: The scientific law that states that rock and soil are deposited in layers, with the youngest layers on top and the oldest layers on the bottom.

Lithification: The process by which the pressure of sediments squeeze extra water out of decaying remains and replace the voids that appear with minerals from the surrounding soil and groundwater.

Luminescence dating: The chronometric dating method based on the buildup of background radiation in pottery, clay, and soils.

Megafauna: Large animals such as mammoths and mastodons.

Mitochondrial DNA: DNA located in the mitochondria of a cell that is only passed down from biological mother to child.

Mya: Million years ago.

Paleopathology: Study of ancient diseases and injuries identified through examining remains.

Periods: Geologic time units that span millions of years and are subdivided into *epochs*.

Permineralization: When minerals from water impregnate or replace organic remains, leaving a fossilized copy of the organism.

Petrified wood: A fossilized piece of wood in which the original organism is completely replaced by minerals through petrifaction.

Potassium-argon (K-Ar) dating: A chronometric dating method that measures the ratio of argon gas in volcanic rock to estimate time elapsed since the volcanic rock cooled and solidified. See also *argon-argon dating*.

Pseudofossils: Natural rocks or mineral formations that can be mistaken for fossils.

Radioactive decay: The process of transforming the atom by spontaneously releasing energy.

Radiocarbon dating: The chronometric dating method based on the radioactive decay of ^{14}C in organic remains.

Relative dating: Dating methods that do not result in numbers of years but, rather, in relative timelines wherein some organisms or artifacts are older or younger than others.

Sediment cores: Core samples taken from lake beds or other water sources for analysis of their pollen.

Stable isotopes: Variants of elements that do not change over time without outside interference.

Stratigraphy: A relative dating method that is based on ordered layers or (strata) that build up over time.

Taphonomy: The study of what happens to an organism after death.

Trace fossils: Fossilized remains of activity such as footprints.

Uniformitarianism: The theoretical perspective that the geologic processes observed today are the same as the processes operating in the past.

Unstable isotopes: Variants of elements that spontaneously change into stable isotopes over time.

Uranium series dating: A radiometric dating method based on the decay chain of unstable isotopes of ^{238}U and ^{235}U.

About the Authors

Sarah S. King, Ph.D.

Cerro Coso Community College, sarah.king1@cerrocoso.edu

Dr. Sarah S. King is an anthropology/sociology professor at Cerro Coso Community College in California. She completed her Ph.D. work at the Division of Archaeological, Geographical and Environmental Sciences at the University of Bradford in West Yorkshire, England. Her thesis was entitled "What Makes War?: Assessing Iron Age Warfare through Mortuary Behavior and Osteological Patterns of Violence." She also holds anthropology degrees from the University of California, Santa Cruz (B.A. hons., 2004), and the University of New Mexico, Albuquerque (M.A., 2006).

Kara Jones, M.A.

PhD student at University of Nevada, Las Vegas, jonesk44@unlv.nevada.edu

Kara Jones received their B.A. in anthropology at California State University, Bakersfield (2018) and their M.A. from University of Nevada, Las Vegas (2023, summer). Their master's thesis is titled "Rockin' at the Lake: Toolstone Use and Procurement along Holocene Lake Ivanpah, CA." Mx Jones is a Mojave Desert archaeologist specializing in stone tool use and manufacture, focusing further on Holocene lakeshore adaptations.

For Further Exploration

Books

Bjornerud, Marcia. 2006. *Reading the Rocks: The Autobiography of the Earth*. New York: Basic Books.

Hazen, Robert M. 2013. *The Story of Earth: The First 4.5 Billion Years, From Stardust to Living Planet*. New York: Viking Penguin.

Holmes, Richard. 2010. *The Age of Wonder: The Romantic Generation and the Discovery of the Beauty and Terror of Science*. New York: Vintage.

Palmer, Douglas. 2005. *Earth Time: Exploring the Deep Past from Victorian England to the Grand Canyon*. New York: John Wiley & Sons.

Prothero, Donald R. 2015. *The Story of Life in 25 Fossils: Tales of Intrepid Fossil Hunters and the Wonder of Evolution*. New York: Columbia University Press.

Pyne, Lydia. 2016. *Seven Skeletons: The Evolution of the World's Most Famous Human Fossils*. New York: Viking Books.

Repcheck, Jack. 2009. *The Man Who Found Time: James Hutton and the Discovery of the Earth's Antiquity*. New York: Basic Books.

Taylor, Paul D., Aaron O'Dea. 2014. *A History of Life in 100 Fossils*. Washington, DC: Smithsonian Books.

Ward, David. 2002. *Smithsonian Handbooks: Fossils*. Washington, DC: Smithsonian Books.

Winchester, Simon. 2009. *The Map That Changed the World: William Smith and the Birth of Modern Geology*. New York: Harper Perennial.

Websites

Amber Museum

East Tennessee State University Center of Excellence in Paleontology

Granger Historical Picture Archive

Indigenous Archaeology Collective

La Brea Tar Pits Museum

Lyme Regis Museum

Natural History Museum (London), on Mary Anning

Pech Merle Cave

Petrified Forest National Park (NE Arizona)

Poozeum: The No. 2 Wonder of the World

Smithsonian National Museum of Natural History, Department of Paleobiology

Smithsonian National Museum of Natural History, on "What Does It Mean to be Human"

Society for American Archaeology, on "Ethics in Professional Archaeology"

Society for American Archaeology, "Principles of Archaeological Ethics"

References

Antoine, Pierre-Oliver, Maeva J. Orliac, Gokhan Atici, Inan Ulusoy, Erdal Sen, H. Evren Çubukçu, Ebru Ibayrak, Neşe Oyal, Erkan Aydar, and Sevket Sen. 2012. "A Rhinocerotid Skull Cooked to Death in a 9.2 Mya-Old Ignimbrite Flow of Turkey." *PLoS ONE* 7 (11): e49997.

Aufderheide, Arthur C. 2003. *The Scientific Study of Mummies*. Cambridge, UK: Cambridge University Press.

Bar-Yosef, O., and M. Belmaker. 2011. "Early and Middle Pleistocene Faunal and Hominins Dispersals through Southwestern Asia." *Quaternary Science Reviews* 30 (11–12): 1318–1337.

Barras, C. 2022. "Lost Footprints of Our Ancestors." *New Scientist* 254 (3381): 40–44.

Blong, John C., Martin E. Adams, Gabriel Sanchez, Dennis L. Jenkins, Ian D. Bull, and Lisa-Marie Shillito. 2020. "Younger Dryas and Early Holocene Subsistence in the Northern Great Basin: Multiproxy Analysis of Coprolites from the Paisley Caves, Oregon, USA." *Archaeological and Anthropological Sciences* 12 (9): 1–29.

Boaz, Noel T., Russel L. Ciochon, Qinqi Xu, and Jinyi Liu. 2004. "Mapping and Taphonomic Analysis of the *Homo erectus* Loci at Locality 1 Zhoukoudian, China." *Journal of Human Evolution* 46 (5): 519–549.

Booth, Thomas J., Andrew T. Chamberlain, and Mike Parker Pearson. 2015. "Mummification in Bronze Age Britain." *Antiquity* 89 (347): 1,155–1,173.

Bradley, Raymond S. 2015. "Chapter 3: Dating Methods I." In *Paleoclimatology*, edited by Raymond S. Bradley, 55–101. Cambridge, MA: Academic Press.

Brown, Theodore L., H. Eugene LeMay Jr., Bruce E. Burston, Catherine J. Murphy, Patrick M. Woodward, and Matthew Stoltzfus. 2018. *Chemistry: The Central Science*. New York: Pearson.

Campbell, Neil A., and Jane B. Reece. 2005. *Biology 7th ed*. New York: Pearson.

Carvajal, Eduar, Luis Montes, and Ovidio A. Almanza. 2011. "Quaternary Dating by Electron Spin Resonance (ESR) Applied to Human Tooth Enamel." *Earth Sciences Research Journal* 15 (2): 115–120.

Chatters, James C., Joaquin Arroyo-Cabrales, and Pilar Luna-Erreguerena. 2022. "The Pre-Ceramic Skeletal Record of Mexico and Central America." In *The Routledge Handbook of Mesoamerican Bioarchaeology,* edited by V. Tieslar, 49–74. New York: Routledge.

Chatters, James C., Douglas J. Kennett, Yemane Asmerom, Brian M. Kemp, Victor Polyak, Alberto Nava Blank, Patricia A. Beddows, et al. 2014. "Late Pleistocene Human Skeleton and mtDNA Link Paleoamericans and Modern Native Americans." *Science* 344 (6185): 750–754.

Clough, Sharon. 2020. "Ethics in Human Osteology." *The Archaeologist* 109 (2020): 3–5.

Cochrane, Grant W. G., Trudy Doelman, and Lyn Wadley. 2013. "Another Dating Revolution for Prehistoric Archaeology?" *Journal of Archaeological Method and Theory* 20 (1): 42–60.

Collins, S. V., E. G. Reinhardt, D. Rissolo, J. C. Chatters, A. Nava-Blank, and P. Luna-Erreguerena. 2015. "Reconstructing Water Level in Hoyo Negro, Quintana Roo, Mexico: Implications for Early Paleoamerican and Faunal Access." *Quaternary Science Reviews* 124: 68–83.

Cook, Harold J. 1928. "Glacial Age Man in New Mexico." *Scientific American* 139 (1): 38–40.

Cook, S. F., and H. C. Ezra-Cohn. 1959. "An Evaluation of the Fluorine Dating Method." *Southwestern Journal of Anthropology* 15 (3): 276–290.

Cooper, Arnie. 2010. "Sticky Situation at the Tar Pits." *LA Weekly*, May 27, 2010. https://www.laweekly.com/sticky-situation-at-the-tar-pits/.

Crompton, Robin H., Todd C. Pataky, Russell Savage, Kristiaan D'Août, Matthew R. Bennett, Michael H. Day, Karl Bates, Sarita Morse, and William I. Sellers. 2012. "Human-like External Function of the Foot, and Fully Upright Gait, Confirmed in the 3.66 Million Year Old Laetoli Hominin Footprints by Topographic Statistics, Experimental Footprint-Formation and Computer Simulation." *Journal of the Royal Society Interface* 9 (69): 707–719. doi: 10.1098/rsif.2011.0258

Crutzen, Paul J., and Eugene F. Stoermer. 2000. "The 'Anthropocene.'" *Global Change Newsletter* 41: 17–18.

Darwin, Charles. 1859. *On the Origin of Species.* London, UK: John Murray.

Dean, Jeffery S. 2009. "One Hundred Years of Dendroarchaeology: Dating, Human Behavior, and Past Climate." In *Tree-rings, Kings, and Old World Archaeology and Environment: Papers Presented in Honor of Peter Ian Kuniholm*, edited by S. Manning and M. J. Bruce, 25–32. Oxford, UK: Oxbow Books.

Dolnick, Edward. 2011. *The Clockwork Universe: Isaac Newton, the Royal Society, and the Birth of the Modern World.* New York: HarperCollins.

Duller, G.A.T. 2008. *Luminescence Dating: Guidelines on Using Luminescence Dating in Archaeology.* Swindon, UK: English Heritage.

Eisenbeiss, Sabine. 2016. "Preserved in Peat: Decoding Bodies from Lower Saxony, Germany." *Expedition* 58 (2): 18–21.

Emling, Shelley. 2009. *The Fossil Hunter: Dinosaurs, Evolution, and the Woman Whose Discoveries Changed the World.* New York: St. Martin's Griffin.

Faux, Jennifer L. 2012. "Hail the Conquering Gods: Ritual Sacrifice of Children in Inca Society." *Journal of Contemporary Anthropology* 3 (1): 1–15.

Feder, Kenneth L. 2017. *The Past in Perspective: An Introduction to Human Prehistory.* 7th ed. New York: Oxford University Press.

Fletcher, Michael-Shawn, Tegan Hall, and Andreas Nicholas Alexandra. 2021. "The Loss of an Indigenous Constructed Landscape Following British Invasion of Australia: An Insight into the Deep Human Imprint on the Australian Landscape." *Ambio* 50 (1): 138–149.

Flowers, Paul, Klaus Theopold, Richard Langley, and William R. Robinson. 2018. *Chemistry.* Houston, TX: Openstax, Rice University.

Fumagalli, Matteo, Ida Moltke, Niels Grarup, Fernando Racimo, Peter Bjerregaard, Marit E. Jørgensen, Thorfinn S. Korneliussen, Pascale Gerbault, Line Skotte, Allan Linneberg, Cramer Christensen, Ivan Brandslund, Torben Jørgensen, Emilia Huerta-Sánchez, Erik B. Schmidt, Oluf Pedersen, Torben Hansen, Anders Albrechtsen, and Rasmus Nielsen. 2015. "Greenlandic Inuit show genetic signatures of diet and climate adaptation." *Science* 349 (6254): 1343-1347.

Funkhouser, J. G., I. L. Barnes, and J. J. Naughton. 1966. "Problems in the Dating of Volcanic Rocks by the Potassium-Argon Method." *Bull Volcanol* 29: 709–717.

Giles, Melanie. 2020. *Bog Bodies: Face to Face with the Past.* Manchester, UK: Manchester University Press.

Goodrum, Matthew R., and Cora Olson. 2009. "The Quest for an Absolute Chronology in Human Prehistory: Anthropologists, Chemists, and the Fluorine Dating Method in Palaeoanthropology." *British Journal for the History of Science* 42 (1): 95–114.

Granger, Darryl E., Ryan J. Gibbon, Kathleen Kuman, Ronald J. Clarke, Laurent Bruxelles, and Marc W. Caffee. 2015. "New Cosmogenic Burial Ages for Sterkfontein Member 2 *Australopithecus* and Member 5 Oldowan." *Nature* 522 (7554): 85–88.

Granger Historical Picture Archive. 2018. *Cro-Magnon Footprint.* Image no. 0167868. Accessed March, 02, 2023. https://www.granger.com/results.asp?image=0167868&itemw=4&itemf=0001&itemstep=1&itemx=11&screenwidth=1085.

Gruhn, R., 2020. "Evidence Grows That Peopling of the Americas Began More Than 20,000 Years Ago." *Nature* 584: 47–48.

Haddy, A., and A. Hanson. 1982. "Research Notes and Application Reports Nitrogen and Fluorine Dating of Moundville Skeletal Samples. *Archaeometry* 24 (1): 37–44.

Hajdas, I., P. Ascough, M. H. Garnett, S. J. Fallon, C. L. Pearson, G. Quarta, K. L. Spalding, H. Yamaguchi, and M. Yoneda. 2021. "Radiocarbon Dating." *Nature Reviews Methods Primers* 1 (62): 1–26.

Hatala, Kevin G., Brigitte Demes, and Brian G. Richmond. 2016. "Laetoli Footprints Reveal Bipedal Gait Biomechanics Different from Those of Modern Humans and Chimpanzees." *Proceedings of the Royal Society B* 283: 20160235. http://dx.doi.org/10.1098/rspb.2016.0235.

Hester, Thomas R., Harry J. Shafer, and Kenneth L. Feder. 1997. *Field Methods in Archaeology*, 7th ed. Mountain View, CA: Mayfield Publishing.

Hillam, J., C. M. Groves, D. M. Brown, M. G. L. Baillie, J. M. Coles, and B. J. Coles. 1990. "Dendrochronology of the English Neolithic." *Antiquity* 64 (243): 210–220.

Holmes, Richard. 2010. *The Age of Wonder: How the Romantic Generation Discovered the Beauty and Terror of Science.* New York: Vintage.

Ingber, Sasha. 2012. "Volcano Eruption Baked Rare Rhino Fossil." *National Geographic News*, November 30, 2012. Accessed July 25, 2018. https://www.nationalgeographic.com/science/article/121130-rare-rhino-fossil-created-by-volcanic-explosion.

Jay, Mandy, B. T. Fuller, Michael P. Richards, Christopher J. Knüsel, and Sarah S. King. 2008. "Iron Age Breastfeeding Practices in Britain: Isotopic Evidence from Wetwang Slack, East Yorkshire." *American Journal of Physical Anthropology* 136 (3): 327–337.

Jones, Nicola. 2020. "Carbon Dating, the Archaeological Workhorse, Is Getting a Major Reboot." *Nature News*, May 19, 2020. doi: https://doi.org/10.1038/d41586-020-01499-y

Klein, Richard G. 1999. *The Human Career: Human Biological and Cultural Origins*, 2nd ed. Chicago: University of Chicago Press.

Komar, Debra A., and Jane E. Buikstra. 2008. *Forensic Anthropology: Contemporary Theory and Practice.* New York: Oxford University Press.

Kuniholm, Peter Ian, and Cecil L. Striker. 1987. "Dendrochronological Investigations in the Aegean and Neighboring Regions, 1983–1986." *Journal of Field Archaeology* 14 (4): 385–398.

Laurenzi, Marinella A., Maria Laura Balestrieri, Giulio Bigazzi, Julio C. Hadler Neto, Pedro J. Iunes, Pio Norelli, Massimo Oddone, Ana Maria

Osorio Araya, and José G. Viramonte. 2007. "New Constraints on Ages of Glasses Proposed as Reference Materials for Fission-Track Dating." *Geostandards & Geoanalytical Research* 31 (2): 105–124.

Lebatard, Anne-Elisabeth, Didier L. Bourlès, Philippe Duringer, Marc Jolivet, Régis Braucher, Julien Carcaillet, Mathieu Schuster, et al. 2008. "Cosmogenic Nuclide Dating of *Sahelanthropus tchadensis* and *Australopithecus bahrelghazali*: Mio-Pliocene Hominids from Chad." *Proceedings of the National Academy of Sciences* 105 (9): 3226–3231.

Lyell, Charles. 1830–1833. *Principles of Geology, Being an Attempt to Explain the Former Changes of the Earth's Surface, by Reference to Causes Now in Operation*. 3 vols. London: John Murray.

Maixner, Frank, Dmitrij Turaev, Amaury Cazenave-Gassiot, Marek Janko, Ben Krause-Kyora, Michael R. Hoopmann, Ulrike Kusebauch, et al. 2018. "The Iceman's Last Meal Consisted of Fat, Wild Meat, and Cereals." *Current Biology* Report 28 (14): 2348–2355.

Masao, Fidelis T., Elgidius B. Ichumbaki, Marco Cherin, Angelo Barili, Giovanni Boschian, David A. Lurino, Sofia Menconero, Jacopo Moggi-Cecchi, and Giorgio Manzi. 2016. "New Footprints from Laetoli (Tanzania) Provide Evidence for Marked Body Size Variation in Early Hominins." *eLife* 5: e19568. https://elifesciences.org/articles/19568.

McDonough, Katelyn, Taryn Johnson, Ted Goebel, and Karl Reinhard. 2022. "Disease, Diet, and Thorny Headed Worm Infection in the Great Basin." Paper presented at 50th Annual Meeting of the Nevada Archaeological Association, Tonopah, Nevada, April 22nd, 2022.

Michels, Joseph W. 1972. "Dating Methods." *Annual Review of Anthropology* 1: 113–126.

Monastersky, Richard. 2015. "Anthropocene: The Human Age." *Nature* 519 (7542): 144–147.

Montgomery, Janet, Jane A. Evans, Dominic Powlesland, and Charlotte A. Roberts. 2005. "Continuity or Colonization in Anglo-Saxon England? Isotope Evidence for Mobility, Subsistence Practice, and Status at West Heslerton." *American Journal of Physical Anthropology* 126 (2): 123–138.

National Park Service. 2022. "Fossilized Footprints." *National Park Service* website, February 1. Accessed May 31, 2022. https://www.nps.gov/whsa/learn/nature/fossilized-footprints.htm.

Pastoors, Andreas, Tilman Lenssen-Erz, Bernd Breuckmann, Tsamkxao Ciqae, Ui Kxunta, Dirk Rieke-Zapp, and Thui Thao. 2017. "Experience Based Reading of Pleistocene Human Footprints in Pech-Merle." *Quaternary International* 430 (A): 155–162.

Potts, Richard. 2012. "Evolution and Environmental Change in Early Human Prehistory." *Annual Review of Anthropology* 41: 151–167.

Raichlen, David A., and Adam D. Gordon. 2017. "Interpretation of Footprints From Site S Confirms Human-like Bipedal Biomechanics in Laetoli Hominins." *Journal of Human Evolution* 107: 134–138.

Ravn, Morten. 2010. "Bronze and Early Iron Age Bog Bodies from Denmark." *Acta Archaeologica* 81 (1): 112–113.

Reimer, Paula J., Edouard Bard, Alex Bayliss, J. Warren Beck, Paul G. Blackwell, Christopher Bronk Ramsey, Caitlin E. Buck, et al. 2013. "INTCAL13 and Marine13 Radiocarbon Age Calibration Curves 0–50,000 Years cal BP." *Radiocarbon* 55 (4): 1869–1887.

Reinhard, Johan. 2006. *Ice Maiden: Inca Mummies, Mountain Gods, and Sacred Sites in the Andes*. Washington, DC.: National Geographic.

Reitz, Elizabeth J., and Elizabeth S. Wing. 1999. *Zooarchaeology*. Cambridge, UK: Cambridge University Press.

Renfrew, Colin, and Paul Bahn. 2016. *Archaeology: Theories, Methods, and Practice*, 7th ed. New York: Thames and Hudson.

Ruddiman, William F., Zhengtang Guo, Xin Zhou, Hanbin Wu, and Yanyan Yu. 2008. "Early Rice Farming and Anomalous Methane Trends." *Quaternary Science Reviews* 27 (13–14): 1291–1295.

Schmidt, Gavin. 1999. "Science Briefs: Cold Climates, Warm Climates: How Can We Tell Past Temperatures?" *National Aeronautics and Space Administration Goddard Institute for Space Studies*. https://www.giss.nasa.gov/research/briefs/1999_schmidt_01/

Shillito, Lisa-Marie, John C. Blong, Eleanor J. Green, and Eline N. van Asperen. 2020a. "The What, How and Why of Archaeological Coprolite Analysis." *Earth-Science Reviews* 207. https://doi.org/10.1016/j.earscirev.2020.103196.

Shillito, Lisa-Marie, Helen L. Whelton, John C. Blong, Dennis L. Jenkins, Thomas J. Connolly, and Ian D. Bull. 2020b. "Pre-Clovis occupation of the Americas Identified by Human Fecal Biomarkers in Coprolites from Paisley Caves, Oregon." *Science Advances* 6 (29). https://www.science.org/doi/10.1126/sciadv.aba6404.

Sims, Douglas., and W. Spaulding. 2017. "Shallow Subsurface Evidence for Postglacial Holocene Lakes at Ivanpah Dry Lake: An Alternative Energy Development Site in the Central Mojave Desert, California, USA." *Journal of Geography and Geology* 9 (1): 1–24. DOI: 10.5539/jgg.v9n1p1.

Slon, Viviane, Fabrizio Mafessoni, Benjamin Vernot, Cesare De Filippo, Steffi Grote, Bence Viola, Mateja Hajdinjak, Stéphane Peyrégne, Sarah Nagel, Samantha Brown, et al. 2018. "The Genome of the Offspring of a Neanderthal Mother and a Denisovan Father." *Nature* 561 (7721): 113–116.

Smithsonian National Museum of Natural History. 2018. Laetoli Footprint Trails. Smithsonian National Museum of History, October 23. Accessed February 14, 2023. http://humanorigins.si.edu/evidence/behavior/footprints/laetoli-footprint-trails.

Snoeck, Christophe, John Pouncett, Philippe Claeys, Steven Goderis, Nadine Mattielli, Mike Parker Pearson, Christie Willis, Antoine Zazzo, Julia A. Lee-Thorp, and Rick J. Schulting. 2018. "Strontium Isotope Analysis on Cremated Human Remains from Stonehenge Support[sic] Links With West Wales." *Scientific Reports* 8. https://www.nature.com/articles/s41598-018-28969-8.

Spaulding, W. G., and D. B. Sims. 2018. "A Glance to the East: Lake Ivanpah—An Isolated Southern Great Basin Paleolake. *The 2018 Desert Symposium Field Guide and Proceedings*, 121-131. https://www.researchgate.net/publication/340493333_A_glance_to_the_east_Lake_Ivanpah-_an_isolated_southern_Great_Basin_paleolake

Spray, Aaron. "La Brea Woman: Only (& Controversial) Human from La Brea Tar Pits." *The Travel*, April 3, 2022. Accessed July 31, 2022. https://www.thetravel.com/what-to-know-of-the-la-brea-woman/.

Steffen, Will, Johan Rockström, Katherine Richardson, Timothy M. Lenton, Carl Folke, Diana Liverman, Colin P. Summerhayes, et al. 2018. "Trajectories of the Earth System in the Anthropocene." *PNAS* 115 (33): 8252–8259.

Stodder, Ann L. W. 2008. "Taphonomy and the Nature of Archaeological Assemblages." In *Biological Anthropology of the Human Skeleton*, edited by M. Anne Katzenberg and Shelley R. Saunders, 71–115. Hoboken, NJ: Wiley Blackwell.

Straus, Lawrence Guy. 1989. "Grave Reservations: More on Paleolithic Burial Evidence." *Current Anthropology* 30 (5): 633–634.

Sullivan, Terry, and Harry Gifford. 1908. *She Sells Sea-Shells*. London: Francis, Day, and Hunter.

Taylor, Anthony, Jarod M. Hutson, Vaughn M. Bryant, and Dennis L. Jenkins. 2020. "Dietary Items in Early to Late Holocene Human Coprolites from Paisley Caves, Oregon, USA." *Palynology* 44 (1): 12–23.

Taylor, Paul D., Aaron O'Dea. 2014. *A History of Life in 100 Fossils*. Washington, D.C.: Smithsonian Books.

Törnqvist, T. E., B. E. Rosenheim, P. Hu, and A. B. Fernandez. 2015. "Radiocarbon Dating and Calibration." In *Handbook of Sea-Level Research*, edited by Ian Shennan, Antony J. Long, and Benjamin P. Horton, 347-360. Oxford, UK: John Wiley & Sons. https://doi.org/10.1002/9781118452547.ch23

University of Arizona. n.d. "Uranium-Thorium Dating: The Uranium 238 Decay Series." Accessed November 21, 2022. https://www.geo.arizona.edu/Antevs/ecol438/uthdating.html

University of the Witwatersrand. 2017. "Little Foot Takes a Bow: South Africa's Oldest and the World's Most Complete *Australopithecus* Skeleton Ever Found, Introduced to the World." *ScienceDaily*, December 6. Accessed February 14, 2023. https://www.sciencedaily.com/releases/2017/12/171206100104.htm.

van Calsteren, Peter, and Louise Thomas. 2006. "Uranium-Series Dating Applications in Natural Environmental Science." *Earth-Science Reviews* 75 (1–4): 155–175.

Vanzetti, A., M. Vidale, M. Gallinaro, D. W. Frayer, and L. Bondioli. 2010. "The Iceman as a Burial." *Antiquity* 84 (325): 681–692. https://doi.org/10.1017/S0003598X0010016X.

Verghese, Namrata. 2021. "What Is Necropolitics? The Political Calculation of Life and Death." *Teen Vogue*. March 10, 2021. Accessed February 14, 2023. https://www.teenvogue.com/story/what-is-necropolitics.

Vidale, M., L. Bondioli, D. W. Frayer, M. Gallinaro, and A. Vanzetti. 2016. "Ötzi the Iceman." *Expedition* 58 (2): 13–17. Accessed February 14, 2023. https://www.penn.museum/sites/expedition/otzi-the-iceman/.

Wade, Lizzie. 2021. "Footprints Support Claim of Early Arrival in the Americas." *Science* 373 (6562): 1426. Accessed February 14, 2023. https://www.sciencemagazinedigital.org/sciencemagazine/24_september_2021/MobilePagedArticle.action?articleId=1727132#articleId1727132.

Waters, Colin N., Jan Zalasiewicz, Anthony D. Barnosky, Alejandro Cearreta, Agieszka Galuszka, Juliana A. Ivar Do Sul, Catherine Jeandel, et al. 2016 "Is the Anthropocene Distinct from the Holocene?" *Science* 351 (6269): aad2622-1-10. DOI:10.1126/science.aad2622

Watson, Traci. 2017. "Ancient Bones Reveal Girl's Tough Life in Early Americas." *Nature* 544 (7648): 15–16.

Wendt, Kathleen, A., Xianglei Li,, and R. Lawrence Edwards. 2021. "Uranium-Thorium Dating of Speleothems." Elements 17 (2): 87–92.

White, Tim D. 1986. "Cut Marks on the Bodo Cranium: A Case of Prehistoric Defleshing." *American Journal of Physical Anthropology* 69 (4): 503–509.

Williams, Linda D. 2004. *Earth Science Demystified*. New York: McGraw-Hill Professional.

Wilson, Andrew S., Timothy Taylor, Maria Constanza Ceruti, Jose Antonio Chavez, Johan Reinhard, Vaughan Grimes, Wolfram Meier-Augenstein, et al. 2007. "Stable Isotope and DNA Evidence for Ritual Sequences in Inca Child Sacrifice." *PNAS* 104 (42): 16456–16461.

Acknowledgments

We are grateful to Lee Anne Zajicek, who coauthored the first edition. Her original contributions continue to be an integral part of this chapter. We thank the staff of the Maturango Museum, Ridgecrest, California. Specifically, for their generous help with photography and fossil images, we acknowledge Debbie Benson, executive director; Alexander K. Rogers, former archaeology curator; Sherry Brubaker, natural history curator; and Elaine Wiley, history curator. We thank Sharlene Paxton, a librarian at Cerro Coso Community College, Ridgecrest, California, for her guidance and expertise with OER and open-source images, and John Stenger-Smith and Claudia Sellers from Cerro Coso Community College, Ridgecrest, California, for their feedback on the chemistry and plant biology content. Finally, we thank William Zajicek and Lauren Zajicek, our community college students, for providing their impressions and extensive feedback on early drafts of the chapter.

Image Descriptions

Figure 7.6: Geologic time scale showing the geologic eons, eras, periods, epochs, and associated dates in millions of years ago (MYA). The time scale also shows the onset of major evolutionary and tectonic events affecting the North American continent and the Northern Cordillera (SCAK, south-central Alaska; SEAK, southeast Alaska; NAK, northern Alaska; CAK central Alaska). The following subdivisions and events are included on the time scale, from oldest to youngest. The oldest subdivision of the time scale is the Precambrian (symbolized by PC, X, Y, or Z in the GRI GIS data). The Precambrian is split into three eons: Hadean (4600-4000 MYA), Archean (4000-2500 MYA), and Proterozoic (2500-541 MYA). Global evolutionary and tectonic events that occurred during the Precambrian include (organized from oldest to youngest and including the eon in which the event occurred): formation of the Earth 4,600 MYA (Hadean); formation of the Earth's crust (Hadean); origin of life (Hadean); oldest known Earth rocks (Archean); early bacteria and algae (stromatolies; Archean); simple multicelled organisms (Proterozoic); Kanektok Metamorphic

Complex (oldest known rocks in Alaska; Proterozoic); and complex multicellular organisms (Proterozoic). The next subdivision of the timescale is the Phanerozoic Eon (541.0 MYA-present). The Phanerozoic Eon is split into three eras: Paleozoic (541.0-252.2 MYA; symbolized by PZ in the GRI GIS data), Mesozoic (252.2-66.0 MYA; symbolized by MZ in the GRI GIS data), and Cenozoic (66.0 MYA-present; symbolized by CZ in the GRI GIS data). The Paleozoic Era is split into seven periods (organized from oldest to youngest and including the geologic map symbol used in the GRI GIS data): Cambrian (541.0-485.4 MYA; C); Ordovician (485.4-443.4 MYA; O); Silurian (443.3-419.2 MYA; S); Devonian (419.2-358.9 MYA; D); Mississippian (358.9-323.2 MYA; M); Pennsylvanian (323.2-298.9 MYA; PN; the Mississippian and Pennsylvanian are also collectively known as the Carboniferous); and Permian (298.9-252.2; P). Major evolutionary and tectonic events that occurred during the Paleozoic include (organized from oldest to youngest and including the period in which the event occurred): Wales Orogeny (SEAK; Cambrian); early shelled organisms (Cambrian); rise of corals (Cambrian); trilobite maximum (Ordovician); primitive fish (Ordovician); mass extinction (Ordovician-Silurian); first land plants (Silurian), Kakas Orogeny (SEAK; Silurian); first forests (evergreens; Devonian); extensive plutonism and volcanism in the Yukon-Tanana and Brooks Range (Devonian); first amphibians (Devonian); mass extinction (Devonian); Ellesemerian Orogeny/Antler Orogeny (Devonian-Mississippian); ancestral Rocky Mountains (Mississippian); first reptiles (Mississippian); sharks abundant (Pennsylvanian); coal-forming swamps (Pennsylvanian); supercontinent Pangaea and Tethys Ocean (Pennsylvanian-Permian); and mass extinction (end Permian). The Mesozoic Era is split into three periods (organized from oldest to youngest and including the geologic map symbol used in the GRI GIS data): Triassic (252.2-201.3 MYA; Tr), Jurassic (201.3-145.0 MYA; J), and Cretaceous (145.0-66.0 MYA; K). Global evolutionary and tectonic events that occurred during the Mesozoic include (organized from oldest to youngest and including the period in which the event occurred): flying reptiles (Triassic); first dinosaurs and first mammals (Triassic); breakup of Pangaea begins (Triassic); mass extinction (end Triassic); Talkeetna arc (Jurassic); dinosaurs diverse and abundant (Jurassic); Brookian Orogeny (Jurassic-Cretaceous); early flowering plants (Cretaceous); opening of the Canada Basin and rotation of Arctic Alaska (Cretaceous); placental mammals (Cretaceous); exhumation of the Nome Complex (Cretaceous); extensive plutonism (Cretaceous), mass extinction (end Cretaceous). The Cenozoic Era is split into three periods (organized from oldest to youngest and including the geologic map symbol used in the GRI GIS data): Paleogene (66.0-23.0 MYA; PG), Neogene (23.0-2.6 MYA; N; together the Paleogene and Neogene are also known as the Tertiary [T]), and Quaternary (2.6 MYA-present; Q). The Paleogene is split into three shorter subdivisions called epochs: Paleocene (66.0-56.0 MYA; EP), Eocene (56.0-33.9 MYA; E), and Oligocene (33.9-23.0 OL). The Neogene is split into two epochs: Miocene (23.0-5.3 MYA; MI), and Pliocene (5.3-2.6 MYA; PL). The Quaternary is split into two epochs: Pleistocene (2.6-0.01 MYA; PE), and Holocene (0.01 MYA-present, H). Global evolutionary and tectonic events that occurred during the Mesozoic include (organized from oldest to youngest and including the epoch in which the event occurred): early primates (Paleocene); slab-window subduction (SCAK; Paleocene-Eocene), start of Bering Sea Volcanic eruptions (Oligocene); Alaska Range uplift (CAK; Oligocene); spread of grassy ecosystems (Miocene-Pliocene); modern humans (Pleistocene); ice age glaciations (Pleistocene); extinction of large mammals and birds (end Pleistocene); end of the ice age (end Pleistocene).

Figure 7.24: A Radiocarbon Date Calibration Curve. X axis: Calendar years ago (cal yr BP) ranging from 25000 (left) to 0 (right). Y axis: Radiocarbon Age (14C yr BP) ranging from 0 (bottom) to over 20000 (top). A slightly wavy line shows the calibration curve that goes from top left (23900 cal, 20000 radiocarbon) to bottom right (0,0). Lines point to other calibrated points: (18000 cal, 15000 radiocarbon), (11400 cal, 10000 radiocarbon), and (5700 cal, 5000 radiocarbon).

Figure 7.26: Graph of averaged oxygen isotope ($\delta18O$) in deep sea sediment carbonate. The Y axis shows isotopic ratio $\delta18O$ permil ranging from -1.2 to +1.2. X axis displays thousands of years before present, ranging from 0 to 600. Data shows large swings from modern climate at -0.8 $\delta18O$ to +.7 $\delta18O$ around 20 thousand years ago (last Ice Age Maximum), back down to -0.8 $\delta18O$ last warm period about 120 thousand years ago. While not as dramatic, nor labeled, the graph also shows additional wide swings of $\delta18O$ measurements through time.

8.

PRIMATE EVOLUTION

Jonathan M. G. Perry, Ph.D., Western University of Health Sciences

Stephanie L. Canington, Ph.D., University of Pennsylvania

This chapter is a revision from "Chapter 8: Primate Evolution" by Jonathan M. G. Perry and Stephanie L. Canington. In Explorations: An Open Invitation to Biological Anthropology, first edition, edited by Beth Shook, Katie Nelson, Kelsie Aguilera, and Lara Braff, which is licensed under CC BY-NC 4.0.

Learning Objectives

- Understand the major trends in primate evolution from the origin of primates to the origin of our own species.
- Learn about primate adaptations and how they characterize major primate groups.
- Discuss the kinds of evidence that anthropologists use to find out how extinct primates are related to each other and to living primates.
- Recognize how the changing geography and climate of Earth have influenced where and when primates have thrived or gone extinct.

The first fifty million years of primate evolution was a series of **adaptive radiations** leading to the diversification of the earliest lemurs, monkeys, and apes. The primate story begins in the canopy and understory of conifer-dominated forests, with our small, furtive ancestors subsisting at night, beneath the notice of day-active dinosaurs.

From the ancient **plesiadapiforms** (archaic primates) to the earliest groups of true primates (**euprimates**) (Bloch and Boyer 2002), the origin of our own order is characterized by the struggle for new food sources and microhabitats in the arboreal setting. Climate change forced major extinctions as the northern continents became increasingly dry, cold, and seasonal and as tropical rainforests gave way to deciduous forests, woodlands, and eventually grasslands. Lemurs, lorises, and tarsiers—once diverse groups containing many species—became rare, except for lemurs in Madagascar, where there were no anthropoid competitors and perhaps few predators. Meanwhile, **anthropoids** (monkeys and apes) likely emerged in Asia and then dispersed across parts of the northern hemisphere, Africa, and ultimately South America. The movement of continents, shifting sea levels, and changing patterns of rainfall and vegetation contributed to the developing landscape of primate biogeography, morphology, and behavior. Today's primates provide modest reminders of the past diversity and remarkable adaptations of their extinct relatives. This chapter explores the major trends in primate evolution from the origin of the Order Primates to the beginnings of our own lineage, providing a window into these stories from our ancient past.

Major Hypotheses About Primate Origins

For many groups of mammals, there is a key feature that led to their success. A good example is powered flight in bats. Primates lack a feature like this (see Chapter 5). Instead, if there is something unique about primates, it is probably a group of features rather than one single thing. Because of this, anthropologists and paleontologists struggle to describe an ecological scenario that could explain the rise and success of our own order. Three major hypotheses have been advanced to consider the origin of primates and to explain what makes our order distinct among mammals (Figure 8.1); these are described below.

Figure 8.1: The three major hypotheses are (a) the arboreal hypothesis, (b) the visual predation hypothesis, and (c) the angiosperm-primate coevolution hypothesis. Credit: Primate origin hypotheses original to Explorations: An Open Invitation to Biological Anthropology (2nd ed.) by Mary Nelson is under a CC BY-NC 4.0 License.

Arboreal Hypothesis

In the 1800s, many anthropologists viewed all animals in relation to humans. That is, animals that were more like humans were considered to be more "advanced" and those lacking humanlike features were considered more "primitive." This way of thinking was particularly obvious in studies of primates. A more modern way of referring to members of a group that lack certain evolutionary innovations seen in other members is to call them **plesiomorphic** (literally "anciently shaped"). The state of their morphological features is sometimes referred to as **ancestral traits**.

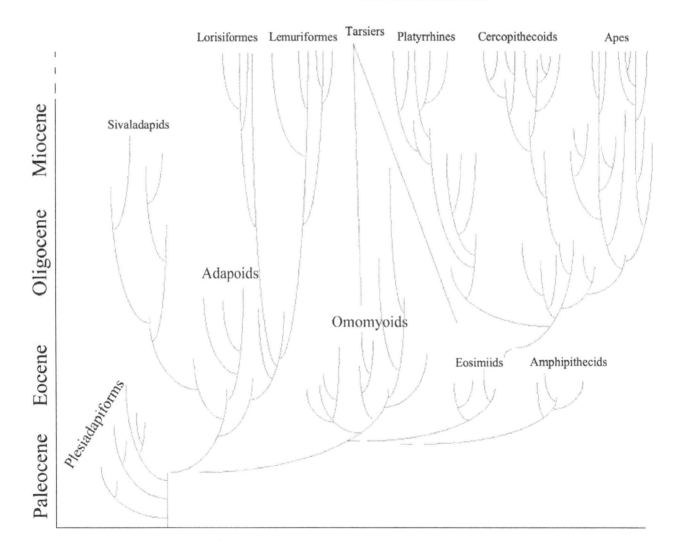

Figure 8.2: Primate family tree showing major groups. Disconnected lines show uncertainty about relationships. Two lines lead to tarsiers from different possible groups of origin. A full text description of this image is available. Credit: Primate family tree (Figure 8.2) by Jonathan M. G. Perry is under a CC BY-NC 4.0 License.

Thus, when anthropologists sought features that separate primates from other mammals, they focused on features that were least developed in lemurs and lorises, more developed in monkeys, and most developed in apes (Figure 8.2). Frederic Wood Jones, one of the leading anatomist-anthropologists of the early 1900s, is usually credited with the Arboreal Hypothesis of primate origins (Jones 1916). This hypothesis holds that many of the features of primates evolved to improve locomotion in the trees; this way of getting around is referred to as arboreal. For example, the grasping hands and feet of primates are well suited to gripping tree branches of various sizes and our flexible joints are good for reorienting the extremities in many different ways. A mentor of Jones, Grafton Elliot Smith, had suggested that the reduced olfactory system, acute vision, and forward-facing eyes of primates are adaptations for making accurate leaps and bounds through a complex, three-dimensional canopy (Smith 1912). The forward orientation of the eyes in primates causes the visual fields to overlap, enhancing depth perception, especially at close range. Evidence to support this hypothesis includes the facts that many extant primates are arboreal, and the plesiomorphic members of most primate groups are dedicated arborealists. The Arboreal Hypothesis was well accepted by most anthropologists at the time and for decades afterward.

Visual Predation Hypothesis

In the late 1960s and early 1970s, Matt Cartmill studied and tested the idea that the characteristic features of primates evolved in the context of arboreal locomotion. Cartmill noted that squirrels climb trees (and even vertical walls) very effectively, even though they lack some of the key adaptations of primates. As members of the Order Rodentia, squirrels also lack the hand and foot anatomy of primates. They have claws instead of flattened nails and their eyes face more laterally than those of primates. Cartmill reasoned that there must be some other explanation for the unique traits of primates. He noted that some nonarboreal animals share at least some of these traits with primates; for example, cats and predatory birds have forward-facing eyes that enable visual field overlap. Cartmill suggested that the unique suite of features in primates is an adaptation to detecting insect prey and guiding the hands (or feet) to catch insects (Cartmill 1972). His hypothesis emphasizes the primary role of vision in prey detection and capture; it is explicitly comparative, relying on form-function relationships in other mammals and nonmammalian vertebrates. According to Cartmill, many of the key features of primates evolved for preying on insects in this special manner (Cartmill 1974).

Angiosperm-Primate Coevolution Hypothesis

The visual predation hypothesis was unpopular with some anthropologists. One reason for this is that many primates today are not especially predatory. Another is that, whereas primates do seem well adapted to moving around in the smallest, terminal branches of trees, insects are not necessarily easier to find there. A counterargument to the visual predation hypothesis is the angiosperm-primate coevolution hypothesis. Primate ecologist Robert Sussman (Sussman 1991) argued that the few primates that eat mostly insects often catch their prey on the ground rather than in tree branches. Furthermore, predatory primates often use their ears more than their eyes to detect prey. Finally, most early primate fossils show signs of having been omnivorous rather than insectivorous. Instead, he argued, the earliest primates were probably seeking fruit. Fruit (and flowers) of angiosperms (flowering plants) often develop in the terminal branches. Therefore, any mammal trying to access those fruits must possess anatomical traits that allow them to maintain their hold on thin branches and avoid falling while reaching for the fruits. Primates likely evolved their distinctive visual traits and extremities in the Paleocene (approximately 65 million to 54 million years ago) and Eocene (approximately 54 million to 34 million years ago) epochs, just when angiosperms were going through a revolution of their own—the evolution of large, fleshy fruit that would have been attractive to a small arboreal mammal. Sussman argued that, just as primates were evolving anatomical traits that made them more efficient fruit foragers, angiosperms were also evolving fruit that would be more attractive to primates to promote better seed dispersal. This mutually beneficial relationship between the angiosperms and the primates was termed coevolution or more specifically **diffuse coevolution.**

At about the same time, D. Tab Rasmussen noted several parallel traits in primates and the South American woolly opossum, *Caluromys*. He argued that early primates were probably foraging on both fruits and insects (Rasmussen 1990). As is true of *Caluromys* today, early primates probably foraged for fruits in the terminal branches of angiosperms, and they probably used their visual sense to aid in catching insects. Insects are also attracted to fruit (and flowers), so these insects represent a convenient opportunity for a primarily fruit-eating primate to gather protein. This solution is a compromise between the visual predation hypothesis and the angiosperm-primate coevolution hypothesis. It is worth noting that other models of primate origins have been proposed, and these include the possibility that no single ecological scenario can account for the origin of primates.

The Origins of Primates

Paleocene: Mammals in the Wake of Dinosaur Extinctions

Placental mammals, including primates, originated in the Mesozoic Era (approximately 251 million to 65.5 million years ago), the Age of Dinosaurs. During this time, most placental mammals were small, probably nocturnal, and probably avoided predators via camouflage and slow, quiet movement. It has been suggested that the success and diversity of the dinosaurs constituted a kind of ecological barrier to Mesozoic mammals. The extinction of the dinosaurs (and many other organisms) at the end of the Cretaceous Period (approximately 145.5–65.5 million years ago) might have opened up these ecological niches, leading to the increased diversity and disparity in mammals of the Tertiary Period (approximately 65.5–2.5 million years ago).

The Paleocene was the first epoch in the Age of Mammals. Soon after the Cretaceous-Tertiary (K-T) extinction event, new groups of placental mammals appear in the fossil record. Many of these groups achieved a broad range of sizes and lifestyles as well as a great number of species before declining sometime in the Eocene (or soon thereafter). These groups were ultimately replaced by the modern orders of placental mammals (Figure 8.3). It is unknown whether these replacements occurred gradually, for example by competitive exclusion, or rapidly, perhaps by sudden geographic dispersals with replacement. In some senses, the Paleocene might have been a time of recovery from the extinction event; it was cooler and more seasonal globally than the subsequent Eocene.

Figure 8.3: A mural of Eocene flora and fauna in North America. Credit: Image from page 27 of "Annual report for the year ended June 30 …" (1951) by Internet Archive Book Images has been designated to the public domain (CC0). This photograph of the mural "Fauna and flora of middle Eocene in the Wyoming area" by Jay Matternes, was originally published by the Smithsonian, and can be viewed in context in the online version of this book.

Plesiadapiforms, the Archaic Primates

The Paleocene epoch saw the emergence of several families of mammals that have been implicated in the origin of primates. These are the plesiadapiforms, which are archaic primates, meaning they possessed some primate features and lacked others. The word *plesiadapiform* means "almost adapiform," a reference to some similarities between some plesiadapiforms and some adapiforms (or adapoids; later-appearing true primates)—mainly in the molar teeth. Because enamel fossilizes better than other parts of the body, the molar teeth are the parts most often found and first discovered for any new species. Thus, dental similarities were often the first to be noticed by early mammalian paleontologists, partly explaining why plesiadapiforms were thought to be primates. Major morphological differences between plesidapiforms and euprimates (true primates) were observed later when more parts of plesiadapiform skeletons were discovered. Many plesiadapiforms have unusual anterior teeth and most have digits possessing claws rather than nails. So far, no plesiadapiform ever discovered has a postorbital bar (seen in extant **strepsirrhines**) or septum (as seen in **haplorhines**), and whether or not the **auditory bulla** was formed by the **petrosal bone** remains unclear for many plesiadapiform specimens. Nevertheless, there are compelling reasons (partly from new skeletal material) for including plesiadapiforms within the Order Primates.

Geographic and Temporal Distribution

Purgatorius is generally considered to be the earliest primate. This Paleocene mammal is known from teeth that are very plesiomorphic for a primate. It has some characteristics that suggest it is a basal plesiadapiform, but there is very little to link it specifically with euprimates (see Clemens 2004). Its ankle bones suggest a high degree of mobility, signaling an arboreal lifestyle (Chester et al. 2015). *Purgatorius* is plesiomorphic enough to have given rise to all primates, including the plesiadapiforms. However, new finds suggest that this genus was more diverse and had more differing tooth morphologies than previously appreciated (Wilson Mantilla et al. 2021). Plesiadapiform families were numerous and diverse during parts of the Paleocene in western North America and western Europe, with some genera (e.g., *Plesiadapis*; see Figure 8.4) living on both continents (Figure

8.5). Thus, there were probably corridors for plesiadapiform dispersal between the two continents, and it stands to reason that these mammals were living all across North America, including in the eastern half of the continent and at high latitudes. A few plesiadapiforms have been described from Asia (e.g., *Carpocristes*), but the affinities of these remain uncertain.

Figure 8.4: Families of plesiadapiforms with example genera and traits: a table. Credit: Plesiadapiforms table original to Explorations: An Open Invitation to Biological Anthropology (2nd ed.) by Jonathan M. G. Perry and Stephanie L. Canington is under a CC BY-NC 4.0 License. Content derived from Fleagle 2013.

Family	Genera	Morphology	Location	Age[1]
Paromomyidae	*Ignacius*	Long, dagger-like, lower incisor.	North America and Europe	Early Paleocene to Late Eocene
Carpolestidae	*Carpolestes*	Plagiaulacoid dentition. Limb adaptations to terminal branch feeding. Grasping big toe.	North America, Europe, and Asia	Middle Paleocene to Early Eocene
Plesiadapidae	*Plesiadapis*	Mitten-like upper incisor. Diastema. Large body size for group.	North America and Europe	Middle Paleocene to Early Eocene

[1] Derived from Fleagle 2013.

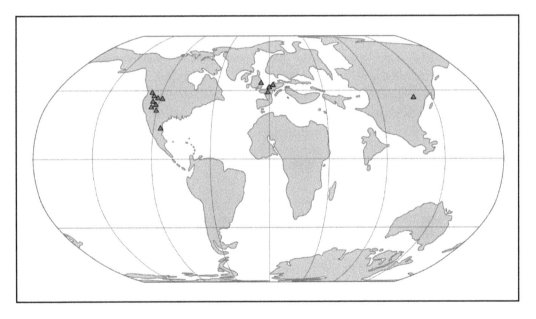

Figure 8.5: Map of the world in the Paleocene, highlighting plesiadapiform localities on lands that would become North America, southern Europe, and eastern Asia. Credit: Paleocene Map with Plesiadapiform Localities (Figure 8.4) original to Explorations: An Open Invitation to Biological Anthropology by Elyssa Ebding at GeoPlace, California State University, Chico is under a CC BY-NC 4.0 License. Localities based on Fleagle 2013, 211.

General Morphological Features

Although there is much morphological variation among the families of plesiadapiforms, some common features unite the group. Most plesiadapiforms were small, the largest being about three kilograms (approximately 7 lbs.; *Plesiadapis cookei*). They had small brains and fairly large snouts, with eyes that faced more laterally than in euprimates. Many species show reduction and/or loss of the canine and anterior premolars, with the resulting formation of a rodent-like **diastema** (a pronounced gap between the premolars and the incisors, with loss of at least the canine); this probably implies a herbivorous diet. Some families appear to have had very specialized diets, as suggested by unusual tooth and jaw shapes.

Arguably the most interesting and unusual family of plesiadapiforms is the Carpolestidae. They are almost exclusively from North America (with a couple of possible members from Asia), and mainly from the Middle and Late Paleocene. Their molars are not very remarkable, being quite similar to those of some other plesiadapiforms (e.g., Plesiadapidae). However, their lower posterior premolars (p4) are laterally compressed and blade-like with vertical serrations topped by tiny cuspules. This unusual dental morphology is termed ***plagiaulacoid*** (Simpson 1933). The upper premolar occlusal surfaces are broad and are covered with many small cuspules; the blade-like lower premolar might have cut across these cuspules, between them, or both.

Figure 8.6: An artistic rendition of Carpolestes simpsoni moving along a small diameter support. Credit: CarpolestesCL by Sisyphos23 is under a CC BY-SA 3.0 License.

Many plesiadapiforms have robust limb bones with hallmarks of arboreality. Instead of having nails, most taxa had sharp claws on most or all of the digits. The extremities show grasping abilities comparable to those of primates and some arboreal marsupials. Nearly complete skeletons have yielded a tremendous wealth of information on locomotor and foraging habits. Many plesiadapiforms appear to have been able to cling to vertical substrates (like a broad tree trunk) using their sharp claws, propelling themselves upward using powerful hindlimbs, bounding along horizontal supports, grasping smaller branches, and moving head-first down tree trunks. In carpolestids in particular, the skeleton appears to have been especially well adapted to moving slowly and carefully in small terminal branches (Figure 8.6).

Debate: Relationship of Plesiadapiforms to True Primates

In the middle of the twentieth century, treeshrews (Order Scandentia) were often considered part of the Order Primates, based on anatomical similarities between some treeshrews and primates. For many people, plesiadapiforms represented intermediates between primates and treeshrews, so plesiadapiforms were included in Primates as well.

Studies of reproduction and brain anatomy in treeshrews and lemurs suggested that treeshrews are not primates (e.g., Martin 1968). This was soon followed by the suggestion to also expel plesiadapiforms (Martin 1972) from the Order Primates. Like treeshrews, plesiadapiforms lack a postorbital bar, nails, and details of the ear region that characterize true primates. Many paleoanthropologists were reluctant to accept this move to banish plesiadapiforms (e.g., F. S. Szalay, P. D. Gingerich).

Later, K. Christopher Beard (1990) found that in some ways, the digits of paromomyid plesiadapiforms are actually more similar to those of dermopterans (Order Dermoptera), the closest living relatives of primates, than they are to those of primates themselves (but see Krause 1991). At the same time, Richard Kay and colleagues (1990) found that cranial circulation patterns and auditory bulla morphology in the paromomyid, *Ignacius* (see Figure 8.4), are more like those of dermopterans than of primates.

For many anthropologists, this one-two punch effectively removed plesiadapiforms from the Order Primates. In the last two decades, the tide of opinion has turned again, with many researchers reinstating plesiadapiforms as members of the Order Primates. New and more complete specimens demonstrate that the postcranial skeletons of plesiadapiforms, including the hands and feet, were primate-like, not dermorpteran-like (Bloch and Boyer 2002, 2007). New fine-grained CT scans of relatively complete plesiadapiform skulls revealed that they share some key traits with primates to the exclusion of other placental mammals (Bloch and Silcox 2006). Most significant was the suggestion that *Carpolestes simpsoni* possessed an auditory bulla formed by the **petrosal bone**, like in all living primates.

The debate about the status of plesiadapiforms continues, owing to a persistent lack of key bones in some species and owing to genuine complexity of the anatomical traits involved. Maybe plesiadapiforms were the ancestral stock from which all primates arose, with some plesiadapiforms (e.g., carpolestids) nearer to the primate **stem** than others.

Adapoids and Omomyoids, the First True Primates

Geographic and Temporal Distribution

The first universally accepted fossil primates are the adapoids (Superfamily **Adapoidea**) and the omomyoids (Superfamily **Omomyoidea**). These groups become quite distinct over evolutionary time, filling mutually exclusive niches for the most part. However, the earliest adapoids are very similar to the earliest omomyoids.

The adapoids were mainly diurnal and herbivorous, with some achieving larger sizes than any plesiadapiforms (10 kg; 22 lbs.). By contrast, the omomyoids were mainly nocturnal, insectivorous and frugivorous, and small.

Both groups appear suddenly at the start of the Eocene, where they are present in western North America, western Europe, and India (Figure 8.7). This wide dispersal of early primates was probably due to the presence of rainforest corridors extending far into northern latitudes.

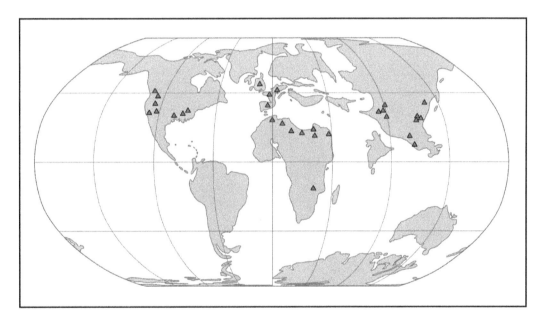

Figure 8.7: Map of the world in the Eocene, highlighting adapoid and omomyoid localities on lands that would become North America, southern Europe, Africa, and Asia. Credit: Eocene Map with Adapoid and Omomyoid Localities (Figure 8.6) original to Explorations: An Open Invitation to Biological Anthropology by Elyssa Ebding at GeoPlace, California State University, Chico is under a CC BY-NC 4.0 License. Localities based on Fleagle 2013, 229.

In North America and Europe, both groups achieved considerable diversity in the Middle Eocene, then mostly died out at the end of that epoch (Figure 8.8). In some Eocene rock formations in the western United States, adapoids and omomyoids make up a major part of the mammalian fauna. The Eocene of India has yielded a modest diversity of euprimates, some of which are so plesiomorphic that it is difficult to know whether they are adapoids or omomyoids (or even early anthropoids).

Figure 8.8: Families of adapoids and omomyoids with example genera and traits: a table. Credit: Adapoids and omomyoids table original to Explorations: An Open Invitation to Biological Anthropology (2nd ed.) by Jonathan M. G. Perry and Stephanie L. Canington is under a CC BY-NC 4.0 License. Content derived from Fleagle 2013.

Family	Genera	Morphology	Location	Age[1]
Cercamoniidae	*Donrussellia*	Variable in tooth number and jaw shape.	Europe and Asia	Early to Late Eocene
Asiadapidae[2]	*Asiadapis*	Plesiomorphic teeth and jaw resemble early Omomyids.	Asia	Early Eocene
Caenopithecidae[3]	*Darwinius*	Robust jaws with crested molars. Fewer premolars.	Europe, Africa, North America, and Asia	Middle to Late Eocene
Adapidae	*Adapis*	Fused mandible. Long molar crests. Large size and large chewing muscles.	Europe	Late Eocene to Early Oligocene
Sivaladapidae	*Sivaladapis*	Some large with robust jaws.	Asia	Middle Eocene to Late Miocene
Notharctidae[4]	*Notharctus*	Canine sexual dimorphism. Lemur-like skull. Clinging and leaping adaptations.	North America and Europe	Early to Middle Eocene
Omomyidae[5]	*Teilhardina*	Small, nocturnal, frugivorous or insectivorous. Tarsier-like skull in some.	North America, Europe, and Asia	Early Eocene to Early Miocene
Microchoeridae[6]	*Necrolemur*	Long bony ear tubes. Tarsier-like lower limb adaptations for leaping.	Europe and Asia	Early Eocene to Early Oligocene

[1] Derived from Fleagle 2013.

[2] See Dunn et al. 2016 and Rose et al. 2018.

[3] See Kirk and Williams 2011 and Seiffert et al. 2009.

[4] See Gregory 1920.

[5] See Beard and MacPhee 1994 and Strait 2001.

[6] See Schmid 1979.

Adapoids and omomyoids barely survived the Eocene-Oligocene extinctions, when colder temperatures, increased seasonality, and the retreat of rainforests to lower latitudes led to changes in mammalian biogeography. In North America, one genus (originally considered an omomyoid but recently reclassified as Adapoidea) persisted until the Miocene: *Ekgmowechashala* (Rose and Rensberger 1983). This taxon has highly unusual teeth and might have been a late immigrant to North America from Asia. In Asia, one family of adapoids, the Sivaladapidae, retained considerable diversity as late as the Late Miocene.

Adapoid Diversity

Adapoids were very diverse, particularly in the Eocene of North America and Europe. They can be divided into six families, with a few species of uncertain familial relationship. As a group, adapoids have some features in common, although much of what they share is plesiomorphic. Important features include the hallmarks of euprimates: postorbital bar, flattened nails, grasping extremities, and a petrosal bulla (Figures 8.9 and 8.10). In addition, some adapoids retain the ancestral dental formula of 2.1.4.3; that is, in each quadrant of the mouth, there are two incisors, one canine, four premolars, and three molars. In general, the incisors are small compared to the molars, but the canines are relatively large, with sexual dimorphism in some species. Cutting crests on the molars are well developed in some species, and the two halves of the mandible were fused at the midline in some species. Some adapoids were quite small (*Anchomomys* at a little over 100 g), and some were quite large (*Magnadapis* at 10 kg; 22 lbs.). Furthermore, the spaces and attachment features for the chewing muscles were truly enormous in some species, suggesting that these muscles were very large and powerful. Taken together, this suggests an overall adaptive profile of diurnal herbivory. The canine sexual dimorphism in some species suggests a possible mating pattern of polygyny, as males in polygynous primate species often compete with each other for mates and have especially large canine teeth.

Figure 8.9: Representative crania of Adapidae from Museum d'Histoire Naturelle Victor Brun, a natural history museum in Montauban, France. The white scale bar is 1 cm long. Credit: **Representative crania of adapids (European adapoids, (Figure 8.7)** from the Museum d'Histoire Naturelle Victor Brun in Montauban, France original to Explorations: An Open Invitation to Biological Anthropology by Jonathan M. G. Perry is under a CC BY-NC 4.0 License.

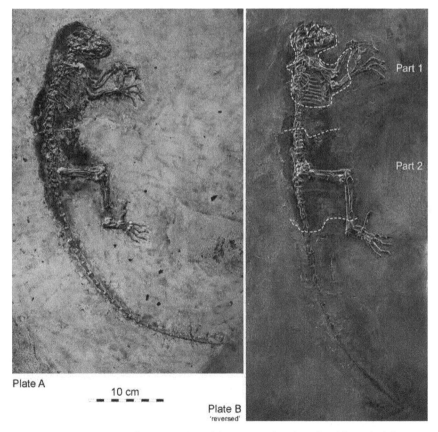

Figure 8.10: Darwinius masillae, a member of the Caenopithecidae. The slab on the left is Plate A and the slab on the right is Plate B. The parts of the skeleton in B that are outside of the dashed lines were fabricated. Credit: **Darwinius masillae holotype slabs** by Jens L. Franzen, Philip D. Gingerich, Jörg Habersetzer1, Jørn H. Hurum, Wighart von Koenigswald, B. Holly Smith is under a **CC BY 2.5 License**. Originally from Franzen et al. 2009.

Omomyoid Diversity

Like adapoids, omomyoids appeared suddenly at the start of the Eocene and then became very diverse with most species dying out before the Oligocene. Omomyoids are known from thousands of jaws with teeth, relatively complete skulls for about a half-dozen species, and very little postcranial material. Omomyoids were relatively small primates, with the largest being less than three kilograms (approximately 7 lbs.; *Macrotarsius montanus*). All known crania possess a postorbital bar, which in some has been described as "incipient closure." Some—but not all—known crania have an elongated bony ear tube extending lateral to the location of the eardrum, a feature seen in living tarsiers and **catarrhines**. The anterior teeth tend to be large, with canines that are usually not much larger than the incisors. Often it is difficult to distinguish closely related species using molar morphology, but the premolars tend to be distinct from one species to another. The postcranial skeleton of most omomyoids shows hallmarks of leaping behavior reminiscent of that of tarsiers. In North America, omomyoids became very diverse and abundant. In fact, omomyoids from Wyoming are sufficiently abundant and from such stratigraphically controlled conditions that they have served as strong evidence for the gradual evolution of anatomical traits over time (Rose and Bown 1984).

Teilhardina (Figure 8.11; see Figure 8.2) is one of the earliest and arguably the most plesiomorphic of omomyoids. *Teilhardina* has several species, most of which are from North America, with one from Europe (*T. belgica*) and one from Asia (*T. asiatica*). The species of this genus are anatomically similar and the deposits from which they are derived are roughly contemporaneous. Thus, this small primate likely dispersed across the northern continents very rapidly (Smith et al. 2006).

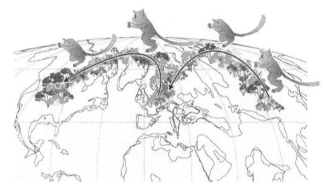

Figure 8.11: A map of the world during the early Eocene showing one hypothesis for the direction of dispersal of the omomyoid Teilhardina. The map depicts primates hopping from continent to continent (East to West) via the forest corridors at high latitudes. Credit: Paleogeographic map showing hypothetical migration routes of Teilhardina (Figure 1) by Thierry Smith, Kenneth D. Rose, and Philip D. Gingerich. 2006. Proceedings of the National Academy of Sciences of the United States of America 103 (30): 11223–11227. Copyright (2006) National Academy of Sciences. Image is used for non-commercial and educational purposes as outlined by PNAS.

The Emergence of Modern Primate Groups

Origins of Crown Strepsirrhines

Until the turn of this century, very little was known about the origins of the **crown** (living) strepsirrhines. The Quaternary record of Madagascar contains many amazing forms of lemurs, including giant sloth-like lemurs, lemurs with perhaps monkey-like habits, lemurs with koala-like habits, and even a giant aye-aye (Godfrey and Jungers 2002). However, in Madagascar, early Tertiary continental sediments are lacking, and there is no record of lemur fossils before the Pleistocene.

The fossil record of galagos is slightly more informative. Namely, there are Miocene African fossils that are very likely progenitors of lorisids (Simpson 1967). However, these are much like modern galagos and do not reveal anything about the relationship between crown strepsirrhines and Eocene fossil primates (but see below regarding *Propotto*). A similar situation exists for lorises in Asia: there are Miocene representatives, but these are substantially like modern lorises. The discovery of the first definite **toothcomb** canine (a hallmark of stresirrhines) in 2003 provided the "smoking gun" for the origin of crown strepsirrhines (Seiffert et al. 2003). Recently, several other African primates have been recognized as having strepsirrhine affinities (Marivaux et al. 2013; Seiffert 2012). The enigmatic Fayum primate *Plesiopithecus* is known from a skull that has been compared to aye-ayes and to lorises (Godinot 2006; Simons and Rasmussen 1994a).

The now-recognized diversity of stem strepsirrhines from the Eocene and Oligocene of Afro-Arabia is strong evidence to suggest that strepsirrhines originated in that geographic area. This implies that lorises dispersed to Asia subsequent to an African origin. It is unknown what the first strepsirrhines in Madagascar were like. However, it seems likely that the lemuriform-lorisiform split occurred in continental Africa, followed by dispersal of lemuriform stock to Madagascar. Recent evidence suggests that *Propotto*, a Miocene primate from Kenya originally described as a potto antecedent, actually forms a clade with *Plesiopithecus* and the aye-aye; this might suggest that strepsirrhines dispersed to Madagascar from continental Africa more than once (Gunnell et al. 2018).

The Fossil Record of Tarsiers

Tarsiers are so unusual that they fuel major debates about primate taxonomy. Tarsiers today are moderately diverse but geographically limited and not very different in their ecological habits—especially considering that the split between them and their nearest living relative probably occurred over 50 million years ago. If omomyoids are excluded, then the fossil record of tarsiers is very limited. Two fossil species from the Miocene of Thailand have been placed in the genus *Tarsius*, as has an Eocene fossil from China (Beard et al. 1994). These, and *Xanthorhysis* from the Eocene of China, are all very tarsier-like. In fact, it is striking that *Tarsius eocaenus* from China was already so tarsier-like as early as the Eocene. This suggests that tarsiers achieved their current morphology very early in their evolution and have remained more or less the same while other primates changed dramatically. Two additional genera, *Afrotarsius* from the Oligocene of Egypt and Libya and *Afrasia* from the Eocene of Myanmar, have also been implicated in tarsier origins, though the relationship between them and tarsiers is unclear (Chaimanee et al. 2012). More recently, a partial skeleton of a small Eocene primate from China, *Archicebus achilles* (dated to approximately 55.8 million to 54.8 million years ago), was described as the most basal tarsiiform (Ni et al. 2013). This primate is reconstructed as a diurnal insectivore and an arboreal quadruped that did some leaping—but not to the specialized degree seen in living tarsiers. The anatomy of the eye in living tarsiers suggests that their lineage passed through a diurnal stage, so *Archicebus* (and diurnal omomyoids) might represent such a stage.

Climate Change and the Paleogeography of Modern Primate Origins

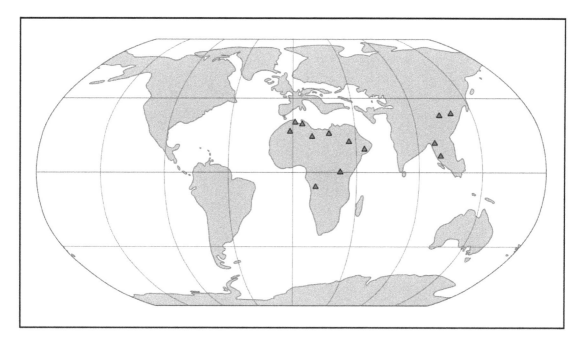

Figure 8.12: Map of key localities of early anthropoids on land that becomes Africa and southern Asia. Credit: Oligocene Map with Key Early Anthropoid Localities (Figure 8.10) original to *Explorations: An Open Invitation to Biological Anthropology* by Elyssa Ebding at GeoPlace, California State University, Chico is under a CC BY-NC 4.0 License. Localities based on Fleagle 2013, 265.

Changing global climate has had profound effects on primate dispersal patterns and ecological habits over evolutionary time. Primates today are strongly tied to patches of trees and particular plant parts such as fruits, seeds, and immature leaves. It is no surprise, then, that the distribution of primates mirrors the distribution of forests. Today, primates are most diverse in the tropics, especially in tropical rainforests. Global temperature trends across the Tertiary have affected primate ranges. Following the Cretaceous-Tertiary extinction event, cooler temperatures and greater seasonality characterized the Paleocene. In the Eocene, temperatures (and probably rainfall) increased globally and rainforests likely extended to very high latitudes. During this time, euprimates became diverse. With cooling and increased aridity at the end of the Eocene, many primate extinctions occurred in the northern continents and the surviving primates were confined to lower latitudes in South America, Afro-Arabia, Asia, and southern

Europe. Among these survivors are the progenitors of the living groups of primates: lemurs and lorises, tarsiers, **platyrrhines** (monkeys of the Americas), and catarrhines (monkeys and apes of Africa and Asia) (Figure 8.12).

Competing Hypotheses for the Origin of Anthropoids

There is considerable debate among paleoanthropologists as to the geographic origins of anthropoids. In addition, there is debate regarding the source group for anthropoids. Three different hypotheses have been articulated in the literature. These are the adapoid origin hypothesis, the omomyoid origin hypothesis, and the tarsier origin hypothesis (Figure 8.13).

Adapoid Origin Hypothesis

Resemblances between some adapoids and some extant anthropoids include fusion of the **mandibular symphysis**, overall robusticity of the chewing system, overall large body size, features that signal a diurnal lifestyle (like relatively small eye sockets), and ankle bone morphology. Another feature in common is canine sexual dimorphism, which is present in some species of adapoids (probably) and in several species of anthropoids.

These features led some paleoanthropologists in the last half of the 20th century to suggest that anthropoids came from adapoid stock (Gingerich 1980; Simons and Rasmussen 1994b). One of the earliest supporters of the link between adapoids and anthropoids was Hans Georg Stehlin, who described much of the best material of adapoids and compared these Eocene primates to South American monkeys (Stehlin 1912). In more recent times, the adapoid origin hypothesis was reinforced by resemblances between these European adapoids (especially *Adapis* and *Leptadapis*) and some early anthropoids from the Fayum Basin (e.g., *Aegyptopithecus*, see below; Figure 8.14).

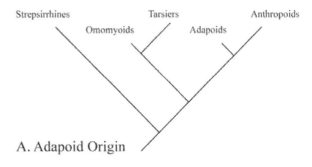

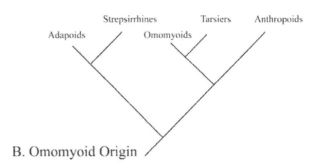

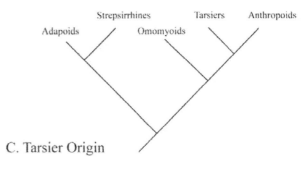

Figure 8.13: Competing models of anthropoid origins. Branch lengths are not to scale. The omomyoid origin model and tarsier origin model do not make specific reference to the evolutionary position of strepsirrhines; however, they were included here for completeness. A full text description of this image is available. Credit: Competing Trees for Anthropoid Origins (Figure 8.11) original to *Explorations: An Open Invitation to Biological Anthropology* by Jonathan M. G. Perry is under a CC BY-NC 4.0 License.

Figure 8.14: Families of early anthropoids with example genera and traits: a table. Credit: Early anthropoids table original to Explorations: An Open Invitation to Biological Anthropology (2nd ed.) by Jonathan M. G. Perry and Stephanie L. Canington is under a CC BY-NC 4.0 License. Content derived from Fleagle 2013.

Family	Genera	Morphology	Location	Age[1]
Propliopithecidae[2]	*Aegyptopithecus*	Large size. Cranial sexual dimorphism, large canines. Robust jaws and rounded molars. Partially ossified ear tube (in some). Robust skeleton; quadruped.	Africa	Late Eocene to Early Oligocene
Parapithecidae[3]	*Apidium*	Medium size. Retention of three premolars per quadrant. Rounded molars and premolars with large central cusps. Adaptations for leaping in the lower limb.	Africa	Late Eocene to Late Oligocene
Proteopithecidae[4]	*Proteopithecus*	Small size. Retention of three premolars per quadrant. Arboreal quadrupeds that ate fruit.	Africa	Late Eocene
Oligopithecidae[5]	*Catopithecus*	Small size. Skull has postorbital septum and unfused mandible. Deep jaws. Diet of fruits. Generalized quadruped.	Africa	Late Eocene
Eosimiidae	*Eosimias*	Deep jaw with vertical unfused symphysis. Pointed incisors and canines. Crowded premolars.	Asia	Middle Eocene
Amphipithecidae[6]	*Pondaungia*	Deep jaws. Molars generally rounded with wide basins.	Asia	Middle Eocene to Early Oligocene

[1] Derived from Fleagle 2013.

[2] See Gebo and Simons 1987 and Simons et al. 2007.

[3] See Feagle and Simons 1995 and Simons 2001.

[4] See Simons and Seiffert 1999.

[5] See Simons and Rasmussen 1996.

[6] See Kay et al. 2004.

Unfortunately for the adapoid hypothesis, most of the shared features listed above probably emerged independently in the two groups as adaptations to a diet of hard and/or tough foods. For example, fusion of the mandibular symphysis likely evolved as a means to strengthen the jaw against forces that would pull the two halves away from each other, in the context of active chewing muscles on both sides of the head generating great bite forces. This context would also favor the development of robust jaws, large chewing muscles, shorter faces, and some other features shared by some adapoids and some anthropoids.

As older and more plesiomorphic anthropoids were found in the Fayum Basin, it became clear that the earliest anthropoids from Africa did not possess these features of jaw robusticity (Seiffert et al. 2009). Furthermore, many adapoids never evolved these features. Fusion of the mandibular symphysis in adapoids is actually quite different from that in anthropoids and probably occurred during juvenile development in the former (Beecher 1983; Ravosa 1996). Eventually, the adapoid origin hypothesis fell out of favor among most paleoanthropologists, although the description of *Darwinius* is a recent revival of that idea (Franzen et al. 2009; but see Seiffert et al. 2009, Williams et al. 2010b).

Omomyoid Origin Hypothesis

Similarities in cranial and hindlimb morphology between some omomyoids and extant tarsiers have led to the suggestion that tarsiers arose from some kind of omomyoid. In particular, *Necrolemur* has many features in common with tarsiers, as does the North American *Shoshonius*, which is known from a few beautifully preserved (although distorted) crania. Tarsiers and *Shoshonius* share exclusively some features of the base of the cranium; however, *Shoshonius* does not have any sign of postorbital closure, and it lacks the bony ear tube of tarsiers. Nevertheless, some of the resemblances between some omomyoids and tarsiers suggest that tarsiers might have originated from within the Omomyoidea (Beard 2002; Beard and MacPhee 1994). In this scenario, although living tarsiers and living anthropoids might be sister taxa, they might have evolved from different omomyoids, possibly separated from each other by more than 50 million years of evolution, or from anthropoids evolved from some non-omomyoid fossil group. The arguments against the omomyoid origin hypothesis are essentially the arguments *for* the tarsier origin hypothesis (see below). Namely, tarsiers and anthropoids share many features (especially of the soft tissues) that must have been retained for many millions of years or must have evolved convergently in the two groups. Furthermore, a key hard-tissue feature shared between the two extant groups, the postorbital septum, was not present in any omomyoid. Therefore, that feature must have arisen convergently in the two extant groups or must have been lost in omomyoids. Neither scenario is very appealing, although recent arguments for **convergent evolution** of the postorbital septum in tarsiers and anthropoids have arisen from embryology and histology of the structure (DeLeon et al. 2016).

Tarsier Origin Hypothesis

Several paleoanthropologists have suggested that there is a relationship between tarsiers and anthropoids to the exclusion of omomyoids and adapoids (e.g., Cartmill and Kay 1978; Ross 2000; Williams and Kay 1995). Tarsiers and anthropoids today share several traits, including many soft-tissue features related to the olfactory system (e.g., the loss of a hairless external nose and loss of the median cleft running from the nose to the mouth, as possessed by strepsirrhines), and aspects of the visual system (e.g., the loss of a reflective layer at the back of the eye, similarities in carotid circulation to the brain, and mode of placentation). Unfortunately, none of these can be assessed directly in fossils. Some bony similarities between tarsiers and anthropoids include an extra air-filled chamber below the middle ear cavity, reduced bones within the nasal cavity, and substantial postorbital closure; these can be assessed in fossils, but the distribution of these traits in omomyoids does not yield clear answers. Furthermore, several similarities between tarsiers and anthropoids are probably due to similarities in sensory systems, which might have evolved in parallel for ecological reasons. Although early attempts to resolve the crown primates with molecular data were sometimes equivocal or in disagreement with one another, more recent analyses (including those of short interspersed elements) suggest that tarsiers and anthropoids are sister groups to the exclusion of lemurs and lorises (Williams et al. 2010a). However, this does not address omomyoids, all of which are far too ancient for DNA extraction.

The above three hypotheses are not the only possibilities for anthropoid origins. It may be that anthropoids are neither the closest sister group of tarsiers, nor evolved from adapoids or omomyoids. In recent years, two new groups of Eocene Asian primates have been implicated in the origin of anthropoids: the eosimiids and the amphipithecids. It is possible that one or the other of these two groups gave rise to anthropoids. Regardless of the true configuration of the tree for crown primates, the three major extant groups probably diverged from each other quite long ago (Seiffert et al. 2004).

Early Anthropoid Fossils in Africa

Figure 8.15: Egyptian workers sweeping Quarry I in the Fayum Basin (2004). This technique, called wind harvesting, removes the desert crust and permits wind to blow out fine sediment and reveal fossils. Credit: **Egyptian workers sweeping Quarry I in the Fayum Basin (2004, Figure 8.12)** by Jonathan M. G. Perry is under a **CC BY-NC 4.0 License**.

The classic localities yielding the greatest wealth of early anthropoid fossils are those from the Fayum Basin in Egypt (Simons 2008; Figure 8.15). The Fayum is a veritable oasis of fossil primates in an otherwise spotty early Tertiary African record. Since the 1960s, teams led by E. L. Simons have discovered several new species of early anthropoids, some of which are known from many parts of the skeleton and several individuals (Figure 8.16).

The Fayum Jebel Qatrani Formation and Birket Qarun Formation between them have yielded a remarkable array of terrestrial, arboreal, and aquatic mammals. These include ungulates, bats, sea cows, elephants, hyraces, rodents, whales, and primates. Also, many other vertebrates, like water birds, were present. The area at the time of deposition (Late Eocene through Early Oligocene) was probably very wet, with slow-moving rivers, standing water, swampy conditions, and lots of trees (see Bown and Kraus 1988). In short, it was an excellent place for primates.

General Morphology of Anthropoids

The anthropoids known from the Fayum (and their close relatives from elsewhere in East Africa and Afro-Arabia) bear many of the anatomical hallmarks of extant anthropoids; however, there are plesiomorphic forms in several families that lack one or more anthropoid traits. All Fayum anthropoids known from skulls possess postorbital closure, most had fused mandibular symphyses, and most had ring-like **ectotympanic** bones. Tooth formulae were generally either 2.1.3.3 or 2.1.2.3. Fayum anthropoids ranged in size from the very small *Qatrania* and *Biretia* (less than 500 g) to the much-larger *Aegyptopithecus* (approximately 7 kg; 15 lbs.). Fruit was probably the main component of the diet for most or all of the anthropoids, with some of them supplementing with leaves (Kay and Simons 1980; Kirk and Simons 2001; Teaford et al. 1996). Most Fayum anthropoids were probably diurnal above-branch quadrupeds. Some of them (e.g., *Apidium*; see Figure 8.14) were probably very good leapers (Gebo and Simons 1987), but none show specializations for gibbon-style suspensory locomotion. Some of the Fayum anthropoids are known from hundreds of individuals, permitting the assessment of individual variation, sexual dimorphism, and in some cases growth and development. The description that follows provides greater detail for the two best known Fayum anthropoid families, the Propliopithecidae and the Parapithecidae; the additional families are summarized briefly.

Figure 8.16: Elwyn Laverne Simons excavating Aegyptopithecus in the Fayum Basin. Credit: Elwyn Laverne Simons in the Fayum Basin (Figure 8.13) used by permission of the Duke Lemur Center, Division of Fossil Primates, is under a CC BY-NC 4.0 License.

Fayum Anthropoid Families

The Propliopithecidae (see Figure 8.14) include the largest anthropoids from the fauna, and they are known from several crania and some postcranial elements. They have been suggested to be stem catarrhines, although perhaps near the split between catarrhines and platyrrhines. The best known propliopithecid is *Aegyptopithecus*, known from many teeth, crania, and postcranial elements (Figure 8.17) .

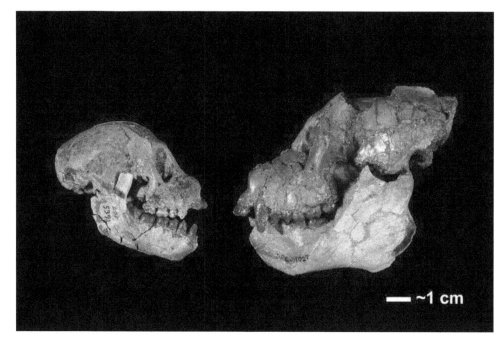

Figure 8.17: Female (left) and male (right) skull material for Aegyptopithecus zeuxis. The mandibles are not associated with the crania. Credit: **Female and male cranium of A. zeuxi (03129Fig5, Supporting Information)** by Elwyn L. Simons, Erik R. Seiffert, Timothy M. Ryan, and Yousry Attia. 2007. **Proceedings of the National Academy of Sciences of the United States of America** 104 (21): 8731–8736. Copyright (2007) National Academy of Sciences. Image is used for non-commercial and educational purposes as outlined by PNAS.

Parapithecidae are an extremely abundant and unusual family of anthropoids from the Fayum. The parapithecid *Apidium* is known from many jaws with teeth, crushed and distorted crania, and several skeletal elements. *Parapithecus* is known from cranial material including a beautiful, undistorted cranium. This genus shows extreme reduction of the incisors, including complete absence of the lower incisors in *P. grangeri* (Simons 2001). This trait is unique among primates. Parapithecids were once thought to be the ancestral stock of platyrrhines; however, their platyrrhine-like features are probably ancestral retentions, so the most conservative approach is to consider them stem anthropoids.

The Proteopithecidae were small frugivores that probably mainly walked along horizontal branches on all fours. TThey are considered stem anthropoids. The best known genus, *Proteopithecus*, is represented by dentitions, crania, and postcranial elements.

The Oligopithecidae share a mixture of traits that makes them difficult to classify more specifically within anthropoids. The best known member, *Catopithecus*, is known from crania that demonstrate a postorbital septum and from mandibles that lack symphyseal fusion. They share the catarrhine tooth formula of 2.1.2.3 and have a canine honing complex that involves the anterior lower premolar. The postcranial elements known for the group suggest generalized arboreal quadrupedalism. The best known member, *Catopithecus*, is known from crania that demonstrate a postorbital septum and from mandibles that lack symphyseal fusion (Simons and Rasmussen 1996). The jaws are deep, with broad muscle attachment areas and crested teeth. *Catopithecus* was probably a little less than a kilogram in weight.

Other genera of putative anthropoids from the Fayum include the very poorly known *Arsinoea*, the contentious *Afrotarsius*, and the enigmatic *Nosmips*. The last of these possesses traits of several major primate **clades** and defies classification (Seiffert et al. 2010).

Early Anthropoid Fossils in Asia

For the last half of the 1900s, researchers believed that Africa was the unquestioned homeland of early anthropoids (see Fleagle and Kay 1994). However, two very different groups of primates from Asia soon began to change that. One was an entirely new discovery (Eosimiidae), and the other was a poorly known group discovered decades prior (Amphipithecidae). Soon, attention on anthropoid origins began to shift eastward (see Ross and Kay 2004; Simons 2004). If anthropoids arose in Asia instead of Africa, then this implies that the African early anthropoids either emigrated from Asia or evolved their anthropoid traits in parallel with living anthropoids.

Eosimiids

First described in the 1990s, the eosimiids are best represented by *Eosimias* (see Figure 8.14; Figure 8.18). This tiny "dawn monkey" is known from relatively complete jaws with teeth, a few small fragments of the face, and some postcranial elements (Beard et al. 1994; Beard et al. 1996; Gebo et al. 2000). *Eosimias* (along with the other less-well-known genera in its family) bears some resemblance to tarsiers as well as anthropoids. Unfortunately, no good crania are known for this family, and the anatomy of, for example, the posterior orbital margin could be very revealing as to higher-level relationships.

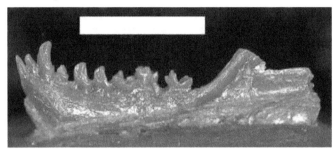

Figure 8.18: Cast of the right half of the mandible of Eosimias centennicus, type specimen. The white scale bar is 1 cm long. Credit: **Cast of the right half of the mandible of *Eosimias centennicus* (Figure 8.15),** type specimen, from K. D. Rose cast collection, photo by Jonathan M. G. Perry is under a **CC BY-NC 4.0 License.**

Amphipithecids

Amphipithecids are small- to medium-size primates (up to 10 kg; 22 lbs.). Most are from the Eocene Pondaung Formation in Myanmar (Early–Middle Eocene), but one genus is known from Thailand. Some dental similarities with anthropoids were noted early on, such as deep jaws and wide basins that separate low molar cusps. The best known genera were *Pondaungia* and *Amphipithecus* (Ciochon and Gunnell 2002; see Figure 8.14). Another amphipithecid, *Siamopithecus* from Thailand, has very rounded molars and was probably a seed-eater (Figure 8.19). In addition to teeth and jaws, some cranial fragments, ankle material, and ends of postcranial bones have been found for *Pondaungia*. There are important resemblances between the postcranial bones of *Pondaungia* and those of adapoids, suggesting adapoid affinities for the amphipithecidae. This would imply that the resemblances with anthropoids in the teeth are convergent, based on similarities in diet (see Ciochon and Gunnell 2002). Unfortunately, the association between postcranial bones and teeth is not definite. With other primates in these faunas (including eosimiids), one cannot be certain that the postcranial bones belong with the teeth. Some researchers suggest that some bones belong to a sivaladapid (or asiadapid) and others to an early anthropoid (Beard et al. 2007; Marivaux et al. 2003). Additional well-associated material of amphipithecids would help to clear up this uncertainty.

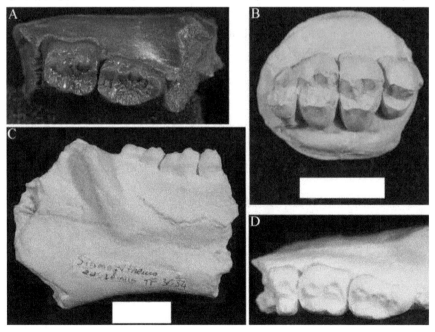

Figure 8.19: Casts of representative amphipithecid material. A. Pondaungia cotteri right lower jaw fragment with m2 and m3. B. Siamopithecus eocaenus right upper jaw fragment with p4-m3. C. S. eocaenus right lower jaw fragment with partial m1, m2, and m3 in lateral view. D. Same as in C but occlusal view. White scale bars are 1 cm long. Credit: **Casts of representative amphipithecid material (Figure 8.16)l** from K. D. Rose cast collection, photo by Jonathan M. G. Perry is under a **CC BY-NC 4.0 License.**

Platyrrhine Dispersal to South America

Today there is an impressive diversity of primates in South and Central America. These are considered to be part of a single clade, the Platyrrhini. Primates colonized South America sometime in the Eocene from an African source. In the first half of the 20th century, the source of platyrrhines was a matter of major debate among paleontologists, with some favoring a North American origin (e.g., Simpson 1940).

Part of the reason for this debate is that South America was an island in the Eocene. Primates needed to cross open ocean to get there from either North America or Africa, although the distance from the former was shorter. Morphology yields clues to platyrrhine origins. The first known primates in South America have more in common morphologically with African primates than with North American ones. At the time, anthropoids were popping up in North Africa, whereas the only euprimates in North America were adapoids and omomyoids. Despite lacking a bony ear tube, early platyrrhines shared a great deal with other anthropoids, including full postorbital closure and fusion of the mandibular symphysis.

The means by which a population of small North African primates managed to disperse across the Atlantic and survive to colonize South America remains a mystery. The most plausible scenario is one of rafting. That is, primates must have been trapped on vegetation that was blown out to sea by a storm. The vegetation then became a sort of life raft, which eventually landed ashore, dumping its passengers in South America. Rodents probably arrived in South America in the same way (Antoine et al. 2012).

Once ashore, platyrrhines must have crossed South America fairly rapidly because the earliest-known primates from that continent are from Peru (Bond et al. 2015). Soon after that, platyrrhines were in Bolivia, namely *Branisella*. By the Miocene, platyrrhines were living in extreme southern Argentina and were exploiting a variety of feeding niches. The Early Miocene platyrrhines were all somewhat plesiomorphic in their morphology, but some features that likely arose by ecological convergence suggest (to some) relationships with extant platyrrhine families. This has led to a lively debate about the pattern of primate evolution in South America (Kay 2015; Kay and Fleagle 2010; Rosenberger 2010). By the Middle Miocene, clear representatives of modern families were present in a diverse fauna from La Venta, Colombia (Wheeler 2010). The Plio-Pleistocene saw the emergence of giant platyrrhines as well as several taxa of platyrrhines living on Caribbean islands (Cooke et al. 2016).

The story of platyrrhines seems to be one of amazing sweepstakes dispersal, followed by rapid diversification and widespread geographic colonization of much of South America. After that, dramatic extinctions resulted in the current, much-smaller geographic distribution of platyrrhines. These extinctions were probably caused by changing climates, leading to the contraction of forests. Platyrrhines dispersed to the Caribbean and to Central America, with subsequent extinctions in those regions that might have been related to interactions with humans. Unlike anthropoids of Africa and Asia, platyrrhines do not seem to have evolved any primarily terrestrial forms and so have always been highly dependent on forests.

Special Topic: Jonathan Perry and Primates of the Extreme South

Many primates are very vulnerable to ecological disturbance because they are heavily dependent on fruit to eat and trees to live in. This is one reason why so many primates are endangered today and why many of them went extinct due to climatic and vegetational changes in the past. I (Jonathan Perry) have conducted paleontological research focusing on primates that lived on the edge of their geographic distribution. This research has taken me to extreme environments in the Americas: southern Patagonia, the Canadian prairies, western Wyoming, and the badlands of eastern Oregon.

Santa Cruz Province in Argentina is as far south as primates have ever lived. The Santa Cruz fauna of the Miocene has yielded a moderate diversity of platyrrhines, each with slightly different dietary adaptations. These include *Homunculus*, first described by Florentino Ameghino in 1891 (Figure 8.20). Recent fieldwork by my colleagues and I in Argentina has revealed several skulls of *Homunculus* as well as many parts of the skeleton (Kay et al. 2012). The emerging profile of this extinct primate is one of a dedicated arboreal quadruped that fed on fruits and leaves. Many of the foods eaten by *Homunculus* must have been very tough and were probably covered and impregnated with grit; we suspect this because the cheek teeth are very worn down, even in young individuals, and because the molar tooth roots were very large, presumably to resist strong bite forces (Perry et al. 2010, 2014).

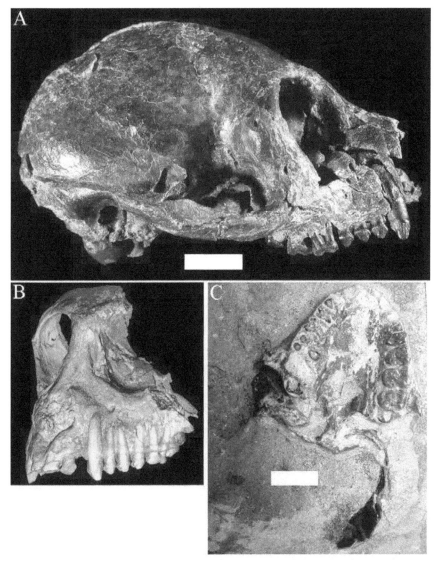

Figure 8.20: Representative specimens of Homunculus patagonicus. A. Adult cranium in lateral view. B. Adult cranium surface reconstructed from microCT scans, with the teeth segmented out. C. Juvenile cranium. White scale bars are 1cm long. Credit: Representative specimens of *Homunculus patagonicus* (Figure 8.17) photo by Jonathan M. G. Perry is under a CC BY-NC 4.0 License.

I began working in Argentina while a graduate student at Duke University. I participated as a field assistant in a team led by my Ph.D. advisor, Richard F. Kay, and Argentine colleagues Sergio F. Vizcaíno and M. Susana Bargo. Most of the localities examined belong to a suite of beach sites known since the 1800s and visited by many field parties from various museums in the early 1900s. Since 2003, our international team of paleontologists from the U.S. and Argentina has visited these localities every single year (Figure 8.21). Over time, new fossils and new students have led to new projects and new approaches, including the use of microcomputed tomography (microCT) to visualize and analyze internal structures of the skeleton.

Figure 8.21: Field localities in Argentina and Canada. A. Cañadon Palos locality, coastal Santa Cruz Province, Argentina. B. Swift Current Creek locality, southwest Saskatchewan, Canada. Credits: A. Cañadon Palos Field Locality in Argentina by Jonathan M. G. Perry is under a CC BY-NC 4.0 License. B. Swift Current Creek locality, Saskatchewan, Canada by Jonathan M. G. Perry is under a CC BY-NC 4.0 License.

Planet of Apes

Geologic Activity and Climate Change in the Miocene

The Miocene Epoch was a time of mammalian diversification and extinction, global climate change, and ecological turnover. In the Miocene, there was an initial warming trend across the globe with the expansion of subtropical forests, followed by widespread cooling and drying with the retreat of tropical forests and replacement with more open woodlands and eventually grasslands. It was also a time of major geologic activity. On one side of the globe, South America experienced the rise of the Andes Mountains. On the other side, the Indian subcontinent collided with mainland Asia, resulting in the rise of the Himalayan Mountains. In Africa, volcanic activity promoted the development of the East African Rift System. Critical to the story of ape evolution was the exposure of an intercontinental landbridge between East Africa and Eurasia, permitting a true planet of apes (Figure 8.22).

PRIMATE EVOLUTION | 259

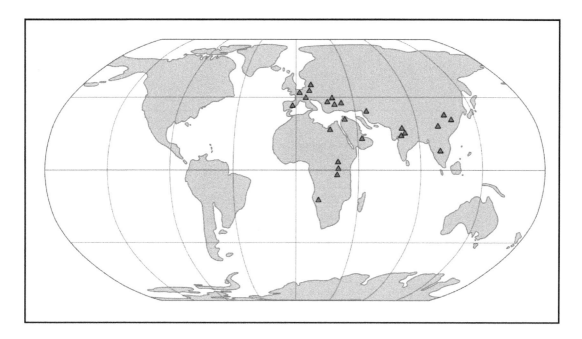

Figure 8.22: Map of the world in the Miocene, highlighting fossil ape localities across Africa, southern Europe, and southern Asia. Credit: Miocene Map with Fossil Ape Localities (Figure 8.19) original to *Explorations: An Open Invitation to Biological Anthropology* by Elyssa Ebding at GeoPlace, California State University, Chico is under a CC BY-NC 4.0 License. Localities based on Fleagle 2013, 311.

Geographic Distribution: Africa, Asia, Europe

The world of the Miocene had tremendous ape diversity compared to today. The earliest records of fossil apes are from Early Miocene deposits in Africa. However, something dramatic happened around 16 million years ago. With the closure of the ancient Tethys Sea, the subsequent exposure of the *Gomphotherium* Landbridge, and a period of global warming, the Middle–Late Miocene saw waves of emigration of mammals (including primates) out of Africa and into Eurasia, with evidence of later African re-entry for some (Harrison 2010). Some of the mammals that dispersed from Africa to Eurasia and back were apes. Though most of these early apes left no modern descendants, some of them gave rise to the ancestors of modern apes—including **hominins**.

Where Are the Monkeys? Diversity in the Miocene

Whereas the Oligocene deposits in the Fayum of Egypt have yielded the earliest-known catarrhine fossils, the Miocene demonstrates some diversification of Cercopithecoidea. However, compared to the numerous and diverse Miocene apes (see below), monkeys of the Miocene are very rare and restricted to a single extinct family, the Victoriapithecidae (Figure 8.23). This family contains the earliest definite cercopithecoids. These monkeys are found from northern and eastern Africa between 20 million and 12.5 million years ago (Miller et al. 2009). The best known early African monkey is *Victoriapithecus* (Figure 8.24), a small-bodied (approximately 7 kg; 15 lbs.), small-brained monkey. **Bilophodonty**, known to be a hallmark of molar teeth of modern cercopithecoid, was present to some extent in Victoriapithecids. *Victoriapithecus* has been reconstructed as being more frugivorous and perhaps spent more time on the ground (terrestrial locomotion) than in the trees (arboreal locomotion; Blue et al. 2006). The two major groups of cercopithecoids today are cercopithecines and colobines. The earliest records demonstrating clear members of each of these two groups are at the end of the Miocene. Examples include the early colobine *Microcolobus* from Kenya and the early cercopithecine *Pliopapio* from Ethiopia.

Figure 8.23: Some families of later anthropoids with example genera and traits: a table. Credit: Late anthropoids table original to Explorations: An Open Invitation to Biological Anthropology (2nd ed.) by Jonathan M. G. Perry and Stephanie L. Canington is under a CC BY-NC 4.0 License. Content derived from Fleagle 2013.

Family	Genera	Morphology	Location	Age[1]
Victoriapithecidae[2]	*Victoriapithecus*	Long, sloping face. Round, narrowly spaced orbits. Deep cheek bones. Well-developed sagittal crest.	Africa	Early to Middle Miocene
Proconsulidae[3]	*Proconsul*	Short face. Generalized dentition. Arboreal quadruped. Probably tailless.	Africa and Arabia	Early to Middle Miocene
Pongidae	*Gigantopithecus*	Largest primate ever. Deep jaws and low rounded molars.	Asia	Miocene to Present

[1] Derived from Fleagle 2013.

[2] See Benefit and McCrossin 1997 and Fleagle 2013.

[3] See Begun 2007.

Figure 8.24: Skull of Victoriapithecus macinnesi. Credit: Victoriapithecus macinnesi skull photo taken at the Musee d'Histoire Naturelle, Paris by Ghedoghedo is under a CC BY-SA 3.0 License.

The Story of Us, the Apes

African Ape Diversity

The Early Miocene of Africa has yielded around 14 genera of early apes (Begun 2003). Many of these taxa have been reconstructed as frugivorous arboreal quadrupeds (Kay 1977). One of the best studied of these genera is the East African *Proconsul* (Family Proconsulidae; see Figure 8.24).

Several species have been described, with body mass reconstructions ranging from 17 to 50 kg (approximately 37–110 lbs.). A paleoenvironmental study reconstructed the habitat of *Proconsul* to be a dense, closed-canopy tropical forest (Michel et al. 2014). No caudal vertebrae (tail bones) have been found in direct association with *Proconsul* postcrania, and the morphology of the sacrum is consistent with *Proconsul* lacking a tail (Russo 2016; Ward et al. 1991).

Overall, the African ape fossil record in the Late Miocene is sparse, with seven fossil localities dating between eleven and five million years ago (Pickford et al. 2009). Nevertheless, most species of great apes live in Africa today. Where did the progenitors of modern African apes arise? Did they evolve in Africa or somewhere else? The paucity of apes in the Late Miocene of Africa stands in contrast to the situation in Eurasia. There, ape diversity was high. Furthermore, several Eurasian ape fossils show morphological affinities with modern hominoids (apes). Because of this, some paleoanthropologists suggest that the ancestors of modern African great apes recolonized Africa from Eurasia toward the end of the Miocene (Begun 2002). However, discoveries of Late Miocene hominoids like the Kenyan *Nakalipithecus* (9.9 million to 9.8 million years ago), the Ethiopian *Chororapithecus* (10.7 million to 10.1 million years ago), and the late-Middle Miocene Namibian *Otavipithecus* (13 million to 12 million years ago) fuel an alternative hypothesis—namely that African hominoid diversity was maintained throughout the Miocene and that one of these taxa might, in fact, be the last common ancestor of extant African apes (Kunimatsu et al. 2007; Mocke et al. 2002). The previously underappreciated diversity of Late Miocene apes in Africa might be due to poor sampling of the fossil record in Africa.

Eurasian Ape Diversity

With the establishment of the *Gomphotherium* Landbridge (a result of the closure of the Eastern Mediterranean seaway; Rögl 1999), the Middle Miocene was an exciting time for hominoid radiations outside of Africa (see Figure 8.23). Eurasian hominoid species exploited their environments in many different ways in the Miocene. Food exploitation ranged from soft-fruit feeding in some taxa to hard-object feeding in others, in part owing to seasonal fluctuations and the necessary adoptions of fallback foods (DeMiguel et al. 2014). For example, the molars of *Oreopithecus bambolii* (Family Hominidae) have relatively long lower-molar shearing crests, suggesting that this hominoid was very folivorous (Ungar and Kay 1995). Associated with variation in diet, there is great variation in the degree to which cranial features (e.g., zygomatic bone or supraorbital tori) are developed across the many taxa (Cameron 1997); however, Middle Miocene fossils tend to exhibit relatively thick molar enamel and relatively robust jaws (Andrews and Martin 1991).

In Spain, the cranium with upper dentition, part of a mandible, and partial skeleton of *Pliobates* (Family Pliobatidae), a small-bodied ape (4–5 kg; 9–11 lbs.), was discovered in deposits dating to 11.6 million years ago (Alba et al. 2015). It is believed to be a frugivore with a relative brain size that overlaps with modern cercopithecoids. The fossilized postcrania of *Pliobates* suggest that this ape might have had a unique style of locomotion, including the tendency to walk across the branches of trees with its palms facing downward and flexible wrists that permitted rotation of the forearm during climbing. However, the anatomy of the distal humerus differs from those of living apes in ways that suggest that *Pliobates* was less efficient at stabilizing its elbow while suspended (Benefit and McCrossin 2015). Two other recently described apes from Spain, *Pierolapithecus* and *Anoiapithecus*, are known from relatively complete skeletons. *Pierolapithecus* had a very projecting face and thick molar enamel as well as some skeletal features that suggest (albeit controversially) a less suspensory locomotor style than in extant apes (Moyà-Solà et al. 2004). In contrast to *Pierolapithecus*, the slightly younger *Anoiapithecus* has a very flat face (Moyà-Solà et al. 2009).

Postcranial evidence for suspensory or well-developed orthograde behaviors in apes does not appear until the Late Miocene of Europe. Primary evidence supporting these specialized locomotor modes includes the relatively short lumbar vertebrae of *Oreopithecus* (Figure 8.25) and *Dryopithecus* (Maclatchy 2004). Further, fossil material of the lower torso of *O. bambolii* (which dates to the *Pan*-hominin divergence) conveys a higher degree of flexion-extension abilities in the lumbar region (lower back) than what is possible in extant apes. Additionally, the hindlimb of *O. bambolii* is suggested to have supported powerful hip adduction during climbing (Hammond et al. 2020). The Late Miocene saw the extinction of most of the Eurasian hominoids in an event referred to as the Vallesian Crisis (Agustí et al. 2003). Among the latest surviving hominoid taxa in Eurasia were *Oreopithecus* and *Gigantopithecus*, the latter of which held out until the Pleistocene in Asia and was probably even sympatric with *Homo erectus* (Cachel 2015).

The Origins of Extant Apes

The fossil record of the extant apes is somewhat underwhelming: it ranges from being practically nonexistent for some taxa (e.g., chimpanzees) to being a little better for others (e.g., humans). There are many possible reasons for these differences in fossil abundance, and many are associated with the environmental conditions necessary for the fossilization of bones. One way to understand the evolution of extant apes that is not so dependent on the fossil record is via molecular evolutionary analyses. This can include counting up the differences in the genetic sequence between two closely related species to estimate the amount of time since these species shared a common ancestor. This is called a molecular clock, and it is often calibrated using fossils of known absolute age that stand in for the last common ancestor of a particular clade. Molecular clock estimates have placed the Hylobatidae and Hominidae split between 19.7 million and 24.1 million years ago, the African ape and Asian ape split between 15.7 million and 19.3 million years ago, and the split of Hylobatidae into its current genera between 6.4 million and 8 million years ago (Israfil et al. 2011).

Small Ape Origins and Fossils

Unfortunately, the fossil record for the small (formerly "lesser") apes is meager, particularly in Miocene deposits. One possible early hylobatid is *Laccopithecus robustus*, a Late Miocene catarrhine from China (Harrison 2016). Although it does share some characteristics with modern gibbons and siamangs (including an overall small body size and a short face), *Laccopithecus* most likely represents a plesiomorphic stem catarrhine and is therefore distantly related to extant apes (Jablonski and Chaplin 2009). A more likely candidate for the hylobatid stem is another Late Miocene taxon from China, *Yuanmoupithecus xiaoyuan*. Interpretation of its phylogenetic standing, however, is complicated by contradicting dental features—some of them quite plesiomorphic—which some believe best place *Yuanmoupithecus* as a stem hylobatid (Harrison 2016). Recently, a Middle Miocene Indian fossil ape, *Kapi ramnagarensis*, has extended the fossil record of small apes by

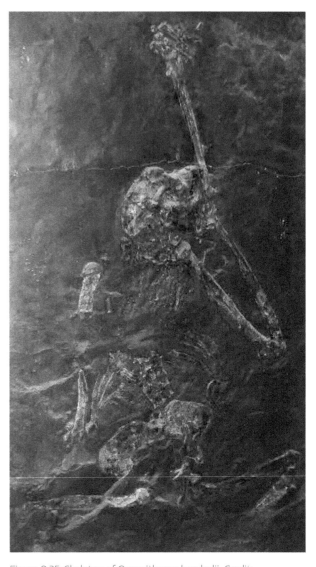

Figure 8.25: Skeleton of Oreopithecus bambolii. Credit: Oreopithecus bambolii 1 by Ghedoghedo is under a CC BY-SA 3.0 License.

approximately five million years. Its teeth are suggestive of a shift to a more frugivorous diet and it is likely a stem hylobatid (Gilbert et al. 2020). The history of Hylobatidae becomes clearer in the Pleistocene, with fossils representing extant genera.

Great Ape Origins and Fossils

The most extensive fossil record of a modern great ape is that of our own genus, *Homo*. The evolution of our own species will be covered in Chapter 9. The evolutionary history of the Asian great ape, the orangutan (*Pongo*), is becoming clearer. Today, orangutans are found only on the islands of Borneo and Sumatra. However, Pleistocene-aged teeth, attributed to *Pongo*, have been found in Cambodia, China, Laos, Peninsular Malaysia, and Vietnam—demonstrating the vastness of the orangutan's previous range (Ibrahim et al. 2013; Wang et al. 2014). *Sivapithecus* from the Miocene of India and Pakistan is represented by many specimens, including parts of the face. *Sivapithecus* is very similar to *Pongo*, especially in the face, and it probably is closely related to ancestral orangutans (Pilbeam 1982). Originally, jaws and teeth belonging to the former genus *Ramapithecus* were thought to be important in the origin of humans (Simons 1961), but now these are recognized as specimens of *Sivapithecus* (Kelley 2002). Postcranial bones of *Sivapithecus*, however, suggest a more generalized locomotor mode—including terrestrial locomotion—than seen in *Pongo* (Pilbeam et al. 1990). Stable carbon and oxygen isotope data from dental enamel have reconstructed the paleoecological space of *Sivapithecus* (as well as the contemporaneous Late Miocene pongine *Khoratpithecus*) within the canopies of forested habitats (Habinger et al. 2022).

A probable close relative of *Sivapithecus* is the amazing *Gigantopithecus*. Known only from teeth and jaws from China and India (e.g., Figure 8.26), this ape probably weighed as much as 270 kg (595 lbs.) and was likely the largest primate ever (Bocherens et al. 2017). Because of unique features of its teeth (including molarized premolars and patterns of wear) and its massive size, it has been reconstructed as a bamboo specialist, somewhat like the modern panda. Small silica particles (phytoliths) from grasses have been found stuck to the molars of *Gigantopithecus* (Ciochon et al. 1990). Recent studies evaluating the carbon isotope composition of the enamel sampled from *Gigantopithecus* teeth suggest that this ape exploited a wide range of vegetation, including fruits, leaves, roots, and bamboo (Bocherens et al. 2017). Its face is reminiscent of that of modern orangutans and it might belong in the same family, Pongidae (Kelley 2002).

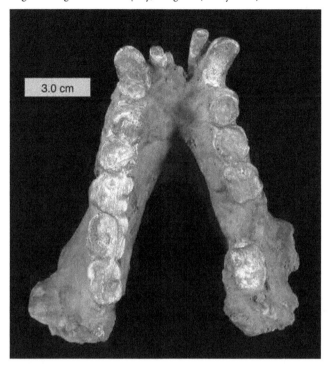

Figure 8.26: Cast of the mandible of Gigantopithecus blacki. Credit: Gigantopithecus blacki mandible 010112 by Wilson44691 is under a CC BY-SA 3.0 License.

In Africa, the first fossil to be confidently attributed to *Pan*, and known to be the earliest evidence of a chimpanzee, was described based on teeth found in Middle Pleistocene deposits in the Eastern Rift Valley of Kenya (McBrearty and Jablonski 2005). Paleoenvironmental reconstructions of this locality suggest that this early chimpanzee was living in close proximity to early *Homo* in a closed-canopy wooded habitat. Similarly, fossil teeth and mandibular remains attributed to two species of Middle-Late Miocene apes—*Chororapithecus abyssinicus* (from Ethiopia; Suwa et al. 2007) and *Nakalipithecus nakayamai* (from Kenya; Kunimatsu et al. 2007)—have been suggested as basal members of the gorilla clade.

While the deposits of Eastern Africa have yielded a profound record of our fossil hominin ancestors, the continent's rainforests remain a "palaeontological desert" (Rosas et al. 2022). Clearly, more work is needed to fill in the large gaps in the fossil record of the nonhuman great apes. The twentieth century witnessed the discovery of many hominin fossils in East Africa, which have been critical for improving our understanding of human evolution. While twenty-first-century conservationists fight to prevent the extinction of the living great apes, perhaps efforts by twenty-first-century paleoanthropologists will yield the evolutionary story of these, our closest relatives.

Review Questions

- Compare three major hypotheses about primate origins, making reference to each one's key ecological reason for primate uniqueness.
- Explain how changes in temperature, rainfall, and vegetation led to major changes in primate biogeography over the Early Tertiary.
- List some euprimate features that plesiadapiforms have and some that they lack.
- Contrast adapoids and omomyoids in terms of life habits.
- Describe one piece of evidence for each of the adapoid, omomyoid, and tarsier origin hypotheses for anthropoids.
- Discuss the biogeography of the origins of African great apes and orangutans using examples from the Miocene ape fossil record.

Key Terms

Adapoidea: Order: Primates. One of the earliest groups of euprimates (true primates; earliest records from the early Eocene).

Adaptive radiations: Rapid diversifications of single lineages into many species which may present unique morphological features in response to different ecological settings.

Ancestral traits: Features that were inherited from a common ancestor and which remain (largely) unchanged.

Anthropoids: Group containing monkeys and apes, including humans.

Auditory bulla: The rounded bony floor of the middle ear cavity.

Bilophodonty: Dental condition in which the cusps of molar teeth form ridges (or lophs) separated from each other by valleys (seen, e.g., in modern catarrhine monkeys).

Catarrhines: Order: Primates; Suborder: Anthropoidea; Infraorder: Catarrhini. Group, with origins in Africa and Asia, that contains monkeys and apes, including humans.

Clade: Group containing all of the descendants of a single ancestor. A portion of a phylogenetic tree represented as a bifurcation (node) in a lineage and all of the branches leading forward in time from that bifurcation.

Convergent evolution: The independent evolution of a morphological feature in animals not closely related (e.g., wings in birds and bats).

Crown: Smallest monophyletic group (clade) containing a specified set of extant taxa and all descendants of their last common ancestor.

Diastema: Space between adjacent teeth.

Diffuse coevolution: The ecological interaction between whole groups of species (e.g., primates) with whole groups of other species (e.g., fruiting trees).

Ectotympanic: Bony ring or tube that holds the tympanic membrane (eardrum).

Euprimates: Order: Primates. True primates or primates of modern aspect.

Haplorhines: Group containing catarrhines, platyrrhines, and tarsiers.

Hominins: Modern humans and any extinct relatives more closely related to us than to chimpanzees.

Mandibular symphysis: Fibrocartilaginous joint between the left and right mandibular segments, located in the midline of the body.

Omomyoidea: Order: Primates; Superfamily: Omomyoidea. One of the earliest groups of euprimates (true primates; earliest record in the early Eocene).

Petrosal bone: The portion of the temporal bone that houses the inner ear apparatus.

Plagiaulacoid: Dental condition where at least one of the lower cheek-teeth (molars or premolars) is a laterally compressed blade.

Platyrrhines: Order: Primates; Suborder: Anthropoidea; Infraorder: Platyrrhini. Group containing monkeys found in the Americas.

Plesiadapiforms: Order: Plesiadapiformes. Archaic primates or primate-like placental mammals (Early Paleocene–Late Eocene).

Plesiomorphic: Having features that are shared by different groups which arose from a common ancestor.

Stem: Taxa that are basal to a given crown group but are more closely related to the crown group than to the closest living sister taxon of the crown group.

Strepsirrhines: Order: Primates; Suborder: Stresirrhini. Group containing lemurs, lorises, and galagos (does not include tarsiers).

Toothcomb: Dental condition found in modern strepsirrhines in which the lower incisors and canines are laterally compressed and protrude forward at a nearly horizontal inclination. This structure is used in grooming.

About the Authors

Jonathan M. G. Perry, Ph.D.

Western University of Health Sciences, Oregon, jperry@westernu.edu

Jonathan Perry was trained as a paleontologist and primatologist at the University of Alberta, Duke University, and Stony Brook University. His research focuses on the relationship between food, feeding, and craniodental anatomy in primates both living and extinct. This work includes primate feeding behavior, comparative anatomy, biomechanics, and field paleontology. He has taught courses on primate evolution at the undergraduate and graduate level.

Stephanie L. Canington, B.A., Ph.D.

University of Pennsylvania, scaning@upenn.edu

Stephanie Canington is a postdoctoral researcher at the University of Pennsylvania. Her current research is on the links between food properties, feeding behavior, and jaw morphology in lemurs that live in varying forms of captivity.

For Further Exploration

Beard, Chris. 2004. *The Hunt for the Dawn Monkey: Unearthing the Origins of Monkeys, Apes, and Humans.* Berkeley: University of California Press.

Begun, David R. 2010. "Miocene Hominids and the Origins of the African Apes and Humans." *Annual Review of Anthropology* 39: 67–84.

Fleagle, John G. 2013. *Primate Adaptation and Evolution.* Third edition. San Diego, CA: Academic Press.

Gebo, Daniel L., ed. 1993. *Postcranial Adaptations in Nonhuman Primates.* Dekalb: Northern Illinois University Press.

Godfrey, Laurie R., and William L. Jungers. 2002. "Quaternary Fossil Lemurs." In *The Primate Fossil Record,* edited by Walter C. Hartwig, 97–121. Cambridge: Cambridge University Press.

Godinot, Marc. 2006. "Lemuriform Origins as Viewed from the Fossil Record." *Folia Primatologica* 77 (6): 446–464.

Kay, Richard F. 2018. "100 Years of Primate Paleontology." *American Journal of Physical Anthropology* 165 (4): 652–676.

Marivaux, Laurent. 2006. "The Eosimiid and Amphipithecid Primates (Anthropoidea) from the Oligocene of the Bugti Hills (Balochistan, Pakistan): New Insight into Early Higher Primate Evolution in South Asia." *Palaeovertebrata, Montpellier* 34 (1–2): 29–109.

Martin, R. D. 1990. *Primate Origins and Evolution: A Phylogenetic Reconstruction.* Princeton: Princeton University Press.

Rose, Kenneth D., Marc Godinot, and Thomas M. Bown. 1994. "The Early Radiation of Euprimates and the Initial Diversification of Omomyidae." In *Anthropoid Origins: The Fossil Evidence,* edited by John G. Fleagle and Richard F. Kay, 1–28. New York: Plenum Press.

Ross, Callum F. 1999. "How to Carry Out Functional Morphology." *Evolutionary Anthropology* 7 (6): 217–222.

Seiffert, Erik R. 2012. "Early Primate Evolution in Afro-Arabia." Evolutionary Anthropology: Issues, News, and Reviews 21(6): 239–253.

Szalay, Frederic S., and Eric Delson. 1979. Evolutionary History of the Primates. New York: Academic Press.

Ungar, Peter S. 2002. "Reconstructing the Diets of Fossil Primates." In *Reconstructing Behavior in the Primate Fossil Record*, edited by Joseph Plavcan, Richard F. Kay, William Jungers, and Carel P. van Schaik, 261–296. New York: Kluwer Academic/Plenum Publishers.

References

Agustí, J., A. Sanz de Siria, and M. Garcés M. 2003. "Explaining the End of the Hominoid Experiment in Europe." *Journal of Human Evolution* 45 (2): 145–153.

Alba, David M., Sergio Almécija, Daniel DeMiguel, Josep Fortuny, Miriam Pérez de los Ríos, Marta Pina, Josep M. Robles, and Salvador Moyà-Solà. 2015. "Miocene Small-Bodied Ape from Eurasia Sheds Light on Hominoid Evolution." *Science* 350 (6260): aab2625.

Andrews, Peter, and Lawrence Martin. 1991. "Hominoid Dietary Evolution." *Philosophical Transactions of the Royal Society of London B: Biological Sciences* 334 (1270): 199–209.

Antoine, Pierre-Oliver, Laurent Marivaux, Darren A. Croft, Guillaume Billet, Morgan Ganerød, Carlos Jaramillo, Thomas Martin, et al. 2012. "Middle Eocene Rodents from Peruvian Amazonia Reveal the Pattern and Timing of Caviomorph Origins and Biogeography." *Proceedings of the Royal Society B: Biological Sciences* 279 (1732): 1319–1326.

Beard, K. Christopher. 1990. "Gliding Behaviour and Palaeoecology of the Alleged Primate Family Paromomyidae (Mammalia, Dermoptera)." *Nature* 345 (6273): 340–341.

Beard, K. Christopher. 2002. "Basal Anthropoids." In *The Primate Fossil Record,* edited by William C. Hartwig, 133–150. Cambridge: Cambridge University Press.

Beard, K. Christopher, and R. D. E. MacPhee. 1994. "Cranial Anatomy of *Shoshonius* and the Antiquity of Anthropoidea." In *Anthropoid Origins: The Fossil Evidence*, edited by John G. Fleagle and Richard F. Kay, 55–98. New York: Plenum Press.

Beard, K. Christopher, Laurent Marivaux, Soe Thura Tun, Aung Naing Soe, Yaowalak Chaimanee, Wanna Htoon, Bernard Marandat, Htun Htun Aung, and Jean-Jacques Jaeger. 2007. "New Sivaladapid Primates from the Eocene Pondaung Formation of Myanmar and the Anthropoid Status of Amphipithecidae." *Bulletin of Carnegie Museum of Natural History* 39: 67–76.

Beard, K. Christopher, Tao Qi, Mary R. Dawson, Banyue Wang, and Chuankuei Li. 1994. "A Diverse New Primate Fauna from Middle Eocene Fissure-Fillings in Southeastern China." *Nature* 368 (6472): 604–609.

Beard, K. Christopher, Yongsheng Tong, Mary R. Dawson, Jingwen Wang, and Xueshi Huang. 1996. "Earliest Complete Dentition of an Anthropoid Primate from the Late Middle Eocene of Shanxi Province, China." *Science* 272 (5258): 82–85.

Beecher, Robert M. 1983. "Evolution of the Mandibular Symphysis in Notharctinae (Adapidae, Primates)." *International Journal of Primatology* 4 (1): 99–112.

Begun, David R. 2002. "European Hominoids." In *The Primate Fossil Record*, edited by William C. Hartwig, 339–368. Cambridge: Cambridge University Press.

Begun, David R. 2003. "Planet of the Apes." *Scientific American* 289 (2): 74–83.

Begun, David R. 2007. "Fossil Record of Miocene Hominoids." In *Handbook of Paleoanthropology*, edited by Winfried Henke and Ian Tattersall, 921–977. New York: Springer.

Benefit, Brenda R., and Monte L. McCrossin. 1997. "Earliest Known Old World Monkey Skull." *Nature* 388 (6640): 368–371.

Benefit, Brenda R., and Monte L. McCrossin. 2015. "A Window into Ape Evolution." *Science* 350 (6260): 515–516.

Bloch, Jonathan I., and David M. Boyer. 2002. "Grasping Primate Origins." *Science* 298 (5598): 1606–1610.

Bloch, Jonathan I., and David M. Boyer. 2007. "New Skeletons of Paleocene-Eocene Plesiadapiformes: A Diversity of Arboreal Positional Behaviors in Early Primates." In *Primate Origins: Adaptations and Evolution*, edited by Matthew J. Ravosa and Marian Dagosto, 535–581. New York: Springer.

Bloch, Jonathan I., and Mary T. Silcox. 2006. "Cranial Anatomy of the Paleocene Plesiadapiform *Carpolestes simpsoni* (Mammalia, Primates) Using Ultra High-Resolution X-ray Computed Tomography, and the Relationships of Plesiadapiforms to Euprimates." *Journal of Human Evolution*: 50 (1): 1–35.

Blue, Kathleen T., Monte L. McCrossin, and Brenda R. Benefit. 2006. "Terrestriality in a Middle Miocene Context: *Victoriapithecus* from Maboko, Kenya." In *Human Origins and Environmental Backgrounds*, edited by Hidemi Ishida, Russell Tuttle, Martin Pickford, Naomichi Ogihara, and Masato Nakatsukasa, 45–58. New York: Springer.

Bocherens, Hervé, Friedemann Schrenk, Yaowalak Chaimanee, Ottmar Kullmer, Doris Mörike, Diana Pushkina, and Jean-Jacques Jaeger. 2017. "Flexibility of Diet and Habitat in Pleistocene South Asian Mammals: Implications for the Fate of the Giant Fossil Ape *Gigantopithecus*." *Quaternary International* 434 (A): 148–155.

Bond, Mariano, Marcelo F. Tejedor, Kenneth E. Campbell Jr., Laura Chornogubsky, Nelson Novo, and Francisco Goin. 2015. "Eocene Primates of South America and the African Origins of New World Monkeys." *Nature* 520 (7548): 539–541.

Bown, T. M., and M. J. Kraus. 1988. "Geology and Paleoenvironment of the Oligocene Jebel Qatrani Formation and Adjacent Rocks, Fayum Depression, Egypt." Professional Paper, 1452. Washington, DC: U.S. Geological Survey Professional Papers.

Cachel, Susan. 2015. *Fossil Primates*. Vol. 69. Cambridge: Cambridge University Press.

Cameron, David W. 1997. "A Revised Systematic Scheme for the Eurasian Miocene Fossil Hominidae." *Journal of Human Evolution* 33 (4): 449–477.

Cartmill, Matt. 1972. "Arboreal Adaptations and the Origin of the Order Primates." In *The Functional and Evolutionary Biology of Primates*, edited by Russell Tuttle, 97–122. Chicago: Aldine-Atherton.

Cartmill, Matt. 1974. "Rethinking Primate Origins." *Science* 184 (4135): 436–443.

Cartmill, Matt, and Richard F. Kay. 1978. "Craniodental Morphology, Tarsier Affinities, and Primate Suborders." In *Recent Advances in Primatology: Evolution*, edited by D. J. Chivers and K. A. Joysey, 205–214. London: Academic Press.

Casanovas-Vilar, Isaac, David M. Alba, Miguel Garcés, Josep M. Robles, and Salvador Moyà-Solà. 2011. "Updated Chronology for the Miocene Hominoid Radiation in Western Eurasia." *Proceedings of the National Academy of Sciences* 108 (14): 5554-5559. https://doi:10.1073/pnas.1018562108.

Chaimanee, Yaowalak, Olivier Chavasseau, K. Christopher Beard, Aung Aung Kyaw, Aung Naing Soe, Chit Sein, Vincent Lazzari, et al. 2012. "Late Middle Eocene Primate from Myanmar and the Initial Anthropoid Colonization of Africa." *Proceedings of the National Academy of Sciences of the United States of America* 109 (26): 10293–10297.

Chester, Stephen G. B., Jonathan I. Bloch, Doug M. Boyer, and William A. Clemens. 2015. "Oldest Known Euarchontan Tarsals and Affinities of Paleocene *Purgatorius* to Primates." *Proceedings of the National Academy of Sciences of the United States of America* 112 (5): 1487–1492.

Ciochon, Russell L., and Gregg F. Gunnell. 2002. "Chronology of Primate Discoveries in Myanmar: Influences on the Anthropoid Origins Debate." *Yearbook of Physical Anthropology* 45 (S35): 2–35.

Ciochon, R. L., D. R. Piperno, and R. G. Thompson. 1990. "Opal Phytoliths Found on the Teeth of the Extinct Ape *Gigantopithecus blacki*: Implications for Paleodietary Studies." *Proceedings of the National Academy of Sciences of the United States of America* 87 (20): 8120–8124.

Clemens, William A. 2004. "*Purgatorius* (Plesiadapiformes, Primates?, Mammalia), a Paleocene Immigrant into Northeastern Montana: Stratigraphic Occurrences and Incisor Proportions." *Bulletin of Carnegie Museum of Natural History* 36: 3–13.

Cooke, Siobhán B., Justin T. Gladman, Lauren B. Halenar, Zachary S. Klukkert, and Alfred L. Rosenberber. 2016. "The Paleobiology of the Recently Extinct Platyrrhines of Brazil and the Caribbean." In *Molecular Population Genetics, Evolutionary Biology and Biological Conservation of Neotropical Primates*, edited by Manuel Ruiz-Garcia and Joseph Mark Shostell, 41–89. New York: Nova Publishers.

DeLeon, Valerie B., Timothy D. Smith, and Alfred L. Rosenberger. 2016. "Ontogeny of the Postorbital Region in Tarsiers and Other Primates." *Anatomical Record: Advances in Integrative Anatomy and Evolutionary Biology* 299 (12): 1631–1645.

DeMiguel, Daniel, David M. Alba, and Salvador Moyà-Solà. 2014. "Dietary Specialization during the Evolution of Western Eurasian Hominoids and the Extinction of European Great Apes." *PLoS ONE* 9 (5): e97442. https://doi.org/10.1371/journal.pone.0097442.

Dunn, Rachel H., Kenneth D. Rose, Rajendra Rana, Kishore Kumar, Ashok Sahni, and Thierry Smith. 2016. "New Euprimate Postcrania from the Early Eocene of Gujarat, India, and the Strepsirrhine–Haplorhine Divergence." *Journal of Human Evolution* 99: 25–51.

Fleagle, John G. 2013. *Primate Adaptation and Evolution*, Third Edition. San Diego, CA: Academic Press.

Fleagle, John G., and Richard F. Kay. 1994. *Anthropoid Origins*. New York: Plenum Press.

Franzen, Jens Lorenz, Phillip D. Gingerich, Jörg Habersetzer, Jørn Hurum, von Wighart Koenigswald, and B. Holly Smith. 2009. "Complete Primate Skeleton from the Middle Eocene of Messel in Germany: Morphology and Paleobiology." *PLoS ONE* 4 (5): e5723. doi:10.1371/journal.pone.0005723.

Gebo, Daniel L., Marian Dagosto, K. Christopher Beard, Tao Qi, and Jingwen Wang. 2000. "The Oldest Known Anthropoid Postcranial Fossils and the Early Evolution of Higher Primates." *Nature* 404 (6775): 276–278.

Gebo, Daniel L., and Elwyn L. Simons. 1987. "Morphology and Locomotor Adaptations of the Foot in Early Oligocene Anthropoids." *American Journal of Physical Anthropology* 74 (1): 83–101.

Gilbert, Christopher C., Alejandra Ortiz, Kelsey D. Pugh, Christopher J. Campisano, Biren A. Patel, Ningthoujam Premjit Singh, John G. Fleagle, and Rajeev Patnaik. 2020. "New Middle Miocene Ape (Primates: Hylobatidae) from Ramnagar, India, Fills Major Gaps in the Hominoid Fossil Record." *Proceedings of the Royal Society B* 287(1934): 20201655.

Gingerich, P. D. 1980. "Eocene Adapidae, Paleobiogeography, and the Origin of South American Platyrrhini." *In Evolutionary Biology of the New World Monkeys and Continental Drift,* edited by Russell L. Ciochon and A. Brunetto Chiarelli, 123–138. New York: Plenum Press.

Godfrey, Laurie R., and William L. Jungers. 2002. "Quaternary Fossil Lemurs." In *The Primate Fossil Record*, edited by Walter C. Hartwig, 97–121. Cambridge: Cambridge University Press.

Godinot, Marc. 2006. "Lemuriform Origins as Viewed from the Fossil Record." *Folia Primatologica* 77 (6): 446–464.

Gregory, William K. 1920. "On the Structure and Relations of *Notharctus*, an American Eocene Primate." *Memoirs of the American Museum of Natural History* (N.S.) 3 (2).

Gunnell, Gregg F., Doug M. Boyer, Anthony R. Friscia, Steven Heritage, Frederik Kyalo Manthi, Ellen R. Miller, Hesham M. Sallam, Nancy B. Simmons, Nancy J. Stevens, and Erik R. Seiffert. 2018. "Fossil Lemurs from Egypt and Kenya Suggest an African Origin for Madagascar's Aye-aye." *Nature Communications* 9 (3193): 1–12.

Habinger, S. G., O. Chavasseau, J. J. Jaeger, Y. Chaimanee, A. N. Soe, C. Sein, and H. Bocherens. 2022. "Evolutionary Ecology of Miocene Hominoid Primates in Southeast Asia." *Scientific Reports* 12 (1): 1–12.

Hammond, Ashley, Lorenzo Rook, Alisha D.Anaya, Elisabetta Cioppi, Loïc Costeur, Salvadore Moyà-Solà, and Sergio Almécija. 2020. "Insights into the Lower Torso in Late Miocene Hominoid Oreopithecus bambolii." *Proceedings of the National Academy of Sciences* 117 (1): 278–284.

Harrison, Terry. 2010. "Apes among the Tangled Branches of Human Origins." *Science* 327 (5965): 532–534.

Harrison, Terry. 2016. "The Fossil Record and Evolutionary History of Hylobatids." In *Evolution of Gibbons and Siamang*, edited by Ullrich H. Reichard, Hirohisa Hirai, and Claudia Barelli, 91–110. New York: Springer.

Ibrahim, Yasamin Kh., Lim Tze Tshen, Kira E. Westaway, Earl of Cranbrook, Louise Humphrey, Ross Fatihah Muhammad, Jian-xin Zhao, and Lee Chai Peng. 2013. "First Discovery of Pleistocene Orangutan (*Pongo* sp.) Fossils in Peninsular Malaysia: Biogeographic and Paleoenvironmental Implications." *Journal of Human Evolution* 65 (6): 770–797.

Israfil, Hulya, Sarah M. Zehr, Alan R. Mootnick, Maryellen Ruvolo, and Michael E. Steiper. 2011. "Unresolved Molecular Phylogenies of Gibbons and Siamangs (Family: Hylobatidae) Based on Mitochondrial, Y-linked, and X-linked Loci Indicate a Rapid Miocene Radiation or Sudden Vicariance Event." *Molecular Phylogenetics and Evolution* 58 (3): 447–455.

Jablonski, Nina G., and George Chaplin. 2009. "The Fossil Record of Gibbons." In *The Gibbons*, edited by Danielle Whittaker and Susan Lappan, 111–130. New York: Springer.

Jones, F. Wood. 1916. *Arboreal Man*. London: Edward Arnold.

Kay, Richard F. 1977. "Diets of Early Miocene African Hominoids." *Nature* 268 (5621): 628–630.

Kay, Richard F. 2015. "Biogeography in Deep Time: What Do Phylogenetics, Geology, and Paleoclimate Tell Us about Early Platyrrhine Evolution?" *Molecular Phylogenetics and Evolution* 82 (B): 358–374.

Kay, Richard F., and John G. Fleagle. 2010. "Stem Taxa, Homoplasy, Long Lineages, and the Phylogenetic Position of *Dolichocebus*." *Journal of Human Evolution* 59 (2): 218–222.

Kay, Richard F., Jonathan M. G. Perry, Michael Malinzak, Kari L. Allen, E. Christopher Kirk, J. Michael Plavcan, and John G. Fleagle. 2012. "Paleobiology of Santacrucian Primates." In *Early Miocene Paleobiology in Patagonia: High-Latitude Paleocommunities of the Santa Cruz Formation*, edited by Sergio F. Vizcaíno, Richard F. Kay, and M. Susana Bargo, 306–330. Cambridge: Cambridge University Press.

Kay, Richard F., Daniel O Schmitt, Christopher J. Vinyard, Jonathan M. G. Perry, Nobuo Shigehara, Masanaru Takai, and Naoko Egi. 2004. "The Paleobiology of Amphipithecidae, South Asian Late Eocene Primates." *Journal of Human Evolution* 46 (1): 3–25.

Kay, Richard F., and Elwyn L. Simons. 1980. "The Ecology of Oligocene African Anthropoidea." *International Journal of Primatology* 1 (1): 21–37.

Kay, Richard F., Richard W. Thorington, and Peter Houde. 1990. "Eocene Plesiadapiform Shows Affinities with Flying Lemurs Not Primates." *Nature* 345 (6273): 342–344.

Kelley, Jay. 2002. "The Hominoid Radiation in Asia." In *The Primate Fossil Record*, edited by Walter C. Hartwig, 369–384. Cambridge: Cambridge University Press.

Kirk, E. Christopher, and Elwyn L. Simons. 2001. "Diets of Fossil Primates from the Fayum Depression of Egypt: A Quantitative Analysis of Molar Shearing." *Journal of Human Evolution* 40 (3): 203–229.

Kirk, E. Christopher, and Blythe A. Williams. 2011. "New Adapiform Primate of Old World Affinities from the Devil's Graveyard Formation of Texas." *Journal of Human Evolution* 61 (2): 156–168.

Krause, David W. 1991. "Were Paromomyids Gliders? Maybe, Maybe Not." *Journal of Human Evolution* 21 (3): 177–188.

Kunimatsu, Yutaka, Masato Nakatsukasa, Yoshihiro Sawada, Tetsuya Sakai, Masayuki Hyodo, Hironobu Hyodo, Tetsumaru Itaya, et al. 2007. "A

New Late Miocene Great Ape from Kenya and Its Implications for the Origins of African Great Apes and Humans." *Proceedings of the National Academy of Sciences of the United States of America* 104 (49): 19220–19225.

Maclatchy, Laura. 2004. "The Oldest Ape." *Evolutionary Anthropology: Issues, News, and Reviews* 13 (3): 90–103.

Marivaux, Laurent, Yaowalak Chaimanee, Stéphane Ducrocq, Bernard Marandat, Jean Sudre, Aung Naing Soe, Soe Thura Tun, Wanna Htoon, and Jean-Jacques Jaeger. 2003. "The Anthropoid Status of a Primate from the Late Middle Eocene Pondaung Formation (Central Myanmar): Tarsal Evidence." *Proceedings of the National Academy of Sciences of the United States of America* 100 (23): 13173–13178.

Marivaux, Laurent, Anusha Ramdarshan, El Mabrouk Essid, Wissem Marzougui, Hayet Khayati Ammar, Renaud Lebrun, Bernard Marandat, Gilles Merzeraud, Rodolphe Tabuce, and Monique Vianey-Liaud. 2013. "*Djebelemur*, a Tiny Pre-ToothCombed Primate from the Eocene of Tunisia: A Glimpse into the Origin of Crown Strepsirrhines." *PLoS ONE* 8 (12): e80778. doi.org/10.1371/journal.pone.0080778.

Martin, R. D. 1968. "Towards a New Definition of Primates." *Man* (N.S.) 3 (3): 377–401.

Martin, R. D. 1972. "Adaptive Radiation and Behaviour of the Malagasy Primates." *Philosophical Transactions of the Royal Society B: Biological Sciences* 264 (862): 295–352.

Martin, R. D. 1990. *Primate Origins and Evolution, a Phylogenetic Reconstruction*. Princeton: Princeton University Press.

McBrearty, Sally, and Nina G. Jablonski. 2005. "First Fossil Chimpanzee." *Nature* 437 (7055): 105–108.

Michel, Lauren A., Daniel J. Peppe, James A. Lutz, Stephen G. Driese, Holly M. Dunsworth, William E. H. Harcourt-Smith, William H. Horner, Thomas Lehmann, Sheila Nightingale, and Kieran P. McNulty. 2014. "Remnants of an Ancient Forest Provide Ecological Context for Early Miocene Fossil Apes." *Nature Communications* 5: 1-9.

Miller, E. R., B. R. Benefit, M. L. McCrossin, J. M. Plavcan, M. G. Leakey, A. N. El-Barkooky, M. A. Hamdan, M. K. A. Gawad, S. M. Hassan, and E. L. Simons. 2009. "Systematics of Early and Middle Miocene Old World Monkeys." *Journal of Human Evolution* 57 (3): 195–211.

Mocke, H., M. Pickford, B. Senut, and D. Gommery. 2022. "New Information about African Late Middle Miocene to Latest Miocene (13–5.5 Ma) Hominoidea. *Communications of the Geological Survey of Namibia* 24: 33–66.

Moyà-Solà, Salvadore, David M. Alba, Sergio Almécija, Isaac Casanovas-Vilar, Meike Köhler, Soledad De Esteban-Trivigno, Josep M. Robles, Jordi Galindo, and Josep Fortuny. 2009. "A Unique Middle Miocene European Hominoid and the Origins of the Great Ape and Human Clade." *Proceedings of the National Academy of Sciences of the United States of America* 106 (24): 9601–9606.

Moyà-Solà, Salvador, Meike Köhler, David M. Alba, Isaac Casanovas-Vilar, and Jordi Galindo. 2004. "*Pierolapithecus catalaunicus*, a New Middle Miocene Great Ape from Spain." *Science* 306 (5700): 1339–1344.

Ni, Xijun, Daniel L. Gebo, Marian Dagosto, Jin Meng, Paul Tafforeau, John J. Flynn, and K. Christopher Beard. 2013. "The Oldest Known Primate Skeleton and Early Haplorhine Evolution." *Nature* 498 (7452): 60–64.

Perry, Jonathan M. G., Richard F. Kay, Sergio F. Vizcaíno, and M. Susana Bargo. 2010. "Tooth Root Size, Chewing Muscle Leverage, and the Biology of *Homunculus patagonicus* (Primates) from the Late Early Miocene of Patagonia." *Ameghiniana* 47 (3): 355–371.

Perry, Jonathan M. G., Richard F. Kay, Sergio F. Vizcaíno, and M. Susana Bargo. 2014. "Oldest Known Cranium of a Juvenile New World Monkey (Early Miocene, Patagonia, Argentina): Implications for the Taxonomy and the Molar Eruption Pattern of Early Platyrrhines." *Journal of Human Evolution* 74: 67–81.

Pickford, Martin, Yves Coppens, Brigitte Senut, Jorge Morales, and José Braga. 2009. "Late Miocene Hominoid from Niger." *Comptes Rendus Palevol* 8 (4): 413–425.

Pilbeam, David. 1982. "New Hominoid Skull Material from the Miocene of Pakistan." *Nature* 295 (5846): 232–234.

Pilbeam, David, Michael D. Rose, John C. Barry, and S. M. Ibrahim Shah. 1990. "New *Sivapithecus* Humeri from Pakistan and the Relationship of *Sivapithecus* and *Pongo*." *Nature* 348 (6298): 237–239.

Rasmussen, D. Tab. 1990. "Primate Origins: Lessons from a Neotropical Marsupial." *American Journal of Primatology* 22 (4): 263–277.

Ravosa, Matthew J. 1996. "Mandibular Form and Function in North American and European Adapidae and Omomyidae." *Journal of Morphology* 229 (2): 171–190.

Rögl, Fred. 1999. "Mediterranean and Paratethys Palaeogeography during the Oligocene and Miocene." In *Hominoid Evolution and Climatic Change in Europe*, edited by Jorge Agustí, Lorenzo Rook, and Peter Andrews, 8–22. Cambridge: Cambridge University Press.

Rosas, A., A. García-Tabernero, D. Fidalgo, M. Fero Meñe, C. Ebana Ebana, F. Esono Mba, and P. Saladie. 2022. "The Scarcity of Fossils in the African Rainforest: Archaeo-Paleontological Surveys and Actualistic Taphonomy in Equatorial Guinea." *Historical Biology* 34 (8): 1–9.

Rose, Kenneth D., and Thomas M. Bown. 1984. "Gradual Phyletic Evolution at the Generic Level in Early Eocene Omomyoid Primates." *Nature* 309 (5965): 250–252.

Rose, Kenneth D., Rachel H. Dunn, Kishor Kumar, Jonathan M. G. Perry, Kristen A. Prufrock, Rajendra S. Rana, and Thierry Smith. 2018. "New Fossils from Tadkeshwar Mine (Gujarat, India) Increase Primate Diversity from the Early Eocene Cambay Shale." *Journal of Human Evolution* 122: 93–107.

Rose, Kenneth D., and John M. Rensberger. 1983. "Upper Dentition of *Ekgmowechashala* (Omomyoid Primate) from the John Day Formation, Oligo-Miocene of Oregon." *Folia Primatologica* 41(1-2): 102–111.

Rosenberger, Alfred L. 2010. "Platyrrhines, PAUP, Parallelism, and the Long Lineage Hypothesis: A Reply to Kay *et al.* (2008)." *Journal of Human Evolution* 59 (2): 214–217.

Ross, Callum F. 2000. "Into the Light: The Origins of Anthropoidea." *Annual Review of Anthropology* 29: 147–194.

Ross, Callum F., and Richard F. Kay, eds. 2004. *Anthropoid Origins: New Visions*. New York: Kluwer Academic/Plenum Publishers.

Russo, Gabrielle A. 2016. "Comparative Sacral Morphology and the Reconstructed Tail Lengths of Five Extinct Primates: *Proconsul heseloni*, *Epipliopithecus vindobonensis*, *Archaeolemur edwardsi*, *Megaladapis grandidieri*, and *Palaeopropithecus kelyus*." *Journal of Human Evolution* 90: 135–162.

Schmid, Peter. 1979. "Evidence of Microchoerine Evolution from Dielsdorf (Zürich Region, Switzerland): A Preliminary Report." *Folia Primatologica* 31 (4): 301–311.

Seiffert, Erik R. 2012. "Early Primate Evolution in Afro-Arabia." *Evolutionary Anthropology: Issues, News, and Reviews* 21 (6): 239–253.

Seiffert, Erik R., Jonathan M. G. Perry, Elwyn L. Simons, and Doug M. Boyer. 2009. "Convergent Evolution of Anthropoid-like Adaptations in Eocene Adapiform Primates." *Nature* 461 (7267): 1118–1121.

Seiffert, Erik R., Elwyn L. Simons, and Yousry Attia. 2003. "Fossil Evidence for an Ancient Divergence of Lorises and Galagos." *Nature* 422 (6930): 421–424.

Seiffert, Erik R., Elwyn L. Simons, Doug M. Boyer, Jonathan M. G. Perry, Timothy M. Ryan, and Hesham M. Sallam. 2010. "A Fossil Primate of Uncertain Affinities from the Earliest Late Eocene of Egypt." *Proceedings of the National Academy of Sciences of the United States of America* 107 (21): 9712–9717.

Seiffert, Erik R., Elwyn L. Simons, and Cornelia V. M. Simons. 2004. "Phylogenetic, Biogeographic, and Adaptive Implications of New Fossil Evidence Bearing on Crown Anthropoid Origins and Early Stem Catarrhine Evolution." In *Anthropoid Origins: New Visions*, edited by Callum F. Ross and Richard F. Kay, 157–182. New York: Kluwer/Plenum Publishing.

Simons, Elwyn L. 1961. "The Phyletic Position of *Ramapithecus*." *Postilla* 57: 1–9.

Simons, Elwyn L. 2001. "The Cranium of *Parapithecus grangeri*, an Egyptian Oligocene Anthropoidean Primate." *Proceedings of the National Academy of Sciences of the United States of America* 98 (4): 7892–7897.

Simons, Elwyn L. 2004. "The Cranium and Adaptations of *Parapithecus grangeri*, a Stem Anthropoid From the Fayum Oligocene of Egypt." In *Anthropoid Origins: New Visions*, edited by Callum F. Ross and Richard F. Kay, 183–204. New York: Kluwer/Plenum Publishing.

Simons, Elwyn L. 2008. "Eocene and Oligocene Mammals of the Fayum, Egypt." In *Elwyn Simons: A Search for Origins*, edited by John G. Fleagle and Christopher C. Gilbert, 87–105. New York: Springer.

Simons, Elwyn L., and D. Tab Rasmussen. 1994a. "A Remarkable Cranium of *Plesiopithecus teras* (Primates, Prosimii) from the Eocene of Egypt." *Proceedings of the National Academy of Sciences of the United States of America* 91(21): 9946–9950.

Simons, Elwyn L., and D. Tab Rasmussen. 1994b. "A Whole New World of Ancestors: Eocene Anthropoideans from Africa." *Evolutionary Anthropology* 3 (4): 128–139.

Simons, Elwyn L., and D. Tab Rasmussen. 1996. "Skull of *Catopithecus browni*, an Early Tertiary Catarrhine." *American Journal of Physical Anthropology* 100 (2): 261–292.

Simons, Elwyn L., and Erik R. Seiffert. 1999. "A Partial Skeleton of *Proteopithecus sylviae* (Primates Anthropoidea): First Associated Dental and Postcranial Remains of an Eocene Anthropoidean." *Comptes Rendus de l'Académie des Sciences, Paris* 329 (12): 921–927.

Simons, Elwyn L., Erik R. Seiffert, Timothy M. Ryan, and Yousry Attia. 2007. "A Remarkable Female Cranium of the Early Oligocene Anthropoid *Aegyptopithecus zeuxis* (Catarrhini, Propliopithecidae)." *Proceedings of the National Academy of Sciences of the United States of America* 104 (21): 8731–8736.

Simpson, George Gaylord. 1933. "The 'Plagiaulacoid' Type of Mammalian Dentition: A Study of Convergence." *Journal of Mammalogy* 14 (2): 97–107.

Simpson, George Gaylord. 1940. "Review of the Mammal-Bearing Tertiary of South America." *Proceedings of the American Philosophical Society* 83 (5): 649–709.

Simpson, George Gaylord. 1967. "The Tertiary Lorisiform Primates of Africa." *Bulletin of the Museum of Comparative Zoology at Harvard University* 136: 39–62.

Smith, G. Elliot. 1912. "The Evolution of Man." *Smithsonian Institute Annual Report* 2012: 553–572.

Smith, Thierry, Kenneth D. Rose, and Philip D. Gingerich. 2006. "Rapid Asia–Europe–North America Geographic Dispersal of Earliest Eocene Primate *Teilhardina* during the Paleocene–Eocene Thermal Maximum." *Proceedings of the National Academy of Sciences of the United States of America* 103 (30): 11223–11227.

Stehlin, Hans G. 1912. "Die säugetiere des schweizerischen Eocaens. Siebenter teil, erst hälfte: *Adapis*" ["The Mammals of the Swiss Eocene. Part Seven, First Half: Adapis"]. *Abhandlungen der Schweizerischen Paläontologischen Gesellschaft* 38: 1165–1298.

Strait, Suzanne G. 2001. "Dietary Reconstruction of Small-Bodied Omomyoid Primates." *Journal of Vertebrate Paleontology* 21 (2): 322–334.

Sussman, Robert W. 1991. "Primate Origins and the Evolution of Angiosperms." *American Journal of Primatology* 23 (4): 209–223.

Suwa, Gen, Reiko T. Kono, Shigehiro Katoh, Berhane Asfaw, and Yonas Beyene. 2007. "A New Species of Great Ape from the Late Miocene Epoch in Ethiopia." *Nature* 448 (7156): 921–924.

Teaford, Mark F., Mary C. Maas, and Elwyn L. Simons. 1996. "Dental Microwear and Microstructure in Early Oligocene Primates from the Fayum, Egypt: Implications for Diet." *American Journal of Physical Anthropology* 101 (4): 527–543.

Ungar, Peter S., and Richard F. Kay. 1995. "The Dietary Adaptations of European Miocene Catarrhines." *Proceedings of the National Academy of Sciences of the United States of America* 92 (12): 5479–5481.

Wang, Cui-Bin, Ling-Xia Zhao, Chang-Zhu Jin, Yuan Wang, Da-Gong Qin, and Wen-Shi Pan. 2014. "New Discovery of Early Pleistocene Orangutan Fossils from Sanhe Cave in Chongzuo, Guangxi, Southern China." *Quaternary International* 354: 68–74.

Ward, C. V., A. Walker, and M. F. Teaford. 1991. "*Proconsul* Did Not Have a Tail." *Journal of Human Evolution* 21 (3): 215–220.

Wheeler, Brandon C. 2010. "Community Ecology of the Middle Miocene Primates of La Venta, Colombia: The Relationship between Ecological Diversity, Divergence Time, and Phylogenetic Richness." *Primates* 51 (2): 131–138.

Williams, Blythe A., and Richard F. Kay. 1995. "The Taxon Anthropoidea and the Crown Clade Concept." *Evolutionary Anthropology* 3 (6): 188–190.

Williams, Blythe A., Richard F. Kay, and E. Christopher Kirk. 2010a. "New Perspectives on Anthropoid Origins." *Proceedings of the National Academy of the United States of America* 107 (11): 4797–4804.

Williams, Blythe A., Richard F. Kay, E. Christopher Kirk, and Callum F. Ross. 2010b. "*Darwinius masillae* Is a European Middle Eocene Stem Strepsirrhine—A Reply to Franzen et al." *Journal of Human Evolution* 59(5): 567–573.

Wilson Mantilla, G. P., S. G. B. Chester, W. A. Clemens, J. R. Moore, C. J. Sprain, B. T. Hovatter, W. S. Mitchell, W. W. Mans, R. Mundil, and P. R. Renne. 2021. "Earliest Palaeocene Purgatoriids and the Initial Radiation of Stem Primates." *Royal Society Open Science* 8(2):210050. doi:10.1098/rsos.210050.

Acknowledgments

We are immensely grateful to the editors of this book, Drs. Beth Shook, Lara Braff, Katie Nelson, and Kelsie Aguilera, for their time and commitment to making this knowledge freely accessible to all, and for giving us the opportunity to participate in this important project.

Image Descriptions

Figure 8.2: A line diagram illustrates the many branches of, and probable relationships between, primates and their primate-like ancestors. Y axis lists time periods (bottom to top): Paleocene, Eocene, Oligocene, Miocene. Across the top are labeled extant primate groups (left to right): lorisiformes, lemuriformes, tarsiers, platyrrhines, cercopithecoids, apes.

From the bottom a vertical line emerges. It has three side branches in the Paleocene labeled Plesiadapiforms. From there it branches into a group labeled Adapoids during the Eocene and Oligocne. A disconnected side-branch leads further to groups of Omomyoids, Eosimiids, and Amphipithecids at roughly the same time period. Branches from Adapoids leads to Sivaladapids (Miocene) and Lorisiformes and Lemuriforms (present day). One disconnected branch connects Omomyoids to Tarsiers (present day). A disconnected branch from Eosimiids also leads to Tarsiers. Other disconnected branches from Eosimiids lead to Platyrrhines, Cercopithecoids, and Apes (all present day).

Figure 8.13: For the adapoid origin model, strepsirrhines, omomyoids, tarsiers, adapoids and anthropoids all share a common ancestor. Strepsirrhines were the first to diverge from the lineage leading to anthropoids, followed by omomyoids. Tarsiers diverged from the lineage leading to Omomyoids. Adapoids were the last to diverge from the lineage leading th anthropoids. For the tarsier origin model, strepsirrhines, omomyoids, tarsiers, adapoids and anthropoids similarly share a common ancestor. However in this model adapoids were the first to diverge from the lineage leading to anthropoids. Strepsirrhines later diverged from the adapoids. Then, omomyoids diverged from the lineage leading to anthropoids, followed by tarsiers. For the omomyoid origin model, like the tarsier model, adapoids first diverged and strepsirrhines later diverging from the lineage leading to adapoids. Omomyoids diverged after the adapoids. However, in this model tarsiers diverged from the lineage leading to omomyoids.

9.

EARLY HOMININS

Kerryn Warren, Ph.D., Grad Coach International

Lindsay Hunter, M.A., University of Iowa

Navashni Naidoo, M.Sc., University of Cape Town

Silindokuhle Mavuso, M.Sc., University of Witwatersrand

This chapter is a revision from "Chapter 9: Early Hominins" by Kerryn Warren, K. Lindsay Hunter, Navashni Naidoo, Silindokuhle Mavuso, Kimberleigh Tommy, Rosa Moll, and Nomawethu Hlazo. In Explorations: An Open Invitation to Biological Anthropology, first edition, edited by Beth Shook, Katie Nelson, Kelsie Aguilera, and Lara Braff, which is licensed under CC BY-NC 4.0.

Learning Objectives

- Understand what is meant by "derived" and "ancestral" traits and why this is relevant for understanding early hominin evolution.
- Understand changing paleoclimates and paleoenvironments as potential factors influencing early hominin adaptations.
- Describe the anatomical changes associated with bipedalism and dentition in early hominins, as well as their implications..
- Describe early hominin genera and species, including their currently understood dates and geographic expanses.
- Describe the earliest stone tool techno-complexes and their impact on the transition from early hominins to our genus.

Defining Hominins

It is through our study of our hominin ancestors and relatives that we are exposed to a world of "might have beens": of other paths not taken by our species, other ways of being human. But to better understand these different evolutionary trajectories, we must first define the terms we are using. If an imaginary line were drawn between ourselves and our closest relatives, the great apes, **bipedalism** (or habitually walking upright on two feet) is where that line would be. **Hominin**, then, means everyone on "our" side of the line: humans and all of our extinct bipedal ancestors and relatives since our divergence from the **last common ancestor (LCA)** we share with chimpanzees.

Historic interpretations of our evolution, prior to our finding of early hominin **fossils**, varied. Debates in the mid-1800s regarding hominin origins focused on two key issues:

- Where did we evolve?
- Which traits evolved first?

Charles Darwin hypothesized that we evolved in Africa, as he was convinced that we shared greater commonality with chimpanzees and gorillas on the continent (Darwin 1871). Others, such as Ernst Haeckel and Eugène Dubois, insisted that we were closer in affinity to orangutans and that we evolved in Eurasia where, until the discovery of the Taung Child in South Africa in 1924, all humanlike fossils (of Neanderthals and *Homo erectus*) had been found (Shipman 2002).

Within this conversation, naturalists and early **paleoanthropologists** (people who study human evolution) speculated about which human traits came first. These included the evolution of a big brain (**encephalization**), the evolution of the way in which we move about on two legs (bipedalism), and the evolution of our flat faces and small teeth (indications of dietary change). Original hypotheses suggested that, in order to be motivated to change diet and move about in a bipedal fashion, the large brain needed to have evolved first, as is seen in the fossil species mentioned above.

However, we now know that bipedal locomotion is one of the first things that evolved in our lineage, with early relatives having more apelike dentition and small brain sizes. While brain size expansion is seen primarily in our genus, *Homo*, earlier hominin brain sizes were highly variable between and within taxa, from 300 cc (cranial capacity, cm^3), estimated in *Ardipithecus*, to 550 cc, estimated in *Paranthropus boisei*. The lower estimates are well within the range of variation of nonhuman extant great apes. In addition, body size variability also plays a role in the interpretation of whether brain size could be considered large or small for a particular species or specimen. In this chapter, we will tease out the details of early hominin evolution in terms of **morphology** (i.e. the study of the form, size, or shape of things; in this case, skeletal parts).

We also know that early human evolution occurred in a very complicated fashion. There were multiple species (multiple genera) that featured diversity in their diets and locomotion. Specimens have been found all along the **East African Rift System (EARS)**; that is, in Ethiopia, Kenya, Tanzania, and Malawi; see Figure 9.1), in limestone caves in South Africa, and in Chad. Dates of these early relatives range from around 7 million years ago (mya) to around 1 mya, overlapping temporally with members of our genus, *Homo*.

Figure 9.1: East African Rift System (EARS). Credit: IMG_1696 Great Rift Valley by Ninara is under a CC BY 2.0 License.

Yet there is still so much to understand. Modern debates now look at the relatedness of these species to us and to one another, and they consider which of these species were able to make and use tools. As a result, every **site** discovery in the patchy hominin fossil record tells us more about our evolution. In addition, recent scientific techniques (not available even ten years ago) provide new insights into the diets, environments, and lifestyles of these ancient relatives.

In the past, **taxonomy** was primarily based on morphology. Today it is tied to known relationships based on molecular **phylogeny** (e.g., based on DNA) or a combination of the two. This is complicated when applied to living **taxa**, but becomes much more difficult when we try to categorize ancestor-descendant relationships for long-extinct species whose molecular information is no longer preserved. We therefore find ourselves falling back on morphological comparisons, often of teeth and partially fossilized skeletal material.

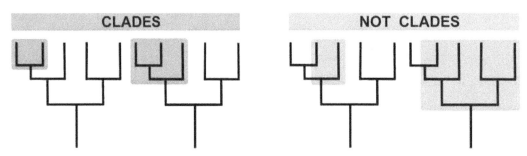

Figure 9.2: Clades refer to groups of species or taxa that share a common ancestor. In a phylogeny, a clade is a complete group of lineages, including their last common ancestor. Groupings that do not include a common ancestor and *all* of its descendants are not clades. Credit: Clades (Figure 9.2) original to Explorations: An Open Invitation to Biological Anthropology by Katie Nelson is under a CC BY-NC 4.0 License.

It is here that we turn to the related concepts of **cladistics** and **phylogenetics.** Cladistics groups organisms according to their last common ancestors based on shared **derived traits**. In the case of early hominins, these are often morphological traits that differ from those seen in earlier populations. These new or modified traits provide evidence of evolutionary relationships, and organisms with the same derived traits are grouped in the same **clade** (Figure 9.2). For example, if we use feathers as a trait, we can group pigeons and ostriches into the clade of birds. In this chapter, we will examine the grouping of the Robust Australopithecines, whose cranial and dental features differ from those of earlier hominins, and therefore are considered derived.

Dig Deeper: Problems Defining Hominin Species

It is worth noting that species designations for early hominin specimens are often highly contested. This is due to the fragmentary nature of the fossil record, the large timescale (millions of years) with which paleoanthropologists need to work, and the difficulty in evaluating whether morphological differences and similarities are due to meaningful phylogenetic or biological differences or subtle differences/variation in niche occupation or time. In other words, do morphological differences really indicate different species? How would classifying species in the paleoanthropological record compare with classifying living species today, for whom we can sequence genomes and observe lifestyles?

There are also broader philosophical differences among researchers when it comes to paleo-species designations. Some scientists, known as "**lumpers,**" argue that large variability is expected among multiple populations in a given species over time. These researchers will therefore prefer to "lump" specimens of subtle differences into single taxa. Others, known as "**splitters**," argue that species variability can be measured and that even subtle differences can imply differences in niche occupation that are extreme enough to mirror modern species differences. In general, splitters would consider geographic differences among populations as meaning that a species is **polytypic** (i.e., capable of interacting and breeding biologically but having morphological population differences). This is worth keeping in mind when learning about why species designations may be contested.

This further plays a role in evaluating ancestry. Debates over which species "gave rise" to which continue to this day. It is common to try to create "lineages" of species to determine when one species evolved into another over time. We refer to these as **chronospecies** (Figure 9.3). Constructed hominin phylogenetic trees are routinely variable, changing with new specimen discoveries, new techniques for evaluating and comparing species, and, some have argued, nationalist or biased interpretations of the record. More recently, some researchers have shifted away from "treelike" models of ancestry toward more nuanced metaphors such as the "braided stream," where some levels of interbreeding among species and populations are seen as natural processes of evolution.

Finally, it is worth considering the process of fossil discovery and publication. Some fossils are easily diagnostic to a species

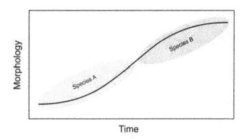

Figure 9.3: This graph demonstrates the concept of a chronospecies, where one species (Species A) "evolves" into another (Species B). Credit: Chronospecies original to Explorations: An Open Invitation to Biological Anthropology, 2nd edition by Kerryn Warren is under a CC BY-NC 4.0 License.

level and allow for easy and accurate interpretation. Some, however, are more controversial. This could be because they do not easily preserve or are incomplete, making it difficult to compare and place within a specific species (e.g., a fossil of a patella or knee bone). Researchers often need to make several important claims when announcing or publishing a find: a secure date (if possible), clear association with other finds, and an adequate comparison among multiple species (both extant and fossil). Therefore, it is not uncommon that an important find was made years before it is scientifically published.

Paleoenvironment and Hominin Evolution

There is no doubt that one of the major selective pressures in hominin evolution is the environment. Large-scale changes in global and regional climate, as well as alterations to the environment, are all linked to hominin diversification, dispersal, and extinction (Maslin et al. 2014). Environmental reconstructions often use modern analogues. Let us take, for instance, the hippopotamus. It is an animal that thrives in environments that have abundant water to keep its skin cool and moist. If the environment for some reason becomes drier, it is expected that hippopotamus populations will reduce. If a drier environment becomes wetter, it is possible that hippopotamus populations may be attracted to the new environment and thrive. Such instances have occurred multiple times in the past, and the bones of some **fauna** (i.e., animals, like the hippopotamus) that are sensitive to these changes give us insights into these events.

Yet reconstructing a **paleoenvironment** relies on a range of techniques, which vary depending on whether research interests focus on local changes or more global environmental changes/reconstructions. For local environments (such as a single site or region), comparing the **faunal assemblages** (collections of fossils of animals found at a site) with animals found in certain modern environments allows us to determine if past environments mirror current ones in the region. Changes in the faunal assemblages, as well as when they occur and how they occur, tell us about past environmental changes. Other techniques are also useful in this regard. Chemical analyses, for instance, can reveal the diets of individual fauna, providing clues as to the relative wetness or dryness of their environment (e.g., nitrogen **isotopes**; Kingston and Harrison 2007).

Global climatic changes in the distant past, which fluctuated between being colder and drier and warmer and wetter on average, would have global implications for environmental change (Figure 9.4). These can be studied by comparing marine core and terrestrial soil data across multiple sites. These techniques are based on chemical analysis, such as examination of the nitrogen and oxygen isotopes in shells and sediments. Similarly, analyzing pollen grains shows which kinds of **flora** survived in an environment at a specific time period. There are multiple lines of evidence that allow us to visualize global climate trends over millions of years (although it should be noted that the direction and extent of these changes could differ by geographic region).

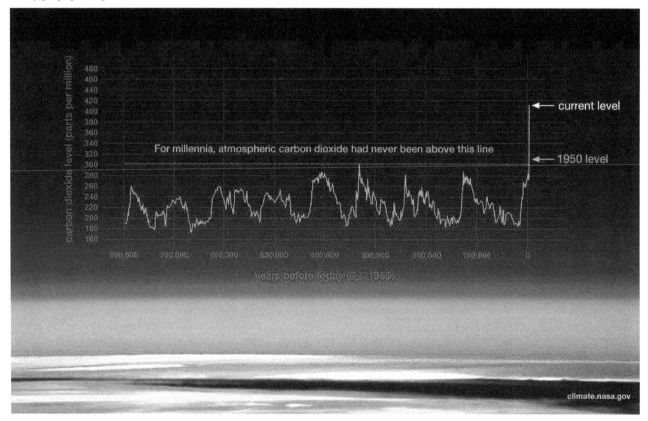

Figure 9.4: This graph, based on the comparison of atmospheric samples contained in ice cores and more recent direct measurements, illustrates how atmospheric CO^2 has fluctuated over time and increased sharply since the Industrial Revolution. The graph also shows that since 800,000ya (and before) atmospheric CO^2 has never exceeded 300 parts per million (ppm). In 1950 it was 310ppm. Today atmospheric CO^2 has spiked to over 410 ppm. Credit: CO^2 increase since the Industrial Revolution by NASA is in the public domain and is used within NASA guidelines on re-use. Original from Luthi, D., et al.. 2008; Etheridge, D.M., et al. 2010; Vostok ice core data/J.R. Petit et al.; NOAA Mauna Loa CO^2 record..

Both local and global climatic/environmental changes have been used to understand factors affecting our evolution (DeHeinzelin et al. 1999; Kingston 2007). Environmental change acts as an important factor regarding the onset of several important hominin traits seen in early hominins and discussed in this chapter. Namely, the environment has been interpreted as the following:

- the driving force behind the evolution of bipedalism,
- the reason for change and variation in early hominin diets, and
- the diversification of multiple early hominin species.

There are numerous hypotheses regarding how climate has driven and continues to drive human evolution. Here, we will focus on just three popular hypotheses.

Savannah Hypothesis (or Aridity Hypothesis)

The hypothesis: This popular theory suggests that the expansion of the savannah (or less densely forested, drier environments) forced early hominins from an **arboreal** lifestyle (one living in trees) to a terrestrial one where bipedalism was a more efficient form of locomotion (Figure 9.5). It was first proposed by Darwin (1871) and supported by anthropologists like Raymond Dart (1925). However, this idea was supported by little fossil or paleoenvironmental evidence and was later refined as the **Aridity Hypothesis**. This hypothesis states that the long-term **aridification** and, thereby, expansion of savannah biomes were drivers in diversification in early hominin evolution (deMenocal 2004; deMenocal and Bloemendal 1995). It advocates for periods of accelerated aridification leading to early hominin speciation events.

Figure 9.5: The African savannah grew during early hominin evolution. This may have forced early hominins from an arboreal lifestyle to a terrestrial one, where bipedalism was a more efficient form of locomotion. Credit: African savannah @ Masai Mara (21308330314) by Leo Li is under a CC BY 2.0 License.

The evidence: While early bipedal hominins are often associated with wetter, more closed environments (i.e., not the Savannah Hypothesis), both marine and terrestrial records seem to support general cooling, drying conditions, with isotopic records indicating an increase in grasslands (i.e., colder and wetter climatic conditions) between 8 mya and 6 mya across the African continent (Cerling et al. 2011). This can be contrasted with later climatic changes derived from aeolian dust records (sediments transported to the site of interest by wind), which demonstrate increases in seasonal rainfall between 3 mya and 2.6 mya, 1.8 mya and 1.6 mya, and 1.2 mya and 0.8 mya (deMenocal 2004; deMenocal and Bloemendal 1995).

Interpretation(s): Despite a relatively scarce early hominin record, it is clear that two important factors occur around the time period in which we see increasing aridity. The first factor is the diversification of taxa, where high morphological variation between specimens has led to the naming of multiple hominin genera and species. The second factor is the observation that the earliest hominin fossils appear to have traits associated with bipedalism and are dated to around the drying period (as based on isotopic records). Some have argued that it is more accurately a combination of bipedalism and arboreal locomotion, which will be discussed later. However, the local environments in which these early specimens are found (as based on the faunal assemblages) do not appear to have been dry.

Turnover Pulse Hypothesis

The hypothesis: In 1985, paleontologist Elisabeth Vbra noticed that in periods of extreme and rapid climate change, **ungulates** (hoofed mammals of various kinds) that had generalized diets fared better than those with specialized diets (Vrba 1988, 1998). **Specialist** eaters (those who rely primarily on specific food types) faced extinction at greater rates than their **generalist** (those who can eat more varied and variable diets) counterparts because they were unable to adapt to new environments (Vrba 2000). Thus, periods with extreme climate change would be associated with high **faunal turnover**: that is, the extinction of many species and the speciation, diversification, and migration of many others to occupy various niches.

The evidence: The onset of the **Quaternary Ice Age**, between 2.5 mya and 3 mya, brought extreme global, cyclical **interglacial** and **glacial** periods (warmer, wetter periods with less ice at the poles, and colder, drier periods with more ice near the poles). Faunal evidence from the Turkana basin in East Africa indicates multiple instances of faunal turnover and extinction events, in which global climatic change resulted in changes from closed/forested to open/grassier habitats at single sites (Behrensmeyer et al. 1997; Bobe and Behrensmeyer 2004). Similarly, work in the Cape Floristic Belt of South Africa shows that extreme changes in climate play a role in extinction and migration in ungulates. While this theory was originally developed for ungulates, its proponents have argued that it can be applied to hominins as well. However, the link between climate and speciation is only vaguely understood (Faith and Behrensmeyer 2013).

Interpretation(s): While the evidence of rapid faunal turnover among ungulates during this time period appears clear, there is still some debate around its usefulness as applied to the paleoanthropological record. Specialist hominin species do appear to exist for long periods of time during this time period, yet it is also true that *Homo*, a generalist genus with a varied and adaptable diet, ultimately survives the majority of these fluctuations, and the specialists appear to go extinct.

Variability Selection Hypothesis

The hypothesis: This hypothesis was first articulated by paleoanthropologist Richard Potts (1998). It links the high amount of climatic variability over the last 7 million years to both behavioral and morphological changes. Unlike previous notions, this hypothesis states that hominin evolution does not respond to habitat-specific changes or to specific aridity or moisture trends. Instead, long-term environmental unpredictability over time and space influenced morphological and behavioral adaptations that would help hominins survive, regardless of environmental context (Potts 1998, 2013). The Variability Selection Hypothesis states that hominin groups would experience varying degrees of natural selection due to continually changing environments and potential group isolation. This would allow certain groups to develop genetic combinations that would increase their ability to survive in shifting environments. These populations would then have a genetic advantage over others that were forced into habitat-specific adaptations (Potts 2013).

The evidence: The evidence for this theory is similar to that for the Turnover Pulse Hypothesis: large climatic variability and higher survivability of generalists versus specialists. However, this hypothesis accommodates for larger time-scales of extinction and survival events.

Interpretation(s): In this way, the Variability Selection Hypothesis allows for a more flexible interpretation of the evolution of bipedalism in hominins and a more fluid interpretation of the Turnover Pulse Hypothesis, where species turnover is meant to be more rapid. In some ways, this hypothesis accommodates both environmental data and our interpretations of an evolution toward greater variability among species and the survivability of generalists.

Paleoenvironment Summary

Some hypotheses presented in this section pay specific attention to habitat (Savannah Hypothesis) while others point to large-scale climatic forces (Variability Selection Hypothesis). Some may be interpreted to describe the evolution of traits such as bipedalism (Savannah Hypothesis), and others generally explain the diversification of early hominins (Turnover Pulse and Variability Selection Hypotheses). While there is no consensus as to how the environment drove our evolution, it is clear that the environment shaped both habitat and resource availability in ways that would have influenced our early ancestors physically and behaviorally.

Derived Adaptations: Bipedalism

The unique form of locomotion exhibited by modern humans, called **obligate bipedalism**, is important in distinguishing our species from the **extant** (living) great apes. The ability to walk habitually upright is thus considered one of the defining attributes of the hominin lineage. We also differ from other animals that walk bipedally (such as kangaroos) in that we do not have a tail to balance us as we move.

The origin of bipedalism in hominins has been debated in paleoanthropology, but at present there are two main ideas:

1. early hominins initially lived in trees, but increasingly started living on the ground, so we were a product of an arboreal last common ancestor (LCA) or,
2. our LCA was a terrestrial quadrupedal knuckle-walking species, more similar to extant chimpanzees.

Most research supports the first theory of an arboreal LCA based on skeletal morphology of early hominin genera that demonstrate adaptations for climbing but not for knuckle-walking. This would mean that both humans and chimpanzees can be considered "derived" in terms of locomotion since chimpanzees would have independently evolved knuckle-walking.

There are many current ideas regarding selective pressures that would lead to early hominins adapting upright posture and locomotion. Many of these selective pressures, as we have seen in the previous section, coincide with a shift in environmental conditions, supported by paleoenvironmental data. In general, however, it appears that, like extant great apes, early hominins thrived in forested regions with dense tree coverage, which would indicate an arboreal lifestyle. As the environmental conditions changed and a savannah/grassland environment became more widespread, the tree cover would become less dense, scattered, and sparse such that bipedalism would become more important.

There are several proposed selective pressures for bipedalism:

1. **Energy conservation:** Modern bipedal humans conserve more energy than extant chimpanzees, which are predominantly knuckle-walking quadrupeds when walking over land. While chimpanzees, for instance, are faster than humans terrestrially, they expend large amounts of energy being so. Adaptations to bipedalism include "stacking" the majority of the weight of the body over a small area around the center of gravity (i.e., the head is above the chest, which is above the pelvis, which is over the knees, which are above the feet). This reduces the amount of muscle needed to be engaged during locomotion to "pull us up" and allows us to travel longer distances expending far less energy.
2. **Thermoregulation:** Less surface area (i.e., only the head and shoulders) is exposed to direct sunlight during the hottest parts of the day (i.e., midday). This means that the body has less need to employ additional "cooling" mechanisms such as sweating, which additionally means less water loss.
3. **Bipedalism:** This method of locomotion freed up our ancestors' hands such that they could more easily gather food and carry tools or infants. This further enabled the use of hands for more specialized adaptations associated with the manufacturing and use of tools.

These selective pressures are not mutually exclusive. Bipedality could have evolved from a combination of these selective pressures, in ways that increased the chances of early hominin survival.

Skeletal Adaptations for Bipedalism

Humans have highly specialized adaptations to facilitate obligate bipedalism (Figure 9.6). Many of these adaptations occur within the soft tissue of the body (e.g., muscles and tendons). However, when analyzing the paleoanthropological record for evidence of the emergence of bipedalism, all that remains is the fossilized bone. Interpretations of locomotion are therefore often based on comparative analyses between fossil remains and the skeletons of extant primates with known locomotor behaviors. These adaptations occur throughout the skeleton and are summarized in Figure 9.7.

The majority of these adaptations occur in the **postcranium** (the skeleton from below the head) and are outlined in Figure 9.7. In general, these adaptations allow for greater stability and strength in the lower limb, by allowing for more shock absorption, for a larger surface area for muscle attachment, and for the "stacking" of the skeleton directly over the center of gravity to reduce energy needed to be kept upright. These adaptations often mean less flexibility in areas such as the knee and foot.

However, these adaptations come at a cost. Evolving from a nonobligate bipedal ancestor means that the adaptations we have are evolutionary compromises. For instance, the valgus knee (angle at the knee) is an essential adaptation to balance the body weight above the ankle during bipedal locomotion. However, the strain and shock absorption at an angled knee eventually takes its toll. For example, runners often experience joint pain. Similarly, the long neck of the

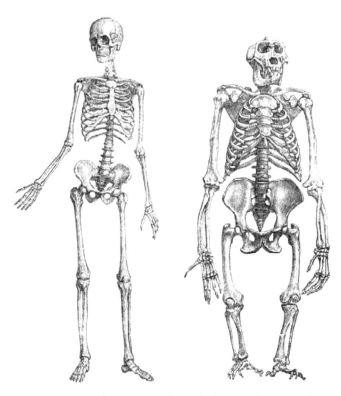

Figure 9.6: Compared to gorillas (right) and other apes, humans (left) have highly specialized adaptations to facilitate bipedal locomotion. Credit: Skeleton of human (1) and gorilla (2), unnaturally sketched by unknown from Brehms Tierleben, Small Edition 1927 is in the public domain.

femur absorbs stress and accommodates for a larger pelvis, but it is a weak point, resulting in hip replacements being commonplace among the elderly, especially in cases where the bone additionally weakens through osteoporosis. Finally, the S-shaped curve in our spine allows us to stand upright, relative to the more curved C-shaped spine of an LCA. Yet the weaknesses in the curves can lead to pinching of nerves and back pain. Since many of these problems primarily are only seen in old age, they can potentially be seen as an evolutionary compromise.

Despite relatively few postcranial fragments, the fossil record in early hominins indicates a complex pattern of emergence of bipedalism. Key features, such as a more anteriorly placed foramen magnum, are argued to be seen even in the earliest discovered hominins, indicating an upright posture (Dart 1925). Some early species appear to have a mix of ancestral (arboreal) and derived (bipedal) traits, which indicates a mixed locomotion and a more **mosaic evolution** of the trait. Some early hominins appear to, for instance, have bowl-shaped pelvises (hip bones) and angled femurs suitable for bipedalism but also have retained an opposable **hallux** (big toe) or curved fingers and longer arms (for arboreal locomotion). These mixed morphologies may indicate that earlier hominins were not fully obligate bipeds and thus thrived in mosaic environments.

Yet the associations between postcranial and the more diagnostic cranial fossils and bones are not always clear, muddying our understanding of the specific species to which fossils belong (Grine et al. 2022).

Region	Feature	Obligate Biped (H. sapiens)	Nonobligate Biped
Cranium	Position of the foramen magnum	Positioned inferiorly (immediately under the cranium) so that the head rests on top of the vertebral column for balance and support (head is perpendicular to the ground).	Posteriorly positioned (to the back of the cranium). Head is positioned parallel to the ground.
Post cranium	Body proportions	Shorter upper limb (not used for locomotion).	Longer upper limbs (used for locomotion).
Post cranium	Spinal curvature	S-curve due to pressure exerted on the spine from bipedalism (lumbar lordosis).	C-curve.
Post cranium	Vertebrae	Robust lumbar (lower-back) vertebrae (for shock absorbance and weight bearing). Lower back is more flexible than that of apes as the hips and trunk swivel when walking (weight transmission).	Gracile lumbar vertebrae compared to those of modern humans.
Post cranium	Pelvis	Shorter, broader, bowl-shaped pelvis (for support); very robust. Broad sacrum with large sacroiliac joint surfaces.	Longer, flatter, elongated ilia; more narrow and gracile; narrower sacrum; relatively smaller sacroiliac joint surface.
Post cranium	Lower limb	In general, longer, more robust lower limbs and more stable, larger joints. • Large femoral head and longer neck (absorbs more stress and increases the mechanical advantage). • Valgus knee, in which the angle of the knee positions it over the ankle and keeps the center of gravity balanced over the stance leg during stride cycle (shock absorbance). • Distal tibia (lower leg) of humans has a large medial malleolus for stability.	In general, smaller, more gracile limbs with more flexible joints. • Femoral neck is smaller in comparison to modern humans and shorter. • The legs bow outward, and there is no valgus angle of the knee (no "knock knees"). • The distal tibia in chimpanzees is trapezoid (wider anteriorly) for climbing and allows more flexibility.
Post cranium	Foot	Rigid, robust foot, without a midtarsal break. Nonopposable and large, robust big toe (for push off while walking) and large heel for shock absorbance.	Flexible foot, midtarsal break present (which allows primates to lift their heels independently from their feet), opposable big toe for grasping.

It is also worth noting that, while not directly related to bipedalism per se, other postcranial adaptations are evident in the hominin fossil record from some of the earlier hominins. For instance, the hand and finger morphologies of many of the earliest hominins indicate adaptations consistent with arboreality. These include longer hands, more curved metacarpals and phalanges (long bones in the hand and fingers, respectively), and a shorter, relatively weaker thumb. This allows for gripping onto curved surfaces during locomotion. The earliest hominins appear to have mixed morphologies for both bipedalism and arborealism. However, among Australopiths (members of the genus, Australopithecus), there are indications for greater reliance on bipedalism as the primary form of locomotion. Similarly, adaptations consistent with tool manufacture (shorter fingers and a longer, more robust thumb, in contrast to the features associated with arborealism) have been argued to appear before the genus *Homo*.

Early Hominins: Sahelanthropus and Orrorin

We see evidence for bipedalism in some of the earliest fossil hominins, dated from within our estimates of our divergence from chimpanzees. These hominins, however, also indicate evidence for arboreal locomotion.

The earliest dated hominin find (between 6 mya and 7 mya, based on radiometric dating of volcanic tufts) has been argued to come from Chad and is named ***Sahelanthropus tchadensis*** (Figure 9.8; Brunet et al. 1995). The initial discovery was made in 2001 by Ahounta Djimdoumalbaye and announced in *Nature* in 2002 by a team led by French paleontologist Michel Brunet. The find has a small cranial capacity (360 cc) and smaller canines than those in extant great apes, though they are larger and pointier than those in humans. This implies strongly that, over evolutionary time, the need for display and dominance among males has reduced, as has our sexual dimorphism. A short cranial base and a foramen magnum that is more humanlike in positioning have been argued to indicate upright walking.

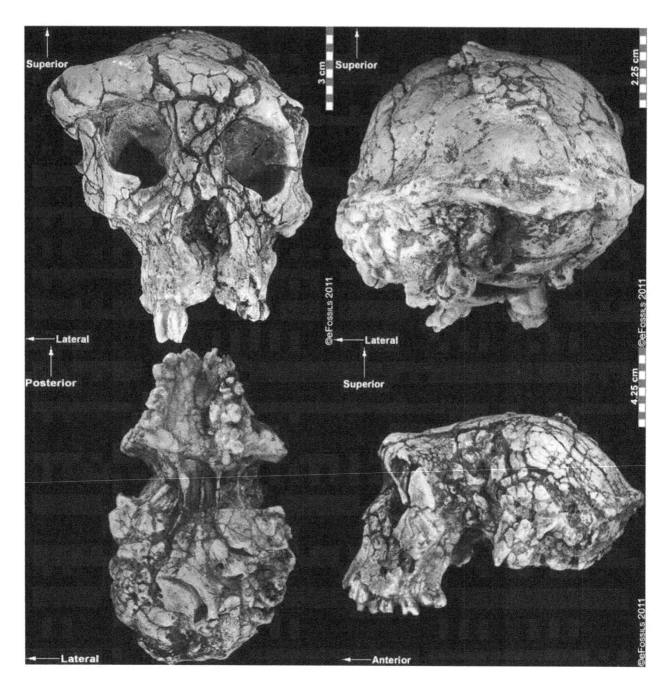

Figure 9.8: Sahelanthropus tchadensis exhibits a set of derived features, including a long, low cranium; a small, ape-sized braincase; and relatively reduced prognathism. Credit: aa Sahelanthropus tchadensis: TM 266-01-060-1 anterior view by ©eFossils is under a CC BY-NC-SA 2.0 License and is used as outlined by eFossils; b Sahelanthropus tchadensis: TM 266-01-060-1 posterior view by ©eFossils is under a CC BY-NC-SA 2.0 License and is used as outlined by eFossils; c Sahelanthropus tchadensis: TM 266-01-060-1 inferior view by ©eFossils is under a CC BY-NC-SA 2.0 License and is used as outlined by eFossils; and d Sahelanthropus tchadensis: TM 266-01-060-1 lateral left view by ©eFossils is under a CC BY-NC-SA 2.0 License and is used as outlined by eFossils.

Initially, the inclusion of *Sahelanthropus* in the hominin family was debated by researchers, since the evidence for bipedalism is based on cranial evidence alone, which is not as convincing as postcranial evidence. Yet, a femur (thigh bone) and ulnae (upper arm bones) thought to belong to *Sahelanthropus* was discovered in 2001 (although not published until 2022). These bones may support the idea that the hominin was in fact a terrestrial biped with arboreal capabilities and behaviors (Daver et al. 2022).

Orrorin tugenensis (Orrorin meaning "original man"), dated to between 6 mya and 5.7 mya, was discovered near Tugen Hills in Kenya in 2000.

Smaller **cheek teeth** (molars and premolars) than those in even more recent hominins, thick enamel, and reduced, but apelike, canines characterize this species. This is the first species that clearly indicates adaptations for bipedal locomotion, with fragmentary leg, arm, and finger bones having been found but few cranial remains. One of the most important elements discovered was a proximal femur, BAR 1002'00. The femur is the thigh bone, and the proximal part is that which articulates with the pelvis; this is very important for studying posture and locomotion. This femur indicates that *Ororrin* was bipedal, and recent studies suggest that it walked in a similar way to later **Pliocene** hominins. Some have argued that features of the finger bones suggest potential tool-making capabilities, although many researchers argue that these features are also consistent with climbing.

Early Hominins: The Genus *Ardipithecus*

Another genus, *Ardipithecus*, is argued to be represented by at least two species: *Ardipithecus (Ar.) ramidus* and *Ar. kadabba*.

Ardipithecus ramidus ("ramid" means root in the Afar language) is currently the best-known of the earliest hominins (Figure 9.9). Unlike *Sahelanthropus* and *Ororrin*, this species has a large sample size of over 110 specimens from Aramis alone. Dated to 4.4 mya, *Ar. ramidus* was found in Ethiopia (in the Middle Awash region and in Gona). This species was announced in 1994 by American palaeoanthropologist Tim White, based on a partial female skeleton nicknamed "Ardi" (ARA-VP-6/500; White et al. 1994). Ardi demonstrates a mosaic of ancestral and derived characteristics in the postcrania. For instance, she had an opposable big toe (hallux), similar to chimpanzees (i.e., more ancestral), which could have aided in climbing trees effectively. However, the pelvis and hip show that she could walk upright (i.e., it is derived), supporting her hominin status. A small brain (300 cc to 350 cc), midfacial projection, and slight prognathism show retained ancestral cranial features, but the cheek bones are less flared and robust than in later hominins.

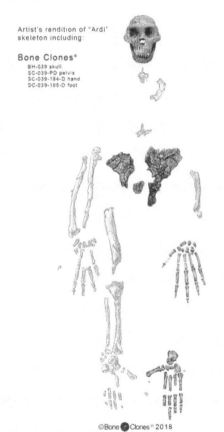

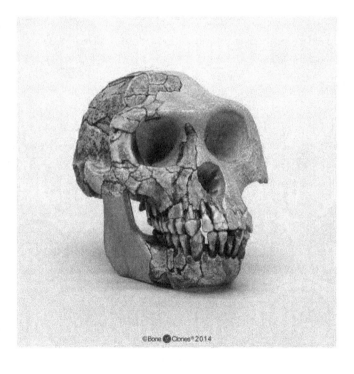

Figure 9.9a and b: Researchers believe that Ardipithecus ramidus was able to walk upright, although not as efficiently as later humans. It possessed the musculature required for tree climbing, and while moving quadrupedally, it likely placed weight on the palms of the hands rather than on the knuckles. Credit: a. Ardipithecus ramidus Skull by ©BoneClones is used by permission and available here under a CC BY-NC 4.0 License; b. Artist's rendition of "Ardi" skeleton by ©BoneClones is used by permission and available here under a CC BY-NC 4.0 License.

Ardipithecus kadabba (the species name means "oldest ancestor" in the Afar language) is known from localities on the western margin of the Middle Awash region, the same locality where *Ar. ramidus* has been found. Specimens include mandibular fragments and isolated teeth as well as a few postcranial elements from the Asa Koma (5.5 mya to 5.77 mya) and Kuseralee Members (5.2 mya), well-dated and understood (but temporally separate) volcanic layers in East Africa. This species was discovered in 1997 by paleoanthropologist Dr. Yohannes Haile-Selassie. Originally these specimens were referred to as a subspecies of *Ar. ramidus*. In 2002, six teeth were discovered at Asa Koma and the dental-wear patterns confirmed that this was a distinct species, named *Ar. kadabba,* in 2004. One of the postcranial remains recovered included a 5.2 million-year-old toe bone that demonstrated features that are associated with toeing off (pushing off the ground with the big toe leaving last) during walking, a characteristic unique to bipedal walkers. However, the toe bone was found in the Kuseralee Member, and therefore some doubt has been cast by researchers about its association with the teeth from the Asa Koma Member.

Bipedal Trends in Early Hominins: Summary

Trends toward bipedalism are seen in our earliest hominin finds. However, many specimens also indicate retained capabilities for climbing. Trends include a larger, more robust hallux; a more compact foot, with an arch; a robust, long femur, angled at the knee; a robust tibia; a bowl-shaped pelvis; and a more anterior foramen magnum. While the level of bipedality in *Salehanthropus tchadenisis* is debated since there are few fossils and no postcranial evidence, *Orrorin tugenensis* and *Ardipithecus kadabba* show clear indications of some of these bipedal trends. However, some retained ancestral traits, such as an opposable hallux in *Ardipithecus*, indicate some retention in climbing ability.

Derived Adaptations: Early Hominin Dentition

The Importance of Teeth

Teeth are abundant in the fossil record, primarily because they are already highly mineralized as they are forming, far more so than even bone. Because of this, teeth preserve readily. And, because they preserve readily, they are well-studied and better understood than many skeletal elements. In the sparse hominin (and primate) fossil record, teeth are, in some cases, all we have.

Teeth also reveal a lot about the individual from whom they came. We can tell what they evolved to eat, to which other species they may be closely related, and even, to some extent, the level of sexual dimorphism, or general variability, within a given species. This is powerful information that can be contained in a single tooth. With a little more observation, the wearing patterns on a tooth can tell us about the diet of the individual in the weeks leading up to its death. Furthermore, the way in which a tooth is formed, and the timing of formation, can reveal information about changes in diet (or even mobility) over infancy and childhood, using isotopic analyses. When it comes to our earliest hominin relatives, this information is vital for understanding how they lived.

The purpose of comparing different hominin species is to better understand the functional morphology as it applies to dentition. In this, we mean that the morphology of the teeth or masticatory system (which includes jaws) can reveal something about the way in which they were used and, therefore, the kinds of foods these hominins ate. When comparing the features of hominin groups, it is worth considering modern analogues (i.e., animals with which to compare) to make more appropriate assumptions about diet. In this way, hominin dentition is often compared with that of chimpanzees and gorillas (our close ape relatives), as well as with that of modern humans.

The most divergent group, however, is humans. Humans around the world have incredibly varied diets. Among hunter-gatherers, it can vary from a honey- and plant-rich diet, as seen in the Hadza in Tanzania, to a diet almost entirely reliant on animal fat and protein, as seen in Inuits in polar regions of the world. We are therefore considered generalists, more general than the largely **frugivorous** (fruit-eating) chimpanzee or the **folivorous** (foliage-eating) gorilla, as discussed in Chapter 5.

One way in which all humans are similar is our reliance on the processing of our food. We cut up and tear meat with tools using our hands, instead of using our front teeth (incisors and canines). We smash and grind up hard seeds, instead of crushing them with our hind teeth (molars). This means that, unlike our ape relatives, we can rely more on developing tools to navigate our complex and varied diets. Our brain, therefore, is our primary masticatory organ. Evolutionarily, our teeth have reduced in size and our faces are flatter, or more **orthognathic,** partially in response to our increased reliance on our hands and brain to process food. Similarly, a reduction in teeth and a more generalist dental morphology could also indicate an increase in softer and more variable foods, such as the inclusion of more meat. These trends begin early on in our evolution. The link has been made between some of the earliest evidence for stone tool manufacture, the earliest members of our genus, and the features that we associate with these specimens.

General Dental Trends in Early Hominins

Several trends are visible in the dentition of early hominins. However, all tend to have the same **dental formula**. The dental formula tells us how many of each tooth type are present in each quadrant of the mouth. Going from the front of the mouth, this includes the square, flat **incisors**; the pointy **canines**; the small, flatter **premolars**; and the larger hind **molars**. In many primates, from Old World monkeys to great apes, the typical dental formula is 2:1:2:3. This means that if we divide the mouth into quadrants, each has two incisors, one canine, two premolars, and three molars. The eight teeth per quadrant total 32 teeth in all (although some humans have fewer teeth due to the absence of their wisdom teeth, or third molars).

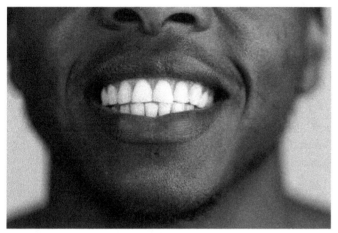

Figure 9.10: In humans, our canines are often a similar size to our incisors. Credit: Adult human teeth by Genusfotografen (Tomas Gunnarsson) through Wikimedia Sverige is under a CC BY-SA 4.0 License.

The morphology of the individual teeth is where we see the most change. Among primates, large incisors are associated with food procurement or preparation (such as biting small fruits), while small incisors indicate a diet that may contain small seeds or leaves (where the preparation is primarily in the back of the mouth). Most hominins have relatively large, flat, vertically aligned incisors that **occlude** (touch) relatively well, forming a "bite." This differs from, for instance, the orangutan, whose teeth stick out (i.e., are **procumbent**).

While the teeth are often aligned with diet, the canines may be misleading in that regard. We tend to associate pointy, large canines with the ripping required for meat, and the reduction (or, in some animals, the absence) of canines as indicative of herbivorous diets. In humans, our canines are often a similar size to our incisors and therefore considered **incisiform** (Figure 9.10). However, our closest relatives all have very long, pointy canines, particularly on their upper dentition. This is true even for the gorilla, which lives almost exclusively on plants. The canines in these instances reveal more about social structure and sexual dimorphism than diet, as large canines often signal dominance.

Early on in human evolution, we see a reduction in canine size. *Sahelanthropus tchadensis* and *Orrorin tugenensis* both have smaller canines than those in extant great apes, yet the canines are still larger and pointier than those in humans or more recent hominins. This implies strongly that, over evolutionary time, the need for display and dominance among males has reduced, as has our sexual dimorphism. In *Ardipithecus ramidus*, there is no obvious difference between male and female canine size, yet they are still slightly larger and pointier than in modern humans. This implies a less sexually dimorphic social structure in the earlier hominins relative to modern-day chimpanzees and gorillas.

Along with a reduction in canine size is the reduction or elimination of a canine **diastema:** a gap between the teeth on the mandible that allows room for elongated teeth on the maxilla to "fit" in the mouth. Absence of a diastema is an excellent indication of a reduction in canine size. In animals with large canines (such as baboons), there is also often a **honing P3**, where the first premolar (also known as P3 for evolutionary reasons) is triangular in shape, "sharpened" by the extended canine from the upper dentition. This is also seen in some early hominins: *Ardipithecus*, for example, has small canines that are almost the same height as its incisors, although still larger than those in recent hominins.

The hind dentition, such as the bicuspid (two cusped) premolars or the much larger molars, are also highly indicative of a generalist diet in hominins. Among the earliest hominins, the molars are larger than we see in our genus, increasing in size to the back of the mouth and angled in such a way from the much smaller anterior dentition as to give these hominins a **parabolic** (V-shaped) dental arch. This differs from our living relatives and some early hominins, such as *Sahelanthropus*, whose molars and premolars are relatively parallel between the left and right sides of the mouth, creating a U-shape.

Among more recent early hominins, the molars are larger than those in the earliest hominins and far larger than those in our own genus, *Homo*. Large, short molars with thick **enamel** allowed our early cousins to grind fibrous, coarse foods, such as sedges, which require plenty of chewing. This is further evidenced in the low **cusps,** or ridges, on the teeth, which are ideal for chewing. In our genus, the hind dentition is far smaller than in these early hominins. Our teeth also have medium-size cusps, which allow for both efficient grinding and tearing/shearing meats.

Understanding the dental morphology has allowed researchers to extrapolate very specific behaviors of early hominins. It is worth noting that while teeth preserve well and are abundant, a slew of other morphological traits additionally provide evidence for many of these hypotheses. Yet there are some traits that are ambiguous. For instance, while there are definitely high levels of sexual dimorphism in *Au. afarensis*, discussed in the next section, the canine teeth are reduced in size, implying that while canines may be useful indicators for sexual dimorphism, it is also worth considering other evidence.

In summary, trends among early hominins include a reduction in procumbency, reduced hind dentition (molars and premolars), a reduction in canine size (more incisiform with a lack of canine diastema and honing P3), flatter molar cusps, and thicker dental enamel. All early hominins have the ancestral dental formula of 2:1:2:3. These trends are all consistent with a generalist diet, incorporating more fibrous foods.

Special Topic: Contested Species

Many named species are highly debated and argued to have specimens associated with a more variable *Au. afarensis* or *Au. anamensis* species. Sometimes these specimens are dated to times when, or found in places in which, there are "gaps" in the palaeoanthropological record. These are argued to represent chronospecies or variants of *Au. afarensis*. However, it is possible that, with more discoveries, the distinct species types will hold.

Australopithecus bahrelghazali is dated to within the time period of *Au. afarensis* (3.6 mya; Brunet et al. 1995) and was the first Australopithecine to be discovered in Chad in central Africa. Researchers argue that the **holotype**, whom discoverers have named "Abel," falls under the range of variation of *Au. afarensis* and therefore that *A. bahrelghazali* does not fall into a new species (Lebatard et al. 2008). If "Abel" is a member of *Au. afarensis*, the geographic range of the species would be greatly extended.

On a different note, ***Australopithecus deyiremada*** (meaning "close relative" in the Ethiopian language of Afar) is dated to 3.5 mya to 3.3 mya and is based on fossil mandible bones discovered in 2011 in Woranso-Mille (in the Afar region of Ethiopia) by Yohannes Haile-Selassie, an Ethiopian paleoanthropologist (Haile-Selassie et al. 2019). The discovery indicated, in contrast to *Au. afarensis*, smaller teeth with thicker enamel (potentially suggesting a harder diet) as well as a larger mandible and more projecting cheekbones. This find may be evidence that more than one closely related hominin species occupied the same region at the same temporal period (Haile-Selassie et al. 2015; Spoor 2015) or that other *Au. afarensis* specimens have been incorrectly designated. However, others have argued that this species has been prematurely identified and that more evidence is needed before splitting the taxa, since the variation appears subtle and may be due to slightly different niche occupations between populations over time.

Australopithecus garhi is another species found in the Middle Awash region of Ethiopia. It is currently dated to 2.5 mya (younger than *Au. afarensis*). Researchers have suggested it fills in a much-needed temporal "gap" between hominin finds in the region, with some anatomical differences, such as a relatively large cranial capacity (450 cc) and larger hind dentition than seen in other gracile Australopithecines. Similarly, the species has been argued to have longer hind limbs than *Au. afarensis*, although it was still able to move arboreally (Asfaw et al. 1999). However, this species is not well documented or understood and is based on only several fossil specimens. More astonishingly, crude stone tools resembling Oldowan (which will be described later) have been found in association with *Au. garhi*. While lacking some of the features of the Oldowan, this is one of the earliest technologies found in direct association with a hominin.

Kenyanthopusplatyops (the name "platyops" refers to its flatter-faced appearance) is a highly contested genus/species designation of a specimen (KNM-WT 40000) from Lake Turkana in Kenya, discovered by Maeve Leakey in 1999 (Figure 9.11). Dated to between 3.5 mya and 3.2 mya, some have suggested this specimen is an *Australopithecus*, perhaps even *Au. afarensis* (with a brain size which is difficult to determine, yet appears small), while still others have placed this specimen in *Homo* (small dentition and flat-orthognathic face). While taxonomic placing of this species is quite divided, the discoverers have argued that this species is ancestral to *Homo*, in particular to *Homo ruldolfensis* (Leakey et al. 2001). Some researchers have additionally associated the earliest tool finds from Lomekwi, Kenya, temporally (3.3 mya) and in close geographic proximity to this specimen.

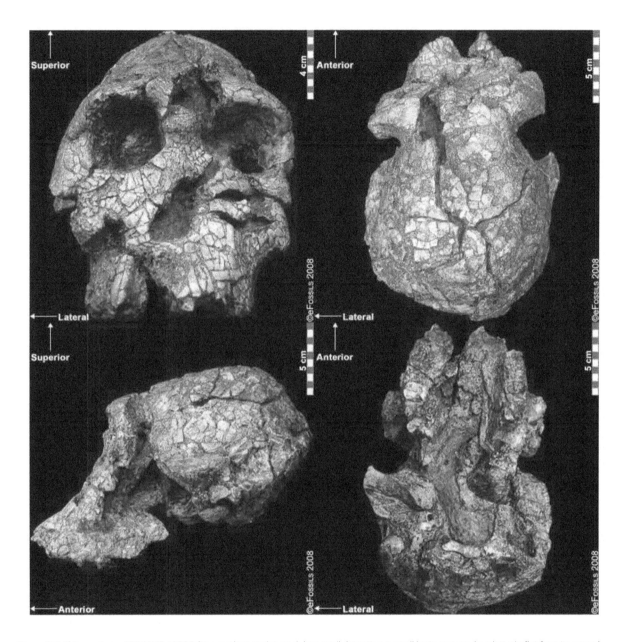

Figure 9.11: This specimen, KNM WT 40000 (Kenyanthopus platyops), has small detention, a small brain case, and a relatively flat face. Its genus/ species designation remains contested. Credit: a. *Kenyanthropus platyops* KNM WT 40000 anterior view by ©eFossils is under a CC BY-NC-SA 2.0 License and is used as outlined by eFossils; b. *Kenyanthropus platyops* KNM WT 40000 superior view by ©eFossils is under a CC BY-NC-SA 2.0 License and is used as outlined by eFossils; c. *Kenyanthropus platyops* KNM WT 40000 lateral left view by ©eFossils is under a CC BY-NC-SA 2.0 License and is used as outlined by eFossils; d. *Kenyanthropus platyops* KNM WT 40000 inferior view by ©eFossils is under a CC BY-NC-SA 2.0 License and is used as outlined by eFossils.

The Genus *Australopithecus*

The Australopithecines are a diverse group of hominins, comprising various species. *Australopithecus* is the given group or genus name. It stems from the Latin word *Australo*, meaning "southern," and the Greek word *pithecus,* meaning "ape." Within this section, we will outline these differing species' geological and temporal distributions across Africa, unique derived and/or shared traits, and importance in the fossil record.

Between 3 mya and 1 mya, there seems to be differences in dietary strategy between different species of hominins designated as Australopithecines. A pattern of larger posterior dentition (even relative to the incisors and canines in the front of the mouth), thick enamel, and cranial evidence for extremely large chewing muscles is far more pronounced in a group known as the robust australopithecines. This pattern is extreme relative to their earlier contemporaries or predecessors, the gracile australopithecines, and is certainly larger than those seen in early *Homo*, which emerged during this time. This pattern of incredibly large hind dentition (and very small anterior dentition) has led people to refer to robust australopithecines as **megadont** hominins (Figure 9.12).

Because of these differences, this section has been divided into "gracile" and "robust" Australopithecines, highlighting the morphological differences between the two groups (which many researchers have designated as separate genera: *Australopithecus* and *Paranthropus*, respectively) and then focusing on the individual species. It is worth noting, however, that not all researchers accept these clades as biologically or genetically distinct, with some researchers insisting that the relative gracile and robust features found in these species are due to parallel evolutionary events toward similar dietary niches.

Despite this genus' ancestral traits and small cranial capacity, all members show evidence of bipedal locomotion. It is generally accepted that *Australopithecus* species display varying degrees of arborealism along with bipedality.

Figure 9.12: Robust Australopithecines such as Paranthropus boisei had large molars and chewing muscles. Credit: Paranthropus boisei skull by Durova is under a CC BY-SA 3.0 License.

Gracile Australopithecines

This section describes individual species from across Africa. These species are called "**gracile** australopithecines" because of their smaller and less robust features compared to the divergent "**robust**" group. Numerous Australopithecine species have been named, but some are only based on a handful of fossil finds, whose designations are controversial.

East African Australopithecines

East African Australopithecines are found throughout the EARS, and they include the earliest species associated with this genus. Numerous fossil-yielding sites, such as Olduvai, Turkana, and Laetoli, have excellent, datable stratigraphy, owing to the layers of **volcanic tufts** that have accumulated over millions of years. These tufts may be dated using absolute dating techniques, such as Potassium-Argon dating (described in Chapter 7). This means that it is possible to know a relatively refined date for any fossil if the **context** (i.e., exact location) of that find is known. Similarly, comparisons between the faunal assemblages of these stratigraphic layers have allowed researchers to chronologically identify environmental changes.

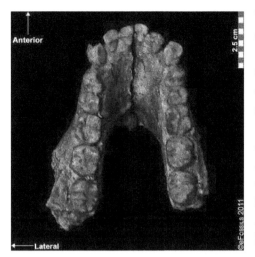

The earliest known Australopithecine is dated to 4.2 mya to 3.8 mya. ***Australopithecus anamensis*** (after "Anam," meaning "lake" from the Turkana region in Kenya; Leakey et al. 1995; Patterson and Howells 1967) is currently found from sites in the Turkana region (Kenya) and Middle Awash (Ethiopia; Figure 9.13). Recently, a 2019 find from Ethiopia, named MRD, after Miro Dora where it was found, was discovered by an Ethiopian herder named Ali Bereino. It is one of the most complete cranial finds of this species (Ward et al. 1999). A small brain size (370 cc), relatively large canines, projecting cheekbones, and earholes show more ancestral features as compared to those of more recent Australopithecines. The most important element discovered with this species is a fragment of a tibia (shinbone), which demonstrates features associated with weight transfer during bipedal walking. Similarly, the earliest found hominin femur belongs to this species. Ancestral traits in the upper limb (such as the humerus) indicate some retained arboreal locomotion.

Figure 9.13: As seen in this mandible of KNM-KP 29281, Australopithecus anamensis had relatively large canine teeth. Credit: Australopithecus anamensis: KNM-KP 29281 occlusal view by ©eFossils is under a CC BY-NC-SA 2.0 License and is used as outlined by eFossils.

Some researchers suggest that *Au. anamensis* is an intermediate form of the chronospecies that becomes *Au. afarensis*, evolving from *Ar. ramidus*. However, this is debated, with other researchers suggesting morphological similarities and affinities with more recent species instead. Almost 100 specimens, representing over 20 individuals, have been found to date (Leakey et al. 1995; McHenry 2009; Ward et al. 1999).

Au. afarensis is one of the oldest and most well-known australopithecine species and consists of a large number of fossil remains. *Au. afarensis* (which means "from the Afar region") is dated to between 2.9 mya and 3.9 mya and is found in sites all along the EARS system, in Tanzania, Kenya, and Ethiopia (Figure 9.14). The most famous individual from this species is a partial female skeleton discovered in Hadar (Ethiopia), later nicknamed "Lucy," after the Beatles' song "Lucy in the Sky with Diamonds," which was played in celebration of the find (Johanson et al. 1978; Kimbel and Delezene 2009). This skeleton was found in 1974 by Donald Johanson and dates to approximately 3.2 mya. In addition, in 2002 a juvenile of the species was found by Zeresenay Alemseged and given the name "Selam" (meaning "peace," DIK 1-1), though it is popularly known as "Lucy's Child" or as the "Dikika Child" (Alemseged et al. 2006). Similarly, the "Laetoli Footprints" (discussed in Chapter 7; Hay and Leakey 1982; Leakey and Hay 1979) have drawn much attention.

Figure 9.14 a-b: Artistic reconstructions of Australopithecus afarensis by artist John Gurche. Female "Lucy" is left and a male is on the right. Credit: a. Australopithecus afarensis, "Lucy," adult female. Reconstruction based on AL-288-1 by artist John Gurche, front view close-up by the Smithsonian [exhibit: "Reconstructed Faces: What Does It Mean to Be Human?"] is copyrighted and used for educational and noncommercial purposes as outlined by the Smithsonian; b. Australopithecus afarensis, adult male. Reconstruction based on AL444-2 by John Gurche by the Smithsonian [exhibit: "Reconstructed Faces: What Does It Mean to Be Human?"] is copyrighted and used for educational and noncommercial purposes as outlined by the Smithsonian.

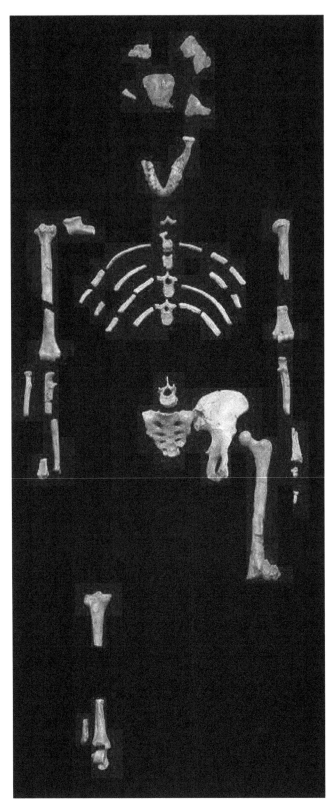

Figure 9.15: The humanlike femoral neck, valgus knee, and bowl-shaped hip seen in the "Lucy" skeleton indicates that *Australopithecus afarensis* was bipedal. Credit: Lucy blackbg [AL 288-1, Australopithecus afarensis, cast from Museum national d'histoire naturelle, Paris] by 120 is under a CC BY-SA 3.0 License.

The canines and molars of *Au. afarensis* are reduced relative to great apes but are larger than those found in modern humans (indicative of a generalist diet); in addition, *Au. afarensis* has a **prognathic** face (the face below the eyes juts anteriorly) and robust facial features that indicate relatively strong chewing musculature (compared with *Homo*) but which are less extreme than in *Paranthropus*. Despite a reduction in canine size in this species, large overall size variation indicates high levels of sexual dimorphism.

Skeletal evidence indicates that this species was bipedal, as its pelvis and lower limb demonstrate a humanlike femoral neck, valgus knee, and bowl-shaped hip (Figure 9.15). More evidence of bipedalism is found in the footprints of this species. *Au. afarensis* is associated with the Laetoli Footprints, a 24-meter trackway of hominin fossil footprints preserved in volcanic ash discovered by Mary Leakey in Tanzania and dated to 3.5 mya to 3 mya. This set of prints is thought to have been produced by three bipedal individuals as there are no knuckle imprints, no opposable big toes, and a clear arch is present. The infants of this species are thought to have been more arboreal than the adults, as discovered through analyses of the foot bones of the Dikika Child dated to 3.32 mya (Alemseged et al. 2006).

Although not found in direct association with stone tools, potential evidence for cut marks on bones, found at Dikika, and dated to 3.39 mya indicates a possible temporal/ geographic overlap between meat eating, tool use, and this species. However, this evidence is fiercely debated. Others have associated the cut marks with the earliest tool finds from Lomekwi, Kenya, temporally (3.3 mya) and in close geographic proximity to this species.

South African Australopithecines

Since the discovery of the Taung Child, there have been numerous Australopithecine discoveries from the region known as "The Cradle of Humankind," which was recently given UNESCO World Heritage Site status as "The Fossil Hominid Sites of South Africa." The limestone caves found in the Cradle allow for the excellent preservation of fossils. Past animals navigating the landscape and falling into cave openings, or caves used as dens by carnivores, led to the accumulation of deposits over millions of years. Many of the hominin fossils, encased in **breccia** (hard, calcareous sedimentary rock), are recently exposed from limestone quarries mined in the previous century. This means that extracting fossils requires excellent and detailed exposed work, often by a team of skilled technicians.

While these sites have historically been difficult to date, with mixed assemblages accumulated over large time periods, advances in techniques such as uranium-series dating have allowed for greater accuracy. Historically, the excellent faunal record from East Africa has been used to compare sites based on **relative dating,** whereby environmental and faunal changes and extinction events allow us to know which hominin finds are relatively younger or older than others.

Figure 9.16: An artistic reconstruction of Australopithecus africanus by John Gurche. Credit: Australopithecus africanus. Reconstruction based on STS 5 by John Gurche by the Smithsonian [exhibit: "Reconstructed Faces: What Does It Mean to Be Human?"] is copyrighted and used for educational and noncommercial purposes as outlined by the Smithsonian.

The discovery of the Taung Child in 1924 (discussed in the Special Topic box "The Taung Child" below) shifted the focus of palaeoanthropological research from Europe to Africa, although acceptance of this shift was slow (Broom 1947; Dart 1925). The species to which it is assigned, ***Australopithecus africanus*** (name meaning "Southern Ape of Africa"), is currently dated to between 3.3 mya and 2.1 mya (Pickering and Kramers 2010), with discoveries from Sterkfontein, Taung, Makapansgat, and Gladysvale in South Africa (Figure 9.16). A relatively large brain (400 cc to 500 cc), small canines without an associated diastema, and more rounded cranium and smaller teeth than *Au. afarensis* indicate some derived traits. Similarly, the postcranial remains (in particular, the pelvis) indicate bipedalism. However, the sloping face and curved phalanges (indicative of retained arboreal locomotor abilities) show some ancestral features. Although not in direct association with stone tools, a 2015 study noted that the trabecular bone morphology of the hand was consistent with forceful tool manufacture and use, suggesting potential early tool abilities.

Another famous *Au. africanus* skull (the skull of "Mrs. Ples") was previously attributed to *Plesianthropus transvaalensis,* meaning "near human from the Transvaal," the old name for Gauteng Province, South Africa (Broom 1947, 1950). The name was shortened by contemporary journalists to "Ples" (Figure 9.17). Due to the prevailing mores of the time, the assumed female found herself married, at least in name, and has become widely known as "Mrs. Ples." It was later reassigned to *Au. africanus* and is now argued by some to be a young male rather than an adult female cranium (Thackeray 2000, Thackeray et al. 2002).

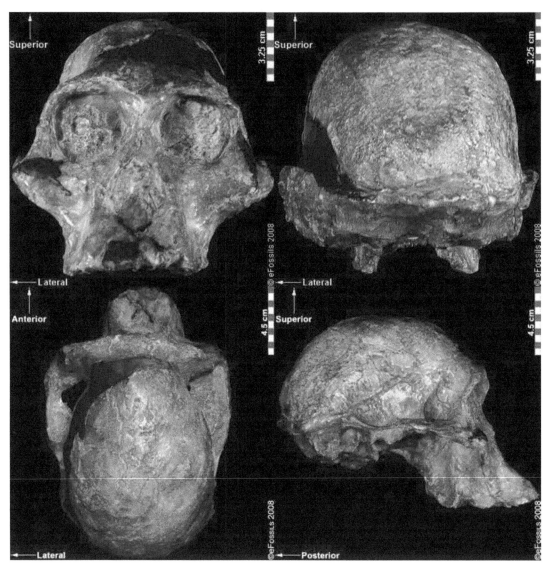

Figure 9.17: The "Mrs. Ples" brain case is small in size (like apes) but its face is less prognathic; its foramen magnum is positioned more like a modern human than an African apes. Credit: a. Australopithecus africanus Sts 5 anterior view by ©eFossils is under a CC BY-NC-SA 2.0 License and is used as outlined by eFossils; b. Australopithecus africanus Sts 5 posterior view by ©eFossils is under a CC BY-NC-SA 2.0 License and is used as outlined by eFossils; c. Australopithecus africanus Sts 5 superior view by ©eFossils is under a CC BY-NC-SA 2.0 License and is used as outlined by eFossils; and d. Australopithecus africanus Sts 5 lateral right view by ©eFossils is under a CC BY-NC-SA 2.0 License and is used as outlined by eFossils.

In 2008, nine-year-old Matthew Berger, son of paleoanthropologist Lee Berger, noted a clavicle bone in some leftover mining breccia in the Malapa Fossil Site (South Africa). After rigorous studies, the species, **Australopithecus sediba** (meaning "fountain" or "wellspring" in the South African language of Sesotho), was named in 2010 (Figure 9.18; Berger et al. 2010). The first type specimen belongs to a juvenile male, Karabo (MH1), but the species is known from at least six partial skeletons, from infants through adults. These specimens are currently dated to 1.97 mya (Dirks et al. 2010). The discoverers have argued that *Au. sediba* shows mosaic features between *Au. africanus* and the genus, *Homo*, which potentially indicates a transitional species, although this is heavily debated. These features include a small brain size (*Australopithecus*-like; 420 cc to 450 cc) but gracile mandible and small teeth (*Homo*-like). Similarly, the postcranial skeletons are also said to have mosaic features: scientists have interpreted this mixture of traits (such as a robust ankle but evidence for an arch in the foot) as a transitional phase between a body previously adapted to arborealism (particularly in evidence from the bones of the wrist) to one that adapted to bipedal ground walking. Some researchers have argued that *Au. sediba* shows a modern hand morphology (shorter fingers and a longer thumb), indicating that adaptations to tool manufacture and use may be present in this species.

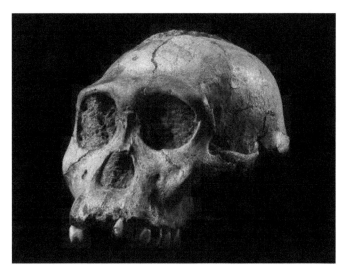

Figure 9.18: Australopithecus sediba shows mosaic features between Au. africanus and Homo. Credit: Australopithecus sediba, photo by Brett Eloff courtesy Profberger and Wits University, is under a CC BY-SA 4.0 License.

Another famous Australopithecine find from South Africa is that of the nearly complete skeleton now known as "Little Foot" (Clarke 1998, 2013). Little Foot (StW 573) is potentially the earliest dated South African hominin fossil, dating to 3.7 mya, based on radiostopic techniques, although some argue that it is younger than 3 mya (Pickering and Kramers 2010). The name is jokingly in contrast to the cryptid species "bigfoot" and is named because the initial discovery of four ankle bones indicated bipedality. Little Foot was discovered by Ron Clarke in 1994, when he came across the ankle bones while sorting through monkey fossils in the University of Witwatersrand collections (Clarke and Tobias 1995). He asked Stephen Motsumi and Nkwane Molefe to identify the known records of the fossils, which allowed them to find the rest of the specimen within just days of searching the Sterkfontein Caves' Silberg Grotto.

The discoverers of Little Foot insist that other fossil finds, previously identified as *Au. Africanus*, be placed in this new species based on shared ancestral traits with older East African Australopithecines (Clarke and Kuman 2019). These include features such as a relatively large brain size (408 cc), robust zygomatic arch, and a flatter midface. Furthermore, the discoverers have argued that the heavy anterior dental wear patterns, relatively large anterior dentition, and smaller hind dentition of this specimen more closely resemble that of *Au. anamensis* or *Au. afarensis*. It has thus been placed in the species ***Australopithecus prometheus***. This species name refers to a previously defunct taxon named by Raymond Dart. The species designation was, through analyzing Little Foot, revived by Ron Clarke, who insists that many other fossil hominin specimens have prematurely been placed into *Au. africanus*. Others say that it is more likely that *Au. africanus* is a more variable species and not representative of two distinct species.

Paranthropus "Robust" Australopithecines

In the robust australopithecines, the specialized nature of the teeth and masticatory system, such as flaring zygomatic arches (cheekbones), accommodate very large temporalis (chewing) muscles. These features also include a large, broad, dish-shaped face and and a large mandible with extremely large posterior dentition (referred to as megadonts) and hyper-thick enamel (Kimbel 2015; Lee-Thorp 2011; Wood 2010). Research has revolved around the shared adaptations of these "robust" australopithecines, linking their morphologies to a diet of hard and/or tough foods (Brain 1967; Rak 1988). Some argued that the diet of the robust australopithecines was so specific that any change in environment would have accelerated their extinction. The generalist nature of the teeth of the gracile australopithecines, and of early *Homo*, would have made them more capable of adapting to environmental change. However, some have suggested that the features of the robust australopithecines might have developed as an effective response to what are known as **fallback foods** in hard times rather than indicating a lack of adaptability.

There are currently three widely accepted robust australopithecus or, *Paranthropus*, species: *P. aethiopicus*, which has more ancestral traits, and *P. boisei and P. robustus*, which are more derived in their features (Strait et al. 1997; Wood and Schroer 2017). These three species have been grouped together by a majority of scholars as a single genus as they share more derived features (are more closely related to each other; or, in other words, are **monophyletic**) than the other australopithecines (Grine 1988; Hlazo 2015; Strait et al. 1997; Wood 2010). While researchers have mostly agreed to use the umbrella term *Paranthropus*, there are those who disagree (Constantino and Wood 2004, 2007; Wood 2010).

As a collective, this genus spans 2.7 mya to 1.0 mya, although the dates of the individual species differ. The earliest of the Paranthropus species, ***Paranthropus aethiopicus***, is dated to between 2.7 mya and 2.3 mya and currently found in Tanzania, Kenya, and Ethiopia in the EARS system (Figure 9.19; Constantino and Wood 2007; Hlazo 2015; Kimbel 2015; Walker et al. 1986; White 1988). It is well known because of one specimen known as the "Black Skull" (KNM–WT 17000), so called because of the mineral manganese that stained it black during fossilization (Kimbel 2015). As with all robust Australopithecines, *P. aethiopicus* has the shared derived traits of large, flat premolars and molars; large, flaring zygomatic arches for accommodating large chewing muscles (the temporalis muscle); a sagittal crest (ridge on the top of the skull) for increased muscle attachment of the chewing muscles to the skull; and a robust mandible and supraorbital torus (brow ridge). However, only a few teeth have been found. A proximal tibia indicates bipedality and similar body size to *Au. afarensis*. In recent years, researchers have discovered and assigned a proximal tibia and juvenile cranium (L.338y-6) to the species (Wood and Boyle 2016).

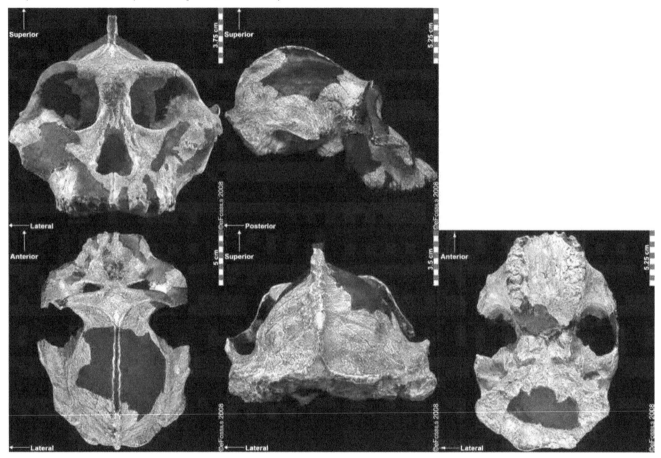

Figure 9.19: The "Black Skull" (Paranthropus aethiopicus) had a large sagittal crest and large, flared zygomatic arches that indicate it had large chewing muscles and a powerful biting force. Credit: a. *Paranthropus aethiopicus*: KNM-WT 17000 anterior view by ©eFossils is under a CC BY-NC-SA 2.0 License and is used as outlined by eFossils; b. *Paranthropus aethiopicus*: KNM-WT 17000 lateral right view by ©eFossils is under a CC BY-NC-SA 2.0 License and is used as outlined by eFossils; c. *Paranthropus aethiopicus*: KNM-WT 17000 superior view by ©eFossils is under a CC BY-NC-SA 2.0 License and is used as outlined by eFossils; d. *Paranthropus aethiopicus*: KNM-WT 17000 posterior view by ©eFossils is under a CC BY-NC-SA 2.0 License and is used as outlined by eFossils; e. *Paranthropus aethiopicus*: KNM-WT 17000 inferior view by ©eFossils is under a CC BY-NC-SA 2.0 License and is used as outlined by eFossils.

Figure 9.20: Artistic reconstruction of a Paranthropus boisei, male, by John Gurche. Credit: Paranthropus boisei, male. Reconstruction based on OH 5 and KNM-ER 406 by John Gurche by the Smithsonian [exhibit: "Reconstructed Faces: What Does It Mean to Be Human?"] is copyrighted and used for educational and noncommercial purposes as outlined by the Smithsonian.

First attributed as *Zinjanthropus boisei* (with the first discovery going by the nickname "Zinj" or sometimes "Nutcracker Man"), **Paranthropus boisei** was discovered in 1959 by Mary Leakey (see Figure 9.20 and 9.21; Hay 1990; Leakey 1959). This "robust" australopith species is distributed across countries in East Africa at sites such as Kenya (Koobi Fora, West Turkana, and Chesowanja), Malawi (Malema-Chiwondo), Tanzania (Olduvai Gorge and Peninj), and Ethiopia (Omo River Basin and Konso). The **hypodigm**, sample of fossils whose features define the group, has been found by researchers to date to roughly 2.4 mya to 1.4 mya. Due to the nature of its exaggerated, larger, and more robust features, *P. boisei* has been termed **hyper-robust**—that is, even more heavily built than other robust species, with very large, flat posterior dentition (Kimbel 2015). Tools dated to 2.5 mya in Ethiopia have been argued to possibly belong to this species. Despite the cranial features of *P. boisei* indicating a tough diet of tubers, nuts, and seeds, isotopes indicate a diet high in C4 foods (e.g., grasses, such as sedges). Another famous specimen from this species is the Peninj mandible from Tanzania, found in 1964 by Kimoya Kimeu.

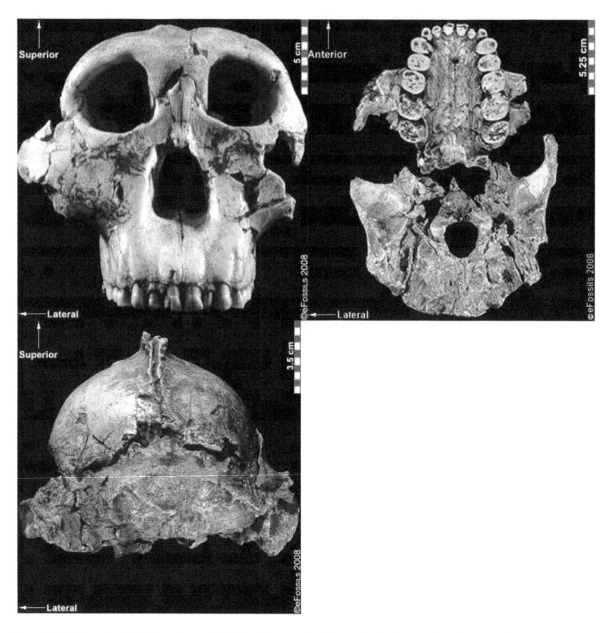

Figure 9.21: "Nutcracker Man" (Paranthropus boisei) had hyper-robust features including very large dentition, flaring zygomatic arches, a broad concave face. It had a powerful and extremely efficient chewing force. Credit: Paranthropus boisei: OH 5 anterior view by ©eFossils is under a CC BY-NC-SA 2.0 License and is used as outlined by eFossils; b. Paranthropus boisei: OH 5 inferior view by ©eFossils is under a CC BY-NC-SA 2.0 License and is used as outlined by eFossils; c. Paranthropus boisei: OH 5 posterior view by ©eFossils is under a CC BY-NC-SA 2.0 License and is used as outlined by eFossils.

Paranthropus robustus was the first taxon to be discovered within the genus in Kromdraai B by a schoolboy named Gert Terblanche; subsequent fossil discoveries were made by researcher Robert Broom in 1938 (Figure 9.22; Broom 1938a, 1938b, 1950), with the holotype specimen TM 1517 (Broom 1938a, 1938b, 1950; Hlazo 2018). *Paranthropus robustus* dates approximately from 2.0 mya to 1 mya and is the only taxon from the genus to be discovered in South Africa. Several of these fossils are fragmentary in nature, distorted, and not well preserved because they have been recovered from quarry breccia using explosives. *P. robustus* features are neither as "hyper-robust" as *P. boisei* nor as ancestral as *P. aethiopicus*; instead, they have been described as being less derived, more general features that are shared with both East African species (e.g., the sagittal crest and zygomatic flaring; Rak 1983; Walker and Leakey 1988). Enamel hypoplasia is also common in this species, possibly because of instability in the development of large, thick-enameled dentition.

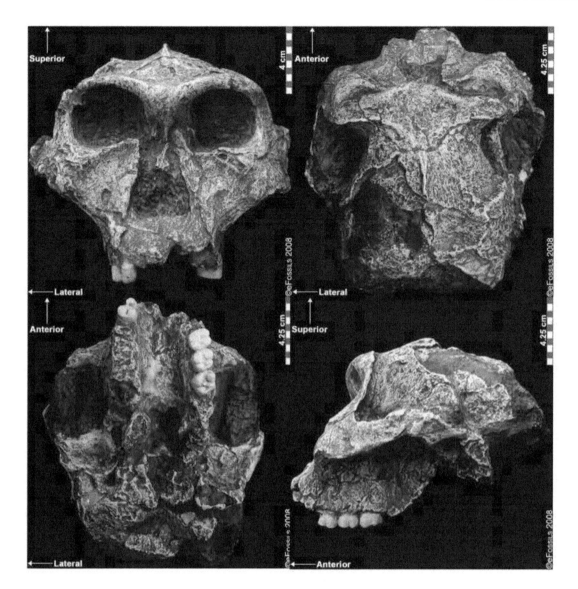

Figure 9.22: SK 48, a Paranthropus robustus specimen, had less derived, more general features that were not as robust as P. boisei and not as ancestral as P. aethiopicus. Credit: a. *Paranthropus robustus*: SK 48 anterior view by ©eFossils is under a CC BY-NC-SA 2.0 License and is used as outlined by eFossils; b. *Paranthropus robustus*: SK 48 superior view by ©eFossils is under a CC BY-NC-SA 2.0 License and is used as outlined by eFossils; c. *Paranthropus robustus*: SK 48 inferior view by ©eFossils is under a CC BY-NC-SA 2.0 License and is used as outlined by eFossils; d. *Paranthropus robustus*: SK 48 lateral left view by ©eFossils is under a CC BY-NC-SA 2.0 License and is used as outlined by eFossils.

Comparisons between Gracile and Robust Australopiths

Comparisons between gracile and robust australopithecines may indicate different phylogenetic groupings or parallel evolution in several species. In general, the robust australopithecines have large temporalis (chewing) muscles, as indicated by flaring zygomatic arches, sagittal crests, and robust mandibles (jawbones). Their hind dentition is large (megadont), with low cusps and thick enamel. Within the gracile australopithecines, researchers have debated the relatedness of the species, or even whether these species should be lumped together to represent more variable or polytypic species. Often researchers will attempt to draw chronospecific trajectories, with one taxon said to evolve into another over time.

Special Topic: The Taung Child

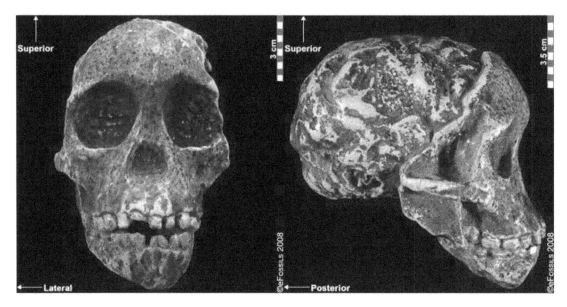

Figure 9.23: The Taung Child has a nearly complete face, mandible, and partial endocranial cast. Credit: a. *Australopithecus africanus*: Taung 1 anterior view by ©eFossils is under a CC BY-NC-SA 2.0 License and is used as outlined by eFossils; b. *australopithecus africanus*: Taung 1 lateral right view by ©eFossils is under a CC BY-NC-SA 2.0 License and is used as outlined by eFossils.

The well-known fossil of a juvenile *Australopithecine*, the "Taung Child," was the first early hominin evidence ever discovered and was the first to demonstrate our common human heritage in Africa (Figure 9.23; Dart 1925). The tiny facial skeleton and natural endocast were discovered in 1924 by a local quarryman in the North West Province in South Africa and were painstakingly removed from the surrounding cement-like breccia by Raymond Dart using his wife's knitting needles. When first shared with the scientific community in 1925, it was discounted as being nothing more than a young monkey of some kind. Prevailing biases of the time made it too difficult to contemplate that this small-brained hominin could have anything to do with our own history. The fact that it was discovered in Africa simply served to strengthen this bias.

Early Tool Use and Technology

Early Stone Age Technology (ESA)

The **Early Stone Age (ESA)** marks the beginning of recognizable technology made by our human ancestors. Stone-tool (or **lithic**) technology is defined by the fracturing of rocks and the manufacture of tools through a process called **knapping**. The Stone Age lasted for more than 3 million years and is broken up into chronological periods called the Early (ESA), Middle (MSA), and Later Stone Ages (LSA). Each period is further broken up into a different **techno-complex**, a term encompassing multiple **assemblages** (collections of artifacts) that share similar traits in terms of artifact production and morphology. The ESA spanned the largest technological time period of human innovation from over 3 million years ago to around 300,000 years ago and is associated almost entirely with hominin species prior to modern *Homo sapiens*. As the ESA advanced, stone tool makers (known as **knappers**) began to change the ways they detached **flakes** and eventually were able to shape artifacts into functional tools. These advances in technology go together with the developments in human evolution and cognition, dispersal of populations across the African continent and the world, and climatic changes.

In order to understand the ESA, it is important to consider that not all assemblages are exactly the same within each techno-complex: one can have multiple phases and traditions at different sites (Lombard et al. 2012). However, there is an overarching commonality between them. Within stone tool assemblages, both flakes or **cores** (the rocks from which flakes are removed) are used as tools. **Large Cutting Tools (LCTs)** are tools that are shaped to have functional edges. It is important to note that the information presented here is a small fraction of what is known about the ESA, and there are ongoing debates and discoveries within archaeology.

Currently, the oldest-known stone tools, which form the techno-complex the Lomekwian, date to 3.3 mya (Harmand et al. 2015; Toth 1985). They were found at a site called Lomekwi 3 in Kenya. This techno-complex is the most recently defined and pushed back the oldest-known date for lithic technology. There is only one known site thus far and, due to the age of the site, it is associated with species prior to *Homo*, such as *Kenyanthropus platyops*. Flakes were produced through indirect percussion, whereby the knappers held a rock and hit it against another rock resting on the ground. The pieces are very chunky and do not display the same fracture patterns seen in later techno-complexes. Lomekwian knappers likely aimed to get a sharp-edged piece on a flake, which would have been functional, although the specific function is currently unknown.

Stone tool use, however, is not only understood through the direct discovery of the tools. Cut marks on fossilized animal bones may illuminate the functionality of stone tools. In one controversial study in 2010, researchers argued that cut marks on a pair of animal bones from Dikika (Ethiopia), dated to 3.4 mya, were from stone tools. The discoverers suggested that they be more securely associated, temporally, with *Au. afarensis*. However, others have noted that these marks are consistent with teeth marks from crocodiles and other carnivores.

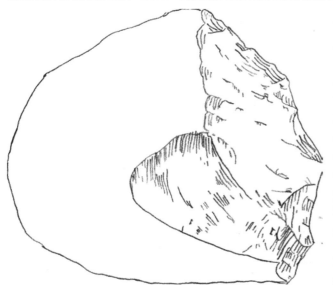

Figure 9.24: Some scholars believe that some genera explored in this chapter were capable of producing more complex stone tools (Oldowan). Credit: **Olduwan Industry Chopper 2** by Emmyanne29 is under a **CC0 1.0 License**.

The Oldowan techno-complex is far more established in the scientific literature (Leakey 1971). It is called the **Oldowan** because it was originally discovered in Olduvai Gorge, Tanzania, but the oldest assemblage is from Gona in Ethiopia, dated to 2.6 mya (Semaw 2000). The techno-complex is defined as a core and flake industry. Like the Lomekwian, there was an aim to get sharp-edged flakes, but this was achieved through a different production method. Knappers were able to actively hold or manipulate the core being knapped, which they could directly hit using a hammerstone. This technique is known as free-hand percussion, and it demonstrates an understanding of fracture mechanics. It has long been argued that the Oldowan hominins were skillful in tool manufacture.

Because Oldowan knapping requires skill, earlier researchers have attributed these tools to members of our genus, *Homo*. However, some have argued that these tools are in more direct association with hominins in the genera described in this chapter (Figure 9.24).

Invisible Tool Manufacture and Use

The vast majority of our understanding of these early hominins comes from fossils and reconstructed paleoenvironments. It is only from 3 mya when we can start "looking into their minds" and lifestyles by analyzing their manufacture and use of stone tools. However, the vast majority of tool use in primates (and, one can argue, in humans) is not with durable materials like stone. All of our extant great ape relatives have been observed using sticks, leaves, and other materials for some secondary purpose (to wade across rivers, to "fish" for termites, or to absorb water for drinking). It is possible that the majority of early hominin tool use and manufacture may be invisible to us because of this preservation bias.

Chapter Summary

The fossil record of our earliest hominin relatives has allowed paleoanthropologists to unpack some of the mysteries of our evolution. We now know that traits associated with bipedalism evolved before other "human-like" traits, even though the first hominins were still very capable of arboreal locomotion. We also know that, for much of this time, hominin taxa were diverse in the way they looked and what they ate, and they were widely distributed across the African continent. And we know that the environments in which these hominins lived underwent many changes over this time during several warming and cooling phases.

Yet this knowledge has opened up many new mysteries. We still need to better differentiate some taxa. In addition, there are ongoing debates about why certain traits evolved and what they meant for the extinction of some of our relatives (like the robust australopiths). The capabilities of these early hominins with respect to tool use and manufacture is also still uncertain.

Hominin Species Summaries

Hominin	*Sahelanthropus tchadensis*
Dates	7 mya to 6 mya
Region(s)	Chad
Famous discoveries	The initial discovery, made in 2001.
Brain size	360 cc average
Dentition	Smaller than in extant great apes; larger and pointier than in humans. Canines worn at the tips.
Cranial features	A short cranial base and a foramen magnum (hole in which the spinal cord enters the cranium) that is more humanlike in positioning; has been argued to indicate upright walking.
Postcranial features	Currently little published postcranial material.
Culture	N/A
Other	The extent to which this hominin was bipedal is currently heavily debated. If so, it would indicate an arboreal bipedal ancestor of hominins, not a knuckle-walker like chimpanzees.

Hominin	*Orrorin tugenensis*
Dates	6 mya to 5.7 mya
Region(s)	Tugen Hills (Kenya)
Famous discoveries	Original discovery in 2000.
Brain size	N/A
Dentition	Smaller cheek teeth (molars and premolars) than even more recent hominins (i.e., derived), thick enamel, and reduced, but apelike, canines.
Cranial features	Not many found
Postcranial features	Fragmentary leg, arm, and finger bones have been found. Indicates bipedal locomotion.
Culture	Potential toolmaking capability based on hand morphology, but nothing found directly.
Other	This is the earliest species that clearly indicates adaptations for bipedal locomotion.

Hominin	*Ardipithecus kadabba*
Dates	5.2 mya to 5.8 mya
Region(s)	Middle Awash (Ethiopia)
Famous discoveries	Discovered by Yohannes Haile-Selassie in 1997.
Brain size	N/A
Dentition	Larger hind dentition than in modern chimpanzees. Thick enamel and larger canines than in later hominins.
Cranial features	N/A
Postcranial features	A large hallux (big toe) bone indicates a bipedal "push off."
Culture	N/A
Other	Faunal evidence indicates a mixed grassland/woodland environment.

Hominin	*Ardipithecus ramidus*
Dates	4.4 mya
Region(s)	Middle Awash region and Gona (Ethiopia)
Famous discoveries	A partial female skeleton nicknamed "Ardi" (ARA-VP-6/500) (found in 1994).
Brain size	300 cc to 350 cc
Dentition	Little differences between the canines of males and females (small sexual dimorphism).
Cranial features	Midfacial projection, slightly prognathic. Cheekbones less flared and robust than in later hominins.
Postcranial features	Ardi demonstrates a mosaic of ancestral and derived characteristics in the postcrania. For instance, an opposable big toe similar to chimpanzees (i.e., more ancestral), which could have aided in climbing trees effectively. However, the pelvis and hip show that she could walk upright (i.e., it is derived), supporting her hominin status.
Culture	None directly associated
Other	Over 110 specimens from Aramis

Hominin	*Australopithecus anamensis*
Dates	4.2 mya to 3.8 mya
Region(s)	Turkana region (Kenya); Middle Awash (Ethiopia)
Famous discoveries	A 2019 find from Ethiopia, named MRD.
Brain size	370 cc
Dentition	Relatively large canines compared with more recent Australopithecines.
Cranial features	Projecting cheekbones and ancestral earholes.
Postcranial features	Lower limb bones (tibia and femur) indicate bipedality; arboreal features in upper limb bones (humerus) found.
Culture	N/A
Other	Almost 100 specimens, representing over 20 individuals, have been found to date.

Hominin	*Australopithecus afarensis*
Dates	3.9 mya to 2.9 mya
Region(s)	Afar Region, Omo, Maka, Fejej, and Belohdelie (Ethiopia); Laetoli (Tanzania); Koobi Fora (Kenya)
Famous discoveries	Lucy (discovery: 1974), Selam (Dikika Child, discovery: 2000), Laetoli Footprints (discovery: 1976).
Brain size	380 cc to 430 cc
Dentition	Reduced canines and molars relative to great apes but larger than in modern humans.
Cranial features	Prognathic face, facial features indicate relatively strong chewing musculature (compared with *Homo*) but less extreme than in *Paranthropus*.
Postcranial features	Clear evidence for bipedalism from lower limb postcranial bones. Laetoli Footprints indicate humanlike walking. Dikika Child bones indicate retained ancestral arboreal traits in the postcrania.
Culture	None directly, but close in age and proximity to controversial cut marks at Dikika and early tools in Lomekwi.
Other	*Au. afarensis* is one of the oldest and most well-known australopithecine species and consists of a large number of fossil remains.

Hominin	*Australopithecus bahrelghazali*
Dates	3.6 mya
Region(s)	Chad
Famous discoveries	"Abel," the holotype (discovery: 1995).
Brain size	N/A
Dentition	N/A
Cranial features	N/A
Postcranial features	N/A
Culture	N/A
Other	Arguably within range of variation of *Au. afarensis*.

Hominin	*Australopithecus prometheus*
Dates	3.7 mya (debated)
Region(s)	Sterkfontein (South Africa)
Famous discoveries	"Little Foot" (StW 573) (discovery: 1994)
Brain size	408 cc (Little Foot estimate)
Dentition	Heavy anterior dental wear patterns, relatively large anterior dentition and smaller hind dentition, similar to *Au. afarensis*.
Cranial features	Relatively larger brain size, robust zygomatic arch, and a flatter midface.
Postcranial features	The initial discovery of four ankle bones indicated bipedality.
Culture	N/A
Other	Highly debated new species designation.

Hominin	*Australopithecus deyiremada*
Dates	3.5 mya to 3.3 mya
Region(s)	Woranso-Mille (Afar region, Ethiopia)
Famous discoveries	First fossil mandible bones were discovered in 2011 in the Afar region of Ethiopia by Yohannes Haile-Selassie.
Brain size	N/A
Dentition	Smaller teeth with thicker enamel than seen in *Au. afarensis*, with a potentially hardier diet.
Cranial features	Larger mandible and more projecting cheekbones than in *Au. afarensis*.
Postcranial features	N/A
Culture	N/A
Other	Contested species designation; arguably a member of *Au. afarensis*.

Hominin	*Kenyanthopus platyops*
Dates	3.5 mya to 3.2 mya
Region(s)	Lake Turkana (Kenya)
Famous discoveries	KNM–WT 40000 (discovered 1999)
Brain size	Difficult to determine but appears within the range of *Australopithecus afarensis*.
Dentition	Small molars/dentition (*Homo*-like characteristic)
Cranial features	Flatter (i.e., orthognathic) face
Postcranial features	N/A
Culture	Some have associated the earliest tool finds from Lomekwi, Kenya, temporally (3.3 mya) and in close geographic proximity to this species/specimen.
Other	Taxonomic placing of this species is quite divided. The discoverers have argued that this species is ancestral to *Homo*, in particular to *Homo ruldolfensis*.

Hominin	*Australopithecus africanus*
Dates	3.3 mya to 2.1 mya
Region(s)	Sterkfontein, Taung, Makapansgat, Gladysvale (South Africa)
Famous discoveries	Taung Child (discovery in 1994), "Mrs. Ples" (discover in 1947), Little Foot (arguable; discovery in 1994).
Brain size	400 cc to 500 cc
Dentition	Smaller teeth (derived) relative to *Au. afarensis*. Small canines with no diastema.
Cranial features	A rounder skull compared with *Au. afarensis* in East Africa. A sloping face (ancestral).
Postcranial features	Similar postcranial evidence for bipedal locomotion (derived pelvis) with retained arboreal locomotion, e.g., curved phalanges (fingers), as seen in *Au. afarensis*.
Culture	None with direct evidence.
Other	A 2015 study noted that the trabecular bone morphology of the hand was consistent with forceful tool manufacture and use, suggesting potential early tool abilities.

Hominin	*Australopithecus garhi*
Dates	2.5 mya
Region(s)	Middle Awash (Ethiopia)
Famous discoveries	N/A
Brain size	450 cc
Dentition	Larger hind dentition than seen in other gracile Australopithecines.
Cranial features	N/A
Postcranial features	A femur of a fragmentary partial skeleton, argued to belong to *Au. garhi*, indicates this species may be longer-limbed than *Au. afarensis*, although still able to move arboreally.
Culture	Crude stone tools resembling Oldowan (described later) have been found in association with *Au. garhi*.
Other	This species is not well documented or understood and is based on only a few fossil specimens.

Hominin	*Paranthropus aethiopicus*
Dates	2.7 mya to 2.3 mya
Region(s)	West Turkana (Kenya); Laetoli (Tanzania); Omo River Basin (Ethiopia)
Famous discoveries	The "Black Skull" (KNM–WT 17000) (discovery 1985).
Brain Size	410 cc
Dentition	*P. aethiopicus* has the shared derived traits of large flat premolars and molars, although few teeth have been found.
Cranial features	Large flaring zygomatic arches for accommodating large chewing muscles (the temporalis muscle), a sagittal crest for increased muscle attachment of the chewing muscles to the skull, and a robust mandible and supraorbital torus (brow ridge).
Postcranial features	A proximal tibia indicates bipedality and similar size to *Au. afarensis*.
Culture	N/A
Other	The "Black Skull" is so called because of the mineral manganese that stained it black during fossilization.

Hominin	*Paranthropus boisei*
Dates	2.4 mya to 1.4 mya
Region(s)	Koobi Fora, West Turkana, and Chesowanja (Kenya); Malema-Chiwondo (Malawi), Olduvai Gorge and Peninj (Tanzania); and Omo River basin and Konso (Ethiopia)
Famous discoveries	"Zinj," or sometimes "Nutcracker Man" (OH5), in 1959 by Mary Leakey. The Peninj mandible from Tanzania, found in 1964 by Kimoya Kimeu.
Brain size	500 cc to 550 cc
Dentition	Very large, flat posterior dentition (largest of all hominins currently known). Much smaller anterior dentition. Very thick dental enamel.
Cranial features	Indications of very large chewing muscles (e.g., flaring zygomatic arches and a large sagittal crest).
Postcranial features	Evidence for high variability and sexual dimorphism, with estimates of males at 1.37 meters tall and females at 1.24 meters.
Culture	Richard Leakey and Bernard Wood have both suggested that *P. boisei* could have made and used stone tools. Tools dated to 2.5 mya in Ethiopia have been argued to possibly belong to this species.
Other	Despite the cranial features of *P. boisei* indicating a tough diet of tubers, nuts, and seeds, isotopes indicate a diet high in C4 foods (e.g., grasses, such as sedges). This differs from what is seen in *P. robustus*.

Hominin	*Australopithecus sediba*
Dates	1.97 mya
Region(s)	Malapa Fossil Site (South Africa)
Famous discoveries	Karabo (MH1) (discovery in 2008)
Brain size	420 cc to 450 cc
Dentition	Small dentition with Australopithecine cusp-spacing.
Cranial features	Small brain size (*Australopithecus*-like) but gracile mandible (*Homo*-like).
Postcranial features	Scientists have interpreted this mixture of traits (such as a robust ankle but evidence for an arch in the foot) as a transitional phase between a body previously adapted to arborealism (tree climbing, particularly in evidence from the bones of the wrist) to one that adapted to bipedal ground walking.
Culture	None of direct association, but some have argued that a modern hand morphology (shorter fingers and a longer thumb) means that adaptations to tool manufacture and use may be present in this species.
Other	It was first discovered through a clavicle bone in 2008 by nine-year-old Matthew Berger, son of paleoanthropologist Lee Berger.

Hominin	*Paranthropus robustus*
Dates	2.3 mya to 1 mya
Region(s)	Kromdraai B, Swartkrans, Gondolin, Drimolen, and Coopers Cave (South Africa)
Famous discoveries	SK48 (original skull)
Brain size	410 cc to 530 cc
Dentition	Large posterior teeth with thick enamel, consistent with other Robust Australopithecines. Enamel hypoplasia is also common in this species, possibly because of instability in the development of large, thick enameled dentition.
Cranial features	*P. robustus* features are neither as "hyper-robust" as *P. boisei* or as ancestral in features as *P. aethiopicus*. They have been described as less derived, more general features that are shared with both East African species (e.g., the sagittal crest and zygomatic flaring).
Postcranial features	Reconstructions indicate sexual dimorphism.
Culture	N/A
Other	Several of these fossils are fragmentary in nature, distorted, and not well preserved, because they have been recovered from quarry breccia using explosives.

Review Questions

- What is the difference between a "derived" versus an "ancestral" trait? Give an example of both, seen in *Au. afarensis*.
- Which of the paleoenvironment hypotheses have been used to describe early hominin diversity, and which have been used to describe bipedalism?
- Which anatomical features for bipedalism do we see in early hominins?
- Describe the dentition of gracile and robust australopithecines. What might these tell us about their diets?
- List the hominin species argued to be associated with stone tool technologies. Are you convinced of these associations? Why/why not?

Key Terms

Arboreal: Related to trees or woodland.

Aridification: Becoming increasingly arid or dry, as related to the climate or environment.

Aridity Hypothesis: The hypothesis that long-term aridification and expansion of savannah biomes were drivers in diversification in early hominin evolution.

Assemblage: A collection demonstrating a pattern. Often pertaining to a site or region.

Bipedalism: The locomotor ability to walk on two legs.

Breccia: Hard, calcareous sedimentary rock.

Canines: The pointy teeth just next to the incisors, in the front of the mouth.

Cheek teeth: Or hind dentition (molars and premolars).

Chronospecies: Species that are said to evolve into another species, in a linear fashion, over time.

Clade: A group of species or taxa with a shared common ancestor.

Cladistics: The field of grouping organisms into those with shared ancestry.

Context: As pertaining to palaeoanthropology, this term refers to the place where an artifact or fossil is found.

Cores: The remains of a rock that has been flaked or knapped.

Cusps: The ridges or "bumps" on the teeth.

Dental formula: A technique to describe the number of incisors, canines, premolars, and molars in each quadrant of the mouth.

Derived traits: Newly evolved traits that differ from those seen in the ancestor.

Diastema: A tooth gap between the incisors and canines.

Early Stone Age (ESA): The earliest-described archaeological period in which we start seeing stone-tool technology.

East African Rift System (EARS): This term is often used to refer to the Rift Valley, expanding from Malawi to Ethiopia. This active geological structure is responsible for much of the visibility of the paleoanthropological record in East Africa.

Enamel: The highly mineralized outer layer of the tooth.

Encephalization: Expansion of the brain.

Extant: Currently living—i.e., not extinct.

Fallback foods: Foods that may not be preferred by an animal (e.g., foods that are not nutritionally dense) but that are essential for survival in times of stress or scarcity.

Fauna: The animals of a particular region, habitat, or geological period.

Faunal assemblages: Collections of fossils of the animals found at a site.

Faunal turnover: The rate at which species go extinct and are replaced with new species.

Flake: The piece knocked off of a stone core during the manufacture of a tool, which may be used as a stone tool.

Flora: The plants of a particular region, habitat, or geological period.

Folivorous: Foliage-eating.

Foramen magnum: The large hole (foramen) at the base of the cranium, through which the spinal cord enters the skull.

Fossil: The remains or impression of an organism from the past.

Frugivorous: Fruit-eating.

Generalist: A species that can thrive in a wide variety of habitats and can have a varied diet.

Glacial: Colder, drier periods during an ice age when there is more ice trapped at the poles.

Gracile: Slender, less rugged, or pronounced features.

Hallux: The big toe.

Holotype: A single specimen from which a species or taxon is described or named.

Hominin: A primate category that includes humans and our fossil relatives since our divergence from extant great apes.

Honing P3: The mandibular premolar alongside the canine (in primates, the P3), which is angled to give space for (and sharpen) the upper canines.

Hyper-robust: Even more robust than considered normal in the Paranthropus genus.

Hypodigm: A sample (here, fossil) from which researchers extrapolate features of a population.

Incisiform: An adjective referring to a canine that appears more incisor-like in morphology.

Incisors: The teeth in the front of the mouth, used to bite off food.

Interglacial: A period of milder climate in between two glacial periods.

Isotopes: Two or more forms of the same element that contain equal numbers of protons but different numbers of neutrons, giving them the same chemical properties but different atomic masses.

Knappers: The people who fractured rocks in order to manufacture tools.

Knapping: The fracturing of rocks for the manufacture of tools.

Large Cutting Tool (LCT): A tool that is shaped to have functional edges.

Last Common Ancestor (LCA): The hypothetical final ancestor (or ancestral population) of two or more taxa before their divergence.

Lithic: Relating to stone (here to stone tools).

Lumbar lordosis: The inward curving of the lower (lumbar) parts of the spine. The lower curve in the human S-shaped spine.

Lumpers: Researchers who prefer to lump variable specimens into a single species or taxon and who feel high levels of variation is biologically real.

Megadont: An organism with extremely large dentition compared with body size.

Metacarpals: The long bones of the hand that connect to the phalanges (finger bones).

Molars: The largest, most posterior of the hind dentition.

Monophyletic: A taxon or group of taxa descended from a common ancestor that is not shared with another taxon or group.

Morphology: The study of the form or size and shape of things; in this case, skeletal parts.

Mosaic evolution: The concept that evolutionary change does not occur homogeneously throughout the body in organisms.

Obligate bipedalism: Where the primary form of locomotion for an organism is bipedal.

Occlude: When the teeth from the maxilla come into contact with the teeth in the mandible.

Oldowan: Lower Paleolithic, the earliest stone tool culture.

Orthognathic: The face below the eyes is relatively flat and does not jut out anteriorly.

Paleoanthropologists: Researchers that study human evolution.

Paleoenvironment: An environment from a period in the Earth's geological past.

Parabolic: Like a parabola (parabola-shaped).

Phalanges: Long bones in the hand and fingers.

Phylogenetics: The study of phylogeny.

Phylogeny: The study of the evolutionary relationships between groups of organisms.

Pliocene: A geological epoch between the Miocene and Pleistocene.

Polytypic: In reference to taxonomy, having two or more group variants capable of interacting and breeding biologically but having morphological population differences.

Postcranium: The skeleton below the cranium (head).

Premolars: The smallest of the hind teeth, behind the canines.

Procumbent: In reference to incisors, tilting forward.

Prognathic: In reference to the face, the area below the eyes juts anteriorly.

Quaternary Ice Age: The most recent geological time period, which includes the Pleistocene and Holocene Epochs and which is defined by the cyclicity of increasing and decreasing ice sheets at the poles.

Relative dating: Dating techniques that refer to a temporal sequence (i.e., older or younger than others in the reference) and do not estimate actual or absolute dates.

Robust: Rugged or exaggerated features.

Site: A place in which evidence of past societies/species/activities may be observed through archaeological or paleontological practice.

Specialist: A specialist species can thrive only in a narrow range of environmental conditions or has a limited diet.

Splitters: Researchers who prefer to split a highly variable taxon into multiple groups or species.

Taxa: Plural of taxon, a taxonomic group such as species, genus, or family.

Taxonomy: The science of grouping and classifying organisms.

Techno-complex: A term encompassing multiple assemblages that share similar traits in terms of artifact production and morphology.

Thermoregulation: Maintaining body temperature through physiologically cooling or warming the body.

Ungulates: Hoofed mammals—e.g., cows and kudu.

Volcanic tufts: Rock made from ash from volcanic eruptions in the past.

Valgus knee: The angle of the knee between the femur and tibia, which allows for weight distribution to be angled closer to the point above the center of gravity (i.e., between the feet) in bipeds.

About the Authors

Kerryn Warren, Ph.D.

Grad Coach International, kerryn.warren@gmail.com

Kerryn Warren is a dissertation coach at Grad Coach International and is passionate about stimulating research thinking in students of all levels. She has lectured on multiple topics, including archaeology and human evolution, with her research and science communication interests including hybridization in the hominin fossil record (stemming from research from her Ph.D.) and understanding how evolution is taught in South African schools. She also worked as one of the "Underground Astronauts," selected to excavate *Homo naledi* remains from the Rising Star Cave System in the Cradle of Humankind.

K. Lindsay Hunter, M.A., Ph.D. candidate

CARTA, k.lindsay.hunter@gmail.com

Lindsay Hunter is a trained palaeoanthropologist who uses her more than 15 years of experience to make sense of the distant past of our species to build a better future. She received her master's degree in biological anthropology from the University of Iowa and is completing her Ph.D. in archaeology at the University of the Witwatersrand in Johannesburg, South Africa. She has studied fossil and human bone collections across five continents with major grant support from the National Science Foundation (United States) and the Wenner-Gren Foundation for Anthropological Research. As a National Geographic Explorer, Lindsay developed and managed the National Geographic–sponsored Umsuka Public Palaeoanthropology Project in the Cradle of Humankind World Heritage Site (CoH WHS) in South Africa from within Westbury Township, Johannesburg, between 2016–2019. She currently serves as the Community Engagement & Advancement Director for CARTA: The UC San Diego/Salk Institute Center for Academic Research and Training in Anthropogeny in La Jolla, California.

Navashni Naidoo, M.Sc.

University of Cape Town, nnaidoo2@illinois.edu

Navashni Naidoo is a researcher at Nelson Mandela University, lecturing on physical geology. She completed her Master's in Science in Archaeology in 2017 at the University of Cape Town. Her research interests include developing paleoenvironmental proxies suited to the African continent, behavioral ecology, and engaging with community-driven archaeological projects. She has excavated at Stone Age sites across Southern Africa and East Africa. Navashni is currently pursuing a PhD in the Department of Anthropology at the University of Illinois.

Silindokuhle Mavuso, M.Sc.

University of Witwatersrand, S.muvaso@ru.ac.za

Silindokuhle has always been curious about the world around him and how it has been shaped. He is a lecturer at Rhodes University of Witwatersrand (Wits), and conducts research on palaeoenvironmental reconstruction and change of the northeastern Turkana Basin's Pleistocene sequence. Silindokuhle began his education with a B.Sc. (Geology, Archaeology, and Environmental and Geographical Sciences) from the University of Cape Town before moving to Wits for a B.Sc. Honors (geology and paleontology) and M.Sc. in geology. He is currently concluding his PhD Studies. During this time, he has gained more training as a Koobi Fora Fieldschool fellow (Kenya) as well as an Erasmus Mundus scholar (France). Silindokuhle is a Plio-Pleistocene geologist with a specific focus on identifying and explaining past environments that are associated with early human life and development through time. He is interested in a wide range of disciplines such as micromorphology, sedimentology, geochemistry, geochronology, and sequence stratigraphy. He has worked with teams from significant eastern and southern African hominid sites including Elandsfontein, Rising Star, Sterkfontein, Gondolin, Laetoli, Olduvai, and Koobi Fora.

For Further Exploration

The Smithsonian Institution website hosts descriptions of fossil species, an interactive timeline, and much more.

The Maropeng Museum website hosts a wealth of information regarding South African Fossil Bearing sites in the Cradle of Humankind.

This quick comparison between *Homo naledi* and *Australopithecus sediba* from the Perot Museum.

This explanation of the braided stream by the Perot Museum.

A collation of 3-D files for visualizing (or even 3-D printing) for homes, schools, and universities.

PBS learning materials, including videos and diagrams of the Laetoli footprints, bipedalism, and fossils.

A wealth of information from the Australian Museum website, including species descriptions, family trees, and explanations of bipedalism and diet.

References

Alemseged, Zeresenay, Fred Spoor, William H. Kimbel, René Bobe, Denis Geraads, Denné Reed, and Jonathan G. Wynn. 2006. "A Juvenile Early Hominin Skeleton from Dikika, Ethiopia." *Nature* 443 (7109): 296–301.

Asfaw, Berhane, Tim White, Owen Lovejoy, Bruce Latimer, Scott Simpson, and Gen Suwa. 1999. "*Australopithecus garhi*: A New Species of Early Hominid from Ethiopia." *Science* 284 (5414): 629–635.

Behrensmeyer, Anna K., Nancy E. Todd, Richard Potts, and Geraldine E. McBrinn. 1997. "Late Pliocene Faunal Turnover in the Turkana Basin, Kenya, and Ethiopia." *Science* 278 (5343): 637–640.

Berger, Lee R., Darryl J. De Ruiter, Steven E. Churchill, Peter Schmid, Kristian J. Carlson, Paul HGM Dirks, and Job M. Kibii. 2010. "*Australopithecus sediba*: A New Species of *Homo*-like Australopith from South Africa." *Science* 328 (5975): 195–204.

Bobe, René, and Anna K. Behrensmeyer. 2004. "The Expansion of Grassland Ecosystems in Africa in Relation to Mammalian Evolution and the Origin of the Genus *Homo*." *Palaeogeography, Palaeoclimatology, Palaeoecology* 207 (3–4): 399–420.

Brain, C. K. 1967. "The Transvaal Museum's Fossil Project at Swartkrans." *South African Journal of Science* 63 (9): 378–384.

Broom, R. 1938a. "More Discoveries of Australopithecus." *Nature* 141 (1): 828–829.

Broom, R. 1938b. "The Pleistocene Anthropoid Apes of South Africa." *Nature* 142 (3591): 377–379.

Broom, R. 1947. "Discovery of a New Skull of the South African Ape-Man, Plesianthropus." *Nature* 159 (4046): 672.

Broom, R. 1950. "The Genera and Species of the South African Fossil Ape-Man." *American Journal of Physical Anthropology* 8 (1): 1–14.

Brunet, Michel, Alain Beauvilain, Yves Coppens, Emile Heintz, Aladji HE Moutaye, and David Pilbeam. 1995. "The First Australopithecine 2,500 Kilometers West of the Rift Valley (Chad)." *Nature* 378 (6554): 275–273.

Cerling, Thure E., Jonathan G. Wynn, Samuel A. Andanje, Michael I. Bird, David Kimutai Korir, Naomi E. Levin, William Mace, Anthony N. Macharia, Jay Quade, and Christopher H. Remien. 2011. "Woody Cover and Hominin Environments in the Past 6 Million Years." *Nature* 476, no. 7358 (2011): 51-56..

Clarke, Ronald J. 1998. "First Ever Discovery of a Well-Preserved Skull and Associated Skeleton of *Australopithecus*." *South African Journal of Science* 94 (10): 460–463.

Clarke, Ronald J. 2013. "Australopithecus from Sterkfontein Caves, South Africa." In *The Paleobiology of Australopithecus*, edited by K. E. Reed, J. G. Fleagle, and R. E. Leakey, 105–123. Netherlands: Springer.

Clarke, Ronald J., and Kathleen Kuman. 2019. "The Skull of StW 573, a 3.67 Ma Australopithecus Prometheus Skeleton from Sterkfontein Caves, South Africa." *Journal of Human Evolution* 134: 102634.

Clarke, R. J., and P. V. Tobias. 1995. "Sterkfontein Member 2 Foot Bones of the Oldest South African Hominid." *Science* 269 (5223): 521–524.

Constantino, P. J., and B. A. Wood. 2004. "Paranthropus Paleobiology". In *Miscelanea en Homenae a Emiliano Aguirre, volumen III: Paleoantropologia*, edited by E. G. Pérez and S. R. Jara, 136–151. Alcalá de Henares: Museo Arqueologico Regional.

Constantino, P. J., and B. A. Wood. 2007. "The Evolution of Zinjanthropus boisei." *Evolutionary Anthropology: Issues, News, and Reviews* 16 (2): 49–62.

Dart, Raymond A. 1925. "Australopithecus africanus, the Man-Ape of South Africa." *Nature* 115: 195–199.

Darwin, Charles. 1871. *The Descent of Man: And Selection in Relation to Sex*. London: J. Murray.

Daver, Guillaume, F. Guy, Hassane Taïsso Mackaye, Andossa Likius, J-R. Boisserie, Abderamane Moussa, Laurent Pallas, Patrick Vignaud, and Nékoulnang D. Clarisse. 2022. "Postcranial Evidence of Late Miocene Hominin Bipedalism in Chad." *Nature* 609 (7925): 94–100.

Heinzelin, Jean de, J. Desmond Clark, Tim White, William Hart, Paul Renne, Giday WoldeGabriel, Yonas Beyene, and Elisabeth Vrba. 1999. "Environment and Behavior of 2.5-Million-Year-Old Bouri Hominids." *Science* 284 (5414): 625–629.

DeMenocal, Peter B. D. 2004. "African Climate Change and Faunal Evolution during the Pliocene–Pleistocene." *Earth and Planetary Science Letters* 220 (1–2): 3–24.

DeMenocal, Peter B. D. and J. Bloemendal, J. 1995. "Plio-Pleistocene Climatic Variability in Subtropical Africa and the Paleoenvironment of Hominid Evolution: A Combined Data-Model Approach." In *Paleoclimate and Evolution, with Emphasis on Human Origins*, edited by E. S. Vrba, G. H. Denton, T. C. Partridge, and L. H. Burckle, 262–288. New Haven: Yale University Press.

Dirks, Paul HGM, Job M. Kibii, Brian F. Kuhn, Christine Steininger, Steven E. Churchill, Jan D. Kramers, Robyn Pickering, Daniel L. Farber, Anne-Sophie Mériaux, Andy I. R. Herries, Geoffrey C. P. King, And Lee R. Berger. 2010. "Geological Setting and Age of *Australopithecus sediba* from Southern Africa." *Science* 328 (5975): 205–208.

Faith, J. Tyler, and Anna K. Behrensmeyer. 2013. "Climate Change and Faunal Turnover: Testing the Mechanics of the Turnover-Pulse Hypothesis with South African Fossil Data." *Paleobiology* 39 (4): 609–627.

Grine, Frederick E. 1988. "New Craniodental Fossils of *Paranthropus* from the Swartkrans Formation and Their Significance in 'Robust' Australopithecine Evolution." In *Evolutionary History of the "Robust" Australopithecines*, edited by F. E. Grine, 223–243. New York: Aldine de Gruyter.

Grine, Frederick E., Carrie S. Mongle, John G. Fleagle, and Ashley S. Hammond. 2022. "The Taxonomic Attribution of African Hominin Postcrania from the Miocene through the Pleistocene: Associations and Assumptions." *Journal of Human Evolution* 173: 103255.

Haile-Selassie, Yohannes, Luis Gibert, Stephanie M. Melillo, Timothy M. Ryan, Mulugeta Alene, Alan Deino, Naomi E. Levin, Gary Scott, and Beverly Z. Saylor. 2015. "New Species from Ethiopia Further Expands Middle Pliocene Hominin Diversity." *Nature* 521 (7553): 432–433.

Haile-Selassie, Yohannes, Stephanie M. Melillo, Antonino Vazzana, Stefano Benazzi, and Timothy M. Ryan. 2019. "A 3.8-Million-Year-Old Hominin Cranium from Woranso-Mille, Ethiopia." *Nature* 573 (7773): 214-219.

Harmand, Sonia, Jason E. Lewis, Craig S. Feibel, Christopher J. Lepre, Sandrine Prat, Arnaud Lenoble, Xavier Boës et al. 2015. "3.3-Million-Year-Old Stone Tools from Lomekwi3, West Turkana, Kenya." *Nature* 521 (7552): 310–316.

Hay, Richard L. 1990. "Olduvai Gorge: A Case History in the Interpretation of Hominid Paleoenvironments." In *East Africa: Establishment of a Geologic Framework for Paleoanthropology*, edited by L. Laporte, 23–37. Boulder: Geological Society of America.

Hay, Richard L., and Mary D. Leakey. 1982. "The Fossil Footprints of Laetoli." *Scientific American* 246 (2): 50–57.

Hlazo, Nomawethu. 2015. "Paranthropus: Variation in Cranial Morphology." Honours thesis, Archaeology Department, University of Cape Town, Cape Town.

Hlazo, Nomawethu. 2018. "Variation and the Evolutionary Drivers of Diversity in the Genus *Paranthropus*." Master's thesis, Archaeology Department, University of Cape Town, Cape Town.

Johanson, D. C., T. D. White, and Y. Coppens. 1978. "A New Species of the Genus *Australopithecus* (Primates: Hominidae) from the Pliocene of East Africa." *Kirtlandia* 28: 1–14.

Kimbel, William H. 2015. "The Species and Diversity of Australopiths." In *Handbook of Paleoanthropology*, 2nd ed., edited by T. Hardt, 2071–2105. Berlin: Springer.

Kimbel, William H., and Lucas K. Delezene. 2009. "'Lucy' Redux: A Review of Research on *Australopithecus afarensis*." *American Journal of Physical Anthropology* 140 (S49): 2–48.

Kingston, John D. 2007. "Shifting Adaptive Landscapes: Progress and Challenges in Reconstructing Early Hominid Environments." *American Journal of Physical Anthropology* 134 (S45): 20–58.

Kingston, John D., and Terry Harrison. 2007. "Isotopic Dietary Reconstructions of Pliocene Herbivores at Laetoli: Implications for Early Hominin Paleoecology." *Palaeogeography, Palaeoclimatology, Palaeoecology* 243 (3–4): 272–306.

Leakey, Louis S. B. 1959. "A New Fossil Skull from Olduvai." *Nature* 184 (4685): 491–493.

Leakey, Mary 1971. *Olduvai Gorge*, Vol. 3. Cambridge: Cambridge University Press.

Leakey, Mary D., and Richard L. Hay. 1979. "Pliocene Footprints in the Laetoli Beds at Laetoli, Northern Tanzania." *Nature* 278 (5702): 317–323.

Leakey, Meave G., Craig S. Feibel, Ian McDougall, and Alan Walker. 1995. "New Four–Million-Year-Old Hominid Species from Kanapoi and Allia Bay, Kenya." *Nature* 376 (6541): 565–571.

Meave G., Fred Spoor, Frank H. Brown, Patrick N. Gathogo, Christopher Kiarie, Louise N. Leakey, and Ian McDougall. 2001. "New Hominin Genus from Eastern Africa Shows Diverse Middle Pliocene Lineages." *Nature* 410 (6827): 433–440.

Lebatard, Anne-Elisabeth, Didier L. Bourlès, Philippe Duringer, Marc Jolivet, Régis Braucher, Julien Carcaillet, Mathieu Schuster et al. 2008.

"Cosmogenic Nuclide Dating of *Sahelanthropus tchadensis* and *Australopithecus bahrelghazali*: Mio-Pliocene Hominids from Chad." *Proceedings of the National Academy of Sciences* 105 (9): 3226–3231.

Lee-Thorp, Julia. 2011. "The Demise of 'Nutcracker Man.'" *Proceedings of the National Academy of Sciences* 108 (23): 9319–9320.

Lombard, Marlize, L. Y. N. Wadley, Janette Deacon, Sarah Wurz, Isabelle Parsons, Moleboheng Mohapi, Joane Swart, and Peter Mitchell. 2012. "South African and Lesotho Stone Age Sequence Updated." *The South African Archaeological Bulletin* 67 (195): 123–144.

Maslin, Mark A., Chris M. Brierley, Alice M. Milner, Susanne Shultz, Martin H. Trauth, and Katy E. Wilson. 2014. "East African Climate Pulses and Early Human Evolution." *Quaternary Science Reviews* 101: 1–17.

McHenry, Henry M. 2009. "Human Evolution." In *Evolution: The First Four Billion Years*, edited by M. Ruse and J. Travis, 256–280. Cambridge: The Belknap Press of Harvard University Press..

Patterson, Bryan, and William W. Howells. 1967. "Hominid Humeral Fragment from Early Pleistocene of Northwestern Kenya." *Science* 156 (3771): 64–66.

Pickering, Robyn, and Jan D. Kramers. 2010. "Re-appraisal of the Stratigraphy and Determination of New U-Pb Dates for the Sterkfontein Hominin Site." *Journal of Human Evolution* 59 (1): 70–86.

Potts, Richard. 1998. "Environmental Hypotheses of Hominin Evolution." *American Journal of Physical Anthropology* 107 (S27): 93–136.

Potts, Richard. 2013. "Hominin Evolution in Settings of Strong Environmental Variability." *Quaternary Science Reviews* 73: 1–13.

Rak, Yoel. 1983. *The Australopithecine Face*. New York: Academic Press.

Rak, Yoel. 1988. "On Variation in the Masticatory System of *Australopithecus boisei*." In *Evolutionary History of the "Robust" Australopithecines*, edited by M. Ruse and J. Travis, 193–198. New York: Aldine de Gruyter.

Semaw, Sileshi. 2000. "The World's Oldest Stone Artefacts from Gona, Ethiopia: Their Implications for Understanding Stone Technology and Patterns of Human Evolution between 2.6 Million Years Ago and 1.5 Million Years Ago." *Journal of Archaeological Science* 27(12): 1197–1214.

Shipman, Pat. 2002. *The Man Who Found the Missing Link: Eugene Dubois and his Lifelong Quest to Prove Darwin Right*. New York: Simon & Schuster.

Spoor, Fred. 2015. "Palaeoanthropology: The Middle Pliocene Gets Crowded." *Nature* 521 (7553): 432–433.

Strait, David S., Frederick E. Grine, and Marc A. Moniz. 1997. A Reappraisal of Early Hominid Phylogeny." *Journal of Human Evolution* 32 (1): 17–82.

Thackeray, J. Francis. 2000. "'Mrs. Ples' from Sterkfontein: Small Male or Large Female?" *The South African Archaeological Bulletin* 55: 155–158.

Thackeray, J. Francis, José Braga, Jacques Treil, N. Niksch, and J. H. Labuschagne. 2002. "'Mrs. Ples' (Sts 5) from Sterkfontein: An Adolescent Male?" *South African Journal of Science* 98 (1–2): 21–22.

Toth, Nicholas. 1985. "The Oldowan Reassessed." *Journal of Archaeological Science* 12 (2): 101–120.

Vrba, E. S. 1988. "Late Pliocene Climatic Events and Hominid Evolution." In *The Evolutionary History of the Robust Australopithecines*, edited by F. E. Grine, 405–426. New York: Aldine.

Vrba, Elisabeth S. 1998. "Multiphasic Growth Models and the Evolution of Prolonged Growth Exemplified by Human Brain Evolution." *Journal of Theoretical Biology* 190 (3): 227–239.

Vrba, Elisabeth S. 2000. "Major Features of Neogene Mammalian Evolution in Africa." In *Cenozoic Geology of Southern Africa*, edited by T. C. Partridge and R. Maud, 277–304. Oxford: Oxford University Press.

Walker, Alan C., and Richard E. Leakey. 1988. "The Evolution of *Australopithecus boisei*." In *Evolutionary History of the "Robust" Australopithecines*, edited by F. E. Grine, 247–258. New York: Aldine de Gruyter.

Walker, Alan, Richard E. Leakey, John M. Harris, and Francis H. Brown. 1986. "2.5-my *Australopithecus boisei* from West of Lake Turkana, Kenya." *Nature* 322 (6079): 517–522.

Ward, Carol, Meave Leakey, and Alan Walker. 1999. "The New Hominid Species *Australopithecus anamensis*." *Evolutionary Anthropology* 7 (6): 197–205.

White, Tim D. 1988. "The Comparative Biology of 'Robust' Australopithecus: Clues from Content." In *Evolutionary History of the "Robust" Australopithecines*, edited by F. E. Grine, 449–483. New York: Aldine de Gruyter.

White, Tim D., Gen Suwa, and Berhane Asfaw. 1994. "*Australopithecus ramidus*, a New Species of Early Hominid from Aramis, Ethiopia." *Nature* 371 (6495): 306–312.

Wood, Bernard. 2010. "Reconstructing Human Evolution: Achievements, Challenges, and Opportunities." *Proceedings of the National Academy of Sciences* 10 (2): 8902–8909.

Wood, Bernard, and Eve K. Boyle. 2016. "Hominin Taxic Diversity: Fact or Fantasy?" *Yearbook of Physical Anthropology* 159 (S61): 37–78.

Wood, Bernard, and Kes Schroer. 2017. "Paranthropus: Where Do Things Stand?" In *Human Paleontology and Prehistory*, edited by A. Marom and E. Hovers, 95–107. New York: Springer, Cham.

Acknowledgements

All of the authors in this section are students and early career researchers in paleoanthropology and related fields in South Africa (or at least have worked in South Africa). We wish to thank everyone who supports young and diverse talent in this field and would love to further acknowledge Black, African, and female academics who have helped pave the way for us.

10.

EARLY MEMBERS OF THE GENUS HOMO

Bonnie Yoshida-Levine Ph.D., Grossmont College

This chapter is a revision from "Chapter 10: Early Members of the Genus Homo" by Bonnie Yoshida-Levine. In Explorations: An Open Invitation to Biological Anthropology, first edition, edited by Beth Shook, Katie Nelson, Kelsie Aguilera, and Lara Braff, which is licensed under CC BY-NC 4.0.

Learning Objectives

- Describe how early Pleistocene climate change influenced the evolution of the genus Homo.
- Identify the characteristics that define the genus Homo.
- Describe the skeletal anatomy of Homo habilis and Homo erectus based on the fossil evidence.
- Assess opposing points of view about how early Homo should be classified.

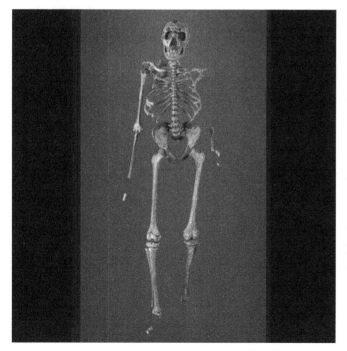

The boy was no older than nine years when he perished by the swampy shores of the lake. After death, his slender, long-limbed body sank into the mud of the lake shallows. His bones fossilized and lay undisturbed for 1.5 million years. In the 1980s, fossil hunter Kamoya Kimeu, working on the western shore of Lake Turkana, Kenya, glimpsed a dark-colored piece of bone eroding in a hillside. This small skull fragment led to the discovery of what is arguably the world's most complete early hominin fossil—a youth identified as a member of the species *Homo erectus*. Now known as Nariokotome Boy, after the nearby lake village, the skeleton has provided a wealth of information about the early evolution of our own genus, *Homo* (see Figure 10.1). Today, a stone monument with an inscription in three languages—English, Swahili, and the local Turkana language—marks the site of this momentous fossil discovery.

Figure 10.1a-b: a. Skeleton of a young male Homo erectus known as "Nariokotome Boy"; b. an artist's depiction of how he may have looked during his life. This is the most complete hominin fossil from this time period ever found. Credit: a. KNM-WT 15000 Turkana Boy Skeleton by Smithsonian [exhibit: Human Evolution Evidence, Human Fossils, Fossils, KNM-WT 15000] is copyrighted and used for educational and non-commercial purposes as outlined by the Smithsonian. b. Homo-erectus Turkana-Boy (Ausschnitt) Fundort Nariokotome, Kenia, Rekonstruktion im Neanderthal Museum by Neanderthal Museum is under a CC BY-SA 4.0 License.

Chapter 9 described our oldest human ancestors, primarily members of the genus *Australopithecus*, who lived between 2 million and 4 million years ago. This chapter introduces the earliest members of the genus *Homo*, focusing on *Homo habilis* and *Homo erectus*.

Defining the Genus *Homo*

Because Anthropology is fundamentally concerned with what makes us human, defining our own genus takes on special significance for anthropologists. Ever since scientists acknowledged the existence of extinct species of humans, they have debated which of them display sufficient "humanness" to merit classification in the genus *Homo*. When grouping species into a common genus, biologists consider criteria such as physical characteristics (morphology), evidence of recent common ancestry, and adaptive strategy (use of the environment). However, there is disagreement about which of those criteria should be prioritized, as well as how specific fossils should be interpreted in light of the criteria.

Nevertheless, there is general agreement that species classified as *Homo* should share characteristics that are broadly similar within our species. These include the following:

- a relatively large brain size, indicating a high degree of intelligence;
- a smaller and flatter face;
- smaller jaws and teeth; and
- increased reliance on culture, particularly the use of stone tools, to exploit a greater diversity of environments (adaptive zone).

Some researchers would include larger overall body size and limb proportions (longer legs/shorter arms) in this list. While these criteria seem relatively clear-cut, evaluating them in the fossil record has proved more difficult, particularly for the earliest members of the genus. There are several reasons for this. First, many fossil specimens dating to this time period are incomplete and poorly preserved. Second, early *Homo* fossils appear quite variable in brain size, facial features, and teeth and body size, and there is not yet consensus about how to best make sense of this diversity. Finally, there is growing evidence that the evolution of the genus *Homo* proceeded in a mosaic pattern: in other words, these characteristics did not appear all at once in a single species; rather, they were patchily distributed in different species from different regions and time periods. Consequently, different researchers have come up with conflicting classification schemes depending on which criteria they think are most important.

In this chapter, we will take several pathways toward examining the origin and evolution of the genus *Homo*. First, we will explore the environmental conditions of the Pleistocene epoch in which the genus *Homo* evolved. Next we will examine the fossil evidence for the two principal species traditionally identified as early Homo: *Homo habilis* and *Homo erectus*. Then we will use data from fossils and archaeological sites to reconstruct the behavior of early members of *Homo*, including tool manufacture, subsistence practices, migratory patterns, and social structure. Finally, we will consider these together in an attempt to characterize the key adaptive strategies of early *Homo* and how they put our early ancestors on the trajectory that led to our own species, *Homo sapiens*.

Climate Change and Human Evolution

A key goal in the study of human origins is to learn about the environmental pressures that may have shaped human evolution. As indicated in Chapter 7, scientists use a variety of techniques to reconstruct ancient environments. These include stable isotopes, core samples from oceans and lakes, windblown dust, analysis of geological formations and volcanoes, and fossils of ancient plant and animal communities. Such studies have provided valuable information about the environmental context of early *Homo*.

The early hominin species covered in Chapter 9, such as *Ardipithecus ramidus* and *Australopithecus afarensis*, evolved during the late **Pliocene** epoch. The Pliocene (5.3 million to 2.6 million years ago) was marked by cooler and drier conditions, with ice caps forming permanently at the poles. Still, Earth's climate during the Pliocene was considerably warmer and wetter than at present.

The subsequent **Pleistocene** epoch (2.6 million years to 11,000 years ago) ushered in major environmental change. The Pleistocene is popularly referred to as the Ice Age. Since the term "Ice Age" tends to conjure up images of glaciers and woolly mammoths, one would naturally assume that this was a period of uniformly cold climate around the globe. But this is not actually the case. Instead, climate became much more variable, cycling abruptly between warm/wet (interglacial) and cold/dry (glacial) cycles. These patterns were influenced by changes in Earth's elliptical orbit around the sun. As is shown in Figure 10.2, each cycle averaged about 41,000 years during the early Pleistocene; the cycles then lengthened to about 100,000 years starting around 1.25 million years ago. Since mountain ranges, wind patterns, ocean currents, and volcanic activity can all influence climate patterns, there were wide-ranging regional and local effects.

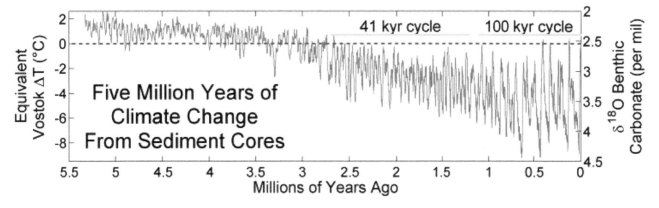

Figure 10.2: Temperature estimates during the last five million years, extrapolated from deep-sea core data. Lower temperatures and increased temperature oscillations start at 2.6 million years ago. Glacial/interglacial cycles during the early part of the epoch are shorter, each averaging about 41,000 years. Credit: Five Myr Climate Change by Dragons flight (Robert A. Rohde), based on data from Lisiechi and Raymo (2005), is under a CC BY-SA 3.0 License.

Data on ancient geography and climate help us understand how our ancestors moved and migrated to different parts of the world—as well as the constraints under which they operated. When periods of global cooling dominated, sea levels were lower as more water was captured as glacial ice. This exposed continental margins and opened pathways between land masses. During glacial periods, the large Indonesian islands of Sumatra, Java, and Borneo were connected to the Southeast Asian mainland, while New Guinea was part of the southern landmass of greater Australia. There was a land bridge connection between Britain and continental Europe, and an icy, treeless plain known as Beringia connected Northern Asia and Alaska.

At the same time, glaciation made some northern areas inaccessible to human habitation. For example, there is evidence that hominin species were in Britain 950,000 years ago, but it does not appear that Britain was continuously occupied during this period. These early humans may have died out or been forced to abandon the region during glacial periods.

In Africa, paleoclimate research has determined that grasslands (shown in Figure 10.3) expanded and shrank multiple times during this period, even as they expanded over the long term (deMenocal 2014). From studies of fossils, paleontologists have been able to reconstruct Pleistocene animal communities and to consider how they were affected by the changing climate. Among the African animal populations, the number of grazing animal species such as antelope increased. Although the African and Eurasian continents are connected by land, the Sahara desert and the mountainous topography of North Africa serve as natural barriers to crossing. But the fossil record shows that at different times animal species have moved back and forth between Africa and Eurasia. During the early Pleistocene, there is evidence of African mammal species such as baboons, hippos, antelope, and African buffalo migrating out of Africa into Eurasia during periods of aridity (Belmaker 2010).

This changing environment was undoubtedly challenging for our ancestors, but it offered new opportunities to make a living. One solution adopted by some hominins was to specialize in feeding on the new types of plants growing in this landscape. The robust australopithecines (described in Chapter 9) likely developed their large molar teeth with thick enamel in order to exploit this particular dietary niche.

Members of the genus *Homo* took a different route. Faced with the unstable African climate and shifting landscape, they evolved bigger brains that enabled them to rely on cultural solutions such as crafting stone tools that opened up new foraging opportunities. This strategy of behavioral flexibility served them well during this unpredictable time and led to new innovations such as increased meat-eating, cooperative hunting, and the exploitation of new environments outside Africa.

Figure 10.3: A savanna grassland in East Africa. Habitats such as this were becoming increasingly common during the Pleistocene. Credit: Savanna grasslands of East Africa by International Livestock Research Institute (ILRI)/Elsworth is under a CC BY-NC-SA 2.0 License.

Homo habilis: The Earliest Members of Our Genus

Homo habilis has traditionally been considered the earliest species placed in the genus *Homo*. However, as we will see, there is substantial disagreement among paleoanthropologists about the fossils classified as *Homo habilis*, including whether they come from a single species or multiple, or even whether they should be part of the genus *Homo* at all.

Homo habilis has a somewhat larger brain size—an average of 650 cubic centimeters (cc)—compared to *Australopithecus* with less than 500 cc. Additionally, the skull is more rounded and the face less prognathic. However, the postcranial remains show a body size and proportions similar to *Australopithecus*.

Known dates for fossils identified as *Homo habilis* range from about 2.5 million years ago to 1.7 million years ago. Recently, a partial lower jaw dated to 2.8 million years from the site of Ledi-Gararu in Ethiopia has been tentatively identified as belonging to the genus *Homo* (Villmoare et al. 2015). If this classification holds up, it would push the origins of our genus back even further.

Discovery and Naming

The first fossils to be named *Homo habilis* were discovered at the site of Olduvai Gorge in Tanzania, East Africa, by members of a team led by Louis and Mary Leakey (Figure 10.4). The Leakey family had been conducting fieldwork in the area since the 1930s and had discovered other hominin fossils at the site, such as the robust *Paranthropos boisei*. The key specimen, a juvenile individual, was actually found by their 20-year-old son Jonathan Leakey. Louis Leakey invited South African paleoanthropologist Philip Tobias and British anatomist John Napier to reconstruct and analyze the remains. The fossil of the juvenile shown in Figure 10.5 (now known as OH-7) consisted of a lower jaw, parts of the parietal bones of the skull, and some hand and finger bones. The fossil was dated by potassium-argon dating to about 1.75 million years. In 1964, the team published their findings in the scientific journal *Nature* (Leakey et al. 1964). As described in the publication, the new fossils had smaller molar teeth that were less "bulgy" than australopithecine teeth. Although the primary specimen was not yet fully grown, an estimate of its anticipated adult brain size would make it somewhat larger-brained than australopithecines such as *Austalopithecus africanus*. The hand bones were capable of a precision grip like a human's hand. This increased the likelihood that stone tools found earlier at Olduvai Gorge were made by this group of hominins. Based on these findings, the authors inferred that it was a new species that should be classified in the genus *Homo*. They gave it the name *Homo habilis*, meaning "handy" or "skilled."

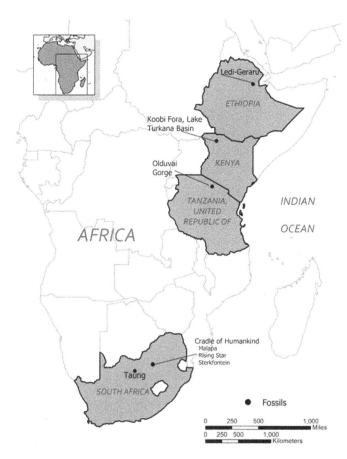

Figure 10.4: Map showing major sites where *Homo habilis* fossils have been found. Ledi-Geraru is located in Ethiopia, Koobi Fora and Lake Turkana Basin are located in Kenya, the Olduvai Gorge is located in Tanzania, and Tuang, Malapa, Rising Star and Sterkfontein are located in South Africa. Credit: *Homo habilis* site map (Figure 10.4) original to *Explorations: An Open Invitation to Biological Anthropology* by Chelsea Barron at GeoPlace, California State University, Chico is under a CC BY-NC 4.0 License.

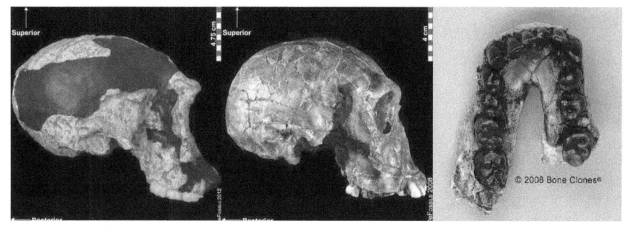

Figure 10.5a-c: Homo habilis fossil specimens. From left to right they are: a. lateral right view of OH-24 (found at Olduvai Gorge), b. lateral right view of KNM-ER-1813 (from Koobi Fora, Kenya), and c. the jaw of OH-7, which was the type specimen found in 1960 at Olduvai Gorge, Tanzania. Credit: a. Homo habilis: OH 24 lateral right view by ©eFossils is under a CC BY-NC-SA 2.0 License and is used as outlined by eFossils. b. Homo habilis: KNM-ER 1813 lateral right view by ©eFossils is under a CC BY-NC-SA 2.0 License and is used as outlined by eFossils. c. Homo habilis OH 7 Jaw by ©BoneClones is used by permission and available here under a CC BY-NC 4.0 License.

Controversies over Classification of *Homo habilis*

Since its initial discovery, many more Homo habilis were discovered in East and South African sites during the 1970s and 1980s (Figure 10.6). As more fossils joined the ranks of *Homo habilis*, several trends became apparent. First, the fossils were quite variable. While some resembled the fossil specimen first published by Leakey and colleagues, others had larger cranial capacity and tooth size. A well-preserved fossil skull from East Lake Turkana labeled KNM-ER-1470 displayed a larger cranial size along with a strikingly wide face. The diversity of the *Homo habilis* fossils prompted some scientists to question whether they displayed too much variation to all belong to the same species. They proposed splitting the fossils into at least two groups. The first group resembling the original small-brained specimen would retain the species name *Homo habilis*; the second group consisting of the larger-brained fossils such as KNM-ER-1470 would be assigned the new name of *Homo rudolfensis* (see Figure 10.7). Researchers who favored keeping all fossils in *Homo habilis* argued that sexual dimorphism, adaptation to local environments, or **developmental plasticity** could be the cause of the differences. For example, modern human body size and body proportions are influenced by variations in climates and nutritional circumstances.

Figure 10.6: Key Homo habilis fossil locations and the corresponding fossils and dates. Credit: Homo habilis table (Figure 10.6) original to Explorations: An Open Invitation to Biological Anthropology by Bonnie Yoshida-Levine is under a CC BY-NC 4.0 License.

Location of Fossils	Dates	Description
Ledi-Gararu, Ethiopia	2.8 mya	Partial lower jaw with evidence of both *Australopithecus* and *Homo* traits; tentatively considered oldest Early *Homo* fossil evidence.
Olduvai Gorge, Tanzania	1.7 mya to 1.8 mya	Several different specimens classified as Homo habilis, including the type specimen found by Leakey, a relatively complete foot, and a skull with a cranial capacity of about 600 cc.
Koobi Fora, Lake Turkana Basin, Kenya	1.9 mya	Several fossils from the Lake Turkana basin show considerable size differences, leading some anthropologists to classify the larger specimen (KNM-ER-1470) as a separate species, *Homo rudolfensis*.
Sterkfontein and other possible South African cave sites	about 1.7 mya	South African caves have yielded fragmentary remains identified as *Homo habilis*, but secure dates and specifics about the fossils are lacking.

Figure 10.7: Cast of the Homo habilis cranium KNM-ER-1470. This cranium has a wide, flat face, larger brain size, and larger teeth than other Homo habilis fossils, leading some scientists to give it a separate species name, Homo rudolfensis. Credit: Homo rudolfensis Cranium KNM-ER 1470 by ©BoneClones is used by permission and available here under a CC BY-NC 4.0 License.

Given the incomplete and fragmentary fossil record from this time period, it is not surprising that classification has proved contentious. As a scholarly consensus has not yet emerged on the classification status of early *Homo*, this chapter makes use of the single (inclusive) *Homo habilis* species designation.

There is also disagreement on whether *Homo habilis* legitimately belongs in the genus *Homo*. Most of the fossils first classified as *Homo habilis* were skulls and teeth. When arm, leg, and foot bones were later found, making it possible to estimate body size, the specimens turned out to be quite small in stature with long arms and short legs. Analysis of the relative strength of limb bones suggested that the species, though bipedal, was much more adapted to arboreal climbing than *Homo erectus* and *Homo sapiens* (Ruff 2009). This has prompted some scientists to assert that *Homo habilis* behaved more like an australopithecine—with a shorter gait and the ability to move around in the trees (Wood and Collard 1999). They were also skeptical of the claim that the brain size of *Homo habilis* was much larger than that of *Australopithecus*. They have proposed reclassifying some or all of the *Homo habilis* fossils into the genus *Australopithecus*, or even placing them into a newly created genus (Wood 2014).

Other scholars have interpreted the fossil evidence differently. A recent reanalysis of *Homo habilis/rudolfensis* fossils concluded that they sort into the genus *Homo* rather than *Australopithecus* (see Hominin Species Summaries at chapter end). In particular, statistical analysis performed indicates that the *Homo habilis* fossils differ significantly in average cranial capacity from the australopithecines. They also note that some australopithecine species such as the recently discovered *Australopithecus sediba* have relatively long legs, so body size may not have been as significant as brain- and tooth-size differences (Anton et al. 2014).

Special Topic: Kamoya Kimeu

Kamoya Kimeu (1938–2022) is arguably the most prolific fossil hunter in the history of paleoanthropology (Figure 10.8). In addition to his many decades of work as a field excavator and project supervisor in East Africa, he also trained field workers and scholars and has served as curator for prehistoric sites for the National Museum of Kenya.

Kamoya Kimeu was born in 1938 in rural southeastern Kenya. Despite a formal education that did not go past the sixth grade, he had an aptitude for languages and familiarity with the plants and animals in the East African bush that led him to a job in Tanzania as a field excavator for Louis and Mary Leakey in 1960. In the years that followed, Kimeu found dozens of major hominin fossils. These included a *Paranthropus boisei* mandible at Olduvai Gorge, *Homo habilis* specimen KNM-ER-1813 from the Turkana Basin (shown in Figure 10.5), and a key early modern *Homo sapiens* fossil from the Omo Valley, Ethiopia. Kimeu's most famous fossil discovery was the skeleton of a young *Homo erectus* by the Nariokotome river bed in 1984. This finding was highly significant because it was a nearly complete early hominin skeleton and provided insight into child development within this species. In recognition of his work, Kimeu was awarded the National Geographic Society La Gorce Medal by U.S. President Ronald Reagan in 1985.

Traditionally, there has been a divide between African field workers and foreign research scientists, who would typically conduct seasonal field work in Africa, then travel back to their home institutions to publish their findings. Although Kimeu received widespread acclaim for the Nariokotome discovery, as well as a personal acknowledgement in the publication of the find in the journal *Nature*, he was not credited as an author. More recently, Kimeu's intellectual contributions to the field of paleoanthropology have been recognized. In 2021, he received an honorary doctorate degree from Case Western Reserve University in Ohio. Kimeu's most lasting legacy may be his mentorship of countless field workers and students. Today, there are a small but growing number of Black African paleoanthropologists taking on principal roles in the science of human origins.

Figure 10.8: Kamoya Kimeu (1938-2022). Credit: Photograph of Kamoya Kimeu by ©Dr. Mark Teaford is used by permission.

Homo habilis Culture and Lifeways

Early Stone Tools

The larger brains and smaller teeth of early *Homo* are linked to a different adaptive strategy than that of earlier hominins: one dependent on modifying rocks to make stone tools and exploit new food sources. As discussed in Chapter 9, the 3.3-million-year-old stone tools from the Lomekwi 3 site in Kenya were made by earlier hominin species than *Homo*. However, stone tools become more frequent at sites dating to about 2 million years ago, the time of *Homo habilis* (Roche et al. 2009). This suggests that these hominins were increasingly reliant on stone tools to make a living.

Stone tools are assigned a good deal of importance in the study of human origins. Examining the form of the tools, the raw materials selected, and how they were made and used can provide insight into the thought processes of early humans and how they modified their environment in order to survive. Paleoanthropologists have traditionally classified collections of stone tools into industries, based on their form and mode of manufacture. There is not an exact correspondence between a tool industry and a hominin species; however, some general associations can be made between tool industries and particular hominins, locations, and time periods.

The **Oldowan** tool industry is named after the site of Olduvai Gorge in Tanzania where the tools were first discovered. The time period of the Oldowan is generally estimated to be 2.5 mya to 1.6 mya. The tools of this industry are described as "flake and chopper" tools—the choppers consisting of stone cobbles with a few flakes struck off them (Figure 10.9). To a casual observer, these tools might not look much different from randomly broken rocks. However, they are harder to make than their crude appearance suggests. The rock selected as the core must be struck by the rock serving as a hammerstone at just the right angle so that one or more flat flakes are removed. This requires selecting rocks that will fracture predictably instead of chunking, as well as the ability to plan ahead and envision the steps needed to create the finished product. The process leaves both the core and the flakes with sharp cutting edges that can be used for a variety of purposes.

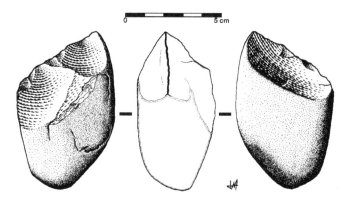

Figure 10.9: Drawing of an Oldowan-style tool. This drawing shows a chopper; the flakes removed from the cores functioned as cutting tools. Credit: **Chopping tool** by José-Manuel Benito Álvarez is under a CC BY-SA 2.5 License.

Stone Tool Use and the Diet of Early *Homo*

What were the hominins doing with the tools? One key activity seems to have been butchering animals. Studies of animal bones at the site show cut marks on bones, and leg bones are often cracked open, suggesting that they were extracting the marrow from the bone cavities. It is interesting to consider whether the hominins hunted these animals or acquired them through other means. The butchered bones come from a variety of African mammals, ranging from small antelope to animals as big as wildebeest and elephants! It is difficult to envision slow, small-bodied *Homo habilis* with their Oldowan tools bringing down such large animals. One possibility is that the hominins were scavenging carcasses from lions and other large cats. Paleoanthropologist Robert Blumenschine has investigated this hypothesis by observing the behavior of present-day animal carnivores and scavengers on the African savanna. When lions abandon a kill after eating their fill, scavenging animals arrive almost immediately to pick apart the carcass. By the time slow-footed hominins arrived on the scene, the carcass would be mostly stripped of meat. However, if hominins could use stone tools to break into the leg bone cavities, they could get to the marrow, a fatty, calorie-dense source of protein (Blumenschine et al. 1987). Reconstructing activities that happened millions of years ago is obviously a difficult undertaking, and paleoanthropologists continue to debate whether scavenging or hunting was more commonly practiced during this time.

Regardless of how they were acquiring the meat, these activities suggest an important dietary shift from the way that the australopithecines were eating. The Oldowan toolmakers were exploiting a new ecological niche that provided them with more protein and calories. And it was not just limited to meat-eating—stone tool use could have made available numerous other subsistence opportunities. A study of microscopic wear patterns on a sample of Oldowan tools indicates that they were used for processing plant materials such as wood, roots or tubers, and grass seeds and stems (Lemorini et al. 2014). In fact, it has been pointed out that the Oldowan toolmakers' cutting ability (whether for the purposes of consuming meat and plants or for making tools, shelters, or clothing) represents a new and unique innovation, never seen before in the natural world (Roche et al. 2009).

Overall, increasing the use of stone tools allowed hominins to expand their ecological niche and exert more control over their environment. As we'll see shortly, this pattern continued and became more pronounced with *Homo erectus*.

Homo erectus: Biological and Cultural Innovations

Two million years ago, a new hominin appeared on the scene. Known as *Homo erectus*, the prevailing scientific view was that this species was much more like us. These hominins were equipped with bigger brains and large bodies with limb proportions similar to our own. Perhaps most importantly, their way of life is now one that is recognizably human, with more advanced tools, hunting, use of fire, and colonizing new environments outside of Africa.

As will be apparent below, new data suggests that the story is not quite as simple. The fossil record for *Homo erectus* is much more abundant than that of *Homo habilis*, but it is also more complex and varied—both with regard to the fossils as well as the geographic context in which they are found. We will first summarize the anatomical characteristics that define *Homo erectus*, and then discuss the fossil evidence from Africa and the primary geographic regions outside Africa where the species has been located.

Homo erectus Anatomy

Compared to *Homo habilis*, *Homo erectus* showed increased brain size, smaller teeth, and a larger body. However, it also displayed key differences from later hominin species including our own. Although the head of *Homo erectus* was less ape-like in appearance than the australopithecines, it did not resemble modern humans (Figure 10.10). Compared to *Homo habilis*, *Homo erectus* had a larger brain size: an average of about 900 cc compared to 650 cc to 750 cc. Instead of a rounded shape like our skulls, the *erectus* skull was long and low like a football, with a receding forehead, and a horizontal ridge called an **occipital torus** that gave the back of the skull a squared-off appearance. The cranial bones are thicker than those of modern humans, and some *Homo erectus* skulls have a slight thickening along the sagittal suture called a **sagittal keel**. Large, shelf-like brow ridges hang over the eyes. The face shows less **prognathism**, and the back teeth are smaller than those of *Homo habilis*. Instead of a pointed chin, like ours, the mandible of *Homo erectus* recedes back.

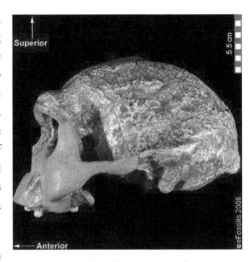

Figure 10.10: Replica of Homo erectus from Java, Indonesia. This cranium (known as Sangiran 17) dates to approximately 1.3 million to 1 million years ago. Note the large brow ridges and the occipital torus that gives the back of the skull a squared-off appearance. Credit: Homo erectus: Sangiran 17 lateral left view by ©eFossils is under a CC BY-NC-SA 2.0 License and is used as outlined by eFossils.

Apart from these features, there is significant variation among *Homo erectus* fossils from different regions. Scientists have long noted differences between the fossils from Africa and those from Indonesia and China. For example, the Asian fossils tend to have a thicker skull and larger brow ridges than the African specimens, and the sagittal keel described above is more pronounced. *Homo erectus* fossils from the Republic of Georgia (described in the next section) also display distinctive characteristics. As with *Homo habilis*, this diversity has prompted a classification debate about whether or not *Homo erectus* should be split into multiple species. When African *Homo erectus* is characterized as a separate species, it is called *Homo ergaster*, while the Asian variant retains the *erectus* species name because it was discovered first. Here, the species name *Homo erectus* will be used for both variants.

Homo erectus was thought to have a body size and proportions more similar to modern humans. Unlike *Homo habilis* and the australopithecines, both of whom were small-statured with long arms and short legs, *Homo erectus* shows evidence of being fully committed to life on the ground. This meant long, powerfully muscled legs that enabled these hominins to cover more ground efficiently. Indeed, studies of the *Homo erectus* body form have linked several characteristics of the species to long-distance running in the more open savanna environment (Bramble and Lieberman 2004). Many experts think that hominins around this time had lost much of their body hair, were particularly efficient at sweating, and had darker-pigmented skin—all traits that would support the active lifestyle of such a large-bodied hominin (see Special Topic box, "How We Became Sweaty, Hairless Primates").

Much of the information about the body form of *Homo erectus* comes from the Nariokotome fossil of the *Homo erectus* youth, described at the beginning of the chapter (see Figure 10.1). However, *Homo erectus* fossils are turning out to be more varied than previously thought. *Homo erectus* fossils from sites in Africa, as well as from Dmanisi, Georgia, show smaller body sizes than the Nariokotome boy. Even the Nariokotome skeleton itself has been reassessed: some now predict he would have been about 5 feet and 4 inches when fully grown rather than over 6 feet as initially hypothesized, although there is still disagreement about which measurement is more accurate. One explanation for the range of body sizes could be adaptation to a range of different local environments, just as humans today show reduced body size in poor nutritional environments (Anton and Snodgrass 2012).

Homo erectus in Africa

Although the earliest discoveries of *Homo erectus* fossils were from Asia, the greatest quantity and best-preserved fossils of the species come from East African sites. The earliest fossils in Africa identified as *Homo erectus* come from the East African site of Koobi Fora, around Lake Turkana in Kenya, and are dated to about 1.8 million years ago. Other fossil remains have been found in East African sites in Kenya, Tanzania, and Ethiopia. Other notable African *Homo erectus* finds are a female pelvis from the site of Gona, Ethiopia (Simpson et al. 2008), and a cranium with massive brow ridges from Olduvai Gorge known as Olduvai 9, thought to be about 1.4 million years old.

Until recently, *Homo erectus*' presence in southern Africa has not been well documented. However, work at the Drimolen cave site in South Africa has yielded new fossils of *Paranthropus robustus*, and the cranium of a 2–3 year old child tentatively identified as *Homo erectus*, dated to about 2 million years (Herries et al. 2020). If substantiated, this would be the oldest discovery to date of *Homo erectus* anywhere.

Regional Discoveries Outside Africa

It is generally agreed that *Homo erectus* was the first hominin to migrate out of Africa and colonize Asia and later Europe (although recent discoveries in Asia may challenge this view). Key locations and discoveries of *Homo erectus* fossils, along with the fossils' estimated ages, are summarized in Figures 10.11 and 10.12.

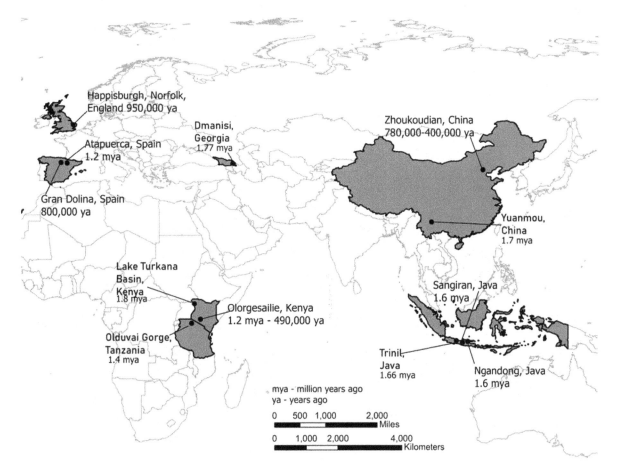

Figure 10.11: Map showing the locations of Homo erectus fossils around Africa and Eurasia. Credit: Homo erectus site map original to Explorations: An Open Invitation to Biological Anthropology by Chelsea Barron at GeoPlace, California State University, Chico is under a CC BY-NC 4.0 License. [Image Description].

Figure 10.12: Regional comparisons of Homo erectus fossils. Credit: Regional comparisons of Homo erectus fossils (Figure 10.12) original to Explorations: An Open Invitation to Biological Anthropology is under a CC BY-NC 4.0 License.

Region	Sites	Dates	Significance of Fossils
East Africa	East and West Lake Turkana, Kenya; Olduvai Gorge, Tanzania	1.8 to 1.4 mya	Earliest evidence of *H. erectus*; significant variation in skull and facial features.
South Africa	Drimolen Cave, South Africa	2 mya	Recent find of a 2–3 year old child would be oldest *H. erectus* anywhere to date.
Western Eurasia	Dmanisi, Republic of Georgia	1.75 mya	Smaller brains and bodies than *H. erectus* from other regions.
Western Europe	Atapuerca, Spain (Sima del Elefante and Gran Dolina caves)	1.2 mya–400,000 ya	Partial jaw from Atapuerca is oldest evidence of *H. erectus* in Western Europe. Fossils from Gran Dolina (dated to about 800,000 years) sometimes referred to as *H. antecessor*.
Indonesia	Ngandong, Java; Sangiran, Java	1.6 mya	Early dispersal of *H. erectus* to East Asia; Asian *H. erectus* features.
China	Zhoukoudian, China; Loess Plateau (Lantian)	780,000–400,000 ya; 2.1 mya	Large sample of *H. erectus* fossils and artifacts. Recent evidence of stone tools from Loess Plateau suggests great antiquity of *Homo* in East Asia.

Indonesia

The first discovery of *Homo erectus* was in the late 1800s in Java, Indonesia. A Dutch anatomist named Eugene Dubois searched for human fossils with the belief that since orangutans lived there, it might be a good place to look for remains of early humans. He discovered a portion of a skull, a femur, and other bone fragments on a riverbank. While the femur looked human, the top of the skull was smaller and thicker than that of a modern person. Dubois named the fossil *Pithecanthropus erectus* ("upright ape-man"), popularized in the media at the time as "Java Man." After later discoveries of similar fossils in China and Africa, they were combined into a single species (retaining the *erectus* name) under the genus *Homo*.

Although *Homo erectus* has a long history in Indonesia, the region's geology has complicated the dating of fossils and sites. Fossils from the Sangiran Dome, Java, had previously been estimated to be as old as 1.8 million years, but scientists using new dating methods have arrived at a later date of about 1.3 mya (Matsu'ura et al. 2020). On the recent end of the timeline, a cache of *H. erectus* fossils from the site of Ngandong in Java has yielded a surprisingly young date of 43,000 years, although a newer study with different dating methods concluded that they were between 117,000 to 108,000 years old (Rizal et al. 2020).

China

There is evidence of *Homo erectus* in China from several regions and time periods. *Homo erectus* fossils from northern China, collectively known as "Peking Man," are some of the most famous human fossils in the world. Dated to about 400,000–700,000 years ago, they were excavated from the site of Zhoukoudian, near the outskirts of Beijing. Hundreds of bones and teeth, including six nearly complete skulls, were excavated from a cave in the 1920s and 1930s. Much of the fossils' fame comes from the fact that they disappeared under mysterious circumstances. As Japan advanced into China during World War II, Chinese authorities, concerned for the security of the fossils, packed up the boxes and arranged for them to be transported to the United States. But in the chaos of the war, they vanished and were never heard about again. Fortunately, an anatomist named Frans Weidenreich had previously studied the bones and made casts and measurements of the skulls, so this valuable information was not lost. More recent excavations at Longgushan "Dragon Bone Cave" at Zhoukoudian—of tools, living sites, and food remains—have revealed much about the lifestyle of *Homo erectus* during this time.

Despite this long history of research, China, compared to Africa, was perceived as somewhat peripheral to the study of hominin evolution. Although *Homo erectus* fossils have been found at several sites in China, with dates that make them comparable to those of Indonesian *Homo erectus*, none seemed to approximate the antiquity of African sites. The notable finds at sites like Nariokotome and Olorgesaille took center stage during the 1970s and 1980s, as scientists focused on elucidating the species' anatomy and adaptations in its African homeland. In contrast, fewer research projects were focused on East Asian sites (Dennell and Roebroeks 2005; Qiu 2016).

However, isolated claims of very ancient hominin occupation kept cropping up from different locations in Asia. While some were dismissed because of problems with dating methods or stratigraphic context, the 2018 publication of the discovery of 2.1-million-year-old stone tools from China caught everyone's attention. Based on paleomagnetic techniques that date the associated soils and windblown dust, these tools indicate that hominins in Asia predated those from the Georgian site of Dmanisi by at least 300,000 years (Zhu et al. 2018). In fact, the tools are older than any *Homo erectus* fossils anywhere. Since no fossils were found with the tools, it isn't known which species made them, but it opens up the intriguing possibility that hominins could have migrated out of Africa earlier than *Homo erectus*. These new discoveries are shaking up previously held views of the East Asian human fossil record.

Western Eurasia

An extraordinary collection of fossils from the site of Dmanisi in the Republic of Georgia has revealed the presence of *Homo erectus* in Western Eurasia between 1.75 million and 1.86 million years ago. Dmanisi is located in the Caucasus mountains in Georgia. When archaeologists began excavating a medieval settlement near the town in the 1980s and came across the bones of extinct animals, they shifted their focus from the historic to the prehistoric era, but they probably did not anticipate going back quite so far in time. The first hominin fossils were discovered in the early 1990s, and since that time, at least five relatively well-preserved crania have been excavated.

There are several surprising things about the Dmanisi fossils. Compared to African *Homo erectus,* they have smaller brains and bodies. However, despite the small brain size, they show clear signs of *Homo erectus* traits such as heavy brow ridges and reduced facial prognathism. Paleoanthropologists have pointed to some aspects of their anatomy (such as the shoulders) that appear rather primitive, although their body proportions seem fully committed to terrestrial bipedalism. One explanation for these differences could be that the Dmanisi hominins represent a very early form of *Homo erectus* that left Africa before increases in brain and body size evolved in the African population.

Second, although the fossils at this location are from the same geological context, they show a great deal of variation in brain size and in facial features. One skull (Skull 5) has a cranial capacity of only 550 cc, smaller than many *Homo habilis* fossils, along with larger teeth and a protruding face. Scientists disagree on what these differences mean. Some contend that the Dmanisi fossils cannot all belong to a single species because each one is so different. Others assert that the variability of the Dmanisi fossils proves that they, along with all early Homo fossils, including *H. habilis* and *H. rudolfensis,* could *all* be grouped into *Homo erectus* (Lordkipanidze et al. 2013). Regardless of which point of view ends up dominating, the Dmanisi hominins are clearly central to the question of how to define the early members of the genus *Homo.*

Europe

Until recently, there was scant evidence of any *Homo erectus* presence in Europe, and it was assumed that hominins did not colonize Europe until much later than East Asia or Eurasia. One explanation for this was that the harsh climate of Western Europe served as a barrier to settlement. However, recent fossil finds from Spain suggest that *Homo erectus* could have made it into Europe over a million years ago. In 2008 a mandible from the Atapuerca region in Spain was discovered, dating to about 1.2 million years ago. A more extensive assemblage of fossils from the site of Gran Dolina in Atapuerca have been dated to about 800,000 years ago. In England in 2013 fossilized hominin footprints of adults and children dated to 950,000 years ago were found at the site of Happisburgh, Norfolk, which would make them the oldest human footprints found outside Africa (Ashton et al. 2014).

At this time, researchers aren't in agreement as to whether the first Europeans belonged to *Homo erectus* proper or to a later descendent species. Some scientists refer to the early fossils from Spain by the species name *Homo antecessor.*

Special Topic: How We Became Hairless, Sweaty Primates

As an anthropology instructor teaching human evolution, my students often ask me about human body hair: When did our ancestors lose it and why? It is assumed that our earliest ancestors were as hairy as modern-day apes. Yet, today, we lack thick hair on most parts of our bodies except in the armpits, pubic regions, and tops of our heads. Humans actually have about the same number of hair follicles per unit of skin as chimpanzees, but, the hairs on most of our body are so thin as to be practically invisible. When did we develop this peculiar pattern of hairlessness? Which selective pressures in our ancestral environment were responsible for this unusual characteristic?

Many experts believe that the driving force behind our loss of body hair was the need to effectively cool ourselves. Along with the lack of hair, humans are also distinguished by being exceptionally sweaty: we sweat larger quantities and more efficiently than any other primate. Humans have a larger amount of eccrine sweat glands than other primates and these glands generate an enormous volume of watery sweat. Sweating produces liquid on the skin that cools the body off as it evaporates. It seems likely that hairlessness and sweating evolved together, as a recent DNA analysis has identified a shared genetic pathway between hair follicles and eccrine sweat gland production (Kamberov et al. 2015).

Which particular environmental conditions led to such adaptations? In this chapter, we learned that the climate was a driving force behind many changes seen in the hominin lineage during the Pleistocene. At that time, the climate was increasingly arid and the forest canopy in parts of Africa was being replaced with a more open grassland environment, resulting in increased sun exposure for our ancestors. Compared to the earlier australopithecines, members of the genus *Homo* were also developing larger bodies and brains, starting to obtain meat by hunting or scavenging carcasses, and crafting sophisticated stone tools.

According to Nina Jablonski, an expert on the evolution of human skin, the loss of body hair and increased sweating capacity are part of the package of traits characterizing the genus *Homo*. While larger brains and long-legged bodies made it possible for humans to cover long distances while foraging, this new body form had to cool itself effectively to handle a more active lifestyle. Preventing the brain from overheating was especially critical. The ability to keep cool may have also enabled hominins to forage during the hottest part of the day, giving them an advantage over savanna predators, like lions, that typically rest during this time (Jablonski 2010).

When did these changes occur? Although hair and soft tissue do not typically fossilize, several indirect methods have been used to explore this question. One method tracks a human skin color gene. Since chimpanzees have light skin under their hair, it is probable that early hominins also had light skin color. Apes and other mammals with thick fur coats have protection against the sun's rays. As our ancestors lost their fur, it is likely that increased melanin pigmentation was selected for as a way to shield our ancestors from harmful ultraviolet radiation. A recent genetic analysis determined that one of the genes responsible for melanin production originated about 1.2 million years ago (Rogers et al 2004).

Another line of evidence tracks the coevolution of a rather unpleasant human companion—the louse. A genetic study identified human body louse as the youngest of the three varieties of lice that infest humans, splitting off as a distinct variety around 70,000 years ago (Kittler et al. 2003). Because human body lice can only spread through clothing, this may have been about the time when humans started to regularly wear clothing. However, the split between human head and pubic lice is estimated to have occurred much earlier, about three million years ago (Bower 2003; Reed et al. 2007). When humans lost much of their body hair, lice that used to roam freely around the body were now confined to two areas: the head and pubic region. As a result of this separation, the lice population split into two distinct groups.

Other explanations have been suggested for the loss of human body hair. For example, being hairless makes it more difficult for skin parasites like lice, fleas, and ticks to live on us. Additionally, after bipedality evolved, hairless bodies would also make reproductive organs and female breasts more visible, suggesting that sexual selection may have played a role.

Homo erectus Lifeways

Now, our examination of *Homo erectus* will turn to its lifeways—how the species utilized its environment in order to survive. This includes making inferences about diet, technology, life history, environments occupied, and perhaps even social organization. As will be apparent, *Homo erectus* shows significant cultural innovations in these areas, some that you will probably recognize as more "human-like" than any of the hominins previously covered.

Tool Technology: Acheulean Tool Industry

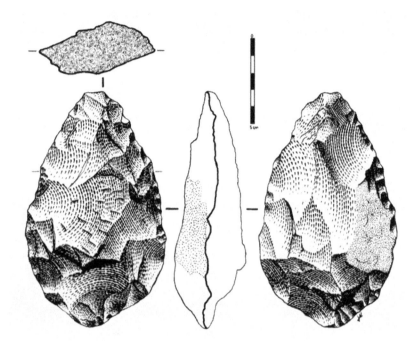

Figure 10.13: Drawing of an Acheulean handaxe. This specimen is from Spain. When drawing a stone tool, artists typically show front and back faces, as well as top and side profiles. Credit: Hand axe spanish by José-Manuel Benito (user: Locutus Borg) has been designated to the public domain (CC0).

In early African sites associated with *Homo erectus*, stone tools such as flakes and choppers identified to the Oldowan Industry dominate. Starting at about 1.5 million years ago, some *Homo erectus* populations began making different forms of tools. These tools—classified together as constituting the **Acheulean** tool industry—are more complex in form and more consistent in their manufacture. Unlike the Oldowan tools, which were cobbles modified by striking off a few flakes, Acheulean toolmakers carefully shaped both sides of the tool. This type of technique, known as bifacial flaking, requires more planning and skill on the part of the toolmaker; he or she would need to be aware of principles of symmetry when crafting the tool. One of the most common tool forms, the handaxe, is shown in Figure 10.13. As with the tool illustrated below, handaxes tend to be thicker at the base and then come to a rounded point at the tip. Besides handaxes, forms such as scrapers, cleavers, and flake tools are present at *Homo erectus* sites.

One striking aspect of Acheulean tools is their uniformity. They are more standardized in form and mode of manufacture than the earlier Oldowan tools. For example, the aforementioned handaxes vary in size, but they are remarkably consistent in regard to their shape and proportions. They were also an incredibly stable tool form over time—lasting well over a million years with little change.

Curiously, the Acheulean tools so prominent at African sites are mostly absent in *Homo erectus* sites in East Asia. Instead, Oldowan-type choppers and scrapers are found at those sites. If this technology seemed to be so important to African *Homo erectus*, why didn't East Asian *Homo erectus* also use the tools? One reason could be environmental differences between the two regions. It has been suggested that *Asian Homo erectus* populations used perishable material such as bamboo to make tools. Another possibility is that *Homo erectus* (or even an earlier hominin) migrated to East Asia before the Acheulean technology developed in Africa. The recent discovery of the 2.1-million-year-old tools in China gives credence to this last explanation.

What (if anything) do the Acheulean tools tell us about the mind of *Homo erectus*? Clearly, they took a fair amount of skill to manufacture. Apart from the actual shaping of the tool, other decisions made by toolmakers can reveal their use of foresight and planning. Did they just pick the most convenient rocks to make their tools, or did they search out a particular raw material that would be ideal for a particular tool? Analysis of Acheulean stone tools suggest that at some sites, the toolmakers selected their raw materials carefully—traveling to particular rock outcrops to quarry stones and perhaps even removing large slabs of rock at the quarries to get at the most desirable material. Such complex activities would require advanced planning and communication with other individuals. However, other *Homo erectus* sites lack evidence of such selectivity; instead of traveling even a short distance for better raw material, the hominins tended to use what was available in their immediate area (Shipton et al. 2018).

In contrast to *Homo erectus* tools, the tools of early modern *Homo sapiens* during the Upper Paleolithic display tremendous diversity across regions and time periods. Additionally, Upper Paleolithic tools and artifacts communicate information such as status and group membership. Such innovation and social signaling seem to have been absent in *Homo erectus*, suggesting that they had a different relationship with their tools than did *Homo sapiens* (Coolidge and Wynn 2017). Some scientists assert that these contrasts in tool form and manufacture may signify key cognitive differences between the species, such as the ability to use a complex language.

Subsistence and Diet

In reconstructing the diet of *Homo erectus*, researchers can draw from multiple lines of evidence. These include stone tools used by *Homo erectus*, animal bones and occasionally plant remains from *Homo erectus* sites, and the bones and teeth of the fossils themselves. These data sources suggest that compared to the australopithecines, *Homo erectus* consumed more animal protein. Coinciding with the appearance of *Homo erectus* fossils in Africa are archaeological sites with much more abundant stone tools and larger concentrations of butchered animal bones.

It makes sense that a larger body and brain would be correlated with a dietary shift to more calorically dense foods. This is because the brain is a very energetically greedy organ. Indeed, our own human brains require more than 20% of one's calorie total intake to maintain. When biologists consider the evolution of intelligence in any animal species, it is often framed as a cost/benefit analysis: For large brains to evolve, there has to be a compelling benefit to having them and a way to generate enough energy to fuel them.

One solution that would allow for an increase in human brain size would be a corresponding reduction in the size of the digestive tract (gut). According to the "expensive tissue hypothesis," initially formulated by Leslie Aiello and Peter Wheeler (1995), a smaller gut would allow for a larger brain without the need for a corresponding increase in the organism's metabolic rate. More meat in the diet could also fuel the larger brain and body size seen in the genus *Homo*. Some researchers also believe that body fat percentages increased in hominins (particularly females) around this time, which would have allowed them to be better buffered against environmental disruption such as food shortages (Anton and Snodgrass 2012).

As indicated above, evidence from archaeology and the inferences about *Homo erectus* body size suggest increased meat eating. How much hunting did *Homo erectus* engage in compared to the earlier Oldowan toolmakers? Although experts continue to debate the relative importance of hunting versus scavenging, there seems to be stronger evidence of hunting for these hominins. For example, at sites such as Olorgesailie in Kenya (Figure 10.14), there are numerous associations of Acheulean tools with butchered remains of large animals.

Figure 10.14: Excavations at the site of Olorgesailie, Kenya. Dated from between 1.2 million years ago and 490,000 years ago, Olorgesailie has some of the most abundant and well-preserved evidence of Homo erectus activity in the world. Fossils of large mammals, such as elephants, along with thousands of Acheulean tools, have been uncovered over the decades. Credit: Elephant Butchery Site Olorgesailie, Kenya by Smithsonian [exhibit: Human Evolution Research, East African Research Projects, Olorgesailie, Kenya] is copyrighted and used for educational and non-commercial purposes as outlined by the Smithsonian.

However, *Homo erectus* certainly ate more than just meat. Studies of the tooth surfaces and microscopic wear patterns on hominin teeth indicate that these hominins ate a variety of foods, including some hard, brittle plant foods (Unger and Scott 2009). This would make sense, considering the environment was changing to be more dominated by grasslands in some areas. Roots, bulbs, and tubers (known as underground storage organs) of open savanna plants may have been a primary food source. Indeed, hunter-gatherer groups such as the Hadza of Tanzania rely heavily on such foods, especially during periods when game is scarce. In the unstable environment of the early Pleistocene, dietary versatility would be a definite advantage.

Tool Use, Cooking, and Fire

One key characteristic of the genus *Homo* is smaller teeth compared to *Australopithecus*. Why would teeth get smaller? In addition to new types of foods, changes in how food was prepared and consumed likely led to a decrease in tooth size. Think about how you would eat if you didn't have access to cutting tools. What you couldn't rip apart with your hands would have to be bitten off with your teeth—actions that would require bigger, more powerful teeth and jaws. As stone tools became increasingly important, hominins began to cut up, tenderize, and process meat and plants, such that they did not have to use their teeth so vigorously.

Cooking food could also have contributed to the reduction in tooth and jaw size. In fact, anthropologist Richard Wrangham (2009) asserts that cooking played a crucial role in human evolution. Cooking provides a head start in the digestive process because of how heat begins to break down food before food even enters the body, and it can help the body extract more nutrients out of meat and plant foods such as starchy tubers.

Obviously cooking requires fire, and the earliest use of fire is a fascinating topic in the study of human evolution. Fire is not only produced by humans; it occurs naturally as a result of lightning strikes. Like other wild animals, early hominins must have been terrified of wildfires, but at some point in time they learned to control fire and put it to good use. Documenting the earliest evidence of fire has been a contentious issue in archaeology because of the difficulty in distinguishing between human-controlled fire and natural burning at hominin sites. Burned areas and ash deposits must have direct associations with human activity to make a case for deliberate fire use. Unfortunately, such evidence is rare at ancient hominin sites, which have been profoundly altered by humans, animals, and geological forces over millions of years. Recently, newer methods—including microscopic analysis of burned rock and bone—have revealed clear evidence of fire use at Koobi Fora, Kenya, dating to 1.5 million years ago (Hlubik et al. 2017).

Migration Out of Africa

Homo erectus is generally thought to be the first hominin species to have left Africa. It is hypothesized that they settled in places in Eurasia, such as the Republic of Georgia, Indonesia, and northern China, where fossil evidence of *Homo erectus* exists. But why would this species have traveled such vast distances to these far-flung regions? To answer this question, we have to consider what we have learned about the biology, culture, and environmental circumstances of *Homo erectus*. The larger brain and body size of *Homo erectus* were fueled by a diet consisting of more meat, and their longer, more powerful legs made it possible to walk and run longer distances to acquire food. Since they were eating higher on the food chain, it was necessary for them to extend their home range to find sufficient game. Cultural developments—including better stone tools and new technology such as fire—gave them greater flexibility in adapting to different environments. Finally, the major Pleistocene climate shift discussed earlier in the chapter certainly played a role. Changes in air temperature, precipitation, access to water sources, and other habitat alteration had far-reaching effects on animal and plant communities; this included *Homo erectus*. If hominins were relying more on hunting, the migration patterns of their prey could have led them to traverse increasingly long distances.

Life History

The **life history** of a species refers to its overall pattern of growth, development, and reproduction during its lifetime, with the assumption that these characteristics have been shaped by natural selection. The field of **human behavioral ecology**, explored in more detail in Appendix C, examines the roots of human behavior and life history. Our species, *Homo sapiens*, is characterized by a unique life history pattern of slow development, an extended period of juvenile dependence, and a long lifespan. Whereas the offspring of great apes achieve self-sufficiency early, human children are dependent on their parents long after weaning. Additionally, human fathers and grandparents (particularly postmenopausal grandmothers) devote substantial time and energy to caring for their children.

Figure 10.15: Hadza men practice bowing. Native to Tanzania, the Hadza have retained many traditional foraging practices. Although most do not subsist entirely upon wild foods today, their way of life may shed light on how humans lived for most of their evolutionary history. Credit: Hadzabe1 by Idobi is under a CC BY-SA 3.0 License.

Human behavioral ecologists who study modern hunter-gatherer societies have observed that foraging is no easy business (Figure 10.15). Members of these groups engage in complex foraging techniques that take many years to master. An extended juvenile period gives children the time to acquire these skills. It also allows time for large human brains to grow and mature. On the back end, a longer developmental period results in skilled, successful adults, capable of living a long time (Hill and Kaplan 1999). Despite the time and energy demands, females could have offspring at more closely spaced intervals if they could depend on help from fathers and grandmothers (Hawkes et al. 1998).

What can the study of *Homo erectus* reveal about its life history pattern? Well-preserved fossils such as the Nariokotome boy can provide some insights. We know that apes such as chimpanzees reach maturity more quickly than humans, and there is some evidence that the australopithecines had a growth rate more akin to that of chimpanzees. Scientists have conducted extensive studies of the Nariokotome skeleton's bones and teeth to assess growth and development. On the one hand, examination of the long bone ends (epiphyses) of the skeleton suggested that he was an early adolescent with a relatively large body mass, though growth had not yet been completed. On the other hand, study of the dentition, including measurement of microscopic layers of tooth enamel called **perikymata**, revealed a much younger age of 8 or 9. According to Christopher Dean and Holly Smith (2009), the best explanation for this discrepancy between the dental and skeletal age is that *Homo erectus* had its own distinct growth pattern—reaching maturity more slowly than chimpanzees but faster than *Homo sapiens*. This suggests that the human life history pattern of slow maturation and lengthy dependency was a more recent development. More work remains on refining this pattern for early *Homo*, but it is an important topic that sheds light on how and when we developed our unique life history characteristics.

The Big Picture of Early *Homo*

We are discovering that the evolution of the genus *Homo* is more complex than what was previously thought. The earlier view of a simple progression from *Australopithecus* to *Homo habilis* to *Homo erectus* as clearly delineated stages in human evolution just doesn't hold up anymore.

As is apparent from the information presented here, there is tremendous variability during this time. While fossils classified as *Homo habilis* show many of the characteristics of the genus *Homo*, such as brain expansion and smaller tooth size, the small body size and long arms are more akin to australopithecines. There is also tremendous variability within the fossils assigned to *Homo habilis*, so there is little consensus on whether it is one or multiple species of *Homo*, a member of the genus *Australopithecus*, or even a yet-to-be-defined new genus. Similarly, there are considerable differences in skull morphology and body size and form of *Homo erectus*, of which some specimens show more similarity to *Homo habilis* than previously thought.

What does this diversity mean for how we should view early *Homo*? First, there isn't an abrupt break between *Australopithecus* and *Homo habilis* or even between *Homo habilis* and *Homo erectus*. Characteristics we define as *Homo* don't appear as a unified package; they appear in the fossil record at different times. This is known as **mosaic evolution**. Indeed, fossil species such as *Australopithecus sediba*, as well as *Homo naledi* and *Homo floresiensis* (who will be introduced in Chapter 11), have displayed unexpected combinations of primitive and derived traits.

We can consider several explanations for the diversity we see within early *Homo* from about 2.5 million to 1.5 million years ago. One possibility is the existence of multiple contemporaneous species of early *Homo* during this period. In light of the pattern of environmental instability discussed earlier, it shouldn't be surprising to see fossils from different parts of Africa and Eurasia display tremendous variability. Multiple hominin forms could also evolve in the same region, as they diversified in order to occupy different ecological niches. However, even the presence of multiple species of hominin does not preclude their interacting and interbreeding with one another. As you'll see in Appendix D, sequencing of ancient hominin genomes has led to deeper understanding of genetic relationships between extinct species such as the Neanderthals and Denisovans.

Diversity of brain and body sizes could also reflect developmental plasticity—short-term adaptations within a lifetime (Anton et al. 2014). These have the advantage of being more flexible than genetic natural selection, which could only occur over many generations. For example, among human populations today, different body sizes are thought to be adaptations to different climate or nutritional environments. Under Pleistocene conditions of intense variability, a more flexible strategy of adaptation would be valuable.

New discoveries are also questioning old assumptions about the behavior of *Homo habilis* and *Homo erectus*. Just as the fossil evidence doesn't neatly separate *Australopithecus* and *Homo*, evidence of the lifeways of early *Homo* show similar diversity. For example, one of the traditional dividing lines between *Homo* and *Australopithecus* was thought to be stone tools: *Homo* made them; *Australopithecus* didn't. However, the recent discovery of stone tools from Kenya dating to 3.3 million years ago challenges this point of view. Similarly, the belief that *Homo erectus* was the first species to settle outside Africa may now come into question with the report of 2.1-million-year-old stone tools from China. If this find is supported by additional evidence, it may cause a reevaluation of *Homo erectus* being the first to leave Africa. Instead, there could have been multiple earlier migrations of hominins such as *Homo habilis* or even *Australopithecus* species.

These various lines of evidence about the genus *Homo* point out the need for a more nuanced view of this period of human evolution. Rather than obvious demarcations between species and their corresponding behavioral advancements, it now looks like many behaviors were shared among species. Earlier hominins that we previously didn't think had the capability could have been doing things like expanding out of Africa or using stone tools. Meanwhile, some other hominins that we had considered more advanced didn't actually have the full suite of "human" characteristics previously expected.

From a student's perspective, all this complexity probably seems frustrating. It would be ideal if the human story were a straightforward, sequential narrative. Unfortunately, it seems that human evolution was not a nice, neat trajectory of increasingly humanlike traits and behaviors; rather, it is emblematic of the untidy but exciting nature of the study of human evolution.

Despite some haziness dominating the early *Homo* narrative, we can identify some overall trends for the million-year period associated with early *Homo*. These trends include brain expansion, a reduction in facial prognathism, smaller jaw and tooth size, larger body size, and evidence of full terrestrial bipedalism. These traits are associated with a key behavioral shift that emphasizes culture as a flexible strategy to adapt to unpredictable environmental circumstances. Included in this repertoire are the creation and use of stone tools to process meat obtained by scavenging and later hunting, a utilization of fire and cooking, and the roots of the human life history pattern of prolonged childhood, cooperation in child raising, and the practice of skilled foraging techniques. In fact, it's apparent that the cultural innovations are driving the biological changes, and vice versa, fueling a feedback loop that continues during the later stages of human evolution.

Hominin Species Summaries

Hominin	*Homo habilis*
Dates	2.5 million years ago to 1.7 million years ago
Region(s)	East and South Africa
Famous discoveries	Olduvai Gorge, Tanzania; Koobi Fora, Kenya; Sterkfontein, South Africa
Brain size	650 cc average (range from 510 cc to 775 cc)
Dentition	Smaller teeth with thinner enamel compared to *Australopithecus*; parabolic dental arcade shape
Cranial features	Rounder cranium and less facial prognathism than *Australopithecus*
Postcranial features	Small stature; similar body plan to *Australopithecus*
Culture	Oldowan tools
Other	N/A

Hominin	*Homo erectus*
Dates	1.8 million years ago to about 110,000 years ago
Region(s)	East and South Africa; West Eurasia; China and Southeast Asia
Famous discoveries	Lake Turkana, Olorgesailie, Kenya; Java, Indonesia; Zhoukoudian, China; Dmanisi, Republic of Georgia
Brain size	Average 900 cc; range between 650 cc and 1,100 cc
Dentition	Smaller teeth than *Homo habilis*
Cranial features	Long, low skull with robust features including thick cranial vault bones and large brow ridge, sagittal keel, and occipital torus
Postcranial features	Larger body size compared to *Homo habilis*; body proportions (longer legs and shorter arms) similar to *Homo sapiens*
Culture	Acheulean tools (in Africa); evidence of increased hunting and meat-eating; use of fire; migration out of Africa
Other	N/A

Review Questions

- Describe the climate during the early Pleistocene. Explain why climate is important for understanding the evolution of early *Homo*.
- List the key anatomical characteristics that are generally agreed to define the genus *Homo*.
- Why has classification of early *Homo* fossils proved difficult? What are some explanations for the variability seen in these fossils?
- Compare and contrast the Oldowan and Acheulean tool industries.
- Name some specific behaviors associated with *Homo erectus* in the areas of tool use, subsistence practices, migration patterns, and other cultural innovations.

Key Terms

Acheulean: Tool industry characterized by teardrop-shaped stone handaxes flaked on both sides.

Developmental plasticity: The capability of an organism to modify its phenotype during development in response to environmental cues.

Human behavioral ecology: The study of human behavior from an evolutionary and ecological perspective.

Life history: The broad pattern of a species' life cycle, including development, reproduction, and longevity.

Mosaic evolution: Different characteristics evolve at different rates and appear at different stages.

Occipital torus: A ridge on the occipital bone in the back of the skull.

Oldowan: Earliest stone-tool industry consisting of simple flakes and choppers.

Perikymata: Microscopic ridges on the surface of tooth enamel that serve as markers of tooth development.

Pleistocene: Geological epoch dating from 2.6 million years ago to about 11,000 years ago.

Pliocene: Geological epoch dating from 5.3 to 2.6 million years ago.

Prognathism: Condition where the lower face and jaw protrude forward from a vertical plane.

Sagittal keel: A thickened area along the top of the skull.

About the Author

Bonnie Yoshida-Levine, Ph.D.

Grossmont College, bonnie.yoshida@gcccd.edu

Bonnie Yoshida-Levine is an instructor of anthropology at Grossmont College, where she teaches biological anthropology and archaeology. She received her bachelor's degree in history from the University of California, Los Angeles, and her M.A. and Ph.D. degrees in anthropology from the University of California, Santa Barbara. Her dissertation research focused on the bioarchaeology of early civilizations in north coastal Peru. Bonnie has also collaborated on archaeological field projects in Bolivia and coastal California.

For Further Exploration

Boaz, Noel Thomas, and Russell L. Ciochon. 2004. *Dragon Bone Hill: An Ice-Age Saga of* Homo erectus. New York: Oxford University Press.

Human Evolution by the Smithsonian Institution. Produced by the Smithsonian National Museum of Natural History, this website covers many aspects of human evolution including 3-D models of hominin fossils.

Lewin, Roger, and Robert A. Foley. 2004. *Principles of Human Evolution*. Oxford, UK: Blackwell Publishing.

Mutu, Kari. "Honour Finds Kenya's Oldest Fossil Hunter Kamoya Kimeu." *The East African*, July 19, 2021.

Nordling, Linda. "Raising Up African Paleoanthropologists." *SAPIENS*, September 28, 2021. Accessed February 24, 2023. *https://www.sapiens.org/ biology/african-paleoanthropologists/*.

Risen, Clay. "Kamoya Kimeu, Fossil-Hunting 'Legend' in East Africa Is Dead." *New York Times*, August 11, 2022. Accessed February 24, 2023. https://www.nytimes.com/2022/08/11/science/kamoya-kimeu-dead.html/.

Stoneking, Mark. 2015. "Of Lice and Men: The Molecular Evolution of Human Lice." Lecture, Center for Academic Research & Training in Anthropogeny, San Diego, California, October 16, 2015. Accessed February 24, 2023. https://carta.anthropogeny.org/events/unique-features-human-skin.

Tarlach, Gemma. 2015. "The First Humans to Know Winter." *Discover*, February 26. https://www.discovermagazine.com/planet-earth/the-first-humans-to-know-winter

Ungar, Peter S. 2017. *Evolution's Bite: A Story of Teeth, Diet, and Human Origins*. Princeton, NJ: Princeton University Press.

References

Aiello, Leslie C., and Peter Wheeler. 1995. "The Expensive-Tissue Hypothesis." *Current Anthropology* 36 (2): 199–221.

Anton, Susan C., Richard Potts, and Leslie C. Aiello. 2014. "Evolution of Early *Homo*: An Integrated Biological Perspective." *Science* 345 (6192) doi: 10.1126/science.1236828.

Anton, Susan C., and J. Josh Snodgrass. 2012. "Origins and Evolution of Genus *Homo*: New Perspectives." *Current Anthropology* 53 (S6): S479–S496.

Ashton, Nick, Simon G. Lewis, Isabelle De Groote, Sarah M. Duffy, Martin Bates, Richard Bates, Peter Hoare, et al. 2014. "Hominin Footprints from Early Pleistocene Deposits at Happisburgh, UK." *PLOS ONE* 9 (2): e88329.

Belmaker, Miriam. 2010. "Early Pleistocene Faunal Connections between Africa and Eurasia: An Ecological Perspective." In *Out of Africa I: The First Hominin Colonization of Eurasia*, edited by John G. Fleagle, John J. Shea, Frederick E. Grine, Andrea L. Baden, and Richard E. Leakey, 183–205. Dordrecht: Springer Netherlands.

Blumenschine, Robert, Henry T. Bunn, Valerius Geist, Fumiko Ikawa-Smith, Curtis W. Marean, Anthony G. Payne, John Tooby, J. Nikolaas, and Van Der Merwe. 1987. "Characteristics of an Early Hominid Scavenging Niche [and Comments and Reply]." *Current Anthropology* 28 (4): 383–407.

Bower, Bruce. 2004. "Evolution's Buggy Ride." *Science News* 166 (15): 230–230.

Bramble, Dennis M., and Daniel E. Lieberman. 2004. "Endurance Running and the Evolution of *Homo*." *Nature* 432 (7015): 345–352.

Coolidge, Frederick L., and Thomas Grant Wynn. 2017. *The Rise of Homo Sapiens: The Evolution of Modern Thinking*. New York: Oxford University Press.

Dean, M. Christopher, and B. Holly Smith. 2009. "Growth and Development of the Nariokotome Youth, KNM-WT 15000." In *The First Humans–Origin and Early Evolution of the Genus Homo: Contributions from the Third Stony Brook Human Evolution Symposium and Workshop October 3–7, 2006*, edited by Frederick E. Grine, John G. Fleagle, and Richard E. Leakey, 101–120. Dordrecht: Springer Netherlands.

deMenocal, Peter B. 2014. "Climate Shocks." *Scientific American* 311 (3): 48–53.

Dennell, Robin, and Wil Roebroeks. 2005. "An Asian Perspective on Early Human Dispersal from Africa." *Nature* 438 (7071): 1099–1104.

Hawkes, Kristen, James F. O'Connell, Nicholas G. Blurton Jones, Helen Alvarez, and Eric L. Charnov. 1998. "Grandmothering, Menopause, and the Evolution of Human Life Histories." *Proceedings of the National Academy of Sciences* 95 (3): 1336–1339.

Herries, A. I. R., J. M. Martin, A. B. Leece, J. W. Adams, G. Boschian, R. Joannes-Boyau, T. R. Edwards, et al. 2020. "Contemporaneity of *Australopithecus*, *Paranthropus*, and early *Homo erectus* in South Africa." *Science* 368 (6486). https://doi.org/10.1126/science.aaw7293

Hill, Kim, and Hillard Kaplan. 1999. "Life History Traits in Humans: Theory and Empirical Studies." *Annual Review of Anthropology* 28: 397–430.

Hlubik, Sarah, Francesco Berna, Craig Feibel, David Braun, and John W. K. Harris. 2017. "Researching the Nature of Fire at 1.5 Mya on the Site of FxJj20 AB, Koobi Fora, Kenya, Using High-Resolution Spatial Analysis and FTIR Spectrometry." *Current Anthropology* 58 (S16): S243–S257.

Jablonski, Nina G. 2010. "The Naked Truth." *Scientific American* 302 (2): 42–49.

Kamberov, Yana G., Elinor K. Karlsson, Gerda L. Kamberova, Daniel E. Lieberman, Pardis C. Sabeti, Bruce A. Morgan, and Clifford J. Tabin. 2015. "A Genetic Basis of Variation in Eccrine Sweat Gland and Hair Follicle Density." *Proceedings of the National Academy of Sciences* 112 (32): 9932–9937.

Kittler, R., M. Kayser, and M. Stoneking. 2003. "Molecular Evolution of Pediculus Humanus and the Origin of Clothing." *Current Biology* 13 (16): 1414–1417.

Leakey, Louis S. B., Phillip V. Tobias, and John R. Napier. 1964. "A New Species of Genus *Homo* from Olduvai Gorge." *Nature* 202: 308–312.

Lemorini, Cristina, Thomas W. Plummer, David R. Braun, Alyssa N. Crittenden, Peter W. Ditchfield, Laura C. Bishop, Fritz Hertel, et al. 2014. "Old Stones' Song: Use-Wear Experiments and Analysis of the Oldowan Quartz and Quartzite Assemblage from Kanjera South (Kenya)." *Journal of Human Evolution* 72: 10–25.

Lisiecki, Lorraine E., and Maureen E. Raymo. 2005. "A Pliocene-Pleistocene stack of 57 globally distributed benthic δ18O records." *Paleoceanography* 20 (1)

Lordkipanidze, David, Marcia S. Ponce de León, Ann Margvelashvili, Yoel Rak, G. Philip Rightmire, Abesalom Vekua, and Christoph P. E. Zollikofer. 2013. "A Complete Skull from Dmanisi, Georgia, and the Evolutionary Biology of Early *Homo*." *Science* 342 (6156): 326–333.

Matsu'ura, S., M. Kondo, T. Danhara, S. Sakata, H. Iwano, T. Hirata, I. Kurniawan, et al. 2020. "Age Control of the First Appearance Datum for Javanese *Homo erectus* in the Sangiran Area." *Science* 367 (6474): 210–214.

Qiu, Jane. 2016. "How China Is Rewriting the Book on Human Origins." *Nature* 535: 22–25.

Reed, David L., Jessica E. Light, Julie M. Allen, and Jeremy J. Kirchman. 2007. "Pair of Lice Lost or Parasites Regained: The Evolutionary History of Anthropoid Primate Lice." *BMC Biology* 5 (1): 7. doi: 10.1186/1741-7007-5-7.

Rizal, Y., K. E. Westaway, Y. Zaim, G. D. van den Bergh, E. A. Bettis, 3rd, M. J. Morwood, O. F. Huffman, R. Grün, et al. 2020. "Last Appearance of *Homo erectus* at Ngandong, Java, 117,000–108,000 Years Ago." *Nature* 577 (7790): 381–385.

Roche, Helene, Robert J. Blumenschine, and John J. Shea. 2009. "Origins and Adaptations of Early *Homo*: What Archeology Tells Us." In *The First Humans: Origin and Early Evolution of the Genus Homo*, edited by Frederick E. Grine, John G. Fleagle, and Richard E. Leakey, 135–147. New York: Springer.

Rogers, Alan R., David Iltis, and Stephen Wooding. 2004. "Genetic Variation at the MC1R l Locus and the Time since Loss of Human Body
Hair." *Current Anthropology* 45 (1): 105–108.

Ruff, Christopher. 2009. "Relative Limb Strength and Locomotion in *Homohabilis*." *American Journal of Physical Anthropology* 138 (1): 90–100.

Shipton, Ceri, James Blinkhorn, Paul S. Breeze, Patrick Cuthbertson, Nick Drake, Huw S. Groucutt, Richard P. Jennings, et al. 2018. "Acheulean Technology and Landscape Use at Dawadmi, Central Arabia." *PloS one* 13 (7): e0200497–e0200497.

Simpson, Scott W., Jay Quade, Naomi E. Levin, Robert Butler, Guillaume Dupont-Nivet, Melanie Everett, and Sileshi Semaw. 2008. "A Female *Homoerectus* Pelvis from Gona, Ethiopia." *Science* 322 (5904): 1089–1092.

Ungar, Peter S., and Robert S. Scott. 2009. "Dental Evidence for Diets of Early *Homo*." In *The First Humans: Origin and Early Evolution of the Genus Homo*, edited by Frederick E. Grine, John G. Fleagle, and Richard E. Leakey, 121–134. New York: Springer.

Villmoare, Brian, William H. Kimbel, Chalachew Seyoum, Christopher J. Campisano, Erin N. DiMaggio, John Rowan, David R. Braun, J. Ramón Arrowsmith, and Kaye E. Reed. 2015. "Early *Homo* at 2.8 Ma From Ledi-Geraru, Afar, Ethiopia." *Science* 347 (6228): 1352–1355.

Wood, Bernard. 2014. "Human Evolution: Fifty Years after *Homohabilis*." *Nature* 508 (7494): 31–33.

Wood, Bernard, and Mark Collard. 1999. "The Changing Face of Genus *Homo*." *Evolutionary Anthropology* 8 (6): 195–207.

Wrangham, Richard. 2009. *Catching Fire: How Cooking Made Us Human*. New York: Basic Books.

Zhu, Zhaoyu, Robin Dennell, Weiwen Huang, Yi Wu, Shifan Qiu, Shixia Yang, and Zhiguo Rao. 2018. "Hominin Occupation of the Chinese Loess Plateau Since about 2.1 Million Years Ago." *Nature* 559: 608–612.

Acknowledgments

The author gratefully acknowledges funding from the California Community Colleges Chancellor's Office Zero Textbook Cost Degree Grant Program—Implementation Phase 2.

Image Description

Figure 10.11: Map showing the locations of Homo erectus fossils around Africa and Eurasia. These include: Happisburgh, Norfolk, English dated to 950,000 ya; Atapuerca, Spain dated to 1.2mya; Gran Dolina, Spain dated to 800,000 ya; Dmanisi, Georgia dated to 1.77 mya; Lake Turkana Basin, Kenya dated to 1.8mya; Olduvai Gorge, Tanzania dated to 1.4mya; Olorgesailie, Kenya dated to 1.2mya to 490,000ya; Zhoukoudian, China dated to 780,000ya to 400,000ya; Yuanmou, China dated to 1.7mya; Sangiran, Java dated to 1.6mya; Trinil, Java dated to 1.66mya; Ngandona, Lava dated to 1.66 mya.

11.

ARCHAIC HOMO

Amanda Wolcott Paskey, M.A., Cosumnes River College

AnnMarie Beasley Cisneros, M.A., American River College

This chapter is a revision from "Chapter 11: Archaic Homo" by Amanda Wolcott Paskey and AnnMarie Beasley Cisneros. In Explorations: An Open Invitation to Biological Anthropology, first edition, edited by Beth Shook, Katie Nelson, Kelsie Aguilera, and Lara Braff, which is licensed under CC BY-NC 4.0.

Learning Objectives

- Identify the main groupings of Archaic *Homo sapiens*, such as Neanderthals.
- Explain how shifting environmental conditions required flexibility of adaptations, both anatomically and behaviorally.
- Describe the unique anatomical and cultural characteristics of Archaic *Homo sapiens*, including Neanderthals, in contrast to other hominins.
- Articulate how Middle Pleistocene hominin fossils fit into evolutionary trends including cranial capacity (brain size) development, cultural innovations, and migration patterns.
- Identify the shared traits, regional variations, and local adaptations among Archaic *Homo sapiens*.
- Detail the increased complexity and debates surrounding the classification of hominins in light of transitional species, species admixture, etc.

Breaking the Stigma of the "Caveman"

What do you think of when you hear the word "caveman"? Perhaps you imagine a character from a film such as *The Croods*, *Tarzan*, and *Encino Man* or from the cartoon *The Flintstones*. Maybe you picture the tennis-playing, therapy-going hairy Neanderthals from Geico Insurance commercials. Or perhaps you imagine characters from *The Far Side* or *B.C.* comics. Whichever you picture, the character in your mind is likely stooped over with a heavy brow, tangled long locks and other body hair, and clothed in animal skins, if anything. They might be holding a club with a confused look on their face, standing at the entrance to a cave or dragging an animal carcass to a fire for their next meal (see Figure 11.1). You might have even signed up to take this course because of what you knew—or expected to learn—about "cavemen."

These images have long been the stigma and expectation about our ancestors at the transition to modern *Homo sapiens*. Tracing back to works as early as Carl Linnaeus, scientists once propagated and advanced this imagery, creating a clear picture in the minds of early scholars that informed the general public, even through today, that Archaic *Homo sapiens*, "cavemen," were somehow fundamentally different and much less intelligent than we are now. Unfortunately, this view is overly simplistic, misleading, and incorrect. Understanding what Archaic *Homo sapiens* were actually like requires a much more complex and nuanced picture, one that comes into sharper focus as continuing research uncovers more about the lives of our not-too-distant (and not-too-different) ancestors.

The first characterizations of Archaic *Homo sapiens* were formed from limited fossil evidence in a time when **ethnocentric** and species-centric perspectives (**anthropocentrism**) were more widely accepted and entrenched in both society and science. Today, scientists are working from a more complete fossil record from three continents (Africa, Asia, and Europe), and genetic evidence informs their analyses and conclusions. The existence of Archaic *Homo sapiens* marks an exciting point in our lineage—a point at which many modern traits had emerged and key refinements were on the horizon. Anatomically, humans today are not that much different from Archaic *Homo sapiens*.

Figure 11.1: Popular perceptions of human ancestors at the transition to modern Homo sapiens often take the form of the stereotypical, and inaccurate, "caveman." Credit: Big head primitive caveman nose man bone cave at Max Pixel has been designated to the public domain (CC0).

This chapter will examine how the environment with which Archaic *Homo sapiens* had to contend shaped their biological and cultural evolution. It will also examine the key anatomical traits that define this group of fossils, focusing on the most well-known of them, including Neanderthals. The chapter will describe cultural innovations that aided their adaptation to the changing environment, as well as their geographic distribution and regional variations. Additionally, exciting new research is examined that suggests even greater nuance and complexity during this time period.

The Changing Environment

While modern climate change is of critical concern today due to its cause (human activity) and pace (unprecedentedly rapid), the existence of global climate change itself is not a recent phenomenon. The focus of this chapter, the Middle Pleistocene (roughly between 780 kya and 125 kya), is the time period in which Archaic *Homo sapiens* appears in the fossil record—a time that witnessed some of the most drastic climatic changes in human existence. During this time period, there were 15 major and 50 minor glacial events in Europe, alone.

What exactly is **glaciation**? When scientists talk about glacial events, they are referring to the climate being in an ice age. This means that the ocean levels were much lower than today, because much of the earth's water was tied up in large glaciers or ice sheets. Additionally, the average temperature would have been much cooler, which would have better supported an Arctic or tundra-adapted plant-and-animal ecosystem in northern latitudes. The most interesting and relevant features of Middle Pleistocene glacial events are the sheer number of them and their repeated bouts: this era alternated between glacial periods and warmer periods, known as **interglacials**. In other words, the planet wasn't in an ice age the whole time.

You can see the dramatic and increasing fluctuations in temperature, recorded through **foraminifera**, in Figure 11.2. The distance between highs and lows demonstrates the severity of temperature shifts. Much as the Richter scale represents more intense earthquakes with more dramatic peaks, so too does this chart, which uses dramatic peaks to demonstrate intense temperature swings.

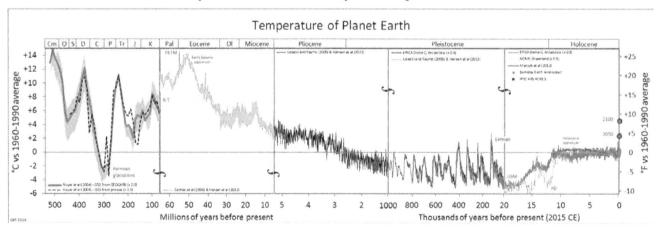

Figure 11.2: The Geologic Timescale and corresponding temperature shifts. Wide and rapid shifts took place during the Pleistocene (the second box from the right). More dramatic fluctuations depict greater severity of temperature shift. The Eocene, Pliocene, and Holocene epochs had more stable temperatures. Credit: All paleotemps by Glen Fergus is under a CC BY-SA 3.0 License.

Glacial periods are defined by Earth's average temperature being lower. Worldwide, temperatures are reduced, with cold areas becoming even colder. Huge portions of the landscape may have become inaccessible during glacial events due to the formation of glaciers and massive ice sheets. In

Europe, the Scandinavian continental glacier covered what is today Ireland, England, Sweden, Norway, Denmark, and some of continental Europe. Plant and animal communities shifted to lower latitudes along the periphery of ice sheets. Additionally, some new land was opened during glacials. Evaporation with little runoff reduced sea levels by as much as almost 150 meters, shifting coastlines outward by in some instances as much as almost 100 kilometers. Additionally, land became exposed that connected what were previously unconnected continents such as Africa into Yemen at the Gulf of Aden.

Glacial periods also affected equatorial regions and other regions that are today thought of as warmer or at least more temperate parts of the globe, including Africa. While these areas were not covered with glaciers, increased global glaciation resulted in lower sea levels and expanded coastlines. Cooler temperatures were accompanied by the drying of the climate, which caused significantly reduced rainfall, increased aridity, and the expansion of deserts. It is an interesting question to consider whether the same plants and animals that lived in these regions prior to the ice ages would be able to survive and thrive in this new climate. Plant and animal communities shifted in response to the changing climate, whenever possible.

Surviving During the Middle Pleistocene

Rather than a single selective force, the Middle Pleistocene was marked by periods of fluctuation, not just cold periods. Interglacials interrupted glaciations, reversing trends in sea level, coastline, temperature, precipitation, and aridity, as well as glacier size and location. Interglacials are marked by increased rainfall and a higher temperature, which causes built-up ice in glaciers to melt. This leads to glacial retreat, which is the shrinking of glaciers and the movement of the glaciers back toward the poles, as we've seen in our lifetime. During interglacials, sea levels increase, flooding some previously exposed coastlines and continental connections. In addition, plant and animal communities shift accordingly, often finding more temperate climates to the north and less arid and more humid climates in the tropics (Van Andel and Tzedakis 1996).

Scientists have found that the Olorgesailie region in southern Kenya was at various times in the Middle Pleistocene a deep lake, a drought-dried lakebed with an area criss-crossed by small streams, and a grassland. While various animal species would have moved in and out of the area as the climate shifted, some animal species went extinct, and new, often related, species took up residence. The trend, scientists noted, was that animals with more specialized features went extinct and animals with more generalized features, such as animals we see today, survived in this changing climatic time period. For example, a zebra with specialized teeth for eating grass was ultimately replaced by a zebra that could eat both grass and other types of vegetation. If this small, localized example shows such a dramatic change in terms of the environment and the plant and animal biocommunities, what would have been the impact on humans?

There is no way humans could have escaped the effects of Middle Pleistocene climate change, no matter what region of the world they were living in. As noted earlier, and as evidenced by what was seen in the other biotic communities, humans would have faced changing food sources as previous sources of food may have gone extinct or moved to a different latitude. Depending on where they were living, fresh water may have been limited. Durial glacials, lower sea levels would have given humans more land to live on, while the interglacials would have reduced the available land through the increase in rainfall and associated sea level rise. Dry land connections between the continents would have made movement from one continent to another by foot easier at times than today, although these passageways were not consistently available through the Middle Pleistocene due to the glacial/interglacial cycle. Finally, as evidenced by the Olorgesailie region in Kenya, during the Middle Pleistocene animal species that were overly specialized to one particular type of environment were less likely to survive when compared to their more generalized counterparts. Evidence suggests that this same pattern may have held true for Archaic *Homo sapiens*, in terms of their ability to survive this dramatic period of climate change.

Defining Characteristics of Archaic *Homo sapiens*

Archaic *Homo sapiens* share our species name but are distinguished by the term "Archaic" as a way of recognizing both the long period of time between their appearance and ours, as well as the way in which human traits have continued to evolve over time—making Archaic *Homo sapiens* look slightly different from us today, despite being considered the same species. Living throughout Africa, and the Middle East during the Middle Pleistocene, Archaic *Homo sapiens* are considered, in many ways, transitional between *Homo erectus* and modern *Homo sapiens* (see Figure 11.3). Archaic *Homo sapiens* share the defining trait of an increased brain size of at least 1,100 cc and averaging 1,200 cc, although there are significant regional and temporal (time) variations. Because of these variations, scientists disagree on whether these fossils represent a single, variable species or multiple, closely related species (sometimes called *Homo antecessor, Homo bodoensis, Homo heidelbergensis, Homo georgicus, Homo neanderthalensis,* and *Homo rhodesiensis*).

An active area of scholarship in the discipline involves reconciling the diversity of species from this time period and establishing the phylogenetic relationships between them. The term "Archaic *Homo sapiens*" can mean different things to different scholars within the discipline. The intent of this chapter is to provide an understanding of the diversity of this time period and provide data used to make interpretations from among the most likely possibilities. Although we recognize that some anthropologists split many of these fossils into separate species, until the issue is resolved at the discipline level, this chapter will rely on the widely used naming conventions that refer to many fossils from this time period as Archaic *Homo sapiens*. We will discuss these contemporaneous fossils as a unit, with the exception of a particularly unique population living in Europe and West Asia known as the Neanderthals, which we will examine separately.

Figure 11.3: A comparison of Homo erectus, Archaic Homo sapiens, and anatomically modern Homo sapiens. This table compares key traits of the crania and postcrania that distinguish these three hominins. Credit: Homo erectus, Archaic Homo sapiens, and anatomically modern Homo sapiens table (Figure 11.3) original to Explorations: An Open Invitation to Biological Anthropology by Amanda Wolcott Paskey and AnnMarie Beasley Cisneros is under a CC BY-NC 4.0 License.

Trait	*Homo erectus*	Archaic *Homo sapiens* (including Neanderthals)	Anatomically Modern *Homo sapiens*
Time	1.8 mya–200,000 ya	600,000–40,000 ya	315,000 ya–today
Brain size	900 cc	1,200 cc (1,500 cc when including Neanderthals)	1,400 cc
Skull Shape	Long and low, angular	Intermediate	Short and high, **globular**
Forehead	Absent	Emerging	Present
Nasal Region	Projecting nasal bones (bridge of the nose), no midfacial prognathism	Wider nasal aperture and some midfacial prognathism, particularly pronounced among Neanderthals	Narrower nasal aperture, no midfacial prognathism
Chin	Absent	Absent	Present
Other Facial Features	Large brow ridge and large projecting face	Intermediate	Small brow ridge and **retracted face**
Other Skull Features	Nuchal torus, sagittal keel, thick cranial bone	Projecting occipital bone, often called occipital bun in Neanderthals; intermediate thickness of cranial bone	Small bump on rear of skull, if anything; thin cranial bone
Dentition	Large teeth, especially front teeth	Slightly smaller teeth; front teeth still large; retromolar gap in Neanderthals	Smaller teeth
Postcranial Features	Robust bones of skeleton	Robust bones of skeleton	More gracile bones of skeleton

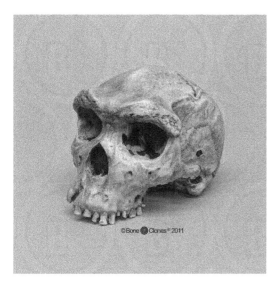

Figure 11.4: "Broken Hill Man," found at Kabwe in Zambia, shows common traits associated with archaic Homo sapiens in Africa, including a large brain, taller cranium, and Homo erectus-like features such as massive brow ridges, a large face, and thick cranial bones. Credit: Homo heidelbergensis Cranium Broken Hill 1 (Rhodesian Man) by ©BoneClones is used by permission and available here under a CC BY-NC 4.0 License.

When comparing *Homo erectus,* Archaic *Homo sapiens,* and anatomically modern *Homo sapiens,* one can see that Archaic *Homo sapiens* are intermediate in their physical form. For some features, this follows the trends first seen in *Homo erectus* with other features having early, less developed forms of traits seen in modern *Homo sapiens.* For example, Archaic *Homo sapiens* trended toward less angular and higher skulls than *Homo erectus.* However, the archaic skulls were not as short and globular and had less developed foreheads compared to anatomically modern *Homo sapiens.* Archaic *Homo sapiens* had smaller brow ridges and a less-projecting face than *Homo erectus* and slightly smaller teeth, although incisors and canines were often about as large as those of *Homo erectus.* Archaic *Homo sapiens* also had a wider **nasal aperture**, or opening for the nose, and a forward-projecting midfacial region, which is later seen more fully developed among Neanderthals and is known as **midfacial prognathism**. The occipital bone often projected and the cranial bone was of intermediate thickness, somewhat reduced from *Homo erectus* but not nearly as thin as that of anatomically modern *Homo sapiens.* The postcrania remained fairly robust. Identifying a set of features that is unique to Archaic *Homo sapiens* is a challenging task, due to both individual and geographic variation—these developments were not all present to the same degree in all individuals. Neanderthals are the exception, as they had several unique traits that made them notably different from modern *Homo sapiens* as well as their closely related Archaic cousins.

The one thing that is clear about Archaic *Homo sapiens* is that, despite general features, there is a lot of regional variation, which is first seen in the different *Homo erectus* specimens across Asia and Africa. While the general features of Archaic *Homo sapiens,* identified earlier, are present in the fossils of this time period, there are significant regional differences. The majority of this regional variation lies in the degree to which fossils have features more closely aligned with *Homo erectus* or with anatomically modern *Homo sapiens.*

To illustrate this point, we will examine three exemplary specimens, one from each of the three continents on which Archaic *Homo sapiens* lived. First, in Africa, a specimen from Broken Hill is one of several individuals found in the Kabwe lead mine in Zambia. It had a large brain (1,300 cc) and taller cranium as well as many *Homo erectus*-like skull features, including massive brow ridges, a large face, and thick cranial bones (Figure 11.4). Second, one partial crania from Dali, China, is representative of Archaic *Homo sapiens* in Asia, with large and robust features with heavy brow ridges, akin to what is seen in *Homo erectus,* and a large cranial capacity intermediate between *Homo erectus* and anatomically modern *Homo sapiens* (Figure 11.5). Third, an almost-complete skeleton was found in northern Spain at Atapuerca. Atapuerca 5 (Figure 11.6) has thick cranial bone, an enlarged cranial capacity, intermediate cranial height, and a more rounded cranium than seen previously. Additionally, Atapuerca 5 demonstrates features that foreshadow Neanderthals, including increased midfacial prognathism. After examining some of the fossils such as those from Kabwe, Dali, and Atapuerca, the transitional nature of Archaic *Homo sapiens* is clear: their features place them squarely between *Homo erectus* and modern *Homo sapiens.*

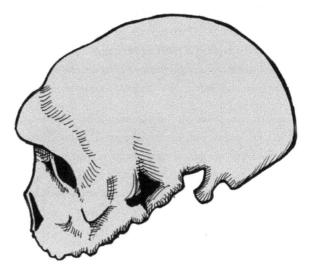

Figure 11.5: Dali cranium, found at Dali, China, is representative of traits seen in archaic Homo sapiens in Asia, including large and robust features with heavy brow ridges like Homo erectus and a large cranial capacity intermediate between Homo erectus and anatomically modern Homo sapiens. Credit: Dali skull original to Explorations: An Open Invitation to Biological Anthropology (2nd ed.) by Mary Nelson is under a CC BY-NC 4.0 License.

Figure 11.6: Atapuerca 5 archaic Homo sapiens, found in northern Spain, is representative of traits seen in archaic Homo sapiens in Europe, including a thick cranial bone, an enlarged cranial capacity, intermediate cranial height, a more rounded cranium, and increased midfacial projection. Credit: Homo heidelbergensis Skull Atapuerca 5 by ©BoneClones is used by permission and available here under a CC BY-NC 4.0 License.

Due to the transitional nature of Archaic *Homo sapiens*, identifying the time period with which they are associated is problematic and complex. Generally, it is agreed that Archaic *Homo sapiens* lived between 600,000 and 200,000 years ago, with regional variation and overlap between *Homo erectus* on the early end of the spectrum and modern *Homo sapiens* and Neanderthals on the latter end. The earliest-known Archaic *Homo sapiens* fossils tentatively date to about 600,000 years ago in Africa, to around 300,000 years ago in Asia, and to about 350,000 years ago in Europe (and potentially as early as 600,000 years ago). Determining the end point of Archaic *Homo sapiens* is also problematic since it largely depends upon when the next subspecies of *Homo sapiens* appears and the classification of highly intermediate specimens. For example, in Africa, the end of Archaic *Homo sapiens* is met with the appearance of modern *Homo sapiens*, while in Europe it is the appearance of Neanderthals that is traditionally seen as marking the transition from other Archaic *Homo sapiens*.

It is important to remember that this time period is represented by many branching relationships and assuming an evolutionary trajectory that follows a single linear path would not be correct. Even still, Archaic *Homo sapiens* mark an important chapter in the human lineage, connecting more ancestral forms, such as *Homo erectus*, to modern *Homo sapiens*. During this period of climatic transition and fluctuation, Archaic *Homo sapiens* mirror the challenges of their environments. Showing increasing regional variation due to the need for local adaptation, there is no single archetype for this group; the defining characteristic seems to be variability.

Neanderthals

One well-known population of Archaic *Homo sapiens* are the Neanderthals, named after the site where they were first discovered in the Neander Valley, or "thal" in German, located near Dusseldorf, Germany. Popularly known as the stereotypical "cavemen" examined at the outset of this chapter, recent research is upending long-held beliefs about this group of Archaics. Neanderthal behavior was increasingly complex, far beyond what was exhibited by even other Archaic *Homo sapiens* discussed throughout this chapter. We implore you to forget the image of the iconic caveman and have an open mind when exploring the fossil evidence of the Neanderthals.

It is important to understand why Neanderthals are separated from other Archaic *Homo sapiens*. Unlike the rest of Archaic *Homo sapiens*, Neanderthals are easily defined and identified in many ways. Evidence suggests the time period when Neanderthals lived was between 150,000 and 40,000 years ago. There is a clear geographic boundary of where Neanderthals lived: western Europe, the Middle East, and western Asia. No

Neanderthal fossils have ever been discovered outside of this area, including Africa. This is a bit curious, as other Archaics seem to have adapted in Africa and then migrated elsewhere, but Neanderthals' regional association makes sense in light of the environment to which they were best adapted: namely, extreme cold weather. Additionally, Neanderthals have a unique and distinct cluster of physical characteristics. While a few aspects of Neanderthals are shared among some Archaic *Homo sapiens*, such as the types of tools, most Neanderthal anatomical and behavioral attributes are unique to them.

Neanderthals lived during some of the coldest times during the last Ice Age and at far northern latitudes. This means Neanderthals were living very close to the glacial edge, rather than in a more temperate region of the globe like some of their Archaic *Homo sapiens* relatives. While able to survive in arctic conditions, most Neanderthal sites dating to the glacial periods were found farther away from the severe cold, in a steppe tundra-like environment, which would have been more hospitable to Neanderthals, and their food sources, both flora and fauna (Ashton 2002; Nicholson 2017; Richter 2006).Their range likely expanded and contracted along with European glacial events, moving into the Middle East during glacial events when Europe became even cooler, and when the animals they hunted would have moved for the same reason. During interglacials, when Europe warmed a bit, Neanderthals and their prey would have been able to move back into Western Europe. Clearly, the true hallmark of Neanderthals is their adaptation to an unstable environment, shifting between warm and cold, as the climate was in constant flux throughout their existence (Adler et al. 2003; Boettger et al. 2009).

Many of the Neanderthals' defining physical features are more extreme and robust versions of traits seen in other Archaic *Homo sapiens*, clustered in this single population. Brain size, namely an enlargement of the cranial capacity, is one such trait. The average Neanderthal brain size is around 1,500 cc, and the range for Neanderthal brains can extend to upwards of 1,700 cc. The majority of the increase in the brain occurs in the occipital region, or the back part of the brain, resulting in a skull that has a large cranial capacity with a distinctly long and low shape that is slightly wider than previous forms at the far back of the skull. Modern humans have a brain size comparable to that of Neanderthals; however, our brain expansion occurred in the frontal region of the brain, not the back, as in Neanderthal brains. This difference is also the main reason why Neanderthals lack the vertical forehead that modern humans possess. They simply did not need an enlarged forehead, because their brain expansion occurred in the rear of their brain. Due to cranial expansion, the back of the Neanderthal skull is less angular (as compared to *Homo erectus*), but not as rounded as *Homo sapiens*, producing an elongated shape, akin to a football.

Another feature that continues the trend noted in previous hominins is the enlargement of the nasal region, or the nose. Neanderthal noses are large and have a wide nasal aperture, which is the opening for the nose. While the nose is only made up of two bones, the nasals, the true size of the nose can be determined by looking at other facial features, including the nasal aperture, and the angle of the nasal and maxillary, or facial bones. In Neanderthals, these indicate a large, forward-projecting nose that appears to be pulled forward away from the rest of the face. This feature is further emphasized by the backward-sloping nature of the cheekbones, or the zygomatic arches. The unique shape and size of the Neanderthal nose is often characterized by the term *midfacial prognathism*—a jutting out of the middle portion of the face, or nose. This is in sharp contrast to the prognathism exhibited by other hominins, who exhibited prognathism, or the jutting out, of their jaws.

The teeth of the Neanderthals follow a similar pattern seen in the Archaic *Homo sapiens*, which is an overall reduction in size, especially as compared to the extremely large teeth seen in the genus *Australopithecus*. However, while the teeth continued to reduce, the jaw size did not keep pace, leaving Neanderthals with an oversized jaw for their teeth, and a gap between their final molar and the end of their jaw. This gap is called a **retromolar gap**.

The projecting occipital bone present in other Archaic *Homo sapiens* is also more prominent in Neanderthals, extending the trend found in Archaics. Among Neanderthals, this projection of bone is easily identified by its bun shape on the back of the skull and is known as an **occipital bun**. This projection appears quite similar to a dinner roll in size and shape. Its purpose, if any, remains unknown.

Continuing the Archaic *Homo sapiens* trend, Neanderthal brow ridges are prominent but somewhat smaller in size than those of *Homo erectus* and earlier Archaic *Homo sapiens*. In Neanderthals, the brow ridges are also often slightly less arched than those of other Archaic *Homo sapiens*.

In addition to extending traits present in Archaic *Homo sapiens*, Neanderthals possess several distinct traits. Neanderthal **infraorbital foramina**, the holes in the maxillae or cheek bones through which blood vessels pass, are notably enlarged compared to other hominins. The Neanderthal postcrania are also unique in that they demonstrate increased robusticity in terms of the thickness of bones and body proportions that show a barrel-shaped chest and short, stocky limbs, as well as increased musculature. These body portions are seen across the spectrum of Neanderthals—in men, women, and children.

Traditionally, many of the unique traits that Neanderthals possess were seen as adaptations to the extreme cold, dry environments in which they often lived and which exerted strong selective forces. For example, Bergmann's and Allen's Rules dictate that an increased body mass and short, stocky limbs are common in animals that live in cold conditions. Neanderthals were said to have matched the predictions of Bergmann's and Allen's Rules perfectly (Churchill 2006). In addition, the Neanderthal skull also exhibits adaptations to the cold. Neanderthals' large infraorbital foramina allow for larger blood vessels, increasing the volume of blood that is found closest to the skin, which helps to keep the skin warmer. Their enlarged noses resulted in longer nasal passages and mucus membranes that warmed and moistened cold air before it reached the lungs. The Neanderthals' larger nose has long been thought to have acted as a humidifier, easing physical exertion in their climate, although research on this particular trait continues to be studied and debated (Rae et al. 2011).

New research, however, seems to suggest that these unique skeletal adaptations might not have been strict adaptations to cold weather (Evteev et al. 2017; Pearce et al. 2013). For example, large brow ridges might have served as a way to shade the face from the sun. The increased occipital portion of the brain, some researchers state, was to support a larger visual system present in Neanderthals. This visual system would have given them increased light sensitivity, which would have been useful in higher latitudes that had dark winters. And, while recent modeling of nostril airflow on reconstructed Neanderthal specimens supports the notion that Neanderthals had extensive mucus membranes inside their noses, the data shows that modern *Homo sapiens* are superior to Neanderthals in our ability to use our noses as a way to warm and cool air. However, Neanderthals were able to snort air through their noses better than we can. Why is this important? When combined with the fact that Neanderthals tended to prefer a more temperate, tundra-like environment, and that other physical traits suggest that Neanderthals had huge bodies that needed massive amounts of calories to sustain them, the picture gets clearer. Massive amounts of energy would have been required to power a Neanderthal body, and anything that might have made them more calorically efficient would have been favored. Efficient breathing, through larger noses into large lungs, meaning deeper breaths, would have been favored. To further save energy expenditure, body sizes might have been sacrificed as well. These same types of adaptations are similar to ones seen in children today who are born in high altitudes, not cold climates. Figure 11.7 provides a summary of these unique features of the Neanderthal.

Figure 11.7: Neanderthal distinguishing features. This table outlines key features associated with Neanderthals. Credit: Neanderthal distinguishing features table (Figure 11.6) original to Explorations: An Open Invitation to Biological Anthropology by Amanda Wolcott Paskey and AnnMarie Beasley Cisneros is under a CC BY-NC 4.0 License.

Distinct Neanderthal Anatomical Features	
Brain Size	1,500 cc average
Skull Shape	Long and low
Brow Ridge Size	Large
Nose Size	Large, with midfacial prognathism
Dentition	Reduced, but large jaw size, creating retromolar gap
Occipital Region	Enlarged occipital region, occipital bun
Other Unique Cranial Features	Large infraorbital foramina
Postcranial Features	Short and stocky body, increased musculature, barrel-shaped chest

A classic example of a Neanderthal with all of the characteristics mentioned above is the nearly complete La Ferrassie 1 Neanderthal, from France. This is a male skeleton, with a brain size of around 1640cc, an extremely large nose and infraorbital foramina, brow ridges that are marked in size, and an overall robust skeleton (Figure 11.8).

Neanderthal Culture: Tool Making and Use

One key Neanderthal adaptation was their cultural innovations, which are an important way that hominins adapt to their environment. As you recall, *Homo erectus*'s tools, Acheulean handaxes, represented an increase in complexity over Oldowan tools, allowing more efficient removal of meat and possibly calculated scavenging. In contrast, Neanderthal tools mark a significant innovation in tool-making technique and use with **Mousterian tools** (named after the Le Moustier site in southwest France). These tools were significantly smaller, thinner, and lighter than Acheulean handaxes and formed a true toolkit. The materials used for Mousterian tools were of higher quality, which allowed for both more precise toolmaking and tool reworking when the tools broke or dulled after frequent reuse. The use of higher-quality materials is also indicative of required forethought and planning to acquire them for tool manufacture. It is noteworthy that the Neanderthals, unlike *Homo erectus*, saved and reused their tools, rather than making new ones each time a tool was needed.

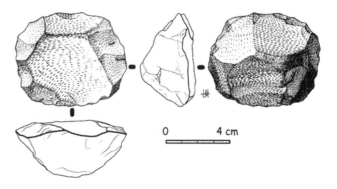

Figure 11.9: The Levallois technique is used to create Mousterian tools. The multistep process involves preparing the core in a specific way to yield flakes that can be used as tools. Credit: Nucléus Levallois La-Parrilla by José-Manuel Benito Álvarez is under a CC BY-SA 2.5 License..

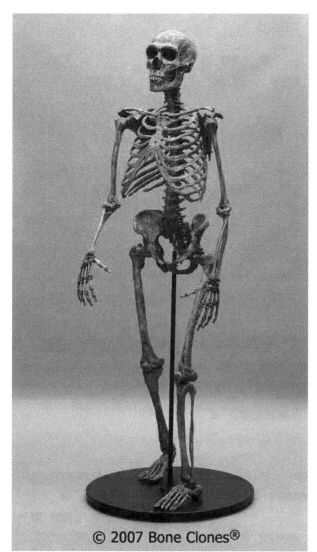

© 2007 Bone Clones®

Figure 11.8: La Ferrassie 1 Neanderthal is representative of many classic Neanderthal features, including a large brain, large nose, large infraorbital foramina, large brow ridges, and robust postcrania. Credit: Neanderthal Skeleton Articulated by ©BoneClones is used by permission and available here under a CC BY-NC 4.0 License.

Mousterian tools are constructed in a very unique manner, utilizing the **Levallois technique** (Figure 11.9), named after the first finds of tools made with this technique, which were discovered in the Levallois-Perret suburb of Paris, France. The Levallois technique is a multistep process that requires preparing the core, or raw material, in a specific way that will yield flakes that are roughly uniform in dimension. The flakes are then turned into individual tools. The preparation of the core is akin to peeling a potato or carrot with a vegetable peeler—when peeling vegetables, you want to remove the skin in long, regular strokes, so that you are taking off the same amount of the vegetable all the way around. In the same way, the Levallois technique requires removing all edges of the **cortex**, or outside surface of the raw material, in a circle before removing the lid. The flakes, which will eventually be turned into the individual tools, can then be removed from the core. The potential yield of tools from one core would be many, as seen in Figure 11.10, compared to all previous tool-making processes, in which one core yielded a single tool. This manufacturing process might be considered the ultimate zero-waste tool-making technique (Delpiano et al. 2018).

Neanderthal tools were used for a variety of purposes, including cutting, butchering, woodworking or antler working, and hide working. Additionally, because the Mousterian tools were lighter than previous stone tools, Neanderthals could **haft**, or attach the tool onto a handle, as the stone would not have been too heavy (Degano et al. 2019). Neanderthals attached small stone blades onto short wood or antler handles to make knives or other small weapons, as well as attached larger blades onto longer shafts to make spears. New research examining tar-covered stones and black lumps at several Neanderthal sites in Europe suggests that Neanderthals may have been making tar by distilling it from birch tree bark, which could have been used to glue the stone tool onto its handle. If Neanderthals were, in fact, manufacturing tar to act as glue, this would predate modern humans in Africa using tree resin or similar adhesives by nearly 100,000 years.

Figure 11.10: Levallois core and flakes for tool production. Using this technique, one core is used to produce many flakes, each of which can be turned into a tool. Credit: NHM – Levalloiskern by Wolfgang Sauber (user: Xenophon) is under a CC BY-SA 4.0 License.

Evidence shows that raw materials used by Neanderthals came from distances as far away as 100 km. This could indicate a variety of things regarding Neanderthal behavior, including a limited trade network with other Neanderthal groups or simply a large area scoured by Neanderthals when collecting raw materials. While research on specific applications continues, it should be clear from this brief discussion that Neanderthal tool manufacturing was much more complex than previous tool-making efforts, requiring technical expertise, patience, and skills beyond toolmaking to carry out.

Neanderthal Culture: Hunting and Diet

With their more sophisticated suite of tools and robust muscular bodies, Neanderthals were better armed for hunting than previous hominins. The animal remains in Neanderthal sites show that, unlike earlier Archaic *Homo sapiens*, Neanderthals were very effective hunters who were able to kill their own prey, rather than relying on scavenging. Though more refined than the tools of earlier hominins, the Neanderthal spear was not the kind of weapon that would have been thrown; rather, it would have been used in a jabbing fashion (Churchill 1998; Kortlandt 2002). This may have required Neanderthals to hunt in groups rather than individually and made it necessary to approach their prey quite closely (Gaudzinski-Windheuser et al. 2018). Remember, the animals living with Neanderthals were very large-bodied due to their adaptations to cold weather; this would have included species of deer, horses, and bovids (relatives of the cow).

Isotopes from Neanderthal bones show that meat was a significant component of their diet, similar to that seen in carnivores like wolves (Bocherens et al. 1999; Jaouen et al. 2019; Richards et al. 2000). In addition to large prey, their diet included ibex, seals, rabbits, and pigeons. Though red meat was a critical component of the Neanderthal diet, evidence shows that at times they also ate limpets, mussels, and pine nuts. Tartar examined from Neanderthal teeth in Iraq and Belgium reveal that they also ate plant material including wheat, barley, date palms, and tubers, first cooking them to make them palatable (Henry et al. 2010). While Neanderthals' diet varied according to the specific environment in which they lived, meat comprised up to 80% of their diet (Wißin et al. 2015).

Neanderthal Culture: Caring for the Injured and Sick

While the close-range style of hunting used by Neanderthals was effective, it also had some major consequences. Many Neanderthal skeletons have been found with significant injuries, which could have caused paralysis or severely limited their mobility. Many of the injuries are to the head, neck, or upper body. Thomas Berger and Erik Trinkaus (1995) conducted a statistical comparative analysis of Neanderthal injuries compared to those recorded in modern-day workers' compensation reports and found that the closest match was between Neanderthal injuries and those of rodeo workers. Rodeo professionals have a high rate of head and neck injuries that are similar to the Neanderthals' injuries. What do Neanderthals and rodeo workers have in common? They were both getting very close to large, strong animals, and at times their encounters went awry.

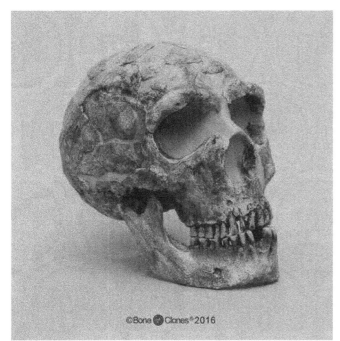

The extensive injuries sustained by Neanderthals are evident in many fossil remains. Shanidar 1 (Figure 11.11), an adult male found at the Shanidar site in northern Iraq and dating to 45,000 ya, has a lifetime of injuries recorded in his bones (Stewart 1977). Shanidar 1 sustained—and healed from—an injury to the face that would have likely caused blindness. His lower right arm was missing and the right humerus shows severe atrophy, likely due to disuse. This pattern has been interpreted to indicate a substantial injury that required or otherwise resulted in amputation or wasting away of the lower arm. Additionally, Shanidar 1 suffered from bony growths in the inner ear that would have significantly impaired his hearing and severe arthritis in the feet. He also exhibited extensive anterior tooth wear, matching the pattern of wear found among modern populations who use their teeth as a tool. Rather than an anomaly, the type of injuries evident in Shanidar 1 are similar to those found in many other Neanderthal fossils, revealing injuries likely sustained from hunting large mammals as well as demonstrating a long life of physical activity.

The pattern of injuries is as significant as the fact that Shanidar 1 and other injured Neanderthals show evidence of having *survived* their severe injuries. One of the earliest-known Neanderthal discoveries—the one on whom misinformed analysis shaped the stereotype of the species for nearly a century—is the La Chapelle-aux-Saints Neanderthal (Trinkaus 1985). The La Chapelle Neanderthal had a damaged eye orbit that likely caused blindness and suffered arthritis of the spine (Dawson and Trinkaus 1997). He had also lost most of his teeth, many of which he had lived without for so long that the mandibular and maxillary bones were partially reabsorbed due to lack of use. The La Chapelle Neanderthal was also thought to be at least in his mid-forties at death, an old age for the rough life of the Late Pleistocene—giving rise to his nickname, "the Old Man." To have survived so long with so many injuries that obviously precluded successful large game hunting, he must have been taken care of by others. Such caretaking behavior is also evident in the survival of other seriously injured Neanderthals, such as Shanidar 1. Long thought to be a hallmark modern human characteristic, taking care of the injured and elderly, for example preparing or pre-chewing food for those without teeth, indicates strong social ties among Neanderthals.

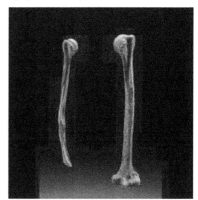

Figure 11.11a-b: a. The Shanidar 1 skull shows an injury to the face that would likely have caused blindness. b. The Shanidar 1 right humerus (on the left side of the image) shows severe atrophy, likely due to disuse. Credit: a. Homo neanderthalensis Shanidar 1 Skull by ©BoneClones is used by permission and available here under a CC BY-NC 4.0 License. b. Shanidar 1 by Chip Clark, Smithsonian Institution [exhibit: Human Evolution Evidence, Human Fossils, Species, Homo neanderthalensis] is used for educational and non-commercial purposes as outlined by the Smithsonian.

Neanderthal Culture: Ritual Life

Such care practices may have been expressed upon death as well. Nearly complete Neanderthal skeletons are not uncommon in the fossil record, and most are well preserved within apparently deliberate burials that involve deep graves and bodies found in specific, often fetal or **flexed positions** (Harrold 1980). Discoveries of pollen in a grave at the Shanidar site in the 1960s led scientists to think that perhaps Neanderthals had placed flowering plants in the grave, an indication of ritual ceremony or spirituality so common in modern humans. But more recent investigations have raised some doubt about this conclusion (Pomeroy et al. 2020). The pollen may have been brought in by burrowing rodents. Claims of **grave goods** or other ornamentation in burials are similarly debated, although possible.

Some tantalizing evidence for symbolism, and debatably, ritual, is the frequent occurrence of natural pigments, such as **ochre** (red) and manganese dioxide (black) in Neanderthal sites that could have been used for art. However, the actual uses of pigments are unclear, as there is very little evidence of art or paintings in Mousterian sites. One exception may be the recent discovery in Spain of a perforated shell that appears to be painted with an orange pigment, which may be evidence of Neanderthal art and jewelry. However, many pigments also have properties that make them good emulsifiers in adhesive (like for attaching a stone tool to a wooden handle) or useful in tanning hides. So the presence of pigment may or may not be associated with symbolic thought; however, it definitely does show a technological sophistication beyond that of earlier Archaic hominins.

The Lasting Gift of Neanderthals: Tantalizing New Directions for Research

Examining the more recent time period in which Neanderthals lived and the extensive excavations completed across Europe allows for a much more complete archaeological record from this time period. Additionally, the increased cultural complexity such as complex tools and ritual behaviors expressed by Neanderthals left a more detailed record than previous hominins. Intentional burials enhanced preservation of the dead and potentially associated ritual behaviors. Such evidence allows for a more complete and nuanced picture of this species.

Figure 11.12: Artistic reconstruction of Neanderthal at The Natural History Museum in Vienna, Austria. Credit: Homo neanderthalensis, The Natural History Museum Vienna, 20210730 1223 1272 by Jakub Hałun is under a CC BY 4.0 License.

Additional analyses are possible on many Neanderthal finds, due to increased preservation of bone, the amount of specimens that have been uncovered, and the recency in which Neanderthals lived. We should be cautious, however, to consider the potential bias of many Neanderthal sites. Overwhelmingly, Neanderthal skeletons are found complete, with injuries or evidence of disease in caves. Does this mean all Neanderthals lived a tough, disease-wrought life? Probably not. It does, however, indicate that the sick were cared for by others, and that they lived in environments that preserved their bodies incredibly well. These additional studies include the examination of dental calculus and even DNA analysis. While limited, samples of Neanderthal DNA have been successfully extracted and analyzed. Research thus far has identified specific genetic markers that show some Neanderthals were light-skinned and probably red-haired with light eyes. Genetic analyses, different from the typical hominin reconstruction done with earlier species, allow scientists to further investigate soft tissue markers of Neanderthals and other more recent hominin species. These studies offer striking conclusions regarding Neanderthal traits, their physical appearance, and their culture, as reflected in these artists' reconstructions (Figure 11.12).

Dr. Svante Pääbo (Figure 11.13), of the Max Planck Institute for Evolutionary Anthropology, has been at the forefront of much of this new research, largely in the form of genomic studies (The Nobel Prize 2022). Awarded the Nobel Prize for Physiology or Medicine in 2022, Pääbo is known primarily for his work with ancient DNA. He has successfully sequenced mitochondrial DNA (mtDNA) as well as the entire Neanderthal genome from nuclear DNA. His genomic work has led to the realization that Denisovans are genetically distinct from Neanderthals, as well as the recent identification of a Neanderthal father and teenage daughter, which he discovered by looking for unique DNA markers in the fossil record. Additionally, Pääbo's genomic work has provided researchers with additional lines of evidence regarding the connections between hominin fossils (such as Neanderthals) and modern people, their time of divergence, and current genetic overlap. The work of Pääbo has even formalized a new field of study within anthropology—paleogenomics. To stay up to date with Dr. Svante Pääbo's work, be sure to follow his lab's website.

Figure 11.13: Nobel Prize winner (2022) and pioneer in paleogenomic research, Dr. Svante Pääbo. Credit: Professor Svante Paabo ForMemRS (cropped) by Duncan.Hull is under a CC BY-SA 3.0 License.

Neanderthal Culture: Communicating through Speech

To successfully live in groups and to foster cultural innovations, Neanderthals would have required at least a basic form of communication in order to function, possibly using a speech-based communication system. The challenge with this line of research is that speech, of course, is not preserved, so indirect evidence must be used to support this conclusion. It is thought that Neanderthals would have possessed some basic speech, as evidenced from a variety of sources, including throat anatomy and genetic evidence (Lieberman 1971). There is only one bone in the human body that could demonstrate if a hominin was able to speak, or produce clear vocalizations like modern humans, and that is the hyoid, a U-shaped bone that is found in the throat and is associated with the ability to precisely control the vocal cords. Very few hyoid bones have been found in the archaeological record; however, a few have been uncovered in Neanderthal burials. The shape of the Neanderthal hyoid is nearly identical to that of modern humans, pointing to the likelihood that they had the same vocal capabilities as modern humans. In addition, geneticists have uncovered a mutation present in both modern humans and Neanderthals—the FOXP2 gene—that is possibly linked to the ability to speak. However, other scientists argue that we cannot make sweeping conclusions that the FOXP2 gene accounts for speech due to small sample size. Finally, scientists have also pointed to the increasingly complex cultural behavior of Neanderthals as a sign that symbolic communication, likely through speech, would have been the only way to pass down the skills needed to make, for example, a Levallois blade or to position a body for intentional burial.

Neanderthal Intelligence

One of the enduring questions about Neanderthals centers on their intelligence, specifically in comparison to modern humans. Brain volume indicates that Neanderthals certainly had a large brain, but it continues to be debated if Neanderthals were of equal intelligence to modern humans. Remember, creatures with larger body sizes tend to have larger brains; however, scaling of the brain is not always associated with greater intelligence (Alex 2018). Brain volume (cranial capacity), cultural complexity, tool use, and compassion toward their kind all point to an increase in intellect among Neanderthals when compared to previous hominins.

Yet, new research is suggesting additional differences between Neanderthal brains and our own. For example, Euluned Pearce and colleagues (2013), from the University of Oxford, noted the frontal lobes of Neanderthals and modern humans are almost identical. However, Neanderthals had a larger visual cortex—the portion of the brain involved in processing visual information. This would have left Neanderthals with less brain tissue for other functions, including those that would have aided them in dealing with large social groupings, one of the differences that has been suggested to exist between Neanderthals and modern humans. Other differences were found when geneticist John Blangero, from the Texas Biomedical Research Institute, compared data from the Neanderthal genome against data from modern study participants. Blangero and his colleagues (Blangero et al. 2014) discovered that some Neanderthal brain components were very different, and smaller, than those in the modern sample. Differences were found in areas associated with the processing of information and controlling emotion and motivation, as well as overall brain connectivity. In short, as Blangero stated, "Neanderthals were certainly cognitively adept," although their specific abilities may have differed from modern humans' in key areas (qtd. in Wong 2015). This point has been echoed in other recent genetic studies comparing Neanderthal and anatomically modern human brains (el-Showk 2019).

Finally, scientists are fairly certain that Neanderthal brain development after birth was not the same as that of modern humans. After birth, anatomically modern *Homo sapiens* babies go through a critical period of brain expansion and cognitive development. It appears that Neanderthal babies' brains and bodies did not follow the same developmental pattern (Smith et al. 2010; Zollikofer and Ponce de León 2013). Modern humans enjoy an extended period of childhood, which allows children to engage in imaginative play and develop creativity that fosters cognitive skills. Neanderthals had a more limited childhood, with less development of the creative mind that may have affected their species' success (Nowell 2016).

The exact nature of Neanderthal intelligence remains under investigation, however. Some studies disagree with the idea that Neanderthal intelligence had limitations compared to our own, noting the extensive evidence of Neanderthals having limb asymmetry. Their tools also have wear marks indicating that they were hand-dominant. This is further supported by marks on Neanderthal teeth that demonstrate hand dominance. The Neanderthal "stuff-and-cut method" of eating, noted by David Frayer and colleagues (Frayer et al. 2012), would have seen Neanderthals hold a piece of meat in their teeth, while pulling it taut with one hand, and then using the other hand, their dominant one, to cut the meat off of the larger slab being held in their teeth. When looking at 17 Neanderthals and their tooth wear, only two do not show markings associated with a right-hand dominant individual eating in this manner. Further, it has been established that favoring the right hand is a key marker between modern humans and chimpanzees, and that handedness also relates to language development, in the form of bilateral brain development. That Neanderthals likely were hand-dominant suggests they had an indicator of bilateral brain development and a precondition for human speech.

The Middle Stone Age: Neanderthal Contemporaries in Africa

While Neanderthals made their home on and adapted to the European and Asian continents, evidence of fossil humans in Africa show they were also adapting to their local environments. These populations in Africa exhibit many more similarities to modern humans than Neanderthals, as well as overall evolutionary success. While the African fossil sample size is smaller and more fragmentary than the number of Neanderthal specimens across Europe and Asia, the African sample is interesting in that it represents a longer time period and larger geographical area. This group of fossils—often represented by the name "Middle Stone Age," or MSA—dates to between 300,000 and 30,000 years ago across the entire continent of Africa. As with Archaic *Homo sapiens*, there is much variability seen in this African set of fossils. There are also a few key consistent elements:

none of them exhibit Neanderthal skeletal features; instead, they demonstrate features that are increasingly consistent with anatomically modern *Homo sapiens*.

Similarities to Neanderthals and MSA contemporaries in Africa are seen, however, in their behavioral adaptations, including stone tools and other cultural elements. The tools associated with the specimens living in Africa during this time period are, like their physical features, varied. In some parts of Africa, namely Northern Africa, stone tools from this time so closely resemble Neanderthal tools that they are classified as Mousterian. In sub-Saharan Africa, the stone tools associated with these specimens are labeled as MSA. Some scholars argue that these could also be a type of Mousterian tools, but they are still typically subdivided based on geographical location.

Recall that Mousterian tools were much more advanced than their Acheulean predecessors in terms of how the stone tools were manufactured, the quality of the stones used, and the ultimate use of the tools that were made. In addition, recent evidence suggests that MSA tools may also have been heat treated—to improve the quality of the stone tool produced (Stolarczyk and Schmidt 2018). Evidence for heat treating is seen not only through advanced analysis of the tool itself but also through the residue of fires from this time period. Fire residues show a shift over time from small, short fires fueled by grasses (probably intended for cooking) to larger, more intensive fires that required the exploitation of dry wood, exactly the type of fire that would have been needed for heat treating stone tools (Esteban et al. 2018).

Other cultural elements seen with MSA specimens include the use of marine (sea-based) resources for their diet (Parkington 2003), manufacture of bone tools, use of adhesive and compound tools (e.g., hafted tools), shell bead production, engraving, use of pigments (such as ochre), and other more advanced tool-making technology (e.g., microlithics). While many of these cultural elements are also seen to a limited extent among Neanderthals, developments at MSA sites appear more complex. This MSA cultural expansion may have been a response to climate change or an increased use of language, complex communication, and/or symbolic thought. Others have suggested that the MSA cultural expansion was due to the increase of marine resources in their diet, which included more fatty acids that may have aided their cognitive development. Still others have suggested that the increased cultural complexity was due to increased interaction among groups, which spurred competition to innovate. Recent studies suggest that perhaps the best explanation for the marked cultural complexity of MSA cultural artifacts is best explained by the simple fact that they lived in diverse habitats (Kandel et al. 2015). This would have necessitated a unique set of cultural adaptations for each habitat type (for example, specialized marine tools would have been needed along coastal sites but not at inland locations). Simply put, the most useful adaptation of MSA was their flexibility of behavior and adaptability to their local environment. As noted previously in this chapter, flexibility of behavior and physical traits, rather than specialization, seems to be a feature that was favored in hominin evolution at this time.

Where Did They Go? The End of Neanderthals

While MSA specimens were increasingly successful and ultimately transitioned into modern *Homo sapiens*, Neanderthals disappeared from the fossil record by around 40,000 years ago. What happened to them? We know, based on genetics, that modern humans come largely from the modern people who occupied Africa around 300,000 to 100,000 years ago, at the same time that Neanderthals were living in northern Europe and Asia. As you will learn in Chapter 12, modern humans expanded out of Africa around 150,000 years ago, rapidly entering areas of Europe and Asia inhabited by Neanderthals and other Archaic hominins. Despite intense interest and speculation in fictional works about possible interactions between these two groups, there is very little direct evidence of either peaceful coexistence or aggressive encounters. It is clear, though, that these two closely related hominins shared Europe for thousands of years, and recent DNA evidence suggests that they occasionally interbred (Fu et al. 2015). Geneticists have found traces of Neanderthal DNA (as much as 1% to 4%) in modern humans of European and Asian descent not present in modern humans from sub-Saharan Africa. This is indicative of limited regional interbreeding with Neanderthals.

While some interbreeding likely occurred, as a whole, Neanderthals did not survive. What is the cause for their extinction? This question has fascinated many researchers and several possibilities have been suggested, including:

- At the time that Neanderthals were disappearing from the fossil record, the climate went through both cooling and warming periods—each of which posed challenges for Neanderthal survival (Defleur and Desclaux 2019; Staubwasser et al. 2018). It has been argued that as temperatures warmed, large-bodied animals, well adapted to cold weather, moved farther north to find colder environments or faced extinction. A shifting resource base could have been problematic for continued Neanderthal existence, especially as additional humans, in the form of modern *Homo sapiens*, began to appear in Europe and compete for a smaller pool of available resources.

- It has been suggested that the eruption of a European volcano 40,000 years ago could have put a strain on available plant resources (Golovanova et al. 2010). The eruption would have greatly affected local microclimates, reducing the overall temperature enough to alter the growing season.

- Possible differences in cognitive development may have limited Neanderthals in terms of their creative problem solving. As much as they were biologically specialized for their environment, the nature of their intelligence might not have offered them the creative problem-solving skills to innovate ways to adapt their culture when faced with a changing environment (Pearce et al. 2013).

- CRISPR gene-editing technology has been used in studies to evaluate potential differences between human and Neanderthal brains, based on differences in the genetic code. Potential differences include a Neanderthal propensity for mutations related to brain development that could account for more rapid brain development, maturation, synapse misfires, and less-orderly neural processes (Mora-Bermúdez et al. 2022; Trujillo et al. 2021). Fundamental differences in brain function at the cellular level may account for the differential survival rates of Neanderthal and modern human populations.

- There is evidence that suggests reproduction may have posed challenges for Neanderthals. Childbirth was thought to have been at least as difficult for female Neanderthals as anatomically modern *Homo sapiens* (Weaver and Hublin 2009). Female Neanderthals may have become sexually mature at an older age, even older than modern humans. This delayed maturation could have kept the Neanderthal population size small. A recent study has further suggested that male Neanderthals might have had a genetic marker on the Y chromosome that could have caused incompatibility between the fetus and mother during gestation; this would have had severe consequences for birth rate and survival (Mendez et al. 2016). Even a small but continuous decrease in fertility would have been enough to result in the extinction of Neanderthals (Degioanni et al. 2019).

- As mentioned above, the end of Neanderthal existence overlaps with modern human expansion into northern Europe and Asia. There is no conclusive direct evidence to indicate that Neanderthals and modern humans lived peacefully side by side, nor that they engaged in warfare, but by studying modern societies and the tendencies of modern humans, it has been suggested that modern humans may not have warmly embraced their close but slightly odd-looking cousins when they first encountered them (Churchill et al. 2009). Nevertheless, direct competition with modern humans for the same resources may have contributed to the Neanderthals' decline (Gilpin et al. 2016); it may also have exposed them to new diseases, brought by modern humans (Houldcroft and Underdown 2016), which further decimated their population. Estimates of energy expenditures suggest Neanderthals had slightly higher caloric needs than modern humans (Venner 2018). When competing for similar resources, the slightly greater efficiency of modern humans might have helped them experience greater success in the face of competition—at a cost to Neanderthals.

As Neanderthal populations were fairly small to begin with (estimated between 5,000 and 70,000 individuals; Bocquet-Appel and Degioanni 2013), one or a combination of these factors could have easily led to their demise. As more research is conducted, we will likely get a better picture of exactly what led to Neanderthal extinction.

Denisovans

While Neanderthals represent one regionally adapted branch of the Archaic *Homo sapiens* family tree, recent discoveries in Siberia and the Tibetan Plateau surprised paleoanthropologists by revealing yet another population that was contemporary with Archaic *Homo sapiens*, Neanderthals, and modern *Homo sapiens*. The genetic analysis of a child's finger bone (Figure 11.14) and an adult upper third molar (Figure 11.15) from Denisova Cave in the Altai Mountains in Siberia by a team including Svante Pääbo discovered that the mitochondrial and nuclear DNA sequences reflected distinct genetic differences from all known Archaic populations. Dubbed "Denisovans" after the cave in which the bones were found, this population is more closely related to Neanderthals than modern humans, suggesting the two groups shared an ancestor who split from modern humans first, then the Neanderthal-Denisovan line diverged more recently (Reich et al. 2010).

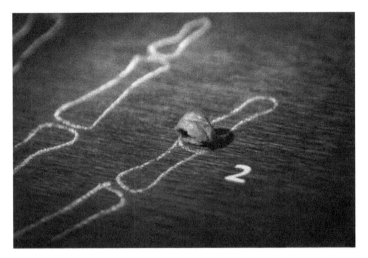

Figure 11.14: Reproduction of Denisovan finger bone. Credit: **Denisova Phalanx distalis** (image from Museum of Natural Sciences, Brussels, Belgium) by **Thilo Parg** is under a **CC BY-SA 3.0 License**.

Denisovans share up to 5% of their DNA with modern Melanesians, aboriginal Australians, and Polynesians, and 0.2% of their DNA with other modern Asian populations and Native Americans. Additional studies have suggested one (Vernot et al. 2018) or two (Browning et al. 2018) separate points of time when interbreeding occurred between modern humans and Denisovans.

Genetic analysis reveals that Denisovans (potentially three distinct populations) had adaptations for life at high altitudes that prevented them from developing altitude sickness and hypoxia in extreme environments such as Tibet, where the average annual temperature is close to 0°C and the altitude is more than a kilometer (about 4,000 feet) above sea level. Through protein analysis of a jawbone, one study (Chen et al. 2019) has placed Denisovans in Tibet as early as 160,000 years ago. Genetic evidence of interbreeding has linked modern Tibetan populations with Denisovans 30,000 to 40,000 years ago, which implies that the unique high-altitude adaptations seen in modern Tibetans may have originated with Denisovans (Huerta-Sanchez et al. 2014).

Figure 11.15: Reproduction of Denisovan molar. Credit: **Denisova Molar** by **Thilo Parg** is under a CC BY-SA 3.0 License.

Other research suggests tantalizing new directions regarding Denisovans. Stone tools similar to those found in Siberia have been uncovered in the Tibetan plateau suggesting a connection between the Denisovan populations in those two areas (Zhang et al. 2018). The molar of a young girl, possibly Denisovan, has been found in Laos and shows strong similarities to specimens from China (Demeter et al. 2022). And DNA sequencing from discoveries in the Denisova Cave have yielded a genome that has been interpreted as the first-generation offspring of a Denisovan father and Neanderthal mother (Slon et al. 2018). While this research is not yet conclusive and is still being interpreted, exciting new possibilities are being revealed. To stay up-to-date with new discoveries, consider following organizations such as the Smithsonian's Human Origins Program on social media.

How Do These Fit In? *Homo naledi* and *Homo floresiensis*

Recently, some fossils have been unearthed that have challenged our understanding of the hominin lineage. The fossils of *Homo naledi* and *Homo floresiensis* are significant for several reasons but are mostly known for how they don't fit the previously held patterns of hominin evolution. While we examine information about these species, we ask you to consider the evidence presented in this chapter and others to draw your own conclusions regarding the significance and placement of these two unusual fossil species in the hominin lineage.

Homo naledi

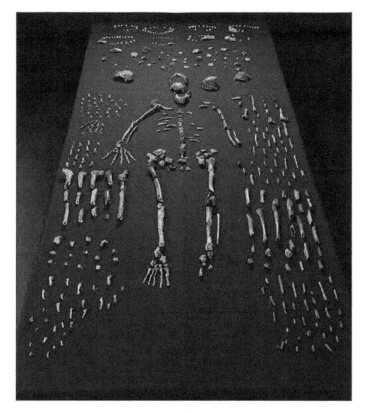

Figure 11.16: A sample of some of the 1,550 bones found representing Homo naledi. Credit: Dinaledi skeletal specimens (Figure 1) by Berger et al. 2015 is under a CC BY 4.0 License.

In 2013 recreational spelunkers uncovered a collection of bones deep in a cave network in Johannesburg, South Africa. The cave system, known as Rising Star, had been well documented by other cavers; however, it appears few people had ever gone as far into the cave as these spelunkers did. Lee Berger, paleoanthropologist at University of Witwatersrand, in Johannesburg, immediately put out a call for what he termed "underground astronauts" to begin recovery and excavation of the fossil materials. Unlike other excavations, Berger and most other paleoanthropologists would not be able to access the elusive site, as it was incredibly difficult to reach, and at some points there was only eight inches of space through which to navigate. The underground astronauts, all petite, slender female anthropologists, were the only ones who were able to access this remarkable site. Armed with small excavation tools and a video camera, which streamed the footage up to the rest of the team at the surface, the team worked together and uncovered a total of 1,550 bones, representing at least 15 individuals, as seen in Figure 11.16. Later, an additional 131 bones, including an almost-complete cranium, were found in a nearby chamber of the cave, representing three more individuals (Figure 11.17). Berger called in a team of specialists to participate in what was dubbed "Paleoanthropology Summer Camp." Each researcher specialized in a different portion of the hominin skeleton. With various specialists working simultaneously, more rapid analysis was possible of *Homo naledi* than most fossil discoveries.

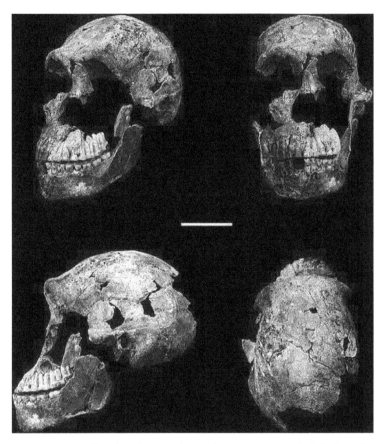

Figure 11.17: Several angles of the nearly complete LES1 Homo naledi skull. Credit: LES1 Cranium (Figure 5) by Hawks et al. 2017 is under a CC BY 4.0 License.

While access to the site, approximately 80 m from any known cave entrance or opening, was treacherous for researchers, it must have been difficult for *Homo naledi* as well. The route included moving through a portion that is just 25 cm wide at some points, known as "Superman's Crawl." The only way to get through this section is by crawling on your stomach with one arm by your side and the other raised above your head. Past Superman's Crawl, a jagged wall known as the Dragon's Back would have been very difficult to traverse. Below that, a narrow vertical chute would have eventually led down to the area where the fossils were discovered. While geology changes over time and the cave system likely has undergone its fair share, it is not likely that these features arose after *Homo naledi* lived (Dirks et al. 2017). This has made scientists curious as to how the bones ended up in the bottom of the cave system in the first place. It has been suggested that *Homo naledi* deposited the bones there, one way or another. If *Homo naledi* did deposit the bones, either through random disposal or intentional burial, this raises questions regarding their symbolic behavior and other cultural traits, including the use of fire, to access a very dark cave system. Another competing idea is that a few individuals may have entered the cave system to escape a predator and then got stuck. To account for the sheer number of fossils, this would have had to happen multiple times.

The features of *Homo naledi* are well-documented due to the fairly large sample, which represents individuals of all sexes and a wide range of ages. The skull shape and features are very much like other members of the genus *Homo*—including a sagittal keel and large brow, like *Homo erectus*, and a well-developed frontal lobe, similar to modern humans—yet the brain size is significantly smaller than its counterparts, at approximately 500 cc (560 cc for males and 465 cc for females). The teeth also exhibit features of later members of the genus *Homo*, such as Neanderthals, including a reduction in overall tooth size. *Homo naledi* also had unique shoulder anatomy and curved fingers, indicating similarities to tree-dwelling primates, which is very different from any other hominin yet found. Perhaps the greatest shock of all is that *Homo naledi* has been dated to 335,000 to 236,000 years ago, placing it as a contemporary to modern *Homo sapiens,* despite its very primitive features. An additional specimen of a child, found in 2021, not only shares many of the unique features found in the adult specimen but will also add insight into the growth and development of individuals of this species (Brophy et al. 2021).

Homo floresiensis

In a small cave called Liang Bua, on the island of Flores, in Indonesia, a small collection of fossils were discovered beginning in 2003 (Figure 11.18). The fossil fragments represent as many as nine individuals, including a nearly complete female skeleton. The features of the skull are very similar to that of *Homo erectus*, including the presence of a sagittal keel, an arching brow ridges and nuchal torus, and the lack of a chin (Figure 11.19). *Homo floresiensis*, as the new species is called, had a brain size that was remarkably small at 400 cc, and recent genetic studies suggest a common ancestor with modern humans that predates *Homo erectus*.

Figure 11.18: Liang Bua Cave on the island of Flores, in Indonesia, where a collection of Homo floresiensis specimens were discovered. Credit: **Homo floresiensis cave** by **Rosino** is under a **CC BY-SA 2.0 License**.

The complete female skeleton, who was an adult, was approximately a meter tall and would have weighed just under 30 kg, which is significantly shorter and just a few kilograms more than the average, modern, young elementary-aged child. A reconstructed comparison between an anatomically modern human and *Homo floresiensis* can be seen in Figure 11.20. The small size of the fossil has earned the species the nickname "the Hobbit." Many questions have been asked about the stature of this species, as all of the specimens found also show evidence of diminutive stature and small brain size. Some explanations include pathology; however, this seems unlikely as all fossils found thus far demonstrate the same pattern. Another possible explanation lies in a biological phenomena seen in other animal species also found on the island, which date to a similar time period. This phenomenon, called **insular dwarfing**, is due to limited food resources on an island, which can create a selective pressure for large-bodied species to be selected for smaller size, as an island would not have been able to support their larger-bodied cousins for a long period of time. This phenomenon is the cause of other unique species known to have lived on the island at the same time, including the miniature stegodon, a dwarf elephant species.

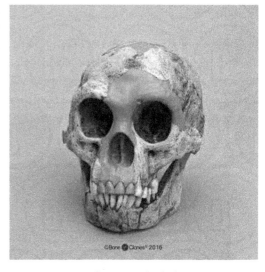

Figure 11.19: Homo floresiensis had a brain that was remarkably small at 400 cc. Recent genetic studies suggest a common ancestor with modern humans that predates Homo erectus. Credit: **Homo floresiensis Skull (Flores Skull LB1)** by ©BoneClones is used by permission and available here under a CC BY-NC 4.0 License.

There is ongoing research and debate regarding *Homo floresiensis'* dates of existence, with some researchers concluding that they lived on Flores until perhaps as recently as 17,000 years ago, although they are more often dated to 100,000 to 60,000 years ago. Stone tools from that time period uncovered at the site are similar to other hominin stone tools found on the island of Flores. *Homo floresiensis* would have hunted a wide range of animals, including the miniature stegodon, giant rats, and other large rodents. Other animals on the island that could have threatened them include the giant komodo dragon. An interesting note about this island chain is that ancestors of *Homo floresiensis* would have had to traverse the open ocean in order to get there, as the nearest island is almost 10 km away, and there is little evidence to support that a land bridge connecting mainland Asia or Australia to the island would have been present. This separation from the mainland would also have limited the number of other animals, including predators and human species, that would have had access to the island. Anatomically modern *Homo sapiens* arrived on the island around 30,000 years ago and, if some researchers' later dates for *Homo floresiensis* are correct, both species may have lived on Flores at the same time. The modern population living on the island of Flores today believes that their ancestors came from the Liang Bua cave; however, recent genetic studies have determined they are not related to *Homo floresiensis* (Tucci et al. 2018).

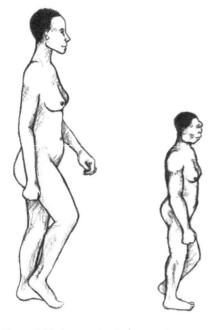

Figure 11.20: A reconstructed comparison between an anatomically modern human and Homo floresiensis. As an adult, Homo floresiensis was approximately 1 meter tall and would have weighed under 30 kg. Credit: **Anatomically modern human and Homo floresiensis (Figure 11.19)** original to Explorations: An Open Invitation to Biological Anthropology by Mary Nelson is under a CC BY-NC 4.0 License.

Conclusion

Research presented in the chapter contributes to why scientists have taken to nicknaming this time period "the muddle in the middle." We know that the Middle Pleistocene picks up from *Homo erectus* and ends with the appearance of anatomically modern *Homo sapiens*. While the start and the end are clear, it's the middle that is messy. As more research is conducted and more data is collected, rather than clarifying our understanding of the hominin lineage during this time period, it only inspires more questions, particularly about the relationships between hominins during this time period, including the oft-misunderstood Neanderthal. Research is painting a more detailed picture of Neanderthal intelligence and both biological and behavioral adaptations. At the same time, their relationship to other Middle Pleistocene hominins, including Denisovans, as well as modern humans, remains unclear.

Homo naledi and *Homo floresiensis* are clear outliers when compared to their contemporary hominin species. Each has surprised paleoanthropologists for both their archaic traits in relatively modern times and their unique combination of traits seen in archaic species and modern humans. While these finds have been exciting, they have also completely upended the assumed trajectory of the human lineage, causing scientists to re-examine assumptions about hominin evolution and what it means to be modern. Add this to the developments being made using ancient DNA, other new fossil discoveries, and other innovations in paleoanthropology, and you see that our understanding of Archaic *Homo sapiens* and others living during this time period is rapidly developing and changing. This is a true testament to the nature of science and the scientific method.

Clearly, hominins of the Middle Pleistocene are distinct from our species today. Yet, understanding the hominins that directly preceded our species and clarifying the evolutionary relationships between us is important to better understanding our own place in nature.

Hominin Species Summaries

Hominin	Archaic *Homo sapiens*
Dates	600,000–200,000 years ago (although some regional variation)
Region(s)	Africa, Europe, and Asia
Famous discoveries	Broken Hill (Zambia), Atapuerca (Spain)
Brain size	1,200 cc average
Dentition	Slightly smaller teeth in back of mouth, larger front teeth
Cranial features	Emerging forehead, no chin, projecting occipital region
Postcranial features	Robust skeleton
Culture	Varied regionally, but some continue to use Acheulean handaxe, others adopt Mousterian tool culture
Other	Lots of regional variation in this species

Species	*Homo naledi*
Dates	335,000–236,000 years ago
Region(s)	South Africa
Famous discoveries	Rising Star Cave
Brain size	500 cc average
Dentition	Reduced tooth size
Cranial features	Sagittal keel, large brow, well-developed frontal region
Postcranial features	Suspensory shoulder
Culture	unknown
Other	N/A

Hominin	Neanderthals
Dates	150,000–40,000 years ago
Region(s)	Western Europe, Middle East, and Western Asia only
Famous discoveries	Shanidar (Iraq), La Chapelle-aux-Saints (France)
Brain size	1500 cc average
Dentition	Retromolar gap
Cranial features	Large brow ridge, midfacial prognathism, large infraorbital foramina, occipital bun
Postcranial features	Robust skeleton with short and stocky body, increased musculature, barrel chest
Culture	Mousterian tools often constructed using the Levallois technique
Other	N/A

Species	*Homo floresiensis*
Dates	100,000–60,000 years ago, perhaps as recently as 17,000 years ago
Region(s)	Liang Bua, island of Flores, Indonesia
Famous discoveries	"The Hobbit"
Brain size	400 cc average
Dentition	unknown
Cranial features	Sagittal keel, arching brow ridges, nuchal torus, no chin
Postcranial features	Very short stature (approximately 3.5 ft.)
Culture	Tools similar to other tools found on the island of Flores
Other	N/A

Hominin	Denisovans
Dates	100,000–30,000 years ago
Region(s)	Siberia
Famous discoveries	Child's finger bone and adult molar
Brain size	unknown
Dentition	Large molars (from limited evidence)
Cranial features	unknown
Postcranial features	unknown
Culture	unknown
Other	Closely related to Neanderthals (genetically)

Review Questions

- What physical and cultural features are unique to Archaic *Homo sapiens*? How are Archaic *Homo sapiens* different in both physical and cultural characteristics from *Homo erectus*?
- Describe the specific changes to the brain and skull first seen in Archaic *Homo sapiens*. Why does the shape of the skull change so dramatically from *Homo erectus*?
- What role did the shifting environment play in the adaptation of Archaic *Homo sapiens*, including Neanderthals? Discuss at least one physical feature and one cultural feature that would have assisted these groups in surviving the changing environment.
- What does the regional variation in Archaic *Homo sapiens* represent in terms of the broader story of our species' evolution?
- Describe the issues raised by the discoveries of *Homo naledi* and *Homo floresiensis* in the understanding of the story of the evolution of *Homo sapiens*.

Key Terms

Allele: Each of two or more alternative forms of a gene that arise by mutation and are found at the same place on a chromosome.

Anthropocentrism: A way of thinking that assumes humans are the most important species and leads to interpreting the world always through a human lens. Species-centric science and thought.

Cortex: The outside, or rough outer covering, of a rock. Usually the cortex is removed during the process of stone tool creation.

Ethnocentric: Applying negative judgments to other cultures based on comparison to one's own.

Exogenous DNA: DNA that originates from sources outside of the specimen you are trying to sequence.

Flexed position: Fetal position, in which the legs are drawn up to the middle of the body and the arms are drawn toward the body center. Intentional burials are often found in the flexed body position.

Foraminifera: Microscopic single-celled organisms with a shell that are common in all marine environments. The fossil record of foraminifera extends back well over 500 million years.

Glaciation: A glacial period, or time when a large portion of the world is covered by glaciers and ice sheets.

Globular: Round-shaped, like a globe.

Grave goods: Items included with a body at burial. Items may signify occupation or hobbies, social status, or level of importance in the community, or they may be items believed necessary for the afterlife.

Haft: A handle. Also used as a verb—to attach a handle to an item, such as a stone tool.

Infraorbital foramina: Small holes on the maxilla bone of the face that allows nerves and blood to reach the skin.

Insular dwarfing: A form of dwarfism that occurs when a limited geographic region, such as an island, causes a large-bodied animal to be selected for a smaller body size.

Interglacial: A warmer period between two glacial time periods.

Levallois technique: A distinctive technique of stone tool manufacturing used by Archaic *Homo sapiens*, including Neanderthals. The technique involves the preparation of a core and striking edges off in a regular fashion around the core. Then a series of similarly sized pieces can be removed, which can then be turned into different tools.

Midfacial prognathism: A forward projection of the nose or the middle facial region. Usually associated with Neanderthals.

Mousterian tools: The stone tool industry of Neanderthals and their contemporaries in Africa and Western Asia. Mousterian tools are known for a diverse set of flake tools, which is different from the large bifacial tools of the Acheulean industry.

Nasal aperture: The opening for the nose visible on a skull. Often pear- or heart-shaped.

Occipital bun: A prominent bulge or projection on the back of the skull, specifically the occipital bone. This is a feature present only on Neanderthal skulls.

Ochre: A natural clay pigment mixed with ferric oxide and clay and sand. Ranges in color from brown to red to orange.

Retracted face: A face that is flatter.

Retromolar gap: A space behind the last molar and the end of the jaw. This is a feature present only on Neanderthals. It also occurs through cultural modification in modern humans who have had their third molars, or wisdom teeth, removed.

About the Authors

Amanda Wolcott Paskey, M.A.

Cosumnes River College, paskeya@crc.losrios.edu

Amanda Wolcott Paskey is an anthropology professor at Cosumnes River College in Sacramento, California. She earned her B.A. and M.A. in anthropology from the University of California, Davis. Her speciality in anthropology is archaeology; however, she was trained in a holistic program and most of her teaching load is in biological anthropology. She is currently working on analyzing a post–gold rush era archaeological site, in Sacramento, with colleagues and students. This project has given her many opportunities to engage in sharing archaeology with a public audience, including local school children and Sacramentans interested in local history.

AnnMarie Beasley Cisneros, M.A.

American River College, beaslea@arc.losrios.edu

AnnMarie Beasley Cisneros is an anthropology professor at American River College in Sacramento, California. Trained as a four-field anthropologist, she earned her B.A. and M.A. in anthropology from California State University, Sacramento. She regularly teaches biological anthropology, among other courses, and is currently engaged in applied anthropology work in community development with historically underserved communities. She most recently has particularly enjoyed facilitating her students' involvement in projects serving Sacramento's Latino and immigrant Mexican populations.

For Further Exploration

Anne and Bernard Spitzer Hall of Human Origins—American Museum of Natural History.

"Dawn of Humanity," PBS documentary, 2015

"DNA Clues to Our Inner Neanderthal," TED Talk by Svante Ibo, 2011.

"The Dirt" Podcast, Episode 30, "The Human Family Tree (Shrub? Crabgrass? Tumbleweed?), Part 3: Very Humany Indeed".

eFossil Games and Activities

Frank, Rebecca. 2021. "The Genus Homo." In *Explorations: Lab and Activity Manual,* edited by Beth Shook, Katie Nelson, Kelsie Aguilera, and Lara Braff. Arlington, VA: American Anthropological Association.

Hobbits on Flores, Indonesia – Smithsonian Human Origins.

Lumping or Splitting in the Fossil Record – UC Berkeley Understanding Evolution.

Neandertals and More – Max Planck Institute for Evolutionary Anthropology.

Neanderthals: Body of Evidence – SAPIENS.

Perash, Rose L., and Kristen A. Broehl. 2021. "Hominin Review: Evolutionary Trends." In *Explorations: Lab and Activity Manual*, edited by Beth Shook, Katie Nelson, Kelsie Aguilera, and Lara Braff. Arlington, VA: American Anthropological Association.

Perkl, Bradley. "Brain, Language, Lithics." In *Explorations: Lab and Activity Manual*, edited by. Beth Shook, Katie Nelson, Kelsie Aguilera, and Lara Braff. CC BY-NC. Arlington, VA: American Anthropological Association.

Shanidar 3 – Neanderthal Skeleton – Smithsonian Human Origins.

Species – Smithsonian Human Origins.

Smithsonian Human Origins Program Facebook page (@smithsonian.humanorigins).

Paleoartist Brings Human Evolution to Life – Elisabeth Dayns.

References

Adler, Daniel S., Timothy J. Prindiville, and Nicholas J. Conard. 2003. "Patterns of Spatial Organization and Land Use During the Eemian Interglacial in the Rhineland: New Data from Wallertheim, Germany." Eurasian Prehistory 1(2): 25–78.

Alex, Bridget. 2018. "Neanderthal Brains: Bigger, Not Necessarily Better." Discover, September 21, 2018. https://www.discovermagazine.com/planet-earth/neanderthal-brains-bigger-not-necessarily-better.

Ashton, Nick M. 2002. "Absence of Humans in Britain during the Last Interglacial Period (Oxygen Isotope Stage 5e)." *Publications du CERP* 8: 93–103.

Berger, Lee R., John Hawks, Darryl J. de Ruiter, Steven E. Churchill, Peter Schmid, Lucas K. Delezene, Tracy L. Kivell, et al. 2015. "*Homo naledi*, a New Species of the Genus *Homo* from the Dinaledi Chamber, South Africa." eLife 4:e09560. https://doi.org/10.7554/eLife.09560.

Berger, Thomas D., and Erik Trinkaus. 1995. "Patterns of Trauma among the Neanderthals." *Journal of Archaeological Science* 22 (6): 841–852.

Blangero, J., E.E. Quillen, M.A. Almeida, D.R. McKay, J.M. Peralta, S. Williams-Blangero, J.E. Curran, R. Duggirala, D.C. Glahn. 2014. "Genomic Reconstruction of Neandertal Brain Structure and Function." Paper presented at the American Association of Physical Anthropologists Annual Meeting, Calgary, Alberta, Canada, 12 April 2014.

Bocherens, Herv, Daniel Billiou, Andr Mariotti, Marylne Patou-Mathis, Marcel Otte, Dominique Bonjean, and Michel Toussaint. 1999. "Palaeoenvionmental and Palaeodietary Implications of Isotopic Biogeochemistry of Last Interglacial Neanderthal and Mammal Bones in Scladina Cave (Belgium)." *Journal of Archaeological Science* 26 (6): 599–607.

Bocquet-Appel, Jean-Pierre and Anna Degioanni. 2013. "Neanderthal Demographic Estimates." *Current Anthropology* 54 (S8): S202–S213.

Boettger, Tatjana, Elena Yu. Novenko, Andrej A. Velichko, Olga K. Borisova, Konstantin V. Kremenetski, Stefan Knetsch, and Frank W. Junge. 2009. "Instability of Climate and Vegetation Dynamics in Central and Eastern Europe during the Final Stage of the Last Interglacial (Eemian, Mikulino) and Early Glaciation." *Quaternary International* 207 (1-2): 137–144. https://doi.org/10.1016/j.quaint.2009.05.006.

Brophy, Juliet K., Marina C. Elliott, Darryl J. De Ruiter, Debra R. Bolter, Steven E. Churchill, Christopher S. Walker, John Hawks, and Lee R. Berger. 2021. "Immature Hominin Craniodental Remains from a New Locality in the Rising Star Cave System, South Africa." *PaleoAnthropology* 1: 1–14. https://doi.org/10.48738/2021.iss1.64.

Browning, Sharon R., Brian L. Browning, Ying Zhou, Serena Tucci, and Josh M. Akey. 2018. "Analysis of Human Sequence Data Reveals Two Pulses of Archaic Denisovan Admixture." *Cell* 173 (1): 53–61.

Chen, Fahu, Frido Welker, Chuan-Chou Shen, Shara E. Bailey, Inga Bergmann, Simon Davis, Huan Xia, et al. 2019. "A Late Middle Pleistocene Denisovan Mandible from the Tibetan Plateau." *Nature* 569: 409–412. https://doi.org/10.1038/s41586-019-1139-x.

Churchill, Steven E. 1998. "Cold Adaptations, Heterochrony, and Neanderthals." *Evolutionary Anthropology* 7 (2): 46–60.

Churchill, Steven E. 2006. "Bioenergetic Perspective on Neanderthal Thermoregulatory and Activity Budgets." In *Neanderthals Revisited: New Approaches and Perspectives*, edited by K. Havarti and T. Harrison, pp. 113–134. Dordrecht, Germany: Springer.

Churchill, Steven E., Robert G. Franciscus, Hilary A. McKean-Peraza, Julie A. Daniel, and Brittany R. Warren. 2009. "Shanidar 3 Neanderthal Rib Puncture Wound and Paleolithic Weaponry." *Journal of Human Evolution* 57 (2): 163–178.

Cook, Rebecca W., Antonio Vazzana, Rita Sorrentino, Stefano Benazzi, Amanda L. Smith, David S. Strait, and Justin A. Ledogar. 2021. "The Cranial Biomechanics and Feeding Performance of *Homo floresiensis*." *Interface Focus* 11 (5). https://doi.org/10.1098/rsfs.2020.0083.

Dawson, James E., and Erik Trinkaus. 1997. "Vertebral Osteoarthritis of La Chapelle-Aux-Saints Neanderthal." *Journal of Archaeological Science* 24 (11): 1015-1021. https://doi.org/10.1006/jasc.1996.0179.

Defleur, Alban R., and Emmanuel Desclaux. 2019. "Impact of the Last Interglacial Climate Change on Ecosystems and Neanderthals Behavior at Baume Moula-Guercy, Ardèche, France." *Journal of Archaeological Science* 104: 114–124. https://doi.org/10.1016/j.jas.2019.01.002.

Degano, Ilaria, Sylvain Soriano, Paola Villa, Luca Pollarolo, Jeannette J. Lucejko, Zenobia Jacobs, Katerina Douka, Silvana Vitagliano, and Carlo Tozzi. 2019. "Hafting of Middle Paleolithic Tools in Latium (Central Italy): New Data from Fossellone and Sant'Agostino Caves." *PLoS ONE* 14(10): 1–29. https://doi.org/10.1371/journal.pone.0213473.

Degioanni Anna, Chritophe Bonenfant, Sandrine Cabut, and Silvana Condemi. 2019. Living on the Edge: Was Demographic Weakness the Cause of Neanderthal Demise? *PLoS ONE* 14 (5): e0216742. https://doi.org/10.1371/journal.pone.0216742.

Delpiano, Davide, Kristin Heasley, and Marci Peresani. 2018. "Assessing Neanderthal Land Use and Lithic Raw Material Management in Discoid Technology." *Journal of Anthropological Sciences* 96: 89–110. https://doi.org/10.4436/jass.96006.

Demeter, Fabrice, Clément Zanolli, Kira E. Westaway, Renaud Joannes-Boyau, Phillippe Duringer, Mike W. Morley, Frido Welker, et al. 2022. "A Middle Pleistocene Denisovan Molar from the Annamite Chain of Northern Laos." *Nature Communications* 13 (1): 2557. https://doi.org/ 10.7554/eLife.24231.

Dirks, Paul H. G. M., Eric M. Roberts, Hannah Hilbert-Wolf, Jan D. Kramers, John Hawks, Anthony Dosseto, Mathieu Duval, et al. 2017. "The Age of *Homo naledi* and Associated Sediments in the Rising Star Cave, South Africa." *eLife* 6: e24231. https://doi.org/10.7554/eLife.24231.

el-Showk, Sedeer. 2019. "Neanderthal Clues to Brain Evolution in Humans." Nature 571: S10–S11. https://doi.org/10.1038/d41586-019-02210-6.

Esteban, Irene, Curtis W. Marean, Erich C. Fisher, Panagiotis Karkanas, Dan Carbanes, and Rosa M. Albert. 2018. "Phytoliths as an Indicator of Early Modern Humans' Plant-Gathering Strategies, Fire, Fuel, and Site-Occupation Intensity During the Middle Stone Age at Pinnacle Point 5-6 (South Coast, South Africa)." *PLoS One* 13 (6): 1–33.

Evteev, Andrej A., Alla A. Movsesian, and Alexandra N. Grosheva. 2017. "The Association between Mid-facial Morphology and Climate in Northeast Europe Differs from That in North Asia: Implications for Understanding the Morphology of Late Pleistocene *Homo sapiens*." *Journal of Human Evolution* 107: 36–48. https://doi.org/10.1016/j.jhevol.2017.02.008.

Frayer, David W., Marina Lozano, Jose M. Bermudez de Castro, Eudald Carbonell, Juan-Luis Arsuaga, Jakov Radovcic, Ivana Fiore, and Luca Bondioli. 2012. "More Than 500,000 Years of Right-handedness in Europeans." *Laterality* 17 (1): 51–69. https://doi.org/10.1080/1357650X.2010.529451.

Fu, Qiaomei, Mateja Hajdinjak, Oana Teodora Moldovan, Silviu Constantin, Swapan Mallick, Pontus Skoglund, Nick Patterson, et al. 2015. "An Early Modern Human from Romania with a Recent Neanderthal Ancestor." *Nature* 524 (7564): 216. https://doi.org/10.1038/nature14558.

Gaudzinski-Windheuser, Sabine, Elizabeth S. Noack, Eduard Pop, Constantin Herbst, Johannes Pfleging, Jonas Buchli, Arne Jacob, et al. 2018. "Evidence for Close-Range Hunting by Last Interglacial Neanderthals." *Nature Ecology and Evolution* 2: 1087–1092. https://doi.org/10.1038/s41559-018-0596-1.

Gilpin, William., Marcus W. Feldman, and Kenichi Aoki. 2016. "An Ecocultural Model Predicts Neanderthal Extinction through Competition with Modern Humans." *Proceedings of the National Academy of Sciences* 113 (8): 2134–2139. https://doi.org/10.1073/pnas.1524861113.

Golovanova, Liubov. Vitaliena, Vladimir B. Doronichev, Naomi E. Cleghorn, Marianna A. Koulkova, Tatiana V. Sapelko, and M. Steven Shackley. 2010. "Significance of Ecological Factors in the Middle to Upper Paleolithic Transition." *Current Anthropology* 51 (5): 655–691. https://doi.org.10.1086/656185.

Harrold, Francis B. 1980. "A Comparative Analysis of Eurasian Paleolithic Burials." *World Archaeology* 12 (2): 195–211.

Hawks, John, Marina Elliott, Peter Schmid, Steven E. Churchill, Darryl J. de Ruiter, Eric M. Roberts, Hannah Hilbert-Wolf, et al. 2017. "New Fossil Remains of *Homo naledi* from the Lesedi Chamber, South Africa." *eLife* 6: e24232. https://doi.org/10.7554/eLife.24232.

Henry, Amanda G., Alison S. Brooks, and Dolores R. Piperno. 2010. "Microfossils and Calculus Demonstrate Consumption of Plants and Cooked Foods in Neanderthal Diets (Shanidar III, Iraq; Spy I and II, Belgium)." *Proceedings of the National Academy of Sciences USA* 108 (2): 486–491. https://doi.org/10.1073/pnas.1016868108.

Houldcroft, Charlotte J., and Simon J. Underdown. 2016. "Neanderthal Genomics Suggests a Pleistocene Time Frame for the First Epidemiologic Transition." *American Journal of Physical Anthropology* 160 (3): 379–388.

Huerta-Sánchez, Emilia, Xin Jin, Asan, Zhuoma Bianba, Benjamin M. Peter, Nicolas Vinckenbosch, Yu Liang, et al. 2014. "Altitude Adaptation in Tibetans Caused by Introgression of Denisovan-like DNA." *Nature* 512 (7513): 194-197.

Jaouen, Klervia, Michael P. Richards, and Adeline Le Cabec. 2019. "Exceptionally High δ^{15}N Values in Collagen Single Amino Acids Confirm Neanderthals as High-Trophic Level Carnivores." *Proceedings of the National Academy of Sciences* 116 (11): 4928–4933. https://doi.org/10.1073/pnas.1814087116.

Kandel, Andrew W., Michael Bolus, Knut Bretzke, Angela A. Bruch, Miriam N. Haidle, Christine Hertler, and Michael Märker. 2015. "Increasing Behavioral Flexibility? An Integrative Macro-Scale Approach to Understanding the Middle Stone Age of Southern Africa." *Journal of Archaeological Method and Theory* 23: 623–668. https://doi.org/10.1007/s10816-015-9254-y.

Kortlandt, Adriaan. 2002. "Neanderthal Anatomy and the Use of Spears." *Evolutionary Anthropology* 11 (5): 183–184.

Kruger, A., P. Randolph-Quinney, and M. Elliott. 2016. "Multimodal Spatial Mapping and Visualization of Dinaledi Chamber and Rising Star Cave." *South African Journal of Science* 112 (5–6). https://doi.org/10.17159/sajs.2016/20160032.

Lieberman, Philip, and Edmund S. Crelin. 1971. "On the Speech of Neanderthal Man." *Linguistic Inquiry* 2 (2): 203–222.

Mendez, Fernando L., G. David Poznik, Sergi Castellano, and Carlos D. Bustamante. 2016. "The Divergence of Neanderthal and Modern Human Y Chromosomes." *American Journal of Human Genetics* 98 (4): 728–734.

Mora-Bermúdez, Felipe, Philipp Kanis, Dominik Macak, Jula Peters, Ronald Naumann, Lei Xing, Mihail Sarov, et al. 2022. "Longer Metaphase and Fewer Chromosome Segregation Errors in Modern Human Than Neanderthal Brain Development." *Science Advances* 8 (30). https://doi.org/10.1126/sciadv.abn7702.

Nicholson, Christopher M. 2017. "Eemian Paleoclimate Zones and Neanderthal Landscape Use: A GIS Model of Settlement Patterning during the Last Interglacial." *Quaternary International* 438 (B): 144–157. https://doi.org/10.1016/j.quaint.2017.04.023.

Nobel Prize, The. 2022. "Press Release: The Nobel Prize in Physiology or Medicine 2022." Nobelförsamlingen The Nobel Assembly at Karolinska Institutet. Press release, November 3, 2022. https://www.nobelprize.org/prizes/medicine/2022/press-release/.

Nowell, April. 2016. "Childhood, Play and the Evolution of Cultural Capacity in Neanderthals and Modern Humans." In *The Nature of Culture: Based on an Interdisciplinary Symposium "The Nature of Culture," Tübingen, Germany*, edited by M. N. Haidle, N. J. Conard, and M. Bolus, 87–97. Heidelberg, Germany: Springer. https://doi.org.10.1007/978-94-017-7426-0_9.

Parkington, John. 2003. "Middens and Moderns: Shellfishing and the Middle Stone Age of the Western Cape, South Africa." *South African Journal of Science* 99 (5–6): 243–274.

Pearce, Eiluned, Chris Stringer, and R. I. M. Dunbar. 2013. "New Insights into Differences in Brain Organizations between Neanderthals and Anatomically Modern Humans." *Proceedings of the Royal Society B: Biological Sciences* 280 (1758): 20130168. https://doi.org/10.1098/rspb.2013.0168.

Pomeroy, Emma, Paul Bennett, Chris O. Hunt, Tim Reynolds, Lucy Farr, Marine Frouin, James Holman, Ross Lane, Charles French, and Graeme Barker. 2020. "New Neanderthal Remains Associated with the 'Flower Burial' at Shanidar Cave." *Antiquity* 94 (373): 11–26. https://doi.org/10.15184/aqy.2019.207.

Rae, Todd, Thomas Koppe, and Chris B. Stringer. 2011. "The Neanderthal Face Is Not Cold-Adapted." *Journal of Human Evolution* 60 (2): 234–239. https://doi.org/10.1016/j.jhevol.2010.10.003.

Reich, David, Richard E. Green, Martin Kircher, Johannes Krause, Nick Patterson, Eric Y. Durand, Bence Viola, et al. 2010. "Genetic History of an Archaic Hominin Group from Denisova Cave in Siberia." *Nature* 468: 1053–1060. https://doi.org/10.1038/nature09710.

Richards, Michael P., Paul B. Pettit, Erik Trinkaus, Fred H. Smith, Maja Paunović, and Ivor Karavanić. 2000. "Neanderthal Diet at Vindija and Neanderthal Predation: The Evidence from Stable Isotopes." *Proceedings of the National Academy of Sciences* 97 (13): 7663–7666. https://doi.org/10.1073/pnas.120178997.

Richter, Jürgen, 2006. "Neanderthals in Their Landscape: Neanderthals in Europe." In *Proceedings of the International Conference held in the Gallo-Roman Museum in Tongeren*, ERAUL 117, edited by B. Demarsin and M. Otte, 17–32. Köln: Universität zu Köln.

Roksandic, Mirjana, Predrag Radovic, Xiu-Jie Wu, and Christopher J. Bae. 2021. "Resolving the 'Muddle in the Middle': The Case for *Homo bodoensis*." *Evolutionary Anthropology: Issues, News, and Reviews*, 31 (1). https://doi.org/10.1002/evan.21929.

Slon, Viviane, Fabrizio Mafessoni, Benjamin Vernot, Cesare de Filippo, Steffi Grote, Bence Viola, Mateja Hajdinjak, et al. 2018. "The Genome of the Offspring of a Neanderthal Mother and a Denisovan Father." *Nature* 561 (7721): 113–116.

Smith, Tanya M., Paul Tafforeau, Donald J. Reid, Joanne Pouech, Vincent Lazzari, John P. Zermeno, Debbi Guatelli-Steinberg, et al. 2010. "Dental Evidence for Ontogenetic Differences Between Modern Humans and Neanderthals." *Proceedings for the National Academy of Sciences* 107 (49): 20923–20928.

Staubwasser, Michael, Virgil Drăguşin, Bogdan P. Onac, Sergey Assonov, Vasile Ersek, Dirk L. Hoffman, and Daniel Veres. 2018. "Impact of

Climate Change on the Transition of Neanderthals to Modern Humans in Europe." *Proceedings of the National Academy of Sciences* 115 (37): 9116–9121. https://doi.org/10.1073/pnas.1808647115.

Stewart, T. D. 1977. "The Neanderthal Skeletal Remains from Shanidar Cave, Iraq: A Summary of Findings to Date." *Proceedings of the American Philosophical Society* 121 (2): 121–165.

Stolarczyk, Regine E., and Patrick Schmidt. 2018. "Is Early Silcrete Heat Treatment a New Behavioural Proxy in the Middle Stone Age?" *PLoS One* 13 (10): 1–21.

Trinkaus, E. 1985. "Pathology and Posture of the La-Chapelle-aux-Saints Neanderthal." *American Journal of Physical Anthropology* 67 (1): 19–41.

Trujillo Cleber A., Edward S. Rice, Nathan K. Schaefer, Isaac A. Chaim, Emily C. Wheeler, Assael A. Madrigal, Justin Buchanan, et al. 2021. "Reintroduction of the Archaic Variant of NOVA1 in Cortical Organoids Alters Neurodevelopment." *Science* 371 (6530): eaax2537. https://doi.org/10.1126/science.aax2537.

Tucci, Serena, Samuel H. Vohr, Rajiv C. McCoy, Benjamin Vernot, Matthew R. Robinson, Chiara Barbieri, Brad J. Nelson, et al. 2018. "Evolutionary History and Adaptation of a Human Pygmy Population of Flores Island, Indonesia." *Science* 361 (6401): 511–516.

Van Andel, T. H., and P. C. Tzedakis. 1996. "Paleolithic Landscapes of Europe and Environs, 150,000–25,000 Years Ago: An Overview." *Quaternary Science Reviews* 15 (5–6): 481–500.

Venner, Stephen J. 2018. "A New Estimate for Neanderthal Energy Expenditure." CUNY Academic Works.

Vernot, Benjamin, Serena Tucci, Janet Kelso, Joshua G. Schraiber, Aaron B. Wolf, Rachel M. Gittelman, Michael Danneman, et al. 2016. "Excavating Neanderthal and Denisovan DNA from the Genomes of Melanesian Individuals." *Science* 352 (6282): 235–239.

Weaver, T. D., and J. Hublin. 2009. "Neanderthal Birth Canal Shape and the Evolution of Human Childbirth." *Proceedings of the National Academy of Sciences* 106 (20): 8151–8156.

Wißing, Christoph, Hélène Rougier, Isabelle Crevecoer, Mietje Germonpré, Yuichi Naito, Patrick Semal, and Hervé Bocherens. 2015. "Isotopic Evidence for Dietary Ecology of Late Neanderthals in Northwestern Europe." *Quaternary International* 411 (A): 327–345. https://doi.org/10.1016/j.quaint.2015.09.091.

Wong, Kate. 2015. "Neanderthal Minds." *Scientific American* (January): 312(2): 36-43. https://doi.org/10.1038/scientificamerican0215-36.

Zhang, X. L., B. B. Ha, S. J. Wang, Z. J. Chen, J. Y. Ge, H. Long, W. He, et al. 2018. "The Earliest Human Occupation of the High-Altitude Tibetan Plateau 40 Thousand to 30 Thousand Years Ago." *Science* 362 (6418): 1049–1051. https://doi.org/10.1126/sciadv.add5582.

Zilhão João, Diego E. Angelucci, Ernestina Badal-García, Francesco d'Errico, Floréal Daniel, Laure Dayet, Katerina Douka, et al. 2010. "Symbolic Use of Marine Shells and Mineral Pigments by Iberian Neandertals." *Proceedings of the National Academy of Sciences* 107 (3): 1023–1028. https://doi.org/10.1073/pnas.0914088107.

Zollikofer, Christopher Peter Edwards, and Marcia Silvia Ponce de León. 2013. "Pandora's Growing Box: Inferring the Evolution and Development of Hominin Brains from Endocasts." Evolutionary Anthropology 22 (1): 20–33. https://doi.org/10.1002/evan.21333.

Acknowledgments

The authors would like to extend their thanks to Cassandra Gilmore and Anna Goldfield for thoughtful and insightful suggestions on the first edition of this chapter.

12.

MODERN HOMO SAPIENS

Keith Chan, Ph.D., Grossmont-Cuyamaca Community College District and MiraCosta College

This chapter is a revision from "Chapter 12: Modern Homo sapiens" by Keith Chan. In Explorations: An Open Invitation to Biological Anthropology, first edition, edited by Beth Shook, Katie Nelson, Kelsie Aguilera, and Lara Braff, which is licensed under CC BY-NC 4.0.

Learning Objectives

- Identify the skeletal and behavioral traits that represent modern *Homo sapiens*.
- Critically evaluate different types of evidence for the origin of our species in Africa and our expansion around the world.
- Understand how the human lifestyle changed when people transitioned from foraging to agriculture.
- Hypothesize how human evolutionary trends may continue into the future.

The walls of a pink limestone cave in the hillside of Jebel Irhoud jutted out of the otherwise barren landscape of the Moroccan desert (Figure 12.1). Miners had excavated the cave in the 1960s, revealing some fossils. In 2007, a re-excavation of the site became a momentous occasion for science. A fossil cranium unearthed by a team of researchers was barely visible to the untrained eye. Just the fossil's robust brows were peering out of the rock. This research team from the Max Planck Institute for Evolutionary Anthropology was the latest to explore the ancient human presence in this part of North Africa after a find by miners in 1960. Excavating near the first discovery, the researchers wanted to learn more about how *Homo sapiens* lived far from East Africa, where we thought our species originated.

Figure 12.1: The excavation of an exposed cave at Jebel Irhoud, Morocco, where hominin fossils were found in the 1960s and in 2007. Dating showed that they could represent the earliest-known modern Homo sapiens. Credit: View looking south of the Jebel Irhoud (Morocco) site by Shannon McPherron, MPI EVA Leipzig, is under a CC BY-SA 2.0 License.

The scientists were surprised when they analyzed the cranium, named Irhoud 10, and other fossils. Statistical comparisons with other human crania concluded that the Irhoud face shapes were typical of recent modern humans while the braincases matched ancient modern humans. Based on the findings of other scientists, the team expected these modern *Homo sapiens* fossils to be around 200,000 years old. Instead, dating revealed that the cranium had been buried for around 315,000 years.

Together, the modern-looking facial dimensions and the older date reshaped the interpretation of our species: modern *Homo sapiens*. Some key evolutionary changes from the archaic *Homo sapiens* (described in Chapter 11) to our species today happened 100,000 years earlier than we had thought and across the vast African continent rather than concentrated in its eastern region.

This revelation in the study of modern *Homo sapiens* is just one of the latest in this continually advancing area of biological anthropology. Researchers today are still discovering amazing fossils and ingenious ways to collect data and test hypotheses about our past. Through the collective work of many scientists, we are building an overall theory of modern human origins. In this chapter, we will first cover the skeletal changes from archaic *Homo sapiens* to modern *Homo sapiens*. Next, we will track how modern *Homo sapiens* expanded around the world. Lastly, we will cover the development of agriculture and how it changed human culture.

Defining Modernity

What defines modern *Homo sapiens* when compared to archaic *Homo sapiens*? Modern humans, like you and me, have a set of derived traits that are not seen in archaic humans or any other hominin. As with other transitions in hominin evolution, such as increasing brain size and bipedal ability, modern traits do not appear fully formed or all at once. In other words, the first modern *Homo sapiens* was not just born one day from archaic parents. The traits common to modern *Homo sapiens* appeared in a **mosaic** manner: gradually and out of sync with one another. There are two areas to consider when tracking the complex evolution of modern human traits. One is the physical change in the skeleton. The other is behavior inferred from the size and shape of the cranium and material culture evidence.

Skeletal Traits

The skeleton of modern *Homo sapiens* is less robust than that of archaic *Homo sapiens*. In other words, the modern skeleton is **gracile**, meaning that the structures are thinner and smoother. Differences related to gracility in the cranium are seen in the braincase, the face, and the mandible. There are also broad differences in the rest of the skeleton.

Cranial Traits

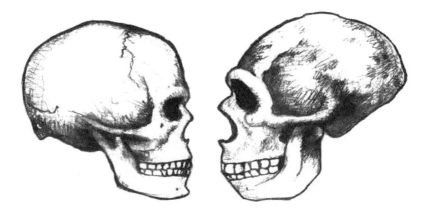

Figure 12.2: Comparison between modern (left) and archaic (right) Homo sapiens skulls. Note the overall gracility of the modern skull, as well as the globular braincase. Credit: Modern human and Neanderthal original to Explorations: An Open Invitation to Biological Anthropology by Mary Nelson is under a CC BY-NC 4.0 License.

Several elements of the braincase differ between modern and archaic *Homo sapiens*. Overall, the shape is much rounder, or more **globular,** on a modern skull (Lieberman, McBratney, and Krovitz 2002; Neubauer, Hublin, and Gunz 2018; Pearson 2008; Figure 12.2). You can feel the globularity of your own modern human skull. Feel the height of your forehead with the palm of your hand. Viewed from the side, the tall vertical forehead of a modern *Homo sapiens* stands out when compared to the sloping archaic version. This is because the frontal lobe of the modern human brain is larger than the one in archaic humans, and the skull has to accommodate the expansion. The vertical forehead reduces a trait that is common to all other hominins: the brow ridge or **supraorbital torus**. The parietal lobes of the brain and the matching parietal bones on either side of the skull both bulge outward more in modern humans. At the back of the skull, the archaic occipital bun is no longer present. Instead, the occipital region of the modern human cranium has a derived tall and smooth curve, again reflecting the globular brain inside.

The trend of shrinking face size across hominins reaches its extreme with our species as well. The facial bones of a modern *Homo sapiens* are extremely gracile compared to all other hominins (Lieberman, McBratney, and Krovitz 2002). Continuing a trend in hominin evolution, technological innovations kept reducing the importance of teeth in reproductive success (Lucas 2007). As natural selection favored smaller and smaller teeth, the surrounding bone holding these teeth also shrank.

Related to smaller teeth, the mandible is also gracile in modern humans when compared to archaic humans and other hominins. Interestingly, our mandibles have pulled back so far from the prognathism of earlier hominins that we gained an extra structure at the most anterior point, called the **mental eminence**. You know this structure as the chin. At the skeletal level, it resembles an upside-down "T" at the centerline of the mandible (Pearson 2008). Looking back at archaic humans, you will see that they all lack a chin. Instead, their mandibles curve straight back without a forward point. What is the chin for and how did it develop? Flora Gröning and colleagues (2011) found evidence of the chin's importance by simulating physical forces on computer models of different mandible shapes. Their results showed that the chin acts as structural support to withstand strain on the otherwise gracile mandible.

Postcranial Gracility

The rest of the modern human skeleton is also more gracile than its archaic counterpart. The differences are clear when comparing a modern *Homo sapiens* with a cold-adapted Neanderthal (Sawyer and Maley 2005), but the trends are still present when comparing modern and archaic humans within Africa (Pearson 2000). Overall, a modern *Homo sapiens* postcranial skeleton has thinner cortical bone, smoother features, and more slender shapes when compared to archaic *Homo sapiens* (Figure 12.3). Comparing whole skeletons, modern humans have longer limb proportions relative to the length and width of the torso, giving us lankier outlines.

Why is our skeleton so gracile compared to those of other hominins? Natural selection can drive the gracilization of skeletons in several ways (Lieberman 2015). A slender frame is adapted for the efficient long-distance running ability that started with *Homo erectus*. Furthermore, slenderness is a genetic adaptation for cooling an active body in hotter climates, which aligns with the ample evidence that Africa was the home continent of our species.

Behavioral Modernity

Aside from physical differences in the skeleton, researchers have also uncovered evidence of behavioral changes associated with increased cultural complexity from archaic to modern humans. How did cultural complexity develop? Two investigations into this question are archaeology and the analysis of reconstructed brains.

Archaeology tells us much about the behavioral complexity of past humans by interpreting the significance of material culture. In terms of advanced culture, items created with an artistic flair, or as decoration, speak of abstract thought processes (Figure 12.4). The demonstration of difficult artistic techniques and technological complexity hints at social learning and cooperation as well. According to paleoanthropologist John Shea (2011), one way to track the complexity of past behavior through artifacts is by measuring the variety of tools found together. The more types of tools constructed with different techniques and for different purposes, the more modern the behavior. Researchers are still working on an archaeological way to measure cultural complexity that is useful across time and place.

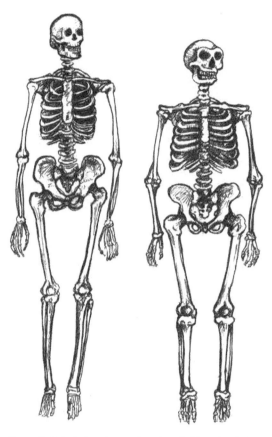

Figure 12.3: Anterior views of modern (left) and archaic (right) Homo sapiens skeletons. The modern human has an overall gracile appearance at this scale as well. Credit: Modern and archaic Homo sapiens skeletons (Figure 12.3) original to Explorations: An Open Invitation to Biological Anthropology by Mary Nelson is under a CC BY-NC 4.0 License.

Figure 12.4: Carved ivory figure called "the Lion-Man of the Hohlenstein-Stadel." It dates to the Aurignacian culture, between 35 and 40 kya. Credit: Loewenmensch1 by Dagmar Hollmann is under a CC BY-SA 3.0 License.

The interpretation of brain anatomy is another promising approach to studying the evolution of human behavior. When looking at investigations on this topic in modern *Homo sapiens* brains, researchers found a weak association between brain size and test-measured intelligence (Pietschnig et al. 2015). Additionally, they found no association between intelligence and biological sex. These findings mean that there are more significant factors that affect tested intelligence than just brain size. Since the sheer size of the brain is not useful for weighing intelligence within a species, paleoanthropologists are instead investigating the differences in certain brain structures. The differences in organization between modern *Homo sapiens* brains and archaic *Homo sapiens* brains may reflect different cognitive priorities that account for modern human culture. As with the archaeological approach, new discoveries will refine what we know about the human brain and apply that knowledge to studying the distant past.

Taken together, the cognitive abilities in modern humans may have translated into an adept use of tools to enhance survival. Researchers Patrick Roberts and Brian A. Stewart (2018) call this concept the **generalist-specialist niche**: our species is an expert at living in a wide array of environments, with populations culturally specializing in their own particular surroundings. The next section tracks how far around the world these skeletal and behavioral traits have taken us.

First Africa, Then the World

What enabled modern *Homo sapiens* to expand its range further in 300,000 years than *Homo erectus* did in 1.5 million years? The key is the set of derived biological traits from the last section. The gracile frame and neurological anatomy allowed modern humans to survive and even flourish in the vastly different environments they encountered. Based on multiple types of evidence, the source of all of these modern humans was Africa. Instead of originating from just one location, evidence shows that modern Homo sapiens evolution occurred in a complex gene flow network across Africa, a concept called **African multiregionalism** (Scerri et al. 2018).

This section traces the origin of modern *Homo sapiens* and the massive expansion of our species across all of the continents (except Antarctica) by 12,000 years ago. While modern *Homo sapiens* first shared geography with archaic humans, modern humans eventually spread into lands where no human had gone before. Figure 12.5 shows the broad routes that our species took expanding around the world. I encourage you to make your own timeline with the dates in this part to see the overall trends.

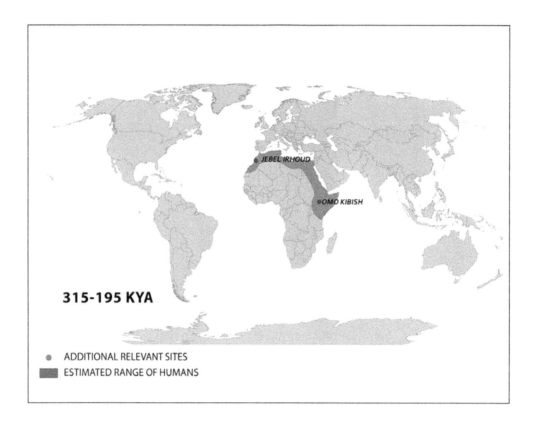

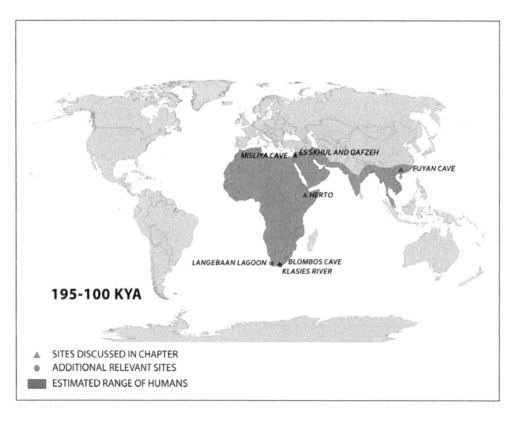

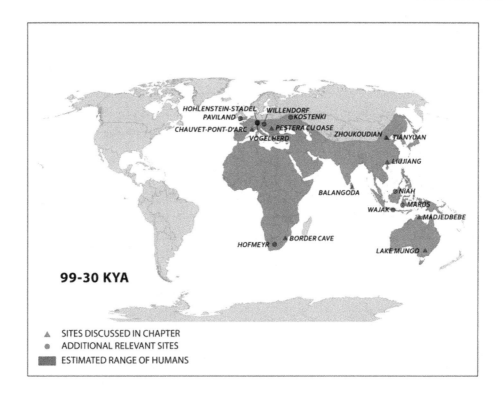

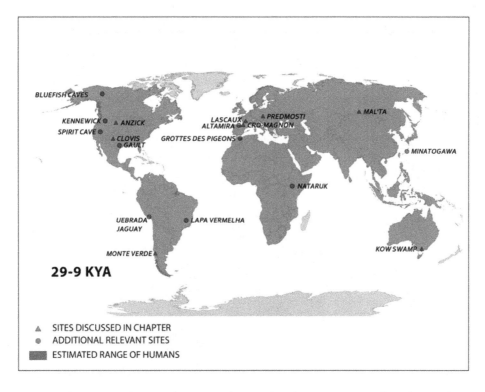

Figure 12.5a-d: Four maps depicting the estimated range of modern Homo sapiens through time. The shaded area is based on geographical connections across known sites. Note the growth in the area starting in Africa and the oftentimes-coastal routes that populations followed. Credit: Four maps depicting the estimated range of modern Homo sapiens through time original to Explorations: An Open Invitation to Biological Anthropology by Elyssa Ebding at GeoPlace, California State University, Chico is under a CC BY-NC 4.0 License.

Modern *Homo sapiens* Biology and Culture in Africa

We start with the ample fossil evidence supporting the theory that modern humans originated in Africa during the Middle Pleistocene, having evolved from African archaic *Homo sapiens*. The earliest dated fossils considered to be modern actually have a mosaic of archaic and modern traits, showing the complex changes from one type to the other. Experts have various names for these transitional fossils, such as **Early Modern *Homo sapiens*** or **Early Anatomically Modern Humans**. However they are labeled, the presence of some modern traits means that they illustrate the origin of the modern type. Three particularly informative sites with fossils of the earliest modern *Homo sapiens* are Jebel Irhoud, Omo, and Herto.

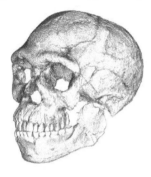

Figure 12.6: Composite rendering of the Jebel Irhoud hominin based on micro-CT scans of multiple fossils from the site. The facial structure is within the modern human range, while the braincase is between the archaic and modern shapes. Credit: A composite reconstruction of the earliest known Homo sapiens fossils from Jebel Irhoud (Morocco) based on micro computed tomographic scans by Philipp Gunz, MPI EVA Leipzig, is under a CC BY-SA 2.0 License.

Recall from the start of the chapter that the most recent finds at Jebel Irhoud are now the oldest dated fossils that exhibit some facial traits of modern *Homo sapiens*. Besides Irhoud 10, the cranium that was dated to 315,000 years ago (Hublin et al. 2017; Richter et al. 2017), there were other fossils found in the same deposit that we now know are from the same time period. In total there are at least five individuals, representing life stages from childhood to adulthood. These fossils form an image of high variation in skeletal traits. For example, the skull named Irhoud 1 has a primitive brow ridge, while Irhoud 2 and Irhoud 10 do not (Figure 12.6). The braincases are lower than what is seen in the modern humans of today but higher than in archaic *Homo sapiens*. The teeth also have a mix of archaic and modern traits that defy clear categorization into either group.

Research separated by nearly four decades uncovered fossils and artifacts from the Kibish Formation in the Lower Omo Valley in Ethiopia. These Omo Kibish hominins were represented by braincases and fragmented postcranial bones of three individuals found kilometers apart, dating back to around 233,000 years ago (Day 1969; McDougall, Brown, and Fleagle 2005; Vidal et al. 2022). One interesting finding was the variation in braincase size between the two more-complete specimens: while the individual named Omo I had a more globular dome, Omo II had an archaic-style long and low cranium.

Also in Ethiopia, a team led by Tim White (2003) excavated numerous fossils at Herto. There were fossilized crania of two adults and a child, along with fragments of more individuals. The dates ranged between 160,000 and 154,000 years ago. The skeletal traits and stone-tool assemblage were both intermediate between the archaic and modern types. Features reminiscent of modern humans included a tall braincase and thinner zygomatic (cheek) bones than those of archaic humans (Figure 12.7). Still, some archaic traits persisted in the Herto fossils, such as the supraorbital tori. Statistical analysis by other research teams concluded that at least some cranial measurements fit just within the modern human range (McCarthy and Lucas 2014), favoring categorization with our own species.

Figure 12.7: This model of the Herto cranium showing its mosaic of archaic and modern traits. Credit: Homo sapiens idaltu BOU-VP-16/1 Herto Cranium by ©BoneClones is used by permission and available here under a CC BY-NC 4.0 License.

The timeline of material culture suggests a long period of relying on similar tools before a noticeable diversification of artifacts types. Researchers label the time of stable technology shared with archaic types the **Middle Stone Age**, while the subsequent time of diversification in material culture is called the **Later Stone Age**.

In the Middle Stone Age, the sites of Jebel Irhoud, Omo, and Herto all bore tools of the same flaked style as archaic assemblages, even though they were separated by almost 150,000 years. The consistency in technology may be evidence that behavioral modernity was not so developed. No clear signs of art dating back this far have been found either. Other hypotheses not related to behavioral modernity could explain these observations. The tool set may have been suitable for thriving in Africa without further innovation. Maybe works of art from that time were made with media that deteriorated or perhaps such art was removed by later humans.

Evidence of what *Homo sapiens* did in Africa from the end of the Middle Stone Age to the Later Stone Age is concentrated in South African cave sites that reveal the complexity of human behavior at the time. For example, Blombos Cave, located along the present shore of the Cape of Africa facing the Indian Ocean, is notable for having a wide variety of artifacts. The material culture shows that toolmaking and artistry were more complex than previously thought for the Middle Stone Age. In a layer dated to 100,000 years ago, researchers found two intact ochre-processing kits made of abalone shells and grinding stones (Henshilwood et al. 2011). Marine snail shell beads from 75,000 years ago were also excavated (Figure 12.8; d'Errico et al. 2005). Together, the evidence shows that the Middle Stone Age occupation at Blombos Cave incorporated resources from a variety of local environments into their culture, from caves (ochre), open land (animal bones and fat), and the sea (abalone and snail shells). This complexity shows a deep knowledge of the region's resources and their use—not just for survival but also for symbolic purposes.

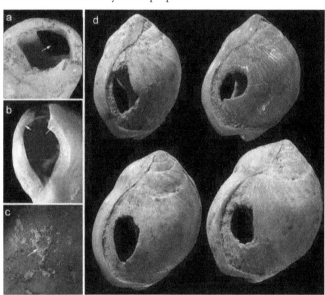

On the eastern coast of South Africa, Border Cave shows new African cultural developments at the start of the Later Stone Age. Paola Villa and colleagues (2012) identified several changes in technology around 43,000 years ago. Stone-tool production transitioned from a slower process to one that was faster and made many **microliths**, small and precise stone tools. Changes in decorations were also found across the Later Stone Age transition. Beads were made from a new resource: fragments of ostrich eggs shaped into circular forms resembling present-day breakfast cereal O's (d'Errico et al. 2012). These beads show a higher level of altering one's own surroundings and a move from the natural to the abstract in terms of design.

Figure 12.8: Examples of the perforated shell beads found in Blombos Cave, South Africa: (a) view of carved hole seen from the inside; (b) arrows indicate worn surfaces due to repetitive contact with other objects, such as with other beads or a connecting string; (c) traces of ochre; and (d) four shell beads showing a consistent pattern of perforation. Credit: BBC-shell-beads by Chenshilwood (Chris Henshilbood and Francesco d'Errico) at English Wikipedia is under a CC BY-SA 3.0 License.

Summary of Modern *H.* sapiens *in Africa*

The combined fossil evidence paints a picture of diversity in geography and traits. Instead of evolving in just East Africa, the Jebel Irhoud find revealed that early modern *Homo sapiens* had a wide range across Middle Pleistocene Africa. Supporting this explanation, fossils have different mosaics of archaic and modern traits in different places and even within the same area. The high level of diversity from just these fossils shows that the modern traits took separate paths toward the set we have today. The connections were convoluted, involving fluctuating gene flow among small groups of regional nomadic foragers across a large continent over a long time.

African culture experienced a long constant phase called the Middle Stone Age until a faster burst of change produced innovation and new styles. The change was not one moment but rather an escalation in development. Later Stone Age culture introduced elements seen across many regions, including the construction of composite tools and even the use of strung decorations such as beads. These developments appear in the Later Stone Age of other regions, such as Europe. Based on the early date of the African artifacts, Later Stone Age culture may have originated in Africa and passed from person to person and region to region, with people adapting the general technique to their local resources and viewing the meaning in their own way.

Expansion into the Middle East and Asia

While modern *Homo sapiens* lived across Africa, some members eventually left the continent. These pioneers could have used two connections to the Middle East or West Asia. From North Africa, they could have crossed the Sinai Peninsula and moved north to the **Levant**, or eastern Mediterranean. Finds in that region show an early modern human presence. Other finds support the **Southern Dispersal model**, with a crossing from East Africa to the southern Arabian Peninsula through the Straits of Bab-el-Mandeb. It is tempting to think of one momentous event in which people stepped off Africa and into the Middle East, never to look back. In reality, there were likely multiple waves of movement producing gene flow back and forth across these regions as the overall range pushed east. The expanding modern human population could have thrived by using resources along the southern coast of the Arabian Peninsula to South Asia, with side routes moving north along rivers. The maximum range of the species then grew across Asia.

Modern Homo sapiens *in the Middle East*

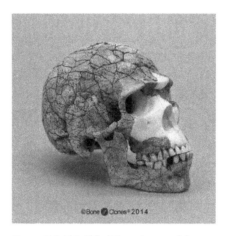

Figure 12.9: This Skhul V cranium model shows the sharp browridges. The contour of a marked occipital bun is barely visible from this angle. Credit: Homo sapiens Skull Skhul 5 by ©BoneClones is used by permission and available here under a CC BY-NC 4.0 License.

Geographically, the Middle East is the ideal place for the African modern *Homo sapiens* population to inhabit upon expanding out of their home continent. In the Eastern Mediterranean coast of the Levant, there is a wealth of skeletal and material culture linked to modern *Homo sapiens*. Recent discoveries from Saudi Arabia further add to our view of human life just beyond Africa.

The Caves of Mount Carmel in present-day Israel have preserved skeletal remains and artifacts of modern *Homo sapiens*, the first-known group living outside Africa. The skeletal presence at Misliya Cave is represented by just part of the left upper jaw of one individual, but it is notable for being dated to a very early time, between 194,000 and 177,000 years ago (Hershkovitz et al. 2018). Later, from 120,000 to 90,000 years ago, fossils of multiple individuals across life stages were found in the caves of Es-Skhul and Qafzeh (Shea and Bar-Yosef 2005). The skeletons had many modern *Homo sapiens* traits, such as globular crania and more gracile postcranial bones when compared to Neanderthals. Still, there were some archaic traits. For example, the adult male Skhul V also possessed what researchers Daniel Lieberman, Osbjorn Pearson, and Kenneth Mowbray (2000) called marked or clear occipital bunning. Also, compared to later modern humans, the Mount Carmel people were more robust. Skhul V had a particularly impressive brow ridge that was short in height but sharply jutted forward above the eyes (Figure 12.9). The high level of preservation is due to the intentional burial of some of these people. Besides skeletal material, there are signs of artistic or symbolic behavior. For example, the adult male Skhul V had a boar's jaw on his chest. Similarly, Qafzeh 11, a juvenile with healed cranial trauma, had an impressive deer antler rack placed over his torso (Figure 12.10; Coqueugniot et al. 2014). Perforated seashells colored with **ochre**, mineral-based pigment, were also found in Qafzeh (Bar-Yosef Mayer, Vandermeersch, and Bar-Yosef 2009).

One remaining question is, what happened to the modern humans of the Levant after 90,000 years ago? Another site attributed to our species did not appear in the region until 47,000 years ago. Competition with Neanderthals may have accounted for the disappearance of modern human occupation since the Neanderthal presence in the Levant lasted longer than the dates of the early modern *Homo sapiens*. John Shea and Ofer Bar-Yosef (2005) hypothesized that the Mount Carmel modern humans were an initial expansion from Africa that failed. Perhaps they could not succeed due to competition with the Neanderthals who had been there longer and had both cultural and biological adaptations to that environment.

Modern Homo sapiens *of China*

A long history of paleoanthropology in China has found ample evidence of modern human presence. Four notable sites are the caves at Fuyan, Liujiang, Tianyuan, and Zhoukoudian. In the distant past, these caves would have been at least seasonal shelters that unintentionally preserved evidence of human presence for modern researchers to discover.

Figure 12.10 This cast of the Qafzeh 11 burial shows the antler's placement over the upper torso. The forearm bones appear to overlap the antler. Credit: Moulage de la sépulture de l'individu "Qafzeh 11" (avec ramure de cervidé), homme de Néandertal (Collections du Muséum national d'histoire naturelle de Paris, France) by Eunostos has been modified (cropped and color modified) and is under a CC BY-SA 4.0 License.

At Fuyan Cave in Southern China, paleoanthropologists found 47 adult teeth associated with cave formations dated to between 120,000 and 80,000 years ago (Liu et al. 2015). It is currently the oldest-known modern human site in China, though other researchers question the validity of the date range (Michel et al. 2016). The teeth have the small size and gracile features of modern *Homo sapiens* dentition.

The fossil Liujiang (or Liukiang) hominin (67,000 years ago) has derived traits that classified it as a modern *Homo sapiens*, though primitive archaic traits were also present. In the skull, which was found nearly complete, the Liujiang hominin had a taller forehead than archaic *Homo sapiens* but also had an enlarged occipital region (Figure 12.11; Brown 1999; Wu et al. 2008). Other parts of the skeleton also had a mix of modern and archaic traits: for example, the femur fragments suggested a slender length but with thick bone walls (Woo 1959).

Another Chinese site to describe here is the one that has been studied the longest. In the Zhoukoudian Cave system (Figure 12.12), where *Homo erectus* and archaic *Homo sapiens* have also been found, there were three crania of modern *Homo sapiens*. These crania, which date to between 34,000 and 10,000 years ago, were all more globular than those of archaic humans but still lower and longer than those of later modern humans (Brown 1999; Harvati 2009). When compared to one another, the crania showed significant differences from one another. Comparison of cranial measurements to other populations past and present found no connection with modern East Asians, again showing that human variation was very different from what we see today.

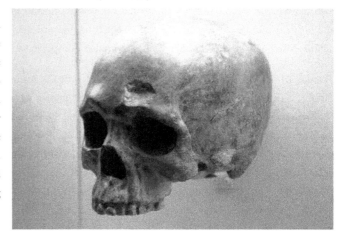

Figure 12.11: The Liujiang cranium shows the tall forehead and overall gracile appearance typical of modern Homo sapiens. Credit: Liujiang cave skull-a. Homo Sapiens 68,000 Years Old (Taken at the David H. Koch Hall of Human Origins, Smithsonian Natural History Museum) by Ryan Somma has been modified (color modified) and is under a CC BY-SA 2.0 License.

Figure 12.12: The entrance to the Upper Cave of the Zhoukoudian complex, where crania of three ancient modern humans were found. Credit: Zhoukoudian Upper Cave by Mutt is under a CC BY-SA 4.0 License.

Summary of Modern *H.* sapiens *in the Middle East and Asia*

As in Africa, the finds of the Middle East have shown that humans were biologically diverse and had complex relationships with their environment. Work in the Levant showed an initial expansion north from the Sinai Peninsula that did not last. Away from the Levant, expansion continued. Local resources were used to make lithics and decorative items.

The early Asian presence of modern *Homo sapiens* was complex and varied as befitting the massive continent. What the evidence shows is that people adapted to a wide array of environments that were far removed from Africa. From the Levant to China, humans with modern anatomy used caves that preserved signs of their presence. Faunal and floral remains found in these shelters speak to the flexibility of the human omnivorous diet as local wildlife and foliage became nourishment. Decorative items, often found as burial goods in planned graves, show a flourishing cultural life.

Eventually, modern humans at the southeastern fringe of the geographical range of the species found their way southeast until some became the first humans in Australia.

Crossing to Australia

Expansion of the first modern human Asians, still following the coast, eventually entered an area that researchers call **Sunda** before continuing on to modern Australia. Sunda was a landmass made up of the modern-day Malay Peninsula, Sumatra, Java, and Borneo. Lowered sea levels connected these places with land bridges, making them easier to traverse. Proceeding past Sunda meant navigating **Wallacea**, the archipelago that includes the Indonesian islands east of Borneo. In the distant past, there were many **megafauna**, large animals that migrating humans would have used for food and materials (such as utilizing animals' hides and bones). Further southeast was another landmass called **Sahul**, which included New Guinea and Australia as one contiguous continent. Based on fossil evidence, this land had never seen hominins or any other primates before modern *Homo sapiens* arrived. Sites along this path offer clues about how our species handled the new environment to live successfully as foragers.

The skeletal remains at Lake Mungo, land traditionally owned by Mutthi Mutthi, Ngiampaa, and Paakantji peoples, are the oldest known in the continent. The now-dry lake was one of a series located along the southern coast of Australia in New South Wales, far from where the first people entered from the north (Barbetti and Allen 1972; Bowler et al. 1970). Two individuals dating to around 40,000 years ago show signs of artistic and symbolic behavior, including intentional burial. The bones of Lake Mungo 1 (LM1), an adult female, were crushed repeatedly, colored with red ochre, and cremated (Bowler et al. 1970). Lake Mungo 3 (LM3), a tall, older male with a gracile cranium but robust postcranial bones, had his fingers interlocked over his pelvic region (Brown 2000).

Kow Swamp, within traditional Yorta Yorta land also in southern Australia, contained human crania that looked distinctly different from the ones at Lake Mungo (Durband 2014; Thorne and Macumber 1972). The crania,

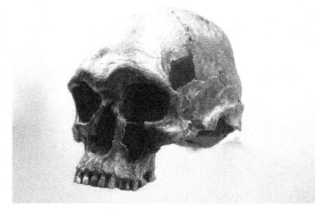

Figure 12.13: Replica of the Kow Swamp 1 cranium. The shape of the braincase could be due to artificial cranial modification. A competing hypothesis is that it reflects the primitive shape of Homo erectus. Credit: Kow Swamp1-Homo sapiens by Ryan Somma from Occoquan, USA, under a CC BY-SA 2.0 License has been modified (background cleaned and color modified) and is available here under a CC BY-NC 4.0 License.

dated between 9,000 and 20,000 years ago, had extremely robust brow ridges and thick bone walls, but these were paired with globular features on the braincase (Figure 12.13).

While no fossil humans have been found at the Madjedbebe rock shelter in the North Territory of Australia, more than 10,000 artifacts found there show both behavioral modernity and variability (Clarkson et al. 2017). They include a diverse array of stone tools and different shades of ochre for rock art, including mica-based reflective pigment (similar to glitter). These impressive artifacts are as far back as 56,000 years old, providing the date for the earliest-known presence of humans in Australia.

Summary of Modern H. sapiens *in Australia*

The overall view of the first modern humans in Australia from a biological perspective shows a high amount of skeletal diversity. This is similar to the trends seen earlier in Africa, the Middle East, and East Asia. The earliest-known arrivals brought with them a multifaceted suite of cultural practices as seen in their material culture.

From the Levant to Europe

The first modern human expansion into Europe occurred after other members of our species settled East Asia and Australia. As the evidence from the Levant suggests, modern human movement to Europe may have been hampered by the presence of Neanderthals. Another obstacle was that the colder climate was incompatible with the biology of African modern *Homo sapiens*, which was adapted for exposure to high temperature and ultraviolet radiation. Still, by 40,000 years ago, modern *Homo sapiens* had a detectable presence. This time was also the start of the Later Stone Age or **Upper Paleolithic**, when there was an expansion in cultural complexity. There is a wealth of evidence from this region due to a Western bias in research, the proximity of these findings to Western scientific institutions, and the desire of Western scientists to explore their own past. This section will cover key evidence of early modern human life in Europe, and the typologies used to view cultural changes in this region.

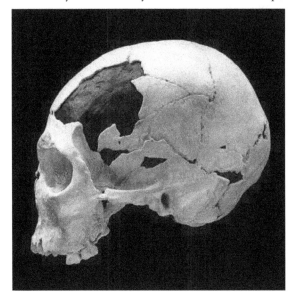

Figure 12.14: This side view of the Oase 2 cranium shows the reduced brow ridges but also occipital bunning that is a sign that modern Homo sapiens interbred with Neanderthals. Credit: **Oase 2** by James Di Loreto & Donald H. Hurlbert, Smithsonian [exhibit: Human Evolution Evidence, Human Fossils] has been modified (sharpened) and is used for educational and non-commercial purposes as outlined by the Smithsonian.

In Romania, the site of Peştera cu Oase (Cave of Bones) had the oldest-known remains of modern *Homo sapiens* in Europe, dated to around 40,000 years ago (Trinkaus et al. 2003a). Among the bones and teeth of many animals were the fragmented cranium of one person and the mandible of another (the two bones did not fit each other). Both bones have modern human traits similar to the fossils from the Middle East, but they also had Neanderthal traits. Oase 1, the mandible, had a mental eminence but also extremely large molars (Trinkaus et al. 2003b). This mandible has yielded DNA that surprisingly is equally similar to DNA from present-day Europeans and Asians (Fu et al. 2015). This means that Oase 1 was not the direct ancestor of modern Europeans. The Oase 2 cranium has the derived traits of reduced brow ridges along with archaic wide zygomatic cheekbones and an occipital bun (Figure 12.14; Rougier et al. 2007).

Dating to around 26,000 years ago, Předmostí near Přerov in the Czech Republic was a site where people buried over 30 individuals along with many artifacts. Eighteen individuals were found in one mass burial area, a few covered by the scapulae of woolly mammoths (Germonpré, Lázničková-Galetová, and Sablin 2012). The Předmostí crania were more globular than those of archaic humans but tended to be longer and lower than in later modern humans (Figure 12.15; Velemínská et al. 2008). The height of the face was in line with modern residents of Central Europe. There was also skeletal evidence of dog domestication, such as the presence of dog skulls with shorter snouts than in wild wolves (Germonpré, Lázničková-Galetová, and Sablin et al. 2012). In total, Předmostí could have been a settlement dependent on mammoths for subsistence and the artificial selection of early domesticated dogs.

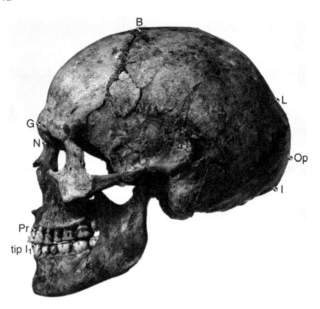

Figure 12.15: This illustration is based upon one of the surviving photographic negatives since the original fossil was lost in World War II. The modern human chin is prominent, as is an archaic occipital bun. Credit: Předmostí 9 by J. Matiegka (1862–1941) has been modified (sharpened) and is in the public domain.

The sequence of modern *Homo sapiens* technological change in the Later Stone Age has been thoroughly dated and labeled by researchers working in Europe. Among them, the Gravettian tradition of 33,000 years to 21,000 years ago is associated with most of the known curvy female figurines, often assumed to be "Venus" figures. Hunting technology also advanced in this time with the first known boomerang, **atlatl** (spear thrower), and archery. The Magdalenian tradition spread from 17,000 to 12,000 years ago. This culture further expanded on fine bone tool work, including barbed spearheads and fishhooks (Figure 12.16).

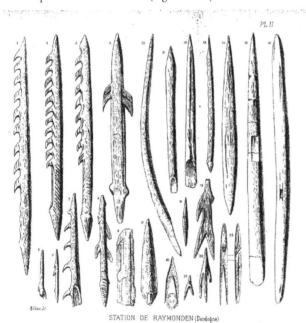

Figure 12.16: This drawing from 1891 shows an array of Magdalenian-style barbed points found in the burial of a reindeer hunter. They were carved from antler. Credit: La station quaternaire de Raymonden (...)Hardy Michel bpt6k5567846s (2) by M. Féauxis, original by Michel Hardy (1891), is in the public domain.

Among the many European sites dating to the Later Stone Age, the famous cave art sites deserve mention. Chauvet-Pont-d'Arc Cave in southern France dates to separate Aurignacian occupations 31,000 years ago and 26,000 years ago. Over a hundred art pieces representing 13 animal species are preserved, from commonly depicted deer and horses to rarer rhinos and owls. Another French cave with art is Lascaux, which is several thousand years younger at 17,000 years ago in the Magdalenian period. At this site, there are over 6,000 painted figures on the walls and ceiling (Figure 12.17). Scaffolding and lighting must have been used to make the paintings on the walls and ceiling deep in the cave. Overall, visiting Lascaux as a contemporary must have been an awesome experience: trekking deeper in the cave lit only by torches giving glimpses of animals all around as mysterious sounds echoed through the galleries.

Summary of Modern H. sapiens *in Europe*

Study of Europe in the Upper Paleolithic gives a more detailed view of the general pattern of biological and cultural change linked with the arrival of modern *Homo sapiens*. The modern humans experienced a rapidly changing culture that went through waves of complexity and refinement. Skeletally, the increasing globularity of the cranium and the gracility of the rest of the skeleton continued, though with unique regional traits, too. The cave art sites showed a deeper exploration of creativity though the exact meaning is unclear. With survival dependent on the surrounding ecology, painting the figures may have connected people to important and impressive wildlife at both a physical and spiritual level. Both reverence for animals and the use of caves for an enhanced sensory experience are common to cultures past and present.

Peopling of the Americas

By 25,000 years ago, our species was the only member of *Homo* left on Earth. Gone were the Neanderthals, Denisovans, *Homo naledi,* and *Homo floresiensis.* The range of modern *Homo sapiens* kept expanding

Figure 12.17: Photograph of just one surface with cave art at Lascaux Cave. The most prominent piece here is the Second Bull, found in a chamber called the Hall of Bulls. Smaller cattle and horses are also visible. Credit: Lascaux cave (document 108435) Prehitoric Sites and Decorated Caves of the Vézère Valley (France) by Francesco Bandarin, © UNESCO, has been modified (color modified) and is under a CC BY-SA 3.0 License.

eastward into—using the name given to this area by Europeans much later—the Western Hemisphere. This section will address what we know about the peopling of the Americas, from the first entry to these continents to the rapid spread of Indigenous Americans across its varied environments.

While evidence points to an ancient land bridge called **Beringia** that allowed people to cross from what is now northeastern Siberia into modern-day Alaska, what people did to cross this land bridge is still being investigated. For most of the 20th century, the accepted theory was the **Ice-Free Corridor model**. It stated that northeast Asians (East Asians and Siberians) first expanded across Beringia inland through a passage between glaciers that opened into the western Great Plains of the United States, just east of the Rocky Mountains, around 13,000 years ago (Swisher et al. 2013). While life up north in the cold environment would have been harsh, migrating birds and an emerging forest might have provided sustenance as generations expanded through this land (Potter et al. 2018).

However, in recent decades, researchers have accumulated evidence against the Ice-Free Corridor model. Archaeologist K. R. Fladmark (1979) brought the alternate **Coastal Route model** into the archaeological spotlight; researcher Jon M. Erlandson has been at the forefront of compiling support for this theory (Erlandson et al. 2015). The new focus is the southern edge of the land bridge instead of its center: About 16,000 years ago, members of our species expanded along the coastline from northeast Asia, east through Beringia, and south down the Pacific Coast of North America while the inland was still sealed off by ice. The coast would have been free of ice at least part of the year, and many resources would have been found there, such as fish (e.g., salmon), mammals (e.g., whales, seals, and otters), and plants (e.g., seaweed).

South through the Americas

When the first modern *Homo sapiens* reached the Western Hemisphere, the spread through the Americas was rapid. Multiple migration waves crossed from North to South America (Posth et al. 2018). Our species took advantage of the lack of hominin competition and the bountiful resources both along the coasts and inland. The Americas had their own wide array of megafauna, which included woolly mammoths (Figure 12.18), mastodons, camels, horses, ground sloths, giant tortoises, and—a favorite of researchers—a two-meter-tall beaver. The reason we cannot see these amazing animals today may be that resources gained from these fauna were crucial to the survival for people over 12,000 years ago (Araujo et al. 2017). Several sites are notable for what they add to our understanding of the distant past in the Americas, including interactions with megafauna and other elements of the environment.

Figure 12.18: Life-size reconstruction of a woolly mammoth at the Page Museum, part of the La Brea Tar Pits complex in Los Angeles, California. Outside of Africa, megafauna such as this went extinct around the time that humans entered their range. Credit: Woolly Mammoth (at La Brea Tar Pits & Museum) by Keith Chan is under a CC BY-NC 4.0 License.

A 2019 discovery may allow researchers to improve theories about the peopling of the Americas. In White Sands National Park, New Mexico, 60 human footprints have been astonishingly dated to around 22,000 years ago (Bennett et al. 2021). This date and location do not match either the Ice-Free Corridor or Coastal Route models. Researchers are now working to verify the find and adjust previous models to account for the new evidence. This groundbreaking find is sparking new theories; it is another example of the fast pace of research performed on our past.

Monte Verde is a landmark site that shows that the human population had expanded down the whole vertical stretch of the Americas to Chile by 14,600 years ago, only a few thousand years after humans first entered the Western Hemisphere from Alaska. The site has been excavated by archaeologist Tom D. Dillehay and his team (2015). The remains of nine distinct edible species of seaweed at the site shows familiarity with coastal resources and relates to the Coastal Route model by showing a connection between the inland people and the sea.

Named after the town in New Mexico, the Clovis stone-tool style is the first example of a widespread culture across much of North America, between 13,400 and 12,700 years ago (Miller, Holliday, and Bright 2013). Clovis points were fluted with two small projections, one on each end of the base, facing away from the head (Figure 12.19). The stone points found at this site match those found as far as the Canadian border and northern Mexico, and from the west coast to the east coast of the United States. Fourteen Clovis sites also contained the remains of mammoths or mastodons, suggesting that hunting megafauna with these points was an important part of life for the Clovis people. After the spread of the Clovis style, it diversified into several regional styles, keeping some of the Clovis form but also developing their own unique touches.

Figure 12.19: The Clovis point has a distinctive structure. It has a wide tip, and its base has two small projections. This example was carved from chert and found in north-central Ohio, dated to around 11,000 years ago. Credit: Clovis Point (15.2012.25) by the Smithsonian [Department of Anthropology; Cooper Hewitt, Smithsonian Design Museum] is used for educational and non-commercial purposes as outlined by the Smithsonian.

Summary of Modern *H. sapiens in the Americas*

Research in Native American origins found some surprising details, refining older models. Genetically, the migration can be considered one long period of movement with splits into regional populations. This finding matches the sudden appearance and diversification of the homegrown Clovis culture. A few thousand years after arrival into the hemisphere, people had already covered the Americas from north to south.

The peopling of the Americas also had a lot of elements in common with the prior spread of humans across Africa, Europe, Asia, and Australia. In all of these expansions, these pioneers explored new lands that tested their ability to adapt, both culturally and biologically. Besides stone-tool technology, the use of ochre as decoration was seen from South Africa to South America. The coasts and rivers were likely avenues in the movement of people, artifacts, and ideas, outlining the land masses while providing access to varied environments. The presence of megafauna aided human success, but this resource was eventually depleted in many parts of the world.

The Big Picture: The Assimilation Hypothesis

How do researchers make sense of all of these modern *Homo sapiens* discoveries that cover over 300,000 years of time and stretch across every continent except Antarctica? How was modern *Homo sapiens* related to archaic *Homo sapiens*?

The **Assimilation hypothesis** proposes that modern *Homo sapiens* evolved in Africa first and expanded out but also interbred with the archaic *Homo sapiens* they encountered outside Africa (Figure 12.20). This hypothesis is powerful since it explains why Africa has the oldest modern human fossils, why early modern humans found in Europe and Asia bear a resemblance to the regional archaics, and why traces of archaic DNA can be found in our genomes today (Dannemann and Racimo 2018; Reich et al. 2010; Reich et al. 2011; Slatkin and Racimo 2016; Smith et al. 2017; Wall and Yoshihara Caldeira Brandt 2016).

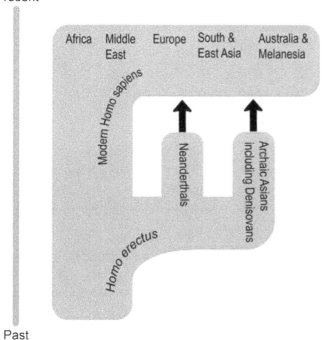

Figure 12.20: This diagram shows archaic humans, having evolved from Homo erectus, expanded from Africa and established the Neanderthal and Denisovan groups. In Africa, archaic humans evolved modern traits and expanded from the continent as well, interbreeding with two archaic groups across Europe and Asia. Credit: Assimilation Model (Figure 12.23)l original to Explorations: An Open Invitation to Biological Anthropology by Keith Chan and Katie Nelson is under a CC BY-NC 4.0 License.

While researchers have produced a model that satisfies the data, there are still a lot of questions for paleoanthropologists to answer regarding our origins. What were the patterns of migration in each part of the world? Why did the archaic humans go extinct? In what ways did archaic and modern humans interact? The definitive explanation of how our species started and what our ancestors did is still out there to be found. You are now in a great place to welcome the next discovery about our distant past—maybe you'll even contribute to our understanding as well.

The Chain Reaction of Agriculture

While it may be hard to imagine today, for most of our species' existence we were nomadic: moving through the landscape without a singular home. Instead of a refrigerator or pantry stocked with food, we procured nutrition and other resources as needed based on what was available in the environment. Instead of collecting and displaying shelves of stuff, we kept our possessions small for mobility. This section gives an overview of how the foraging lifestyle enabled the expansion of our species and how the invention of a new way of life caused a chain reaction of cultural change.

The Foraging Tradition

There are a variety of possible **subsistence strategies**, or methods of finding sustenance and resources. To understand our species is to understand the subsistence strategy of **foraging**, or the search for resources in the environment. While most (but not all) humans today live in cultures that practice **agriculture** (whereby we greatly shape the environment to mass produce what we need), we have spent far more time as nomadic foragers than as settled agriculturalists. As such, our traits have evolved to be primarily geared toward foraging. For instance, our efficient bipedalism allows persistence-hunting across long distances as well as movement from resource to resource.

How does human foraging, also known as hunting and gathering, work? Anthropologists have used all four fields to answer this question (see Ember n.d.). Typically, people formed **bands**, or kin-based groups of around 50 people or less (rarely over 100). A band's organization would be **egalitarian**, with a flexible hierarchy based on an individual's age, level of experience, and relationship with others. Everyone would have a general knowledge of the skills assigned to their gender roles, rather than specializing in different occupations. A band would be able to move from place to place in the environment, using knowledge of the area to forage (Figure 12.21). In varied environments—from savannas to tropical forests, deserts, coasts, and the Arctic circle—people found sustenance needed for survival. Our species's omnivorousness and cultural abilities led us to excel in the generalist-specialist niche.

Figure 12.21: A present-day San man in Namibia demonstrates hunting using archery. Anthropologists study the San today to learn about the persistence of foraging as a viable lifestyle, while noting how these cultures have changed over time and how they interact with other groups. Credit: **San hunter with bow and arrow** by CharlesFred has been modified (color modified) and is under a CC BY-NC-SA 2.0 License.

Humans made extensive use of the foraging subsistence strategy, but this lifestyle did have limitations. The ease of foraging depended on the richness of the environment. Due to the lack of storage, resources had to be dependably found when needed. While a bountiful environment would require just a few hours of foraging a day and could lead to a focus on one location, the level and duration of labor increased greatly in poor or unreliable environments. Labor was also needed to process the acquired resources, which contributed to the foragers' daily schedule (Crittenden and Schnorr 2017).

The adaptations to foraging found in modern *Homo sapiens* may explain why our species became so successful both within Africa and in the rapid expansion around the world. Overcoming the limitations, each generation at the edge of our species's range would have found it beneficial to expand a little further, keeping contact with other bands but moving into unexplored territory where resources were more plentiful. The cumulative effect would have been the spread of modern *Homo sapiens* across continents and hemispheres.

Why Agriculture?

After hundreds of thousands of years of foraging, some groups of people around 12,000 years ago started to practice agriculture. This transition, called the **Neolithic Revolution,** occurred at the start of the **Holocene** epoch. While the reasons for this global change are still being investigated, two likely co-occurring causes are a growing human population and natural global climate change.

Overcrowding could have affected the success of foraging in the environment, leading to the development of a more productive subsistence strategy (Cohen 1977). Foraging works best with low population densities since each band needs a lot of space to support itself. If too many people occupy the same environment, they deplete the area faster. The high population could exceed the **carrying capacity**, or number of people a location can reliably support. Reaching carrying capacity on a global level due to growing population and limited areas of expansion would have been an increasingly pressing issue after the expansion through the major continents by 14,600 years ago.

A changing global climate immediately preceded the transition to agriculture, so researchers have also explored a connection between the two events. Since the **Last Glacial Maximum** of 23,000 years ago, the Earth slowly warmed. Then, from 13,000 to 11,700 years ago, the temperature in most of the Northern Hemisphere dropped suddenly in a phenomenon called the **Younger Dryas.** Glaciers returned in Europe, Asia, and North America. In Mesopotamia, which includes the Levant, the climate changed from warm and humid to cool and dry. The change would have occurred over decades, disrupting the usual nomadic patterns and subsistence of foragers around the world. The disruption to foragers due to the temperature shift could have been a factor in spurring a transition to agriculture. Researchers Gregory K. Dow and colleagues (2009) believe that foraging bands would have clustered in the new resource-rich places where people started to direct their labor to farming the limited area. After the Younger Dryas ended, people expanded out of the clusters with their agricultural knowledge (Figure 12.22).

Figure 12.22: The map shows the areas where agriculture was independently invented around the world and where they spread. Blue arrows show the spread of agriculture from these zones to other regions. Credit: Centres of origin and spread of agriculture by Joe Roe is under a CC BY-SA 3.0 License. [Image Description].

The double threat of the limitation of human continental expansion and the sudden global climate change may have placed bands in peril as more populations outpaced their environment's carrying capacity. Not only had a growing population led to increased competition with other bands, but environments worldwide shifted to create more uncertainty. As people in different areas around the world faced this unpredictable situation, they became the independent inventors of agriculture.

Agriculture around the World

Due to global changes to the human experience starting from 12,000 years ago, cultures with no knowledge of each other turned toward intensely farming their local resources (see Figure 12.22). The first farmers engaged in artificial selection of their domesticates to enhance useful traits over generations. The switch to agriculture took time and effort with no guarantee of success and constant challenges (e.g. fires, droughts, diseases, and pests). The regions with the most widespread impact in the face of these obstacles became the primary centers of agriculture (Figure 12.23; Fuller 2010):

- Mesopotamia: The Fertile Crescent from the Tigris and Euphrates rivers through the Levant was where bands started to domesticate plants and animals around 12,000 years ago. The connection between the development of agriculture and the Younger Dryas was especially strong here. Farmed crops included wheat, barley, peas, and lentils. This was also where cattle, pigs, sheep, and goats were domesticated.
- South and East Asia: Multiple regions across this land had varieties of rice, millet, and soybeans by 10,000 years ago. Pigs were farmed with no connection to Mesopotamia. Chickens were also originally from this region, bred for fighting first and food second.
- New Guinea: Agriculture started here 10,000 years ago. Bananas, sugarcane, and taro were native to this island. Sweet potatoes were brought back from voyages to South America around the year C.E. 1000. No known animal farming occurred here.
- Mesoamerica: Agriculture from Central Mexico to northern South America also occurred from 10,000 years ago; it was also only plant based. Maize was a crop bred from teosinte grass, which has become one of the global staples. Beans, squash, and avocados were also grown in this region.
- The Andes: Starting around 8,000 years ago, local domesticated plants started with squash but later included potatoes, tomatoes, beans, and quinoa. Maize was brought down from Mesoamerica. The main farm animals were llamas, alpacas, and guinea pigs.
- Sub-Saharan Africa: This region went through a change 5,000 years ago called the Bantu expansion. The Bantu agriculturalists were established in West Central Africa and then expanded south and east. Native varieties of rice, yams, millet, and sorghum were grown across this area. Cattle were also domesticated here.
- Eastern North America: This region was the last major independent agriculture center, from 4,000 years ago. Squash and sunflower are the

produce from this region that are most known today, though sumpweed and pitseed goosefoot were also farmed. Hunting was still the main source of animal products.

Figure 12.23: Rice farmers in the present day using draft cattle to prepare their field. Credit: Plowing muddy field using cattle by IRRI Photos (International Rice Research Institute) has been modified (color modified) and is under a CC BY-NC-SA 2.0 License.

By 5,000 years ago, our species was well within the Neolithic Revolution. Agriculturalists spread to neighboring parts of the world with their domesticates, further expanding the use of this subsistence strategy. From this point, the human species changed from being primarily foragers to primarily agriculturalists with skilled control of their environments. The planet changed from mostly unaffected by human presence to being greatly transformed by humans. The revolution took millennia, but it was a true revolution as our species' lifestyle was dramatically reshaped.

Cultural Effects of Agriculture

The worldwide adoption of agriculture altered the course of human culture and history forever. The core change in human culture due to agriculture is the move toward not moving: rather than live a nomadic lifestyle, farmers had to remain in one area to tend to their crops and livestock. The term for living bound to a certain location is **sedentarism**. This led to new aspects of life that were uncommon among foragers: the construction of permanent shelters and agricultural infrastructure, such as fields and irrigation, plus the development of storage technology, such as pottery, to preserve extra resources in case of future instability.

The high productivity of successful agriculture sparked further changes (Smith 2009). Since successful agriculture produced a much-greater amount of food and other resources per unit of land compared to foraging, the population growth rate skyrocketed. The surplus of a bountiful harvest also provided insurance for harder times, reducing the risk of famine. Changes happened to society as well. With a few farming households producing enough food to feed many others, other people could focus on other tasks. So began specialization into different occupations such as craftspeople, traders, religious figures, and artists, spurring innovation in these areas as people could now devote time and effort toward specific skills. These interdependent people would settle an area together for convenience. The growth of these settlements led to **urbanization**, the founding of cities that became the foci of human interaction (Figure 12.24).

The formation of cities led to new issues that sparked the growth of further specializations, called **institutions**. These are cultural constructs that exist beyond the individual and have wide control over a population. Leadership of these cities became hierarchical with different levels of rank and control.

Figure 12.24: View of downtown San Diego taken by the author at a shopping complex during a break from jury duty. Here, people live amongst structures that facilitate commerce, government, tourism, and art. Credit: Downtown San Diego (October 13, 2016; Figure 12.28) original to Explorations: An Open Invitation to Biological Anthropology by Keith Chan is under a CC BY-NC 4.0 License.

The stratification of society increased social inequality between those with more or less power over others. Under leadership, people built impressive **monumental architecture**, such as pyramids and palaces, that embodied the wealth and power of these early cities. Alliances could unite cities, forming the earliest states. In several regions of the world, state organization expanded into empires, wide-ranging political entities that covered a variety of cultures.

Urbanization brought new challenges as well. The concentration of sedentary peoples was ideal for infectious diseases to thrive since they could jump from person to person and even from livestock to person (Armelagos, Brown, and Turner 2005). While successful agriculture provided a large surplus of food to thwart famine, the food produced offered less diverse food sources than foragers' diets (Cohen and Armelagos 1984; Cohen and Crane-Kramer 2007). This shift in nutrition caused other diseases to flourish among those who adopted farming, such as dental cavities and malocclusion (the misalignment of teeth caused by soft, agricultural diets). The need to extract "wisdom teeth" or third molars seen in agricultural cultures today stems from this misalignment between the environment our ancestors adapted to and our lifestyles today.

As the new disease trends show, the adoption of agriculture and the ensuing cultural changes were not entirely positive. It is also important to note that this is not an absolutely linear progression of human culture from simple to complex. In many cases, empires have collapsed and, in some cases, cities dispersed to low-density bands that rejected institutions. However, a global trend has emerged since the adoption of agriculture, wherein population and social inequality have increased, leading to the massive and influential nation-states of today.

The rise of states in Europe has a direct impact on many of this book's topics. Science started as a European cultural practice by the upper class that became a standardized way to study the world. Education became an institution to provide a standardized path toward producing and gaining knowledge. The scientific study of human diversity, embroiled in the race concept that still haunts us today, was connected to the European slave trade and colonialism.

Figure 12.25: This combine harvester can collect and process grain at a massive scale. Our food now commonly comes from enormous farms located around the world. Credit: **Combine CR9060** by Hertzsprung is under a CC BY-SA 3.0 License.

Also starting in Europe, the Industrial Revolution of the 19th century turned cities into centers of mass manufacturing and spurred the rapid development of inventions (Figure 12.25). In the technologically interconnected world of today, human society has reached a new level of complexity with **globalization**. In this system, goods are mass-produced and consumed in different parts of the world, weakening the reliance on local farms and factories. The imbalanced relationship between consumers and producers of goods further increases economic inequality.

As states based on agriculture and industry keep exerting influence on humanity today, there are people, like the Hadzabe of Tanzania, who continue to live a lifestyle centered on foraging. Due to the overwhelming force that agricultural societies exert, foragers today have been marginalized to live in the least habitable parts of the world—the areas that are not conducive to farming, such as tropical rainforests, deserts, and the Arctic (Headland et al. 1989). Foragers can no longer live in the abundant environments that humans would have enjoyed before the Neolithic Revolution. Interactions with agriculturalists are typically imbalanced, with trade and other exchanges heavily favoring the larger group. One of anthropology's important roles today is to intelligently and humanely manage equitable interactions between people of different backgrounds and levels of influence.

Special Topic: Indigenous Land Management

Insight into the lives of past modern humans has evolved as researchers revise previous theories and establish new connections with Indigenous knowledge holders.

The outdated view of foraging held that people lived off of the land without leaving an impact on the environment. Accompanying this idea was anthropologist Marshall Sahlins's (1968) proposal that foragers were the "original affluent society" since they were meeting basic needs and achieving satisfaction with less work hours than agriculturalists and city-dwellers. This view countered an earlier idea that foragers were always on the brink of starvation. Sahlins's theory took hold in the public eye as an attractive counterpoint to our busy contemporary lives in which we strive to meet our endless wants.

A fruitful type of study involving researchers collaborating with Indigenous experts has found that foragers did not just live off the land with minimal effort nor were they barely surviving in unchanging environments. Instead, they shaped the landscape to their needs using labor and strategies that were more subtle than what European colonizers and subsequent researchers were used to seeing. Research from two regions shows the latest developments in understanding Indigenous land management.

In British Columbia, Canada, the bridging of scientific and Indigenous perspectives has shown that the forests of the region are not untouched wilderness but, rather, have been crafted by Indigenous peoples thousands of years ago. Forest gardens adjacent to archaeological sites show higher plant diversity than unmanaged places even after 150 years (Armstrong et al. 2021). On the coast, 3,500-year-old archaeological sites are evidence of constructed clam gardens, according to Indigenous experts (Lepofsky et al. 2015). Another project, in consultation with Elders of the T'exelc (William Lakes First Nation) in British Columbia, introduced researchers to explanations of how forests were managed before the practice was disrupted by European colonialism (Copes-Gerbitz et al. 2021). Careful management of controlled fires reduced the density of the forest to favor plants such as raspberries and allow easier movement through the landscape.

Similarly, the study of landscapes in Australia, in consultation with Aboriginal Australians today, shows that areas previously considered wilderness by scientists were actually the result of controlling fauna and fires. The presence of grasslands with adjacent forests were purposely constructed to attract kangaroos for hunting (Gammage 2008). People also managed other animal and insect life, from emus to caterpillars. In Tasmania, a shift from productive grassland to wildfire-prone rainforest occurred after Aboriginal Australian land management was replaced by British colonial rule (Fletcher, Hall, and Alexander 2021). The site of Budj Bim of the Gunditjmara people has archaeological features of **aquaculture**, or the farming of fish, that date back 6,600 years (McNiven et al. 2012; McNiven et al. 2015). These examples show that Indigenous knowledge of how to manipulate the environment may be invaluable at the state level, such as by creating an Aboriginal ranger program to guide modern land management.

Conclusion

Modern *Homo sapiens* is the species that took the hominin lifestyle the furthest to become the only living member of that lineage. The largest factor that allowed us to persist while other hominins went extinct was likely our advanced ability to culturally adapt to a wide variety of environments. Our species, with its skeletal and behavioral traits, was well-suited to be generalist-specialists who successfully foraged across most of the world's environments. The biological basis of this adaptation was our reorganized brain that facilitated innovation in cultural adaptations and intelligence for leveraging our social ties and finding ways to acquire resources from the environment. As the brain's ability increased, it shaped the skull by reducing the evolutionary pressure to have large teeth and robust cranial bones to produce the modern *Homo sapiens* face.

Our ability to be generalist-specialists is seen in the geographical range that modern *Homo sapiens* covered in 300,000 years. In Africa, our species formed from multiregional gene flow that loosely connected archaic humans across the continent. People then expanded out to the rest of the continental Eurasia and even further to the Americas.

For most of our species's existence, foraging was the general subsistence strategy within which people specialized to culturally adapt to their local environment. With omnivorousness and mobility, people found ways to extract and process resources, shaping the environment in return. When resource uncertainty hit the species, people around the world focused on agriculture to have a firmer control of sustenance. The new strategy shifted human history toward exponential growth and innovation, leading to our high dependence on cultural adaptations today.

While a cohesive image of our species has formed in recent years, there is still much to learn about our past. The work of many driven researchers shows that there are amazing new discoveries made all the time that refine our knowledge of human evolution. Technological innovations such as DNA analysis enable scientists to approach lingering questions from new angles. The answers we get allow us to ask even more insightful questions that will lead us to the next revelation. Like the pink limestone strata at Jebel Irhoud, previous effort has taken us so far and you are now ready to see what the next layer of discovery holds.

Special Topic: The Future of Humanity

A common question stemming from understanding human evolution is: What will the genetic and biological traits of our species be hundreds of thousands of years in the future? When faced with this question, people tend to think of directional selection. Maybe our braincases will be even larger, resembling the large-headed and small-bodied aliens of science fiction (Figure 12.26). Or, our hands could be specialized for interacting with our touch-based technology with less risk of repetitive injury. These ideas do not stand up to scrutiny. Since natural selection is based on adaptations that increase reproductive success, any directional change must be due to a higher rate of producing successful offspring compared to other alleles. Larger brains and more agile fingers would be convenient to possess, but they do not translate into an increase in the underlying allele frequencies.

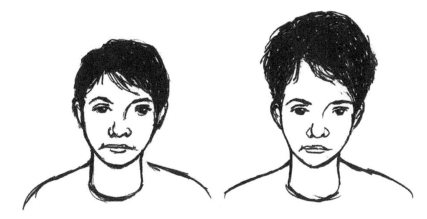

Figure 12.26: Will we evolve toward even more globular brains? Actually, this trend is not likely to continue for our species. Credit: Hypothetical image of future human evolution (Figure 12.30) original to Explorations: An Open Invitation to Biological Anthropology by Mary Nelson is under a CC BY-NC 4.0 License.

Scientists are hesitant to professionally speculate on the unknowable, and we will never know what is in store for our species one thousand or one million years from now, but there are two trends in human evolution that may carry on into the future: increased genetic variation and a reduction in regional differences.

Rather than a directional change, genetic variation in our species could expand. Our technology can protect us from extreme environments and pathogens, even if our biological traits are not tuned to handle these stressors. The rapid pace of technological advancement means that biological adaptations will become less and less relevant to reproductive success, so nonbeneficial genetic traits will be more likely to remain in the gene pool. Biological anthropologist Jay T. Stock (2008) views environmental stress as needing to defeat two layers of protection before affecting our genetics. The first layer is our cultural adaptations. Our technology and knowledge can reduce pressure on one's genotype to be "just right" to pass to the next generation. The second defense is our flexible physiology, such as our acclimatory responses. Only stressors not handled by these powerful responses would then cause natural selection on our alleles. These shields are already substantial, and cultural adaptations will only keep increasing in strength.

The increasing ability to travel far from one's home region means that there will be a mixing of genetic variation on a global level in the future of our species. In recent centuries, gene flow of people around the world has increased, creating admixture in populations that had been separated for tens of thousands of years. For skin color, this means that populations all around the world could exhibit the whole range of skin colors, rather than the current pattern of decreasing melanin pigment farther from the equator. The same trend of intermixing would apply to all other traits, such as blood types. While our genetics will become more varied, the variation will be more intermixed instead of regionally isolated.

Our distant descendants will not likely be dextrous ultraintellectuals; more likely, they will be a highly variable and mobile species supported by novel cultural adaptations that make up for any inherited biological limitations. Technology may even enable the editing of DNA directly, changing these trends. With the uncertainty of our future, these are just the best-educated guesses for now. Our future is open and will be shaped little by little by the environment, our actions, and the actions of our descendants.

Hominin Species Summary

Hominin	Modern *Homo sapiens*
Dates	315,000 years ago to present
Region(s)	Starting in Africa, then expanding around the world
Famous discoveries	Cro-Magnon individuals, discovered 1868 in Dordogne, France. Otzi the Ice Man, discovered 1991 in the Alps between Austria and Italy. Kennewick man, discovered 1996 in Washington state.
Brain size	1400 cc average
Dentition	Extremely small with short cusps.
Cranial features	An extremely globular brain case and gracile features throughout the cranium. The mandibular symphysis forms a chin at the anterior-most point.
Postcranial features	Gracile skeleton adapted for efficient bipedal locomotion at the expense of the muscular strength of most other large primates.
Culture	Extremely extensive and varied culture with many spoken and written languages. Art is ubiquitous. Technology is broad in complexity and impact on the environment.
Other	The only living hominin. Chimpanzees and bonobos are the closest living relatives.

Review Questions

- What are the skeletal and behavioral traits that define modern *Homo sapiens*? What are the evolutionary explanations for its presence?
- What are some creative ways that researchers have learned about the past by studying fossils and artifacts?
- How do the discoveries mentioned in "First Africa, Then the World" fit the Assimilation model?
- What is foraging? What adaptations do we have for this subsistence strategy? Could you train to be a skilled forager?
- What are aspects of your life that come from dependence on agriculture and its cultural effects? Where did the ingredients of your favorite foods originate from?

Key Terms

African multiregionalism: The idea that modern *Homo sapiens* evolved as a complex web of small regional populations with sporadic gene flow among them.

Agriculture: The mass production of resources through farming and domestication.

Aquaculture: The farming of fish using techniques such as trapping, channels, and artificial ponds.

Assimilation hypothesis: Current theory of modern human origins stating that the species evolved first in Africa and interbred with archaic humans of Europe and Asia.

Atlatl: A handheld spear thrower that increased the force of thrown projectiles.

Band: A small group of people living together as foragers.

Beringia: Ancient landmass that connected Siberia and Alaska. The ancestors of Indigenous Americans would have crossed this area to reach the Americas.

Carrying capacity: The amount of organisms that an environment can reliably support.

Coastal Route model: Theory that the first Paleoindians crossed to the Americas by following the southern coast of Beringia.

Early Modern *Homo sapiens*, Early Anatomically Modern Human: Terms used to refer to transitional fossils between archaic and modern *Homo sapiens* that have a mosaic of traits. Humans like ourselves, who mostly lack archaic traits, are referred to as Late Modern *Homo sapiens* and simply Anatomically Modern Humans.

Egalitarian: Human organization without strict ranks. Foraging societies tend to be more egalitarian than those based on other subsistence strategies.

Foraging: Lifestyle consisting of frequent movement through the landscape and acquiring resources with minimal storage capacity.

Generalist-specialist niche: The ability to survive in a variety of environments by developing local expertise. Evolution toward this niche may have been what allowed modern *Homo sapiens* to expand past the geographical range of other human species.

Globalization: A recent increase in the interconnectedness and interdependence of people that is facilitated with long-distance networks.

Globular: Having a rounded appearance. Increased globularity of the braincase is a trait of modern *Homo sapiens*.

Gracile: Having a smooth and slender quality; the opposite of robust.

Holocene: The epoch of the Cenozoic Era starting around 12,000 years ago and lasting arguably through the present.

Ice-Free Corridor model: Theory that the first Native Americans crossed to the Americas through a passage between glaciers.

Institutions: Long-lasting and influential cultural constructs. Examples include government, organized religion, academia, and the economy.

Last Glacial Maximum: The time 23,000 years ago when the most recent ice age was the most intense.

Later Stone Age: Time period following the Middle Stone Age with a diversification in tool types, starting around 50,000 years ago.

Levant: The eastern coast of the Mediterranean. The site of early modern human expansion from Africa and later one of the centers of agriculture.

Megafauna: Large ancient animals that may have been hunted to extinction by people around the world.

Mental eminence: The chin on the mandible of modern *H. sapiens*. One of the defining traits of our species.

Microlith: Small stone tool found in the Later Stone Age; also called a bladelet.

Middle Stone Age: Time period known for Mousterian lithics that connects African archaic to modern *Homo sapiens*.

Monumental architecture: Large and labor-intensive constructions that signify the power of the elite in a sedentary society. A common type is the pyramid, a raised crafted structure topped with a point or platform.

Mosaic: Composed from a mix or composite of traits.

Neolithic Revolution: Time of rapid change to human cultures due to the invention of agriculture, starting around 12,000 years ago.

Ochre: Iron-based mineral pigment that can be a variety of yellows, reds, and browns. Used by modern human cultures worldwide since at least 80,000 years ago.

Sahul: Ancient landmass connecting New Guinea and Australia.

Sedentarism: Lifestyle based on having a stable home area; the opposite of nomadism.

Southern Dispersal model: Theory that modern *H. sapiens* expanded from East Africa by crossing the Red Sea and following the coast east across Asia.

Subsistence strategy: The method an organism uses to find nourishment and other resources.

Sunda: Ancient Asian landmass that incorporated modern Southeast Asia.

Supraorbital torus: The bony brow ridge across the top of the eye orbits on many hominin crania.

Upper Paleolithic: Time period considered synonymous with the Later Stone Age.

Urbanization: The increase of population density as people settled together in cities.

Wallacea: Archipelago southeast of Sunda with different biodiversity than Asia.

Younger Dryas: The rapid change in global climate—notably a cooling of the Northern Hemisphere—13,000 years ago.

About the Author

Keith Chan, Ph.D.

Grossmont-Cuyamaca Community College District and MiraCosta College, drkeithcchan@gmail.com, Dr. Keith Chan is an instructor of anthropology at Grossmont-Cuyamaca Community College District and MiraCosta College in San Diego County. He reached this step of his anthropological path after many memorable experiences across the country and the hemisphere. He earned a bachelor's degree in anthropology from the University of California, Berkeley, in 2001. As a graduate student at the University of Missouri, he traveled to Perú with teams of students to study skeletons in the archaeological record to understand the lives of ancient Andeans. He completed his dissertation and earned a Ph.D. in 2011. Inspired by many educators in his journey, Dr. Chan turned his career toward teaching anthropology and helping students understand and appreciate humanity.

For Further Exploration

Websites

First-person virtual tour of Lascaux cave with annotated cave art: Ministère de la Culture and Musée d'Archéologie Nationale. "Visit the cave" Lascaux website.

Online anthropology magazine articles related to paleoanthropology and human evolution: SAPIENS. "Evolution." *SAPIENS* website.

Various presentations of information about hominin evolution: Smithsonian Institution. "What does it mean to be human?" *Smithsonian National Museum of Natural History* website.

Magazine-style articles on archaeology and paleoanthropology: ThoughtCo. "Archaeology." ThoughtCo. Website.

Database of comparisons across hominins and primates: University of California, San Diego. "MOCA Domains." *Center for Academic Research & Training in Anthropogeny* website.

Books

Engaging book that covers human-made changes to the environment with industrialization and globalization: Kolbert, Elizabeth. 2014. *The Sixth Extinction: An Unnatural History*. New York: Bloomsbury.

Overview of what human life was like among the environmental shifts of the Ice Age: Woodward, Jamie. 2014. *The Ice Age: A Very Short Introduction*. Oxford: OUP Press.

Articles

Recent review paper about the current state of paleoanthropology research: Stringer, C. 2016. "The Origin and Evolution of *Homo sapiens*." *Philosophical Transactions of the Royal Society B* 371 (1698).

Overview of the history of American paleoanthropology and the many debates that have occurred over the years: Trinkaus, E. 2018. "One Hundred Years of Paleoanthropology: An American Perspective." *American Journal of Physical Anthropology* 165 (4): 638–651.

Amazing magazine article that synthesizes hominin evolution and why it is important to study this subject: Wheelwright, Jeff. 2015. "Days of Dysevolution." *Discover* 36 (4): 33–39.

Fascinating research on Ötzi, a mummy from 5,000 years ago: Wierer, Ursula, Simona Arrighi, Stefano Bertola, Günther Kaufmann, Benno Baumgarten, Annaluisa Pedrotti, Patrizia Pernter, and Jacques Pelegrin. 2018. "The Iceman's Lithic Toolkit: Raw Material, Technology, Typology and Use." *PLOS One* 13 (6): e0198292. https://doi.org/10.1371/journal.pone.0198292.

Documentaries

PBS NOVA series covering the expansion of modern *Homo sapiens* and interbreeding with archaic humans: Brown, Nicholas, dir. 2015. *First Peoples*. Edmonton: Wall to Wall Television. Amazon Prime Video.

PBS NOVA special featuring the footprints found in White Sands National Park: Falk, Bella, dir. 2016. *Ice Age Footprints*. Boston: Windfall Films. https://www.pbs.org/wgbh/nova/video/ice-age-footprints/.

PBS NOVA special about how modern humans evolved adaptations to different environments. Shows how present-day people live around the world: Thompson, Niobe, dir. 2016. *Great Human Odyssey*. Edmonton: Clearwater Documentary. http://www.pbs.org/wgbh/nova/evolution/great-human-odyssey.html.

References

Araujo, Bernardo B. A., Luiz Gustavo R. Oliveira-Santos, Matheus S. Lima-Ribeiro, José Alexandre F. Diniz-Filho, and Fernando A. S. Fernandez. 2017. "Bigger Kill Than Chill: The Uneven Roles of Humans and Climate on Late Quaternary Megafaunal Extinctions." *Quaternary International* 431: 216–222.

Armelagos, George J., Peter J. Brown, and Bethany Turner. 2005. "Evolutionary, Historical, and Political Economic Perspectives on Health and Disease." *Social Science & Medicine* 61 (4): 755–765.

Armstrong, C. G., J. E. D. Miller, A. C. McAlvay, P. M. Ritchie, and D. Lepofsky. 2021. "Historical Indigenous Land-Use Explains Plant Functional Trait Diversity. *Ecology and Society* 26 (2): 6.

Bar-Yosef Mayer, Daniella E., Bernard Vandermeersch, and Ofer Bar-Yosef. 2009. "Shells and Ochre in Middle Paleolithic Qafzeh Cave, Israel: Indications for Modern Behavior." *Journal of Human Evolution* 56 (3): 307–314.

Barbetti, M., and H. Allen. 1972. "Prehistoric Man at Lake Mungo, Australia, by 32,000 Years Bp." *Nature* 240 (5375): 46–48.

Bennett, M. R., D. Bustos, J. S. Pigati, K. B. Springer, T. M. Urban, V. T. Holliday, Sally C. Reynolds, et al. (2021). "Evidence of Humans in North America during the Last Glacial Maximum." *Science* 373 (6562): 1528–1531.

Bowler, J. M., Rhys Jones, Harry Allen, and A. G. Thorne. 1970. "Pleistocene Human Remains from Australia: A Living Site and Human Cremation from Lake Mungo, Western New South Wales." *World Archaeology* 2 (1): 39–60.

Brown, Peter. 1999. "The First Modern East Asians? Another Look at Upper Cave 101, Liujiang and Minatogawa 1." In *Interdisciplinary Perspectives on the Origins of the Japanese*, edited by K. Omoto, 105–131. Kyoto: International Research Center for Japanese Studies.

Brown, Peter. 2000. "Australian Pleistocene Variation and the Sex of Lake Mungo 3." *Journal of Human Evolution* 38 (5): 743–749.

Clarkson, Chris, Zenobia Jacobs, Ben Marwick, Richard Fullagar, Lynley Wallis, Mike Smith, Richard G. Roberts, et al. 2017. "Human Occupation of Northern Australia by 65,000 Years Ago." *Nature* 547 (7663): 306–310.

Cohen, Mark Nathan. 1977. *The Food Crisis in Prehistory: Overpopulation and the Origins of Agriculture.* New Haven, CT: Yale University Press.

Cohen, Mark Nathan, and George J. Armelagos, eds. 1984. *Paleopathology at the Origins of Agriculture.* Orlando, FL: Academic Press.

Cohen, Mark Nathan, and Gillian M. M. Crane-Kramer, eds. 2007. *Ancient Health: Skeletal Indicators of Agricultural and Economic Intensification.* Gainesville, FL: University Press of Florida.

Copes-Gerbitz, K., S. Hagerman, and L. Daniels. 2021. "Situating Indigenous Knowledge for Resilience in Fire-Dependent Social-Ecological Systems." *Ecology and Society* 26(4): 25. https://www.ecologyandsociety.org/vol26/iss4/art25/.

Coqueugniot, Hélène, Olivier Dutour, Baruch Arensburg, Henri Duday, Bernard Vandermeersch, and Anne-Marie Tillier. 2014. "Earliest Cranio-Encephalic Trauma from the Levantine Middle Palaeolithic: 3-D Reappraisal of the Qafzeh 11 Skull, Consequences of Pediatric Brain Damage on Individual Life Condition and Social Care." *PLOS ONE* 9 (7): e102822.

Crittenden, Alyssa N., and Stephanie L. Schnorr. 2017. "Current Views on Hunter-Gatherer Nutrition and the Evolution of the Human Diet." *American Journal of Physical Anthropology* 162 (S63): 84–109.

d'Errico, Francesco, Lucinda Backwell, Paola Villa, Ilaria Degano, Jeannette J. Lucejko, Marion K. Bamford, Thomas F. G. Higham, Maria Perla Colombini, and Peter B. Beaumont. 2012. "Early Evidence of San Material Culture Represented by Organic Artifacts from Border Cave, South Africa." *Proceedings of the National Academy of Sciences* 109 (33): 13214–13219.

d'Errico, Francesco, Christopher Henshilwood, Marian Vanhaeren, and Karen Van Niekerk. 2005. "Nassarius Kraussianus Shell Beads from Blombos Cave: Evidence for Symbolic Behaviour in the Middle Stone Age." *Journal of Human Evolution* 48 (1): 3–24.

Dannemann, Michael, and Fernando Racimo. 2018. "Something Old, Something Borrowed: Admixture and Adaptation in Human Evolution." *Current Opinion in Genetics & Development* 53: 1–8.

Day, M. H. 1969. "Omo Human Skeletal Remains." *Nature* 222: 1135–1138.

Dillehay, Tom D., Carlos Ocampo, José Saavedra, Andre Oliveira Sawakuchi, Rodrigo M. Vega, Mario Pino, Michael B. Collins, et al. 2015. "New Archaeological Evidence for an Early Human Presence at Monte Verde, Chile." *PLOS ONE* 10 (11): e0141923. doi:10.1371/journal.pone.0141923.

Dow, Gregory K., Clyde G. Reed, and Nancy Olewiler. 2009. "Climate Reversals and the Transition to Agriculture." *Journal of Economic Growth* 14 (1): 27–53.

Durband, Arthur C. 2014. "Brief Communication: Artificial Cranial Modification in Kow Swamp and Cohuna." *American Journal of Physical Anthropology* 155 (1): 173–178.

Ember, Carol R. N.d. "Hunter-Gatherers." *Explaining Human Culture. Human Relations Area Files*. Accessed March 4, 2023. http://hraf.yale.edu/ehc/summaries/hunter-gatherers.

Erlandson, Jon M., Todd J. Braje, Kristina M. Gill, and Michael H. Graham. 2015. "Ecology of the Kelp Highway: Did Marine Resources Facilitate Human Dispersal from Northeast Asia to the Americas?" *The Journal of Island and Coastal Archaeology* 10 (3): 392–411.

Fladmark, K. R. 1979. "Routes: Alternate Migration Corridors for Early Man in North America." *American Antiquity* 44 (1): 55–69.

Fletcher, M. S., T. Hall, and A. N. Alexandra. 2021. "The Loss of an Indigenous Constructed Landscape Following British Invasion of Australia: An Insight into the Deep Human Imprint on the Australian Landscape." *Ambio* 50(1): 138–149.

Fu, Qiaomei, Mateja Hajdinjak, Oana Teodora Moldovan, Silviu Constantin, Swapan Mallick, Pontus Skoglund, Nick Patterson, et al. 2015. "An Early Modern Human from Romania with a Recent Neanderthal Ancestor." *Nature* 524 (7564): 216–219.

Fuller, Dorian Q. 2010. "An Emerging Paradigm Shift in the Origins of Agriculture." *General Anthropology* 17 (2): 1, 8–11.

Gammage, B. 2008. "Plain Facts: Tasmania under Aboriginal Management." *Landscape Research* 33 (2): 241–254.

Germonpré, Mietje, Martina Lázničková-Galetová, and Mikhail V. Sablin. 2012. "Palaeolithic Dog Skulls at the Gravettian Předmostí Site, the Czech Republic." *Journal of Archaeological Science* 39 (1): 184–202.

Gröning, Flora, Jia Liu, Michael J. Fagan, and Paul O'Higgins. 2011. "Why Do Humans Have Chins? Testing the Mechanical Significance of Modern Human Symphyseal Morphology with Finite Element Analysis." *American Journal of Physical Anthropology* 144 (4): 593–606.

Harvati, Katerina. 2009. "Into Eurasia: A Geometric Morphometric Reassessment of the Upper Cave (Zhoukoudian) Specimens." *Journal of Human Evolution* 57 (6): 751–762.

Headland, Thomas N., Lawrence A. Reid, M. G. Bicchieri, Charles A. Bishop, Robert Blust, Nicholas E. Flanders, Peter M. Gardner, Karl L. Hutterer, Arkadiusz Marciniak, and Robert F. Schroeder. 1989. "Hunter-Gatherers and Their Neighbors from Prehistory to the Present." *Current Anthropology* 30 (1): 43–66.

Henshilwood, Christopher S., Francesco d'Errico, Karen L. van Niekerk, Yvan Coquinot, Zenobia Jacobs, Stein-Erik Lauritzen, Michel Menu, and Renata García-Moreno. 2011. "A 100,000-Year-Old Ochre-Processing Workshop at Blombos Cave, South Africa." *Science* 334 (6053): 219–222.

Hershkovitz, Israel, Gerhard W. Weber, Rolf Quam, Mathieu Duval, Rainer Grün, Leslie Kinsley, Avner Ayalon, et al. 2018. "The Earliest Modern Humans Outside Africa." *Science* 359 (6374): 456–459.

Hublin, Jean-Jacques, Abdelouahed Ben-Ncer, Shara E. Bailey, Sarah E. Freidline, Simon Neubauer, Matthew M. Skinner, Inga Bergmann, et al. 2017. "New Fossils from Jebel Irhoud, Morocco, and the Pan-African Origin of *Homo sapiens*." *Nature* 546 (7657): 289–292.

Lepofsky, D., N. F. Smith, N. Cardinal, J. Harper, M. Morris, M., Gitla (Elroy White), Randy Bouchard, et al. 2015. "Ancient Shellfish Mariculture on the Northwest Coast of North America." *American Antiquity* 80 (2): 236–259.

Lieberman, Daniel E. 2015. "Human Locomotion and Heat Loss: An Evolutionary Perspective." *Comprehensive Physiology* 5 (1): 99–117.

Lieberman, Daniel E., Brandeis M. McBratney, and Gail Krovitz. 2002. "The Evolution and Development of Cranial Form in *Homo sapiens*." *Proceedings of the National Academy of Sciences* 99 (3): 1134–1139.

Lieberman, Daniel E., Osbjorn M. Pearson, and Kenneth M. Mowbray. 2000. "Basicranial Influence on Overall Cranial Shape." *Journal of Human Evolution* 38 (2): 291–315.

Liu, Wu, María Martinón-Torres, Yan-jun Cai, Song Xing, Hao-wen Tong, Shu-wen Pei, Mark Jan Sier, Xiao-hong Wu, R. Lawrence Edwards, and Hai Cheng. 2015. "The Earliest Unequivocally Modern Humans in Southern China." *Nature* 526 (7575): 696-699.

Lucas, Peter W. 2007. "The Evolution of the Hominin Diet from a Dental Functional Perspective." In *Evolution of the Human Diet: The Known, the Unknown, and the Unknowable*, edited by Peter S. Ungar, 31–38 Oxford, UK: Oxford University Press.

McCarthy, Robert C., and Lynn Lucas. 2014. "A Morphometric Reassessment of Bou-Vp-16/1 from Herto, Ethiopia." *Journal of Human Evolution* 74: 114–117.

McDougall, Ian, Francis H. Brown, and John G. Fleagle. 2005. "Stratigraphic Placement and Age of Modern Humans from Kibish, Ethiopia." *Nature* 433 (7027): 733–736.

McNiven, I. J., J. Crouch, T. Richards, N. Dolby, and G. Jacobsen. 2012. "Dating Aboriginal Stone-Walled Fishtraps at Lake Condah, Southeast Australia." *Journal of Archaeological Science* 39 (2): 268–286.

McNiven, I., J. Crouch, T. Richards, K. Sniderman, N. Dolby, and G. Mirring. 2015. "Phased Redevelopment of an Ancient Gunditjmara Fish Trap over the Past 800 Years: Muldoons Trap Complex, Lake Condah, Southwestern Victoria." *Australian Archaeology* 81 (1): 44–58.

Michel, Véronique, Hélène Valladas, Guanjun Shen, Wei Wang, Jian-xin Zhao, Chuan-Chou Shen, Patricia Valensi, and Christopher J. Bae. 2016. "The Earliest Modern *Homo sapiens* in China?" *Journal of Human Evolution* 101: 101–104.

Miller, D. Shane, Vance T. Holliday, and Jordon Bright. 2013. "Clovis across the Continent." In *Paleoamerican Odyssey*, edited by Kelly E. Graf, Caroline V. Ketron, and Michael R. Waters, 207–220. College Station: Texas A&M University Press.

Neubauer, Simon, Jean-Jacques Hublin, and Philipp Gunz. 2018. "The Evolution of Modern Human Brain Shape." *Science Advances* 4 (1): eaao5961. https://doi.org/10.1126/sciadv.aao5961.

Pearson, Osbjorn M. 2000. "Postcranial Remains and the Origin of Modern Humans." *Evolutionary Anthropology* 9: 229–247.

Pearson, Osbjorn M. 2008. "Statistical and Biological Definitions of 'Anatomically Modern' Humans: Suggestions for a Unified Approach to Modern Morphology." *Evolutionary Anthropology: Issues, News, and Reviews* 17 (1): 38–48.

Pietschnig, Jakob, Lars Penke, Jelte M. Wicherts, Michael Zeiler, and Martin Voracek. 2015. "Meta-Analysis of Associations between Human Brain Volume and Intelligence Differences: How Strong Are They and What Do They Mean?" *Neuroscience & Biobehavioral Reviews* 57: 411–432.

Posth, Cosimo, Nathan Nakatsuka, Iosif Lazaridis, Pontus Skoglund, Swapan Mallick, Thiseas C. Lamnidis, Nadin Rohland, et al. 2018. "Reconstructing the Deep Population History of Central and South America." *Cell* 175 (5): 1185–1197.

Potter, Ben A., James F. Baichtal, Alwynne B. Beaudoin, Lars Fehren-Schmitz, C. Vance Haynes, Vance T. Holliday, Charles E. Holmes, et al. 2018. "Current Evidence Allows Multiple Models for the Peopling of the Americas." *Science Advances* 4 (8): eaat5473. https://doi.org/10.1126/sciadv.aat5473.

Reich, David, Richard E. Green, Martin Kircher, Johannes Krause, Nick Patterson, Eric Y. Durand, Bence Viola, et al. 2010. "Genetic History of an Archaic Hominin Group from Denisova Cave in Siberia." *Nature* 468 (7327): 1053–1060.

Reich, David, Nick Patterson, Martin Kircher, Frederick Delfin, Madhusudan R. Nandineni, Irina Pugach, Albert Min-Shan Ko, et al. 2011. "Denisova Admixture and the First Modern Human Dispersals into Southeast Asia and Oceania." *American Journal of Human Genetics* 89 (4): 516–528.

Richter, Daniel, Rainer Grün, Renaud Joannes-Boyau, Teresa E. Steele, Fethi Amani, Mathieu Rué, Paul Fernandes, et al. 2017. "The Age of the Hominin Fossils from Jebel Irhoud, Morocco, and the Origins of the Middle Stone Age." *Nature* 546 (7657): 293–296.

Roberts, Patrick, and Brian A. Stewart. 2018. "Defining the 'Generalist-Specialist' Niche for Pleistocene *Homo sapiens*." *Nature Human Behaviour* 2: 542–550.

Rougier, Helene, Ştefan Milota, Ricardo Rodrigo, Mircea Gherase, Laurenţiu Sarcină, Oana Moldovan, João Zilhão, et al. 2007. "Peştera Cu Oase 2 and the Cranial Morphology of Early Modern Europeans." *Proceedings of the National Academy of Sciences* 104 (4): 1165–1170.

Sahlins, Marshall. 1968. "Notes on the Original Affluent Society." In *Man the Hunter*, edited by R. B. Lee and I. DeVore, 85–89. New York: Aldine Publishing Company.

Sawyer, G. J., and Blaine Maley. 2005. "Neanderthal Reconstructed." *The Anatomical Record (Part B: New Anat.)* 283 (1): 23–31.

Scerri, Eleanor M. L., Mark G. Thomas, Andrea Manica, Philipp Gunz, Jay T. Stock, Chris Stringer, Matt Grove, et al. 2018. "Did Our Species Evolve in Subdivided Populations Across Africa, and Why Does It Matter?" *Trends in Ecology & Evolution* 33 (8): 582–594.

Shea, John J. 2011. "Refuting a Myth about Human Origins." *American Scientist* 99 (2): 128–135.

Shea, John J., and Ofer Bar-Yosef. 2005. "Who Were the Skhul/Qafzeh People? An Archaeological Perspective on Eurasia's Oldest Modern Humans." *Journal of the Israel Prehistoric Society* 35: 451–468.

Slatkin, Montgomery, and Fernando Racimo. 2016. "Ancient DNA and Human History." *Proceedings of the National Academy of Sciences* 113 (23): 6380–6387.

Smith, Fred H., James C. M. Ahern, Ivor Janković, and Ivor Karavanić. 2017. "The Assimilation Model of Modern Human Origins in Light of Current Genetic and Genomic Knowledge." *Quaternary International* 450: 126–136.

Smith, Michael. 2009. "V. Gordon Childe and the Urban Revolution: A Historical Perspective on a Revolution in Urban Studies." *Town Planning Review* 80 (1): 3–29.

Stock, Jay T. 2008. "Are Humans Still Evolving?" *EMBO Reports* 9 (Suppl 1): S51–S54.

Swisher, Mark E., Dennis L. Jenkins, Lionel E. Jackson Jr., and Fred M. Phillips. 2013. "A Reassessment of the Role of the Canadian Ice-Free Corridor in Light of New Geological Evidence." Poster Symposium 5B: Geology, Geochronology and Paleoenvironments of the First Americans at the Paleoamerican Odyssey Conference, Santa Fe, New Mexico, October 16–19.

Thorne, A. G., and P. G. Macumber. 1972. "Discoveries of Late Pleistocene Man at Kow Swamp, Australia." *Nature* 238 (5363): 316–319.

Trinkaus, Erik, Ştefan Milota, Ricardo Rodrigo, Gherase Mircea, and Oana Moldovan. 2003a. "Early Modern Human Cranial Remains from the Peştera Cu Oase, Romania." *Journal of Human Evolution* 45 (3): 245–253.

Trinkaus, Erik, Oana Moldovan, Adrian Bîlgăr, Laurenţiu Sarcina, Sheela Athreya, Shara E Bailey, Ricardo Rodrigo, Gherase Mircea, Thomas Higham, and Christopher Bronk Ramsey. 2003b. "An Early Modern Human from the Peştera Cu Oase, Romania." *Proceedings of the National Academy of Sciences* 100 (20): 11231–11236.

Velemínská, J., J. Brůzek, P. Velemínský, L. Bigoni, A. Sefcáková, and S. Katina. 2008. "Variability of the Upper-Palaeolithic Skulls from Predmostí Near Prerov (Czech Republic): Craniometric Comparison with Recent Human Standards." *Homo* 59 (1): 1–26.

Vidal, Céline M., Christine S. Lane, Asfawossen Asrat, Dan N. Barfod, Darren F. Mark, Emma L. Tomlinson, Ambdemichael Zafu Tadesse, et al. (2022). "Age of the Oldest Known *Homo sapiens* from Eastern Africa. *Nature* 601 (7894): 579–583.

Villa, Paola, Sylvain Soriano, Tsenka Tsanova, Ilaria Degano, Thomas F. G. Higham, Francesco d'Errico, Lucinda Backwell, Jeannette J. Lucejko, Maria Perla Colombini, and Peter B. Beaumont. 2012. "Border Cave and the Beginning of the Later Stone Age in South Africa." *Proceedings of the National Academy of Sciences* 109 (33): 13208–13213.

Wall, Jeffrey D., and Deborah Yoshihara Caldeira Brandt. 2016. "Archaic Admixture in Human History." *Current Opinion in Genetics & Development* 41: 93–97.

White, Tim D., Berhane Asfaw, David DeGusta, Henry Gilbert, Gary D. Richards, Gen Suwa, and F. Clark Howell. 2003. "Pleistocene *Homo sapiens* from Middle Awash, Ethiopia." *Nature* 423 (6641): 742–747.

Woo, Ju-Kang. 1959. "Human Fossils Found in Liukiang, Kwangsi, China." *Vertebrata PalAsiatica* 3 (3): 109–118.

Wu, XiuJie, Wu Liu, Wei Dong, JieMin Que, and YanFang Wang. 2008. "The Brain Morphology of Homo Liujiang Cranium Fossil by Three-Dimensional Computed Tomography." *Chinese Science Bulletin* 53 (16): 2513–2519.

Acknowledgments

I could not have undertaken this project without the help of many who got me to where I am today. I extend sincere thank yous to the many colleagues and former students who have inspired me to keep learning and talking about anthropology. Thank you also to all who are involved in this textbook project. The anonymous reviewers truly sparked improvements to the chapter. Lastly, the staff of Starbucks #5772 also contributed immensely to this text.

Image Description

Figure 12.22: The map shows the areas where agriculture was independently invented around the world and where they spread. These include: 1. the southeastern United States, which spread northwest and northeast; central Mexico, which spread north and south through Central America; the northwestern coast of South America, which spread to the caribbean, south, and east; the middle east, which spread to Europe, North Africa, and East Africa; central China, which spread north, south, west and south east; New Guinea, which spread northwest and southeast. The Sahel region around sub-Saharan Africa Africa is another probable site.

13.

RACE AND HUMAN VARIATION

Michael B. C. Rivera, Ph.D., University of Cambridge

This chapter is a revision from "Chapter 13: Race and Human Variation" by Michael B. C. Rivera. In Explorations: An Open Invitation to Biological Anthropology, first edition, edited by Beth Shook, Katie Nelson, Kelsie Aguilera, and Lara Braff, which is licensed under CC BY-NC 4.0.

Learning Objectives

- Illustrate the troubling history of "race" concepts.
- Explain human variation and evolution as the thematic roots of biological anthropology as a discipline.
- Critique earlier "race" concepts based on a contemporary understanding of the apportionment of human genetic variation.
- Explain how biological variation in humans is distributed clinally and in accordance with both isolation-by-distance and Out-of-Africa models.
- Identify phenotypic traits that reflect selective and neutral evolution.
- Extend this more-nuanced view of human variation to today's research, the implications for biomedical studies, applications in forensic anthropology, and other social/cultural/political concerns.

Humans exhibit biological variation. Humans also have a universal desire to categorize other humans in order to make sense of the world around them. Since the birth of the discipline of **biological anthropology** (or **physical anthropology**, as referred to back then), we have been interested in studying how humans vary biologically and what the sources of this variation are. Before we tackle these big problems, first consider this question: Why *should* we study human variation?

There are certainly academic reasons for studying human variation. First, it is highly interesting and important to consider the evolution of our species (see Chapters 9–12) and how our biological variation may be similar to (or different from) that of other species (e.g., other primates and apes; see Chapters 5 and 6). Second, anthropologists study modern human variation to understand how different biological traits developed over evolutionary time (see Figure 13.1). Suppose we are able to grasp the evolutionary processes that produce the differences in biology, physiology, body chemistry, behavior, and culture (**human variation**). In that case, we can make more accurate inferences about evolution and adaptation among our hominin ancestors, complementing our study of fossil evidence and the archaeological record. Third, as will be discussed in more detail later on, it is important to consider that biological variation among humans has biomedical, forensic, and sociopolitical implications. For these reasons, the study of human variation and evolution has formed the basis of anthropological inquiry for centuries and continues to be a major source of intrigue and inspiration for scientific research conducted today.

An even-more-important role of the biological anthropologist is to improve public understanding of human evolution and variation—outside of academic circles. Terms such as **race** and **ethnicity** are used in everyday conversations and in formal settings within and outside academia. The division of humankind into smaller, discrete categories is a regular occurrence in day-to-day life. This can be seen regularly when governments acquire census data with a heading like "geographic origin" or "ethnicity." Furthermore, such checkboxes and drop-down lists are commonly seen as part of the identifying information required for surveys and job applications.

According to professors of anthropology, ethnic studies, and sociology, race is often understood as rooted in biological differences, ranging from such familiar traits as skin color or eye shape to variations at the genetic level. However, race can also be studied as an "ideological construct" that goes beyond biological and genetic bases (Fuentes et al. 2019), at different times relating to our ethnicities, languages, religious beliefs, and cultural practices. Sometimes people associate racial identity with the concept of socioeconomic status or position, or they link ideas about race to what passport someone has, how long they have been in a country, or how well they have "integrated" into a population.

Some of these ideas about ethnicity have huge social and political impacts, and notions of race have been part of the motivation behind various forms of racism and prejudice today, as well as many wars and genocides throughout history. **Racism** manifests in many ways—from instances of bullying between kids on school playgrounds to underpaid minorities in the workforce, and from verbal abuse hurled at people of color to violent physical behaviors against those of a certain race. **Prejudice** can be characterized as negative views toward another group based on some perceived characteristic that makes all members of that group worthy of disdain, disrespect, or exclusion (not solely along racial lines but also according to [dis]ability, gender, sexual orientation, or socioeconomic background, for example). According to Shay-Akil McLean (2014), "Racism is not something particular to the United States and race is not the same everywhere in the world. Racial categories serve particular contextual purposes depending on the

Figure 13.1: Humans are culturally diverse (in that cultural differences contribute to a great degree of variation between individuals), but those shown are genetically undiverse. (Top left: Hadzabe members in Tanzania; top right: Inuit family; bottom left: Andean man in Peru; bottom right: English woman.) Credit: Humans are diverse (Figure 13.1) original to Explorations: An Open Invitation to Biological Anthropology by Michael Rivera is a collective work under a CC BY-NC-SA 4.0 license. [Includes Tanzania – Hadzabe hunter (14533536392) by A_Peach, CC BY 2.0; Inuit-Kleidung 1 by Ansgar Walk, CC BY-SA 3.0; Andean Man by Cacophony, CC BY-SA 4.0; Jane Goodall GM by Floatjon, CC BY-SA 3.0.

society they are used in, but generally follow the base logic of the supremacy of one type of human body over all others (ordering these human bodies in a hierarchical fashion)." Choosing which biological or nonbiological features to use when discussing race is always a social process (Omi and Winant 2014). Race concepts have no validity to them unless people continue to use them in their daily lives—and, in the worst cases, to use them to justify racist behaviors and problematic ideas about racial difference or superiority/inferiority. Recent work in anthropological genetics has revealed the similarities amongst humans on a molecular level and the relatively few differences that exist between populations (Omi and Winant 2014).

The role of the biological anthropologist becomes crucial in the public sphere, because we may be able to debunk myths surrounding human variation and shed light, for the nonanthropologists around us, on how human variation is actually distributed worldwide (see Figure 13.1). Rooted in scientific observations, our work can help nonanthropologists recognize how common ideas about "race" often have no biological or genetic basis. Many anthropologists work hard to educate students on the history of where race concepts come from, why and how they last in public consciousness, and how we become more conscious of racial issues and the need to fight against racism in our societies. Throughout this chapter, I will highlight how humans cannot actually be divided into discrete "races," because most traits vary on a continuous basis and human biology is, in fact, very **homogenous** compared to the greater genetic variation we observe in closely related species. Molecular anthropology, or anthropological genetics, continues to add new layers to our understanding of human biological variation and the evolutionary processes that gave rise to the contemporary patterns of human variation. The study of human variation has not always been unbiased, and thinkers and scientists have always worked in their particular sociohistorical context. For this reason, this chapter opens with a brief overview of race concepts throughout history, many of which relied on unethical and unscientific notions about different human groups.

Special Topic: My Experiences as an Asian Academic

Figure 13.2: Michael B. C. Rivera in Hong Kong. Credit: Michael B. C. Rivera in Hong Kong original to Explorations: An Open Invitation to Biological Anthropology (2nd ed.) is under a CC BY-NC 4.0 License.

My name is Michael, and I am a biological anthropologist and archaeologist (Figure 13.2). What strikes me as most interesting to investigate is human biological variation today and the study of past human evolution. For instance, some of my research on ancient coastal populations has revealed positive effects of coastal living on dietary health and many unique adaptations in bones and teeth when living near rivers and beaches. I love talking to students and nonscientists about bioanthropologists' work, through teaching, science communication events, and writing book chapters like this one. I grew up in Hong Kong, a city in southern China. My father is from the Philippines and my mother is from Hong Kong, which makes me a mixed Filipino-Chinese academic. Growing up, I noticed that people came in all shapes, sizes, and colors. My life is very different now in that I have gained the expertise to explain those differences, and I feel a great responsibility to guide those new to anthropology toward their own understandings of diversity.

Biological anthropology is not taught extensively in Hong Kong, so I moved to the United Kingdom to earn my bachelor's, master's, and doctorate degrees. It was fascinating to me that we could answer important questions about human variation and history using scientific methods. However, I did not have many minority academic role models to look up to while I was at university. My department was made up almost exclusively of white westerner faculty, and it was hard to imagine I could one day get a job at these western institutions. While pursuing my degrees, I also remember several instances of my research contributions being overlooked or dismissed. Sometimes professors and fellow students would make racist comments toward Asian scholars (including me) and other Black, Indigenous and researchers of color, making us greatly uncomfortable in those spaces. When one of us would work up the courage to tell university leaders our experiences of being stereotyped, dismissed, or insulted, we received little support and were further excluded from research and teaching activities. This is a common experience for Black, Indigenous, and other people of color who pursue biological anthropology, and we face the difficult choice between leaving the field or bearing with such unsafe spaces.

It became important to me at that time to find other academics of color with whom to share experiences and form community. I feel inspired by all my colleagues who advocate for greater representation and diversity in universities (whether they are minority academics or not). I admire many of my fellow researchers who are underrepresented and do a great job of representing minority groups through their cutting-edge research and quality teaching at the undergraduate and graduate levels. Although I no longer work in the West, it has remained my great hope that those in the West and the "Global North" will continue to improve university culture, and I support any efforts there to welcome all scholars.

My current work is based in Hong Kong, where I am deeply dedicated to helping develop biological anthropology in East and Southeast Asia and promoting research from our home regions on the international scene. The study of anthropology really highlights how we share a common humanity and history. Being somebody who is "mixed race" and Asian likely played a key role in steering me toward the study of human variation. As this chapter hopefully shows, there is a lot to discuss about race and ethnicity regarding the discipline's history and current understandings of **human diversity**. Some scientific and technological advancements today are misused for reasons to do with money, politics, or the continuation of antiquated ideas. It is my belief, alongside many of my friends and fellow anthropologists, that science should be more about empathy toward all members of our species and contributing to the intellectual and technological nourishment of society. After speaking to many members of the public, as well as my own undergraduate students, I have received lovely messages from other individuals of color expressing thanks and appreciation for my presence and understanding as a minority scientist and mentor figure. Anthropology needs much more diversity as well as to make room for those who have traveled different routes into the discipline. All paths taken into anthropology are valid and valuable. I would encourage everyone to study anthropology—it is a field for understanding and celebrating the intricacies of human diversity.

The History of "Race" Concepts

"Race" in the Classical Era

Figure 13.3: (From left to right) Depicting a Berber (Libyan), a Nubian, an Asiatic (Levantine), and an Egyptian, copied from a mural on the tomb of Seti I. Credit: Egyptian races drawing by Heinrich von Minutoli (1820) of a mural by an unknown artist from the tomb of Seti I is in the public domain.

The earliest classification systems used to understand human variation are evidenced by ancient manuscripts, scrolls, and stone tablets recovered through archaeological, historical, and literary research. The Ancient Egyptians had the *Book of Gates*, dated to the New Kingdom between 1550 B.C.E. and 1077 B.C.E (Figure 13.3). In one part of this tome dedicated to depictions of the underworld, scribes used pictures and hieroglyphics to illustrate a division of Egyptian people into the four categories known to them at the time: the Aamu (Asiatics), the Nehesu (Nubians), the Reth (Egyptians), and the Themehu (Libyans). Though not rooted in any scientific basis like our current understandings of human variation today, the Ancient Egyptians believed that each of these groups were made of a distinctive category of people, distinguishable by their skin color, place of origin, and even behavioral traits.

Another well-known early document is the Bible, where it is written that all humankind descends from one of three sons of Noah: Shem (the ancestor to all olive-skinned Asians), Japheth (the ancestor to pale-skinned Europeans), and Ham (the ancestor to darker-skinned Africans). Similar to the Ancient Egyptians, these distinctions were based on behavioral traits and skin color. More recent work in historiography and linguistics suggest that the branches of "Hamites," "Japhethites," and "Shemites" may also relate to the formation of three independent language groups some time between 1000 and 3000 B.C.E. With the continued proliferation of Christianity, this concept of approximately three racial groupings lasted until the Middle Ages and spread as far across Eurasia as crusaders and missionaries ventured at the time.

Figure 13.4: The Great Chain of Being from the Rhetorica Christiana by Fray Diego de Valades (1579). Credit: **Great Chain of Being** by Didacus Valades (Diego Valades 1579), print from Rhetorica Christiana (via **Getty Research**), is in the **public domain**.

There is also the "Great Chain of Being," conceived by ancient Greek philosophers like Plato (427–348 B.C.E.) and Aristotle (384–322 B.C.E.). They played a key role in laying the foundations of empirical science, whereby observations of everything from animals to humans were noted with the aim of creating taxonomic categories. Aristotle describes the Great Chain of Being as a ladder along which all objects, plants, animals, humans, and celestial bodies can be mapped in an overall hierarchy (in the order of existential importance, with humans placed near the top, just beneath divine beings; see Figure 13.4). When he writes about humans, Aristotle expressed the belief that certain people are inherently (or genetically) more instinctive rulers, while others are more natural fits for the life of a worker or enslaved person. Based on research by biological anthropologists, we currently recognize that these early systems of classification and hierarchization are unhelpful in studying human biological variation. Both behavioral traits and physical traits are coded for by multiple genes each, and how we exhibit those traits based on our genetics can vary significantly even between individuals of the same population.

"Race" during the Scientific Revolution

The 1400s to 1600s saw the beginnings of the **Scientific Revolution** in Western societies, with thinkers like Nicholas Copernicus, Galileo Galilei, and Leonardo Da Vinci publishing some of their most important findings. While by no means the first or only scholars globally to use observation and experimentation to understand the world around them, early scientists living at the end of the medieval period in Europe increasingly employed more experimentation, quantification, and rational thought in their work. This is the main difference between the work of the ancient Egyptians, Romans, and Greeks and that of later scientists such as Isaac Newton and Carl Linnaeus in the 1600s and 1700s.

Linnaeus is the author of *Systema Naturae* (1758), in which he classified all plants and animals under the formalized naming system known as **binomial nomenclature** (Figure 13.5). This system is **typological**, in that organisms are placed into groups according to how they are similar or different to others under study. What was most anthropologically notable about Linnaeus's typological system was that he was one of the first to group humans with apes and monkeys, based on the anatomical similarities between humans and nonhuman primates. However, Linnaeus viewed the world in line with **essentialism**, a problematic concept that dictates that there are a unique set of characteristics that organisms of a specific kind *must* have and that would remove organisms from taxonomic categorizations if they lacked any of the required criteria.

Figure 13.5: Carl Linnaeus. Credit: **Carl von Linné** by Alexander Roslin (1718-1793) is in the **public domain**.

Figure 13.6: A painting depicting the colonization of the Mississippi River environs by Spaniard Hernando DeSoto in 1541 (painted in 1853 by William H. Powell). Credit: Discovery of the Mississippi by William Henry Powell (photograph courtesy of Architect of the Capitol) is in the public domain.

Linnaeus subdivided the human species into four varieties, with overtly racist categories based on skin color and "inherent" behaviors. Some European scientists during this period were not aware of their own biases skewing their interpretations of biological variation, while others deliberately worked to shape public perceptions of human variation in ways that established "**otherness**" and enforced European domination and the subordination of non-European people. The conclusions and claims at which they arrived, consciously or subconsciously, often fit the times they were living through—the so-called **Age of Discovery**, when the superiority of European cultures over others was a pervasive idea throughout people's social and political lives. Although much of Eurasia was linked by spice- and silk-trading routes, the European colonial period between the 1400s and 1700s was marked by many new and unfortunately violent encounters overseas (Figure 13.6). When Europeans arrived by ship on the shores of continents that were already inhabited, it was their first meeting with the Indigenous peoples of the Americas and Australasia, who looked, spoke, and behaved differently from peoples with whom they were familiar. Building on the idea of species and "subspecies," natural historians of this time invented the term *race*, from the French *rasse* meaning "local strain."

Another scientist of the times, Johann Friedrich Blumenbach (1752–1840), classified humans into five races based on his observations of cranial form variation as well as skin color. He thus dubbed the "original" form of the human cranium the "Caucasian" form, with the idea that the ideal climate conditions for early humans would have been in the Caucasus region near the Caspian Sea. The key insight Blumenbach presented was that human variation in any particular trait should be more accurately viewed as falling along a gradation (Figure 13.7). While some of his theories were correct according to what we observe today with more knowledge in genetics, they erroneously believed that human "subspecies" were "degenerated" or "transformed" varieties of an ancestral Caucasian or European race. According to them, the Caucasian cranial dimensions were the least changed over human evolutionary time, while the other skull forms represented geographic variants of this "original." As will be discussed in greater detail later in this chapter, we have genetic and craniometric evidence for sub-Saharan Africa being the origin of the human species instead (see Chapter 12 on the fossil record that places the origins of modern *Homo sapiens* in north and east Africa). Based on work that shows how most biological characteristics are coded for by nonassociated genes, it is not reasonable to draw links between individuals' personalities and their skull shapes.

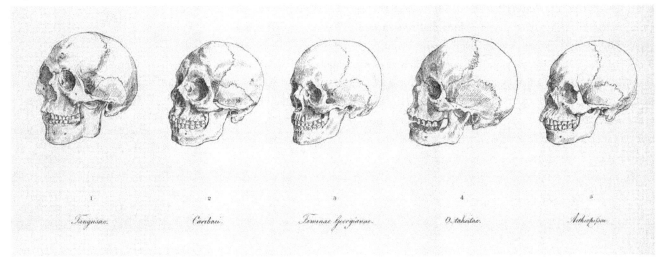

Figure 13.7: Five skull drawings representing specimens for Blumenbach's "Mongolian," "American," "Caucasian," "Malayan," and "Aethiopian" races. Credit: Blumenbach's five races by Johann Friedrich Blumenbach is in the public domain. Original in the 1795 Treatise on "De generis humani varietate nativa," unnumbered page at the end of the book titled "Tab II".

"Race" and the Dawn of Scientific Racism

Between the 1800s and mid-1900s, and contrary to what you might expect, an increased use of scientific methods to justify racial schemes developed in scholarship. Differing from earlier views, which saw all humans as environmentally deviated from one "original" humankind, classification systems after 1800 became more **polygenetic** (viewing all people as having separate origins) rather than **monogenetic** (viewing all people as having a single origin). Instead of moving closer to our modern-day understandings of human variation, there was increased support for the notion that each race was created separately and with different attributes (intelligence, temperament, and appearance).

The 1800s were an important precursor to modern biological anthropology as we know it, given that this was when the scientific measurement of human physical features (anthropometry) truly became popularized. However, empirical studies in the 1800s pushed even further the idea that Europeans were culturally and biologically superior to others. While considered one of the pioneers of American "physical" anthropology, Samuel George Morton (1799–1851) was a scholar who had a large role in perpetuating 1800s scientific racism. By measuring cranial size and shape, he calculated that "Caucasians," on average, have greater cranial volumes than other groups, such as the Indigenous peoples of the Americas and peoples Morton referred to collectively as "Negros." Today, we know that cranial size variation depends on such factors as Allen's and Bergmann's rules, which give a more likely explanation: in colder environments, it is advantageous for those living there to have larger and rounder heads because they conserve heat more effectively than more slender heads (Beals et al. 1984). The leading figures in craniometry during the 1800s instead were linked heavily with powerful individuals and wealthy sociopolitical institutions and financial bodies. Theories in support of hierarchical racial schemes using "scientific" bases certainly helped continue the exploitative and unethical trafficking and enslavement of Africans between the 1500s and 1800s.

Morton went on to write in his publication *Crania Americana* (1839) a number of views that fit with a concept called **biological determinism**. The idea behind biological determinism is that an association exists between people's physical characteristics and their behavior, intelligence, ability, values, and morals. If the idea is that some groups of people are essentially superior to others in cognitive ability and temperament, then it is easier to justify the unequal treatment of certain groups based on outward appearances. Another such problematic thinker was Paul Broca (1824–1880), after whom a region of the frontal lobe related to language use is named (Broca's area). Influenced by Morton, Broca likewise claimed that internal skull capacities could be linked with skin color and cognitive ability. He went on to justify the European colonization of other global territories by purporting it was noble for a biologically more "civilized" population to improve the "humanity" of more "barbaric" populations. Today, these theories of Morton, Broca, and others like them are known to have no scientific basis. If we could speak with them today, they would likely try to emphasize that their conclusions were based on empirical evidence and not *a priori* reasoning. However, we now can clearly see that their reasoning was biased and affected by prevailing societal views at the time.

"Race" and the Beginnings of Physical Anthropology

In the early 20th century, we saw a number of new figures coming into the science of human variation and shifting the theoretical focus within. Most notably, these included Aleš Hrdlička and Franz Boas.

Aleš Hrdlička (1869–1943) was a Czech anthropologist who moved to the United States. In 1903, he established the physical anthropology section of the National Museum of Natural History (Figure 13.8). In 1918, he founded the *American Journal of Physical Anthropology*, which remains one of the foremost scientific journals disseminating bioanthropological research. As part of his work and the scope of the journal, he differentiated **"physical anthropology"** from other kinds of anthropology: he wrote that physical anthropology is "the study of racial anatomy, physiology, and pathology" and "the study of man's variation" (Hrdlička 1918). In some ways, although the scope and technological capabilities of biological anthropologists have changed significantly, Hrdlička established an area of inquiry that has continued and prospered for over a hundred years.

Figure 13.8: Aleš Hrdlička (1869–1943), a Czech anthropologist who founded the American Journal of Physical Anthropology. Credit: (Ales Hrdlicka) SIA2009-4246 (1903) by an unknown photographer is used for educational and non-commercial purposes as outlined by the Smithsonian.. [Smithsonian Institution Archives, Record Unit 9521, Box 1, T. Dale Stewart Oral History Interview; and Record Unit 9528, Box 1, Henry B. Collins Oral History Interview.]

Franz Boas (1858–1942) was a German American anthropologist who established the four-field anthropology system in the United States and founded the American Anthropological Association in 1902. He argued that the scientific method should be used in the study of human cultures and the comparative method for looking at human biology worldwide. One of Boas's significant contributions to biological anthropology was the study of skull dimensions with respect to race. After a long-term research project, he demonstrated how cranial form was highly dependent on cultural and environmental factors and that human behaviors were influenced primarily not by genes but by social learning. He wrote in one essay for the journal *Science*: "While individuals differ, biological differences between races are small. There is no reason to believe that one race is by nature so much more intelligent, endowed with great willpower, or emotionally more stable than another, that the difference would materially influence its culture" (Boas 1931:6). This conclusion directly contrasted with the theories of the past that relied on biological determinism. Biological anthropologists today have found evidence that corroborates Boas's explanations: societies do not exist on a hierarchy or gradation of "civilizedness" but instead are shaped by the world around them, their demographic histories, and the interactions they have with other groups.

The first half of the 1900s still involved some research that was essentialist and focused on proving racial determinism. Anthropologists like Francis Galton (1822–1911) and Earnest A. Hooton (1887–1954) created the field of **eugenics** as an attempt to formalize the social scientific study of "fitness" and "superiority" among members of 19th-century Europe. As a way of "dealing with" criminals, diseased individuals, and "uncivilized" people, eugenicists recommended prohibiting parts of the population from being married or sterilizing these members of society so they could no longer procreate (Figure 13.9). They instead encouraged "reproduction in individual families with sound physiques, good mental endowments, and demonstrable social and economic capability" (Hooton 1936). In the 1930s, Nazi Germany used this false idea of there being "pure races" to highly destructive effect. The need to be protected against admixture from "unfit" groups was their justification for their blatant racism and purging of citizens that fell under their subjective criteria.

It should be noted that eugenicist ideas were popularly discussed and debated in many non-European contexts, as in the U.S., China, and South Africa, too. The Immigration Restriction Act of 1924 was passed in the United States, with the explicit aim of reducing the country's "burden" of people considered inferior by restricting immigration of eastern European Jews, Italians, Africans, Arabs, and Asians. In the early 1900s, Chinese scientists and politicians showed great interest in eugenic ideologies, which came to dictate decisions in law-making, family life, and the medical field. Noted American anthropologist Ruth Benedict wrote extensively on Japanese culture and society during and after World War II. Her essentialist portrayals of Japanese people were heavily cited in popular discourse at the time. In 1950s South Africa, interracial marriages and sexual relations were banned by law; antimiscegenation became one of the huge focuses of apartheid resistance activists in later years. We still see the continuation of eugenics-based logic today around the world—in exclusionary immigration laws, cases of incarcerated prison inmates being forcibly sterilized, and the persistence of intelligence testing as a form of measuring people's "fitness" in a society.

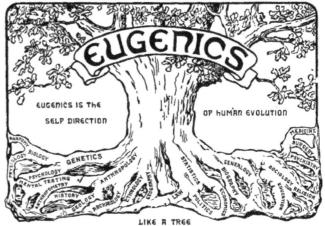

Figure 13.9: Logo of the Second International Exhibition of Eugenics, held in 1921. The text of the logo states: "Eugenics is the self-direction of human evolution. Like a tree, eugenics draws its materials from many sources and organizes them into an harmonious entity." Credit: Eugenics congress logo scanned from Harry H. Laughlin, The Second International Exhibition of Eugenics held September 22 to October 22, 1921, is in the public domain.

Shortly after World War II and the Nazi Holocaust, the full extent of essentialist, eugenicist thinking became clear. Social constructions of race, and the notion that one can predict psychological or behavioral traits based on external appearance, had become unpopular both within and outside the discipline. It was up to those in the field of physical anthropology at the time to separate physical anthropology from race concepts that supported unscientific and socially damaging agendas. This does not mean that there are no physiological or behavioral differences between different members of the human species. However, going forward, a number of physical anthropologists saw human biological variation as more complicated than simple typologies could describe.

"The New Physical Anthropology"

After 1950, focus steered away from the concept of "race" as a unit of variation and toward understanding why variation exists in **populations** from an evolutionary perspective. This was outlined by those pioneering the "new physical anthropology," such as Sherwood Washburn, Theodosius Dobzhansky (Figure 13.10), and Julian Huxley, who borrowed this approach from contemporary population geneticists. Whether using genetic or phenotypic markers as the units of study, "groups" or "clusters" of humans differentiated by these became defined as populations that differ in the frequency of some gene or genes. Anthropologists consider what "makes" a population—a group of individuals potentially capable of or actually interbreeding due to shared geographic proximity, language, ethnicity, culture, and/ or values. Put another way, a population is a local interbreeding group with reduced gene flow between themselves and other groups of humans. Members of the same population may be expected to share many genetic traits (and, as a result, many phenotypic traits that may or may not be visible outwardly).

Figure 13.10: Theodosius Dobzhansky, an important scientist who formulated the 20th-century "modern synthesis" reconciling Charles Darwin's theory of evolution and Gregor Mendel's ideas on heredity. Credit: Dobzhansky no Brasil em 1943 by unknown photographer via Flickr user Cely Carmo is in the public domain.

Figure 13.11: Julian Huxley (1942). Credit: Julian Huxley 1-2 by unknown photographer is in the public domain.

Thinking of humans in terms of populations was part of Julian Huxley's (1942) "Modern Synthesis"—so named because it helped to reconcile two fundamental principles about evolution that had not been made sense of together before (Figure 13.11). As discussed in Chapter 3, Gregor Mendel (1822–1884) was able to show that inheritance was mediated by discrete particles (or genes) and not blended in the offspring. However, it was difficult for some 19th-century scientists to accept this model of genetic inheritance at the time because much of biological variation appeared to be continuous and not particulate (take skin color or height as examples). In the 1930s, it was demonstrated that traits could be polygenic and that multiple alleles could be responsible for any one phenotypic trait, thus producing the continuous variation in traits such as eye color that we see today. Thus, Huxley's "Modern Synthesis" outlines not only how human populations are capable of exchanging genes at the microevolutionary level but also how multiple alleles for one trait (polygenic exchanges) can cause gradual macroevolutionary changes.

Human Variation in Biological Anthropology Today

Many Human Traits Are Nonconcordant

In our studies of human (genetic) variation today, we understand most human traits to be nonconcordant (Figure 13.12). "**Nonconcordance**" is a term used to describe how biological traits vary independent of each other—that is, they do not get inherited in a correlative manner with other genetically controlled traits. For example, if you knew an individual had genes that coded for tall height, you would not be able to predict if they are lighter-skinned or have red hair. This is different from earlier essentialist views of human variation: the idea that skin color could predict one's brain function or even "temperament" and tendencies toward criminal behavior.

Figure 13.12: Most human biological traits are non-concordant, meaning traits vary independently and each trait has its own pattern of distribution around the world. In this image, different colors and patterns represent trait varieties. For example, the color and pattern of the head may represent hair color (dark to light), but sharing dark hair with another person does not mean you will share other traits (e.g. ability to digest lactose or ABO blood type). Credit: Nonconcordance original to Explorations: An Open Invitation to Biological Anthropology (2nd ed.) by Katie Nelson is under a CC BY-NC 4.0 License.

Human Variation Is Clinal/Continuous (Not Discrete)

Frank B. Livingstone (1928–2005) wrote: "There are no races, only clines" (1962: 279). A **cline** is a gradation in the frequency of an allele/trait between populations living in different geographic regions. Human variation cannot be broken into discrete "races," because most physical traits vary on a continuous or "clinal" basis. One obvious example of this is how human height does not only come in three values ("short," "medium," and "tall") but instead varies across a spectrum of vertical heights achievable by humans all over the world. On the one hand, we can describe human height as exhibiting **continuous variation**, forming a continuous pattern, but height does not vary according to where people live across the globe and does not exhibit a clinal pattern. On the other hand, skin color variation between populations does show patterning that fits quite well on to how near or far they are from each other on a world map. This makes a trait like skin color clinally distributed worldwide. When large numbers of genetic loci for large numbers of samples were sampled from human populations distributed worldwide during the 1960s and 1970s, the view that certain facets of human diversity were clinally distributed was further supported by genetic data.

To study human traits that are clinally distributed, genetic tests must be performed to uncover the true frequencies of an allele or trait across a certain geographic space. One easily visible example of a clinal distribution seen worldwide is the patterning of human variation in skin color. Whether in southern Asia, sub-Saharan Africa, or Australia, dark brown skin is found. Paler skin tones are found in higher-latitude populations such as those who have lived in areas like Europe, Siberia, and Alaska for millennia. Skin color is easily observable as a phenotypic trait exhibiting continuous variation.

A clinal distribution still derives from genetic inheritance; however, clines often correspond to some gradually changing environmental factor. Clinal patterns arise when selective pressures in one geographic area differ from those in another as well as when people procreate and pass on genes together with their most immediate neighbors. There are several mechanisms, selective and neutral, that can lead to the clinal distribution of an allele or a biological trait. **Natural selection** is the mechanism that produced a global cline of skin color, whereby darker skin color protects equatorial populations from high amounts of UV radiation; there is a transition of lessening pigmentation in individuals that reside further and further away from the tropics (Jablonski 2004; Jablonski and Chaplin 2000; see Figure 13.13). The ability and inability to digest lactose (milk sugar) among different world communities varies according to differential practices and histories of milk and dairy-product consumption (Gerbault et al.

2011; Ingram et al. 2009). Where malaria seems to be most prevalent as a disease stressor on human populations, a clinal gradient of increasing sickle cell anemia experience toward these regions has been studied extensively by genetic anthropologists (Luzzatto 2012). Sometimes culturally defined mate selection based on some observable trait can lead to clinal variation between populations as well.

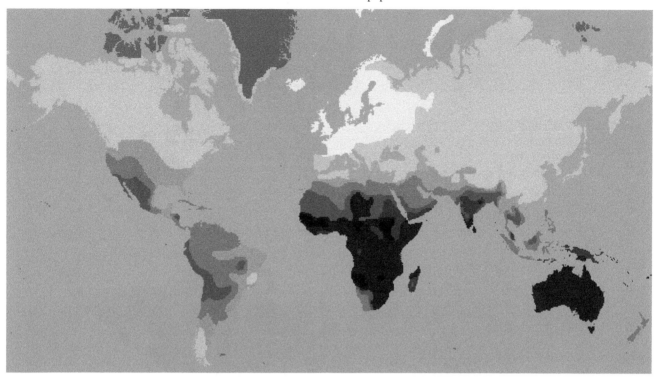

Figure 13.13: A global map of skin colors shows that dark skin pigmentation is more common in areas that receive more UV radiation (near the equator and in high altitude areas). Light skin is more common at northern and southern latitudes. It is worth bearing in mind, though, that these do not tell the full story of how human skin pigmentation varies worldwide. Each region will contain populations that exhibit a range of skin tones. In this way, this map is not perfect as an illustration of skin-color distribution. Credit: Mercator style projection map showing human skin color according to Biasutti 1940.png by Dark Tichondrias at English Wikipedia, modified (cropped) by Tuvalkin, is under a CC BY-SA 4.0 License.

Two neutral microevolutionary processes that may produce a cline in a human allele or trait are **gene flow** and **genetic drift** (see Chapter 4). The ways in which neutral processes can produce clinal distributions is seen clearly when looking at clinal maps for different blood groups in the human ABO blood group system (Figure 13.14). For instance, scientists have identified an East-to-West cline in the distribution of the blood type *B* allele across Eurasia. The frequency of *B* allele carriers decreases gradually westward when we compare the blood groups of East and Southeast Asian populations with those in Europe. This shows how populations residing nearer to one another are more likely to interbreed and share genetic material (i.e., undergo gene flow). We also see 90%–100% of native South American individuals, as well as between 70%–90% of Aboriginal Australian groups, carrying the *O* allele (Mourant, Kopeć, and Domaniewska-Sobczak 1976). These high frequencies are likely due to random genetic drift and founder effects, in which population sizes were severely reduced by the earliest *O* allele-carrying individuals migrating into those areas. Over time, the *O* blood type has remained predominant.

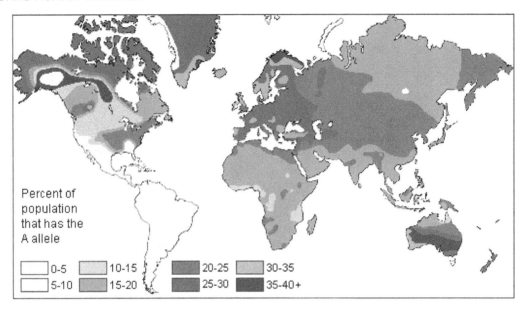

Percent of
population
that has the
A allele

0-5	10-15	20-25	30-35
5-10	15-20	25-30	35-40+

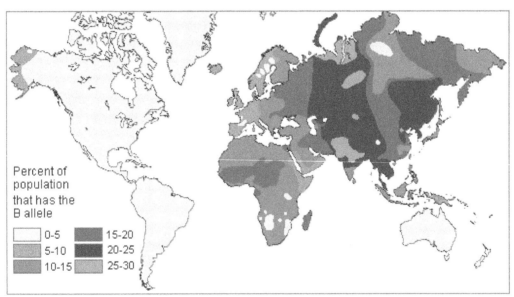

Percent of
population
that has the
B allele

0-5	15-20
5-10	20-25
10-15	25-30

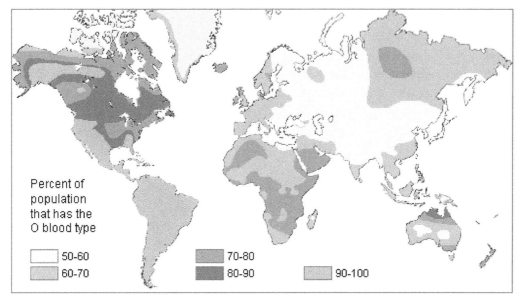

Figure 13.14a–c: a. Global distribution of blood type A. b. Global distribution of blood type B. c. Global distribution of blood type O. Credit: a. Map of blood group a by Muntuwandi at en.wikipedia is under a CC BY-SA 3.0 License. b. Map of blood group b by Muntuwandi at en.wikipedia is under a CC BY-SA 3.0 License. c. Map of blood group o is based on diagrams from http://anthro.palomar.edu/vary/vary_3.htm, reproduced from A. E. Mourant et al. (1976), and is under a CC BY-SA 3.0 License. [Image Description].

Genetic Variation Is Greater Within Group than Between Groups

One problem with race-based classifications is they relied on an erroneous idea that individuals with particular characteristics would share more similar genes with each other within a particular "race" and share less with individuals of other "races" possessing different traits and genetic makeups. However, since around 50 years ago, scientific studies have shown that the majority of human genetic differences worldwide exist *within* groups (or "races") individually rather than *between* groups. Indeed, most genetic variation we see occurs in Africa, and many variants are shared among individuals on all continents (Figure 13.15).

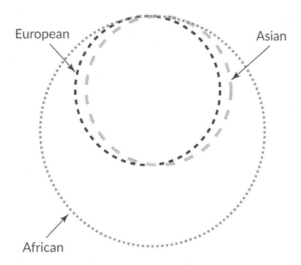

Figure 13.15: Circles represent human genetic variation. Most variants are shared among individuals on all continents. There are more variants in Africa, some of which are not found in Europe or Asia. Credit: Human Genetic Variation original to Explorations: An Open Invitation to Biological Anthropology (2nd ed.) by Katie Nelson is under a CC BY-NC 4.0 License.

In 2002, a landmark article by Noah Rosenberg and colleagues explored worldwide human genetic variation using an even-greater genetic data set. They used 377 highly variable markers in the human genome and sampled from 1,056 individuals representative of 52 populations. The markers chosen for study were not ones that code for any expressed genes. Because these regions of the human genome were made of unexpressed genes, we may understand these markers as neutrally derived (as opposed to selectively derived) because they do not code for functional advantages or disadvantages. These neutral genetic markers likely reflect an intricate combination of regional founder effects and population histories. Analyses of these neutral markers allowed scientists to identify that 93%–95% of global genetic differences, referred to as **variance**, can be accounted for by within-population differences, while only a small proportion of genetic variance (3%–5%) can be attributed to differences among major groups (Rosenberg et al. 2002). This research supports the theory that distinct biological races do not exist, even though misguided concepts of race may still have real social and political consequences.

Biological Data Fit Isolation-By-Distance and Out-of-Africa Models

One further note is that the world's population may be genetically divided into "groups," "subsets," "clumps," or "clusters" that reflect some degree of genetic similarity. These identifiable clusters reflect genetic or geographic distances—either with gene flow facilitated by proximity between populations or impeded by obstacles like oceans or environmentally challenging habitats (Rosenberg et al. 2005). Sometimes, inferred clusters using multiple genetic loci are interpreted by nongeneticists literally as "ancestral populations." However, it would be wrong to assume from these genetic results that highly differentiated and "pure" ancestral groups ever existed. These groupings reflect differences that have arisen over time due to clinal patterning, genetic drift, and/or restricted or unrestricted gene flow (Weiss and Long 2009). The clusters identified by scientists are arbitrary and the parameters used to split up the global population into groups is subjective and dependent on the particular questions or distinctions being brought into focus (Relethford 2009).

Additionally, research on worldwide genetic variation has shown that human variation decreases with increasing distance from sub-Saharan Africa, where there is evidence for this vast region being the geographical origin of anatomically modern humans (Liu et al. 2006; Prugnolle, Manica, and Balloux 2005; see Figures 13.16 and 13.17). Genetic differentiation decreases in human groups the further you sample data from relative to sub-Saharan Africa because of serial founder effects (Relethford 2004). Over the course of human colonization of the rest of the world outside Africa, populations broke away in expanding waves across continents into western Asia, then Europe and eastern Asia, followed by Oceania and the Americas. As a result, founder events occurred whereby genetic variation was lost, as the colonization of each new geographical region involved a smaller number of individuals moving from the original larger population to establish a new one (Relethford 2004). The most genetic variation is found across populations residing in different parts of sub-Saharan Africa, while other current populations in places like northern Europe and the southern tip of South America exhibit some of the least genetic differentiation relative to all global populations (Campbell and Tishkoff 2008).

Figure 13.16: Sub-Saharan Africa (shaded dark/green). Credit: Sub-Saharan Africa by Ezeu has been designated to the public domain (CC0).

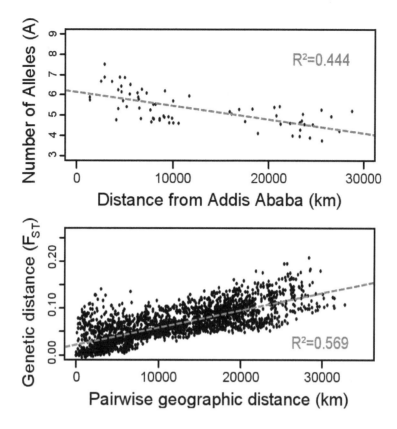

Figure 13.17: Comparison of the genetic distance and geographical distance between populations. In the top graph, the pattern reveals that genetic variation conforms to an Out-of-Africa model, as those populations further away from Addis Ababa in Ethiopia share a smaller number of alleles; in the bottom graph, we see the populations follow an isolation-by-distance model, as pairs of populations further apart geographically seem to have greater genetic distance (Kanitz et al. 2018). Credit: **Complex genetic patterns (figure 1)** by Kanitz et al. (2018) is under a CC BY 4.0 License.

Besides fitting nicely into the **Out-of-Africa model**, worldwide human genetic variation conforms to an **isolation-by-distance model**, which predicts that genetic similarity between groups will decrease exponentially as the geographic distance between them increases (Kanitz et al. 2018). This is because of the greater and greater restrictions to gene flow presented by geographic distance, as well as cultural and linguistic differences that occur as a result of certain degrees of isolation. Since genetic data conform to isolation-by-distance and Out-of-Africa models, these findings support the abolishment of "race" groupings. This research demonstrates that human variation is continuous and cannot be differentiated into geographically discrete categories. There are no "inherent" or "innate" differences between human groups; instead, variation derives from some degree of natural selection, as well as neutral processes like **population bottle-necking** (Figure 13.18), random **mutations** in the DNA, genetic drift, and gene flow through between-mate interbreeding.

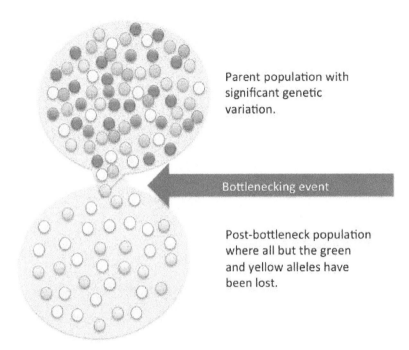

Parent population with significant genetic variation.

Bottlenecking event

Post-bottleneck population where all but the green and yellow alleles have been lost.

Figure 13.18: The founder effect is a change in a small population's gene pool due to a limited number of individuals breaking away from a parent population. Credit: Bottleneck effect by Tsaneda is under a CC BY 3.0 License.

Humans Have Higher Homogeneity Compared to Many Other Species

An important fact to bear in mind is that humans are 99.9% identical to one another. This means that the apportionments of human variation discussed above only concern that tiny 0.1% of difference that exists between all humans globally. Compared to other mammalian species, including the other great apes, human variation is remarkably lower. This may be surprising given that the worldwide human population has already exceeded seven billion, and, at least on the surface level, we appear to be quite phenotypically diverse. Molecular approaches to human and primate genetics tells us that external differences are merely superficial. For a proper appreciation of human variation, we have to look at our closest relatives in the primate order and mammalian class. Compared to chimpanzees, bonobos, gorillas and other primates, humans have remarkably low average genome-wide **heterogeneity** (Osada 2005).

When we look at chimpanzee genetic variation, it is fascinating that western, central, eastern, and Cameroonian chimpanzee groups have substantially more genetic variation between them than large global samples of human DNA (Bowden et al. 2012; Figure 13.19). This is surprising given that all of these chimpanzee groups live relatively near one another in Africa, while measurements of human genetic variation have been conducted using samples from entirely different continents. First, geneticists suppose that this could reflect differential experiences of the founder effect between humans and chimpanzees. Because all non-African human populations descended from a small number of anatomically modern humans who left Africa, it would be expected that all groups descended from that smaller ancestral group would be similar genetically. Second, our species is really young, given that we have only existed on the planet for around 150,000 to 300,000 years. This gave humans little time for random genetic mutations to occur as genes get passed down through genetic interbreeding and meiosis. Chimpanzees, however, have inhabited different **ecological niches**, and less interbreeding has occurred between the four chimpanzee groups over the past six to eight million years compared to the amount of gene flow that occurred between worldwide human populations (Bowden et al. 2012).

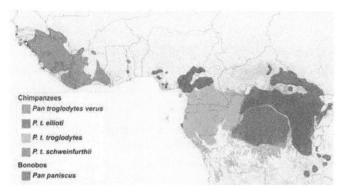

Figure 13.19: Distribution of the genus Pan, including bonobos and the four subspecies of chimpanzee, across western and central Africa (Clee et al. 2015). Credit: Chimpanzee subspecies ranges (Figure 1) by Clee et al. 2015 is under a CC BY 4.0 License. [Image Description].

Recent advances have now enabled the attainment of genetic samples from the larger family of great apes and the evaluation of genetic variation among bonobos, orangutans, and gorillas alongside that of chimpanzees and humans (Prado-Martinez et al. 2013). Collecting such data and analyzing primate genetic variation has been important not only to elucidate how different ecological, demographic, and climatic factors have shaped our evolution but also to inform upon conservation efforts and medical research. Genes that may code for genetic susceptibilities to tropical diseases that affect multiple primates can be studied through genome-wide methods. Species differences in the genomes associated with speech, behavior, and cognition could tell us more about how human individuals may be affected by genetically derived neurological or speech-related disorders and conditions (Prado-Martinez et al. 2013; Staes et al. 2017). In 2018, a great ape genomic study also reported genetic differences between chimpanzees and humans related to brain cell divisions (Kronenberg et al. 2018). From these results, it may be inferred that cognitive or behavioral variation between humans and the great apes might relate to an increased number of cortical neurons being formed during human brain development (Kronenberg et al. 2018). Comparative studies of human and nonhuman great ape genetic variation highlight the complex interactions of population histories, environmental changes, and natural selection between and within species. When viewed in the context of overall great ape variation, we may reconsider how variable the human species is relatively and how unjustified previous "race" concepts really were.

Phenotypic Traits That Reflect Neutral Evolution

Depending on the trait being observed, different patterns of phenotypic variation may be found within and among groups worldwide. In this subsection, some phenotypic traits that reflect the aforementioned patterns of genetic variation will be discussed.

Looking beyond genetic variation briefly, recent studies have revisited biological anthropology's earlier themes of externally observable traits, such as skull shape. In the last 20 or so years, anthropologists have evaluated the level to which human cranial shape variation reflects the results from genetic markers, such as those used previously to fit against Out-of-Africa models (Relethford 2004) or those used in the apportionment of human variation between and within groups (Lewontin 1972; Rosenberg et al. 2002). Using larger sample sizes of cranial data collected from thousands of skulls worldwide and a long list of cranial measurements, studies demonstrate a similar decrease in variation with distance from Africa and show that a majority of cranial variation occurs within populations rather than between populations (Betti et al. 2009; Betti et al. 2010; Manica et al. 2007; Relethford 2001; von Cramon-Taubadel and Lycett 2008; see Figure 13.20). The greatest cranial variation is found among skulls of sub-Saharan African origin, while the least variation is found among populations inhabiting places like Tierra del Fuego at the southern tip of Argentina and Chile. While ancient and historical thinkers previously thought "race" categories could reasonably be determined based on skull dimensions, modern-day analyses using more informative sets of cranial traits simply show that migrations out of Africa and the relative distances between populations can explain a majority of worldwide cranial variation (Betti et al. 2009).

Figure 13.20: Contemporary anthropologists who use many types of skeletal markers have demonstrated that a majority of cranial variation occurs within populations rather than between populations and that there is a decrease in variation with distance from Africa. Credit: Dental Anthropologist Heart Necklace by Anthro Illustrated is under a CC BY-NC 4.0 License.

Figure 13.21: Diagram of the bony labyrinth in the inner ear. Credit: Bony labyrinth by Selket has been designated to the public domain (CC0).

This same patterning in phenotypic variation has even been found in studies examining shape variation of the pelvis (Betti et al. 2013; Betti et al. 2014), the teeth (Rathmann et al. 2017), and the human **bony labyrinth** of the ear (Ponce de León et al. 2018;Figure 13.21). The skeletal morphology of these bones still varies worldwide, but a greater proportion of that variation can still be attributed to the ways in which human populations migrated across the world and exchanged genes with those closer to them rather than those further away. Human skeletal variation in these parts of the body is continuous and nondiscrete. Given the important functions of the cranium and these other skeletal parts, we may infer that the genes that underpin their development have been relatively conserved by neutral evolutionary processes such as genetic drift and gene flow. It is also important to note that while some traits such as height, weight, cranial dimensions, and body composition are determined, in part, by genes, the underlying developmental processes behind these traits are underpinned by complex polygenic mechanisms that have led to the continuous spectrum of variation in such variables among modern-day human populations.

Phenotypic Traits That Reflect Natural Selection

Even though 99.9% of our DNA is the same across all humans worldwide, and many traits reflect neutral processes, there are parts of that remaining 0.1% of the human genome that code for individual and regional differences. Similarly to craniometric analyses that have been conducted in recent decades, human variation in skin color has also been reassessed using new methods and in light of greater knowledge of biological evolution.

New technologies allow scientists to use color photometry to sample and quantify the visible wavelength of skin color, in a way 19th- and 20th-century readers could not. In one report, it was found that 87.9% of global skin color variation can be attributed to genetic differences *between* groups, 3.2% to those among local populations within regions, and 8.9% *within* local populations (Relethford 2002). This apportionment differs significantly and is the reverse situation found in the distribution of genetic differences we see when we examine genetic markers such as blood type–related alleles. However, this pattern of human skin color worldwide is not surprising, given that we now understand that past selection has occurred for darker skin near the equator and lighter skin at higher latitudes (Jablonski 2004; Jablonski and Chaplin 2000). While most genetic variation reflects neutral variation due to population migrations, geographic isolation, and restricted gene flow dynamics, some human genetic/phenotypic variation is best explained as local adaptation to environmental conditions (i.e., selection). Given that skin color variation is atypical compared to other genetic markers and biological traits, this, in fact, goes against earlier "race" typologies. This is because recent studies ironically show how so much of genetic variation relates to neutral processes, while skin color does not. It follows that skin color *cannot* be viewed as useful in making inferences about other human traits.

It is also true that some populations have not been studied extensively in skin pigmentation genetics (e.g., African, Austronesian, Melanesian, Southeast Asian, Indigenous American, and Pacific Islander populations, according to Lasisi and Shriver 2018). Earlier dispersals of these populations, and their local genetic varition, will have contributed to worldwide genetic variation, inclusive of skin pigmentation variation. Gene loci we did not previously appreciate as being linked to pigmentation are now being recognized thanks to better tools, more diverse genetic samples, and more accessible datasets (Quillen et al. 2018). Biological anthropologists look forward to further discoveries elucidating the different selective pressures and population dynamics that influence skin pigmentation evolution.

Figure 13.22: Genomicists and biological anthropologists have dedicated efforts to improving quantitative methods of measuring hair and skin variation over the last twenty years. Dr. Nina Jablonski is one such biological anthropologist specializing in the evolution and variation of human skin pigmentation. Credit: Nina Jablonski 2016 The Skin of Homo sapiens 01 (cropped) by Ptolusque is under a CC BY-SA 4.0 license.

Social Implications

To finish this chapter, we will consider the social, economic, political, and biological implications of poor understandings of race and the deliberate perpetuation of social and medical racism.

The Black Lives Matter movement (BLM) of 2013 began with the work of racial justice activists and community organizers Alicia Garza, Opal Tometi, and Patrissa Cullors. First incited by the murder of Trayvon Martin, a 17-year-old African American, and the acquittal of the man who shot him, BLM went on to protest against the deaths of numerous Black individuals, most of whom were killed by police officers (for example, Ahmaud Arbery was killed in February of 2020 by two white non-police officers). Some key characteristics of BLM from the start were its decentralized grassroots structure, the role of university students and social media in spreading awareness of the movement, and its embrace of other movements (e.g., climate justice, ending police brutality, feminist campaigns, queer activism, immigration reform, etc.). When George Floyd was murdered by a white police officer on May 25, 2020, the BLM gained new momentum, across 2,000-plus cities in the United States, and among many protesting against historic racism and police brutality in other contexts around the globe. Many in the biological anthropology community have responded to these events with a great dedication to working against systemic racism in society and institutions (American Association of Biological Anthropologists 2020).

BLM continues to be an important movement, as is evidenced in the degree of community organizing, mutual aid efforts, calls for political reform, progress toward curriculum reform and equality, inclusion and diversity (EDI) work in businesses and universities, the removal of monuments honoring historical figures associated with slavery and racism, and many other important actions. Garza (2016) writes: "The reality is that race in the United States operates on a spectrum from black to white ... the closer you are to white on that spectrum, the better off you are." Tometi (2016) has stated: "We need [a human rights movement that challenges systemic racism] because the global reality is that Black people are subject to all sorts of disparities in most of our challenging issues of our day. I think about climate change, and how six of the ten worst impacted nations by climate change are actually on the continent of Africa." In the words of Cullors (2016), "Black Lives Matter is our call to action. It is a tool to reimagine a world where Black people are free to exist, free to live. It is a tool for our allies to show up differently for us." We gather from their words the importance of learning from the egregious role that anthropologists have played in the past, recognizing the legacies of "scientific" justifications for eugenics and racism in our society today, and proactively working toward environmental and social equity.

Another major industry that engages in the quantification and interpretation of human variation is medical and clinical work (National Research Council [U.S.] Committee on Human Genome Diversity 1997). Large-scale genomic studies sampling from human populations distributed worldwide have produced detailed knowledge on variation in disease resistance or susceptibility between and within populations. Let's think about drug companies who develop medicines for Black patients particularly. The predispositions to particular diseases are higher among people of African descent than some pharmaceutical businesses have taken into account. Through targeted sampling of various world groups, clinical geneticists may also identify genetic risk factors of certain common disorders such as chronic heart disease, asthma, diabetes, autoimmune diseases, and behavioral disorders. Having an understanding of population-specific biology is crucial in the development of therapies, medicines, and vaccinations, as not all treatments may be suitable for every human, depending on their genotype. During diagnosis and treatment, it is important to have an evolutionary perspective on gene-environment relationships in patients. Typological concepts of "race" are not useful, given that most racial groups (whether self-identified or not) popularly recognized lack homogeneity and are, in fact, variable. **Cystic fibrosis**, for instance, occurs in all world populations but can often be underdiagnosed in populations with African ancestry because it is thought of as a "white" disease (Yudell et al. 2016).

Sociologists, law scholars, and professors of race studies have written extensively on how genetic/technological/medical revolutions impact people of color. In her book, *Fatal Invention: How Science, Politics, and Big Business Re-create Race in the Twenty-First Century* (2013), Professor Dorothy E. Roberts writes about how technological advances have been used in resuscitating race as a biological category for dividing humans in essentialist ways (Figure 13.23). She notes how members of law enforcement have engaged in racial profiling, sometimes with the use of machine-learning and facial-recognition technologies. Ancestry-testing services also purport to tell us "what" we are and to insist that this information is "written" in our genes. Such advertising campaigns obscure the nuances of genetic variation with the primary motive of tapping into people's desire to "know themselves" and driving up profits for their businesses. Commercial genetic testing reinforces the idea that genes map neatly onto race, all while generating massive stores of data in DNA databases. In Roberts's view, the myth of the biological concept of race being perpetuated in these ways undermines a just society and reproduces racial inequalities.

Figure 13.23: Professor Dorothy E. Roberts is a sociologist, legal scholar, and expert on the relationships among technology, medicine, bioethics, policymaking, race, and racism. Credit: Dorothy Roberts author of Fatal Invention by https://kpfa.org/ is copyrighted and used with permission.

The COVID-19 pandemic has had a significant impact on the world's population, particularly people living in the economic Global South and many Black, Indigenous and communities of color residing in the Global North. We have witnessed disproportionately high numbers of COVID-related deaths and infection cases among marginalized groups. Many immigrants and ethnic minorities in various societies have also experienced scapegoating and blame directed at them for being the source of COVID-19 spread.

To inform us on how to interpret this current worldwide pandemic, historians and anthropologists are looking back at the lessons learned from past instances of racist medicine (discriminatory practices based on broader social discrimination) and medical racism (application of discriminatory practices justified on medical grounds). Historically, who could become doctors and medical professionals was often racialized, gendered, and class specific. This made it difficult for many to overcome prejudices against women, Black people, Indigenous individuals, or other people of color from becoming doctors and clinical researchers in places such as South Africa and the United States. This, in turn, affects the sorts of information we know about health levels and health outcomes among these very groups. In the past decade, long-overdue attention is finally being paid to how race affects biological outcomes. For instance, researchers have focused on the negative legacies of racial discrimination and racism-induced stress on hormone (im)balances, mental health disorders, cardiovascular disease prevalence, and other health outcomes (Kuzawa and Sweet 2009; Shonkoff, Slopen, and WIlliams 2021; Williams 2018). The technology and standards of protocol in medical testing have been scrutinized (for more on how pulse oximeters were not designed with nonwhite patients in mind, for example, see Sjoding et al. 2020). Scholars of race and medicine have also written on how illness and disease spread have often been used to perpetuate societal prejudices. This manifests as xenophobic tendencies at a societal level, such as the blaming of "outgroups" and increased "in-group" protectiveness. Overreliance on the idea that people are "inherently" disease carriers due to genetic or biological reasons leads to improper accounting for socioeconomic or infrastructural issues that lead to differential disease prevalence amongst minority communities. (For more on race and COVID, see Tsai 2021 as well as this textbook's Chapter 16: Contemporary Topics: Human Biology and Health.)

Lastly, consider the changing field of forensic anthropology. In the past, forensic anthropologists ascribed **ancestry** or racial categories to sets of skeletons, reliant on the belief that different human groups will exhibit biologically "discrete" assortments so as to divide along culturally constructed categories (Sauer 1992). Now, a number of forensic anthropologists have argued that we should abandon these methods, both because it is unscientific and because it further validates and perpetuates this idea that race is biologically meaningful. As scientists, whether we affirm biological race as real has huge influence on the beliefs of members of the public, the judicolegal system, and law enforcement. Not all forensic experts agree with abandoning ancestry estimation. Some prefer to refocus on the neutral or selective *causes* of human biological variation, and assess how *probabilistic* it may be to assign bones of certain dimensions to one of several identified racial categories. These debates continue today as this textbook chapter is being written. More details on population affinity may be found in Chapter 15: Bioarchaeology and Forensic Anthropology.

It is important to remember that while it is possible to look for clues about one's ancestry or geographic origin based on skull morphology, again, the amount of distinctiveness in any given sample makes it impossible to distinguish whether a cranium belongs to one group (Relethford 2009). Individuals can vary in their skeletal dimensions by continental origin, country origin, regional origin, sex, age, environmental factors, and the time period in which they lived, making it difficult to assign individuals to particular categories in a completely meaningful way (Ousley, Jantz, and Freid 2009). When forensic reports and scientific journal articles give an estimation of ancestry, it is crucial to keep in mind that responsible assignments of ancestry will be done through robust statistical testing and stated as a probability estimate. Today, we also live in a more globalized world where a skeletal individual may have been born originally to parents of two separate traditional racial categories. In contexts of great heterogeneity within populations, this definitely adds difficulty to the work of forensic scientists and anthropologists preparing results for the courtroom (genetic testing may be comparatively more helpful in such situations).

Did Deeper: Measuring F$_{ST}$

Richard Lewontin (1929–) is a biologist and evolutionary geneticist who authored an article evaluating where the total genetic variation in humans lies. Titled "The Apportionment of Human Diversity" (Lewontin 1972), the article addressed the following question: On average, how genetically similar are two randomly chosen people from the same group when compared to two randomly chosen people from different groups?

Lewontin studied this problem by using genetic data. He obtained data for a large number of different human populations worldwide using 17 genetic markers (including alleles that code for various important enzymes and proteins, such as blood-group proteins). The statistical analysis he ran used a measure of human genetic differences in and among populations known as the fixation index (F$_{ST}$).

Technically, F$_{ST}$ can be defined as the proportion of total genetic variance within a *subpopulation* relative to the total genetic variance from an *entire population*. Therefore, F$_{ST}$ values range from 0 to 1 (or, sometimes you will see this stated as a percentage between 0% and 100%). The closer the F$_{ST}$ value of a population (e.g., the world's population) approaches 1, the higher the degree of genetic differentiation among subpopulations relative to the overall population (see Figure 13.24 for a detailed illustration).

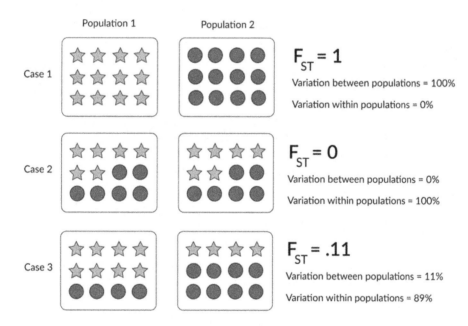

Figure 13.24: This diagram shows a range of different case studies with which we may understand how FST is calculated in different populations. In Case 1, the gene pools of Populations 1 and 2 are 100% different from each other but possess 0% variation within themselves, so FST has a value of 1. When there is no genetic variation at all between two populations and 100% variation within them, as in Case 2, we see that FST is calculated as 0. When we look at Case 3, where variation between and within are some values between 0% and 100%, we will get a decimal figure for FST dependent upon how much variation there is between and within populations. It is through such comparisons of population genetic data that we may quantify the relative similarities or differences between and within populations, and we may thus speak to the nonexistence of "racial groups" that divide up our species into broad continental or racial categories. Credit: FST original to Explorations: An Open Invitation to Biological Anthropology (2nd ed.) by Katie Nelson is under a CC BY-NC 4.0 License.

In his article, Lewontin (1972) identified that most of human genetic differences (85.4%) were found within local subpopulations (e.g., the Germans or Easter Islanders), whereas 8.3% were found between populations within continental human groups, and 6.3%

were attributable to traditional "race" groups (e.g., "Caucasian" or "Amerind"). These findings have been important for scientifically rejecting the existence of biological races (Long and Kittles 2003).

Talking About Human Biological Variation Going Forward

To conclude, utilizing the term *races* to describe human biological variation is not accurate or productive. Using a select few hundred genetic loci, or perhaps a number of phenotypic traits, it may be possible to assign individuals to a geographic ancestry, but what constitutes a bounded genetic or geographical grouping is both arbitrary and potentially harmful owing to ethical and historical reasons. The discipline of biological anthropology has moved past typological frameworks that shoehorn continuously variable human populations into discrete and socially constructed subsets. Improvements in the number of markers, the genetic technologies used to study variation, and the number of worldwide populations sampled have led to more nuanced understandings of human variation. It is of utmost importance that scientists make the following points clear to the public:

- Today, we refer to different local human groups as "populations." What constitutes a population should be carefully defined in scientific reports based on some geographical, linguistic, or cultural criteria and some degree of relativity to other closely or distantly related human groups.
- Humans have significantly less genetic variation than other primates and mammals, and all human beings on Earth share 99.9% of their overall DNA. Some of the remaining 0.1% of human variation varies on a clinal or continuous basis, such as can be seen when looking at ABO blood-type **polymorphisms** worldwide.
- Many biological characteristics in humans are actually determined nonconcordantly and/or polygenically. Therefore, superiority or inferiority in human behavior or body form cannot justifiably be linked to fixed and innate differences between groups.
- Genetic distances are correlated with geographic distances among the global human population. This is especially apparent when we consider that genetic variation is highest in sub-Saharan Africa, and average genetic heterogeneity decreases in populations further away from the African continent in accordance with the migratory history of anatomically modern *Homo sapiens*.
- The effects of gene flow, genetic drift, and population bottlenecking are reflected in some phenotypic traits, such as cranial shape.
- We recognize other traits, like skin color and lactase persistence, to be the products of many millennia of natural selective pressures influencing human biology from the external environment.

Taken together, genetic analyses of human variation do not support 20th-century (or even-earlier) concepts of race. In discussions about human variation, these genomic results help clarify how biological variation is distributed across the human population today. Taking care to think about and debate the nature of human variation is important, because although the effects and events that produced genetic differences among groups occurred in the ancient past, sociocultural concepts about race and ethnicity continue to have real social, economic, and political consequences.

Beyond talking about variation in the university setting, it is important that teachers, researchers, and students of anthropology recognize and assume the responsibility of influencing public perspectives of human variation. Race-based classification systems were developed during the colonial era, the transatlantic trafficking of kidnapped Africans and the so-called "Scientific Revolution" by the first "anthropologists" and scholars of humankind's variation. Unfortunately, some of their early ideas have persisted and evolved into present-day lived realities. Some of today's politicians and socioeconomic bodies have racially charged agendas that promote racism or certain kinds of economic or racial inequalities. As anthropologists, we must acknowledge that while human "races" are not a biological reality, their status as a (misguided) social construction does have real consequences for many people (Antrosio 2011).

In other words, while "race" is a sociocultural invention, the treatment different individuals receive due to their perceived "race" can have significant financial, emotional, sociopolitical, and physiological costs. However—and importantly assuming a "color-blind" position when it comes to the topics of "race" and ethnicity (especially in political discussions) is actually counterproductive, because the negative social consequences of modern "race" ideas could be ignored, making it harder to examine and address instances of discrimination properly (Wise 2010). Rather than shy away from these topics, we can use our scientific findings to establish socially relevant and biologically accurate ideas concerning human diversity.

Today, research into genetic and phenotypic differentiation among and within various human populations continues to expand in its scope, its technological capabilities, its sample sizes, and its ethical concerns. It is thanks to such scientific work done in the past few decades that we now have a deeper understanding not only of how humans vary but also of how we are biologically a rather homogenous, intermixing world population.

Review Questions

- How is the genetic variation of the human species distributed worldwide?
- What evolutionary processes are responsible for producing genotypic/phenotypic variation within and between human populations?
- Should we continue to attribute any value to "race" concepts older than 1950, based on our current understandings of human biological variation?
- How should we communicate scientific findings about human biological variation more accurately and responsibly to those outside the anthropological discipline?

Key Terms

Age of Discovery: A period between the late 1400s and late 1700s when European explorers and ships sailed extensively across the globe in pursuit of new trading routes and territorial conquest.

Ancestry: Biogeographical information about an individual, traced either through the study of an individual's genome, skeletal characteristics, or some other form of forensic/archaeological evidence. Anthropologists carry out probabilistic estimates of ancestry. They attribute sets of human remains to distinctive "ancestral" groups using careful statistical testing and should report ancestry estimations with statistical probability values.

Binomial nomenclature: A system of naming living things developed by Linnaeus in the 1700s. It employs a scientific name made up of two italicized Latin or Greek words, with the first word capitalized and representative of an organism's genus and the second word indicating an organism's species (e.g., *Homo sapiens*, *Australopithecus afarensis*, *Pongo tapanuliensis*, etc.).

Biological anthropology: A branch of study under anthropology (the study of humankind) that focuses on when and where humans and our human ancestors first originated, how we have evolved and adapted globally over time, and the reasons why we see biological variation among humans worldwide today.

Biological determinism: The erroneous concept that an individual's behavioral characteristics are innate and determined by genes, brain size, or other physiological attributes—and, notably, without the influence of social learning or the environment around the individual during development.

Bony labyrinth: A system of interconnected canals within the auditory (ear- or hearing-related) apparatus, located in the inner ear and responsible for balance and the reception of sound waves.

Cline: A gradient of physiological or morphological change in a single character or allele frequency among a group of species across environmental or geographical lines (e.g., skin color varies clinally, as, over many generations, human groups living nearer the equator have adapted to have more skin pigmentation).

Continuous variation: This term refers to variation that exists between individuals and cannot be measured using distinct categories. Instead, differences between individuals within a population in relation to one particular trait are measurable along a smooth, continuous gradient.

Cystic fibrosis: A genetic disorder in which one defective gene causes overproduction and buildup of mucus in the lungs and other bodily organs. It is most common in northern Europeans (but also occurs in other world populations).

Ecological niche: The position or status of an organism within its community and/or ecosystem, resulting from the organism's structural and functional adaptations (e.g., bipedalism, omnivorous diets, lactose digestion, etc.).

Essentialism: A belief or view that an entity, organism, or human grouping has a specific set of characteristics that are fundamentally necessary to its being and classification into definitive categories.

Ethnicity: A term used commonly in an interchangeable way with the term *race*, complicated because how different people define this term depends on the qualities and characteristics they use to assign a label or identity to themselves and/or others (which may include aspects of family background, skin color, language(s) spoken, religion, physical proportions, behavior and temperament, etc.).

Eugenics: A set of beliefs and practices that involves the controlled selective breeding of human populations with the hope of improving their heritable qualities, especially through surgical procedures like sterilization and legal rulings that affect marriage rights for interracial couples.

Gene flow: A neutral (or nonselective) evolutionary process that occurs when genes get shared between populations.

Genetic drift: A neutral evolutionary process in which allele frequencies change from generation to generation due to random chance.

Heterogeneity: The quality of being diverse genetically.

Homogenous: The quality of being uniform genetically.

Human diversity: Human diversity is a measure of variation that may describe how many different forms of human there are, separated or clustered into groups according to some genetic, phenotypic, or cultural trait(s). The term can be applied to culture (in which case humans can be described as significantly diverse) or genetics (in which case humans are not diverse because all humans on Earth share a majority of their genes).

Human variation: Differences in biology, physiology, body chemistry, behavior, and culture. By measuring these differences, we understand the degrees of variation between individuals, groups, populations, or species.

Isolation-by-distance model: A model that predicts a positive relationship between genetic distances and geographical distances between pairs of populations.

Monogenetic: Pertaining to the idea that the origin of a species is situated in one geographic region or time (as opposed to *polygenetic*).

Mutation: A gene alteration in the DNA sequence of an organism. As a random, neutral evolutionary process that occurs over the course of meiosis and early cell development, gene mutations are possible sources of variation in any given human gene pool. Genetic mutations that occur in more than 1% of a population are termed *polymorphisms*.

Natural selection: An evolutionary process whereby certain traits are perpetuated through successive generations, likely owing to the advantages they give organisms in terms of chances of survival and/or reproduction.

Nonconcordance: The fact of genes or traits not varying with one another and instead being inherited independently.

Otherness: In postcolonial anthropology, we now understand "othering" to mean any action by someone or some group that establishes a division between "us" and "them" in relation to other individuals or populations. This could be based on linguistic or cultural differences, and it has largely been based on external characteristics throughout history.

Out-of-Africa model: A model that suggests that all humans originate from one single group of *Homo sapiens* in (sub-Saharan) Africa who lived between 100,000 and 315,000 years ago and who subsequently diverged and migrated to other regions across the globe.

Physical anthropology: This used to be the more common name given to the subdiscipline of anthropology centered upon the study of human origins, evolution and variation (also see *biological anthropology* above). This name for the field has gradually become less popular due to two reasons: first, it may not reflect our interests in other aspects of humankind that are not physical (such as those behavioral, cultural and spiritual), and second, using this term popular in the early decades of our field may be viewed by some as harkening back to a time when biological anthropologists conducted their work in unethical ways.

Polygenetic: Having many different ancestries, as in older theories about human origins that involved multiple traditional groupings of humans evolving concurrently in different parts of the world before they merged into one species through interbreeding and/or intergroup warfare. These earlier suggestions have now been overwhelmed by insurmountable evidence for a single origin of the human species in Africa (see the "Out-of-Africa model").

Polymorphism: A genetic variant within a population (caused either by a single gene or multiple genes) that occurs at a rate of over 1% among the population. Polymorphisms are responsible for variation in phenotypic traits such as blood type and skin color.

Population: A group of humans living in a particular geographical area, with more local interbreeding within-group than interbreeding with other groups. A limited or restricted amount of gene flow between populations can occur due to geographical, cultural, linguistic, or environmental factors.

Population bottlenecking: An event in which genetic variation is significantly reduced owing to a sharp reduction in population size. This can occur when environmental disaster strikes or as a result of human activities (e.g., genocides or group migrations). An important example of this loss in genetic variation occurred over the first human migrations out of Africa and into other continental regions.

Prejudice: An unjustified attitude toward an individual or group that is not based on reason, whether positive (and showing preference for one group of people over another) or negative (and resulting in harm or injury to others).

Race: The identification of a group based on a perceived distinctiveness that makes that group more similar to each other than they are to others outside the group. This may be based on cultural differences, genetic parentage, physical characteristics, behavioral attributes, or something arbitrarily and socially constructed. As a social or demographic category, perceptions of "race" can have real and serious consequences for different groups of people. This is despite the fact that biological anthropologists and geneticists have demonstrated that all humans are genetically homogenous and that more differences can be found within populations than between them in the overall apportionment of human biological variation. This term is sometimes used interchangeably with *ethnicity*.

Racism: Any action or belief that discriminates against someone based on perceived differences in race or ethnicity.

Scientific Revolution: A period between the 1400s and 1600s when substantial shifts occurred in the social, technological, and philosophical sense, when a scientific method based on the collection of empirical evidence through experimentation was emphasized and inductive reasoning was used to test hypotheses and interpret their results.

Typological: Of or describing an assortment system that relies on the interpretation of qualitative similarities or differences in the study of variation among objects or people. The categorization of cultures or human groups according to "race" was performed with a typological approach in the earliest practice of anthropology, but this practice has since been discredited and abandoned.

Variance: In statistics, variance measures the dispersal of a set of data around the mean or average value.

About the Author

Michael B. C. Rivera, Ph.D.

University of Hong Kong, mrivera@hku.hk

Michael B. C. Rivera is a biological anthropologist and human bioarchaeologist who studies human evolution and history and works to develop these disciplines in Hong Kong, East/Southeast Asia, and the "Global South." His doctoral thesis focused on the transition into agriculture in coastal environments and adaptations of ancient people along the beach. He is the only biological anthropologist working at the University of Hong Kong and the lead archaeologist managing the excavation of a WWII military aircraft that crashed in Hong Kong in 1945.

Michael is also an advocate for greater inclusion, diversity, equality, and access to learning in academia. Much of his work also includes science communication and public engagement activities online, in schools, and in collaboration with museums.

For Further Exploration

Videos

American Medical Association (AMA). 2020. "Examining Race-Based Medicine." YouTube, October 29. Accessed June 4, 2023.

Crenshaw, Kimberlé. 2016. "The Urgency of Intersectionality." YouTube, December 7. Accessed June 4, 2023.

Golash-Boza, Tanya. 2018. "What Is Race? What Is Ethnicity? Is There a Difference?." YouTube, October 28. Accessed June 4, 2023.

Lasisi, Tina. 2020. "How Hair Reveals the Futility of Race Categories." National Museum of Natural History webinar, October 21.

Lasisi, Tina. 2022. "Where Does My Skin Color Come From?." PBS Terra, August 18. Accessed June 4, 2023.

PBS Origins. 2018. "The Origin of Race in the USA." YouTube, April 3. Accessed June 4, 2023.

Roberts, Dorothy. 2016. "The Problem with Race-Based Medicine." YouTube, March 4. Accessed June 4, 2023.

Vox. 2015. "The Myth of Race, Debunked in 3 Minutes." YouTube, January 13. Accessed June 4, 2023.

Podcast Episodes

Kwong, Emily, and Rebecca Ramirez. 2021. "Here's a Better Way to Talk about Hair: A 16 Minute Listen with Tina, Lasisi" NPR Short Wave, October 6. Accessed June 4, 2023.

Speaking of Race. 2020. "Race and Health series." Speaking of Race, April 10. Accessed June 4, 2023.

Websites

Choices Program. 2023. "An Interactive Timeline: Black Activism and the Long Fight for Racial Justice." *Choices Program, Brown University* [Interactive Timeline], Updated February, 2023.

References

American Association of Biological Anthropologists. 2020. "An Open Letter to Our Community in Response to Police Brutality against African-Americans and a Call to Antiracist Action". *American Association of Biological Anthropologists*, June 10, 2020. Accessed June 4, 2023.

Antrosio, Jason. 2011. "'Race Reconciled': Race Isn't Skin Color, Biology, or Genetics." *Living Anthropologically* (website), June 5, 2011; updated May 20, 2020. Accessed June 4, 2023.

Beals, Kenneth L., Courtland L. Smith, Stephen M. Dodd, J. Lawrence Angel, Este Armstrong, Bennett Blumenberg, Fakhry G. Girgis, et al. 1984. "Brain Size, Cranial Morphology, Climate, and Time Machines [and Comments and Reply]." *Current Anthropology* 25 (3): 301–330.

Betti, Lia, François Balloux, Tsunehiko Hanihara, and Andrea Manica. 2010. "The Relative Role of Drift and Selection in Shaping the Human Skull." *American Journal of Physical Anthropology* 141 (1): 76–82. https://doi.org/10.1002/ajpa.21115.

Betti, Lia, François Balloux, William Amos, Tsunehiko Hanihara, and Andrea Manica. 2009. "Distance from Africa, Not Climate, Explains Within-Population Phenotypic Diversity in Humans." *Proceedings: Biological Sciences* 276 (1658): 809–814. https://doi.org/10.1098/rspb.2008.1563.

Betti, Lia, Noreen von Cramon-Taubadel, Andrea Manica, and Stephen J. Lycett. 2013. "Global Geometric Morphometric Analyses of the Human Pelvis Reveal Substantial Neutral Population History Effects, Even across Sexes." *PLoS ONE* 8 (2): e55909. https://doi.org/10.1371/journal.pone.0055909.

Betti, Lia, Noreen von Cramon-Taubadel, Andrea Manica, and Stephen J. Lycett. 2014. "The Interaction of Neutral Evolutionary Processes with Climatically Driven Adaptive Changes in the 3D Shape of the Human Os Coxae." *Journal of Human Evolution* 73 (August): 64–74. https://doi.org/10.1016/j.jhevol.2014.02.021.

Boas, Franz. 1931. "Race and Progress." *Science* 74 1905): 1–8.

Bowden, Rory, Tammie S. MacFie, Simon Myers, Garrett Hellenthal, Eric Nerrienet, Ronald E. Bontrop, Colin Freeman, Peter Donnelly, and Nicholas I. Mundy. 2012. "Genomic Tools for Evolution and Conservation in the Chimpanzee: *Pan troglodytes ellioti* Is a Genetically Distinct Population." *PLoS Genetics* 8 (3): e1002504. https://doi.org/10.1371/journal.pgen.1002504.

Campbell, Michael C., and Sarah A. Tishkoff. 2008. "African Genetic Diversity: Implications for Human Demographic History, Modern Human Origins, and Complex Disease Mapping." *Annual Review of Genomics and Human Genetics* 9: 403–433.

Clee, Paul R. Sesink, Ekwoge E. Abwe, Ruffin D. Ambahe, Nicola M. Anthony, Roger Forso, Sabrina Locatelli, Fiona Maisels, et al. 2015. "Chimpanzee Population Structure in Cameroon and Nigeria Is Associated with Habitat Variation That May Be Lost Under Climate Change." *BMC Evolutionary Biology* 15: 2. https://doi.org/10.1186/s12862-014-0275-z.

Cullors, Patrisse. 2016. "An Interview with the Founders of Black Lives Matter." TED Talks 2016, October 26–28. Accessed June 15, 2023. https://www.ted.com/talks/alicia_garza_patrisse_cullors_and_opal_tometi_an_interview_with_the_founders_of_black_lives_matter/up-next.

Fuentes, Agustín, Rebecca Rogers Ackermann, Sheela Athreya, Deborah Bolnick, Tina Lasisi, Sang-Hee Lee, Shay-Akil McLean, and Robin Nelson. 2019. "AAPA Statement on Race and Racism." *American Journal of Physical Anthropology* 169 (3): 400–402.

Garza, Alicia. 2016. "An Interview with the Founders of Black Lives Matter." TED Talks 2016, October 26–28. Accessed June 15, 2023. https://www.ted.com/talks/alicia_garza_patrisse_cullors_and_opal_tometi_an_interview_with_the_founders_of_black_lives_matter/up-next.

Gerbault, Pascale, Anke Liebert, Yuval Itan, Adam Powell, Mathias Currat, Joachim Burger, Dallas M. Swallow, and Mark G. Thomas. 2011. "Evolution of Lactase Persistence: An Example of Human Niche Construction." *Philosophical Transactions of the Royal Society B* 366 (1566): 863–877. https://doi.org/10.1098/rstb.2010.0268.

Hooton, Earnest A. 1936. "Plain Statements about Race." *Science* 83 (2161): 511–513.

Hrdlička, Aleš. 1918. "Physical Anthropology: Its Scope and Aims; Its History and Present Status in America. A: Physical Anthropology; Its Scopes and Aims." *American Journal of Physical Anthropology* 1 (1): 3–23.

Huxley, Julian. 1942. *Evolution: The Modern Synthesis*. London: Allen and Unwin.

Ingram, Catherine J. E., Charlotte A. Mulcare, Yuval Itan, Mark G. Thomas, and Dallas M. Swallow. 2009. "Lactose Digestion and the Evolutionary Genetics of Lactase Persistence." *Human Genetics* 124 (6): 579–591. https://doi.org/10.1007/s00439-008-0593-6.

Jablonski, Nina G. 2004. "The Evolution of Human Skin and Skin Color." *Annual Review of Anthropology* 33: 585–623. https://doi.org/10.1146/annurev.anthro.33.070203.143955.

Jablonski, Nina G., and George Chaplin. 2000. "The Evolution of Human Skin Coloration." *Journal of Human Evolution* 39 (1): 57–106. https://doi.org/10.1006/jhev.2000.0403.

Kanitz, Ricardo, Elsa G. Guillot, Sylvain Antoniazza, Samuel Neuenschwander, and Jérôme Gedout. 2018. "Complex Genetic Patterns in Human Arise from a Simple Range-Expansion Model over Continental Landmasses." *PLoS ONE* 13 (2): e0192460.

Kronenberg, Zev N., Ian T. Fiddes, David Gordon, Shwetha Murali, Stuart Cantsilieris, Olivia S. Meyerson, Jason G. Underwood, et al. 2018. "High-Resolution Comparative Analysis of Great Ape Genomes." *Science* 360 (6393): eaar6343. https://doi.org/10.1126/science.aar6343.

Kuzawa, Christopher W., and Elizabeth Sweet. 2009. "Epigenetics and the Embodiment of Race: Development Origins of US Racial Disparities in Cardiovascular Health." *American Journal of Human Biology* 21 (1) : 2–15.

Lasisi, Tina, and Mark D. Shriver. 2018. "Focus on African Diversity Confirms Complexity of Skin Pigmentation Genetics." *Genomic Biology* 19: 13.

Lewontin, Richard. 1972. "The Apportionment of Human Diversity." In *Evolutionary Biology*, vol. 6, edited by Theodosius Dobzhansky, Max K. Hecht, and William C. Steere, 381–398. New York: Springer.

Linnaeus, Carl. 1758. *Systema Naturae*. Stockholm: Laurentius Salvius. http://www.cabdirect.org/abstracts/20057000018.html.

Liu, Hua, Franck Prugnolle, Andrea Manica, and François Balloux. 2006. "A Geographically Explicit Genetic Model of Worldwide Human-Settlement History." *American Journal of Human Genetics* 79 (2): 230–237.

Livingstone, Frank B. 1962. "On the Nonexistence of Human Races." *Current Anthropology* 3 (3): 279–281.

Long, Jeffery C., and Rick A. Kittles. 2003. "Human Genetic Diversity and the Nonexistence of Biological Races." *Human Biology* 75 (4): 449–471.

Luzzatto, Lucio. 2012. "Sickle Cell Anaemia and Malaria." *Mediterranean Journal of Hematology and Infectious Diseases* 4 (1). https://doi.org/10.4084/MJHID.2012.065.

Manica, Andrea, William Amos, François Balloux, and Tsunehiko Hanihara. 2007. "The Effect of Ancient Population Bottlenecks on Human Phenotypic Variation." *Nature* 448 (7151): 346–348. https://doi.org/10.1038/nature05951.

McLean, Shay-Akil. 2014. "'Race, Ethnicity, & Racism." Decolonize ALL The Things Website, Accessed January 10, 2023. https://decolonizeallthethings.com/learning-tools/race-ethnicity-racism/.

Morton, Samuel George. 1839. *Crania Americana, or, A Comparative View of the Skulls of Various Aboriginal Nations of North and South America*. Philadelphia: J. Dobson.

Mourant, A. E., Ada C. Kopeć, and Kazimiera Domaniewska-Sobczak. 1976. *The Distribution of the Human Blood Groups and Other Polymorphisms*, 2nd edition. Oxford: Oxford University Press.

National Research Council (U.S.) Committee on Human Genome Diversity. 1997. *Evaluating Human Genetic Diversity*. Washington, D.C.: National Academies Press.

Omi, Michael, and Howard Winant. 2014. "The Theory of Racial Formation." In *Racial Formation in the United States*,3rd edition, edited by Michael Omi and Howard Winant, 105–126. Routledge: New York.

Osada, Naoki. 2015. "Genetic Diversity in Humans and Non-Human Primates and Its Evolutionary Consequences." *Genes and Genetic Systems* 90 (3): 133–145.

Ousley, Stephen D., Richard L. Jantz, and Donna Freid. 2009. "Understanding Race and Human Variation: Why Forensic Anthropologists Are Good at Identifying Race." *American Journal of Physical Anthropology* 139 (1): 68–76. https://doi.org/10.1002/ajpa.21006.

Ponce de León, Marcia S., Toetik Koesbardiati, John David Weissmann, Marco Millela, Carlos S. Reyna-Blanco, Gen Suwa, Osamu Kondo, Anna-Sapfo Malaspinas, Tim D. White, and Christoph P. E. Zollikofer. 2018. "Human Bony Labyrinth Is an Indicator of Population History and Dispersal from Africa." *Proceedings of the National Academy of Sciences* 115 (16): 4128–4133. https://doi.org/10.1073/pnas.1808125115.

Prado-Martinez, Javier, Peter H. Sudmant, Jeffrey M. Kidd, Heng Li, Joanna L. Kelley, Belen Lorente-Galdos, Krishna R. Veeramah, et al. 2013. "Great Ape Genetic Diversity and Population History." *Nature* 499 (7459): 471–475. https://doi.org/10.1038/nature12228.

Prugnolle, Franck, Andrea Manica, and François Balloux. 2005. "Geography Predicts Neutral Genetic Diversity of Human Populations." *Current Biology* 15 (5): 159–160.

Quillen, Ellen E., Heather L. Norton, Esteban J. Parra, Frida Lona-Durazo, Khai C. Ang, Florin Mircea Illiescu, Laurel N. Pearson, et al. 2018. "Shades of Complexity: New Perspectives on the Evolution and Genetic Architecture of Human Skin." *American Journal of Physical Anthropology* 168 (S67): 4–26.

Rathmann, Hannes, Hugo Reyes-Centeno, Silvia Ghirotto, Nicole Creanza, Tsunehiko Hanihara, and Katerina Harvati. 2017. "Reconstructing Human Population History from Dental Phenotypes." *Scientific Reports* 7: 12495. https://doi.org/10.1038/s41598-017-12621-y.

Relethford, John H. 2001. "Global Analysis of Regional Differences in Craniometric Diversity and Population Substructure." *Human Biology* 73 (5): 629–636. https://doi.org/10.1353/hub.2001.0073.

Relethford, John H. 2002. "Apportionment of Global Human Genetic Diversity Based on Craniometrics and Skin Color." *American Journal of Physical Anthropology* 118 (4): 393–398. https://doi.org/10.1002/ajpa.10079.

Relethford, John H. 2004. "Global Patterns of Isolation by Distance Based on Genetic and Morphological Data." *Human Biology* 76 (4): 499–513. https://doi.org/10.1353/hub.2004.0060.

Relethford, John H. 2009. "Race and Global Patterns of Phenotypic Variation." *American Journal of Physical Anthropology* 139 (1): 16–22. https://doi.org/10.1002/ajpa.20900.

Roberts, Dorothy. 2013. *Fatal Invention: How Science, Politics, and Big Business Re-Create Race in the Twenty-First Century*. New York: The New Press.

Rosenberg, Noah A., Saurabh Mahajan, Sohini Ramachandran, Chengfeng Zhao, Jonathan K. Pritchard, and Marcus W. Feldman. 2005. "Clines, Clusters, and the Effect of Study Design on the Inference of Human Population Structure." *PLoS Genetics* 1 (6): e70. https://doi.org/10.1371/journal.pgen.0010070.

Rosenberg, Noah A., Jonathan K. Pritchard, James L. Weber, Howard M. Cann, Kenneth K. Kidd, Lev A. Zhivotovsky, and Marcus W. Feldman. 2002. "Genetic Structure of Human Populations." *Science* 298 (5602): 2381–2385.

Sauer, Norman J. 1992. "Forensic Anthropology and the Concept of Race: If Races Don't Exist, Why Are Forensic Anthropologists So Good at Identifying Them?" *Social Science and Medicine* 34 (2): 107–111. https://doi.org/10.1016/0277-9536(92)90086-6.

Shonkoff, Jack P., Natalie Slopen, and David R. Williams. 2021. "Early Childhood Adversity, Toxic Stress, and the Impacts of Racism on the Foundations of Health." *Annual Review of Public Health* 42: 115–134.

Sjoding, Michael W., Robert P. Dickson, Theodore J. Iwashyna, Steven E. Gay, and Thomas S. Valley. 2020. "Racial Bias in Pulse Oximetry Measurement." *The New England Journal of Medicine* 383: 2477-2478.

Staes, Nicky, Chet C. Sherwood, Katharine Wright, Marc de Manuel, Elaine E. Guevara, Tomas Marques-Bonet, Michael Krützen, et al. 2017. "FOXP2 Variation in Great Ape Populations Offers Insight into the Evolution of Communication Skills." *Scientific Reports* 7 (1): 1–10. https://doi.org/10.1038/s41598-017-16844-x.

Tomati, Opal. 2016. "An Interview with the Founders of Black Lives Matter." TED Talks 2016, October 26–28. Accessed June 15, 2023. https://www.ted.com/talks/alicia_garza_patrisse_cullors_and_opal_tometi_an_interview_with_the_founders_of_black_lives_matter/up-next.

Tsai, Jennifer. 2021. "COVID-19 Is Not a Story of Race, but a Record of Racism—Our Scholarship Should Reflect That Reality." *The American Journal of Bioethics* 21 (2): 43–47. https://doi.org/10.1080/15265161.2020.1861377.

von Cramon-Taubadel, Noreen, and Stephen J. Lycett. 2008. "Brief Communication: Human Cranial Variation Fits Iterative Founder Effect Model with African Origin." *American Journal of Physical Anthropology* 136 (1): 108–113. https://doi.org/10.1002/ajpa.20775.

Weiss, Kenneth M., and Jeffrey C. Long. 2009. "Non-Darwinian Estimation: My Ancestors, My Genes' Ancestors." *Genome Research* 19: 703–710. https://doi.org/10.1101/gr.076539.108.19.

Williams, David W. 2018. "Stress and the Mental Health of Populations of Color: Advancing Our Understanding of Race-related Stressors." *Journal of Health and Social Behavior* 59 (4): 466–485.

Wise, Tim. 2010. *Colorblind: The Rise of Post-Racial Politics and the Retreat from Racial Equity*. San Francisco: City Lights.

Yudell, Michael, Dorothy Roberts, Rob DeSalle, and Sarah Tishkoff. 2016. "Taking Race out of Human Genetics." *Science* 351 (6273): 564–565. https://doi.org/10.1126/science.aac4951.

Image Descriptions

Figure 13.14a: This world map is colored in to reflect the percent of populations that have the A allele (for ABO bloodtypes). The lightest color reflects populations with 0-5% allele A, and these increase at 5% intervals to the darkest color for 35-40% allele A. The lightest colors are in the Americas, particularly in South America. The darkest colors are in Europe, Australia, and very northern North America.

Figure 13.14b: This world map is colored in to reflect the percent of populations that have the B allele (for ABO bloodtypes). The lightest color reflects populations with 0-5% allele B, and these increase at 5% intervals to the darkest color for 25-30% allele B. The lightest color covers most of North and South America and Australia. The darkest colors are found in central Asia.

Figure 13.14c: This world map is colored in to reflect the percent of populations that have the O allele (the most common allele for ABO bloodtypes). The lightest color reflects populations with 50-60% allele O, and these increase at 10% intervals to the darkest color for 90-100% allele O. The lightest color is in central Asia, and the darkes colors are in North and South America.

Figure 13.19: This map shows the distribution of the four subspecies of chimpanzees and bonobos across west and central Africa.

Chimpanzees:

- Pan troglodytes verus: found across many nations in West Africa including Guinea, Sierra Leone, Liberia, and the Ivory Coast
- Pan troglodytes ellioti: found only in Nigeria and Cameroon
- Pan troglodytes troglodytes: found in Cameroon and Congo Basin
- Pan troglodytes schweinfurthii: found in Burundi, Central African Republic, Congo, Democratic Republic of Congo, Rwanda, South Sudan, Tanzania, and Uganda.

Bonobos:

- Pan paniscus: Found in the Democratic Republic of Congo

14.

HUMAN VARIATION: AN ADAPTIVE SIGNIFICANCE APPROACH

Leslie E. Fitzpatrick, Ph.D., Independent Archaeological Consultants

This chapter is a revision from "Chapter 14: Human Variation: An Adaptive Significance Approach" by Leslie E. Fitzpatrick. In Explorations: An Open Invitation to Biological Anthropology, first edition, edited by Beth Shook, Katie Nelson, Kelsie Aguilera, and Lara Braff, which is licensed under CC BY-NC 4.0.

Learning Objectives

- Distinguish between adaptations and adjustments as ways of coping with environmental stressors.
- Provide examples of adjustments humans use to cope with thermal stressors.
- Describe how specific patterns of human adaptations and adjustments are correlated to natural selection processes.
- Summarize the role of solar radiation in variations of human skin tone, and explain why reduced pigmentation is advantageous in northern latitudes.
- Compare and contrast the various genetic mutations present in Tibetan and Ethiopian populations that allow them to survive at high altitudes.
- Define the relationship between specific genetic mutations in some human populations and certain infectious diseases, such as the sickle-cell trait mutation and malarial infection.

As early humans left Africa and spread across the globe, they faced numerous challenges related to their new environments. Beyond genetically influenced changes in physiology as a result of evolution, humans have developed lifestyle strategies to cope with and even thrive in a wide range of habitats. The ways populations of humans met such challenges, coupled with their geographic separation throughout the majority of the last two hundred thousand years, have led to the many forms of adaptation in our species. This chapter focuses on the complexities of modern human variation through the lens of human evolutionary history.

Stress and Homeostasis

All organisms, including humans, must maintain a baseline of normal functions within their cells, tissues, and organs to survive. This constancy of internal functions is referred to as **homeostasis.** Homeostatic regulation, however, may be disrupted by a variety of both external and internal stimuli known as **stressors.** Within limits, all organisms have evolved certain physiological mechanisms to respond to stressors in an effort to maintain homeostasis. The range of changes in the physiology (function), morphology (form), and/or behavior of organisms in response to their environments and potential stressors is regulated by its **phenotypic plasticity**. Coping with these stressors led to the development of both **adjustments** (behavioral, acclimatory, and developmental) and **adaptations**, which are explained in detail in the following sections.

Adjustments and Adaptations

Adjustments

The term *adjustment* refers to an organism's nongenetic way of coping with the stressors of its environment. Although adjustments themselves are nongenetic in nature, the ability of an organism to experience or develop an adjustment is based on its phenotypic plasticity, which is linked to its evolutionarily guided genetic potential. Adjustments occur exclusively on the individual level. As such, different individuals within a population may experience a wide range of possible adjustments in response to a similar stressor. In general, the three main forms of adjustment are: behavioral, acclimatory, and developmental.

Behavioral Adjustments

Figure 14.1: Notice the lack of full-spectrum color in this photo of a deep-water diver as well as the diver's use of specialized equipment, such as a breathing apparatus to deliver gasses for respiration, a bodysuit to ensure thermal regulation, and a flashlight to increase visibility in the low-light setting. Credit: Deep water diver by Leslie E. Fitzpatrick is under a CC BY-NC 4.0 License.

When you are cold, do you reach for a blanket? When you are warm, do you seek out shelter cooled by an air-conditioning system? If so, you have likely been influenced to do so by the culture in which you were raised. As noted earlier in this textbook, the term *culture* refers to a collection of shared, learned beliefs and behaviors among individuals within a discrete population. **Behavioral adjustments** are regarded as cultural responses to environmental stressors. These adjustments are temporary in nature and, since they are nongenetic, must be constantly altered to meet novel situations posed by the environment. For example, divers are able to reach extraordinary depths (in excess of 300 meters below the surface) within the water through the use of a specialized mixture of gasses for breathing, an apparatus for the delivery of the gasses, protective clothing, and gear to increase visibility. The deeper a diver descends, the more atmospheric pressure the diver experiences, resulting in increased levels of potentially toxic byproducts of respiration within the body. In addition, with increased depth there is a decrease in the ambient temperature of the water and a decrease in the availability of light within the visible spectrum. Deep-water divers are well-versed in the environmental stressors of open waters and employ a variety of strategies based on behavioral adjustments to meet such demands. From wearing protective clothing to help maintain the body's core temperature to waiting at a specific depth for a prescribed period of time to facilitate the expulsion of nitrogen gas that may have accumulated within the bloodstream, divers employ numerous behavioral adjustments to ensure their safety (Figure 14.1). Without these culturally mediated behavioral adjustments, a deep-water diver's first dive would also be their last.

In many developing countries, the use of refrigeration for the storage of perishable food products is uncommon; therefore, individuals within these cultures have developed a variety of behavioral adjustment strategies related to food preparation to address possible food spoilage. Through a cross-cultural analysis of spice use in recipes, Paul Sherman and Jennifer Billing (1999) determined that cultures closest to the equator, where temperatures are hotter, tend to use both a greater number and a wider variety of plant-based spices with bacteria-inhibiting phytochemical properties (e.g., garlic and onion). Antimicrobial properties of spices permits the consumption of foods, particularly animal-based protein sources, for a period of time beyond that which would be considered safe. There are some acclimatory adjustment benefits to the use of some pungent spices as well, which are explored in the following section.

Acclimatory Adjustments: Thermal Stressors

Acclimatory adjustments are temporary, reversible changes in an organism's physiology in response to environmental stressors. Although they are not genetically determined, the range of acclimatory adjustments that an organism is capable of producing is linked to its underlying phenotypic plasticity and the duration and severity of the stressor. A good example of this is the human response to varying ambient temperatures.

To understand human adjustments, we must first understand the thermodynamic mechanisms through which heat may be gained or lost. The four pathways for this are conduction, convection, evaporation, and radiation (Figure 14.2).

Through **conduction** processes, heat will move from a warmer body to a cooler one through direct contact. An example of this is when you accidentally touch a hot cooktop with your hand and the heat is transferred from the cooktop to your skin.

With **convection**, when a warm body is surrounded by a cooler fluid (e.g., air or water), heat will be transferred from the warmer body to the cooler fluid. This is why we will often employ the behavioral adjustment of wearing multiple layers of clothing during the winter in an effort to prevent heat loss to the cooler atmosphere. Conversely, if your body temperature is cooler than that of the air surrounding you, your body will absorb heat.

Depending on your physical condition, most people will begin to sweat around 37.2°C to 37.7°C (98.9°F–99.9°F). Sweating is an example of **evaporation**, which occurs when a liquid, such as the water within our bodies, is converted to a gas. Phase conversions, such as those underlying the evaporative processes of transforming liquids to gasses, require energy. In evaporation, this energy is in the form of heat, and the effect is to cool the body.

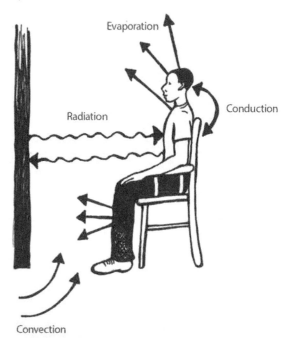

The final mechanism for heat loss within the human body is **radiation**, through which energy in the form of electromagnetic waves is produced at a wavelength that typically lies below that which is visible to the human eye. Although humans gain and lose heat from their bodies through radiation, this form of heat transfer is not visible. Humans are capable of losing and gaining heat through conduction, convection, and radiation; however, heat may not be gained through evaporation.

Figure 14.2: Various thermodynamic mechanisms related to heat gain and loss in the human body. This process is decribed in the text below. Credit: Mechanisms of heat transfer (Figure 14.2) original to Explorations: An Open Invitation to Biological Anthropology by Mary Nelson is under a CC BY-NC 4.0 License.

As the ambient temperature decreases, it becomes increasingly difficult for the human body to regulate its core temperature, which is central to the maintenance of homeostasis. When an individual's body temperature falls below 34.4°C (93.9°F), the brain's **hypothalamus** becomes impaired, leading to issues with body temperature control. A total loss of the ability to regulate body temperature occurs around 29.4°C (84.9°F), which may result in death. When the ambient temperature falls below the critical temperature of 31°C (87.8°F), a nude human body that is at rest will respond with a series of physiological changes to preserve homeostasis (Figure 14.3).

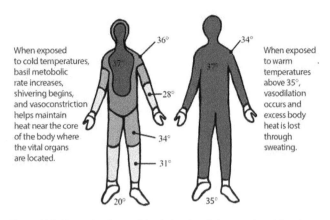

When exposed to cold temperatures, basil metabolic rate increases, shivering begins, and vasoconstriction helps maintain heat near the core of the body where the vital organs are located.

When exposed to warm temperatures above 35°, vasodilation occurs and excess body heat is lost through sweating.

Figure 14.3: Example of overall body heat maintenance in cold and warm ambient environments. Credit: Body heat maintenance in cold and warm (Figure 14.3) original to Explorations: An Open Invitation to Biological Anthropology by Mary Nelson is under a CC BY-NC 4.0 License. [Image Description].

The human body experiences two main types of physiological responses to colder temperatures: those that increase the production of heat and those that seek to retain heat. The production of heat within the body is accomplished through short-term increases in the body's basal metabolic rate, such as shivering to increase muscular metabolism. An organism's basic metabolic rate is a measure of the energy required to maintain necessary body processes when the organism is at rest. Increases in basal metabolic rates, such as when we shiver from the cold, require increased consumption of energy-providing nutrients. Of course, such increases in metabolic rates are not infinite, as we may only consume a finite amount of nutrients. As with all **acclimatory adjustments**, an increase in the basal metabolic rate is merely temporary.

Of the physiological mechanisms to preserve heat already in the body, the most notable is **vasoconstriction**, or the constriction of peripheral capillaries in the skin. The decreased surface area of the capillaries through vasoconstriction results in less heat reaching the surface of the skin where it would be dissipated into the atmosphere. Vasoconstriction also leads to the maintenance of heat near the core of the body where the vital organs are located. As a trade-off, though, individuals are more at risk of cold-related injuries, such as frost-bite, which can lead to tissue necrosis (tissue death) in regions of the body that are most distant from the core (e.g., fingers, toes, nose, ears, cheeks, chin, etc.).

Just as cold stress presents challenges to maintaining homeostasis, heat does as well. In hot climates, the body will absorb heat from its surroundings (through conduction, convection, and radiation), resulting in potential heat-related disorders, such as heat exhaustion. When the human body is exposed to ambient temperatures above 35°C (95°F), excess body heat will be lost primarily through evaporative processes, specifically through sweating. All humans, regardless of their environment, have approximately the same number of sweat glands within their bodies. Over time, individuals living in hot, arid environments will develop more sensitive forms of sweat glands resulting in the production of greater quantities of sweat (Best, Lieberman, and Kamilar 2019; Pontzer et al. 2021). In an effort to prevent dehydration due to this form of acclimatory adjustment, there will be an additional reduction in the volume of urine produced by the individual (Pontzer et al. 2021).

As noted in the previous section, some cultural groups, particularly those in equatorial regions, add pungent spices to their foods to inhibit the colonization of bacteria (Sherman and Billing 1999). Although adding spices to decrease spoilage rates is a behavioral adjustment, the application of some forms of peppers triggers an acclimatory adjustment as well. Compounds referred to as capsaicinoids are the secondary byproducts of chili pepper plants' metabolism and are produced to deter their consumption by some forms of fungi and mammals. When mammals, such as humans, consume the capsaicinoids from chili peppers, a burning sensation may occur within their mouths and along their digestive tracts. This burning sensation is the result of the activation of capsaicin receptors along the body's nerve pathways. Although the peppers themselves may be at ambient temperature so their consumption is not causing any form of body temperature increase, the human body perceives the pepper as elevating its core temperature due to the activation of the capsaicin receptors. This causes the hypothalamus to react, initiating sweating in an attempt to lower body temperature and maintain homeostasis. The increased piquancy (application of pungent spices to food) as a means of inhibiting food-borne bacterial colonization in warm climates, as well as spices' ability to trigger sweating processes as a method for cooling the body, is an example of the intersection between behavioral and acclimatory adjustments that utilized within certain populations.

In addition to increased sweat production to maintain homeostasis in excess heat, **vasodilation** may occur (Figure 14.4). Vasodilation is an expansion of the capillaries within the skin leading to a more effective transfer of heat from within the body to the exterior to allow conductive, convective, radiative, and evaporative (sweating) processes to occur.

Physiologically based acclimatory adjustments to hot, dry climates may be complemented by behavioral adjustments as well. For example, individuals in such climates may limit their physical activity during the times of day when the temperature is typically the hottest. Additionally, these individuals may wear loose-fitting clothing that covers much of their skin. The looseness of the clothing allows for air to flow between the clothing and the skin to permit the effective evaporation of sweat. Although it may seem counterintuitive to cover one's body completely in a hot climate, the covering of the skin keeps the sun's rays from directly penetrating the skin and elevating the body's core temperature.

Acclimatory Adjustments: Altitudinal Stressors

The challenges posed by thermal conditions are but one form of environmental stressor humans must face. High-altitude environments, which are defined as altitudes in excess of 2,400 meters above sea level (masl) or 7,874 feet above sea level (fasl), pose additional challenges to the maintenance of homeostasis in humans. Some of the main stressors encountered by those living within high-altitude environments include decreased oxygen availability, cold temperatures, low humidity, high wind speed, a reduced nutritional base, and increased solar radiation levels. Of these challenges, the most significant is the decreased availability of oxygen.

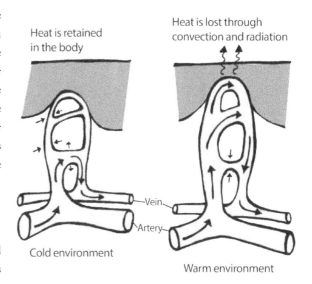

Figure 14.4: The vasoconstriction processes occur within the peripheral vascular system when an individual is exposed to cold ambient temperatures and the vasodilation that occurs in warmer environments. Credit: Vasoconstriction and vasodilation (Figure 14.4) original to Explorations: An Open Invitation to Biological Anthropology by Mary Nelson is under a CC BY-NC 4.0 License. [Image Description].

To visualize how altitude affects the availability of oxygen, imagine two balloons that are each filled with the same quantity of oxygen molecules. One of these balloons is positioned at sea-level and the other is placed high upon a mountain peak. For the balloon at sea level, there is more atmospheric pressure pressing down on the molecules within this balloon. This leads to the oxygen molecules within the sea level balloon being forced into a more compact organization. In contrast, the mountain peak balloon has less atmospheric pressure pressing down on it. This leads to the oxygen molecules within that balloon spreading out from each other since they are not being forced together quite as strongly. This example highlights the availability of oxygen molecules in each breath than we take in low- versus high-altitude environments. At 5,500 masl (approximately 18,000 fasl), the atmospheric pressure is approximately 50% of its value at sea level (Peacock 1998). At the peak of Mount Everest (8,900 masl or approximately 29,200 fasl), the atmospheric pressure is equivalent to only about 30% of their sea level amounts (Peacock 1998; Figure 14.5).

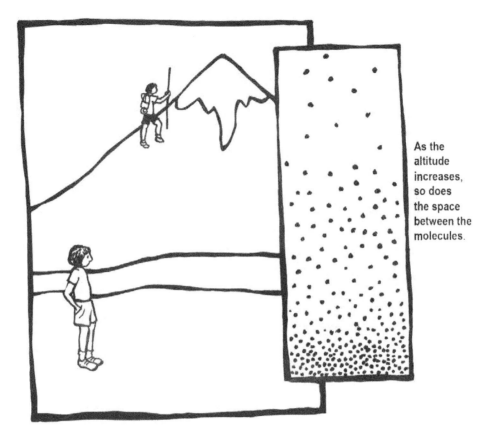

Figure 14.5: As altitude increases, atmospheric pressure decreases, which allows for more space between air molecules. Credit: Atmospheric pressure (Figure 14.5) original to Explorations: An Open Invitation to Biological Anthropology by Mary Nelson is under a CC BY-NC 4.0 License.

Due to decreased availability of oxygen at higher altitudes, certain acclimatory adjustments are required to ensure the maintenance of homeostasis for individuals other than those who were gestated, born, and raised at high altitude. For these people, their rate of breathing will increase to permit greater quantities of air containing oxygen into the lungs when they ascend into higher altitude environments. An increased speed and depth of breathing, which is referred to as **hyperpnea**, is not sustainable indefinitely; thus, the rate of breathing begins to decrease as the person becomes acclimatized to the altitude. During the initial phases of high-altitude-related hyperpnea, the heart begins to beat faster but the amount of blood pushed through during each beat decreases slightly. In addition, the body will divert energy from noncritical bodily functions, such as digestive processes.

Once the atmospheric oxygen reaches the alveoli (small air sacs) in the lungs, it spreads across the alveolar membrane and enters **erythrocytes** (red blood cells). As oxygen reaches the alevoli's erythrocytes, it loosely binds with hemoglobin (an iron-rich protein) contained in the erythrocytes. When the erythrocytes carrying the hemoglobin-bound oxygen molecules reach capillaries where the partial pressure of oxygen is relatively low, oxygen will be released by the hemoglobin so that it is free for diffusion into body cells. Similar to acclimatory adjustments related to thermal conditions (e.g., shivering or sweating), those related to high altitude may not be infinitely sustained due to their energetically expensive nature.

Although the long-term acclimatory adjustments that an individual from low altitude experiences in a high-altitude environment may permit them to reside there successfully, reproduction within such settings is frequently complicated. With increased altitude comes an increased risk of miscarriage, lower birth weights, and higher infant mortality rates. As the pregnant person's body seeks to preserve its own homeostasis, there is often a decreased rate and volume of blood flow to the uterus as compared to a pregnant person of similar physiological condition at a lower altitude (Moore, Niermeyer, and Zamudio 1998). This results in a decrease in the amount of oxygen that will be passed through the uterus and placenta to the developing fetus. In addition, pregnant people who experience pregnancy at higher altitudes are more prone to developing preeclampsia (severe elevation of blood pressure), which is linked to increased rates of both fetal and maternal death (Moore, Niermeyer, and Zamudio 1998; Figure 14.6).

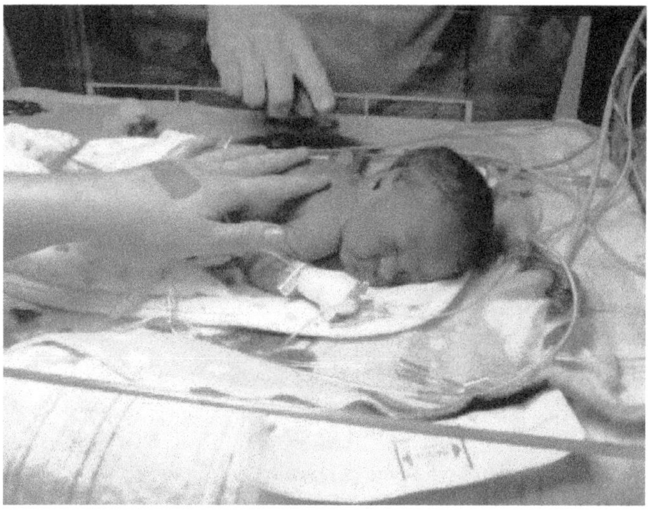

Figure 14.6: Premature infant born at 30 weeks, 4 days gestation to a mother with altitudinal-induced preeclampsia. Blue light assists the infant's liver with processing high levels of bilirubin. Credit: Premature infant by Leslie E. Fitzpatrick is under a CC BY-NC 4.0 License.

Developmental Adjustments

Developmental adjustments occur only in individuals who spent their developmental period (i.e., childhood and adolescence) within a high-altitude environment; they do not apply to those who moved into these environments in the post developmental (i.e., adult) phase. Furthermore, the degree of developmental adjustment within an individual is directly related to their underlying phenotypic plasticity as well as the amount of time during the crucial growth and development period that the individual resides within the challenging environment. Although humans have the remarkable capacity to develop and survive within environments that are not overly conducive to the successful maintenance of homeostasis, there are definitely physiological costs associated with this ability.

Figure 14.7: Two individuals from a high-altitude region of the Peruvian Andes. Credit: Andahuaylas Peru-two women walking down street by Thayne Tuason has been modified (cropped) and is under a CC BY 4.0 License.

In general, high-altitude natives tend to grow more slowly and physically mature later than their low-altitude counterparts (Figure 14.7). Lowered growth and maturity rates are linked not only to the increased physiological demands placed on the body due to the decreased partial pressure of oxygen but also to reductions in the quality of the nutritional base at higher altitudes. Increased terrain complexity, elevated solar radiation levels, and higher wind speeds coupled with the lower temperatures and humidity levels found at high altitudes leads to difficulties with growing and maintaining crops and raising livestock. Overall, as altitude rises, the quality of the available nutritional base goes down, which is correlated to a lack of the nutrients necessary to ensure proper physiological growth and development in humans. Thus, even though individuals may be able to develop and grow within high-altitude environments, they may not reach their full genetically mediated growth potential as they would in a lower-altitude environment.

Not all developmental adjustments are linked to environmental pressures such as climate or altitude; rather, some of these adjustments are correlated to sociocultural or behavioral practices. Some of these adjustments may affect the physiological appearance of an individual when they are practiced consistently during the development and growth phases.

Sudden infant death syndrome (SIDS) has no definitive cause; however, the American Academy of Pediatrics published a report in 1992 linking SIDS to infants (under the age of one) sleeping on their stomachs. The "Back to Sleep" campaign championed by the American Academy of Pediatrics helped educate members of the medical community as well as the public that the best sleep position for infants is on their backs (American Academy of Pediatrics 2000).

Figure 14.8: These sketches illustrate a top and side view of brachycephaly (left and middle images, respectively) and plagiocephaly (right image). Credit: Brachycephaly and plagiocephaly original to Explorations: An Open Invitation to Biological Anthropology (2nd ed.) by Mary Nelson is under a CC BY-NC 4.0 License.

Placing infants on their backs to sleep has led to decreased infant mortality (death) rates due to SIDS; however, it has led to an unintended consequence: infant cranial deformation. The cranial deformations experienced by infants who sleep solely on their back tend to manifest in one of two forms: brachycephaly and plagiocephaly (Roby et al. 2012; Figure 14.8). With positional brachycephaly, the back of the infant's head appears rather uniformly flattened due to repetitive contact with a flat surface, such as a crib mattress or car seat back. In cases of positional plagiocephaly, the back of the infant's head appears asymmetrically flattened. This asymmetry is typically due to an uneven distribution of mechanical forces resulting from the manner in which the infant's head is in contact with a flat surface. The forms of cranial deformation resulting from sleep positioning do not affect the infant's brain development. For many individuals, the appearance of the deformation is minimized during later development. Still, some individuals will maintain the pattern of cranial deformation acquired during their infancy throughout their lives. The unintentional cranial deformation resulting from placing infants on their backs to sleep as a means of preventing SIDS-related deaths is a physiological indicator of a behavioral adjustment.

Adaptations

As we have just explored, survival and reproduction at high altitudes present numerous physiological challenges for most humans. The behavioral, acclimatory, and developmental adjustments discussed above are all related to the phenotypic plasticity of the individual; however, most adjustments are temporary in nature and they affect a single individual rather than all individuals within a population. But what if the physiological changes were permanent? What if they affected all members of a population rather than just a single individual? The long-term, microevolutionary (i.e., genetic) changes that occur within a population in response to an environmental stressor are referred to as an adaptation. From an evolutionary standpoint, the term *adaptation* refers to a phenotypic trait (i.e., physiological/morphological feature or behavior) that has been acted upon by natural selection processes to increase a species' ability to survive and reproduce within a specific environment. Within the field of physiology, the term *adaptation* refers to traits that serve to restore homeostasis. The physiology-based interpretation of adaptations presumes that all traits serve a purpose and that all adaptations are beneficial in nature; however, this may be a fallacy, since some traits may be present without clear evidence as to their purpose. As such, during the following discussion of various forms of adaptations in human populations, we will focus our attention on phenotypic traits with an evidence-based purpose.

Adaptation: Altitudinal Adaptation

As mentioned in the previous section, there is genomic research supporting the evolutionary selection of certain phenotypes and their corresponding genotypes within indigenous high-altitude populations across the globe. The following discussion focuses on two high-altitude indigenous populations from Tibet and Ethiopia (Figure 14.9). Although these populations share many common genetic traits based on relatively similar evolutionary histories influenced by similar environmental stressors, there is support for local genetically based adaptation as well, based on different genes being acted upon by environmental stressors that may be unique to Tibet and Ethiopia (Bigham 2016).

Figure 14.9: Highlighted regions feature (from left to right) the Simian (Ethiopian) and Tibetan Plateau high-altitude regions. Credit: World Map of HVR adaptation in high altitude populations by Chkuu has been modified (cropped, Andean region color change) and is under CC BY-SA 4.0 License.

Tibetan populations have resided in the Tibetan Plateau and Himalayan Mountain regions at elevations exceeding 4,000 masl (13,100 fasl) for at least the past 7,400 years (Meyer et al. 2017). There is evidence of a genetic exchange event involving Tibetan populations and Denisovans around 48,700 years ago, which introduced a haplogroup involving mutations of the *EPAS1* gene (Zhang et al. 2021). The *EPAS1* is involved in the regulation of erythrocytes and hemoglobin. For individuals originating in lower-altitude environments, *EPAS1* stimulates increased erythrocyte production in high-altitude environments as a temporary acclimatory adjustment. For indigenous high-altitude populations of Tibet, the *EPAS1* gene mutation introduced by Denisovan introgression inhibits increased erythrocyte production, which reduces potential negative effects (e.g., stroke or heart attack) associated with long-term high levels of erythrocyte production (Gray et al. 2022; Zhang et al. 2021). The erythrocyte count of high-altitude Tibetans with the *EPAS1* point mutation is about the same as for individuals residing at sea level.

Populations indigenous to the Semien Plateau of Ethiopia, such as the Oromo and Amhara, share a similar but not identical *EPAS1* point mutation with the Tibetan population (Bigham 2016); however, there is no indication that this mutation was derived from Denisovan introgression. The *EPAS1* mutations occurred independently from each other; however, their effects are still similar in that they permit the Tibetan and Ethiopian populations to survive at high altitudes. Not all adaptations are related to life in high-altitude environments, however. In the following sections, we will address two more general examples of adaptation in human populations: variations in skin color and differences in body build.

Adaptation: Skin Tone Basics

When you think about your own skin tone and compare it to members of your family, do you all possess exactly the same shade? Are some members of your family darker than others? What about your friends? Your classmates? Skin tone occurs along a continuum, which is a reflection of the complex evolutionary history of our species. The expression of skin tone is regulated primarily by melanin and hemoglobin. **Melanin** is a dark brown-black pigment that is produced by the oxidation of certain amino acids (e.g., tyrosine, cysteine, phenylalanine) in melanocytes. **Melanocytes** are specialized cells located in the base layer (stratum basale) of the skin's epidermis as well as several other areas within the body (Figure 14.10). Within the melanocytes, melanin is produced in the special organelle called a melanosome. Melanosomes serve as sites for the synthesis, storage, and transportation of melanin. Melanosomes transport the melanin particles through cellular projections to epidermal skin cells (keratinocytes) as well as to the base of the growing hair root. In the eye, however, melanin particles produced by the melanosomes remain present within the iris and are not transported beyond their origin location. The two main forms of melanin related to skin, hair, and eye color are eumelanin and pheomelanin. All humans contain both eumelanin and pheomelanin within their bodies; however, the relative expression of these two forms of melanin determines an individual's overall coloring. Eumelanin is a brown-to-black colored melanin particle while pheomelanin is more pink-to-red colored. Individuals with darker skin or hair color have a greater expression of eumelanin than those with lighter-colored skin and blonde or red hair.

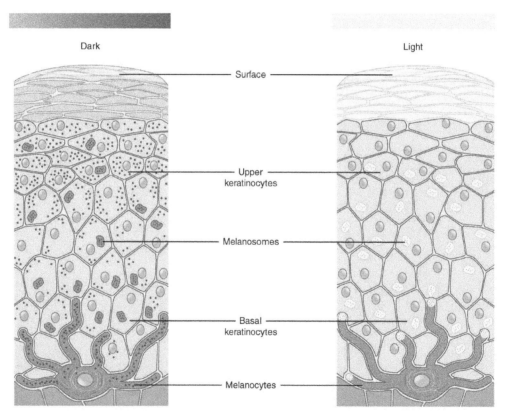

Figure 14.10: Diagram featuring the relative numbers of melanocytes and melanosomes in light and dark shades of skin tone. Credit: Skin Pigmentation (Anatomy and Physiology, Figure 5.8) by OpenStax is under a CC BY 4.0 License. [Image Description].

Adaptation: Melanogenesis

Although all humans have approximately the same number of melanocytes within their epidermis, the production of melanin by these melanocytes varies. There are two forms of melanogenesis (the process through which melanocytes generate melanin): basal and activated. As discussed previously, the expression of eumelanin and pheomelanin by the melanocytes is genetically regulated through the expression of specific receptors (e.g., *MC1R*) or other melanocyte components (e.g., *MFSD12*). **Basal melanogenesis** is dependent upon an individual's inherent genetic composition and is not influenced by external factors. **Activated melanogenesis** occurs in response to ultraviolet radiation (UV) exposure, specifically UV-B (short UV wave) exposure. Increased melanogenesis in response to UV-B exposure serves to provide protection to the skin's innermost layer called the hypodermis, which lies below the epidermis and dermis (Figure 14.11). Melanin in the skin, specifically eumelanin, effectively absorbs UV-B radiation from light—meaning that it will not reach the hypodermal layer. This effect is often more apparent during periods of the year when people tend to be outside more and the weather is warmer, which leads to most donning fewer protective garments. The exposure of skin to sunlight is, of course, culturally mediated with some cultures encouraging the covering of skin at all times.

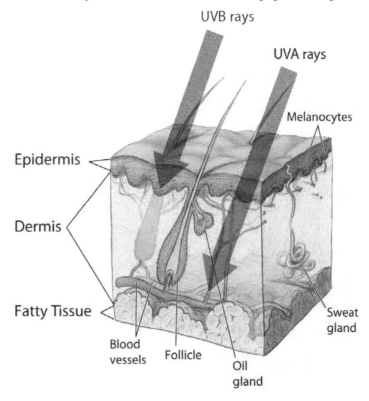

Figure 14.11: Penetration of skin layers by UVA and UVB rays. UVB rays penetrate only through the epidermis. UVA rays penetrate much deeper, through the dermis. Credit: Skin Pigmentation (Anatomy and Physiology, Figure 5.8) by OpenStax is under a CC BY 4.0 License.

As previously noted in this chapter, hemoglobin is an iron-rich protein that binds with oxygen in the bloodstream. For individuals with lighter-colored skin, blood vessels near the surface of the skin and the hemoglobin contained within those vessels is more apparent than in individuals with darker skin. The visible presence of hemoglobin coupled with the pink-to-red tone of the pheomelanin leads to lighter-skinned individuals having a pale pink skin tone. Individuals with lighter skin more readily absorb UV radiation as their basal melanin expression is directed more toward the production of pheomelanin than eumelanin. But why are there so many variations in skin tone in humans? To answer this question, we now turn toward an exploration of an evolutionary-based adaptation of skin tone as a function of the environment.

Adaptation: Evolutionary Basis for Skin Tone Variation

Evolution of Skin Color Variation

HAIR AND SKIN

Once hominins lost most of their body hair they likely had dark pigmented skin. In environments with high UV radiation, dark skin protected early humans against skin damage.

FOLATE & UV RAYS

UV rays penetrate the skin and can break down folate in the blood stream. Folate is necessary for sperm production and for fetal development.

LEAVING AFRICA

Once some humans left Africa, they encountered environments with different levels of UV radiation. New selective pressures began to shape human skin color among these groups.

VITAMIN D

In low UV environments, people with dark skin could not synthesize enough vitamin D resulting in rickets and other health problems. People with dark skin had a lower chance of survival in most of these environments.

SELECTIVE PRESSURES

Vitamin D, folate and changing UV environments were the selective pressures that resulted in the development of a variety of skin colors in different populations throughout the world.

Figure 14.12: Evolutionary basis for human skin color variation. Credit: Evolutionary basis for human skin color variation (Figure 14.12) original to *Explorations: An Open Invitation to Biological Anthropology* by Katie Nelson is under a CC BY-NC 4.0 License. [Image Description].

Skin cancer is a significant concern for many individuals with light skin tone as the cumulative exposure of the epidermis and underlying skin tissues to UV radiation may result in the development of abnormal cells within those tissues, leading to malignancies. Although darker-skinned individuals are at risk for skin cancer as well, they are less likely to develop it due to increased levels of melanin, specifically eumelanin, in their skin. Even though skin cancer is a serious health concern for some individuals, most skin cancers occur in the postreproductive years; therefore, it is improbable that evolutionary forces favoring varying melanin expression levels are related to a selective pressure to avoid such cancers. Furthermore, if avoiding skin cancer were the primary factor driving the evolution of various skin tones, then it reasons that everyone would have the most significant expression of eumelanin possible. So, why do we have different skin tones (Figure 14.12)?

The term **cline** (introduced in Chapter 13) refers to the continuum or spectrum of gradations (i.e., levels or degrees) from one extreme to another. With respect to skin tone, the various tonal shades occur clinally with darker skin being more prevalent near the equator and gradually decreasing in tone (i.e., decreased melanin production) in more distant latitudes. For individuals who are indigenous to equatorial regions, the increased levels of melanin within their skin provides them with a measure of protection against both sunburn and sunstroke because the melanin is more reflective of UV radiation than hemoglobin. In cases of severe sunburn, eccrine glands are affected, resulting in an individual's ability to sweat being compromised. As sweat is the body's most effective means of reducing its core temperature to maintain homeostasis, damage to the eccrine glands may lead to numerous physiological issues related to heat that may ultimately result in death.

Even though avoiding severe sunburn and sunstroke is of great importance to individuals within equatorial regions, this is likely not the primary factor driving the evolutionary selection of darker skin within these regions. It has been proposed that UV radiation's destruction of **folic acid**, which is a form of B-complex vitamin, may have led to the selection of darker skin in equatorial regions. For pregnant people, low levels of folic acid within the body during gestation may lead to defects in the formation of the brain and spinal cord of the fetus. This condition, which is referred to as spina bifida (Figure 14.13), often significantly reduces an infant's chances of survival without medical intervention. In people producing sperm, low levels of folic acid within the body reduce sperm quantity and quality. Thus, in geographic regions with high UV radiation levels (i.e., equatorial regions), there appears to be an evolutionarily driven correlation between darker skin and fertility.

If darker skin tone is potentially correlated to more successful reproduction, then why do lighter shades of skin exist? One hypothesis is that there is a relationship between lighter skin tone and vitamin D synthesis within the body. When skin is exposed to the UV-B radiation waves in sunlight, a series of chemical reactions occur within the epidermis leading to the production of vitamin D3, which is a fat-soluble vitamin that assists the body with absorbing calcium and phosphorus in the small intestine. These nutrients are among those that are critical for the proper growth and maintenance of bone tissue within the body. In the absence of adequate minerals, particularly calcium, bone structure and strength will be compromised, leading to the development of rickets during the growth phase. Rickets is a disease affecting children during their growth phase. It is characterized by inadequately calcified bones that are softer and more flexible than normal. Individuals with rickets will develop a true bowing of their legs, which may affect their mobility (Figure 14.14). In addition, deformation of pelvic bones in people who may become pregnant may occur as a result of rickets, leading to complications with reproduction. In adults, a deficiency in vitamin D3 will often result in osteomalacia, which is a general softening of the bones due to inadequate mineralization. As noted, a variety of maladies may occur due to the

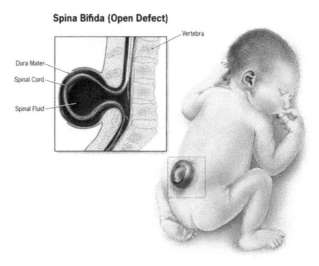

Figure 14.13: Infant with open neural tube defect in lower (lumbar) region of the spine (right). A close-up of the open neural tube defect within the spinal column (left) shows the dura matter, which is ordinarily protected within the spine, is exposed on the surface of the skin. The spinal cord sits near the surface, when it should be protected within the spinal column. Credit: Spina-bifida by the Centers for Disease Control and Prevention is in the public domain.

inadequate production or absorption of vitamin D3, as well as the destruction of folate within the human body. Therefore, from an evolutionary perspective, natural selection should favor a skin tone that is best suited to a given environment.

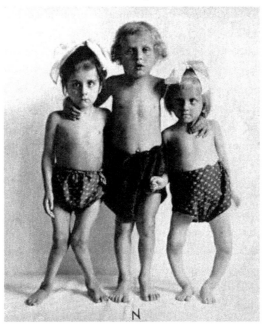

Figure 14.14: Children with rickets in various developmental stages. Credit: Rachitis, stages of development for children [slide numbers 7181 and 7182; photo number: M0003399] by Wellcome Collection is under a CC BY 4.0 License.

In general, the trend related to lighter skin pigmentation further from the equator follows a principle called **Gloger's Rule**. This rule states that within the same species of mammals the more heavily pigmented individuals tend to originate near the equator while lighter-pigmented members of the species will be found in regions further from the equator. Gloger's Rule applies latitudinally; however, it does not appear to hold for certain human populations near the poles. Specifically, it does not apply to the Inuit people (Figure 14.15), who are indigenous to regions near the North Pole and currently reside in portions of Canada, Greenland, Alaska, and Denmark. The Inuit have a darker skin tone that would not be anticipated under the provisions of Gloger's Rule. The high reflectivity of light off of snow and ice, which is common in polar regions, necessitates the darker skin tone of these individuals to prevent folic acid degradation just as it does for individuals within equatorial regions. The consumption of vitamin D–rich foods, such as raw fish, permits the Inuit to reside at high latitudes with darker skin tone while preventing rickets.

Adaptation: Shape and Size Variations

Figure 14.15: Copper Inuk (from Bernard Harbour, Nunavut) with lake trout on his back (1915). Credit: **Copper Inuk with lake trout on his back near Bernard Harbour, Northwest Territories (Nunavut) (1915)** by George H. Wilkins is under a **CC BY-SA 4.0 License**. This image is part of the Photographic Archives of the Canadian Museum of History.

In addition to natural selection playing a role in the determination of melanin expression, it plays a significant role in the determination of the shape and size of the human body. As previously discussed, the most significant thermodynamic mechanism of heat loss from the body is radiation. At temperatures below 20°C (68°F), the human body loses around 65% of its heat to radiative processes; however, the efficiency of radiation is correlated to the overall body shape and size of the individual. There is a direct correlation between the ratio of an object's surface area to mass and the amount of heat that may be lost through radiation. For example, two objects of identical composition and mass are heated to the same temperature. One object is a cube and the other is a sphere. Which object will cool the fastest? Geometrically, a sphere has the smallest surface area per unit mass of any three-dimensional object, so the sphere will cool more slowly than the cube. In other words, the smaller the ratio of the surface area to mass an object has, the more it will retain heat. With respect to the cube in our example, mass increases by the cube, but surface area may increase only by the square, so size will affect the mass to surface area ratio. This, in general, holds true for humans, as well.

In regions where temperatures are consistently cold, the body shape and size of individuals indigenous to the area tend to be more compact. These individuals have a relatively higher body mass to surface area (i.e., skin) than their counterparts from equatorial regions where the average temperatures are considerably warmer. Individuals from hot climates, such as the Fulani (Figure 14.16a) of West Africa, have limbs that are considerably longer than those of individuals from cold climates, such as the Inuit of Greenland (Figure 14.16b). Evolutionarily, the longer limbs of individuals from equatorial regions (e.g., the Fulani) provide a greater surface area (i.e., lower body mass to surface area ratio) for the dissipation of heat through radiative processes. In contrast, the relatively short limbs of Arctic-dwelling people, such as the Inuit, allows for the retention of heat because there is a decreased surface area through which heat may radiate away from the body.

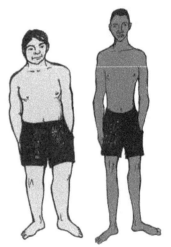

Figure 14.16: The individual on the left is typical of one adapted to a cold environment where the conservation of heat in the body's core is of critical importance. The individual on the right could be adapted to a tropical environment where the rapid dispersal of heat is necessary to maintain homeostasis. Credit: **Greenland 1999 (01)** by Vadeve has been designated to the **public domain (CC0)**.

As described above, there are certain trends related to the general shape and size of human bodies in relation to the thermal conditions. To better describe these trends, we turn to a couple of general principles that are applicable to a variety of species beyond humans. **Bergmann's Rule** predicts that as average environmental temperature decreases, populations are expected to exhibit an increase in weight and a decrease in surface area (Figure 14.17a). Also, within the same species of homeothermic animals, the relative length of projecting body parts (e.g., nose, ears, and limbs) increases in relation to the average environmental temperature (Figure 14.17b). This principle, referred to as **Allen's Rule**, notes that longer, thinner limbs are advantageous for the radiation of excess heat in hot environments and shorter, stockier limbs assist with the preservation of body heat in cold climates. A measure of the crural index (crural index = tibia length ÷ femur length) of individuals from various human populations provides support for Allen's Rule since this value is lower in individuals from colder climates than it is for those from hot climates. The crural indices for human populations vary directly with temperature, so individuals with higher crural index values are generally from regions with a warmer average environmental temperature. Conversely, the crural indices are lower for individuals from regions where there are colder average temperatures.

Figure 14.17a: These organisms are representative of Bergmann's rule. The animal on the left depicts an ungulate from a cooler environment with increased body weight and decreased surface area, compared to the slender ungulate on the right. Credit: **Bergmann's Rule (Figure 14.16a)** original to **Explorations: An Open Invitation to Biological Anthropology** by Mary Nelson is under a **CC BY-NC 4.0 License.**

Figure 14.17b: These animals are representative of Allen's rule. The rabbit on the left comes from a cooler environment and is compact with short limbs and ears. The rabbit on the right comes from a warm environment and has long and lanky limbs and ears. The rabbit in the middle has ears and limbs that are in-between the other two. Rabbits do not sweat like humans; heat is dissipated primarily through their ears. Credit: **Allen's Rule (Figure 14.16b)** original to **Explorations: An Open Invitation to Biological Anthropology** by Mary Nelson is under a **CC BY-NC 4.0 License.**

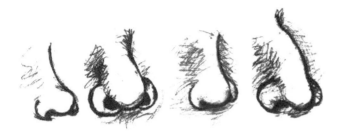

Figure 14.18: Human nasal morphological variation as influenced by four major climate-based adaptive zones: hot-dry, hot-wet, cold-dry, and cold-wet. The four noses in this figure vary in shape in relation to their respective climate-based adaptive zones. Credit: **Human nasal morphological variation (Figure 14.17)** original to Explorations: An Open Invitation to Biological Anthropology by Mary Nelson is under a CC BY-NC 4.0 License.

Nasal shape and size (Figure 14.18) is another physiological feature affected by our ancestors' environments. The selective role of climate in determining human nasal variation is typically approached by dividing climates into four adaptive zones: hot-dry, hot-wet, cold-dry, and cold-wet (Maddux et al. 2016). A principal role of the nasal cavity is to condition (i.e., warm and humidify) ambient air prior to its reaching the lungs. Given this function of the nasal cavity, it is anticipated that different nasal shapes and sizes will be related to varying environments. In cold-dry climates, an individual's nasal cavity must provide humidification and warmth to the dry air when breathing in through the nose (Noback et al. 2011). Also, in that type of climate, the nasal cavity must conserve moisture and minimize heat loss during when the individual exhales through the nose (Noback et al. 2011). From a physiological stress perspective, this is a stressful event.

Conversely, in hot-wet environments, there is no need for the nasal cavity to provide additional moisture to the inhaled air nor is there a need to warm the air or to preserve heat within the nasal cavity (Noback et al. 2011). So, in hot-wet climates, the body is under less physiological stress related to the inhalation of ambient air than in cold-dry climates. As with most human morphological elements, the shape and size of the nasal cavity occurs along a cline. Due to the environmental stressors of cold-dry environments requiring the humidification and warming of air through the nasal cavity, individuals indigenous to such environments tend to have taller (longer) noses with a reduced nasal entrance (nostril opening) size (Noback et al. 2011). This general shape is referred to as leptorrhine, and it allows for a larger surface area within the nasal cavity itself for the air to be warmed and humidified prior to entering the lungs (Maddux et al. 2016). In addition, the relatively small nasal entrance of leptorrhine noses serves as a means of conserving moisture and heat (Noback et al. 2011). Individuals indigenous to hot-wet climates tend to have platyrrhine nasal shapes, which are shorter with broader nasal entrances (Maddux et al. 2016). Since individuals in hot-wet climates do not need to humidify and warm the air entering the nose, their nasal tract is shorter and the nasal entrance wider to permit the effective cooling of the nasal cavity during respiratory processes.

Adaptation: Infectious Disease

Throughout our evolutionary journey, humans have been exposed to numerous infectious diseases. In the following section, we will explore some of the evolutionary-based adaptations that have occurred in certain populations in response to the stressors presented by select infectious diseases. One of the primary examples of natural selection processes acting on the human genome in response to the presence of an infectious disease is the case of the relationship between the sickle-cell anemia trait and malaria, introduced in Chapter 4.

Malaria is a zoonotic disease (an infectious disease transmitted between animals and humans; it is covered in more detail in Chapter 16). It is caused by the spread of the parasitic protozoa from the genus *Plasmodium* (Figure 14.19). These unicellular, eukaryotic protozoa are transmitted through the bite of a female *Anopheles* mosquito. During the bite process, the protozoan parasites present within an infected mosquito's saliva enter a host's bloodstream where they are transported to the liver. Within the liver, the parasites multiply and are eventually released into the bloodstream, where they infect erythrocytes. Once inside the erythrocytes, the parasites reproduce until they exceed the cell's storage capacity, causing it to burst and release the parasites into the bloodstream once again. This replication cycle continues as long as there are viable erythrocytes within the host to infect.

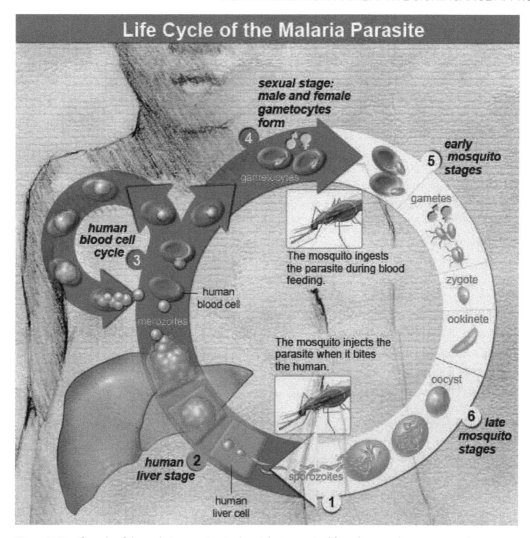

Figure 14.19: Life cycle of the malaria parasite. Credit: Malaria parasite life cycle-NIAID by NIH National Institute of Allergy and Infectious Diseases is in the public domain. [Image Description].

General complications from malaria infections include the following: enlargement of the spleen (due to destruction of infected erythrocytes); lower number of thrombocytes (also called platelets, required for coagulation/clotting of blood); high levels of bilirubin (a byproduct of hemoglobin breakdown in the liver) in the blood; jaundice (yellowing of the skin and eyes due to increased blood bilirubin levels); fever; vomiting; retinal (eye) damage; and convulsions (seizures). In 2020, there were 241 million cases of malaria reported globally, with 95% of those cases originating in Africa (World Health Organization 2021). In sub-Saharan Africa, where incidents of malaria are the highest in the world, 125 million pregnancies are affected by malaria, resulting in 200,000 infant deaths (Hartman, Rogerson, and Fischer 2013). Pregnant people who become infected during the gestational process are more likely to have low-birthweight infants due to prematurity or growth restriction inside the uterus (Hartman, Rogerson, and Fischer 2013). After birth, infants born to malaria-infected pregnant people are more likely to develop infantile anemia (low red-blood cell counts), a malaria infection that is not related to the maternal malarial infection, and they are more likely to die than infants born to non-malaria-infected pregnant people (Hartman, Rogerson, and Fischer 2013).

For children and adolescents whose brains are still developing, there is a risk of cognitive (intellectual) impairment associated with some forms of malaria infections (Fernando, Rodrigo, and Rajapakse 2010). Given the relatively high rates of morbidity (disease) and mortality (number of deaths) associated with malaria, it is plausible that this disease may have served as a selective pressure during human evolution. Support for natural selection related to malaria resistance is related to genetic mutations associated with sickle cell, thalassemia, glucose-6-phosphate dehydrogenase (G6PD) deficiency, and the absence of certain antigens (molecules capable of inducing an immune response from the host) on erythrocytes. For the purposes of this text, we will focus our discussion on the relationship between sickle cell disease and malaria.

Sickle cell disease is a group of genetically inherited blood disorders characterized by an abnormality in the shape of the hemoglobin within erythrocytes. It is important to note that there are multiple variants of hemoglobin, including, but not limited to the following: A, D, C, E, F, H, S, Barts, Portland, Hope, Pisa, and Hopkins. Each of these variants of hemoglobin may result in various conditions within the body; however, for the following explanation we will focus solely on variants A and S.

Individuals who inherit a mutated gene (hemoglobin with a sickled erythrocyte variety, HbS) on chromosome 11 from both parents will develop sickle cell anemia, which is the most severe form of the sickle cell disease family (Figure 14.20). The genotype of an individual with sickle cell anemia is HbSS; whereas, an individual without sickle cell alleles has a genotype of HbAA representing two normal adult hemoglobin type A variants. Manifestations of sickle cell anemia (HbSS) range from mild to severe, with some of the more common symptoms being anemia, blood clots, organ failure, chest pain, fever, and low blood-oxygen levels. In high-income countries with advanced medical care, the median life expectancy of an HbSS individual is around 60 years; however, in low-income countries where advanced medical care is scarce, as many as 90% of children with sickle cell disease perish before the age of five (Longo et al. 2017).

Considering that advanced medical care was not available during much of human evolutionary history, it stands to reason that the majority of individuals with the HbSS genotype died before the age of reproduction. If that is the case though, why do we still have the HbS variant present in modern populations? As covered earlier in this textbook, the genotype of an individual is composed of genes from both biological parents. In the case of an individual with an HbSS genotype, the sickle cell allele (HbS) was inherited from each of the parents. For individuals with the heterozygous genotype of HbSA, they have inherited both a sickle cell allele (HbS) and a normal hemoglobin allele (HbA). Heterozygous (HbSA) individuals who reside in regions where malaria is endemic may have a selective advantage. They will experience a sickling of some, but not all, of their erythrocytes. As

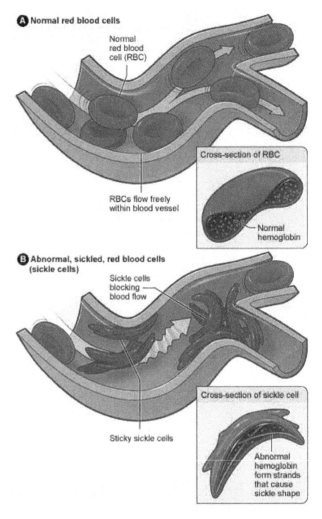

Figure 14.20: Normal and sickled erythrocytes. Normal red blood cells are round and can easily flow freely through blood vessels. Abnormal, or cicle, blood cells are half moon shaped and can easily become entangled and block blood flow. Sickle cells have abnormal hemoglobin that form strands that cause the sickle shape. The Credit: Sickle cell 01 by The National Heart, Lung, and Blood Institute (NHLBI) is in the public domain.

discussed in the following paragraph, HbSA heterozygous individuals are less likely to die from malaria infections than their HbAA counterparts. Unlike an individual with the HbSS genotype, someone with HbSA may experience some of the symptoms listed above; however, they are generally less severe.

As noted earlier, the mechanism through which *Plasmodium* protozoan parasites replicate involves human erythrocyte cells. However, due to their sickled shape, as well as the presence of an abnormally shaped protein within the cell, the parasites are unable to replicate effectively in the erythrocyte cells coded for by the HbS allele (Cyrklaff et al. 2011). An individual who has an HbSA genotype and an active malaria infection will become ill with the disease to a lesser extent than someone with an HbAA genotype, which increases their chances of survival. Although normal erythrocytes (regulated by the HbA allele) allow for parasite replication, they are not able to replicate in HbS erythrocytes of the heterozygote. So, individuals with the HbSA genotype are more likely to survive a malaria infection than an individual who is HbAA. Although individuals with the HbSA genotype may endure some physiological complications related to the sickling of some of their erythrocytes, their morbidity and mortality rates are lower than they are for HbSS members of the population. The majority of individuals who are heterozygous or homozygous for the HbS trait have ancestors who originated in sub-Saharan Africa, India, Saudi Arabia, and regions in South and Central America, the Mediterranean (Turkey, Greece, and Italy), and the Caribbean (Centers for Disease Control and Prevention 2017; Figure 14.21).

With respect to the history of these regions, during the early phases of settlement horticulture was the primary method of crop cultivation. Typically performed on a small scale, horticulture is based on manual labor and relatively simple hand tools rather than the use of draft animals or irrigation technologies. Common in horticulture is *swidden*, or the cutting and burning of plants in woodland and grassland regions. The swidden is the prepared field that results following a slash-and-burn episode. This practice fundamentally alters the soil chemistry, removes plants that provide shade, and increases the areas where water may pool. This anthropogenically altered landscape provides the perfect breeding ground for the *Anopheles* mosquito, as it prefers warm, stagnant pools of water (Figure 14.22).

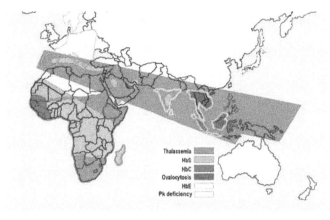

Figure 14.21: Distribution of sickle cell and associated erythrocytic abnormalities for Africa and Asia. Credit: Red Blood Cell abnormalities by Armando Moreno Vranich has been designated to the public domain (CC0). [Image Description].

Humans arrive and clear the land to grow crops. Slash and burn horticulture leads to pools of stagnant water.

Mosquitos flourish in the pools of water. Malaria increases as a result.

Balancing selection occurs in populations with both malaria and high incidences of sickle cell disease (from the HbSS genotype).

Individuals with the sickle cell allele HbS are better at fighting malaria, leading to its increased frequency.

Figure 14.22: The effects of human horticultural activities on the balancing selection of populations in relation to sickle cell disease genotype variants. Credit: Sickle cell disease (Figure 14.21) original to Explorations: An Open Invitation to Biological Anthropology by Katie Nelson is a collective work under a CC BY-NC 4.0 License. [Includes two horticulture illustrations by Mary Nelson, CC BY-NC 4.0; Sickle cell anemia by Pkleong at English Wikibooks (modified), public domain (CC0).] [Image Description].

Although swidden agriculture was historically practiced across the globe, it became most problematic in the regions where the *Anopheles* mosquito is endemic. These areas have the highest incidence rates of malaria infection. Over time, the presence of the *Anopheles* mosquito and the *Plasmodium* parasite that it transmitted acted as a selective pressure, particularly in regions where swidden agricultural practices were common, toward the selection of individuals with some modicum of resistance against the infection. In these regions, HbSS and HbSA individuals would have been more likely to survive and reproduce successfully. Although individuals and populations are far more mobile now than they have been throughout much of history, there are still regions where we can see higher rates of malaria infection as well as greater numbers of individuals with the HbS erythrocyte variant. The relationship between malaria and the selective pressure for the HbS variant is one of the most prominent examples of natural selection in the human species within recent evolutionary history.

Adaptation: Lactase Persistence

With the case of sickled erythrocytes and their resistance to infection by malaria parasites, there is strong support for a cause-and-effect-style relationship linked to natural selection. Although somewhat less apparent, there is a correlation between lactase persistence and environmental challenges. Lactase-phlorizin hydrolase (LPH) is an enzyme that is primarily produced in the small intestine and permits the proper digestion of lactose, a disaccharide (composed of two simple sugars: glucose and galactose) found in the milk of mammals. Most humans will experience a decrease in the expression of LPH following weaning, leading to an inability to properly digest lactose. Generally, LPH production decreases between the ages of two and five and is completely absent by the age of nine (Dzialanski et al. 2016). For these individuals, the ingestion of lactose may lead to a wide variety of gastrointestinal ailments, including abdominal bloating, increased gas, and diarrhea. Although the bloating and gas are unpleasant, the diarrhea caused by a failure to properly digest lactose can be life-threatening if severe enough due to the dehydration it can cause. Some humans, however, are able to produce LPH far beyond the weaning period.

Individuals who continue to produce LPH have what is referred to as the **lactase persistence** trait. The lactase persistence trait is encoded for a gene called *LCT*, which is located on human chromosome 2 (Ranciaro et al. 2014; see also Chapter 3). From an evolutionary and historical perspective, this trait is most commonly linked to cultures that have practiced cattle domestication (Figure 14.23). For individuals in those cultures, the continued expression of LPH may have provided a selective advantage. During periods of environmental stress, such as a drought, if an individual is capable of successfully digesting cow's milk, they have a higher chance of survival than someone who suffers from diarrhea-linked dehydration due to a lack of LPH. Although the frequency of the lactase persistence trait is relatively low among African agriculturalists, it is high among pastoralist populations that are traditionally associated with cattle domestication, such as the Tutsi and Fulani, who have frequencies of 90% and 50%, respectively (Tishkoff et al. 2007).

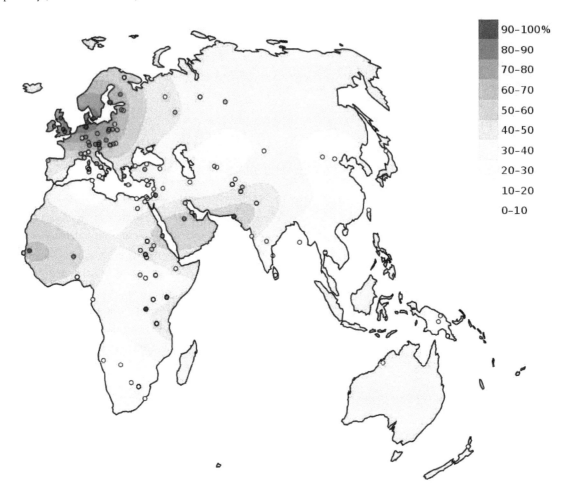

Figure 14.23: Interpolated map depicting the percentage of adults with the lactase persistence genotype in indigenous populations of Africa, Europe, Asia, and Australia. Circles denote sample locations. Credit: Lactose tolerance in the Old World by Joe Roe is under a CC BY 4.0 License. [Image Description].

Cattle domestication began around 11,000 years ago in Europe (Beja-Pereira et al. 2006) and 7,500 to 9,000 years ago in the Middle East and North Africa (Tishkoff et al. 2007). Based on human genomic studies, it is estimated that the mutation for the lactase persistence trait occurred around 2,000 to 20,000 years ago for European populations (Tishkoff et al. 2007). For African populations, the lactase persistence trait emerged approximately 1,200 to 23,000 years ago (Gerbault et al. 2011). This begs the question: Is this mutation the same for both populations? It appears that the emergence of the lactase persistence mutation in non-European populations, specifically those in East Africa (e.g., Tutsi and Fulani), is a case of **convergent evolution**. With convergent evolution events, a similar mutation may occur in species of different lineages through independent evolutionary processes. Based on our current understanding of the genetic mutation pathways for the lactase persistence trait in European and African populations, these mutations are not representative of a shared lineage. In other words, just because a person of European origin and a person of African origin can each digest milk due to the presence of the lactase-persistence trait in their genotypes, it does not mean that these two individuals inherited it due to shared common ancestry.

Is it possible that the convergent evolution of similar lactase-persistence traits in disparate populations is merely a product of genetic drift? Or is there evidence for natural selection? Even though 23,000 years may seem like a long time, it is but a blink of the proverbial evolutionary eye. From the perspective of human evolutionary pathways, mutations related to the *LCT* gene have occurred relatively recently. Similar genetic changes in multiple populations through genetic drift processes, which are relatively slow and directionless, fail to accumulate as rapidly as lactase-persistence traits (Gerbault et al. 2011). The widespread accumulation of these traits in a relatively short period of time supports the notion that an underlying selective pressure must be driving this form of human evolution. Although to date no definitive factors have been firmly identified, it is thought that environmental pressures are likely to credit for the rapid accumulation of the lactase-persistence trait in multiple human populations through convergent evolutionary pathways.

Special Topic: Skin Tone Genetic Regulation

The melanocortin 1 receptor (*MC1R*) gene acts to control which types of melanin (eumelanin or pheomelanin) are produced by melanocytes. The *MC1R* receptor is located on the surface of the melanocyte cells (Quillen et al. 2018). Activation of the *MC1R* receptors may occur through exposure to specific environmental stimuli or due to underlying genetic processes. Inactive or blocked *MC1R* receptors result in melanocytes producing pheomelanin. If the *MC1R* gene receptors are activated, then the melanocytes will produce eumelanin. Thus, individuals with activated *MC1R* receptors tend to have darker-pigmented skin and hair than individuals with inactive or blocked receptors.

The alleles of another gene, the major facilitator, superfamily domain-containing protein 12 (*MFSD12*) gene, affect the expression of melanocytes in a different way than the *MC1R* gene. Instead of affecting the activation of melanocyte receptors, the *MFSD12* alleles indirectly affect the membranes of melanocyte lysosomes (Quillen et al. 2018). The melanocyte's lysosomes are organelles containing digestive enzymes, which ultimately correlate to varying degrees of pigmentation in humans. Variations in the membranes of the melanocyte lysosomes ultimately correlate to differing degrees of pigmentation in humans.

Ancestral *MFSD12* allele variants are present in European and East Asian populations and are associated with lighter pigmentation of the skin (Crawford et al. 2017; Quillen et al. 2018). In addition, this ancestral variant is also associated with Tanzanian, San, and Ethiopian populations of Afro-Asiatic ancestry (Crawford et al. 2017; Quillen et al. 2018). In contrast, the more derived (i.e., more recent) allele variants that are linked to darker skin tones are more commonly present in East African populations, particularly those of Nilo-Saharan descent (Crawford et al. 2017; Quillen et al. 2018). The notion that ancestral alleles of *MFSD12* are associated with lighter skin pigmentation is in opposition to the commonly accepted idea that our pigmentation was likely darker throughout early human evolution (Crawford et al. 2017; Quillen et al. 2018). Due to the complexity of the human genome, *MFSD12* and *MC1R* are but two examples of alleles affecting human skin tone. Furthermore, there is genetic evidence suggesting that certain genomic variants associated with both darker and lighter skin color have been subject to directional selection processes for as long as 600,000 years, which far exceeds the evolutionary span of *Homo sapiens sapiens* (Crawford et al. 2017; Quillen et al. 2018).

Human Variation: Our Story Continues

From the time that the first of our species left Africa, we have had to adjust and adapt to numerous environmental challenges. The remarkable ability of human beings to maintain homeostasis through a combination of both nongenetic (adjustments) and genetic (adaptations) means has allowed us to occupy a remarkable variety of environments, from high-altitude mountainous regions to the tropics near the equator. From adding piquant, pungent spices to our foods as a means of inhibiting food-borne illnesses due to bacterial growth to donning garments specially suited to local climates, behavioral adjustments have provided us with a nongenetic means of coping with obstacles to our health and well-being. Acclimatory adjustments, such as sweating when we are warm in an attempt to regulate our body temperature or experiencing increased breathing rates as a means of increasing blood oxygen levels in regions where the partial pressure of oxygen is low, have been instrumental in our survival with respect to thermal and altitudinal environmental challenges. For some individuals, developmental adjustments that were acquired during their development and growth phases (e.g., increased heart and lung capacities for individuals from high-altitude regions) provide them with a form of physiological advantage not possible for someone who ventures to such an environmentally challenging region as an adult. Genetically mediated adaptations, such as variations in the pigmentation of our skin, have ensured our evolutionary fitness across all latitudes.

Will the human species continue to adjust and adapt to new environmental challenges in the future? If past performance is any measure of future expectations, then the human story will continue as long as we do not alter our environment to the point that the plasticity of our behavior, physiological, and morphological boundaries is exceeded. In the following chapters, you will explore additional information about our saga as a species. From the concept of race as a sociocultural construct to our epidemiological history, the nuances of evolutionary-based human variation are always present and provide the basis for understanding our history and our future as a species.

Review Questions

- Detail at least two examples of how natural selection has influenced human variation. Specifically, what was the selective pressure that may have led to a preference for a specific trait and how is that trait related to an increased level of fitness?
- Why is reduced pigmentation of the skin advantageous for individuals from northern latitudes? What role does darker skin pigmentation serve for individuals near the equator? What is the relationship between skin pigmentation and fitness?
- What are some of the risks associated with pregnancy at high altitude? Compare and contrast the various genetic mutations of the indigenous Tibetan and Ethiopian high-altitude populations. In your answer, specifically address the issue of pregnancy at high altitudes.
- What is the relationship between the sickle cell mutation and the *Plasmodium* parasite? Would having the HbSA genotype still be advantageous in a region where such parasites are not common? Why or why not?

Key Terms

Acclimatory adjustments: Processes by which an individual organism adjusts in order to maintain homeostasis in response to environmental challenges.

Activated melanogenesis: Increase in melanin production in response to ultraviolet radiation (UV) exposure.

Adaptation: Alteration in population-level gene frequencies related to environmentally induced selective pressures; leads to a greater level of fitness for a population related to a specific environment.

Adjustment: Nongenetic-based ways in which organisms adjust to environmental stressors.

Allen's Rule: Due to thermal adaptation, homeothermic animals have body volume-to-surface ratios that vary inversely with the average temperature of their environment. In cold climates, the anticipated ratio is high; in warm climates, it is low.

Basal melanogenesis: Genetically mediated, non-environmentally influenced base melanin level.

Behavioral adjustments: An individual's culturally mediated responses to an environmental stressor in an effort to maintain homeostasis.

Bergmann's Rule: For a broadly distributed monophyletic group, species and populations of smaller size tend to be found in environments with warmer climates and those of larger size tend to be found in ones that are colder.

Cline: A continuum of gradations (i.e., degrees or levels) of a specific trait.

Conduction: Mechanism of heat transfer between objects through direct contact.

Convection: Movement of heat away from a warm object to the cooler surrounding fluid (i.e., gas or liquid).

Convergent evolution: Evolutionary process whereby organisms that are not closely related independently evolve similar traits as a product of adaptation to similar evolutionary parameters.

Erythrocyte: Red blood cell; most common form of blood cell; the principle means of transporting oxygen throughout the circulatory system.

Evaporation: Mechanism of heat transfer whereby liquid is transformed into a gas, utilizing energy (e.g., heat).

Folic acid: Form of B complex vitamin necessary for proper fetal development.

Gloger's Rule: For mammals of the same species, those with more darkly pigmented forms tend to be found closer to the equator and those with lighter forms are found in regions further from the equator.

Homeostasis: Condition of optimal functioning for an organism.

Hyperpnea: Increased depth and rate of respiration.

Hypothalamus: Small portion of the human brain responsible for body temperature regulation.

Lactase persistence: Genetic mutation permitting the continued production of lactase-phlorizin hydrolase enzyme in the small intestine past the weaning period.

Melanin: Black-brown pigment produced by melanocytes; one of the primary pigments in skin.

Melanocytes: Specialized cells that produce melanin.

Phenotypic plasticity: Ability of one genotype to produce more than one phenotype dependent on environmental conditions.

Radiation: Mechanism of heat transfer involving electromagnetic energy being emitted from an object.

Sickle cell disease: A group of genetically inherited blood disorders characterized by an abnormality in the shape of the hemoglobin within erythrocytes (red blood cells).

Stressor: Any stimulus resulting in an imbalance in an organism's homeostatic balance.

Vasoconstriction: Narrowing of the blood vessels due to contractions of the muscular vessel walls.

Vasodilation: Dilation of the blood vessels due to relaxation of the muscular vessel walls.

About the Author

Leslie E. Fitzpatrick, Ph.D., RPA

Independent Archaeological Consultants

Lfitzpatrick@iac-llc.net

Leslie Fitzpatrick is an historical archaeologist with Independent Archaeological Consultants based in Dover, New Hampshire. She earned a PhD in Anthropology from the University of Wyoming (2017), an MA in Anthropology from Georgia State (2012), and a BS in Mechanical Engineering from Georgia Tech (2000). Her primary research focus is the stable-isotope analysis of human remains as a means of interpreting past mobility and diet profiles for both modern and archaeological populations. In addition to her work as a historical archaeologist in New England, she has worked as a bioarchaeologist at field sites in Germany, Spain, Croatia, Mexico, Peru, and throughout the United States.

For Further Exploration

Homeostasis

Baptista, Vander. 2006. "Starting Physiology: Understanding Homeostasis." *Advances in Physiology Education* 30: 263–264.

Goldstein, David S., and Bruce McEwen. 2002. "Allostasis, Homeostats, and the Nature of Stress." *The International Journal on the Biology of Stress* 5 (1): 55–58.

General Clinal Variation and Genetic Exchange

Delhey, Kaspar. 2019. "A Review of Gloger's Rule, an Ecogeographical Rule of Colour: Definitions, Interpretations and Evidence." *Biological Reviews* 94 (4): 1294–1316.

Feng, Yuanqing, Michael A. McQuillan, and Sarah A. Tishkoff. 2021. "Evolutionary Genetics of Skin Pigmentation in African Populations." *Human Molecular Genetics* 30 (R1): R88–R97.

Hu, Hao, Nayia Petousi, Gustavo Glusman, Yao Yu, Ryan Bohlender, Tsewang Tashi, Jonathan M. Downie, et al. 2017. "Evolutionary History of Tibetans Inferred from Whole-Genome Sequencing." *PLoS Genetics* 13 (4): e1006675. .

Jablonski, Nina G. 2021. "Skin Color and Race." Special issue, "Race Reconciled II: Interpreting and Communicating Biological Variation and Race in 2021," *American Journal of Physical Anthropology* 175 (2): 437–447.

Pritchard, Jonathan K., Joseph K. Pickrell, and Graham Coop. 2010. "The Genetics of Human Adaptation: Hard Sweeps, Soft Sweeps, and Polygenic Adaptation." *Current Biology* 20 (4): R208–R215.

Sankararaman, Sriram, Swapan Mallick, Nick Patterson, and David Reich. 2016. "The Combined Landscape of Denisovan and Neanderthal Ancestry in Present-Day Humans." *Current Biology* 26 (9): 1241–1247.

Lactase Persistence

HHMI BioInteractive. 2021. "The Making of the Fittest: Got Lactase? The Co-evolution of Genes and Culture." Accessed April 7, 2023.

Malaria and Sickle Cell Anemia

Bill and Melinda Gates Foundation. 2022. "Malaria." Accessed April 7, 2023.

Centers for Disease Control and Prevention. 2022. "Malaria." Accessed April 7, 2023.

HHMI BioInteractive. 2020. "The Making of the Fittest: Natural Selection in Humans." 2020. Accessed April 7, 2023.

National Institutes of Health: National Center for Advancing Translational Sciences. "Sickle Cell Anemia." Accessed April 7, 2023.

World Health Organization. 2022. "Malaria." Accessed April 7, 2023.

Rickets and Bone Health

National Institutes of Health: National Center for Advancing Translational Sciences. "Rickets." Accessed April 7, 2023.

Talmadge, D. W., and R. V. Talmadge. 2007. "Calcium Homeostasis: How Bone Solubility Relates to All Aspects of Bone Physiology." *Journal of Musculoskeletal and Neuronal Interactions* 7 (2): 108–112.

Skin Color

HHMI BioInteractive. 2020. "The Biology of Skin Color." Accessed April 7, 2023

References

American Academy of Pediatrics, Task Force on Infant Sleep Position and Sudden Infant Death Syndrome. 2000. "Changing Concepts of Sudden Infant Death Syndrome: Implications for Infant Sleeping Environment and Sleep Position." *Pediatrics* 105 (3): 650–656.

Beja-Pereira, Albano, David Caramelli, Carles Lalueza-Fox, Cristiano Vernesi, Nuno Ferrand, Antonella Casoli, Felix Goyache, et al. 2006. "The Origin of European Cattle: Evidence from Modern and Ancient DNA." *PNAS* 103 (21): 8113–8118.

Best, Andre, Daniel E. Lieberman, and Jason M. Kamilar. 2019. "Diversity and Evolution of Human Eccrine Sweat Gland Density." *Journal of Thermal Biology* 84: 331–338.

Bigham, Abigail W. 2016. "Genetics of Human Origin and Evolution: High-Altitude Adaptations." *Current Opinion in Genetics & Development* 41: 8–13.

Centers for Disease Control and Prevention. 2017. "Data & Statistics on Sickle Cell Disease." *Centers for Disease Control and Prevention* website, August 9. Accessed April 7, 2023. .

Crawford, Nicholas G., Derek E. Kelly, Matthew E. B. Hansen, Marcia H. Beltrame, Shaohua Fan, Shanna L. Bowman, Ethan Jewett, et al. 2017. "Loci Associated with Skin Pigmentation Identified in African Populations." *Science* 358 (6365): 1–49.

Cyrkalff, Marek, Cecilia P. Sanchez, Nicole Kilian, Curille Bisseye, Jacques Simpore, Friedrich Frischknecht, and Michael Lanzer. 2011. "Hemoglobins S and C Interfere with Actin Remodeling in *Plasmodium falciparum*-Infected Erythrocytes." *Science* 334 (6060): 1283–1286.

Dzialanski, Zbigniew, Michael Barany, Peter Engfeldt, Anders Magnuson, Lovisa A. Olsson, and Torbjörn K. Nilsson. 2016. "Lactase Persistence versus Lactose Intolerance: Is There an Intermediate Phenotype?" *Clinical Biochemistry* 49 (2016): 248–252.

Fernando, Sumadya D., Chaturaka Rodrigo, and Senaka Rajapakse. 2010. "The 'Hidden' Burden of Malaria: Cognitive Impairment Following Infection." *Malaria Journal* 9 (366): 1–11.

Gerbault, Pascale, Anke Liebert, Yuval Itan, Adam Powell, Mathias Currat, Joachim Burger, Dallas M. Swallow, and Mark G. Thomas. 2011. "Evolution of Lactase Persistence: An Example of Human Niche Construction." *Philosophical Transactions of the Royal Society B: Biological Sciences* 366 (1566): 863–877.

Gray, Olivia A., Jennifer Yoo, Débora R. Sobriera, Jordan Jousma, David Witnosky, Noboru J. Sakabe, Ying-Jie Ping, et al. 2022. "A Pleiotropic Hypoxia-Sensitive *EPAS1* Enhancer Is Disrupted by Adaptive Alleles in Tibetans." *Science Advances* 8 (47): 1–13.

Hartman, T. K., S. J. Rogerson, and P. R. Fischer. 2013. "The Impact of Maternal Malaria on Newborns." *Annals of Tropical Paediatrics* 30 (4): 271–282.

Longo, Dan L., Frédéric B. Piel, Martin H. Steinberg, and David C. Rees. 2017. "Sickle Cell Disease." *The New England Journal of Medicine* 376 (16): 1561–1573.

Maddux, Scott D., Todd R. Yokley, Bohumil M. Svoma, and Robert G. Franciscus. 2016. "Absolute Humidity and the Human Nose: A Reanalysis of Climate Zones and Their Influence on Nasal Form and Function." *American Journal of Physical Anthropology* 161 (2): 309–320.

Meyer, M. C., M. S. Alexander, Z. Wang, D. L. Hoffmann, J. A. Dahl, D. Degering, W. R. Haas, and F. Schlütz. 2017. "Permanent Human Occupation of the Central Tibetan Plateau in the Early Holocene." *Science* 355 (6320): 64–67.

Moore, Lorna G., Susan Niermeyer, and Stacy Zamudio. 1998. "Human Adaptation to High Altitude: Regional and Life-Cycle Perspectives." *Yearbook of Physical Anthropology* 41: 25–64.

Noback, Marlijn L., Katerina Harvati, and Fred Spoor. 2011. "Climate-Related Variation of the Human Nasal Cavity." *American Journal of Physical Anthropology* 145 (4): 599–614.

Peacock, A. J. 1998. "ABC of Oxygen: Oxygen at High Altitude." *BMJ* 317 (7165): 1063–1066.

Pontzer, Herman, Mary H. Brown, Brian M. Wood, David A. Raichlen, Audax Z.P. Madbulla, Jacob A. Harris, Holly Dunsworth, et al. 2021. "Evolution of Water Conservation in Humans." *Current Biology* 31 (8): 1804–1810.

Quillen, Ellen E., Heather L. Norton, Esteban J. Parra, Frida Loza-Durazo, Khai C. Ang, Florin Mircea Illiescu, Laurel N. Pearson, et al. 2019. "Shades of Complexity: New Perspectives on the Evolution and Genetic Architecture of Human Skin." *Yearbook of Physical Anthropology* 168 (S67): 4–26.

Ranciaro, Alessia, Michael C. Campbell, Jibril B. Hirbo, Wen-Ya Ko, Alain Froment,

Paolo Anagnostou, Maritha J. Kotze,

et al. 2014. "Genetic Origins of Lactase Persistence and the Spread of Pastoralism in Africa." *American Journal of Human Genetics* 94 (4): 496–510.

Roby, Brianne Barnett, Marsha Finkelstein, Robert J. Tibesar, and James D. Sidman. 2012. "Prevalence of Positional Plagiocephaly in Teens Born after the 'Back to Sleep' Campaign." *Otolaryngology—Head and Neck Surgery* 146 (5): 823–828.

Sherman, Paul W., and Jennifer Billing. 1999. "Darwinian Gastronomy: Why We Use Spices." *BioScience* 49 (6): 453–463.

Tishkoff, Sarah A., Floyd A. Reed, Alessia Ranciaro, Benjamin F. Voight, Courtney C. Babbitt, Jesse S. Silverman, Kweli Powell, et al. 2007. "Convergent Adaptation of Human Lactase Persistence in Africa and Europe." *Nature Genetics* 39 (1): 31–40.

World Health Organization. 2021. "World Malaria Report 2021." *World Health Organization* website, December 4, 2022. Accessed April 7, 2023.

Zhang, Xinjun, Kelsey E. Witt, Mayra M. Bañuelos, Amy Ko, Kai Yuan, Shuhua Xu, Rasmus Nielsen, and Emilia Huerta-Sanchez. 2021. "The History and Evolution of Denisovan-*EPAS1* Haplotype in Tibetans." *PNAS Biological Sciences* 118 (22): 1–9.

Image Descriptions

Figure 14.3: When exposed to cold temperatures, basal metabolic rate increases, shivering begins and vasoconstriction helps maintain heat near the core of the body where the vital organs are located. When exposed to warm temperatures above 35 degrees celsius, vasodilation occurs and excess body heat is lost through sweating.

Figure 14.4: Vasoconstriction is the constriction of peripheral capillaries in the skin. The decreased surface area of the capillaries through vasoconstriction results in less heat reaching the surface of the skin where it would be dissipated into the atmosphere. The opposite happens with vasodilation, where the peripheral capillaries in the skin are closer to the surface of the skin so that heat can be dissipated into the atmosphere, thereby cooling the body.

Figure 14.10: Melanocytes are melanin-producing cells located in the bottom layer of the skin's epidermis. Located in the central part of the epidermis, melanosomes are packets of color made by melanocytes. In light skin, melanosomes are small, with little pigmentation. In larger skin, they are larger and darkly pigmented. The differences in pigmentation are also due to differences in the distribution of melanosomes within the keratinocytes.

Figure 14.12: Evolution of Skin Color Variation:

1. Hair and Skin: Once hominins lost most of their body hair they likely had dark pigmented skin. In environments with high UV radiation, dark skin protected early humans against skin damage.
2. Folate and UV Rays: UV rays penetrate the skin and can break down folate in the bloodstream. Folate is necessary for sperm production and for fetal development.
3. Leaving Africa: Once some humans left Africa, they encountered environments with different levels of UV radiation. New selective pressures began to shape human skin color among these groups.

4. Vitamin D: In low UV environments, people with dark skin could not synthesize enough vitamin D resulting in rickets and other health problems. People with dark skin had a lower chance of survival in most of these environments.
5. Selective Pressures: Vitamin D, folate and changing UV environments were the selective pressures that resulted in the development of a variety of skin colors in different populations throughout the world.

Figure 14.19: Life cycle of the malaria parasite: The mosquito injects the parasites when it bites the human. The parasites grow and multiply first in the liver cells and then in the red cells of the blood. In the blood, successive broods of parasites grow inside the red cells and destroy them, releasing daughter parasites ("merozoites") that continue the cycle by invading other red cells. The blood stage parasites are those that cause the symptoms of malaria. When certain forms of blood stage parasites (gametocytes, which occur in male and female forms) are ingested during blood feeding by a female mosquito, they mate in the gut of the mosquito and begin a cycle of growth and multiplication in the mosquito. After 10-18 days, a form of the parasite called a sporozoite migrates to the mosquito's salivary glands. When the Anopheles mosquito takes a blood meal on another human, anticoagulant saliva is injected together with the sporozoites, which migrate to the liver, thereby beginning a new cycle. (Adapted from Malaria: Biology: Lifecycle by the CDC).

Figure 14.21: Map of the eastern hemisphere shows locations of different red blood cell abnormalities:

- Thalassemia: most of Africa, Mediterranean, and SE Asia,
- HbS: most of sub-Saharan Africa and smaller regions of the Mediterranean, Middle East, and India,
- HbC: western Africa,
- Ovalocytosis: parts of southeast Asia,
- HbE: parts of south Asia, and
- Pk deficiency: much of Europe.

Figure 14.22: The effects of human horticultural activities on the balancing selection of populations in relation to sickle cell disease genotype variants: Humans arrive and clear the land to grow crops. Slash and burn horticulture leads to pools of stagnant water. Mosquitos flourish in the pools of water. Malaria increases as a result. Individuals with the sickle cell allele HbS are better at fighting malaria, leading to its increased frequency in the population. Balancing selection occurs in populations with both malaria and high incidences of sickle cell disease (from the HbSS genotype).

Figure 14.23: A map of the eastern hemisphere with shading illustrating the population frequencies of adults with lactase persistence. Shades range from very light in populations with little lactase persistence (0-10%) to very dark (90-100%). Low frequencies were more common in southern Africa and southeastern mainland Asia. Frequencies were higher in western Africa, the Arabian Peninsula, and most of Europe. The highest frequencies were in northern Europe.

15.

FORENSIC ANTHROPOLOGY

Ashley Kendell, Ph.D., California State University, Chico

Alex Perrone, M.A., M.S.N, R.N., P.H.N., Butte Community College

Colleen Milligan, Ph.D., California State University, Chico

This chapter is a revision from "Chapter 15: Bioarchaeology and Forensic Anthropology" by Ashley Kendell, Alex Peronne, and Colleen Milligan. In Explorations: An Open Invitation to Biological Anthropology, first edition, edited by Beth Shook, Katie Nelson, Kelsie Aguilera, and Lara Braff, which is licensed under CC BY-NC 4.0.

Content Warning and Disclaimer: This chapter includes images of human remains as well as discussions centered on human skeletal analyses. All images are derived from casts, sketches, nonhuman skeletal material, as well as non-Indigenous skeletal materials curated within the CSU, Chico Human Identification Lab, and the Hartnett-Fulginiti donated skeletal collection.

Learning Objectives

- Define forensic anthropology as a subfield of biological anthropology.
- Describe the seven steps carried out during skeletal analysis.
- Outline the four major components of the biological profile.
- Contrast the four categories of trauma.
- Explain how to identify the different taphonomic agents that alter bone.
- Discuss ethical considerations for forensic anthropology.

Forensic anthropology is a subfield of biological anthropology and an applied area of anthropology. Forensic anthropologists use skeletal analysis to gain information about humans in the present or recent past, then they apply this information within a medicolegal context. This means that forensic anthropologists specifically conduct their analysis on recently deceased individuals (typically within the last 50 years) as part of investigations by law enforcement. Forensic anthropologists can assist law enforcement agencies in several different ways, including aiding in the identification of human remains whether they are complete, fragmentary, burned, scattered, or decomposed. Additionally, forensic anthropologists can help determine what happened to the deceased at or around the time of death as well as what processes acted on the body after death (e.g., whether the remains were scattered by animals, whether they were buried in the ground, or whether they remained on the surface as the soft tissue decomposed).

Many times, because of their expertise in identifying human skeletal remains, forensic anthropologists are called to help with outdoor search-and-recovery efforts, such as locating remains scattered across the surface or carefully excavating and documenting buried remains. In other cases, forensic anthropologists recover remains after natural disasters or accidents, such as fire scenes, and can help identify whether each bone belongs to a human or an animal. Forensic anthropology spans a wide scope of contexts involving the law, including incidences of mass disasters, genocide, and war crimes.

A point that can be somewhat confusing for students is that although the term *forensic* is included in this subfield of biological anthropology, there are many forensic techniques that are not included in the subfield. Almost exclusively, forensic anthropology deals with skeletal analysis. While this can include the comparison of antemortem (before death) and postmortem (after death) radiographs to identify whether remains belong to a specific person, or using photographic superimposition of the cranium, it does not include analyses beyond the skeleton. For example, blood-spatter analysis, DNA analysis, fingerprints, and material evidence collection do not fall under the scope of forensic anthropology.

So, what can forensic anthropologists glean from bones alone? Forensic anthropologists can address a number of questions about a human individual based on their skeletal remains. Some of those questions are as follows: How old was the person? Was the person biologically male or female? How tall was the person? What happened to the person at or around their time of death? Were they sick? The information from the skeletal analysis can then be matched with missing persons records, medical records, or dental records, aiding law enforcement agencies with identifications and investigations.

Skeletal Analysis

Forensic anthropology relies on skeletal analysis to reveal information about the deceased. The methodology and approaches outlined below are specific to the United States. Forensic anthropological methods differ depending on the country conducting an investigation. In the United States, there are typically seven steps or questions to the process:

- Is it bone?
- Is it human?
- Is it modern or archaeological?
- How many individuals are present or what is the minimum number of individuals (MNI)?
- Who is it?
- Is there evidence of trauma before or around the time of death?
- What happened to the remains after death?

Is It Bone?

One of the most important steps in any skeletal analysis starts with determining whether or not material suspected to be bone is in fact bone. Though it goes without saying that a forensic anthropologist would only carry out analysis on bone, this step is not always straightforward. Whole bones are relatively easy to identify, but determining whether or not something is bone becomes more challenging once it becomes fragmentary. As an example, in high heat such as that seen on fire scenes, bone can break into pieces. During a house fire with fatalities, firefighters watered down the burning home. After the fire was extinguished, the sheetrock (used to construct the walls of the home) was drenched and crumbled. The crumbled sheetrock was similar in color and form to burned, fragmented bone, therefore mistakable for human remains (Figure 15.1). Forensic anthropologists on scene were able to separate the bones from the construction material, helping to confirm the presence of bone and hence the presence of individual victims of the fire. In this case, forensic anthropologists were able to recognize the anatomical and layered structure of bone and were able to distinguish it from the uniform and unlayered structure of sheetrock.

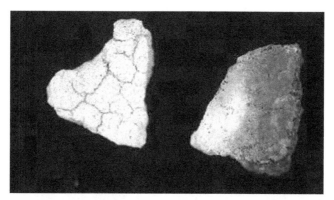

Figure 15.1: Burned sheetrock used as building material appears similar to human bone but can be differentiated by the fact that it is the same density throughout. Credit: **Example of burned sheetrock (Figure 15.1)** original to *Explorations: An Open Invitation to Biological Anthropology* by Alex Perrone is under a CC BY-NC 4.0 License.

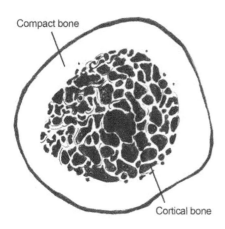

Figure 15.2: Cross section of human long bone with compact and cortical bone layers visible. Credit: **Cross section of human long bone (Figure 15.2)** original to *Explorations: An Open Invitation to Biological Anthropology* by Mary Nelson is under a CC BY-NC 4.0 License.

As demonstrated by the example above, both the macrostructure (visible with the naked eye) and microstructure (visible with a microscope) of bone are helpful in bone identification. Bones are organs in the body made up of connective tissue. The connective tissue is hardened by a mineral deposition, which is why bone is rigid in comparison to other connective tissues such as cartilage (Tersigni-Tarrant and Langley 2017, 82–83; White and Folkens 2005, 31). In a living body, the mineralized tissue does not make up the only component of bone—there are also blood, bone marrow, cartilage, and other types of tissues. However, in dry bone, two distinct layers of the bone are the most helpful for identification. The outer layer is made up of densely arranged osseous (bone) tissue called **compact (cortical) bone**. The inner layer is composed of much more loosely organized, porous bone tissue whose appearance resembles that of a sponge, hence the name **spongy (trabecular) bone**. Knowing that most bone contains both layers helps with the macroscopic identification of bone (Figures 15.2, 15.3). For example, a piece of coconut shell might look a lot like a fragment of a human skull bone. However, closer inspection will demonstrate that coconut shell only has one very dense layer, while bone has both the compact and spongy layers.

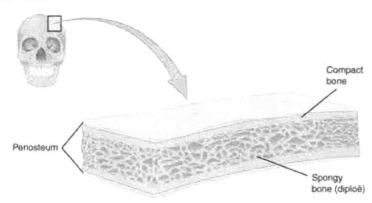

Figure 15.3: Cranial anatomy is slightly different as compared to that of a long bone in cross section. The compact (cortical) bone layers sandwich the spongy (trabecular) bone. One layer of compact bone forms the very outer surface of the skull and the other lines the internal surface of the skull. Credit: Anatomy of a Flat Bone (Anatomy & Physiology, Figure 6.3.3) by OpenStax is under a CC BY 4.0 License.

The microscopic identification of bone relies on knowledge of **osteons**, or bone cells (Figure 15.4). Under magnification, bone cells are visible in the outer, compact layer of bone. The bone cells are arranged in a concentric pattern around blood vessels for blood supply. The specific shape of the cells can help differentiate, for example, a small piece of PVC (white plastic) pipe from a human bone fragment (Figure 15.5).

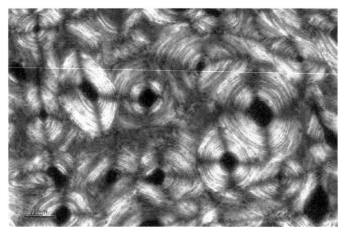

Figure 15.4: Bone microstructure (osteons). Credit: Bone (248 12) Bone cross section by Doc. RNDr. Josef Reischig, CSc. is under a CC BY-SA 3.0 License.

Figure 15.5: Fragments of plastic PVC pipe, such as those seen in this photo, may be mistaken for human bone. Credit: **Example of PVC pipe** original to **Explorations: An Open Invitation to Biological Anthropology** by Alex Perrone is under a **CC BY-NC 4.0 License.**

Is It Human?

Once it has been determined that an object is bone, the next logical step is to identify whether the bone belongs to a human or an animal. Forensic anthropologists are faced with this question in everyday practice because human versus nonhuman bone identification is one of the most frequent requests they receive from law enforcement agencies.

There are many different ways to distinguish human versus nonhuman bone. The morphology (the shape/form) of human bone is a good place for students to start. Identifying the 206 bones in the adult human skeleton and each bone's distinguishing features (muscle attachment sites, openings and grooves for nerves and blood vessels, etc.) is fundamental to skeletal analysis.

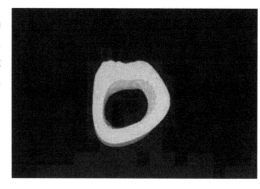

Figure 15.6: The compact layer of this animal bone is very thick, with almost no spongy bone visible. Compare with Figure 15.2 to visualize the difference in structure between human and nonhuman bone. Credit: **Animal bone cross section (Figure 15.6)** original to **Explorations: An Open Invitation to Biological Anthropology** by Alex Perrone is under a **CC BY-NC 4.0 License.**

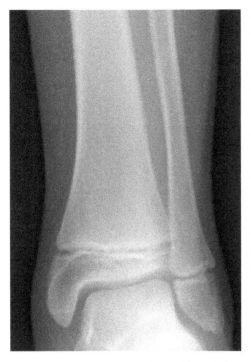

Figure 15.7: An x-ray of a subadult's ankle with the epiphyses of the tibia and fibula visible. The gap between the shaft of the bone and the end of the bone (epiphysis) is the location of the growth plate. Therefore, the growth plate gap is what separates the shafts from the epiphyses in the image. Credit: Tib fib growth plates by Gilo1969 at English Wikipedia is under a CC BY 3.0 License.

Nevertheless, there are many animal bones and human bones that look similar. For example, the declawed skeleton of a bear paw looks a lot like a human hand, pig molars appear similar to human molars, and some smaller animal bones might be mistaken for those of an infant. To add to the confusion, fragmentary bone may be even more difficult to identify as human or nonhuman. However, several major differences between human and nonhuman vertebrate bone help distinguish the two.

Forensic anthropologists pay special attention to the density of the outer, compact layer of bone in both the cranium and in the long bones. Human cranial bone has three distinctive layers. The spongy bone is sandwiched between the outer (ectocranial) and inner (endocranial) compact layers. In most other mammals, the distinction between the spongy and compact layers is not always so definite. Secondly, the compact layer in nonhuman mammal long bones can be much thicker than observed in human bone. Due to the increased density of the compact layer, nonhuman bone tends to be heavier than human bone (Figure 15.6).

The size of a bone can also help determine whether it belongs to a human. Adult human bones are larger than subadult or infant bones. However, another major difference between human adult bones and those of a young individual or infant human can be attributed to development and growth of the **epiphyses** (ends of the bone). The epiphyses of human subadult bones are not fused to the shaft (Figure 15.7). Therefore, if a bone is small and it is suspected to belong to a human subadult or infant, the epiphyses would not be fused. Many small animal bones appear very similar in form compared to adult human bones, but they are much too small to belong to an adult human. Yet they can be eliminated as subadult or infant bones if the epiphyses are fused to the shaft.

Is It Modern or Archaeological?

Forensic anthropologists work with modern cases that fall within the scope of law enforcement investigations. Accordingly, it is important to determine whether discovered human remains are **archaeological** or forensic in nature. Human remains that are historic are considered archeaological. The scientific study of human remains from archaeological sites is called **bioarchaeology**.

Dig Deeper: Bioarchaeology

For readers who are interested in the sister subfield of bioarchaeology, which studies human remains and material culture from the past, please refer to chapter 8 of *Bioarchaeology: Interpreting Human Behavior from Skeletal Remains*, in *TRACES: An Open Invitation to Archaeology* (Blatt, Michael, and Bright forthcoming).

A forensic anthropologist should begin their analysis by reviewing the context in which the remains were discovered. This will help them understand a great deal about the remains, including determining whether they are archaeological or forensic in nature as well as considering legal and ethical issues associated with the collection, analysis, and storage of human remains (see "Ethics and Human Rights" section of this chapter for more information).

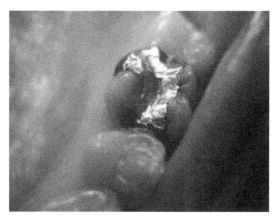

Figure 15.8: A human tooth with a filling. Credit: Filling by Kauzio has been designated to the public domain (CC0).

The "context" refers to the relationship the remains have to the immediate area in which they were found. This includes the specific place where the remains were found, the soil or other organic matter immediately surrounding the remains, and any other objects or artifacts in close proximity to the body. For example, imagine that a set of remains has been located during a house renovation. The remains are discovered below the foundation. Do the remains belong to a murder victim? Or was the house built on top of an ancient burial ground? Observing information from the surroundings can help determine whether the remains are archaeological or modern. How long ago was the foundation of the house erected? Are there artifacts in close proximity to the body, such as clothing or stone tools? These are questions about the surroundings that will help determine the relative age of the remains.

Clues directly from the skeleton may also indicate whether the remains are archaeological or modern. For example, tooth fillings can suggest that the individual was alive recently (Figure 15.8). In fact, filling material has changed over the decades, so the specific type of material used to fix a cavity can be matched with specific time periods. Gold was used in dental work in the past, but more recently composite (a mixture of plastic and fine glass) fillings have become more common.

How Many Individuals Are Present?

What Is MNI?

Another assessment that an anthropologist can perform is the calculation of the number of individuals in a mixed burial assemblage. Because not all burials consist of a single individual, it is important to **burial assemblage** be able to estimate the number of individuals in a forensic context. Quantification of the number of individuals in a **burial assemblage** can be done through the application of a number of methods, including the following: the Minimum Number of Individuals (MNI), the Most Likely Number of Individuals (MLNI), and the Lincoln Index (LI). The most commonly used method in biological anthropology, and the focus of this section, is determination of the MNI.

The MNI presents "the minimum estimate for the number of individuals that contributed to the sample" (Adams and Konigsberg 2008, 243). Many methods of calculating MNI were originally developed within the field of zooarchaeology for use on calculating the number of individuals in faunal or animal assemblages (Adams and Konigsberg 2008, 241). What MNI calculations provide is a lowest possible count for the total number of individuals contributing to a skeletal assemblage. Traditional methods of calculating MNI include separating a skeletal assemblage into categories according to the individual bone and the side the bone comes from and then taking the highest count per category and assigning that as the minimum number (Figure 15.9).

Figure 15.9: Skeletal elements from a commingled faunal assemblage. Credit: Commingled animal remains from Eden-Farson Pre-Contact site in southwest Wyoming by Matt O'Brien original to Explorations: An Open Invitation to Biological Anthropology (2nd ed.) is under a CC BY-NC 4.0 License.

Why Calculate MNI?

In a forensic context, the determination of MNI is most applicable in cases of mass graves, **commingled burials**, and mass fatality incidents. The term *commingled* is applied to any burial assemblage in which individual skeletons are not separated into separate burials. As an example, the authors of this chapter have observed commingling of remains resulting from mass fatality wildfire events. Commingled remains may also be encountered in events such as a plane or vehicle crash. It is important to remember that in any forensic context, MNI should be referenced and an MNI of one should be substantiated by the fact that there was no repetition of elements associated with the case.

Constructing the Biological Profile

Who Is It?

"Who is it?" is one of the first questions that law enforcement officers ask when they are faced with a set of skeletal remains. To answer this question, forensic anthropologists construct a biological profile (White and Folkens 2005, 405). A **biological profile** is an individual's identifying characteristics, or biological information, which include the following: biological sex, age at death, stature, population affinity, skeletal variation, and evidence of trauma and pathology.

Forensic anthropologists typically construct a biological profile to help positively identify a deceased person. The following section will lay out each component of the biological profile and briefly review standard methodology used for each.

Assessing Biological Sex

Assessment of biological sex is often one of the first things considered when establishing a biological profile because several other parts, such as age and stature estimations, rely on an assessment of biological sex to make the calculations more accurate.

Assessment of biological sex focuses on differences in both morphological (form or structure) and metric (measured) traits in individuals. When assessing morphological traits, the skull and the pelvis are the most commonly referenced areas of the skeleton. These differences are related to sexual dimorphism usually varying in the amount of robusticity seen between males and females. **Robusticity** deals with strength and size; it is frequently used as a term to describe a large size or thickness. In general, males will show a greater degree of robusticity than females. For example, the length and width of the mastoid process, a bony projection located behind the opening for the ear, is typically larger in males. The mastoid process is an attachment point for muscles of the neck, and this bony projection tends to be wider and longer in males. In general, cranial features tend to be more robust in males (Figure 15.10).

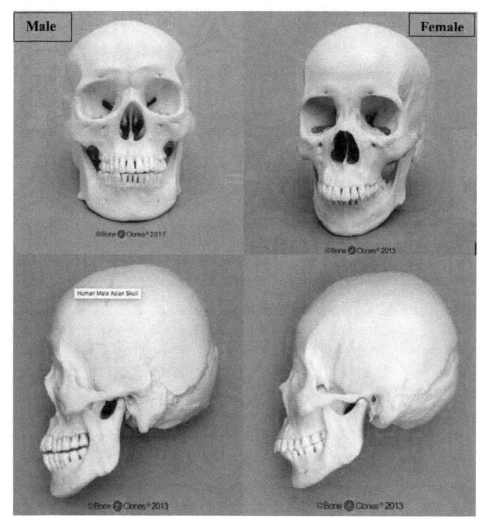

Figure 15.10: Anterior and lateral view of a male and female cranium. Credit: Anterior and lateral view of a male and female cranium (Figure 15.10) original to Explorations: An Open Invitation to Biological Anthropology by Ashley Kendell is a collective work under a CC BY-NC-SA 4.0 License. [Includes Human Female Asian Skull and Human Male Asian Skull by ©BoneClones, used by permission.]

When considering the pelvis, the features associated with the ability to give birth help distinguish females from males. During puberty, estrogen causes a widening of the female pelvis to allow for the passage of a baby. Several studies have identified specific features or bony landmarks associated with the widening of the hips, and this section will discuss one such method. The Phenice Method (Phenice 1969) is traditionally the most common reference used to assess morphological characteristics associated with sex. The Phenice Method specifically looks at the presence or absence of (1) a ventral arc, (2) the presence or absence of a subpubic concavity, and (3) the width of the medial aspect of the ischiopubic ramus (Figure 15.11). When present, the ventral arc, a ridge of bone located on the ventral surface of the pubic bone, is indicative of female remains. Likewise the presence of a subpubic concavity and a narrow medial aspect of the ischiopubic ramus is associated with a female sex estimation. Assessments of these features, as well as those of the skull (when both the pelvis and skull are present), are combined for an overall estimation of sex.

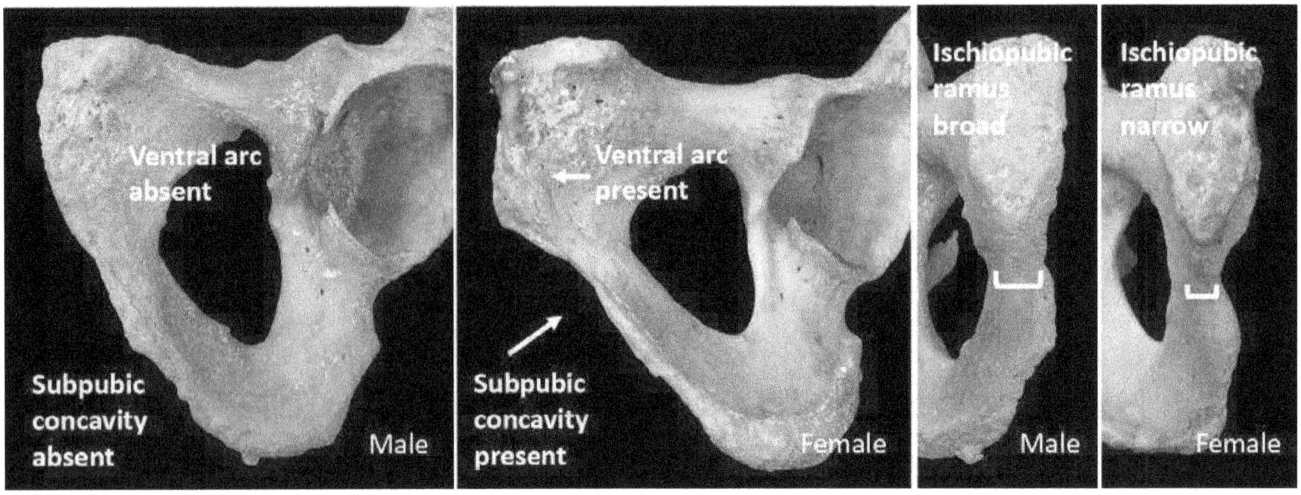

Figure 15.11: Features associated with the Phenice Method. Images derived from CSU-HIL donated skeletal collection. Credit: Features associated with the Phenice Method (Figure 15.11) original to Explorations: An Open Invitation to Biological Anthropology by Colleen Milligan is under a CC BY-NC 4.0 License.

Metric analyses are also used in the estimation of sex. Measurements taken from every region of the body can contribute to estimating sex through statistical approaches that assign a predictive value of sex. These approaches can include multiple measurements from several skeletal elements in what is called multivariate (multiple variables) statistics. Other approaches consider a single measurement, such as the diameter of the head of the femur, of a specific element in a univariate (single variable) analysis (Berg 2017, 152–156).

It is important to note that, although forensic anthropologists usually begin assessment of biological profile with biological sex, there is one major instance in which this is not appropriate. The case of two individuals found in California, on July 8, 1979, is one example that demonstrates the effect age has on the estimation of sex. The identities of the two individuals were unknown; therefore, law enforcement sent them to a lab for identification. A skeletal analysis determined that the remains represented one adolescent male and one adolescent female, both younger than 18 years of age. This information did not match with any known missing children at the time.

In 2015, the cold case was reanalyzed, and DNA samples were extracted. The results indicated that the remains were actually those of two girls who went missing in 1978. The girls were 15 years old and 14 years old at the time of death. It is clear that the 1979 results were incorrect, but this mistake also provides the opportunity to discuss the limitations of assessing sex from a subadult skeleton.

Assessing sex from the human skeleton is based on biological and genetic traits associated with females and males. These traits are linked to differences in sexual dimorphism and reproductive characteristics between females and males. The link to reproductive characteristics means that most indicators of biological sex do not fully manifest in prepubescent individuals, making estimations of sex unreliable in younger individuals (SWGANTH 2010b). This was the case in the example of the 14-year-old girl. When examined in 1979, her remains were misidentified as male because she had not yet fully developed female pelvic traits.

Sex vs. Gender

Biological sex is a different concept than **gender**. While biological anthropologists can estimate sex from the skeleton, estimating an individual's gender would require a greater context because gender is defined culturally rather than biologically. Take, for example, an individual who identifies as transgender. This individual has a gender identity that is different from their biological sex. The gender identity of any individual depends on factors related to self-identification, situation or context, and cultural factors. While in the U.S. we have historically thought of sex and gender as binary concepts (male or female), many cultures throughout the world recognize several possible gender identities. In this sense, gender is seen as a continuous or fluid variable rather than a fixed one.

Historically, forensic anthropologists have used a binary construct to categorize human skeletal remains as either male or female (with the accompanying categories of probable male, probable female, and indeterminate). In the case of transgender and gender nonconforming individuals, the binary approach to sex assessment may delay or hinder identification efforts (Buchanan 2014; Schall, Rogers, and Deschamps-Braly 2020; Tallman, Kincer, and Plemons 2021). As such, many forensic anthropologists have begun to address the inherent problems associated with a binary approach to sex identification and to explore ways of assessing social identity and self-identified gender using skeletal remains and forensic context.

For the duration of this section, the term *transgender* refers to individuals whose gender identity differs from the sex assigned at birth (Schall, Rogers, and Deschamps-Braly 2020:2). Transgender individuals transition from one gender binary to another, such as male-to-female (MTF) or female-to-male (FTM). While many of the gender-affirming procedures available to trans and gender-nonconforming individuals are focused on soft tissue modifications (e.g., breast augmentation, genital reconstruction, hormone therapies, etc.), there are a number of gender-affirmation surgeries that do leave a permanent record on the skeleton. Generally speaking, FTM transgender people are reported to undergo fewer surgical procedures than do MTF transgender people (Buchanan 2014). The discussion below focuses on Facial Feminization Surgery (FFS), which leaves a permanent record on the human skeleton that may be used to help make an identification.

FFS refers to a combination of procedures focused on sexually dimorphic features of the face, with the intent of transforming typically male facial features into more feminine forms. Facial Feminization Surgery procedures were developed by Dr. Douglas Ousterhout, a San Francisco based cranio-maxillofacial surgeon, in the mid-1980s (Schall, Rogers, and Deschamps-Braly 2020:2). FFS can include one or a combination of the following: hairline lowering, forehead reduction and contouring, brow lift, reduction rhinoplasty, cheek enhancement, lift lift, lip filling, chin contouring, jaw contouring, and/or tracheal shave (Buchanan 2014; Schall, Rogers, and Deschamps-Braly 2020:2). Of the procedures outlined previously, four are known to directly affect the facial skeleton: forehead contouring, rhinoplasty, chin contouring, and jaw contouring (Buchanan 2014; Schall, Rogers, and Deschamps-Braly 2020:2).

Because FFS procedures have been widely documented in the medical (and more recently the forensic anthropological) literature, there are a number of indicators that a forensic anthropologist can use to make more informed evaluations of gender, including evidence of bone remodeling in sexually dimorphic regions of the skull (e.g., forehead, chin, jawline), as well as the presence of plates, pins, or other surgical hardware that may be evidence of FFS (Buchanan 2014; Schall, Rogers, and Deschamps-Braly 2020; Tallman, Kincer, and Plemons 2021). Additionally, some forensic anthropologists suggest cautiously integrating contextual information from the scene, such as personal effects, material evidence, and recovery scene information, into their evaluation of an individual's social identity (Beatrice and Soler 2016; Birkby, Fenton, and Anderson 2008; Soler and Beatrice 2018; Soler et al. 2019; Tallman, Kincer, and Plemons 2021; Winburn, Schoff, and Warren 2016). The ultimate goal of many skeletal analyses is to make a positive identification on a set of unidentified remains.

Special Topic: Trans Doe Task Force

The Trans Doe Task Force (TDTF) is a Trans-led nonprofit organization that investigates cases involving LGBTQ+ missing and murdered persons. The organization specifically focuses on transgender and gender-variant cases, providing connections between law enforcement agencies, medical examiner offices, forensic anthropologists, and forensic genetic genealogists to increase the chances of identification. Additionally, the TDTF curates a data repository of missing, murdered, and unclaimed LGBTQ+ individuals, and they continuously try innovative approaches to identify these individuals, whose lived gender identity may not match their biological sex.

For more information visit transdoetaskforce.org

Assessment of Population Affinity

Population affinity is another component of the biological profile. We use the term *population affinity* to refer to the variation seen among modern populations—variation that is both genetic and environmentally driven. The word *affinity* refers to similarities or relationships between individuals. As forensic anthropologists, we compare an unknown individual to multiple reference groups and look for the degree of similarity in observable traits with those groups. As noted previously, population affinity can aid law enforcement in their identification of missing persons or unknown skeletal remains.

Within the field of anthropology, the estimation of population affinity has a contentious history, and early attempts at classification were largely based on the erroneous assumption that an individual's **phenotype** (outward appearance) was correlated with their innate intelligence and abilities (see Chapter 13 for a more in-depth discussion of the history of the race concept). The use of the term *race* is deeply embedded in the social context of the United States. In any other organism/living thing, groups divided according to the biological race concept would be defined as a separate subspecies. The major issue with applying the biological race concept to humans is that there are not enough differences between any two populations to separate on a genetic basis. In other words, *biological races do not exist in human populations.* However, the concept of race has been perpetuated and upheld by sociocultural constructs of race.

The conundrum for forensic anthropologists is the fact that while races do not exist on a biological level, we still socially recognize and categorize individuals based on their phenotype. Clearly, our phenotype is an important factor in not only how we are viewed by others but also how we identify ourselves. It is also a commonly reported variable. Often labeled as "race," we are asked to report how we self-identify on school applications, government identification, surveys, census reports, and so forth. It follows then that when a person is reported missing, the information commonly collected by law enforcement and sometimes entered into a missing person's database includes their age, biological sex, stature, and "race." Therefore, the more information a forensic anthropologist can provide regarding the individual's physical characteristics, the more he or she can help to narrow the search.

As an exercise, create a list of all of the women you know who are between the ages of 18 and 24 and approximately 5' 4" to 5' 9" tall. You probably have several dozen people on the list. Now, consider how many females you know who are between the ages of 18 and 24, are approximately 5' 4" to 5' 9" tall, and are Vietnamese. Your list is going to be significantly shorter. That's how missing persons searches go as well. The more information you can provide regarding a decedent's phenotype, the fewer possible matches law enforcement are left to investigate. This is why population affinity has historically been included as a part of the biological profile.

In an effort to combat the erroneous assumptions tied to the race concept, forensic anthropologists have attempted to reframe this component of the biological profile. The term *race* is no longer used in casework and teaching. Historically, the word *ancestry* is and was deemed a more appropriate way to describe an individual's phenotype. However, in more recent years, forensic anthropologists have begun using the term *population affinity,* recognizing that we are basing our analysis on the similarities we see based on the reference samples we have available (Winburn and Algee-Hewitt 2021). An important note here is that it is possible to hinder identifications and harm individuals when tools like estimations of population affinity are misapplied, misinterpreted, or misused. For this reason, the field of forensic anthropology has ongoing conversations about the appropriateness of this analysis in the biological profile (Bethard and DiGangi 2020; Stull et al. 2021).

Traditionally, population affinity was accomplished through a visual inspection of morphological variants of the skull (morphoscopics). These methods focused on elements of the facial skeleton, including the nose, eyes, and cheek bones. However, in an effort to reduce subjectivity, nonmetric cranial traits are now assessed within a statistical framework to help anthropologists better interpret their distribution among living populations (Hefner and Linde 2018). Based on the observable traits, a macromorphoscopic analysis will allow the practitioner to create a statistical prediction of geographic origin. In essence, forensic anthropologists are using human variation in the estimation of geographic origin, by referencing documented frequencies of nonmetric skeletal indicators or macromorphoscopic traits.

Population affinity is also assessed through metric analyses. The computer program Fordisc is an anthropological tool used to estimate different components of the biological profile, including ancestry, sex, and stature. When using Fordisc, skeletal measurements are input into the computer software, and the program employs multivariate statistical classification methods, including discriminant function analysis, to generate a statistical prediction for the geographic origin of unknown remains based on the comparison of the unknown to the reference samples in the software program. Fordisc also calculates the likelihood of the prediction being correct, as well as how typical the metric data is for the assigned group.

Estimating Age-at-Death

Estimating age-at-death from the skeleton relies on the measurement of two basic physiological processes: (1) growth and development and (2) degeneration (or aging). From fetal development on, our bones and teeth grow and change at a predictable rate. This provides for relatively accurate age estimates. After our bones and teeth cease to grow and develop, they begin to undergo structural changes, or degeneration, associated with aging. This does not happen at such predictable rates and, therefore, results in less accurate or larger age-range estimations.

During growth and development stages, two primary methods used for estimations of age of subadults (those under the age of 18) are **epiphyseal union** and **dental development.** Epiphyseal union (or **epiphyseal fusion**) refers to the appearance and closure of the epiphyseal plates between the primary centers of growth in a bone and the subsequent centers of growth (see Figure 15.7). Prior to complete union, the cartilaginous area between the primary and secondary centers of growth is also referred to as the growth plates (Schaefer, Black, and Scheuer 2009). Different areas of the skeleton have documented differences in the appearance and closure of epiphyses, making this a reliable method for aging subadult remains (SWGANTH 2013).

As an example of its utility in the identification process, epiphyseal development was used to identify two subadult victims of a fatal fire in Flint, Michigan, in February 2010. The remains represented two young girls, ages three and four. Due to the intensity of the fire, the subadult victims were differentiated from each other through the appearance of the patella, the kneecap. The patella is a bone that develops within the tendon of the quadriceps muscle at the knee joint. The patella begins to form around three to four years of age (Cunningham, Scheuer, and Black 2016, 407–409). In the example above, radiographs of the knees showed the presence of a patella in the four-year-old girl and the absence of a clearly discernible patella in the three-year-old.

Dental development begins during fetal stages of growth and continues until the complete formation and eruption of the adult third molars (if present). The first set of teeth to appear are called deciduous or baby teeth. Individuals develop a total of 20 deciduous teeth, including incisors, canines, and molars. These are generally replaced by adult dentition as an individual grows (Figure 15.12). A total of 32 teeth are represented in the adult dental arcade, including incisors, canines, premolars, and molars. When dental development is used for age estimations, researchers use both tooth-formation patterns and eruption schedules as determining evidence. For example, the crown of the tooth forms first followed by the formation of the tooth root. During development, an individual can exhibit a partially formed crown or a complete crown with a partially formed root. The teeth generally begin the eruption process once the crown of the tooth is complete. The developmental stages of dentition are one of the most reliable and consistent aging methods for subadults (Langley, Gooding, and Tersigni-Tarrant 2017, 176–177).

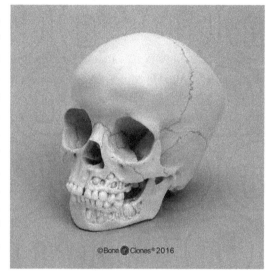

Figure 15.12: Dental development in a subadult. Credit: 5-year-old Human Child Skull with Mixed Dentition Exposed by ©BoneClones is used by permission and available here is under a CC BY-NC 4.0 License.

Degenerative changes in the skeleton typically begin after 18 years of age, with more prominent changes developing after an individual reaches middle adulthood (commonly defined as after 35 years of age in osteology). These changes are most easily seen around joint surfaces of the pelvis, the cranial vault, and the ribs. In this chapter, we focus on the pubic symphysis surfaces of the pelvis and the sternal ends of the ribs, which show metamorphic changes from young adulthood to older adulthood. The **pubic symphysis** is a joint that unites the left and right halves of the pelvis. The surface of the pubic symphysis changes during adulthood, beginning as a surface with pronounced ridges (called billowing) and flattening with a more distinct rim to the pubic symphysis as an individual ages. As with all metamorphic age changes, older adults tend to develop lipping around the joint surfaces as well as a breakdown of the joint surfaces. The most commonly used method for aging adult skeletons from the pubic symphysis is the Suchey-Brooks method (Brooks and Suchey 1990; Katz and Suchey 1986). This method divides the changes seen with the pubic symphysis into six phases based on macroscopic age-related changes to the surface. Figure 15.13 provides a visual of the degenerative changes that typically occur on the pubic symphysis.

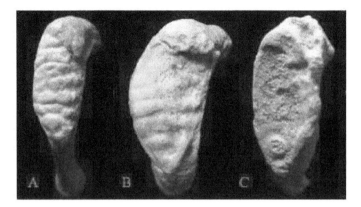

Figure 15.13: Examples of degenerative changes to the pubic symphysis: (A) young adult; (B) middle adult; (C) old adult. Credit: **Example of the progression of degenerative changes to the pubic symphysis (Figure 15.14)** original to **Explorations: An Open Invitation to Biological Anthropo logy** by Ashley Kendell is under a **CC BY-NC-SA 4.0 License.** [Original photos by Dr. Julie Fleischman used by permission. Pubic symphyses are curated in the Hartnett-Fulginiti donated skeletal collection. Donation and research consent was provided by next of kin.]

The sternal end of the ribs, the **anterior** end of the rib that connects via cartilage to the sternum, is also used in age estimations of adults. This method, first developed by M. Y. İşcan and colleagues, considers both the change in shape of the sternal end as well as the quality of the bone (İşcan, Loth, and Wright 1984; İşcan, Loth, and Wright 1985). The sternal end first develops a billowing appearance in young adulthood. The bone typically develops a wider and deeper cupped end as an individual ages. Older adults tend to exhibit bony extensions of the sternal end rim as attaching cartilage ossifies. Figure 15.14 provides a visual of the degenerative changes that typically occur in sternal rib ends.

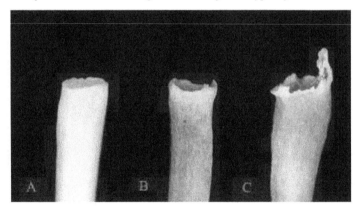

Figure 15.14: Examples of degenerative changes to the sternal rib end: (A) young adult; (B) middle adult; (C) old adult. Images derived from CSU, Chico HIL donated skeletal collection. Credit: **Examples of degenerative changes to the sternal rib end (Figure 15.15)** original to **Explorations: An Open Invitation to Biological Anthropology** by Alex Perrone is under a **CC BY-NC 4.0 License.**

Estimating Stature

Stature, or height, is one of the most prominently recorded components of the biological profile. Our height is recorded from infancy through adulthood. Doctor's appointments, driver's license applications, and sports rosters all typically involve a measure of stature for an individual. As such, it is also a component of the biological profile nearly every individual will have on record. Bioarchaeologists and forensic anthropologists use stature estimation methods to provide a range within which an individual's biological height would fall. **Biological height** is a person's true anatomical height. However, the range created through these estimations is often compared to **reported stature**, which is typically self-reported and based on an approximation of an individual's true height (Ousley 1995).

In June 2015, two men were shot and killed in Granite Bay, California, in a double homicide. Investigators were able to locate surveillance camera footage from a gas station where the two victims were spotted in a car with another individual believed to be the perpetrator in the case. The suspect, sitting behind the victims in the car, hung his right arm out of the window as the car drove away. The search for the perpetrator was eventually narrowed down to two suspects. One suspect was 5' 8" while the other suspect was 6' 4", representing almost a foot difference in height reported stature between the two. Forensic anthropologists were given the dimensions of the car (for proportionality of the arm) and were asked to calculate the stature of the suspect in the car from measurements of the suspect's forearm hanging from the window. Approximate lengths of the bones of the forearm were established from the video footage and used to create a predicted stature range. Stature estimations from skeletal remains typically look at the correlation between the measurements of any individual bone and the overall measurement of body height. In the case above, the length of the right forearm pointed to the taller of the two suspects who was subsequently arrested for the homicide.

Certain bones, such as the long bones of the leg, contribute more to our overall height than others and can be used with mathematical equations known as regression equations. **Regression methods** examine the relationship between variables such as height and bone length and use the correlation between the variables to create a prediction interval (or range) for estimated stature. This method for calculating stature is the most commonly used method (SWGANTH 2012). Figure 15.15 shows the measurement of the bicondylar length of the femur for stature estimations.

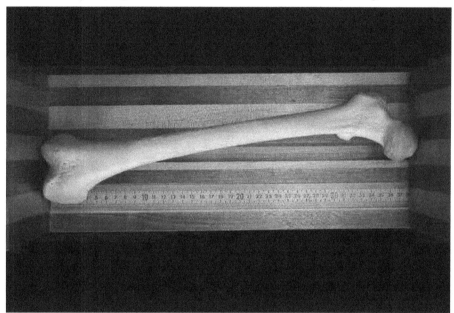

Figure 15.15: Image of measurement of the bicondylar length of the femur, often used in the estimation of living stature. Image derived from CSU, Chico HIL donated skeletal collection. Credit: Measurement of the bicondylar length of the femur original to Explorations: An Open Invitation to Biological Anthropology by Alex Perrone is under a CC BY-NC 4.0 License.

Identification Using Individualizing Characteristics

One of the most frequently requested analyses within the forensic anthropology laboratory is assistance with the identification of unidentified remains. While all components of a biological profile, as discussed above, can assist law enforcement officers and medical examiners to narrow down the list of potential identifications, a biological profile will not lead to a **positive identification**. The term *positive identification* refers to a scientifically validated method of identifying previously unidentified remains. Presumptive identifications, however, are not scientifically validated; rather, they are based on circumstances or scene context. For example, if a decedent is found in a locked home with no evidence of forced entry but the body is no longer visually identifiable, it may be presumed that the remains belong to the homeowner. Hence, a presumptive identification.

The medicolegal system ultimately requires that a positive identification be made in such circumstances, and a presumptive identification is often a good way to narrow down the pool of possibilities. Biological profile information also assists with making a presumptive identification based on an individual's phenotype in life (e.g., what they looked like). As an example, a forensic anthropologist may establish the following components of a biological profile: white male, between the ages of 35 and 50, approximately 5' 7" to 5' 11." While this seems like a rather specific description of an individual, you can imagine that this description fits dozens, if not hundreds, of people in an urban area. Therefore, law enforcement can use the biological profile information to narrow their pool of possible identifications to include only white males who fit the age and height outlined above. Once a possible match is found, the decedent can be identified using a method of positive identification.

Positive identifications are based on what we refer to as individualizing traits or characteristics, which are traits that are unique at the individual level. For example, brown hair is not an individualizing trait as brown is the most common hair color in the U.S. But, a specific pattern of dental restorations or surgical implants can be individualizing, because it is unlikely that you will have an exact match on either of these traits when comparing two individuals.

A number of positive methods are available to forensic anthropologists, and for the remainder of this section we will discuss the following methods: comparative medical and dental radiography and identification of surgical implants.

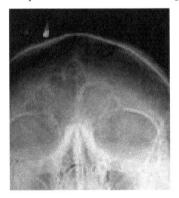

Figure 15.16: Example of the unique shape of the frontal sinus. Credit: Frontal bone sinuses by Alex Khimich is under a CC BY-SA 4.0 License.

Comparative medical and dental radiography is used to find consistency of traits when comparing antemortem records (medical and dental records taken during life) with images taken postmortem (after death). Comparative medical radiography focuses primarily on features associated with the skeletal system, including trabecular pattern (internal structure of bone that is honeycomb in appearance), bone shape or cortical density (compact outer layer of bone), and evidence of past trauma, skeletal pathology, or skeletal anomalies. Other individualizing traits include the shape of various bones or their features, such as the frontal sinuses (Figure 15.16).

Comparative dental radiography focuses on the number, shape, location, and orientation of dentition and dental restorations in antemortem and postmortem images. While there is not a minimum number of matching traits that need to be identified for an identification to be made, the antemortem and postmortem records should have enough skeletal or dental consistencies to conclude that the records did in fact come from the same individual (SWGANTH 2010a). Consideration should also be given to population-level frequencies of specific skeletal and dental traits. If a trait is particularly common within a given population, it may not be a good trait to utilize for positive identification.

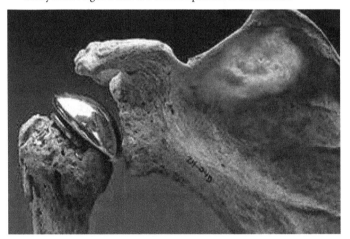

Figure 15.17: Image of joint replacement in the right shoulder. Credit: Shoulder replacement by Smithsonian [exhibit: Written in Bone, Today's Bones] is used for educational and non-commercial purposes as outlined by the Smithsonian.

Surgical implants or devices can also be used for identification purposes (Figure 15.17). These implements are sometimes recovered with human remains. One of the ways forensic anthropologists can use surgical implants to assist in decedent identification is by providing a thorough analysis of the implant and noting any identifying information such as serial numbers, manufacturer symbols, and so forth. This information can then sometimes be tracked directly to the manufacturer or the place of surgical intervention, which may be used to identify unknown remains (SWGANTH 2010a).

Trauma Analysis

Types of Trauma

Within the field of anthropology, **trauma** is defined as an injury to living tissue caused by an extrinsic force or mechanism (Lovell 1997:139). Forensic anthropologists can assist a forensic pathologist by providing an interpretation of the course of events that led to skeletal trauma. Typically, traumatic injury to bone is classified into one of four categories, defined by the trauma mechanism. A trauma mechanism refers to the force that produced the skeletal modification and can be classified as (1) sharp force, (2) blunt force, (3) projectile, or (4) thermal (burning). Each type of trauma, and the characteristic pattern(s) associated with that particular categorization, will be discussed below.

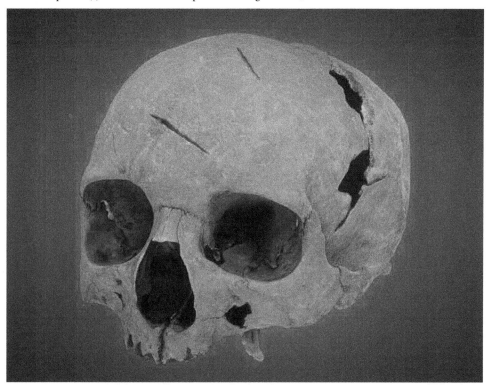

Figure 15.18: Example of sharp-force trauma (sword wound) to the frontal bone. The skull appears sliced with thin lines in two places across the top of the skull. Credit: **Female skull injured by a medieval sword** by Provinciaal depot voor archeologie Noord-Holland is under a CC BY 4.0 License. The original image is a 3D model that can be manipulated on the **openverse website**.

First, let's consider *sharp-force trauma*, which is caused by a tool that is edged, pointed, or beveled—for example, a knife, saw, or machete (SWGANTH 2011). The patterns of injury resulting from sharp-force trauma include linear incisions created by a sharp, straight edge; punctures; and chop marks (Figure 15.18; SWGANTH 2011). When observed under a microscope, an anthropologist can often determine what kind of tool created the bone trauma. For example, a power saw cut will be discernible from a manual saw cut.

Second, *blunt-force trauma* is defined as "a relatively low-velocity impact over a relatively large surface area" (Galloway 1999, 5). Blunt-force injuries can result from impacts from clubs, sticks, fists, and so forth. Blunt-force impacts typically leave an injury at the point of impact but can also lead to bending and deformation in other regions of the bone. Depressions, fractures, and deformation at and around the site of impact are all characteristics of blunt-force trauma (Figure 15.19). As with sharp-force trauma, an anthropologist attempts to interpret blunt-force injuries, providing information pertaining to the type of tool used, the direction of impact, the sequence of impacts, if more than one, and the amount of force applied.

Third, *projectile trauma* refers to high-velocity trauma, typically affecting a small surface area (Galloway 1999, 6). Projectile trauma results from fast-moving objects such as bullets or shrapnel. It is typically characterized by penetrating defects or embedded materials (Figure 15.20). When interpreting injuries resulting from projectile trauma, an anthropologist can often offer information pertaining to the type of weapon used (e.g., rifle vs. handgun), relative size of the bullet (but not the caliber of the bullet), the direction the projectile was traveling, and the sequence of injuries if there are multiple present.

Finally, *thermal trauma* is a bone alteration that results from bone exposure to extreme heat. Thermal trauma can result in cases of house or car fires, intentional disposal of a body in cases of homicidal violence, plane crashes, and so on. Thermal trauma is most often characterized by color changes to bone, ranging from yellow to black (charred) or white (calcined). Other bone alterations characteristic of thermal trauma include delamination (flaking or layering due to bone failure), shrinkage, fractures, and heat-specific burn patterning. When interpreting injuries resulting from thermal damage, an anthropologist can differentiate between thermal fractures and fractures that occurred before heat exposure, thereby contributing to the interpretation of burn patterning (e.g., was the individual bound or in a flexed position prior to the fire?).

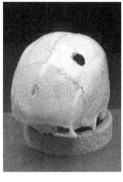

Figure 15.19: Example of multiple blunt force impacts to the left parietal and frontal bones. There is one hole in the skull with fractured bone around the edges. There are also multiple spots across the back of the skull with depressions of various sizes. Credit: **Skull hammer trauma** by the **National Institutes of Health**, Health & Human Services, is in the **public domain**. [Exhibit: Visible Proofs: Forensic Views of the Body, U.S. National Library of Medicine, 19th Century Collection, National Museum of Health and Medicine, Armed Forces Institute of Pathology, Washington, D.C.]

While there are characteristic patterns associated with the four categories of bone trauma, it is also important to note that these bone alterations do not always occur independently of different trauma types. An individual's skeleton may present with multiple different types of trauma, such as a projectile wound and thermal trauma. Therefore, it is important that the anthropologist recognize the different types of trauma and interpret them appropriately.

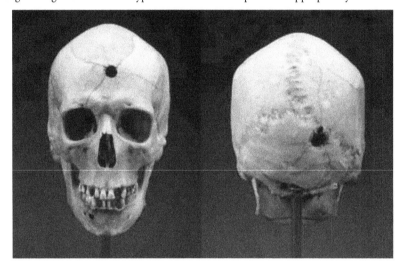

Figure 15.20: Example of projectile trauma with an entrance wound to the frontal bone and exit wound visible on the occipital. A small circular hole is visible in the front of the skull with cracks radiating out from the point of impact. There is a larger hole visible in the back of the skull that is irregular yet circular in shape. Credit: **Trauma: Gunshot Wounds** by **Smithsonian** [exhibit: Written in Bone, How Bone Biographies Get Written] is used for educational and non-commercial purposes as outlined by the Smithsonian.

Timing of Injury

Another important component of any anthropological trauma analysis is the determination of the timing of injury (e.g., when did the injury occur). Timing of injury is traditionally split into one of three categories: **antemortem** (before death), **perimortem** (at or around the time of death), and **postmortem** (after death). This classification system differs slightly from the classification system used by the pathologist because it specifically references the qualities of bone tissue and bone response to external forces. Therefore, the perimortem interval (at or around the time of death) means that the bone is still fresh and has what is referred to as a green bone response, which can extend past death by several weeks or even months. For example, in cold or freezing temperatures a body can be preserved for extended periods of time, increasing the perimortem interval, while in desert climates decomposition is accelerated, thereby significantly decreasing the postmortem interval (Galloway 1999, 12). Antemortem injuries (occurring well before death and not related to the death incident) are typically characterized by some level of healing, in the form of a fracture callus or unification of fracture margins. Finally, postmortem injuries (occurring after death, while bone is no longer fresh) are characterized by jagged fracture margins, resulting from a loss of moisture content during the decomposition process (Galloway 1999, 16). In general, all bone traumas should be classified according to the timing of injury, if possible. This information will help the medical examiner or pathologist better understand the circumstances surrounding the decedent's death, as well as events occurring during life and after the final disposition of the body.

The Role of the Forensic Anthropologist in Trauma Analysis

Within the medicolegal system, forensic anthropologists are often called upon by the medical examiner, forensic pathologist, or coroner to assist with an interpretation of trauma. The forensic anthropologist's main focus in any trauma analysis is the underlying skeletal system—as well as, sometimes, cartilage. Analysis and interpretation of soft tissue injuries fall within the purview of the medical examiner or pathologist. It is also important to note that the main role of the forensic anthropologist is to provide information pertaining to skeletal injury to assist the medical examiner/pathologist in their final interpretation of injury. Forensic anthropologists do not hypothesize as to the cause of death of an individual. Instead, a forensic anthropologist's report should include a description of the injury (e.g., trauma mechanism, number of injuries, location, timing of injury); documentation of the injury, which may be utilized in court testimony (e.g., photographs, radiographs, measurements); and, if applicable, a statement as to the condition of the body and state of decomposition, which may be useful for understanding the depositional context (e.g., how long has the body been exposed to the elements; was it moved or in its original location; are any of the alterations to bone due to environmental or faunal exposure instead of intentional human modification).

Taphonomy

What Happened to the Remains After Death?

The majority of the skeletal analysis process revolves around the identity of the deceased individual. However, there is one last, very important question that forensic anthropologists should ask: What happened to the remains after death? Generally speaking, processes that alter the bone after death are referred to as taphonomic changes (refer to Chapter 7 for a discussion regarding taphonomy and the fossil record).

The term *taphonomy* was originally used to refer to the processes through which organic remains mineralize, also known as fossilization. Within the context of biological anthropology, the term *taphonomy* is better defined as the study of what happens to human remains after death (Komar and Buikstra 2008). Initial factors affecting a body after death include processes such as decomposition and scavenging by animals. However, taphonomic processes encompass much more than the initial period after death. For example, plant root growth can leach minerals from bone, leaving a distinctive mark. Sunlight can bleach human remains, leaving exposed areas whiter than those that remained buried. Water can wear the surface of the bone until it becomes smooth.

Some taphonomic processes can help a forensic anthropologist estimate the relative amount of time that human remains have been exposed to the elements. For example, root growth through a bone would certainly indicate a body was buried for more than a few days. Forensic anthropologists must be very careful when attempting to estimate time since death based on taphonomic processes because environmental conditions can greatly influence the rate at which taphonomic processes progress. For example, in cold environments, tissue may decay slower than in warm, moist environments.

Forensic anthropologists must contend with taphonomic processes that affect the preservation of bones. For example, high acidity in the soil can break down human bone to the point of crumbling. In addition, when noting trauma, they must be very careful not to confuse postmortem (after death) bone damage with trauma.

Figure 15.21: Table showing taphonomic processes that affect the preservation of bones. A. Rodent gnawing. B. Carnivore damage. C. Burned bone. D. Root etching. E. Weathering. F. Cut marks. Credit: A. Rodent gnawing (Figure 15.26), B. Carnivore damage (Figure 15.27), C. Burned bone (Figure 15.28), D. Root etching (Figure 15.29), E. Weathering (Figure 15.30), and F. Cut marks (Figure 15.30), all original to Explorations: An Open Invitation to Biological Anthropology by Alex Perrone are under a CC BY-NC 4.0 License.

Taphonomic Process	Definition
Rodent Gnawing 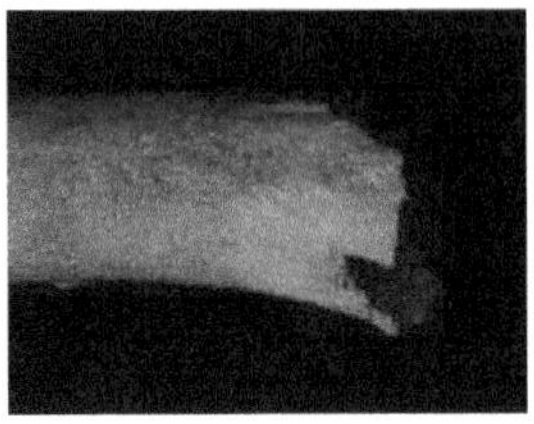	When rodents, such as rats and mice, chew on bone, they leave sets of parallel grooves. The shallow grooves are etched by the rodent's incisors.
Carnivore Damage 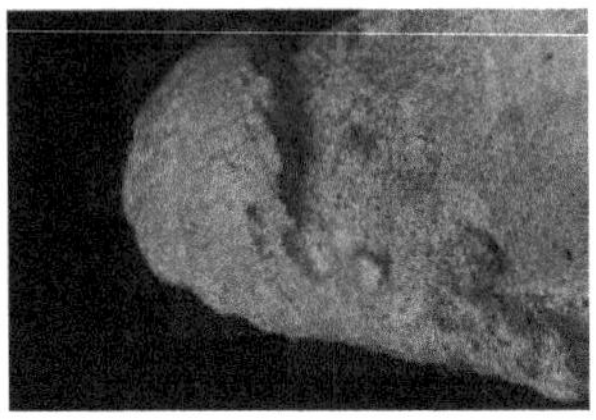	Carnivores may leave destructive dental marks on bone. The tooth marks may be visible as pit marks or punctures from the canines, as well as extensive gnawing or chewing of the ends of the bones to retrieve marrow.
Burned Bone 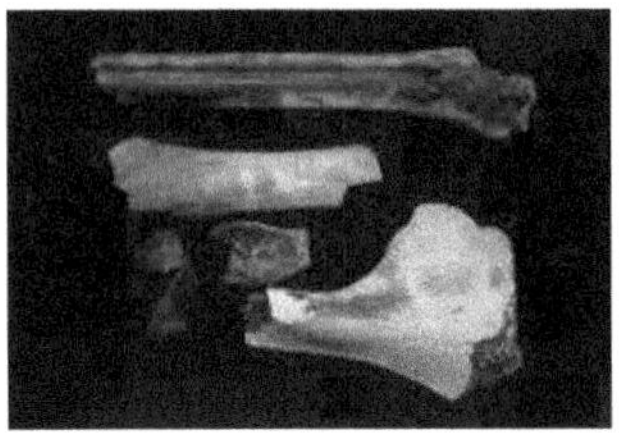	Fire causes observable damage to bone. Temperature and the amount of time bone is heated affect the appearance of the bone. Very high temperatures can crack bone and result in white coloration. Color gradients are visible in between high and lower temperatures, with lower temperatures resulting in black coloration from charring. Cracking can also reveal information about the directionality of the burn.

Taphonomic Process	Definition
Root Etching 	Plant roots can etch the outer surface of bone, leaving grooves where the roots attached as they leached nutrients. During this process, the plant's roots secrete acid that breaks down the surface of the bone.
Weathering 	Many different environmental conditions affect bone. River transport can smooth the surface of the bone due to water abrasion. Sunlight can bleach the exposed surface of bone. Dry and wet environments or the mixture of both types of environments can cause cracking and exfoliation of the surface. Burial in different types of soil can cause discoloration, and exposure can cause degreasing.
Cut Marks 	Humans may alter bone by cutting, scraping, or sawing it directly or in the process of removing tissue. The groove pattern—that is, the depth and width of the cuts—can help identify the tool used in the cutting process.

Ethics and Human Rights

Working with human remains requires a great deal of consideration and respect for the dead. Forensic anthropologists have to think about the ethics of our use of human remains for scientific purposes. How do we conduct casework in the most respectable manner possible? While there are a wide range of ethical considerations to consider when contemplating a career in forensic anthropology, this chapter will focus on two major categories: working with human remains and acting as an expert within the medicolegal system.

Working with Human Remains

Forensic anthropologists work with human remains in a number of contexts, including casework, excavation, research, and teaching. When working with human remains, it is always important to use proper handling techniques. To prevent damage to skeletal remains, bones should be handled over padded surfaces. Skulls should never be picked up by placing fingers in the eye orbits, foramen magnum (hole at the base of the skull for entry of the spinal cord), or through the zygomatic arches (cheekbones). Human remains, whether related to casework, fieldwork, donated skeletal collections, or research, were once living human beings. It is important to always bear in mind that work with remains should be ingrained with respect for the individual and their relatives. In addition to fieldwork, casework, and teaching, anthropologists are often invited to work with remains that come from a bioarchaeological context or from a human rights violation. While this discussion of ethics is not comprehensive, two case examples will be provided below in which an anthropologist must consider the ethical standards outlined above.

Modern Human Rights Violations

Forensic anthropologists may also be called to participate in criminal investigations involving human rights violations. Anthropological investigations may include assistance with identifications, determination of the number of victims, and trauma analyses. In this role, forensic anthropologists play an integral part in promoting human rights, preventing future human rights violations, and providing the evidence necessary to prosecute those responsible for past events. A few ethical considerations for the forensic anthropologist involved in human rights violations include the use of appropriate standards of identification, presenting reliable and unbiased testimony, and maintaining preservation of evidence. For a more comprehensive history of forensic anthropological contributions to human rights violations investigations, see Ubelaker 2018.

Acting as an Expert in the Medicolegal System

In addition to the ethical considerations involved in working with human skeletal remains, forensic anthropologists must abide by ethical standards when they act as experts within the medicolegal system. The role of the forensic anthropologist within the medicolegal system is primarily to provide information to the medical examiner or coroner that will aid in the identification process or determination of cause and manner of death. Forensic anthropologists also may be called to testify in a court of law. In this capacity, forensic anthropologists should always abide by a series of ethical guidelines that pertain to their interpretation, presentation, and preservation of evidence used in criminal investigations. First and foremost, practitioners should never misrepresent their training or education. When appropriate, outside opinions and assistance in casework should be requested (e.g., consulting a radiologist for radiological examinations or odontologist for dental exams). The best interest of the decedent should always take precedence. All casework should be conducted in an unbiased way, and financial compensation should never be accepted as it can act as an incentive to take a biased stance regarding casework. All anthropological findings should be kept confidential, and release of information is best done by the medical examiner or coroner. Finally, while upholding personal ethical standards, forensic anthropologists are also expected to report any perceived ethical violations committed by their peers.

Ethical standards for the field of forensic anthropology are outlined by the Organization of Scientific Area Committees (OSAC) for Forensic Science, administered by the National Institute of Standards and Technology (NIST). OSAC and NIST recently began an initiative to develop standards that would strengthen the practice of forensic science both in the United States and internationally. OSAC's main objective is to "strengthen the nation's use of forensic science by facilitating the development of technically sound forensic science standards and by promoting the adoption of those standards by the forensic science community" (NIST n.d.). Additionally, OSAC promotes the establishment of best practices and other guidelines to ensure that forensic science findings and their presentation are reliable and reproducible (NIST 2023).

Special Topic: Native American Graves Protection and Repatriation Act (NAGPRA)

There is a long history in the United States of systematic disenfranchisement of Native American people, including lack of respect for tribal sovereignty. This includes the egregious treatment of Native American human remains. Over several centuries, thousands of Native American remains were removed from tribal lands and held at institutions in the United States, such as museums and universities.

In 1990, a landmark human rights federal law, the Native American Graves Protection and Repatriation Act (NAGPRA), spurred change in the professional standards and practice of biological anthropology and archaeology. NAGPRA established a legal avenue to provide protection for and repatriation of Native American remains, cultural items, and sacred objects removed from Federal or tribal lands to Native American lineal descendants, Indian tribes, and Native Hawaiian organizations. Human remains and associated artifacts, curated in museum collections and federally funded institutions, are subject to three primary provisions outlined by the NAGPRA statute: (1) protection for Native graves on federal and private land; (2) recognition of tribal authority on such lands; and (3) the requirement that all Native skeletal remains and associated artifacts be inventoried and culturally affiliated groups be consulted concerning decisions related to ownership and final disposition (Rose, Green, and Green 1996). NAGPRA legislation was enacted to ensure ethical consideration and treatment of Native remains and to improve dialogue between scientists and Native groups.

- For more information about NAGPRA, visit the Bureau of Reclamation NAGPRA website
- To read the text of the law, visit the US Congress NAGPRA law website.
- For further discussion of NAGPRA history, please see *TRACES: An Open Invitation to Archaeology* open textbook website

Becoming a Forensic Anthropologist

What does it take to be a forensic anthropologist? Forensic anthropologists are first and foremost anthropologists. While many forensic anthropologists have an undergraduate degree in anthropology, they may also major in biology, criminal justice, pre-law, pre-med, and many other related fields. Practicing forensic anthropologists typically have an advanced degree, either a Master's or Doctoral degree in Anthropology. Additional training and experience in archaeology, the medico-legal system, rules of evidence, and expert witness testimony are also common. Practicing forensic anthropologists are also encouraged to be board-certified through the American Board of Forensic Anthropology (ABFA). Learn more about the field and educational opportunities on the ABFA website.

Review Questions

- What is forensic anthropology? What are the seven primary steps involved in a skeletal analysis?
- What are the major components of a biological profile? Why are forensic anthropologists often-tasked with creating biological profiles for unknown individuals?
- What are the four major types of skeletal trauma?
- What is taphonomy, and why is an understanding of taphonomy often critical in forensic anthropology analyses?
- What are some of the ethical considerations faced by forensic anthropologists?

About the Authors

Ashley Kendell, Ph.D.

California State University, Chico, akendell@csuchico.edu

Dr. Ashley Kendell is currently an associate professor and forensic anthropologist at Chico State. Prior to beginning her position at Chico State, she was a visiting professor at the University of Montana and the forensic anthropologist for the state of Montana. Dr. Kendell obtained her doctorate from Michigan State University, and her research interests include skeletal trauma analysis and digitization and curation methods for digital osteological data. She is also a Registry Diplomate of the American Board of Medicolegal Death Investigators. Throughout her doctoral program, she worked as a medicolegal death investigator for the greater Lansing, Michigan, area and was involved in the investigation of over 200 forensic cases.

Alex Perrone, M.A., M.S.N, R.N., P.H.N.

Butte Community College, perroneal@butte.edu

Alex Perrone is a lecturer in anthropology at Butte Community College. She is also a Registered Nurse and a certified Public Health Nurse. She is a former Supervisor of the Human Identification Laboratory in the Department of Anthropology at California State University, Chico. Her research interests include bioarchaeology, paleopathology, forensic anthropology, skeletal biology, California prehistory, and public health. She has worked on bioarchaeological and archaeological projects in Antigua, California, Hawaii, Greece, and the UK, and was an archaeological technician for the USDA Forest Service. She assisted with training courses for local and federal law enforcement agencies and assisted law enforcement agencies with the recovery and analysis of human remains.

Colleen Milligan, Ph.D.

California State University, Chico, cfmilligan@csuchico.edu

Dr. Colleen Milligan is a biological and forensic anthropologist with research interests in bioarchaeology, skeletal biology, and forensic anthropology. She has been a Fellow with the Department of Homeland Security and has assisted in forensic anthropology casework and recoveries in the State of Michigan and California. She has also assisted in community outreach programs in forensic anthropology and forensic science, as well as recovery training courses for local, state, and federal law enforcement officers. She is a certified instructor through Peace Officers Standards and Training (POST). Dr. Milligan serves as the current co-director of the Chico State Human Identification Laboratory.

For Further Exploration

The American Board of Forensic Anthropology (ABFA)

The American Academy of Forensic Sciences (AAFS)

The Organization of Scientific Area Committees for Forensic Science (OSAC)

TRACES Bioarchaeology

Trans Doe Task Force

References

Adams, Bradley J., and Lyle W. Konigsberg, eds. 2008. *Recovery, Analysis, and Identification of Commingled Remains.* Totowa, NJ: Humana Press.

Beatrice, Jared S., and Angela Soler. 2016. "Skeletal Indicators of Stress: A Component of the Biocultural Profile of Undocumented Migrants in Southern Arizona." *Journal of Forensic Sciences* 61 (5): 1164–1172.

Berg, Gregory E. 2017. "Sex Estimation of Unknown Human Skeletal Remains." In *Forensic Anthropology: A Comprehensive Introduction, Second Edition*, edited by Natalie R. Langley and MariaTeresa A. Tersigni-Tarrant, 143–159. Boca Raton, FL: CRC Press.

Bethard, Jonathan D., and Elizabeth A. DiGangi. 2020. "Letter to the Editor—Moving Beyond a Lost Cause: Forensic Anthropology and Ancestry Estimates in the United States." *Journal of Forensic Sciences* 65 (5): 1791–1792.

Birkby, Walter H., Todd W. Fenton, and Bruce E. Anderson. 2008. "Identifying Southwest Hispanics Using Nonmetric Traits and the Cultural Profile." *Journal of Forensic Sciences* 53 (1): 29–33.

Blatt, Samantha, Amy Michael, and Lisa Bright. Forthcoming. "Bioarchaeology: Interpreting Human Behavior from Skeletal Remains." In *TRACES: An Open Invitation to Archaeology.* https://textbooks.whatcom.edu/tracesarchaeology/.

Brooks, S., and J. M. Suchey. 1990. "Skeletal Age Determination Based on the Os Pubis: A Comparison of the Acsádi-Nemeskéri and Suchey-Brooks Methods." *Human Evolution* 5 (3): 227–238.

Buchanan, Shelby. 2014. "Bone Modification in Male to Female Transgender Surgeries: Considerations for the Forensic Anthropologist." MA thesis, Department of Geography and Anthropology, Louisiana State University, Baton Rouge.

Cunningham, Craig, Louise Scheuer, and Sue Black. 2016. *Developmental Juvenile Osteology, Second Edition.* London: Elsevier Academic Press.

Galloway, Alison, ed. 1999. *Broken Bones: Anthropological Analysis of Blunt Force Trauma.* Springfield, IL: Charles C. Thomas Publisher, LTD.

Hefner, Joseph T., and Kandus C. Linde. 2018. *Atlas of Human Cranial Macromorphoscopic Traits.* San Diego: Academic Press.

İşcan, M. Y., S. R. Loth, and R. K. Wright. 1984. "Age Estimation from the Rib by Phase Analysis: White Males." *Journal of Forensic Sciences* 29 (4): 1094–1104.

İşcan, M. Y., S. R. Loth, and R. K. Wright. 1985. "Age Estimation from the Rib by Phase Analysis: White Females." *Journal of Forensic Sciences* 30 (3): 853–863.Katz, Darryl, and Judy Myers Suchey. 1986. "Age Determination of the Male Os Pubis." *American Journal of Physical Anthropology* 69 (4): 427–435.

Komar, Debra A., and Jane E. Buikstra. 2008. *Forensic Anthropology: Contemporary Theory and Practice.* New York: Oxford University Press.

Langley, Natalie R., Alice F. Gooding, and MariaTeresa Tersigni-Tarrant. 2017. "Age Estimation Methods." In *Forensic Anthropology: A Comprehensive Introduction, Second Edition*, edited by Natalie R. Langley and MariaTeresa A. Tersigni-Tarrant, 175–191. Boca Raton, FL: CRC Press.

Lovell, Nancy C. 1997. "Trauma Analysis in Paleopathology." *Yearbook of Physical Anthropology* 104 (S25): 139–170.

Native American Graves Protection and Repatriation Act (NAGPRA) 1990 (25 U.S. Code 3001 et seq.)

NIST (National Institute of Standards and Technology). N.d. "The Organization of Scientific Area Committees for Forensic Science." Accessed April 18, 2023. https://www.nist.gov/topics/organization-scientific-area-committees-forensic-science.

Ousley, Stephen. 1995. "Should We Estimate Biological or Forensic Stature?" *Journal of Forensic Sciences* 40(5): 768–773.

Phenice, T. W. 1969. "A Newly Developed Visual Method of Sexing the Os Pubis." *American Journal of Physical Anthropology* 30 (2): 297–302.

Rose, Jerome C., Thomas J. Green, and Victoria D. Green. 1996. "NAGPRA Is Forever: Osteology and the Repatriation of Skeletons." *Annual Review of Anthropology* 25: 81–103.

Schaefer, Maureen, Sue Black, and Louise Scheuer. *Juvenile Osteology: A Laboratory and Field Manua*l. 2009. San Diego: Elsevier Academic Press.

Schall, Jenna L., Tracy L. Rogers, and Jordan D. Deschamps-Braly. 2020. "Breaking the Binary: The Identification of Trans-women in Forensic Anthropology." *Forensic Science International* 309: 110220. https://doi.org/10.1016/j.forsciint.2020.110220.

Scientific Working Group for Forensic Anthropology (SWGANTH). 2010a. "Personal Identification." Last modified June 3, 2010. https://www.nist.gov/sites/default/files/documents/2018/03/13/swganth_personal_identification.pdf.

Scientific Working Group for Forensic Anthropology (SWGANTH). 2010b. "Sex Assessment." Last modified June 3, 2010. https://www.nist.gov/sites/default/files/documents/2018/03/13/swganth_sex_assessment.pdf.

Scientific Working Group for Forensic Anthropology (SWGANTH). 2011. "Trauma Analysis." Last modified May 27, 2011. https://www.nist.gov/sites/default/files/documents/2018/03/13/swganth_trauma.pdf.

Scientific Working Group for Forensic Anthropology (SWGANTH). 2012. "Stature Estimation." Last modified August 2, 2012. https://www.nist.gov/sites/default/files/documents/2018/03/13/swganth_stature_estimation.pdf.

Scientific Working Group for Forensic Anthropology (SWGANTH). 2013. "Age Estimation." Last modified January 22, 2013. https://www.nist.gov/sites/default/files/documents/2018/03/13/swganth_age_estimation.pdf.

Soler, Angela, and Jared S. Beatrice. 2018. "Expanding the Role of Forensic Anthropology in Humanitarian Crisis: An Example from the USA-Mexico Border. In *Sociopolitics of Migrant Death and Repatriation: Perspectives from Forensic Science*, edited by Krista E. Latham and Alyson J. O'Daniel, 115–128. New York: Springer.

Soler, Angela, Robin Reineke, Jared Beatrice, and Bruce E. Anderson. 2019. "Etched in Bone: Embodied Suffering in the Remains of Undocumented Migrants." *In The Border and Its Bodies: The Embodiment of Risk along the U.S.-México Line*, edited by Thomas E. Sheridan and Randall H. McGuire, 173–207. Tucson: University of Arizona Press.

Stull, Kyra E., Eric J. Bartelink, Alexandra R. Klales, Gregory E. Berg, Michael W. Kenyhercz, Erica N. L'Abbé, Matthew C. Go, et al.. 2021. "Commentary on: Bethard JD, DiGangi EA. Letter to the Editor—Moving Beyond a Lost Cause: Forensic Anthropology and Ancestry Estimates in the United States. J Forensic Sci. 2020;65(5):1791–2. doi: 10.1111/1556-4029.14513." *Journal of Forensic Sciences* 66 (1): 417–420.

Tallman, Sean D., Caroline D. Kincer, and Eric D. Plemons. 2022. "Centering Transgender Individuals in Forensic Anthropology and Expanding Binary Sex Estimation in Casework and Research." Special issue, "Diversity and Inclusion," *Forensic Anthropology* 5 (2): 161–180.

Tersigni-Tarrant, MariaTeresa A., and Natalie R. Langley. 2017. "Human Osteology." In *Forensic Anthropology: A Comprehensive Introduction, Second Edition*, edited by Natalie R. Langley and MariaTeresa A. Tersigni-Tarrant, 81–109. Boca Raton, FL: CRC Press.

Ubelaker, Douglas H. 2018. "A History of Forensic Anthropology." Special issue, "Centennial Anniversary Issue of AJPA," *American Journal of Physical Anthropology* 165 (4): 915–923.

White, Tim D., and Pieter A. Folkens. 2005. *The Human Bone Manual*. Burlington, MA: Elsevier Academic Press.

Winburn, Allysha P., and Bridget Algee-Hewitt. 2021. "Evaluating Population Affinity Estimates in Forensic Anthropology: Insights from the Forensic Anthropology Database for Assessing Methods Accuracy (FADAMA)." *Journal of Forensic Sciences* 66 (4): 1210–1219.

Winburn, Allysha Powanda, Sarah Kiley Schoff, and Michael W. Warren. 2016. "Assemblages of the Dead: Interpreting the Biocultural and Taphonomic Signature of Afro- Cuban Palo Practice in Florida." *Journal of African Diaspora Archaeology and Heritage* 5 (1): 1–37.

16.

CONTEMPORARY TOPICS: HUMAN BIOLOGY AND HEALTH

Joylin Namie, Ph.D., Truckee Meadows Community College

This chapter is a revision from "Chapter 16: Contemporary Topics: Human Biology and Health" by Joylin Namie. In Explorations: An Open Invitation to Biological Anthropology, first edition, edited by Beth Shook, Katie Nelson, Kelsie Aguilera, and Lara Braff, which is licensed under CC BY-NC 4.0.

Learning Objectives

- Describe the major transitions in patterns of disease that have occurred throughout human evolution.
- Describe what is meant by a "mismatch" between our evolved biology and contemporary lifestyles and how this is reflected in modern disease patterns.
- Explain how the human stress response can positively and negatively have an impact on health.
- Explain what a "syndemic" is and why the COVID-19 pandemic represents one.
- Describe the ways institutionalized racism and bias in the medical field contributed to different rates of exposure, differential treatment, morbidity, and mortality from COVID-19 for different ethnic groups in the United States.

When was the last time you needed to do research for an upcoming paper? I bet you started by looking for information online. How did you go about your search? Which websites looked promising? Which ones did not entice you to click past the home page? Once you found one you thought might be useful, how much time did you spend searching for information? At what point did you decide to leave that site and move on? I would wager money that you never once thought your behavior had anything to do with human evolution, but it does.

Although we may not often stop to think about it, our evolutionary past is reflected in many aspects of modern life. The ways we "forage" for information on the internet mimics the ways we once foraged for food during our several-million-year history as hunter-gatherers (Chin et al. 2015). Humans are visual hunters (Lieberman 2006). We practice optimal foraging strategy, meaning we make decisions based on energy return for investment (McElroy and Townsend 2009). When we search for information online, we locate a "patch," in this case a website or research article, then quickly scan the contents to discern how much of it is useful to us. Like our hominin ancestors, we spend more time in "patches" with abundant resources and abandon sites quickly once we have exhausted the available goods. As with internet searches, our evolutionary past is also reflected in the kinds of landscapes we find appealing, the foods that taste good to us, why we break a sweat at the gym, and why we have to go to the gym at all (Bogin 1991; Dutton 2009; Lieberman 2015). Many of the health problems facing humans in the 21st century also have their beginnings in the millions of years we roamed the earth as foragers.

This chapter addresses contemporary health issues from an evolutionary perspective. It begins with a review of diet, activity patterns, and causes of **morbidity** (sickness) and **mortality** (death) among our preagricultural ancestors, which form the foundation for the ways our bodies function today. This is followed by a brief review of the health consequences of the transition to agriculture (see "Cultural Effects of Agriculture" in Chapter 12 for more detail), marking the first of several major **epidemiological transitions** (changes in disease patterns) experienced by humankind. It then addresses health conditions affecting modern, industrialized societies, including **obesity**, diabetes, heart disease, **cancer**, and the effect of stress on health. The environments in which we now live and the choices we make put a strain on biological systems that came about in response to selective pressures in our past, meaning the ways our bodies evolved are, in many ways, a mismatch for the conditions of modern life.

Preagricultural Humans

Diet

Humans may be the species with the longest list of nutritional requirements (Bogin 1991). This is due to the fact that we evolved in environments where there was a high diversity of edible species but low densities of any given species. *Homo sapiens sapiens* require 45–50 essential nutrients for growth, maintenance, and repair of cells and tissues. These include protein, carbohydrates, fats, vitamins, minerals, and water. As a species, we are (or were) physically active with high metabolic demands. We are also **omnivorous** and evolved to choose foods that are dense in essential nutrients. One of the ways we identified high-calorie resources in our evolutionary past was through taste, and it is no accident that humans find sweet, salty, fatty foods appealing.

The human predisposition toward sugar, salt, and fat is innate (Farb and Armelagos 1980). Receptors for sweetness are found in every one of our mouth's 10,000 taste buds (Moss 2013). Preference for sweet makes sense in an ancestral environment where sweetness signaled high-value resources like ripe fruits. Likewise, "the long evolutionary path from sea-dwelling creatures to modern humans has given us salty body fluids, the exact salinity of which must be maintained" (Farb and Armelagos 1980), drawing us to salty-tasting things. Cravings for fat are also inborn, with some archaeological evidence suggesting that hominins collected animal bones for their fatty marrow, which contains two essential fatty acids necessary for brain development (Richards 2002), rather than for any meat remaining on the surface (Bogin 1991).

Bioarchaeological studies indicate Paleolithic peoples ate a wider variety of foods than many people eat today (Armelagos et al. 2005; Bogin 1991; Larsen 2014; Marciniak and Perry 2017). Foragers took in more protein, less fat, much more fiber, and far less sodium than modern humans typically do (Eaton, Konner, and Shostak 1988). Changes in tooth and intestinal morphology illustrate that animal products were an important part of human diets from the time of *Homo erectus* onward (Baltic and Boskovic 2015; Richards 2002; Wrangham 2009). Once cooking became established, it opened up a wider variety of both plant and animal resources to humans. However, the protein, carbohydrates, and fats preagricultural peoples ate were much different from those we eat today. Wild game lacked the antibiotics, growth hormones, and high levels of cholesterol and saturated fat associated with industrialized meat production today (Walker et al. 2005). Wild game was also protein dense, providing only 50% of energy as fat (Lucock et al. 2014). The ways meat is prepared and eaten today also have implications for disease.

Meats cooked well done over high heat and/or over an open flame, including hamburgers and barbecued meats, are highly carcinogenic due to compounds formed during the cooking process (Trafialek and Kolanowski 2014). Processed meats that have been preserved by smoking, curing, salting, or by adding chemical preservatives such as sodium nitrite (e.g., ham, bacon, pastrami, salami, and beef jerky) have been linked to cancers of the colon, lung, and prostate (Abid, Cross, and Sinha 2014; Figure 16.1). Nitrites/nitrates have additionally been linked to cancers of the ovaries, stomach, esophagus, bladder, pancreas, and thyroid (Abid, Cross, and Sinha 2014). In addition, studies analyzing the diets of 103,000 Americans for up to 16 years indicate that those who ate grilled, broiled, or roasted meats more than 15 times per month were 17% more likely to develop high blood pressure than those who ate meat fewer than four times per month, and participants who preferred their meats well done were 15% more likely to suffer from **hypertension** (high blood pressure) than those who ate their meats rare (Liu 2018). A previous study of the same cohort indicated "independent of consumption amount, open-flame and/or high-temperature cooking for both red meat and chicken is associated with an increased risk of type 2 diabetes among adults who consume animal flesh regularly" (Liu et al. 2018). Although meat has been argued to be crucial to cognitive and physical development among hominins (Wrangham 2009), there has been an evolutionary trade-off between the ability to preserve protein through cooking and the health risks of cooked meat and chemical preservatives.

Although carbohydrates represent half of the diet on average for both ancient foragers and modern humans, the types of carbohydrates consumed are very different. Ancient foragers ate fresh fruits, vegetables, grasses, legumes, and tubers, rather than the processed carbohydrates common in industrialized economies (Moss 2013). Their diets also lacked the refined white sugar and corn syrup found in many modern foods that contribute to the development of diabetes (Pontzer et al. 2012).

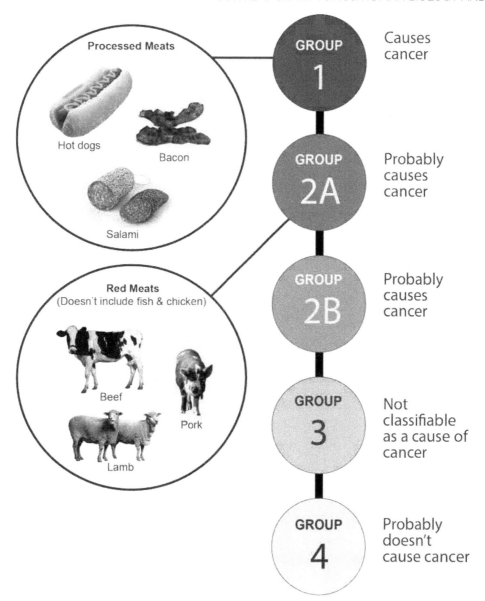

Figure 16.1: Positive associations have been observed between meat consumption and some types of cancer. The International Agency for Research on Cancer (2018) categorized four groupings of cancer risk. The first group is labeled "causes cancer", and the second group "probably causes cancer". Group 1 includes processed meats such as bacon, salami and hot dogs. Group 2A includes red meat such as beef, pork and lamb. Credit: Carcinogenic Meats (Figure 16.1) original to Explorations: An Open Invitation to Biological Anthropology by Katie Nelson is under a CC BY-NC 4.0 License. [Includes Hot dog PNG image by unknown, CC BY-NC 4.0; Rasher of Bacon by unknown, public domain (CC0); Salami aka by André Karwath Aka, CC BY-SA 2.5; Cow PNG image by unknown, CC BY-NC 4.0; sheep PNG image by unknown, CC BY-NC 4.0; Pig on white background by unknown, public domain (CC0).

Physical Activity Patterns

How do we know how active our ancestors were? Hominin morphology and physiology provide us with clues. Adaptations to heat discussed in Chapter 14 evolved in response to the need for physical exertion in the heat of the day in equatorial Africa. Human adaptations for preventing hyperthermia (overheating) suggest an evolutionary history of regular, strenuous physical activity. Research with modern foraging populations also offers clues to ancient activity patterns. Although subject to sampling biases and marginal environments (Marlowe 2005), modern foragers provide the only direct observations of human behavior in the absence of agriculture (Lee 2013). From such studies, we know foragers cover greater distances in single-day foraging bouts than other living primates, and these treks require high levels of cardiovascular endurance (Raichlen and Alexander 2014). Recent research with the Hadza in Tanzania indicates they walk up to 11 kilometers (6.8 miles) daily while hunting and gathering (Pontzer et al. 2012), engaging in moderate-to-vigorous physical activity for over two hours each day—meeting the U.S. government's weekly requirements for physical activity in just two days (Raichlen et al. 2016; Figure 16.2). The fact that humans were physically active in our evolutionary past is also supported by the fact that regular physical exercise has been shown to be protective against a variety of health conditions found in modern humans, including **cardiovascular disease** (Raichlen and Alexander 2014) and Alzheimer's dementia (Mandsager, Harb, and Cremer 2018), even in the presence of brain pathologies indicative of cognitive decline (Buchman et al. 2019).

Figure 16.2: Hadza foragers hunting on foot. Credit: Hadazbe returning from hunt by Andreas Lederer has been modified (cropped) and is under a CC BY 2.0 License.

Infectious Disease

Population size and density remained low throughout the Paleolithic, by some estimates only 0.4 inhabitants per square kilometer (McClellan and Dorn 2006). This limited morbidity and mortality from infectious diseases, which sometimes require large populations to sustain epidemics. Our earliest ancestors had primarily two types of infections with which to contend (Armelagos 1990). The first were organisms that adapted to our prehominin ancestors and have been problems ever since. Examples include head lice, pinworms, and yaws. A second set of diseases were **zoonoses**, diseases that originate in animals and mutate into a form infectious to humans. One example is the Human Immunodeficiency Virus (HIV) that originated in nonhuman primates and was likely passed to humans through the butchering of hunted primates for food (Sharp and Hahn 2011). Zoonoses that could have infected ancient hunter-gatherers include tetanus and **vector-borne diseases** transmitted by flies, mosquitoes, fleas, midges, ticks, and the like. Many of these diseases are slow acting, chronic, or latent, meaning they can last for weeks, months, or even decades, causing low levels of sickness and allowing victims to infect others over long periods of time. Survival or cure does not result in lasting immunity, with survivors returning to the pool of potential victims. Such diseases often survive in animal reservoirs, reinfecting humans again and again (Wolfe et al. 2012). A study of bloodsucking insects preserved in samples of amber dating from 15 to 100 million years ago indicates that they carried microorganisms that today cause diseases such as river blindness, typhus, Lyme disease, and malaria (Poinar 2018). Such diseases may have been infecting humans throughout our history and may have had significant impacts on small foraging communities because they more often infected adults, who provided the food supply (Armelagos et al. 2005).

Health

Given their diets, levels of physical activity, and low population densities, nomadic preagricultural humans were likely in better health than many modern populations. This assertion is supported by comparative research conducted with modern foraging and industrialized populations. Measures of health taken from 20th-century foraging populations demonstrate excellent aerobic capacity, as measured by oxygen uptake during exertion, and low body-fat percentages, with **triceps skinfold measurements** half those of white Canadians and Americans. Serum cholesterol levels were also low, and markers for diabetes, hypertension, and cardiovascular disease were missing among them (Eaton, Konner, and Shostak 1988; Raichlen et al. 2016).

Health Consequences of the Transition to Agriculture and Animal Domestication

The shift from foraging to food production occurred relatively recently in our evolutionary history (Larsen 2014), and there are indications our biology has not yet caught up (Pritchard 2010). Beginning around 12,000 BCE in several parts of the globe, humans began to move toward a diet based on domesticated plants and animals (Armelagos et al. 2005). This involved manipulating the natural landscape to facilitate intensive food production, including the clearing of forest and construction of wells, irrigation canals, and ditches, exposing humans to water-borne illnesses and parasites and attracting mosquitos and other vectors of disease to human settlements. The heavy, repetitive physical labor of early agricultural production resulted in negative impacts on articular joints, including **osteoarthritis** (Larsen 2014). At the same time, nutritional diversity became restricted, focused on major cereal crops that continue to dominate agricultural production today, including corn, wheat, and rice (Jain 2012). This represented a major shift in diet from a wide variety of plant and animal foods to dependence on starchy carbohydrates, leading to increases in dental caries (cavities), reductions in stature and growth rates, and nutritional deficiencies (Larsen 2014). Domesticated animals added new foods to the human diet, including meat that was higher in fat and cholesterol than wild game as well as dairy products (Lucock et al. 2014). Agriculture provided the means to produce a storable surplus for the first time in human history, leading to the beginnings of economic inequality (see Chapter 12). Social hierarchies led to the unequal distribution of resources, concentrating infectious disease among the poor and malnourished (Zuckerman et al. 2014), a situation that continues to plague humanity today (Marmot 2005).

Sedentism and a rise in population density accompanied the move to agriculture, increasing the risk of infectious disease. Agriculture often provided enough calories, if not enough nutrition, to increase fertility. Although diets were worse and people unhealthier, populations continued to grow, even in the midst of high levels of child and maternal mortality and short life expectancies (Omran 2005). Hygiene became an issue as large settlements increased the problem of removing human waste and providing uncontaminated water (Armelagos et al. 2005). Domesticated animals provided reservoirs of zoonotic pathogens, which affected farmers more than foragers, as farmers were in closer proximity to their animals on a daily basis (Marciniak and Perry 2017). Many of these diseases became major killers of humankind, including influenza, tuberculosis, malaria, plague, syphilis, and smallpox, functioning as selective pressures in and of themselves (Cooling 2015). As these diseases encountered large human populations, they caused major epidemics that traveled along newly established routes for trade, warfare, and colonization.

Epidemiological Transitions

Changes in diet and physical-activity patterns, population densities, and exposure to zoonoses associated with agriculture resulted in an epidemiological transition, a shift in the causes of morbidity (sickness) and mortality (death) among humankind (Omran 2005). The first epidemiological transition from foraging to food production resulted in increases in dental caries (see Chapter 12), nutritional deficiencies, infectious disease, and skeletal conditions like osteoarthritis, as well as decreases in growth and height (Larsen 2014). A second epidemiological transition occurred following the Industrial Revolution in Western Europe and the United States when improved standards of living, hygiene, and nutrition minimized the effects of infectious disease, after which people began to experience higher rates of **noncommunicable diseases**, such as cancer, heart disease, and diabetes due to the changes in lifestyle, diet, and activity levels that are the subject of this chapter (Omran 2005). With the addition of immunizations and other public health initiatives, modified forms of this transition remain ongoing in many low- and middle-income countries (Zuckerman et al. 2014), with several now facing a **"double burden"** of disease, with poor, often rural, populations struggling with infectious diseases due to malnutrition, lack of sanitation, and access to health care, while more affluent citizens are victims of chronic illnesses. A third epidemiological transition is now underway as infectious diseases, including new, re-emergent, and multidrug-resistant diseases, have once again become major health concerns (Harper and Armelagos 2010; Zuckerman et al. 2014). These include COVID-19, Ebola, HIV/AIDS, tuberculosis, malaria, dengue, Lyme disease, and West Nile virus—all zoonoses that initially spread to humans through contact with animals.

Patterns of morbidity and mortality continue to shift across the globe. As with the first epidemiological transition resulting from the adoption of large-scale agriculture, such shifts can be the direct, if unintended, result of human interactions with the environment. For example, there has been a rise in chronic inflammatory diseases (CIDs) in developed countries (Versini et al. 2015). This includes increased rates of allergic conditions like asthma and autoimmune diseases like rheumatoid arthritis, multiple sclerosis, Crohn's disease, and inflammatory bowel disease. This has coincided with the decrease in infectious disease associated with the second epidemiological transition, and the two are related. The "hygiene hypothesis" postulates the rise in CIDs is a result of limited exposure to nonlethal environmental pathogens in utero and early childhood (Zuckerman and Armelagos 2014). Modern human societies have become so sanitized that we are no longer exposed to microorganisms that stimulate the development of a healthy immune system (Versini et al. 2015). "In effect, the lifestyle changes—sanitary improvements, pasteurization, use of antibiotics, and improved hygiene—that contributed to the second transition may have produced a substantial trade-off, with developed nations exchanging a high burden of infectious disease for a higher burden of CIDs" (Zuckerman et al. 2014).

The third epidemiological transition, the re-emergence of infectious disease, reflects the continuing relationship between humans, animals, and pathogens. Over 60% of **emerging infectious diseases (EIDs)** since 1940 have been of zoonotic origin, with over 70% stemming from human contact with wildlife (Jones et al. 2008), including COVID-19. The crossover of COVID to humans is believed to have involved transmission from bats to an intermediate species then to humans, with infected humans then passing it to other humans in a wet market in Wuhan, China in late 2019 (Worobey et al. 2022). Two COVID variants, representing two distinct crossover events from animals to humans, were circulating in the market by February 2020. Similarly, the global bushmeat trade currently devastating Africa's wildlife is a continuing source of Ebola infection (Asher 2017), as well as the original source of HIV and viruses related to leukemia and lymphoma among humans (Zuckerman et al. 2014). New strains of avian (bird) flu, some with mortality rates as high as 60% among humans (WHO n.d.), are transmitted to humans through poultry production and contact with wild birds (Davis 2005). Lastly, the use of antibiotics in commercial meat production is directly related to the rise of drug-resistant strains of previously controlled infectious diseases. An estimated 80% of antibiotics in the U.S. are used to promote growth and prevent infection in livestock, and drug-resistant bacteria from these animals are transmitted to humans through meat consumption (Ventola 2015).

Figure 16.3: Flooding in Sindh, Pakistan, in 2022. Credit: Flood in Pakistan by Ali Hyder Junejo is under a CC BY 2.0 License.

A fourth epidemiological transition is currently underway in which some parts of the globe are suffering from a **"triple burden"** of infectious and chronic diseases combined with injuries and diseases related to intensifying globalization, urbanization, deforestation, and climate change (Karn and Sharma 2021). Massive flooding in Pakistan in 2022 (Figure 16.3) will serve to illustrate the concept. Following a severe heat wave in June 2022, Pakistan experienced extremely heavy seasonal monsoon rains, in some provinces 700% above normal. Combined with water flow from melting glaciers, this caused the worst flooding in the country's history, putting one third of the nation under water (Sheerazi 2022). The heat wave, glacial melt, and extreme rainfall were all attributable to global climate change, inflicting destruction and disease on Pakistan, which produces less than 1% of total global carbon emissions (Government of Pakistan 2021).

As a direct result of the flooding, infrastructure, including roads, homes, and bridges, was destroyed, and 1,700 people died, nearly 13,000 were injured, and over 33 million were displaced. In addition to their initial injuries and trauma, displaced people lacked food, health care, safe water, and basic sanitation, leading to starvation and exposure to infectious diseases like malaria and dengue fever, as well as skin conditions like scabies, caused by mites. Pakistan also has a poverty rate of 30–40%, contributing to already-high rates of HIV, tuberculosis, and hepatitis. At the same time, the leading causes of death are heart disease, cancer, lower respiratory diseases, and stroke (CDC n.d), all chronic conditions.

These examples illustrate continuing interaction between humans, our evolved biology, and the physical and cultural environments in which we live. The remainder of this chapter will focus on selected diseases and the social, cultural, and environmental factors that contribute to their **prevalence** in modern, industrialized economies. We begin with the health condition that affects all of the others—obesity.

Obesity

According to the World Health Organization (2017), 1.9 billion of the world's people are overweight and 650 million of these are obese. In the United States, 70% of Americans are overweight, and 40% of these meet the criteria for obesity. For the first time in human history, most of the world's population lives in countries where overweight and obesity kill more people than hunger (Figure 16.4). Improvements in public health and food production have allowed a greater number of people to live past childhood and to have enough to eat. This does not include everyone. Many people still struggle with poverty, hunger, and disease, even in the wealthiest of nations, including the United States. On a global scale, however, many people not only have enough food to survive but also to gain weight—enough extra weight to cause health problems.

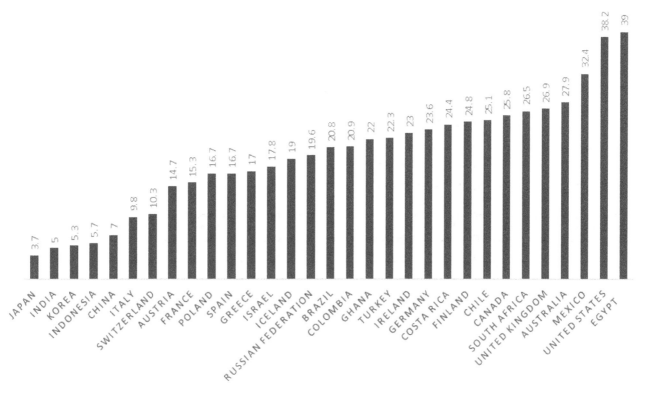

PERCENTAGE OF POPULATION WITH BMI OVER 30

Figure 16.4: Obesity rates by country, 2017. Credit: Obesity rates by country (Figure 16.3) original to Explorations: An Open Invitation to Biological Anthropology by Katie Nelson is under a CC BY-NC 4.0 License. Based on Obesity Update 2017. [Image Description].

Although studies show differences in daily energy expenditure between foraging and farming populations compared with industrialized peoples, the major contributor to obesity in Western populations is energy intake (Pontzer et al. 2012). Many people not only eat too much but too much of the wrong things. Biological anthropologist Leslie Lieberman (2006) argues that contemporary humans continue to rely on cues from foraging strategies of our evolutionary past that are now counterproductive in the **obesogenic** environments in which we now live.

Examine your own eating habits in the context of how humans once hunted and gathered. Humans once relied on visual cues to find food, often traveled long distances to obtain it, then transported it back to our home base. There they may have had to process it by hand to render it edible. Think of how much less energy it takes to find food now. If we have the financial resources, we can acquire big energy payoffs by simply sitting at home and using an app on our mobile phone to place an order for delivery. And, voila! High-calorie (if not highly nutritious) food arrives at our door. Should we venture out for food, search time is reduced by signage and advertising directing us toward high-density "patches" where food is available 24 hours a day. These include vending machines, gas stations, and fast-food outlets. Travel time is minimal and little human energy is used in the process (Lieberman 2006).

Foods are also prepackaged and prepared in ways that allow us to eat large quantities quickly. Think French fries or chicken nuggets, which we can easily eat with our hands while doing other things, like driving or watching television, rendering eating mindless and allowing us to take in food faster than our **endocrine systems** can tell us we are getting full. Modern "patches" offer low-fiber, calorie-dense resources, which allow us to eat larger quantities, a problem already encouraged by larger portion sizes (Lieberman 2006). Processed foods are also engineered to appeal to human preferences for sweet tastes and fatty, creamy textures (Moss 2013). Remember from earlier chapters that natural selection favored depth perception, color vision, grasping hands, and coordinated eye-hand movements as general primate traits. Advertising and packaging now use our color vision against us, attracting us to products that have little nutritional value but that play to our evolutionary predisposition toward variety. Remember those 50 different nutrients we require? That variety is now presented to us in the form of 55 different flavors of Oreo cookies (Cerón 2017), which we take out of the package and dip in milk using our hand-eye coordination and depth perception.

Even if we are ostensibly eating the same things our ancestors did, these foods are nothing alike. Take potatoes, for example. One medium-sized, plain, baked potato is a healthy food, especially if we eat the skin too. It contains 110 calories, 0 grams of fat, 26 grams of carbohydrates, and 3 grams of protein, plus 30% of the U.S. Recommended Daily Allowance (RDA) of vitamin C, 10% of vitamin B6, 15% of potassium, and no sodium (Potato USA). In contrast, a medium order of McDonald's fries, which takes the potato and adds salt and fat, contains 340 calories, 16 grams of fat, 44 grams of carbohydrates, 4 grams of protein, and 230 mg of sodium (McDonalds). Potato chips take food processing to a whole new level, removing even more nutrition and adding a host of additional ingredients, including oils, preservatives, and artificial flavorings and colors (Moss 2013). Take Ruffles Loaded Bacon and Cheddar Potato Skins Potato Chips as an example (St. Pierre 2018). The number of ingredients increases from one to 11 to 35 as we move from the potato to the potato chip, moving further from nature with each step (Figure 16.5). It should be noted that the nutritional information for the potato chips is based on a serving size of 11 chips, an amount likely smaller than many people eat. Many sweet, fatty, salty foods like fries and chips are cheap, which is why many people choose to eat them (Moss 2013). The price of a medium-sized order of McDonald's fries as of this writing is US$1.79, and the potato chips are $2.98 for an 8.5-ounce bag. A single potato prewrapped for microwaving is available in many supermarkets for US$1.99 but requires access to a microwave and eating utensils, making it less convenient.

Figure 16.5: The potato in three modern forms. Credit: The potato in three modern forms (Figure 16.4) original to Explorations: An Open Invitation to Biological Anthropology by Joylin Namie and Katie Nelson is a collective work under a CC BY-NC 4.0 License. [Includes Potato by Charles Rondeau, public domain (CC0); McDonalds-French-Fries-Plate by Evan-Amos, public domain (CC0); Potato chips bowl by pdpics.com, public domain (CC0).]

	Baked Potato [based, skin on, plain]	French Fries [Medium order]	Potato Chips [1 oz. serving of 11 chips]
Calories	110	340	
Calories from fat	0	144	
Fat	0g	16g	
Carbohydrates	26g	44g	
Protein	3g	4g	
Sodium	0g	230mg	
Dietary fiber	2g	4g	
Sugars	1g	0g	
Cholesterol	0g	0g	
Ingredients	Potato	Potatoes, vegetable oil (canola oil), soybean oil, hydrogenated soybean oil, natural beef flavor (wheat and milk derivatives), citric acid (preservative), dextrose, sodium acid pyrophosphate (main color), salt.	Potatoes, vegetable oil (sunflower, corn, and/or canola oil), bacon and chedder loaded potato skins seasoning (maltodextrin – made from corn) salt, cheddar cheese (milk, cheese cultures, salt enzymes), sour cream (cultured cream, skin milk), whey, dried onion, monosodium.

Not only have we transformed the food supply and our eating in ways that are detrimental to our health, but these changes have been accompanied by reductions in physical activity. **Sedentarism** is built into contemporary lifestyles. Think of how much time you spent sitting down today. Some of it may have been in class or at work, some may have been driving a car or perhaps binge-watching your favorite show, playing a video game, or checking in on social media. An inactive lifestyle is almost dictated by the digital age (Lucock et al. 2014). Levels of physical activity in many countries are now so low that large portions of the population are completely sedentary, including one in five Americans (CDC 2022). For a species whose biology evolved in an environment where walking, lifting, and carrying were part of daily life, this is unhealthy and often leads to weight gain.

Biology and Genetics of Weight

Research indicates multiple genetic variants influence weight gain, and they are not spread evenly among human populations. Tuomo Rankinen and colleagues (2006) identified 127 genes associated with obesity, of which 22 contributed to weight gain. Claude Bouchard (2007) then identified five categories of obesity-promoting genotypes. These genotypes promote sedentarism, result in low metabolism, and lead to poor regulation of appetite, and a propensity to overeat. An example of the impact such genotypes can have in an environment of plenty is found among the population of the Micronesian island of Nauru. Historically, the island was geographically isolated and the food supply was unpredictable. These conditions favored genotypes that promoted the ability to rapidly build up and store fat in times of food availability. In Nauruans, there are two genetic variants favoring weight gain and insulin resistance, and both are associated with obesity and type 2 diabetes. One variant is also associated with hypertension. One of these variants is also found in Pima Indians, who live in parts of Arizona and Mexico. In the Pima, this variant is associated with a high **body mass index (BMI)** and type 2 diabetes, although it is not associated with the same outcomes in Japanese and British subjects (de Silva et al. 1999). The other variant was analyzed in Finnish and South Indian populations, neither of whom experienced the same outcome as Nauruans. This suggests these alleles may act as modifying genes for type 2 diabetes in some population groups (Baker et al. 1994). Unfortunately, Nauruans are one of those groups. Eventually, they became wealthy through phosphate mining on the island, gaining access to a calorie-rich Western diet of imported foods and developing a sedentary lifestyle. This resulted in rates of type 2 diabetes as high as 30–40% in Nauruans over the age of 15, which became the leading cause of death (Lucock et al. 2014), something Nauruans are taking seriously (Figure 16.6).

Figure 16.6: Participants of a walk against diabetes and for general fitness around Nauru airport. Credit: Participants of a walk against Diabetes and for general fitness around Nauru airport by Lorrie Graham, Department of Foreign Affairs and Trade, is under a CC BY 2.0 License.

Factors other than biology influence which populations that carry a genetic predisposition to diabetes actually express it. The Pima Indians of Arizona, for example, were seriously impacted by U.S. government policies that affected water rights, forcing the population away from subsistence farming to dependence on government handouts and convenience food. This resulted in a significant loss of physical activity, malnutrition, and obesity. The Pima continue to experience hardship due to high rates of unemployment, poverty, and depression, sometimes made worse by alcoholism. In the absence of these pressures, the Pima were diabetes free for centuries prior, even though they relied on agriculture for subsistence, suggesting genetics alone is not responsible for high rates of obesity and diabetes in current Pima Indian populations (Smith-Morris 2004).

Medical Complications of Obesity

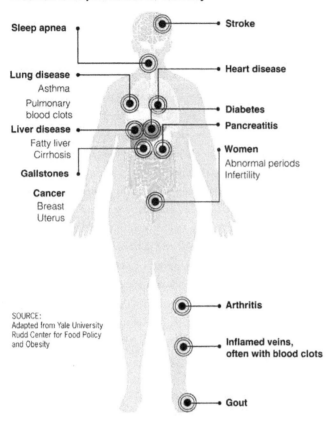

Sleep apnea

Lung disease
Asthma
Pulmonary
blood clots

Liver disease
Fatty liver
Cirrhosis

Gallstones

Cancer
Breast
Uterus

Stroke

Heart disease

Diabetes

Pancreatitis

Women
Abnormal periods
Infertility

Arthritis

Inflamed veins,
often with blood clots

Gout

SOURCE:
Adapted from Yale University
Rudd Center for Food Policy
and Obesity

Figure 16.7: Medical complications of obesity include stroke, sleep apnea, lung disease, liver disease, gallstones, cancer, heart disease, diabetes, pancreatitis, abnormal periods and infertility, arthritis, inflamed veins, and gout. Credit: **Medical complications of obesity** by the **Centers for Disease Control and Prevention (CDC)** has been modified (color changed and cancer list shortened) and is in the **public domain**.

Obesity also has an epigenetic component. You learned about epigenetics in Chapter 3. With regard to obesity, epigenetics is counterintuitive in that mothers who do not take in enough calories during pregnancy often give birth to babies who grow up to be fat. What takes place is the fetus receives signals during pregnancy from its mother through the placenta and intrauterine environment about environmental conditions outside of the womb, in this case food insecurity. These signals encourage the turning on and off of genes related to metabolism. This alters the phenotype of the fetus so that if the child is born into an environment where food is plentiful, it will put on weight rapidly whenever possible, leading to obesity and related diseases later in life. If the child is a girl, her own eggs are formed in utero with the same genetic changes coded in, meaning she will pass along this same genetic predisposition to gain weight to her children. Hence, a biological propensity toward obesity can continue across generations (Worthman and Kuzara 2005). Epigenetic changes to genes that promote weight gain are argued to be partly responsible for the rapid rise in obesity and diabetes in developing countries gaining access to Western diets (Stearns, Nesse, and Haig 2008).

Obesity and overweight put a strain on several biological systems of the body, including the **circulatory**, endocrine, and skeletal systems, contributing to hypertension, heart disease, **stroke**, diabetes, and osteoarthritis (Figure 16.7). Obesity also elevates the risk of cancers of the breast, endometrium, kidney, colon, esophagus, stomach, pancreas, and gallbladder (National Institutes of Health 2017; Vucenik and Stains 2012). Diabetes—one of the fastest-growing health conditions around the globe (WHO 2016) and one tightly connected to obesity and overweight—is the focus of the following Special Topics box.

Special Topic: Diabetes

Diabetes mellitus is an endocrine disorder characterized by excessively high blood glucose levels (Martini et al. 2013). According to a report released by the World Health Organization, the number of people living with diabetes is growing in all regions of the world. Rates of diabetes have nearly doubled in the past three decades, largely due to increases in obesity and sugary diets (WHO 2016). One in 10 people around the world, 537 million people, now have diabetes, and three out of four live in low- and middle-income countries (IDF 2022). In the United States, 37 million people have diabetes (CDC 2020), where the disease is rising fastest among millennials (those ages 20–40) (BCBSA 2017), and one in every two adults with diabetes is undiagnosed (IDF 2022). Obesity and diabetes are linked: obesity causes a diet-related disease (diabetes) because of humans' evolved metabolic homeostasis mechanism, which is poorly suited to contemporary energy environments (Lucock et al. 2014).

To function properly, cells need a steady fuel supply. Blood sugar (glucose) is the fuel for most cells in the body, and the body produces the hormone **insulin** to help move glucose into cells that need it (Figure 16.8). Foods that most readily supply glucose to your bloodstream are carbohydrates, especially starchy foods like potatoes or sweet, sugary foods like candy and soda. The body can also convert other types of foods, including protein-rich foods (e.g., lean meats) and fatty foods (e.g., vegetable oils and butter), into blood sugar in the liver via gluconeogenesis. Insulin's main job is to tell your cells when to take up glucose. The cell also has to listen to the signal and mobilize the glucose transporters. This not only allows your cells to get the energy they need, but it also keeps blood sugar from building up to dangerously high levels when you are at rest.

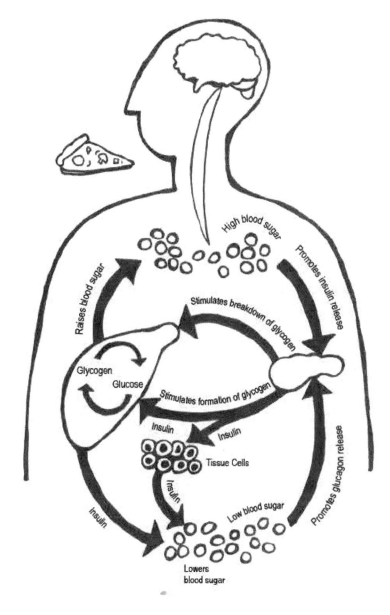

Figure 16.8: Carbohydrates are eaten and broken down into simple sugars (e.g., glucose). Glucose enters the bloodstream from the intestines, and the increase in glucose stimulates the pancreas to release insulin into the bloodstream. Insulin deposits glucose in the muscles and fat cells, where it is stored and used for energy. Credit: Glucose metabolism (Figure 16.7) original to Explorations: An Open Invitation to Biological Anthropology by Mary Nelson is under a CC BY-NC 4.0 License.

This system has limits. Like the rest of our biology, it evolved during several million years when sugar was hard to come by and carbohydrates took the form of fresh foods with a low **glycemic index (GI)**. Our ancestors were also active throughout the day, taking pressure off of the endocrine system. Now, sedentary lifestyles and processed-food diets cause many of us to take in more calories—and especially more carbohydrates—than our bodies can handle. There is only so much blood sugar your cells can absorb. Many modern populations are taxing those limits. After years of being asked by insulin to take in more glucose than they can use, cells eventually stop responding (McKee and McKee 2015). This is called type 2 diabetes or insulin resistance, which accounts for 90–95% of diabetes cases in the United States (Figure 16.9). type 1 diabetes is believed to be caused by an autoimmune response in which your immune system is attacking and destroying the insulin-producing cells in your pancreas (Figure 16.9). type 1 diabetes is a genetic condition that often shows up early in life, while type 2 is more lifestyle-related and develops over time.

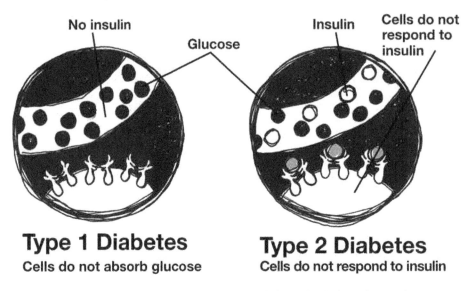

Figure 16.9: Type 1 and type 2 diabetes. For Type 1 Diabetes, cells do not absorb glucose becuase there is no insulin. For Type 2 Diabetes, although there is insulin available, cells do not respond to it. Credit: Type 1 and Type 2 Diabetes (Figure 16.8) original to Explorations: An Open Invitation to Biological Anthropology by Mary Nelson has been modified (text) and is under a CC BY-NC 4.0 License.

Cardiovascular Disease

Cardiovascular disease (CVD)—which includes coronary heart disease, hypertension (high blood pressure), and stroke—is the leading cause of death globally, and heart disease remains the number one cause of death in the United States (American Heart Association 2018). Risk factors for cardiovascular disease include diet, obesity/overweight, diabetes, smoking and alcohol consumption, and physical inactivity.

The connections between these factors and heart disease may not seem obvious and will be addressed here beginning with diet. Diets high in saturated fat and cholesterol can lead to atherosclerosis, a condition in which fat and cholesterol form plaque inside the arteries, eventually building up and hardening to the point that blood flow is blocked. Too much salt in the diet leads to fluid retention, which increases blood volume and thereby blood pressure, taxing the heart. Obesity/overweight contribute to cardiovascular disease directly through increases in total blood volume, cardiac output, and cardiac workload. In other words, the heart has to work much harder if one is overweight (Akil and Ahmad 2011). Obesity also relates to CVD indirectly through elevation of blood pressure (hypertension) and diabetes. High levels of blood glucose from diabetes can damage blood vessels and the nerves that control the heart and blood vessels. Alcohol consumption can raise blood pressure and triglyceride levels, a type of fat found in the blood. Alcohol also adds extra calories, which may cause weight gain, especially around the abdomen, which is directly associated with risk of a heart attack (Akil and Ahmad 2011). Cigarette smoking also increases the risk of coronary heart disease. Nicotine increases blood pressure; in addition, cigarette smoke causes fatty buildup in the main artery in the neck and thickens blood, making it more likely to clot. It also decreases levels of HDL ("good") cholesterol (American Heart Association 2018). Even secondhand smoke can have an adverse effect if exposure occurs on a regular basis. Chronic psychological stress also elevates the risk of heart disease (Dimsdale 2008). The repeated release of stress hormones like adrenaline elevates blood pressure and may eventually damage artery walls. The human **stress response** and its connections to health and disease are discussed in more detail below.

However, physical activity alters the likelihood of having heart disease, both directly and indirectly. Regular exercise of moderate to vigorous intensity strengthens the heart muscle and allows capillaries, tiny blood vessels in your body, to widen, improving blood flow. Regular exercise can also lower blood pressure and cholesterol levels and manage blood sugar levels, all of which reduce the risk of CVD.

Cancer

Cancer is the second-leading cause of death globally, causing one in every six deaths and killing nearly nine million people in 2015 (WHO 2018). Lifetime cancer risk in developed Western populations is now one in two, or 50% (Greaves 2015). Approximately one-third of deaths from cancer are due to behavioral and dietary factors, including high body mass index (BMI), low fruit and vegetable intake, lack of physical activity, and the use of tobacco and alcohol. Depending on the type of cancer and one's own genetic inheritance, these factors can increase cancer risk from 2- to 100-fold (Greaves 2015). Cancer is the result of interactions between a person's genes and three categories of external agents: physical carcinogens (e.g., ultraviolet radiation), chemical carcinogens (e.g., tobacco smoke, asbestos), and biological carcinogens, such as infections from certain viruses, bacteria, or parasites (WHO 2018). Obesity is also a risk factor for cancer, including of the breast, endometrium, kidney, colon, esophagus, stomach, pancreas, and gallbladder (National Institutes of Health 2017; Vucenik and Stains 2012).

Cancer has been regarded as a relatively recent affliction for humans that became a problem after we were exposed to modern carcinogens and lived long enough to express the disease (David and Zimmerman 2010). Given the long history that humans share with many oncogenic (cancer-causing) parasites and viruses (Ewald 2018), and the recent discovery of cancer in the metatarsal bone of a 1.8-million-year-old hominin (Odes et al. 2016), this view is being challenged (See "Special Topic: Life Choices and Reproductive Cancers in Women"). The difficulties of identifying cancer in archaeological populations are many. Most cancer occurs in soft tissue, which rarely preserves, and fast-growing cancers would likely kill victims before leaving evidence in bone. It is also difficult to distinguish cancer from benign growths and inflammatory disease in ancient fossils, and there is often postmortem damage to fossil evidence from scavenging and erosion. However, using 3-D images, South African researchers recently diagnosed a type of cancer called osteosarcoma in a toe bone belonging to a human relative who died in Swartkrans Cave between 1.6 and 1.8 million years ago (Randolph-Quinney et al. 2016). This study provides the earliest evidence of cancer in hominins.

Special Topic: Life Choices and Reproductive Cancers in Women

Behavioral or "lifestyle" choices have an impact on cancer risk. Breast cancer is one example. It is the most common cancer in women worldwide, but **incidence** of new cases varies from 19.3 per 100,000 women in Eastern Africa to 89.7 per 100,000 women in Western Europe (WHO 2018). These differences are attributable to cultural changes among women in Western, industrialized countries that are a mismatch for our evolved reproductive biology. Age at **menarche**, the onset of menstrual periods, has dropped over the course of the last century from 16 to 12 years of age in the U.S. and Europe, with some girls getting their periods and developing breasts as young as eight years old (Greenspan and Deardorff 2014, Figure 16.10). A World Health Organization study involving 34 countries in Europe and North America suggests the primary reason for the increase in earlier puberty is obesity, with differences in BMI accounting for 40% of individual- and country-level variance (Currie et al. 2012). Early puberty in girls is associated with increased risk of breast cancer, ovarian cancer, diabetes, and high cholesterol in later life (Pierce and Hardy 2012).

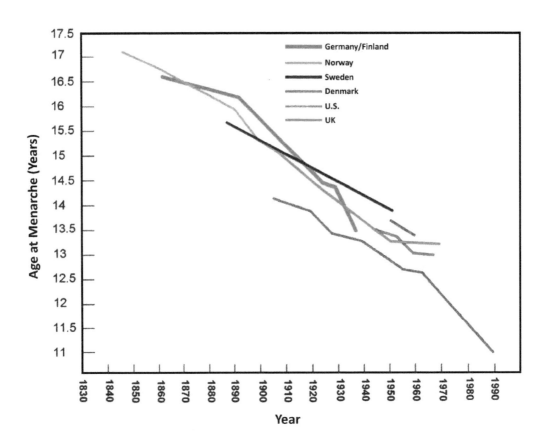

Figure 16.10: Decreasing ages at time of first menstruation in selected countries. Credit: Acceleration1.jpg by Yahadzija is under a CC BY-SA 3.0 Unported License. [Image Description].

At the same time that age at puberty is dropping for girls in Western nations, age at birth of the first child is later, at 26 years old (Mathews and Hamilton 2016). Women are also having fewer children, two on average (Gao 2015), with 15% of women choosing to remain childless (Livingston 2015). Rates of breastfeeding have risen in recent decades but drop to only 27% of infants once babies reach 12 months of age (CDC 2014). In contrast, data from modern foraging populations (Eaton et al. 1994) indicate that age at menarche is around 16 years old, age at birth of the first child is 19, breastfeeding on-demand continues for three years for each child, and the number of children averages six. These differences relate to elevated risk for reproductive cancers, including breast cancer, among women in developed countries.

Other than an established genetic risk (e.g., BRCA gene), the primary risk factor for breast cancer is exposure to estrogen. For women living in modern, industrialized economies, this exposure now often comes from women's own ovaries rather than from external environmental sources (Stearns, Nesse, and Haig 2008). There is nothing biologically normal about regular monthly periods. Women in cultures without contraception are pregnant or breastfeeding for much of their reproductive lives, resulting in 100 or so menstrual cycles per lifetime. In contrast, Western women typically experience 400 or more (Strassmann 1997). This is partly due to early puberty. From menarche to the birth of a woman's first child can be 14 years or longer in Western populations, after which breastfeeding, if undertaken at all, lasts for a few weeks or months. Oral contraceptives or other hormonal methods to control reproduction induce monthly periods. Age at menopause (the cessation of menstrual cycles) is 50–55 years old across human populations. For Western women, this translates into forty years of menstrual cycling. Each month the body prepares for a pregnancy that never occurs, experiencing cell divisions that put women at risk for cancers of the breast, endometrium, ovaries, and uterus (Strassmann 1999). Obesity adds to risk, as adipose (fat) tissues are the main source of estrogen biosynthesis. Thus, weight gain during the postmenopausal stage means higher exposure to estrogen and a greater risk of cancer (Ali 2014).

Women cannot return to our evolutionary past, and there are important social and economic reasons for delaying pregnancy and having fewer children. These include achieving educational and career goals, greater earning power, a reduction in the gender pay gap, more enduring marriages, and a decrease in the number of women needing public assistance (Sonfield et al. 2013). There are also cultural means by which we might reduce the risk of reproductive cancers. These include reformulating hormonal contraceptives with enough estrogen to maintain bone density but reducing the number of menstrual periods over the reproductive lifespan (Stearns, Nesse, and Haig 2008). Reducing fat intake may also lower estrogen levels. High-fat diets contribute to breast tumor development, while high fiber diets are beneficial in decreasing intestinal resorption of estrogenic hormones. Exercise also appears protective. Studies of former college athletes demonstrate risks of breast, uterine, and ovarian cancers later in life two to five times lower than those of nonathletes (Eaton et al. 1994).

Stress

Have you ever been "stressed out" in class? Say you're in a large lecture hall with a hundred other people, or even in a small class where you don't know anyone. You're not sure about something the professor just said and you would really like to ask about it, so you start to raise your hand. Does your heart begin to pound and your mouth become dry? Do you get so nervous that you choose to ask a classmate after lecture instead? If so, you are not alone. Fear of speaking in public is one of the most common social phobias (APA 2013). It has been estimated that 75% of all people experience some degree of anxiety or nervousness when it comes to public speaking (Hamilton 2011), and surveys have shown that most people fear public speaking more than they fear death (Croston 2012).

We have evolution to thank for this.

Humans, like other primates, are social animals. Being part of a group helped us to survive predation, get enough to eat, and successfully raise our young. When faced with standing up in front of a group, or even speaking up in class, we break into a sweat because we are afraid of rejection. Psychologist Glenn Croston (2012) writes, "The fear is so great because we are not merely afraid of being embarrassed or judged. We are afraid of being rejected from the social group, ostracized and left to defend ourselves all on our own. We fear ostracism still so much today it seems, fearing it more than death, because not so long ago getting kicked out of the group probably really was a death sentence." Hence, it is no surprise that public speaking triggers a stress response among much of humankind.

The human nervous system evolved in a context where quick responses to perceived threats presented an evolutionary advantage. The "fight or flight" response was honed during millions of years when threats more often took the form of an approaching lion than an approaching deadline. Our body's stress response, however, is triggered by a wide variety of stressors that produce the same general pattern of hormonal and physiological adjustments (Martini et al. 2013). In today's world, the system is often stuck in the "on" position due to the constant pressures of modern life, and this is a significant influence on health and disease.

It is important to recognize that there are different types of stress and the time in life when adult coping mechanisms are formed is in childhood. In children, some stressors can be positive—for example, stressors that are mild to moderate in magnitude, and accompanied by the support of a caring adult, which help children develop pathways by which stress is dealt with by the body throughout life. In a young child, a positive stress response might be going to the pediatrician to receive a vaccination and receiving encouragement and comfort from both parent and practitioner. A tolerable stress response is more serious, precipitated by something like a divorce or death of a relative. Again, buffered by positive support from surrounding adults, these types of stressors can be successfully managed by children. Toxic stress, however, "results from strong, frequent or prolonged activation of the stress response in the absence of the buffering protection of a supportive adult relationship" (Shonkoff and Garner 2012). Examples include child abuse or neglect, parental substance abuse, homelessness, and violence. In the absence of adequate psychological and physical support, the biological pathways of a child's physiological stress response are altered and lead to reduced abilities to cope with life's challenges as an adult.

The negative effects of sustained, elevated cortisol levels on health are well documented. These include higher levels of infectious disease and slowed growth in childhood (Flinn and England 2003) and increased incidence of heart disease, obesity, and diabetes in adults (Worthman and Kuzara 2005). Contrary to our evolutionary past, many causes of sustained stress in contemporary societies are psychosocial rather than physical threats. These can include an unhappy marriage or frustrations at work (Dimsdale 2008). Stressors can also be more subtle. For example, a review of research into the effects of stress on health indicated that experiencing racism was a significant stressor that was associated with alcohol consumption, psychological distress, overweight, abdominal obesity, and higher fasting-glucose levels among minority groups (Williams and Mohammed 2013). Chronic, everyday racial discrimination is also associated with the hardening of coronary arteries, elevated blood pressure, giving birth to lower-birth-weight infants, cognitive impairment, poor sleep, and visceral fat, which is fat stored deep inside the belly, wrapped around the organs, including the liver and intestines. Visceral fat is a sign of **metabolic syndrome**, increasing the risk of stroke, heart disease, and type 2 diabetes. These effects have been shown to increase morbidity and mortality among members of affected groups.

Epigenetics can also be a factor in how a person is able to deal with stressful situations. Maternal experiences of stress during pregnancy have the potential to permanently alter the physiology of mothers' offspring, especially the hypothalamic-pituitary-adrenal (HPA) axis. The HPA axis regulates metabolism, blood pressure, and the immune response, and these alterations can predispose prenatally stressed individuals to suffer metabolic, cardiovascular, and mental disorders in adulthood (Palma-Gudiel et al. 2015). These experiences carry across generations, with children of Holocaust survivors who experienced PTSD demonstrating similar changes in neurochemistry in the absence of a sustained, traumatic event, as did infant offspring of mothers who developed PTSD during pregnancy after witnessing the traumatic events of 9/11 (Yehuda and LeDoux 2007).

Syndemics and the Ecological Model

It is important to recognize that disease risk is not spread evenly within or between populations. Diseases combine and interact to create a **syndemic**, where the coexistence of two or more conditions exacerbates the effects of one or all conditions. A syndemic (versus a pandemic, for example) takes into account social, political, economic, and environmental factors that increase risk for the clustering of two or more diseases (Singer et al. 2017). One of the first syndemics identified involved substance abuse, violence, and AIDS. In inner cities in the U.S., the health crisis around HIV/AIDS was related to tuberculosis, sexually transmitted infections, hepatitis, cirrhosis, infant mortality, drug abuse, suicide, and homicide. These were connected to poverty, homelessness, unemployment, poor nutrition, lack of social support, and social and ethnic inequality (Singer et al. 2017). Together, these factors and others, like health policy and unequal access to health care, form an **ecological model** of health and disease, one that moves beyond biology and medical intervention (Sallis et al. 2008).

The COVID-19 pandemic represents a syndemic in which systemic racism in the healthcare system, differential access to diagnosis and treatment, income, employment, housing, family structure, pre existing conditions, and public health policies combined to result in higher rates of infection and death for African Americans, Native Americans, Asians, and Hispanic populations in the United States (Figure 16.11).

Figure 16.11: Risk for COVID-19 infection, hospitalization, and death by race/ethnicity. Race and ethnicity are risk markers for other underlying conditions that affect health, including socioeconomic status, access to health care, and exposure to the virus related to occupation, e.g., frontline, essential, and critical infrastructure workers. Credit: Risk for COVID-19 Infection, Hospitalization, and Death by Race/Ethnicity by the Centers for Disease Control and Prevention is in the public domain.

Rate ratios compared to White, Non-Hispanic persons	American Indian or Alaska Native, Non-Hispanic persons	Asian, Non-Hispanic persons	Black or African American, Non-Hispanic persons	Hispanic or Latino persons
Cases	1.6x	.8x	1.1x	1.5x
Hospitalization	2.7x	.8x	2.3x	2.0x
Death	2.1x	.8x	1.7x	1.8x

COVID-19 was the third leading cause of death in the U.S. in 2020 and 2021 (NIH 2022; Figure 16.12), but morbidity and mortality was not equally spread across the population. Working-class people and people of color in the U.S. are more likely to live in poverty, in areas with high rates of crime and violence, and in close proximity to freeways and environmental threats like petrochemical plants and waste incinerators (Singer and Baer 2012). Many such neighborhoods are also food "deserts" without ready access to a healthy, affordable diet, made more challenging by residents not owning a car (Food Empowerment Project n.d.). Low-income people also often lack access to high-quality health care and delay or avoid preventive care and health screenings (Ross et al. 2007). These factors contributed to higher rates of preexisting conditions, including obesity, diabetes, hypertension, asthma, heart disease, chronic obstructive pulmonary disease (COPD), and smoking behavior, which then led to more complications and higher death rates from COVID (Ghosh et al. 2021).

Family structure also affected COVID exposure and severity. Many Americans live in multigenerational households, including 27% of Hispanics, 29% of Asians, 26% of African Americans, and 20% of Whites (Cohn and Passel 2018). Not all multigenerational households are equal, however. Over twice as many African Americans as Whites are in multigenerational families in which at least one family member is unemployed, and over three times as many African Americans are in multigenerational families in which everyone is simultaneously unemployed (Park, Wiemers, and Seltzer 2019). Family members in multigenerational households were at a much higher risk of developing more severe forms of COVID due to decreased personal space and multiple exposures to the virus, as well as higher rates of diabetes, smoking, and residents living below the poverty line (Ghosh et al. 2021). While aimed at reducing overall infection rates from COVID, public health measures such as mandatory lockdowns only exacerbated the situation in overcrowded and multigenerational housing, resulting in higher rates of infection and death in these communities.

Figure 16.12: Top five causes of death in the U.S. and worldwide since 2020. Credit: Top five causes of death in the U.S. and worldwide original to Explorations: An Open Invitation to Biological Anthropology (2nd ed.) by Joylin Namie is under a CC BY-NC 4.0 License. Based on data from Shiels et al. 2022 and Traeger 2022.

United States	Worldwide
1. Heart disease	1. Heart disease
2. Cancer	2. Stroke
3. COVID-19	3. COVID-19
4. Accidents	4. Chronic Obstructive Pulmonary Disease
5. Stroke	5. Lower respiratory infections

There is a long history of systemic racism and discrimination in the medical system in the United States (Washington 2006). African Americans have been subjected to medical testing and experimentation without their consent or knowledge since the time of slavery. They continue to routinely receive care of poorer quality than whites (Williams and Wyatt 2015), less pain medication during treatment and hospitalization (Green et al. 2003), and differential treatment during pregnancy and childbirth (Washington 2006). Many Americans, including 50% of White medical students and residents in one recent study (Hoffman et al. 2016), hold at least one false belief about African Americans, including "Black people's skin is thicker than white people's skin," "Blacks have stronger immune systems than whites," and "Blacks' nerve endings are less sensitive than whites'." Such beliefs affect health care for African Americans in medical emergencies and for chronic conditions.

During the COVID-19 pandemic, patients with darker skin in the United States were negatively affected by the very medical device most commonly used to assess oxygen levels in their blood. The pulse oximeter, a small device that clips onto the tip of your index finger and measures blood oxygen levels, experienced increased use in home, clinical, and hospital settings during the COVID-19 pandemic. Decisions regarding treatment and hospital admission for patients infected with COVID were often based on pulse oximeter readings (Valbuena, Merchant, and Hough 2022). The problem is the device overestimates oxygen saturation in patients with darker skin, an issue which has been recognized for over thirty years (Valbuena, Merchant, and Hough 2022). It would be as if a standard thermometer reported lower body temperatures for patients of color, making it seem as if they did not have a fever when they actually did. In the case of COVID-19, Asians, Hispanics, and African Americans experienced inaccurately high readings of their oxygen levels (with African Americans and darker-skinned Hispanics having the highest), resulting in delays in treatment, hospital admission, and access to medications to treat COVID and contributing to higher severity of illness and higher death rates among these populations in comparison to whites (Fawzi et al. 2022).

Employment was also a factor in unequal exposure to and death from COVID-19 (Raifman, Skinner, and Sojourner 2022), with many low-income workers making the choice (which, realistically, may not be a choice at all) to expose themselves to COVID in order to earn the funds necessary to purchase food, housing, and other necessities. Many such workers were then forced to miss work due to COVID infection. With only 35% of low-wage workers (as opposed to 95% of high-wage workers) having paid sick leave, this left many families struggling financially. Three years into the pandemic, low-wage workers continue to have the least access to COVID vaccines and boosters. The U.S. also lacks federal workplace-safety regulations with regard to vaccine and masking mandates that other nations enforce in times of high transmission, and it does not provide high-quality masks to its essential workers. Many occupations deemed essential by the CDC during the height of the pandemic—such as health care, emergency services, meat packing, agricultural work, teaching, and jobs in the hospitality sector—experienced higher rates of morbidity and mortality from COVID. Many of these fields disproportionately employ people of color (McKinsey and Company 2021). Given this, future policies that address the pandemic at a structural level—for example, providing monetary assistance to people who work in environments with a high risk of infection, such as cleaning, nursing, transportation, retail, restaurant work, and factory work, so that they can remain at home—may function more effectively to prevent transmission and curb future outbreaks (Arnot et al. 2020).

Food for Thought

This chapter focused primarily on health conditions prevalent in contemporary, industrialized societies that are due, in part, to the mismatch between our evolved biology and modern environments. These are the built environment and the social environment, which together form the obesogenic environment in which unhealthy behaviors are encouraged. This chapter will close by examining each of these in a college context.

Figure 16.13: Students walking around a campus. Credit: Row four man woman people walking together 3755342 by MaxPixel has been designated to the public domain (CC0).

Consider your campus from an evolutionary perspective. To what degree does the built environment lend itself to physical activity as part of daily life? Is your campus constructed in ways that promote driving at the expense of walking or biking? If driving is necessary, is parking available close to the buildings or do you need to walk a fair distance from the parking lot to your destination? Do the buildings have stairs or ramps or is it necessary to take the elevator? Is it possible to negotiate safely around campus on foot or by bike in all weather? After dark? How about the classrooms and computer labs? Do they have standing or treadmill desks? Does your class schedule encourage walking from building to building between classes, or are most courses in your major scheduled in the same location? Most college majors also lack a physical education requirement, leaving it up to students to incorporate exercise into already-challenging schedules (Figure 16.13).

Sociocultural factors that contribute to obesity include food advertising, ubiquitous fast-food and junk food options, and social pressure to consume, all of which are present on college campuses. Although nutrition on campuses has improved in recent years, many students find eating healthy in the dining halls and dorms challenging (Plotnikoff et al. 2015), and students who live off campus fare even worse (Small et al. 2013). There are also parties and other social events, a normal part of college life, that involve unhealthy food and encourage behaviors like alcohol consumption and smoking. Give some thought to the social atmosphere on your campus and the ways it may contribute to obesity. My own freshman orientation involved a succession of pizza parties, ice cream socials, and barbecues, followed by late-night runs to the nearest fast-food outlet. The purpose of these events was to encourage people to make friends and feel comfortable living away from home, but the foods served were unhealthy, and there was social pressure to join in and be part of the group. Such activities set students up for the "freshman fifteen" and then some. They also reinforce the idea that being social involves eating (and sometimes drinking and/or smoking).

Sedentarism and inactivity are also built into the academics of college life. Digital technology is a significant contributor to obesity. Students use laptops and cell phones to take notes, complete their work outside of class, and access social media. There are also video games, virtual reality headsets, and streaming television and movies for entertainment. The built environment of college already necessitates that students sit in class for hours each day, then sit at computers to complete work outside of class. The social environment enabled by digital technology encourages sitting around for entertainment. It is telling that we call it "binge watching" when we spend hours watching our favorite shows. Doing so often involves eating, as well as multiple exposures to food advertising embedded in the shows themselves. In these ways, college contributes to the development of obesity-causing behaviors that can have negative health ramifications long after college is over (Small et al. 2013).

In the U.S., the greatest increase in obesity is among young adults aged 18–29 years, a significant percentage of whom are college students (Plotnikoff et al. 2015). Analyses of college students' behavior across semesters shows consumption of fruits and vegetables drops over time, as does the amount of physical activity, while consumption of sugar-sweetened beverages and fast-food goes up, leading to weight gain at nearly six times the rate of the general public (Small et al. 2013). In response, many colleges and universities have instituted programs to encourage healthier eating and more physical activity among students (Plotnikoff et al. 2015). It is important to emphasize that neither changes in diet or exercise are effective on their own.. A 2022 study of over 340,000 British participants demonstrated that physical activity and diet quality did not individually have an impact on cardiovascular disease or cancers (Ding et al. 2022). That is, hitting the gym won't counteract the consequences of consuming high-calorie, fatty foods, and eating kale all day can't cancel out sedentary habits.

Just as no one fad diet is going to prove healthier than another, no one type of exercise is better than another. Anything that raises your heart rate and that you enjoy doing for at least an hour each day will work. Take advantage of opportunities to build exercise into everyday life. Take the stairs, park as far away from buildings as possible, ride a bike or walk instead of driving, and take walks between classes instead of sitting down and checking your phone. As far as diets go, eating a few less unhealthy calories each day, one less soda, no sugar in your coffee, or letting that last slice of pizza go to someone else, make a difference in the long run. Little changes add up to bigger ones. We cannot change our biology, but we can certainly change our habits.

Review Questions

- Why do humans like foods that are "bad" for them? Describe the evolutionary underpinnings of our tastes for sugar, salt, and fat.
- How might understanding contemporary disease from an evolutionary perspective benefit medical practitioners in treating their patients?
- Several risk factors for conditions like heart disease, diabetes, and cancer are referred to as "lifestyle factors," implying these are behavioral choices people make that put them at risk. These include unhealthy eating, lack of physical activity, smoking, and alcohol consumption. To what degree is unhealthy behavior structured by the physical and social environment? For example, how does being a college student influence your eating habits, physical activity patterns, smoking, and consumption of alcohol?
- Who benefits from the global obesity epidemic? Think about how the following industries and institutions might profit from it: The medical establishment? The fitness industry? The diet industry? Fashion? Pharmaceutical companies? Food manufacturers? Advertisers?

Key Terms

Body mass index (BMI): A person's weight in kilograms divided by the square of their height in meters. This is the most widely used measure for identifying obesity. The formula using kilograms and meters (or centimeters) is: weight (kg) / [height (m)]^2 . The formula using pounds and inches is: 703 x weight (lbs) / [height (in)]^2 . Use of the BMI is controversial for several reasons, including that it does not take into account age, bone structure, muscle mass, fat distribution, or ethnic and racial differences in body type.

Cancer: A collection of related diseases in which some of the body's cells begin to divide without stopping and spread into surrounding tissues.

Cardiovascular disease (CVD): A disease of the heart and blood vessels, often related to atherosclerosis. CVD is a condition in which a substance called plaque builds up in the walls of the arteries, the blood vessels that carry blood away from the heart, which compromises the flow of blood to the heart or brain.

Central nervous system: The complex of nerve tissues stemming from the brain and spinal cord that controls the activities of the body.

Circulatory (system): The biological system that circulates blood around the body via the heart, arteries, and veins, delivering oxygen and nutrients to organs and cells and carrying waste products away.

Diabetes mellitus: An endocrine disorder in which high glucose (blood sugar) levels occur over a prolonged period of time. Blood glucose is your body's main source of energy and comes from the food you eat. Insulin, a hormone made by the pancreas, helps glucose from food get into your cells to be used for energy. Sometimes your body does not make enough—or any—insulin (type 1 diabetes) or does not take up insulin well (type 2 diabetes). Glucose then stays in your blood and does not reach your cells.

"Double burden": Refers to parts of the world in which there is a prevalence of chronic disease (e.g., cancer, heart disease) while, at the same time, there are also high rates of infectious disease due to poverty, malnutrition, poor sanitation, and lack of access to health care, often accompanied by high rates of maternal and child mortality.

Ecological model: Ecological models of health and disease emphasize environmental and policy contexts of behavior, while incorporating social and psychological influences, rather than focusing on individual behaviors. These models encompass multiple levels of influence and can lend themselves to more comprehensive health interventions.

Emerging infectious diseases (EIDs): Infections that have recently appeared within a population or those whose incidence or geographic range is rapidly increasing or threatens to increase in the near future. Examples include Covid-19, Ebola, Zika, SARS, and avian (bird) flu.

Endocrine system: Those organs in the body whose primary function is the production of hormones.

Epidemiological transition: A transformation in patterns of disease (morbidity) and death (mortality) among a population.

Glycemic index (GI): A system that ranks foods on a scale from 1 to 100 based on their effect on blood-sugar levels. Carbohydrates with a low GI value (55 or less) are more slowly digested and metabolized causing a lower, slower rise in blood glucose and insulin levels.

Hypertension: High blood pressure. Blood pressure is the force exerted by the blood against the walls of the blood vessels. In a blood pressure reading, the top number (usually higher) refers to the systolic pressure, the amount of pressure in your arteries during the contraction of your heart muscle when your heart beats. The bottom number is the diastolic pressure when your heart muscle is resting between beats. Hypertension can lead to severe health complications and increases the risk of heart attack and stroke.

Incidence: The rate at which new cases of a disease occur in a population over a given period of time.

Insulin: A hormone produced in the pancreas that regulates the amount of glucose in the blood. Lack of insulin or the inability to absorb insulin causes diabetes.

Metabolic syndrome: A cluster of conditions, including increased blood pressure, high blood sugar, excess body fat around the waist, and abnormal cholesterol levels that occur together, increasing the risk of heart disease, stroke, and diabetes. Lifestyle changes like losing weight, exercising regularly, and making dietary changes can help prevent or reverse metabolic syndrome.

Menarche: The first occurrence of menstruation.

Morbidity: The number of cases of disease per unit of population occurring over a unit of time.

Mortality: The number of deaths attributable to a particular cause per unit of population over a unit of time.

Noncommunicable diseases (NCDs): Also known as chronic diseases, NCDs tend to be of long duration and are the result of a combination of genetic, physiological, environmental, and behavior factors. The main types of NCDs are cardiovascular diseases (like heart attacks and stroke), cancers, chronic respiratory diseases (such as chronic obstructive pulmonary disease and asthma), and diabetes.

Obesity: A medical condition in which excess body fat has accumulated to the point that it has adverse effects on health. Although controversial due to its lack of ethnic and racial specificity, the most widely used measure for identifying obesity is the body mass index (BMI), a person's weight in kilograms divided by the square of their height in meters. A measure of 30 kg/m^2 is considered obese and 25–29 kg/m^2 is considered overweight. Distribution of body fat also matters. Fat in the abdominal region has a stronger association with type 2 diabetes and cardiovascular disease, meaning waist-to-hip ratio and waist circumference are also important indicators of obesity-related health risk.

Obesogenic: Promoting excessive weight gain.

Omnivorous: Able to eat and digest foods of both plant and animal origins.

Osteoarthritis: Refers to the degeneration of joint cartilage and underlying bone, causing pain and stiffness. In the absence of previous injury, it is most common in modern populations from middle age onward.

Prevalence: The proportion of individuals in a population who have a particular disease or condition at a given point in time.

Sedentarism: A way of life characterized by much sitting and little physical activity.

Sedentism: Living in groups settled permanently in one place.

Stress response: A predictable response to any significant threat to homeostasis. The human stress response involves the **Central Nervous System** and the endocrine system acting together. Sudden and severe stress incites the "flight or flight" response from the autonomic nervous system in conjunction with hormones secreted by the adrenal and pituitary glands, increasing our heart rate and breathing and releasing glucose from the liver for quick energy.

Stroke: A stroke occurs when a blood vessel leading to the brain is blocked or bursts, preventing that part of the brain from receiving blood and oxygen, leading to cell death.

Syndemic: The aggregation (grouping together) of two or more diseases or health conditions in a population in which there is some level of harmful biological or behavioral interface that exacerbates the negative health effects of any or all of the diseases involved. Syndemics involve the adverse interaction of diseases of all types, including infections, chronic noncommunicable diseases, mental health problems, behavioral conditions, toxic exposure, and malnutrition.

Tricep skinfold measurement: The triceps skinfold site is a common location used for the assessment of body fat using skinfold calipers. A section of skin on the posterior (back) surface of the arm that lays atop the tricep muscle is pinched between calipers. The resulting measurement is matched against a chart standardized for age and gender.

"Triple burden": A fourth epidemiological transition currently underway in which some parts of the globe are suffering from the "double burden" of infectious and chronic diseases combined with injuries and diseases related to intensifying globalization, urbanization, deforestation, and climate change.

Vector-borne diseases: Human illnesses caused by parasites, viruses, and bacteria that are transmitted by mosquitoes, flies, ticks, mites, snails, and lice.

Zoonoses: Diseases that can be transmitted from animals to humans.

About the Author

Joylin Namie, Ph.D.

Truckee Meadows Community College, jnamie@tmcc.edu

Joylin Namie is Professor of Anthropology at Truckee Meadows Community College, where she teaches courses in biological and cultural anthropology. Her current research interest is in culturally and environmentally sustainable tourism in desert environments, particularly in the country of Jordan and the U.S. state of Nevada. She was awarded a fellowship to Jordan from the Council of American Overseas Research Centers (CAORC) in 2020 to explore this topic, including visiting Petra and other important tourism destinations in Jordan. Dr. Namie's favorite things in life are teaching, competing in sports, and traveling.

For Further Exploration

Lents, Nathan H. 2018. *Human Errors: A Panorama of Our Glitches, from Pointless Bones to Broken Genes*. Boston: Houghton Mifflin Harcourt.

Stearns, Stephen C., and Jacob C. Koella, eds. 2008. *Evolution in Health and Disease*. 2nd edition. United Kingdom: Oxford University Press.

Zuk, Marlene. 2013. *Paleofantasy: What Evolution Really Tells Us about Sex, Diet, and How We Live*. New York: W. W. Norton & Company.

References

Abid, Zaynah, Amanda J. Cross, and Rashmi Sinha. 2014. "Meat, Dairy, and Cancer." *The American Journal of Clinical Nutrition* 100 (S1): 386S–393S.

Akil, Luma, and H. Anwar Ahmad. 2011. "Relationships between Obesity and Cardiovascular Diseases in Four Southern States and Colorado." *Journal of Health Care for the Poor and Underserved* 22 (S4): 61–72.

Ali, Aus Tariq. 2014. "Reproductive Factors and the Risk of Endometrial Cancers." *International Journal of Gynecological Cancer* 24 (3): 384–393.

American Heart Association. 2018. "Heart Disease and Stroke Statistics-2018 Update: A Report." *Circulation 137* (12). Accessed April 7, 2023. https://www.ahajournals.org/doi/10.1161/cir.0000000000000558.

American Psychiatric Association (APA). 2013. *Diagnostic and Statistical Manual of Mental Disorder*. 5th Edition: DSM-5. Washington, DC: APA.

Armelagos, George J. 1990. "Health and Disease in Prehistoric Populations in Transition." *Disease in Populations in Transition: Anthropological and Epidemiological Perspectives*, edited by George J. Armelagos and Alan C. Swedland, 127–144. New York: Bergin & Garvey.

Armelagos, George J., Peter J. Brown, and Bethany Turner. 2005. "Evolutionary, Historical and Political Economic Perspectives on Health and Disease." *Social Science and Medicine 61* (4): 755-765.

Arnot, Megan, Eva Brandl, O. L. K. Campbell, Yuan Chen, Mark Dyble, Emily H. Emmott, et al. 2020. *Evolution, Medicine, and Public Health* 2020 (1): 264–278. https://doi.org/10.1093/emph/eoaa038.

Asher, Claire. 2017. "Illegal Bushmeat Trade Threatens Human Health and Great Apes." *Mongabay* April 6. Accessed April 4, 2023. https://news.mongabay.com/2017/04/illegal-bushmeat-trade-threatens-human-health-and-great-apes/.

Baker, W. A., G. A. Hitman, K. Hawrami, M .I. McCarthy, A. Riikonen, E. Tuomilehto-Wolf, A. Nissinen, et al. 1994. "Apolipoprotein D Gene Polymorphism: A New Genetic Marker for Type 2 Diabetic Subjects in Nauru and South India." *Diabetic Medicine* 11 (10): 947–952.

Baltic, Milan Z., and Marija Boskovic. 2015. "When Man Met Meat: Meat in Human Nutrition from Ancient Times Till Today." *Procedia Food Science 5*: 6- 9.

Blue Cross Blue Shield Association (BCBSA). 2017. "Diabetes and the Commercially Insured U.S. Population." *The Health of America Report*, August 1. Accessed April 4, 2023. https://www.bcbs.com/the-health-of-america/reports/diabetes-and-commercially-insured-us-population.

Bogin, Barry. 1991. "The Evolution of Human Nutrition." In *The Anthropology of Medicine: From Culture to Method*, edited by Lola Romanucci-Ross, Daniel E. Moerman, and Laurence R. Tancredi, 158–195. New York: Bergin & Garvey.

Bouchard, Claude. 2007. "The Biological Predisposition to Obesity: Beyond the Thrifty Genotype Scenario." *International Journal of Obesity* 31 (9): 1337–1339.

Buchman, Aron S., Lei Yu, Robert S. Wilson, Andrew Lim, Robert J. Dawe, Chris Gaiteri, Sue E. Leurgans, Julie A. Schneider, and David A. Bennett. 2019. "Physical Activity, Common Brain Pathologies, and Cognition in Community-Dwelling Older Adults." *Neurology* 98 (2). http://doi.org/10.1212/WNL.0000000000006954.

Centers for Disease Control and Prevention (CDC). N.d. "Global Health – Pakistan." Accessed April 4, 2023. https://www.cdc.gov/globalhealth/countries/pakistan/default.htm.

Centers for Disease Control and Prevention (CDC). 2014. "Breastfeeding Report Card: United States/2014." Atlanta, GA: Centers for Disease Control and Prevention.

Centers for Disease Control and Prevention (CDC). 2020. *National Diabetes Statistics Report: Estimates of Diabetes and Its Burden in the United States*. Accessed April 7, 2023 from https://diabetesresearch.org/wp-content/uploads/2022/05/national-diabetes-statistics-report-2020.pdf.

Centers for Disease Control and Prevention (CDC). 2022. "CDC Releases Updated Maps of America's High Levels of Inactivity." January 20. https://www.cdc.gov/media/releases/2022/p0120-inactivity-map.html.

Cerón, Ella. 2017. "Here's Every Oreo Flavor Ever Created." *TeenVogue.com*, June 19. Accessed April 4, 2023. https://www.teenvogue.com/story/every-oreo-flavor-ranked.

Chin, Jessie, Brennan R. Payne, Wai-Tat Fu, Daniel G. Morrow, and Elizabeth A. L. Stine-Morrow. 2015. "Information Foraging across the Life Span: Search and Switch in Unknown Patches." *Topics in Cognitive Science* 7 (3): 428–450.

Cohn, D'Vera, and Jeffrey S. Passel. 2018. "A Record 64 Million Americans Live In Multigenerational Households." *Pew Research Center,* April 5. Accessed April 4, 2023. https://www.pewresearch.org/fact-tank/2018/04/05/a-record-64-million-americans-live-in-multigenerational-households/.

Cooling, Laura. 2015. "Blood Groups in Infection and Host Susceptibility." *Clinical Microbiology Reviews* 28 (3): 801–870.

Croston, Glenn. 2012. "The Thing We Fear More Than Death: Why Predators Are Responsible for Our Fear of Public Speaking." *Psychology Today* blog, November 29. Accessed April 4, 2023. https://www.psychologytoday.com/us/blog/the-real-story-risk/201211/the-thing-we-fear-more-death.

Currie, Candace, Naman Ahluwalia, Emmanuelle Godeau, Saoirse Nic Gabhainn, Pernille Due, and Dorothy B. Mille. 2012. "Is Obesity at Individual and National Level Associated with Lower Age at Menarche? Evidence from 34 Countries in the Health Behaviour in School-Aged Children Study." *Journal of Adolescent Health* 50 (6): 621–626.

David, A. Rosalie, and Michael Zimmerman. 2010. "Cancer: An Old Disease, A New Disease or Something In Between?" *Nature Reviews: Cancer* 10 (10): 728–733.

Davis, Mike. 2005. *The Monster at Our Door: The Global Threat of Avian Flu*. New York: Owl Books.

de Silva, A. M., K. R. Walder, T. J. Aitman, T. Gotoda, A. P. Goldstone, A. M. Hodge, M. P. de Courten, P. Z. Zimmet, and G. R. Collier. 1999. "Combination of Polymorphisms in OB-R and the OB Gene Associated with Insulin Resistance in Nauruan Males." *International Journal of Obesity* 23 (8): 816–822.

Dimsdale, Joel E. 2008. "Psychological Stress and Cardiovascular Disease." Journal of the American College of Cardiology 51 (13): 1237–1246.

Ding, Ding, Joe Van Buskirk, Binh Nguyen, Emmanuel Stammotakis, Mona Elbarbary, Nicole Veronese, Philip J. Clare, et al. 2022. "Physical Activity, Diet Quality and All-Cause Cardiovascular Disease and Cancer Mortality: A Prospective Study of 346,627 UK Biobank Participants." *British Journal of Sports Medicine* 56 (20): 1148–1156.

Dutton, Denis. 2009. *The Art Instinct: Beauty, Pleasure, and Human Evolution*. New York: Bloomsbury.

Eaton, S. Boyd, Melvin Konner, and Marjorie Shostak. 1988. "Stone Agers in the Fast Lane: Chronic Degenerative Diseases in Evolutionary Perspective." *American Journal of Medicine* 84 (4): 739–749.

Eaton, S. Boyd, Malcolm C. Pike, Roger V. Short, Nancy C. Lee, James Trussell, Robert A. Hatcher, James W. Wood, et al. 1994. "Women's Reproductive Cancers in Evolutionary Context." *The Quarterly Review of Biology* 69 (3): 353–367.

Ewald, Paul W. 2018. "Ancient Cancers and Infection-Induced Oncogenesis." *International Journal of Paleopathology* 21: 178–185. http://dx.doi.org/10.1016/J.ijpp.2017.08.007.

Farb, Peter, and George Armelagos. 1980. *Consuming Passions: The Anthropology of Eating*. New York: Washington Square Press.

Fawzi, Ashraf, Tianshi David Wu, Kunbo Wang, Matthew L. Robinson, Jad Farha, Amanda Bradke, Sherita H. Golden, et al. 2022. "Racial and Ethnic Discrepancy in Pulse Oximetry and Delayed Identification of Treatment Eligibility among Patients With COVID-19." *JAMA Internal Medicine* 182 (7): 730–738.

Flinn, Mark V., and Barry G. England. 2003. "Childhood Stress: Endocrine and Immune Responses to Psychosocial Events." In *Social and Cultural Lives of Immune Systems: Theory and Practice in Medical Anthropology and International Health*, edited by James M. Wilce Jr., 105–146. London: Routledge.

Food Empowerment Project. N.d. "Food Deserts." Accessed April 4, 2023. https://foodispower.org/access-health/food-deserts/.

Gao, George. 2015. "Americans' Ideal Family Size Is Smaller Than It Used to Be." Pew Research Center, May 8. Accessed April 4, 2023. http://www.pewresearch.org/fact-tank/2015/05/08/ideal-size-of-the-american-family/.

Ghosh, A. K., S. Venkatraman, O. Soroka, E. Reshetnyak, M. Rajan, A. An, J. K. Chae, et al. 2021. "Association between Overcrowded Households, Multigenerational Households, and COVID-19: A Cohort Study." *Public Health* 198: 273–279.

Government of Pakistan. "Pakistan: Updated Nationally Determined Contributions." 2021. Accessed October 12, 2022. https://unfccc.int/sites/default/files/NDC/2022-06/Pakistan%20Updated%20NDC%202021.pdf.

Greaves, Mel. 2015. "Evolutionary Determinants of Cancer." *Cancer Discovery* 5 (8): 806–820.

Green, Carmen R., Karen O. Anderson, Tamara A. Baker, Lisa C. Campbell, Sheila Decker, Robert B. Fillingim, Donna A. Kalukalani, et al. 2003. "The Unequal Burden of Pain: Confronting Racial and Ethnic Disparities in Pain." *Pain Medicine* 4 (3): 277–294.

Greenspan, Louise, and Julianna Deardorff. 2014. *The New Puberty: How to Navigate Early Development in Today's Girls*. New York: Rodale.

Hamilton, Cheryl. 2011. *Communicating for Results, a Guide for Business and the Professions, 9th Edition*. Belmont, CA: Thomson Wadsworth.

Harper, Kristin, and George Armelagos. 2010. "The Changing Disease-Scape in the Third Epidemiological Transition." *International Journal of Environmental Research and Public Health* 7 (2): 675–697.

Hoffman, Kelly M., Sophie Trawalter, Jordan R. Axt, and M. Norman Oliver. 2016. "Racial Bias in Pain Assessment and Treatment Recommendations, and False Beliefs about Biological Differences among Blacks and Whites." *PNAS* 113 (16): 4296–4301.

International Agency for Research on Cancer (IARC). 2018. *Red Meat and Processed Meat IARC Monographs on the Evaluation of Carcinogenic Risks to Humans, Volume 114.* ISBN-13: 978-92-832-0152-6.

International Diabetes Federation (IDF). 2022. *IDF Diabetes Atlas 2022 Reports.* 10th edition. https://diabetesatlas.org/.

Jain, H. K. 2012. "Transition to Twenty-First Century Agriculture: Change of Direction." *Agricultural Research* 1 (1): 12–17.

Jones, Kate E., Nikkita G. Patel, Mark A. Levy, Adam Storeygard, Deborah Balk, John L. Gittleman, and Peter Daszak. 2008. "Global Trends in Emerging Infectious Disease." *Nature* 451 (7181): 990–993.

Karn, Mitesh, and Muna Sharma. 2021. "Climate Change, Natural Calamities, and the Triple Burden of Disease." *Nature Climate Change* 11: 796–797.

Larsen, Clark Spencer. 2014. "Foraging to Farming Transition: Global Health Impacts, Trends, and Variation." In *Encyclopedia of Global Archaeology*, edited by Claire Smith, 2818–2824. New York: Springer.

Lee, Richard B. 2013. *The Dobe Ju/'hoansi.* 4th edition. Belmont, CA: Wadsworth/Cengage Learning.

Lieberman, Daniel E. 2015. "Human Locomotion and Heat Loss: An Evolutionary Perspective." *Comprehensive Physiology* 5 (1): 99–117.

Lieberman, Leslie Sue. 2006. "Evolutionary and Anthropological Perspectives on Optimal Foraging in Obesogenic Environments." *Appetite* 47 (1): 3–9.

Liu, Gang. 2018. "Abstract P184: Meat Cooking Methods and Risk of Hypertension: Results From Three Prospective Cohort Studies." *Circulation* 137 (S1): AP184.

Liu, Gang, Geng Zong, Kana Wu, Yang Hu, Yanping Li, Walter C. Willett, David M. Eisenberg, Frank B. Hu, and Qi Sun. 2018. "Meat Cooking Methods and Risk of Type 2 Diabetes: Results from Three Prospective Cohort Studies." *Diabetes Care* 41 (5): 1049–1060.

Livingston, Gretchen. 2015. "Childlessness." Pew Research Center, May 7. Accessed April 4, 2023. http://www.pewsocialtrends.org/2015/05/07/childlessness/.

Lucock, Mark D., Charlotte E. Martin, Zoe R. Yates, and Martin Veysey. 2014. "Diet and Our Genetic Legacy in the Recent Anthropocene: A Darwinian Perspective to Nutritional Health." *Journal of Evidence-Based Complementary and Alternative Medicine* 19 (1): 68–83.

Mandsager, Kyle, Serge Harb, and Paul Cremer. 2018. "Association of Cardiorespiratory Fitness with Long-term Mortality among Adults Undergoing Exercise Treadmill Testing." *JAMA Network Open* 1 (6): e183605. http://doi.org/10.1001/jamanetworkopen.2018.3605.

Marciniak, Stephanie, and George H. Perry. 2017. "Harnessing Ancient Genomes to Study the History of Human Adaptation." *Nature Reviews Genetics* 18: 659–674.

Marlowe, Frank W. 2005. "Hunter-Gatherers and Human Evolution." *Evolutionary Anthropology* 14 (2): 54–67.

Marmot, Michael. 2005. "Social Determinants of Health Inequality." *The Lancet* 365 (9464): 1099–1104.

Martini, Frederic H., William C. Ober, Edwin F. Bartholomew, and Judi L. Nath. 2013. *Visual Essentials of Anatomy & Physiology.* Boston, MA: Pearson.

Mathews, T. J., and Brady E. Hamilton. 2016. "Mean Age of Mothers Is on the Rise: United States, 2000–2014." National Center for Health Statistics (CHS) Data Brief. No. 232. Accessed April 4, 2023. https://www.cdc.gov/nchs/data/databriefs/db232.pdf.

McClellan, James E., and Harold Dorn. 2006. *Science and Technology in World History: An Introduction*. 2nd edition. Baltimore, MD: The Johns Hopkins University Press.

McElroy, Ann, and Patricia Townsend. 2009. *Medical Anthropology in Ecological Perspective*. 5th edition. Boulder, CO: Westview Press.

McKee, Trudy, and James R. McKee. 2015. *Biochemistry: The Molecular Basis of Life*. 6th edition. Oxford, UK: Oxford University Press.

McKinsey and Company. 2021. "Race in the Workplace: Black Workers in the U.S. Private Sector." February 21. Accessed April 4, 2023. https://www.mckinsey.com/featured-insights/diversity-and-inclusion/race-in-the-workplace-the-black-experience-in-the-us-private-sector.

Moss, Michael. 2013. *Salt, Sugar, Fat: How the Food Giants Hooked Us*. New York: Random House.

National Institutes of Health (NIH). 2022. "COVID-19 Was Third Leading Cause of Death in the United States in Both 2020 and 2021." Media Advisory. July 5. Accessed April 4, 2023. https://www.nih.gov/news-events/news-releases/covid-19-was-third-leading-cause-death-united-states-both-2020-2021.

National Institutes of Health (NIH). 2017. "Obesity and Cancer Fact Sheet." Last modified January, 2017. Accessed April 4, 2023. https://www.cancer.gov/about-cancer/causes-prevention/risk/obesity/obesity-fact-sheet.

Odes, Edward J., Patrick S. Randolph-Quinney, Maryna Steyn, Zach Throckmorton, Jacqueline S. Smilg, Bernhard Zipfel, Tanya N. Augustine, et al. 2016. "Earliest Hominin Cancer: 1.7-Million-Year-Old Osteosarcoma from Swartkrans Cave, South Africa." *South African Journal of Science* 112 (7–8): 1–5.

Omran, Abdel R. 2005. "The Epidemiologic Transition: A Theory of the Epidemiology of Population Change." *The Milbank Quarterly*, December 83 (4): 731-757. Accessed April 7, 2023. https://www.ncbi.nlm.nih.gov/pmc/articles/PMC2690264/.

Palma-Gudiel, H., A. Córdova-Palomera, E. Eixarch, M. Deuschle, and L. Fañanás. 2015. "Maternal Psychosocial Stress during Pregnancy Alters the Epigenetic Signature of the Glucocorticoid Receptor Gene Promoter in Their Offspring: A Meta-Analysis." *Epigenetics* 10 (10): 893–902.

Park, Sung S., Emily E. Wiemers, and Judith A. Seltzer. 2019. "The Family Safety Net of Black and White Multigenerational Families." *Population and Development Review* 45 (2): 351–378.

Pierce, Mary, and Rebecca Hardy. 2012. "Commentary: The Decreasing Age of Puberty—As Much a Psychosocial as Biological Problem?" *International Journal of Epidemiology* 41 (1): 300–302.

Plotnikoff, Ronald C., Sarah A. Costigan, Rebecca L. Williams, Melinda J. Hutchesson, Sarah G. Kennedy, Sara L. Robards, Jennifer Allen, Clare E. Collins, Robin Callister, and John Germov. 2015. "Effectiveness of Interventions Targeting Physical Activity, Nutrition and Healthy Weight for University and College Students: A Systematic Review and Meta-analysis." *International Journal of Behavioral Nutrition and Physical Activity* 12 (1): 1–10.

Poinar, George. 2018. "Vertebrate Pathogens Vectored by Ancient Hematophagous Arthropods." *Historical Biology*, November 7. http://doi.org/ 10.1080/08912963.2018.1545018.

Pontzer, Herman, David A. Raichlen, Brian M. Wood, Audax Z. P. Mabulla, Susan B. Racette, and Frank W. Marlowe. 2012. "Hunter-Gatherer Energetics and Obesity." *PLoS ONE* 7 (7): e40503. http://doi.org/10.1371/journal.pone.0040503.

Pritchard, Jonathan K. 2010. "How We Are Evolving." *Scientific American* 303 (4): 4047.

Raichlen, David A., and Gene E. Alexander. 2014. "Exercise, APOE Genotype, and the Evolution of the Human Lifespan." *Trends in Neurosciences* 37 (5): 247–255.

Raichlen, David A., Herman Pontzer, Jacob A. Harris, Audax Z. P. Mabulla, Frank W. Marlowe, J. Josh Snodgrass, Geeta Eick, J. Colette Berbesque, Amelia Sancilio, and Brian M. Wood. 2016. "Physical Activity Patterns and Biomarkers of Cardiovascular Disease Risk in Hunter-Gatherers." *American Journal of Human Biology* 29 (2): e22919. https://doi.org/10.1002/ajhb.22919.

Raifman, Julia, Alexander Skinner, and Aaron Sojourner. 2022. "The Unequal Toll of COVID-19 On Workers." Working Economics Blog (of the Economic Policy Institute), February 7. Accessed April 4, 2023. https://www.epi.org/blog/the-unequal-toll-of-covid-19-on-workers/.

Randolph-Quinney, Patrick S., Scott A. Williams, Maryna Stein, Mark R. Meyer, Jacqueline S. Smilg, Steven E. Churchill, Edward J. Odes, Tanya Augustine, Paul Tafforeau and Lee Berger. 2016. "Osteogenic Tumour in *Australopithecus sediba*: Earliest Hominin Evidence for Neoplastic Disease." South African Journal of Science 112 (7-8). Accessed April 7, 2023. http://www.scielo.org.za/scielo.php?script=sci_arttext&pid=S0038-23532016000400013. http://dx.doi.org/10.17159/sajs.2016/20150470

Rankinen, Tuomo, Aamir Zuberi, Yvon C. Chagnon, S. John Weisnagel, George Argyropoulos, Brandon Walts, Louis Pérusse, and Claude Bouchard. 2006. "The Human Obesity Gene Map: The 2005 Update." *Obesity* 14 (4): 529–644.

Richards, M. P. 2002. "A Brief Review of the Archaeological Evidence for Palaeolithic and Neolithic Subsistence." *European Journal of Clinical Nutrition* 56 (12): 1270–1278.

Ross, Joseph S., Susannah M. Bernheim, Elizabeth H. Bradley, Hsun-Mei Teng, and William T. Gallo. 2007. "Use of Preventive Care by the Working Poor in the United States." *Preventive Medicine* 44 (3): 254–259.

Sallis, James F., Neville Owen, and Edwin B. Fisher. 2008. "Chapter 20: Ecological Models of Health Behavior." In *Health Behavior and Health Education: Theory, Research, and Practice*, edited by Karen Glanz, Barbara K. Rimer, and K. Viswanath, 465–485. 4th edition. San Francisco, CA: Jossey-Bass.

Sharp, Paul M., and Beatrice H. Hahn. 2011. "Origins of HIV and the AIDS Pandemic." *Cold Springs Harbor Perspectives in Medicine* 1 (1): a006841.

Sheerazi, Hadia A. 2022. "The Flood Seen from Space: Pakistan's Apocalyptic Crisis." *State of the Planet* (news from the Columbia Climate School), September 12. Accessed April 4, 2023. https://news.climate.columbia.edu/2022/09/12/the-flood-seen-from-space-pakistans-apocalyptic-crisis/.

Shiels, Meredith S., Anika T. Haque, Amy Berrington de González, and Neal D. Freedman. 2022. "Leading Causes of Death in the US During the COVID-19 Pandemic, March 2020 to October 2021." *JAMA* 182 (8): 883-886. doi:10.1001/jamainternmed.2022.2476.

Shonkoff, Jack P., and Andrew S. Garner. 2012. "The Lifelong Effects of Early Childhood Adversity and Toxic Stress." *Pediatrics* 129 (1): e232–e246. https://doi.org/10.1542/peds.2011-2663.

Singer, Merrill, and Hans Baer. 2012. "Health Disparity, Health Inequality." In *Introducing Medical Anthropology: A Discipline in Action*, 2nd edition, edited by Merrill Singer and Hans Baer, 175–205. Lanham, MD: AltaMira.

Singer, Merrill, Nicola Bulled, Bayla Ostrach, and Emily Mendenhall. 2017. "Syndemics and the Biosocial Conception of Health." *Lancet* 389 (10072): 941–950.

Small, Meg, Lisa Bailey-Davis, Nicole Morgan, and Jennifer Maggs. 2013. "Changes in Eating and Physical Activity Behaviors across Seven Semesters of College: Living On or Off Campus Matters." *Health Education and Behavior* 40 (4): 435–441.

Smith-Morris, Carolyn M. 2004. "Reducing Diabetes in Indian Country: Lessons from the Three Domains Influencing Pima Diabetes." *Human Organization* 63 (1): 34–46.

Sonfield, Adam, Kinsey Hasstedt, Megan L. Cavanaugh, and Ragnar Anderson. 2013. "The Social and Economic Benefits of Women's Ability to Determine Whether and When to Have Children." Report, March 13. New York: Guttmacher Institute. Accessed April 4, 2023. https://www.guttmacher.org/report/social-and-economic-benefits-womens-ability-determine-whether-and-when-have-children.

St. Pierre, Danielle. 2018. "The 15 Best Potato Chips for Every Flavor Craving." *Best*, April 6. Accessed June 13, 2018. https://www.bestproducts.com/eats/food/g972/best-potato-chips/.

Stearns, Stephen C., Randolph M. Nesse, and David Haig. 2008. "Introducing Evolutionary Thinking into Medicine." In *Evolution in Health and Disease*, edited by Stephen C. Stearns and Jacob C. Koella, 3–15. United Kingdom: Oxford University Press.

Strassmann, Beverly I. 1997. "The Biology of Menstruation in Homo Sapiens: Total Lifetime Menses, Fecundity, and Nonsynchrony in a Natural-Fertility Population." *Current Anthropology* 38 (1): 123–129.

Strassmann, Beverly I. 1999. "Menstrual Cycling and Breast Cancer: An Evolutionary Perspective." *Journal of Women's Health* 8 (2): 193–202.

Trafialek, Joanna, and Wojciech Kolanowski. 2014. "Dietary Exposure to Meat-Related Carcinogenic Substances: Is There a Way to Estimate the Risk?" *International Journal of Food Sciences and Nutrition* 65 (6): 774–780.

Troeger, Christopher. 2023. "Just How Do Deaths Due to COVID-19 Stack Up?" *Think Global Health*. February 15. Accessed April 8, 2023. https://www.thinkglobalhealth.org/article/just-how-do-deaths-due-covid-19-stack#:~:text=Looking%20at%20official%20statistics%20alone,since%20the%20beginning%20of%202020.

Valbuena, Valeria S.M., Raina M. Merchant, and Catherine L. Hough. 2022. "Racial and Ethnic Bias in Pulse Oximetry and Clinical Outcomes." Editorial. JAMA Internal Medicine 182 (7): 699–700.

Ventola, C. Lee. 2015. "The Antibiotic Resistance Crisis: Part I: Causes and Threats." *Pharmacy & Therapeutics* 40 (4): 277–283.

Versini, Mathilde, Pierre-Yves Jeandel, Tomer Bashi, Giorgia Bizzaro, Miri Blank, and Yahuda Shoenfeld. 2015. "Unraveling the Hygiene Hypothesis of Helminthes and Autoimmunity: Origins, Pathophysiology, and Clinical Applications." BMC Medicine, 13: 81. https://doi.org/10.1186/s12916-015-0306-7.

Vucenik, Ivana, and Joseph P. Stains. 2012. "Obesity and Cancer Risk: Evidence, Mechanisms, and Recommendations." Special issue, "Nutrition and Physical Activity in Aging, Obesity, and Cancer," *Annals of the New York Academy of Sciences* 1271 (1): 37–43.

Walker, Polly, Pamela Rhubart-Berg, Shawn McKenzie, Kristin Kelling, and Robert S. Lawrence. 2005. "Public Health Implications of Meat Production and Consumption." *Public Health Nutrition* 8 (4): 348–356.

Washington, Harriet A. 2006. *Medical Apartheid: The Dark History of Medical Experimentation on Black Americans from Colonial Times to the Present*. New York: Anchor Books.

Williams, David R., and Selina A. Mohammed. 2013. "Racism and Health I: Pathways and Scientific Evidence." *American Behavioral Scientist* 57 (8). http://doi.org/10.1177/0002764213487340.

Williams, David R., and Ronald Wyatt. 2015. "Racial Bias in Health Care and Health: Challenges and Opportunities." *JAMA* 314 (6): 555–556. http://doi.org10.1001/jama.2015.9260.

Wolfe, Nathan, Claire P. Dunavan, and Jared Diamond. 2012. "Origins Of Major Human Infectious Diseases." In *Institute of Medicine: Improving Food Safety through a One Health Approach: Workshop Summary*, A16. Washington, DC: National Academies Press. Accessed April 4, 2023. https://www.ncbi.nlm.nih.gov/books/NBK114494/.

World Health Organization (WHO). 2016. *Global Report on Diabetes*. Accessed April 4, 2023. http://apps.who.int/iris/bitstream/handle/10665/204871/9789241565257_eng.pdf.

World Health Organization (WHO). 2017. "Obesity and Overweight." Fact Sheet. Last modified June 9, 2021; accessed April 4, 2023. http://www.who.int/mediacentre/factsheets/fs311/en/.

World Health Organization (WHO). 2018. "Cancer." Fact Sheet. Last modified February 3, 2022; accessed April 5, 2023. http://www.who.int/news-room/fact-sheets/detail/cancer.

Worobey, Michael, Joshua I. Levy, Lorena Malpica Serrano, Alexander Crits-Christoph, Jonathan E. Pekar, Stephan A. Goldstein, Angela L.

Rassmussen, et al. July 26, 2022. "The Huanan Seafood Wholesale Market in Wuhan was the Early Epicenter of the COVID-19 Pandemic." *SCIENCE* 26 (377): 951–959. http://doi.org/10.1126/science.abp8715.

Worthman, Carol M., and Jennifer Kuzara. 2005. "Life History and the Early Origins of Health Differentials." *American Journal of Human Biology* 17 (1): 95–112.

Wrangham, Richard. 2009. *Catching Fire: How Cooking Made Us Human*. New York: Basic Books.

Yehuda, Rachel, and Joseph LeDoux. 2007. "Response Variation Following Trauma: A Translational Neuroscience Approach to Understanding PTSD." *Neuron* 56 (1): 19–32.

Zuckerman, Molly K., and George J. Armelagos. 2014. "The Hygiene Hypothesis and the Second Epidemiologic Transition." In *Modern Environments and Human Health: Revisiting the Second Epidemiologic Transition*, edited by Molly K. Zuckerman, 301–320. Hoboken, NJ: Wiley-Blackwell.

Zuckerman, Molly Kathleen, Kristin Nicole Harper, Ronald Barrett, and George John Armelagos. 2014. "The Evolution of Disease: Anthropological Perspectives on Epidemiologic Transitions." Special issue, "Epidemiological Transitions: Beyond Omran's Theory," *Global Health Action* 7 (1): 23303. http://doi.org/10.3402/gha.v7.23303.

Image Descriptions

Figure 16.4: Obesity rates by country, 2017. The following are the rates as percentages of the total population of these countries:

1. Japan, 3.7%
2. India, 5%
3. Korea, 5.3%
4. Indonesia, 5.7%
5. China, 7%
6. Italy, 9.8%
7. Switzerland, 10.2%
8. Austria, 14.7%
9. France, 15.3%
10. Poland, 16.7%
11. Spain, 16.7%
12. Greece, 17%
13. Israel, 17.8%
14. Iceland, 19%
15. Russian Federation, 19.6%
16. Brazil, 20.8%
17. Columbia, 20.9%
18. Ghana, 22%
19. Turkey, 22.3%
20. Iceland, 23%
21. Germany, 23.6%
22. Costa Rica, 24.4%
23. Finland, 24.8%
24. Chile, 25.1%
25. Canada, 25.8%
26. South Africa, 26.5%
27. United Kingdom, 26.9%

28. Australia, 26.9%
29. Mexico, 27.9%
30. United States, 38.2%
31. Egypt, 39%

Figure 16.10: This chart depicts decreasing ages at time of first menstruation (menarche) in seven countries:

1. In Germany/Finland, the age of menarche was approximately 16.5 years in 1860. This dropped to approximately 13.5 years by 1940.
2. In Norway, the age of menarche was approximately 17 years of age in 1850. This dropped to approximately 13.3 by 1950, where it remained for 30 more years.
3. In Sweden, the age of menarche was approximately 15.7 in 1890, dropping to approximately 14 years by 1950.
4. There appears to be less data for Denmark. For Denmark, menarche was 13.7 in 1950 and dropped to approximately 13.3 by 1960.
5. In the US, the age of menarche was 14 years in 1905. This dropped to 11 by 1990. This is the lowest data point on the chart.
6. In the UK, the age of menarche was 13.3 in 1945, dropping to approximately 12.7 by 1970.

17.

SOCIAL AND BIOPOLITICAL DIMENSIONS OF EVOLUTIONARY THINKING

Jonathan Marks, Ph.D., University of North Carolina at Charlotte

Adam P. Johnson, M.A., University of North Carolina at Charlotte/University of Texas at San Antonio

This chapter is an adaptation of "Chapter 2: Evolution" by Jonathan Marks. In Explorations: An Open Invitation to Biological Anthropology, first edition, edited by Beth Shook, Katie Nelson, Kelsie Aguilera, and Lara Braff, which is licensed under CC BY-NC 4.0.

Learning Objectives

- Explain the relationship among genes, bodies, and organismal change.
- Discuss the shortcomings of simplistic understandings of genetics.
- Describe what is meant by the "biopolitics of heredity."
- Discuss issues caused by misuse of ideas about adaptations and natural selection.
- Examine and correct myths about evolution.

The Human Genome Project, an international initiative launched in 1990, sought to identify the entire genetic makeup of our species. For many scientists, it meant trying to understand the genetic underpinnings of what made humans uniquely human. James Watson, a codiscoverer of the helical shape of DNA, wrote that "when finally interpreted, the genetic messages encoded within our DNA molecules will provide the ultimate answers to the chemical underpinnings of human existence" (Watson 1990, 248). The underlying message is that what makes humans unique can be found in our **genes**. The Human Genome Project hoped to find the core of who we are and where we come from.

Despite its lofty goal, the Human Genome Project—even after publishing the entire human genome in January 2022—could not fully account for the many factors that contribute to what it is to be human. Richard Lewontin, Steven Rose, and Leon Kamin (2017) argue that genetic determinism of the sort assumed by the Human Genome Project neglects other essential dimensions that contribute to the development and evolution of human bodies, not to mention the role that culture plays. They use an apt metaphor of a cake to illustrate the incompleteness of reductive models. Consider the flavor of a cake and think of the ingredients listed in the recipe. The recipe includes ingredients such as flour, sugar, shortening, vanilla extract, eggs, and milk. Does raw flour taste like cake? Does sugar, vanilla extract, or any of the other ingredients taste like cake? They do not, and knowing the individual flavors of each ingredient does not tell us much about what cake tastes like. Even mixing all of the ingredients in the correct proportions does not get us cake. Instead, external factors such as baking at the right temperature, for the right amount of time, and even the particularities of our evolved sense of taste and smell are all necessary components of experiencing the cake.

Lewontin, Rose, and Kamin (2017) argue that the same is true for humans and other organisms.

Knowing everything about cake ingredients does not allow us to fully know cake. Equally so, knowing everything about the genes found in our DNA does not allow us to fully know humans. Different, interacting levels are implicated in the development and evolution of all organisms, including humans. Genes, the structure of chromosomes, developmental processes, epigenetic tags, environmental factors, and still-other components all play key roles such that genetically reductive models of human development and evolution are woefully inadequate.

The complex interactions across many levels—genetic, developmental, and environmental—explain why we still do not know how our one-dimensional DNA nucleotide sequence results in a four-dimensional organism. This was the unfulfilled promise of the inception of the Human Genome Project in the 1980s and 1990s: the project produced the complete DNA sequence of a human cell in the hopes that it would reveal how human bodies are built and how to cure them when they are built poorly. Yet, that information has remained elusive. Presumably, the knowledge of how organisms are produced from DNA sequences will one day permit us to reconcile the discrepancies between patterns in anatomical evolution and molecular evolution.

In this chapter, we will consider multilevel evolution and explore evolution as a complex interaction between genetic and epigenetic factors as well as the environments in which organisms live. Next, we will examine the biopolitical nature of human evolution. We will then investigate problems that arise from attributing all traits to an adaptive function. Finally, we will address common misconceptions about evolution. The goal of this chapter is to provide you with the necessary toolkit for understanding the molecular, anatomical, and political dimensions of evolution.

Evolution Happens at Multiple Levels

Following Richard Dawkins's publication of *The Selfish Gene* in 1976, the scientific imagination was captured by the potential of genomics to reveal how genes are copied by Darwinian selection. Dawkins argues that the genes in individuals that contribute to greater reproductive success are the units of selection. His conception of evolution at the molecular level undercuts the complex interactions between organisms and their environments, which are not expressed genomically but are nevertheless key drivers in evolution.

By the 1980s, the acknowledgment among most biologists that even though genes construct bodies, genes and bodies evolve at different rates and with distinct patterns. This realization led to a renewed focus on how bodies change. The Evolutionary Synthesis of the 1930s–1970s had reduced organisms to their **genotypes** and species to their **gene pools**, which provided valuable insights about the processes of biological change, but it was only a first approximation. Animals are in fact reactive and adaptable beings, not passive and inert genotypes. Species are clusters of socially interacting and reproductively compatible organisms.

Figure 17.1: A painting by Donald E. Davis representing the Chicxulub asteroid impact off the Yucatan Peninsula that contributed to the mass extinction that included the dinosaurs about 65 million years ago. Credit: Chicxulub impact – artist impression by Donald E. Davis, NASA, is in the public domain.

Once we accept that evolutionary change is fundamentally genetic change, we can ask: How do bodies function and evolve? How do groups of animals come to see one another as potential mates or competitors for mates, as opposed to just other creatures in the environment? Are there evolutionary processes that are not explicable by population genetics? These questions—which lead us beyond reductive assumptions—were raised in the 1980s by Stephen Jay Gould, the leading evolutionary biologist of the late 20th century (see: Gould 2003; 1996).

Gould spearheaded a movement to identify and examine higher-order processes and features of evolution that were not adequately explained by population genetics. For example, **extinction**, which was such a problem for biologists of the 1600s, could now be seen as playing a more complex role in the history of life than population genetics had been able to model. Gould recognized that there are two kinds of extinctions, each with different consequences: background extinctions and mass extinctions. Background extinctions are those that reflect the balance of nature, because in a competitive Darwinian world, some things go extinct and other things take their place. Ecologically, your species may be adapted to its niche, but if another species comes along that's better adapted to the same niche, eventually your species will go extinct. It sucks, but it is the way of all life: you come into existence, you endure, and you pass out of existence. But mass extinctions are quite different. They reflect not so much the balance of nature as the wholesale disruption of nature: many species from many different lineages dying off at roughly the same time—presumably as the result of some kind of rare ecological disaster. The situation may not be survival of the fittest as much as survival of the luckiest. The result, then, would be an ecological scramble among the survivors. Having made it through the worst, the survivors could now simply divide up the new ecosystem amongst themselves, since their competitors were gone. Something like this may well have happened about 65 million years ago, when a huge asteroid hit the Yucatan Peninsula, which mammals survived but dinosaurs did not (Figure 17.1). Something like this may be happening now, due to human expansion and environmental degradation. Note, though, that there is only a limited descriptive role here for population genetics: the phenomena we are describing are about organisms and species in ecosystems.

Another question involved the disconnect between properties of *species* and the properties of *gene pools*. For example, there are upwards of 15 species of gibbons but only two species of chimpanzees. Why? There are upwards of 20 species of guenons but fewer than ten of baboons. Why? Are there genes for that? It seems unlikely. Gould suggested that species, as units of nature, might have properties that are not reducible to the genes in their cells. For example, rates of speciation and extinction might be properties of their ecologies and histories rather than their genes. Thus, relationships between environmental contexts and variability within a species result in degrees of resistance to extinction and affect the frequency and rates at which clades diversify (Lloyd and Gould 1993). Consistent biases of speciation rates might well produce patterns of macroevolutionary diversity that are difficult to explain genetically and better understood ecologically. Gould called such biases in speciation rates **species selection**—a higher-order process that invokes competition between species, in addition to the classic Darwinian competition between individuals.

One of Gould's most important studies involved the very nature of species. In the classical view, a species is continually adapting to its environment until it changes so much that it is a different species than it was at the beginning of this sentence (Eldredge and Gould 1972). That implies that the species is a fundamentally unstable entity through time, continuously changing to fit in. But suppose, argued Gould along with paleontologist Niles Eldredge, a species is more stable through time and only really adapts during periods of ecological instability and change. Then we might expect to find in the fossil record long equilibrium periods—a few million years or so—in which species don't seem to change much, punctuated by relatively brief periods in which they change a bit and then stabilize again as new species. They called this idea **punctuated equilibria**. The idea helps to explain certain features of the fossil record, notably the existence of small anatomical "gaps" between closely related fossil forms (Figure 17.2). Its significance lies in the fact that although it incorporates genetics, punctuated equilibria is not really a theory of genetics but one of types bodies in deep time.

Punctuated equilibria is seen across taxa, with long periods in the fossil record representing little phenotypic change. These periods of stability are disrupted by shorter periods of rapid **adaptation**, the process through which populations of organisms become suited to living in their environments. Phenotypic changes are often coupled with drastic climatic or ecological changes that affect the milieu in which organisms live. For example, throughout much of hominin evolutionary history, brain size was closely associated with body size and thus remained mostly stable. However, changes occurred in average hominin brain size at around 100 thousand years ago, 1 million years ago, and 1.8 million years ago. Several hypotheses have been put forth to explain these changes, including unpredictability in climate and environment (Potts 1998), social development (Barton 1996), and the evolution of language (Deacon 1998). Evidence from the fossil record, paleoclimate models, and comparative anatomy suggests that the changes observed in hominin lineage result from biocultural processes—that is, the coalescence of environmental and cultural factors that selected for larger brains (Marks 2015; Shultz, Nelson, and Dunbar 2012).

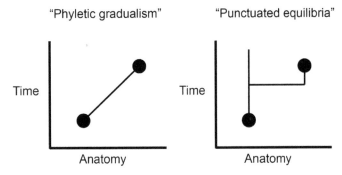

Figure 17.2: Different ways of conceptualizing the evolutionary relationship between an earlier and a later species. With phyletic gradualism, species are envisioned transforming continually in a direct line over time. With punctuated equilibria species branch off at particular points over time. Credit: Phyletic gradualism vs. punctuated equilibria (Figure 2.12) original to Explorations: An Open Invitation to Biological Anthropology is under a CC BY-NC 4.0 License.

In response to the call for a theory of the evolution of form, the field of **evo-devo**—the intersection of evolutionary and developmental biology—arose. The central focus here is on how changes in form and shape arise. An embryo matures by the stimulation of certain cells to divide, forming growth fields. The interactions and relationships among these growth fields generate the structures of the body. The **hox genes** that regulate these growth fields turn out to be highly conserved across the animal kingdom. This is because they repeatedly turn on and off the most basic genes guiding the animal's development, and thus any changes to them would be catastrophic. Indeed, these genes were first identified by manipulating them in fruit flies, such that one could produce a bizarre mutant fruit fly that grew a pair of legs where its antennae were supposed to be (Kaufman, Seeger, and Olsen 1990).

Certain genetic changes can alter the fates of cells and the body parts, while other genetic changes can simply affect the rates at which neighboring groups of cells grow and divide, thus producing physical bumps or dents in the developing body. The result of altering the relationships among these fields of cellular proliferation in the growing embryo is **allometry**, or the differential growth of body parts. As an animal gets larger—either over the course of its life or over the course of macroevolution—it often has to change shape in order to live at a different size. Many important physiological functions depend on properties of geometric area: the strength of a bone, for example, is proportional to its cross-sectional area. But area is a two-dimensional quality, while growing takes place in three dimensions—as an increase in mass or volume. As an animal expands, its bones necessarily weaken, because volume expands faster than area does. Consequently a bigger animal has more stress on its bones than a smaller animal does and must evolve bones even thicker than they would be by simply scaling the animal up proportionally. In other words, if you expand a mouse to the size of an elephant, it will nevertheless still have much thinner bones than the elephant does. But those giant mouse bones will unfortunately not be adequate to the task. Thus, a giant mouse would have to change aspects of its form to maintain function at a larger size (see Figure 17.3).

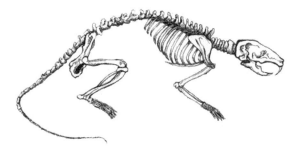

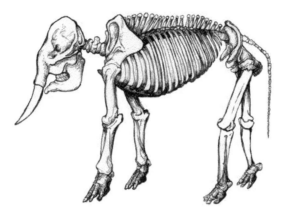

Figure 17.3: Mouse (top) and elephant (bottom) skeletons. Notice the elephant's bones are more robust when the two animals are the same size. Credit: **Mouse and elephant skeletons (Figure 2.13)** original to Explorations: An Open Invitation to Biological Anthropology is under a CC BY-NC 4.0 License.

Physiologically, we would like to know how the body "knows" when to turn on and off the genes that regulate growth to produce a normal animal. Evolutionarily, we would like to know how the body "learns" to alter the genetic on/off switch (or the genetic "slow down/speed up" switch) to produce an animal that looks different. Moreover, since organisms differ from one another, we would like to know how the developing body distinguishes a range of normal variation from abnormal variation. And, finally, how does abnormal variation eventually become normal in a descendant species?

Taking up these questions, Gould invoked the work of a British geneticist named Conrad H. Waddington, who thought about genetics in less reductive ways than his colleagues. Rather than isolate specific DNA sites to analyze their function, Waddington instead studied the inheritance of an organism's reactivity—its ability to adapt to the circumstances of its life. In a famous experiment, he grew fruit fly eggs in an atmosphere containing ether. Most died, but a few survived somehow by developing a weird physical feature: a second thorax with a second pair of wings. Waddington bred these flies and soon developed a stable line of flies who would reliably develop a second thorax when grown in ether. Then he began to lower the concentration of ether, while continuing to selectively breed the flies that developed the strange appearance. Eventually he had a line of flies that would stably develop the "bithorax" **phenotype**–the suite of traits of an organism–even when there was no ether; it had become the "new normal." The flies had genetically assimilated the bithorax condition.

Waddington was thus able to mimic the **inheritance of acquired characteristics**: what had been a trait stimulated by ether a few generations ago was now a normal part of the development of the descendants. Waddington recognized that while he had performed a selection experiment on genetic variants, he had not selected for particular traits. Rather, he helped produce the physiological tendency to develop particular traits when appropriately stimulated. He called that tendency **plasticity** and its converse, the tendency to stay the same even under weird environmental circumstances, **canalization.** Waddington had initially selected for plasticity, the tendency to develop the bithorax phenotype under weird conditions, and then, later, for canalization, the developmental normalization of that weird physical trait. Although Waddington had high stature in the community of geneticists, evolutionary biologists of the 1950s and 1960s regarded him with suspicion because he was not working within the standard mindset of reductionism, which saw evolution as the spread of genetic variants that coded for favorable traits. Both Waddington and Gould resisted contemporary intellectual paradigms that favored reductive accounts of evolutionary processes. They conceived of evolution as an emergent process in which many external factors (e.g. climate, environment, predation) and internal factors (e.g., genotypes, plasticity, canalization) coalesce to produce the evolutionary trends that we observe in the fossil record and our genome.

While Gould and Waddington both looked beyond the genome to understand evolution, the Human Genome Project—an international project with the goal of identifying each base pair in the human genome in the 1990s—generated a great deal of public interest in analyzing the human DNA sequence from the standpoint of medical genetics. Some of the rhetoric aimed to sell the public on investing a lot of money and resources in sequencing the human genome in order to show the genetic basis of heritable traits, cure genetic diseases, and learn what it means ultimately to be biologically human. However, the Human Genome Project was not actually able to answer those questions through the use of genetics alone, and thus a broader, more holistic account was required.

This holistic account came from decades of research in human biology and anthropology, which understood the human body as highly adaptable, dynamic, and emergent. For example, in the early 20th century, anthropologist Franz Boas measured the skulls of immigrants to the U.S., revealing that environmental, not merely genetic, factors affected skull shape. The growing human body adjusts itself to the conditions of life, such as diet, sunshine, high altitude, hard labor, population density, how babies are carried—any and all of which can have subtle but consistent effects upon its development. There can thus be no normal human form, only a context-specific range of human forms.

However, what the human biologists called human adaptability, evolutionary biologists called developmental plasticity, and evidence quickly began to mount for its cause being **epigenetic** modifications to DNA. Epigenetic modifications are changes to how genes are used by the body (as opposed to changes in the DNA sequences; see Chapter 3). Scientific interest shifted from the focus of the Human Genome Project to the ways that bodies are made by evolutionary-developmental processes, including epigenetics. What is meant by "epigenetic modification"? Evolution is about how descendants diverge from their ancestors. Inheritance from parent to offspring is still critical to this process, which occurs through genetic recombination: the pairing of homologous chromosomes and sharing of genetic material during meiosis (see Chapter 3). However, in the 21st century, the link between evolution and inheritance has broadened with a clearer understanding of how environmental and developmental factors shape bodies and the expression of genes, including epigenetic inheritance patterns. While offspring inherit their genes through random assortment during meiosis, environmental factors also shape how genes are used. When these epigenetic modifications occur in germ cells, they can be passed onto offspring. In these cases, there is no change in the DNA sequence but rather in how genes are used by the body due to DNA methylation and the structure of chromosomes due to histone acetylation (see Chapter 3).

In addition, we now recognize that evolution is affected by two other forms of intergenerational transmission and inheritance (in addition to genetics and epigenetics). These forms include behavioral variation and culture. That is, behavioral information can be transmitted horizontally (intragenerationally), permitting more rapid ways for organisms to adjust to the environment. And, then there is the fourth mode of transmission: the cultural or symbolic mode. Humans are the only species that horizontally transmits an arbitrary set of rules to govern communication, social interaction, and thought. This shared information is symbolic and has resulted in what we recognize as "culture": locally emergent worlds of names, words, pictures, classifications, revered pasts, possible futures, spirits, dead ancestors, unborn descendants, in-laws, politeness, taboo, justice, beauty, and story, all accompanied by practices and a material world of tools.

Consequently our contemporary ideas about evolution see the evolutionary processes as hierarchically organized and not restricted to the differential transmission of DNA sequences into the next generation. While that is indeed a significant part of evolution, the organism and species are nevertheless crucial to understanding how those DNA sequences get transmitted. Further, the transmission of epigenetic, behavioral, and symbolic information play a complex role in perpetuating our genes, bodies, and species. In the case of human evolution, one can readily see that symbolic information and cultural adaptation are far more central to our lives and our survival today than DNA and genetic adaptation. It is thus misleading to think of humans passively occupying an environmental niche. Rather, humans are actively engaged in constructing our own niches, as well as adapting to them and using them to adapt. The complex interplay between a species and its active engagement in creating its own ecology is known as **niche construction**. If we understand **natural selection**–the process by which populations adapt to their specific environments–as the effects that environmental context has on the reproductive success of organisms, then niche construction is the process through which organisms shape their own selective pressures.

The Biopolitics of Heredity

"Science isn't political" is a sentiment that you have likely heard before. Science is supposed to be about facts and objectivity. It exists, or at least ought to, outside of petty human concerns. However, the sorts of questions we ask as scientists, the problems we choose to study, the categories and concepts we use, who gets to do science, and whose work gets cited are all shaped by culture. Doing science is a political act. This fact is markedly true for human evolution. While it is easier to create intellectual distance between us and fruit flies and viruses, there is no distance when we are studying ourselves. The hardest lesson to learn about human evolution is that it is intensely political. Indeed, to see it from the opposite side, as it were, the history of creationism—the belief that the universe was divinely created around 6,000 years ago—is essentially a history of legal decisions.

For instance, in *Tennessee v. John T. Scopes* (1925), a schoolteacher was prosecuted for violating a law in Tennessee that prohibited the teaching of human evolution in public schools, where teachers were required by law to teach creationism.

More recently, legal decisions aimed at legislating science education have shaped how students are exposed to evolutionary theory. For instance, *McLean v. Arkansas* (1982) dispatched "scientific creationism" by arguing that the imposition of balanced teaching of evolution and creationism in science classes violates the Establishment Clause, separating church and state. Additionally, *Kitzmiller v. Dover (Pennsylvania) Area School District* (2005) dispatched the teaching of "intelligent design" in public school classrooms as it was deemed to not be science. In some cases, people see unbiblical things in evolution, although most Christian theologians are easily able to reconcile science to the Bible. In other cases, people see immoral things in evolution, although there is morality and immorality everywhere. And some people see evolution as an aspect of alt-religion, usurping the authority of science in schools to teach the rejection of the Christian faith, which would be unconstitutional due to the protected separation of church and state.

Clearly, the position that politics has nothing to do with science is untenable. But is the politics in evolution an aberration or is it somehow embedded in science? In the early 20th century, scientists commonly promoted the view that science and politics were separate: science was seen as a pure activity, only rarely corrupted by politics. And yet as early as World War I, the politics of nationalism made a hero of the German chemist Fritz Haber for inventing poison gas. And during World War II, both German doctors and American physicists, recruited to the war effort, helped to end many civilian lives. Therefore, we can think of the apolitical scientist as a self-serving myth that functions to absolve scientists of responsibility for their politics. The history of science shows how every generation of scientists has used evolutionary theory to rationalize political and moral positions. In the very first generation of evolutionary science, Darwin's *Origin of Species* (1859) is today far more readable than his *Descent of Man* (1871). The reason is that Darwin consciously purged *The Origin of Species* of any discussion of people. And when he finally got around to talking about people, in *The Descent of Man*, he simply imbued them with the quaint Victorian prejudices of his age, and the result makes you cringe every few pages. There is plenty of politics in there—sexism, racism, and colonialism—because *you cannot talk about people apolitically*.

One immediate faddish deduction from Darwinism, popularized by Herbert Spencer (1864) as "survival of the fittest," held that unfettered competition led to advancement in nature and to human history. Since the poor were purported losers in that struggle, anything that made their lives easier would go against the natural order. This position later came to be known ironically as "Social Darwinism." Spencer was challenged by fellow Darwinian Thomas Huxley (1863), who agreed that struggle was the law of the jungle but observed that we don't live in jungles anymore. The obligation to make lives better for others is a moral, not a natural, fact. We simultaneously inhabit a natural universe of descent from apes and a moral universe of injustice and inequality, and science is not well served by ignoring the latter.

Concurrently, the German biologist Ernst Haeckel's 1868 popularization of Darwinism was translated into English a few years later as *The History of Creation*. As we saw earlier, Haeckel was determined to convince his readers that they were descended from apes, even in the absence of fossil evidence attesting to it. When he made non-Europeans into the missing links that connected his readers to the apes, and depicted them as ugly caricatures, he knew precisely what he was doing. Indeed, even when the degrading racial drawings were deleted from the English translation of his book, the text nevertheless made his arguments quite clear. And a generation later, when the Americans had not yet entered the Great War in 1916, a biologist named Vernon Kellogg visited the German High Command as a neutral observer and found that the officers knew a lot about evolutionary biology, which they had gotten from Haeckel and which rationalized their military aggressions. Kellogg went home and wrote a bestseller about it, called *Headquarters Nights* (1917). World War I would have been fought with or without evolutionary theory, but as a source of scientific authority, evolution—even if a perversion of the Darwinian theory—had very quickly attained global geopolitical relevance.

Oftentimes, politics in evolutionary science is subtle, due to the pervasive belief in the advancement of science. We recognize the biases of our academic ancestors and modify our scientific stories accordingly. But we can never be free of our own cultural biases, which are invisible to us, as much as our predecessors' biases were invisible to them. In some cases, the most important cultural issues resurface in different guises each generation, like scientific racism. **Scientific racism** is the recruitment of science for the evil political ends of racism, and it has proved remarkably impervious to evolution. Before Darwin, there was creationist scientific racism, and after Darwin, there was evolutionist scientific racism. And there is still scientific racism today, self-justified by recourse to evolution, which means that scientists have to be politically astute and sensitive to the uses of their work to counter these social tendencies.

Consider this: Are you just your ancestry, or can you transcend it? If that sounds like a weird question, it was actually quite important to a turn-of-the-20th-century European society in which an old hereditary aristocracy was under increasing threat from a rising middle class. And that is why the very first English textbook of Mendelian genetics concluded with the thought that "permanent progress is a question of breeding rather than of pedagogics; a matter of gametes, not of training ... the creature is not made but born" (Punnett 1905, 60). *Translation: Not only do we now know a bit about how heredity works, but it's also the most important thing about you. Trust me, I'm a scientist.*

Yet evolution is about how descendants come to differ from ancestors. Do we really know that your heredity, your DNA, your ancestry, is the most important thing about you? That you were born, not made? After all, we do know that you could be born into slavery or as a peasant, and come from a long line of enslaved people or peasants, and yet not have slavery or peasantry be the most important thing about you. Whatever your ancestors were may unfortunately constrain what you can become, but as a moral precept, it should not. But just as science is not purely "facts and objectivity," ancestry is not a strictly biological concept. Human ancestry is biopolitics, not biology.

Evolution is fundamentally a theory about ancestry, and yet ancestors are, in the broad anthropological sense, sacred: ancestors are often more meaningful symbolically than biologically. Just a few years after *The Origin of Species* (Darwin 1859), the British politician and writer Benjamin Disraeli declared himself to be on the side of the angels, not the apes, and to "repudiate with indignation and abhorrence those new-fangled theories" (Monypenny, Flavelle, and Buckle 1920, 105). He turned his back on an ape ancestry and looked to the angel; yet, he did so as a prominent Jew-turned-Anglican, who had personally transcended his humble roots and risen to the pinnacle of the Empire. Ancestry was certainly important, and Disraeli was famously proud of his, but it was also certainly not the most important thing, not the primary determinant of his place in the world. Indeed, quite the opposite: Disraeli's life was built on the transcendence of many centuries of Jewish poverty and oppression in Europe. Humble ancestry was there to be superseded and nobility was there to be earned; Disraeli would later become the Earl of Beaconsfield. Clearly, "are you just your ancestry" is not a value-neutral question, and "the creature is not made, but born" is not a value-neutral answer.

Figure 17.4: Eugenic and Health Exhibit, Fitter Families exhibit, and examination building, Kansas State Free Fair. Credit: Gallery 14: Eugenics Exhibit at the Kansas State Free Fair, 1920 ID (ID 16328) by Cold Spring Harbor (Courtesy American Philosophical Society) is under a CC BY-NC-ND 3.0 License.

Ancestry being the most important thing about a person became a popular idea twice in 20th century science. First, at the beginning of the century, when the **eugenics** movement in America called attention to "feeble-minded stocks," which usually referred to the poor or to immigrants (see Figure 17.4; and see Chapter 2). This movement culminated in Congress restricting the immigration of "feeble-minded races" (said to include Jews and Italians) in 1924, and the Supreme Court declaring it acceptable for states to sterilize their "feeble-minded" citizens involuntarily in 1927. After the Nazis picked up and embellished these ideas during World War II, Americans moved swiftly away from them in some contexts (e.g., for most people of European descent) while still strictly adhering in other contexts (e.g., Japanese internment camps and immigration restrictions).

Ancestry again became paramount in the drumming up of public support for the Human Genome Project in the 1990s. Public support for sequencing the human genome was encouraged by a popular science campaign that featured books titled *The Book of Man* (Bodmer and McKie 1997), *The Human Blueprint* (Shapiro 1991), and *The Code of Codes* (Kevles and Hood 1993). These books generally promised cures for genetic diseases and a deeper understanding of the human condition. We can certainly identify progress in molecular genetics over the last couple of decades since the human genome was sequenced, but that progress has notably not been accompanied by cures for genetic diseases, nor by deeper understandings of the human condition.

Even at the most detailed and refined levels of genetic analysis, we still don't have much of an understanding of the actual basis by which things seem to "run in families." While the genetic basis of simple, if tragic, genetic diseases have become well-known—such as sickle-cell anemia, cystic fibrosis, and Tay-Sachs' Disease—we still haven't found the ostensible genetic basis for traits that are thought to have a strong genetic component. For example, a recent genetic summary found over 12,000 genetic sites that contributed to height yet still explained only about 40-50 percent of the variation in height among European ancestry but no more than 10-20 percent of variation of other ancestries, which we know strongly runs in families (Yengo et al. 2022).

Partly in reaction to the reductionistic hype of the Human Genome Project, the study of epigenetics has become the subject of great interest. One famous natural experiment involves a Nazi-imposed famine in Holland over the winter of 1944–1945. Children born during and shortly after the famine experienced a higher incidence of certain health problems as adults, many decades later. Apparently, certain genes had been down-regulated early in development and remained that way throughout the course of life. Indeed, this modified regulation of the genes in response to the severe environmental conditions may have been passed on to their children.

Obviously one's particular genetic constitution may play an important role in one's life trajectory. But overvaluing that role may have important social and political consequences. In the first place, genotypes are rendered meaningful in a cultural universe. Thus, if you live in a strongly patriarchal society and are born without a Y chromosome (since human males are chromosomally XY and females XX), your genotype will indeed have a strong effect upon your life course. So even though the variation is natural, the consequences are political. The mediating factors are the cultural ideas about how people of different sexes ought to be treated, and the role of the state in permitting certain people to develop and thrive. More broadly, there are implications for public education if variation in intelligence is genetic. There are implications for the legal system if criminality is genetic. There are implications for the justice system if sexual preference, or sexual identity, is genetic. There are implications for the development of sports talent if that is genetic. And yet, even for the human traits that are more straightforward to measure and known to be strongly heritable, the DNA base sequence variation seems to explain little.

Genetic determinism or **hereditarianism** is the idea that "the creature is made, not born"—or, in a more recent formulation by James Watson, that "our fate is in our genes." One of the major implications drawn from genetic determinism is that the feature in question must inevitably express itself; therefore, we can't do anything about it. Therefore, we might as well not fund the social programs designed to ameliorate economic inequality and improve people's lives, because their courses are fated genetically. And therefore, they don't deserve better lives.

All of the "therefores" in the preceding paragraph are open to debate. What is important is that the argument relies on a very narrow understanding of the role of genetics in human life, and it misdirects the causes of inequality from cultural to natural processes. By contrast, instead of focusing on genes and imagining them to place an invisible limit upon social progress, we can study the ways in which your DNA sequence does *not* limit your capability for self-improvement or fix your place in a social hierarchy. In general, two such avenues exist. First, we can examine the ways in which the human body responds and reacts to environmental variation: human adaptability and plasticity. This line of research began with the anthropometric studies of immigrants by Franz Boas in the early 20th century and has now expanded to incorporate the epigenetic inheritance of modified human DNA. And second, we can consider how human lives are shaped by social histories—especially the structural inequalities within the societies in which they grow up.

Although it arises and is refuted every generation, the radical hereditarian position (genetic determinism) perennially claims to speak for both science and evolution. It does not. It is the voice of a radical fringe—perhaps naive, perhaps evil. It is not the authentic voice of science or of evolution. Indeed, keeping Charles Darwin's name unsullied by protecting it from association with bad science often seems like a full-time job. Culture and epigenetics are very much a part of the human condition, and their roles are significant parts of the complete story of human evolution.

Adaptationism and the Panglossian Paradigm

The story of human evolution, and the evolution of all life for that matter, is never settled because evolution is ongoing. Additionally, because the conditions that shape evolutionary trajectories are not predetermined, evolution itself is emergent. Even during periods of ecological stability, when fewer macroevolutionary changes occur, populations of organisms continue to experience change. When ecological stability is disrupted, populations must adapt to the changes. Darwin explained in naturalistic terms how animals adapt to their environments: traits that contribute to an organism's ability to survive and reproduce in specific environments will become more common. The most "fit"—those organisms best suited to the *current* environmental conditions in which they live—have survived over eons of the history of life on earth to cocreate ecosystems full of animals and plants. Our own bodies are full of evident adaptations: eyes for seeing, ears for hearing, feet for walking on, and so forth.

But what about hands? Feet are adapted to be primarily weight-bearing structures (rather than grasping structures, as in the apes) and that is what we primarily use them for. But we use our hands in many ways: for fine-scale manipulation, greeting, pointing, stimulating a sexual partner, writing, throwing, and cooking, among other uses. So which of these uses express what hands are "for," when all of them express what hands do?

Gould and Lewontin (1979) illustrate the problem with assuming that the function of a trait defines its evolutionary cause. Consider the case of Dr. Pangloss—the protagonistic of Voltaire's *Candide*—who believed that we lived in the best of all possible worlds. Gould and Lewontin use his pronouncement that "noses were made for spectacles and so we have spectacles" to demonstrate the problem with assuming any trait has evolved for a specific purpose. Identifying a function of a trait does not necessitate that the function is the ultimate cause of the trait. Individual traits are not under selection pressures in isolation; in fact, an entire organism must be able to survive and reproduce in their environment. When natural selection results in adaptations, changes that occur in some traits can have cascading effects throughout the phenotype and features that are not under selection pressure can also change.

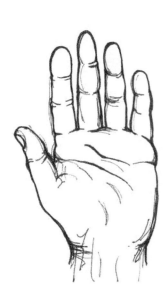

Figure 17.5: Drawings of a human hand (left) and a chimpanzee hand (right). Credit: Human and chimpanzee hand (Figure 2.16) by Mary Nelson original to Explorations: An Open Invitation to Biological Anthropology is under a CC BY-NC 4.0 License.

There is an important lesson in recognizing that what things do in the present is not a good guide to understanding why they came to exist. Gunpowder was invented for entertainment—only later was it adopted for killing people. The Internet was invented to decentralize computers in case of a nuclear attack—and only later adopted for social media. Apes have short thumbs and use their hands in locomotion; our ancestors stopped using their hands in locomotion by about six million years ago and had fairly modern-looking hands by about two million years ago. We can speculate that a combination of selection for abstract thought and dexterity led to evolution of the human hand, with its capability for toolmaking that exceeds what apes can do (see Figure 17.5). But let's face it—how many tools have you made today?

Consequently, we are obliged to see the human foot as having a purpose to which it is adapted and the human hand as having multiple purposes, most of which are different from what it originally evolved for. Paleontologists Gould and Elisabeth Vrba suggested that an original use be regarded as an adaptation and any additional uses be called "**exaptations.**" Thus, we would consider the human hand to be an adaptation for toolmaking and an exaptation for writing. So how do we know whether any particular feature is an adaptation, like the walking foot, rather than an exaptation, like the writing hand? Or more broadly, how can we reason rigorously from what a feature does to what it evolved for?

The answer to the question "what did this feature evolve for?" creates an origin myth. This origin myth contains three assumptions: (1) features can be isolated as evolutionary units; (2) there is a specific reason for the existence of any particular feature; and (3) there is a clear and simplistic explanation for why the feature evolved.

The first assumption was appreciated a century ago as the "unit-character problem." Are the units by which the body grows and evolves the same as units we name? This is clearly not the case: we have genes and we have noses, and we have genes that affect noses, but we don't have "nose genes." What is the relationship between the evolving elements that we see, identify, and name, and the elements that biologically exist and evolve? It is hard to know, but we can use the history of science as a guide to see how that fallacy has been used by earlier generations. Back in the 19th century, the early anatomists argued that since the brain contained the mind, they could map different mental states (acquisitiveness, punctuality, sensitivity) onto parts of the brain. Someone who was very introspective, say, would have an enlarged introspection part of the brain, a cranial bulge to represent the hyperactivity of this mental state. The anatomical science was known as **phrenology**, and it was predicated on the false assumption that units of thought or personality or behavior could be mapped to distinct parts of the brain and physically observed (see Figure17.6). This is the fallacy of reification, imagining that something named is something real.

Long alt text: Side view of human head. At the top are the words "Know Thyself." On the upper head are small illustrations and word qualities such as "friendship," "self-esteem," and "secretiveness." On the lower part of the man's man's face are the words *The Phrenological Journal and Science of Health, A First Class Monthly*. The caption at the bottom reads: "Specially devoted to the '.' Contains PHRENOLOGY and PHYSIOGNOMY, with all the SIGNS OF CHARACTER, and how to read them; ETHNOLOGY, or the Natural History of Man in all his relations." (All emphases in original.)

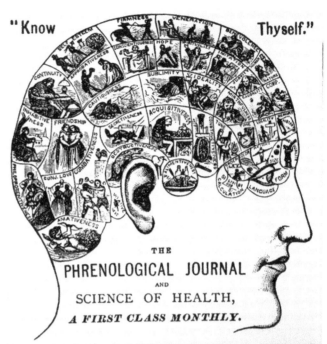

Figure 17.6: According to the early 19th century science of phrenology, units of personality could be mapped onto units in the head, as shown on this cover of The Phrenology Journal. Credit: Phrenology; Chart [slide number 5278, photo number: L0000992, original print from Dr. E. Clark, The Phrenological Journal (Know Thyself)] by Wellcome Collection, is under a CC BY 4.0 License.

Figure 17.7: Chimpanzees have big ears. Credit: Chimpanzee head sketch by Roger Zenner, original by Brehms Tierleben (1887), is in the public domain.

The second assumption, that everything has a reason, has long been recognized as a core belief of religion. Our desire to impose order and simplicity on the workings of the universe, however, does not constrain it to obey simple and orderly causes. Magic, witchcraft, spirits, and divine agency are all powerful explanations for why things happen. Consequently, it is probably not a good idea to lump natural selection in with those. Sometimes things do happen for a reason, of course, but other times things happen as byproducts of other things, or for very complicated and entangled reasons, or for no reason at all. What phenomena have reasons and thereby merit explanation? Chimpanzees have very large testicles, and we think we know why: their promiscuous sexual behavior triggers intense competition for high sperm count. But chimpanzees also have very large ears, but much less scientific attention has been paid to this trait (see Figure 17.7). Why not? Why should there be a reason for chimp testicles but not for chimp ears? What determines the kinds of features that we try to explain, as opposed to the ones that we do not? Again, the assumption that any specific feature has a reason is metaphysical; that is to say, it may be true in any particular case, but to assume it in all cases is gratuitous.

And third, the possibility of knowing what the reason for any particular feature is, assuming that it has one, is a challenge for evolutionary epistemology (the theory of how we know things). Consider the big adaptations of our lineage: bipedalism and language. Nobody doubts that they are good, and they evolved by natural selection, and we know how they work. But why did they evolve? If talking and walking are simply better than not talking and not walking, then why did they evolve in just a single branch of the ape lineage in the primate family tree? We don't know what bipedalism evolved for, although there are plenty of speculations: walking long distances, running long distances, cooling the head, seeing over tall grass, carrying babies, carrying food, wading, threatening, counting calories, sexual display, and so on. Neither do we know what language evolved for, although there are speculations: coordinating hunting, gossiping, manipulating others. But it is also possible that bipedality is simply the way that a small arboreal ape travels on the ground, if it isn't in the treetops. Or that language is simply the way that a primate with small canine teeth and certain mental propensities comes to communicate. If that were true, then there might be no reason for bipedality or language: having the unique suite of preconditions and a fortuitous set of circumstances simply set them in motion, and natural selection elaborated and explored their potentials. It is possible that walking and talking simply solved problems that no other lineage had ever solved; but even if so, the fact remains that the rest of the species in the history of life have done pretty well without having solved them.

It is certainly very optimistic to think that all three assumptions (that organisms can be meaningfully atomized, that everything has a reason, and that we can know the reason) would be simultaneously in effect. Indeed, just as there are many ways of adapting (genetically, epigenetically, behaviorally, culturally), there are also many ways of being nonadaptive, which would imply that there is no reason at all for the feature in question.

First, there is the element of randomness of population histories. There are more cases of sickle-cell anemia among sub-Saharan Africans than other peoples, and there is a reason for it: carriers of sickle-cell anemia have a resistance to malaria, which is more frequent in parts of Africa (as discussed in Chapters 4 and 14). But there are more cases of a blood disease called variegated porphyria, a rare genetic metabolic disorder, in the Afrikaners of South Africa (descendants of mostly Dutch settlers in the 17th century) than in other peoples, and there is no reason for it. Yet we know the cause: One of the founding Dutch colonial settlers had the **allele**–a variant of a gene–and everyone in South Africa with it today is her descendant. But that is not a reason—that is simply an accident of history.

Second, there is the potential mismatch between the past and the present. The value of a particular feature in the past may be changed as the environmental circumstances change. Our species is diurnal, and our ancestors were diurnal. But beginning around a few hundred thousand years ago, our ancestors could build fires, which extended the light period, which was subsequently further amplified by lamps and candles. And over the course of the 20th century, electrical power has made it possible for people to stay up very late when it is dark—working, partying, worrying—to a greater extent than any other closely related species. In other words, we evolved to be diurnal, yet we are now far more nocturnal than any of our recent ancestors or close relatives. Are we adapting to nocturnality? If so, why? Does it even make any sense to speak of the human occupation of a nocturnal ape niche, despite the fact that we empirically seem to be doing just that? And if so, does it make sense to ask what the reason for it is?

Third, there is a genetic phenomenon known as a selective sweep, or the hitchhiker effect. Imagine three genes—A, B, and C—located very closely together on a chromosome. They each have several variants, or alleles, in the population. Now, for whatever reason, it becomes beneficial to have one of the B alleles, say B4; this B4 allele is now under strong positive selection. Obviously, we will expect future generations to be characterized by mostly B4. But what was B4 attached to? Because whatever A and C alleles were adjacent to it will also be quickly spread, simply by virtue of the selection for B4. Even if the A and C alleles are not very good, they will spread because of the good B4 allele between them. Eventually the linkage groups will break up because of genetic crossing-over in future generations. But in the meantime, some random version of genes A and C are proliferating in the species simply because they are joined to superior allele B4. And clearly, the A and C alleles are there because of selection—but not because of selection *for* them!

Fourth, some features are simply consequences of other properties rather than adaptations to external conditions. We already noted the phenomenon of allometric growth, in which some physical features have to outgrow others to maintain function at an increased size. Can we ask the reason for the massive brow ridges of *Homo erectus*, or are brow ridges simply what you get when you have a conjunction of thick skull bones, a large face, and a sloping forehead—and, thus, again would have a cause but no reason?

Fifth, some features may be underutilized and on the way out. What is the reason for our two outer toes? They aren't propulsive, they don't do anything, and sometimes they're just in the way. Obviously they are there because we are descended from ancestors with five digits on their hands and feet. Is it possible that a million years from now, we will just have our three largest toes, just as the ancestors of the horse lost their digits in favor of a single hoof per limb? Or will our outer toes find another use, such as stabilizing the landings in our personal jet-packs? For the time being, we can just recognize vestigiality as another nonadaptive explanation for the presence of a given feature.

Finally, Darwin himself recognized that many obvious features do not help an animal survive. Some things may instead help an animal breed. The peacock's tail feathers do not help it eat, but they do help it mate. There is competition, but only against half of the species. Darwin called this

sexual selection. Its result is not a fit to the environment but, rather, a fit to the opposite sex. In some species, that is literally the case, as the male and female genitalia have specific ways of anatomically fitting together. The specific form is less important than the specific match, so inquiring about the reason for a particular form of the reproductive anatomy may be misleading. The specific form may be effectively random, as long as it fits the opposite sex and is different from the anatomies of other species. Nor is sexual selection the only form of selection that can affect the body differently from natural selection. Competition might also take place between biological units other than organisms—perhaps genes, perhaps cells, or populations, or species. The spread of cultural things, such as head-binding or cheap refined fructose or forced labor, can have significant effects upon bodies, which are also not adaptations produced by natural selection. They are often adaptive physiological responses to stresses but not the products of natural selection.

With so many paths available by which a physical feature might have organically arisen without having been the object of natural selection, it is unwise to assume that any individual trait is an adaptation. And that generalization applies to the best-known, best-studied, and most materially based evolutionary adaptations of our lineage. But our cultural behaviors are also highly adaptive, so what about our most familiar social behaviors? Patriarchy, hierarchy, warfare—are these adaptations? Do they have reasons? Are they good for something?

This is where some sloppy thinking has been troublesome. What would it mean to say that patriarchy evolved by natural selection in the human species? If, on the one hand, it means that the human mind evolved by natural selection to be able to create and survive in many different kinds of social and political regimes, of which patriarchy is one, then biological anthropologists will readily agree. If, on the other hand, it means that patriarchy evolved by natural selection, that implies that patriarchy is genetically determined (since natural selection is a genetic process) and out-reproduced the alleles for other, more egalitarian, social forms. This in turn would imply that patriarchy is an adaptation and therefore of some beneficial value in the past and has become an ingrained part of human nature today. This would be bad news, say, if you harbored ambitions of dismantling it. Dismantling patriarchy in that case would be to go against nature, a futile gesture. In other words, this latter interpretation would be a naturalistic manifesto for a conservative political platform: don't try to dismantle the patriarchy, because it is within us, the product of evolution—suck it up and live with it.

Here, evolution is being used as a political instrument for transforming the human genome into an imaginary glass ceiling against equality. There is thus a convergence between the pseudo-biology of crude **adaptationism** (the idea that everything is the product of natural selection) and the pseudo-biology of hereditarianism. Naturalizing inequality is not the business of evolutionary theory, and it represents a difficult moral position for a scientist to adopt, as well as a poor scientific position.

Concluding Thoughts

Now that you have finished reading this chapter, you are equipped to understand the historical and political dimensions of evolution. Evolution is an ongoing process of change and diversification. Evolutionary theory is a tool that we use to understand this process. The development of evolutionary theory is shaped both by scientific innovation and political engagement. Since Darwin first articulated natural selection as an observable mechanism by which species adapt to their environments, our understanding of evolution has grown. Initially, scientists focused on the adaptive aspects of evolution. However, with the emergence of genetics, our understanding of heredity and the level at which evolution acts has changed. Genetics led to a focus on the molecular dimensions of evolution. For some, this focus resulted in reductive accounts of evolution. Further developments in our understanding of evolution shifted our view to epigenetic processes and how organisms shape their own evolutionary pressures (e.g., niche construction).

Evolutionary theory will continue to develop in the future as we invent new technologies, describe new dimensions of biology, and experience cultural changes. Current innovations in evolutionary theory are asking us to consider evolutionary forces beyond natural selection and genetics to include the ways organisms shape their environments (niche construction), inheritances beyond genetics (inclusive inheritance), constraints on evolutionary change (developmental bias), and the ability of bodies to change in response to external factors (plasticity). The future of evolutionary theory looks bright as we continue to explore these and other dimensions. Biological anthropology is well-positioned to be a lively part of this conversation, as it extends standard evolutionary theory by considering the role of culture, social learning, and human intentionality in shaping the evolutionary trajectories of humans (Zeder 2018). Remember, at root, human evolutionary theory consists of two propositions: (1) the human species is descended from other similar species and (2) natural selection has been the primary agent of biological adaptation. Pretty much everything else is subject to some degree of contestation.

Review Questions

- How is the study of your ancestors biopolitical, not just biological? Does that make it less scientific or differently scientific?
- What was gained by reducing organisms to genotypes and species to gene pools? What is gained by reintroducing bodies and species into evolutionary studies?
- How do genetic or molecular studies complement anatomical studies of evolution?
- How are you reducible to your ancestry? If you could meet your ancestors from the year 1700 (and you would have well over a thousand of them!), would their lives be meaningfully similar to yours? Would you even be able to communicate with them?
- The molecular biologist François Jacob argued that evolution is more like a tinkerer than an engineer. In what ways do we seem like precisely engineered machinery, and in what ways do we seem like jerry-rigged or improvised contraptions?
- How might biological anthropology contribute to future developments in evolutionary theory?

Key Terms

Adaptation: A fit between the organism and environment.

Adaptationism: The idea that everything is the product of natural selection.

Allele: A genetic variant.

Allometry: The differential growth of body parts.

Canalization: The tendency of a growing organism to be buffered toward normal development.

Epigenetics: The study of how genetically identical cells and organisms (with the same DNA base sequence) can nevertheless differ in stably inherited ways.

Eugenics: An idea that was popular in the 1920s that society should be improved by breeding "better" kinds of people.

Evo-devo: The study of the origin of form; a contraction of "evolutionary developmental biology."

Exaptation: An additional beneficial use for a biological feature.

Extinction: The loss of a species from the face of the earth.

Gene: A stretch of DNA with an identifiable function (sometimes broadened to include any DNA with recognizable structural features as well).

Gene pool: Hypothetical summation of the entire genetic composition of population or species.

Genotype: Genetic constitution of an individual organism.

Hereditarianism: The idea that genes or ancestry is the most crucial or salient element in a human life. Generally associated with an argument for natural inequality on pseudo-genetic grounds.

Hox genes: A group of related genes that control for the body plan of an embryo along the head-tail axis.

Inheritance of acquired characteristics: The idea that you pass on the features that developed during your lifetime, not just your genes; also known as Lamarckian inheritance.

Natural selection: A consistent bias in survival and fertility, leading to the overrepresentation of certain features in future generations and an improved fit between an average member of the population and the environment.

Niche construction: The active engagement by which species transform their surroundings in favorable ways, rather than just passively inhabiting them.

Phenotype: Observable manifestation of a genetic constitution, expressed in a particular set of circumstances. The suite of traits of an organism.

Phrenology: The 19th-century anatomical study of bumps on the head as an indication of personality and mental abilities.

Plasticity: The tendency of a growing organism to react developmentally to its particular conditions of life.

Punctuated equilibria: The idea that species are stable through time and are formed very rapidly relative to their duration. (The opposite theory, that species are unstable and constantly changing through time, is called phyletic gradualism.)

Scientific racism: The use of pseudoscientific evidence to support or legitimize racial hierarchy and inequality.

Sexual selection: Natural selection arising through preference by one sex for certain characteristics in individuals of the other sex.

Species selection: A postulated evolutionary process in which selection acts on an entire species population, rather than individuals.

About the Authors

Jonathan Marks, Ph.D.

University of North Carolina at Charlotte, jmarks@uncc.edu

Jonathan Marks is Professor of Anthropology at the University of North Carolina at Charlotte. He has published many books and articles on broad aspects of biological anthropology. In 2006 he was elected a Fellow of the American Association for the Advancement of Science. In 2012 he was awarded the First Citizen's Bank Scholar's Medal from UNC Charlotte. In recent years he has been a Visiting Research Fellow at the ESRC Genomics Forum in Edinburgh, a Visiting Research Fellow at the Max Planck Institute for the History of Science in Berlin, and a Templeton Fellow at the Institute for Advanced Study at Notre Dame. His work has received the W. W. Howells Book Prize and the General Anthropology Division Prize for Exemplary Cross-Field Scholarship from the American Anthropological Association as well as the J. I. Staley Prize from the School for Advanced Research. Two of his books are titled *What It Means to Be 98% Chimpanzee* and *Why I Am Not a Scientist*, but actually he is about 98 percent scientist and not a chimpanzee.

Adam P. Johnson, M.A.

University of North Carolina at Charlotte/University of Texas at San Antonio, ajohn344@uncc.edu

Adam Johnson is a doctoral candidate at the University of Texas at San Antonio and part-time lecturer at the University of North Carolina at Charlotte. He earned his M.A. in anthropology at UNC-Charlotte in 2017 and will complete his Ph.D. in anthropology at UTSA by 2024. His interests include human-animal relations, science studies, primate behavior, ecology, and the history of anthropology. His recent research project analyzes the social, historical, political, and evolutionary dimensions that shape human-javelina encounters. His goal is to understand how humans and animals find ways to get along in a precarious world.

For Further Exploration

Ackermann, Rebecca Rogers, Alex Mackay, and Michael L. Arnold. 2016. "The Hybrid Origin of 'Modern' Humans." *Evolutionary Biology* 43 (1): 1–11.

Bateson, Patrick, and Peter Gluckman. 2011. *Plasticity, Robustness, Development and Evolution*. New York: Cambridge University Press.

Cosans, Christopher E. 2009. *Owen's Ape and Darwin's Bulldog: Beyond Darwinism and Creationism*. Bloomington, IN: Indiana University Press.

Desmond, Adrian, and James Moore. 2009. *Darwin's Sacred Cause: How a Hatred of Slavery Shaped Darwin's Views on Human Evolution*. New York: Houghton Mifflin Harcourt.

Dobzhansky, Theodosius, Francisco J. Ayala, G. Ledyard Stebbins, and James W. Valentine. 1977. *Evolution*. San Francisco: W.H. Freeman and Company.

Fuentes, Agustín. 2017. *The Creative Spark: How Imagination Made Humans Exceptional*. New York: Dutton.

Gould, Stephen J. 2003. *The Structure of Evolutionary Theory*. Cambridge, MA: Harvard University Press.

Haraway, Donna J. 1989. *Primate Visions: Gender, Race, and Nature in the World of Modern Science*. New York: Routledge.

Huxley, Thomas. 1863. *Evidence as to Man's Place in Nature*. London: Williams & Norgate.

Jablonka, Eva, and Marion J. Lamb. 2005. *Evolution in Four Dimensions: Genetic, Epigenetic, Behavioral, and Symbolic Variation in the History of Life*. Cambridge, MA: The MIT Press.

Kuklick, Henrika, ed. 2008. *A New History of Anthropology*. New York: Blackwell.

Laland, Kevin N., Tobias Uller, Marcus W. Feldman, Kim Sterelny, Gerd B. Muller, Armin Moczek, Eva Jablonka, and John Odling-Smee. 2015. "The Extended Evolutionary Synthesis: Its Structure, Assumptions and Predictions." *Proceedings of the Royal Society, Series B* 282 (1813): 20151019.

Lamarck, Jean Baptiste. 1809. *Philosophie Zoologique*. Paris: Dentu.

Landau, Misia. 1991. *Narratives of Human Evolution*. New Haven: Yale University Press.

Lee, Sang-Hee. 2017. *Close Encounters with Humankind: A Paleoanthropologist Investigates Our Evolving Species*. New York: W. W. Norton.

Livingstone, David N. 2008. *Adam's Ancestors: Race, Religion, and the Politics of Human Origins*. Baltimore: Johns Hopkins University Press.

Marks, Jonathan. 2015. *Tales of the Ex-Apes: How We Think about Human Evolution*. Berkeley, CA: University of California Press.

Pigliucci, Massimo. 2009. "The Year in Evolutionary Biology 2009: An Extended Synthesis for Evolutionary Biology." *Annals of the New York Academy of Sciences* 1168: 218–228.

Simpson, George Gaylord. 1949. *The Meaning of Evolution: A Study of the History of Life and of Its Significance for Man*. New Haven: Yale University Press.

Sommer, Marianne. 2016. *History Within: The Science, Culture, and Politics of Bones, Organisms, and Molecules*. Chicago: University of Chicago Press.

Stoczkowski, Wiktor. 2002. *Explaining Human Origins: Myth, Imagination and Conjecture*. New York: Cambridge University Press.

Tattersall, Ian, and Rob DeSalle. 2019. *The Accidental Homo sapiens: Genetics, Behavior, and Free Will*. New York: Pegasus.

References

Barton, Robert A. 1996. "Neocortex Size and Behavioural Ecology in Primates." *Proceedings of the Royal Society of London. Series B: Biological Sciences* 263 (1367): 173–177.

Bodmer, Walter, and Robin McKie. 1997. *The Book of Man: The Hman Genome Project and the Quest to Discover our Genetic Heritage.* Oxford University Press.

Darwin, Charles. 1859. *On the Origin of Species by Means of Natural Selection, or, the Preservation of Favoured Races in the Struggle for Life.* London: J. Murray.

Darwin, Charles. 1871. *The Descent of Man, and Selection in Relation to Sex.* London: J. Murray.

Dawkins, Richard. 1976. *The Selfish Gene.* Oxford University Press.

Deacon, T. W. 1998. *The Symbolic Species: The Co-evolution of Language and the Brain.* W. W. Norton & Company.

Eldredge, N., and S. J. Gould. 1972. "Punctuated Equilibria: An Alternative to Phyletic Gradualism." In *Models in Paleobiology*, edited by T. J. Schopf, 82–115. San Francisco: W. H. Freeman.

Gould, Stephen J. 2003. *The Structure of Evolutionary Theory.* Cambridge, MA: Harvard University Press.

Gould, Stephen J. 1996. *Mismeasure of Man.* New York: WW Norton & Company.

Gould, Stephen Jay, and Richard C. Lewontin. 1979. "The Spandrels of San Marco and the Panglossian Paradigm: A Critique of the Adaptationist Programme." *Proceedings of the Royal Society of London. Series B: Biological Sciences* 205 (1151): 581–598.

Haeckel, Ernst. 1868. *Natürliche Schöpfungsgeschichte.* Berlin: Reimer.

Huxley, Thomas Henry. 1863. *Evidence as to Man's Place in Nature.* London: Williams and Norgate.

Kaufman, Thomas C., Mark A. Seeger, and Gary Olsen. 1990. "Molecular and Genetic Organization of the Antennapedia Gene Complex of *Drosophila melanogaster*." *Advances in Genetics* 27: 309–362.

Kellogg, Vernon. 1917. *Headquarters Nights.* Boston: The Atlantic Monthly Press.

Kevles, Daniel J., and Leroy Hood. 1993. *The Code of Codes: Scientific and Social Issues in the Human Genome Project.* Cambridge, MA: Harvard University Press.

Lewontin, Richard, Steven Rose, and Leon Kamin. 2017. *Not in Our Genes: Biology, Ideology, and Human Nature*, 2nd ed. Chicago: Haymarket Books.

Lloyd, Elisabeth A., and Stephen J. Gould. 1993. "Species Selection on Variability." *Proceedings of the National Academy of Sciences* 90 (2): 595–599.

Marks, Jonathan. 2015. "The Biological Myth of Human Evolution." In *Biologising the Social Sciences: Challenging Darwinian and Neuroscience Explanations*, edited by David Canter and David A. Turner, 59–78. London: Routledge.

Monypenny, William Flavelle, and George Earle Buckle. 1929. *The Life of Benjamin Disraeli, Earl of Beaconsfield, Volume II: 1860–1881.* London: John Murray.

Potts, Rick. 1998. "Variability Selection in Hominid Evolution." *Evolutionary Anthropology* 7: 81–96.

Punnett, R. C. 1905. *Mendelism.* Cambridge: Macmillan and Bowes.

Shapiro, Robert. 1991. *The Human Blueprint: The Race to Unlock the Secrets of Our Genetic Script.* New York: St. Martin's Press.

Shultz, Susanne, Emma Nelson, and Robin Dunbar. 2012. "Hominin Cognitive Evolution: Identifying Patterns and Processes in the Fossil and Archaeological Record." *Philosophical Transactions of the Royal Society B: Biological Sciences* 367 (1599): 2130–2140.

Spencer, Herbert. 1864. *Principles of Biology.* London: Williams and Norgate.

Watson, James D. 1990. "The Human Genome Project: Past, Present, and Future." *Science* 248 (4951): 44–49.

Yengo, L., Vedantam, S., Marouli, E., Sidorenko, J., Bartell, E., Sakaue, S., Graff, M., Eliasen, A.U., Jiang, Y., Raghavan, S. and Miao, J., 2022. A saturated map of common genetic variants associated with human height. *Nature, 610* (7933): 704-712.

Zeder, Melinda A. 2018. "Why Evolutionary Biology Needs Anthropology: Evaluating Core Assumptions of the Extended Evolutionary Synthesis." *Evolutionary Anthropology: Issues, News, and Reviews* 27 (6): 267–284.

APPENDIX A: OSTEOLOGY

Jason M. Organ, Ph.D., Indiana University School of Medicine

Jessica N. Byram, Ph.D., Indiana University School of Medicine

This chapter is a revision from "Appendix A: Osteology" by Jason M. Organ and Jessica N. Byram. In Explorations: An Open Invitation to Biological Anthropology, *first edition, edited by Beth Shook, Katie Nelson, Kelsie Aguilera, and Lara Braff, which is licensed under CC BY-NC 4.0.*

Learning Objectives

- Identify anatomical position and anatomical planes, and use directional terms to describe relative positions of bones and teeth.
- Describe the different regions of the human skeleton and identify (by name) all of the bones within them.
- Distinguish major bony features of the human skeleton like muscle attachment sites and passages for nerves and/or arteries and veins.
- Identify the bony features relevant to estimating age and sex in forensic and bioarchaeological contexts.

Introduction to Osteology

Osteology, or the study of bones, is central to biological anthropology because every person's skeleton tells a story of how that person has lived. Bones from archaeological sites can be used to understand what animals people ate, how stressful and strenuous their lives were, and how they died—by natural or unnatural causes. This appendix introduces the basics of anatomical terminology and describes the different regions and bones of the skeleton. It also highlights some skeletal features that are used frequently by forensic anthropologists to estimate the age and sex of recovered remains. The authors note that sex is not binary but exists on a spectrum based on influences of chromosomes, genes, and hormones. These biological influences affect the size and shape of bone, which is sometimes useful in classifying skeletal remains into one of the two most common sex categories: female and male.

Bone Structure and Function

Bone is a composite of organic collagen and an inorganic mineral (hydroxyapatite, a calcium phosphate salt), which help make it strong enough to support the body under the force of gravity without collapsing. When bone is mature (fully mineralized as in adults), it comprises an outer dense region of bone called **cortical (or compact) bone** and an inner spongy region of bone called **cancellous (or trabecular) bone** (Figure A.1).

Bone performs both metabolic and mechanical functions for the body. On the metabolic side, bone is required to maintain mineral (i.e., calcium) homeostasis and for the production of red and white blood cells (Figure A.2), which develop in the diaphyseal marrow cavity and the cancellous region of the metaphysis and epiphysis. But it is undeniable that the mechanical functions of bone are primary because bone is critically responsible for protecting internal organs, providing support against the force of gravity, and serving as a network of rigid levers for muscles to act upon during movement.

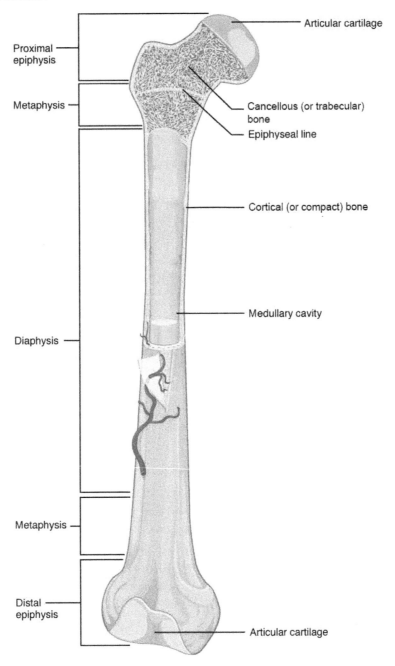

Figure A.1: A typical long bone shows the gross anatomical characteristics of bone. Credit: Anatomy of a Long Bone (Anatomy & Physiology, Figure 6.7) by OpenStax has been modified (some labels modified or removed) and is under a CC BY 4.0 License. [Image Description].

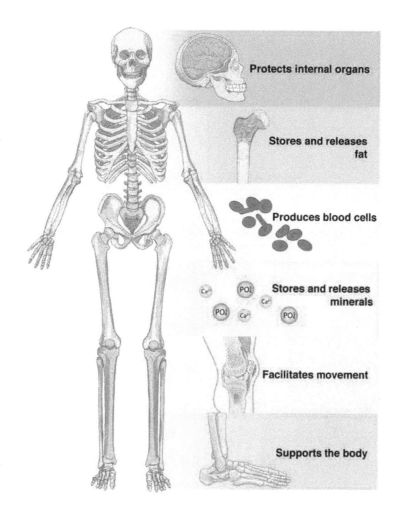

Figure A.2: Functions of the skeletal system include support and protection, storage and release of fat, production of red blood cells, storage and release of calcium and phosphates, and facilitating movement. Credit: Functions of the Skeletal System (Anatomy & Physiology, Figure 6.1.1) by Open Oregon State is under a CC BY 4.0 License. [Image Description].

Bone Shape

Bones have different shapes that largely relate to their specific function within the skeletal system. Additionally, the ratio of cortical to cancellous bone, and which muscles are attached to the bone and how, affect the shape of the whole bone. Generally there are five recognized bone shapes: long bones, short bones, flat bones, sesamoid bones, and irregular bones. **Long bones** are longer than they are wide and consist of three sections: diaphysis, epiphysis, and metaphysis (see Figure A.1). The **diaphysis** of a long bone is simply the shaft of the bone, and it comprises mostly cortical bone with a thin veneer of internal cancellous bone lining a **medullary cavity**. At both the proximal and distal ends of every long bone, there is an **epiphysis**, which consists of a thin shell of cortical bone surrounding a high concentration of cancellous bone. The epiphysis is usually coated with cartilage to facilitate joint articulation with other bones. The junction between diaphysis and epiphysis is the **metaphysis**, which has a more equal ratio of cortical to cancellous bone. Examples of long bones are the humerus, the femur, and the metacarpals and metatarsals.

The other three bone shapes are simpler. **Short bones** are defined as being equal in length and width, and they possess a mix of cortical and cancellous bone (Figure A.3). They are usually involved in forming movable joints with adjacent bones and therefore often have surfaces covered with cartilage. Examples of short bones are the carpals of the wrist and the tarsals of the ankle. **Flat bones** are flat and consist of two layers of thick cortical bone with an intermediate layer of cancellous bone referred to as diploë. Most of the bones of the skull are flat bones, such as the frontal and parietal bones, as well as all parts of the sternum (Figure A.3). Sometimes bones develop within the tendon of a muscle in order to reduce friction on the joint surface and to increase leverage of the muscle to move a joint. These types of bones are called **sesamoid bones**, and these include the patella (or knee cap) and the pisiform (a bone of the wrist). **Irregular bones** are bones that don't fit into any of the other four categories. The shapes of these bones are often more complex than the others, and examples include the vertebrae and certain bones of the skull, like the ethmoid and sphenoid bones (Figure A.3).

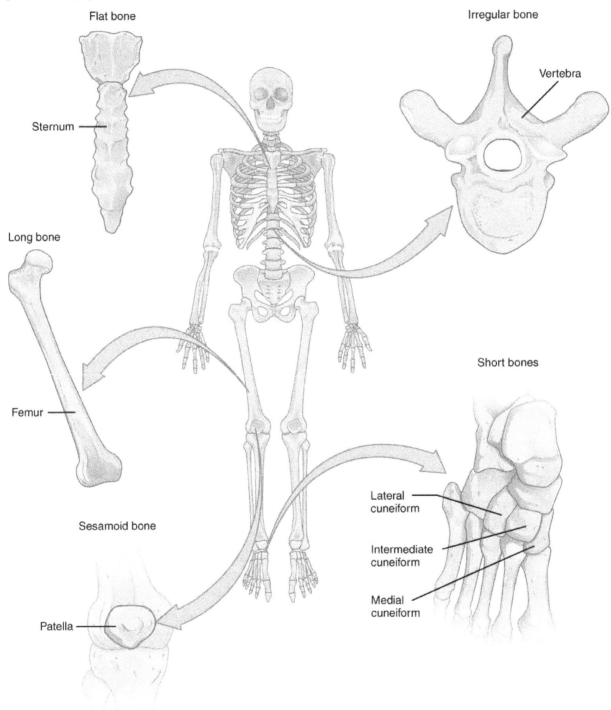

Figure A.3: Bones are classified according to their shape and include long, short, flat, sesamoid, and irregular bones. Credit: Classifications of Bones (Anatomy & Physiology, Figure 6.6) by OpenStax is under a CC BY 4.0 License. [Image Description].

Dig Deeper: Bone Functional Adaptation

Each time we move our muscles, we bend, twist, compress, and tense our bones, and this causes them to develop microscopic cracks that weaken them. These may even lead to a bone fracture. Bone cells called **osteocytes** can sense when these microcracks form. Osteocytes then signal **osteoclasts** to remove the cracked bone and **osteoblasts** to lay down new bone—a process known as skeletal remodeling. **Osteogenic cells** are stem cells that are able to differentiate into osteoblasts and osteocytes (Figure A.4).

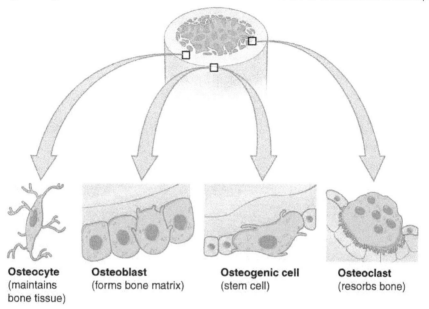

Osteocyte
(maintains
bone tissue)

Osteoblast
(forms bone matrix)

Osteogenic cell
(stem cell)

Osteoclast
(resorbs bone)

Figure A.4: Four types of cells are found within bone tissue. Osteogenic cells are stem cells that develop into osteoblasts. Osteoblasts lay down new bone while osteoclasts remove bone. Osteoblasts that get trapped in calcified matrix become osteocytes. Credit: Bone Cells (Anatomy & Physiology, Figure 6.11) by OpenStax is under a CC BY 4.0 License. [Image Description].

Did Deeper: How Do Bones Develop?

Bones develop via one of two mechanisms: intramembranous or endochondral bone formation. During **intramembranous bone formation** connective tissue (mesenchymal) stem cells form a tissue layer and then differentiate into osteoblasts, which begin to synthesize new bone along the tissue layer (Figure A.5). Only a few bones develop through intramembranous bone formation, mostly bones of the skull and the clavicle (collar bone). In **endochondral bone formation**, instead of developing directly from connective tissue stem cells, osteoblasts develop from an intermediate cartilage "model" that is then replaced by synthesized new bone (Figure A.6). Most bones of the skeleton develop through endochondral bone formation (Burr and Organ 2017).

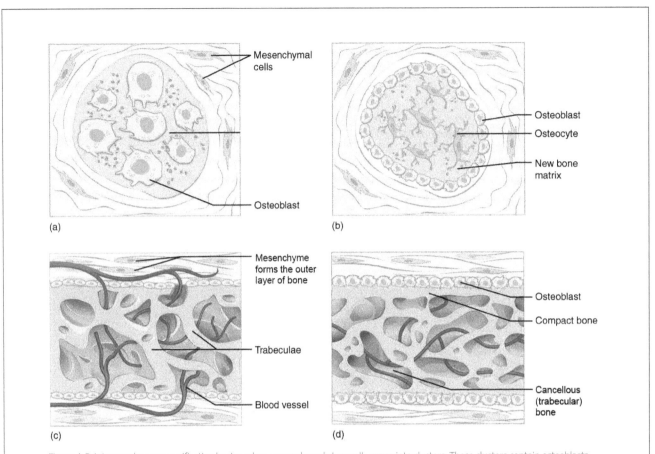

Figure A.5: Intramembranous ossification begins when mesenchymal stem cells group into clusters. These clusters contain osteoblasts, which lay down the initial trabecular bone. Compact bone develops superficial to the trabecular bone, and the initial structure of the bone is complete. Credit: Intramembranous Ossification (Anatomy & Physiology, Figure 6.16) by OpenStax has been modified (some labels modified or removed) and is under a CC BY 4.0 License. [Image Description].

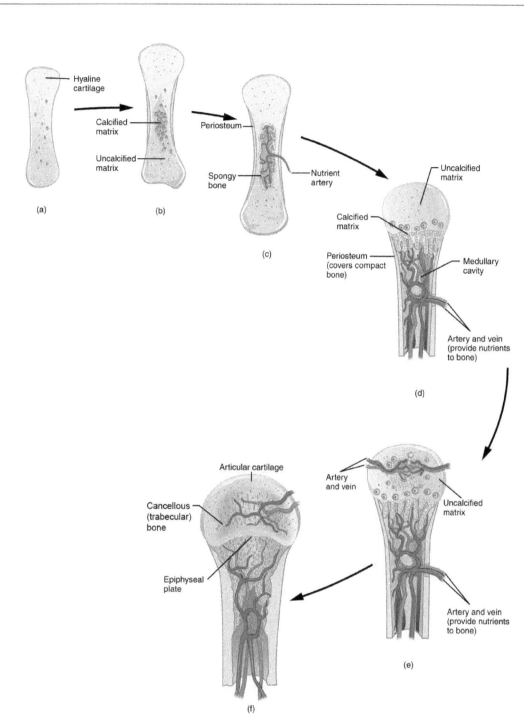

Figure A.6: Endochondral ossification begins when mesenchymal cells differentiate into cartilage cells, which lay down a cartilage model of the future bony skeleton. Cartilage is then replaced by bone, except at the (epiphyseal) growth plates (which fuse at the end of postnatal growth) and the hyaline (articular) cartilage on the joint surface. Credit: Endochondral Ossification (Anatomy & Physiology, Figure 6.17) by OpenStax has been modified (some labels modified or removed) and is under a CC BY 4.0 License. [Image Description].

Anatomical Terminology

Anatomical Planes

A body in **anatomical position** is situated as if the individual is standing upright; with head, eyes, and feet pointing forward; and with arms at the side and palms facing forward. In anatomical position, the bones of the forearm are not crossed (Figure A.7).

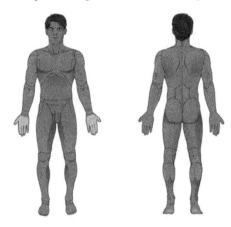

In anatomical position, specific organs are situated within specific anatomical planes (Figure A.8). These imaginary planes divide the body into equal or subequal halves, depending on which plane is described. **Coronal (frontal) planes** divide the body vertically into anterior (front) and posterior (back) halves. **Transverse planes** divide the body horizontally into superior (upper) and inferior (lower) halves. **Sagittal planes** divide the body vertically into left and right halves. The plane that divides the body vertically into equal left and right halves is called the **midsagittal plane**. The midsagittal plane is also called the median plane because it is in the midline of the body. Every other sagittal plane divides the body into unequal right and left halves; these planes are called **parasagittal planes**.

Figure A.7: A human body is shown in anatomical position in an (left) anterior view and a (right) posterior view. Credit: Regions of the Human Body (Anatomy & Physiology, Figure 1.12) by OpenStax has been modified (labels removed) and is under a CC BY 4.0 License. [Image Description].

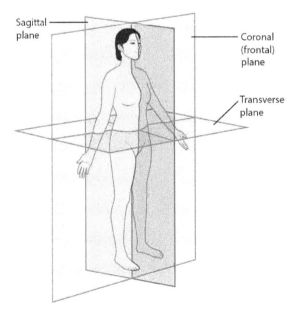

Figure A.8: The three planes most commonly used in anatomical and medical imaging are the sagittal, coronal (or frontal), and transverse planes. A full text description of this image is available. Credit: Planes of the Body (Anatomy & Physiology, Figure 1.14) by OpenStax has been modified (some labels modified) and is under a CC BY 4.0 License. [Image Description].

Directional Terms

An anatomical feature that is **anterior (or ventral)** is located toward the front of the body, and a bone that is **posterior (or dorsal)** is located toward the back of the body (Figure A.9). For example, the sternum (breastbone) is anterior to the vertebral column ("backbone"). A feature that is **medial** is located closer to the midline (midsagittal plane) than a feature that is **lateral**, or located further from the midline. For example, the thumb is lateral to the index finger. A structure that is **proximal** is closer to the trunk of the body (usually referring to limb bones) than a **distal** structure, which is further from the trunk of the body. For example, the femur (thigh bone) is proximal to the tibia (leg bone). Finally, a structure that is **superior (or cranial)** is located closer to the head than a structure that is **inferior (or caudal)**. For example, the rib cage is superior to the pelvis, and the foot is inferior to the knee.

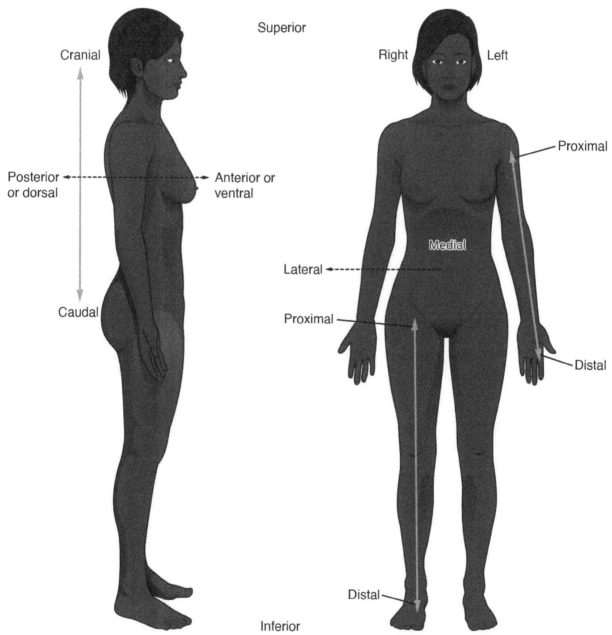

Figure A.9: Paired directional terms are shown as applied to a human body. Credit: Directional Terms Applied to the Human Body (Anatomy & Physiology, Figure 1.13) by OpenStax is under a CC BY 4.0 License. [Image Description].

Human Skeletal System

The skeletal system is divided into two regions: axial and appendicular (Figure A.10). The **axial skeleton** consists of the skull, vertebral column, and the thoracic cage formed by the ribs and sternum (breastbone). The **appendicular skeleton** comprises the pectoral girdle, the pelvic girdle, and all the bones of the upper and lower limbs.

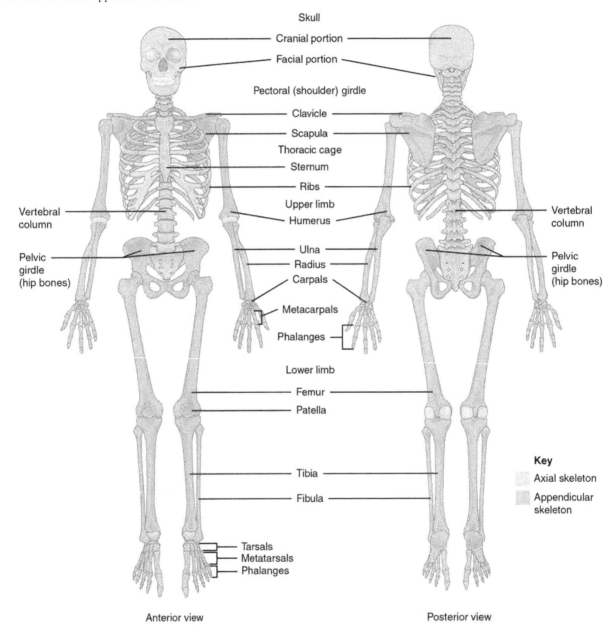

Figure A.10: The axial skeleton consists of the skull, vertebral column, and the thoracic cage. The appendicular skeleton is made up of all bones of the upper and lower limbs. Credit: Axial and Appendicular Skeleton (Anatomy & Physiology, Figure 7.2) by OpenStax is under a CC BY 4.0 License. [Image Description].

Axial Skeleton

Skull

The skull comprises numerous bones (some paired and others that are unpaired) and is divided into two major portions: the **mandible** (or lower jaw) and the **cranium** (the remainder of the skull). The cranium is further subdivided into the **neurocranium** (or cranial vault), which houses the brain, and the **viscerocranium** (or facial skeleton; Figure A.11), which houses the organs responsible for special senses like sight, smell, taste, hearing, and balance.

Where two bones of the cranium come together, they form articulations called **cranial sutures**, which fuse (or close) with increasing age. Degree of suture closure can be used to broadly estimate age at death (Boldsen et al. 2002; Meindl and Lovejoy 1985).

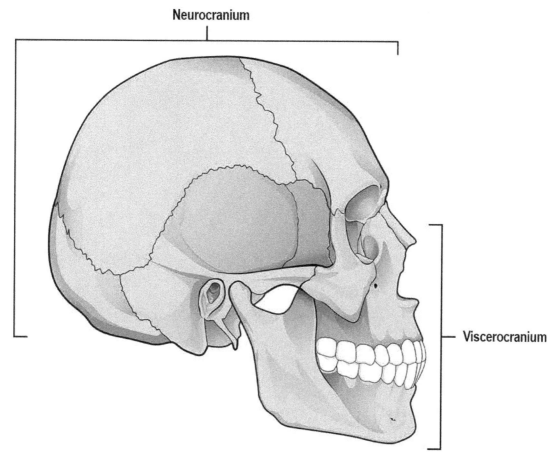

Figure A.11: The skull consists of the cranium and the mandible (jawbone). The cranium is further divided into the neurocranium and viscerocranium. Credit: Parts of the Skull (Anatomy & Physiology, Figure 7.3) by OpenStax has been modified (some labels modified or removed) and is under a CC BY 4.0 License. [Image Description].

Bones and Some Features of the Neurocranium

Frontal bone: an unpaired bone consisting of two parts: a superior, vertically oriented portion called the squama and an inferior, horizontally oriented portion that forms the roof of the **orbit** (eye socket; Figures A.12 and A.13).

The **coronal suture** is the articulation between the frontal bone and the two parietal bones posterior and lateral to the frontal.

The frontal bone develops initially as two separate bones that fuse together during growth. Occasionally this fusion is incomplete, resulting in a **metopic suture** that persists between the two halves (left and right) of the frontal bone (Cunningham, Scheuer, and Black 2017).

The **glabella** is a bony projection between the brow ridges. The glabella in females tends to be flat while it is more rounded and protruding in males (Walker 2008).

The **supraorbital margin** is the upper edge of the orbit. The thickness of the edge may be used as an indicator of sex. The border tends to be thin and sharp in females and blunt and thick in males.

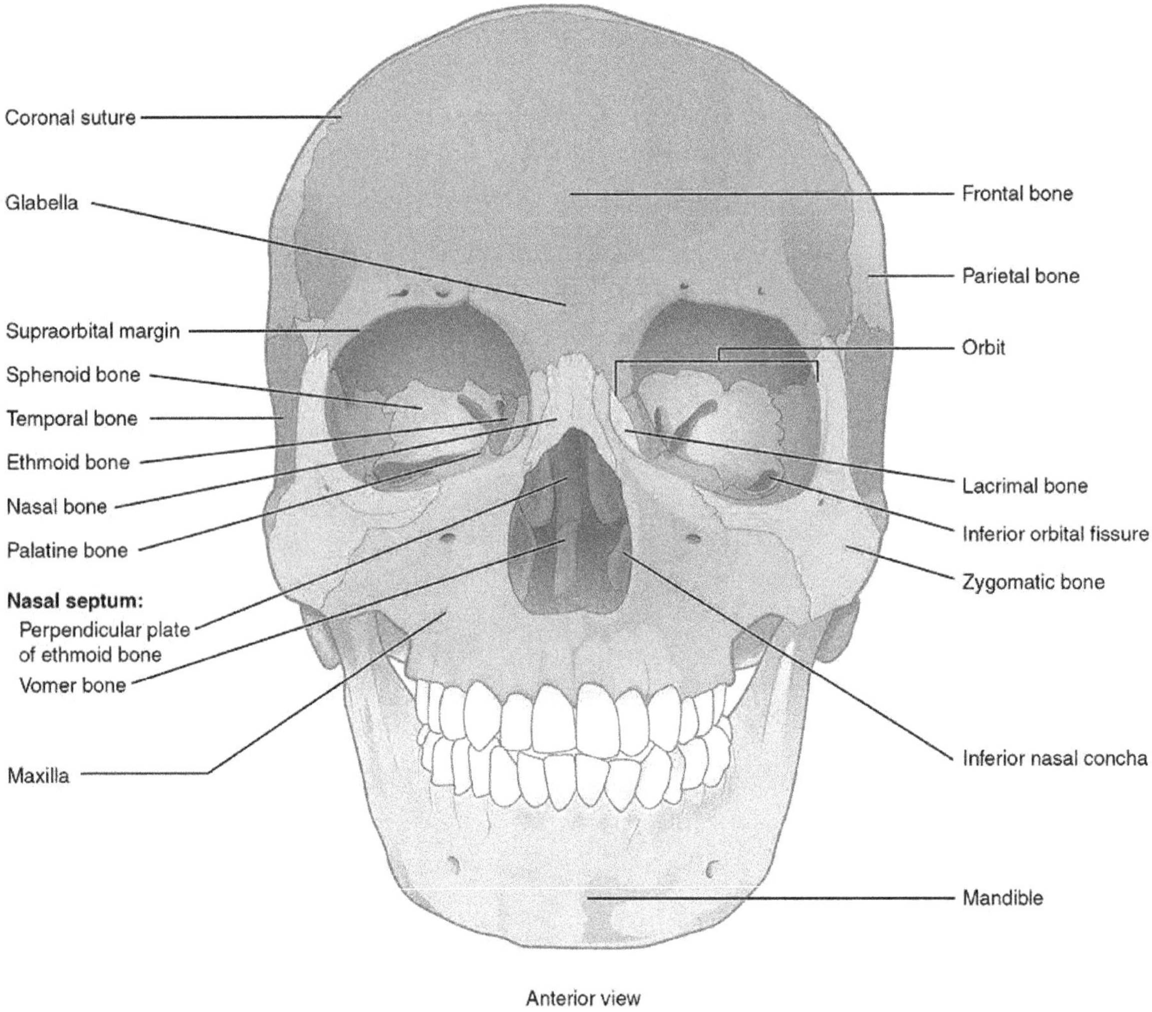

Coronal suture

Glabella

Supraorbital margin

Sphenoid bone

Temporal bone

Ethmoid bone

Nasal bone

Palatine bone

Nasal septum:

Perpendicular plate
of ethmoid bone

Vomer bone

Maxilla

Frontal bone

Parietal bone

Orbit

Lacrimal bone

Inferior orbital fissure

Zygomatic bone

Inferior nasal concha

Mandible

Anterior view

Figure A.12: Anterior view of the skull. Credit: **Anterior View of Skull (Anatomy & Physiology, Figure 7.4)** by OpenStax has been modified (some labels removed) and is under a **CC BY 4.0 License**. [Image Description].

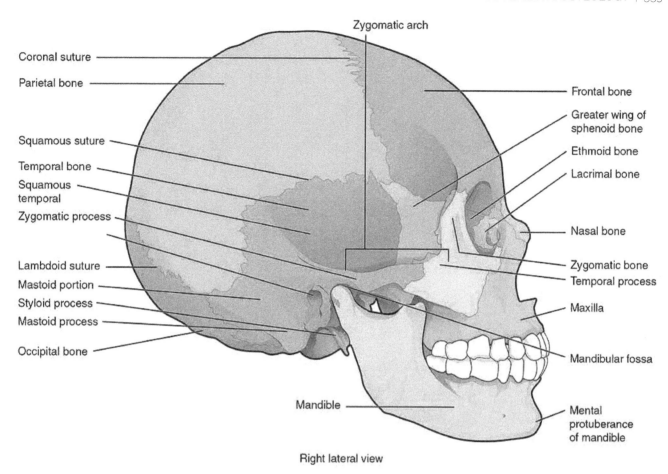

Right lateral view

Figure A.13: The lateral view of the skull. Credit: Lateral View of Skull (Anatomy & Physiology, Figure 7.5) by OpenStax has been modified (some labels removed) and is under a CC BY 4.0 License. [Image Description].

Parietal bone: Paired bones that form the majority of the roof and sides of the neurocranium (Figures A.12 and A.13).

The **sagittal suture** is the articulation between the right and left parietal bones. It extends from the coronal suture to the lambdoidal suture, which separates the parietal bones from the occipital bone posteriorly.

Each parietal bone is marked by two **temporal lines** (superior and inferior), which are anterior-posterior arching lines that serve as attachment sites for a major chewing muscle (temporalis) and its associated connective tissue.

Temporal bone: Paired bones on the lateral side of the neurocranium that are divided into two portions: squamous (or flat) portion that forms the lateral side of the neurocranium and the petrous (or rock-like) portion that houses the special sense organs of the ear for hearing and balance as well as the three tiny bones of the middle ear: incus, malleus, and stapes (Figures A.13, A.14, and A.15).

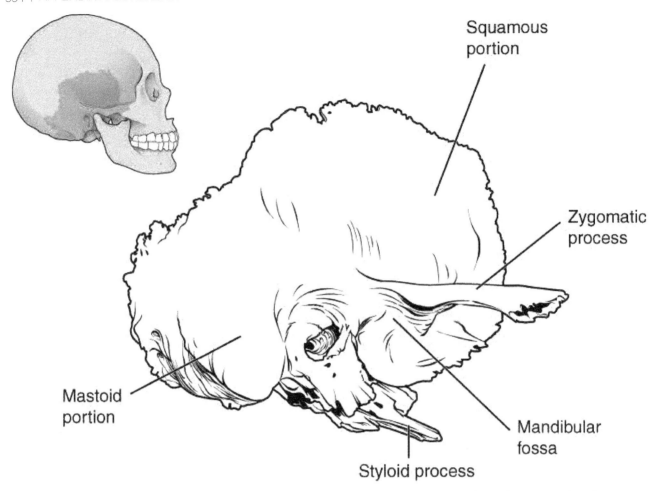

Figure A.14: A lateral view of the isolated temporal bone shows the squamous portion. Credit: Temporal Bone (Anatomy & Physiology, Figure 7.7) by OpenStax has been modified (some labels removed) and is under a CC BY 4.0 License. [Image Description].

The **squamosal suture** is the articulation between the squamous portion of the temporal bone and the inferior border of the parietal bone.

The **mastoid process** is a prominent muscle attachment site for several muscles including the large sternocleidomastoid muscle. Males tend to have longer and wider mastoid processes compared to females (Walker 2008).

The **styloid process** is a thin, pointed, inferior projection of the temporal bone that serves as an attachment site for several muscles and a ligament of the throat.

The **zygomatic process of the temporal bone** is a long thin, arch-like process that originates from the squamous portion of the temporal bone. The zygomatic process articulates with the temporal process of the zygomatic bone to form the **zygomatic arch** (or cheekbone).

The **mandibular fossa** is the depression in the temporal bone where the mandibular condyle (see below, under mandible) articulates to form the temporomandibular (or jaw) joint.

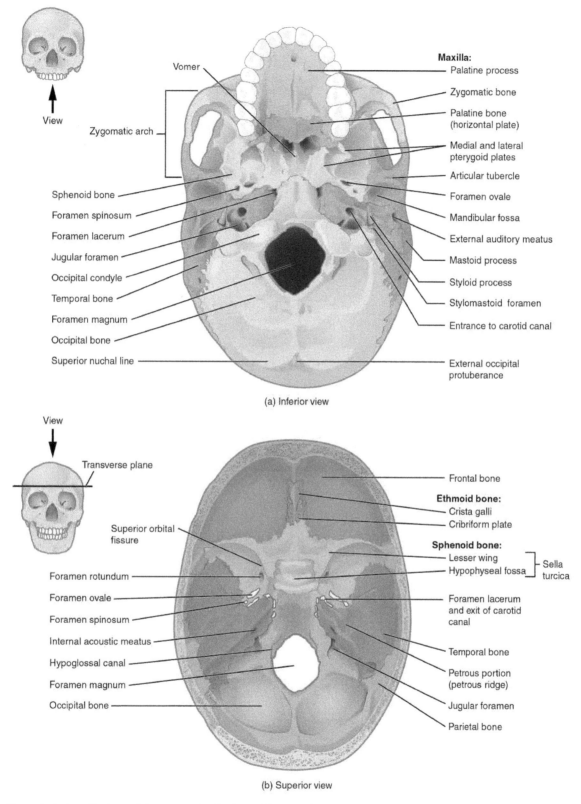

Figure A.15a–b: a. The base of the cranium. b. The floor of the cranial cavity. Credit: External and Internal Views of Base of Skull (Anatomy & Physiology, Figure 7.8) by OpenStax has been modified (some labels modified or removed) and is under a CC BY 4.0 License. [Image Description].

Occipital bone: Unpaired bone that forms the posterior and inferior portions of the neurocranium (see Figures A.13 and A.15).

The **lambdoidal suture** is the articulation between the occipital bone and the two parietal bones. It resembles the shape of the Greek letter lambda.

The **external occipital protuberance** (EOP) is a bump along the posterior margin of the occipital bone where the nuchal ligament attaches.

The **nuchal lines** are parallel ridges that meet on the midline at the EOP and serve as attachment sites for neck muscles. Nuchal lines are usually more pronounced in males.

The occipital bone contains a large circular opening called the **foramen magnum**, which provides a space for passage of the brainstem/spinal cord from the neurocranium into the vertebral canal of the spine.

Sphenoid bone: Unpaired, butterfly-shaped bone that forms the central portion of the bottom of the neurocranium. The sphenoid is divided into several regions, including the body, greater wings, lesser wings, and pterygoid processes (with pterygoid plates; see Figures A.15 and A.16). This bone is critical to supporting the brain and several nerves and blood vessels supplying this region.

Pterygoid plates are flat projections of the pterygoid processes that serve as attachment sites for chewing muscles and muscles of the throat.

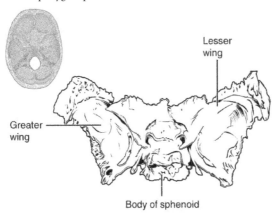

(a) Superior view

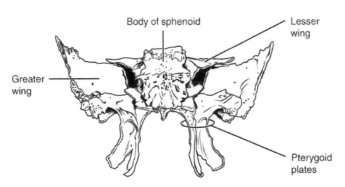

(b) Posterior view

Figure A.16: Shown in isolation in (a) superior and (b) posterior views, the sphenoid forms the central portion of the neurocranium. The sphenoid has multiple openings for the passage of nerves and blood vessels. Credit: Sphenoid Bone (Anatomy & Physiology, Figure 7.10) by OpenStax has been modified (some labels removed) and is under a CC BY 4.0 License. [Image Description].

Ethmoid bone: Unpaired bone consisting of a median vertical plate that forms part of the bony nasal septum and a horizontal plate (cribriform plate) with many small **cribriform foramina** (holes) that transmit olfactory nerves (special sense of smell; Figure A.17).

Bones of the Viscerocranium

Maxilla bone: Paired bones that form the upper jaw, support the upper teeth, and form the inferior margin of the cheek (Figures A.12, A.15, and A.18).

The **nasal spine** is a thin projection on the midline at the inferior border of the nasal aperture.

The **zygomatic process of the maxilla** is the portion of the bone that articulates with the zygomatic bone to form the anterior portion of the zygomatic arch.

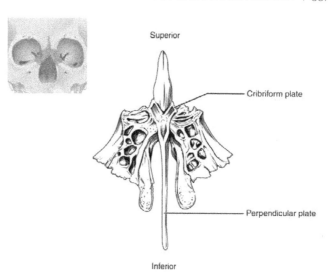

Figure A.17: The unpaired ethmoid bone is located at the midline within the central skull. It forms the upper nasal septum and contains foramina to convey olfactory nerves. Credit: Ethmoid Bone (Anatomy & Physiology, Figure 7.12) by OpenStax has been modified (some labels removed) and is under a CC BY 4.0 License. [Image Description].

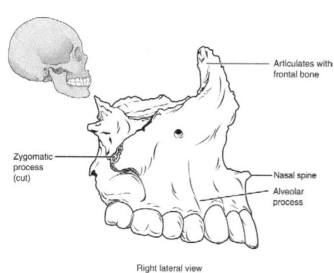

Figure A.18: The maxilla forms the upper jaw and supports the upper teeth. Credit: Maxillary Bone (Anatomy & Physiology, Figure 7.14) by OpenStax has been modified (some labels modified or removed) and is under a CC BY 4.0 License. [Image Description].

Nasal bone: Small, paired, flat, rectangular bones that form the bridge of the nose (Figure A.19).

Nasal aperture is the anterior opening into the nasal cavity.

Zygomatic bone: Paired bones that form the anterolateral portion of the cheekbone and contribute to the lateral and inferior wall of the orbit (Figure A.19).

The **temporal process of the zygomatic bone** is the portion of the bone that articulates with the temporal bone to form the anterior portion of the zygomatic arch.

Palatine bone: Paired L-shaped bones that form the posterior portion of the roof of the mouth, floor of the orbit, and the floor and lateral walls of the nasal cavity (Figures A.15 and A.19).

Lacrimal bone: Small, flat, paired bones that form the anterior portion of the medial wall of the orbit (Figure A.19).

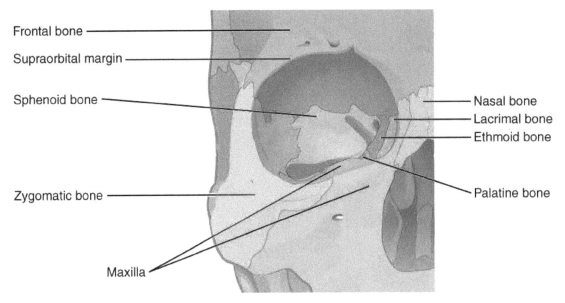

Figure A.19: Seven skull bones contribute to the walls of the orbit: frontal, zygomatic, maxilla, lacrimal, ethmoid, palatine, and sphenoid. Credit: Bones of the Orbit (Anatomy & Physiology, Figure 7.16) by OpenStax has been modified (some labels removed) and is under a CC BY 4.0 License. [Image Description].

Vomer bone: Unpaired thin bone that forms the inferior portion of the bony nasal septum. It articulates with the ethmoid superiorly (Figure A.20).

Inferior nasal concha bone: Paired bones that project and curl like a scroll from the lateral wall of the nasal cavity (Figure A.21).

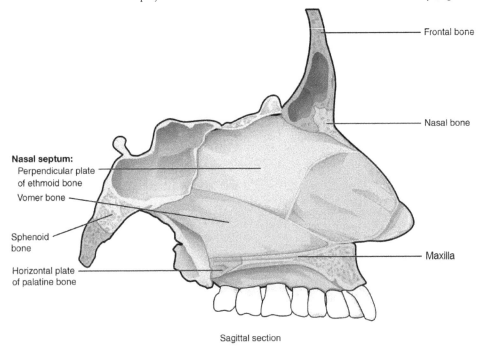

Sagittal section

Figure A.20: The nasal septum is formed by the perpendicular plate of the ethmoid bone and the vomer bone. Credit: Nasal Septum (Anatomy & Physiology, Figure 7.17) by OpenStax has been modified (some labels modified or removed) and is under a CC BY 4.0 License. [Image Description].

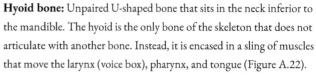

Hyoid bone: Unpaired U-shaped bone that sits in the neck inferior to the mandible. The hyoid is the only bone of the skeleton that does not articulate with another bone. Instead, it is encased in a sling of muscles that move the larynx (voice box), pharynx, and tongue (Figure A.22).

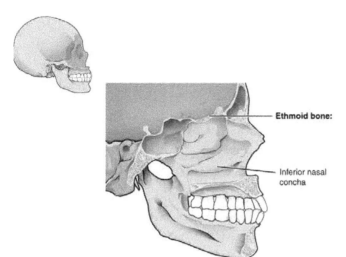

Medial view

Figure A.21: Inferior nasal concha scroll from the lateral wall of the nasal cavity. Credit: Lateral Wall of Nasal Cavity (Anatomy & Physiology, Figure 7.13) by OpenStax has been modified (some labels removed) and is under a CC BY 4.0 License. [Image Description].

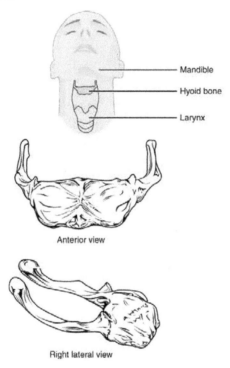

Anterior view

Right lateral view

Figure A.22: The hyoid bone is located in the upper neck and does not join with any other bone. It provides attachments for muscles that move the tongue, larynx, and pharynx. Credit: Hyoid Bone (Anatomy & Physiology, Figure 7.19) by OpenStax has been modified (some labels removed) and is under a CC BY 4.0 License. [Image Description].

Mandible: Unpaired bone with a horizontal (and anteriorly arched) body and a vertical ramus that articulates with the mandibular fossa to form the temporomandibular (jaw) joint. The body of the mandible houses the lower teeth (Figure A.13 and A.23).

The **mental protuberance (eminence)** is the most anteriorly projecting point on the mandible—the so-called "chin." Males tend to have a more prominent mental protuberance than females (Walker 2008).

The **ramus of the mandible** projects superiorly from the body of the mandible and ascends to one of two features on the superior aspect: coronoid process or mandibular condyle.

The **coronoid process** is a bony projection off the anterior and superior aspect of the mandibular ramus. The inferior attachment of the temporalis muscle (a chewing muscle) attaches here.

The **mandibular condyle**, a rounded projection off the posterior and superior aspect of the mandibular ramus. It articulates with the temporal (mandibular) fossa of the temporal bone at the temporomandibular (TMJ) joint.

The **gonial (or mandibular) angle** is the rounded posteroinferior border of the mandible. It tends to be smooth in females with a more obtuse angle but is laterally flared in males and closer to a right angle in shape (Christensen, Passalacqua, and Bartelink 2019).

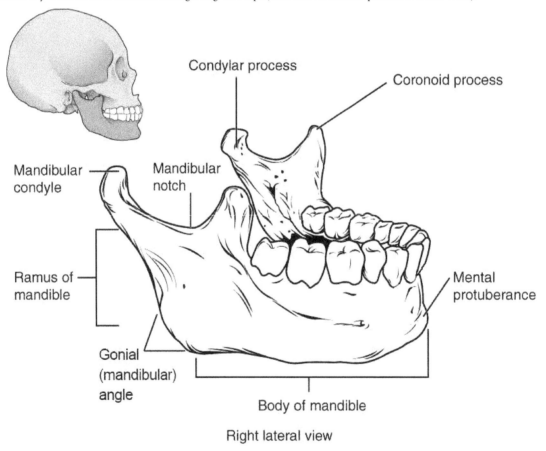

Figure A.23: Isolated view of the mandible, the only moveable bone of the skull. Credit: Isolated Mandible (Anatomy & Physiology, Figure 7.15) by OpenStax has been modified (some labels modified or removed) and is under a CC BY 4.0 License. [Image Description].

Teeth: Adults normally have 32 teeth, distributed among four quadrants of the mouth (upper left, upper right, lower left, lower right). In each quadrant, there are eight teeth: two incisors (central and lateral), one canine, two premolars, and three molars. Each of these types of teeth has a different shape that reflects its function during chewing:

Incisors are flat and shovel shaped and are used to bite into a food item.

Canines are conical, with a single pointed cusp used to puncture a food item.

Premolars have two rounded cusps and are used to grind and mash a food item.

Molars have four (upper molars) or five (lower molars) flatter cusps and are used to grind food prior to swallowing.

The teeth have their own set of directional terms that help differentiate the different parts of the tooth. For example, the anterior portion of the tooth is called **mesial**, while the posterior portion of the tooth is called distal. In the case of teeth in the front of the mouth, mesial refers to the aspect toward the midline of the body; distal refers to the aspect away from the midline. Similarly, the side of the tooth facing the lips is called the **buccal** surface and the side facing the tongue is called the **lingual** surface. Finally, we can talk about the **occlusal surface** of the tooth, which is the surface that comes in contact with food or the teeth from the other jaw when the jaw is closed. Sometimes the occlusal surface of the incisors is called the **incisal surface**.

Vertebral Column

The adult vertebral column consists of 32–33 individual vertebrae, divided into five regions: cervical, thoracic, lumbar, sacral, and coccygeal.

General Structure of a Vertebra

A typical vertebra consists of an anteriorly situated **centrum** (body)—the main weight-bearing element of the vertebra—and a posteriorly projecting **vertebral arch** (Figure A.24). The vertebral arch consists of the paired pedicles and paired laminae. The **pedicle** connects the **transverse process**—a laterally projecting process that serves as an attachment site for muscles and ligaments—to the vertebral body; the **lamina** connects the **spinous process**—a posteriorly projecting process that serves as an attachment site for muscles and ligaments—to the transverse process. Projecting inferiorly off the vertebral arch is the **inferior articular process,** and projecting superiorly off the vertebral arch is the **superior articular process**. Between the vertebral body anteriorly and the vertebral arch posteriorly is an open space called the **vertebral foramen**.

Vertebrae articulate with one another through two major types of joints: **intervertebral disc joints** between adjacent vertebral bodies and **zygapophyseal (facet) joints** between the inferior articular process of one vertebra and the superior articular process of the vertebra immediately inferior to it. When all vertebrae are articulated into a column, the adjacent vertebral foramina form the **vertebral canal**, through which the spinal cord travels from the foramen magnum of the occipital bone to approximately the level of the second lumbar vertebra. At the level of each vertebra, the spinal cord gives off a pair (left and right) of spinal nerves that exit between vertebrae through the intervertebral foramen formed by adjacent vertebral arches. Even though the spinal cord ends in the lumbar region, the spinal nerves emanating from the spinal cord continue all the way to the sacral (and sometimes coccygeal) region, culminating in a total of 30–31 pairs of spinal nerves.

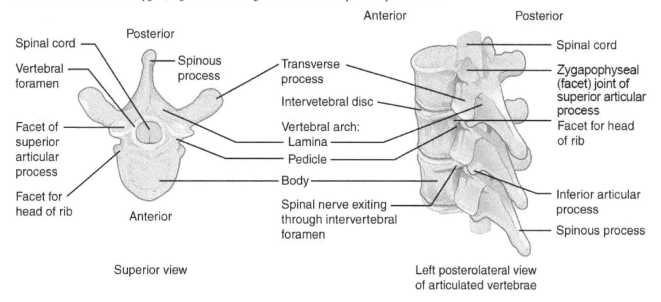

Figure A.24: A typical vertebra consists of a body and a vertebral arch. The arch is formed by the paired pedicles and paired laminae. Arising from the vertebral arch are the transverse, spinous, superior articular, and inferior articular processes. The vertebral foramen provides for passage of the spinal cord. Each spinal nerve exits through an intervertebral foramen, located between adjacent vertebrae. Credit: Parts of a Typical Vertebra (Anatomy & Physiology, Figure 7.23) by OpenStax has been modified (some labels removed) and is under a CC BY 4.0 License. [Image Description].

Regional Differences in Vertebral Shape

In the **cervical region** of the vertebral column, there are seven vertebrae (named C1–C7 from superior to inferior; Figure A.25). The first two cervical vertebrae are unique from each other and all other cervical vertebrae, and they get special names: atlas (C1) and axis (C2). The atlas lacks a vertebral body (having only two large articular facets for articulation with the occipital bone of the skull: the **atlanto-occipital joint** for nodding the head) and does not have a spinous process. The axis is notable for the superiorly projecting **dens** (or **odontoid process**), which articulates with the atlas to create the **atlanto-axial joint** for head rotation. Otherwise, a typical cervical vertebra has a small vertebral body, a bifid (split) spinous process, a transverse process with a transverse foramen on it for passage of the vertebral artery and vein, and a triangular-shaped vertebral foramen.

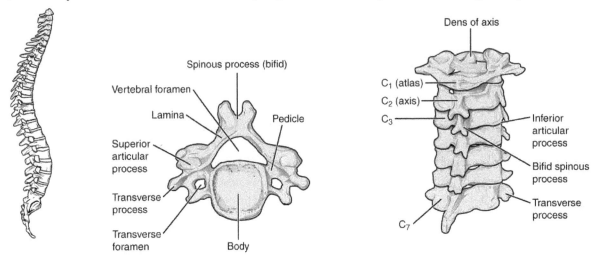

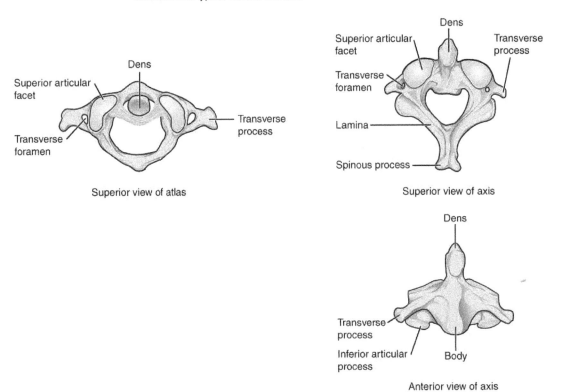

Figure A.25: A typical cervical vertebra has a small body, a bifid spinous process, transverse processes that have a transverse foramen, and a triangular vertebral foramen. The atlas (C1 vertebra) does not have a body or spinous process. The axis (C2 vertebra) has the upward projecting dens, which articulates with the atlas. Credit: Cervical Vertebra (Anatomy & Physiology, Figure 7.25) by OpenStax has been modified (some labels removed) and is under a CC BY 4.0 License. [Image Description].

The vertebrae in the other regions of the spinal column are less variable in shape than the cervical region vertebrae. There are 12 **thoracic region** vertebrae (T1–T12), and they can be easily distinguished from the vertebrae in other regions because they have articular facets on their vertebral bodies for articulation with the head of a rib, as well as articular facets on the transverse process for articulation with the rib tubercle (Figure A.26). In particular, the vertebral bodies of T2–T9 have two pairs of articular facets called **demifacets** (superior and inferior), for articulation with multiple ribs; T1 and T10–T12 have single facets for articulation with a single rib. All five **lumbar region** vertebrae (L1–L5) are distinguished by their large vertebral body and rounded spinous process (Figure A.27). Finally, there is the **sacrum**, which is a bone of the pelvis that forms from the fusion of all five sacral region vertebrae (S1–S5), and there is the **coccyx**, which comprises three to four fused coccygeal region vertebrae that form the tailbone (Figure A.28).

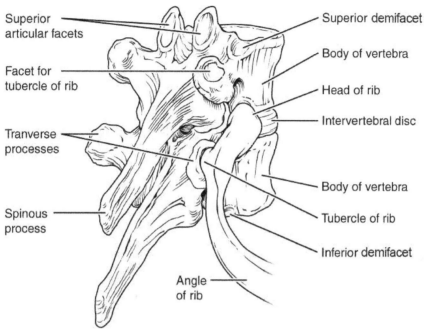

Figure A.26: Thoracic vertebrae have superior and inferior articular facets on the vertebral body for articulation with the head of a rib, as well as a transverse process facet for articulation with the rib tubercle. Credit: Rib Articulation in Thoracic Vertebrae (Anatomy & Physiology, Figure 7.27) by OpenStax has been modified (some labels removed) and is under a CC BY 4.0 License. [Image Description].

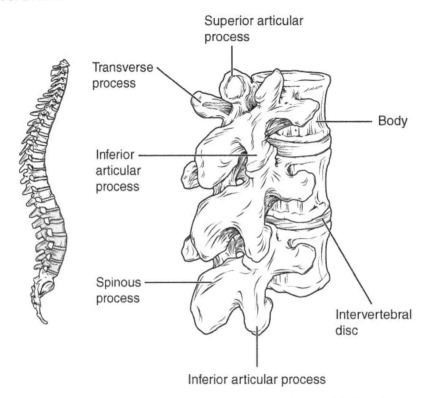

Figure A.27: Lumbar vertebrae are characterized by having a large, thick body and a short, rounded spinous process. Credit: Lumbar Vertebrae (Anatomy & Physiology, Figure 7.28) by OpenStax is under a CC BY 4.0 License. [Image Description].

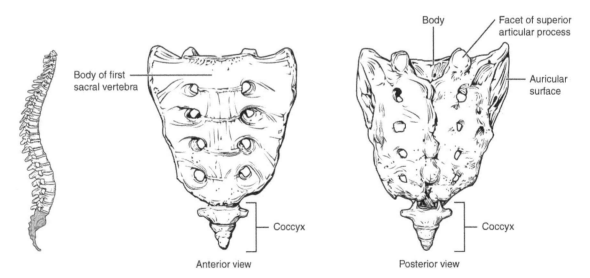

Figure A.28: The sacrum is formed from the fusion of five sacral vertebrae, whose lines of fusion are indicated by the transverse ridges. The coccyx is formed by the fusion of three to four coccygeal vertebrae. Credit: Sacrum and Coccyx (Anatomy & Physiology, Figure 7.29) by OpenStax has been modified (some labels removed) and is under a CC BY 4.0 License. [Image Description].

Curvatures of the Vertebral Column

The adult spine is curved in the midsagittal plane in four regions of the vertebral column (cervical, thoracic, lumbar, and sacral; Figure A.29). During the fetal period of development, the vertebral column forms an anteriorly concave curvature called a **kyphosis**. But during the postnatal period, when an infant learns to hold its head up and then again when it learns to walk, it develops secondary curvatures called lordoses (singular: **lordosis**) that are posteriorly concave in the cervical and lumbar vertebral regions, while the kyphoses remain in the thoracic and sacral regions. The end result is an S-shaped curvature to our spine that enables us to keep our head and torso above our center of mass (near our pelvis) while walking around on two legs.

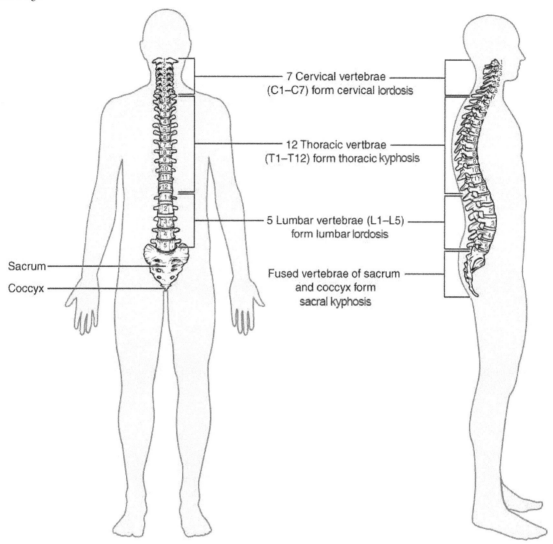

Figure A.29: The adult vertebral column is curved in the midsagittal plane, with two primary curvatures (thoracic and sacral kyphoses) and two secondary curvatures (cervical and lumbar lordoses). Credit: Vertebral Column (Anatomy & Physiology, Figure 7.20) by OpenStax has been modified (some labels modified or removed) and is under a CC BY 4.0 License. [Image Description].

Thoracic Cage

The thoracic cage is formed from the sternum, the 12 ribs and their cartilages (costal cartilages), and the 12 thoracic vertebrae with which the ribs articulate (Figure A.30). The **sternum** comprises the **manubrium** (superior portion), the **body of the sternum,** and the **xiphoid process**

. Each rib has a head and neck (with rib tubercle) at the vertebral end of the rib as well as a flattened shaft that extends to articulate with the sternum. All ribs articulate with the vertebral column at two points: the transverse process facet (**rib tubercle**) and vertebral body articular facet (**head of rib**). But articulations between the ribs and the sternum vary, where some ribs (1–7, the "true ribs") attach directly to the sternum via their costal cartilages, other ribs (8–10, the "false ribs") attach indirectly to the sternum via the costal cartilage of the rib above, and some ribs (11–12, the "floating ribs") do not attach to the sternum at all. With increasing age, the **sternal end of the rib** becomes thinner and irregularly shaped compared to the smooth, rounded shape seen in young adults (Hartnett 2010).

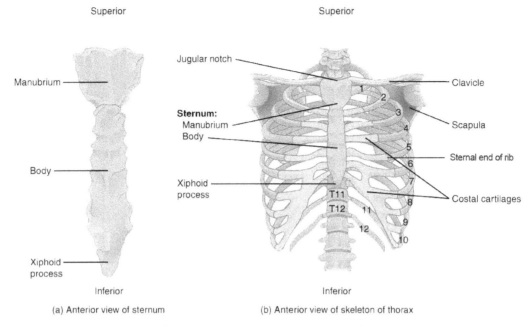

(a) Anterior view of sternum   (b) Anterior view of skeleton of thorax

Figure A.30: The thoracic cage is formed by the (a) sternum and (b) 12 pairs of ribs with their costal cartilages. The ribs are anchored posteriorly to the 12 thoracic vertebrae. The sternum consists of the manubrium, body, and xiphoid process. The ribs are classified as true ribs (1–7) and false ribs (8–12). The last two pairs of false ribs are also known as floating ribs (11–12). Credit: **Thoracic Cage (Anatomy & Physiology, Figure 7.32)** by **OpenStax** has been modified (some labels modified or removed) and is under a **CC BY 4.0 License.** [Image Description].

Appendicular Skeleton

Pectoral Girdle

The pectoral girdle consists of the **clavicle** and the **scapula**, and it serves as the proximal base of the upper limb as well as the anchor for the upper limb to the axial skeleton. The clavicle is an S-shaped bone, and it forms the strut that connects the scapula to the sternum (Figure A.31). The scapula is a large, flat bone with three angles (superior, inferior, and lateral) and three borders (medial, lateral, and superior). The lateral angle is noteworthy because it serves as the articulation for the head of the humerus of the upper limb at the **glenoid cavity (or fossa)** (Figure A.32). The borders and the anterior and posterior surfaces of the scapula are sites of muscle attachment. The scapula also has three important projections for muscle and ligament attachments: the **coracoid process** anteriorly and superiorly; the **acromion**, which articulates with the lateral end of the clavicle; and the **spine** on the posterior aspect of the scapula.

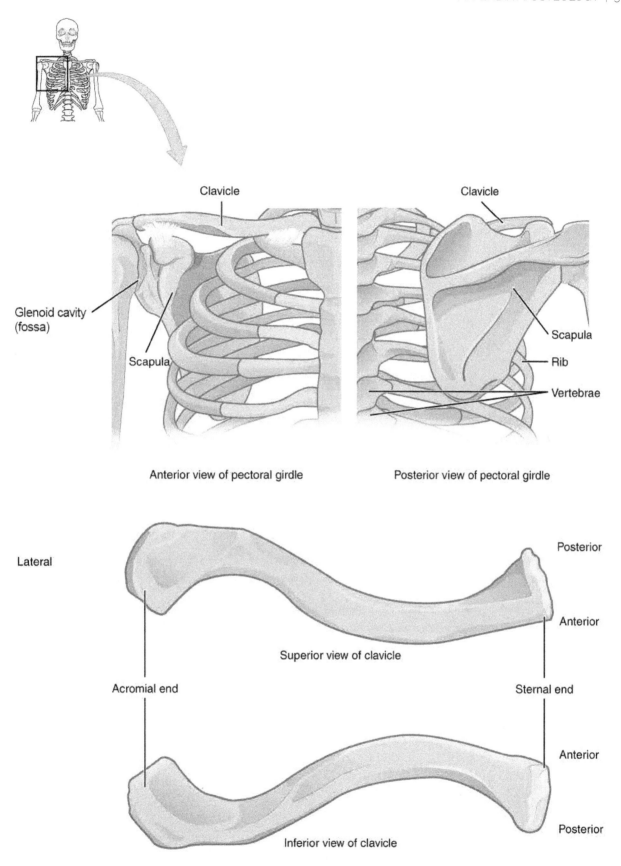

Clavicle

Clavicle

Glenoid cavity
(fossa)

Scapula

Scapula

Rib

Vertebrae

Anterior view of pectoral girdle

Posterior view of pectoral girdle

Lateral

Posterior

Anterior

Superior view of clavicle

Acromial end

Sternal end

Anterior

Posterior

Inferior view of clavicle

Figure A.31: The pectoral girdle consists of the clavicle and the scapula, which serve to attach the upper limb to the axial skeleton at the sternum. Credit: Pectoral Girdle (Anatomy & Physiology, Figure 8.3) by OpenStax has been modified (some labels modified or removed) and is under a CC BY 4.0 License. [Image Description].

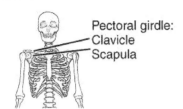

Pectoral girdle:
Clavicle
Scapula

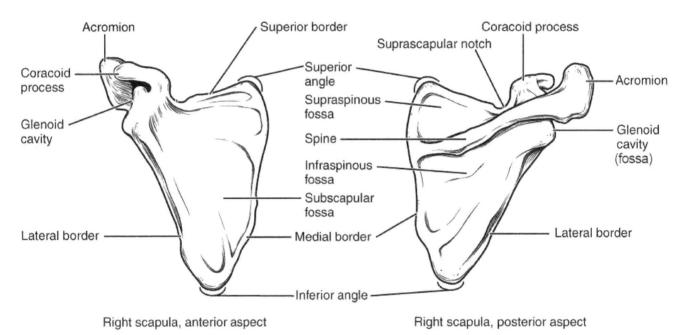

Figure A.32: The scapula is shown from its anterior (deep) side and its posterior (superficial) side. Credit: Scapula (Anatomy & Physiology, Figure 8.4) by OpenStax has been modified (some labels modified or removed) and is under a CC BY 4.0 License. [Image Description].

Upper Limb

The bones of the upper limb skeleton include the humerus, radius, ulna, eight carpal (wrist) bones, five metacarpal (hand) bones, and 14 phalanges (finger bones). Each of these bones is described below along with several of the prominent features.

The **humerus** is the bone of the arm. On the proximal epiphysis of the humerus are attachment sites for muscles of the rotator cuff (**greater tubercle and lesser tubercle**). A major shoulder muscle (deltoid muscle) attaches to the humerus along the lateral aspect of the diaphysis at the **deltoid tuberosity**. On the distal epiphysis of the humerus, the medial epicondyle is an attachment site for muscles that flex the forearm, and the lateral epicondyle is an attachment site for muscles that extend the forearm (Figure A.33).

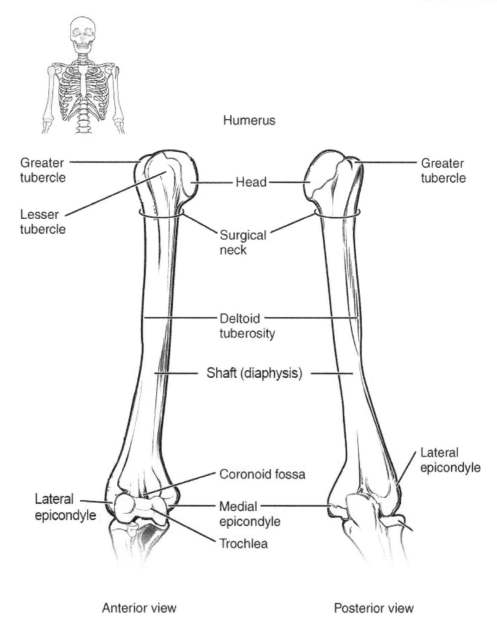

Figure A.33: The humerus is the single bone of the upper arm region. It articulates with the radius and ulna bones of the forearm to form the elbow joint. Credit: Humerus and Elbow Joint (Anatomy & Physiology, Figure 8.5) by OpenStax has been modified (some labels modified or removed) and is under a CC BY 4.0 License. [Image Description].

There are two bones of the forearm, attached to each other by a thick connective tissue interosseous membrane: the radius and the ulna (Figure A.34). The **radius** is lateral to the ulna in anatomical position (this is called supination of the forearm), but it crosses over the ulna when the wrist is rotated so that the thumb points medially (this is called pronation of the forearm). On the proximal end of the radius is the **radial tuberosity**, an attachment site for the biceps brachii muscle that will help supinate and flex the forearm; on the distal end of the radius is the **styloid process of radius**, an attachment site for ligaments of the wrist. The **ulna** also has a styloid process (**styloid process of ulna**), but unlike the one on the radius it does not have a relevant function. Instead, the important processes on the ulna are located proximally, and they include the **olecranon process** for the attachment of the triceps brachii muscle (a muscle that extends the forearm and arm) and the coronoid process for the attachment of the brachialis muscle (a muscle that flexes the forearm).

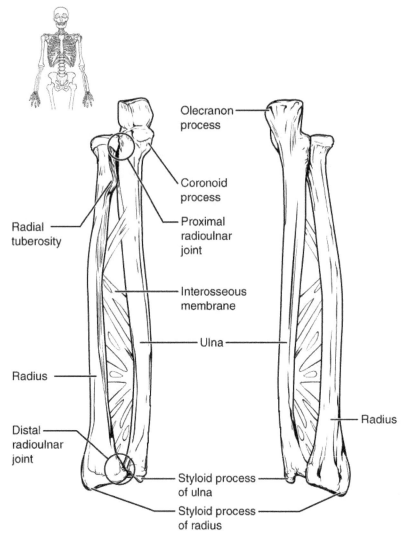

Figure A.34: The ulna is located on the medial side of the forearm, and the radius is on the lateral side. These bones are attached to each other by an interosseous membrane. Credit: Ulna and Radius (Anatomy & Physiology, Figure 8.6) by OpenStax has been modified (some labels removed) and is under a CC BY 4.0 License. [Image Description].

There are eight **carpal bones** that comprise the wrist, and they are organized into two rows: proximal and distal (Figure A.35). The proximal row of carpals (from lateral to medial) includes the scaphoid, lunate, triquetrum, and pisiform. The distal row (from lateral to medial) includes the trapezium, trapezoid, capitate, and hamate with its distinctive hamulus (hook) for muscle and ligament attachments. Distal to the carpal bones are the digital rays, each of which contains a **metacarpal** (hand) bone and three **phalanges** (proximal, middle, and distal) or finger bones. The exception to this rule is the thumb, which has fewer phalanges (proximal and distal, but no middle) than the other digits.

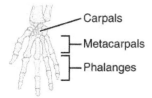

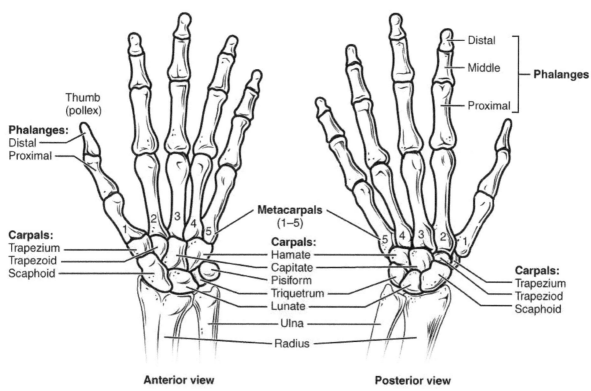

Figure A.35: The eight carpal bones form the base of the hand. These are arranged into proximal and distal rows of four bones each. The five metacarpal bones form the palm of the hand. The thumb and fingers contain a total of 14 phalanges. Credit: **Bones of the Wrist and Hand** (Anatomy & Physiology, Figure 8.7) by OpenStax has been modified (some labels removed) and is under a CC BY 4.0 License. [Image Description].

Pelvic Girdle

The pelvic girdle consists of the two **os coxae** and the sacrum that articulates with both, and it serves as the proximal base and anchor of the lower limb to the axial skeleton. Each os coxa comprises three bones that fuse together during growth: ilium, ischium, and pubis. These three bones fuse in a region called the **acetabulum**, which is the socket for the ball-and-socket hip joint (Figure A.36). The **ilium**, the flared superior portion of the pelvis, is the largest bone of the os coxa and serves as a major site of attachments for muscles from the abdomen, back, and lower limb. The ilium has several important features including the **auricular surface**, the surface where the ilium articulates with the sacrum. The auricular surface is used to estimate age at death as the surface progressively deteriorates with increasing age to appear coarse and porous. The **greater sciatic notch** is a large notch in the ilium that allows for several structures to leave the pelvis and enter the lower extremity, including the sciatic nerve. In females, the notch tends to be symmetrical whereas in males it tends to curve posteriorly (Nawrocki et al. 2018).

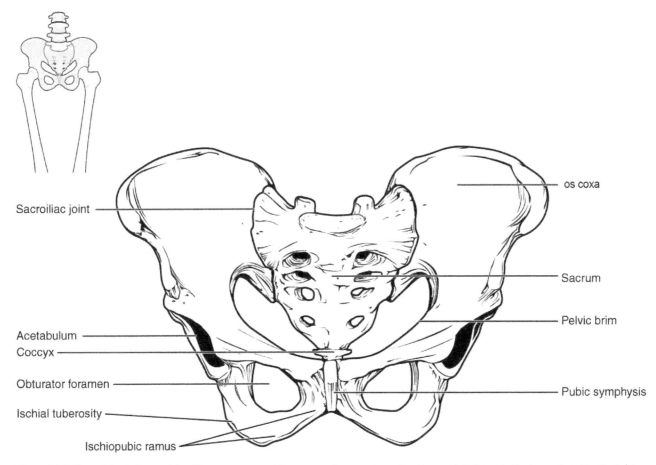

Figure A.36: The pelvic girdle consists of two os coxae and the sacrum. It serves to anchor the axial skeleton to the lower limb. Credit: Pelvis (Anatomy & Physiology, Figure 8.12) by OpenStax has been modified (some labels modified or removed) and is under a CC BY 4.0 License. [Image Description].

The **ischium** forms the posterior and inferior portion of the os coxa. There are two significant projections of note on the ischium: the ischial spine and tuberosity. The **ischial spine** is the attachment point for a major pelvic ligament and is located inferior to the greater sciatic notch of the ilium. The **ischial tuberosity** is the proximal attachment site for the hamstring muscles of the lower limb.

The anterior and medial portions of the os coxa are formed by the **pubis**. The pubis is a useful bone with which to sex a skeleton in a forensic context (Bass 2005; Buikstra and Ubelaker 1994). The **body of pubis** is the superior and medial portion (Figure A.37). The body tends to be rectangular in cross-section in females and triangular in males. The bony projection that unites the ischium and pubis anteriorly is called the **ischiopubic ramus**. Females tend to display a thin and sharp ramus on the medial surface while the surface in males tends to be broad and blunt. The joint that unites the two pubic bones in the front of the pelvis is called the **pubic symphysis**, which is a structure commonly used in age estimation. In young adults, the surface is billowed, but it transitions to being smooth and porous with increasing age (Hartnett 2010). The **subpubic concavity** is a depression inferior to the ischiopubic ramus. Female pelves tend to exhibit this concavity while male pelves tend not to. Finally, the large opening encircled by the pubis and ischium is called the **obturator foramen**. The shape of the foramen in females has been described as triangular while it is more likely to appear oval in males (Bass 2005).

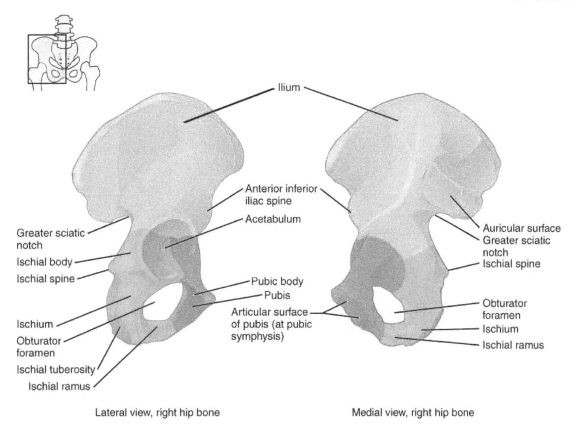

Lateral view, right hip bone   Medial view, right hip bone

Figure A.37: The os coxae consist of three bones that fuse during development. The ilium forms the large, fan-shaped superior portion, the ischium forms the posteroinferior portion, and the pubis forms the anteromedial portion. Credit: The Hip Bone (Anatomy & Physiology, Figure 8.13) by OpenStax has been modified (some labels removed) and is under a CC BY 4.0 License. [Image Description].

Lower Limb

The bones of the lower limb skeleton include the femur, patella, tibia, fibula, seven tarsal (ankle) bones, five **metatarsal** (foot) bones, and 14 phalanges (toe bones). Each of these bones is described below along with several of the prominent features.

The **femur** is the bone of the thigh. On the proximal epiphysis of the femur are attachment sites for major hip and thigh muscles on the **greater trochanter**, **lesser trochanter**, and **gluteal tuberosity** (Figure A.38). The raised ridge on the posterior aspect of the femoral diaphysis is called the **linea aspera**, and it is a major attachment site for the quadriceps femoris muscles and other muscles, and it terminates distally by splitting into medial and lateral epicondyles, additional sites of muscle attachment. The distal epiphysis of the femur is marked by two rounded condyles that articulate with the proximal part of the tibia. The anterior surface of the distal femur articulates with the **patella** (kneecap), a bone that develops within the tendon of the quadriceps femoris muscle to enhance the function of the muscle. The patella does not articulate with the tibia.

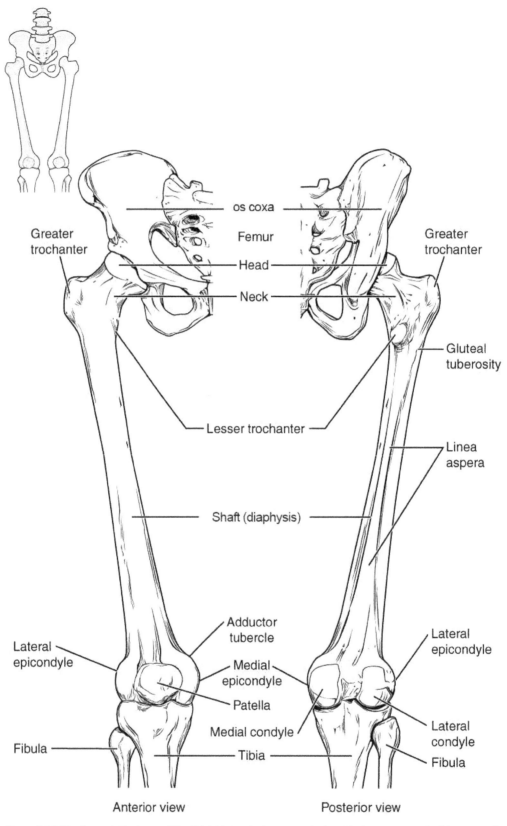

Anterior view   Posterior view

Figure A.38: The femur is the bone of the thigh that articulates superiorly with the os coxa at the hip joint and inferiorly with the tibia at the knee joint. The patella only articulates with the distal end of the femur. Credit: Femur and Patella (Anatomy & Physiology, Figure 8.16) by OpenStax has been modified (some labels modified or removed) and is under a CC BY 4.0 License. [Image Description].

There are two bones of the leg: **tibia** and **fibula**. The tibia is the robust, medial bone of the leg, and it is connected to the laterally positioned fibula by an interosseous membrane like in the forearm (Figure A.39). The proximal epiphysis of the tibia has two articular facets called tibial condyles that articulate with the femoral condyles. On the anterior surface of the proximal tibia is a raised projection called the **tibial tuberosity**, where the quadriceps muscle tendon attaches distally after containing the patella. On the distal epiphysis of the tibia is the **medial malleolus**, which articulates with the talus in the ankle joint. The **lateral malleolus** is a feature of the distal end of the fibula; the proximal end of the fibula articulates with the lateral portion of the proximal tibia.

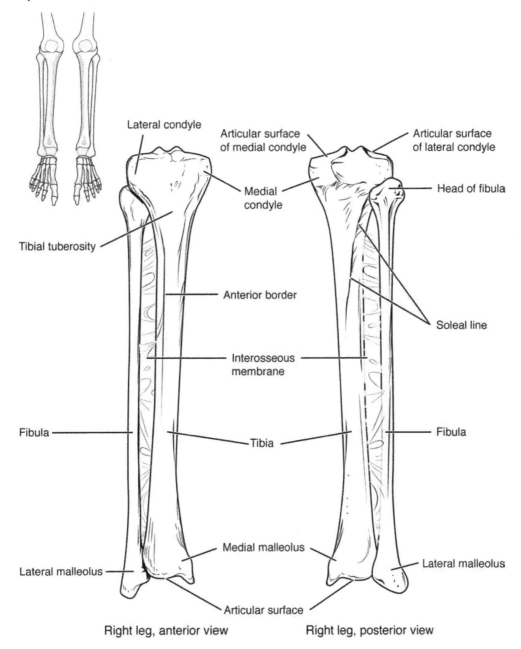

Figure A.39: The tibia is the larger, weight-bearing bone located on the medial side of the leg. It is connected to the laterally positioned fibula by an interosseous membrane. Credit: Tibia and Fibula (Anatomy & Physiology, Figure 8.18) by OpenStax has been modified (label removed) and is under a CC BY 4.0 License. [Image Description].

There are seven **tarsal bones** that comprise the ankle (Figure A.40). The **talus** is the most superior of the tarsals, and it articulates with the distal tibia and distal fibula superiorly and with the calcaneus inferiorly. The **calcaneus** is the heel of the foot; it is the largest of the tarsals. On the posterior-most aspect of the calcaneus is the **calcaneal tuberosity**, which is the attachment site for the Achilles tendon of the posterior leg. Distal to the talus is the medially positioned navicular, the three cuneiform bones (medial, intermediate, and lateral), and the laterally positioned cuboid. Distal to the tarsals are the digital rays, each of which contains a metatarsal (foot) bone and three phalanges (proximal, middle, and distal) or toe bones. The exception to this rule is the big toe, which has fewer phalanges (proximal and distal, but no middle) than the other digits.

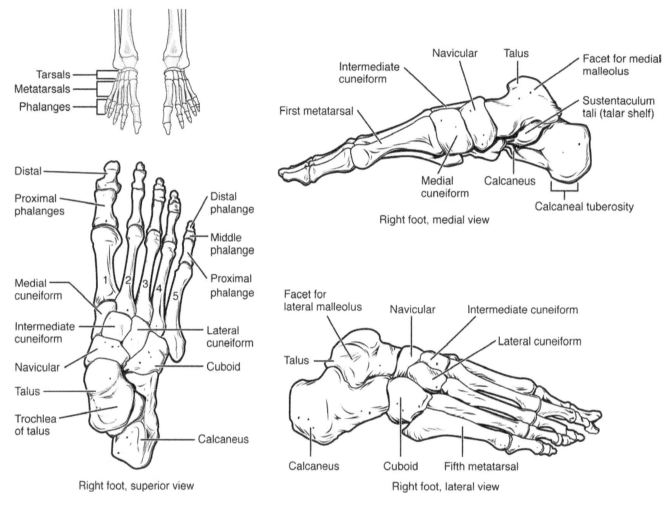

Figure A.40: The bones of the foot are divided into three groups. The posterior foot is formed by the seven tarsal bones. The mid-foot has the five metatarsal bones. The toes contain 14 phalanges. Credit: **Bones of the Foot (Anatomy & Physiology, Figure 8.19)** by OpenStax has been modified (some labels modified or removed) and is under a CC BY 4.0 License. [Image Description].

Review Questions

- Which bony features of the pelvic girdle are relevant to estimating age and/or sex in forensic and bioarchaeological contexts? Give specific examples of how these features differ among sexes.
- What is the mechanistic difference between endochondral and intramembranous bone formation?
- Which bones articulate with the calcaneus? Which bones articulate with the humerus?
- Which elements of the skeleton belong to the axial skeleton versus the appendicular skeleton?

Key Terms

Acetabulum: Shallow cavity of the coxa for articulation of the head of the femur.

Acromion: Lateral projection of the spine of scapula.

Anatomical position: Standing upright, facing forward with arms at the side and palms facing forward.

Anterior (ventral): Toward the front.

Appendicular skeleton: Part of the skeleton that consists of the bones of the pectoral and pelvic girdls, arms, and legs.

Atlanto-axial joint: Joint between the atlas (C1 vertebrae) and the axis (C2 vertebrae), used for turning the head side to side.

Atlanto-occipital joint: Joint between the atlas (C1 vertebrae) and occipital bone, used for nodding the head.

Auricular surface: Roughened joint surface for articulation of the sacrum.

Axial skeleton: Part of the skeleton that consists of the bones of the head and trunk.

Body of pubis: Superior bar of the pubis.

Body of the sternum: Central portion of the sternum where ribs articulate.

Buccal: Toward the cheek.

Calcaneal tuberosity: Roughened attachment site at the posterior calcaneus.

Calcaneus: Large bone that forms the heel.

Cancellous (or trabecular) bone: Porous bone found at the ends of long bones and within flat and irregular bones.

Canines: Conical teeth with a single pointed cusp used to puncture a food item.

Carpal bones: The 8 bones of the wrist: scaphoid, lunate, triquetrum, pisiform, trapezium, trapezoid, capitate, and hamate.

Centrum: Anterior body of vertebra; the main weight-bearing element of the vertebra.

Cervical region: Neck region that contains 7 vertebrae.

Clavicle: The collarbone, which connects the sternum to the scapula to form the pectoral girdle.

Coccyx: Small triangular bone that projects from the inferior part of sacrum.

Coracoid process: Hook-shaped projection from the anterior surface of the scapula.

Coronal (frontal) plane: An imaginary line that divides the body into anterior and posterior halves.

Coronal suture: Joint that connects the frontal bone to the paired parietal bones.

Coronoid process: Triangular eminence from the superior part of the mandibular ramus.

Coronoid process of ulna: Triangular projection from the anterior surface of proximal ulna.

Cortical (or compact) bone: Dense, outer surface of bone.

Cranial sutures: Fibrous joints that connect bones of the skull and face.

Cranium: Bones of the head that support the brain and face.

Cribriform foramina: Small openings in the superior plate of the ethmoid that transmit olfactory nerves.

Deltoid tuberosity: Lateral projection for attachment of deltoid muscle.

Demifacets: Partial joint surfaces on the lateral surface of the centrum of thoracic vertebrae.

Dens (or odontoid process): Projection from superior surface of centrum of C2.

Diaphysis: Shaft or central part of a long bone.

Distal: Further away from the center of the body or point of attachment.

Endochondral bone formation: Process of bone formation that occurs from a cartilage model.

Epiphysis: End of long bones.

Ethmoid bone: Unpaired bone of the skull that separates the nasal cavity from the brain.

External occipital protuberance (EOP): Projection from the occipital superior to nuchal lines.

Femur: Long bone of the thigh.

Fibula: Lateral bone of the leg.

Flat bone: Bones that are flat with thin layers of cortical bone surrounding cancellous bone.

Foramen magnum: Large opening in the occipital where the spinal cord passes.

Frontal bone: An unpaired bone that forms the anterior and superior part of the cranium.

Glabella: Part of the forehead between the eyebrows.

Glenoid cavity (or fossa): Shallow depression for the articulation of the head of the humerus.

Gluteal tuberosity: Roughened attachment site for the gluteus maximus muscle.

Gonial (or mandibular) angle: Posterior border of the mandible at the junction of the ramus and body.

Greater sciatic notch: Large indentation of the ilium.

Greater trochanter: Large projection from the lateral surface of the proximal femur.

Greater tubercle: Large projection on the superior and lateral surface of the humerus.

Head of rib: Posterior part of the rib that articulates with the centrum.

Humerus: Long bone of the arm.

Hyoid bone: U-shaped bone in the neck that does not articulate with another bone.

Ilium: Large flat bone of the superior part of the coxa.

Incisal surface: Toward the cutting edge.

Incisors: Flat and shovel shaped teeth that are used to bite into a food item.

Inferior (caudal): Away from the head or downward.

Inferior articular process: Inferior projections from the vertebral arch that connect to superior articular processes of the inferior vertebra.

Inferior nasal concha: Scroll-like paired bones that attach to the lateral part of the nasal cavity.

Intervertebral disc joints: Fibrocartilaginous joints that connect adjacent centra of vertebrae.

Intramembranous bone formation: Process of bone formation that occurs in mesenchyme and gives rise to flat bones of the skull.

Irregular bone: Bones that have a complex appearance.

Ischial spine: Thin, square projection from the ischium.

Ischial tuberosity: Large, round protrusion of the posterior and inferior ischium.

Ischiopubic ramus: Thin bar of bone that unites the pubis and ischium.

Ischium: The posterior and inferior portion of the os coxae.

Kyphosis: Anterior curvature of the spine.

Lacrimal bone: Paired bones that form the anterior and medial part of the orbit.

Lambdoidal suture: Joint that connects the parietal and occipital bones.

Lamina: Flattened portion of the vertebral arch.

Lateral: Further away from the midline.

Lateral malleolus: Prominence of the distal fibula that forms the outer part of the ankle.

Lesser trochanter: Projection from the medial surface of the proximal femur.

Lesser tubercle: Projection on the anterior and superior surface of the humerus.

Linea aspera: Elongated projection of the posterior surface of the femur.

Lingual: Toward the tongue.

Long bone: Bones that are longer than they are wide.

Lordosis: Posterior curvature of the spine.

Lumbar region: Lower back region that consists of 5 vertebrae.

Mandible: Lower jaw bone.

Mandibular condyle: Rounded projection of the mandibular ramus.

Mandibular fossa: Depression at the base of the temporal bone where the mandibular condyle articulates to form the temporomandibular (or jaw) joint.

Manubrium: Upper part of the sternum.

Mastoid process: Bony projection from the back of the temporal bone.

Maxilla bone: Upper jaw bone.

Medial: Toward the midline.

Medial malleolus: Prominence of the distal tibia that forms the inner part of the ankle.

Medullary cavity: Central cavity in the diaphysis of long bones that contains bone marrow.

Mental protuberance (eminence): Triangular projection at the front of the mandible.

Mesial: Toward the middle.

Metacarpal: The 5 bones of the palm of the hand.

Metaphysis: Junction between diaphysis and epiphysis where bone growth occurs.

Metatarsal: The 5 bones at the distal part of the foot.

Metopic suture: Joint that connects paired frontal bones and usually fuses early in childhood.

Midsagittal plane: Plane that divides the body vertically into equal left and right halves. It is also called the medial plane, because it occurs on the midline of the body.

Molars: Teeth with flatter cusps that are used to grind food prior to swallowing.

Nasal aperture: Anterior opening of the nasal cavity.

Nasal bone: Paired bones that form the bridge of the nose and the roof of the nasal cavity.

Nasal spine: Bony projection from the inferior part of the nasal aperture.

Neurocranium: Bones of the cranium that protects the brain.

Nuchal lines: Ridges on occipital from attachment of neck and back muscles.

Obturator foramen: Irregularly shaped opening within the pubis and ischium.

Occipital bone: Unpaired bone at the posterior and base of the skull.

Occlusal: Toward the chewing surface.

Olecranon process: Posterior projection of the proximal ulna.

Orbit: Bony cavity that houses the eye and associated structures.

Os coxa: Hip bone, forms from the fusion of the ilium, ischium, and pubis.

Osteoblast: Cell that secretes the matrix for bone formation.

Osteoclast: A multinucleated bone cell that resorbs bone tissue during growth and repair.

Osteocyte: Mature bone cell that lies within the bone matrix.

Osteogenic cells: Stem cells that differentiate into osteoblasts.

Osteology: The study of bones.

Palatine bone: Paired bones that form the posterior part of the hard palate.

Parasagittal plane: A vertical imaginary line adjacent to the sagittal plane that divides the body into unequal halves.

Parietal bone: Paired bones forming the lateral walls of the cranium.

Patella: Knee cap; a bone that forms in the tendon of the quadriceps femoris muscle.

Pedicle: Projection that connects the lamina to the centrum.

Phalanges: The 14 bones of the digits.

Posterior (or dorsal): Toward the back.

Premolars: Teeth with two rounded cusps that are used to grind and mash a food item.

Proximal: Closer to the center of the body or point of attachment.

Pterygoid plates: Flat projections of the sphenoid that serve as attachment sites for chewing muscles and muscles of the throat.

Pubic symphysis: Joint surface that unites the two pubic bones anteriorly.

Pubis: Anterior and inferior portion of the coxa.

Radial tuberosity: Rough projection for attachment of biceps brachii muscle.

Radius: Lateral bone of the forearm.

Ramus of the mandible: Bar-like portion of the posterior mandible.

Rib tubercle: Posterior part of the rib that articulates with the transverse process.

Sacrum: Triangular bone at the base of the spine that consists of 5 fused vertebrae.

Sagittal plane: An imaginary line that divides the body into left and right halves.

Sagittal suture: Joint that connects the parietal bones.

Scapula: Flat, triangular bone that connects the upper limb to the pectoral girdle.

Sesamoid bone: Bones that form within a tendon.

Short bone: Bones that are as wide as they are long.

Sphenoid bone: Unpaired bone that forms the anterior part of the base of the skull.

Spine: Elongated ridge on posterior surface.

Spinous process: Posterior projection of vertebral arch at the junction of the lamina.

Squamosal suture: Joint that connects the parietal and temporal bones.

Sternal end of the rib: Anterior part of rib that connects to the sternal body through costal cartilage.

Sternum: Breastbone; flat bone of the anterior chest wall.

Styloid process: Thin projection from the base of the temporal bone.

Styloid process of radius: Projection from the distal radius.

Styloid process of ulna: Projection from the distal ulna.

Subpubic concavity: Depression below the pubic symphysis to the ischiopubic rami.

Superior (or cranial): Toward the head.

Superior articular process: Superior projections from the vertebral arch that connect to inferior articular processes of the superior vertebra.

Supraorbital margin: External ridge at the superior part of the orbit.

Talus: Ankle bone that articulates with the tibia.

Tarsal bones: The 7 bones at the proximal end of foot; talus, calcaneus, navicular, cuneiforms (medial, intermediate, lateral), and cuboid.

Temporal bone: Paired bones at the lateral and base of the skull that contain the middle and inner ear.

Temporal lines: Ridges on the parietal bone from attachments of temporalis muscle and fascia.

Temporal process of zygomatic bone: Long process that forms the anterior half of the zygomatic arch.

Thoracic region: Trunk region that consists of 12 vertebrae that attach to ribs.

Tibia: Medial bone of the leg.

Tibial tuberosity: Roughened attachment site on the anterior surface of the proximal tibia.

Transverse plane: An imaginary line that divides the body into superior and inferior halves.

Transverse process: Lateral projection at the junction of the pedicle and lamina.

Ulna: Medial bone of the forearm.

Vertebral arch: Circular ring of bone at the posterior vertebra.

Vertebral canal: Cavity that contains the spinal cord.

Vertebral foramen: Opening formed by the vertebral arch.

Viscerocranium: Bones of the cranium that make up the face skeleton.

Vomer: Unpaired bone that forms the inferior part of the bony nasal septum.

Xiphoid process: Lower part of the sternum.

Zygapophyseal (facet) joints: Synovial joints between the superior and inferior articular processes.

Zygomatic arch: Bridge of bone at the cheek.

Zygomatic bone: Paired bones that form the anterior and lateral parts of the mid-face.

Zygomatic process of temporal bone: Long process that forms the posterior half of the zygomatic arch.

Zygomatic process of the maxilla: Portion of the bone that articulates with the zygomatic bone to form the anterior portion of the zygomatic arch.

About the Authors

Jason M. Organ, Ph.D.

Indiana University School of Medicine, jorgan@iu.edu

Jason M. Organ is an associate professor of anatomy, cell biology, and physiology at the Indiana University School of Medicine (IUSM) and Editor-in-Chief of *Anatomical Sciences Education*, the premier peer-reviewed journal for anatomy education research. Jason earned an M.A. in anthropology from the University of Missouri and a PhD in functional anatomy and evolution from Johns Hopkins University School of Medicine, and he completed a postdoctoral research fellowship in physical medicine and rehabilitation at the Johns Hopkins Kennedy Krieger Institute. He is the director of the IUSM clinical anatomy and physiology M.S. program and was the 2018 recipient of the prestigious Basmajian Award from the American Association for Anatomy for excellence in teaching gross anatomy and outstanding accomplishments in biomedical research and scholarship in education. Follow him on Twitter: @OrganJM.

Jessica N. Byram, Ph.D.

Indiana University School of Medicine, jbyram@iu.edu

Jessica N. Byram is an assistant professor of anatomy, cell biology, and physiology at the Indiana University School of Medicine (IUSM). Jessica earned her M.S. in human biology with a focus in forensic anthropology from the University of Indianapolis and her Ph.D. in anatomy education at IUSM. Jessica is the director of the anatomy education track Ph.D. program at IUSM. Her research interests include medical professionalism, investigating professional identity formation in medical students and residents, and exploring how to improve the learning environments at medical institutions.

References

Bass, William M. 2005. *Human Osteology: A Laboratory and Field Manual, 5th edition*. Columbia, MO: Missouri Archaeological Society.

Boldsen, Jesper L., George R. Milner, Lyle W. Konigsberg, and James W. Wood. 2002. "Transition Analysis: A New Method for Estimating Age from Skeletons." In *Paleodemography: Age Distributions from Skeletal Samples*, edited by Robert D. Hoppa and James W. Vaupel, 73–106. Cambridge UK: Cambridge University Press.

Buikstra, Jane E., and Douglas H. Ubelaker. 1994. *Standards for Data Collection From Human Skeletal Remains*. Arkansas Archaeological Survey Research Series, 44. Fayetteville, AR: Arkansas Archeological Survey.

Burr, David B., and Jason M. Organ. 2017. "Postcranial Skeletal Development and Its Evolutionary Implications." In *Building Bones: Bone Formation and Development in Anthropology*, edited by Christopher J. Percival and Joan T. Richtsmeier, 148–174. Cambridge, UK: Cambridge University Press.

Christensen, Angi M., Nicholas V. Passalacqua, and Eric J. Bartelink. 2019. *Forensic Anthropology: Current Methods and Practice*. London: Academic Press.

Cunningham, Craig, Louise Scheuer, and Sue Black. 2017. *Developmental Juvenile Osteology, 2nd Edition*. London: Elsevier.

Hartnett, Kristen M. 2010 "Analysis of Age-at-Death Estimation Using Data from a New, Modern Autopsy Sample—Part II: Sternal End of the Fourth Rib. *Journal of Forensic Sciences* 55 (5): 1152–1156.

Meindl, Richard S., and C. Owen Lovejoy. 1985. "Ectocranial Suture Closure: A Revised Method for the Determination of Skeletal Age at Death Based on the Lateral-Anterior Sutures." *American Journal of Physical Anthropology* 68 (1): 57–66.

Nawrocki, Stephen P., Krista E. Latham, Thomas Gore, Rachel M. Hoffman, Jessica N. Byram, and Justin Maiers. 2018. "Using Elliptical Fourier Analysis to Interpret Complex Morphological Features in Global Populations." In *New Perspectives in Forensic Human Skeletal Identification*, edited by Krista E. Latham, Eric J. Bartelink, and Michael Finnegan, 301–312. London: Elsevier/Academic Press.

Walker, Phillip L. 2008. "Sexing Skulls Using Discriminant Function Analysis of Visually Assessed Traits." *American Journal of Physical Anthropology* 136 (1): 39–50.

Image Descriptions

Figure A.1: This illustration depicts an anterior view of the right femur, or thigh bone. The inferior end that connects to the knee is at the bottom of the diagram and the superior end that connects to the hip is at the top of the diagram. The bottom end of the bone contains a smaller lateral bulge and a larger medial bulge. A blue articular cartilage covers the inner half of each bulge as well as the small trench that runs between the bulges. This area of the inferior end of the bone is labeled the distal epiphysis. Above the distal epiphysis is the metaphysis, where the bone tapers from the wide epiphysis into the relatively thin shaft. The entire length of the shaft is the diaphysis. The superior half of the femur is cut away to show its internal contents. The bone is covered with an outer translucent sheet called the periosteum. At the midpoint of the diaphysis, a nutrient artery travels through the periosteum and into the inner layers of the bone. The periosteum surrounds a white cylinder of solid bone labeled compact bone. The cavity at the center of the compact bone is called the medullary cavity. The inner layer of the compact bone that lines the medullary cavity is called the endosteum. Within the diaphysis, the medullary cavity contains a cylinder of yellow bone marrow that is penetrated by the nutrient artery. The superior end of the femur is also connected to the diaphysis by a metaphysis. In this upper metaphysis, the bone gradually widens between the diaphysis and the proximal epiphysis. The proximal epiphysis of the femur is roughly hexagonal in shape. However, the upper right side of the hexagon has a large, protruding knob. The femur connects and rotates within the hip socket at this knob. The knob is covered with a blue colored articular cartilage. The internal anatomy of the upper metaphysis and proximal epiphysis are revealed. The medullary cavity in these regions is filled with the mesh-like spongy bone. Red bone marrow occupies the many cavities within the spongy bone. There is a clear, white line separating the spongy bone of the upper metaphysis with that of the proximal epiphysis. This line is labeled the epiphyseal line."

Figure A.2: On the left side is an anterior view of a complete human skeleton. PRojecting from it to the right are six different colored rows with six functions of the human skeleton and a smaller corresponding image:

- Protects internal organs (image of crania with brain inside)
- Stores and releases fat (image of the proximal half of a femur with yellow marrow drawn in the shaft's medullary cavity and red specs in the cancellous bone of the proximal femur.
- Produces blood cells (image of red blood cells)
- Stores and releases minerals (image of bubbles with either Ca2+ or PO43- written on them.)
- Facilitates movement (image of the bones in a knee)
- Supports the body (image of the lower leg and foot bones)

Figure A.3: This illustration shows an anterior view of a human skeleton with call outs of five bones. The first call out is the sternum, or breast bone, which lies along the midline of the thorax. The sternum is the bone to which the ribs connect at the front of the body. It is classified as a flat bone and appears somewhat like a tie, with an enlarged upper section and a thin, tapering, lower section. The next callout is the right femur, which is the thigh bone. The inferior end of the femur is broad where it connects to the knee while the superior edge is ball-shaped where it attaches to the hip socket. The femur is an example of a long bone. The next callout is of the patella or kneecap. It is a small, wedge-shaped bone that sits on the anterior side of the knee. The kneecap is an example of a sesamoid bone. The next callout is a dorsal view of the right foot. The lateral, intermediate and medial cuneiform bones are small, square-shaped bones of the top of the foot. These bones lie between the proximal edge of the toe bones and the inferior edge of the shin bones. The lateral cuneiform is proximal to the fourth toe while the medial cuneiform is proximal to the great toe. The intermediate cuneiform lies between the lateral and medial cuneiform. These bones are examples of short bones. The fifth callout shows a superior view of one of the lumbar vertebrae. The vertebra has a kidney-shaped body connected to a triangle of bone that projects above the body of the vertebra. Two spines project off of the triangle at approximately 45 degree angles. The vertebrae are examples of irregular bones.

Figure A.4: The top of this diagram shows the cross section of a generic bone with three zoom in boxes. The first box is on the periosteum. The second box is on the middle of the compact bone layer. The third box is on the inner edge of the compact bone where it transitions into the spongy bone. The callout in the periosteum points to two images. In the first image, four osteoblast cells are sitting end to end on the periosteum. The osteoblasts are roughly square shaped, except for one of the cells which is developing small, finger like projections. The caption says, "Osteoblasts form the matrix of the bone." The second image called out from the periosteum shows a large, amorphous osteogenic cell sitting on the periosteum. The osteogenic cell is surrounded on both sides by a row of much smaller osteoblasts. The cell is shaped like a mushroom cap and also has finger like projections. The cell is a stem cell that develops into other bone cells. The box in the middle of the compact bone layer is pointing to an osteocyte. The osteocyte is a thin cell, roughly diamond shaped, with many branching, finger-like projections. The osteoctyes maintain bone tissue. The box at the inner edge of the compact bone is pointing to an osteoclast. The osteoclast is a large, round cell with multiple nuclei. It also has rows of fine finger like projections on its lower surface where it is sitting on the compact bone. The osteoclast reabsorbs bone.

Figure A.5: Image A shows seven osteoblasts, cells with small, finger like projections. They are surrounded by granules of osteoid. Both the cells and the osteoid are contained within a blue, circular, ossification center that is surrounded by a "socket" of dark, string-like collagen fibers and gray mesenchymal cells. The cells are generally amorphous, similar in appearance to an amoeba. In image B, the ossification center is no longer surrounded by a ring of osteoblasts. The osteoblasts have secreted bone into the ossification center, creating a new bone matrix. There are also five osteocytes embedded in the new bone matrix. The osteocytes are thin, oval-shaped cells with many fingerlike projections. Osteoid particles are still embedded in the bony matrix in image B. In image C, the ring of osteoblasts surrounding the ossification center has separated, forming an upper and lower layer of osteoblasts sandwiched between the two layers of mesenchyme cells. A label indicates that the mesenchyme cells and the surrounding collagen fibers form the periosteum. The osteoblasts secrete spongy bone into the space between the two osteoblast rows. Therefore, the accumulating spongy bone pushes the upper and lower rows of osteoblasts away from each other. In this image, most of the spongy bone has been secreted by the osteoblasts, as the trabeculae are visible. In addition, an artery has already broken through the periosteum and invaded the spongy bone. Image D looks similar to image C, except that the rows of osteoblasts are now secreting layers of compact bone between the spongy bone and the periosteum. The artery has now branched and spread throughout the spongy bone. A label indicates that the cavities between the trabeculae now contain red bone marrow.

Figure A.6: Image A shows a small piece of hyaline cartilage that looks like a bone but without the characteristic enlarged ends. The hyaline cartilage is surrounded by a thin perichondrium. In image B, the hyaline cartilage has increased in size and the ends have begun to bulge outwards. A group of dark granules form at the center of the cartilage. This is labeled the calcified matrix, as opposed to the rest of the cartilage, which is uncalcified matrix. In image C, the hyaline cartilage has again increased in size and spongy bone has formed at the calcified matrix. This is now called the primary ossification center. A nutrient artery has invaded the ossification center and is growing through the cavities of the new spongy bone. In image D, the cartilage now looks like a bone, as it has greatly increased in size and each end has two bulges. Only the proximal half of the bone is shown in all of the remaining images. In image D, spongy bone has completely developed in the medullary cavity, which is surrounded, on both sides, by compact bone. Now, the calcified matrix is located at the border between the proximal metaphysis and the proximal epiphysis. The epiphysis is still composed of uncalcified matrix. In image E, arteries and veins have now invaded the epiphysis, forming a calcified matrix at its center. This is called a secondary ossification center. In image F, the interior of the epiphysis is now completely calcified into bone. The outer edge of the epiphysis remains as cartilage, forming the articular cartilage at the joint. In addition, the border between the epiphysis and the metaphysis remains uncalcified, forming the epiphyseal plate.

Figure A.8: This illustration shows a female viewed from her right, front side. The anatomical planes are depicted as blue rectangles passing through the woman's body. The frontal or coronal plane enters through the right side of the body, passes through the body, and exits from the left side. It divides the body into front (anterior) and back (posterior) halves. The sagittal plane enters through the back and emerges through the front of the body. It divides the body into right and left halves. The transverse plane passes through the body perpendicular to the frontal and sagittal planes. This plane is a cross section which divides the body into upper and lower halves.

Figure A.10: This diagram shows the human skeleton and identifies the major bones. The left panel shows the anterior view (from the front) and the right panel shows the posterior view (from the back).

Figure A.11: In this image, the lateral view of the human skull is shown and the brain case and facial bones are labeled.

Figure A.12: This image shows the anterior view (from the front) of the human skull. The major bones on the skull are labeled.

Figure A.13: This image shows the lateral view of the human skull and identifies the major parts.

Figure A.14: This image shows the location of the temporal bone. A small image of the skull on the top left shows the temporal bone highlighted in pink and a magnified view of this region then highlights the important parts of the temporal bone.

Figure A.15: This image shows the superior and inferior view of the skull base. In the top panel, the inferior view is shown. A small image of the skull shows the viewing direction on the left. In the inferior view, the maxilla and the associated bones are shown. In the bottom panel, the superior view shows the ethmoid and sphenoid bones and their subparts.

Figure A.16: This image shows the location and structure of the sphenoid bone. A small image of the skull on the top left shows the sphenoid bone highlighted in ochre yellow. The top panel shows the superior view of the sphenoid bone and the bottom panel shows the posterior view of the sphenoid bone.

Figure A.17: This image shows the location and structure of the ethmoid bone. A small image of the skull on the top left shows the ethmoid bone colored in pink. A magnified image shows the inferior view of the ethmoid bone.

Figure A.18: This image shows the location and structure of the maxilla. A small image of the skull on the top left shows the maxilla in ochre yellow. A magnified view shows the detailed structure of the maxilla.

Figure A.19: In this image, the different bones forming the orbit for the eyes are shown and labeled.

Figure A.20: This image shows the sagittal section of the bones that comprise the nasal cavity.

Figure A.21: This figure shows the structure of the nasal cavity. A lateral view of the human skull is shown on the top left with the nasal cavity highlighted in purple. A magnified view of the nasal cavity shows the various bones present and their location.

Figure A.22: In this image, the location and structure of the hyoid bone are shown. The top panel shows a person's face and neck, with the hyoid bone highlighted in gray. The middle panel shows the anterior view and the bottom panel shows the right anterior view.

Figure A.23: This image shows the structure of the mandible. On the top left, a lateral view of the skull shows the location of the mandible in purple. A magnified image shows the right lateral view of the mandible with the major parts labeled.

Figure A.24: This image shows the detailed structure of each vertebra. The left panel shows the superior view of the vertebra and the right panel shows the left posterolateral view.

Figure A.25: This figure shows the structure of the cervical vertebrae. The left panel shows the location of the cervical vertebrae in green along the vertebral column. The middle panel shows the structure of a typical cervical vertebra and the right panel shows the superior and anterior view of the axis.

Figure A.26: This diagram shows how the thoracic vertebra connects to the angle of the rib. The major parts of the vertebra and the processes connecting the vertebra to the rib are labeled.

Figure A.27: This figure shows the structure of the thoracic vertebra. The left panel shows the vertebral column with the thoracic vertebrae highlighted in blue. The right panel shows the detailed structure of a single thoracic vertebra.

Figure A.28: This figure shows the structure of the sacrum and coccyx. The left panel shows the vertebral column with the sacrum and coccyx highlighted in pink. The middle panel shows the anterior view and the right panel shows the posterior view of the sacrum and coccyx.

Figure A.29: This image shows the structure of the vertebral column. The left panel shows the front view of the vertebral column and the right panel shows the side view of the vertebral column.

Figure A.30: This figure shows the skeletal structure of the rib cage. The left panel shows the anterior view of the sternum and the right panel shows the anterior panel of the sternum including the entire rib cage.

Figure A.31: This figure shows the rib change. The top left panel shows the anterior view, and the top right panel shows the posterior view. The bottom panel shows two bones.

Figure A.32: This diagram shows the anterior and posterior view of the scapula.

Figure A.33: This diagram shows the bones of the upper arm and the elbow joint. The left panel shows the anterior view, and the right panel shows the posterior view.

Figure A.34: This figure shows the bones of the lower arm.

Figure A.35: This figure shows the bones in the hand and wrist joints. The left panel shows the anterior view, and the right panel shows the posterior view.

Figure A.36: This figure shows the bone of the pelvis.

Figure A.37: This figure shows the right hip bone. The left panel shows the lateral view, and the right panel shows the medial view.

Figure A.38: This diagram shows the bones of the femur and the patella. The left panel shows the anterior view, and the right panel shows the posterior view.

Figure A.39: This diagram shows the bones of the tibia and the fibula. The left panel shows the anterior view, and the right panel shows the posterior view.

Figure A.40: This diagram shows the bones of the foot from three different perspectives. The upper right panel shows the medial view, the lower right panel shows the lateral view, and the bottom left shows the superior view.

APPENDIX B: PRIMATE CONSERVATION

Mary P. Dinsmore, Ph.D., Loyola University Chicago

Ilianna E. Anise, M.S.

Rebekah J. Ellis, M.S.

Jacob B. Kraus, Ph.D. Candidate, University of Wisconsin–Madison

Karen B. Strier, Ph.D., University of Wisconsin–Madison

This chapter is a revision from "Appendix B: Primate Conservation" by Mary P. Dinsmore, Ilianna E. Anise, Rebekah J. Ellis, Amanda J. Hardie, Jacob B. Kraus, and Karen B. Strier. In Explorations: An Open Invitation to Biological Anthropology, first edition, edited by Beth Shook, Katie Nelson, Kelsie Aguilera, and Lara Braff, which is licensed under CC BY-NC 4.0.

Learning Objectives

- Describe the current conservation status of the world's primates and the criteria that researchers and conservationists use to make these assessments.
- Recognize the many threats that negatively impact primate survival.
- Identify how these threats uniquely affect primates because of characteristics like slow growth rates, long interbirth intervals, strong social bonds, and cultural behavior.
- Distinguish the many ways in which primates are significant to ecological processes, our understanding of human evolution, human cultures, and local economies.
- Illustrate the ways that people, wherever they may live, can work to protect primates.

We are field primatologists interested in understanding nonhuman primates (henceforth, simply "primates") in their natural environments and in contributing to their conservation. Our research has focused on a diversity of primate species that occur in a wide range of habitats throughout the tropics; however, these species and their habitats are subject to many similar threats. As human populations continue to grow (Figure B.1), primates are being pushed out of their natural home ranges and forced to occupy increasingly smaller and more isolated patches of land. Humans and primates are sharing more spaces with one another, making it easier for primates to be hunted or captured and for diseases to spread from humans to primates (and vice versa). Even when primates are not directly threatened by human activities, human-induced climate change is altering local ecosystems at an alarming rate. Local political instability exacerbates all of these problems. Our research has caused us to think about these issues on a daily basis, both in the field and at home. Understanding how these threats affect the primates we have studied is a very important part of what we do. Ultimately, the research of field primatologists is important for documenting the status of wild primate populations and for understanding how primates respond to these threats in order to gain insight into efforts that can help improve their chances of survival in an uncertain future.

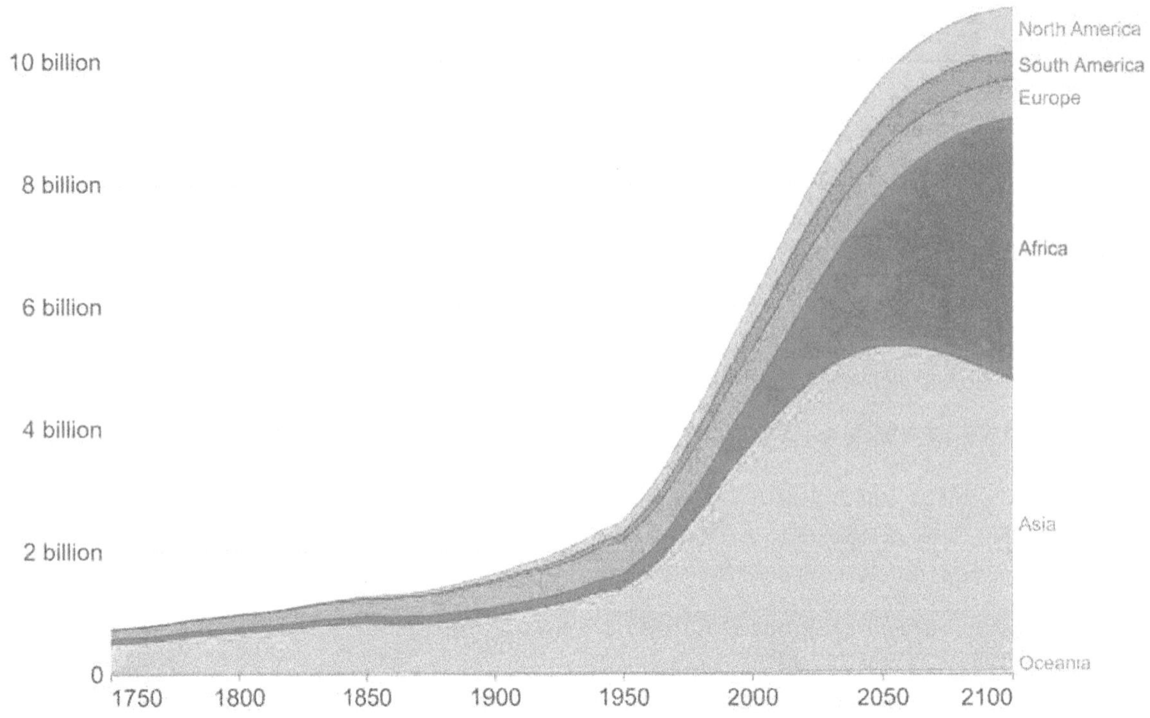

Figure B1: Caption: World population growth by region. Global populations are projected to approach 11 billion people by 2100 (UN Population Division 2019). Credit: **World population by region** by **Our World in Data** [Source Gapminder (v6), HYDE (v3.2) & UN (2019)] accessed June 6, 2022 is used under a **CC BY 4.0 License.** [Image Description].

This appendix begins with a review of the current status of primates and the criteria used in these assessments. We then describe the major threats to primates, explain why primates are important, and consider what can be done to improve their chances of survival. We conclude with a brief consideration of the future for primates.

Current Conservation Status of Nonhuman Primates

Diversity of Primates

The order Primates is one of the most diverse groups of mammals on the planet, with over 528 species in 81 different genera currently recognized (IUCN SSC Primate Specialist Group 2022). In the last few decades new genera, species, and subspecies of primates have been recognized—sometimes as a result of new discoveries and new data but also because of revisions to taxonomic classification systems based on different species concepts (Groves 2014; Lynch Alfaro et al. 2012; Rylands and Mittermeier 2014).

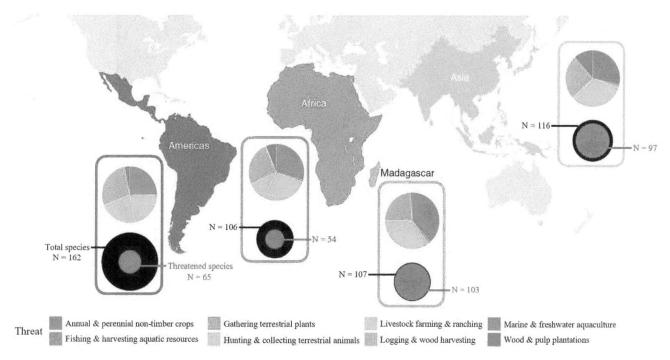

Threat				
▦ Annual & perennial non-timber crops	▦ Gathering terrestrial plants	▦ Livestock farming & ranching	▦ Marine & freshwater aquaculture
▦ Fishing & harvesting aquatic resources	▦ Hunting & collecting terrestrial animals	▦ Logging & wood harvesting	▦ Wood & pulp plantations

Figure B.2: Global distribution of primates and their main threats within the four major primate regions. For each region, the top circle represents the proportion of species impacted by specific threat types; the bottom circle represents the total number of species (in black) and threatened species (in red). Credit: Main threats and conservation status within each of the four primate regions based on IUCN data (Figure 2) by Fernández et al. (2022) is used with permission under a CC BY 4.0 License. [Image Description].

Figure B.3: Mountain gorilla (Gorilla beringei beringei) in Bwindi Impenetrable National Park, Uganda. This endangered species has suffered tremendously due to habitat destruction, poaching, political unrest, and war (Kalpers et al. 2003). Credit: **Mountain Gorilla Bwindi** by **Rod Waddington** is used under a **CC BY-SA 2.0 License**.

Wild primates occur in 90 countries around the world, but two-thirds of all species are found in only four countries: Brazil, Madagascar, Democratic Republic of Congo, and Indonesia (Estrada et al. 2017; Estrada et al. 2018). An estimated 66% of primate species are threatened with extinction (Fernández et al. 2022; Figure B.2). Yet despite this discouraging statistic, there are a growing number of populations recovering as a result of research and conservation efforts. For example, the population of mountain gorillas (Figure B.3) initially studied by Dian Fossey in Rwanda in 1967 has grown from 250 gorillas in 1981 to 339 in 2008. The increase is a result of ongoing research and conservation efforts that include highly controlled ecotourism (Robbins et al. 2011). Similarly, one population of northern muriqui monkeys (Figure B.4)—which inhabits a small, privately owned forest fragment in southeastern Brazil's Atlantic Forest—increased from about 50 individuals to nearly 350 individuals as a result of increased habitat protection over the course of the Muriqui Project of Caratinga, a long-term field study initiated nearly 40 years ago by one of the authors of this appendix (Strier and Mendes 2012). Although the population has declined by about ⅓ in the past five years, it is still 4–5 times larger than it was 40 years ago (Strier 2021a).

Figure B.4: A female northern muriqui (Brachyteles hypoxanthus) with infant at the Feliciano Miguel Abdala Private Natural Heritage Reserve near Caratinga, Minas Gerais, Brazil. Credit: A female northern muriqui (Brachyteles hypoxanthus) with infant at the Feliciano Miguel Abdala Private Natural Heritage Reserve outside of Caratinga, Brazil by A.J. Hardie, courtesy of **Projeto Muriqui de Caratinga**, is used by permission and available here under a CC BY-NC 4.0 License.

International Union for the Conservation of Nature (IUCN)

In conservation, it is crucial to have a global standard to assess and recognize the conservation status of species. The International Union for the Conservation of Nature (IUCN) formed the Red List for Threatened Species in 1994 to determine species extinction risks (IUCN 2022). Scientists submit assessments of species to the IUCN, which are subsequently categorized based on the size and distribution of species' numbers and available habitat. The categories range from "data deficient," when not enough is known, to "least concern," "near threatened," "vulnerable," "endangered," "critically endangered," "extinct in the wild," and "extinct." Threatened species are classified as "vulnerable," "endangered," or "critically endangered," with the most critically endangered species being those whose numbers are fewer than 250 mature individuals and continuing to decline or whose habitats are severely fragmented (Figure B.5; IUCN 2022).

Critically Endangered (CR): Facing an extremely high risk of extinction in the wild due to any of the following:

- Reduction in population size of 80%–90% over the last ten years or three generations, depending on the causes and reversibility of the reductions;
- Extent of occurrence <100 km^2 or area of occupancy <10 km^2 or both;
- Population size estimated to number fewer than 250 mature individuals and to be declining or unevenly distributed;
- Population size estimated to number fewer than 50 mature individuals;
- Probability of extinction within ten years or three generations is at least 50%.

Endangered (EN): Facing a very high risk of extinction in the wild due to any of the following:

- Reduction in population size of 50%–70% over the last ten years or three generations, depending on the causes and reversibility of the reductions;

- Extent of occurrence <5000 km^2 or area of occupancy <500 km^2 or both;
- Population size estimated to number fewer than 2,500 mature individuals and to be declining or unevenly distributed;
- Population size estimated to number fewer than 250 mature individuals;
- Probability of extinction within 20 years or five generations is at least 20%.

Vulnerable (VU): Facing a high risk of extinction in the wild due to any of the following:

- Reduction in population size of 30%–50% over the last ten years or three generations, depending on the causes and reversibility of the reductions;
- Extent of occurrence <20,000 km^2 or area of occupancy <2000 km^2 or both;
- Population size estimated to number fewer than 10,000 mature individuals and to be declining or unevenly distributed;
- Population size estimated to number fewer than 1,000 mature individuals;
- Probability of extinction within 100 years is at least 10%.

Figure B.5: International Union for Conservation of Nature (IUCN) Criteria for Threatened Taxa. Credit: International Union for Conservation of Nature (IUCN) Criteria for Threatened Taxa by Mary P. Dinsmore et al., updated from Strier 2011, with data simplified and condensed from IUCN Species Survival Commission (2012), is under a CC BY-NC 4.0 License.

The IUCN has a committee specifically dedicated to primates, the IUCN Species Survival Commission (SSC) Primate Specialist Group. This group collaborates with the International Primatological Society (IPS), Conservation International (CI), and the Bristol Zoological Society (BZS) every two years to publish "Primates in Peril: The World's 25 Most Endangered Primates." These lists are created at IPS open meetings and are intended to focus attention on all endangered primates by highlighting the plights of some of the most critically endangered (Mittermeier et al. 2022).

Identifying Priorities in Primate Conservation

It is important to consider extinction risk in making conservation decisions, thus the IUCN Red list and the "Primates in Peril" reports are factors in deciding how to allocate resources and funding. Some primate species are found only in biodiversity hot spots or in areas that contain high levels of species diversity and include primates that are endemic to the area and genetically unique (Sechrest et al. 2002). Hot spots are often considered conservation priorities because protecting these areas can result in the protection of large numbers of species. In addition, some conservation organizations focus on highly charismatic primate species (e.g., primates that are large, closely related to humans, or well-known from zoos) to garner attention and resources for conservation (Figure B.6). However, dramatic declines of charismatic species indicate that charisma is not enough (Estrada et al. 2017). In making conservation decisions, primatologists may also consider the importance of genetically unique primates—such as the aye-aye (*Daubentonia madagascariensis*), the last remaining species within its genus—in order to preserve evolutionary history (Strier 2011a).

Figure B.6: A male Bornean orangutan (Pongo pygmaeus). This species's large size and close genetic relatedness to humans make them appealing to the public, such that they are categorized as a "charismatic species." Credit: Bornean Orangutan Wide Face by Eric Kilby is used under a CC BY-SA 2.0 License.

Threats to Primates

Hunting, Poaching, and Wildlife Trade

Hunting represents one of the most critical threats to primates (Figure B.7). Bushmeat, which is the meat of wild animals, has historically been a staple diet in many societies. However, human population growth and economic development have increased the commercialization of bushmeat hunting (Estrada et al. 2017). The availability and use of shotguns has also dramatically increased the quantity of carcasses that hunters capture (Cronin et al. 2015). A study in the Ivory Coast indicated that primates are preferentially targeted for bushmeat hunting by economically reliant hunters, as primate meat is more likely to be sold in markets compared to smaller species (such as rodents), possibly due to its demand as a luxury product for those in nearby urban environments (Bachman et al. 2020). In one market on the Liberia/Ivory Coast border, Ryan Covey and Scott McGraw (2014) estimated that the carcasses of nearly 9,500 primates (from at least nine different species) were sold per year, resulting in an almost 3% annual reduction in the local primate population.

Figure B.7: A female gelada (*Theropithecus gelada*) with a snare around its neck in central Ethiopia. Many rural hunters rely on snare traps, which are easier to construct and more affordable than firearms and can be equally lethal (Noss 1998; Tumusiime et al. 2010). Credit: A female gelada (*Theropithecus gelada*) with a snare around its neck in central Ethiopia by Kadie Callingham is used by permission and available here under a CC BY-NC 4.0 License.

Not all primates are hunted specifically for food. Biomedical researchers use primates as models for understanding human biology and as test subjects for the development of vaccines, drugs, and hormones (Conaway 2011). Many of these experiments require large numbers of primates; therefore biomedical facilities often require a continuous supply of primates. Between 2007 and 2008, a single biomedical laboratory purchased roughly 4,000 nocturnal monkeys for over 100,000 USD through a network of 43 traders across Brazil, Colombia, and Peru (Maldonado, Nijman, and Bearder 2009). Although the use of apes in biomedical research has been severely reduced and/or banned in many countries, such as Austria, New Zealand, the United Kingdom, and the United States (Aguilera, Perez Gomez, and DeGrazia 2021), the use of other primates to study disease transmission, incubation, vaccine effectiveness, and similar topics is still ongoing and has recently been widespread in studying SARS-CoV-2 (Corbett et al. 2020; Lu et al. 2020; Stammes et al. 2021).

Aside from biomedical research, captured primates are both legally and illegally sold to pet owners, zoos, tourist centers, and circuses. In Peru, it is estimated that, as recently as 2015, hundreds of thousands of primates are illegally traded every year, comparable to levels of trade prior to a 1973 national ban on primate exportation (Shanee, Mendoza, and Shanee 2017). Once captured, primates may spend over a week in transit from a rural village to a coastal market. To make the transportation of primates more manageable, common trafficking strategies include sedation, asphyxiation, electrocution, and the removal of teeth. As these conditions severely affect the health of the trafficked primates, many perish during the journey while others die within the hands of authorities. Out of the 77 greater slow lorises (*Nycticebus coucang*) confiscated from a single wildlife trader in Indonesia, 22 died from either trauma or from the severity of their wounds (Fuller et al. 2018). Even when primates are successfully confiscated from wildlife traders, authorities sometimes resell or gift these animals to friends and family (Shanee, Mendoza, and Shanee 2017).

A growing concern of primate conservationists is the use of social media to convey harmful images of primates. People posting on social media sites, such as Instagram, TikTok, Facebook, and YouTube, who show videos and photos of primates dressed in human clothing, tourists engaging with primates while traveling, and "funny" or "cute" photos of primates as pets, may not realize the negative impact their posts can have. The sharing of this content, coupled with comments expressing the desire to own the subject as a pet, can motivate further harvesting of these species from the wild (Clarke et al. 2019; Norconk et al. 2019). After a video depicting a pygmy slow loris (*Nycticebus pygmaeus*) being "tickled" went viral in 2009, and another depicting a slow loris eating rice went viral in 2012, international confiscations of slow lorises increased (Nekaris et al. 2013).

To help curb illegal trafficking of animals, the Convention on International Trade in Endangered Species of Wild Fauna and Flora (CITES) was established in 1973 and ratified in 1975. Under this treaty, the 183 participating countries work together to both regulate the international trade of wildlife and to prevent the overexploitation of wild populations. While only some primates are listed as endangered or threatened under the Endangered Species Act (ESA), all primates are listed under CITES. According to the CITES database, more than 450,000 live primates were traded over the past 15 years (CITES n.d.). However, as the CITES database only includes information formally reported by each country, the real number of primates involved is likely to be much higher.

Disease

Disease has become a critical threat to human and nonhuman primates alike (Nunn and Altizer 2006). Shifting temperatures, unpredictable precipitation, crowding in fragmented habitats, and more frequent human contact can contribute to increased disease transmission among primates (Nunn and Gillespie 2016). Mosquito populations often thrive in this environment and are vectors of diseases that affect both humans and primates, such as Zika virus, yellow fever, and malaria (Lafferty 2009). Disease outbreaks have the potential to severely reduce primate populations. In 2016 and 2017, a large yellow fever outbreak devastated several populations of the brown howler monkeys (*Alouatta guariba*) and other species in the Atlantic forest of Brazil (Fernandes et al. 2017; Strier et al. 2017; Possamai et al. 2022). Ebola outbreaks have similarly diminished populations of African apes; in 2003 and 2004, an outbreak killed up to 5,000 endangered western gorillas (*Gorilla gorilla*; Bermejo et al. 2006) and severely reduced populations of chimpanzees (*Pan troglodytes*; Leroy et al. 2004) in Gabon and the Republic of Congo.

Human encroachment into primate habitats as a result of agricultural expansion, resource extraction, or even through irresponsible ecotourism or research practices can introduce novel pathogens into both human and primate populations (Strier 2017). Due to our close shared lineage, many diseases are communicable between humans and primates, such as Ebola, HIV, tuberculosis, herpes, and other common ailments. Close contact and primate handling are often the most direct ways in which these diseases are transmitted. However, poor hygiene practices, improper waste disposal, and primate provisioning (*e.g.* providing food resources to primates) contribute to disease susceptibility in primates (Wallis and Lee 1999). For example, two groups of olive baboons (*Papio cynocephalus anubis*) living in the Masai Mara Game Reserve in Kenya contracted tuberculosis from foraging at contaminated garbage dumps near the tourist lodge (Tarara et al. 1985). Recently with the proliferation of social media, tourists are coming into close contact with charismatic primate species, such as orangutans, in an effort to capture engaging photographs. Such close contact with varied populations is yet another driver for possible increased disease transmission (Molyneaux et al. 2021). Transmission of diseases through increased human contact can have devastating effects on primate populations that have not built any resistance (Laurance 2015).

Habitat Loss, Fragmentation, and Degradation

Figure B.8: Cattle graze in a newly formed papaya plantation, which was once forested land in Montagne des Français, Madagascar. Credit: Cattle graze in papaya plantation, once forested land, in Montagne des Français, Madagascar by Mary P. Dinsmore is under a CC BY-NC 4.0 License.

The geographic distribution of many primate species has been severely limited by habitat loss. A recent analysis showed human demands for biological resources threaten 81% of primate species, followed by demands for agricultural land (80%) and residential and commercial development (32%; see Fernández et al. 2022). Habitat loss is not new and has affected the distribution of some primate species, including golden snub-nosed monkeys (*Rhinopithecus roxellana*), for thousands of years (Wang et al. 2014). However, our ever-growing need for food, water, and other natural resources has drastically decreased primate habitats globally (Figure B.8). From 2000 to 2013, roughly 220,000 km^2 of tropical forest have been completely deforested in the Brazilian Amazon alone (Tyukavina et al. 2017). Since the start of oil palm development in Indonesia's Ketapang District in 1994, over 65% of habitats without government protection have been allocated to the oil palm industry (Carlson et al. 2012). Habitat loss can lead to increased human-primate conflict. After a 2004 tsunami destroyed large areas of natural habitat on India's Nicobar Islands, local farmers witnessed increased crop raiding by long-tailed macaques (*Macaca fascicularis*;

Velankar et al. 2016). In Saudi Arabia, expanding cities and improper waste disposal practices contributed to the formation of unusually large urban troops of Hamadryas baboons (*Papio hamadryas*) that are less fearful of humans than troops surveyed in rural areas (Biquand et al. 1994). Even within protected areas, primate habitats are rapidly declining. In South Asia, 36% of surveyed protected areas had more than half of their habitat modified for human use, many of which experienced near-total habitat transformation (Clark et al. 2013). In a protected area in northern Madagascar that houses the last remaining population of the critically endangered Northern sportive lemur (*Lepilemur septentrionalis*), forest cover was reduced from 76% to 24% in a 60-year time frame (Dinsmore et al. 2021a).

Habitat fragmentation compounds the effects of habitat loss. Whereas habitat loss reduces the total area in which primates can survive, habitat fragmentation divides large, contiguous primate habitats into smaller isolated patches (Figure B.9). The construction of road networks cutting through savannas, forests, and other primate habitats is a key driver of this fragmentation. Within the next half-century, over 25,000,000 km of new roads are expected to be built, many of which will be located in developing nations through primate habitats (Laurance et al. 2014). By fragmenting habitats, it becomes increasingly challenging for primates (particularly arboreal primates) to disperse between isolated habitat patches. While only 0.1% of black-and-white snub-nosed monkey (*Rhinopithecus bieti*) habitat was lost to the construction of China National Highway 214, movement between habitat patches on either side of the highway was reduced by over 20% (Clauzel et al. 2015). In the long run, habitat fragmentation can force primate populations into genetic bottlenecks, which occur when populations become so small that genetic diversity in them is severely reduced. In the forest fragments of Manaus, Brazil, groups of pied tamarins (*Sanguins bicolor*) that historically formed one biological

Figure B.9: Forest cleared for cattle ranching in the province of Manabí, Ecuador. Cattle ranching is currently the main driver of deforestation in South American countries (Steinweg et al. 2016). Credit: Forest cleared for cattle ranching in the province of Manabí, Ecuador, by Irene Duch-Latorre, courtesy of **Proyecto Washu**, is used by permission and available here under a CC BY-NC 4.0 License.

population were found to harbor only a subset of the genetic diversity previously exhibited in the region (Farias et al. 2015). Furthermore, primates living in fragments with scarce resources experience elevated levels of stress, which can also have long-term consequences on the health of individuals and populations (Rimbach et al. 2014).

Figure B.10: An industrial-sized truck leaves the Montagne des Français region in Madagascar, with dozens of bags of charcoal in tow to be delivered to a nearby town. Much of sub-Saharan Africa still relies on fuelwoods as a main source of energy for cooking and heating, acting as strong drivers of forest degradation (Hosonuma et al. 2012). Credit: An industrial-sized truck with charcoal leaves Montagne des Français region, Madagascar, by Mary P. Dinsmore is under a CC BY-NC 4.0 License.

Aside from habitat loss, other drivers of habitat degradation may affect primate populations. For example, streams can carry toxic chemicals used for agriculture into local habitats where they are either directly or indirectly consumed by primates. In Uganda, chimpanzees (*Pan troglodytes*) living within the Sebitoli Forest have been spotted with facial and limb deformities that are suspected of being related to their exposure to pesticides and herbicides used by local tea farmers (Krief et al. 2017). Additionally, invasive species that outcompete native species and alter habitats can affect primate behaviors. In Madagascar, southern bamboo lemurs (*Hapalemur meridionalis*) spent less time feeding in forests dominated by invasive Melaleuca trees (*Melaleuca quinquenervia*) than in forests without these trees (Eppley et al. 2015). Lastly, fuelwood and charcoal are still widely used throughout sub-Saharan Africa to produce heat and energy for cooking. Heavy reliance on these resources can result in degradation of primate habitat, fragmentation, and overall forest loss (Figure B.10).

Climate Change

The ramifications of climate change, many of which are just beginning to be documented, can be unpredictable and cause a range of consequences for biodiversity, compounding preexisting threats facing primates, as each decade is warmer than the last (IPCC 2022). On a large scale, the deleterious effects of climate change can make primates' current environments inhospitable. Additionally, climate change alters the flowering and fruiting seasons of many plants, requiring dietary flexibility from the organisms that rely on their production (Anderson et al. 2012). Many primates are not capable of this adjustment and would need to shift their habitat range to cope. Arboreal primates have already been observed to shift the utilization of their habitats due to climate change, especially by spending more time on the ground (Eppley et al. 2022). Unfortunately, habitat loss and fragmentation make these range shifts impossible for many species without human assistance in the form of translocations. Compounding this, primates have relatively slow life-histories, often producing only one offspring at a time, and their extended juvenile period results in minimal evolutionary adaptation to change (Campos et al. 2017; Bernard and Marshall 2020). Primates are projected to have some of the most restricted ranges due to climate change (Schloss, Nuñez, and Lawler 2012), forcing them to utilize a variety of possible, nonpreferred habitats.

Figure B.11: An old-growth tree is uprooted after Cyclone Enawo made landfall in northeast Madagascar in March 2017. Hurricanes and cyclones may become stronger with global climate change and often alter ecosystems in ways that negatively affect primates in these regions (Dinsmore, Strier, and Louis 2018). Credit: Old-growth tree uprooted after Cyclone Enawo, Madagascar, by Mary P. Dinsmore is under a CC BY-NC 4.0 License.

Figure B. 12: A northern sportive lemur (Lepilemur septentrionalis), a Critically Endangered species, rests in a tree at Montagne des Français, Madagascar. Credit: A northern sportive lemur (*Lepilemur septentrionalis*), Montagne des Français, Madagascar, by Mary P. Dinsmore is under a CC BY-NC 4.0 License.

Rapidly changing climate also causes other extreme weather events in primate areas. Due to climate change, hurricanes and cyclones are increasing in severity. On a small or local scale, these stochastic environmental events are more fine-tuned and the severity can differ depending on the primate species, which can directly impact populations or their habitats (Figure B.11). For example, spider monkeys (*Ateles geoffroyi yucatanensis*) were not severely affected after two hurricanes hit Mexico but still exhibited behavioral plasticity by spending more time resting, feeding on leaves, and gathering in smaller subgroups than they did before the hurricanes (Schaffner et al. 2012). Some species, such as the critically endangered northern sportive lemur (*Lepilemur septentrionalis*), which has an estimated population of ~87 individuals, exhibited behavioral plasticity after a Category 4 cyclone (Figure B.12; Bailey et al. 2020; Dinsmore et al. 2021b). However, stochastic weather events can still severely impact the species by causing the direct death of individuals in an already-small population, reducing overall population totals and genetic diversity (Dinsmore et al. 2021b). Species that are not threatened or that have large, intact ranges are not likely to be greatly affected by localized climatic conditions, but they may nonetheless experience local devastation and even extinction (Strier 2017).

Dig Deeper: The COVID-19 Pandemic

Severe acute respiratory syndrome coronavirus 2 (SARS-CoV-2), the virus that causes COVID-19, was first recorded in December of 2019 and has infected millions of people since then. Although humans have been the primary focus during this global pandemic, other animals, such as minks, cats, fruit bats, and nonhuman primates can also be infected (Oude Munnink et al. 2021). Human-to-animal transmission of diseases like COVID-19 is a process most commonly known as "zooanthroponosis" or "reverse zoonosis" (Messenger, Barnes, and Gray 2014). For example, in January 2021, western lowland gorillas at the San Diego Zoo in California were confirmed to have contracted SARS-CoV-2 (USDA 2021).

Apart from the direct risks that respiratory viruses bring to nonhuman primates, the COVID-19 pandemic also brought economic crisis and limited human presence in conservation areas. The reduction in human mobility due to the pandemic is being referred to as "anthropause"—a term coined to represent the temporary diminishment of the human footprint. However, this reduction in movement halted conservation action on the ground, potentially increasing poaching and the wildlife trade by people who rely more heavily on natural resources due to global market stress (Rutz et al. 2020). Given the interactions among the multiple consequences of the COVID-19 pandemic, many scientists fear that increased poaching pressure could push some primates, especially the great apes, closer to extinction (Casal and Singer 2021).

Dig Deeper: Extinction Vortex

The many threats facing primates that we have listed here are interrelated: as they interact with one another, they create what is known as an *extinction vortex* (Figure B.13; Gilpin and Soulé 1986). Habitat fragmentation and loss, hunting, climate change, and disease compound to reduce primate populations at a greater rate than when any one factor acts alone. Small populations living in isolated fragments of habitat are disconnected from the rest of their species and are therefore more vulnerable to inbreeding effects. Daniel Brito and colleagues (2008) found that many populations of the critically endangered northern muriqui (*Brachyteles hypoxanthus*) residing in the remaining fragments of the Atlantic Forest would experience genetic decay with the possibility of extinction over the next 50 generations if management practices are not put into place. Slow life histories resulting in long interbirth intervals push many primate species farther into the extinction vortex. Shifting demographics can have dire consequences for primates, thrusting them into a cycle that is hard to break once entered. With the continued presence of threats, many species have a difficult time recovering (Brook et al. 2008; Strier 2011a).

Extinction Vortex

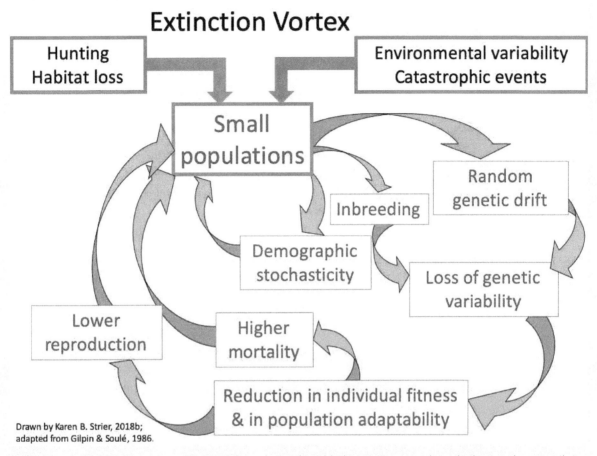

Drawn by Karen B. Strier, 2018b;
adapted from Gilpin & Soulé, 1986.

Figure B.13: A model of the extinction vortex (Strier 2021b: see ch. 4 study guide). The extinction vortex shows the threats and pressures that work simultaneously to threaten populations. These pressures are often exacerbated by the compounding effects they have on each other. Once a population has entered the vortex, this cascade of events can prevent recovery, resulting in extinction. Credit: A model of the extinction vortex drawn by Karen B. Strier (Strier 2021b), adapted from Gilpin and Soulé 1986, is available here under a CC BY-NC 4.0 License. [Image Description].

Primate Significance

As threats to primates continue to widen in scale, increase in severity, and compound with each other, it is imperative to highlight the variety of ways that primates are important not only to their ecosystems but to humans as well. Below we denote four specific areas of primate significance: ecological, bioanthropological, cultural, and economic. Understanding the value of primates can help strengthen conservation actions.

Ecological Significance of Primates

Primates play a key role within their ecosystems, often acting as important contributors to forest community structure by aiding in seed dispersal and pollination of angiosperms and other plant species. Variability in traits such as diet, gut anatomy, and movement patterns influence the spatial landscape of dispersed seeds (Russo and Chapman 2011). Frugivorous primates that range widely are considered the greatest contributors to the dispersal of seeds, as they often either swallow seeds whole, as is common for most Neotropical frugivorous primates (Figure B.14), or spit seeds out, as is common for primates with cheek pouches in Africa and Asia. These primates can augment the diversification and regeneration of forest communities by traveling long distances after consuming fruit and depositing seeds away from the parent plant within heterogeneous landscapes (Strier 2017; Terborgh 1983). Frugivory and seed dispersal are critical plant-animal relationships (Russo 2017). Bach Thanh Hai and colleagues

(2018) found that yellow-cheeked crested gibbons (*Nomascus gabriellae*) in Southeast Asia were the most effective seed disperser for the Pacific walnut tree. Gibbons dispersed seeds via consumption anywhere from 4 m to 425 m from the parent tree. Seeds defecated by gibbons had higher germination and success rates than those spit by macaques in the same forest.

Figure B.14: Fecal matter with seeds from the large-bodied northern muriqui (Brachyteles hypoxanthus). When primates consume fruit, they often swallow whole seeds that they then disperse via their dung. Credit: Fecal matter with seeds from the large-bodied northern muriqui (*Brachyteles hypoxanthus*) by Amanda J. Hardie, courtesy of Projeto Muriqui de Caratinga, is used by permission and available here under a CC BY-NC 4.0 License.

Some species of primate may also act as pollinators for local plant species. These primates are attracted to the nectar and flowers of the plant, which often leave pollen on their faces and fur, subsequently spreading pollen to conspecifics when the primate moves to a new location. Some primates may have coevolved a plant-pollinator relationship. Data indicate that the black-and-white ruffed lemur (*Varecia variegata*) is reliant on the nectar of the traveler's palm (*Ravenala madagascariensis*) during specific times of the year when food is scarce. When eating this nectar, pollen can stick to the ruff of these lemurs' necks. This, along with the notion that no other species visit the travel's palm during these times of the year, indicate that this plant species may be dependent on nonflying mammals for pollination (Kress et al. 1994).

By acting as seed dispersers and pollinators, primates can aid in the reproductive success, regeneration, and diversification of plants within their ecosystems. The significance of these relationships is only becoming more apparent as habitats continue to be fragmented and destroyed. As habitats dwindle, the ability to regenerate healthy forest systems is crucial to the health and survival of tropical forest systems worldwide (Stier 2017).

Bioanthropological Significance of Primates

The study of nonhuman primates has been an integral component of anthropology for many decades (Riley 2020). Even before Sherwood Washburn advocated in *The New Physical Anthropology* (1951) that primates could be studied as living reference for hominin behaviors, anthropologists like Margaret Mead recognized that studies of wild primates contribute to biological and sociocultural anthropology in many ways (Strier 2011b). Primatology in Japan, the U.S., and Europe grew out of a desire to better understand ourselves. Thus, research in the 1960s and 1970s largely focused on species such as chimpanzees (*Pan spp.*) or baboons (*Papio spp.*) that are closely related to humans phylogenetically or live in environments similar to those occupied by early hominins (Haraway 1991; Strum and Fedigan 1999; Washburn 1973). Since those early days, biological anthropological primatology has broadened to include primates from around the world (Strier 2003, 2018a). The inclusion of diverse taxa from what were then-understudied regions challenged notions of "typical" primate behavior.

Anthropologists draw from primate studies to explore the many facets of human behavior and evolution. For example, studies demonstrating the tool-using capabilities of wild chimpanzees (*Pan troglodytes*) and capuchin monkeys (*Sapajus spp.*, formerly *Cebus spp.*) show that similar ecological pressures and intelligence (not just phylogenetic relatedness to humans) contribute to tool-using behaviors (Fragaszy et al. 2004; Inoue-Nakamura and Matsuzawa 1997). Similarly, studies of modern primate morphology are frequently used to assess how locomotor style or behaviors (such as foraging) are related to anatomy, and this knowledge can then be used to assess the skeletal and dental anatomy of fossil hominins. Living primates provide a comparative sample with which we deepen our understanding of the evolutionary mechanisms that shaped human evolution.

Cultural Significance of Primates

For as long as our species has existed, groups of people have lived alongside nonhuman primates and engaged with them in varying ways (Fuentes 2012). The development and expansion of the field of ethnoprimatology, the study of the human-primate interface, has encouraged researchers from sociocultural anthropology and primatology to investigate these points where primates and humans interact and influence each other in surprising ways (Fuentes 2012; Riley 2020; Sponsel 1997). Primates are viewed by many as exceptional animals for the ways in which they reflect elements of humanness, enticing thousands of people to observe their exhibits at zoos and sanctuaries throughout the world. However, the significance of these animals to diverse cultures goes beyond anthropocentrism and touches on aspects of ecology, religion, and social systems. Primates are common figures in religion and myth, appearing sometimes as gods or deities themselves (e.g., the Hindu deity Hanuman) and sometimes as mediators between the human and spirit realms (Alves, Barboza, and de Medeiros Silva Souto 2017; Peterson 2017; Wheatley 1999).

Primates have additional cultural significance as figures in folklore and legend, and they are often ascribed human-like characteristics in many of these narratives (Cormier 2017). These stories often inform local taboos that may discourage the consumption of particular species or deforestation of particular areas (Osei-Tutu 2017; Roncal, Bowler, and Gilmore 2018; Sicotte 2017).

The role that primates play in human cultures is complex and varies significantly with local history, religious practice, and economies. Among the Awa Guajá of eastern Amazonia, for example, primates are considered a part of the humans' extended kin network and are protected as such, yet they also constitute an important source of dietary protein and are hunted regularly (Cormier 2003). In other primate habitat countries, such as Bali, primates play a significant role in religious practice. Long-tailed macaques (*Macaca fascicularis*) in Bali are frequently found in the forests surrounding Hindu temples and will consume offerings left by residents and tourists once festivals or rituals are concluded (Fuentes 2010; Wheatley 1999). These macaques are seen by some as mediators between the natural world and the spiritual world that transports offerings from one realm to another (Wheatley 1999). Investigating how local residents view primates—for example, whether species are considered sacred or not—is a vital component of conservation programs in these areas (Peterson and Riley 2017). Studying the interface between human and nonhuman primates, as well as considering what factors (e.g., local religious practices, taboos, etc.) influence these interactions, can lead to more holistic conservation planning and implementation.

Economic Significance of Primates

One of the most concrete ways that primates can benefit people is through the potential to stimulate local economies from ecotourism. Ecotourism differs from traditional tourism in three main ways: it focuses on nature-based attractions, it provides learning opportunities, and its tourism management practices adhere to economic and ecological sustainability (Fennell and Weaver 2005). Primates are charismatic megafauna, meaning that they are large animals (oftentimes mammals) that elicit mass appeal. They have the possibility to draw tourists, which can in turn bring revenue to lower-income communities found near primate habitats. This attraction from tourists, along with revenue-sharing, can then stimulate local populations to have more positive attitudes toward protected areas and become more invested in the well-being and protection of primates and their habitats (Archabald and Naughton-Treves 2001).

Perhaps one of the greatest success stories of nature-based tourism revolves around the mountain gorillas (*Gorilla beringei beringei*) of Rwanda. After internal conflict plagued Rwanda during the 1990s, the Virungas area developed gorilla-based tourism as a means to aid in socioeconomic development and to bring stability to the region. This process not only helped to increase mountain gorilla populations but was also able to generate enough income to cover the operation costs of three national parks (Maekawa et al. 2013). Research indicated that low-income individuals living around Parc National des Volcans in Rwanda could garner direct income as well as nonfinancial benefits (such as the development of schools and hospitals) from gorilla tourism in the region (Spenceley et al. 2010). Ecotourism success has also been preliminarily observed in the Amazonias region in Brazil. The Mamirauá Sustainable Development Reserve began to let tourists visit groups of uakaris (*Cacajao* spp.) in 2019. Data indicated that although the program was new, tourists had a high success rate (>70%) of observing these rare primates, and researchers believe that these educational encounters will help promote uakari conservation while also driving economic possibilities for the local human populations (Lebrão et al. 2021).

Figure B.15: Tourists observing a black-and-white snub-nosed monkey (Rhinopithecus bieti) from a distance, in southwest China. Although nature-based tourism generates revenue for local communities and primate conservation, it can overhabituate primates, changing their natural behaviors. Credit: Tourists observing a black-and-white snub-nosed monkey (*Rhinopithecus bieti*) in southwest China by Danhe Yang is used by permission and available here under a CC BY-NC 4.0 License.

Although ecotourism has the potential to alleviate poverty situations for local populations and aid in the overall sustainability of natural habitats, it can also bring a suite of new problems to areas. It can overcrowd national parks and overhabituate primates (Figure B.15), increase potential disease transfer between humans and primates, and exacerbate corruption, which often pulls money away from local communities (Hvenegaard 2014; Muehlenbein et al. 2010).

What Can Be Done?

Role of Research

Systematic and long-term research studies provide some of the most foundational and necessary information for the conservation of endangered primates (Kappeler and Watts 2012). Research provides critical data on essential and preferred feeding resources, life history parameters and reproduction rates, territoriality, the carrying capacity of habitats, and solitary or group social dynamics. Within the last few decades, researchers have also begun to stress the acute need for studies investigating how various primates are responding to human disturbances; how climate change is affecting the behavior, range, and habitat of these species; and the significance of primate biodiversity hotspots (Brown and Yoder 2015; Chapman and Peres 2001; Estrada et al. 2018). Understanding these aspects will provide crucial information for practitioners to make the most effective and species-specific conservation decisions.

Long-term studies on primate species provide some of the most conclusive information on changes occurring to populations in the face of anthropogenic disturbances and climate change. They also provide a suite of direct and indirect conservation contributions to endangered species, and the continual monitoring of populations can deter deleterious anthropogenic actions, allowing for population growth and forest regeneration. For example, the Northern Muriqui Project of Caratinga in Minas Gerais, Brazil, has documented growth of both the muriqui population and the regeneration of the forest via secondary succession (Strier 2010). The project has also invested in future research and conservation by training more than 65 Brazilian students, as well as providing stable jobs for local people, stimulating the local community, and alleviating reliance on forest products for income and survival (Strier 2010; Strier and Boubli 2006; Strier and Mendes 2012). Several other long-term primate studies all over the world have seen similar positive impacts and conservation successes (Kappeler and Watts 2012).

The implementation of novel research techniques can also aid in the conservation of primates and their ecosystems. Remote sensing, a technique that gathers information about the environment using satellites, aircraft, or drones, has recently been applied in primate conservation efforts (reviewed in Strier 2021b: see Box 1.3). Another remote-sensing method called LiDAR (Light Detection and Ranging) has been used to generate 3D images of a forest canopy and quantify how canopy height and forest maturity influences movement patterns of three neotropical primates (McLean et al. 2016). The use of high-resolution camera traps both on the ground and in the canopy have become widespread and invaluable in their ability to aid primatologists and conservationists in surveying rare populations, establishing population counts, and assessing behavior (Pebsworth and LaFleur 2014). Camera traps became particularly important in allowing field research to continue during the "anthropause" of 2020, as human mobility was limited during the onset of the COVID-19 pandemic (Blount et al. 2021).

Research is also imperative for making important decisions regarding translocations and reintroductions of animals. Without knowledge of the species' social ecology, demography, and unique learned behaviors—also known as primate traditions or cultures—successful translocations and reintroductions from captive populations would not be possible. Researchers and conservationists must recognize these dynamics when making the difficult decision to reintroduce or move populations and factor in how these dynamics may shift or affect the resident population after management. The most notable case of effective translocation and reintroduction is that of the golden lion tamarin (*Leontopithecus rosalia*). Over 30 zoos contributed 146 captive-born individuals to be reintroduced into Brazil, providing essential information on nutrition and health that aided in reintroduction strategies. Additionally, in 1994, isolated individuals in forest fragments were successfully translocated into protected regions in order to increase gene flow, which through the exchange of genes, introduces more genetic variation into the next generation (Kierulff et al. 2012).

Nongovernmental Organizations (NGOs) and Community-Based Conservation Work

Conservation NGOs have a long-standing history of working to save endangered species from going extinct. These organizations often target primates for their work because of their ability to act as umbrella species, supporting the conservation of many species found within their ecosystems. Over the past 30 years, conservation NGOs have begun to move away from a preservation-based mindset that focused on excluding humans from using protected areas. The 1990s ushered in a shift toward community-based conservation (CBC), which instead aimed to work with local people living near targeted natural environments to establish sustainable practices (Horwich and Lyon 2007). CBC strategies involving the installation of visual and acoustic deterrents, barriers, and buffers around human settlements can also help reduce human-primate conflict (Hockings 2016). CBC has shown success in terms of reducing hunting and deforestation in many regions including the Manas Biosphere Reserve in Assam, India, as well as in the cloud forests of Peru from the work of the Yellow Tailed Woolly Monkey Project (Horwich et al. 2012; Shanee et al. 2007). Although CBC has seen conservation successes, many warn that it should not be a panacea for all conservation goals but, rather, one mechanism among many when attempting to conserve endangered species (Reibelt and Nowack 2015; Scales 2014).

Reforestation is widely becoming one of the most practical ways in which NGOs aid in primate conservation. Organizations often collaborate with communities to establish nurseries to grow saplings, which can then be transplanted strategically to reforest certain parts of primate habitats or create habitat corridors between forest fragments. Madagascar Biodiversity Partnership, an NGO with four field sites throughout Madagascar, has planted over 5,166,000 trees from 2010 to August of 2022 (Edward E. Louis Jr., personal communication, 7,15,22). These efforts have been shown to be successful, as lemurs have been observed in reforested regions where they had previously not been seen when trees were more sparse.

Special Topic: What Can Readers of this Book Do?

It may be difficult to imagine how an individual living thousands of miles away can aid in the conservation of primates and their habitats, but in fact there are several small steps that people all over the world can take to make a difference. Many local zoos contribute to in situ conservation work as well as maintain species survival plans in order to increase diversity among zoo populations. We recommend readers visit their local zoos to learn about what actions zoos take to aid in the conservation of primates and how they can get involved in these activities.

One tangible action that can be done is to reduce the purchasing of products that contain nonsustainable ingredients. The demand for cheap oil has increased in recent years for commercial products such as peanut butter, chocolate, soaps, and shampoos, among many others. As such, palm oil plantations have expanded into wildlife habitat throughout Southeast Asia, especially in Borneo and Sumatra, the last remaining habitats of orangutans (*Pongo spp.*) and many other species of primates. This, coupled with other local pressures such as hunting and peat fires, resulted in the IUCN upgrading the Borneo orangutan's (*Pongo pygmaeus*) conservation status to Critically Endangered in 2016. Although data suggest that orangutans will nest within agroindustrial environments, they will only do so with natural forest patches nearby (Ancrenaz et al. 2014). Reducing individual consumption of palm oil or choosing sustainable oil products can help reduce the overall demand and drive producers to commit to more environmentally friendly practices. This can hopefully slow the conversion of naturally forested landscapes into agroindustrial environments.

As previously noted, the proliferation of social media has spurred the desire to photograph animals in close proximity (Pearce and Moscardo 2015). We recommend that readers who visit native primate environments resist engaging with primates in an attempt to take "selfies" with animals. Repeated encounters with travelers and tourists can overhabituate primates and put them in danger of contracting (and transmitting) diseases (Geffroy et al. 2015). Paying for photos with primates can also exacerbate the illegal pet trade because local people will be incentivized to harvest primate infants from wild populations, adversely affecting primate densities and social group dynamics. While it may be popular to try to take the most engaging "selfie" with a wild animal, it is best to just admire these animals from afar (Figure B.16).

Figure B.16: Students on a field course observe and record data on primates in the canopy at El Zota field station in Costa Rica. Credit: Students in the canopy at El Zota field station, Costa Rica, by Mary P. Dinsmore, courtesy of Broadreach Global Summer Adventures, Inc., is used by permission and available here under a CC BY-NC 4.0 License.

Lastly, readers can aid in primate conservation by resisting sharing social media videos depicting primates in nonnative habitats. Videos of primates engaging with humans often spark the popularity of these animals as pets. The desire for these animals can lead to an influx in illegal pet harvesting and trading, the mistreatment of wild animals in domestic settings, and the belief that these animals are not endangered since others own them as pets (Nekaris et al. 2013). Educating one's self and others, coupled with a refusal to share these 'cute' videos, can help reduce the market for primates to be captured for the illegal pet trade.

Further Perspectives

As anthropogenic and natural disturbances continue to intensify in range and scale, the future status of the world's primates is increasingly dire. However, researchers, conservationists, and the general public are attempting to understand how primates respond to these disturbances, what actions can be done to mitigate further disturbances, how to establish sustainable relationships between humans and primates, and what small actions each individual can do to aid these processes.

Regardless of our cultural or political views, we think it is valid to ask ourselves as researchers, conservationists, and students: What is the value of Earth's biological diversity, and what are our obligations to nonhuman primates, our closest living ancestors? Although scientists and conservationists often argue that there is inherent value in maintaining the world's biodiversity, we propose that primates have a special significance that goes beyond their intrinsic contribution to biodiversity. The concept that species and systems can provide a suite of benefits to humans is known as ecosystem services (Cardinale et al. 2012; Kremen 2005). These services are often classified into four categories: provisioning (e.g., food), regulating (e.g., water-quality regulating), cultural (e.g., recreation and aesthetic), and supporting services (e.g., nutrient cycling) (Harrison et al. 2014; Mace et al. 2011; Millennium Ecosystem Assessment 2005). Following this approach, we propose that understanding the value of primates and their habitats in terms of their ecological, bioanthropological, cultural–historical, and economic contributions can aid in the long-term conservation of these endangered species. Recognizing the connections and continuities between ourselves and other primates is the first critical step toward caring about their future and making it part of our own.

Review Questions

- What criteria do researchers and conservationists use to identify the conservation status of primate populations and species?
- What are the main threats facing primates today, and how do the combined impacts of these threats uniquely affect primates?
- What do you think a world without primates would look like? Consider their unique significance and the various roles they play in ecology, human evolutionary and cultural history, and local economies. How would the absence of primates affect ecosystems, other animals, and humans?
- Considering all the other problems in the world today, should primate conservation be a high priority? What are the arguments to support prioritizing primate conservation?
- How can you contribute to primate conservation in your everyday life?

About the Authors

Mary P. Dinsmore, Ph.D

Loyola University Chicago, mdinsmore@luc.edu

Mary P. Dinsmore, Ph.D. is an Assistant Teaching Professor in the School of Environmental Sustainability at Loyola University Chicago. Mary's interest in primatology began when she was working as a research assistant in Peru with saddleback tamarins (*Saguinus fuscicollis*) and in Madagascar with greater bamboo lemurs (*Prolemur simus*). It was during these experiences that she saw firsthand the immense impacts that humans had on primate habitats and became interested in human-wildlife conflict and conservation. Her dissertation work explored the consequences of anthropogenic and natural disturbances on the habitat and behavior of the northern sportive lemur (*Lepilemur septentrionalis*). She received funding for her work from the Primate Action Fund of Conservation International and African Studies Department of UW–Madison.

Mary received her BS and BA from the University of Portland in 2009, her MS from the University of Wisconsin–Madison in 2014, and her Ph.D. from the University of Wisconsin-Madison in 2020. She currently teaches courses at Loyola University Chicago on Biodiversity and Biogeography, Mammalogy, and Human Dimensions of Conservation.

Ilianna E. Anise, M.S.

University of Wisconsin–Madison, ilianna.anise@wisc.edu

Ilianna E. Anise received her M.S. in Integrative Biology at the University of Wisconsin–Madison in 2022. In her masters research, she used social network analysis to detect the timing of a group fission using behavioral data that had been collected on wild northern muriquis and considered the implications of this method for conservation management. During the writing of the first edition of this appendix, she was supported by an Advanced Opportunity Fellowship, the Department of Integrative Biology, and Teaching Assistantships at University of Wisconsin-Madison.

Ilianna received her BA in biology and environmental science from Drew University. She found her passion for fieldwork while participating in a small mammal demography research project as an undergraduate student.

Rebekah J. Ellis, M.S.

Rebekah J. Ellis received her M.S degree from the Department of Anthropology at the University of Wisconsin–Madison. Rebekah received her BA in anthropology and psychology from the University of Texas at Austin. She has studied the behavior of neotropical primates at field sites in Eastern Costa Rica and the Ecuadorian Amazon. At her time at UW–Madison, Rebekah assisted in teaching an introductory course covering the subdisciplines of cultural, archeological, and biological anthropology and her research utilized social network analysis to explore the social behavior of neotropical primates.

Jacob B. Kraus, B.A., Ph.D. student

University of Wisconsin–Madison, jbkraus2@wisc.edu

Jacob B. Kraus is a Ph.D. candidate and teaching assistant in the Department of Integrated Biology at the University of Wisconsin–Madison and a member of the Strier Lab. His interest in primatology began while studying the ecology and behavior of Gelada monkeys (*Theropithecus gelada*) as a field assistant for the Guassa Gelada Research Project (GGRP) in Ethiopia. He is broadly interested in the behavioral thermoregulation strategies that primates, and other social mammals, employ in high-altitude habitats. Jacob's current research is focused on how the sociality of Yunnan snub-nosed monkeys (*Rhinopithecus bieti*) affects their microhabitat selection and grooming behaviors. His work has been funded by the Department of Integrative Biology.

Jacob received his BA in Biology from Reed College. Prior to attending UW–Madison, Jacob interned at the Smithsonian Conservation Biology Institute (SCBI), where he worked on various remote-sensing and habitat-survey projects.

Karen B. Strier, Ph.D.

University of Wisconsin–Madison, kbstrier@wisc.edu

https://strierlab.anthropology.wisc.edu/

Karen B. Strier is Vilas Research Professor and Irven DeVore Professor of Anthropology at the University of Wisconsin–Madison. She received her BA (1980) from Swarthmore College, and MA (1981) and PhD (1986) from Harvard University. She has been studying the endangered northern muriqui monkey in the Brazilian Atlantic forest since 1982. She is a fellow of the U.S. National Academy of Sciences, the American Academy of Arts and Sciences, and the American Association for the Advancement of Science. She was awarded an Honorary Doctorate of Science from the University of Chicago and Distinguished Primatologist Awards from the American Primatological Society and the Midwestern Primate Interest Group. She has received various research, teaching, and service awards from the University of Wisconsin–Madison. She holds Lifetime Honorary Memberships from the Brazilian Primatological Society, the Latin American Primatological Society, the Margot Marsh Biodiversity Foundation Award for Excellence in Primate Conservation, and the Premio Muriqui from the Reserva Biosfera da Mata Atlantica. She has authored or coauthored more than 100 publications; and authored two books, including *Primate Behavioral Ecology, 6th edition* (2021b). She served as the President of the International Primatological Society from 2016 to 2022.

For Further Exploration

For those interested in gaining hands-on experience with primates, we recommend visiting Primate Info Net, where a list of field school opportunities and professional, educational, and volunteer positions are posted regularly. These listings can be found here:

To learn more about reducing the spread of potentially harmful images of primates, access *Best Practice Guidelines for Responsible Images of Non-Human Primates*, written by The Primate Specialist Group of the International Union for the Conservation of Nature (IUCN):

References

Aguilera, Bernardo, Javiera Perez Gomez, and David DeGrazia. 2021. "Should Biomedical Research with Great Apes Be Restricted? A Systematic Review of Reasons." *BMC Medical Ethics* 22. doi: https://doi.org/10.1186/s12910-021-00580-z.

Alves, Rômulo Romeu Nóbrega, Raynner Rilke Duarte Barboza, and Wedson de Medeiros Silva Souto. 2017. "Primates in Mythology." In *The International Encyclopedia of Primatology*, edited by Agustín Fuentes, 1149–1154. Hoboken, NJ: John Wiley and Sons. https://doi.org/10.1002/9781119179313.wbprim0173.

Ancrenaz, Marc, Felicity Oram, Laurentius Ambu, Isabelle Lackman, Eddie Ahmad, Hamisah Elahan, Harjinder Kler, Nicola K. Abram, and Erik Meijaard. 2014. "Of Pongo, Palms, and Perceptions: A Multidisciplinary Assessment of Bornean Orangutans *Pongo pygmaeus* in an Oil Palm Context." *Oryx* 49 (3): 465–472. https://doi.org/10.1017/S0030605313001270.

Archabald, Karen, and Lisa Naughton-Treves. 2001. "Tourism Revenue-Sharing around National Parks in Uganda: Early Efforts to Identify and Reward Local Communities." *Environmental Conservation* 28 (2): 135–149. https://doi.org/10.1017/S0376892901000145.

Bachmann, Mona Estrella, Martin Reinhardt Nielsen, Heather Cohen, Dagmar Haase, Joseph A. K. Kouassi, Roger Mundry, and Hjalmar S. Kuehl. 2020. "Saving Rodents, Losing Primates: Why We Need Tailored Bushmeat Management Strategies." *People and Nature* 2: 889–902. https://doi.org/10.1002/pan3.10119.

Bailey, Carolyn A., Timothy M. Sefczek, Brittani A. D. Robertson, Lucile Rasoamazava, Valérie F. Rakotomalala, Jean D. N. Andriamadison, François Randrianasolo,

Aubin Andriajaona, and Edward E. Louis, Jr. 2020. "A Re-evaluation of the Northern Sportive Lemur (*Lepilemur septentrionalis*) Population at Montagne des Français, and a Review of Its Current State of Conservation in the Protected Area." *Primate Conservation* 34: 53–59.

Bermejo, Magdalena, Jose Domingo Rodriguez-Teijeiro, German Illera, and Peter D. Walsh. 2006. "Ebola Outbreak Killed 5,000 Gorillas." *Science* 314 (5805): 1564. https://doi.org/10.1126/science.1133105.

Bernard, Andrew M., and Andrew J. Marshall. 2020. "Assessing the State of Knowledge of Contemporary Climate Change and Primates." *Evolutionary Anthropology* 29 (6): 317–331. https://doi.org/10.1002/evan.21874.

Biquand, S., A. Boug, V. Biquand-Guyot, and J. P. Gautier. 1994. "Management of Commensal Baboons in Saudi Arabia." *Revue d'Ecologie, Terre et Vie, Société nationale de protection de la nature* 49 (3): 213–222.

Blount, J. David., Mark W. Chynoweth, Austin M. Green, and Çağan H. Şekercioğlu. 2021.

"Review: COVID-19 Highlights the Importance of Camera Traps for Wildlife Conservation Research and Management." *Biological Conservation* 256: 108984. https://doi.org/10.1016/j.biocon.2021.108984.

Brito, Daniel, Carlos E. V. Grelle, and Jean Phillipe Boubli. 2008. "Is the Atlantic Forest Protected Area Network Efficient in Maintaining Viable Populations of *Brachyteles hypoxanthus*?" *Biodiversity and Conservation* 17 (13): 3255–3268. https://doi.org/10.1007/s10531-008-9427-z.

Brook, Barry W., Navjot S. Sodhi, and Corey J. A. Bradshaw. 2008. "Synergies among Extinction Drivers under Global Change." *Trends in Ecology and Evolution* 23 (8): 453–460. https://doi.org/10.1016/j.tree.2008.03.011.

Brown, Jason L., and Anne D. Yoder. 2015. "Shifting Ranges and Conservation Challenges for Lemurs in the Face of Climate Change." *Ecology and Evolution* 5 (6): 1131–1142. https://doi.org/10.1002/ece3.1418.

Campos, Fernando A., William F. Morris, Susan C. Alberts, Jeanne Altmann, Diane K. Brockman, Marina Cords, Anne Pusey, Tara S. Stoinski, Karen B. Strier, and Linda M. Fedigan. 2017. "Does Climate Variability Influence the Demography of Wild Primates? Evidence from Long-Term Life-History Data in Seven Species." *Globe Change Biology* 23 (11): 1–15. https://doi.org/10.1111/gcb.13754.

Cardinale, B. J., J. Emmett Duffy, Andrew Gonzalez, David U. Hopper, Charles Perrings, Patrick Venail, Anita Narwani, et al. 2012. "Biodiversity Loss and Its Impact on Humans." *Nature* 486 (7401): 59–67. https://doi.org/10.1038/nature11148.

Carlson, Kimberly M., Lisa M. Curran, Dessy Ratnasari, Alice M. Pittman, Britaldo S. Soares-Filho, Gregory P. Asner, Simon N. Trigg, David A. Gaveau, Deborah Lawrence, and Herman O. Rodrigues. 2012. "Committed Carbon Emissions, Deforestation, and Community Land Conversion from Oil Palm Plantation Expansion in West Kalimantan, Indonesia." *Proceedings of the National Academy of Sciences* 109 (19): 7559–7564. https://doi.org/10.1073/pnas.1200452109.

Casal, Paula, and Peter Singer. 2021. "The Threat of Great Ape Extinction from COVID-19." *Journal of Animal Ethics* 11 (2): 6–11. https://doi.org/10.5406/janimalethics.11.2.0006.

Chapman, Colin A., and Carlos A. Peres. 2001. "Primate Conservation in the New Millennium: The Role of Scientists." *Evolutionary Anthropology* 10 (1): 16–33. https://doi.org/10.1002/1520-6505(2001)10:1<16::AID-EVAN1010>3.0.CO;2-O.CITES. N.d. "CITES Trade Database." Accessed July 22, 2018. https://trade.cites.org/en/cites_trade/#.

Clark, Natalie E., Elizabeth H. Boakes, Philip J. K. McGowan, Georgina M. Mace, and Richard A. Fuller. 2013. "Protected Areas in South Asia Have Not Prevented Habitat Loss: A Study Using Historical Models of Land-Use Change." *PLoS ONE* 8 (5):e65298. https://doi.org/10.1371/journal.pone.0065298.

Clarke, Tara A., Kim E. Reuter, Marni LaFleur, and Melissa S. Schaefer. 2019. "A Viral Video and Pet Lemurs on Twitter." *PLoS ONE* 14(1): e0208577. https://doi.org/10.1371/journal.pone.0208577.

Clauzel, Celine, Deng Xiqing, Wu Gongsheng, Patrick Giraudoux, and Li Li. 2015. "Assessing the Impact of Road Developments on Connectivity across Multiple Scales: Application to Yunnan Snub-Nosed Monkey Conservation." *Biological Conservation* 192: 207–217. https://doi.org/10.1016/j.biocon.2015.09.029.

Conaway, Eileen. 2011. "Bioidentical Hormones: An Evidence-Based Review for Primary Care Providers." *The Journal of the American Osteopathic Association* 111 (3): 153–164.

Corbett, Kizzmekia S., Barbara Flynn, Kathryn E. Foulds, Joseph R. Francica, Seyhan Boyoglu-Barnum, Anne P. Werner, Britta Flach, et al. 2020. "Evaluation of the mRNA-1273 Vaccine against SARS-CoV-2 in Nonhuman Primates." *The New England Journal of Medicine* 383: 1544–1555. https://doi.org/10.1056/NEJMoa2024671.

Cormier, Loretta A. 2003. *Kinship with Monkeys: The Guajá Foragers of Eastern Amazonia*. New York: Columbia University Press.

Cormier, Loretta A. 2017. "Primates in Folklore." In *The International Encyclopedia of Primatology*, edited by Agustín Fuentes, 1139–1146. Hoboken, NJ: John Wiley and Sons. https://doi.org/10.1002/9781119179313.wbprim0285.

Covey, Ryan, and W. Scott McGraw. 2014. "Monkeys in a West African Bushmeat Market: Implications for Cercopithecid Conservation in Eastern Liberia." *Tropical Conservation Science* 7 (1): 115–125. https://doi.org/10.1177/194008291400700103.

Cronin, Drew T., Stephen Woloszynek, Wayne A. Morra, Shaya Honarvar, Joshua M. Linder, Mary Katherine Gonder, Michael P. O'Connor, and Gail W. Hearn. 2015. "Long-term Urban Market Dynamics Reveal Increased Bushmeat Carcass Volume Despite Economic Growth and Proactive Environmental Legislation on Bioko Island, Equatorial Guinea." *PLoS ONE* 10 (7): e0134464. https://doi.org/10.1371/journal.pone.0134464.

Dinsmore, Mary P., Edward E. Louis Jr., Daniel Georges Randriamahazomana, Ali Hachim, John R. Zaonarivelo, and Karen B. Strier. 2016. "Variation in Habitat and Behavior of the Northern Sportive Lemur (*Lepilemur septentrionalis*) at Montagne des Français, Madagascar." *Primate Conservation* 30: 73–88.

Dinsmore, Mary P., Karen B. Strier, and Edward E. Louis Jr. 2018. "The Impacts of Cyclone Enawo and Anthropogenic Disturbances on the Habitat of Northern Sportive Lemurs (*Lepilemur septentrionalis*) in Northern Madagascar." *American Journal of Physical Anthropology* 165 (2): 68.

Dinsmore, Mary P., Karen B. Strier, and Edward E. Louis Jr. 2021a. "Anthropogenic Disturbances and Deforestation of Northern Sportive Lemur (*Lepilemur septentrionalis*) Habitat at Montagne des Français, Madagascar." *Primate Conservation* 35: 125–138.

Dinsmore, Mary P., Karen B. Strier, and Edward E. Louis Jr. 2021b. "The Influence of Seasonality, Anthropogenic Disturbances, and Cyclonic Activity on the Behavior of Northern Sportive Lemurs (*Lepilemur septentrionalis*) at Montagne des Français, Madagascar." American Journal of Primatology 83: e23333. https://doi.org/10.1002/ajp.23333.

Eppley, Timothy M., Giuseppe Donati, Jean Baptiste Ramanamanjato, Faly Randriatafika, Laza N. Andriamandimbiarisoa, David Rabehevitra, Robertin Ravelomanantsoa, and Jörg U. Ganzhorn. 2015. "The Use of an Invasive Species Habitat by a Small Folivorous Primate: Implications for Lemur Conservation in Madagascar." *PLoS ONE* 10 (11): e0140981. https://doi.org/10.1371/journal.pone.0140981.

Eppley, Timothy M., Selwyn Hoeks, Colin A. Chapman, Jörg U. Ganzhorn, Katie Hall, Megan E. Owen, Dara B. Adams, et al. 2022. "Factors influencing terrestriality in primates of the Americas and Madagascar." PNAS 119 (42): e2121105119. https://doi.org/10.1073/pnas.2121105119.

Estrada, Alejandro, Paul A. Garber, Russell A. Mittermeier, Serge Wich, Sidney Gouveia, Ricardo Dobrovolski, K. A. I. Nekaris, et al. 2018. "Primates in Peril: The Significance of Brazil, Madagascar, Indonesia, and the Democratic Republic of the Congo for Global Primate Conservation." *PeerJ* 6: e4869. https://doi.org/10.7717/peerj.4869.

Estrada, Alejandro, Paul A. Garber, Anthony B. Rylands, Christian Roos, Eduardo Fernandez-Duque, Anthony Di Fiore, K. Anne-Isola Nekaris, et al. 2017. "Impending Extinction Crisis of the World's Primates: Why Primates Matter." *Science Advances* 3 (229): 1–16. https://doi.org/10.1126/sciadv.1600946.

Farias, Izeni P., Wancley G. Santos, Marcelo Gordo, and Tomas Hrbek. 2015. "Effects of Forest Fragmentation on Genetic Diversity of the Critically Endangered Primate, the Pied Tamarin (*Saguinus Bicolor*): Implications for Conservation." *Journal of Heredity* 106 (S1): 512–521. https://doi.org/10.1093/jhered/esv048.

Fennell, David, and David Weaver. 2005. "The Ecotourium Concept and Tourism-Conservation Symbiosis." *Journal of Sustainable Tourism* 13(4): 373–390. https://doi.org/10.1080/09669580508668563.

Fernandes, Natalia C. C. A., Mariana Sequetin Cunha, Juliana Mariotti Guerra, Rodrigo Albergaria Ressio, Cinthya dos Santos Cirqueira, Silvia D'Andretta Iglezias, Julia de Carvalho, Emerson L. L. Aruajo, Jose-Luiz Catao-Dias, and Josue Diaz-Delgado. 2017. "Outbreak of Yellow Fever among Nonhuman Primates, Espirito Santo, Brazil, 2017." *Emerging Infectious Diseases* 23 (12): 2038–2041. https://doi.org/10.3201/eid2312.170685.

Fernández, David, Daphne Kerhoas, Andrea Dempsey, Josephine Billany, Gráinne McCabe, and Elitsa Argirova. 2022. "The Current Status of the World's Primates: Mapping Threats to Understand Priorities." *International Journal of Primatology* 433: 15–39. https://doi.org/10.1007/s10764-021-00242-2.

Fragaszy, Dorothy, Patrícia Izar, Elisabetta Visalberghi, Eduardo B. Ottoni, and Marino Gomes de Oliveira. 2004. "Wild Capuchin Monkeys (*Cebus libidinosus*) Use Anvils and Stone-Pounding Tools." *American Journal of Primatology* 64 (4): 359–366. https://doi.org/10.1002/ajp.20085.

Fuentes, Agustín. 2010. "Natural Cultural Encounters in Bali: Monkeys, Temples, Tourists, and Ethnoprimatology." *Cultural Anthropology* 25 (4): 600–624. https://doi.org/10.1111/j.1548-1360.2010.0170.x.

Fuentes, Agustín. 2012. "Ethnoprimatology and the Anthropology of the Human-Primate Interface." *Annual Review of Anthropology* 41: 101–117. https://doi.org/10.1148/annurev-anthro-092611-145808.

Fuller, Grace, Wilhelmina Frederica Eggen, Wirdateti Wirdateti, and K. A. I. Nekaris. 2018. "Welfare Impacts of the Illegal Wildlife Trade in a Cohort of Confiscated Greater Slow Lorises, Nycticebus Coucang." *Journal of Applied Animal Welfare Science* 21 (3): 224–238. https://doi.org/10.1080/10888705.2017.1393338.

Geffroy, Benjamin, Diogo S. M. Samia, Eduardo Bessa, and Daniel T. Blumstein. 2015. "How Nature-Based Tourism Might Increase Prey Vulnerability to Predators." *Trends in Ecology & Evolution* 30 (12): 755–765.

Gilpin, Michael E., and Michael E. Soulé. 1986. "Minimum Viable Populations: Processes of Species Extinction." In *Conservation Biology: The Science of Scarcity and Diversity*, edited by Michael E. Soulé, 19–34. Sunderland, UK: Sinauer and Associates.

Groves, Colin P. 2014. "Primate Taxonomy: Inflation or Real?" *Annual Review of Anthropology* 43: 27–36. https://doi.org/10.1146/annurev-anthro-102313-030232.

Hai, Bach Thanh, Jin Chen, Kim R. McConkey, and Salindra K. Dayananda. 2018. "Gibbons (*Nomascus gabriellae*) Provide Key Seed Dispersal for the Pacific Walnut (*Dracontomelon dao*), in Asia's Lowland Tropical Forest." *Acta Oecologica* 88: 71–79. https://doi.org/10.1016/j.actao.2018.03.011.

Haraway, Donna. 1991. *Simians, Cyborgs, and Women: The Reinvention of Nature*. New York: Routledge.

Harrison, P. A., P. M. Barry, G. Simpson, J. R. Haslett, M. Blicharska, M. Bucur, R. Dunford, et al. 2014. "Linkages between Biodiversity Attributes and Ecosystem Services: A Systematic Review." *Ecosystem Services* 9: 191–203. https://doi.org/10.1016/j.ecoser.2014.05.006.

Hockings, Kimberly J. 2016. "Mitigating Human-Nonhuman Primate Conflict." In *The International Encyclopedia of Primatology*, edited by Agustín Fuentes, 820–828. Hoboken, NJ: John Wiley and Sons. https://doi.org/10.1002/9781119179313.wbprim0053.

Horwich, Robert H., and Jonathan Lyon. 2007. "Community Conservation: Practitioners' Answer to Critics." *Oryx* 41 (3): 376–385. https://doi.org/10.1017/S0030605307001010.

Horwich, R. H., J. Lyon, and A. Bose. 2012. "Preserving Biodiversity and Ecosystems: Catalyzing Conservation Contagion." In *Deforestation around the World*, edited by P. Moutinho, 283–318. Rijeka, Croatia: InTech.

Hosonuma, Noriko, Martin Herold, Veronique de Sy, Ruth S. de Fries, Maria Brockhaus, Louis Verchot, Arild Angelsen, and Erika Romijn. 2012. "An Assessment of Deforestation and Forest Degradation Drivers in Developing Countries." *Environmental Research Letters* 7 (4). https://doi.org/10.1088/1748-9326/7/4/044009.

Hvenegaard, Glen. 2014. "Economic Aspects of Primate Tourism Associated with Primate Conservation." In *Primate Tourism: A Tool for Conservation?*, edited by Anne E. Russon and Janette Wallis, 259–277. Cambridge, UK: Cambridge University Press.

Inoue-Nakamura, Noriko, and Tetsuro Matsuzawa. 1997. "Development of Stone Tool Use by Wild Chimpanzees (*Pan troglodytes*)." *Journal of Comparative Psychology* 111 (2): 159–173.

IPCC. 2022. "Climate Change 2022: Impacts, Adaptation and Vulnerability. Contribution of Working Group II to the Sixth Assessment Report of the Intergovernmental Panel on Climate Change," edited by H.-O. Pörtner, D. C. Roberts, M. Tignor, E. S. Poloczanska, K. Mintenbeck, A. Alegría, M. Craig, S. Langsdorf, S. Löschke, V. Möller, A. Okem, B. Rama. Cambridge, UK: Cambridge University Press. https://doi.org/10.1017/9781009325844.

IUCN. 2012. "IUCN Red List Categories and Criteria: Version 3.1." Technical Report, 32. Gland, Switzerland and Cambridge, UK: IUCN.

IUCN. 2022. "The IUCN Red List of Threatened Species: Version 2021-3." Accessed June 6, 2022. http://www.iucnredlist.org.

IUCN SSC Primate Specialist Group. 2022. "Global Non-Human Primate Diversity." Accessed June 6, 2022. http://www.primate-sg.org/primate_diversity_by_region/.

Kalpers, José, Elizabeth A. Williamson, Martha M. Robbins, Alastair Mcneilage, Augustin Nzamurambaho, Ndakasi Lola, and Ghad Mugiri. 2003. "Gorillas in the Crossfire: Population Dynamics of the Virunga Mountain Gorillas over the Past Three Decades." *Oryx* 37 (3): 326–337. https://doi.org/10.1017/S0030605303000589.

Kappeler, Peter M., and David P. Watts. 2012. *Long-term Field Studies of Primates*. New York: Springer.

Kierulff, M. C. M., C. R. Ruiz-Miranda, P. Procopio de Oliveira, B. B. Beck, A. Martins, J. M. Dietz, D. M. Rambaldi, and A. J. Baker. 2012. "The

Golden Lion Tamarin *Leontopithecus rosalia*: A Conservation Success Story." *International Zoo Yearbook* 46 (1): 36–45. https://doi.org/10.1111/j.1748-1090.2012.00170.x.

Kremen, Claire. 2005. "Managing Ecosystem Services: What Do We Need to Know about Their Ecology?" *Ecology Letters* 8 (5): 468–479. https://doi.org/10.1111/j.1461-0248.2005.00751.x.

Kress, John, George E. Schatz, Michael Andrianifahanana, and Hilary Simons Morland. 1994. "Pollination of *Ravenala madagascariensis* (*Strelitziaceae*) by Lemurs in Madagascar: Evidence for an Archaic Coevolution System?" *American Journal of Botany* 81 (5): 542–551. https://doi.org/10.1002/j.1537-2197.1994.tb15483.x.

Krief, Sabrina, Philippe Berny, Francis Gumisiriza, Régine Gross, Barbara Demeneix, Jean Baptiste Fini, Colin A. Chapman, Lauren J. Chapman, Andrew Seguya, and John Wasswa. 2017. "Agricultural Expansion as Risk to Endangered Wildlife: Pesticide Exposure in Wild Chimpanzees and Baboons Displaying Facial Dysplasia." *Science of the Total Environment* 598: 647–656. https://doi.org/10.1016/j.scitotenv.2017.04.113.

Lafferty, Kevin D. 2009. "The Ecology of Climate Change and Infectious Diseases." *Ecology* 90 (4): 888–900. doi: https://doi.org/10.1890/08-0079.1.

Laurance, William F. 2015. "Emerging Threats to Tropical Forests." *Annals of the Missouri Botanical Garden* 100 (3): 159–169. doi: https://doi.org/10.3417/2011087.

Laurance, William F., Gopalasamy Reuben Clements, Sean Sloan, Christine S. O'Connell, Nathan D. Mueller, Miriam Goosem, Oscar Venter, et al. 2014. "A Global Strategy for Road Building." *Nature* 513 (7517): 229–232. https://doi.org/10.1038/nature13717.

Lebrão, Cynthia, Lana Mignone Viana Rosa, Fernanda P. Paim, Pedro M. Nassar, Hani R. El Bizri, and Felipe Ennes Silva. 2021. "Community-Based Ecotourism and Primate Watching as a Conservation Tool in the Amazon Rainforest." *International Journal of Primatology* 42: 523–527. doi: https://doi.org/10.1007/s10764-021-00226-2.

Leroy, Eric M., Pierre Rouquet, Pierre Formenty, Sandrine Souquiere, Annelisa Kilbourne, Jean-Marc Froment, Magdalena Bermejo, et al. 2004. "Multiple Ebola Virus Transmission Events and Rapid Decline of Central African Wildlife." *Science* 303 (5656): 387–390. https://doi.org/10.1126/science.1092528.

Lu, Shuaiyao, Yuan Zhao, Wenhai Yu, Yun Yang, Jiahong Gao, Junbin Wang, Dexuan Kuang, et al. 2020. "Comparison of Nonhuman Primates Identified the Suitable Model for COVID-19." *Signal Transduction and Targeted Therapy* 5: 157. https://doi.org/10.1038/s41392-020-00269-6.

Lynch Alfaro, Jessica W., José de Sousa E. Silva Jr., and Anthony B. Rylands. 2012. "How Different Are Robust and Gracile Capuchin Monkeys? An Argument for the Use of *Sapajus* and *Cebus*." *American Journal of Primatology* 74 (4): 273–286. https://doi.org/10.1002/ajp.22007.

Mace, Georgina M., Ken Norris, and Alastair H. Fitter. 2011. "Biodiversity and Ecosystem Services: A Multilayered Relationship." *Trends in Ecology and Evolution* 27 (1): 19–26. https://doi.org/10.1016/j.tree.2011.08.006.

Maekawa, Miko, Annette Lanjouw, Eugene Rutagarama, and Douglas Sharp. 2013. "Mountain Gorilla Tourism Generating Wealth and Peace in Post-Conflict Rwanda." *Natural Resources Forum* 37 (2): 127–137. https://doi.org/10.1111/1477-8947.12020.

Maldonado, Angela M., Vincent Nijman, and Simon K. Bearder. 2009. "Trade in Night Monkeys *Aotus Spp.* in the Brazil-Colombia-Peru Tri-Border Area: International Wildlife Trade Regulations Are Ineffectively Enforced." *Endangered Species Research* 9 (2): 143–149. https://doi.org/10.3354/esr00209.

McLean, Kevin A., Anne M. Trainor, Gregory P. Asner, Margaret C. Crofoot, Mariah E. Hopkins, Christina J. Campbell, Roberta E. Martin, et al. 2016. "Movement Patterns of Three Arboreal Primates in a Neotropical Moist Forest Explained by LiDAR Estimated Canopy Structure." *Landscape Ecology* 31: 1849–1862. https://doi.org/10.1007/s10980-016-0367-9.

Messenger, Ali M., Amber N. Barnes, and Gregory C. Gray. 2014. "Reverse Zoonotic Disease Transmission (Zooanthroponosis): A Systematic Review of Seldom-Documented Human Biological Threats to Animals." *PLoS One* 9 (2): e89055. https://doi.org/10.1371/journal.pone.0089055.

Millenium Ecosystem Assessment. 2005. *Ecosystems and Human Well-Being: Synthesis*. Washington, DC: World Resources Institute.

Mittermeier, Russel A., Kim E. Reuter, Anthony B. Rylands, Leonardo Jerusalinsky, Christoph Schwitzer, Karen B. Strier, Jonah Ratsimbazafy, and Tatyana Humle, eds. 2022.*Primates in Peril: The World's 25 Most Endangered Primates 2022–2023*. Washington, DCVA: IUCN SSC Primate Specialist Group (PSG), International Primatological Society (IPS), Re:wild.

Molyneaux, A., E. Hankinson, M. Kaban, M. S. Svensson, S. M. Cheyne, and V. Nijman. 2021. "Primate Selfies and Anthropozoonotic Diseases: Lack of Rule Compliance and Poor Risk Perception Threatens Orangutans." *Folia Primatologica* 92: 296–305. https://doi.org/10.1159/000520371.

Muehlenbein, Michael P., Leigh A. Martinez, Andrea A. Lemke, Laurentius Ambu, Senthilvel Nathan, Sylvia Alsisto, and Rosman Sakong. 2010. "Unhealthy Travelers Present Challenges to Sustainable Primate Ecotourism." *Travel Medicine and Infectious Disease* 8 (3): 169–175. https://doi.org/10.1016/j.tmaid.2010.03.004.

Nekaris, Anne-Isola, Nicola Campbell, Tim G. Coggins, E. Johanna Rode, and Vincent Nijman. 2013. "Tickled to Death: Analysing Public Perceptions of 'Cute' Videos of Threatened Species (Slow Loris–*Nycticebus spp.*) on Web 2.0 Sites." *PLoS ONE* 8(7): e69215. https://doi.org/10.1371/journal.pone.0069215.

Norconk, Marilyn A., Sylvia Atsalis, Gregg Tully, Ana Maria Santillan, Siân Waters, Cheryl D. Knott, Stephan R. Ross, Sam Shanee, and Daniel Stiles. 2019. "Reducing the Primate Pet Trade: Actions of Primatologists." *American Journal of Primat*ology 82: e23079. https://doi.org/10.1002/ajp.23079.

Noss, Andrew J. 1998. "The Impacts of Cable Snare Hunting on Wildlife Populations in the Forests of the Central African Republic." *Conservation Biology* 12 (2): 390–398.

Nunn, Charles L., and Sonia Altizer. 2006. *Infectious Diseases in Primates*. Oxford, UK: Oxford University Press.

Nunn, Charles L., and Thomas R. Gillespie. 2016. "Infectious Disease and Primate Conservation." In *An Introduction to Primate Conservation*, edited by Serge A. Wich and Andrew J. Marshall, 157–174. Oxford, UK: Oxford University Press.

Osei-Tutu, Paul. 2017. "Taboos as Informal Institutions of Local Resource Management in Ghana: Why They Are Complied With or Not." *Forest Policy and Economics* 85 (1): 114–123. https://doi.org/10.1016/j.forpol.2017.09.009.

Oude Munnink, Bas B., Reina S. Sikkema, David F. Nieuwenhuijse, Robert Jan Molenaar, Emmanuelle Munger, Richard Molenkamp, Arco van der Spek, et al. 2021. "Transmission of SARS-CoV-2 on Mink Farms Between Humans and Mink and Back to Humans." *Science* 371 (6525): 172–177. https://doi.org/10.1126/science.abe5901.

Pearce, John, and Gianna Moscardo. 2015. "Social Representations of Tourist Selfies: New Challenges for Sustainable Tourism." In *BEST EN Think Tank X, The Environment-People Nexus in Sustainable Tourism: Finding the Balance*, 59–73. BEST EN Think Tank XV, 17–21 June 2015, Skukuza, Mpumalanga, South Africa.

Pebsworth, Paula A., and Marni LaFleur. 2014. "Advancing Primate Research and Conservation through the Use of Camera Traps: Introduction to the Special Issue." *International Journal of Primatology* 35 (5): 825–840. https://doi.org/10.1007/s10764-014-9802-4.

Peterson, Jeffrey V. 2017. "Primates in World Religions (Buddhism, Christianity, Hinduism, Islam)." In *The International Encyclopedia of Primatology*, edited by Agustín Fuentes, 1171–1177. Hoboken, NJ: John Wiley and Sons. https://doi.org/10.1002/9781119179313.wbprim0122.

Peterson, Jeffrey V., and Erin P. Riley. 2017. "Sacred Monkeys? An Ethnographic Perspective on Macaque Sacredness in Balinese Hinduism." In *Ethnoprimatology: A Practical Guide to Research at the Human-Nonhuman Primate Interface*, edited by Kerry M. Dore, Erin P. Riley, and Agustín Fuentes, 206–218. Cambridge, UK: Cambridge University Press.

Possamai, Carla B., Fabiano Rodrigues de Melo, Sérgio Lucena Mendes, and Karen B. Strier. 2022. "Demographic Changes in an Atlantic Forest Primate Community Following a Yellow Fever Outbreak." *American Journal of Primatology* 84 (9): e23425. https://doi.org/10.1002/ajp.23425.

Reibelt, L. M., and J. Nowack. 2015. "Editorial: Community-Based Conservation in Madagascar, the 'Cure-All' Solution? *Madagascar Conservation & Development* 10 (1): 3–5. https://doi.org/10.4314/mcd.v10i1.S1.

Riley, Erin P. 2020. *The Promise of Contemporary Primatology*. New York: Routledge.

Rimbach, Rebecca, Andrés Link, Andrés Montes-Rojas, Anthony Di Fiore, Michael Heistermann, and Eckhard W. Heymann. 2014. "Behavioral and Physiological Responses to Fruit Availability of Spider Monkeys Ranging in a Small Forest Fragment." *American Journal of Primatology* 76 (11): 1049–1061. https://doi.org/10.1002/ajp.22292.

Robbins, Martha M., Markye Gray, Katie A. Fawcett, Felicia B. Nutter, Prosper Uwingeli, Innocent Mburanumwe, Edwin Kagoda, et al. 2011. "Extreme Conservation Leads to Recovery of the Virunga Mountain Gorillas." *PLoS ONE* 6 (6): e19788. https://doi.org/10.1371/journal.pone.0019788.

Roncal, Carla Mere, Mark Bowler, and Michael P. Gilmore. 2018. "The Ethnoprimatology of the Maijuna of the Peruvian Amazon and Implications for Primate Conservation." *Journal of Ethnobiology and Ethnomedicine* 14 (19). https://doi.org/10.1186/s13002-018-0207-x.

Russo, Sabrina E. 2017. "Seed Dispersal." In *The International Encyclopedia of Primatology*, edited by Agustín Fuentes, 1265–1269. Hoboken, NJ: John Wiley and Sons.

Russo, Sabrina, and Colin Chapman. 2011. "Primate Seed Dispersal: Linking Behavioral Ecology with Forest Community Structure." In *Primates in Perspective*, edited by Christina Campbell, Agustín Fuentes, Katherine McKinnon, Simon Bearder, and Rebecca Stumpf, 523–534. New York: Oxford University Press.

Rutz, Christian, Matthias-Claudio Loretto, Amanda E. Bates, Sarah C. Davidson, Carlos M. Duarte, Walter Jetz, Mark Johnson, et al. 2020. "COVID-19 Lockdown Allows Researchers to Quantify Effects of Human Activity on Wildlife." *Nature Ecology & Evolution* 4: 1156–1159. https://doi.org/10.1038/s41559-020-1237-z.

Rylands, Anthony B., and Russell A. Mittermeier. 2014. "Primate Taxonomy: Species and Conservation." *Evolutionary Anthropology* 23 (1): 8–10. https://doi.org/10.1002/evan.21387.

Scales, I. R. 2014. "The Future of Biodiversity Conservation and Environmental Management in Madagascar: Lessons from the Past and Challenges Ahead." In *Conservation and Environmental Management in Madagascar*, edited by I. R. Scales, 342–360. London: Routledge.

Schaffner, Colleen M., Luisa Rebecchini, Gabriel Ramos-Fernandez, Laura G. Vick, and Filippo Aureli. 2012. "Spider Monkeys (*Ateles geoffroyi yucatenensis*) Cope with the Negative Consequences of Hurricanes Through Changes in Diet, Activity Budget, and Fission-Fusion Dynamics." *International Journal of Primatology* 33: 922-936. https://doi.org/10.1007/s10764-012-9621-4.

Schloss, Carrie A., Tristan A. Nuñez, and Joshua J. Lawler. 2012. "Dispersal Will Limit Ability of Mammals to Track Climate Change in the Western Hemisphere." *PNAS* 109 (22): 8606–8611. https://doi.org/10.1073/pnas.1116791109.

Sechrest, W., Thomas M. Brooks, Gustavo A. B. da Fonseca, William R. Konstant, Russel A. Mittermeier, Andy Purvis, Anthony B. Rylands, and John L. Gittleman. 2002. "Hot Spots and the Conservation of Evolutionary History." *Proceedings of the National Academy of Sciences* 99 (4): 2067–2071. https://doi.org/10.1073/pnas.251680798.

Shanee, Noga, A. Patricia Mendoza, and Sam Shanee. 2017. "Diagnostic Overview of the Illegal Trade in Primates and Law Enforcement in Peru." *American Journal of Primatology* 79 (11): 1–12. https://doi.org/10.1002/ajp.22516.

Shanee, N., S. Shanee, and A. M. Maldonado. 2007. "Conservation Assessment and Planning for the Yellow-Tailed Woolly Monkey (*Oreonax flavicauda*) in Peru." *Wildlife Biology in Practice* 3 (2): 73–82. https://doi.org/10.2461/wbp.2007.3.9.

Sicotte, Pascale. 2017. "Social Taboos." In *The International Encyclopedia of Primatology*, edited by Agustín Fuentes, 1319–1321. Hoboken, NJ: John Wiley and Sons. https://doi.org/10.1002/9781119179313.wbprim0117.

Spenceley, Anna, Straton Habyalimana, Ritah Tusabe, and Donnah Mariza. 2010. "Benefits to the Poor from Gorilla Tourism in Rwanda." *Development Southern Africa* 27 (5): 647–662. https://doi.org/10.1080/0376835X.2010.522828.

Sponsel, Leslie E. 1997. "The Human Niche in Amazonia: Explorations in Ethnoprimatology." In *New World Primates: Ecology, Evolution, and Behavior,* edited by W. Kinzey, 143–165. New York: Aldine de Gruyter.

Stammes, Marieke A., Ji Hyun Lee, Lisette Meijer, Thibaut Naninck, Lara A. Doyle-Meyers, Alexander G. White, H. Jacob Borish, et al. 2021. "Medical Imaging of Pulmonary Disease in SARS-CoV-2-Exposed Non-human Primates." *Trends in Molecular Medicine* 28 (2): 123–142. https://doi.org/10.1016/j.molmed.2021.12.001.

Steinweg, Tim, Barbara Kuepper, and Gabriel Thoumi. 2016. *Economic Drivers of Deforestation.* Washington, DC: Chain Reaction Research. Accessed March 12, 2023. http://chainreactionresearch.com/wp-content/uploads/2016/08/economic-drivers-of-deforestation-crr-160803-final1.pdf.

Strier, Karen B. 1994. "Myth of the Typical Primate." *American Journal of Physical Anthropology* 37 (S19): 233–271. https://doi.org/10.1002/ajpa.13303700609.

Strier, Karen B. 2003. "Primatology Comes of Age: 2002 AAPA Luncheon Address." *Yearbook of Physical Anthropology* 46: 2–13.

Strier, Karen B. 2010. " Long-term Field Studies: Positive Impacts and Unintended Consequences." *American Journal of Primatology* 72 (9): 772–778. https://doi.org/10.1002/ajp.20830.

Strier, Karen B. 2011a. "Conservation." In *Primates in Perspective*, edited by Christina Campbell, Agustín Fuentes, Katherine C. MacKinnon, Simon K. Bearder, and Rebecca M. Stumpf, 664–675. New York: Oxford University Press.

Strier, Karen B. 2011b. "Why Anthropology Needs Primatology." *General Anthropology* 18 (1): 1–8.

Strier, Karen B. 2017. *Primate Behavioral Ecology: Fifth Edition.* New York: Routledge.

Strier, Karen B. 2018a. "Primate Social Behavior." *American Journal of Physical Anthropology* 165 (4): 801–812.

Strier, Karen B. 2018b. "What Climate Change Means for Primates and Primatology." Paper presented at the 87th Annual Meeting of American Association of Physical Anthropologists, Austin, Texas, April 11–14, 2018.

Strier, Karen B. 2021a. "The Limits of Resilience." *Primates* 62: 861–868. https://doi.org/10.1007/s10329-021-00953-3.

Strier, Karen B. 2021b. *Primate Behavioral Ecology.* 6th ed. New York: Routledge.

Strier, Karen B., and Jean Philippe Boubli. 2006. "A History of Long-term Research and Conservation of Northern Muriquis (*Brachyteles hypoxanthus*) at the Estação Biológica de Caratinga/RPPN-FMA." *Primate Conservation* 20: 53–63. https://doi.org/10.1896/0898-6207.20.1.53.

Strier, Karen B., and Sérgio L. Mendes. 2012. "The Northern Muriqui (*Brachyteles hypoxanthus*):Lessons on Behavioral Plasticity and Population Dynamics from a Critically Endangered Species." In *Long-term Field Studies of Primates*, edited by Peter M. Kappeler and David P. Watts, 125–140. Berlin, Heidelberg: Springer.

Strier, Karen B., Carla B. Possamai, Fernanda P. Tabacow, Alcides Pissinatti, Andre M. Lanna, Fabiano Rodrigues de Melo, Leandro Moreira, et al. 2017. "Demographic Monitoring of Wild Muriqui Populations: Criteria for Defining Priority Areas and Monitoring Intensity." *PLoS ONE* 12 (12): e0188922. https://doi.org/10.1371/journal.pone.0188922.

Strum, Shirley C., and Linda M. Fedigan. 1999. "Theory, Method, Gender, and Culture: What Changed Our Views of Primate Society." In *The New Physical Anthropology: Science, Humanism, and Critical Reflection,* edited by S. C. Strum, D. G. Lindburg, and D. A. Hamburg, 67–105. New Jersey: Prentice Hall.

Tarara, R., M. A. Suleman, R. Sapolsky, M. J. Wabomba, and J. G. Else. 1985. "Tuberculosis in Wild Olive Baboons (*Papio cynocephalus anubis*) in Kenya." *Journal of Wildlife Diseases* 21 (2): 137–140. https://doi.org/10.7589/0090-3558-21.2.137.

Terborgh, J. 1983. *Five New World Primates: A Study in Comparative Ecology*. Princeton: Princeton University Press.

Tumusiime, David Mwesigye, Gerald Eilu, Mnason Tweheyo, Mnason Tweheyo, and Fred Babweteera. 2010. "Wildlife Snaring in Budongo Forest Reserve, Uganda." *Human Dimensions of Wildlife* 15 (2): 129–144. https://doi.org/10.1080/10871200903493899.

Tyukavina, Alexandra, Matthew C. Hansen, Peter V. Potapov, Stephen V. Stehman, Kevin Smith-Rodriguez, Chima Okpa, and Ricardo Aguilar. 2017. "Types and Rates of Forest Disturbance in Brazilian Legal Amazon, 2000–2013." *Science Advances* 3 (4): 1–16. https://doi.org/10.1126/sciadv.1601047.

UN Population Division. 2017. "World Population Prospects: The 2017 Revision." Accessed January 2, 2019. https://esa.un.org/unpd/wpp/publications/files/wpp2017_keyfindings.pdf.

USDA [United States Department of Agriculture]. 2021. "Confirmation of COVID-19 in Gorillas at California Zoo." *Animal and Plant Health Inspection Service* website. Accessed June 15, 2022. https://www.aphis.usda.gov/aphis/newsroom/stakeholder-info/sa_by_date/sa-2021/sa-01/ca-gorillas-sars-cov-2.

Velankar, Avadhoot D., Honnavalli N. Kumara, Arijit Pal, Partha Sarathi Mishra, and Mewa Singh. 2016. "Population Recovery of Nicobar Long-tailed Macaque *Macaca fascicularis umbrosus* following a Tsunami in the Nicobar Islands, India." *PLoS ONE* 11(2): e0148205. https://doi.org/10.1371/journal.pone.0148205.

Wallis, Janette, and D. Rick Lee. 1999. "Primate Conservation: The Prevention of Disease Transmission." *International Journal of Primatology* 20 (6): 803–826. https://doi.org/10.1023/A:1020879700286.

Wang, Chengliang, Xiaowei Wang, Xiaoguang Qi, Songtao Guo, Haitao Zhao, Wei Wei, and Baoguo Li. 2014. "Influence of Human Activities on the Historical and Current Distribution of Sichuan Snub-Nosed Monkeys in the Qinling Mountains, China." *Folia Primatologica* 85 (6): 343–357.

Washburn, Sherwood L. 1951. "Section of Anthropology: The New Physical Anthropology." *Transactions of the New York Academy of Sciences* 13 (7): 298–304.

Washburn, Sherwood L. 1973. "The Promise of Primatology." *American Journal of Physical Anthropology* 38 (2): 177–182.

Wheatley, Bruce P. 1999. *The Sacred Monkeys of Bali*. New York: Waveland.

Acknowledgments

We are grateful to the University of Wisconsin–Madison for the various sources of funding that enabled us to write this Appendix, including Teaching Assistantships from the department of Integrative Biology (to JBK) and a Vilas Research Professorship (to KBS). We are grateful to A.J. Hardy for their significant contributions to the previous addition of this appendix, Irene Duch Latorre for her photograph and helpful additions, and to Kadie Callingham and Danhe Yang for the use of their photographs. We thank the editors of this volume for inviting our contribution and for the helpful comments that they and anonymous reviewers provided.

Image Descriptions

Figure B.1: In 1750 the world population was less than 1 billion. 1950 marks a point in which all regions of the world begin to rapidly accelerate population growth. Global populations are projected to approach 11 billion people by 2100. At this time, it is projected that the majority of the population will live in Asia, followed by Africa, North America, Europe, South America and Oceania. Populations in Asian and African will both far exceed those in all other regions of the world combined.

Figure B.2: Global distribution of primates and their main threats within the four major primate regions.

1. There are a total of 162 primate species in Central and South America, of which 65 are threatened. These primates are threatened by 1. logging and wood harvesting, 2. annual and perennial non-timber crops, 3. hunting and collecting terrestrial animals, 4. livestock farming and ranching, and 5. wood and pulp plantations.

2. There are a total of 106 primate species in Africa, of which 54 are threatened. These primates are threatened by 1. annual and perennial non-timber crops, 2. hunting and collecting terrestrial animals, 3. logging and wood harvesting, 4. livestock farming and ranching, wood and pulp plantations, and gathering terrestrial plants.

3. There are a total of 107 primate species on Madagascar, of which 103 are threatened. These primates are threatened by 1. annual and perennial non-timber crops, 2. hunting and collecting terrestrial animals, 3. logging and wood harvesting, 4. livestock farming and ranching, 5. gathering terrestrial plants, and 6. wood and pulp plantations.

4. There are a total of 116 primate species in Asia, of which 97 are threatened. These primates are threatened by 1. hunting and collecting terrestrial animals, 2. annual and perennial non-timber crops, 3. logging and wood harvesting, 4. livestock farming and ranching, and 5. gathering terrestrial plants.

Figure B.13: A word diagram illustrates the extinction vortex. Threats and pressures such as hunting, habitat loss, environmental variability, and catastrophic events can directly decrease the population size of primates. Small populations can trigger the extinction vortex, a cascade of events that exacerbate problems, can prevent recovery, resulting in extinction. For example, small population size increases demographic stochasticity, inbreeding, and random genetic drift. All of these can lead to further problems such as loss of genetic variability, reduction of individual fitness and population adaptability, higher mortality, and lower reproduction. Ultimately all these problems result in ever smaller populations.

APPENDIX C: HUMAN BEHAVIORAL ECOLOGY

Kristin Snopkowski, Ph.D., Boise State University

This chapter is a revision from "Appendix C:Human Behavioral Ecology" by Kristin Snopkowski. In Explorations: An Open Invitation to Biological Anthropology, first edition, edited by Beth Shook, Katie Nelson, Kelsie Aguilera, and Lara Braff, which is licensed under CC BY-NC 4.0.

Learning Objectives

- Define human behavioral ecology.
- Describe the types of behaviors that human behavioral ecologists study.
- Explain why humans share food.
- Identify how human behavioral ecology contributes to contemporary world issues.

On December 26, 2004, an earthquake in the Indian Ocean resulted in a tsunami that killed over 200,000 people in at least a dozen different countries (Figure C.1; Editors of Encyclopedia Britannica 2018). In the aftermath, 30% of households in the United States donated an estimated $2.78 billion to help the victims (Center on Philanthropy at Indiana University 2008). At the same time, despite being one of the wealthiest countries in the world, the United States has over a million children who experience homelessness each year (National Center for Homeless Education 2017). Why is it that sometimes humans work together to help those in need, but at other times, humans struggle to solve basic problems? The field of Human Behavioral Ecology seeks to understand this and many other questions to learn why humans behave the way they do. **Human Behavioral Ecology** is the field of anthropology that explores how evolutionary history and ecological factors combine to influence human behavior.

Figure C.1: Aftermath of the 2004 Asian Tsunami in Sri Lanka. Credit: Pictures from bus 13 by Sarvodaya Shramadana is under a CC BY 2.0 License.

Human Behavioral Ecology

Evolutionary History

Natural selection is the force of evolution by which individuals with heritable traits that result in greater survival and reproduction have more offspring than individuals without those traits. By having more offspring (specifically, offspring who themselves survive and reproduce), these heritable traits become more common in future generations. As an example, hominin brain size has increased dramatically over the past two million years. Our ancestors with larger brains were better able to survive and reproduce than those with smaller brains, possibly because they were better able to acquire food or navigate the social complexities of living in a large group (Dunbar 1998; Parker and Gibson 1979).

Figure C.2: Sample of sweets to celebrate Diwali, a Hindu festival of lights. Credit: Diwali sweets India 2009 by robertsharp is under a CC BY 2.0 License.

Human behavioral ecology uses the theory of evolution by natural selection to understand how modern behaviors were advantageous in our **evolutionary history**. For most of human history, humans lived as hunter-gatherers, meaning they collected or hunted food; they typically resided in small communities with individuals related through blood or marriage; and they had no access to modern medicines or other modern conveniences. It is useful to think about this environment—which is much different than how humans live today—to help us understand how current behaviors may have evolved. For example, humans today enjoy consuming food high in fats and sugars (Figure C.2; see Chapter 16). In the past, eating fatty and sugary food was a good survival strategy since food was limited in this environment and these foods contained a lot of calories. Over time, those individuals who sought out these foods were probably better able to survive and reproduce, resulting in a population of people today who have preferences for these foods. In modern environments, where food is abundant, this preference has likely contributed to the obesity epidemic, which increases people's risk of cardiovascular diseases and no longer improves people's ability to survive and reproduce.

Ecology

In addition to evolutionary history, the field of human behavioral ecology also focuses on the influence of ecology. **Ecology** is defined as one's physical environment, including types of resources, predators, terrain, and weather, as well as one's social environment, including the behaviors of other individuals and cultural rules. For example, if one lives in an environment where there are abundant fruit trees, then the diet likely includes fruit. Since fruits are easy to acquire, children can engage in food gathering at young ages. In contrast, in environments like the Arctic, where there are fewer plant resources, the diet focuses more on hunting and fishing. Since these skills take longer to acquire, children may only be able to contribute to their own subsistence at older ages. One's environment influences the behaviors in which individuals engage, such as children's foraging.

Another component of ecology is one's social environment, including cultural rules. Throughout the world, different cultures have quite different norms of behavior. For instance, in some societies marriages are required to be monogamous, meaning that a marriage is between just two individuals. This is a cultural norm in the United States, and it is illegal to violate this rule. In other societies, marriages can occur between one man and several women or one woman and several men, referred to as polygyny and polyandry respectively. Across the world, polyandry tends to be quite rare, and in cultures with polyandrous marriage, polygynous and monogamous marriages also occur. The age difference of married people frequently depends on the type of marriages allowed in their culture. In cultures with polygynous marriage, the age difference between husbands and wives tends to be larger than it is in monogamous cultures, as the men who are able to attract additional wives tend to have high status or wealth and are typically older than the women who are available for marriage. In cultures with fraternal polyandry, defined as the marriage of one woman to a set of brothers, marriage typically occurs when the eldest brother is ready to marry and he typically marries a woman close in age. This results in the wife being older than some of her husbands, with the exception of the eldest one. The environment (both physical and social) influences one's behavioral options, and human behavioral ecologists examine how one's ecology influences people's behavior. In Figure C.3, we see a visual depiction of the field of human behavioral ecology, using evolutionary history and ecology (physical environment plus culture) to explain modern human behavior.

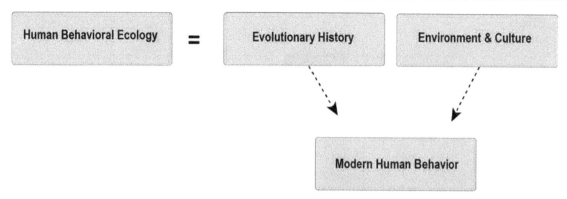

Figure C.3: Human Behavioral Ecology. Credit: Human Behavioral Ecology (Figure C.3) original to Explorations: An Open Invitation to Biological Anthropology by Katie Nelson is under a CC BY-NC 4.0 License.

Both Genes and Environment Influence Behavior

While physical characteristics (like height) are clearly heritable, we also know that they depend on the environment. When children grow up with poor nutrition and do not ingest enough calories, their growth is stunted. At the same time, if parents are both tall, then their child is more likely to be tall as well. Physical traits are the result of both genes and environment. Behavior is the same—dependent on both genes and environment. While there are no genes for specific behaviors, behavioral tendencies do show some level of heritability. Personality disorders, for instance, may be partially heritable, but it also depends on the environment in which a child is raised, where child neglect or sexual abuse may increase the risk of personality disorders (Johnson et al. 1999).

Human behavioral ecologists assume that even though there are not genes for specific behaviors, genes may influence behavioral tendencies. Additionally, behaviors are flexible and people use information from the environment to determine under which conditions they should behave in particular ways. For example, the *ability* to cooperate has evolved over evolutionary time, but whether or not an individual cooperates in a particular instance likely depends on the situation. Research shows that people are more likely to cooperate if: (1) their behavior is known to others (that is to say their identity is *not* anonymous); (2) it will improve their reputation; or (3) they will be punished for not cooperating (Andreoni and Petrie 2004; Fehr and Fischbacher 2003; Milinski, Semmann, and Krambeck 2002).

How Can Human Behavioral Ecology Help Us Understand Altruism?

Altruism is defined as providing a benefit to someone without expecting anything in return. A perfect example is donating money to tsunami victims. From an evolutionary perspective, it seems that providing benefits to others would be disadvantageous for one's own survival and reproduction, as resources given to others are resources that cannot be used for oneself. But people do engage in altruistic behaviors, so how can the field of human behavioral ecology help us understand this behavior? We will use the example of food sharing to think about different ways that human behavioral ecologists have examined this question. In many small-scale hunter-gatherer societies, people share food extensively with other people living in their communities. This sharing is most widespread when the item is a hunted animal, which can typically feed many people. Just as giving away money seems counterintuitive, so does giving away food. So, why do people in these foraging communities share so much food with each other?

Kin Selection

Figure C.4: Lao family eating together. Credit: Lao Mangkong family eats together by BigBrotherMouse is modified (faces blurred) and under a CC BY-NC-SA 4.0 License.

One of the first explanations for why humans share food is that they are sharing with their close family members. **Kin selection** proposes that individuals help kin, even at a cost to themselves, because this help is directed at individuals with whom they share genes. Genes that result in a person acting altruistically toward close kin would have become more frequent over time if individuals sharing that gene are more successful than those not sharing that gene (Hamilton 1964). Taking this perspective is described as a *gene's eye view*. Since family members share genes, this may explain why kin help one another. Figure C.4 shows a Lao family eating together. It is very common around the world for families to share food with one another. In many small-scale societies, people share food with family members but also with those who are not family members. Kin selection helps explain some food sharing, but it doesn't explain all food sharing.

Reciprocal Altruism

Another potential explanation for why humans share food is that they are engaging in **reciprocal altruism**, meaning that an individual shares food today with the expectation of repayment at some point in the future (Trivers 1971). This can work well, unless the person who receives the help chooses not to reciprocate in the future. In this case, the original sharer does not obtain anything in return. To maintain these relationships, it is important that individuals have the opportunity to share with one another repeatedly and that if one person chooses not to reciprocate, the original sharer terminates their sharing.

Reciprocal altruism is even more likely to occur if the value of the food is greater to the person receiving the food than the person sharing the food. For instance, imagine that you have an entire pizza. After you eat several slices, you are no longer hungry and the next piece of pizza has little value to you. In contrast, if you are hungry, receiving a slice of pizza from a friend would mean a lot to you. In this case, the person giving a piece of pizza after already eating their fill is giving away something of little value, but the person receiving a slice of pizza when they are hungry is receiving something with substantial value. If the following week the roles are reversed, then in both cases, the person receiving the food has received something of greater value than the person who gave it away.

This makes sense in the case of sharing hunted meat as well. In environments without refrigeration technology or in highly mobile groups where food storage is not feasible, the killing of a large animal will result in leftover meat. Sharing that meat with hungry community members has a lot of value to those receiving the meat. Then, at some point in the future, the person who received the meat may successfully hunt and share with others. Figure C.5 displays an Indigenous hunting party from Malaysia. Food is widely shared in small-scale societies, particularly when the item is large in size and when there is a lot of uncertainty around when the next successful hunt will occur (Gurven 2004). But, as with other skilled activities, some individuals are better hunters than others and acquire more meat than others consistently, so why would highly skilled hunters give more food to low-skilled hunters than will be reciprocated (e.g., Gurven et al. 2000)? Again, reciprocal altruism is one piece of the story but cannot explain all sharing behavior.

Figure C.5: A Lamalera whale-spearer jumps from a boat, spearing a whale in Lembata Island, East Nusa Tenggara Province. Credit: Lamafa (spearer) jumping from peledang boat to a whale by Bambang Budi Utomo is in the public domain in Indonesia.

Costly Signaling

Another possible explanation for why people share food, particularly meat in small-scale societies, is because they want to signal their foraging abilities and generosity (Smith and Bliege Bird 2000). One way to communicate to others your inherent qualities is to do something that is hard to fake. For instance, telling someone that you are a good hunter is not as convincing as hunting a difficult-to-acquire animal and sharing it with them. If someone is a poor hunter, it will be difficult for them to successfully hunt, so sharing hunted meat demonstrates one's abilities. The hunter who provides resources to the community is likely viewed as generous, allowing them to attract mates, friends, and allies. **Costly signaling theory** argues that a signaller produces a costly display (e.g., shares hunted meat) to communicate honest information about themselves to others (e.g., I am a generous, skilled hunter). Costly signals can occur across species for a variety of purposes, but this example may help us understand why people share food with unrelated others who are unlikely to reciprocate.

Among the Melanesian Meriam Islanders, turtles (Figure C.6) are hunted at two times of year; during the turtles' feeding/mating season, which is risky and unpredictable, and during the turtles' nesting season, which is low risk and relatively easier. Turtles hunted during the feeding/mating season are typically shared widely in the community, while turtles hunted during the nesting season are consumed by a small number of households. This suggests that more people know about high-risk hunts, which may result in hunters gaining more prestige for their successful hunts. Evidence also shows that hunters involved in high-risk hunting gain social and reproductive benefits, such as having children earlier and having more sexual (or reproductive) partners (Smith, Bliege Bird, and Bird 2003). While some sharing behavior may be best explained by a desire to display one's skills to gain reputational benefits, it cannot explain all sharing behavior and likely works in conjunction with the other hypotheses described above.

Figure C.6: Green turtle. Credit: Green turtle Palmyra Atoll National Wildlife Refuge by Kydd Pollock, The Nature Conservancy, US Fish and Wildlife Service Pacific Region is under a CC BY-NC 2.0 License.

What Does Food Sharing Tell Us about Altruism?

Examining these three explanations of sharing behavior—kin selection, reciprocal altruism, and costly signaling (Figure C.7)—helps explain a lot of sharing seen around the world, but donating money to tsunami victims is still hard to understand. Most donors from the United States were not related to the victims of the tsunami; donors probably did not expect reciprocation; and because the donors and receivers did not know each other, reputational benefits would have been limited to people who were made aware of the donation. While some charitable giving may be explained by the tax incentives, the donations to the tsunami victims were so extensive that it seems unlikely to be the main explanation. There are other hypotheses that have not been discussed here, but they also suffer from the inability to fully explain all examples of altruistic behavior. People commonly state that they donate because "it makes them feel good." While helping others does make people feel good, this likely evolved because those that had the feel-good sensation helped others (like their family members) resulting in greater survival and reproduction. The "feel good" sensation is a **proximate explanation**, the immediate reason for the behavior, while human behavioral ecology seeks to understand the **ultimate explanation**, the deep evolutionary reason that this trait led to increased survival and reproduction. In the case of donating money to people living on the other side of the world, our modern environment (allowing us to help people living so far away) may lead us to act in ways that were adaptive in our evolutionary past but may not improve our survival or reproduction today.

Explanations of food sharing:

1. **Kin selection:** Helping family members who share the same genes.
2. **Reciprocal altruism:** Sharing food with someone with the expectation that they will reciprocate at some point in the future.
3. **Costly signaling:** Providing food to others to display one's foraging skill and generosity to improve one's reputation or social standing.

At the same time, we struggle to solve the problem of homelessness across the United States. Using evolutionary theory may help us understand why people are unable to come together to eliminate this problem. Eradicating homelessness would be costly, would require the cooperation of lots of individuals (no single individual or small group can solve it on their own), and would be ongoing. This type of long-lasting commitment to help unrelated strangers may be difficult to acquire from large numbers of people.

How Can Human Behavioral Ecology Help Us Understand the World?

Throughout this appendix, I have been discussing one of the main research areas in Human Behavioral Ecology: cooperation and sharing. Two other prominent areas of research for Human Behavioral Ecologists include production and reproduction. Production research explores how people acquire the resources that they need. Some research in this area has examined which items people choose to include in their diets and how long people spend foraging. This research has shown that people do not simply acquire any food resource in their environment; instead they make strategic decisions based on the food options available and the possible nutrients gained. Research on reproduction includes an examination of how people choose mates, make reproductive choices, invest in children, and acquire help to raise offspring. This line of research has shown that human mothers need help from others to raise offspring, and this help can come from a variety of sources, including the child's father, grandmothers, older siblings, grandfathers, or others (Hrdy 2009; Sear and Mace 2008). This is quite different from our nonhuman primate relatives, for whom almost all offspring care is given by mothers. These research areas capture many behaviors we faced in our evolutionary history: How did we obtain food, how did we distribute that food once we had it, and how did we make mating and reproductive decisions? All of the topics examined in the field of human behavioral ecology are closely linked to survival and reproduction and to understanding how the environment influences decision making.

Some common misperceptions about human behavioral ecology cause skepticism of this type of research. Some critiques have argued that studying the evolution of human behavior is problematic because of **biological determinism**, the idea that all behaviors are innate, determined by our genes. If behaviors are innate, then we cannot hold people accountable for their actions. But this is a misunderstanding. As mentioned previously, both genes and the environment influence behavior. Individuals may have a tendency to behave in a particular way, but behaviors are flexible. Also, there is no guarantee that everyone behaves in perfectly optimal ways. Over evolutionary time, those who behaved in ways that resulted in more successful offspring had a greater representation of genes in the next generation, but in each generation we have variation in environments, genotypes, phenotypes, and behaviors on which selection can act.

Another common misconception is that by studying human behavior, human behavioral ecologists are providing justifications for those behaviors. The **naturalistic fallacy** describes the incorrect belief that what occurs in nature is what *ought to be*. This is a fallacy because it is absolutely not the goal of researchers in this field. For instance, some researchers study human violence. It is wrong to assume that by studying violence, the researchers believe that violence is an acceptable behavior or is justifiable. It is easy to slip into this misconception.

Modern Applications

While it may seem that the field of human behavioral ecology is more concerned about our evolutionary past than our present, there are many contemporary issues that human behavioral ecology can help us solve. One area that human behavioral ecologists have focused on is climate change (Schradin 2021). In many ways, solving the climate crisis is similar to that of homelessness; it requires many people to come together and sacrifice for the benefit of all. Evidence has shown that people are more likely to sacrifice for others' benefit when their good deeds are known, their actions improve their reputation, or their failure to act produces negative consequences, like increased taxes (Milinski et al. 2002). By focusing on these motivators, policy makers may be able to leverage people to minimize their carbon usage, although current progress achieving targets has seen limited success. Researchers have also used evolutionary theory to improve handwashing rates around the world (Curtis 2013), reduce the obesity epidemic (Pepper and Nettle 2014), ease conflicts (de Waal 2000), and improve cooperation (Boyd and Richerson 1992).

Special Topic: Fertility Research in Human Behavioral Ecology

To understand how human behavior has evolved through time and responds to local environments, human behavioral ecologists collect data on populations across the world. Globally, people are choosing to have fewer children than in the past. Some countries are still dealing with overpopulation, but an even larger number are dealing with **population aging** and fear of depopulation. Understanding decisions about how many children to have is important in today's world and is the focus of my research. To examine how family size is changing, researchers calculate **total fertility rate**, which is specific to a given year and is calculated as the total number of children that would be born to a female if she were to give birth at that particular year's age-specific fertility rate for each age. This is a value that represents the fertility of females at all ages in a particular year but does not represent any particular person (since a real person experiences fertility across many years). I conducted fieldwork in rural Bolivia, a place where the total fertility rate was approximately 6 children per woman in 1970 but fell to only 3 children per woman by 2013 (World Bank 2022). By interviewing people who live in communities that are undergoing rapid changes in fertility rates, I attempt to understand how people make decisions about family size.

Figure C.7: Conducting fieldwork in Bolivia. Credit: Conducting fieldwork in Bolivia original to Explorations: An Open Invitation to Biological Anthropology (2nd ed.) by Kristin Snopkowski is under a CC BY-NC 4.0 License.

Figure C.8 shows me walking from house to house during my fieldwork in Bolivia. My interviews with over 500 Bolivian women found that those who had more education or those who expected their children to go further in school had fewer children and that family size was similar across groups of friends (Snopkowski and Kaplan 2014). While the conflict between work and childcare is particularly difficult for parents in postindustrialized contexts, in this rural Bolivian community, most women were able to integrate their daily work with childcare. For instance, a woman may own a shop where she could engage in childcare and run the shop simultaneously. To fully understand human behavior cross-culturally, we need to examine many different societies. Using large datasets collected in 45 different countries, my collaborator and I were able to examine how factors such as education and wealth may have different effects on fertility across the world (Colleran and Snopkowski 2018). Our results showed that in every country surveyed, more education for women was associated with having fewer children, but the effect of wealth varied. In countries with high fertility, more wealth typically associated with more children, but in countries with low fertility, more wealth was typically associated with fewer children. These results show that as people have access to more education and choose to educate themselves and their children, small families will become the norm everywhere in the world.

Review Questions

- In human behavioral ecology, human behavior is the result of the interaction among which two factors?
- What are the three main explanations for why people in small-scale societies share food extensively?
- Describe the difference between a proximate and an ultimate explanation and include an example of each.
- What are two misconceptions about human behavioral ecology?
- What contemporary world issues can human behavioral ecology help us solve?

Key Terms

Altruism: Providing a benefit to someone else at a cost to oneself, without expecting future reciprocation.

Biological determinism: The idea that behaviors are determined exclusively by genes.

Costly signaling theory: A theory by which individuals provide honest signals about personal attributes through costly displays.

Ecology: The physical and social environment, including food resources, predators, terrain, weather, social rules, behavior of other people, and cultural rules.

Evolutionary history: An understanding of how traits (including behaviors) may be the result of natural selection in our hominin past.

Human Behavioral Ecology: The field of anthropology that explores how ecological factors and evolutionary history combine to influence how humans behave.

Kin selection: A type of natural selection whereby people help relatives, which can evolve because people are helping other individuals with whom they share genes.

Naturalistic fallacy: The incorrect belief that what occurs is what ought to be.

Population aging: An increase in the number and proportion of people who are over the age of 60.

Proximate explanation: The mechanism that is immediately responsible for an event.

Reciprocal altruism: Helping behavior that occurs because individuals expect that any help they provide will be reciprocated in the future.

Total fertility rate: the number of children a hypothetical female would have at the end of their reproductive period if they experienced fertility rates of a given year for each year of their reproductive period and were not subject to mortality. It represents the fertility of all females in a given year. It is reported as children per woman.

Ultimate explanation: An explanation for an event that is further removed than a proximate explanation but provides a greater insight or understanding. In human behavioral ecology, ultimate explanations usually describe how a behavior is linked to reproduction and survival.

About the Author

Kristin Snopkowski, Ph.D.

Boise State University, kristinsnopkowski@boisestate.edu

Kristin Snopkowski is Associate Professor of Anthropology at Boise State University specializing in human behavioral ecology. Her research examines reproductive decisions, including how many children people have, how other family members influence fertility decisions, and the interaction between females and males in negotiating these decisions. She has conducted field work in Bolivia and Peru, interviewing women about their reproductive choices, and has been analyzing data sets from around the world to understand how environmental factors influence these decisions worldwide. She has published more than 15 peer-reviewed journal articles and co-edited the special issue *The Behavioral Ecology of the Family*.

For Further Exploration

Barrett, Louise, Robin Dunbar, and John Lycett. 2002. *Human Evolutionary Psychology*. Princeton: Princeton University Press.

Cronk, Lee, and Beth L. Leech. 2013. *Meeting at Grand Central: Understanding the Social and Evolutionary Roots of Cooperation*. Princeton: Princeton University Press.

Low, Bobbi S. 2015. *Why Sex Matters: A Darwinian Look at Human Behavior*. Princeton: Princeton University Press.

Raihani, Nichola. 2021. *The Social Instinct: How Cooperation Shaped the World*. New York: St. Martin's Press.

References

Andreoni, James, and Ragan Petrie. 2004. "Public Goods Experiments without Confidentiality: A Glimpse into Fund-Raising." *Journal of Public Economics* 88 (7-8): 1605–1623. https://doi.org/10.1016/S0047-2727(03)00040-9.

Boyd, Robert, and Peter J. Richerson. 1992. "Punishment Allows the Evolution of Cooperation (or Anything Else) in Sizable Groups." *Ethology and Sociobiology* 13 (3): 171–195. Center on Philanthropy at Indiana University. 2008. "Key Findings about Charitable Giving." Accessed June 26, 2023. https://scholarworks.iupui.edu/bitstream/handle/1805/5775/copps_2005_key_findings.pdf?sequence=1&isAllowed=y.

Colleran, Heidi, and Kristin Snopkowski. 2018. "Variation in Wealth and Educational Drivers of Fertility Decline across 45 Countries." *Population Ecology* 60: 155–169. https://doi.org/10.1007/s10144-018-0626-5.

Curtis, Valerie. 2013. *Don't Look, Don't Touch, Don't Eat*. Chicago: University of Chicago Press.

de Waal, Frans B. M. 2000. "Primates—A Natural Heritage of Conflict Resolution." *Science* 289 (5479): 586–590. https://doi.org/10.1126/science.289.5479.586.

Dunbar, Robin I. M. 1998. "The Social Brain Hypothesis." *Evolutionary Anthropology* 6 (5): 178–190.

Editors of Encyclopaedia Britannica. 2018. "Indian Ocean Tsunami of 2004." *Encyclopaedia Britannica*. Accessed June 26, 2023. https://www.britannica.com/event/Indian-Ocean-tsunami-of-2004.

Fehr, Ernst, and Urs Fischbacher. 2003. "The Nature of Human Altruism." *Nature* 425: 785–791.

Gurven, Michael. 2004. "Reciprocal Altruism and Food-Sharing Decisions among Hiwi and Ache Hunter-Gatherers." *Behavioral Ecology and Sociobiology* 56 (4): 366–380. https://doi.org/10.1007/s00265-004-0793-6.

Gurven, Michael, Wesley Allen-Arave, Kim Hill, and Magdalena Hurtado. 2000. "'It's a Wonderful Life': Signaling Generosity among the Ache of Paraguay." *Evolution and Human Behavior* 21 (4): 263–282.

Hamilton, W. D. 1964. "The Genetical Evolution of Social Behaviour I & II." *Journal of Theoretical Biology* 7 (1): 1–52.

Hrdy, Sarah Blaffer. 2009. *Mothers and Others: The Evolutionary Origins of Mutual Understanding.* Cambridge, MA: The Belknap Press of Harvard University Press.

Johnson, Jeffrey G., Patricia Cohen, Jocelyn Brown, Elizabeth M. Smailes, and David P. Bernstein. 1999. "Childhood Maltreatment Increases Risk for Personality Disorders during Early Adulthood." *Archives of General Psychiatry* 56 (7): 600–606. https://doi.org/10.1001/archpsyc.56.7.600.

Milinski, Manfred, Dirk Semmann, and Hans-Jürgen Krambeck. 2002. "Reputation Helps Solve the 'Tragedy of the Commons.'" *Nature* 415: 424–426.

National Center for Homeless Education. 2017. "Federal Data Summary: School Years 2013–2014 to 2015–2016." Accessed June 26, 2023. https://nche.ed.gov/wp-content/uploads/2018/11/data-comp-1314-1516.pdf.

Parker, Sue Taylor, and Kathleen Rita Gibson. 1979. "A Developmental Model for the Evolution of Language and Intelligence in Early Hominids." *Behavioral and Brain Sciences* 2 (3): 367–381. https://doi.org/10.1017/S0140525X0006307X.

Pepper, Gillian V., and Daniel Nettle. 2014. "Out-of-Control Mortality Matters: The Effect of Perceived Uncontrollable Mortality Risk on a Health-Related Decision." *PeerJ* 2: e459. https://doi.org/10.7717/peerj.459.

Schradin, Carsten. 2021. "Corona, Climate Change, and Evolved Human Behavior" *Trends in Ecology & Evolution* 36 (7): 569-572.

Sear, Rebecca, and Ruth Mace. 2008. "Who Keeps Children Alive? A Review of the Effects of Kin on Child Survival." *Evolution and Human Behavior* 29 (1): 1–18. https://doi.org/10.1016/j.evolhumbehav.2007.10.001.

Smith, Eric Alden, and Rebecca L. Bliege Bird. 2000. "Turtle Hunting and Tombstone Opening: Public Generosity as Costly Signaling." *Evolution and Human Behavior* 21 (4): 245–261. https://doi.org/10.1016/S1090-5138(00)00031-3.

Smith, Eric Alden, Rebecca Bliege Bird, and Douglas W. Bird. 2003. "The Benefits of Costly Signaling: Meriam Turtle Hunters." *Behavioral Ecology* 14 (1): 116–126. https://doi.org/10.1093/beheco/14.1.116.

Snopkowski, Kristin, and Hillard Kaplan. 2014. "A Synthetic Biosocial Model of Fertility Transition: Testing the Relative Contribution of Embodied Capital Theory, Changing Cultural Norms, and Women's Labor Force Participation." *American Journal of Physical Anthropology* 154 (3): 322–333. https://doi.org/10.1002/ajpa.22512.

Trivers, Robert L. 1971. "The Evolution of Reciprocal Altruism." *The Quarterly Review of Biology* 46 (1): 35–57. https://doi.org/10.1086/406755.

World Bank. 2022. "Fertility Rate, Total (Births per Woman): Bolivia." The World Bank Group. Accessed November 15, 2022. https://data.worldbank.org/indicator/SP.DYN.TFRT.IN?locations=BO.

APPENDIX D: ANCIENT DNA

Robyn Humphreys, MSc., University of Cape Town

This appendix is a revision of the "Chapter 11 Special Topics: Ancient DNA" by Robyn Humphreys. In Explorations: An Open Invitation to Biological Anthropology, *first edition, edited by Beth Shook, Katie Nelson, Kelsie Aguilera, and Lara Braff, which is licensed under CC BY-NC 4.0.*

Learning Objectives

- Describe the challenges in recovering and sequencing ancient DNA.
- Explain how the Denisovans were discovered and what we have learned about them based on their aDNA.
- Describe the relationships between Neanderthals, Denisovans, and modern humans based on aDNA evidence.
- Explain how DNA can provide insights into the population structure of hominin groups of the past.

Ancient DNA (aDNA) has provided us with new insights into our evolutionary history that cannot be garnered from the fossil record alone. For example, it has assisted with the discovery of the Denisovans, for whom little fossil evidence is available. It has helped us better understand, and make inferences about, the evolution of and relationships among Neanderthals, Denisovans, and modern humans. It has also helped to answer some very important questions about what happened when modern humans migrated out of Africa and encountered these European/Asian hominins, as we will discuss in this appendix.

Sequencing Ancient Genomes

The first successful sequencing of aDNA from an archaic hominin took place in 1997 with the sequencing of mitochondrial DNA (mtDNA) from a Neanderthal-type specimen from Feldhofer Cave. mtDNA is ideal for aDNA studies because it is more abundant than nuclear DNA in our cells. This mitochondrial sequence provided evidence that Neanderthals belonged in a clade separate from modern humans and that their mtDNA was four times more different from modern humans than modern human mtDNA was from each other (Krings et al. 1997).

Sequencing of nuclear DNA would not occur until more than ten years later. The first nuclear genomic sequence representing Neanderthals was produced by sequencing three individuals and using their sequences to create a composite draft Neanderthal genome (Green et al. 2010). The first high-coverage sequence of a single Neanderthal was that of a female Neanderthal who lived in Siberia, followed by another high-coverage sequence from a female Neanderthal whose remains were found in the Vidja cave in Croatia (Prüfer et al. 2014). **High-coverage sequences** are produced when the genome has been sequenced multiple times, which ensures that the sequences are a true reflection of the genomic sequence and not due to errors that occur during the process of sequencing.

Collecting and Sequencing aDNA

While aDNA can be collected from many different sources (e.g., soft tissue, hair, paleo feces, soils, and sediments), when studying ancient hominins it is most often collected from bone and teeth. Because extraction of aDNA requires destruction of part of the tissue, and the morphology of the skeletal element might be informative, care needs to be taken when deciding what is sampled. Multiple samples are often taken to allow repeat sequencing and demonstrate reproducibility of results. All samples must be minimally handled to avoid contamination.

Endogenous aDNA, or DNA that was present in the tissue before the body decomposed, are usually in fragments 100 to 300 base pairs (bp) long due to degradation, and thus difficult to study. Sometimes DNA from other sources, known as **exogenous DNA,** are also found in samples. Some examples include DNA from microbes or modern human contamination (Figure D.1).

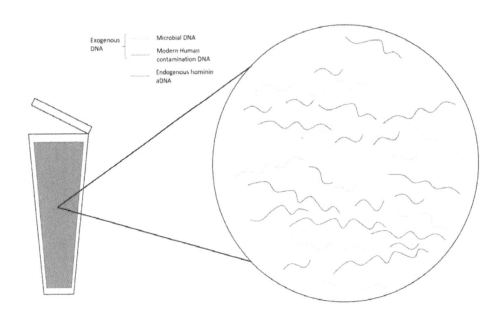

Figure D.1: The different types of DNA you may find after DNA extraction is performed on bone or other samples. In the sample you can see microbial DNA, modern human contamination DNA (both exogenous DNA), and endogenous hominin aDNA. Credit: DNA extraction (Figure 11.12) original to Explorations: An Open Invitation to Biological Anthropology by Robyn Humphreys is under a CC BY-NC 4.0 License.

There are also modifications that occur to aDNA due to chemical reactions. For example, **deamination** results in Cytosine (C) to Thymine (T) conversions, which occur mostly at the 5' end **(5 prime end)** of the DNA fragment. This in turn results in Guanine (G) to Adenine (A) substitutions on the 3' end **(3 prime end)** of the DNA fragment. These sequence changes in aDNA might not reflect the original hominin sequence, yet these changes can be helpful when differentiating between aDNA and modern human DNA contamination. The environment plays a significant role, as DNA preserves well in cold conditions such as permafrost. aDNA has also been recovered from material found in drier environments under special conditions. Factors such as water percolation, salinity, pH, and microbial growth all affect the preservation of aDNA.

The bone that best preserves DNA after death is the petrous portion of the temporal bone. This forms part of the skull and protects the inner ear. Due to its high density, the petrous portion preserves DNA very well. Thus, it is possible to get DNA from older and less well-preserved individuals when using the petrous portion. Compared to other bones, the petrous portion not only preserves DNA better but also allows for the extraction of more DNA. The petrous portion can yield up to 100 times more DNA than other bones (Pinhasi et al. 2015)

Initially the short fragments and degraded nature of aDNA posed a big problem with the usual polymerase chain reaction (PCR) procedures used to sequence DNA. But, the advent of **high-throughput sequencing** has revolutionized sequencing the genomes of ancient hominins. High-throughput sequencing allows for the parallel sequencing of many fragments of DNA in one reaction, without prior knowledge of the target sequence. In this way, the maximum amount of available aDNA can be sequenced. Because the high-throughput sequencing method does not discriminate between endogenous aDNA and exogenous DNA, it is important to either ensure that there is as little contamination as possible and/or use methods that allow for differentiation of the target aDNA.

The Discovery of Denisovans

Denisovans, named after the Siberian cave in which they were discovered, are a distinct group of hominins that were identified through aDNA.

Analysis of the ancient mtDNA from teeth and bone fragments revealed they had haplotypes outside the range of variation of modern humans and Neanderthals. The phalanx bone from which the DNA of the Denisovan was recovered did not have traits that indicated that it was another species. A **haplotype** is a set of genetic variants located on a single stretch of the genome. Shared or similar haplotypes can be used to identify ancestral relationships and to differentiate groups. Dubbed lineage X, the mtDNA sequence from these fossils suggested that Denisovans diverged from modern humans and Neanderthals.

Subsequent high-coverage sequence of a Denisovan (Denisovan 3) nuclear genome showed that Denisovans are a sister group to Neanderthals and thus more closely related to them than indicated by the mtDNA data (Brown et al. 2016). Because mtDNA and nuclear DNA have different patterns of inheritance, they can paint different pictures about the relationships between two groups. The Denisovans are now thought to have a mtDNA sequence derived from an ancient hominin group that hybridized with Denisovans and introduced the mtDNA sequence.

Sequences from three other Denisovans (Denisovan 2, 4, and 8) that provide insight into how old the specimens are, along with the usual dating methods (such as radio carbon dating and uranium dating), show that Denisovans occupied the Denisovan cave from around 195 kya to 52 kya to 76 kya. DNA can assist with dating because, compared to older sequences, younger sequences will have accumulated more mutations from the putative common ancestral sequence. Thus, it is possible to conclude from sequence data, that Denisovan 2 is 54.2 kya to 99.4 kya older than Denisovan 3, and 20.6 kya to 37.7 kya older than Denisovan 8. Molecular data indicates that Neanderthals and Denisovans separated between 381 kya and 473 kya and that the branch leading to Denisovans and modern humans diverged around 800 kya. Denisovans are also more closely related to another set of fossils found in the cave Sima de los Huesos dated to 430 kya. Thus, the split between Neanderthals and Denisovans must have occurred before 430 kya (Meyer et al. 2016).

What Can We Learn About Population Structure of the Neanderthals and Denisovans from aDNA?

Ancient DNA has helped us understand the demographics of Neanderthals and Denisovans and make inferences about population size and history. Three lines of evidence suggest that these groups had small populations toward the end of their existence.

The first line of evidence uses **coalescent** methods. This process is used to determine which population dynamics in the past are most likely to give rise to the genetic sequences we have, and it allows us to understand population changes of the past, including recombination, population subdivision, and variable population size.

The second indicator that Neanderthals and Denisovans had smaller population sizes is that these groups carried many deleterious (or harmful) genomic variants. Genomic variants are considered deleterious when the change in genomic sequence alters the amino acid sequence of a protein and affects the function of the protein; such variants are known as **nonsynonymous mutations**. By contrast, **synonymous mutations** that occur in protein-coding regions of the genome do not change the amino acid sequence nor affect the proteins produced. Denisovans and Neanderthals have a higher ratio of nonsynonymous to synonymous mutations when compared to contemporary modern human populations. This is indicative of a small population size, because if the population were larger, natural selection would have acted on these deleterious variants and weeded them out.

A third indicator of small population size is that the Neanderthals sequenced thus far have low levels of **heterozygosity**. Heterozygosity is measured by looking at how often two different **alleles** are found within a certain stretch of DNA. When you find many regions on the genome with different alleles, there is a high level of heterozygosity. When you find very few positions where there are two different alleles, this indicates a low level of heterozygosity. Both Neanderthals and Denisovans appear to have low levels of heterozygosity, indicating smaller population sizes. Ancient Neanderthal genomes also revealed that there were consanguineous relations (mating relationships between two closely related Neanderthals). This was determined by looking at the stretches of **homozygosity** in a female neanderthal's genome that were longer than expected and could not be explained by small population size alone.

Sequencing Archaic Genomes to Understand Modern Humans

Not only did the sequencing of archaic genomes allow us to learn more about Neanderthals and Denisovans, it gave us important insights into our own evolution. Previously the human genome was only compared to our closest living relatives, the great apes, which helped us identify unique derived genomic changes that occurred since humans split from our last common ancestor with chimpanzees. Neanderthal and Denisovan genomes provide another set of comparative samples that might help us identify changes unique to modern humans that occurred after our split from the last common ancestor with Neanderthals/Denisovans. These changes may help account for our success as a species.

Hybridization Between Hominin Groups

aDNA also provides insight into interactions between modern humans migrating out of Africa and other hominins that evolved in Europe and Asia. One of the hypotheses tested was this: if **hybridization** between modern humans and Neanderthals occurred, Neanderthals would have shared more genomic variants with some modern human populations than with others. When this was tested, the data showed that Neanderthals shared more genomic variants with Europeans and Asians than with African individuals (Sankararaman 2016). This difference in relatedness was significant, indicating that there had been hybridization between Neanderthals and modern humans.

From the genetic data, we know that Europeans have a smaller proportion of Neanderthal-derived genes than East Asians do (Prüfer et al. 2017). Thus, there was more admixture into ancestral East Asian populations than into ancestral European populations. Oceanians (Melanesians, Australian aborigines, and other Southeast Asian islanders) have a higher proportion of their DNA derived from Denisovans and longer stretches of Denisovan DNA. DNA in chromosomes get exchanged and experience **genetic recombination,** whereby **introgressed** regions (inherited from different species or taxon) are broken down into smaller segments each generation. Thus, longer stretches of introgressed DNA indicate that hybridization occurred more recently. Genetic analysis shows that the admixture event between the Denisovan and human ancestors of these populations is more recent than the admixture events between Neanderthals and modern humans.

To determine whether shared sequences are a result of introgression or more ancient substructure, researchers use **divergence time:** a measure of how long two sequences have been changing independently. The longer the two sequences have been changing independently, the more differences they will accumulate, which will result in a longer divergence time. By measuring the divergence time between the introgressed regions in modern human genomes and the Neanderthal sequences, researchers can calculate that the shared sequences are recent as well as date to when the two taxa made secondary contact. This is well after the initial population split between modern humans and Neanderthals. There has been gene flow from Neanderthals and Denisovans into modern human populations, between Neanderthals and Denisovans, and from modern humans into Neanderthals.

There is variation in how much of the Neanderthal genome is represented in the modern human population. Individuals outside of Africa usually have 1% to 4% of their genome derived from Neanderthals. Approximately 30% of the Neanderthal genome is represented in modern human genomes, altogether.

Introgressed genes have signatures that allow us to identify them and differentiate them from parts of the genome that are not introgressed. This can be identified in at least three ways. First, in this case, if the sequence is more similar to the Neanderthal sequence (i.e.,fewer sequence differences from the Neanderthal than the African modern human), it is likely that it is derived from a Neanderthal. Second, what is the divergence time between the allele and the same allele in a Neanderthal? If it is shorter than the divergence time between humans and Neanderthal, then the gene is most likely introgressed. An example of this can be seen in Figure D.2. Third, consider whether the allele that meets the first two criteria and is identified as possibly being introgressed can be found at higher frequencies in populations outside of Africa.

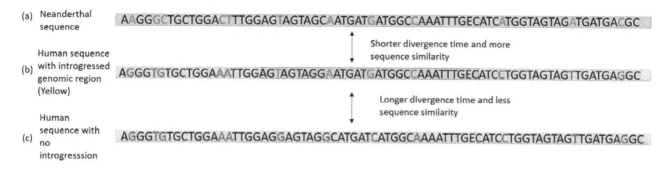

(a) Neanderthal sequence

AAGGGCTGCTGGACTTTGGAGTAGTAGCAATGATGATGGCCAAATTTGCATCATGGTAGTAGATGATGACGC

Shorter divergence time and more sequence similarity

(b) Human sequence with introgressed genomic region (Yellow)

AGGGTGCTGGAAATTGGAGTAGTAGGAATGATGATGGCCAAATTTGCATCCTGGTAGTAGTTGATGAGGC

Longer divergence time and less sequence similarity

(c) Human sequence with no introgresssion

AGGGTGTGCTGGAAATTGGAGGAGTAGGCATGATCATGGCAAAATTTGCATCCTGGTAGTAGTTGATGAGGC

Figure D.2: The middle (b) DNA sequence is that of a modern human with an introgressed genomic region (DNA inherited from a more recent Neanderthal ancestor, highlighted in yellow). This DNA sequence is compared to (c) a human sequence with no introgression and (a) a Neanderthal sequence. The introgressed region of DNA can be recognized because it has more sequence similarity with that of neanderthal DNA, indicating that region has had a shorter divergence time from a Neanderthal ancestor. Credit: Introgressed Neanderthal DNA in a modern human genome (Figure 11.14) original to Explorations: An Open Invitation to Biological Anthropology by Robyn Humphreys is under a CC BY-NC 4.0 License.

Examining the genomes of modern humans, we can see that there are regions of the genome with no Neanderthal and Denisovan genomic variants. These are known as Neanderthal or Denisovan introgression deserts. There are also overlaps between regions in the human genome that are Neanderthal and Denisovan deserts, which might indicate genomic incompatibilities between modern humans and these groups, resulting in those genes being selected against in the modern human genome. We can also infer that hybridization may itself have been a barrier to gene flow because there is a significant reduction in introgression on the X chromosome and around genes that are disproportionately expressed in the testes compared to other tissue groups. This could indicate that hybridization between modern humans and Neanderthals may have resulted in male hybrid infertility.

Because of the climate in Africa, it has been difficult or impossible to extract aDNA from African fossil remains. However, analysis of genomes of modern African populations indicate that there was admixture between modern humans and other hominins within Africa (see Figure D.2).

Confirmed Fossil Hybrids

Another line of evidence concerns hybrids. A first-generation hybrid is called an F1 hybrid; it is the direct offspring of two lineages that have been evolving independently over an extended period. A second-generation hybrid (F2) would be the offspring of two F1 hybrids. A backcrossed individual is the result of an F1 or F2 hybrid mating with an individual from one of the parental populations. An example of a backcross would be when a Neanderthal-human hybrid produces offspring with a human; their offspring would be considered a first-generation backcrossed hybrid (B1). Sequencing of aDNA from fossil material has confirmed that hybridization between different hominins has occurred, supporting the introgression data from recent populations.

The sequencing of Oase 1, a suspected hybrid based on skeletal morphology, showed that it had a Neanderthal ancestor as recently as six to eight generations back. He would thus be considered a backcrossed individual. The recent sequencing of a 13-year-old Denisovan female showed that she was the F1 hybrid offspring of a Neanderthal mother (from whom she inherited Neanderthal mtDNA) and a Denisovan father. While these are only two examples of individuals who are confirmed hybrids, many other remains show some indication of gene flow between hominins.

The Future of Genetic Studies

We are continuing to learn how introgressed genes affect modern humans. Combining phenotypic and genetic information, Neanderthal-derived genes have been associated with diverse traits, ranging from thes skin's sun sensitivity to excessive blood clotting by certain individuals. Interesting research has also shown that introgressed alleles might produce different gene expression profiles when compared to non-introgressed alleles. However, there is a lot of research still to be done to fully understand the effects of introgression on modern populations and how it might have assisted modern humans who migrated out of Africa.

Review Questions

- What are three reasons that ancient DNA is so difficult to study?
- What are introgressed regions of DNA? What insights do studying introgression provide about early hominins?
- Diagram our current understanding of Denisovan, Neanderthal, and modern human lineages based on ancient DNA.
- How can ancient DNA help us understand Neanderthal demographics?

Key Terms

5 prime end: A nucleic acid strand that terminates at the chemical group attached to the fifth carbon in the sugar-ring.

3 prime end: A nucleic acid strand that terminates at the hydroxyl (-OH) chemical group attached to the third carbon in the sugar-ring.

Allele: Each of two or more alternative forms of a gene that arise by mutation and are found at the same place on a chromosome.

Coalescent methods: These are models which allow for inference of how genetic variants sampled from a population may have originated from a common ancestor

Deamination: The chemical process that results in the conversion of Cytosine to uracil, which results in Cytosine to Thymine conversions during sequencing.

Divergence time: A measure of how long two genomic sequences have been changing independently.

Endogenous aDNA: A form of ancient DNA in which DNA originates from the specimen being examined.

Exogenous DNA: DNA that originates from sources outside of the specimen you are trying to sequence.

Genetic recombination: This is the process of exchange of DNA between two strands to produce new sequence arrangements.

Haplotype: A set of genetic variants located on a single stretch of the genome. This unique combination of variants on a stretch of the genome can be used to differentiate groups that will have different combinations of variants.

Heterozygosity: A measure of how many genes within a diploid genome are made up of more than one variant for a gene.

High-coverage sequences: These are genomic sequences which have been sequenced multiple times to ensure that the sequence produced is a true reflection of the genomic sequence, and reduce the likelihood that the sequence has sequencing errors as a result of the sequencing process.

High–throughput sequencing: DNA sequencing technologies developed in the early 21st century that are capable of sequencing many DNA molecules at a time.

Homozygosity: A measure of how many genes within a diploid genome are made up of more than the same variant for a gene.

Hybridization: Mating between two genetically differentiated groups (or species).

Introgressed genes: This is the movement of genes from one species to the gene pool of another species through hybridization between the species and backcross into the parental population by hybrid offspring.

Nonsynonymous mutations: These are changes that occur in the protein-coding region of the genome and result in a change in amino acid sequence of the protein being produced.

Synonymous mutations: Mutations that occur in the protein-coding region of the genome but do not result in a change in amino acid sequence of the protein being produced.

About the Author

Robyn Humphreys, MSc.

University of the Western Cape, rhumphreys@uwc.ac.za

Robyn Humphreys is a biological anthropologist based in the archaeology department at the University of Cape Town. Her MSc focused on the role of hybridization in human evolution. She is now pursuing her Ph.D., which will involve looking at the relationship between archaeologists and communities in relation to research on human remains from historical sites in Cape Town.

For Further Exploration

Fu, Qiaomei, Mateja Hajdinjak, Oana Teodora Moldovan, Silviu Constantin, Swapan Mallick, Pontus Skoglund, Nick Patterson, et al. 2015. "An Early Modern Human from Romania with a Recent Neanderthal Ancestor." *Nature* 524 (7564): 216.

Pääbo, Svante. 2011. "DNA Clues to Our Inner Neanderthal.," TED Talk by Svante Pääbo, August 2011. Last accessed May 7, 2023. https://www.ted.com/talks/svante_paeaebo_dna_clues_to_our_inner_neanderthal?language=en.

References

Beyin, Amanuel. 2011. "Upper Pleistocene Human Dispersals out of Africa: A Review of the Current State of the Debate." *International Journal of Evolutionary Biology* 2011: Article ID 615094. https://doi.org/10.4061/2011/615094.

Brown, Samantha, Thomas Higham, Viviane Slon, Svante Pääbo, Matthias Meyer, Katerina Douka, Fiona Brock, et al. 2016. "Identification of a New Hominin Bone from Denisova Cave, Siberia, Using Collagen Fingerprinting and Mitochondrial DNA Analysis." *Science Reports* 6: 23559. https://doi.org/10.1038/srep23559.

Green, Richard E., Johannes Krause, Adrian W. Briggs, Tomislav Maricic, Udo Stenzel, Martin Kircher, Nick Patterson, et al. 2010. "A Draft Sequence of the Neanderthal Genome." *Science* 328 (5979): 710–722.

Krings, Matthias, Anne Stone, Ralf W. Schmitz, Heike Krainitzki, Mark Stoneking, and Svante Pääbo. 1997. "Neanderthal DNA Sequences and the Origin of Modern Humans." *Cell* 90 (1): 19–30.

Meyer, Matthias, Juan-Luis Arsuaga, Cesare de Filippo, Sarah Nagel, Ayinuer Aximu-Petri, Birgit Nickel, Ignacio Martínez, et al. 2016. "Nuclear DNA Sequences from the Middle Pleistocene Sima de los Huesos Hominins." *Nature* 531: 504–507.

Pinhasi, Ron, Daniel Fernandes, Kendra Sirak, Mario Novak, Sarah Connell, Songül Alpaslan-Roodenberg, Fokke Gerritsen, et al. 2015. "Optimal Ancient DNA Yields from the Inner Ear Part of the Human Petrous Bone." *PLoS One* 10 (6): e0129102. https://doi.org/10.1371/journal.pone.0129102.

Prüfer, Kay, Fernando Racimo, Nick Patterson, Flora Jay, Sriram Sankararaman, Susanna Sawyer, Anja Heinze, et al. 2014. "The Complete Genome Sequence of a Neanderthal from the Altai Mountains." *Nature* 505 (7481): 43–49.

Prüfer, Kay, Cesare De Filippo, Steffi Grote, Fabrizio Mafessoni, Petra Korlević, Mateja Hajdinjak, Benjamin Vernot, et al. 2017. "A High-Coverage Neandertal Genome from Vindija Cave in Croatia." Science *358 (6363):* 655–658.

Sankararaman, Sriram, Swapan Mallick, Nick Patterson, and David Reich. 2016. "The Combined Landscape of Denisovan and Neanderthal Ancestry in Present-Day Humans." *Current Biology* 26 (9): 1241–1247.

Printed in the USA
CPSIA information can be obtained
at www.ICGtesting.com
CBHW080916080924
14103CB00037B/609